הַסִּדּוּר הַשָּׁלֵם

מְתֻרְגָּם וּמְפֹרָשׁ
בְּתוֹסֶפֶת מָבוֹא
מֵאֵת

פַּלְטִיאֵל בִּירֶנְבּוֹים

הִיבְּרוּ פּוּבְּלִישִׁינְג קוֹמְפַּנִי
נְיוּ-יוֹרְק

DAILY
PRAYER BOOK

HA-SIDDUR HA-SHALEM

Cheryl Sorosky F/B
783-7005

Translated and Annotated
with an Introduction

by

PHILIP BIRNBAUM

HEBREW PUBLISHING COMPANY
NEW YORK

Ha-Siddur Ha-Shalem

Dedicated
to the Memory of
DAVID WERBELOWSKY

הַתֹּכֶן

CONTENTS

INTRODUCTION

I

The Siddur is the most popular book in Jewish life. No book so completely unites the dispersed people of Israel. If any single volume can tell us what it means to be a Jew, it is the Siddur which embodies the visions and aspirations, the sorrows and joys of many generations. The whole gamut of Jewish history may be traversed in its pages; it is a mirror that reflects the development of the Jewish spirit throughout the ages. Interwoven into the texture of the prayers are passages from the Bible, the Mishnah, the Talmud and the Zohar. The poetic and philosophic creations of numerous known and unknown authors constitute a considerable part of the Siddur. No other book so thoroughly expresses the creative genius of our people across the centuries.

The Siddur passed through a long process of evolution until it finally emerged as a rich anthology of our literary classics. It abounds in quotations from every book of the Bible; it includes half the Book of Psalms, the entire Song of Songs, and lengthy excerpts from each of the Five Books of Moses. The *Ethics of the Fathers* and other chapters of the Mishnah have become particularly popular because they form part of the Siddur, which contains also extensive selections from the vast Hebrew literature that was written after the Talmud. Though its language is largely biblical Hebrew, it embodies a great deal of post-biblical diction. Aramaic, too, the common Jewish tongue that once replaced Hebrew for a long period, is prominently featured in prayers like the *Kaddish* and the *Yekum Purkan*.

Judaism demands from its adherents a knowledge of the Bible and the traditions based upon it. Many, however, lack the leisure or the aptitude for such study; hence, the Siddur has developed in a way that enables every worshiper to become familiar with the various forms of Jewish learning and religious expression. Since the

Siddur is designed for all Jews, individual needs and private interests are often disregarded in the prescribed prayers. These are
phrased in plural form and are meant to be the voice of all Israel.
The diversified authorship of the Siddur, embracing prophets and
psalmists, legalists and poets, proclaims that all Israel has a share
in its making. For nearly two thousand years, the Hebrew prayers
have helped to keep the Jews alive, saving them from losing their
language and their identity.

There is profound truth in the statement that from a man's
prayers we can discover whether he is cultured or not.[1] It is regret-
table that the Siddur, over which many generations have brooded
and wept, has never been sufficiently appreciated as a vehicle of
Jewish knowledge. People have learned to recite it by heart without giving adequate attention to its fine beauty and deep significance. Many have recited *Ashre*, for instance, three times a day
for decades without knowing what it means. In the schools, where
the Siddur is used as a text for the study of the mechanics of reading, the pupils are seldom taught to appreciate its contents.

The Siddur cannot be understood correctly unless it is read
thoughtfully. Talmudic authorities have invariably laid stress on
mental concentration as the chief requirement in praying. Maimonides writes: "Prayer without devotion is not prayer . . . He
whose thoughts are wandering or occupied with other things ought
not to pray . . . Before engaging in prayer, the worshiper ought . . .
to bring himself into a devotional frame of mind, and then he must
pray quietly and with feeling, not like one who carries a load, un-
loads it and departs."[2] Clearly, this is said because by means of the
traditional prayers the ideals of Judaism are ever brought afresh
to the consciousness of the worshiper.

---

[1] Tosefta, Berakhoth 1:8: מברכותיו של אדם ניכר אם בור הוא ואם תלמיד חכם הוא.

[2] Mishneh Torah, *Tefillah* 4:16: ואחר...המחשבות מכל לבו שיפנה ?הכוונה היא כיצד
כך יתפלל בנחת ובתחנונים; ולא יעשה תפלתו כמי שהיה נושא משאוי ומשליכו והולך לו.

The sages of Israel constantly emphasized the importance of uniformity in synagogue service. In order to link the people closely together, they reconciled variant forms of prayer and sought to bring them into harmonious union. The well-known *Modim d'Rabbanan*, a constituent part of the *Shemoneh Esreh*, is so named because it consists of variant readings reported by a number of talmudic rabbis.[1] The formula "who healest all creatures and doest wonders" is a combination of two readings.[2] As a compromise between two competing phrasings, אַהֲבָה רַבָּה is used in the morning service and אַהֲבַת עוֹלָם in the evening service.[3] A similar reconciliation was effected between the versions שִׂים שָׁלוֹם and שָׁלוֹם רָב.[4] The purpose of all this co-ordination and unification of the prescribed prayers was to prevent the formation of separate religious factions.

The Siddur should never become a source of contention among any segments of our people. One must not fail to realize that the Siddur is a classic similar to the Bible and the Talmud, to which the terms orthodox, conservative or reform do not apply. No one, of course, has ever attempted to prepare a reform edition of the Bible by removing the so-called "objectionable" expressions from the Torah or the Prophets. Editors of the Siddur should not take liberties with the original, eliminating a phrase here and adding one there, each according to his own beliefs. Such a procedure is liable to breed as many different kinds of public worship as there are synagogues and temples. The danger of rising sects is obvious, sects that are likely to weaken still more our harassed people. The ever-increasing modifications in the text of the Siddur are apt to destroy this unique source book of Judaism, designed for old and young, scholars and laymen.

---

[1] Sotah 40a. [2] Berakhoth 60b. [3] Tosafoth, Berakhoth 11b. [4] Baer, *Avodath Yisrael*, page 103.

II

A great many editions of the Siddur have suffered from gross carelessness. In the first place, the Hebrew text has not been adequately provided with punctuation to indicate the logical relation of words to one another. The prayers have therefore remained unclear even to those who have a fair knowledge of Hebrew. Opinions are still divided as to the groupings of the words of one of the most popular prayers, the *Kaddish*.[1]

For no sound reason the pages of the Siddur are broken up by several type sizes which have a confusing effect on the eyes of the reader. Those who learn the contents of the prayers soon discover that the emphasis suggested by the larger type is in most cases no emphasis at all. Why, for instance, should one part of the *Shema* be made to appear more prominent than the other? Why give the impression that certain psalms or the *Ethics of the Fathers* are of negligible importance? The variation of type sizes frequently causes mental stumbling and interferes with the proper appreciation of the Siddur. Our school children, generally trained in the reading of the larger type in the Siddur, gradually develop a prejudice against whatever appears in the smaller print; they imagine it as too hard to read or too unimportant to learn.

A cursory glance at the complicated directions, frequently attended by a strange mixture of Hebrew and English characters, will suffice to explain the confusion created in the mind of the average worshiper. These directions have "the New Moon" instead of *Rosh Ḥodesh*, "Pentecost" instead of *Shavuoth*, "Tabernacles" instead of *Sukkoth*, "the Eighth Day of Solemn Assembly and the Rejoicing of the Law" instead of *Shemini Atsereth and Simḥath Torah*, "the Ten Days of Penitence" instead of *between Rosh Hashanah and Yom Kippur*. During the High Holyday period one is misdirected into reciting twenty instead of the prescribed nineteen

---

[1] De Sola Pool, *The Kaddish*, page 60.

benedictions of the *Shemoneh Esreh*. Instructed to add the special paragraph בְּסֵפֶר חַיִּים, he is puzzled by the improper arrangement of the text so that he combines two variant formulas and says: "Blessed art thou . . . Author of peace" and "Blessed art thou . . . who blessest thy people with peace." As many as forty-five cumber‑ some words are employed merely to indicate that שֶׁהֶחֱיָנוּ is omitted from the *Kiddush* on the last two nights of *Pesaḥ*. The direction is phrased obscurely enough to perplex the reader whenever he recites the *Kiddush* for festivals. The well-known blessing over cakes and pastry bears a heading of no less than twenty-two words such as "the five species of grain . . . oats and spelt." What does it all mean? The answer can be put in one word: confusion. As a result of poor arrangement and inadequate instructions, comparatively few worshipers ever succeed in properly reciting the full *Musaf* for *Ḥol ha-Mo'ed Sukkoth*.

Some translators, unfortunately, have failed in their task of making intelligible the meaning of the prayers. In their careless‑ ness, they have imitated the antiquated versions of the Bible that abound in phrases like "yielded up the ghost" instead of *died*, and filled the Siddur with a mass of words which convey little meaning to the mind of the modern Jew. The general complaint that "we do not understand what we say" is an indictment against many translations of the Siddur.

"Bible English" has inevitably hindered many from gaining a wholesome appreciation of the Siddur. If translation is to facilitate a proper understanding of the original, it must be freed from archaic forms like this: "Thou sawest the afflictions of our fathers . . . and heardest their cry . . . and shewedst signs and wonders." Unquestionably irritating are expressions such as "he gathereth the outcasts of Israel"; "he hath lifted up a horn for his people"; "as for me, in the abundance of thy lovingkindness will I come into thy house." To the modern reader, *dispersed* is undoubtedly better than "outcasts," and *raised the strength* more idiomatic than "lifted up a horn." Since the future tense in Hebrew often denotes repeated acts in the present, the correct form is *by thy abundant grace I enter thy house.* אֲנִי אָבוֹא simply means *I enter.* The circumlocution "and as for me," repeated four times in מַה־טֹּבוּ, is not implied in וַאֲנִי.

The fault of some translations is their literalness. Good translators should seek to make the original as clearly understood as possible; they cannot avoid being also interpreters. Words should be translated according to their context. It is decidedly wrong to use invariably the same English word to represent the same Hebrew word. Utterly misleading is a rendering such as "precious in the sight of the Lord is the death of his saints" (Psalm 116:15). The adjective יָקָר in this verse does not mean "precious" but *grievous.* The verb אָסַף is not restricted to one connotation only and does not always mean "to gather." Thus, וַאֲסַפְתּוֹ אֶל תּוֹךְ בֵּיתֶךָ (Deuteronomy 22:2) signifies *you shall take it home,* and אֱסֹף יָדֶךָ (I Samuel 14:19) means *withdraw your hand.* Hence, the rendering "he gathered up his feet into the bed" (Genesis 49:33) is more ludicrous than authentic.

Every student of Hebrew knows that בֶּן is not always the equivalent of *a son.* It frequently denotes age, membership in a definite class, or the possession of some quality. Similarly, אִישׁ and בַּעַל are often used interchangeably to characterize a person. Thus, אִישׁ לָשׁוֹן (Psalm 140:12) means *a slanderer,* and אִישׁ מִלְחָמָה (Exodus 15:3) *a warrior.* Hence, the rendering "the Lord is a man of war" is erroneous and nothing short of sacrilegious. "The children of thy covenant" is a mistranslation for *thy people of the covenant.* The term בַּר מִצְוָה is applied in the Talmud to every adult Israelite in the sense of *man of duty* and not "son of the commandment."[1] Similarly, בַּר דַּעַת is the counterpart of אִישׁ דַּעַת

---

[1] Baba Metsi'a 96a.

and signifies *a sensible man*. A telling argument against literalness is the awkward rendering of four Hebrew words (וּגְאָלוֹ מִיַּד חָזָק מִמֶּנּוּ): "and redeemed him from the hand of him that was stronger than he" (Jeremiah 31:10), meaning *he saved him from a stronger power*. This is typical of what has crept into the Siddur's translation as a result of copying from men unfamiliar with idiomatic Hebrew.

Herder, the famous poet and philosopher of the 18th century, declared that it is worthwhile studying the Hebrew language for ten years in order to read Psalm 104 in the original. This statement is applicable to all biblical poetry, which is highly figurative and does not readily lend itself to translation. "Let his horn be exalted"; "that my glory may sing praise unto thee . . ." What precisely can these convey to the English reader? The term "horn" in Hebrew frequently signifies strength or dignity. The word "glory" is occasionally used to denote soul.

In examining the translations of the Siddur one encounters expressions like "As for me, may my prayer unto thee be in an acceptable time" instead of *I offer my prayer to thee at a time of grace*, alluding to the time of public worship.[1] "The habitation of thy house," as redundant as "the tent of my house" (Psalm 132:3), simply means *thy abode* (אֹהֶל בֵּיתִ=מְעוֹן בַּיִת). "Answer me in the truth of thy salvation" hardly makes any sense. Proper translation would give *answer me with thy saving truth*. The word "truth" is often identical with mercy and kindness; for example, "thy kindness and thy truth shall ever preserve me" (Psalm 40:12).

In the opening sentence of the *Kedushah* one is puzzled by "the mystic utterance," a mistranslation of שִׂיחַ סוֹד.[2] The reference is of course to the phrase *holy, holy, holy*, chanted by the assembly of angels in the vision of Isaiah. The word סוֹד occurs here and

---

[1] Berakhoth 8a. [2] Compare the Sephardic version of the *Kedushah*.

there in the sense of *council, assembly,* and has nothing to do with mystery.[1] סוֹד שַׂרְפֵי קֹדֶשׁ in the *Kedushah* is the equivalent of סוֹד קְדוֹשִׁים in Psalm 89:8. Similarly, in the *Hymn of Glory* "the mystic utterance of thy servants" should be corrected to *amidst thy servants.*

The famous poem *Adon Olam* celebrates the eternity of God, and yet the initial phrase אֲדוֹן עוֹלָם is invariably translated "Lord of the universe" instead of *Eternal Lord.* The terms חַגִּים and זְמַנִּים are frequently used synonymously in the sense of *festivals,* and yet זְמַן חֵרוּתֵנוּ is generally rendered "the Season of our Freedom" instead of *our Festival of Freedom.* גֵּרֵי הַצֶּדֶק means *the true proselytes,* that is, those who have accepted Judaism out of inner conviction; it does not mean "strangers of righteousness" or "proselytes of righteousness." הַמְיַחֲדִים בָּתֵּי כְנֵסִיּוֹת signifies *who dedicate synagogues,* and nct "who unite to form synagogues."[2]

The oft-repeated "Blessed be the name of his glorious kingdom" is incorrectly translated. Equally incorrect is "Blessed be his name, whose glorious kingdom" or "Blessed be his glorious kingdom." *His glorious Majesty*—God himself—is here the object of praise, and not his kingdom. The response בָּרוּךְ שֵׁם כְּבוֹד מַלְכוּתוֹ, which was used in the Temple in place of Amen,[3] is the equivalent of the *Kaddish* response יְהֵא שְׁמֵהּ רַבָּא מְבָרַךְ ("may his great name be blessed").[4] שֵׁם כְּבוֹד מַלְכוּתוֹ connotes *His Majesty the King,* a circumlocution for the name of God and similar to שֵׁם כְּבוֹדוֹ (Psalm 72:19).

Translators have rendered the *Modim* passage variously: "We give thanks unto thee, for thou art . . . the God of our fathers for ever and ever"; "We acknowledge thee that thou art the Lord our God to all eternity and God of our fathers"; "We thankfully acknowledge thee . . . our fathers' God to all eternity." Closer in-

---

[1] Genesis 49:6; Psalms 89:8; 111:1; Jeremiah 15:17. [2] Singer, *Daily Prayer Book,* page 152. [3] Ta'anith 16b. [4] Compare Daniel 2:20. Targum Yerushalmi (Deuteronomy 6:4) interchanges the two formulas.

spection shows that this sentence is based on Psalm 79:13 and should read: *We ever thank thee, who art the Lord our God and the God of our fathers.* Unaware that the phrase "evening, morning and noon" refers to the three daily services, they have construed it as if it were a dangling modifier of another phrase. Correctly translated, the third sentence of *Modim* ought to read: *In every generation we will thank thee . . . evening, morning and noon.* Others apparently thought that the original text was in need of some repair, so they paraphrased it: "We thank thee . . . for the wonderful gifts which thou dost dispense unto us morning, noon, and night."

There are translators who indulge in periphrastic and verbose locutions like "in the flowering of thy saving power gives life"; "even as in the prophet's vision the choir of holy Seraphim in triple consecration call with sweet word one unto another." A good translation ought to be authentic and free from deceptions. One must not read into the original what is not there. No new poetry should be introduced into the Siddur presumably as the translation of the Hebrew text. The meaning ought to be preserved as close to to the original as possible. The poem "Rock of Ages," for example, is certainly not a translation of the familiar *Ḥanukkah* hymn *Ma'oz Tsur.*

The Siddur contains prayer-poems which should be annotated but not translated. Such are the הוֹשַׁעֲנוֹת, replete with historical and midrashic allusions and constructed in an involved poetic fashion. They comprise many intricate acrostics and a variety of Hebrew synonyms which, if translated, are likely to create a wrong impression and confuse the reader. One of these prayer-poems is composed of an interesting alphabetic list of twenty-two Hebrew synonyms for the Temple; another presents an alphabetic description of Israel's qualities; a third enumerates types of locusts and destructive forces of nature mentioned in the Bible. It may well be

said that the editions that have included the available English
translation of the *Hoshanoth* have not been enhanced by it. The
Hoshanoth can be appreciated only in the Hebrew.

III

The present edition of the complete Siddur abides by the wise
counsel of Rabbi Judah of Regensburg, who wrote in the twelfth
century: "He who copies a prayerbook . . . ought to copy every
recurrent passage to the end, thereby dispensing with the worshiper's need of searching for it . . . "[1] In this volume each of the
services is arranged as a completely integrated unit so that the worshiper is not called upon to search from page to page and to com-
mute from reference to reference. The directions are explicit, brief
and to the point. The traditional text is left intact, carefully
vocalized, and divided into sentences and clauses by the use of
modern punctuation marks.

Festival services such as *Tal* and *Geshem*, *Akdamuth* and *Hoshanoth*, have been included in this edition in view of the fact that
copies of the special prayerbooks for *Pesaḥ*, *Shavuoth* and *Sukkoth*
are not always available in sufficient numbers. On the other hand,
portions of the High Holyday services have not been made part of
this edition. Their inclusion is unwise and even misleading; because
of their wide range and variety, the prayers recited on *Rosh Hashanah* and *Yom Kippur* are properly situated in the *Maḥzor* and
should not be embodied in the regular daily Siddur.

Obvious errors found in current editions of the Siddur have been
removed. Instead of לְכָל, the variant וְכָל has been adopted as
the correct reading in the fifth verse of *Yigdal*.[2] This verse is the
poetic counterpart of Maimonides' fifth principle that the Creator
is the only one to whom it is proper to address our prayers; hence,

---

[1] Sefer Ḥasidim, 881. [2] The curious statement in the Jewish Encyclopedia
that the poet devoted eight years to improving and perfecting the excellent
poem *Yigdal* is based on a misunderstanding of a Hebrew passage quoted by
S. D. Luzzatto (see my article in ספר השנה ליהודי אמריקה, 1946, page 335).

it is wrong to translate here: "To every creature he teacheth his greatness and his sovereignty." Through the change of a single character (וְכָל in place of לְכָל), the fifth verse of *Yigdal* corresponds exactly to the fifth principle of faith formulated by Maimonides: *Every creature must declare his greatness and his kingship;* that is, everyone must pray to God.

In the Baraitha of Rabbi Ishmael, enumerating the thirteen principles upon which the talmudic exposition of the Bible is based, the ninth principle as well as the tenth contains the word אַחֵר and not אֶחָד. The correct reading is found on the first page of *Sifra* and in some rare *Siddurim*, thus: כל דבר שהיה בכלל ויצא מן הכלל לטעון טען אחר שהוא כעניגו ... כל דבר שהיה בכלל ויצא מן הכלל לטעון טען אחר שלא כעניגו.

לְעֵלָּא לְעֵלָּא, the phrase used in the *Kaddish* during the High Holyday period, is a reproduction of the Targum on מַעְלָה מָעְלָה (Deuteronomy 28:43). Though it means *higher and higher*, it is analogous to all adverbs which are repeated without the use of a conjunction for the purpose of intensification and emphasis; examples: מְאֹד מְאֹד, מַטָּה מַטָּה, מְעַט מְעַט, סָבִיב סָבִיב. In none of these instances does the Targum add the letter ו as a conjunction.

The phrasing וּלְעוֹלָם לֹא נֵבוֹשׁ כִּי בְךָ בָּטָחְנוּ in the *Shemoneh Esreh* corresponds to בְּךָ חָסִיתִי, אַל אֵבוֹשָׁה לְעוֹלָם in Psalm 71:1. It means *may we never come to shame, for in thee we trust.* This reading has been adopted here on the basis of *Maḥzor Vitry* (page 67) and the Sephardic editions. Additional support for this reading is offered by the expression שֶׁלֹּא נֵבוֹשׁ לְעוֹלָם וָעֶד in the grace recited after meals.

In the prayer וּבָא לְצִיּוֹן, the correct reading ... הוּא יִפְתַּח לִבֵּנוּ לַעֲשׂוֹת רְצוֹנוֹ ("may he open our heart... to do his will") is found in the Spanish Siddur. The reading וְלַעֲשׂוֹת ("and to do") is the result of a dittography; that is, the last letter of the preceding word has been erroneously repeated.

In the *Zemiroth*, or Sabbath Hymns, the following necessary emendations have been made. In *Yah Ribbon*, the phrase שְׁפַר קֳדָמֵי לְהַחֲוָיָה is borrowed from Daniel 3:32 and signifies *it is my pleasure to declare*. The variants קֳדָמָךְ לְהַחֲוָיָא and שַׁפִּיר קֳדָמָךְ are without basis. עַד אָנָה תּוֹגְיוּן נֶפֶשׁ ("how long will you torment a soul") is taken from Job 19:2. The author of בָּרוּךְ אֵל עֶלְיוֹן un-deniably employed תּוֹגְיוּן as a verb, exactly as in the biblical phrase, and did not coin a new noun תּוּגְיוֹן.

In the grace, the phrase הָנִיחַ לָנוּ has been corrected to הָנַח לָנוּ, a reading based on several texts, including those of Saadyah Gaon and of Maimonides.[1] The use of הָנִיחַ as an imperative in the singular is an obvious error.

Rabbi Jacob Emden of the 18th century called attention to a printer's error in the case of the parenthetical clause, "Our God and God of our fathers, be pleased with our rest," inserted in the passage וְהַשִּׂיאֵנוּ on festivals occurring on a Sabbath. Only the two words רְצֵה בִמְנוּחָתֵנוּ ("be pleased with our rest") directly apply to the Sabbath; the address to God applies to the remainder of the passage as well and should not be inserted within parentheses.

Every effort has been exerted to make the new translation of the Siddur readily intelligible to the modern reader. Wherever necessary, an interpretive phrase has been inserted within square brackets, so that the student may apprehend the thought immedi-ately. No pronouns have been capitalized, because the frequent use of capitals makes for confusion. The example of English Bibles has been followed in this respect. The pronouns *thou* and *thee* have been retained where they are addressed to God, since they convey a more reverent feeling than the common *you*. The diction has not been allowed to reach the level of everyday English in view of the exalted literary tone of the Siddur.

---

[1]Baer, *Avodath Yisrael* (page 557), quotes the correct reading from Saadyah Gaon, Maimonides and others, but decides against it because he misreads הַנַּח in place of הָנַח.

The following parallel columns will illustrate the difference between the old English translation and the new. The extracts for comparison are taken from the grace after meals.

THE NEW TRANSLATION

Blessed art thou ... who sustainest the whole world with goodness, kindness and mercy. Thou givest food to all creatures.

Through thy abundant goodness we have never yet been in want; may we never be in want of sustenance for thy great name's sake. Thou sustainest all, doest good to all, and providest food for all ...

We thank thee ... for having given a lovely and spacious land to our fathers as a heritage ... for thy covenant ... for the life, grace and kindness thou hast bestowed on us; and for the sustenance thou grantest us continuously.

May the Merciful One bless ... their entire family and all that is theirs. May he bless all alike with a perfect blessing even as our forefathers ... were blessed in every way.

THE OLD TRANSLATION

Blessed art thou ... who feedest the whole world with thy goodness, with grace, with loving kindness and tender mercy; thou givest food to all flesh.

Through thy great goodness food hath never failed us; O may it not fail us for ever and ever for thy great name's sake, since thou nourishest and sustainest all beings, and doest good unto all, and ...

We thank thee ... because thou didst give as an heritage unto our fathers a desirable, good and ample land ... as well as for thy covenant ... the life, grace and loving kindness which thou hast vouchsafed unto us, and for the food wherewith thou dost constantly feed and sustain us on every day, in every season, at every hour.

May the All-merciful bless ... them, their household, their seed and all that is theirs, us also and all that is ours, as our fathers ... were blessed each with his own comprehensive blessing; even thus may he bless all of us together.

Here and there new interpretations have been given to biblical passages. The usual translation of Song of Songs 5:8, for example, is not satisfactory. It reads: "If you find my beloved, what will ye tell him? that I am love-sick." This has been corrected to read: *If you find my beloved, do not tell him that I am love-sick.* Thus, the word מַה has been rendered in the sense of *not.* In the Arabic, the same particle is constantly used as a negative. Similarly, מַה תָּעִירוּ וּמַה תְּעוֹרְרוּ אֶת הָאַהֲבָה, being the exact counterpart of אִם תָּעִירוּ וְאִם תְּעוֹרְרוּ אֶת הָאַהֲבָה (Song of Songs 2:7; 8:4) is here translated: *Do not stir up, do not rouse love;* that is, it must come spontaneously.

Where a given verse is quoted for homiletical purposes, the entire passage would lack coherence should that verse be translated literally. For instance, the phrase לְמַעַן צִדְקוֹ (Isaiah 42:21) literally refers to God's righteousness, but in a Mishnah passage it is taken as an allusion to the potential righteousness of Israel. Hence, the biblical verse cited by Rabbi Ḥananya ben Akashya has been translated here: "The Lord was pleased, for the sake of [Israel's] righteousness, to render the Torah great and glorious" (page 484).

The benedictions are phrased essentially in biblical style. "Blessed art thou, O Lord" is a phrase borrowed from Psalm 119:12, while "King of the universe" is taken from Jeremiah 10:10. Since the verb בּרך originally connotes *to bend the knees,* that is, to worship (Psalm 95:6), it would certainly be better to translate בָּרוּךְ אַתָּה *worshiped art thou;* but this would be too much of a deviation from the long established "blessed art thou." Abrupt transitions from the second person to the third person occur in the benedictions as in all biblical poetry. English syntax, on the other hand, does not tolerate such transitions. For this reason, the benedictions must be rendered consistently in the second person.

A running commentary has been provided in the present edition of the Siddur to explain various points of interest. Without accompanying illustrations even the best and most lucid translation cannot make clear, for example, the well-known tannaitic passage that lists the thirteen principles upon which the talmudic interpretation of the Bible is based. Included in the Siddur in order to complete the daily minimum of study required of every Jew, they are on the lips of countless worshipers. Yet very few have learned precisely what these important principles are, because the old translation is too obscurely worded for the student to make out its meaning.

Designed for laymen, the footnotes are written in non-technical style and contain no abbreviations. To save space they include references only to original sources which do not bear long titles. Great authorities like Amram Gaon, Saadyah Gaon, Rashi, Maimonides and their works on the Siddur are mentioned only on rare occasions. The footnotes embody illuminating information derived from a wide range of commentaries and works of scholars.

The biblical references at the bottom of the English pages serve to indicate the central source of whatever has gone into the composition of the Siddur. The biblical phrases and expressions woven into the texture of the liturgical poems are indicated in the notes which, at the same time, contain biographical sketches of the authors.

It is hoped that a better and more widely disseminated understanding of our religious resources will result from this edition. It remains only to emphasize that such an inspiring book as the Siddur does not become the real possession of a person unless its contents are impressed upon his mind and influence his everyday life.

PHILIP BIRNBAUM

January, 1949.

שַׁחֲרִית לִילָדִים

Upon awakening in the morning:

מוֹדֶה אֲנִי לְפָנֶיךָ, מֶלֶךְ חַי וְקַיָּם, שֶׁהֶחֱזַרְתָּ בִּי נִשְׁמָתִי בְּחֶמְלָה; רַבָּה אֱמוּנָתֶךָ.

When washing the hands:

בָּרוּךְ אַתָּה, יְיָ אֱלֹהֵינוּ, מֶלֶךְ הָעוֹלָם, אֲשֶׁר קִדְּשָׁנוּ בְּמִצְוֹתָיו וְצִוָּנוּ עַל נְטִילַת יָדָיִם.

When putting on the *arba kanfoth*:

בָּרוּךְ אַתָּה, יְיָ אֱלֹהֵינוּ, מֶלֶךְ הָעוֹלָם, אֲשֶׁר קִדְּשָׁנוּ בְּמִצְוֹתָיו וְצִוָּנוּ עַל מִצְוַת צִיצִת.

When dressed:

תּוֹרָה צִוָּה לָנוּ מֹשֶׁה, מוֹרָשָׁה קְהִלַּת יַעֲקֹב. בְּרָכוֹת יָחֹלוּ עַל רֹאשִׁי. שְׁמַע בְּנִי מוּסַר אָבִיךָ, וְאַל תִּטֹּשׁ תּוֹרַת אִמֶּךָ. תּוֹרָה תְּהִי אֱמוּנָתִי, וְאֵל שַׁדַּי בְּעֶזְרָתִי. אֵל מֶלֶךְ נֶאֱמָן. שְׁמַע יִשְׂרָאֵל, יְיָ אֱלֹהֵינוּ, יְיָ אֶחָד. בָּרוּךְ שֵׁם כְּבוֹד מַלְכוּתוֹ לְעוֹלָם וָעֶד. וְאַתֶּם הַדְּבֵקִים בַּיְיָ אֱלֹהֵיכֶם, חַיִּים כֻּלְּכֶם הַיּוֹם. לִישׁוּעָתְךָ קִוִּיתִי, יְיָ.

אֱלֹהַי, נְצֹר לְשׁוֹנִי מֵרָע, וּשְׂפָתַי מִדַּבֵּר מִרְמָה. פְּתַח לִבִּי בְּתוֹרָתֶךָ, וּבְמִצְוֹתֶיךָ תִּרְדּוֹף נַפְשִׁי. יִהְיוּ לְרָצוֹן אִמְרֵי פִי וְהֶגְיוֹן לִבִּי לְפָנֶיךָ, יְיָ, צוּרִי וְגוֹאֲלִי.

תורה צוה לנו (Deuteronomy 33:4) is the first Hebrew verse which a father is directed to teach his child at a very early age (Sukkah 42a; Maimonides, *Talmud Torah* 1:6). Although the child is held to be free from religious duties, his father is required to make him amenable to them.

1

MORNING PRAYER FOR CHILDREN

Upon awakening in the morning:

I render thanks to thee, everlasting King, who hast mercifully restored my soul within me; thy faithfulness is great.

When washing the hands:

Blessed art thou, Lord our God, King of the universe, who hast sanctified us with thy commandments, and commanded us concerning the washing of the hands.

When putting on the arba kanfoth:

Blessed art thou, Lord our God, King of the universe, who hast sanctified us with thy commandments, and commanded us concerning the precept of tsitsith.

When dressed:

The Torah which Moses handed down to us is the heritage of the community of Jacob. May blessings rest on my head. Hear, my son, your father's instruction, and reject not your mother's teaching. The Torah shall be my trust, and the Almighty my help. God is a faithful King. Hear, O Israel, the Lord is our God, the Lord is One. Blessed be the name of his glorious majesty forever and ever. You who cling to the Lord are all alive today. For thy salvation I hope, O Lord.

My God, guard my tongue from evil, and my lips from speaking falsehood. Open my heart to thy Torah, that my soul may follow thy commands. May the words of my mouth and the meditation of my heart be pleasing before thee, O Lord, my Stronghold and my Redeemer.

תורה תהי אמונתי brings to mind the prayer quoted in the Talmud (Bera. khoth 16b) to the effect that we were favored with making the Torah our occupation: יהי רצון מלפניך שתהא תורתך אומנותו. However, the reading אֱמוּנָתִי (my trust), instead of אֻמְנוּתִי (my occupation), is well-established in the morning prayer for children and should not be changed.

בִּרְכוֹת הַשַּׁחַר

Upon entering the synagogue:

מַה טֹּבוּ אֹהָלֶיךָ יַעֲקֹב, מִשְׁכְּנֹתֶיךָ יִשְׂרָאֵל. וַאֲנִי בְּרֹב חַסְדְּךָ אָבֹא בֵיתֶךָ, אֶשְׁתַּחֲוֶה אֶל הֵיכַל קָדְשְׁךָ בְּיִרְאָתֶךָ. יְיָ, אָהַבְתִּי מְעוֹן בֵּיתֶךָ, וּמְקוֹם מִשְׁכַּן כְּבוֹדֶךָ. וַאֲנִי אֶשְׁתַּחֲוֶה וְאֶכְרָעָה, אֶבְרְכָה לִפְנֵי יְיָ עֹשִׂי. וַאֲנִי תְפִלָּתִי לְךָ, יְיָ, עֵת רָצוֹן; אֱלֹהִים, בְּרָב־חַסְדֶּךָ, עֲנֵנִי בֶּאֱמֶת יִשְׁעֶךָ.

סֵדֶר עֲטִיפַת טַלִּית

Before putting on the *tallith*:

בָּרְכִי נַפְשִׁי אֶת יְיָ; יְיָ אֱלֹהַי, גָּדַלְתָּ מְאֹד, הוֹד וְהָדָר לָבָשְׁתָּ. עֹטֶה אוֹר כַּשַּׂלְמָה, נוֹטֶה שָׁמַיִם כַּיְרִיעָה.

הִנְנִי מִתְעַטֵּף בְּטַלִּית שֶׁל צִיצִת כְּדֵי לְקַיֵּם מִצְוַת בּוֹרְאִי, כַּכָּתוּב בַּתּוֹרָה: וְעָשׂוּ לָהֶם צִיצִת עַל כַּנְפֵי בִגְדֵיהֶם לְדֹרֹתָם. וּכְשֵׁם שֶׁאֲנִי מִתְכַּסֶּה בְּטַלִּית בָּעוֹלָם הַזֶּה, כֵּן תִּזְכֶּה נִשְׁמָתִי לְהִתְלַבֵּשׁ בְּטַלִּית נָאָה לְעוֹלָם הַבָּא בְּגַן עֵדֶן. אָמֵן.

משכנותיך, אהליך are interpreted in the Talmud (Sanhedrin 105b) to refer to synagogues and schools. עת רצון is taken to mean the time of public worship (Berakhoth 8a).

ציצית is a continual reminder of our obligation to keep God's commands. The purple-blue thread (פתיל תכלת) entwined in the *tsitsith* was originally its chief distinction. When, however, it became impossible to procure the special dye required, it was made permissible to use white threads alone. Why blue? "Because this color resembles the sea, the sea resembles the sky . . ." (Menahoth 43b).

Four threads are taken, of which one (the *shammash*) is considerably longer than the rest, for each of the four corners of the *tallith*. The four threads are drawn through a small hole or eyelet and the ends brought together. A double knot is tied close to the margin of the *tallith;* the *shammash* is then

3

PRELIMINARY MORNING SERVICE

Upon entering the synagogue:

How goodly are your tents, O Jacob, your habitations, O Israel! By thy abundant grace I enter thy house; I worship before thy holy shrine with reverence. O Lord, I love thy abode, the place where thy glory dwells. I will worship and bow down; I will bend the knee before the Lord my Maker. I offer my prayer to thee, O Lord, at a time of grace. O God, in thy abundant kindness, answer me with thy saving truth.[1]

PUTTING ON THE TALLITH

Before putting on the tallith:

Bless the Lord, O my soul! Lord my God, thou art very great; thou art robed in glory and majesty. Thou wrappest thyself in light as in a garment; thou spreadest the heavens like a curtain.[2]

I am enwrapping myself in the fringed garment in order to fulfill the command of my Creator, as it is written in the Torah: "They shall make fringes for themselves on the corners of their garments throughout their generations."[3] Even as I cover myself with the tallith in this world, so may my soul deserve to be robed in a beautiful garment in the world to come, in Paradise. Amen.

---

twisted tightly 7 times round the remaining 7 threads, and another double knot is tied; then round 8 times, and a double knot; then round 11 times, and a double knot; and finally round 13 times, and a double knot. 7 and 8=15 equals the numerical value of יה, 11=וה, and 13=אחד, meaning: The Lord is One. Furthermore, the numerical value of the word ציצית is 600, which with the 8 threads and the 5 knots makes a total of 613, the exact number of the positive (248) and negative (365) precepts of the Torah. This explains the talmudic statement that the wearing of the *tsitsith* is of equal merit with the observance of the whole Torah (Nedarim 25a).

[1] *Numbers* 24:5; *Psalms* 5:8; 26:8; 95:6; 69:14. [2] *Psalm* 104:1-2. [3] *Numbers* 15:38.

4

When putting on the *tallith*:

בָּרוּךְ אַתָּה, יְיָ אֱלֹהֵינוּ, מֶלֶךְ הָעוֹלָם, אֲשֶׁר קִדְּשָׁנוּ בְּמִצְוֹתָיו וְצִוָּנוּ לְהִתְעַטֵּף בַּצִּיצִת.

תהלים לו, ח—יא

מַה יָּקָר חַסְדְּךָ, אֱלֹהִים, וּבְנֵי אָדָם בְּצֵל כְּנָפֶיךָ יֶחֱסָיוּן. יִרְוְיֻן מִדֶּשֶׁן בֵּיתֶךָ, וְנַחַל עֲדָנֶיךָ תַשְׁקֵם. כִּי עִמְּךָ מְקוֹר חַיִּים, בְּאוֹרְךָ נִרְאֶה אוֹר. מְשֹׁךְ חַסְדְּךָ לְיֹדְעֶיךָ, וְצִדְקָתְךָ לְיִשְׁרֵי לֵב. יְהִי רָצוֹן מִלְּפָנֶיךָ, יְיָ אֱלֹהֵינוּ וֵאלֹהֵי אֲבוֹתֵינוּ, שֶׁתְּהֵא חֲשׁוּבָה מִצְוַת צִיצִת זוֹ כְּאִלּוּ קִיַּמְתִּיהָ בְּכָל פְּרָטֶיהָ וְדִקְדּוּקֶיהָ וְכַוָּנוֹתֶיהָ וְתַרְיַ"ג מִצְוֹת הַתְּלוּיִים בָּהּ. אָמֵן סֶלָה.

סֵדֶר הֲנָחַת תְּפִלִּין

Meditation before putting on the tefillin

הִנְנִי מְכַוֵּן בַּהֲנָחַת תְּפִלִּין לְקַיֵּם מִצְוַת בּוֹרְאִי שֶׁצִּוָּנוּ לְהָנִיחַ תְּפִלִּין, כַּכָּתוּב בַּתּוֹרָה: וּקְשַׁרְתָּם לְאוֹת עַל יָדֶךָ, וְהָיוּ לְטֹטָפֹת בֵּין עֵינֶיךָ. וְהֵם אַרְבַּע פָּרָשִׁיּוֹת אֵלּוּ: שְׁמַע, וְהָיָה אִם שָׁמֹעַ, קַדֶּשׁ, וְהָיָה כִּי יְבִיאֲךָ, שֶׁיֵּשׁ בָּהֶם יִחוּדוֹ וְאַחְדוּתוֹ יִתְבָּרַךְ שְׁמוֹ בָּעוֹלָם; וְשֶׁנִּזְכֹּר נִסִּים וְנִפְלָאוֹת שֶׁעָשָׂה עִמָּנוּ בְּהוֹצִיאוֹ אוֹתָנוּ

The תפלין, known as של ראש (head-phylactery) and של יד (hand-phylactery), are made of the skins of clean animals. *Shel rosh* consists of four compartments containing four separate strips of parchment on which are written four biblical passages (Exodus 13:1–10, 11–16; Deuteronomy 6:4–9 and 11:13–21). *Shel yad* consists of a single compartment, and contains the same four passages written in four parallel columns on a single piece of parchment. *Shel rosh* has on the outside two *shins* (ש), one with three strokes being to the right of the wearer, and one with four strokes to the left. The *shin* together with the letters formed by the knots of the two straps make up the letters of שדי (Almighty). The seven strokes of the two *shins* equal the number of times the *retsuah* is wound around the arm.

There was a difference of opinion between Rashi and his grandson Rabbi Jacob ben Meir (*Rabbenu Tam*) as to the order in which the four biblical se-

When putting on the tallith:

Blessed art thou, Lord our God, King of the universe, who hast sanctified us with thy commandments, and commanded us to enwrap ourselves in the fringed garment.

Psalm 36:8–11

How precious is thy kindness, O God! The children of men take refuge in the shadow of thy wings. They have their fill of the choice food of thy house, and thou givest them drink of thy stream of delights. For with thee is the fountain of life; by thy light do we see light. Continue thy kindness to those who know thee, and thy righteousness to the upright in heart.

May it be thy will, Lord our God and God of our fathers, that my observance of this precept of tsitsith be considered as if I fulfilled it with all its particulars, details and implications, together with the six hundred and thirteen precepts that are related to it. Amen.

PUTTING ON THE TEFILLIN

Meditation before putting on the tefillin

By putting on the tefillin I intend to fulfill the command of my Creator, who has commanded us to wear tefillin, as it is written in the Torah: You shall bind them as a sign on your hand, and they shall be as frontlets between your eyes.[1] The tefillin contain four sections of the Torah[2] which proclaim the absolute unity of God, blessed be his name, and remind us of the miracles and wonders which he did for us when he brought us out from

---

lections should be arranged and inserted in the compartments of the *tefillin*. We follow the opinion of Rashi. However, some people wear two types of *tefillin*, prepared according to Rashi and according to *Rabbenu Tam*, in order to be certain of performing their duty properly.

The *tefillin* are not worn on Sabbaths and festivals because, like the *tefillin*, Sabbaths and festivals are themselves regarded as signs of the covenant relation between God and Israel.

... הנני מכון is derived from the Siddur of Rabbi Isaiah Horowitz (1555–1630), author of שני לוחות הברית (של"ה). This meditation contains the thought that by wearing the *tefillin* on the head and near the heart we are made conscious of our duty to employ our thoughts and emotions in the service of God.

---

[1] *Deuteronomy 6:8.* [2] *Deuteronomy 6:4–9; 11:13–21; Exodus 13:1–10; 11–16.*

מִמִּצְרַיִם, וַאֲשֶׁר לוֹ הַכֹּחַ וְהַמֶּמְשָׁלָה בָּעֶלְיוֹנִים וּבַתַּחְתּוֹנִים לַעֲשׂוֹת בָּהֶם כִּרְצוֹנוֹ. וְצִוָּנוּ לְהַנִּיחַ עַל הַיָּד לְזִכָּרוֹן זְרוֹעַ הַנְּטוּיָה; וְשֶׁהִיא נֶגֶד הַלֵּב, לְשַׁעְבֵּד בָּזֶה תַּאֲוֺת וּמַחְשְׁבוֹת לִבֵּנוּ לַעֲבוֹדָתוֹ, יִתְבָּרַךְ שְׁמוֹ; וְעַל הָרֹאשׁ נֶגֶד הַמֹּחַ, שֶׁהַנְּשָׁמָה שֶׁבְּמֹחִי עִם שְׁאָר חוּשַׁי וְכֹחוֹתַי כֻּלָּם יִהְיוּ מְשֻׁעְבָּדִים לַעֲבוֹדָתוֹ, יִתְבָּרַךְ שְׁמוֹ. וּמִשֶּׁפַע מִצְוַת תְּפִלִּין יִתְמַשֵּׁךְ עָלַי לִהְיוֹת לִי חַיִּים אֲרֻכִּים וְשֶׁפַע קֹדֶשׁ וּמַחֲשָׁבוֹת קְדוֹשׁוֹת, בְּלִי הַרְהוֹר חֵטְא וְעָוֹן כְּלָל, וְשֶׁלֹּא יְפַתֵּנוּ וְלֹא יִתְגָּרֶה בָּנוּ יֵצֶר הָרָע, וְיַנִּיחֵנוּ לַעֲבוֹד אֶת יְיָ כַּאֲשֶׁר עִם לְבָבֵנוּ. אָמֵן.

When placing the *tefillin* on the left arm:

בָּרוּךְ אַתָּה, יְיָ אֱלֹהֵינוּ, מֶלֶךְ הָעוֹלָם, אֲשֶׁר קִדְּשָׁנוּ בְּמִצְוֺתָיו וְצִוָּנוּ לְהַנִּיחַ תְּפִלִּין.

When placing the *tefillin* on the forehead:

בָּרוּךְ אַתָּה, יְיָ אֱלֹהֵינוּ, מֶלֶךְ הָעוֹלָם, אֲשֶׁר קִדְּשָׁנוּ בְּמִצְוֺתָיו וְצִוָּנוּ עַל מִצְוַת תְּפִלִּין.

בָּרוּךְ שֵׁם כְּבוֹד מַלְכוּתוֹ לְעוֹלָם וָעֶד.

וּמֵחָכְמָתְךָ, אֵל עֶלְיוֹן, תַּאֲצִיל עָלַי, וּמִבִּינָתְךָ תְּבִינֵנִי; וּבְחַסְדְּךָ תַּגְדִּיל עָלַי, וּבִגְבוּרָתְךָ תַּצְמִית אוֹיְבַי וְקָמַי, וְשֶׁמֶן הַטּוֹב תָּרִיק עַל שִׁבְעָה קְנֵי הַמְּנוֹרָה לְהַשְׁפִּיעַ טוּבְךָ לִבְרִיּוֹתֶיךָ. פּוֹתֵחַ אֶת יָדֶךָ, וּמַשְׂבִּיעַ לְכָל חַי רָצוֹן.

When winding the *retsuah* three times round the middle finger:

וְאֵרַשְׂתִּיךְ לִי לְעוֹלָם, וְאֵרַשְׂתִּיךְ לִי בְּצֶדֶק וּבְמִשְׁפָּט וּבְחֶסֶד וּבְרַחֲמִים. וְאֵרַשְׂתִּיךְ לִי בֶּאֱמוּנָה, וְיָדַעַתְּ אֶת יְיָ.

וִיהִי רָצוֹן מִלְּפָנֶיךָ, יְיָ אֱלֹהֵינוּ וֵאלֹהֵי אֲבוֹתֵינוּ, שֶׁתְּהֵא

וּמֵחָכְמָתְךָ is taken from **הֵיכַל הַקֹּדֶשׁ**, a kabbalistic commentary on the *Siddur* by Moses Albas (sixteenth century), who lived in northwest Africa.

Egypt, he who has the power and the dominion over the heavenly and the earthly creatures to deal with them as he pleases. He has commanded us to wear tefillin on the arm in memory of his outstretched arm; opposite the heart, to intimate that we ought to subject our heart's desires and designs to the service of God, blessed be he; and on the head opposite the brain, to intimate that the mind which is in the brain, and all senses and faculties, ought to be subjected to his service, blessed be he. May my observance of the tefillin precept bring me long life, holy inspiration and sacred thoughts, and free me from any sinful reflection whatever. May the evil impulse never tempt us, but leave us to serve the Lord as our heart desires.

When placing the tefillin on the left arm:

Blessed art thou, Lord our God, King of the universe, who hast sanctified us with thy commandments, and commanded us to wear tefillin.

When placing the tefillin on the forehead:

Blessed art thou, Lord our God, King of the universe, who hast sanctified us with thy commandments, and commanded us concerning the precept of tefillin.

Blessed be the name of his glorious majesty forever and ever.

Supreme God, thou wilt imbue me with thy wisdom and thy intelligence; in thy grace thou wilt do great things for me; by thy might thou wilt cut off my foes and my adversaries. Thou wilt pour the good oil into the seven branches of the *Menorah* so as to bestow thy goodness upon thy creatures. Thou openest thy hand, and satisfiest every living thing with favor.[1]

When winding the retsuah three times round the middle finger:

I will betroth you to myself forever; I will betroth you to myself in righteousness and in justice, in kindness and in mercy. I will betroth you to myself in faithfulness; and you shall know the Lord.[2]

May it be thy will, Lord our God and God of our fathers, that

---

קני המנורה symbolically represent the continents of the earth.

[1] *Psalm* 145:16   [2] *Hosea* 2:21-22.

חֲשׁוּבָה מִצְוַת הַנָּחַת תְּפִלִּין זוֹ כְּאִלּוּ קִיַּמְתִּיהָ בְּכָל פְּרָטֶיהָ
וְדִקְדּוּקֶיהָ וְכַוָּנוֹתֶיהָ וְתַרְיַ״ג מִצְוֹת הַתְּלוּיִים בָּהּ. אָמֵן סֶלָה.

שמות יג, א–טז

וַיְדַבֵּר יְיָ אֶל מֹשֶׁה לֵּאמֹר: קַדֶּשׁ־לִי כָל בְּכוֹר, פֶּטֶר כָּל
רֶחֶם בִּבְנֵי יִשְׂרָאֵל, בָּאָדָם וּבַבְּהֵמָה, לִי הוּא. וַיֹּאמֶר מֹשֶׁה אֶל
הָעָם: זָכוֹר אֶת הַיּוֹם הַזֶּה אֲשֶׁר יְצָאתֶם מִמִּצְרַיִם, מִבֵּית
עֲבָדִים, כִּי בְּחֹזֶק יָד הוֹצִיא יְיָ אֶתְכֶם מִזֶּה; וְלֹא יֵאָכֵל חָמֵץ.
הַיּוֹם אַתֶּם יֹצְאִים, בְּחֹדֶשׁ הָאָבִיב. וְהָיָה כִי יְבִיאֲךָ יְיָ אֶל אֶרֶץ
הַכְּנַעֲנִי, וְהַחִתִּי וְהָאֱמֹרִי וְהַחִוִּי וְהַיְבוּסִי, אֲשֶׁר נִשְׁבַּע לַאֲבֹתֶיךָ
לָתֶת לָךְ, אֶרֶץ זָבַת חָלָב וּדְבָשׁ, וְעָבַדְתָּ אֶת הָעֲבֹדָה הַזֹּאת
בַּחֹדֶשׁ הַזֶּה. שִׁבְעַת יָמִים תֹּאכַל מַצֹּת, וּבַיּוֹם הַשְּׁבִיעִי חַג לַיְיָ.
מַצּוֹת יֵאָכֵל אֵת שִׁבְעַת הַיָּמִים, וְלֹא יֵרָאֶה לְךָ חָמֵץ וְלֹא יֵרָאֶה
לְךָ שְׂאֹר בְּכָל גְּבֻלֶךָ. וְהִגַּדְתָּ לְבִנְךָ בַּיּוֹם הַהוּא לֵאמֹר: בַּעֲבוּר
זֶה עָשָׂה יְיָ לִי בְּצֵאתִי מִמִּצְרָיִם. וְהָיָה לְךָ לְאוֹת עַל יָדְךָ,
וּלְזִכָּרוֹן בֵּין עֵינֶיךָ, לְמַעַן תִּהְיֶה תּוֹרַת יְיָ בְּפִיךָ, כִּי בְּיָד חֲזָקָה
הוֹצִאֲךָ יְיָ מִמִּצְרָיִם. וְשָׁמַרְתָּ אֶת הַחֻקָּה הַזֹּאת לְמוֹעֲדָהּ מִיָּמִים
יָמִימָה. וְהָיָה, כִּי יְבִאֲךָ יְיָ אֶל אֶרֶץ הַכְּנַעֲנִי, כַּאֲשֶׁר נִשְׁבַּע לְךָ
וְלַאֲבֹתֶיךָ, וּנְתָנָהּ לָךְ. וְהַעֲבַרְתָּ כָל פֶּטֶר רֶחֶם לַיְיָ; וְכָל פֶּטֶר
שֶׁגֶר בְּהֵמָה אֲשֶׁר יִהְיֶה לְךָ, הַזְּכָרִים, לַיְיָ. וְכָל פֶּטֶר חֲמֹר
תִּפְדֶּה בְשֶׂה, וְאִם לֹא תִפְדֶּה וַעֲרַפְתּוֹ; וְכֹל בְּכוֹר אָדָם בְּבָנֶיךָ
תִּפְדֶּה. וְהָיָה, כִּי יִשְׁאָלְךָ בִנְךָ מָחָר לֵאמֹר מַה זֹּאת, וְאָמַרְתָּ
אֵלָיו: בְּחֹזֶק יָד הוֹצִיאָנוּ יְיָ מִמִּצְרַיִם, מִבֵּית עֲבָדִים. וַיְהִי כִּי
הִקְשָׁה פַרְעֹה לְשַׁלְּחֵנוּ, וַיַּהֲרֹג יְיָ כָּל בְּכוֹר בְּאֶרֶץ מִצְרַיִם,

my observance of this precept of tefillin be considered as if I fulfilled it with all its particulars, details and implications, together with the six hundred and thirteen precepts that are related to it. Amen.

Exodus 13:1–16

The Lord spoke to Moses, saying: "Consecrate all the first-born to me, whatever is first-born in Israel, of man or of beast, for it belongs to me."

Moses said to the people: "Remember this day, in which you came out of Egypt, out of a house of slavery; for by a strong hand the Lord brought you out of this place; no leavened bread shall be eaten. This day you are leaving, in the month of Aviv. And when the Lord will bring you into the land of the Canaanite, the Hittite, the Amorite, the Hivvite, and the Jebusite, which he swore to your fathers he would give you, a land flowing with milk and honey, then you shall perform this service in this month: For seven days you shall eat unleavened bread, and on the seventh day there shall be a festival in honor of the Lord. Unleavened bread shall be eaten throughout the seven days; no leavened bread shall be seen in your possession, nor any leaven, anywhere in your territory. And you shall tell your son on that day, saying: This is on account of what the Lord did for me when I left Egypt. It shall serve you as a sign on your hand, and as frontlets between your eyes, so that the Lord's teaching may be ever in your mouth; for by a strong hand the Lord brought you out of Egypt. You shall observe this ordinance at its proper time from year to year.

"And when the Lord will bring you into the land of the Canaanite, as he swore to you and to your fathers, and will give it to you, you shall make over to the Lord whatever is first-born; all the firstlings of the young animals that you will have, the males, shall be the Lord's. Every firstling ass, however, you shall redeem with a lamb; but if you will not redeem it, then you shall break its neck; and every first-born son of yours you shall redeem. And when your son asks you in time to come: What does this mean? You shall tell him: By a strong hand the Lord brought us out of Egypt, out of a house of slavery; and when Pharaoh made difficulties about letting us go, the Lord slew every first-born in the

מִבְּכוֹר אָדָם וְעַד בְּכוֹר בְּהֵמָה, עַל כֵּן אֲנִי זֹבֵחַ לַיְיָ כָּל פֶּטֶר
רֶחֶם, הַזְּכָרִים, וְכָל בְּכוֹר בָּנַי אֶפְדֶּה. וְהָיָה לְאוֹת עַל יָדְכָה,
וּלְטוֹטָפֹת בֵּין עֵינֶיךָ, כִּי בְּחֹזֶק יָד הוֹצִיאָנוּ יְיָ מִמִּצְרָיִם.

בְּטֶרֶם כָּל יְצִיר נִבְרָא.	אֲדוֹן עוֹלָם אֲשֶׁר מָלַךְ
אֲזַי מֶלֶךְ שְׁמוֹ נִקְרָא.	לְעֵת נַעֲשָׂה בְחֶפְצוֹ כֹּל
לְבַדּוֹ יִמְלוֹךְ נוֹרָא.	וְאַחֲרֵי כִּכְלוֹת הַכֹּל
וְהוּא יִהְיֶה בְּתִפְאָרָה.	וְהוּא הָיָה וְהוּא הֹוֶה
לְהַמְשִׁיל לוֹ לְהַחְבִּירָה.	וְהוּא אֶחָד וְאֵין שֵׁנִי
וְלוֹ הָעֹז וְהַמִּשְׂרָה.	בְּלִי רֵאשִׁית בְּלִי תַכְלִית
וְצוּר חֶבְלִי בְּעֵת צָרָה.	וְהוּא אֵלִי וְחַי גֹּאֲלִי
מְנָת כּוֹסִי בְּיוֹם אֶקְרָא.	וְהוּא נִסִּי וּמָנוֹס לִי
בְּעֵת אִישַׁן וְאָעִירָה.	בְּיָדוֹ אַפְקִיד רוּחִי
יְיָ לִי וְלֹא אִירָא.	וְעִם רוּחִי גְּוִיָּתִי

נִמְצָא וְאֵין עֵת אֶל מְצִיאוּתוֹ.	יִגְדַּל אֱלֹהִים חַי וְיִשְׁתַּבַּח
נֶעְלָם וְגַם אֵין סוֹף לְאַחְדּוּתוֹ.	אֶחָד וְאֵין יָחִיד כְּיִחוּדוֹ
לֹא נַעֲרוֹךְ אֵלָיו קְדֻשָׁתוֹ.	אֵין לוֹ דְּמוּת הַגּוּף וְאֵינוֹ גוּף
רִאשׁוֹן וְאֵין רֵאשִׁית לְרֵאשִׁיתוֹ.	קַדְמוֹן לְכָל דָּבָר אֲשֶׁר נִבְרָא
יוֹרֶה גְדֻלָּתוֹ וּמַלְכוּתוֹ.	הִנּוֹ אֲדוֹן עוֹלָם וְכָל נוֹצָר

אדון עולם treats of God's omnipotence and providence. This noble hymn
has been attributed to various poets, particularly to Solomon ibn Gabirol
who flourished in Spain during the eleventh century. It has been part of the
morning service since the fifteenth century. It is composed of ten lines, each
of which consists of twelve syllables. A single rhyme runs through it.

יגדל is a summary of the thirteen principles of faith formulated by Maimonides in his commentary on the Mishnah (Sanhedrin 10:1). This poem
was composed by Daniel ben Judah of Rome (fourteenth century). One rhyme
runs through all its thirteen lines, each of which consists of sixteen syllables.
The variant reading **וכל נוצר** in the fifth line brings out the full meaning of
Maimonides' fifth principle that God alone must be worshiped. **יורה** is used

land of Egypt, the first-born of both man and beast; that is why
I sacrifice to the Lord every first-born male animal, but I redeem
all my first-born sons. This shall serve as a sign on your hand,
and as frontlets between your eyes; for the Lord brought you out
of Egypt by a strong hand."

ADON OLAM

He is the eternal Lord who reigned
Before any being was created.
At the time when all was made by his will,
He was at once acknowledged as King.
And at the end, when all shall cease to be,
The revered God alone shall still be King.
He was, he is, and he shall be
In glorious eternity.
He is One, and there is no other
To compare to him, to place beside him.
He is without beginning, without end;
Power and dominion belong to him.
He is my God, my living Redeemer,
My stronghold in times of distress.
He is my guide and my refuge,
My share of bliss the day I call.
To him I entrust my spirit
When I sleep and when I wake.
As long as my soul is with my body
The Lord is with me; I am not afraid.

YIGDAL

1. Exalted and praised be the living God!
   He exists; his existence transcends time.
2. He is One—there is no oneness like his;
   He's unknowable—his Oneness is endless.
3. He has no semblance—he is bodiless;
   Beyond comparison is his holiness.
4. He preceded all that was created;
   The First he is though he never began.
5. He is the eternal Lord; every creature
   Must declare his greatness and his kingship.

---

here in the sense of יגיד, יספר (see Job 12:7–8; Psalm 145:6–12). In Erubin 65a,
יורה is taken as the equivalent of יתפלל.

שֶׁפַע נְבוּאָתוֹ נְתָנוֹ אֵל   אַנְשֵׁי סְגֻלָתוֹ וְתִפְאַרְתּוֹ.

לֹא קָם בְּיִשְׂרָאֵל כְּמֹשֶׁה עוֹד   נָבִיא וּמַבִּיט אֶת תְּמוּנָתוֹ.

תּוֹרַת אֱמֶת נָתַן לְעַמּוֹ אֵל   עַל יַד נְבִיאוֹ נֶאֱמַן בֵּיתוֹ.

לֹא יַחֲלִיף הָאֵל וְלֹא יָמִיר   דָּתוֹ לְעוֹלָמִים לְזוּלָתוֹ.

צוֹפֶה וְיוֹדֵעַ סְתָרֵינוּ   מַבִּיט לְסוֹף דָּבָר בְּקַדְמָתוֹ.

גּוֹמֵל לְאִישׁ חֶסֶד כְּמִפְעָלוֹ   נוֹתֵן לְרָשָׁע רָע כְּרִשְׁעָתוֹ.

יִשְׁלַח לְקֵץ יָמִין מְשִׁיחֵנוּ   לִפְדּוֹת מְחַכֵּי קֵץ יְשׁוּעָתוֹ.

מֵתִים יְחַיֶּה אֵל בְּרֹב חַסְדּוֹ   בָּרוּךְ עֲדֵי עַד שֵׁם תְּהִלָּתוֹ.

מסכת ברכות יא, א; ס, ב

בָּרוּךְ אַתָּה, יְיָ אֱלֹהֵינוּ, מֶלֶךְ הָעוֹלָם, אֲשֶׁר קִדְּשָׁנוּ בְּמִצְוֹתָיו וְצִוָּנוּ עַל נְטִילַת יָדָיִם.

בָּרוּךְ אַתָּה, יְיָ אֱלֹהֵינוּ, מֶלֶךְ הָעוֹלָם, אֲשֶׁר יָצַר אֶת הָאָדָם בְּחָכְמָה, וּבָרָא בוֹ נְקָבִים נְקָבִים, חֲלוּלִים חֲלוּלִים. גָּלוּי וְיָדוּעַ לִפְנֵי כִסֵּא כְבוֹדֶךָ, שֶׁאִם יִפָּתֵחַ אֶחָד מֵהֶם אוֹ יִסָּתֵם אֶחָד מֵהֶם אִי אֶפְשָׁר לְהִתְקַיֵּם וְלַעֲמוֹד לְפָנֶיךָ. בָּרוּךְ אַתָּה, יְיָ, רוֹפֵא כָל בָּשָׂר וּמַפְלִיא לַעֲשׂוֹת.

בָּרוּךְ אַתָּה, יְיָ אֱלֹהֵינוּ, מֶלֶךְ הָעוֹלָם, אֲשֶׁר קִדְּשָׁנוּ בְּמִצְוֹתָיו וְצִוָּנוּ לַעֲסוֹק בְּדִבְרֵי תוֹרָה.

וְהַעֲרֶב־נָא, יְיָ אֱלֹהֵינוּ, אֶת דִּבְרֵי תוֹרָתְךָ בְּפִינוּ, וּבְפִי עַמְּךָ בֵּית יִשְׂרָאֵל, וְנִהְיֶה אֲנַחְנוּ וְצֶאֱצָאֵינוּ, וְצֶאֱצָאֵי עַמְּךָ בֵּית יִשְׂרָאֵל, כֻּלָּנוּ יוֹדְעֵי שְׁמֶךָ וְלוֹמְדֵי תוֹרָתֶךָ לִשְׁמָהּ. בָּרוּךְ אַתָּה, יְיָ, הַמְלַמֵּד תּוֹרָה לְעַמּוֹ יִשְׂרָאֵל.

בָּרוּךְ אַתָּה, יְיָ אֱלֹהֵינוּ, מֶלֶךְ הָעוֹלָם, אֲשֶׁר בָּחַר בָּנוּ מִכָּל הָעַמִּים, וְנָתַן לָנוּ אֶת תּוֹרָתוֹ. בָּרוּךְ אַתָּה, יְיָ, נוֹתֵן הַתּוֹרָה.

6. His abundant prophecy he granted
   To the men of his choice and his glory.
7. Never has there arisen in Israel
   A prophet like Moses beholding God's image.
8. The Torah of truth God gave to his people
   Through his prophet, his own faithful servant.
9. God will never amend, nor ever change
   His eternal Law for any other law.
10. He inspects, he knows all our secret thoughts;
    He foresees the end of things at their birth.
11. He rewards the godly man for his deeds;
    He repays the evil man for his evil.
12. At time's end he will send our Messiah
    To save all who wait for his final help.
13. God, in his great mercy, will revive the dead;
    Blessed be his glorious name forever.

Talmud Berakhoth 11a; 60b

Blessed art thou, Lord our God, King of the universe, who hast sanctified us with thy commandments, and commanded us concerning the washing of the hands.

Blessed art thou, Lord our God, King of the universe, who hast formed man in wisdom, and created in him a system of ducts and tubes. It is well known before thy glorious throne that if but one of these be opened, or if one of those be closed, it would be impossible to exist in thy presence. Blessed art thou, O Lord, who healest all creatures and doest wonders.

Blessed art thou, Lord our God, King of the universe, who hast sanctified us with thy commandments, and commanded us to study the Torah.

Lord our God, make the words of thy Torah pleasant in our mouth and in the mouth of thy people, the house of Israel, so that we and our descendants and the descendants of thy people, the house of Israel, may all know thy name and study the Torah for its own sake. Blessed art thou, O Lord, who teachest the Torah to thy people Israel.

Blessed art thou, Lord our God, King of the universe, who hast chosen us from all peoples and given us thy Torah. Blessed art thou, O Lord, Giver of the Torah.

במדבר ו, כד-כו

יְבָרֶכְךָ יְיָ וְיִשְׁמְרֶךָ. יָאֵר יְיָ פָּנָיו אֵלֶיךָ וִיחֻנֶּךָּ. יִשָּׂא יְיָ פָּנָיו אֵלֶיךָ, וְיָשֵׂם לְךָ שָׁלוֹם.

פאה א, משנה א; מסכת שבת קכז, א

אֵלּוּ דְבָרִים שֶׁאֵין לָהֶם שִׁעוּר: הַפֵּאָה, וְהַבִּכּוּרִים, וְהָרֵאָיוֹן, וּגְמִילוּת חֲסָדִים, וְתַלְמוּד תּוֹרָה אֵלּוּ דְבָרִים. שֶׁאָדָם אוֹכֵל פֵּרוֹתֵיהֶם בָּעוֹלָם הַזֶּה וְהַקֶּרֶן קַיֶּמֶת לוֹ לָעוֹלָם הַבָּא, וְאֵלּוּ הֵן: כִּבּוּד אָב וָאֵם, וּגְמִילוּת חֲסָדִים, וְהַשְׁכָּמַת בֵּית הַמִּדְרָשׁ שַׁחֲרִית וְעַרְבִית, וְהַכְנָסַת אוֹרְחִים, וּבִקּוּר חוֹלִים, וְהַכְנָסַת כַּלָּה, וּלְוָיַת הַמֵּת, וְעִיּוּן תְּפִלָּה, וַהֲבָאַת שָׁלוֹם בֵּין אָדָם לַחֲבֵרוֹ; וְתַלְמוּד תּוֹרָה כְּנֶגֶד כֻּלָּם.

מסכת ברכות ס, ב

אֱלֹהַי, נְשָׁמָה שֶׁנָּתַתָּ בִּי טְהוֹרָה הִיא. אַתָּה בְרָאתָהּ, אַתָּה יְצַרְתָּהּ, אַתָּה נְפַחְתָּהּ בִּי, וְאַתָּה מְשַׁמְּרָהּ בְּקִרְבִּי, וְאַתָּה עָתִיד לִטְּלָהּ מִמֶּנִּי וּלְהַחֲזִירָהּ בִּי לֶעָתִיד לָבֹא. כָּל זְמַן שֶׁהַנְּשָׁמָה בְקִרְבִּי מוֹדֶה אֲנִי לְפָנֶיךָ, יְיָ אֱלֹהַי וֵאלֹהֵי אֲבוֹתַי, רִבּוֹן כָּל הַמַּעֲשִׂים, אֲדוֹן כָּל הַנְּשָׁמוֹת. בָּרוּךְ אַתָּה, יְיָ, הַמַּחֲזִיר נְשָׁמוֹת לִפְגָרִים מֵתִים.

בָּרוּךְ אַתָּה, יְיָ אֱלֹהֵינוּ, מֶלֶךְ הָעוֹלָם, אֲשֶׁר נָתַן לַשֶּׂכְוִי בִינָה לְהַבְחִין בֵּין יוֹם וּבֵין לָיְלָה.

בָּרוּךְ אַתָּה, יְיָ אֱלֹהֵינוּ, מֶלֶךְ הָעוֹלָם, שֶׁלֹּא עָשַׂנִי גּוֹי.

פאה part of the crop which the owner was required to leave for the benefit of the poor (Leviticus 23:22). According to tradition, the minimum was one-sixtieth of the harvest (Mishnah Peah 1:2).

בכורים the earliest gathered fruits of the season brought to the Temple.

ראיון The nature and value of the offering which all male Israelites were required to present at the Temple is not defined in Deuteronomy 16:16–17.

גמילות חסדים There is no fixed limit to personal service and charity to all men. *Gemiluth ḥasadim* includes every kind of help.

Numbers 6:24–26

May the Lord bless you and protect you; may the Lord countenance you and be gracious to you; may the Lord favor you and grant you peace.

Mishnah Peah 1:1; *Talmud Shabbath* 127a

These are the things for which no limit is prescribed: the corner of the field, the first-fruits, the pilgrimage offerings, the practice of kindness, and the study of the Torah. These are the things of which a man enjoys the fruits in this world, while the principal remains for him in the hereafter, namely: honoring father and mother, practice of kindness, early attendance at the schoolhouse morning and evening, hospitality to strangers, visiting the sick, dowering the bride, attending the dead to the grave, devotion in prayer, and making peace between fellow men; but the study of the Torah excels them all.

Talmud Berakhoth 60b

My God, the soul which thou hast placed within me is pure. Thou hast created it; thou hast formed it; thou hast breathed it into me. Thou preservest it within me; thou wilt take it from me, and restore it to me in the hereafter. So long as the soul is within me, I offer thanks before thee, Lord my God and God of my fathers, Master of all creatures, Lord of all souls. Blessed art thou, O Lord, who restorest the souls to the dead.

Blessed art thou, Lord our God, King of the universe, who hast given the cock intelligence to distinguish between day and night.

Blessed art thou, Lord our God, King of the universe, who hast not made me a heathen.

תלמוד תורה is one of the duties to which there is no prescribed limit. We are to engage in Torah study at all times. The readings from the Bible and the Talmud which form part of the morning service are meant to enable every Jew to have a daily share in the study of the Torah.

לשכוי בינה is taken from Job 38:36, where שכוי is derived from שכה ("to see"). According to Berakhoth 60b and Rosh Hashanah 26a, שכוי signifies "cock", that is, the bird which foresees the approaching day. The worshiper expresses his appreciation of nature's super-senses and the exact timing of animals, for there are many kinds of "knowingness" in which animals far surpass us by means of their exquisite ability to "feel" things.

בָּרוּךְ אַתָּה, יְיָ אֱלֹהֵינוּ, מֶלֶךְ הָעוֹלָם, שֶׁלֹּא עָשַׂנִי עָבֶד.

Men say:	Women say:

בָּרוּךְ אַתָּה, יְיָ אֱלֹהֵינוּ, מֶלֶךְ   בָּרוּךְ אַתָּה, יְיָ אֱלֹהֵינוּ, מֶלֶךְ
הָעוֹלָם, שֶׁעָשַׂנִי כִּרְצוֹנוֹ.   הָעוֹלָם, שֶׁלֹּא עָשַׂנִי אִשָּׁה.

בָּרוּךְ אַתָּה, יְיָ אֱלֹהֵינוּ, מֶלֶךְ הָעוֹלָם, פּוֹקֵחַ עִוְרִים.

בָּרוּךְ אַתָּה, יְיָ אֱלֹהֵינוּ, מֶלֶךְ הָעוֹלָם, מַלְבִּישׁ עֲרֻמִּים.

בָּרוּךְ אַתָּה, יְיָ אֱלֹהֵינוּ, מֶלֶךְ הָעוֹלָם, מַתִּיר אֲסוּרִים.

בָּרוּךְ אַתָּה, יְיָ אֱלֹהֵינוּ, מֶלֶךְ הָעוֹלָם, זוֹקֵף כְּפוּפִים.

בָּרוּךְ אַתָּה, יְיָ אֱלֹהֵינוּ, מֶלֶךְ הָעוֹלָם, רוֹקַע הָאָרֶץ עַל הַמָּיִם.

בָּרוּךְ אַתָּה, יְיָ אֱלֹהֵינוּ, מֶלֶךְ הָעוֹלָם, שֶׁעָשָׂה לִי כָּל צָרְכִּי.

בָּרוּךְ אַתָּה, יְיָ אֱלֹהֵינוּ, מֶלֶךְ הָעוֹלָם, הַמֵּכִין מִצְעֲדֵי גָבֶר.

בָּרוּךְ אַתָּה, יְיָ אֱלֹהֵינוּ, מֶלֶךְ הָעוֹלָם, אוֹזֵר יִשְׂרָאֵל בִּגְבוּרָה.

בָּרוּךְ אַתָּה, יְיָ אֱלֹהֵינוּ, מֶלֶךְ הָעוֹלָם, עוֹטֵר יִשְׂרָאֵל בְּתִפְאָרָה.

בָּרוּךְ אַתָּה, יְיָ אֱלֹהֵינוּ, מֶלֶךְ הָעוֹלָם, הַנּוֹתֵן לַיָּעֵף כֹּחַ.

בָּרוּךְ אַתָּה, יְיָ אֱלֹהֵינוּ, מֶלֶךְ הָעוֹלָם, הַמַּעֲבִיר שֵׁנָה מֵעֵינַי
וּתְנוּמָה מֵעַפְעַפָּי.

וִיהִי רָצוֹן מִלְּפָנֶיךָ, יְיָ אֱלֹהֵינוּ וֵאלֹהֵי אֲבוֹתֵינוּ, שֶׁתַּרְגִּילֵנוּ
בְּתוֹרָתֶךָ וְדַבְּקֵנוּ בְּמִצְוֹתֶיךָ; וְאַל תְּבִיאֵנוּ לֹא לִידֵי חֵטְא, וְלֹא
לִידֵי עֲבֵרָה וְעָוֹן, וְלֹא לִידֵי נִסָּיוֹן, וְלֹא לִידֵי בִזָּיוֹן; וְאַל תַּשְׁלֵט־
בָּנוּ יֵצֶר הָרָע; וְהַרְחִיקֵנוּ מֵאָדָם רָע וּמֵחָבֵר רָע; וְדַבְּקֵנוּ בְּיֵצֶר

שלא עשני אשה and the following two blessings are taken from Menaḥoth
43b. Men thank God for the privilege of performing many precepts which
are incumbent only on male Israelites.

שעשני כרצונו is mentioned by David Abudarham (fourteenth century) as
a recently introduced blessing to be recited by women.

הנותן ליעף כח is not derived from the Talmud but is found in Maḥzor
Vitry, the liturgical work which was compiled in the eleventh century by
Rabbi Simḥah of Vitry, France, a pupil of Rashi.

Blessed art thou, Lord our God, King of the universe, who hast not made me a slave.

Men say:	*Women say:*
Blessed art thou, Lord our God, King of the universe, who hast not made me a woman.	Blessed art thou, Lord our God, King of the universe, who hast made me according to thy will.

Blessed art thou, Lord our God, King of the universe, who openest the eyes of the blind.

Blessed art thou, Lord our God, King of the universe, who clothest the naked.

Blessed art thou, Lord our God, King of the universe, who settest the captives free.

Blessed art thou, Lord our God, King of the universe, who raisest up those who are bowed down.

Blessed art thou, Lord our God, King of the universe, who spreadest forth the earth above the waters.

Blessed art thou, Lord our God, King of the universe, who hast provided for all my needs.

Blessed art thou, Lord our God, King of the universe, who guidest the steps of man.

Blessed art thou, Lord our God, King of the universe, who girdest Israel with might.

Blessed art thou, Lord our God, King of the universe, who crownest Israel with glory.

Blessed art thou, Lord our God, King of the universe, who givest strength to the weary.

Blessed art thou, Lord our God, King of the universe, who removest sleep from my eyes and slumber from my eyelids.

May it be thy will, Lord our God and God of our fathers, to make us familiar with thy Torah, and to cause us to adhere to thy precepts. Lead us not into sin, transgression, iniquity, temptation, or disgrace; let not the evil impulse have power over us; keep us far from an evil man and a bad companion; make us cling to

---

In the Talmud, the first יהי רצון is phrased in the singular (שתרגילני...ודבקני) while the second יהי רצון is reported in singular and plural (Berakhoth 60b; Shabbath 39b).

הַטּוֹב וּבְמַעֲשִׂים טוֹבִים; וְכֹף אֶת יִצְרֵנוּ לְהִשְׁתַּעְבֶּד־לָךְ.

Reader וּתְנֵנוּ הַיּוֹם וּבְכָל יוֹם לְחֵן וּלְחֶסֶד וּלְרַחֲמִים בְּעֵינֶיךָ וּבְעֵינֵי כָל רוֹאֵינוּ, וְתִגְמְלֵנוּ חֲסָדִים טוֹבִים. בָּרוּךְ אַתָּה, יְיָ, גּוֹמֵל חֲסָדִים טוֹבִים לְעַמּוֹ יִשְׂרָאֵל.

יְהִי רָצוֹן מִלְּפָנֶיךָ, יְיָ אֱלֹהַי וֵאלֹהֵי אֲבוֹתַי, שֶׁתַּצִּילֵנִי הַיּוֹם וּבְכָל יוֹם מֵעַזֵּי פָנִים וּמֵעַזּוּת פָּנִים, מֵאָדָם רָע וּמֵחָבֵר רָע, וּמִשָּׁכֵן רָע וּמִפֶּגַע רָע וּמִשָּׂטָן הַמַּשְׁחִית, מִדִּין קָשֶׁה וּמִבַּעַל דִּין קָשֶׁה, בֵּין שֶׁהוּא בֶן־בְּרִית וּבֵין שֶׁאֵינוֹ בֶן־בְּרִית.

אֱלֹהֵינוּ וֵאלֹהֵי אֲבוֹתֵינוּ, זָכְרֵנוּ בְּזִכָּרוֹן טוֹב לְפָנֶיךָ, וּפָקְדֵנוּ בִּפְקֻדַּת יְשׁוּעָה וְרַחֲמִים מִשְּׁמֵי שְׁמֵי קֶדֶם; וּזְכָר־לָנוּ, יְיָ אֱלֹהֵינוּ, אַהֲבַת הַקַּדְמוֹנִים, אַבְרָהָם יִצְחָק וְיִשְׂרָאֵל עֲבָדֶיךָ, אֶת הַבְּרִית וְאֶת הַחֶסֶד, וְאֶת הַשְּׁבוּעָה שֶׁנִּשְׁבַּעְתָּ לְאַבְרָהָם אָבִינוּ בְּהַר הַמּוֹרִיָּה, וְאֶת הָעֲקֵדָה שֶׁעָקַד אֶת יִצְחָק בְּנוֹ עַל גַּבֵּי הַמִּזְבֵּחַ, כַּכָּתוּב בְּתוֹרָתֶךָ:

בראשית כב, א-יט

וַיְהִי אַחַר הַדְּבָרִים הָאֵלֶּה, וְהָאֱלֹהִים נִסָּה אֶת אַבְרָהָם, וַיֹּאמֶר אֵלָיו: אַבְרָהָם, וַיֹּאמֶר הִנֵּנִי. וַיֹּאמֶר: קַח נָא אֶת בִּנְךָ, אֶת יְחִידְךָ, אֲשֶׁר אָהַבְתָּ, אֶת יִצְחָק, וְלֶךְ לְךָ אֶל אֶרֶץ הַמֹּרִיָּה, וְהַעֲלֵהוּ שָׁם לְעֹלָה עַל אַחַד הֶהָרִים אֲשֶׁר אֹמַר אֵלֶיךָ. וַיַּשְׁכֵּם אַבְרָהָם בַּבֹּקֶר, וַיַּחֲבֹשׁ אֶת חֲמֹרוֹ, וַיִּקַּח אֶת שְׁנֵי נְעָרָיו אִתּוֹ וְאֵת יִצְחָק בְּנוֹ; וַיְבַקַּע עֲצֵי עֹלָה, וַיָּקָם וַיֵּלֶךְ אֶל הַמָּקוֹם אֲשֶׁר אָמַר לוֹ הָאֱלֹהִים. בַּיּוֹם הַשְּׁלִישִׁי, וַיִּשָּׂא אַבְרָהָם אֶת עֵינָיו וַיַּרְא אֶת הַמָּקוֹם מֵרָחֹק. וַיֹּאמֶר אַבְרָהָם אֶל נְעָרָיו: שְׁבוּ לָכֶם פֹּה עִם הַחֲמוֹר, וַאֲנִי וְהַנַּעַר נֵלְכָה עַד כֹּה, וְנִשְׁתַּחֲוֶה וְנָשׁוּבָה

<hr>

נסה את אברהם Abraham's faith was put to the supreme test when he was commanded to sacrifice Isaac. This was the tenth and the greatest of the trials.

the good impulse and to good deeds, and bend our will to submit to thee. Grant us today, and every day, grace, favor and mercy, both in thy sight and in the sight of all men, and bestow loving-kindness on us. Blessed art thou, O Lord, who bestowest loving-kindness on thy people Israel.

May it be thy will, Lord my God and God of my fathers, to deliver me today, and every day, from impudent men and from insolence; from an evil man, a bad companion, and a bad neighbor; from an evil occurrence and from the destructive adversary; from an oppressive lawsuit and from a hard opponent, be he a man of the covenant or not.

Our God and God of our fathers, remember us favorably, and visit us with mercy and salvation from the eternal high heavens. Remember in our favor, Lord our God, the love of our ancestors Abraham, Isaac and Israel thy servants. Remember the covenant, the kindness, and the oath which thou didst swear to our father Abraham on Mount Moriah, and the binding of Isaac his son on the altar, as it is written in thy Torah:

Genesis 22:1–19

And it came to pass after these things that God put Abraham to the test, and said to him: "Abraham"; and he answered: "Here I am." Then he said: "Take your son, your only son, Isaac, whom you love; go to the land of Moriah and offer him there as a burnt-offering on one of the mountains that I will tell you." So Abraham rose early in the morning, saddled his ass, and took with him his two servants and his son Isaac; he cut wood for the burnt-offering and started for the place about which God had told him.

On the third day Abraham looked up and saw the place at a distance. Then Abraham said to his servants: "You stay here with the ass while I and the boy go yonder; we will worship and

---

he had to face, to prove that he was worthy of being the founder of the Jewish people. This narrative portrays also the faith and obedience of Isaac.

משטן המשחית is an allusion to the corrupting influence of Satan, the great adversary of man, who is often identical with the lower passions.

זכרנו בזכרון טוב and רבונו של עולם which immediately follows the biblical account of Abraham's willingness to sacrifice his son are both taken from the *Musaf* service for *Rosh Hashanah*. The *Akedah*, the intended sacrifice of Isaac, is regarded as a symbol of Israel's martyrdom.

אֲלֵיכֶם. וַיִּקַּח אַבְרָהָם אֶת עֲצֵי הָעֹלָה וַיָּשֶׂם עַל יִצְחָק בְּנוֹ,
וַיִּקַּח בְּיָדוֹ אֶת הָאֵשׁ וְאֶת הַמַּאֲכֶלֶת, וַיֵּלְכוּ שְׁנֵיהֶם יַחְדָּו. וַיֹּאמֶר
יִצְחָק אֶל אַבְרָהָם אָבִיו, וַיֹּאמֶר: אָבִי, וַיֹּאמֶר הִנֶּנִּי בְנִי;
וַיֹּאמֶר: הִנֵּה הָאֵשׁ וְהָעֵצִים, וְאַיֵּה הַשֶּׂה לְעֹלָה. וַיֹּאמֶר אַבְרָהָם:
אֱלֹהִים יִרְאֶה לּוֹ הַשֶּׂה לְעֹלָה, בְּנִי; וַיֵּלְכוּ שְׁנֵיהֶם יַחְדָּו. וַיָּבֹאוּ
אֶל הַמָּקוֹם אֲשֶׁר אָמַר לוֹ הָאֱלֹהִים, וַיִּבֶן שָׁם אַבְרָהָם אֶת
הַמִּזְבֵּחַ, וַיַּעֲרֹךְ אֶת הָעֵצִים, וַיַּעֲקֹד אֶת יִצְחָק בְּנוֹ, וַיָּשֶׂם אֹתוֹ
עַל הַמִּזְבֵּחַ מִמַּעַל לָעֵצִים. וַיִּשְׁלַח אַבְרָהָם אֶת יָדוֹ וַיִּקַּח אֶת
הַמַּאֲכֶלֶת לִשְׁחֹט אֶת בְּנוֹ. וַיִּקְרָא אֵלָיו מַלְאַךְ יְיָ מִן הַשָּׁמַיִם,
וַיֹּאמֶר: אַבְרָהָם, אַבְרָהָם, וַיֹּאמֶר הִנֵּנִי. וַיֹּאמֶר: אַל תִּשְׁלַח
יָדְךָ אֶל הַנַּעַר וְאַל תַּעַשׂ לוֹ מְאוּמָה, כִּי עַתָּה יָדַעְתִּי כִּי יְרֵא
אֱלֹהִים אַתָּה, וְלֹא חָשַׂכְתָּ אֶת בִּנְךָ אֶת יְחִידְךָ מִמֶּנִּי. וַיִּשָּׂא
אַבְרָהָם אֶת עֵינָיו וַיַּרְא וְהִנֵּה אַיִל, אַחַר, נֶאֱחַז בַּסְּבַךְ בְּקַרְנָיו;
וַיֵּלֶךְ אַבְרָהָם וַיִּקַּח אֶת הָאַיִל, וַיַּעֲלֵהוּ לְעֹלָה תַּחַת בְּנוֹ. וַיִּקְרָא
אַבְרָהָם שֵׁם הַמָּקוֹם הַהוּא: יְיָ יִרְאֶה, אֲשֶׁר יֵאָמֵר הַיּוֹם: בְּהַר יְיָ
יֵרָאֶה. וַיִּקְרָא מַלְאַךְ יְיָ אֶל אַבְרָהָם שֵׁנִית מִן הַשָּׁמָיִם. וַיֹּאמֶר:
בִּי נִשְׁבַּעְתִּי, נְאֻם יְיָ, כִּי יַעַן אֲשֶׁר עָשִׂיתָ אֶת הַדָּבָר הַזֶּה, וְלֹא
חָשַׂכְתָּ אֶת בִּנְךָ, אֶת יְחִידֶךָ. כִּי בָרֵךְ אֲבָרֶכְךָ, וְהַרְבָּה אַרְבֶּה
אֶת זַרְעֲךָ כְּכוֹכְבֵי הַשָּׁמַיִם, וְכַחוֹל אֲשֶׁר עַל שְׂפַת הַיָּם, וְיִרַשׁ
זַרְעֲךָ אֵת שַׁעַר אֹיְבָיו. וְהִתְבָּרְכוּ בְזַרְעֲךָ כֹּל גּוֹיֵי הָאָרֶץ, עֵקֶב
אֲשֶׁר שָׁמַעְתָּ בְּקֹלִי. וַיָּשָׁב אַבְרָהָם אֶל נְעָרָיו, וַיָּקֻמוּ וַיֵּלְכוּ יַחְדָּו
אֶל בְּאֵר שָׁבַע; וַיֵּשֶׁב אַבְרָהָם בִּבְאֵר שָׁבַע.

רִבּוֹנוֹ שֶׁל עוֹלָם, יְהִי רָצוֹן מִלְּפָנֶיךָ, יְיָ אֱלֹהֵינוּ וֵאלֹהֵי

בהר ה׳ יראה refers to the Temple which was afterwards established on this
mountain (II Chronicles 3:1).

come back to you." So Abraham took the wood for the burnt-offering and laid it on his son Isaac, while he took in his hand the fire and the knife; and the two of them went off together.

Then Isaac spoke to Abraham his father and said: "My father"; and he answered: "Here I am, my son." And he said: "Here are the fire and the wood, but where is the lamb for a burnt-offering?" Abraham answered: "God will provide himself with the lamb for a burnt-offering, my son." So the two of them went on together. They came to the place of which God had told him, and Abraham built the altar there, arranged the wood, bound his son Isaac and laid him on the altar on top of the wood. Then Abraham put out his hand and took the knife to slay his son. But the angel of the Lord called to him from the heavens: "Abraham, Abraham," and he answered: "Here I am." He said: "Do not lay your hand on the boy, and do nothing to him; for I know now that you revere God, seeing that you have not refused me your son, your only son." Then Abraham looked up and saw behind him a ram caught in the thicket by its horns; so Abraham went and took the ram, and offered it as a burnt-offering instead of his son. Abraham called the name of that place Adonai-yireh, as it is said to this day: "The mount where the Lord reveals himself."

The angel of the Lord called to Abraham a second time from the heavens, and said: "By myself I swear," says the Lord, "that since you have done this, since you have not withheld your son, your only son, I will indeed bless you, and will surely make your descendants as numerous as the stars in the sky or as the sands on the seashore; your descendants shall possess the cities of their enemies, and through your descendants shall all the nations of the earth be blessed—because you have obeyed my voice." Abraham then returned to his servants, and they started together for Beersheba, for Abraham dwelt in Beersheba.

Master of the world! May it be thy will, Lord our God and

אֲבוֹתֵינוּ, שֶׁתִּזְכָּר־לָנוּ בְּרִית אֲבוֹתֵינוּ. כְּמוֹ שֶׁכָּבַשׁ אַבְרָהָם
אָבִינוּ אֶת רַחֲמָיו מִבֶּן־יְחִידוֹ, וְרָצָה לִשְׁחֹט אוֹתוֹ כְּדֵי לַעֲשׂוֹת
רְצוֹנֶךָ, כֵּן יִכְבְּשׁוּ רַחֲמֶיךָ אֶת כַּעַסְךָ מֵעָלֵינוּ, וְיָגֹלּוּ רַחֲמֶיךָ
עַל מִדּוֹתֶיךָ, וְתִכָּנֵס אִתָּנוּ לִפְנִים מִשּׁוּרַת דִּינֶךָ, וְתִתְנַהֵג עִמָּנוּ,
יְיָ אֱלֹהֵינוּ, בְּמִדַּת הַחֶסֶד וּבְמִדַּת הָרַחֲמִים. וּבְטוּבְךָ הַגָּדוֹל,
יָשׁוּב חֲרוֹן אַפְּךָ מֵעַמְּךָ וּמֵעִירְךָ וּמֵאַרְצְךָ וּמִנַּחֲלָתֶךָ. וְקַיֶּם־
לָנוּ, יְיָ אֱלֹהֵינוּ, אֶת הַדָּבָר שֶׁהִבְטַחְתָּנוּ עַל יְדֵי מֹשֶׁה עַבְדֶּךָ,
כָּאָמוּר: וְזָכַרְתִּי אֶת בְּרִיתִי יַעֲקוֹב, וְאַף אֶת בְּרִיתִי יִצְחָק, וְאַף
אֶת בְּרִיתִי אַבְרָהָם אֶזְכֹּר, וְהָאָרֶץ אֶזְכֹּר.

לְעוֹלָם יְהֵא אָדָם יְרֵא שָׁמַיִם בַּסֵּתֶר וּבַגָּלוּי, וּמוֹדֶה עַל
הָאֱמֶת, וְדוֹבֵר אֱמֶת בִּלְבָבוֹ, וְיַשְׁכֵּם וְיֹאמַר:

רִבּוֹן כָּל הָעוֹלָמִים, לֹא עַל צִדְקוֹתֵינוּ אֲנַחְנוּ מַפִּילִים
תַּחֲנוּנֵינוּ לְפָנֶיךָ, כִּי עַל רַחֲמֶיךָ הָרַבִּים. מָה אֲנַחְנוּ, מֶה חַיֵּינוּ,
מֶה חַסְדֵּנוּ, מַה צִּדְקֵנוּ, מַה יְּשׁוּעָתֵנוּ, מַה כֹּחֵנוּ, מַה גְּבוּרָתֵנוּ.
מַה נֹּאמַר לְפָנֶיךָ, יְיָ אֱלֹהֵינוּ וֵאלֹהֵי אֲבוֹתֵינוּ, הֲלֹא כָּל הַגִּבּוֹרִים
כְּאַיִן לְפָנֶיךָ, וְאַנְשֵׁי הַשֵּׁם כְּלֹא הָיוּ, וַחֲכָמִים כִּבְלִי מַדָּע,
וּנְבוֹנִים כִּבְלִי הַשְׂכֵּל, כִּי רֹב מַעֲשֵׂיהֶם תֹּהוּ, וִימֵי חַיֵּיהֶם הֶבֶל
לְפָנֶיךָ; וּמוֹתַר הָאָדָם מִן הַבְּהֵמָה אָיִן, כִּי הַכֹּל הָבֶל.

אֲבָל אֲנַחְנוּ עַמְּךָ בְּנֵי בְרִיתֶךָ, בְּנֵי אַבְרָהָם אֹהַבְךָ שֶׁנִּשְׁבַּעְתָּ
לוֹ בְּהַר הַמּוֹרִיָּה, זֶרַע יִצְחָק יְחִידוֹ שֶׁנֶּעֱקַד עַל גַּב הַמִּזְבֵּחַ,
עֲדַת יַעֲקֹב בִּנְךָ בְּכוֹרֶךָ, שֶׁמֵּאַהֲבָתְךָ שֶׁאָהַבְתָּ אוֹתוֹ, וּמִשִּׂמְחָתְךָ
שֶׁשָּׂמַחְתָּ בּוֹ, קָרָאתָ אֶת שְׁמוֹ יִשְׂרָאֵל וִישֻׁרוּן.

לְעוֹלָם יְהֵא and onwards forms an impressive setting for the *Shema*, the
acknowledgment of the unity of God. During the reign of Yezdejerd II (fifth
century) it was made unlawful for the Babylonian Jews to recite the *Shema*
as being a challenge to the Zoroastrian religion. Special government officials

God of our fathers, to remember in our favor the covenant of our fathers. Even as Abraham our father held back his compassion from his only son and desired to slay him in order to do thy will, so may thy mercy hold back thy anger from us; let thy compassion prevail over thy acts of retaliation. Be lenient with us, Lord our God, and deal with us kindly and mercifully. In thy great goodness, may thy fierce wrath turn away from thy people, thy city, thy land, and thy heritage. Fulfill, Lord our God, what thou hast promised us through Moses thy servant, as it is said: "I will remember my covenant with Jacob; also my covenant with Isaac and my covenant with Abraham will I remember; and I will remember the land."[1]

Man should ever be God-fearing in private as well as in public. He should acknowledge the truth, and speak the truth in his heart. Let him rise early and say:

Master of all worlds! It is not on account of our own righteousness that we offer our supplications before thee, but on account of thy great compassion. What are we? What is our life? What is our goodness? What our righteousness? What our helpfulness? What our strength? What our might? What can we say in thy presence, Lord our God and God of our fathers? Indeed, all the heroes are as nothing before thee, the men of renown as though they never existed, the wise as if they were without knowledge, the intelligent as though they lacked understanding; for most of their doings are worthless, and the days of their life are vain in thy sight; man is not far above beast, for all is vanity.

However, we are thy people, thy people of the covenant, the children of Abraham thy friend, to whom thou didst make a promise on Mount Moriah; we are the descendants of his only son Isaac, who was bound on the altar; we are the community of Jacob thy first-born, whom thou didst name Israel and Jeshurun because of thy love for him and thy delight in him.

---

were posted in the synagogues to watch the services. The rabbis of the time impressed upon the people the duty of reciting at least the first verse of *Shema* privately, in their homes, before proceeding to the synagogue for the morning service. לעולם יהא is an exhortation to the effect that Judaism must be practised in secrecy (בסתר) during religious persecution. The additional word ובגלוי is not found in early texts.

רבון כל העולמים is mentioned in Yoma 87b as a *Yom Kippur* prayer.

[1] *Leviticus* 26:42.

לְפִיכָךְ אֲנַחְנוּ חַיָּבִים לְהוֹדוֹת לְךָ וּלְשַׁבֵּחֲךָ וּלְפָאֶרְךָ,
וּלְבָרֵךְ וּלְקַדֵּשׁ וְלָתֵת שֶׁבַח וְהוֹדָיָה לִשְׁמֶךָ. אַשְׁרֵינוּ, מַה טּוֹב
חֶלְקֵנוּ וּמַה נָּעִים גּוֹרָלֵנוּ וּמַה יָּפָה יְרֻשָּׁתֵנוּ. Reader אַשְׁרֵינוּ,
שֶׁאֲנַחְנוּ מַשְׁכִּימִים וּמַעֲרִיבִים, עֶרֶב וָבֹקֶר, וְאוֹמְרִים פַּעֲמַיִם
בְּכָל יוֹם:

שְׁמַע, יִשְׂרָאֵל, יְיָ אֱלֹהֵינוּ, יְיָ אֶחָד.

בָּרוּךְ שֵׁם כְּבוֹד מַלְכוּתוֹ לְעוֹלָם וָעֶד.

אַתָּה הוּא עַד שֶׁלֹּא נִבְרָא הָעוֹלָם, אַתָּה הוּא מִשֶּׁנִּבְרָא
הָעוֹלָם, אַתָּה הוּא בָּעוֹלָם הַזֶּה וְאַתָּה הוּא לָעוֹלָם הַבָּא. קַדֵּשׁ
אֶת שִׁמְךָ עַל מַקְדִּישֵׁי שְׁמֶךָ, וְקַדֵּשׁ אֶת שִׁמְךָ בְּעוֹלָמֶךָ,
וּבִישׁוּעָתְךָ תָּרוּם וְתַגְבִּיהַּ קַרְנֵנוּ. בָּרוּךְ אַתָּה, יְיָ, מְקַדֵּשׁ Reader
אֶת שִׁמְךָ בָּרַבִּים.

אַתָּה הוּא, יְיָ אֱלֹהֵינוּ, בַּשָּׁמַיִם וּבָאָרֶץ וּבִשְׁמֵי הַשָּׁמַיִם
הָעֶלְיוֹנִים. אֱמֶת, אַתָּה הוּא רִאשׁוֹן וְאַתָּה הוּא אַחֲרוֹן,
וּמִבַּלְעָדֶיךָ אֵין אֱלֹהִים. קַבֵּץ קֹוֶיךָ מֵאַרְבַּע כַּנְפוֹת הָאָרֶץ;
יַכִּירוּ וְיֵדְעוּ כָּל בָּאֵי עוֹלָם כִּי אַתָּה הוּא הָאֱלֹהִים לְבַדְּךָ לְכֹל
מַמְלְכוֹת הָאָרֶץ. אַתָּה עָשִׂיתָ אֶת הַשָּׁמַיִם וְאֶת הָאָרֶץ, אֶת
הַיָּם, וְאֶת כָּל אֲשֶׁר בָּם, וּמִי בְּכָל מַעֲשֵׂה יָדֶיךָ, בָּעֶלְיוֹנִים אוֹ
בַתַּחְתּוֹנִים, שֶׁיֹּאמַר לְךָ מַה תַּעֲשֶׂה. אָבִינוּ שֶׁבַּשָּׁמַיִם, עֲשֵׂה
עִמָּנוּ חֶסֶד בַּעֲבוּר שִׁמְךָ הַגָּדוֹל שֶׁנִּקְרָא עָלֵינוּ, וְקַיֶּם-לָנוּ, יְיָ
אֱלֹהֵינוּ, מַה שֶּׁכָּתוּב: בָּעֵת הַהִיא אָבִיא אֶתְכֶם, וּבָעֵת קַבְּצִי
אֶתְכֶם, כִּי אֶתֵּן אֶתְכֶם לְשֵׁם וְלִתְהִלָּה בְּכֹל עַמֵּי הָאָרֶץ, בְּשׁוּבִי
אֶת שְׁבוּתֵיכֶם לְעֵינֵיכֶם, אָמַר יְיָ.

קַדֵּשׁ אֶת שִׁמְךָ–בָּרַבִּים God manifests his saving power to the entire world by delivering those who suffer martyrdom for his sake (Ezekiel 36:23; 39:7).

Therefore, it is our duty to give thanks to thee, to praise and glorify thee, to bless and hallow thy name, and to offer many thanksgivings to thee. Happy are we! How good is our destiny, how pleasant our lot, how beautiful our heritage! Happy are we who, early and late, morning and evening, twice every day, proclaim:

Hear, O Israel, the Lord is our God, the Lord is One.

Blessed be the name of his glorious majesty forever and ever.

Thou wast the same before the world was created; thou hast been the same since the world has been created; thou art the same in this world, and thou wilt be the same in the world to come. Reveal thy holiness to those who sanctify thy name; manifest thy holiness throughout thy world. May our strength rise and be exalted through thy deliverance. Blessed art thou, O Lord, who sanctifiest thy name in the presence of all men.

Thou, Lord our God, art in heaven and on earth and in the highest heavens. Truly, thou art the first and thou art the last; besides thee there is no God. O gather those who yearn for thee from the four corners of the earth. Let all mankind realize and know that thou alone art God over all the kingdoms of the earth. Thou hast made the heavens, the earth, the sea, and all that is in them. Who is there among all the works of thy hands, among the heavenly or the earthly creatures, that can say to thee, "What doest thou?" Our Father who art in heaven, deal kindly with us for the sake of thy great name by which we are called, and fulfill for us, Lord our God, that which is written: "At that time I will bring you home; at that time I will gather you; indeed, I will grant you fame and praise among all the peoples of the earth, when I bring back your captivity before your own eyes, says the Lord."[1]

---

[1] *Zephaniah* 3:20.

שמות ל, יז–כא

וַיְדַבֵּר יְיָ אֶל מֹשֶׁה לֵּאמֹר: וְעָשִׂיתָ כִּיּוֹר נְחֹשֶׁת, וְכַנּוֹ נְחֹשֶׁת,
לְרָחְצָה. וְנָתַתָּ אֹתוֹ בֵּין אֹהֶל מוֹעֵד וּבֵין הַמִּזְבֵּחַ, וְנָתַתָּ שָׁמָּה
מָיִם. וְרָחֲצוּ אַהֲרֹן וּבָנָיו מִמֶּנּוּ אֶת יְדֵיהֶם וְאֶת רַגְלֵיהֶם. בְּבֹאָם
אֶל אֹהֶל מוֹעֵד יִרְחֲצוּ מַיִם וְלֹא יָמֻתוּ; אוֹ בְגִשְׁתָּם אֶל הַמִּזְבֵּחַ
לְשָׁרֵת, לְהַקְטִיר אִשֶּׁה לַיְיָ. וְרָחֲצוּ יְדֵיהֶם וְרַגְלֵיהֶם וְלֹא יָמֻתוּ;
וְהָיְתָה לָהֶם חָק־עוֹלָם, לוֹ וּלְזַרְעוֹ לְדֹרֹתָם.

יְהִי רָצוֹן מִלְּפָנֶיךָ, יְיָ אֱלֹהֵינוּ וֵאלֹהֵי אֲבוֹתֵינוּ, שֶׁתְּרַחֵם
עָלֵינוּ וְתִמְחָל־לָנוּ עַל כָּל חַטֹּאתֵינוּ, וּתְכַפֶּר־לָנוּ עַל כָּל
עֲוֹנוֹתֵינוּ, וְתִסְלַח לְכָל פְּשָׁעֵינוּ, וְתִבְנֶה בֵּית הַמִּקְדָּשׁ בִּמְהֵרָה
בְיָמֵינוּ, וְנַקְרִיב לְפָנֶיךָ קָרְבַּן הַתָּמִיד שֶׁיְּכַפֵּר בַּעֲדֵנוּ, כְּמוֹ
שֶׁכָּתַבְתָּ עָלֵינוּ בְּתוֹרָתֶךָ עַל יְדֵי מֹשֶׁה עַבְדֶּךָ, מִפִּי כְבוֹדֶךָ,
כָּאָמוּר:

במדבר כח, א–ח

וַיְדַבֵּר יְיָ אֶל מֹשֶׁה לֵּאמֹר: צַו אֶת בְּנֵי יִשְׂרָאֵל וְאָמַרְתָּ
אֲלֵהֶם: אֶת קָרְבָּנִי לַחְמִי לְאִשַּׁי, רֵיחַ נִיחֹחִי, תִּשְׁמְרוּ לְהַקְרִיב
לִי בְּמוֹעֲדוֹ. וְאָמַרְתָּ לָהֶם: זֶה הָאִשֶּׁה אֲשֶׁר תַּקְרִיבוּ לַיְיָ:
כְּבָשִׂים בְּנֵי שָׁנָה תְמִימִם, שְׁנַיִם לַיּוֹם, עֹלָה תָמִיד. אֶת הַכֶּבֶשׂ
אֶחָד תַּעֲשֶׂה בַבֹּקֶר, וְאֵת הַכֶּבֶשׂ הַשֵּׁנִי תַּעֲשֶׂה בֵּין הָעַרְבָּיִם.
וַעֲשִׂירִית הָאֵיפָה סֹלֶת לְמִנְחָה, בְּלוּלָה בְּשֶׁמֶן כָּתִית רְבִיעִת
הַהִין. עֹלַת תָּמִיד, הָעֲשֻׂיָה בְּהַר סִינַי, לְרֵיחַ נִיחֹחַ, אִשֶּׁה לַיְיָ.
וְנִסְכּוֹ רְבִיעִת הַהִין לַכֶּבֶשׂ הָאֶחָד; בַּקֹּדֶשׁ הַסֵּךְ נֶסֶךְ שֵׁכָר לַיְיָ.

וידבר ... ועשית כיור According to the Talmud, God said: "Whenever they
recite the order of sacrifices, I will deem it as if they offered them before me
and I will forgive them all their sins" (Ta'anith 27b). The sacrificial system
symbolized self-surrender and devotion to the will of God. The peace-offering
with its communion-feast showed the idea of fellowship. It served to keep
alive the sense of dependence on God for the natural blessings of life, while

Exodus 30:17-21

The Lord spoke to Moses, saying: You shall make a bronze laver with a bronze base for washing, and place it between the tent of meeting and the altar, and put water in it, so that Aaron and his sons may wash their hands and feet in it. Whenever they enter the tent of meeting they must wash themselves with water, that they die not; or whenever they approach the altar to minister by burning a sacrifice to the Lord. They must wash their hands and feet, that they die not; this shall be a perpetual statute for them, for him and his descendants, throughout their generations.

May it be thy will, Lord our God and God of our fathers, to have mercy on us and pardon all our sins, iniquities and transgressions; and rebuild the Temple speedily in our days, that we may offer before thee the daily burnt-offering to atone for us, as thou hast written in thy Torah through Moses thy servant, as it is said:

Numbers 28:1-8

The Lord spoke to Moses, saying: Command the children of Israel, and say to them: My food-offering, consumed by fire, a sweet savor to me, you shall be careful to offer me at its proper time. Say also to them: This is the fire-offering which you shall bring to the Lord: two yearling lambs without blemish, every day, as a daily burnt-offering. The one lamb you shall offer in the morning, and the other lamb towards evening, along with a tenth of an *ephah* of fine flour as a meal-offering, mixed with a fourth of a *hin* of oil from crushed olives. This is a daily burnt-offering, as instituted at Mount Sinai, for a sweet savor, a sacrifice to the Lord. Its drink-offering shall be the fourth part of a *hin* for the one lamb; in the holy place shall you pour out a libation of

---

it had the social value of promoting the solidarity of the nation. The *Tamid*, or daily offering, symbolized Israel's pledge of unbroken service to God. The fragrant smoke of incense rising towards heaven was a natural symbol of prayer ascending to God. From Psalm 141:2 ("Let my prayer rise like incense before thee") it appears that the incense-offering symbolized prayer.

An *ephah* (a little over a bushel) was equivalent to three *seahs*, and a *seah* was equivalent to six *kabs*. A *hin* was equivalent to nearly two gallons. A *mina*, or *maneh*, was equal to 341 grams.

וְאֵת הַכֶּבֶשׂ הַשֵּׁנִי תַּעֲשֶׂה בֵּין הָעַרְבָּיִם; כְּמִנְחַת הַבֹּקֶר וּכְנִסְכּוֹ תַּעֲשֶׂה, אִשֵּׁה רֵיחַ נִיחֹחַ לַיָי.

ויקרא א, יא

וְשָׁחַט אֹתוֹ עַל יֶרֶךְ הַמִּזְבֵּחַ צָפֹנָה לִפְנֵי יְיָ; וְזָרְקוּ בְּנֵי אַהֲרֹן הַכֹּהֲנִים אֶת דָּמוֹ עַל הַמִּזְבֵּחַ סָבִיב.

יְהִי רָצוֹן מִלְפָנֶיךָ, יְיָ אֱלֹהֵינוּ וֵאלֹהֵי אֲבוֹתֵינוּ, שֶׁתְּהֵא אֲמִירָה זוֹ חֲשׁוּבָה וּמְקֻבֶּלֶת וּמְרֻצָה לְפָנֶיךָ, כְּאִלּוּ הִקְרַבְנוּ קָרְבַּן הַתָּמִיד בְּמוֹעֲדוֹ וּבִמְקוֹמוֹ וּכְהִלְכָתוֹ.

אַתָּה הוּא יְיָ אֱלֹהֵינוּ שֶׁהִקְטִירוּ אֲבוֹתֵינוּ לְפָנֶיךָ אֶת קְטֹרֶת הַסַּמִּים בִּזְמַן שֶׁבֵּית הַמִּקְדָּשׁ הָיָה קַיָּם, כַּאֲשֶׁר צִוִּיתָ אוֹתָם עַל יְדֵי מֹשֶׁה נְבִיאֶךָ, כַּכָּתוּב בְּתוֹרָתֶךָ:

שמות ל, לד–לו; ל ז–ח

וַיֹּאמֶר יְיָ אֶל מֹשֶׁה: קַח לְךָ סַמִּים, נָטָף וּשְׁחֵלֶת וְחֶלְבְּנָה, סַמִּים וּלְבֹנָה זַכָּה; בַּד בְּבַד יִהְיֶה. וְעָשִׂיתָ אֹתָהּ קְטֹרֶת, רֹקַח מַעֲשֵׂה רוֹקֵחַ, מְמֻלָּח, טָהוֹר קֹדֶשׁ. וְשָׁחַקְתָּ מִמֶּנָּה הָדֵק, וְנָתַתָּה מִמֶּנָּה לִפְנֵי הָעֵדֻת בְּאֹהֶל מוֹעֵד אֲשֶׁר אִוָּעֵד לְךָ שָׁמָּה; קֹדֶשׁ קָדָשִׁים תִּהְיֶה לָכֶם. וְנֶאֱמַר: וְהִקְטִיר עָלָיו אַהֲרֹן קְטֹרֶת סַמִּים בַּבֹּקֶר בַּבֹּקֶר, בְּהֵיטִיבוֹ אֶת הַנֵּרֹת יַקְטִירֶנָּה. וּבְהַעֲלֹת אַהֲרֹן אֶת הַנֵּרֹת בֵּין הָעַרְבַּיִם יַקְטִירֶנָּה; קְטֹרֶת תָּמִיד לִפְנֵי יְיָ לְדֹרֹתֵיכֶם.

תלמוד בבלי, כריתות ו, א; תלמוד ירושלמי, יומא ד, ה

תָּנוּ רַבָּנָן, פִּטּוּם הַקְּטֹרֶת כֵּיצַד. שְׁלֹשׁ מֵאוֹת וְשִׁשִּׁים וּשְׁמוֹנָה מָנִים הָיוּ בָהּ: שְׁלֹשׁ מֵאוֹת וְשִׁשִּׁים וַחֲמִשָּׁה כְּמִנְיַן יְמוֹת הַחַמָּה, מָנֶה לְכָל יוֹם, פְּרַס בְּשַׁחֲרִית וּפְרַס בֵּין הָעַרְבַּיִם, וּשְׁלֹשָׁה מָנִים יְתֵרִים שֶׁמֵּהֶם מַכְנִיס כֹּהֵן גָּדוֹל מְלֹא חָפְנָיו בְּיוֹם הַכִּפּוּרִים, וּמַחֲזִירָם לְמַכְתֶּשֶׁת בְּעֶרֶב יוֹם הַכִּפּוּרִים, וְשׁוֹחֲקָן

strong drink unto the Lord. The other lamb you shall offer towards evening, with the same meal-offering and the same libation as in the morning, to be a burnt-offering of sweet savor to the Lord.

Leviticus 1:11

He shall slaughter it on the north side of the altar before the Lord; and Aaron's sons, the priests, shall sprinkle its blood all around the altar.

May it be thy will, Lord our God and God of our fathers, that this recital be favorably regarded and accepted by thee as if we offered the daily offering at its proper time, its right place, and according to rule.

Thou art the Lord our God before whom our forefathers burned the incense of fragrant spices when the Temple was in existence, as thou didst command them through Moses thy prophet, as it is written in thy Torah:

Exodus 30:34–36; 30:7–8

The Lord said to Moses: "Take fragrant spices, stacte, onycha, and galbanum, aromatics along with pure frankincense; of each shall there be a like weight. And you shall make of it incense, a compound after the art of the apothecary, seasoned with salt, pure and holy. You shall pulverize some of it very fine, and place some of it in front of the ark in the tent of meeting, where I will meet with you; it shall be to you most holy." It is also said: "Aaron shall burn the incense of fragrant spices on the altar every morning; when he trims the lamps, he shall burn it. And when Aaron lights the lamps toward evening, he shall again burn it; this is a regular incense-offering before the Lord throughout your generations."

Babylonian Talmud, Kerithoth 6a; *Palestinian Talmud, Yoma* 4:5

The Rabbis have taught: How was the compounding of the incense performed? The [annual amount of] incense weighed three hundred and sixty-eight minas: three hundred and sixty-five corresponding to the number of the days of the solar year, one mina for each day—half a mina of incense being offered in the morning and half in the afternoon—and of the surplus three minas the high priest took two handfuls [to the Holy of Holies] on the Day of Atonement. These were ground again in a mortar on the eve

יָפֶה יָפֶה כְּדֵי שֶׁתְּהֵא דַקָּה מִן הַדַּקָּה. וְאַחַד עָשָׂר סַמָּנִים הָיוּ
בָּהּ, וְאֵלּוּ הֵן: הַצֳּרִי וְהַצִּפֹּרֶן, הַחֶלְבְּנָה, וְהַלְּבוֹנָה, מִשְׁקַל
שִׁבְעִים שִׁבְעִים מָנֶה; מוֹר וּקְצִיעָה, שִׁבֹּלֶת נֵרְדְּ, וְכַרְכֹּם,
מִשְׁקַל שִׁשָּׁה עָשָׂר שִׁשָּׁה עָשָׂר מָנֶה; הַקֹּשְׁטְ שְׁנֵים עָשָׂר, וְקִלּוּפָה
שְׁלֹשָׁה, וְקִנָּמוֹן תִּשְׁעָה. בֹּרִית כַּרְשִׁינָה תִּשְׁעָה קַבִּין; יֵין
קַפְרִיסִין סְאִין תְּלָתָא וְקַבִּין תְּלָתָא; וְאִם אֵין לוֹ יֵין קַפְרִיסִין,
מֵבִיא חֲמַר חִוַּרְיָן עַתִּיק; מֶלַח סְדוֹמִית רֹבַע הַקָּב; מַעֲלֶה
עָשָׁן כָּל שֶׁהוּא. רַבִּי נָתָן אוֹמֵר: אַף כִּפַּת הַיַּרְדֵּן כָּל שֶׁהוּא.
וְאִם נָתַן בָּהּ דְּבַשׁ, פְּסָלָהּ; וְאִם חִסַּר אַחַת מִכָּל סַמָּנֶיהָ, חַיָּב
מִיתָה.

רַבָּן שִׁמְעוֹן בֶּן גַּמְלִיאֵל אוֹמֵר: הַצֳּרִי אֵינוֹ אֶלָּא שְׂרָף הַנּוֹטֵף
מֵעֲצֵי הַקְּטָף. בֹּרִית כַּרְשִׁינָה לָמָה הִיא בָאָה, כְּדֵי לְיַפּוֹת בָּהּ
אֶת הַצִּפֹּרֶן, כְּדֵי שֶׁתְּהֵא נָאָה. יֵין קַפְרִיסִין לָמָה הוּא בָא, כְּדֵי
לִשְׁרוֹת בּוֹ אֶת הַצִּפֹּרֶן, כְּדֵי שֶׁתְּהֵא עַזָּה. וַהֲלֹא מֵי רַגְלַיִם יָפִין
לָהּ, אֶלָּא שֶׁאֵין מַכְנִיסִין מֵי רַגְלַיִם בָּעֲזָרָה מִפְּנֵי הַכָּבוֹד.

תַּנְיָא, רַבִּי נָתָן אוֹמֵר: כְּשֶׁהוּא שׁוֹחֵק, אוֹמֵר הָדֵק הֵיטֵב,
הֵיטֵב הָדֵק, מִפְּנֵי שֶׁהַקּוֹל יָפֶה לַבְּשָׂמִים. פִּטְּמָהּ לַחֲצָאִין,
כְּשֵׁרָה; לִשְׁלִישׁ וְלִרְבִיעַ, לֹא שָׁמָעְנוּ. אָמַר רַבִּי יְהוּדָה: זֶה
הַכְּלָל: אִם כְּמִדָּתָהּ, כְּשֵׁרָה לַחֲצָאִין; וְאִם חִסַּר אַחַת מִכָּל
סַמָּנֶיהָ, חַיָּב מִיתָה.

תַּנְיָא, בַּר קַפָּרָא אוֹמֵר: אַחַת לְשִׁשִּׁים אוֹ לְשִׁבְעִים שָׁנָה
הָיְתָה בָאָה שֶׁל שִׁירַיִם לַחֲצָאִין. וְעוֹד תָּנֵי בַּר קַפָּרָא: אִלּוּ
הָיָה נוֹתֵן בָּהּ קֹרְטוֹב שֶׁל דְּבַשׁ, אֵין אָדָם יָכוֹל לַעֲמוֹד מִפְּנֵי

of the Day of Atonement so as to make the incense extremely thin.

The incense was composed of the following eleven kinds of spices: balm, onycha, galbanum, and frankincense, seventy minas' weight of each; myrrh, cassia, spikenard, and saffron, sixteen minas' weight of each; twelve minas of costus; three minas of an aromatic bark; and nine minas of cinnamon. [Added to the spices were] nine *kabs* of Karsina lye, three *seahs* and three *kabs* of Cyprus wine—if Cyprus wine could not be obtained, strong white wine might be substituted for it—a fourth of a *kab* of Sodom salt, and a minute quantity of *ma'aleh ashan* [a smoke-producing ingredient]. Rabbi Nathan says: A minute quantity of Jordan amber was also required. If one added honey to the mixture, he rendered the incense unfit for sacred use; and if he left out any of its ingredients, he was subject to the penalty of death.

Rabbi Simeon ben Gamaliel says: The balm required for the incense is a resin exuding from the balsam trees. Why was Karsina lye used? To refine the onycha. Why was Cyprus wine employed? To steep the onycha in it so as to make it more pungent. Though *mei raglayim* might have been good for that purpose, it was not decent to bring it into the Temple.

It has been taught: Rabbi Nathan says: While the priest was grinding the incense, his superintendent would say: "Grind it very thin, grind it very thin," because the [rhythmic] sound is good for the compounding of the spices. If the incense was compounded in two instalments, it is fit for use; but we have not heard that it is permissible to prepare it in portions of one-third or one-fourth [of the total required annually]. Rabbi Judah says: The general rule is that if it was well-proportioned, the incense was fit for use even though it was prepared in two instalments; if, however, one left out any of its ingredients he would be subject to the penalty of death.

It has been taught: Bar Kappara says: Once in sixty or seventy years a total of half the required amount came from the accumulated surpluses [the extra three minas of which the high priest took two handfuls on the Day of Atonement]. Bar Kappara moreover has taught: Had one mixed with the incense the smallest amount of honey, nobody could have resisted the scent. Then

רֵיחָהּ; וְלָמָּה אֵין מְעָרְבִין בָּהּ דְּבַשׁ, מִפְּנֵי שֶׁהַתּוֹרָה אָמְרָה:
כִּי כָל שְׂאֹר וְכָל דְּבַשׁ לֹא תַקְטִירוּ מִמֶּנּוּ אִשֶּׁה לַייָ.

יְיָ צְבָאוֹת עִמָּנוּ, מִשְׂגָּב לָנוּ אֱלֹהֵי יַעֲקֹב, סֶלָה.
יְיָ צְבָאוֹת, אַשְׁרֵי אָדָם בֹּטֵחַ בָּךְ.
יְיָ, הוֹשִׁיעָה; הַמֶּלֶךְ יַעֲנֵנוּ בְיוֹם קָרְאֵנוּ.

אַתָּה סֵתֶר לִי, מִצַּר תִּצְּרֵנִי; רָנֵּי פַלֵּט תְּסוֹבְבֵנִי, סֶלָה.
וְעָרְבָה לַייָ מִנְחַת יְהוּדָה וִירוּשָׁלָיִם, כִּימֵי עוֹלָם וּכְשָׁנִים
קַדְמֹנִיּוֹת.

מסכת יומא לג, א

אַבַּיֵּי הֲוָה מְסַדֵּר סֵדֶר הַמַּעֲרָכָה מִשְּׁמָא דִגְמָרָא וְאַלִּבָּא
דְאַבָּא שָׁאוּל: מַעֲרָכָה גְדוֹלָה קוֹדֶמֶת לְמַעֲרָכָה שְׁנִיָּה שֶׁל
קְטֹרֶת, וּמַעֲרָכָה שְׁנִיָּה שֶׁל קְטֹרֶת קוֹדֶמֶת לְסִדּוּר שְׁנֵי גִזְרֵי
עֵצִים, וְסִדּוּר שְׁנֵי גִזְרֵי עֵצִים קוֹדֵם לְדִשּׁוּן מִזְבֵּחַ הַפְּנִימִי,
וְדִשּׁוּן מִזְבֵּחַ הַפְּנִימִי קוֹדֵם לַהֲטָבַת חָמֵשׁ נֵרוֹת, וַהֲטָבַת חָמֵשׁ
נֵרוֹת קוֹדֶמֶת לְדַם הַתָּמִיד, וְדַם הַתָּמִיד קוֹדֵם לַהֲטָבַת שְׁתֵּי
נֵרוֹת, וַהֲטָבַת שְׁתֵּי נֵרוֹת קוֹדֶמֶת לִקְטֹרֶת, וּקְטֹרֶת קוֹדֶמֶת
לְאֵבָרִים, וְאֵבָרִים לְמִנְחָה, וּמִנְחָה לַחֲבִתִּין, וַחֲבִתִּין לִנְסָכִין,
וּנְסָכִין לְמוּסָפִין, וּמוּסָפִין לְבָזִיכִין, וּבָזִיכִין קוֹדְמִין לְתָמִיד
שֶׁל בֵּין הָעַרְבָּיִם, שֶׁנֶּאֱמַר: וְעָרַךְ עָלֶיהָ הָעֹלָה, וְהִקְטִיר עָלֶיהָ
חֶלְבֵי הַשְּׁלָמִים. עָלֶיהָ הַשְּׁלֵם כָּל הַקָּרְבָּנוֹת כֻּלָּם.

אָנָּא, בְּכֹחַ גְּדֻלַּת יְמִינְךָ תַּתִּיר צְרוּרָה.
קַבֵּל רִנַּת עַמְּךָ, שַׂגְּבֵנוּ, טַהֲרֵנוּ, נוֹרָא.

מֵעֲרֹכָה גדולה, the large pile of burning wood, was used for the sacrificial
offerings; the second pile of burning wood was used for the supply of coal to
burn the incense twice every day; the third pile was in keeping with this command: "The fire must be kept burning on the altar, never allowed to go out"
(Leviticus 6:6).

שלמים is here interpreted to imply completion (from שלם, "to be finished").

אנא בכח is a rhymed prayer. It has six words to each of its seven lines.

why was no honey mixed with it? Because the Torah says: "You shall not present any leaven or honey as a fire-offering to the Lord."[1]

The Lord of hosts is with us; the God of Jacob is our fortress. Lord of hosts, happy is the man who trusts in thee.

O Lord, save us; may the King answer us when we call.

Thou art my shelter; from the foe thou wilt preserve me; with songs of deliverance thou wilt surround me.[2]

The offering of Judah and Jerusalem will be pleasing to the Lord, as in the days of old and as in former years.[3]

Talmud Yoma 33a

Abbaye recounted the daily order of the Temple service on the authority of tradition and according to Abba Saul: The large pile of wood was set on the altar prior to the second pile which supplied coal to be used for the incense; the second pile was arranged before placing two [additional] logs of wood [on the large pile]; the placing of the two logs of wood preceded the removing of the ashes from the inner altar; the removing of the ashes from the inner altar came before the trimming of the five lamps; the trimming of the five lamps preceded the sprinkling of the blood of the daily offering; the blood of the daily offering was sprinkled before the trimming of the two remaining lamps; the trimming of the two lamps preceded the incense offering; the incense offering preceded the offering of the sacrificial parts; the offering of the sacrificial parts preceded the meal-offering; the meal-offering preceded the offering of pancakes; the pancakes came before the libations; the libations preceded the additional offerings on Sabbaths and festivals; the additional offerings preceded the removal of the two bowls of frankincense; the frankincense bowls preceded the daily afternoon-offering, as it is said: "And the priest shall arrange the burnt-offering on the altar, and burn on it the fat of the *shelamim*,"[4] which means that with the afternoon-offering all the offerings of the day are to be completed.

By the great power of thy right hand, O set the captive free.

Revered God, accept thy people's prayer; strengthen us, cleanse us.

---

[1] *Leviticus* 2:11. [2] *Psalms* 46:8; 84:13; 20:10; 32:7. [3] *Malachi* 3:4. [4] *Leviticus* 6:5.

נָא, גִּבּוֹר, דּוֹרְשֵׁי יִחוּדְךָ כְּבָבַת שָׁמְרֵם.

בָּרְכֵם, טַהֲרֵם, רַחֲמֵם, צִדְקָתְךָ תָּמִיד גָּמְלֵם.

חֲסִין קָדוֹשׁ, בְּרֹב טוּבְךָ נַהֵל עֲדָתֶךָ.

יָחִיד גֵּאֶה, לְעַמְּךָ פְּנֵה, זוֹכְרֵי קְדֻשָּׁתֶךָ.

שַׁוְעָתֵנוּ קַבֵּל וּשְׁמַע צַעֲקָתֵנוּ, יוֹדֵעַ תַּעֲלֻמוֹת.

בָּרוּךְ שֵׁם כְּבוֹד מַלְכוּתוֹ לְעוֹלָם וָעֶד.

רִבּוֹן הָעוֹלָמִים, אַתָּה צִוִּיתָנוּ לְהַקְרִיב קָרְבַּן הַתָּמִיד
בְּמוֹעֲדוֹ, וְלִהְיוֹת כֹּהֲנִים בַּעֲבוֹדָתָם, וּלְוִיִּם בְּדוּכָנָם, וְיִשְׂרָאֵל
בְּמַעֲמָדָם; וְעַתָּה בַּעֲוֹנוֹתֵינוּ חָרַב בֵּית הַמִּקְדָּשׁ וּבָטֵל הַתָּמִיד,
וְאֵין לָנוּ לֹא כֹהֵן בַּעֲבוֹדָתוֹ. וְלֹא לֵוִי בְּדוּכָנוֹ, וְלֹא יִשְׂרָאֵל
בְּמַעֲמָדוֹ. וְאַתָּה אָמַרְתָּ: וּנְשַׁלְּמָה פָרִים שְׂפָתֵינוּ, לָכֵן יְהִי רָצוֹן
מִלְּפָנֶיךָ, יְיָ אֱלֹהֵינוּ וֵאלֹהֵי אֲבוֹתֵינוּ, שֶׁיְּהֵא שִׂיחַ שִׂפְתוֹתֵינוּ
חָשׁוּב וּמְקֻבָּל וּמְרֻצֶּה לְפָנֶיךָ כְּאִלּוּ הִקְרַבְנוּ קָרְבַּן הַתָּמִיד
בְּמוֹעֲדוֹ וְעָמַדְנוּ עַל מַעֲמָדוֹ.

On Sabbath say:

במדבר כח, ט-י

וּבְיוֹם הַשַּׁבָּת שְׁנֵי כְבָשִׂים בְּנֵי שָׁנָה תְּמִימִם, וּשְׁנֵי עֶשְׂרֹנִים
סֹלֶת מִנְחָה בְּלוּלָה בַשֶּׁמֶן, וְנִסְכּוֹ. עֹלַת שַׁבַּת בְּשַׁבַּתּוֹ עַל עֹלַת
הַתָּמִיד וְנִסְכָּהּ.

On Rosh Ḥodesh say:

במדבר כח, יא-מו

וּבְרָאשֵׁי חָדְשֵׁיכֶם תַּקְרִיבוּ עֹלָה לַיְיָ: פָּרִים בְּנֵי בָקָר שְׁנַיִם,
וְאַיִל אֶחָד, כְּבָשִׂים בְּנֵי שָׁנָה שִׁבְעָה, תְּמִימִם. וּשְׁלֹשָׁה עֶשְׂרֹנִים
סֹלֶת מִנְחָה בְּלוּלָה בַשֶּׁמֶן לַפָּר הָאֶחָד, וּשְׁנֵי עֶשְׂרֹנִים סֹלֶת
מִנְחָה בְּלוּלָה בַשֶּׁמֶן לָאַיִל הָאֶחָד. וְעִשָּׂרֹן עִשָּׂרוֹן, סֹלֶת מִנְחָה
בְּלוּלָה בַשֶּׁמֶן, לַכֶּבֶשׂ הָאֶחָד, עֹלָה רֵיחַ נִיחֹחַ, אִשֶּׁה לַיְיָ.

Almighty God, guard as the apple of the eye those who seek thee.
Bless them, cleanse them, pity them; ever grant them thy truth.
Mighty, holy God, in thy abundant grace, guide thy people.
Exalted God, turn to thy people who proclaim thy holiness.
Accept our prayer, hear our cry, thou who knowest secret thoughts.
Blessed be the name of his glorious majesty forever and ever.

Lord of the universe, thou hast commanded us to sacrifice the
daily offering at its proper time with priests officiating, Levites
[singing] on the platform, and lay representatives of Israel attending the Temple service. Now, through our sins the Temple
is destroyed, the daily offering is abolished, and we have neither
priest officiating, nor Levite [singing] on the platform, nor Israelite attending the Temple service. However, thou hast declared
that we may substitute the prayer of our lips for the sacrifice of
bullocks.[1] Therefore, may it be thy will, Lord our God and God
of our fathers, that the prayer of our lips be favorably regarded
and accepted by thee as if we offered the daily offering at its
proper time and attended at its service.

On Sabbath say (Numbers 28:9–10):

On the Sabbath day two yearling male lambs without blemish
[are to be offered], with two-tenths of an *ephah* of fine flour mixed
with oil as a meal-offering, along with its libation. This is the
burnt-offering of every Sabbath, in addition to the daily burnt-
offering and its libation.

On Rosh Ḥodesh say (Numbers 28:11–15):

And on your new moon festivals you shall offer as a burnt-
offering to the Lord two young bullocks, one ram, seven yearling
male lambs without blemish, along with three-tenths of an *ephah*
of fine flour mixed with oil as a meal-offering for each bullock,
and two-tenths of fine flour mixed with oil as a meal-offering for
the one ram, and a tenth of an *ephah* of fine flour mixed with oil
as a meal-offering for each lamb; this is to be a burnt-offering of a
sweet savor—a burnt-offering to the Lord. Their libations are to

---

[1] *Hosea* 14:3.

וְנִסְכֵּיהֶם, חֲצִי הַהִין יִהְיֶה לַפָּר, וּשְׁלִישִׁת הַהִין לָאַיִל, וּרְבִיעַת הַהִין לַכֶּבֶשׂ, יָיִן; זֹאת עֹלַת חֹדֶשׁ בְּחָדְשׁוֹ לְחָדְשֵׁי הַשָּׁנָה. וּשְׂעִיר עִזִּים אֶחָד לְחַטָּאת לַיְיָ; עַל עֹלַת הַתָּמִיד יֵעָשֶׂה, וְנִסְכּוֹ.

משנה זבחים, פרק ה

א. אֵיזֶהוּ מְקוֹמָן שֶׁל זְבָחִים. קָדְשֵׁי קָדָשִׁים שְׁחִיטָתָן בַּצָּפוֹן, פַּר וְשָׂעִיר שֶׁל יוֹם הַכִּפּוּרִים שְׁחִיטָתָן בַּצָּפוֹן, וְקִבּוּל דָּמָן בִּכְלִי שָׁרֵת בַּצָּפוֹן. וְדָמָן טָעוּן הַזָּיָה עַל בֵּין הַבַּדִּים וְעַל הַפָּרֹכֶת וְעַל מִזְבַּח הַזָּהָב; מַתָּנָה אַחַת מֵהֶן מְעַכָּבֶת. שְׁיָרֵי הַדָּם הָיָה שׁוֹפֵךְ עַל יְסוֹד מַעֲרָבִי שֶׁל מִזְבֵּחַ הַחִיצוֹן; אִם לֹא נָתַן, לֹא עִכֵּב.

ב. פָּרִים הַנִּשְׂרָפִים וּשְׂעִירִים הַנִּשְׂרָפִים שְׁחִיטָתָן בַּצָּפוֹן, וְקִבּוּל דָּמָן בִּכְלִי שָׁרֵת בַּצָּפוֹן. וְדָמָן טָעוּן הַזָּיָה עַל הַפָּרֹכֶת וְעַל מִזְבַּח הַזָּהָב; מַתָּנָה אַחַת מֵהֶן מְעַכָּבֶת. שְׁיָרֵי הַדָּם הָיָה שׁוֹפֵךְ עַל יְסוֹד מַעֲרָבִי שֶׁל מִזְבֵּחַ הַחִיצוֹן; אִם לֹא נָתַן, לֹא עִכֵּב. אֵלּוּ וָאֵלּוּ נִשְׂרָפִין בְּבֵית הַדָּשֶׁן.

ג. חַטֹּאת הַצִּבּוּר וְהַיָּחִיד, אֵלּוּ הֵן חַטֹּאת הַצִּבּוּר: שְׂעִירֵי רָאשֵׁי חֳדָשִׁים וְשֶׁל מוֹעֲדוֹת, שְׁחִיטָתָן בַּצָּפוֹן, וְקִבּוּל דָּמָן בִּכְלִי שָׁרֵת בַּצָּפוֹן. וְדָמָן טָעוּן אַרְבַּע מַתָּנוֹת עַל אַרְבַּע קְרָנוֹת. כֵּיצַד, עָלָה בַכֶּבֶשׁ וּפָנָה לַסּוֹבֵב וּבָא־לוֹ לְקֶרֶן דְּרוֹמִית מִזְרָחִית, מִזְרָחִית צְפוֹנִית, צְפוֹנִית מַעֲרָבִית, מַעֲרָבִית דְּרוֹמִית. שְׁיָרֵי הַדָּם הָיָה שׁוֹפֵךְ עַל יְסוֹד דְּרוֹמִי. וְנֶאֱכָלִין לִפְנִים מִן הַקְּלָעִים לְזִכְרֵי כְהֻנָּה, בְּכָל מַאֲכָל, לְיוֹם וָלַיְלָה, עַד חֲצוֹת.

be half a *hin* of wine per bullock, a third of a *hin* for the ram, and a fourth of a *hin* per lamb. This is to be the burnt-offering of every month throughout the months of the year. Moreover, one he-goat is to be offered as a sin-offering to the Lord, in addition to the daily burnt-offering and its libation.

Mishnah Zebaḥim, Chapter 5

1. Which were the places of sacrifice in the Temple? The most holy offerings were slaughtered on the north side of the altar, as were also the bullock and the he-goat for the Day of Atonement. Their blood, which was there received in a sacred vessel, had to be sprinkled over the space between the poles of the ark, towards the curtain of the Holy of Holies, and upon the golden altar. The omission of one of these sprinklings rendered the atonement ceremony invalid. The priest poured out the rest of the blood at the western base of the outer altar, if, however, he failed to do so, the omission did not invalidate the ceremony.

2. The bullocks and the he-goats which were to be burned were slaughtered on the north side of the altar; their blood, which was there received in a sacred vessel, had to be sprinkled towards the curtain and upon the golden altar. The omission of either of these sprinklings rendered the ceremony invalid. The priest poured out the rest of the blood at the western base of the outer altar; if, however, he failed to do so, the omission did not invalidate the ceremony. All these offerings were burnt at the place where the ashes were deposited.

3. The communal sin-offerings and those of individuals—the goats offered on new moon festivals and on major feasts are the communal sin-offerings—were slaughtered on the north side of the altar. Their blood, which was there received in a sacred vessel, required four sprinklings on the four corners of the altar. How was this done? The priest went up the ascent, and, having turned to the ledge bordering the altar, walked along it to the southeast, northeast, northwest and southwest corners, successively. The rest of the blood he poured out at the southern base. These offerings, prepared for food in any fashion, were eaten within the Temple court only by the males of the priesthood during that day and evening—until midnight.

ד. הָעוֹלָה קֹדֶשׁ קָדָשִׁים. שְׁחִיטָתָהּ בַּצָּפוֹן, וְקִבּוּל דָּמָהּ בִּכְלִי שָׁרֵת בַּצָּפוֹן. וְדָמָהּ טָעוּן שְׁתֵּי מַתָּנוֹת שֶׁהֵן אַרְבַּע; וּטְעוּנָה הַפְשֵׁט, וְנִתּוּחַ, וְכָלִיל לָאִשִּׁים.

ה. זִבְחֵי שַׁלְמֵי צִבּוּר וַאֲשָׁמוֹת, אֵלּוּ הֵן אֲשָׁמוֹת: אֲשַׁם גְּזֵלוֹת, אֲשַׁם מְעִילוֹת, אֲשַׁם שִׁפְחָה חֲרוּפָה, אֲשַׁם נָזִיר, אֲשַׁם מְצֹרָע, אָשָׁם תָּלוּי. שְׁחִיטָתָן בַּצָּפוֹן, וְקִבּוּל דָּמָן בִּכְלִי שָׁרֵת בַּצָּפוֹן, וְדָמָן טָעוּן שְׁתֵּי מַתָּנוֹת שֶׁהֵן אַרְבַּע. וְנֶאֱכָלִין לִפְנִים מִן הַקְּלָעִים לְזִכְרֵי כְהֻנָּה, בְּכָל מַאֲכָל, לְיוֹם וָלַיְלָה, עַד חֲצוֹת.

ו. הַתּוֹדָה וְאֵיל נָזִיר קָדָשִׁים קַלִּים. שְׁחִיטָתָן בְּכָל מָקוֹם בָּעֲזָרָה, וְדָמָן טָעוּן שְׁתֵּי מַתָּנוֹת שֶׁהֵן אַרְבַּע. וְנֶאֱכָלִין בְּכָל הָעִיר, לְכָל אָדָם, בְּכָל מַאֲכָל, לְיוֹם וָלַיְלָה, עַד חֲצוֹת. הַמּוּרָם מֵהֶם כַּיּוֹצֵא בָהֶם, אֶלָּא שֶׁהַמּוּרָם נֶאֱכָל לַכֹּהֲנִים, לִנְשֵׁיהֶם וְלִבְנֵיהֶם וּלְעַבְדֵיהֶם.

ז. שְׁלָמִים קָדָשִׁים קַלִּים. שְׁחִיטָתָן בְּכָל מָקוֹם בָּעֲזָרָה, וְדָמָן טָעוּן שְׁתֵּי מַתָּנוֹת שֶׁהֵן אַרְבַּע. וְנֶאֱכָלִין בְּכָל הָעִיר, לְכָל אָדָם, בְּכָל מַאֲכָל, לִשְׁנֵי יָמִים וְלַיְלָה אֶחָד. הַמּוּרָם מֵהֶם כַּיּוֹצֵא בָהֶם, אֶלָּא שֶׁהַמּוּרָם נֶאֱכָל לַכֹּהֲנִים, לִנְשֵׁיהֶם וְלִבְנֵיהֶם וּלְעַבְדֵיהֶם.

ח. הַבְּכוֹר וְהַמַּעֲשֵׂר וְהַפֶּסַח קָדָשִׁים קַלִּים. שְׁחִיטָתָן בְּכָל מָקוֹם בָּעֲזָרָה, וְדָמָן טָעוּן מַתָּנָה אֶחָת, וּבִלְבַד שֶׁיִּתֵּן כְּנֶגֶד הַיְסוֹד. שָׁנָה בַאֲכִילָתָן: הַבְּכוֹר נֶאֱכָל לַכֹּהֲנִים, וְהַמַּעֲשֵׂר לְכָל

4.   The burnt-offering was one of the most holy sacrifices. It was slaughtered on the north side of the altar. Its blood, which was there received in a sacred vessel, required two sprinklings [at opposite angles of the altar] making four in all. This offering had to be flayed, severed into parts, and consumed by fire.

5.   As to the communal peace-offerings and the guilt-offerings—the following are the guilt-offerings: for robbery, for making improper use of sacred objects, for violating a betrothed handmaid, the offering of a nazirite who has become ritually unclean, the offering of a leper at his cleansing, and the offering of a person in doubt whether an act he has committed requires a sin-offering—all these were slaughtered on the north side of the altar. Their blood, which was there received in a sacred vessel, required two sprinklings [at opposite angles of the altar] making four in all. These offerings, prepared for food in any fashion, were eaten within the Temple court only by the males of the priesthood that day and evening—until midnight.

6.   The thanksgiving-offering and the ram offered by a nazirite [at the termination of his vow] were holy in a minor degree. These might be slaughtered anywhere in the Temple court. Their blood required two sprinklings [at opposite angles of the altar] making four in all. They might be eaten, prepared for food in any fashion, anywhere in the city by anyone during that day and evening—until midnight. The same rule applied to the priests' share, except that the priests' share might be eaten only by the priests, their wives, their children and their servants.

7.   The peace-offerings also were holy in a minor degree. These might be slaughtered anywhere in the Temple court. Their blood required two sprinklings [at opposite angles of the altar] making four in all. They might be eaten, prepared for food in any fashion, anywhere in the city by anyone during two days and one night. The same rule applied to the priests' share, except that the priests' share might be eaten only by the priests, their wives, their children and their servants.

8.   The firstlings of animals, the tithe of cattle, and the paschal lamb were likewise holy in a minor degree. These might be slaughtered anywhere in the Temple court. Their blood required one sprinkling only; this, however, had to be done at the base of the altar. The following difference prevailed as to the eating of them: the firstborn animal might be eaten only by the priests,

אָדָם. וְנֶאֱכָלִין בְּכָל הָעִיר, בְּכָל מַאֲכָל, לִשְׁנֵי יָמִים וְלַיְלָה
אֶחָד. הַפֶּסַח אֵינוֹ נֶאֱכָל אֶלָּא בַלַּיְלָה, וְאֵינוֹ נֶאֱכָל אֶלָּא עַד
חֲצוֹת, וְאֵינוֹ נֶאֱכָל אֶלָּא לִמְנוּיָיו, וְאֵינוֹ נֶאֱכָל אֶלָּא צָלִי.

ספרא, פתיחה

רַבִּי יִשְׁמָעֵאל אוֹמֵר: בִּשְׁלֹשׁ עֶשְׂרֵה מִדּוֹת הַתּוֹרָה נִדְרָשֶׁת:

א) מִקַּל וָחֹמֶר;

ב) וּמִגְּזֵרָה שָׁוָה;

ג) מִבִּנְיַן אָב מִכָּתוּב אֶחָד, וּמִבִּנְיַן אָב מִשְּׁנֵי כְתוּבִים;

ד) מִכְּלָל וּפְרָט;

ה) וּמִפְּרָט וּכְלָל;

ו) כְּלָל וּפְרָט וּכְלָל אִי אַתָּה דָן אֶלָּא כְּעֵין הַפְּרָט;

רבי ישמעאל בן אלישע, a contemporary of Rabbi Akiba, died as a martyr in the year 135 during the Roman persecutions. The *Baraitha d'Rabbi Ishmael*, which constitutes the introduction to the *Sifra* (tannaitic commentary on Leviticus), has been inserted here to complete the daily minimum of Bible and Talmud study required of every Jew. This section is prefaced (on page 13) by two blessings concerning Torah study.

ILLUSTRATIONS

1. If, for example, a certain act is forbidden on an ordinary festival, it is so much the more forbidden on Yom Kippur; if a certain act is permissible on Yom Kippur, it is so much the more permissible on an ordinary festival.

2. The phrase "Hebrew slave" (Exodus 21:2) is ambiguous, for it may mean a heathen slave owned by a Hebrew, or else, a slave who is a Hebrew. That the latter is the correct meaning is proved by a reference to the phrase "your Hebrew brother" in Deuteronomy 15:12, where the same law is mentioned (... "If your Hebrew brother is sold to you...").

3. (a) From Deuteronomy 24:6 ("No one shall take a handmill or an upper millstone in pledge, for he would be taking a life in pledge") the Rabbis concluded: "Everything which is used for preparing food is forbidden to be taken in pledge." (b) From Exodus 21:26-27 ("If a man strikes the eye of his slave ... and destroys it, he must let him go free in compensation for his eye. If he knocks out the tooth of his slave ... he must let him go free ...") the Rabbis concluded that when *any* part of the slave's body is mutilated by the master, the slave shall be set free.

4. In Leviticus 18:6 the law reads: "None of you shall marry anyone

while the tithe might be eaten by anyone. Both the firstling and the tithe might be eaten, prepared for food in any fashion, anywhere in the city during two days and one night. The paschal lamb, however, had to be eaten on that night only—and not later than midnight. It might be eaten only by those numbered for it; nor might it be eaten except when roasted.

TALMUDIC EXPOSITION OF THE SCRIPTURES

Sifra, Introduction

Rabbi Ishmael says: The Torah is interpreted by means of thirteen rules:

1. Inference is drawn from a minor premise to a major one, or from a major premise to a minor one.

2. From the similarity of words or phrases occurring in two passages it is inferred that what is expressed in the one applies also to the other.

3. A general principle, as contained in one or two biblical laws, is applicable to all related laws.

4. When a generalization is followed by a specification, only what is specified applies.

5. When a specification is followed by a generalization, all that is implied in the generalization applies.

6. If a generalization is followed by a specification and this in turn by a generalization, one must be guided by what the specification implies.

---

related to him." This generalization is followed by a specification of forbidden marriages. Hence, this prohibition applies only to those expressly mentioned.

5.   In Exodus 22:9 we read: "If a man gives to his neighbor an ass, or an ox, or a sheep, to keep, or *any* animal, and it dies . . ." The general phrase "any animal," which follows the specification, includes in this law all kinds of animals.

6.   In Exodus 22:8 we are told that an embezzler shall pay double to his neighbor "for anything embezzled [generalization], for ox, or ass, or sheep, or clothing [specification], or any article lost" [generalization]. Since the specification includes only movable property, and objects of intrinsic value, the fine of double payment does not apply to embezzled real estate, nor to notes and bills, since the latter represent only a symbolic value.

ז) מִכְּלָל שֶׁהוּא צָרִיךְ לִפְרָט, וּמִפְּרָט שֶׁהוּא צָרִיךְ לִכְלָל;

ח) כָּל דָּבָר שֶׁהָיָה בִּכְלָל וְיָצָא מִן הַכְּלָל לְלַמֵּד, לֹא לְלַמֵּד עַל עַצְמוֹ יָצָא, אֶלָּא לְלַמֵּד עַל הַכְּלָל כֻּלּוֹ יָצָא;

ט) כָּל דָּבָר שֶׁהָיָה בִּכְלָל וְיָצָא לִטְעוֹן טָעַן אַחֵר שֶׁהוּא כְעִנְיָנוֹ, יָצָא לְהָקֵל וְלֹא לְהַחֲמִיר;

י) כָּל דָּבָר שֶׁהָיָה בִּכְלָל וְיָצָא לִטְעוֹן טָעַן אַחֵר שֶׁלֹּא כְעִנְיָנוֹ, יָצָא לְהָקֵל וּלְהַחֲמִיר;

יא) כָּל דָּבָר שֶׁהָיָה בִּכְלָל וְיָצָא לִדּוֹן בַּדָּבָר הֶחָדָשׁ, אִי אַתָּה יָכוֹל לְהַחֲזִירוֹ לִכְלָלוֹ עַד שֶׁיַּחֲזִירֶנּוּ הַכָּתוּב לִכְלָלוֹ בְּפֵרוּשׁ;

יב) דָּבָר הַלָּמֵד מֵעִנְיָנוֹ, וְדָבָר הַלָּמֵד מִסּוֹפוֹ;

---

7. In Leviticus 17:13 we read: "He shall pour out its blood, and *cover* it with *dust*." The verb "to cover" is a general term, since there are various ways of covering a thing; "with dust" is specific. If we were to apply rule 4 to this passage, the law would be that the blood of the slaughtered animal must be covered with nothing except dust. Since, however, the general term "to cover" may also mean "to hide," our present passage necessarily requires the specific expression "with dust"; otherwise, the law might be interpreted to mean that the blood is to be concealed in a closed vessel. On the other hand, the specification "with dust" without the general expression "to cover" would have been meaningless.

8. In Deuteronomy 22:1 we are told that the finder of lost property must return it to its owner. In a next verse the Torah adds: "You shall do the same . . . with his *garment* and with anything lost by your brother . . . which you have found . . ." *Garment*, though included in the general expression "anything lost," is specifically mentioned in order to indicate that the duty to announce the finding of lost articles applies only to such objects which are likely to have an owner, and which have, as in the case of clothing, some marks by which they can be identified.

9. In Exodus 35:2-3 we read: "Whoever does any work on the Sabbath shall be put to death; you shall not light a fire on the sabbath day." The law against lighting a fire on the Sabbath, though already implied in "any work", is mentioned separately in order to indicate that the penalty for lighting a fire on the Sabbath is not as drastic.

10. According to Exodus 21:29-30, the proprietor of a vicious animal which has killed a man or woman must pay such compensation as may be im-

7. When, however, for the sake of clearness, a generalization necessarily requires a specification, or when a specification requires a generalization, rules 4 and 5 do not apply.

8. Whatever is first implied in a generalization and afterwards specified to teach us something new, is expressly stated not only for its own sake, but to teach something additional concerning all the instances implied in the generalization.

9. Whatever is first implied in a general law and afterwards specified to add another provision similar to the general law, is specified in order to alleviate, and not to increase, the severity of that particular provision.

10. Whatever is first implied in a general law and afterwards specified to add another provision which is not similar to the general law, is specified in order to alleviate in some respects, and in others to increase the severity of that particular provision.

11. Whatever is first implied in a general law and is afterwards specified to determine a new matter, the terms of the general law can no longer apply to it, unless Scripture expressly declares that they do apply.

12. A dubious word or passage is explained from its context or from a subsequent expression.

---

posed on him by the court. In a succeeding verse the Torah adds: "If the ox gores a slave, male or female, he must pay the master thirty shekels of silver." The case of a slave, though already included in the preceding general law of the slain man or woman, contains a different provision, the *fixed* amount of compensation, with the result that whether the slave was valued at more than thirty shekels or less than thirty shekels, the proprietor of the animal must invariably pay thirty shekels.

11. The guilt-offering which a cured leper had to bring was unlike all other guilt-offerings in this, that some of its blood was sprinkled on the person who offered it (Leviticus 14:13–14). On account of this peculiarity none of the rules connected with other offerings would apply to that brought by a cured leper, had not the Torah expressly added: "As the sin-offering so is the guilt-offering."

12. (a) The noun *tinshemeth* occurs in Leviticus 11:18 among the unclean birds, and again (verse 30) among the reptiles. Hence, it becomes certain that *tinshemeth* is the name of a certain bird as well as of a certain reptile. (b) In Deuteronomy 19:6, with regard to the cities of refuge where the manslayer is to flee, we read: "So that the avenger of blood may not pursue the manslayer . . . and slay him, *and he is not deserving of death.*" That the last clause refers to the slayer, and not to the blood avenger, is made clear by the subsequent clause: "inasmuch as he hated him not in time past."

יג) וְכֵן שְׁנֵי כְתוּבִים הַמַּכְחִישִׁים זֶה אֶת זֶה, עַד שֶׁיָּבוֹא
הַכָּתוּב הַשְּׁלִישִׁי וְיַכְרִיעַ בֵּינֵיהֶם.

אבות ה, כג; מלאכי ג, ד

יְהִי רָצוֹן מִלְּפָנֶיךָ, יְיָ אֱלֹהֵינוּ וֵאלֹהֵי אֲבוֹתֵינוּ, שֶׁיִּבָּנֶה בֵּית
הַמִּקְדָּשׁ בִּמְהֵרָה בְיָמֵינוּ, וְתֵן חֶלְקֵנוּ בְּתוֹרָתֶךָ. וְשָׁם נַעֲבָדְךָ
בְּיִרְאָה, כִּימֵי עוֹלָם וּכְשָׁנִים קַדְמוֹנִיּוֹת.

קַדִּישׁ דְּרַבָּנָן

Mourners:

יִתְגַּדַּל וְיִתְקַדַּשׁ שְׁמֵהּ רַבָּא בְּעָלְמָא דִי בְרָא כִרְעוּתֵהּ;
וְיַמְלִיךְ מַלְכוּתֵהּ בְּחַיֵּיכוֹן וּבְיוֹמֵיכוֹן, וּבְחַיֵּי דְכָל בֵּית יִשְׂרָאֵל,
בַּעֲגָלָא וּבִזְמַן קָרִיב, וְאִמְרוּ אָמֵן.
יְהֵא שְׁמֵהּ רַבָּא מְבָרַךְ לְעָלַם וּלְעָלְמֵי עָלְמַיָּא.

---

13. In Exodus 13:6 we read: "Seven days you shall eat unleavened bread," and in Deuteronomy 16:8 we are told: 'Six days you shall eat unleavened bread." The contradiction between these two passages is explained by a reference to a third passage (Leviticus 23:14), where the use of the new produce is forbidden until the second day of Passover, after the offering of the *Omer*. If, therefore, the unleavened bread was prepared of the new grain, it could only be eaten six days of Passover. Hence, the passage in Exodus 13:6 must refer to unleavened bread prepared of the produce of a previous year.

קדיש דרבנן (Scholars' Kaddish) is recited after the reading of talmudic or midrashic passages. על ישראל ועל רבנן is a prayer for the welfare of the scholars.

THE KADDISH

The essential part of the Kaddish consists of the congregational response: "May his great name be blessed forever and ever." Around this response, which is found almost verbatim in Daniel 2:20, the whole Kaddish developed. Originally, it was recited at the close of sermons delivered in Aramaic, the language spoken by the Jews for about a thousand years after the Babylonian captivity. Hence the Kaddish was composed in Aramaic, the language in which the religious discourses were held. At a later period the Kaddish was

13.   Similarly, if two biblical passages contradict each other, they can be harmonized only by a third passage.

Mishnah Avoth 5:23; *Malachi* 3:4

May it be thy will, Lord our God and God of our fathers, that the Temple be speedily rebuilt in our days; and grant us a portion in thy Torah. There we will serve thee with reverence, as in the days of old and as in former years.

KADDISH D'RABBANAN

Mourners:

Glorified and sanctified be God's great name throughout the world which he has created according to his will. May he establish his kingdom in your lifetime and during your days, and within the life of the entire house of Israel, speedily and soon; and say, Amen.

May his great name be blessed forever and to all eternity.

---

introduced into the liturgy to mark the conclusion of sections of the service or of the reading of the biblical and talmudic passages.

The Kaddish contains no reference to the dead. The earliest allusion to the Kaddish as a mourners' prayer is found in Maḥzor Vitry, dated 1208, where it is said plainly: "The lad rises and recites Kaddish." One may safely assume that since the Kaddish has as its underlying thought the hope for the redemption and ultimate healing of suffering mankind, the power of redeeming the dead from the sufferings of *Gehinnom* came to be ascribed in the course of time to the recitation of this sublime doxology. Formerly the Kaddish was recited the whole year of mourning, so as to rescue the soul of one's parents from the torture of *Gehinnom* where the wicked are said to spend no less than twelve months. In order not to count one's own parents among the wicked, the period for reciting the Kaddish was later reduced to eleven months.

The observance of the anniversary of parents' death, the Jahrzeit, originated in Germany, as the term itself well indicates. Rabbi Isaac Luria, the celebrated Kabbalist of the sixteenth century, explains that "while the orphan's Kaddish within the eleven months helps the soul to pass from *Gehinnom* to *Gan-Eden*, the Jahrzeit Kaddish elevates the soul every year to a higher sphere in Paradise." The Kaddish has thus become a great pillar of Judaism. No matter how far a Jew may have drifted away from Jewish life, the Kaddish restores him to his people and to the Jewish way of living.

יִתְבָּרַךְ וְיִשְׁתַּבַּח, וְיִתְפָּאַר וְיִתְרוֹמַם, וְיִתְנַשֵּׂא וְיִתְהַדָּר,
וְיִתְעַלֶּה וְיִתְהַלָּל שְׁמֵהּ דְּקֻדְשָׁא, בְּרִיךְ הוּא, לְעֵלָּא (לְעֵלָּא)
מִן כָּל בִּרְכָתָא וְשִׁירָתָא, תֻּשְׁבְּחָתָא וְנֶחֱמָתָא, דַּאֲמִירָן בְּעָלְמָא,
וְאִמְרוּ אָמֵן.

עַל יִשְׂרָאֵל וְעַל רַבָּנָן וְעַל תַּלְמִידֵיהוֹן, וְעַל כָּל תַּלְמִידֵי
תַלְמִידֵיהוֹן, וְעַל כָּל מָן דְּעָסְקִין בְּאוֹרַיְתָא, דִּי בְּאַתְרָא הָדֵן
וְדִי בְּכָל אֲתַר וַאֲתַר, יְהֵא לְהוֹן וּלְכוֹן שְׁלָמָא רַבָּא, חִנָּא
וְחִסְדָּא וְרַחֲמִין, וְחַיִּין אֲרִיכִין, וּמְזוֹנֵי רְוִיחֵי, וּפֻרְקָנָא מִן קֳדָם
אֲבוּהוֹן דִּבִשְׁמַיָּא וְאַרְעָא, וְאִמְרוּ אָמֵן.

יְהֵא שְׁלָמָא רַבָּא מִן שְׁמַיָּא, וְחַיִּים טוֹבִים, עָלֵינוּ וְעַל כָּל
יִשְׂרָאֵל, וְאִמְרוּ אָמֵן.

עֹשֶׂה שָׁלוֹם בִּמְרוֹמָיו, הוּא בְּרַחֲמָיו יַעֲשֶׂה שָׁלוֹם עָלֵינוּ וְעַל
כָּל יִשְׂרָאֵל, וְאִמְרוּ אָמֵן.

On Sabbaths and on major festivals the service is continued on page 299.

During the geonic period it was suggested that the ten synonyms of praise contained in the Kaddish, glorifying "God's great name throughout the world which he has created according to his will," correspond to the ten divine utterances by which the world was created (Avoth 5:1). The seven words of the congregational response (... יְהֵא שְׁמֵיהּ רַבָּא) are composed of twenty-eight letters, the numerical value of the word כֹּחַ (power). This alludes to the first verse of the Torah, which consists of seven words composed of twenty-eight letters.

The prayer עַל הַכֹּל, recited on Sabbaths before the reading of the Torah, embodies part of the Kaddish in pure Hebrew. Genizah fragments have been found to contain a larger proportion of Hebrew in the Kaddish.

The Kaddish, like צִדּוּק הַדִּין ("acknowledgment of divine justice"), recited on the occasion of a death, seems to express the sentiment: "The Lord gave and the Lord has taken away; blessed be the name of the Lord" (Job 1:21).

The Kaddish has five different forms: 1) קַדִּישׁ דְּרַבָּנָן, recited after the reading of passages from the Talmud; 2) קַדִּישׁ שָׁלֵם, the full-Kaddish, recited by the Reader at the end of the service; 3) חֲצִי קַדִּישׁ, the half-Kaddish, recited by the Reader between sections of the service; 4) קַדִּישׁ יָתוֹם, the mourners' Kad-

Blessed and praised, glorified and exalted, extolled and honored, adored and lauded be the name of the Holy One, blessed be he, beyond all the blessings and hymns, praises and consolations that are ever spoken in the world; and say, Amen.

[We pray] for Israel, for our teachers and their disciples and the disciples of their disciples, and for all who study the Torah, here and everywhere. May they have abundant peace, loving-kindness, ample sustenance and salvation from their Father who is in heaven; and say, Amen.

May there be abundant peace from heaven, and life, for us and for all Israel; and say, Amen.

He who creates peace in his celestial heights, may he in his mercy create peace for us and for all Israel; and say, Amen.

On Sabbaths and on major festivals the service is continued on page 300.

---

dish, recited by the mourners after the service and after the recitation of certain psalms, such as the Psalm of the Day (pages 139–147); 5) קדיש לאתחדתא, an expanded form of the mourners' Kaddish, recited at the cemetery after a burial.

לעלא מן כל ...ושירתא תשבחתא refers to the hymns of praise contained in the Psalms of David; compare the expression על כל דברי שירות ותשבחות דוד.

לעלא לעלא is said between *Rosh Hashanah* and *Yom Kippur*; otherwise only לעלא is said. In the Italian ritual לעלא is repeated throughout the year. לעלא לעלא is the Targum's rendering of מעלה מעלה (Deuteronomy 28:43).

נחמתא ("consolations"), occurring in the Kaddish as a synonym of praise, probably refers to prophetic works such as the Book of Isaiah, called Books of Consolation, which contain hymns of praise as well as Messianic prophecies.

עושה שלום, which repeats in Hebrew the thought expressed in the preceding Aramaic paragraph, seems to have been added from the meditation recited at the end of the *Shemoneh Esreh*. The same sentence is also added at the end of the grace recited after meals. The three steps backwards, which formed the respectful manner of retiring from a superior, were likewise transferred from the concluding sentence of the *Shemoneh Esreh*. On the other hand, the phrase "and say Amen", added at the end of the silent meditation after the *Shemoneh Esreh*, must have been borrowed from the Kaddish which is always recited in the hearing of no fewer than ten men.

תְּפִלַּת שַׁחֲרִית

תהלים ל

מִזְמוֹר שִׁיר חֲנֻכַּת הַבַּיִת לְדָוִד. אֲרוֹמִמְךָ, יְיָ, כִּי דִלִּיתָנִי,
וְלֹא שִׂמַּחְתָּ אֹיְבַי לִי. יְיָ אֱלֹהָי, שִׁוַּעְתִּי אֵלֶיךָ וַתִּרְפָּאֵנִי. יְיָ,
הֶעֱלִיתָ מִן שְׁאוֹל נַפְשִׁי, חִיִּיתַנִי מִיָּרְדִי בוֹר. זַמְּרוּ לַיְיָ חֲסִידָיו,
וְהוֹדוּ לְזֵכֶר קָדְשׁוֹ. כִּי רֶגַע בְּאַפּוֹ, חַיִּים בִּרְצוֹנוֹ; בָּעֶרֶב יָלִין
בֶּכִי, וְלַבֹּקֶר רִנָּה. וַאֲנִי אָמַרְתִּי בְשַׁלְוִי, בַּל אֶמּוֹט לְעוֹלָם. יְיָ,
בִּרְצוֹנְךָ הֶעֱמַדְתָּה לְהַרְרִי עֹז; הִסְתַּרְתָּ פָנֶיךָ, הָיִיתִי נִבְהָל.
אֵלֶיךָ יְיָ אֶקְרָא, וְאֶל אֲדֹנָי אֶתְחַנָּן. מַה בֶּצַע בְּדָמִי, בְּרִדְתִּי
אֶל שָׁחַת; הֲיוֹדְךָ עָפָר, הֲיַגִּיד אֲמִתֶּךָ. שְׁמַע יְיָ וְחָנֵּנִי; יְיָ, הֱיֵה
עֹזֵר לִי. הָפַכְתָּ מִסְפְּדִי לְמָחוֹל לִי; פִּתַּחְתָּ שַׂקִּי וַתְּאַזְּרֵנִי
שִׂמְחָה. Reader לְמַעַן יְזַמֶּרְךָ כָבוֹד, וְלֹא יִדֹּם; יְיָ אֱלֹהַי, לְעוֹלָם
אוֹדֶךָּ.

MOURNERS' KADDISH

יִתְגַּדַּל וְיִתְקַדַּשׁ שְׁמֵהּ רַבָּא בְּעָלְמָא דִּי בְרָא כִרְעוּתֵהּ;
וְיַמְלִיךְ מַלְכוּתֵהּ בְּחַיֵּיכוֹן וּבְיוֹמֵיכוֹן, וּבְחַיֵּי דְכָל בֵּית יִשְׂרָאֵל,
בַּעֲגָלָא וּבִזְמַן קָרִיב, וְאִמְרוּ אָמֵן.

יְהֵא שְׁמֵהּ רַבָּא מְבָרַךְ לְעָלַם וּלְעָלְמֵי עָלְמַיָּא.

יִתְבָּרַךְ וְיִשְׁתַּבַּח, וְיִתְפָּאַר וְיִתְרוֹמַם, וְיִתְנַשֵּׂא וְיִתְהַדָּר,
וְיִתְעַלֶּה וְיִתְהַלָּל שְׁמֵהּ דְּקֻדְשָׁא, בְּרִיךְ הוּא, לְעֵלָּא (לְעֵלָּא)
מִן כָּל בִּרְכָתָא וְשִׁירָתָא, תֻּשְׁבְּחָתָא וְנֶחֱמָתָא, דַּאֲמִירָן בְּעָלְמָא,
וְאִמְרוּ אָמֵן.

מִזְמוֹר שִׁיר is a hymn of gratitude for recovery from a grave sickness. The
psalmist relates that trouble came to him when he thought that he could be

49

MORNING SERVICE

Psalm 30

A psalm, a song for the dedication of the house; by David.

I extol thee, O Lord, for thou hast lifted me, and hast not let my foes rejoice over me. Lord my God, I cried to thee, and thou didst heal me. O Lord, thou hast lifted me up from the grave; thou hast let me live, that I should not go down to the pit. Sing to the Lord, you who are godly, and give thanks to his holy name. For his anger only lasts a moment, but his favor lasts a lifetime; weeping may lodge with us at evening, but in the morning there are shouts of joy. I thought in my security I never would be shaken. O Lord, by thy favor thou hadst established my mountain as a stronghold; but when thy favor was withdrawn, I was dismayed. To thee, O Lord, I called; I appealed to my God: "What profit would my blood be, if I went down to the grave? Will the dust praise thee? Will it declare thy faithfulness? Hear, O Lord, and be gracious to me; Lord, be thou my helper." Thou hast changed my mourning into dancing; thou hast put off my sackcloth and girded me with joy; so that my soul may praise thee, and not be silent. Lord my God, I will thank thee forever.

MOURNERS' KADDISH

Glorified and sanctified be God's great name throughout the world which he has created according to his will. May he establish his kingdom in your lifetime and during your days, and within the life of the entire house of Israel, speedily and soon; and say, Amen.

May his great name be blessed forever and to all eternity.

Blessed and praised, glorified and exalted, extolled and honored, adored and lauded be the name of the Holy One, blessed be he, beyond all the blessings and hymns, praises and consolations that are ever spoken in the world; and say, Amen.

---

independent of God's aid. In his distress he pleaded that his life might be spared, and his prayer was answered. He is determined to spend the rest of his life in thanksgiving.

יְהֵא שְׁלָמָא רַבָּא מִן שְׁמַיָּא, וְחַיִּים, עָלֵינוּ וְעַל כָּל יִשְׂרָאֵל, וְאִמְרוּ אָמֵן.

עֹשֶׂה שָׁלוֹם בִּמְרוֹמָיו, הוּא יַעֲשֶׂה שָׁלוֹם עָלֵינוּ וְעַל כָּל יִשְׂרָאֵל, וְאִמְרוּ אָמֵן.

הֲרֵינִי מְזַמֵּן אֶת פִּי לְהוֹדוֹת וּלְהַלֵּל וּלְשַׁבֵּחַ אֶת בּוֹרְאִי.

בָּרוּךְ שֶׁאָמַר וְהָיָה הָעוֹלָם, בָּרוּךְ הוּא. בָּרוּךְ עֹשֶׂה בְרֵאשִׁית, בָּרוּךְ אוֹמֵר וְעוֹשֶׂה, בָּרוּךְ גּוֹזֵר וּמְקַיֵּם, בָּרוּךְ מְרַחֵם עַל הָאָרֶץ, בָּרוּךְ מְרַחֵם עַל הַבְּרִיּוֹת, בָּרוּךְ מְשַׁלֵּם שָׂכָר טוֹב לִירֵאָיו, בָּרוּךְ חַי לָעַד וְקַיָּם לָנֶצַח, בָּרוּךְ פּוֹדֶה וּמַצִּיל, בָּרוּךְ שְׁמוֹ. בָּרוּךְ אַתָּה, יְיָ אֱלֹהֵינוּ, מֶלֶךְ הָעוֹלָם, הָאֵל, הָאָב הָרַחֲמָן, הַמְהֻלָּל בְּפִי עַמּוֹ, מְשֻׁבָּח וּמְפֹאָר בִּלְשׁוֹן חֲסִידָיו וַעֲבָדָיו. וּבְשִׁירֵי דָוִד עַבְדְּךָ נְהַלֶּלְךָ, יְיָ אֱלֹהֵינוּ; בִּשְׁבָחוֹת וּבִזְמִרוֹת נְגַדֶּלְךָ וּנְשַׁבֵּחֲךָ וּנְפָאֶרְךָ, וְנַזְכִּיר שִׁמְךָ וְנַמְלִיכְךָ, מַלְכֵּנוּ, אֱלֹהֵינוּ. Reader יָחִיד, חֵי הָעוֹלָמִים, מֶלֶךְ, מְשֻׁבָּח וּמְפֹאָר עֲדֵי עַד שְׁמוֹ הַגָּדוֹל. בָּרוּךְ אַתָּה, יְיָ, מֶלֶךְ מְהֻלָּל בַּתִּשְׁבָּחוֹת.

דברי הימים א טז, ח—לו

הוֹדוּ לַייָ, קִרְאוּ בִשְׁמוֹ, הוֹדִיעוּ בָעַמִּים עֲלִילוֹתָיו. שִׁירוּ לוֹ, זַמְּרוּ לוֹ, שִׂיחוּ בְּכָל נִפְלְאוֹתָיו. הִתְהַלְלוּ בְּשֵׁם קָדְשׁוֹ; יִשְׂמַח לֵב מְבַקְשֵׁי יְיָ. דִּרְשׁוּ יְיָ וְעֻזּוֹ, בַּקְּשׁוּ פָנָיו תָּמִיד. זִכְרוּ נִפְלְאֹתָיו אֲשֶׁר עָשָׂה, מֹפְתָיו וּמִשְׁפְּטֵי פִיהוּ. זֶרַע יִשְׂרָאֵל עַבְדּוֹ, בְּנֵי יַעֲקֹב בְּחִירָיו. הוּא יְיָ אֱלֹהֵינוּ, בְּכָל הָאָרֶץ מִשְׁפָּטָיו. זִכְרוּ לְעוֹלָם בְּרִיתוֹ, דָּבָר צִוָּה לְאֶלֶף דּוֹר. אֲשֶׁר כָּרַת אֶת אַבְרָהָם,

---

ברוך שאמר is composed of eighty-seven words, a number suggesting the numerical value of פז ("refined gold"). This hymn introduces the biblical se-

May there be abundant peace from heaven, and life, for us and for all Israel; and say, Amen.

He who creates peace in his celestial heights, may he create peace for us and for all Israel; and say, Amen.

Blessed be he who spoke, and the world came into being; blessed be he. Blessed be he who created the universe. Blessed be he who says and performs. Blessed be he who decrees and fulfills. Blessed be he who has mercy on the world. Blessed be he who has mercy on all creatures. Blessed be he who grants a fair reward to those who revere him. Blessed be he who lives forever and exists eternally. Blessed be he who redeems and saves; blessed be his name. Blessed art thou, Lord our God, King of the universe, O God, merciful Father, who art praised by the mouth of thy people, lauded and glorified by the tongue of thy faithful servants. With the songs of thy servant David will we praise thee, Lord our God; with his hymns and psalms will we exalt, extol and glorify thee. We will call upon thy name and proclaim thee King, our King, our God. Thou who art One, the life of the universe, O King, praised and glorified be thy great name forever and ever. Blessed art thou, O Lord, King extolled with hymns of praise.

I Chronicles 16:8–36

Give thanks to the Lord, call upon his name; make known his deeds among the peoples. Sing to him, sing praises to him; speak of all his wonders. Take pride in his holy name; let the heart of those who seek the Lord rejoice. Inquire of the Lord and his might; seek his presence continually. Remember the wonders he has done, his marvels, and the judgments of his mouth, O descendants of Israel his servant, children of Jacob, his chosen. He is the Lord our God; his judgments are over all the earth. Remember his covenant forever, the word which he pledged for a thousand generations, the covenant he made with Abraham, and his oath to

---

lections entitled פסוקי דזמרה ("verses of praise"). It is included in the ninth century *Siddur* of Amram Gaon.

הודו is the hymn which David sang when the ark was brought to Jerusalem. The first fifteen verses of Psalm 105 are almost identical with the first half of this passage.

וּשְׁבוּעָתוֹ לְיִצְחָק. וַיַּעֲמִידֶהָ לְיַעֲקֹב לְחֹק, לְיִשְׂרָאֵל בְּרִית
עוֹלָם. לֵאמֹר, לְךָ אֶתֵּן אֶרֶץ כְּנָעַן, חֶבֶל נַחֲלַתְכֶם. בִּהְיוֹתְכֶם
מְתֵי מִסְפָּר, כִּמְעַט וְגָרִים בָּהּ. וַיִּתְהַלְּכוּ מִגּוֹי אֶל גּוֹי, וּמִמַּמְלָכָה
אֶל עַם אַחֵר. לֹא הִנִּיחַ לְאִישׁ לְעָשְׁקָם, וַיּוֹכַח עֲלֵיהֶם מְלָכִים.
אַל תִּגְּעוּ בִמְשִׁיחָי, וּבִנְבִיאַי אַל תָּרֵעוּ. שִׁירוּ לַיְיָ כָּל הָאָרֶץ,
בַּשְּׂרוּ מִיּוֹם אֶל יוֹם יְשׁוּעָתוֹ. סַפְּרוּ בַגּוֹיִם אֶת כְּבוֹדוֹ, בְּכָל
הָעַמִּים נִפְלְאוֹתָיו. כִּי גָדוֹל יְיָ וּמְהֻלָּל מְאֹד, וְנוֹרָא הוּא עַל כָּל
אֱלֹהִים. כִּי כָּל אֱלֹהֵי הָעַמִּים אֱלִילִים, וַיְיָ שָׁמַיִם עָשָׂה. הוֹד
וְהָדָר לְפָנָיו, עֹז וְחֶדְוָה בִּמְקֹמוֹ. הָבוּ לַיְיָ מִשְׁפְּחוֹת עַמִּים, הָבוּ
לַיְיָ כָּבוֹד וָעֹז. הָבוּ לַיְיָ כְּבוֹד שְׁמוֹ, שְׂאוּ מִנְחָה וּבֹאוּ לְפָנָיו,
הִשְׁתַּחֲווּ לַיְיָ בְּהַדְרַת קֹדֶשׁ. חִילוּ מִלְּפָנָיו כָּל הָאָרֶץ, אַף תִּכּוֹן
תֵּבֵל בַּל תִּמּוֹט. יִשְׂמְחוּ הַשָּׁמַיִם וְתָגֵל הָאָרֶץ, וְיֹאמְרוּ בַגּוֹיִם יְיָ
מָלָךְ. יִרְעַם הַיָּם וּמְלֹאוֹ, יַעֲלֹץ הַשָּׂדֶה וְכָל אֲשֶׁר בּוֹ. אָז יְרַנְּנוּ
עֲצֵי הַיָּעַר, מִלְּפְנֵי יְיָ, כִּי בָא לִשְׁפּוֹט אֶת הָאָרֶץ. הוֹדוּ לַיְיָ כִּי
טוֹב, כִּי לְעוֹלָם חַסְדּוֹ. וְאִמְרוּ, הוֹשִׁיעֵנוּ אֱלֹהֵי יִשְׁעֵנוּ, וְקַבְּצֵנוּ
וְהַצִּילֵנוּ מִן הַגּוֹיִם, לְהֹדוֹת לְשֵׁם קָדְשֶׁךָ, לְהִשְׁתַּבֵּחַ בִּתְהִלָּתֶךָ.
בָּרוּךְ יְיָ אֱלֹהֵי יִשְׂרָאֵל מִן הָעוֹלָם וְעַד הָעֹלָם; וַיֹּאמְרוּ כָל
הָעָם אָמֵן וְהַלֵּל לַיְיָ.

רוֹמְמוּ יְיָ אֱלֹהֵינוּ, וְהִשְׁתַּחֲווּ לַהֲדֹם רַגְלָיו, קָדוֹשׁ הוּא.
Reader רוֹמְמוּ יְיָ אֱלֹהֵינוּ, וְהִשְׁתַּחֲווּ לְהַר קָדְשׁוֹ, כִּי קָדוֹשׁ יְיָ
אֱלֹהֵינוּ.

וְהוּא רַחוּם, יְכַפֵּר עָוֹן וְלֹא יַשְׁחִית, וְהִרְבָּה לְהָשִׁיב אַפּוֹ,
וְלֹא יָעִיר כָּל חֲמָתוֹ. אַתָּה, יְיָ, לֹא תִכְלָא רַחֲמֶיךָ מִמֶּנִּי, חַסְדְּךָ
וַאֲמִתְּךָ תָּמִיד יִצְּרוּנִי. זְכֹר רַחֲמֶיךָ יְיָ, וַחֲסָדֶיךָ, כִּי מֵעוֹלָם

The passage beginning with רוממו is composed of a variety of biblical verses.

Isaac. He confirmed the same to Jacob as a statute, to Israel as an everlasting covenant, saying: "To you I give the land of Canaan as the portion of your possession." While they were but a few men, very few, and strangers in it; when they went about from nation to nation and from realm to realm, he permitted no man to oppress them, and warned kings concerning them: "Touch not my anointed, and do my prophets no harm!" Sing to the Lord, all the earth; proclaim his salvation day after day. Recount his glory among the nations, and his wonders among all the peoples. For great is the Lord and most worthy of praise; he is to be feared above all gods. For all the gods of the peoples are mere idols, but the Lord made the heavens. Majesty and beauty are in his presence; strength and joy are in his sanctuary. Ascribe to the Lord, O families of peoples, ascribe to the Lord glory and strength. Give to the Lord the honor due to his name; bring an offering and come before him; worship the Lord in holy array. Tremble before him, all the earth; indeed, the world is firm that it cannot be shaken. Let the heavens rejoice, let the earth exult, and let them say among the nations: "The Lord is King!" Let the sea and its fulness roar; let the field and all that is therein rejoice. Then let the trees of the forest sing before the Lord, for he comes to rule the world. Praise the Lord, for he is good; for his kindness endures forever. And say: "Save us, O God of our salvation, gather us and deliver us from the nations, to give thanks to thy holy name, to glory in thy praise." Blessed be the Lord, the God of Israel, from eternity to eternity. Then all the people said "Amen" and praised the Lord.

Exalt the Lord our God, and worship at his footstool—holy is he. Exalt the Lord our God, and worship at his holy mountain, for holy is the Lord our God. He, being merciful, forgives iniquity, and does not destroy; frequently he turns his anger away, and does not stir up all his wrath. Thou, O Lord, wilt not hold back thy mercy from me; thy kindness and thy faithfulness will always protect me. Remember thy mercy, O Lord, and thy kindness, for

הֵמָּה. תְּנוּ עֹז לֵאלֹהִים, עַל יִשְׂרָאֵל גַּאֲוָתוֹ, וְעֻזּוֹ בַּשְּׁחָקִים. נוֹרָא
אֱלֹהִים מִמִּקְדָּשֶׁיךָ; אֵל יִשְׂרָאֵל, הוּא נוֹתֵן עֹז וְתַעֲצֻמוֹת לָעָם;
בָּרוּךְ אֱלֹהִים. אֵל נְקָמוֹת, יְיָ, אֵל נְקָמוֹת, הוֹפִיעַ. הִנָּשֵׂא, שֹׁפֵט
הָאָרֶץ, הָשֵׁב גְּמוּל עַל גֵּאִים. לַיְיָ הַיְשׁוּעָה, עַל עַמְּךָ בִרְכָתֶךָ
סֶּלָה. יְיָ צְבָאוֹת עִמָּנוּ, מִשְׂגָּב לָנוּ אֱלֹהֵי יַעֲקֹב, סֶלָה. Reader יְיָ
צְבָאוֹת, אַשְׁרֵי אָדָם בֹּטֵחַ בָּךְ. יְיָ, הוֹשִׁיעָה; הַמֶּלֶךְ יַעֲנֵנוּ בְיוֹם
קָרְאֵנוּ.

הוֹשִׁיעָה אֶת עַמֶּךָ, וּבָרֵךְ אֶת נַחֲלָתֶךָ, וּרְעֵם וְנַשְּׂאֵם עַד
הָעוֹלָם. נַפְשֵׁנוּ חִכְּתָה לַיְיָ, עֶזְרֵנוּ וּמָגִנֵּנוּ הוּא. כִּי בוֹ יִשְׂמַח
לִבֵּנוּ, כִּי בְשֵׁם קָדְשׁוֹ בָטָחְנוּ. יְהִי חַסְדְּךָ יְיָ עָלֵינוּ, כַּאֲשֶׁר יִחַלְנוּ
לָךְ. הַרְאֵנוּ יְיָ חַסְדֶּךָ, וְיֶשְׁעֲךָ תִּתֶּן־לָנוּ. קוּמָה עֶזְרָתָה לָּנוּ,
וּפְדֵנוּ לְמַעַן חַסְדֶּךָ. אָנֹכִי יְיָ אֱלֹהֶיךָ הַמַּעַלְךָ מֵאֶרֶץ מִצְרָיִם,
הַרְחֶב־פִּיךָ וַאֲמַלְאֵהוּ. אַשְׁרֵי הָעָם שֶׁכָּכָה לּוֹ, אַשְׁרֵי הָעָם שֶׁיְיָ
אֱלֹהָיו. Reader וַאֲנִי בְּחַסְדְּךָ בָטַחְתִּי, יָגֵל לִבִּי בִּישׁוּעָתֶךָ;
אָשִׁירָה לַיְיָ, כִּי גָמַל עָלָי.

The following psalm is omitted on *Erev Yom Kippur, Erev Pesaḥ*
and *Ḥol ha-Mo'ed Pesaḥ.*

תהלים ק

מִזְמוֹר לְתוֹדָה; הָרִיעוּ לַיְיָ כָּל הָאָרֶץ. עִבְדוּ אֶת יְיָ
בְּשִׂמְחָה, בֹּאוּ לְפָנָיו בִּרְנָנָה. דְּעוּ כִּי יְיָ הוּא אֱלֹהִים; הוּא עָשָׂנוּ
וְלוֹ אֲנַחְנוּ, עַמּוֹ וְצֹאן מַרְעִיתוֹ. בֹּאוּ שְׁעָרָיו בְּתוֹדָה, חֲצֵרוֹתָיו
בִּתְהִלָּה; הוֹדוּ לוֹ, בָּרְכוּ שְׁמוֹ. Reader כִּי טוֹב יְיָ, לְעוֹלָם חַסְדּוֹ,
וְעַד דֹּר וָדֹר אֱמוּנָתוֹ.

יְהִי כְבוֹד יְיָ לְעוֹלָם; יִשְׂמַח יְיָ בְּמַעֲשָׂיו. יְהִי שֵׁם יְיָ מְבֹרָךְ,

---

מזמור לתודה was recited in the Temple on weekdays when thank-offerings
were presented. The psalmist invites the whole world to join Israel in the
worship of God and to acknowledge him as the merciful Father of all mankind.

they have been since eternity. Give honor to God, whose majesty is over Israel, whose glory is in the skies. Feared art thou, O Lord, from thy sanctuary; the God of Israel gives strength and power to his people. Blessed be God! God of vengeance, O Lord, God of vengeance, appear! Arise, O Ruler of the world, and render to the arrogant what they deserve. Salvation belongs to the Lord; thy blessing be upon thy people. The Lord of hosts is with us; the God of Jacob is our Stronghold. O Lord of hosts, happy is the man who trusts in thee. O Lord, save us; may the King answer us when we call. Save thy people and bless thy heritage; tend them and sustain them forever. Our soul waits for the Lord; he is our help and our shield. Indeed, our heart rejoices in him, for in his holy name we trust. May thy kindness, O Lord, rest on us, as our hope rests on thee. Show us thy kindness, O Lord, and grant us thy salvation. Arise for our help, and set us free for thy goodness' sake. I am the Lord your God, who brought you up from the land of Egypt; open your mouth and I will fill it. Happy the people that is so situated; happy the people whose God is the Lord. I have trusted in thy kindness; may my heart rejoice in thy salvation; I will sing to the Lord, because he has treated me kindly.[1]

The following Psalm is omitted on Erev Yom Kippur, Erev Pesaḥ and Ḥol ha-Mo'ed Pesaḥ.

Psalm 100

A psalm for the thank-offering.

Shout praise to the Lord, all the earth. Serve the Lord with joy; come before him with singing. Know that the Lord is God; he has made us, and we are his, his people and the flock of his pasture. Enter into his gates with thanksgiving, and into his courts with praise; give thanks to him, bless his name. For the Lord is good; his kindness is forever; his faithfulness endures to all generations.

May the glory of the Lord be forever; may the Lord rejoice in his works. Blessed be the name of the Lord henceforth and for-

---

... יהי כבוד that is, may the glory of the Lord, the universe, remain forever; may God always be pleased with his creation and preserve it.

[1] *Psalms* 99:5, 9; 78:38; 40:12; 25:6; 68:35–36; 94:1–2; 3:9; 46:8; 84:13; 20:10; 28:9; 33:20–22; 85:8; 44:27; 81:11; 144:15; 13:6.

מֵעַתָּה וְעַד עוֹלָם. מִמִּזְרַח שֶׁמֶשׁ עַד מְבוֹאוֹ, מְהֻלָּל שֵׁם יְיָ. רָם
עַל כָּל גּוֹיִם יְיָ, עַל הַשָּׁמַיִם כְּבוֹדוֹ. יְיָ, שִׁמְךָ לְעוֹלָם; יְיָ, זִכְרְךָ
לְדֹר וָדֹר. יְיָ בַּשָּׁמַיִם הֵכִין כִּסְאוֹ, וּמַלְכוּתוֹ בַּכֹּל מָשָׁלָה.
יִשְׂמְחוּ הַשָּׁמַיִם וְתָגֵל הָאָרֶץ, וְיֹאמְרוּ בַגּוֹיִם יְיָ מָלָךְ. יְיָ מֶלֶךְ,
יְיָ מָלָךְ, יְיָ יִמְלֹךְ לְעֹלָם וָעֶד. יְיָ מֶלֶךְ עוֹלָם וָעֶד, אָבְדוּ גוֹיִם
מֵאַרְצוֹ. יְיָ הֵפִיר עֲצַת גּוֹיִם, הֵנִיא מַחְשְׁבוֹת עַמִּים. רַבּוֹת
מַחֲשָׁבוֹת בְּלֶב־אִישׁ, וַעֲצַת יְיָ הִיא תָקוּם. עֲצַת יְיָ לְעֹלָם
תַּעֲמֹד, מַחְשְׁבוֹת לִבּוֹ לְדֹר וָדֹר. כִּי הוּא אָמַר וַיֶּהִי, הוּא צִוָּה
וַיַּעֲמֹד. כִּי בָחַר יְיָ בְּצִיּוֹן, אִוָּהּ לְמוֹשָׁב לוֹ. כִּי יַעֲקֹב בָּחַר לוֹ
יָהּ, יִשְׂרָאֵל לִסְגֻלָּתוֹ. כִּי לֹא יִטֹּשׁ יְיָ עַמּוֹ, וְנַחֲלָתוֹ לֹא יַעֲזֹב.
Reader וְהוּא רַחוּם, יְכַפֵּר עָוֹן וְלֹא יַשְׁחִית, וְהִרְבָּה לְהָשִׁיב
אַפּוֹ, וְלֹא יָעִיר כָּל חֲמָתוֹ. יְיָ, הוֹשִׁיעָה; הַמֶּלֶךְ יַעֲנֵנוּ בְיוֹם
קָרְאֵנוּ.

אַשְׁרֵי יוֹשְׁבֵי בֵיתֶךָ; עוֹד יְהַלְלוּךָ סֶּלָה.
אַשְׁרֵי הָעָם שֶׁכָּכָה לּוֹ; אַשְׁרֵי הָעָם שֶׁיְיָ אֱלֹהָיו.

תהלים קמה

תְּהִלָּה לְדָוִד

אֲרוֹמִמְךָ, אֱלוֹהַי הַמֶּלֶךְ, וַאֲבָרְכָה שִׁמְךָ לְעוֹלָם וָעֶד.
בְּכָל יוֹם אֲבָרְכֶךָּ, וַאֲהַלְלָה שִׁמְךָ לְעוֹלָם וָעֶד.
גָּדוֹל יְיָ וּמְהֻלָּל מְאֹד, וְלִגְדֻלָּתוֹ אֵין חֵקֶר.
דּוֹר לְדוֹר יְשַׁבַּח מַעֲשֶׂיךָ, וּגְבוּרֹתֶיךָ יַגִּידוּ.

אשרי The first two verses, which are taken from Psalms 84:5 and 144:15
and prefixed to Psalm 145, contain the word **אשרי** three times. *Ashre* is recited
twice in the morning service and once in the Minḥah service. The Talmud
asserts that "whoever recites this psalm three times a day is assured of his
share in the world to come" (Berakhoth 4b). This noble hymn of praise, calling
upon all mankind to glorify God's greatness, celebrates his providential care
for all his creation. It is an acrostic psalm, the successive lines beginning with

ever. From the rising of the sun to its setting let the Lord's name be praised. High above all nations is the Lord; above the heavens is his glory. O Lord, thy name is forever; O Lord, thy fame is through all generations. The Lord has set up his throne in the heavens, and his kingdom rules over all. Let the heavens rejoice, let the earth exult, and let them say among the nations, "The Lord is King!" The Lord is King, the Lord was King, the Lord shall be King forever and ever. The Lord is King for evermore; the heathen have vanished from his land. The Lord annuls the counsel of nations; he foils the plans of peoples. Many are the plans in a man's heart, but it is the Lord's purpose that shall stand. The Lord's purpose stands forever; his plans are through all generations. For he spoke, and the world came into being; he commanded, and it stood firm. Surely, the Lord has chosen Zion; he has desired it for his habitation. Surely, the Lord has chosen Jacob to be his, and Israel as his prized possession. Surely, the Lord will not abandon his people, nor forsake his heritage. He, being merciful, forgives iniquity, and does not destroy; frequently he turns his anger away, and does not stir up all his wrath. O Lord, save us; may the King answer us when we call.[1]

Happy are those who dwell in thy house; they are ever praising thee. Happy the people that is so situated; happy the people whose God is the Lord.[2]

Psalm 145

A hymn of praise by David.

I extol thee, my God the King,
And bless thy name forever and ever.
Every day I bless thee,
And praise thy name forever and ever.
Great is the Lord and most worthy of praise;
His greatness is unsearchable.
One generation to another praises thy works;
They recount thy mighty acts.

---

the letters of the Hebrew alphabet taken in order. However, the letter *nun* is missing. The alphabetic arrangement is probably intended as an aid to memory.

[1] *Psalms* 104:31; 113:2–4; 135:13; 103:19; *I Chronicles* 16:31; *Psalms* 10:16; 33:10; *Proverbs* 19:21; *Psalm* 33:11, 9; 132:13; 135:4; 94:14; 78:38; 20:10. [2] *Psalms* 84:5; 144:15.

הֲדַר כְּבוֹד הוֹדֶךָ, וְדִבְרֵי נִפְלְאֹתֶיךָ אָשִׂיחָה.

וֶעֱזוּז נוֹרְאֹתֶיךָ יֹאמֵרוּ, וּגְדֻלָּתְךָ אֲסַפְּרֶנָּה.

זֵכֶר רַב טוּבְךָ יַבִּיעוּ, וְצִדְקָתְךָ יְרַנֵּנוּ.

חַנּוּן וְרַחוּם יְיָ, אֶרֶךְ אַפַּיִם וּגְדָל־חָסֶד.

טוֹב יְיָ לַכֹּל, וְרַחֲמָיו עַל כָּל מַעֲשָׂיו.

יוֹדוּךָ יְיָ כָּל מַעֲשֶׂיךָ, וַחֲסִידֶיךָ יְבָרְכוּכָה.

כְּבוֹד מַלְכוּתְךָ יֹאמֵרוּ, וּגְבוּרָתְךָ יְדַבֵּרוּ.

לְהוֹדִיעַ לִבְנֵי הָאָדָם גְּבוּרֹתָיו, וּכְבוֹד הֲדַר מַלְכוּתוֹ.

מַלְכוּתְךָ מַלְכוּת כָּל עֹלָמִים, וּמֶמְשַׁלְתְּךָ בְּכָל דּוֹר וָדֹר.

סוֹמֵךְ יְיָ לְכָל הַנֹּפְלִים, וְזוֹקֵף לְכָל הַכְּפוּפִים.

עֵינֵי כֹל אֵלֶיךָ יְשַׂבֵּרוּ, וְאַתָּה נוֹתֵן לָהֶם אֶת אָכְלָם בְּעִתּוֹ.

פּוֹתֵחַ אֶת יָדֶךָ, וּמַשְׂבִּיעַ לְכָל חַי רָצוֹן.

צַדִּיק יְיָ בְּכָל דְּרָכָיו, וְחָסִיד בְּכָל מַעֲשָׂיו.

קָרוֹב יְיָ לְכָל קֹרְאָיו, לְכֹל אֲשֶׁר יִקְרָאֻהוּ בֶאֱמֶת.

רְצוֹן יְרֵאָיו יַעֲשֶׂה, וְאֶת שַׁוְעָתָם יִשְׁמַע וְיוֹשִׁיעֵם.

שׁוֹמֵר יְיָ אֶת כָּל אֹהֲבָיו, וְאֵת כָּל הָרְשָׁעִים יַשְׁמִיד.

תְּהִלַּת יְיָ יְדַבֶּר־פִּי; וִיבָרֵךְ כָּל בָּשָׂר שֵׁם קָדְשׁוֹ לְעוֹלָם וָעֶד.

<u>וַאֲנַחְנוּ נְבָרֵךְ</u> יָהּ מֵעַתָּה וְעַד עוֹלָם; הַלְלוּיָהּ. Reader

תהלים קמו

הַלְלוּיָהּ; הַלְלִי נַפְשִׁי אֶת יְיָ. אֲהַלְלָה יְיָ בְּחַיָּי, אֲזַמְּרָה לֵאלֹהַי בְּעוֹדִי. אַל תִּבְטְחוּ בִנְדִיבִים, בְּבֶן־אָדָם שֶׁאֵין לוֹ תְשׁוּעָה. תֵּצֵא רוּחוֹ יָשֻׁב לְאַדְמָתוֹ; בַּיּוֹם הַהוּא אָבְדוּ עֶשְׁתֹּנֹתָיו.

וַאֲנַחְנוּ נְבָרֵךְ is added from Psalm 115:18 so that אשרי, like the five subsequent psalms, may end with *Halleluyah*.

On the splendor of thy glorious majesty
And on thy wondrous deeds I meditate.
They speak of thy awe-inspiring might,
And I tell of thy greatness.
They spread the fame of thy great goodness,
And sing of thy righteousness.
Gracious and merciful is the Lord,
Slow to anger and of great kindness.
The Lord is good to all,
And his mercy is over all his works.
All thy works praise thee, O Lord,
And thy faithful followers bless thee.
They speak of thy glorious kingdom,
And talk of thy might,
To let men know thy mighty deeds,
And the glorious splendor of thy kingdom.
Thy kingdom is a kingdom of all ages,
And thy dominion is for all generations.
The Lord upholds all who fall,
And raises all who are bowed down.
The eyes of all look hopefully to thee,
And thou givest them their food in due season.
Thou openest thy hand,
And satisfiest every living thing with favor.
The Lord is righteous in all his ways,
And gracious in all his deeds.
The Lord is near to all who call upon him,
To all who call upon him sincerely.
He fulfills the desire of those who revere him;
He hears their cry and saves them.
The Lord preserves all who love him,
But all the wicked he destroys.
My mouth speaks the praise of the Lord;
Let all creatures bless his holy name forever and ever.
[1]We will bless the Lord henceforth and forever.
Praise the Lord!

Psalm 146

Praise the Lord! Praise the Lord, O my soul! I will praise the
Lord as long as I live; I will sing to my God as long as I exist.
Put no trust in princes, in mortal man who can give no help. When
his breath goes, he returns to the dust, and on that very day his

---
[1] *Psalm* 115:18.

אַשְׁרֵי שֶׁאֵל יַעֲקֹב בְּעֶזְרוֹ, שִׂבְרוֹ עַל יְיָ אֱלֹהָיו. עֹשֶׂה שָׁמַיִם
וָאָרֶץ, אֶת הַיָּם, וְאֶת כָּל אֲשֶׁר בָּם; הַשֹּׁמֵר אֱמֶת לְעוֹלָם. עֹשֶׂה
מִשְׁפָּט לַעֲשׁוּקִים, נֹתֵן לֶחֶם לָרְעֵבִים; יְיָ מַתִּיר אֲסוּרִים. יְיָ
פֹּקֵחַ עִוְרִים, יְיָ זֹקֵף כְּפוּפִים, יְיָ אֹהֵב צַדִּיקִים. יְיָ שֹׁמֵר אֶת
גֵּרִים; יָתוֹם וְאַלְמָנָה יְעוֹדֵד, וְדֶרֶךְ רְשָׁעִים יְעַוֵּת. Reader יִמְלֹךְ
יְיָ לְעוֹלָם, אֱלֹהַיִךְ צִיּוֹן לְדֹר וָדֹר; הַלְלוּיָהּ.

תהלים קמז

הַלְלוּיָהּ; כִּי טוֹב זַמְּרָה אֱלֹהֵינוּ, כִּי נָעִים, נָאוָה תְהִלָּה.
בּוֹנֵה יְרוּשָׁלַיִם יְיָ; נִדְחֵי יִשְׂרָאֵל יְכַנֵּס. הָרוֹפֵא לִשְׁבוּרֵי לֵב,
וּמְחַבֵּשׁ לְעַצְּבוֹתָם. מוֹנֶה מִסְפָּר לַכּוֹכָבִים, לְכֻלָּם שֵׁמוֹת
יִקְרָא. גָּדוֹל אֲדוֹנֵינוּ וְרַב כֹּחַ, לִתְבוּנָתוֹ אֵין מִסְפָּר. מְעוֹדֵד
עֲנָוִים יְיָ, מַשְׁפִּיל רְשָׁעִים עֲדֵי אָרֶץ. עֱנוּ לַיְיָ בְּתוֹדָה, זַמְּרוּ
לֵאלֹהֵינוּ בְכִנּוֹר. הַמְכַסֶּה שָׁמַיִם בְּעָבִים, הַמֵּכִין לָאָרֶץ מָטָר,
הַמַּצְמִיחַ הָרִים חָצִיר. נוֹתֵן לִבְהֵמָה לַחְמָהּ, לִבְנֵי עֹרֵב אֲשֶׁר
יִקְרָאוּ. לֹא בִגְבוּרַת הַסּוּס יֶחְפָּץ, לֹא בְשׁוֹקֵי הָאִישׁ יִרְצֶה.
רוֹצֶה יְיָ אֶת יְרֵאָיו, אֶת הַמְיַחֲלִים לְחַסְדּוֹ. שַׁבְּחִי, יְרוּשָׁלַיִם,
אֶת יְיָ; הַלְלִי אֱלֹהַיִךְ, צִיּוֹן. כִּי חִזַּק בְּרִיחֵי שְׁעָרָיִךְ, בֵּרַךְ בָּנַיִךְ
בְּקִרְבֵּךְ. הַשָּׂם גְּבוּלֵךְ שָׁלוֹם, חֵלֶב חִטִּים יַשְׂבִּיעֵךְ. הַשֹּׁלֵחַ
אִמְרָתוֹ אָרֶץ; עַד מְהֵרָה יָרוּץ דְּבָרוֹ. הַנֹּתֵן שֶׁלֶג כַּצָּמֶר; כְּפוֹר
כָּאֵפֶר יְפַזֵּר. מַשְׁלִיךְ קַרְחוֹ כְפִתִּים; לִפְנֵי קָרָתוֹ מִי יַעֲמֹד.
יִשְׁלַח דְּבָרוֹ וְיַמְסֵם; יַשֵּׁב רוּחוֹ, יִזְּלוּ מָיִם. מַגִּיד דְּבָרָיו לְיַעֲקֹב,
חֻקָּיו וּמִשְׁפָּטָיו לְיִשְׂרָאֵל. Reader לֹא עָשָׂה כֵן לְכָל גּוֹי,
וּמִשְׁפָּטִים בַּל יְדָעוּם; הַלְלוּיָהּ.

תהלים קמח

הַלְלוּיָהּ; הַלְלוּ אֶת יְיָ מִן הַשָּׁמַיִם, הַלְלוּהוּ בַּמְּרוֹמִים.
הַלְלוּהוּ כָל מַלְאָכָיו, הַלְלוּהוּ כָל צְבָאָיו. הַלְלוּהוּ שֶׁמֶשׁ

designs perish. Happy is he who has the God of Jacob as his help, whose hope rests upon the Lord his God, Maker of heaven and earth and sea and all that is therein; who keeps faith forever, renders justice to the oppressed, and feeds those who are hungry. The Lord sets the captives free. The Lord opens the eyes of the blind, raises those who are bowed down, and loves the righteous. The Lord protects the strangers, and upholds the fatherless and the widow; but the way of the wicked he thwarts. The Lord shall reign forever; your God, O Zion, for all generations. Praise the Lord!

Psalm 147

Praise the Lord! It is good to sing to our God, it is pleasant; praise is comely. The Lord rebuilds Jerusalem; he gathers together the dispersed people of Israel. He heals the broken-hearted, and binds up their wounds. He counts the number of the stars, and gives a name to each. Great is our Lord and abundant in power; his wisdom is infinite. The Lord raises the humble; he casts the wicked down to the ground. Sing thanks to the Lord; make melody upon the harp to our God, who covers the sky with clouds, provides rain for the earth, and causes grass to grow upon the hills. He gives food to the cattle and to the crying young ravens. He cares not for [those who rely on] the strength of the horse; he delights not in [those who rely on] a warrior's legs. The Lord is pleased with those who revere him, those who yearn for his kindness. Praise the Lord, O Jerusalem! Praise your God, O Zion! He has indeed fortified your gates; he has blessed your children within. He establishes peace within your territory, and fills you with the finest of wheat. He sends forth his command to the earth; his word runs very swiftly. He gives snow like wool; he scatters hoarfrost like ashes. He casts forth his ice like crumbs; who can stand before his cold? He sends forth his word and melts them; he causes his wind to blow, and the waters flow. He declares his word to Jacob, his statutes and ordinances to Israel. He has not dealt so with heathen nations; his ordinances they do not know. Praise the Lord!

Psalm 148

Praise the Lord! Praise the Lord from the heavens; praise him in the heights. Praise him, all his angels; praise him, all his hosts.

לבני עורב that is, God sends food to the abandoned young birds that are unable to provide for themselves. The raven turns its young out of the nest at an early period.

וְיָרֵחַ, הַלְלוּהוּ כָּל כּוֹכְבֵי אוֹר. הַלְלוּהוּ שְׁמֵי הַשָּׁמָיִם, וְהַמַּיִם אֲשֶׁר מֵעַל הַשָּׁמָיִם. יְהַלְלוּ אֶת שֵׁם יְיָ, כִּי הוּא צִוָּה וְנִבְרָאוּ. וַיַּעֲמִידֵם לָעַד לְעוֹלָם, חָק־נָתַן וְלֹא יַעֲבוֹר. הַלְלוּ אֶת יְיָ מִן הָאָרֶץ, תַּנִּינִים וְכָל תְּהֹמוֹת. אֵשׁ וּבָרָד, שֶׁלֶג וְקִיטוֹר, רוּחַ סְעָרָה עֹשָׂה דְבָרוֹ. הֶהָרִים וְכָל גְּבָעוֹת, עֵץ פְּרִי וְכָל אֲרָזִים, הַחַיָּה וְכָל בְּהֵמָה, רֶמֶשׂ וְצִפּוֹר כָּנָף. מַלְכֵי אֶרֶץ וְכָל לְאֻמִּים, שָׂרִים וְכָל שֹׁפְטֵי אָרֶץ. בַּחוּרִים וְגַם בְּתוּלוֹת, זְקֵנִים עִם נְעָרִים. יְהַלְלוּ אֶת שֵׁם יְיָ, כִּי נִשְׂגָּב שְׁמוֹ לְבַדּוֹ; הוֹדוֹ עַל אֶרֶץ וְשָׁמָיִם. Reader וַיָּרֶם קֶרֶן לְעַמּוֹ, תְּהִלָּה לְכָל חֲסִידָיו, לִבְנֵי יִשְׂרָאֵל עַם קְרֹבוֹ; הַלְלוּיָהּ.

תהלים קמט

הַלְלוּיָהּ; שִׁירוּ לַיְיָ שִׁיר חָדָשׁ, תְּהִלָּתוֹ בִּקְהַל חֲסִידִים. יִשְׂמַח יִשְׂרָאֵל בְּעֹשָׂיו, בְּנֵי צִיּוֹן יָגִילוּ בְמַלְכָּם. יְהַלְלוּ שְׁמוֹ בְמָחוֹל, בְּתֹף וְכִנּוֹר יְזַמְּרוּ לוֹ. כִּי רוֹצֶה יְיָ בְּעַמּוֹ, יְפָאֵר עֲנָוִים בִּישׁוּעָה. יַעְלְזוּ חֲסִידִים בְּכָבוֹד, יְרַנְּנוּ עַל מִשְׁכְּבוֹתָם. רוֹמְמוֹת אֵל בִּגְרוֹנָם, וְחֶרֶב פִּיפִיּוֹת בְּיָדָם. לַעֲשׂוֹת נְקָמָה בַּגּוֹיִם, תּוֹכֵחוֹת בַּלְאֻמִּים. Reader לֶאְסֹר מַלְכֵיהֶם בְּזִקִּים, וְנִכְבְּדֵיהֶם בְּכַבְלֵי בַרְזֶל. לַעֲשׂוֹת בָּהֶם מִשְׁפָּט כָּתוּב; הָדָר הוּא לְכָל חֲסִידָיו; הַלְלוּיָהּ.

תהלים קנ

הַלְלוּיָהּ; הַלְלוּ אֵל בְּקָדְשׁוֹ, הַלְלוּהוּ בִּרְקִיעַ עֻזּוֹ. הַלְלוּהוּ בִגְבוּרֹתָיו, הַלְלוּהוּ כְּרֹב גֻּדְלוֹ. הַלְלוּהוּ בְּתֵקַע שׁוֹפָר, הַלְלוּהוּ בְּנֵבֶל וְכִנּוֹר. הַלְלוּהוּ בְּתֹף וּמָחוֹל, הַלְלוּהוּ בְּמִנִּים וְעֻגָב.

המים ... מעל השמים According to Genesis 1:6–7, there are waters above the heavens.

שיר חדש a new song, in acknowledgment of a fresh act of deliverance by God which merits a new song of thanksgiving. יפאר ענוים God restores the

Praise him, sun and moon; praise him, all you stars of light. Praise him, highest heavens and waters that are above the heavens. Let them praise the name of the Lord; for he commanded and they were created. He fixed them fast forever and ever; he gave a law which none transgresses. Praise the Lord from the earth, you sea-monsters and all depths; fire and hail, snow and vapor, stormy wind, fulfilling his word; mountains and all hills, fruit-trees and all cedars; wild animals and all cattle, crawling things and winged fowl; kings of the earth and all nations, princes and all earthly rulers; young men and maidens, old men and children; let them praise the name of the Lord, for his name alone is exalted; his majesty is above earth and heaven. He has raised the honor of his people, the glory of his faithful followers, the children of Israel, the people near to him. Praise the Lord!

Psalm 149

Praise the Lord! Sing a new song to the Lord; praise him in the assembly of the faithful. Let Israel rejoice in his Maker; let the children of Zion exult in their King. Let them praise his name with dancing; let them make music to him with drum and harp. For the Lord is pleased with his people; he adorns the meek with triumph. Let the faithful exult in glory; let them sing upon their beds. Let the praises of God be in their mouth, and a double-edged sword in their hand, to execute vengeance upon the nations, punishment upon the peoples; to bind their kings with chains, and their nobles with fetters of iron; to execute upon them the written judgment. He is the glory of all his faithful. Praise the Lord!

Psalm 150

Praise the Lord! Praise God in his sanctuary; praise him in his glorious heaven. Praise him for his mighty deeds; praise him for his abundant greatness. Praise him with the blast of the horn; praise him with the harp and the lyre. Praise him with the drum and dance; praise him with strings and flute. Praise him with re-

---

dignity and honor to those who have been humiliated and degraded. ירננו על משכבותם that is, they can lie down in peace, their foes having been defeated. ... רוממות–וחרב The Maccabean warriors were described as "fighting with their hands and praying with their hearts."

According to Josephus, the נבל had twelve strings and the כנור ten. מחול The dance was an important part of religious ceremonies. "David danced before the Lord with all his might" (II Samuel 6:14). עוגב was a wind instrument, a flute, which was called אבוב in the period of the second Temple.

הַלְלוּהוּ בְצִלְצְלֵי שָׁמַע, הַלְלוּהוּ בְּצִלְצְלֵי תְרוּעָה. Reader בֹּל
הַנְּשָׁמָה תְּהַלֵּל יָהּ; הַלְלוּיָהּ. כֹּל הַנְּשָׁמָה תְּהַלֵּל יָהּ; הַלְלוּיָהּ.

בָּרוּךְ יְיָ לְעוֹלָם, אָמֵן וְאָמֵן. בָּרוּךְ יְיָ מִצִּיּוֹן, שֹׁכֵן יְרוּשָׁלָיִם;
הַלְלוּיָהּ. בָּרוּךְ יְיָ אֱלֹהִים, אֱלֹהֵי יִשְׂרָאֵל, עֹשֵׂה נִפְלָאוֹת לְבַדּוֹ.
Reader וּבָרוּךְ שֵׁם כְּבוֹדוֹ לְעוֹלָם; וְיִמָּלֵא כְבוֹדוֹ אֶת כָּל הָאָרֶץ,
אָמֵן וְאָמֵן.

דברי הימים א כט, י-יג

וַיְבָרֶךְ דָּוִיד אֶת יְיָ לְעֵינֵי כָּל הַקָּהָל, וַיֹּאמֶר דָּוִיד: בָּרוּךְ
אַתָּה יְיָ, אֱלֹהֵי יִשְׂרָאֵל אָבִינוּ, מֵעוֹלָם וְעַד עוֹלָם. לְךָ יְיָ
הַגְּדֻלָּה וְהַגְּבוּרָה וְהַתִּפְאֶרֶת וְהַנֵּצַח וְהַהוֹד, כִּי כֹל בַּשָּׁמַיִם
וּבָאָרֶץ; לְךָ יְיָ הַמַּמְלָכָה, וְהַמִּתְנַשֵּׂא לְכֹל לְרֹאשׁ. וְהָעֹשֶׁר
וְהַכָּבוֹד מִלְּפָנֶיךָ, וְאַתָּה מוֹשֵׁל בַּכֹּל, וּבְיָדְךָ כֹּחַ וּגְבוּרָה,
וּבְיָדְךָ לְגַדֵּל וּלְחַזֵּק לַכֹּל. וְעַתָּה אֱלֹהֵינוּ, מוֹדִים אֲנַחְנוּ לָךְ,
וּמְהַלְלִים לְשֵׁם תִּפְאַרְתֶּךָ.

נחמיה ט, ו-יא

אַתָּה הוּא יְיָ לְבַדֶּךָ, אַתָּה עָשִׂיתָ אֶת הַשָּׁמַיִם, שְׁמֵי הַשָּׁמַיִם
וְכָל צְבָאָם, הָאָרֶץ וְכָל אֲשֶׁר עָלֶיהָ, הַיַּמִּים וְכָל אֲשֶׁר בָּהֶם,
וְאַתָּה מְחַיֶּה אֶת כֻּלָּם, וּצְבָא הַשָּׁמַיִם לְךָ מִשְׁתַּחֲוִים. Reader אַתָּה
הוּא יְיָ הָאֱלֹהִים, אֲשֶׁר בָּחַרְתָּ בְּאַבְרָם וְהוֹצֵאתוֹ מֵאוּר כַּשְׂדִּים
וְשַׂמְתָּ שְׁמוֹ אַבְרָהָם. וּמָצָאתָ אֶת לְבָבוֹ נֶאֱמָן לְפָנֶיךָ—

וְכָרוֹת עִמּוֹ הַבְּרִית לָתֵת אֶת אֶרֶץ הַכְּנַעֲנִי, הַחִתִּי, הָאֱמֹרִי,
וְהַפְּרִזִּי וְהַיְבוּסִי וְהַגִּרְגָּשִׁי, לָתֵת לְזַרְעוֹ; וַתָּקֶם אֶת דְּבָרֶיךָ, כִּי
צַדִּיק אָתָּה. וַתֵּרֶא אֶת עֳנִי אֲבֹתֵינוּ בְּמִצְרָיִם, וְאֶת זַעֲקָתָם
שָׁמַעְתָּ עַל יַם סוּף. וַתִּתֵּן אֹתֹת וּמֹפְתִים בְּפַרְעֹה וּבְכָל עֲבָדָיו

צלצלי שמע cymbals of soft sound, castanets or metal discs fixed to two fingers
of the hand. צלצלי תרועה cymbals of loud sound, constructed of copper.

sounding cymbals; praise him with clanging cymbals. Let everything that has breath praise the Lord. Praise the Lord!

Blessed be the Lord forever. Amen, Amen. Blessed out of Zion
be the Lord who dwells in Jerusalem. Praise the Lord! Blessed be
the Lord God, the God of Israel, who alone works wonders; blessed
be his glorious name forever. May the whole earth be filled with
his glory. Amen, Amen.[1]

I Chronicles 29:10–13

David blessed the Lord before all the assembly, and David
said: Blessed art thou, O Lord, God of Israel our father, forever
and ever. Thine, O Lord, is the greatness and the power, the glory
and the victory and the majesty, for all that is in heaven and on
earth is thine; thine, O Lord, is the kingdom, and thou art supreme
over all. Riches and honor come from thee; thou rulest over all;
in thy hand are power and might, and it is in thy power to make
all great and strong. Hence, our God, we ever thank thee and praise
thy glorious name.

Nehemiah 9:6–11

Thou art the Lord, thou alone. Thou hast made the heavens
and the heaven of heavens with all their host, the earth and all
the things upon it, the seas and all that is in them, and thou preservest them all; the host of the heavens worships thee. Thou art
the Lord God, who didst choose Abram, and didst bring him out
of Ur of the Chaldeans, and gavest him the name of Abraham.
Thou didst find his heart faithful before thee, and didst make a
covenant with him to give the land of the Canaanite, the Hittite,
the Amorite, the Perizzite, the Jebusite, and the Girgashite—to
give it to his descendants, and hast fulfilled thy words, for thou
art righteous. Thou didst see the distress of our fathers in Egypt
and hear their cry by the Red Sea; thou didst show signs and
wonders on Pharaoh and all his servants and all the people of his

---

כל הנשמה is repeated because this verse marks the end of the Book of
Psalms.

וכרות is recited responsively on the occasion of a *Brith Milah;* hence it
has been arranged as a new paragraph. וכרות is part of the preceding verse.

[1] *Psalms* 89:53; 135:21; 72:18–19.

וּבְכָל עַם אַרְצוֹ, כִּי יָדַעְתָּ כִּי הֵזִידוּ עֲלֵיהֶם; וַתַּעַשׂ לְךָ שֵׁם כְּהַיּוֹם הַזֶּה. Reader וְהַיָּם בָּקַעְתָּ לִפְנֵיהֶם, וַיַּעַבְרוּ בְתוֹךְ הַיָּם בַּיַּבָּשָׁה; וְאֶת רֹדְפֵיהֶם הִשְׁלַכְתָּ בִמְצוֹלֹת, כְּמוֹ אֶבֶן בְּמַיִם עַזִּים.

שמות יד, ל-לא

וַיּוֹשַׁע יְיָ בַּיּוֹם הַהוּא אֶת יִשְׂרָאֵל מִיַּד מִצְרָיִם; וַיַּרְא יִשְׂרָאֵל אֶת מִצְרַיִם מֵת עַל שְׂפַת הַיָּם. Reader וַיַּרְא יִשְׂרָאֵל אֶת הַיָּד הַגְּדֹלָה אֲשֶׁר עָשָׂה יְיָ בְּמִצְרַיִם, וַיִּירְאוּ הָעָם אֶת יְיָ, וַיַּאֲמִינוּ בַּיְיָ וּבְמֹשֶׁה עַבְדּוֹ.

שמות טו, א-יח

אָז יָשִׁיר מֹשֶׁה וּבְנֵי יִשְׂרָאֵל אֶת הַשִּׁירָה הַזֹּאת לַיְיָ, וַיֹּאמְרוּ לֵאמֹר: אָשִׁירָה לַיְיָ כִּי גָאֹה גָּאָה, סוּס וְרֹכְבוֹ רָמָה בַיָּם. עָזִּי וְזִמְרָת יָהּ, וַיְהִי לִי לִישׁוּעָה; זֶה אֵלִי וְאַנְוֵהוּ, אֱלֹהֵי אָבִי וַאֲרֹמְמֶנְהוּ. יְיָ אִישׁ מִלְחָמָה, יְיָ שְׁמוֹ. מַרְכְּבֹת פַּרְעֹה וְחֵילוֹ יָרָה בַיָּם, וּמִבְחַר שָׁלִשָׁיו טֻבְּעוּ בְיַם סוּף. תְּהֹמֹת יְכַסְיֻמוּ: יָרְדוּ בִמְצוֹלֹת כְּמוֹ אָבֶן. יְמִינְךָ יְיָ נֶאְדָּרִי בַּכֹּחַ, יְמִינְךָ יְיָ תִּרְעַץ אוֹיֵב. וּבְרֹב גְּאוֹנְךָ תַּהֲרֹס קָמֶיךָ; תְּשַׁלַּח חֲרֹנְךָ, יֹאכְלֵמוֹ כַּקַּשׁ. וּבְרוּחַ אַפֶּיךָ נֶעֶרְמוּ מַיִם, נִצְּבוּ כְמוֹ נֵד נֹזְלִים; קָפְאוּ תְהֹמֹת בְּלֶב יָם. אָמַר אוֹיֵב: אֶרְדֹּף אַשִּׂיג, אֲחַלֵּק שָׁלָל, תִּמְלָאֵמוֹ נַפְשִׁי, אָרִיק חַרְבִּי, תּוֹרִישֵׁמוֹ יָדִי. נָשַׁפְתָּ בְרוּחֲךָ, כִּסָּמוֹ יָם; צָלֲלוּ כַּעוֹפֶרֶת בְּמַיִם אַדִּירִים. מִי כָמֹכָה בָּאֵלִם, יְיָ; מִי כָּמֹכָה, נֶאְדָּר בַּקֹּדֶשׁ, נוֹרָא תְהִלֹּת, עֹשֵׂה פֶלֶא. נָטִיתָ יְמִינְךָ, תִּבְלָעֵמוֹ אָרֶץ. נָחִיתָ בְחַסְדְּךָ עַם־זוּ גָּאָלְתָּ; נֵהַלְתָּ בְעָזְּךָ אֶל נְוֵה קָדְשֶׁךָ. שָׁמְעוּ עַמִּים, יִרְגָּזוּן; חִיל אָחַז יֹשְׁבֵי פְּלָשֶׁת. אָז נִבְהֲלוּ אַלּוּפֵי

land, for thou knewest that they dealt viciously against them; and so hast thou made a name for thyself to this day. The sea thou didst divide before them, so that they went through the middle of the sea on dry ground; and their pursuers thou didst cast into the depths, like a stone into the mighty waters.

Exodus 14:30–31

Thus did the Lord save Israel that day from the power of the Egyptians; and Israel saw the Egyptians dead on the seashore. Israel saw the mighty act which the Lord had performed against the Egyptians, and the people revered the Lord; they believed in the Lord and in his servant Moses.

Exodus 15:1–18

Then Moses and the children of Israel sang this song to the Lord; they said: I will sing to the Lord, for he has completely triumphed; the horse and its rider he has hurled into the sea. The Lord is my strength and song, for he has come to my aid. This is my God, and I will glorify him; my father's God, and I will extol him. The Lord is a warrior—Lord is his name. Pharaoh's chariots and his army he has cast into the sea, and his picked captains are engulfed in the Red Sea. The depths cover them; they went down into the depths like a stone. Thy right hand, O Lord, glori-ous in power, thy right hand, O Lord, crushes the enemy. By thy great majesty thou destroyest thy opponents. Thou sendest forth thy wrath—it consumes them like stubble. By the blast of thy nostrils the waters piled up—the floods stood upright like a wall; the depths were congealed in the heart of the sea. The enemy said: "I will pursue them, I will overtake them, I will divide the spoil, my lust shall be glutted with them; I will draw my sword, my hand shall destroy them." Thou didst blow with thy wind—the sea covered them; they sank like lead in the mighty waters. Who is there like thee among the mighty, O Lord? Who is like thee, glorious in holiness, awe-inspiring in renown, doing marvels? Thou didst stretch out thy right hand—the earth swallowed them. In thy grace thou hast led the people whom thou hast redeemed; by thy power thou hast guided them to thy holy habitation. The peoples have heard of it and trembled; pangs have seized the in-habitants of Philistia. Then were the chieftains of Edom in agony;

אֱדוֹם; אֵילֵי מוֹאָב יֹאחֲזֵמוֹ רָעַד; נָמֹגוּ כֹּל יֹשְׁבֵי כְנָעַן. תִּפֹּל
עֲלֵיהֶם אֵימָתָה וָפַחַד; בִּגְדֹל זְרוֹעֲךָ יִדְּמוּ כָּאָבֶן; עַד יַעֲבֹר
עַמְּךָ יְיָ, עַד יַעֲבֹר עַם־זוּ קָנִיתָ. תְּבִאֵמוֹ וְתִטָּעֵמוֹ בְּהַר נַחֲלָתְךָ,
מָכוֹן לְשִׁבְתְּךָ פָּעַלְתָּ, יְיָ; מִקְדָּשׁ, אֲדֹנָי, כּוֹנְנוּ יָדֶיךָ. יְיָ יִמְלֹךְ
לְעֹלָם וָעֶד. יְיָ יִמְלֹךְ לְעֹלָם וָעֶד.

כִּי לַיְיָ הַמְּלוּכָה, וּמֹשֵׁל בַּגּוֹיִם. Reader. וְעָלוּ מוֹשִׁיעִים בְּהַר
צִיּוֹן לִשְׁפֹּט אֶת הַר עֵשָׂו, וְהָיְתָה לַיְיָ הַמְּלוּכָה. וְהָיָה יְיָ לְמֶלֶךְ
עַל כָּל הָאָרֶץ; בַּיּוֹם הַהוּא יִהְיֶה יְיָ אֶחָד וּשְׁמוֹ אֶחָד.

יִשְׁתַּבַּח שִׁמְךָ לָעַד, מַלְכֵּנוּ, הָאֵל הַמֶּלֶךְ הַגָּדוֹל וְהַקָּדוֹשׁ,
בַּשָּׁמַיִם וּבָאָרֶץ. כִּי לְךָ נָאֶה, יְיָ אֱלֹהֵינוּ וֵאלֹהֵי אֲבוֹתֵינוּ, שִׁיר
וּשְׁבָחָה, הַלֵּל וְזִמְרָה, עֹז וּמֶמְשָׁלָה, נֶצַח, גְּדֻלָּה וּגְבוּרָה, תְּהִלָּה
וְתִפְאֶרֶת, קְדֻשָּׁה וּמַלְכוּת, Reader בְּרָכוֹת וְהוֹדָאוֹת, מֵעַתָּה
וְעַד עוֹלָם. בָּרוּךְ אַתָּה, יְיָ, אֵל מֶלֶךְ גָּדוֹל בַּתִּשְׁבָּחוֹת, אֵל
הַהוֹדָאוֹת, אֲדוֹן הַנִּפְלָאוֹת, הַבּוֹחֵר בְּשִׁירֵי זִמְרָה, מֶלֶךְ, אֵל,
חֵי הָעוֹלָמִים.

Reader:

יִתְגַּדַּל וְיִתְקַדַּשׁ שְׁמֵהּ רַבָּא בְּעָלְמָא דִי בְרָא כִרְעוּתֵהּ;
וְיַמְלִיךְ מַלְכוּתֵהּ בְּחַיֵּיכוֹן וּבְיוֹמֵיכוֹן, וּבְחַיֵּי דְכָל בֵּית יִשְׂרָאֵל,
בַּעֲגָלָא וּבִזְמַן קָרִיב, וְאִמְרוּ אָמֵן.

יְהֵא שְׁמֵהּ רַבָּא מְבָרַךְ לְעָלַם וּלְעָלְמֵי עָלְמַיָּא.

יִתְבָּרַךְ וְיִשְׁתַּבַּח, וְיִתְפָּאַר וְיִתְרוֹמַם, וְיִתְנַשֵּׂא וְיִתְהַדָּר,
וְיִתְעַלֶּה וְיִתְהַלָּל שְׁמֵהּ דְּקֻדְשָׁא, בְּרִיךְ הוּא, לְעֵלָּא (לְעֵלָּא)
מִן כָּל בִּרְכָתָא וְשִׁירָתָא, תֻּשְׁבְּחָתָא וְנֶחֱמָתָא, דַּאֲמִירָן בְּעָלְמָא,
וְאִמְרוּ אָמֵן.

יְיָ ה' יִמְלֹךְ is said twice to mark the end of שירת הים (Abudarham).
יִשְׁתַּבַּח and בָּרוּךְ שֶׁאָמַר form the prologue and the epilogue to *Pesuke d'Zim-*

trembling seized the lords of Moab; all the inhabitants of Canaan melted away. Terror and dread fell on them. Under the great sweep of thy arm they are as still as a stone, till thy people pass over, O Lord, till the people thou hast acquired pass over. Thou wilt bring them in and plant them in the highlands of thy own, the place which thou, O Lord, hast made for thy dwelling, the sanctuary, O Lord, which thy hands have established. The Lord shall reign forever and ever. The Lord shall reign forever and ever.

For sovereignty is the Lord's, and he governs the nations. Deliverers shall go up to Mount Zion to rule the hill country of Esau, and dominion shall be the Lord's. The Lord shall be King over all the earth; on that day shall the Lord be One and his name One.[1]

Praised be thy name forever, our King, great and holy God and King, in heaven and on earth; for to thee, Lord our God and God of our fathers, pertain song and praise, hymn and psalm, power and dominion, victory, greatness and might, renown and glory, holiness and kingship, blessings and thanks, henceforth and forever. Blessed art thou, O Lord, most exalted God and King, Lord of wonders, who art pleased with hymns, thou God and King, the life of the universe.

Reader:

Glorified and sanctified be God's great name throughout the world which he has created according to his will. May he establish his kingdom in your lifetime and during your days, and within the life of the entire house of Israel, speedily and soon; and say, Amen.

May his great name be blessed forever and to all eternity.

Blessed and praised, glorified and exalted, extolled and honored, adored and lauded be the name of the Holy One, blessed be he, beyond all the blessings and hymns, praises and consolations that are ever spoken in the world; and say, Amen.

---

rah. It has been suggested that the name of the author of *Yishtabah* was Solomon, since the initial letters of the words שמך לעד מלכנו האל form the acrostic שלמה. According to some, the fifteen synonyms of praise correspond to the fifteen psalms known as שיר המעלות.

[1] *Psalm* 22:29; *Obadiah* 1:21; *Zechariah* 14:9.

Reader:

בָּרְכוּ אֶת יְיָ הַמְבֹרָךְ.

Silent meditation:

יִתְבָּרַךְ וְיִשְׁתַּבַּח, וְיִתְפָּאַר וְיִתְרוֹמַם וְיִתְנַשֵּׂא שְׁמוֹ שֶׁל מֶלֶךְ מַלְכֵי הַמְּלָכִים, הַקָּדוֹשׁ בָּרוּךְ הוּא, שֶׁהוּא רִאשׁוֹן וְהוּא אַחֲרוֹן, וּמִבַּלְעָדָיו אֵין אֱלֹהִים. סֹלּוּ

Congregation and Reader:

בָּרוּךְ יְיָ הַמְבֹרָךְ לְעוֹלָם וָעֶד.

לָרֹכֵב בָּעֲרָבוֹת, בְּיָהּ שְׁמוֹ, וְעִלְזוּ לְפָנָיו; וּשְׁמוֹ מְרוֹמָם עַל כָּל בְּרָכָה וּתְהִלָּה. בָּרוּךְ שֵׁם כְּבוֹד מַלְכוּתוֹ לְעוֹלָם וָעֶד. יְהִי שֵׁם יְיָ מְבֹרָךְ מֵעַתָּה וְעַד עוֹלָם.

בָּרוּךְ אַתָּה, יְיָ אֱלֹהֵינוּ, מֶלֶךְ הָעוֹלָם, יוֹצֵר אוֹר וּבוֹרֵא חֹשֶׁךְ, עֹשֶׂה שָׁלוֹם, וּבוֹרֵא אֶת הַכֹּל.

הַמֵּאִיר לָאָרֶץ וְלַדָּרִים עָלֶיהָ בְּרַחֲמִים, וּבְטוּבוֹ מְחַדֵּשׁ בְּכָל יוֹם תָּמִיד מַעֲשֵׂה בְרֵאשִׁית. מָה רַבּוּ מַעֲשֶׂיךָ, יְיָ, כֻּלָּם בְּחָכְמָה עָשִׂיתָ, מָלְאָה הָאָרֶץ קִנְיָנֶךָ. הַמֶּלֶךְ הַמְרוֹמָם לְבַדּוֹ מֵאָז, הַמְשֻׁבָּח וְהַמְפֹאָר וְהַמִּתְנַשֵּׂא מִימוֹת עוֹלָם. אֱלֹהֵי עוֹלָם, בְּרַחֲמֶיךָ הָרַבִּים רַחֵם עָלֵינוּ, אֲדוֹן עֻזֵּנוּ, צוּר מִשְׂגַּבֵּנוּ, מָגֵן יִשְׁעֵנוּ, מִשְׂגָּב בַּעֲדֵנוּ.

אֵל בָּרוּךְ גְּדוֹל דֵּעָה, הֵכִין וּפָעַל זָהֳרֵי חַמָּה, טוֹב יָצַר כָּבוֹד לִשְׁמוֹ, מְאוֹרוֹת נָתַן סְבִיבוֹת עֻזּוֹ, פִּנּוֹת צְבָאָיו קְדוֹשִׁים, רוֹמְמֵי שַׁדַּי, תָּמִיד מְסַפְּרִים כְּבוֹד אֵל וּקְדֻשָּׁתוֹ. תִּתְבָּרַךְ, יְיָ אֱלֹהֵינוּ, עַל שֶׁבַח מַעֲשֵׂה יָדֶיךָ, וְעַל מְאוֹרֵי אוֹר שֶׁעָשִׂיתָ; יְפָאֲרוּךָ סֶּלָה.

תִּתְבָּרַךְ צוּרֵנוּ, מַלְכֵּנוּ וְגוֹאֲלֵנוּ, בּוֹרֵא קְדוֹשִׁים; יִשְׁתַּבַּח שִׁמְךָ לָעַד מַלְכֵּנוּ, יוֹצֵר מְשָׁרְתִים, וַאֲשֶׁר מְשָׁרְתָיו כֻּלָּם עוֹמְדִים בְּרוּם עוֹלָם, וּמַשְׁמִיעִים בְּיִרְאָה, יַחַד בְּקוֹל, דִּבְרֵי אֱלֹהִים חַיִּים וּמֶלֶךְ עוֹלָם. כֻּלָּם אֲהוּבִים, כֻּלָּם בְּרוּרִים, כֻּלָּם

ברכו introduces the main part of the service, consisting of the *Shema* and the *Shemoneh Esreh*. The silent meditation, found in Maḥzor Vitry, includes a sentence of the Aramaic Kaddish rendered into Hebrew and parts of Isaiah 44:6, Psalms 68:5 and 113:2.

Reader:

Bless the Lord who is blessed.

Congregation and Reader:

Blessed be the Lord who is blessed
forever and ever.

Silent meditation:

Blessed, praised, glorified, extolled and exalted be the name
of the supreme King of kings,
the Holy One, blessed be he,
who is the first and the last, and

besides him there is no God. Extol him who is in the heavens—Lord is his
name, and rejoice before him. His name is exalted above all blessing and
praise. Blessed be the name of his glorious majesty forever and ever. Let the
name of the Lord be blessed henceforth and forever.

Blessed art thou, Lord our God, King of the universe, who
formest light and createst darkness, who makest peace and createst
all things.

In mercy thou givest light to the earth and to those who dwell
on it; in thy goodness thou renewest the work of creation every
day, constantly. How great are thy works, O Lord! In wisdom
hast thou made them all; the earth is full of thy creations. Thou
alone, O King, hast ever been exalted, lauded and glorified and
extolled from days of old. Eternal God, show us thy great mercy!
Thou art Lord of our strength, our defending Stronghold, our
saving Shield, our Protector.

The blessed God, great in knowledge, designed and made the
brilliant sun. The Beneficent One created glory for his name. He
placed luminaries round about his majesty. His chief hosts are
holy beings that extol the Almighty. They constantly recount
God's glory and holiness. Be thou blessed, Lord our God, for thy
excellent handiwork and for the luminaries which thou hast made;
they ever render thee glory.

Be thou blessed, our Stronghold, our King and Redeemer,
Creator of holy beings; praised be thy name forever, our King,
Creator of ministering angels, all of whom stand in the heights
of the universe and reverently proclaim in unison, aloud, the

---

יוצר אור is a modified form of Isaiah 45:7, where the text has ובורא רע.
This variation is explained to be due to a desire of using a more auspicious
expression (Berakhoth 11b).

אל ברוך is an alphabetical acrostic, the words beginning with the letters
of the alphabet in regular order.

גְּבוֹרִים, וְכֻלָּם עֹשִׂים בְּאֵימָה וּבְיִרְאָה רְצוֹן קוֹנָם. Reader וְכֻלָּם
פּוֹתְחִים אֶת פִּיהֶם בִּקְדֻשָּׁה וּבְטָהֳרָה, בְּשִׁירָה וּבְזִמְרָה,
וּמְבָרְכִים וּמְשַׁבְּחִים, וּמְפָאֲרִים וּמַעֲרִיצִים, וּמַקְדִּישִׁים
וּמַמְלִיכִים—

אֶת שֵׁם הָאֵל הַמֶּלֶךְ הַגָּדוֹל, הַגִּבּוֹר וְהַנּוֹרָא, קָדוֹשׁ הוּא.
וְכֻלָּם מְקַבְּלִים עֲלֵיהֶם עֹל מַלְכוּת שָׁמַיִם זֶה מִזֶּה, וְנוֹתְנִים
רְשׁוּת זֶה לָזֶה Reader לְהַקְדִּישׁ לְיוֹצְרָם. בְּנַחַת רוּחַ, בְּשָׂפָה
בְרוּרָה וּבִנְעִימָה קְדֻשָּׁה, כֻּלָּם כְּאֶחָד עוֹנִים וְאוֹמְרִים בְּיִרְאָה:
קָדוֹשׁ, קָדוֹשׁ, קָדוֹשׁ יְיָ צְבָאוֹת;

מְלֹא כָל הָאָרֶץ כְּבוֹדוֹ.

וְהָאוֹפַנִּים וְחַיּוֹת הַקֹּדֶשׁ, בְּרַעַשׁ גָּדוֹל מִתְנַשְּׂאִים לְעֻמַּת
שְׂרָפִים. Reader לְעֻמָּתָם מְשַׁבְּחִים וְאוֹמְרִים:

בָּרוּךְ כְּבוֹד יְיָ מִמְּקוֹמוֹ.

לְאֵל בָּרוּךְ נְעִימוֹת יִתֵּנוּ; לַמֶּלֶךְ, אֵל חַי וְקַיָּם, זְמִרוֹת
יֹאמֵרוּ, וְתִשְׁבָּחוֹת יַשְׁמִיעוּ; כִּי הוּא לְבַדּוֹ פּוֹעֵל גְּבוּרוֹת, עֹשֶׂה
חֲדָשׁוֹת, בַּעַל מִלְחָמוֹת, זוֹרֵעַ צְדָקוֹת, מַצְמִיחַ יְשׁוּעוֹת, בּוֹרֵא
רְפוּאוֹת, נוֹרָא תְהִלּוֹת, אֲדוֹן הַנִּפְלָאוֹת, הַמְחַדֵּשׁ בְּטוּבוֹ בְּכָל
יוֹם תָּמִיד מַעֲשֵׂה בְרֵאשִׁית, כָּאָמוּר: לְעֹשֵׂה אוֹרִים גְּדֹלִים, כִּי
לְעוֹלָם חַסְדּוֹ. Reader אוֹר חָדָשׁ עַל צִיּוֹן תָּאִיר, וְנִזְכֶּה כֻלָּנוּ
מְהֵרָה לְאוֹרוֹ. בָּרוּךְ אַתָּה, יְיָ, יוֹצֵר הַמְּאוֹרוֹת.

אַהֲבָה רַבָּה אֲהַבְתָּנוּ, יְיָ אֱלֹהֵינוּ; חֶמְלָה גְדוֹלָה וִיתֵרָה
חָמַלְתָּ עָלֵינוּ. אָבִינוּ מַלְכֵּנוּ, בַּעֲבוּר אֲבוֹתֵינוּ שֶׁבָּטְחוּ בְךָ
וַתְּלַמְּדֵם חֻקֵּי חַיִּים, כֵּן תְּחָנֵּנוּ וּתְלַמְּדֵנוּ. אָבִינוּ, הָאָב הָרַחֲמָן,

---

אהבה רבה, one of the most beautiful prayers in the liturgies of the world,
is very old and was probably instituted by the men of the Great Assembly
in the early period of the second Temple. A profound love for God and the

words of the living God and everlasting King. All of them are beloved, all of them are pure, all of them are mighty; they all perform with awe and reverence the will of their Creator; they all open their mouth with holiness and purity, with song and melody, while they bless and praise, glorify and reverence, sanctify and acclaim—

The name of the great, mighty and revered God and King; holy is he. They all accept the rule of the kingdom of heaven, one from the other, granting permission to one another to hallow their Creator. In serene spirit, with pure speech and sacred melody, they all exclaim in unison and with reverence:

Holy, holy, holy is the Lord of hosts;
The whole earth is full of his glory.[1]

Then the celestial ofannim and the holy beings, rising with a loud sound toward the seraphim, respond with praise and say:

Blessed be the glory of the Lord from his abode.[2]

To the blessed God they offer melodies; to the King, the living and eternal God, they utter hymns and praises. Truly, he alone performs mighty acts and creates new things; he is a warrior who sows justice, produces triumphs, and creates healing. Revered in renown, Lord of wonders, in his goodness he renews the creation every day, constantly, as it is said: "He makes the great lights; truly, his mercy endures forever."[3] O cause a new light to shine upon Zion, and may we all be worthy soon to enjoy its brightness. Blessed art thou, O Lord, Creator of the lights.

With a great love hast thou loved us, Lord our God; great and abundant mercy hast thou bestowed upon us. Our Father, our King, for the sake of our forebears who trusted in thee, whom thou didst teach laws of life, be gracious to us and teach us likewise. Our Father, merciful Father, thou who art ever compas-

---

Torah is echoed in this prayer, in which the merciful Father is entreated to enlighten our eyes and our minds to understand his teachings. This is the second of the two blessings preceding the *Shema,* יוצר אור being the first. As Psalm 19 praises God first for the sun and then for the Torah which enlightens the mind, so have we in these two blessings first a thanksgiving for natural light, then a thanksgiving for spiritual enlightenment. As in the case with all the prayers, occasional variations have been introduced here in the course of many centuries.

[1] *Isaiah* 6:3.   [2] *Ezekiel* 3:12.   [3] *Psalm* 136:7.

הַמְרַחֵם, רַחֵם עָלֵינוּ וְתֵן בְּלִבֵּנוּ לְהָבִין וּלְהַשְׂכִּיל, לִשְׁמֹעַ
לִלְמֹד וּלְלַמֵּד, לִשְׁמֹר וְלַעֲשׂוֹת וּלְקַיֵּם אֶת כָּל דִּבְרֵי תַלְמוּד
תוֹרָתֶךָ, בְּאַהֲבָה. וְהָאֵר עֵינֵינוּ בְּתוֹרָתֶךָ, וְדַבֵּק לִבֵּנוּ בְּמִצְוֹתֶיךָ,
וְיַחֵד לְבָבֵנוּ לְאַהֲבָה וּלְיִרְאָה אֶת שְׁמֶךָ, וְלֹא נֵבוֹשׁ לְעוֹלָם
וָעֶד. כִּי בְשֵׁם קָדְשְׁךָ הַגָּדוֹל וְהַנּוֹרָא בָּטָחְנוּ, נָגִילָה וְנִשְׂמְחָה
בִּישׁוּעָתֶךָ. Reader וַהֲבִיאֵנוּ לְשָׁלוֹם מֵאַרְבַּע כַּנְפוֹת הָאָרֶץ,
וְתוֹלִיכֵנוּ קוֹמְמִיּוּת לְאַרְצֵנוּ. כִּי אֵל פּוֹעֵל יְשׁוּעוֹת אָתָּה, וּבָנוּ
בָחַרְתָּ מִכָּל עַם וְלָשׁוֹן, וְקֵרַבְתָּנוּ לְשִׁמְךָ הַגָּדוֹל סֶלָה בֶּאֱמֶת,
לְהוֹדוֹת לְךָ וּלְיַחֶדְךָ בְּאַהֲבָה. בָּרוּךְ אַתָּה, יְיָ, הַבּוֹחֵר בְּעַמּוֹ
יִשְׂרָאֵל בְּאַהֲבָה.

(When praying in private, add: אֵל מֶלֶךְ נֶאֱמָן)

דברים ו, ד–ט

שְׁמַע יִשְׂרָאֵל, יְיָ אֱלֹהֵינוּ, יְיָ אֶחָד.

בָּרוּךְ שֵׁם כְּבוֹד מַלְכוּתוֹ לְעוֹלָם וָעֶד.

וְאָהַבְתָּ אֵת יְיָ אֱלֹהֶיךָ בְּכָל לְבָבְךָ וּבְכָל נַפְשְׁךָ וּבְכָל
מְאֹדֶךָ. וְהָיוּ הַדְּבָרִים הָאֵלֶּה, אֲשֶׁר אָנֹכִי מְצַוְּךָ הַיּוֹם, עַל
לְבָבֶךָ. וְשִׁנַּנְתָּם לְבָנֶיךָ, וְדִבַּרְתָּ בָּם בְּשִׁבְתְּךָ בְּבֵיתֶךָ, וּבְלֶכְתְּךָ
בַדֶּרֶךְ, וּבְשָׁכְבְּךָ וּבְקוּמֶךָ. וּקְשַׁרְתָּם לְאוֹת עַל יָדֶךָ, וְהָיוּ
לְטֹטָפֹת בֵּין עֵינֶיךָ. וּכְתַבְתָּם עַל מְזֻזוֹת בֵּיתֶךָ וּבִשְׁעָרֶיךָ.

יחד לבבנו let our heart be concentrated upon God, and not distracted by
worldly desires. Such singleheartedness is frequently expressed by the phrases
"a whole heart", "a perfect heart."

The initial letters of אל מלך נאמן form the word אמן. There are 245 words
in the *Shema*. When the Reader repeats ה' אלהיכם אמת the number of words is
raised to 248, corresponding to the 248 parts of the human frame. On reciting
the *Shema* privately, however, one is required to add the three words אל מלך
נאמן in order to complete the number 248.

The last letters of שמע and אחד form the word עד ("witness"), that is,
he who recites the *Shema* bears witness that God is One.

sionate, have pity on us and inspire us to understand and discern, to perceive, learn and teach, to observe, do, and fulfill gladly all the teachings of thy Torah. Enlighten our eyes in thy Torah; attach our heart to thy commandments; unite our heart to love and reverence thy name, so that we may never be put to shame. In thy holy, great and revered name we trust—may we thrill with joy over thy salvation. O bring us home in peace from the four corners of the earth, and make us walk upright to our land, for thou art the God who performs triumphs. Thou hast chosen us from all peoples and nations, and hast forever brought us near to thy truly great name, that we may eagerly praise thee and acclaim thy Oneness. Blessed art thou, O Lord, who hast graciously chosen thy people Israel.

SHEMA

(*When praying in private, add:* God is a faithful King.)

Deuteronomy 6:4-9

Hear, O Israel, the Lord is our God, the Lord is One.

Blessed be the name of his glorious majesty forever and ever.

You shall love the Lord your God with all your heart, and with all your soul, and with all your might. And these words which I command you today shall be in your heart. You shall teach them diligently to your children, and you shall speak of them when you are sitting at home and when you go on a journey, when you lie down and when you rise up. You shall bind them for a sign on your hand, and they shall be for frontlets between your eyes. You shall inscribe them on the doorposts of your house and on your gates.

The *Shema*, Israel's confession of faith, expresses the duty of loving and serving God with our whole being. The second paragraph demands that we give living expression to our love of God by careful observance of his precepts which are designed to assure our happiness. The third section contains the law of *tsitsith*, intended to remind us constantly of our duties towards God, and a warning against following the evil impulses of the heart. The *Shema*, sounding the keynote of Judaism, is the oldest prayer of the *Siddur*. In the morning service the *Shema* is preceded by two blessings and followed by one; in the evening service it is preceded by two blessings and followed by two. This is in keeping with the expression: "Seven times a day I praise thee" (Psalm 119:164; Berakhoth 11b).

ברוך שם כבוד was regularly used in the Temple. It is attributed to Jacob,

דברים יא, יג–כא

וְהָיָה אִם שָׁמֹעַ תִּשְׁמְעוּ אֶל מִצְוֹתַי, אֲשֶׁר אָנֹכִי מְצַוֶּה אֶתְכֶם הַיּוֹם, לְאַהֲבָה אֶת יְיָ אֱלֹהֵיכֶם, וּלְעָבְדוֹ בְּכָל לְבַבְכֶם וּבְכָל נַפְשְׁכֶם. וְנָתַתִּי מְטַר אַרְצְכֶם בְּעִתּוֹ, יוֹרֶה וּמַלְקוֹשׁ; וְאָסַפְתָּ דְגָנֶךָ, וְתִירֹשְׁךָ וְיִצְהָרֶךָ. וְנָתַתִּי עֵשֶׂב בְּשָׂדְךָ לִבְהֶמְתֶּךָ; וְאָכַלְתָּ וְשָׂבָעְתָּ. הִשָּׁמְרוּ לָכֶם פֶּן יִפְתֶּה לְבַבְכֶם, וְסַרְתֶּם וַעֲבַדְתֶּם אֱלֹהִים אֲחֵרִים, וְהִשְׁתַּחֲוִיתֶם לָהֶם. וְחָרָה אַף יְיָ בָּכֶם, וְעָצַר אֶת הַשָּׁמַיִם וְלֹא יִהְיֶה מָטָר, וְהָאֲדָמָה לֹא תִתֵּן אֶת יְבוּלָהּ; וַאֲבַדְתֶּם מְהֵרָה מֵעַל הָאָרֶץ הַטֹּבָה אֲשֶׁר יְיָ נֹתֵן לָכֶם. וְשַׂמְתֶּם אֶת דְּבָרַי אֵלֶּה עַל לְבַבְכֶם וְעַל נַפְשְׁכֶם; וּקְשַׁרְתֶּם אֹתָם לְאוֹת עַל יֶדְכֶם, וְהָיוּ לְטוֹטָפֹת בֵּין עֵינֵיכֶם. וְלִמַּדְתֶּם אֹתָם אֶת בְּנֵיכֶם לְדַבֵּר בָּם, בְּשִׁבְתְּךָ בְּבֵיתֶךָ, וּבְלֶכְתְּךָ בַדֶּרֶךְ, וּבְשָׁכְבְּךָ וּבְקוּמֶךָ. וּכְתַבְתָּם עַל מְזוּזוֹת בֵּיתֶךָ וּבִשְׁעָרֶיךָ.

לְמַעַן יִרְבּוּ יְמֵיכֶם וִימֵי בְנֵיכֶם, עַל הָאֲדָמָה אֲשֶׁר נִשְׁבַּע יְיָ לַאֲבֹתֵיכֶם לָתֵת לָהֶם, כִּימֵי הַשָּׁמַיִם עַל הָאָרֶץ.

במדבר טו, לז–מא

וַיֹּאמֶר יְיָ אֶל מֹשֶׁה לֵּאמֹר: דַּבֵּר אֶל בְּנֵי יִשְׂרָאֵל וְאָמַרְתָּ אֲלֵהֶם, וְעָשׂוּ לָהֶם צִיצִת עַל כַּנְפֵי בִגְדֵיהֶם לְדֹרֹתָם; וְנָתְנוּ עַל צִיצִת הַכָּנָף פְּתִיל תְּכֵלֶת. וְהָיָה לָכֶם לְצִיצִת, וּרְאִיתֶם אֹתוֹ וּזְכַרְתֶּם אֶת כָּל מִצְוֹת יְיָ, וַעֲשִׂיתֶם אֹתָם; וְלֹא תָתוּרוּ אַחֲרֵי לְבַבְכֶם וְאַחֲרֵי עֵינֵיכֶם, אֲשֶׁר אַתֶּם זֹנִים אַחֲרֵיהֶם. לְמַעַן תִּזְכְּרוּ וַעֲשִׂיתֶם אֶת כָּל מִצְוֹתָי; וִהְיִיתֶם קְדֹשִׁים לֵאלֹהֵיכֶם. אֲנִי יְיָ אֱלֹהֵיכֶם, אֲשֶׁר הוֹצֵאתִי אֶתְכֶם מֵאֶרֶץ מִצְרַיִם לִהְיוֹת לָכֶם לֵאלֹהִים; אֲנִי Reader יְיָ אֱלֹהֵיכֶם–

אֱמֶת וְיַצִּיב, וְנָכוֹן וְקַיָּם, וְיָשָׁר וְנֶאֱמָן, וְאָהוּב וְחָבִיב, וְנֶחְמָד

אמת ויציב is mentioned in the Mishnah (Tamid 5:1) among the prayers

Deuteronomy 11:13–21

And if you will carefully obey my commands which I give you today, to love the Lord your God and to serve him with all your heart and with all your soul, I will give rain for your land at the right season, the autumn rains and the spring rains, that you may gather in your grain, your wine and your oil. And I will produce grass in your fields for your cattle, and you will eat and be satisfied. Beware lest your heart be deceived, and you turn and serve other gods and worship them; for then the Lord's anger will blaze against you, and he will shut up the skies so that there will be no rain, and the land will yield no produce, and you will quickly perish from the good land which the Lord gives you. So you shall place these words of mine in your heart and in your soul, and you shall bind them for a sign on your hand, and they shall be for frontlets between your eyes. You shall teach them to your children, speaking of them when you are sitting at home and when you go on a journey, when you lie down and when you rise up. You shall inscribe them on the doorposts of your house and on your gates—that your life and the life of your children may be prolonged in the land, which the Lord promised he would give to your fathers, for as long as the sky remains over the earth.

Numbers 15:37–41

The Lord spoke to Moses, saying: Speak to the children of Israel and tell them to make for themselves fringes on the corners of their garments throughout their generations, and to put on the fringe of each corner a blue thread. You shall have it as a fringe, so that when you look upon it you will remember to do all the commands of the Lord, and you will not follow the desires of your heart and your eyes which lead you astray. It is for you to remember and do all my commands and be holy for your God. I am the Lord your God who brought you out of the land of Egypt to be your God; I am the Lord your God.

True and certain, established and enduring, right and steadfast, beloved and precious, pleasant and sweet, revered and glorious,

---

used in the Temple. The fifteen synonyms, ויפה-ויציב, correspond to the fifteen words in the last sentence of the *Shema*, beginning with אני and ending with אמת. The rule is not to interrupt the connection between ה' אלהיכם and אמת, as if these three words formed one sentence, meaning: "The Lord your God is true" (Mishnah Berakhoth 2:2).

וְנָעִים, וְנוֹרָא וְאַדִּיר, וּמְתֻקָּן וּמְקֻבָּל, וְטוֹב וְיָפֶה הַדָּבָר הַזֶּה
עָלֵינוּ לְעוֹלָם וָעֶד. אֱמֶת, אֱלֹהֵי עוֹלָם מַלְכֵּנוּ, צוּר יַעֲקֹב מָגֵן
יִשְׁעֵנוּ. Reader לְדֹר וָדֹר הוּא קַיָּם, וּשְׁמוֹ קַיָּם, וְכִסְאוֹ נָכוֹן,
וּמַלְכוּתוֹ וֶאֱמוּנָתוֹ לָעַד קַיֶּמֶת. וּדְבָרָיו חָיִים וְקַיָּמִים, נֶאֱמָנִים
וְנֶחֱמָדִים, לָעַד וּלְעוֹלְמֵי עוֹלָמִים, עַל אֲבוֹתֵינוּ וְעָלֵינוּ, עַל
בָּנֵינוּ וְעַל דּוֹרוֹתֵינוּ, וְעַל כָּל דּוֹרוֹת זֶרַע יִשְׂרָאֵל עֲבָדֶיךָ.

עַל הָרִאשׁוֹנִים וְעַל הָאַחֲרוֹנִים דָּבָר טוֹב וְקַיָּם לְעוֹלָם
וָעֶד, אֱמֶת וֶאֱמוּנָה, חֹק וְלֹא יַעֲבֹר. Reader אֱמֶת, שָׁאַתָּה הוּא
יְיָ אֱלֹהֵינוּ וֵאלֹהֵי אֲבוֹתֵינוּ, מַלְכֵּנוּ מֶלֶךְ אֲבוֹתֵינוּ, גֹּאֲלֵנוּ גֹּאֵל
אֲבוֹתֵינוּ, יוֹצְרֵנוּ צוּר יְשׁוּעָתֵנוּ, פּוֹדֵנוּ וּמַצִּילֵנוּ; מֵעוֹלָם שְׁמֶךָ,
אֵין אֱלֹהִים זוּלָתֶךָ.

עֶזְרַת אֲבוֹתֵינוּ אַתָּה הוּא מֵעוֹלָם, מָגֵן וּמוֹשִׁיעַ לִבְנֵיהֶם
אַחֲרֵיהֶם בְּכָל דּוֹר וָדוֹר. בְּרוּם עוֹלָם מוֹשָׁבֶךָ, וּמִשְׁפָּטֶיךָ
וְצִדְקָתְךָ עַד אַפְסֵי אָרֶץ. אַשְׁרֵי אִישׁ שֶׁיִּשְׁמַע לְמִצְוֹתֶיךָ,
וְתוֹרָתְךָ וּדְבָרְךָ יָשִׂים עַל לִבּוֹ. אֱמֶת, אַתָּה הוּא אָדוֹן לְעַמֶּךָ,
וּמֶלֶךְ גִּבּוֹר לָרִיב רִיבָם. אֱמֶת, אַתָּה הוּא רִאשׁוֹן וְאַתָּה הוּא
אַחֲרוֹן, וּמִבַּלְעָדֶיךָ אֵין לָנוּ מֶלֶךְ גּוֹאֵל וּמוֹשִׁיעַ. מִמִּצְרַיִם
גְּאַלְתָּנוּ, יְיָ אֱלֹהֵינוּ, וּמִבֵּית עֲבָדִים פְּדִיתָנוּ. כָּל בְּכוֹרֵיהֶם
הָרָגְתָּ, וּבְכוֹרְךָ גָּאָלְתָּ, וְיַם סוּף בָּקַעְתָּ, וְזֵדִים טִבַּעְתָּ, וִידִידִים
הֶעֱבַרְתָּ; וַיְכַסּוּ מַיִם צָרֵיהֶם, אֶחָד מֵהֶם לֹא נוֹתָר. עַל זֹאת
שִׁבְּחוּ אֲהוּבִים וְרוֹמְמוּ אֵל, וְנָתְנוּ יְדִידִים זְמִירוֹת שִׁירוֹת
וְתִשְׁבָּחוֹת, בְּרָכוֹת וְהוֹדָאוֹת לַמֶּלֶךְ, אֵל חַי וְקַיָּם. רָם וְנִשָּׂא,
גָּדוֹל וְנוֹרָא, מַשְׁפִּיל גֵּאִים וּמַגְבִּיהַּ שְׁפָלִים, מוֹצִיא אֲסִירִים

הדבר הזה refers to the *Shema* as a solemn profession of the Oneness of God.
The *Shema* is the watchword of Israel's faith, and it is the desire of every
loyal Jew to have it upon his lips when he dies.

correct and acceptable, good and beautiful is this faith to us forever and ever. True it is that the eternal God is our King, the Stronghold of Jacob and our saving Shield. He exists throughout all generations; his name endures; his throne is firm; his kingship and his truth are forever established. His words are living and enduring, faithful and precious, forever and to all eternity, as for our fathers so also for us, for our children and future generations, and for all generations of the seed of Israel his servants.

Alike for the first and the last generations this faith is good and valid forever and ever; it is true and trustworthy, a law that will not pass away. True it is that thou art the Lord our God and the God of our fathers, our King and the King of our fathers, our Redeemer and the Redeemer of our fathers, our Maker and saving Stronghold, our Deliverer and Rescuer. Thou art eternal; there is no God besides thee.

Thou wast the help of our fathers from of old, and hast been a Shield and Savior to their children after them in every generation. In the heights of the universe is thy habitation, and thy justice and righteousness reach to the furthest ends of the earth. Happy is the man who obeys thy commands and takes thy Torah and thy word to heart. True it is that thou art the Lord of thy people, and a mighty King to champion their cause. True it is that thou art the first and thou art the last, and besides thee we have no King who redeems and saves. From Egypt thou didst redeem us, Lord our God, and from the house of slavery thou didst deliver us; all their first-born thou didst slay, but thy first-born thou didst redeem; thou didst divide the Red Sea and drown the arrogant, but thy beloved people thou didst take across; the water covered their enemies, not one of them was left.

For this, the beloved people praised and extolled God; they offered hymns, blessings and thanksgivings to the King, the living and eternal God. He is high and exalted, great and revered; he brings low the arrogant, and raises up the lowly; he frees the

וּפוֹדֶה עֲנָוִים, וְעוֹזֵר דַּלִּים, וְעוֹנֶה לְעַמּוֹ בְּעֵת שַׁוְּעָם אֵלָיו.
תְּהִלּוֹת לְאֵל עֶלְיוֹן, בָּרוּךְ הוּא וּמְבֹרָךְ.

מֹשֶׁה וּבְנֵי יִשְׂרָאֵל לְךָ עָנוּ שִׁירָה בְּשִׂמְחָה רַבָּה, וְאָמְרוּ כֻלָּם:

מִי כָמֹכָה בָּאֵלִם, יְיָ; מִי כָּמֹכָה נֶאְדָּר בַּקֹּדֶשׁ, נוֹרָא תְהִלֹּת,
עֹשֵׂה פֶלֶא.

שִׁירָה חֲדָשָׁה שִׁבְּחוּ גְאוּלִים לְשִׁמְךָ עַל שְׂפַת הַיָּם; יַחַד
כֻּלָּם הוֹדוּ וְהִמְלִיכוּ וְאָמְרוּ:

יְיָ יִמְלֹךְ לְעוֹלָם וָעֶד.

צוּר יִשְׂרָאֵל, קוּמָה בְּעֶזְרַת יִשְׂרָאֵל, וּפְדֵה כִנְאֻמְךָ יְהוּדָה
וְיִשְׂרָאֵל. Reader. גֹּאֲלֵנוּ יְיָ צְבָאוֹת שְׁמוֹ, קְדוֹשׁ יִשְׂרָאֵל. בָּרוּךְ
אַתָּה, יְיָ, גָּאַל יִשְׂרָאֵל.

The *Shemoneh Esreh* is recited in silent devotion while standing, facing east.
The Reader repeats the *Shemoneh Esreh* aloud when a *minyan* holds service.

אֲדֹנָי, שְׂפָתַי תִּפְתָּח, וּפִי יַגִּיד תְּהִלָּתֶךָ.

בָּרוּךְ אַתָּה, יְיָ אֱלֹהֵינוּ וֵאלֹהֵי אֲבוֹתֵינוּ, אֱלֹהֵי אַבְרָהָם,
אֱלֹהֵי יִצְחָק, וֵאלֹהֵי יַעֲקֹב, הָאֵל הַגָּדוֹל הַגִּבּוֹר וְהַנּוֹרָא, אֵל
עֶלְיוֹן, גּוֹמֵל חֲסָדִים טוֹבִים, וְקוֹנֵה הַכֹּל, וְזוֹכֵר חַסְדֵי אָבוֹת,
וּמֵבִיא גוֹאֵל לִבְנֵי בְנֵיהֶם לְמַעַן שְׁמוֹ בְּאַהֲבָה.

שמונה עשרה is spoken of in the Talmud as *Tefillah*, the prayer par excellence, on account of its importance and its antiquity. According to tradition,
it was drawn up by the men of the Great Assembly. Originally, the *Shemoneh
Esreh* consisted of eighteen blessings; in its present form, however, there are
nineteen. The addition of the paragraph concerning the slanderers was made
toward the end of the first century at the direction of Rabban Gamaliel II,
head of the Sanhedrin of Yabneh. The Talmud offers a variety of reasons for
the number eighteen. It corresponds to the eighteen times God is mentioned
in Psalm 29 as well as in the *Shema*. The three patriarchs, Abraham, Isaac
and Jacob are mentioned eighteen times in the Bible. This number also corresponds to the eighteen vertebrae of the spinal column (Berakhoth 28b).

Because it is recited in a standing posture, the *Shemoneh Esreh* is now
generally known as the *Amidah*, a name which accurately describes this

captives, and delivers the afflicted; he helps the poor, and answers his people whenever they cry to him. Praised be the supreme God; be he ever blessed.

Moses and the children of Israel sang a song to thee with great joy; all of them said:

> "Who is like thee, O Lord, among the mighty?
> Who is like thee, glorious in holiness,
> Awe-inspiring in renown, doing wonders?"[1]

The redeemed people sang a new song of praise to thy name at the seashore; they all, in unison, gave thanks and proclaimed thy sovereignty, and said:

> "The Lord shall reign forever and ever."[2]

Stronghold of Israel, arise to the help of Israel; deliver Judah and Israel, as thou hast promised. Our Redeemer, thou art the Lord of hosts, the Holy One of Israel. Blessed art thou, O Lord, who hast redeemed Israel.

SHEMONEH ESREH

The Shemoneh Esreh is recited in silent devotion while standing, facing east.
The Reader repeats the Shemoneh Esreh aloud when a minyan holds service.

O Lord, open thou my lips, that my mouth may declare thy praise.[3]

Blessed art thou, Lord our God and God of our fathers, God of Abraham, God of Isaac and God of Jacob; great, mighty and revered God, sublime God, who bestowest lovingkindness, and art Master of all things; who rememberest the good deeds of our fathers, and who wilt graciously bring a redeemer to their children's children for the sake of thy name.

---

prayer for Sabbaths and festivals, when it includes only seven blessings. The Reader repeats this principal prayer aloud for the benefit of those who cannot read it for themselves.

The nineteen benedictions of the *Amidah* are designated in the Talmud as follows: 1) אבות; 2) גבורות; 3) קדושת השם; 4) בינה; 5) תשובה; 6) סליחה; 7) סליחה; 7) ברכת המינים (12); רפואה (8); גאולה (9); ברכת השנים (10); קבוץ גליות (11); ברכת משפט (12) ברכת המינים; 13) ברכת צדיקים (14); ברכת ירושלים (15); ברכת דוד (16); תפלה (17); עבודה (18); הודאה; 19) ברכת כהנים.

אבות, the first benediction naming the three patriarchs, contains phrases from Exodus 3:15; Deuteronomy 10:17; Genesis 14:19; 15:1.

[1] *Exodus* 15:11.   [2] *Exodus* 15:18.   [3] *Psalm* 51:17.

Between *Rosh Hashanah* and *Yom Kippur* add:

(זָכְרֵנוּ לְחַיִּים, מֶלֶךְ חָפֵץ בַּחַיִּים,

וְכָתְבֵנוּ בְּסֵפֶר הַחַיִּים, לְמַעַנְךָ אֱלֹהִים חַיִּים.)

מֶלֶךְ עוֹזֵר וּמוֹשִׁיעַ וּמָגֵן. בָּרוּךְ אַתָּה, יְיָ, מָגֵן אַבְרָהָם.

אַתָּה גִבּוֹר לְעוֹלָם, אֲדֹנָי; מְחַיֵּה מֵתִים אַתָּה, רַב לְהוֹשִׁיעַ.

Between *Sukkoth* and *Pesaḥ* add:

(מַשִּׁיב הָרוּחַ וּמוֹרִיד הַגָּשֶׁם.)

מְכַלְכֵּל חַיִּים בְּחֶסֶד, מְחַיֵּה מֵתִים בְּרַחֲמִים רַבִּים, סוֹמֵךְ

נוֹפְלִים, וְרוֹפֵא חוֹלִים, וּמַתִּיר אֲסוּרִים, וּמְקַיֵּם אֱמוּנָתוֹ לִישֵׁנֵי

עָפָר. מִי כָמוֹךָ, בַּעַל גְּבוּרוֹת, וּמִי דוֹמֶה לָּךְ, מֶלֶךְ מֵמִית

וּמְחַיֶּה וּמַצְמִיחַ יְשׁוּעָה.

Between *Rosh Hashanah* and *Yom Kippur* add:

(מִי כָמוֹךָ, אַב הָרַחֲמִים, זוֹכֵר יְצוּרָיו לְחַיִּים בְּרַחֲמִים.)

וְנֶאֱמָן אַתָּה לְהַחֲיוֹת מֵתִים. בָּרוּךְ אַתָּה, יְיָ, מְחַיֵּה הַמֵּתִים.

When the Reader repeats the *Shemoneh Esreh*, the following *Kedushah* is said:

נְקַדֵּשׁ אֶת שִׁמְךָ בָּעוֹלָם כְּשֵׁם שֶׁמַּקְדִּישִׁים אוֹתוֹ בִּשְׁמֵי מָרוֹם,

כַּכָּתוּב עַל יַד נְבִיאֶךָ: וְקָרָא זֶה אֶל זֶה וְאָמַר:

קָדוֹשׁ, קָדוֹשׁ, קָדוֹשׁ יְיָ צְבָאוֹת; מְלֹא כָל הָאָרֶץ כְּבוֹדוֹ.

Reader —לְעֻמָּתָם בָּרוּךְ יֹאמֵרוּ

בָּרוּךְ כְּבוֹד יְיָ מִמְּקוֹמוֹ.

Reader וּבְדִבְרֵי קָדְשְׁךָ כָּתוּב לֵאמֹר:

יִמְלֹךְ יְיָ לְעוֹלָם, אֱלֹהַיִךְ צִיּוֹן לְדֹר וָדֹר; הַלְלוּיָהּ.

זכרנו and the other special prayers, added between *Rosh Hashanah* and *Yom Kippur*, are not mentioned in the Talmud. They were inserted during the geonic period.

גבורות, the second benediction recounting the omnipotence of God, includes phrases from Psalms 145:14; 146:7; Daniel 12:2; I Samuel 2:6.

משיב הרוח, referring to God's control of the forces of nature, is added in winter, during the rainy season in *Eretz Yisrael*. Rain is considered as great

Between Rosh Hashanah and Yom Kippur add:

(Remember us to life, O King who delightest in life; inscribe us in the book of life for thy sake, O living God.)

O King, Supporter, Savior and Shield! Blessed art thou, O Lord, Shield of Abraham.

Thou, O Lord, art mighty forever; thou revivest the dead; thou art powerful to save.

Between Sukkoth and Pesaḥ add:

(Thou causest the wind to blow and the rain to fall.)

Thou sustainest the living with kindness, and revivest the dead with great mercy; thou supportest all who fall, and healest the sick; thou settest the captives free, and keepest faith with those who sleep in the dust. Who is like thee, Lord of ʹⁿower? Who resembles thee, O King? Thou bringest death and restorest life, and causest salvation to flourish.

Between Rosh Hashanah and Yom Kippur add:

(Who is like thee, merciful Father? In mercy thou rememberest thy creatures to life.)

Thou art faithful to revive the dead. Blessed art thou, O Lord, who revivest the dead.

KEDUSHAH

When the Reader repeats the Shemoneh Esreh, the following Kedushah is said:

We sanctify thy name in this world even as they sanctify it in the highest heavens, as it is written by thy prophet: "They keep calling to one another:

Holy, holy, holy is the Lord of hosts;
The whole earth is full of his glory."[1]

Those opposite them say: Blessed—
Blessed be the glory of the Lord from his abode.[2]

And in thy holy Scriptures it is written:
The Lord shall reign forever,
Your God, O Zion, for all generations.
Praise the Lord![3]

---

a manifestation of the divine power as the resurrection of the dead (Ta'anith 2a); hence משיב הרוח is inserted in the passage מחיה מתים ... אתה גבור.

קדושה, to which the Talmud (Sotah 49a) attaches unusual importance, is recited only when a *minyan* is present because it is said: "I shall be sanctified

[1] *Isaiah* 6:3.   [2] *Ezekiel* 3:12.   [3] *Psalm* 146:10.

Reader לְדוֹר וָדוֹר נַגִּיד גָּדְלֶךָ, וּלְנֵצַח נְצָחִים קְדֻשָּׁתְךָ
נַקְדִּישׁ, וְשִׁבְחֲךָ אֱלֹהֵינוּ מִפִּינוּ לֹא יָמוּשׁ לְעוֹלָם וָעֶד, כִּי אֵל
מֶלֶךְ גָּדוֹל וְקָדוֹשׁ אָתָּה. * בָּרוּךְ אַתָּה, יְיָ, הָאֵל הַקָּדוֹשׁ.

*Between *Rosh Hashanah* and *Yom Kippur* substitute:

(בָּרוּךְ אַתָּה, יְיָ, הַמֶּלֶךְ הַקָּדוֹשׁ.)

אַתָּה קָדוֹשׁ וְשִׁמְךָ קָדוֹשׁ, וּקְדוֹשִׁים בְּכָל יוֹם יְהַלְלוּךָ סֶּלָה.
*בָּרוּךְ אַתָּה, יְיָ, הָאֵל הַקָּדוֹשׁ.

*Between *Rosh Hashanah* and *Yom Kippur* substitute:

(בָּרוּךְ אַתָּה, יְיָ, הַמֶּלֶךְ הַקָּדוֹשׁ.)

אַתָּה חוֹנֵן לְאָדָם דַּעַת, וּמְלַמֵּד לֶאֱנוֹשׁ בִּינָה. חָנֵּנוּ מֵאִתְּךָ
דֵּעָה, בִּינָה וְהַשְׂכֵּל. בָּרוּךְ אַתָּה, יְיָ, חוֹנֵן הַדָּעַת.

הֲשִׁיבֵנוּ אָבִינוּ לְתוֹרָתֶךָ, וְקָרְבֵנוּ מַלְכֵּנוּ לַעֲבוֹדָתֶךָ;
וְהַחֲזִירֵנוּ בִּתְשׁוּבָה שְׁלֵמָה לְפָנֶיךָ. בָּרוּךְ אַתָּה, יְיָ, הָרוֹצֶה
בִּתְשׁוּבָה.

סְלַח לָנוּ אָבִינוּ כִּי חָטָאנוּ, מְחַל לָנוּ מַלְכֵּנוּ כִּי פָשָׁעְנוּ, כִּי
מוֹחֵל וְסוֹלֵחַ אָתָּה. בָּרוּךְ אַתָּה, יְיָ, חַנּוּן הַמַּרְבֶּה לִסְלֹחַ.

רְאֵה נָא בְעָנְיֵנוּ וְרִיבָה רִיבֵנוּ, וּגְאָלֵנוּ מְהֵרָה לְמַעַן שְׁמֶךָ,
כִּי גוֹאֵל חָזָק אָתָּה. בָּרוּךְ אַתָּה, יְיָ, גּוֹאֵל יִשְׂרָאֵל.

On fast days the Reader adds here:

(עֲנֵנוּ, יְיָ, עֲנֵנוּ בְּיוֹם צוֹם תַּעֲנִיתֵנוּ, כִּי בְצָרָה גְדוֹלָה אֲנָחְנוּ. אַל תֵּפֶן אֶל רִשְׁעֵנוּ,
וְאַל תַּסְתֵּר פָּנֶיךָ מִמֶּנּוּ, וְאַל תִּתְעַלַּם מִתְּחִנָּתֵנוּ. הֱיֵה נָא קָרוֹב לְשַׁוְעָתֵנוּ, יְהִי נָא
חַסְדְּךָ לְנַחֲמֵנוּ; טֶרֶם נִקְרָא אֵלֶיךָ עֲנֵנוּ, כַּדָּבָר שֶׁנֶּאֱמַר: וְהָיָה טֶרֶם יִקְרָאוּ, וַאֲנִי
אֶעֱנֶה; עוֹד הֵם מְדַבְּרִים, וַאֲנִי אֶשְׁמָע. כִּי אַתָּה, יְיָ, הָעוֹנֶה בְּעֵת צָרָה, פּוֹדֶה וּמַצִּיל
בְּכָל עֵת צָרָה וְצוּקָה. בָּרוּךְ אַתָּה, יְיָ, הָעוֹנֶה בְּעֵת צָרָה.)

---

among the children of Israel" (Leviticus 22:32), which implies that the proclamation of the holiness and kingship of God is to be made in public service only.

Reader:

Through all generations we will declare thy greatness; to all eternity we will proclaim thy holiness; thy praise, our God, shall never depart from our mouth, for thou art a great and holy God and King. *Blessed art thou, O Lord, holy God.

Between Rosh Hashanah and Yom Kippur substitute:
(Blessed art thou, O Lord, holy King.)

Thou art holy and thy name is holy, and holy beings praise thee daily. * Blessed art thou, O Lord, holy God.

Between Rosh Hashanah and Yom Kippur substitute:
(Blessed art thou, O Lord, holy King.)

Thou favorest man with knowledge, and teachest mortals understanding. O grant us knowledge, understanding and insight. Blessed art thou, O Lord, gracious Giver of knowledge.

Restore us, our Father, to thy Torah; draw us near, our King, to thy service; cause us to return to thee in perfect repentance. Blessed art thou, O Lord, who art pleased with repentance.

Forgive us, our Father, for we have sinned; pardon us, our King, for we have transgressed; for thou dost pardon and forgive. Blessed art thou, O Lord, who art gracious and ever forgiving.

Look upon our affliction and champion our cause; redeem us speedily for thy name's sake, for thou art a mighty Redeemer. Blessed art thou, O Lord, Redeemer of Israel.

On fast days the Reader adds here:

(Answer us, O Lord, answer us on the day of our fast, for we are in great distress. Regard not our wickedness; conceal not thy presence from us, and hide not thyself from our supplication. Be near to our cry, and let thy kindness comfort us; even before we call to thee answer us, as it is said: "Before they call, I will answer; while they are yet speaking, I will hear."[1] For thou, O Lord, art he who answers in time of trouble, who redeems and delivers in all times of woe and stress. Blessed art thou, O Lord, who answerest in time of distress.)

אתה חונן begins the group of thirteen petitions which are replaced on Sabbaths and festivals by one petition appropriate for the occasion.

---

[1]*Isaiah* 65:24.

רְפָאֵנוּ יְיָ וְנֵרָפֵא, הוֹשִׁיעֵנוּ וְנִוָּשֵׁעָה, כִּי תְהִלָּתֵנוּ אָתָּה;
וְהַעֲלֵה רְפוּאָה שְׁלֵמָה לְכָל מַכּוֹתֵינוּ, כִּי אֵל מֶלֶךְ רוֹפֵא נֶאֱמָן
וְרַחֲמָן אָתָּה. בָּרוּךְ אַתָּה, יְיָ, רוֹפֵא חוֹלֵי עַמּוֹ יִשְׂרָאֵל.

בָּרֵךְ עָלֵינוּ, יְיָ אֱלֹהֵינוּ, אֶת הַשָּׁנָה הַזֹּאת וְאֶת כָּל מִינֵי
תְבוּאָתָהּ לְטוֹבָה,

<table>
<tr><td>From December 4th till Pesaḥ say:</td><td>From Pesaḥ till December 4th say:</td></tr>
<tr><td>וְתֵן בְּרָכָה</td><td>וְתֵן טַל וּמָטָר לִבְרָכָה</td></tr>
</table>

עַל פְּנֵי הָאֲדָמָה, וְשַׂבְּעֵנוּ מִטּוּבֶךָ, וּבָרֵךְ שְׁנָתֵנוּ כַּשָּׁנִים הַטּוֹבוֹת.
בָּרוּךְ אַתָּה, יְיָ, מְבָרֵךְ הַשָּׁנִים.

תְּקַע בְּשׁוֹפָר גָּדוֹל לְחֵרוּתֵנוּ, וְשָׂא נֵס לְקַבֵּץ גָּלֻיּוֹתֵינוּ,
וְקַבְּצֵנוּ יַחַד מֵאַרְבַּע כַּנְפוֹת הָאָרֶץ. בָּרוּךְ אַתָּה, יְיָ, מְקַבֵּץ
נִדְחֵי עַמּוֹ יִשְׂרָאֵל.

הָשִׁיבָה שׁוֹפְטֵינוּ כְּבָרִאשׁוֹנָה, וְיוֹעֲצֵינוּ כְּבַתְּחִלָּה; וְהָסֵר
מִמֶּנּוּ יָגוֹן וַאֲנָחָה; וּמְלוֹךְ עָלֵינוּ, אַתָּה יְיָ לְבַדְּךָ, בְּחֶסֶד
וּבְרַחֲמִים, וְצַדְּקֵנוּ בַּמִּשְׁפָּט. * בָּרוּךְ אַתָּה, יְיָ, מֶלֶךְ אוֹהֵב
צְדָקָה וּמִשְׁפָּט.

*Between Rosh Hashanah and Yom Kippur substitute:
(בָּרוּךְ אַתָּה, יְיָ, הַמֶּלֶךְ הַמִּשְׁפָּט.)

וְלַמַּלְשִׁינִים אַל תְּהִי תִקְוָה, וְכָל הָרִשְׁעָה כְּרֶגַע תֹּאבֵד,
וְכָל אוֹיְבֶיךָ מְהֵרָה יִכָּרֵתוּ; וְהַזֵּדִים מְהֵרָה תְעַקֵּר וּתְשַׁבֵּר,
וּתְמַגֵּר וְתַכְנִיעַ בִּמְהֵרָה בְיָמֵינוּ. בָּרוּךְ אַתָּה, יְיָ, שׁוֹבֵר אֹיְבִים
וּמַכְנִיעַ זֵדִים.

עַל הַצַּדִּיקִים וְעַל הַחֲסִידִים, וְעַל זִקְנֵי עַמְּךָ בֵּית יִשְׂרָאֵל
וְעַל פְּלֵיטַת סוֹפְרֵיהֶם, וְעַל גֵּרֵי הַצֶּדֶק וְעָלֵינוּ, יֶהֱמוּ נָא
רַחֲמֶיךָ, יְיָ אֱלֹהֵינוּ; וְתֵן שָׂכָר טוֹב לְכָל הַבּוֹטְחִים בְּשִׁמְךָ

Heal us, O Lord, and we shall be healed; save us and we shall be saved; for thou art our praise. Grant a perfect healing to all our wounds; for thou art a faithful and merciful God, King and Healer. Blessed art thou, O Lord, who healest the sick among thy people Israel.

Bless for us, Lord our God, this year and all kinds of its produce for the best.

From Pesaḥ till December 4th say: *From December 4th till Pesaḥ say:*

Bestow a blessing   Bestow dew and rain for a blessing upon the face of the earth. Satisfy us with thy goodness, and bless our year like other good years. Blessed art thou, O Lord, who blessest the years.

Sound the great Shofar for our freedom; lift up the banner to bring our exiles together, and assemble us from the four corners of the earth. Blessed art thou, O Lord, who gatherest the dispersed of thy people Israel.

Restore our judges as at first, and our counselors as at the beginning; remove from us sorrow and sighing; reign thou alone over us, O Lord, in kindness and mercy, and clear us in judgment. *Blessed art thou, O Lord, King, who lovest righteousness and justice.

     * Between Rosh Hashanah and Yom Kippur substitute:

(Blessed art thou, O Lord, King of Justice.)

May the slanderers have no hope; may all wickedness perish instantly; may all thy enemies be soon cut down. Do thou speedily uproot and crush the arrogant; cast them down and humble them speedily in our days. Blessed art thou, O Lord, who breakest the enemies and humblest the arrogant.

May thy compassion, Lord our God, be aroused over the righteous and over the godly; over the leaders of thy people, the house of Israel, and over the remnant of their sages; over the true proselytes and over us. Grant a good reward to all who truly trust

---

נֵרי צֶדֶק proselytes who have accepted Judaism out of inner conviction.

בֶּאֱמֶת, וְשִׂים חֶלְקֵנוּ עִמָּהֶם, וּלְעוֹלָם לֹא נֵבוֹשׁ, כִּי בְךָ בָּטָחְנוּ.
בָּרוּךְ אַתָּה, יְיָ, מִשְׁעָן וּמִבְטָח לַצַּדִּיקִים.

וְלִירוּשָׁלַיִם עִירְךָ בְּרַחֲמִים תָּשׁוּב, וְתִשְׁכּוֹן בְּתוֹכָהּ כַּאֲשֶׁר
דִּבַּרְתָּ; וּבְנֵה אוֹתָהּ בְּקָרוֹב בְּיָמֵינוּ בִּנְיַן עוֹלָם; וְכִסֵּא דָוִד
מְהֵרָה לְתוֹכָהּ תָּכִין. בָּרוּךְ אַתָּה, יְיָ, בּוֹנֵה יְרוּשָׁלַיִם.

אֶת צֶמַח דָּוִד עַבְדְּךָ מְהֵרָה תַצְמִיחַ, וְקַרְנוֹ תָּרוּם
בִּישׁוּעָתֶךָ, כִּי לִישׁוּעָתְךָ קִוִּינוּ כָּל הַיּוֹם. בָּרוּךְ אַתָּה, יְיָ,
מַצְמִיחַ קֶרֶן יְשׁוּעָה.

שְׁמַע קוֹלֵנוּ, יְיָ אֱלֹהֵינוּ; חוּס וְרַחֵם עָלֵינוּ, וְקַבֵּל בְּרַחֲמִים
וּבְרָצוֹן אֶת תְּפִלָּתֵנוּ, כִּי אֵל שׁוֹמֵעַ תְּפִלּוֹת וְתַחֲנוּנִים אָתָּה;
וּמִלְּפָנֶיךָ מַלְכֵּנוּ רֵיקָם אַל תְּשִׁיבֵנוּ, כִּי אַתָּה שׁוֹמֵעַ תְּפִלַּת
עַמְּךָ יִשְׂרָאֵל בְּרַחֲמִים. בָּרוּךְ אַתָּה, יְיָ, שׁוֹמֵעַ תְּפִלָּה.

רְצֵה, יְיָ אֱלֹהֵינוּ, בְּעַמְּךָ יִשְׂרָאֵל וּבִתְפִלָּתָם; וְהָשֵׁב אֶת
הָעֲבוֹדָה לִדְבִיר בֵּיתֶךָ, וְאִשֵּׁי יִשְׂרָאֵל וּתְפִלָּתָם בְּאַהֲבָה
תְקַבֵּל בְּרָצוֹן, וּתְהִי לְרָצוֹן תָּמִיד עֲבוֹדַת יִשְׂרָאֵל עַמֶּךָ.

On *Rosh Ḥodesh* and *Ḥol ha-Moʻed* add:

(אֱלֹהֵינוּ וֵאלֹהֵי אֲבוֹתֵינוּ, יַעֲלֶה וְיָבֹא, וְיַגִּיעַ וְיֵרָאֶה, וְיֵרָצֶה
וְיִשָּׁמַע, וְיִפָּקֵד וְיִזָּכֵר זִכְרוֹנֵנוּ וּפִקְדוֹנֵנוּ, וְזִכְרוֹן אֲבוֹתֵינוּ,
וְזִכְרוֹן מָשִׁיחַ בֶּן דָּוִד עַבְדֶּךָ, וְזִכְרוֹן יְרוּשָׁלַיִם עִיר קָדְשֶׁךָ,
וְזִכְרוֹן כָּל עַמְּךָ בֵּית יִשְׂרָאֵל לְפָנֶיךָ, לִפְלֵיטָה וּלְטוֹבָה, לְחֵן
וּלְחֶסֶד וּלְרַחֲמִים, לְחַיִּים וּלְשָׁלוֹם, בְּיוֹם

Sukkoth	*Pesaḥ*	*Rosh Ḥodesh*
חַג הַסֻּכּוֹת	חַג הַמַּצּוֹת	רֹאשׁ הַחֹדֶשׁ

הַזֶּה. זָכְרֵנוּ, יְיָ אֱלֹהֵינוּ, בּוֹ לְטוֹבָה, וּפָקְדֵנוּ בּוֹ לִבְרָכָה,

רְצֵה, as well as מוֹדִים and שִׂים שָׁלוֹם. was daily recited by the priests in the

in thy name, and place our lot among them; may we never come to shame, for in thee we trust. Blessed art thou, O Lord, who art the stay and trust of the righteous.

Return in mercy to thy city Jerusalem and dwell in it as thou hast promised; rebuild it soon, in our days, as an everlasting structure, and speedily establish in it the throne of David. Blessed art thou, O Lord, Builder of Jerusalem.

Speedily cause the offspring of thy servant David to flourish, and let his glory be exalted by thy help, for we hope for thy deliverance all day. Blessed art thou, O Lord, who causest salvation to flourish.

Hear our voice, Lord our God; spare us and have pity on us; accept our prayer in mercy and favor, for thou art God who hearest prayers and supplications; from thy presence, our King, dismiss us not empty-handed, for thou hearest in mercy the prayer of thy people Israel. Blessed art thou, O Lord, who hearest prayer.

Be pleased, Lord our God, with thy people Israel and with their prayer; restore the worship to thy most holy sanctuary; accept Israel's offerings and prayer with gracious love. May the worship of thy people Israel be ever pleasing to thee.

On Rosh Ḥodesh and Ḥol ha-Mo·ed add:

(Our God and God of our fathers, may the remembrance of us, of our fathers, of Messiah the son of David thy servant, of Jerusalem thy holy city, and of all thy people the house of Israel, ascend and come and be accepted before thee for deliverance and happiness, for grace, kindness and mercy, for life and peace, on this day of

Rosh Ḥodesh	*Pesaḥ*	*Sukkoth*
the New Moon.	the Feast of Un-leavened Bread.	the Feast of Tabernacles.

Remember us this day, Lord our God, for happiness; be mind-

Temple. However, the phrase "restore the worship to thy sanctuary" could not be used when the Temple was still in existence.

יעלה ויבא is mentioned in Sofrim 19:7, and is based on the following passage: "On your feasts and new moon festivals you shall sound the trumpets . . . they will serve as a reminder of you before your God" (Numbers 10:10).

וְהוֹשִׁיעֵנוּ בוֹ לְחַיִּים; וּבִדְבַר יְשׁוּעָה וְרַחֲמִים חוּס וְחָנֵּנוּ, וְרַחֵם עָלֵינוּ וְהוֹשִׁיעֵנוּ, כִּי אֵלֶיךָ עֵינֵינוּ, כִּי אֵל מֶלֶךְ חַנּוּן וְרַחוּם אָתָּה.)

וְתֶחֱזֶינָה עֵינֵינוּ בְּשׁוּבְךָ לְצִיּוֹן בְּרַחֲמִים. בָּרוּךְ אַתָּה, יְיָ, הַמַּחֲזִיר שְׁכִינָתוֹ לְצִיּוֹן.

מוֹדִים אֲנַחְנוּ לָךְ, שָׁאַתָּה הוּא יְיָ אֱלֹהֵינוּ וֵאלֹהֵי אֲבוֹתֵינוּ לְעוֹלָם וָעֶד. צוּר חַיֵּינוּ, מָגֵן יִשְׁעֵנוּ אַתָּה הוּא. לְדוֹר וָדוֹר נוֹדֶה לְּךָ, וּנְסַפֵּר תְּהִלָּתֶךָ, עַל חַיֵּינוּ הַמְּסוּרִים בְּיָדֶךָ, וְעַל נִשְׁמוֹתֵינוּ הַפְּקוּדוֹת לָךְ, וְעַל נִסֶּיךָ שֶׁבְּכָל יוֹם עִמָּנוּ, וְעַל נִפְלְאוֹתֶיךָ וְטוֹבוֹתֶיךָ שֶׁבְּכָל עֵת, עֶרֶב וָבֹקֶר וְצָהֳרָיִם. הַטּוֹב כִּי לֹא כָלוּ רַחֲמֶיךָ, וְהַמְרַחֵם כִּי לֹא תַמּוּ חֲסָדֶיךָ, מֵעוֹלָם קִוִּינוּ לָךְ.

When the Reader repeats the She-moneh Esreh, the Congregation responds here by saying:

(מוֹדִים אֲנַחְנוּ לָךְ, שָׁאַתָּה הוּא יְיָ אֱלֹהֵינוּ וֵאלֹהֵי אֲבוֹתֵינוּ. אֱלֹהֵי כָל בָּשָׂר, יוֹצְרֵנוּ, יוֹצֵר בְּרֵאשִׁית, בְּרָכוֹת וְהוֹדָאוֹת לְשִׁמְךָ הַגָּדוֹל וְהַקָּדוֹשׁ עַל שֶׁהֶחֱיִיתָנוּ וְקִיַּמְתָּנוּ. כֵּן תְּחַיֵּנוּ וּתְקַיְּמֵנוּ, וְתֶאֱסוֹף גָּלֻיּוֹתֵינוּ לְחַצְרוֹת קָדְשֶׁךָ לִשְׁמוֹר חֻקֶּיךָ וְלַעֲשׂוֹת רְצוֹנֶךָ, וּלְעָבְדְּךָ בְּלֵבָב שָׁלֵם, עַל שֶׁאֲנַחְנוּ מוֹדִים לָךְ. בָּרוּךְ אֵל הַהוֹדָאוֹת.)

On Ḥanukkah add:

(עַל הַנִּסִּים וְעַל הַפֻּרְקָן, וְעַל הַגְּבוּרוֹת וְעַל הַתְּשׁוּעוֹת, וְעַל הַמִּלְחָמוֹת, שֶׁעָשִׂיתָ לַאֲבוֹתֵינוּ בַּיָּמִים הָהֵם בַּזְּמַן הַזֶּה—

בִּימֵי מַתִּתְיָהוּ בֶּן יוֹחָנָן כֹּהֵן גָּדוֹל, חַשְׁמוֹנַי וּבָנָיו, כְּשֶׁעָמְדָה מַלְכוּת יָוָן הָרְשָׁעָה עַל עַמְּךָ יִשְׂרָאֵל לְהַשְׁכִּיחָם תּוֹרָתֶךָ, וּלְהַעֲבִירָם מֵחֻקֵּי רְצוֹנֶךָ. וְאַתָּה בְּרַחֲמֶיךָ הָרַבִּים עָמַדְתָּ לָהֶם

ful of us for blessing; save us to enjoy life. With a promise of salvation and mercy spare us and be gracious to us; have pity on us and save us, for we look to thee, for thou art a gracious and merciful God and King.)

May our eyes behold thy return in mercy to Zion. Blessed art thou, O Lord, who restorest thy divine presence to Zion.

We ever thank thee, who art the Lord our God and the God of our fathers. Thou art the strength of our life and our saving shield. In every generation we will thank thee and recount thy praise—for our lives which are in thy charge, for our souls which are in thy care, for thy miracles which are daily with us, and for thy continual wonders and favors— evening, morning and noon. Beneficent One, whose mercies never fail, Merciful One, whose kindnesses never cease, thou hast always been our hope.

When the Reader repeats the Shemoneh Esreh, the Congregation responds here by saying:

(We thank thee, who art the Lord our God and the God of our fathers. God of all mankind, our Creator and Creator of the universe, blessings and thanks are due to thy great and holy name, because thou hast kept us alive and sustained us; mayest thou ever grant us life and sustenance. O gather our exiles to thy holy courts to observe thy laws, to do thy will, and to serve thee with a perfect heart. For this we thank thee. Blessed be God to whom all thanks are due.)

On Ḥanukkah add:

(We thank thee for the miracles, for the redemption, for the mighty deeds and triumphs, and for the battles which thou didst perform for our fathers in those days, at this season—

In the days of the Hasmonean, Mattathias ben Yoḥanan, the High Priest, and his sons, when a wicked Hellenic government rose up against thy people Israel to make them forget thy Torah and transgress the laws of thy will. Thou in thy great mercy didst

---

מודים is based on נודה לך לעולם, לדור ודור נספר תהלתך and נודה לך לעולם, לדור ודור נספר תהלתך **אשיחה** (Psalms 79:13; 55:18).

מודים דרבנן, recited by the Congregation in an undertone while the Reader repeats aloud the eighteenth benediction, is a composite of several phrases suggested by a number of talmudic rabbis (Sotah 40a).

בְּעֵת צָרָתָם, רַבְתָּ אֶת רִיבָם, דַּנְתָּ אֶת דִּינָם, נָקַמְתָּ אֶת נִקְמָתָם;
מָסַרְתָּ גִבּוֹרִים בְּיַד חַלָּשִׁים, וְרַבִּים בְּיַד מְעַטִּים, וּטְמֵאִים בְּיַד
טְהוֹרִים, וּרְשָׁעִים בְּיַד צַדִּיקִים, וְזֵדִים בְּיַד עוֹסְקֵי תוֹרָתֶךָ.
וּלְךָ עָשִׂיתָ שֵׁם גָּדוֹל וְקָדוֹשׁ בְּעוֹלָמֶךָ, וּלְעַמְּךָ יִשְׂרָאֵל עָשִׂיתָ
תְּשׁוּעָה גְדוֹלָה וּפֻרְקָן כְּהַיּוֹם הַזֶּה. וְאַחַר כֵּן בָּאוּ בָנֶיךָ לִדְבִיר
בֵּיתֶךָ, וּפִנּוּ אֶת הֵיכָלֶךָ, וְטִהֲרוּ אֶת מִקְדָּשֶׁךָ, וְהִדְלִיקוּ נֵרוֹת
בְּחַצְרוֹת קָדְשֶׁךָ, וְקָבְעוּ שְׁמוֹנַת יְמֵי חֲנֻכָּה אֵלּוּ לְהוֹדוֹת וּלְהַלֵּל
לְשִׁמְךָ הַגָּדוֹל.)

On *Purim* add:

(עַל הַנִּסִּים וְעַל הַפֻּרְקָן, וְעַל הַגְּבוּרוֹת וְעַל הַתְּשׁוּעוֹת, וְעַל
הַמִּלְחָמוֹת, שֶׁעָשִׂיתָ לַאֲבוֹתֵינוּ בַּיָּמִים הָהֵם בַּזְּמַן הַזֶּה—

בִּימֵי מָרְדֳּכַי וְאֶסְתֵּר בְּשׁוּשַׁן הַבִּירָה, כְּשֶׁעָמַד עֲלֵיהֶם הָמָן
הָרָשָׁע. בִּקֵּשׁ לְהַשְׁמִיד לַהֲרֹג וּלְאַבֵּד אֶת כָּל הַיְּהוּדִים, מִנַּעַר
וְעַד זָקֵן, טַף וְנָשִׁים, בְּיוֹם אֶחָד, בִּשְׁלוֹשָׁה עָשָׂר לְחֹדֶשׁ שְׁנֵים
עָשָׂר, הוּא חֹדֶשׁ אֲדָר, וּשְׁלָלָם לָבוֹז. וְאַתָּה בְּרַחֲמֶיךָ הָרַבִּים
הֵפַרְתָּ אֶת עֲצָתוֹ, וְקִלְקַלְתָּ אֶת מַחֲשַׁבְתּוֹ, וַהֲשֵׁבוֹתָ גְּמוּלוֹ
בְרֹאשׁוֹ, וְתָלוּ אוֹתוֹ וְאֶת בָּנָיו עַל הָעֵץ.)

וְעַל כֻּלָּם יִתְבָּרַךְ וְיִתְרוֹמַם שִׁמְךָ, מַלְכֵּנוּ, תָּמִיד לְעוֹלָם
וָעֶד.

Between *Rosh Hashanah* and *Yom Kippur* add:

(וּכְתוֹב לְחַיִּים טוֹבִים כָּל בְּנֵי בְרִיתֶךָ.)

וְכֹל הַחַיִּים יוֹדוּךָ סֶּלָה, וִיהַלְלוּ אֶת שִׁמְךָ בֶּאֱמֶת, הָאֵל,
יְשׁוּעָתֵנוּ וְעֶזְרָתֵנוּ סֶלָה. בָּרוּךְ אַתָּה, יְיָ, הַטּוֹב שִׁמְךָ, וּלְךָ נָאֶה
לְהוֹדוֹת.

Priestly blessing recited by Reader:

אֱלֹהֵינוּ וֵאלֹהֵי אֲבוֹתֵינוּ, בָּרְכֵנוּ בַבְּרָכָה הַמְשֻׁלֶּשֶׁת בַּתּוֹרָה

ברכה המשולשת the blessing which consists of three biblical verses. The variant reading הכתובה בתורה clarifies the meaning of this passage.

stand by them in the time of their distress. Thou didst champion their cause, defend their rights and avenge their wrong; thou didst deliver the strong into the hands of the weak, the many into the hands of the few, the impure into the hands of the pure, the wicked into the hands of the righteous, and the arrogant into the hands of the students of thy Torah. Thou didst make a great and holy name for thyself in thy world, and for thy people Israel thou didst perform a great deliverance unto this day. Thereupon thy children entered the shrine of thy house, cleansed thy Temple, purified thy sanctuary, kindled lights in thy holy courts, and designated these eight days of Ḥanukkah for giving thanks and praise to thy great name.)

On Purim add:

(We thank thee for the miracles, for the redemption, for the mighty deeds and triumphs, and for the battles which thou didst perform for our fathers in those days, at this season—

In the days of Mordecai and Esther, in Shushan the capital [of Persia], when the wicked Haman rose up against them and sought to destroy, slay and wipe out all the Jews, young and old, infants and women, in one day, on the thirteenth of the twelfth month Adar, and to plunder their wealth. Thou in thy great mercy didst frustrate his counsel and upset his plan; thou didst cause his mischief to recoil on his own head, so that he and his sons were hanged upon the gallows.)

For all these acts may thy name, our King, be blessed and exalted forever and ever.

Between Rosh Hashanah and Yom Kippur add:

(Inscribe all thy people of the covenant for a happy life.)

All the living shall ever thank thee and sincerely praise thy name, O God, who art always our salvation and help. Blessed art thou, O Lord, Beneficent One, to whom it is fitting to give thanks.

Priestly blessing recited by Reader:

Our God and God of our fathers, bless us with the threefold

הַכְּתוּבָה עַל יְדֵי מֹשֶׁה עַבְדֶּךָ, הָאֲמוּרָה מִפִּי אַהֲרֹן וּבָנָיו, כֹּהֲנִים עַם קְדוֹשֶׁךָ, כָּאָמוּר: יְבָרֶכְךָ יְיָ וְיִשְׁמְרֶךָ. יָאֵר יְיָ פָּנָיו אֵלֶיךָ וִיחֻנֶּךָּ. יִשָּׂא יְיָ פָּנָיו אֵלֶיךָ, וְיָשֵׂם לְךָ שָׁלוֹם.

שִׂים שָׁלוֹם, טוֹבָה וּבְרָכָה, חֵן וָחֶסֶד וְרַחֲמִים, עָלֵינוּ וְעַל כָּל יִשְׂרָאֵל עַמֶּךָ. בָּרְכֵנוּ אָבִינוּ, כֻּלָּנוּ כְּאֶחָד, בְּאוֹר פָּנֶיךָ; כִּי בְאוֹר פָּנֶיךָ נָתַתָּ לָּנוּ, יְיָ אֱלֹהֵינוּ, תּוֹרַת חַיִּים וְאַהֲבַת חֶסֶד, וּצְדָקָה וּבְרָכָה וְרַחֲמִים, וְחַיִּים וְשָׁלוֹם. וְטוֹב בְּעֵינֶיךָ לְבָרֵךְ אֶת עַמְּךָ יִשְׂרָאֵל בְּכָל עֵת וּבְכָל שָׁעָה בִּשְׁלוֹמֶךָ. * בָּרוּךְ אַתָּה, יְיָ, הַמְבָרֵךְ אֶת עַמּוֹ יִשְׂרָאֵל בַּשָּׁלוֹם.

*Between *Rosh Hashanah* and *Yom Kippur* say:

(בְּסֵפֶר חַיִּים, בְּרָכָה וְשָׁלוֹם וּפַרְנָסָה טוֹבָה, נִזָּכֵר וְנִכָּתֵב לְפָנֶיךָ, אֲנַחְנוּ וְכָל עַמְּךָ בֵּית יִשְׂרָאֵל, לְחַיִּים טוֹבִים וּלְשָׁלוֹם. בָּרוּךְ אַתָּה, יְיָ, עוֹשֵׂה הַשָּׁלוֹם.)

After the *Shemoneh Esreh* add the following meditation:

אֱלֹהַי, נְצֹר לְשׁוֹנִי מֵרָע, וּשְׂפָתַי מִדַּבֵּר מִרְמָה, וְלִמְקַלְלַי נַפְשִׁי תִדּוֹם, וְנַפְשִׁי כֶּעָפָר לַכֹּל תִּהְיֶה. פְּתַח לִבִּי בְּתוֹרָתֶךָ, וּבְמִצְוֹתֶיךָ תִּרְדּוֹף נַפְשִׁי; וְכָל הַחוֹשְׁבִים עָלַי רָעָה, מְהֵרָה הָפֵר עֲצָתָם וְקַלְקֵל מַחֲשַׁבְתָּם. עֲשֵׂה לְמַעַן שְׁמֶךָ, עֲשֵׂה לְמַעַן יְמִינֶךָ, עֲשֵׂה לְמַעַן קְדֻשָּׁתֶךָ, עֲשֵׂה לְמַעַן תּוֹרָתֶךָ. לְמַעַן יֵחָלְצוּן יְדִידֶיךָ, הוֹשִׁיעָה יְמִינְךָ וַעֲנֵנִי. יִהְיוּ לְרָצוֹן אִמְרֵי פִי וְהֶגְיוֹן לִבִּי לְפָנֶיךָ, יְיָ, צוּרִי וְגוֹאֲלִי. עֹשֶׂה שָׁלוֹם בִּמְרוֹמָיו, הוּא יַעֲשֶׂה שָׁלוֹם עָלֵינוּ וְעַל כָּל יִשְׂרָאֵל, וְאִמְרוּ אָמֵן.

יְהִי רָצוֹן מִלְּפָנֶיךָ, יְיָ אֱלֹהֵינוּ וֵאלֹהֵי אֲבוֹתֵינוּ, שֶׁיִּבָּנֶה בֵּית הַמִּקְדָּשׁ בִּמְהֵרָה בְיָמֵינוּ, וְתֵן חֶלְקֵנוּ בְּתוֹרָתֶךָ. וְשָׁם נַעֲבָדְךָ

אלהי נצור עשה is taken substantially from the Talmud (Berakhoth 17a). עושה שלום and למען שמך are later insertions.

blessing written in thy Torah by thy servant Moses and spoken by Aaron and his sons the priests, thy holy people, as it is said: "May the Lord bless you and protect you; may the Lord countenance you and be gracious to you; may the Lord favor you and grant you peace."[1]

O grant peace, happiness, blessing, grace, kindness and mercy to us and to all Israel thy people. Bless us all alike, our Father, with the light of thy countenance; indeed, by the light of thy countenance thou hast given us, Lord our God, a Torah of life, lovingkindness, charity, blessing, mercy, life and peace. May it please thee to bless thy people Israel with peace at all times and hours. * Blessed art thou, O Lord, who blessest thy people Israel with peace.

* Between Rosh Hashanah and Yom Kippur say:

(May we and all Israel thy people be remembered and inscribed before thee in the book of life and blessing, peace and prosperity, for a happy life and for peace. Blessed art thou, O Lord, Author of peace.)

After the Shemoneh Esreh add the following meditation:

My God, guard my tongue from evil, and my lips from speaking falsehood. May my soul be silent to those who insult me; be my soul lowly to all as the dust. Open my heart to thy Torah, that my soul may follow thy commands. Speedily defeat the counsel of all those who plan evil against me, and upset their design. Do it for the glory of thy name; do it for the sake of thy power; do it for the sake of thy holiness; do it for the sake of thy Torah. That thy beloved may be rescued, save with thy right hand and answer me. May the words of my mouth and the meditation of my heart be pleasing before thee, O Lord, my Stronghold and my Redeemer.[2] May he who creates peace in his high heavens create peace for us and for all Israel. Amen.

May it be thy will, Lord our God and God of our fathers, that the Temple be speedily rebuilt in our days, and grant us a share in thy Torah. There we will serve thee with reverence, as in the

---

[1] *Numbers* 6:24–26.   [2] *Psalms* 60:7; 19:15.

בְּיִרְאָה, כִּימֵי עוֹלָם וּכְשָׁנִים קַדְמוֹנִיּוֹת. וְעָרְבָה לַיָי מִנְחַת
יְהוּדָה וִירוּשָׁלֵָם, כִּימֵי עוֹלָם וּכְשָׁנִים קַדְמוֹנִיּוֹת.

Hallel (page 565) is recited here on *Rosh Ḥodesh, Ḥol ha-Mo'ed* and *Ḥanukkah.*

ABRIDGED SHEMONEH ESREH
Used when one is unable to recite the complete *Amidah*

הֲבִינֵנוּ, יְיָ אֱלֹהֵינוּ, לָדַעַת דְּרָכֶיךָ; וּמוֹל אֶת לְבָבֵנוּ
לְיִרְאָתֶךָ; וְתִסְלַח לָנוּ לִהְיוֹת גְּאוּלִים; וְרַחֲקֵנוּ מִמַּכְאוֹב;
וְדַשְּׁנוּ בִּנְאוֹת אַרְצֶךָ; וּנְפוּצוֹתֵינוּ מֵאַרְבַּע כַּנְפוֹת הָאָרֶץ
תְּקַבֵּץ. וְהַתּוֹעִים עַל דַּעְתְּךָ יִשָּׁפֵטוּ; וְעַל הָרְשָׁעִים תָּנִיף יָדֶךָ;
וְיִשְׂמְחוּ צַדִּיקִים בְּבִנְיַן עִירֶךָ, וּבְתִקּוּן הֵיכָלֶךָ, וּבִצְמִיחַת קֶרֶן
לְדָוִד עַבְדֶּךָ, וּבַעֲרִיכַת נֵר לְבֶן יִשַׁי מְשִׁיחֶךָ; טֶרֶם נִקְרָא אַתָּה
תַעֲנֶה. בָּרוּךְ אַתָּה, יְיָ, שׁוֹמֵעַ תְּפִלָּה.

Between *Rosh Hashanah* and *Yom Kippur* and on fast days:

אָבִינוּ מַלְכֵּנוּ, חָטָאנוּ לְפָנֶיךָ.

אָבִינוּ מַלְכֵּנוּ, אֵין לָנוּ מֶלֶךְ אֶלָּא אָתָּה.

אָבִינוּ מַלְכֵּנוּ, עֲשֵׂה עִמָּנוּ לְמַעַן שְׁמֶךָ.

On fast days:	From *Rosh Hashanah* to *Yom Kippur*:
אָבִינוּ מַלְכֵּנוּ,	אָבִינוּ מַלְכֵּנוּ,
בָּרֵךְ עָלֵינוּ שָׁנָה טוֹבָה.	חַדֵּשׁ עָלֵינוּ שָׁנָה טוֹבָה.

אָבִינוּ מַלְכֵּנוּ, בַּטֵּל מֵעָלֵינוּ כָּל גְּזֵרוֹת קָשׁוֹת.

הביננו, called מעין שמונה עשרה ("abstract of the *Shemoneh Esreh*"), was composed by Rabbi Samuel, one of the first generation of the Babylonian authors
of the Talmud, who lived in the third century. This prayer (Berakhoth 29a)
is a synopsis of the middle thirteen petitions of the *Shemoneh Esreh*, from
אתה חונן until רצה. When recited on urgent occasions, הביננו is preceded by the
opening three blessings and concluded by the last three blessings of the original *Shemoneh Esreh*.

days of old and as in former years. Then the offering of Judah and Jerusalem will be pleasing to the Lord, as in the days of old and as in former years.[1]

Hallel (page 566) is recited here on Rosh Ḥodesh, Ḥol ha-Mo'ed and Ḥanukkah.

ABRIDGED SHEMONEH ESREH

Used when one is unable to recite the complete Amidah

Grant us, Lord our God, wisdom to learn thy ways; subject our heart to thy worship; forgive us so that we may be redeemed; keep us from suffering; satisfy us with the products of thy earth; gather our dispersed people from the four corners of the earth. Judge those who stray from thy faith; punish the wicked; may the righteous rejoice over the rebuilding of thy city, the reconstruction of thy Temple, the flourishing dynasty of thy servant David and the continuance of the offspring of thy anointed, the son of Jesse. Answer us before we call. Blessed art thou, O Lord, who hearest prayer.

Between Rosh Hashanah and Yom Kippur and on fast days:

Our Father, our King, we have sinned before thee.

Our Father, our King, we have no king except thee.

Our Father, our King, deal with us kindly for the sake of thy name.

From Rosh Hashanah to Yom Kippur:	*On fast days:*
Our Father, our King,	Our Father, our King,
renew for us a good year.	bestow on us a good year.

Our Father, our King, abolish all evil decrees against us.

אבינו מלכנו is mentioned in the Talmud (Ta'anith 25b) as the prayer of Rabbi Akiba on a fast day. There is a close resemblance between some of its phrases and the *Shemoneh Esreh*. In the ninth century *Siddur* of Amram Gaon there are only twenty-five verses of *Avinu Malkenu*. In the course of time the number has been increased on account of disaster and persecution.

---

[1] *Malachi* 3:4.

אָבִינוּ מַלְכֵּנוּ, בַּטֵּל מַחְשְׁבוֹת שׂוֹנְאֵינוּ.

אָבִינוּ מַלְכֵּנוּ, הָפֵר עֲצַת אוֹיְבֵינוּ.

אָבִינוּ מַלְכֵּנוּ, כַּלֵּה כָּל צַר וּמַשְׂטִין מֵעָלֵינוּ.

אָבִינוּ מַלְכֵּנוּ, סְתוֹם פִּיוֹת מַשְׂטִינֵינוּ וּמְקַטְרִגֵינוּ.

אָבִינוּ מַלְכֵּנוּ, כַּלֵּה דֶבֶר וְחֶרֶב וְרָעָב, וּשְׁבִי וּמַשְׁחִית וְעָוֹן
וּשְׁמַד, מִבְּנֵי בְרִיתֶךָ.

אָבִינוּ מַלְכֵּנוּ, מְנַע מַגֵּפָה מִנַּחֲלָתֶךָ.

אָבִינוּ מַלְכֵּנוּ, סְלַח וּמְחַל לְכָל עֲוֹנוֹתֵינוּ.

אָבִינוּ מַלְכֵּנוּ, מְחֵה וְהַעֲבֵר פְּשָׁעֵינוּ וְחַטֹּאתֵינוּ מִנֶּגֶד עֵינֶיךָ.

אָבִינוּ מַלְכֵּנוּ, מְחוֹק בְּרַחֲמֶיךָ הָרַבִּים כָּל שִׁטְרֵי חוֹבוֹתֵינוּ.

אָבִינוּ מַלְכֵּנוּ, הַחֲזִירֵנוּ בִּתְשׁוּבָה שְׁלֵמָה לְפָנֶיךָ.

אָבִינוּ מַלְכֵּנוּ, שְׁלַח רְפוּאָה שְׁלֵמָה לְחוֹלֵי עַמֶּךָ.

אָבִינוּ מַלְכֵּנוּ, קְרַע רֹעַ גְּזַר דִּינֵנוּ.

אָבִינוּ מַלְכֵּנוּ, זָכְרֵנוּ בְּזִכָּרוֹן טוֹב לְפָנֶיךָ.

On fast days:	From *Rosh Hashanah* to *Yom Kippur:*
אָבִינוּ מַלְכֵּנוּ, זָכְרֵנוּ לְחַיִּים טוֹבִים.	אָבִינוּ מַלְכֵּנוּ, כָּתְבֵנוּ בְּסֵפֶר חַיִּים טוֹבִים.
אָבִינוּ מַלְכֵּנוּ, זָכְרֵנוּ לִגְאֻלָּה וִישׁוּעָה.	אָבִינוּ מַלְכֵּנוּ, כָּתְבֵנוּ בְּסֵפֶר גְּאֻלָּה וִישׁוּעָה.
אָבִינוּ מַלְכֵּנוּ, זָכְרֵנוּ לְפַרְנָסָה וְכַלְכָּלָה.	אָבִינוּ מַלְכֵּנוּ, כָּתְבֵנוּ בְּסֵפֶר פַּרְנָסָה וְכַלְכָּלָה.
אָבִינוּ מַלְכֵּנוּ, זָכְרֵנוּ לִזְכֻיּוֹת.	אָבִינוּ מַלְכֵּנוּ, כָּתְבֵנוּ בְּסֵפֶר זְכֻיּוֹת.
אָבִינוּ מַלְכֵּנוּ, זָכְרֵנוּ לִסְלִיחָה וּמְחִילָה.	אָבִינוּ מַלְכֵּנוּ, כָּתְבֵנוּ בְּסֵפֶר סְלִיחָה וּמְחִילָה.

Our Father, our King, annul the plans of our enemies.

Our Father, our King, frustrate the counsel of our foes.

Our Father, our King, rid us of every oppressor and adversary.

Our Father, our King, close the mouths of our adversaries and accusers.

Our Father, our King, remove pestilence, sword, famine, captivity, destruction, iniquity and persecution from thy people of the covenant.

Our Father, our King, keep the plague back from thy heritage.

Our Father, our King, forgive and pardon all our sins.

Our Father, our King, blot out and remove our transgressions and sins from thy sight.

Our Father, our King, cancel in thy abundant mercy all the records of our sins.

Our Father, our King, bring us back in perfect repentance to thee.

Our Father, our King, send a perfect healing to the sick among thy people.

Our Father, our King, tear up the evil sentence decreed against us.

Our Father, our King, remember us favorably.

Our Father, our King, * inscribe us in the book of happy life.

Our Father, our King, * inscribe us in the book of redemption and salvation.

Our Father, our King, * inscribe us in the book of maintenance and sustenance.

Our Father, our King, * inscribe us in the book of merit.

Our Father, our King, * inscribe us in the book of pardon and forgiveness.

* On fast days, instead of "inscribe us" the phrase "remember us" is used.

אָבִינוּ מַלְכֵּנוּ, הַצְמַח לָנוּ יְשׁוּעָה בְּקָרוֹב.

אָבִינוּ מַלְכֵּנוּ, הָרֵם קֶרֶן יִשְׂרָאֵל עַמֶּךָ.

אָבִינוּ מַלְכֵּנוּ, הָרֵם קֶרֶן מְשִׁיחֶךָ.

אָבִינוּ מַלְכֵּנוּ, מַלֵּא יָדֵינוּ מִבִּרְכוֹתֶיךָ.

אָבִינוּ מַלְכֵּנוּ, מַלֵּא אֲסָמֵינוּ שָׂבָע.

אָבִינוּ מַלְכֵּנוּ, שְׁמַע קוֹלֵנוּ, חוּס וְרַחֵם עָלֵינוּ.

אָבִינוּ מַלְכֵּנוּ, קַבֵּל בְּרַחֲמִים וּבְרָצוֹן אֶת תְּפִלָּתֵנוּ.

אָבִינוּ מַלְכֵּנוּ, פְּתַח שַׁעֲרֵי שָׁמַיִם לִתְפִלָּתֵנוּ .

אָבִינוּ מַלְכֵּנוּ, נָא אַל תְּשִׁיבֵנוּ רֵיקָם מִלְּפָנֶיךָ.

אָבִינוּ מַלְכֵּנוּ, זְכוֹר כִּי עָפָר אֲנָחְנוּ.

אָבִינוּ מַלְכֵּנוּ, תְּהֵא הַשָּׁעָה הַזֹּאת שְׁעַת רַחֲמִים וְעֵת רָצוֹן מִלְּפָנֶיךָ.

אָבִינוּ מַלְכֵּנוּ, חֲמוֹל עָלֵינוּ וְעַל עוֹלָלֵינוּ וְטַפֵּנוּ.

אָבִינוּ מַלְכֵּנוּ, עֲשֵׂה לְמַעַן הֲרוּגִים עַל שֵׁם קָדְשֶׁךָ.

אָבִינוּ מַלְכֵּנוּ, עֲשֵׂה לְמַעַן טְבוּחִים עַל יִחוּדֶךָ.

אָבִינוּ מַלְכֵּנוּ, עֲשֵׂה לְמַעַן בָּאֵי בָאֵשׁ וּבַמַּיִם עַל קִדּוּשׁ שְׁמֶךָ.

אָבִינוּ מַלְכֵּנוּ, נְקוֹם נִקְמַת דַּם עֲבָדֶיךָ הַשָּׁפוּךְ.

אָבִינוּ מַלְכֵּנוּ, עֲשֵׂה לְמַעַנְךָ אִם לֹא לְמַעֲנֵנוּ.

אָבִינוּ מַלְכֵּנוּ, עֲשֵׂה לְמַעַנְךָ וְהוֹשִׁיעֵנוּ.

אָבִינוּ מַלְכֵּנוּ, עֲשֵׂה לְמַעַן רַחֲמֶיךָ הָרַבִּים.

אָבִינוּ מַלְכֵּנוּ, עֲשֵׂה לְמַעַן שִׁמְךָ הַגָּדוֹל הַגִּבּוֹר וְהַנּוֹרָא שֶׁנִּקְרָא עָלֵינוּ.

אָבִינוּ מַלְכֵּנוּ, חָנֵּנוּ וַעֲנֵנוּ, כִּי אֵין בָּנוּ מַעֲשִׂים; עֲשֵׂה עִמָּנוּ צְדָקָה וָחֶסֶד וְהוֹשִׁיעֵנוּ.

Our Father, our King, cause our salvation soon to flourish.

Our Father, our King, raise the strength of Israel thy people.

Our Father, our King, raise the strength of thy anointed one.

Our Father, our King, fill our hands with thy blessings.

Our Father, our King, fill our storehouses with plenty.

Our Father, our King, hear our voice, spare us and have mercy on us.

Our Father, our King, receive our prayer with mercy and favor.

Our Father, our King, open the gates of heaven to our prayer.

Our Father, our King, dismiss us not empty-handed from thy presence.

Our Father, our King, remember that we are but dust.

Our Father, our King, may this hour be an hour of mercy and a time of grace with thee.

Our Father, our King, have compassion on us, on our children and our infants.

Our Father, our King, act for the sake of those who were slain for thy holy name.

Our Father, our King, act for the sake of those who were slaughtered for proclaiming thy Oneness.

Our Father, our King, act for the sake of those who went through fire and water for the sanctification of thy name.

Our Father, our King, avenge the spilt blood of thy servants.

Our Father, our King, do it for thy sake, if not for ours.

Our Father, our King, do it for thy sake and save us.

Our Father, our King, do it for the sake of thy abundant mercy.

Our Father, our King, do it for the sake of thy great, mighty and revered name by which we are called.

Our Father, our King, be gracious to us and answer us, though we have no merits; deal charitably and kindly with us and save us.

תַּחֲנוּן

Except Mondays and Thursdays, the following *Taḥanun* is recited daily. On Mondays and Thursdays, the long *Taḥanun* is said (pages 105–117). *Taḥanun* is omitted on the following occasions: *Rosh Ḥodesh*, the entire month of *Nisan*, *Lag b'Omer*, the first eight days of *Sivan*, the 9th and 15th of *Av*, *Erev Rosh Hashanah*, from *Erev Yom Kippur* until the second day after *Sukkoth*, *Ḥanukkah*, the 15th of *Shevat*, the 14th and 15th of *Adar* and *Adar Sheni*. *Taḥanun* is also omitted in the house of a mourner during the week of mourning, and on the occasion of a *Brith Milah*.

וַיֹּאמֶר דָּוִד אֶל גָּד: צַר לִי מְאֹד; נִפְּלָה נָּא בְיַד יְיָ, כִּי רַבִּים רַחֲמָיו, וּבְיַד אָדָם אַל אֶפֹּלָה.

רַחוּם וְחַנּוּן, חָטָאתִי לְפָנֶיךָ; יְיָ מָלֵא רַחֲמִים, רַחֵם עָלַי וְקַבֵּל תַּחֲנוּנָי.

תהלים ו

יְיָ, אַל בְּאַפְּךָ תוֹכִיחֵנִי, וְאַל בַּחֲמָתְךָ תְיַסְּרֵנִי. חָנֵּנִי, יְיָ, כִּי אֻמְלַל אָנִי; רְפָאֵנִי, יְיָ, כִּי נִבְהֲלוּ עֲצָמָי. וְנַפְשִׁי נִבְהֲלָה מְאֹד; וְאַתָּה יְיָ, עַד מָתָי. שׁוּבָה, יְיָ, חַלְּצָה נַפְשִׁי; הוֹשִׁיעֵנִי לְמַעַן חַסְדֶּךָ. כִּי אֵין בַּמָּוֶת זִכְרֶךָ; בִּשְׁאוֹל מִי יוֹדֶה לָּךְ. יָגַעְתִּי בְּאַנְחָתִי, אַשְׂחֶה בְכָל לַיְלָה מִטָּתִי; בְּדִמְעָתִי עַרְשִׂי אַמְסֶה. עָשְׁשָׁה מִכַּעַס עֵינִי; עָתְקָה בְּכָל צוֹרְרָי. סוּרוּ מִמֶּנִּי, כָּל פֹּעֲלֵי אָוֶן, כִּי שָׁמַע יְיָ קוֹל בִּכְיִי. שָׁמַע יְיָ תְּחִנָּתִי; יְיָ תְּפִלָּתִי יִקָּח. יֵבֹשׁוּ וְיִבָּהֲלוּ מְאֹד כָּל אֹיְבָי; יָשֻׁבוּ יֵבֹשׁוּ רָגַע.

שׁוֹמֵר יִשְׂרָאֵל, שְׁמוֹר שְׁאֵרִית יִשְׂרָאֵל, וְאַל יֹאבַד יִשְׂרָאֵל, הָאוֹמְרִים שְׁמַע יִשְׂרָאֵל.

תחנון ("petition") is recited in a sitting posture known as נפילת אפים ("falling on the face"), which is a modified form of the complete prostration with the face to the ground practised in the early days of the Talmud (Megillah 22b). This custom originates from Moses, who "fell down before the Lord" (Deuteronomy 9:18), and Joshua, who "fell on the earth upon his face before the ark of the Lord" (Joshua 7:6). Hence, נפילת אפים is performed only where there is a *Sefer Torah*. It consists of merely resting the head on the arm. During

TAḤANUN

Except Mondays and Thursdays, the following Taḥanun is recited daily. **On**
Mondays and Thursdays, the long Taḥanun is said (pages 106–118).
Taḥanun is omitted on the following occasions: Rosh Ḥodesh, the entire month of
Nisan, Lag b'Omer, the first eight days of Sivan, the 9th and 15th of Av, Erev Rosh
Hashanah, from Erev Yom Kippur until the second day after Sukkoth, Ḥanukkah,
the 15th of Shevat, the 14th and 15th of Adar and Adar Sheni. Taḥanun is also
omitted in the house of a mourner during the week of mourning, and on the occasion
of a Brith Milah.

And David said to Gad: "I am deeply distressed; let us fall
into the hand of the Lord, for his mercy is great, but let me not
fall into the hand of man.[1]

Merciful and gracious God, I have sinned before thee; O Lord,
who art full of compassion, have mercy on me and accept my
supplications.

Psalm 6

O Lord, punish me not in thy anger; chastise me not in thy
wrath. Have pity on me, O Lord, for I languish away; heal me,
O Lord, for my health is shaken. My soul is severely troubled;
and thou, O Lord, how long? O Lord, deliver my life once again;
save me because of thy grace. For in death there is no thought of
thee; in the grave who gives thanks to thee? I am worn out with
my groaning; every night I flood my bed with tears; I cause my
couch to melt with my weeping. My eye is dimmed from grief; it
grows old because of all my foes. Depart from me, all you evildoers, for the Lord has heard the sound of my weeping. The Lord
has heard my supplication; the Lord receives my prayer. All my
foes shall be utterly ashamed and terrified; they shall turn back;
they shall be suddenly ashamed.

Guardian of Israel, preserve the remnant of Israel; let not
Israel perish, who say: "Hear, O Israel."

the morning service, when the *tefillin* are on the left arm, the right arm is used;
at the *Minḥah* service, however, the left arm is used. Since the verse ויאמר דוד
contains the phrase נפלה נא ("let us fall") it precedes נפילת אפים, the falling
posture assumed during the *Taḥanun* prayer.

גד was the name of the prophet who offered to David a choice of punish-
ments, coming directly from God or through the agency of man. David replied
that he preferred to be punished by the gracious God rather than by man.

[1] *II Samuel* 24:14.

שׁוֹמֵר גּוֹי אֶחָד, שְׁמוֹר שְׁאֵרִית עַם אֶחָד, וְאַל יֹאבַד גּוֹי
אֶחָד, הַמְיַחֲדִים שְׁמְךָ, יְיָ אֱלֹהֵינוּ, יְיָ אֶחָד.

שׁוֹמֵר גּוֹי קָדוֹשׁ, שְׁמוֹר שְׁאֵרִית עַם קָדוֹשׁ, וְאַל יֹאבַד גּוֹי
קָדוֹשׁ, הַמְשַׁלְּשִׁים בְּשָׁלֹשׁ קְדֻשּׁוֹת לְקָדוֹשׁ.

מִתְרַצֶּה בְּרַחֲמִים וּמִתְפַּיֵּס בְּתַחֲנוּנִים, הִתְרַצֵּה וְהִתְפַּיֵּס
לְדוֹר עָנִי, כִּי אֵין עוֹזֵר. אָבִינוּ מַלְכֵּנוּ, חָנֵּנוּ וַעֲנֵנוּ, כִּי אֵין בָּנוּ
מַעֲשִׂים; עֲשֵׂה עִמָּנוּ צְדָקָה וָחֶסֶד וְהוֹשִׁיעֵנוּ.

וַאֲנַחְנוּ לֹא נֵדַע מַה נַּעֲשֶׂה, כִּי עָלֶיךָ עֵינֵינוּ. זְכֹר רַחֲמֶיךָ יְיָ,
וַחֲסָדֶיךָ, כִּי מֵעוֹלָם הֵמָּה. יְהִי חַסְדְּךָ יְיָ עָלֵינוּ, כַּאֲשֶׁר יִחַלְנוּ
לָךְ. אַל תִּזְכָּר־לָנוּ עֲוֹנוֹת רִאשֹׁנִים; מַהֵר יְקַדְּמוּנוּ רַחֲמֶיךָ, כִּי
דַלּוֹנוּ מְאֹד. חָנֵּנוּ יְיָ חָנֵּנוּ, כִּי רַב שָׂבַעְנוּ בוּז. בְּרֹגֶז רַחֵם תִּזְכּוֹר.
כִּי הוּא יָדַע יִצְרֵנוּ, זָכוּר כִּי עָפָר אֲנָחְנוּ. Reader. עָזְרֵנוּ, אֱלֹהֵי
יִשְׁעֵנוּ, עַל דְּבַר כְּבוֹד שְׁמֶךָ, וְהַצִּילֵנוּ וְכַפֵּר עַל חַטֹּאתֵינוּ
לְמַעַן שְׁמֶךָ.

The service is continued with the Reader's recital of the Kaddish on page 117.

TAḤANUN FOR MONDAYS AND THURSDAYS

The following is omitted during the occasions enumerated on page 103.

וְהוּא רַחוּם, יְכַפֵּר עָוֹן וְלֹא יַשְׁחִית; וְהִרְבָּה לְהָשִׁיב אַפּוֹ,
וְלֹא יָעִיר כָּל חֲמָתוֹ. אַתָּה, יְיָ, לֹא תִכְלָא רַחֲמֶיךָ מִמֶּנּוּ; חַסְדְּךָ
וַאֲמִתְּךָ תָּמִיד יִצְּרוּנוּ. הוֹשִׁיעֵנוּ, יְיָ אֱלֹהֵינוּ, וְקַבְּצֵנוּ מִן הַגּוֹיִם
לְהוֹדוֹת לְשֵׁם קָדְשֶׁךָ, לְהִשְׁתַּבֵּחַ בִּתְהִלָּתֶךָ. אִם עֲוֹנוֹת תִּשְׁמָר־
יָהּ, אֲדֹנָי, מִי יַעֲמֹד. כִּי עִמְּךָ הַסְּלִיחָה, לְמַעַן תִּוָּרֵא. לֹא
כַחֲטָאֵינוּ תַּעֲשֶׂה לָּנוּ, וְלֹא כַעֲוֹנוֹתֵינוּ תִּגְמֹל עָלֵינוּ. אִם עֲוֹנֵינוּ

והוא רחום was composed, according to legend, soon after the destruction
of the second Temple. It is suggested, however, that it was written during the
persecutions of the seventh century. It has been said that whoever can read
this long prayer without emotion has lost all feeling for what is great and

Guardian of a unique people, preserve the remnant of a unique people; let not a unique people perish, who proclaim thy Oneness, saying: "The Lord is our God, the Lord is One."

Guardian of a holy people, preserve the remnant of a holy people; let not a holy people perish, who repeat the threefold sanctification to the Holy One.

O thou who art reconciled by prayers and conciliated by supplications, be thou reconciled and conciliated to an afflicted generation, for there is none to help.

Our Father, our King, be gracious to us and answer us, for we have no merits; deal charitably and kindly with us and save us.

We know not what to do, but our eyes are upon thee. Remember thy mercy and thy kindness, O Lord, for they are eternal. May thy kindness rest on us, O Lord, as our hope rests on thee. O mind not our former iniquities; may thy compassion hasten to our aid, for we are brought very low. Take pity on us, O Lord, take pity on us, for we are exceedingly sated with contempt. When in wrath, remember to be merciful. He knows what we are made of, remembering that we are but dust. Help us, our saving God, for the sake of thy glorious name; rescue us and pardon our sins for thy name's sake.[1]

The service is continued with the Reader's recital of the Kaddish on page 118.

The service is continued with the Reader's recital of the Kaddish on page 118.

TAHANUN FOR MONDAYS AND THURSDAYS

The following is omitted during the occasions enumerated on page 104.

The following is omitted during the occasions enumerated on page 104.

He, being merciful, forgives iniquity, and does not destroy; frequently he turns his anger away, and does not stir up all his wrath.[2]

Thou, O Lord, wilt not hold back thy mercy from us; thy kindness and thy truth will always protect us. Save us, Lord our God, and gather us from among the nations, that we may give thanks to thy holy name, that we may glory in thy praise. If thou, O Lord, shouldst record iniquities—O Lord, who could live on? But with thee there is forgiveness, that thou mayest be revered. Deal not with us according to our sins; requite us not according to our iniquities. If our sins, O Lord, testify against us, act for

---

noble. The soul of an entire people utters these elegies and supplications, and gives voice to its woe of a thousand years.

[1] *II Chronicles* 20:12; *Psalms* 25:6; 33:22; 79:8; 123:3; *Habakkuk* 3:2; *Psalm* 103:14. [2] *Psalm* 78:38.

עֲנֵנוּ בָנוּ, יְיָ, עֲשֵׂה לְמַעַן שְׁמֶךָ. זְכֹר רַחֲמֶיךָ יְיָ, וַחֲסָדֶיךָ, כִּי
מֵעוֹלָם הֵמָּה. יַעֲנֵנוּ יְיָ בְּיוֹם צָרָה. יְשַׂגְּבֵנוּ שֵׁם אֱלֹהֵי יַעֲקֹב. יְיָ,
הוֹשִׁיעָה; הַמֶּלֶךְ יַעֲנֵנוּ בְיוֹם קָרְאֵנוּ. אָבִינוּ מַלְכֵּנוּ, חָנֵּנוּ וַעֲנֵנוּ,
כִּי אֵין בָּנוּ מַעֲשִׂים; צְדָקָה עֲשֵׂה עִמָּנוּ לְמַעַן שְׁמֶךָ. אֲדוֹנֵנוּ
אֱלֹהֵינוּ, שְׁמַע קוֹל תַּחֲנוּנֵינוּ, וּזְכָר־לָנוּ אֶת בְּרִית אֲבוֹתֵינוּ,
וְהוֹשִׁיעֵנוּ לְמַעַן שְׁמֶךָ. וְעַתָּה אֲדֹנָי אֱלֹהֵינוּ, אֲשֶׁר הוֹצֵאתָ אֶת
עַמְּךָ מֵאֶרֶץ מִצְרַיִם בְּיָד חֲזָקָה וַתַּעַשׂ לְךָ שֵׁם כַּיּוֹם הַזֶּה,
חָטָאנוּ רָשָׁעְנוּ. אֲדֹנָי, כְּכָל צִדְקוֹתֶיךָ יָשָׁב־נָא אַפְּךָ וַחֲמָתְךָ
מֵעִירְךָ יְרוּשָׁלַיִם, הַר קָדְשֶׁךָ; כִּי בַחֲטָאֵינוּ וּבַעֲוֹנוֹת אֲבוֹתֵינוּ,
יְרוּשָׁלַיִם וְעַמְּךָ לְחֶרְפָּה לְכָל סְבִיבוֹתֵינוּ. וְעַתָּה שְׁמַע, אֱלֹהֵינוּ,
אֶל תְּפִלַּת עַבְדְּךָ וְאֶל תַּחֲנוּנָיו, וְהָאֵר פָּנֶיךָ עַל מִקְדָּשְׁךָ
הַשָּׁמֵם, לְמַעַן אֲדֹנָי.

הַטֵּה אֱלֹהַי אָזְנְךָ וּשֲׁמָע; פְּקַח עֵינֶיךָ וּרְאֵה שׁוֹמְמוֹתֵינוּ,
וְהָעִיר אֲשֶׁר נִקְרָא שִׁמְךָ עָלֶיהָ; כִּי לֹא עַל צִדְקוֹתֵינוּ אֲנַחְנוּ
מַפִּילִים תַּחֲנוּנֵינוּ לְפָנֶיךָ, כִּי עַל רַחֲמֶיךָ הָרַבִּים. אֲדֹנָי, שְׁמָעָה;
אֲדֹנָי, סְלָחָה; אֲדֹנָי, הַקְשִׁיבָה וַעֲשֵׂה, אַל תְּאַחַר, לְמַעַנְךָ
אֱלֹהַי, כִּי שִׁמְךָ נִקְרָא עַל עִירְךָ וְעַל עַמֶּךָ. אָבִינוּ, הָאָב
הָרַחֲמָן, הַרְאֵנוּ אוֹת לְטוֹבָה וְקַבֵּץ נְפוּצוֹתֵינוּ מֵאַרְבַּע כַּנְפוֹת
הָאָרֶץ; יַכִּירוּ וְיֵדְעוּ כָּל הַגּוֹיִם כִּי אַתָּה יְיָ אֱלֹהֵינוּ. וְעַתָּה יְיָ,
אָבִינוּ אָתָּה; אֲנַחְנוּ הַחֹמֶר וְאַתָּה יוֹצְרֵנוּ, וּמַעֲשֵׂה יָדְךָ כֻּלָּנוּ.
הוֹשִׁיעֵנוּ לְמַעַן שְׁמֶךָ, צוּרֵנוּ, מַלְכֵּנוּ וְגוֹאֲלֵנוּ. חוּסָה יְיָ עַל עַמֶּךָ,
וְאַל תִּתֵּן נַחֲלָתְךָ לְחֶרְפָּה לִמְשָׁל־בָּם גּוֹיִם; לָמָּה יֹאמְרוּ
בָעַמִּים אַיֵּה אֱלֹהֵיהֶם. יָדַעְנוּ כִּי חָטָאנוּ, וְאֵין מִי יַעֲמֹד בַּעֲדֵנוּ;
שִׁמְךָ הַגָּדוֹל יַעֲמָד־לָנוּ בְּעֵת צָרָה. יָדַעְנוּ כִּי אֵין בָּנוּ מַעֲשִׂים:
צְדָקָה עֲשֵׂה עִמָּנוּ לְמַעַן שְׁמֶךָ. כְּרַחֵם אָב עַל בָּנִים, כֵּן תְּרַחֵם

thy name's sake. Remember, O Lord, thy mercy and thy kindness, for they are eternal. May the Lord answer us on the day of trouble; may the name of the God of Jacob protect us. O Lord, save us; may the King answer us when we call.[1]

Our Father, our King, take pity on us and answer us, for we have no merits; deal charitably with us for thy name's sake. Our Lord God, hear our supplications; remember in our favor the covenant of our fathers, and save us for thy name's sake. And now, Lord our God, who hast brought thy people out of the land of Egypt with a mighty hand, and hast made for thyself a name unto this day, we have sinned, we have acted wickedly. O Lord, in accordance with all thy righteous deeds, pray let thy anger and thy fury turn from Jerusalem thy city, thy holy mountain; for through our sins, and through the iniquities of our fathers, Jerusalem and thy people are held in disgrace by all who surround us. And now, our God, listen to thy servant's prayer and supplications, and let thy favor shine upon thy desolate sanctuary for thy own sake, O Lord.[2]

Bend thy ear, my God, and hear; open thy eyes and see our ruins, and the city which is called by thy name. Indeed, it is not because of our own righteousness that we plead before thee, but because of thy great mercy. O Lord, hear; O Lord, forgive; O Lord, listen and take action, do not delay, for thy own sake, my God; for thy city and thy people are called by thy name.[3] Our Father, merciful Father, show us a sign for happiness, and gather our dispersed from the four corners of the earth; let all the nations realize and know that thou art the Lord our God. And now, O Lord, thou art our Father; we are the clay, and thou art our potter; all of us are the work of thy hands.[4] Save us for thy name's sake, our Stronghold, our King, our Redeemer. Spare thy people, O Lord, and let not thy heritage be an object of contempt, a byword among nations. Why should it be said among the peoples: "Where is their God?"[5] We know that we have sinned, and there is none to stand up for us, so let thy great name protect us in time of trouble; we know that we have no merits, so deal with us charitably for thy name's sake. As a father has compassion on his children, so, O Lord, have compassion on us, and save us for thy

[1] *Psalms* 40:12; 106:47; 130:3–4; 103:10; *Jeremiah* 14:7; *Psalms* 25:6; 20:2. 10.   [2] *Daniel* 9:15–17.   [3] *Daniel* 9:18–19.   [4] *Isaiah* 64:7.   [5] *Joel* 2:17.

יְיָ עָלֵינוּ, וְהוֹשִׁיעֵנוּ לְמַעַן שְׁמֶךָ. חֲמוֹל עַל עַמֶּךָ, רַחֵם עַל נַחֲלָתֶךָ, חוּסָה נָא כְּרֹב רַחֲמֶיךָ, חָנֵּנוּ וַעֲנֵנוּ, כִּי לְךָ יְיָ הַצְּדָקָה, עֹשֵׂה נִפְלָאוֹת בְּכָל עֵת.

הַבֶּט־נָא, רַחֶם־נָא עַל עַמְּךָ מְהֵרָה לְמַעַן שְׁמֶךָ. בְּרַחֲמֶיךָ הָרַבִּים, יְיָ אֱלֹהֵינוּ, חוּס וְרַחֵם וְהוֹשִׁיעָה צֹאן מַרְעִיתֶךָ, וְאַל יִמְשָׁל־בָּנוּ קָצֶף, כִּי לְךָ עֵינֵינוּ תְלוּיוֹת; הוֹשִׁיעֵנוּ לְמַעַן שְׁמֶךָ. רַחֵם עָלֵינוּ לְמַעַן בְּרִיתֶךָ; הַבִּיטָה וַעֲנֵנוּ בְּעֵת צָרָה, כִּי לְךָ יְיָ הַיְשׁוּעָה, בְּךָ תוֹחַלְתֵּנוּ, אֱלוֹהַּ סְלִיחוֹת. אָנָּא, סְלַח נָא, אֵל טוֹב וְסַלָּח, כִּי אֵל מֶלֶךְ חַנּוּן וְרַחוּם אָתָּה.

אָנָּא, מֶלֶךְ חַנּוּן וְרַחוּם, זְכוֹר וְהַבֵּט לִבְרִית בֵּין הַבְּתָרִים, וְתֵרָאֶה לְפָנֶיךָ עֲקֵדַת יָחִיד לְמַעַן יִשְׂרָאֵל. אָבִינוּ מַלְכֵּנוּ, חָנֵּנוּ וַעֲנֵנוּ, כִּי שִׁמְךָ הַגָּדוֹל נִקְרָא עָלֵינוּ; עֹשֵׂה נִפְלָאוֹת בְּכָל עֵת, עֲשֵׂה עִמָּנוּ כְּחַסְדֶּךָ; חַנּוּן וְרַחוּם, הַבִּיטָה וַעֲנֵנוּ בְּעֵת צָרָה, כִּי לְךָ יְיָ הַיְשׁוּעָה. אָבִינוּ מַלְכֵּנוּ, מַחֲסֵנוּ, אַל תַּעַשׂ עִמָּנוּ כְּרַע מַעֲלָלֵינוּ. זְכֹר רַחֲמֶיךָ יְיָ, וַחֲסָדֶיךָ, וּכְרֹב טוּבְךָ הוֹשִׁיעֵנוּ, וְחָמֹל־נָא עָלֵינוּ, כִּי אֵין לָנוּ אֱלוֹהַּ אַחֵר מִבַּלְעָדֶיךָ. צוּרֵנוּ, אַל תַּעַזְבֵנוּ; יְיָ אֱלֹהֵינוּ, אַל תִּרְחַק מִמֶּנּוּ; כִּי נַפְשֵׁנוּ קָצְרָה מֵחֶרֶב וּמִשֶּׁבִי, וּמִדֶּבֶר וּמִמַּגֵּפָה, וּמִכָּל צָרָה וְיָגוֹן. הַצִּילֵנוּ, כִּי לְךָ קִוִּינוּ, וְאַל תַּכְלִימֵנוּ, יְיָ אֱלֹהֵינוּ; וְהָאֵר פָּנֶיךָ בָּנוּ, וּזְכָר־לָנוּ אֶת בְּרִית אֲבוֹתֵינוּ, וְהוֹשִׁיעֵנוּ לְמַעַן שְׁמֶךָ. רְאֵה בְצָרוֹתֵינוּ, וּשְׁמַע קוֹל תְּפִלָּתֵנוּ, כִּי אַתָּה שׁוֹמֵעַ תְּפִלַּת כָּל פֶּה.

אֵל רַחוּם וְחַנּוּן, רַחֵם עָלֵינוּ וְעַל כָּל מַעֲשֶׂיךָ, כִּי אֵין כָּמוֹךָ, יְיָ אֱלֹהֵינוּ. אָנָּא, שָׂא נָא פְשָׁעֵינוּ, אָבִינוּ מַלְכֵּנוּ, צוּרֵנוּ וְגוֹאֲלֵנוּ, אֵל חַי וְקַיָּם, הַחָסִין בַּכֹּחַ, חָסִיד וְטוֹב עַל כָּל מַעֲשֶׂיךָ, כִּי אַתָּה הוּא יְיָ אֱלֹהֵינוּ. אֵל אֶרֶךְ אַפַּיִם וּמָלֵא רַחֲמִים, עֲשֵׂה עִמָּנוּ

name's sake. Have compassion on thy people; have mercy on thy heritage; spare us in thy great mercy; take pity on us and answer us, for righteousness is thine, O Lord, who doest wonders at all times.

O look down and speedily have mercy on thy people for the sake of thy name; in thy great compassion, Lord our God, mercifully spare and save thy own flock; let no wrath prevail against us, for our eyes are lifted to thee; save us for thy name's sake. Have mercy on us for the sake of thy covenant; look down and answer us in time of distress, for salvation is thine, O Lord; our hope rests with thee, God of forgiveness. O forgive, beneficent and forgiving God, for thou art a gracious and merciful God and King.

O gracious and merciful King, remember thy covenant with Abraham; let the attempted sacrifice of his only son appear before thee for Israel's sake. Our Father, our King, be gracious to us and answer us, for we bear thy great name; thou who doest wonders at all times, deal with us according to thy kindness. Thou who art gracious and merciful, look down and answer us in time of distress, for salvation is thine, O Lord. Our Father, our King, our Refuge, deal not with us according to our evil deeds; remember, O Lord, thy mercy and thy kindness; save us, in thy great goodness, and have compassion on us, for we have no other God besides thee. Our Rock, forsake us not; Lord our God, be not far from us; for we are exhausted from war and captivity, pestilence and plague, and from every trouble and sorrow. Rescue us, for thou art our hope; put us not to shame, Lord our God; let thy favor shine upon us; remember the covenant of our fathers, and save us for thy name's sake. Look at our troubles, and hear the voice of our prayer, for thou hearest the prayer of every mouth.

Merciful and gracious God, have compassion on us and on all that thou hast made, for there is none like thee, Lord our God. O forgive our transgressions, our Father, our King, our Rock and Redeemer, thou everlasting and almighty God, who art kind and good to all that thou hast made; truly, thou art the Lord our God. O God, who art slow to anger and full of compassion, deal with us

כְּרֹב רַחֲמֶיךָ, וְהוֹשִׁיעֵנוּ לְמַעַן שְׁמֶךָ. שְׁמַע מַלְכֵּנוּ תְּפִלָּתֵנוּ, וּמִיַּד אוֹיְבֵינוּ הַצִּילֵנוּ; שְׁמַע מַלְכֵּנוּ תְּפִלָּתֵנוּ, וּמִכָּל צָרָה וְיָגוֹן הַצִּילֵנוּ. אָבִינוּ מַלְכֵּנוּ אָתָּה, וְשִׁמְךָ עָלֵינוּ נִקְרָא, אַל תַּנִּיחֵנוּ· אַל תַּעַזְבֵנוּ אָבִינוּ, וְאַל תִּטְּשֵׁנוּ בּוֹרְאֵנוּ, וְאַל תִּשְׁכָּחֵנוּ יוֹצְרֵנוּ, כִּי אֵל מֶלֶךְ חַנּוּן וְרַחוּם אָתָּה·

אֵין כָּמְוֹךָ חַנּוּן וְרַחוּם, יְיָ אֱלֹהֵינוּ; אֵין כָּמְוֹךָ אֵל אֶרֶךְ אַפַּיִם וְרַב חֶסֶד וֶאֱמֶת. הוֹשִׁיעֵנוּ בְּרַחֲמֶיךָ הָרַבִּים; מֵרַעַשׁ וּמֵרֹגֶז הַצִּילֵנוּ. זְכוֹר לַעֲבָדֶיךָ, לְאַבְרָהָם לְיִצְחָק וּלְיַעֲקֹב; אַל תֵּפֶן אֶל קָשְׁיֵנוּ וְאֶל רִשְׁעֵנוּ וְאֶל חַטָּאתֵנוּ. שׁוּב מֵחֲרוֹן אַפֶּךָ, וְהִנָּחֵם עַל הָרָעָה לְעַמֶּךָ, וְהָסֵר מִמֶּנּוּ מַכַּת הַמָּוֶת, כִּי רַחוּם אָתָּה; כִּי כֵן דַּרְכֶּךָ, עֹשֶׂה חֶסֶד חִנָּם בְּכָל דּוֹר וָדוֹר. חוּסָה יְיָ עַל עַמֶּךָ, וְהַצִּילֵנוּ מִזַּעְמֶךָ; וְהָסֵר מִמֶּנּוּ מַכַּת הַמַּגֵּפָה וּגְזֵרָה קָשָׁה, כִּי אַתָּה שׁוֹמֵר יִשְׂרָאֵל. לְךָ אֲדֹנָי הַצְּדָקָה, וְלָנוּ בֹּשֶׁת הַפָּנִים· מַה נִּתְאוֹנֵן, מַה נֹּאמַר, מַה נְּדַבֵּר, וּמַה נִּצְטַדָּק. נַחְפְּשָׂה דְרָכֵינוּ וְנַחְקֹרָה וְנָשׁוּבָה אֵלֶיךָ, כִּי יְמִינְךָ פְּשׁוּטָה לְקַבֵּל שָׁבִים. אָנָּא, יְיָ, הוֹשִׁיעָה נָּא; אָנָּא, יְיָ, הַצְלִיחָה נָא. אָנָּא, יְיָ, עֲנֵנוּ בְיוֹם קָרְאֵנוּ· לְךָ יְיָ חִכִּינוּ, לְךָ יְיָ קִוִּינוּ, לְךָ יְיָ נְיַחֵל, אַל תֶּחֱשֶׁה וּתְעַנֵּנוּ, כִּי נְאֻמוּ גוֹיִם אָבְדָה תִקְוָתָם. כָּל בֶּרֶךְ וְכָל קוֹמָה לְךָ לְבַד תִּשְׁתַּחֲוֶה·

הַפּוֹתֵחַ יָד בִּתְשׁוּבָה לְקַבֵּל פּוֹשְׁעִים וְחַטָּאִים, נִבְהֲלָה נַפְשֵׁנוּ מֵרֹב עִצְּבוֹנֵנוּ, אַל תִּשְׁכָּחֵנוּ נֶצַח; קוּמָה וְהוֹשִׁיעֵנוּ, כִּי חָסִינוּ בָךְ· אָבִינוּ מַלְכֵּנוּ, אִם אֵין בָּנוּ צְדָקָה וּמַעֲשִׂים טוֹבִים, זְכָר־לָנוּ אֶת בְּרִית אֲבוֹתֵינוּ וְעֵדוּתֵנוּ בְּכָל יוֹם יְיָ אֶחָד· הַבִּיטָה בְעָנְיֵנוּ, כִּי רַבּוּ מַכְאוֹבֵינוּ וְצָרוֹת לְבָבֵנוּ. חוּסָה יְיָ עָלֵינוּ בְּאֶרֶץ שֶׁבְיֵנוּ, וְאַל תִּשְׁפּוֹךְ חֲרוֹנְךָ עָלֵינוּ, כִּי אֲנַחְנוּ עַמְּךָ בְּנֵי בְרִיתֶךָ·

in thy great mercy, and save us for the sake of thy name. Hear our prayer, O our King, and deliver us from the hand of our ene- mies; hear our prayer, O our King, and save us from all trouble and sorrow. Thou art our Father, our King, and we bear thy name, desert us not. Forsake us not, our Father; abandon us not, our Creator; forget us not, our Maker; for thou art a gracious and merciful God and King.

There is none gracious and merciful like thee, Lord our God; there is none like thee, a God slow to anger and rich in kindness and truth. Save us in thy great mercy; deliver us from storm and rage. Remember thy servants Abraham, Isaac and Jacob; con- sider not our stubbornness, our wickedness and sinfulness. Turn from thy fierce anger, and change thy mind about doing evil to thy people. Remove from us the scourge of death, for thou art merciful, for such is thy way—showing undeserved kindness in every generation. Spare thy people, O Lord, and deliver us from thy wrath; remove from us the scourge of plague and cruel per- secution, for thou art the guardian of Israel. Righteousness is thine, O Lord, and confusion is ours. How can we complain? What can we say? What can we urge? How can we justify ourselves? Let us search and examine our ways and return to thee, for thy right hand is stretched out to receive those who repent.

O Lord, save us; O Lord, make us prosper; O Lord, answer us when we call. For thee, O Lord, we wait; for thee, O Lord, we hope; in thee, O Lord, we trust; afflict us not by thy silence, for the nations say: "Their hope is lost." To thee alone everyone shall bend the knee and bow down.

O thou who openest thy hand to receive [repentant] trans- gressors and sinners—our soul is crushed by our great sorrow— forget us not forever; arise and save us, for we trust in thee. Our Father, our King, though we be without righteousness and good deeds, remember in our favor the covenant of our fathers and our daily testimony: "The Lord is One." Look at our plight, for our pangs and miseries of heart are numerous. Have pity on us, O Lord, in the land of our captivity; pour not out thy anger on us, for we are thy people, thy people of the covenant. O God, look!

אֵל, הַבִּיטָה, דַּל כְּבוֹדֵנוּ בַּגּוֹיִם; וְשִׁקְּצוּנוּ כְּטֻמְאַת הַנִּדָּה. עַד
מָתַי עֻזְּךָ בַּשְּׁבִי, וְתִפְאַרְתְּךָ בְּיַד צָר. עוֹרְרָה גְבוּרָתְךָ וְקִנְאָתְךָ
עַל אוֹיְבֶיךָ; הֵם יֵבֹשׁוּ וְיֵחַתּוּ מִגְּבוּרָתָם, וְאַל יִמְעֲטוּ לְפָנֶיךָ
תְלָאוֹתֵינוּ. מַהֵר יְקַדְּמוּנוּ רַחֲמֶיךָ בְּיוֹם צָרָתֵנוּ; וְאִם לֹא
לְמַעֲנֵנוּ, לְמַעַנְךָ פְּעַל, וְאַל תַּשְׁחִית זֵכֶר שְׁאֵרִיתֵנוּ. Reader וְחֹן
אִם הַמְיַחֲדִים שִׁמְךָ פַּעֲמַיִם בְּכָל יוֹם תָּמִיד בְּאַהֲבָה, וְאוֹמְרִים:
שְׁמַע יִשְׂרָאֵל, יְיָ אֱלֹהֵינוּ, יְיָ אֶחָד.

וַיֹּאמֶר דָּוִד אֶל גָּד: צַר לִי מְאֹד; נִפְּלָה נָּא בְיַד יְיָ, כִּי רַבִּים
רַחֲמָיו, וּבְיַד אָדָם אַל אֶפֹּלָה.

רַחוּם וְחַנּוּן, חָטָאתִי לְפָנֶיךָ; יְיָ מָלֵא רַחֲמִים, רַחֵם עָלַי
וְקַבֵּל תַּחֲנוּנָי.
תהלים ו

יְיָ, אַל בְּאַפְּךָ תוֹכִיחֵנִי, וְאַל בַּחֲמָתְךָ תְיַסְּרֵנִי. חָנֵּנִי, יְיָ, כִּי
אֻמְלַל אָנִי; רְפָאֵנִי, יְיָ, כִּי נִבְהֲלוּ עֲצָמָי. וְנַפְשִׁי נִבְהֲלָה מְאֹד;
וְאַתָּה יְיָ, עַד מָתָי. שׁוּבָה, יְיָ, חַלְּצָה נַפְשִׁי; הוֹשִׁיעֵנִי לְמַעַן
חַסְדֶּךָ. כִּי אֵין בַּמָּוֶת זִכְרֶךָ; בִּשְׁאוֹל מִי יוֹדֶה לָּךְ. יָגַעְתִּי
בְּאַנְחָתִי, אַשְׂחֶה בְכָל לַיְלָה מִטָּתִי; בְּדִמְעָתִי עַרְשִׂי אַמְסֶה.
עָשְׁשָׁה מִכַּעַס עֵינִי; עָתְקָה בְּכָל צוֹרְרָי. סוּרוּ מִמֶּנִּי, כָּל פֹּעֲלֵי
אָוֶן, כִּי שָׁמַע יְיָ קוֹל בִּכְיִי. שָׁמַע יְיָ תְּחִנָּתִי; יְיָ תְּפִלָּתִי יִקָּח.
יֵבֹשׁוּ וְיִבָּהֲלוּ מְאֹד כָּל אֹיְבָי; יָשֻׁבוּ יֵבֹשׁוּ רָגַע.

יְיָ אֱלֹהֵי יִשְׂרָאֵל, שׁוּב מֵחֲרוֹן אַפֶּךָ, וְהִנָּחֵם עַל הָרָעָה לְעַמֶּךָ.
הַבֵּט מִשָּׁמַיִם וּרְאֵה, כִּי הָיִינוּ לַעַג וָקֶלֶס בַּגּוֹיִם, נֶחְשַׁבְנוּ
כַּצֹּאן לַטֶּבַח יוּבָל, לַהֲרוֹג וּלְאַבֵּד וּלְמַכָּה וּלְחֶרְפָּה.

On נפילת אפים, the posture assumed during the recital of *Taḥanun*, see page 103.

Our glory has waned among the nations; they utterly detest us.
How long shall thy glory remain in captivity, and thy splendor in
the hand of the foe? Arouse thy might and thy zeal against thy
enemies, that they may be put to shame and crushed despite their
power; let not our sufferings seem trivial to thee. May thy compassion hasten to our aid in the day of our trouble; if not for our
sake, act for thy own sake, and destroy not our mere remnant.
Be gracious to a people, who fervently proclaim thy Oneness twice
a day, saying: "Hear, O Israel, the Lord is our God, the Lord is
One."[1]

And David said to Gad: "I am deeply distressed; let us fall
into the hand of the Lord, for his mercy is great, but let me not
fall into the hand of man."[2]

Merciful and gracious God, I have sinned before thee; O Lord,
who art full of compassion, have mercy on me and accept my
supplications.   *Psalm 6*

O Lord, punish me not in thy anger; chastise me not in thy
wrath. Have pity on me, O Lord, for I languish away; heal me,
O Lord, for my health is shaken. My soul is severely troubled;
and thou, O Lord, how long? O Lord, deliver my life once again;
save me because of thy grace. For in death there is no thought of
thee; in the grave who gives thanks to thee? I am worn out with
my groaning; every night I flood my bed with tears; I cause my
couch to melt with my weeping. My eye is dimmed from grief; it
grows old because of all my foes. Depart from me, all you evildoers, for the Lord has heard the sound of my weeping. The Lord
has heard my supplication; the Lord receives my prayer. All my
foes shall be utterly ashamed and terrified; they shall turn back;
they shall be suddenly ashamed.

Lord God of Israel, turn from thy fierce anger, and change
thy mind about doing evil to thy people.

Look down from heaven and see how we have become an
object of contempt and derision among the nations; we are counted as sheep led to the slaughter, to be slain and destroyed, or to
be beaten and disgraced.

Deuteronomy 6:4.   [2] *II Samuel* 24:14.

וּבְכָל זֹאת שִׁמְךָ לֹא שָׁכָחְנוּ; נָא אַל תִּשְׁכָּחֵנוּ. יְיָ אֱלֹהֵי יִשְׂרָאֵל, שׁוּב מֵחֲרוֹן אַפֶּךָ, וְהִנָּחֵם עַל הָרָעָה לְעַמֶּךָ.

זָרִים אוֹמְרִים אֵין תּוֹחֶלֶת וְתִקְוָה; חֹן אִם לְשִׁמְךָ מְקַוֵּה. טָהוֹר, יְשׁוּעָתֵנוּ קָרְבָה; יְגַעְנוּ וְלֹא הוּנַח לָנוּ. רַחֲמֶיךָ יִכְבְּשׁוּ אֶת כַּעַסְךָ מֵעָלֵינוּ.

אָנָּא, שׁוּב מֵחֲרוֹנֶךָ, וְרַחֵם סְגֻלָּה אֲשֶׁר בָּחָרְתָּ. יְיָ אֱלֹהֵי יִשְׂרָאֵל, שׁוּב מֵחֲרוֹן אַפֶּךָ, וְהִנָּחֵם עַל הָרָעָה לְעַמֶּךָ.

חוּסָה יְיָ עָלֵינוּ בְּרַחֲמֶיךָ, וְאַל תִּתְּנֵנוּ בִּידֵי אַכְזָרִים, לָמָּה יֹאמְרוּ הַגּוֹיִם אַיֵּה נָא אֱלֹהֵיהֶם. לְמַעַנְךָ עֲשֵׂה עִמָּנוּ חֶסֶד, וְאַל תְּאַחַר.

אָנָּא, שׁוּב מֵחֲרוֹנֶךָ, וְרַחֵם סְגֻלָּה אֲשֶׁר בָּחָרְתָּ. יְיָ אֱלֹהֵי יִשְׂרָאֵל, שׁוּב מֵחֲרוֹן אַפֶּךָ, וְהִנָּחֵם עַל הָרָעָה לְעַמֶּךָ.

קוֹלֵנוּ תִשְׁמַע וְתָחֹן, וְאַל תִּטְּשֵׁנוּ בְּיַד אוֹיְבֵינוּ לִמְחוֹת אֶת שְׁמֵנוּ. זְכֹר אֲשֶׁר נִשְׁבַּעְתָּ לַאֲבוֹתֵינוּ; כְּכוֹכְבֵי הַשָּׁמַיִם אַרְבֶּה אֶת זַרְעֲכֶם; וְעַתָּה נִשְׁאַרְנוּ מְעַט מֵהַרְבֵּה.

וּבְכָל זֹאת שִׁמְךָ לֹא שָׁכָחְנוּ, נָא אַל תִּשְׁכָּחֵנוּ. יְיָ אֱלֹהֵי יִשְׂרָאֵל, שׁוּב מֵחֲרוֹן אַפֶּךָ, וְהִנָּחֵם עַל הָרָעָה לְעַמֶּךָ.

עָזְרֵנוּ, אֱלֹהֵי יִשְׁעֵנוּ, עַל דְּבַר כְּבוֹד שְׁמֶךָ, וְהַצִּילֵנוּ וְכַפֵּר עַל חַטֹּאתֵינוּ לְמַעַן שְׁמֶךָ.

יְיָ אֱלֹהֵי יִשְׂרָאֵל, שׁוּב מֵחֲרוֹן אַפֶּךָ, וְהִנָּחֵם עַל הָרָעָה לְעַמֶּךָ.

שׁוֹמֵר יִשְׂרָאֵל, שְׁמוֹר שְׁאֵרִית יִשְׂרָאֵל, וְאַל יֹאבַד יִשְׂרָאֵל, הָאוֹמְרִים שְׁמַע יִשְׂרָאֵל.

שׁוֹמֵר גּוֹי אֶחָד, שְׁמוֹר שְׁאֵרִית עַם אֶחָד, וְאַל יֹאבַד גּוֹי אֶחָד, הַמְיַחֲדִים שִׁמְךָ, יְיָ אֱלֹהֵינוּ, יְיָ אֶחָד.

Yet, despite all this, we have not forgotten thy name; O forget us not. Lord God of Israel, turn from thy fierce anger, and change thy mind about doing evil to thy people.

Strangers say to us: "There is no hope for you." Be gracious to a people that yearns for thy name. Pure One, hasten our salvation; we are worn out, and no rest is granted us. May thy mercy hold back thy anger from us.

O turn from thy wrath, and have pity on the people thou hast chosen. Lord God of Israel, turn from thy fierce anger, and change thy mind about doing evil to thy people.

Spare us, O Lord, in thy mercy, and deliver us not into the hands of the cruel oppressors. Why should the nations say: "Where is their God?" For thy own sake, deal kindly with us, and delay not.

O turn from thy wrath and have pity on the people thou hast chosen. Lord God of Israel, turn from thy fierce anger, and change thy mind about doing evil to thy people.

Hear our voice and have pity; leave us not in the power of our enemies to blot out our name. Remember that thou hast sworn to our fathers: "I will make your descendants as numerous as the stars in the sky"; and now, we are left but a few out of many.

Yet, despite all this, we have not forgotten thy name; O forget us not. Lord God of Israel, turn from thy fierce anger, and change thy mind about doing evil to thy people.

Help us, our saving God, for the sake of thy glorious name; rescue us, and pardon our sins for thy name's sake.

Lord God of Israel, turn from thy fierce anger, and change thy mind about doing evil to thy people.

Guardian of Israel, preserve the remnant of Israel; let not Israel perish, who say: "Hear, O Israel."

Guardian of a unique people, preserve the remnant of a unique people; let not a unique people perish, who proclaim thy Oneness, saying: "The Lord is our God, the Lord is One."

שׁוֹמֵר גּוֹי קָדוֹשׁ, שְׁמוֹר שְׁאֵרִית עַם קָדוֹשׁ, וְאַל יֹאבַד גּוֹי
קָדוֹשׁ, הַמְשַׁלְּשִׁים בְּשָׁלֹשׁ קְדֻשּׁוֹת לְקָדוֹשׁ.

מִתְרַצֶּה בְּרַחֲמִים וּמִתְפַּיֵּס בְּתַחֲנוּנִים, הִתְרַצֵּה וְהִתְפַּיֵּס
לְדוֹר עָנִי, כִּי אֵין עוֹזֵר. אָבִינוּ מַלְכֵּנוּ, חָנֵּנוּ וַעֲנֵנוּ, כִּי אֵין בָּנוּ
מַעֲשִׂים; עֲשֵׂה עִמָּנוּ צְדָקָה וָחֶסֶד וְהוֹשִׁיעֵנוּ.

וַאֲנַחְנוּ לֹא נֵדַע מַה נַּעֲשֶׂה, כִּי עָלֶיךָ עֵינֵינוּ. זְכֹר רַחֲמֶיךָ יְיָ,
וַחֲסָדֶיךָ, כִּי מֵעוֹלָם הֵמָּה. יְהִי חַסְדְּךָ יְיָ עָלֵינוּ, כַּאֲשֶׁר יִחַלְנוּ
לָךְ. אַל תִּזְכָּר־לָנוּ עֲוֹנוֹת רִאשֹׁנִים; מַהֵר יְקַדְּמוּנוּ רַחֲמֶיךָ, כִּי
דַלּוֹנוּ מְאֹד. חָנֵּנוּ יְיָ חָנֵּנוּ, כִּי רַב שָׂבַעְנוּ בוּז. בְּרֹגֶז רַחֵם תִּזְכּוֹר.
כִּי הוּא יָדַע יִצְרֵנוּ, זָכוּר כִּי עָפָר אֲנָחְנוּ. Reader עָזְרֵנוּ, אֱלֹהֵי
יִשְׁעֵנוּ, עַל דְּבַר כְּבוֹד שְׁמֶךָ, וְהַצִּילֵנוּ וְכַפֵּר עַל חַטֹּאתֵינוּ
לְמַעַן שְׁמֶךָ.

Reader:

יִתְגַּדַּל וְיִתְקַדַּשׁ שְׁמֵהּ רַבָּא בְּעָלְמָא דִּי בְרָא כִרְעוּתֵהּ;
וְיַמְלִיךְ מַלְכוּתֵהּ בְּחַיֵּיכוֹן וּבְיוֹמֵיכוֹן, וּבְחַיֵּי דְכָל בֵּית יִשְׂרָאֵל,
בַּעֲגָלָא וּבִזְמַן קָרִיב, וְאִמְרוּ אָמֵן.

יְהֵא שְׁמֵהּ רַבָּא מְבָרַךְ לְעָלַם וּלְעָלְמֵי עָלְמַיָּא.

יִתְבָּרַךְ וְיִשְׁתַּבַּח, וְיִתְפָּאַר וְיִתְרוֹמַם, וְיִתְנַשֵּׂא וְיִתְהַדָּר,
וְיִתְעַלֶּה וְיִתְהַלָּל שְׁמֵהּ דְּקֻדְשָׁא, בְּרִיךְ הוּא, לְעֵלָּא (לְעֵלָּא)
מִן כָּל בִּרְכָתָא וְשִׁירָתָא, תֻּשְׁבְּחָתָא וְנֶחֱמָתָא, דַּאֲמִירָן בְּעָלְמָא,
וְאִמְרוּ אָמֵן.

The following paragraph is said on Mondays and Thursdays, except on *Rosh Hodesh, Erev Pesah, Tish'ah b'Av, Hanukkah,* the 14th and 15th of *Adar* and *Adar Sheni.*

אֵל אֶרֶךְ אַפַּיִם וְרַב חֶסֶד וֶאֱמֶת, אַל בְּאַפְּךָ תוֹכִיחֵנוּ. חוּסָה
יְיָ עַל עַמֶּךָ, וְהוֹשִׁיעֵנוּ מִכָּל רָע. חָטָאנוּ לָךְ, אָדוֹן; סְלַח נָא
כְּרֹב רַחֲמֶיךָ, אֵל.

Guardian of a holy people, preserve the remnant of a holy people; let not a holy people perish, who repeat the threefold sanctification to the Holy One.

O thou who art reconciled by prayers and conciliated by supplications, be thou reconciled and conciliated to an afflicted generation, for there is none to help.

Our Father, our King, be gracious to us and answer us, for we have no merits; deal charitably and kindly with us and save us.

We know not what to do, but our eyes are upon thee. Remember thy mercy and thy kindness, O Lord, for they are eternal. May thy kindness rest on us, O Lord, as our hope rests on thee. O mind not our former iniquities; may thy compassion hasten to our aid, for we are brought very low. Take pity on us, O Lord, take pity on us, for we are exceedingly sated with contempt. When in wrath, remember to be merciful. He knows what we are made of, remembering that we are but dust. Help us, our saving God, for the sake of thy glorious name; rescue us and pardon our sins for thy name's sake.[1]   *Reader:*

Glorified and sanctified be God's great name throughout the world which he has created according to his will. May he establish his kingdom in your lifetime and during your days, and within the life of the entire house of Israel, speedily and soon; and say, Amen.

May his great name be blessed forever and to all eternity.

Blessed and praised, glorified and exalted, extolled and honored, adored and lauded be the name of the Holy One, blessed be he, beyond all the blessings and hymns, praises and consolations that are ever spoken in the world; and say, Amen.

The following paragraph is said on Mondays and Thursdays, except on Rosh Hodesh, Erev Pesah, Tish'ah b'Av, Hanukkah, the 14th and 15th of Adar and Adar Sheni.

O God who art slow to anger and abounding in kindness and truth, rebuke us not in thy anger. Have pity on thy people, O Lord, and save us from all evil. We have sinned against thee, O Lord; forgive us, O God, in thy great mercy.

---

[1] *II Chronicles* 20:12; *Psalms* 25:6; 33:22; 79:8; 123:3; *Habakkuk* **3:2;** *Psalm* 103:14.

קְרִיאַת הַתּוֹרָה

The Torah is read on Mondays and Thursdays, *Rosh Ḥodesh*, *Ḥol ha-Mo'ed*, *Ḥanukkah*, *Purim*, and on fast days.

The ark is opened.

Reader and Congregation:

וַיְהִי בִּנְסֹעַ הָאָרֹן וַיֹּאמֶר מֹשֶׁה: קוּמָה יְיָ, וְיָפֻצוּ אֹיְבֶיךָ, וְיָנֻסוּ מְשַׂנְאֶיךָ מִפָּנֶיךָ. כִּי מִצִּיּוֹן תֵּצֵא תוֹרָה, וּדְבַר יְיָ מִירוּשָׁלָיִם. בָּרוּךְ שֶׁנָּתַן תּוֹרָה לְעַמּוֹ יִשְׂרָאֵל בִּקְדֻשָּׁתוֹ.

זוהר, ויקהל

בְּרִיךְ שְׁמֵהּ דְּמָרֵא עָלְמָא, בְּרִיךְ כִּתְרָךְ וְאַתְרָךְ. יְהֵא רְעוּתָךְ עִם עַמָּךְ יִשְׂרָאֵל לְעָלַם, וּפֻרְקַן יְמִינָךְ אַחֲזֵי לְעַמָּךְ בְּבֵית מִקְדְּשָׁךְ; וּלְאַמְטוּיֵי לָנָא מִטּוּב נְהוֹרָךְ, וּלְקַבֵּל צְלוֹתָנָא בְּרַחֲמִין. יְהֵא רַעֲוָא קֳדָמָךְ, דְּתוֹרִיךְ לָן חַיִּין בְּטִיבוּתָא. וְלֶהֱוֵא אֲנָא פְּקִידָא בְּגוֹ צַדִּיקַיָּא, לְמִרְחַם עֲלַי וּלְמִנְטַר יָתִי וְיָת כָּל דִּי לִי וְדִי לְעַמָּךְ יִשְׂרָאֵל. אַנְתְּ הוּא זָן לְכֹלָּא וּמְפַרְנֵס לְכֹלָּא; אַנְתְּ הוּא שַׁלִּיט עַל כֹּלָּא; אַנְתְּ הוּא דְּשַׁלִּיט עַל מַלְכַיָּא, וּמַלְכוּתָא דִּילָךְ הִיא. אֲנָא עַבְדָּא דְקֻדְשָׁא בְּרִיךְ הוּא, דְּסָגְדְנָא קַמֵּהּ וּמִקַּמָּא דִּיקַר אוֹרַיְתֵהּ בְּכָל עִדָּן וְעִדָּן. לָא עַל אֱנָשׁ רָחִצְנָא, וְלָא עַל בַּר אֱלָהִין סָמְכְנָא, אֶלָּא בֵּאלָהָא דִשְׁמַיָּא, דְּהוּא אֱלָהָא קְשׁוֹט, וְאוֹרַיְתֵהּ קְשׁוֹט, וּנְבִיאוֹהִי קְשׁוֹט, וּמַסְגֵּא לְמֶעְבַּד טַבְוָן וּקְשׁוֹט. בֵּהּ אֲנָא רָחֵץ, וְלִשְׁמֵהּ קַדִּישָׁא יַקִּירָא אֲנָא אָמַר תֻּשְׁבְּחָן. יְהֵא רַעֲוָא קֳדָמָךְ, דְּתִפְתַּח לִבָּאִי

קְרִיאַת הַתּוֹרָה on Mondays and Thursdays was instituted by Ezra, according to tradition, in order not to let three days go by without the instruction of the Torah. Originally, the persons called to the Torah read the passages apportioned to them. This custom was abandoned in order not to embarrass those who lacked proper training.

בְּרִיךְ שְׁמֵהּ is taken from the *Zohar*, the fundamental book of *Kabbalah*,

READING OF THE TORAH

The Torah is read on Mondays and Thursdays, Rosh Ḥodesh, Ḥol ha-Moʿed, Ḥanukkah, Purim, and on fast days.

The ark is opened.

Reader and Congregation:

And it came to pass, whenever the ark started, Moses would say: "Arise, O Lord, and let thy enemies be scattered; let those who hate thee flee before thee."[1] Truly, out of Zion shall come forth Torah, and the word of the Lord out of Jerusalem.[2]

Blessed be he who in his holiness gave the Torah to his people Israel.

Zohar, Wayyakhel

Blessed be the name of the Lord of the universe! Blessed be thy crown and thy dominion. May thy good will ever abide with thy people Israel. Reveal thy saving power to thy people in thy sanctuary; bestow on us the good gift of thy light, and accept our prayer in mercy. May it be thy will to prolong our life in happiness.

Let me also be counted among the righteous, so that thou mayest have compassion on me and shelter me and mine and all that belong to thy people Israel. Thou art he who nourishes and sustains all; thou art he who rules over all; thou art he who rules over kings, for dominion is thine. I am the servant of the Holy One, blessed be he, before whom and before whose glorious Torah I bow at all times. Not in man do I put my trust, nor do I rely on any angel, but only in the God of heaven who is the God of truth, whose Torah is truth and whose Prophets are truth, and who performs many deeds of goodness and truth. In him I put my trust, and to his holy and glorious name I utter praises. May it be thy will to

---

which was first made known in the thirteenth century and ascribed to Rabbi Simeon ben Yoḥai of the second century. The *Zohar* introduces this inspiring and uplifting prayer as follows: "When the Torah is taken out to be read before the congregation, the heavenly gates of mercy are opened and the divine love is aroused; therefore one should recite: בריך שמיה . . ." The term בר אלהין ("angel") is found in Daniel 3:25.

[1] *Numbers* 10:35–36.   [2] *Isaiah* 2:3.

בְּאוֹרַיְתָא, Reader וְתַשְׁלֵם מִשְׁאֲלִין דְּלִבָּאִי וְלִבָּא דְכָל עַמָּךְ יִשְׂרָאֵל לְטַב וּלְחַיִּין וְלִשְׁלָם.

The Reader takes the Torah and says:

גַּדְּלוּ לַיְיָ אִתִּי, וּנְרוֹמְמָה שְׁמוֹ יַחְדָּו.

Congregation:

לְךָ יְיָ הַגְּדֻלָּה וְהַגְּבוּרָה, וְהַתִּפְאֶרֶת וְהַנֵּצַח וְהַהוֹד, כִּי כֹל בַּשָּׁמַיִם וּבָאָרֶץ. לְךָ, יְיָ, הַמַּמְלָכָה וְהַמִּתְנַשֵּׂא לְכֹל לְרֹאשׁ. רוֹמְמוּ יְיָ אֱלֹהֵינוּ, וְהִשְׁתַּחֲווּ לַהֲדֹם רַגְלָיו, קָדוֹשׁ הוּא. רוֹמְמוּ יְיָ אֱלֹהֵינוּ, וְהִשְׁתַּחֲווּ לְהַר קָדְשׁוֹ, כִּי קָדוֹשׁ יְיָ אֱלֹהֵינוּ.

אַב הָרַחֲמִים, הוּא יְרַחֵם עַם עֲמוּסִים, וְיִזְכֹּר בְּרִית אֵיתָנִים, וְיַצִּיל נַפְשׁוֹתֵינוּ מִן הַשָּׁעוֹת הָרָעוֹת, וְיִגְעַר בְּיֵצֶר הָרָע מִן הַנְּשׂוּאִים, וְיָחֹן אוֹתָנוּ לִפְלֵיטַת עוֹלָמִים, וִימַלֵּא מִשְׁאֲלוֹתֵינוּ בְּמִדָּה טוֹבָה, יְשׁוּעָה וְרַחֲמִים.

The Torah is placed on the desk. The Reader unrolls it and says:

וְתִגָּלֶה וְתֵרָאֶה מַלְכוּתוֹ עָלֵינוּ בִּזְמַן קָרוֹב, וְיָחֹן פְּלֵיטָתֵנוּ וּפְלֵיטַת עַמּוֹ בֵּית יִשְׂרָאֵל לְחֵן וּלְחֶסֶד, לְרַחֲמִים וּלְרָצוֹן, וְנֹאמַר אָמֵן. הַכֹּל הָבוּ גֹדֶל לֵאלֹהֵינוּ, וּתְנוּ כָבוֹד לַתּוֹרָה. כֹּהֵן, קְרָב; יַעֲמֹד (פלוני בן פלוני) הַכֹּהֵן. בָּרוּךְ שֶׁנָּתַן תּוֹרָה לְעַמּוֹ יִשְׂרָאֵל בִּקְדֻשָּׁתוֹ. תּוֹרַת יְיָ תְּמִימָה, מְשִׁיבַת נָפֶשׁ; עֵדוּת יְיָ נֶאֱמָנָה, מַחְכִּימַת פֶּתִי. פִּקּוּדֵי יְיָ יְשָׁרִים, מְשַׂמְּחֵי לֵב; מִצְוַת יְיָ בָּרָה, מְאִירַת עֵינָיִם. יְיָ עֹז לְעַמּוֹ יִתֵּן; יְיָ יְבָרֵךְ אֶת עַמּוֹ בַשָּׁלוֹם. הָאֵל תָּמִים דַּרְכּוֹ; אִמְרַת יְיָ צְרוּפָה, מָגֵן הוּא לְכֹל הַחוֹסִים בּוֹ.

Congregation and Reader:

וְאַתֶּם הַדְּבֵקִים בַּיְיָ אֱלֹהֵיכֶם, חַיִּים כֻּלְּכֶם הַיּוֹם.

open my heart to thy Torah, and to fulfill the wishes of my heart and of the heart of all thy people Israel for happiness, life and peace.

The Reader takes the Torah and says:

Exalt the Lord with me, and let us extol his name together.[1]

Congregation:

Thine, O Lord, is the greatness and the power, the glory and the victory and the majesty; for all that is in heaven and on earth is thine; thine, O Lord, is the kingdom, and thou art supreme over all.[2] Exalt the Lord our God, and worship at his footstool; holy is he. Exalt the Lord our God, and worship at his holy mountain, for holy is the Lord our God.[3]

May the merciful Father have compassion on the people who have been upheld by him, and remember the covenant with the patriarchs; may he deliver us from evil times, and check the evil impulse in those who have been tended by him; may he graciously grant us everlasting deliverance, and in his goodness fulfill our petitions for salvation and mercy.

The Torah is placed on the desk. The Reader unrolls it and says:

May his kingdom soon be revealed and made visible to us; may he be gracious to our remnant, the remnant of his people, the house of Israel, granting them grace and kindness, mercy and favor; and let us say, Amen. Let us all ascribe greatness to our God, and give honor to the Torah. Let the *Kohen* come forward [*the Reader names the first person called to the Torah*]. Blessed be he who in his holiness gave the Torah to his people Israel. The Lord's Torah is perfect, refreshing the soul; the Lord's testimony is trustworthy, teaching the simple man wisdom. The Lord's precepts are right, gladdening the heart; the Lord's commandment is clear, enlightening the eyes. The Lord will give strength to his people; the Lord will bless his people with peace. The way of God is perfect; the word of the Lord is pure; he is a shield to all who trust in him.[4]

Congregation and Reader:

And you who cling to the Lord your God are all alive today.[5]

---

[1] *Psalm* 34:3.   [2] *I Chronicles* 29:11.   [3] *Psalm* 99:5. 9.   [4] *Psalms* 19:8–9; 29:11; 18:31.   [5] *Deuteronomy* 4:4.

The person called to the Torah recites:

בָּרְכוּ אֶת יְיָ הַמְבֹרָךְ.

Congregation responds:

בָּרוּךְ יְיָ הַמְבֹרָךְ לְעוֹלָם וָעֶד.

He repeats the response and continues:

בָּרוּךְ אַתָּה, יְיָ אֱלֹהֵינוּ, מֶלֶךְ הָעוֹלָם, אֲשֶׁר בָּחַר בָּנוּ מִכָּל הָעַמִּים וְנָתַן לָנוּ אֶת תּוֹרָתוֹ. בָּרוּךְ אַתָּה, יְיָ, נוֹתֵן הַתּוֹרָה.

The Torah is read. Then he recites:

בָּרוּךְ אַתָּה, יְיָ אֱלֹהֵינוּ, מֶלֶךְ הָעוֹלָם, אֲשֶׁר נָתַן לָנוּ תּוֹרַת אֱמֶת וְחַיֵּי עוֹלָם נָטַע בְּתוֹכֵנוּ. בָּרוּךְ אַתָּה, יְיָ, נוֹתֵן הַתּוֹרָה.

בִּרְכַּת הַגּוֹמֵל

One who has come safely through a dangerous experience recites:

בָּרוּךְ אַתָּה, יְיָ אֱלֹהֵינוּ, מֶלֶךְ הָעוֹלָם, הַגּוֹמֵל לְחַיָּבִים טוֹבוֹת, שֶׁגְּמָלַנִי כָּל טוֹב.

Congregation responds:

מִי שֶׁגְּמָלְךָ כָּל טוֹב, הוּא יִגְמָלְךָ כָּל טוֹב סֶלָה.

When the reading of the Torah is concluded, the Reader recites:

יִתְגַּדַּל וְיִתְקַדַּשׁ שְׁמֵהּ רַבָּא בְּעָלְמָא דִי בְרָא כִרְעוּתֵהּ; וְיַמְלִיךְ מַלְכוּתֵהּ בְּחַיֵּיכוֹן וּבְיוֹמֵיכוֹן, וּבְחַיֵּי דְכָל בֵּית יִשְׂרָאֵל, בַּעֲגָלָא וּבִזְמַן קָרִיב, וְאִמְרוּ אָמֵן.

יְהֵא שְׁמֵהּ רַבָּא מְבָרַךְ לְעָלַם וּלְעָלְמֵי עָלְמַיָּא.

יִתְבָּרַךְ וְיִשְׁתַּבַּח, וְיִתְפָּאַר וְיִתְרוֹמַם, וְיִתְנַשֵּׂא וְיִתְהַדָּר, וְיִתְעַלֶּה וְיִתְהַלָּל שְׁמֵהּ דְּקֻדְשָׁא, בְּרִיךְ הוּא, לְעֵלָּא (לְעֵלָּא) מִן כָּל בִּרְכָתָא וְשִׁירָתָא, תֻּשְׁבְּחָתָא וְנֶחֱמָתָא, דַּאֲמִירָן בְּעָלְמָא, וְאִמְרוּ אָמֵן.

ברכת הגומל, known as "gomel benshen," is derived from Berakhoth 54b,

The person called to the Torah recites:

Bless the Lord who is blessed.

Congregation responds:

Blessed be the Lord who is blessed forever and ever.

He repeats the response and continues:

Blessed art thou, Lord our God, King of the universe, who hast chosen us from all peoples, and hast given us thy Torah. Blessed art thou, O Lord, Giver of the Torah.

The Torah is read. Then he recites:

Blessed art thou, Lord our God, King of the universe, who hast given us the Torah of truth, and hast planted everlasting life in our midst. Blessed art thou, O Lord, Giver of the Torah.

THANKSGIVING

One who has come safely through a dangerous experience recites:

Blessed art thou, Lord our God, King of the universe, who bestowest favors on the undeserving, and hast shown me every kindness.

Congregation responds:

May he who has shown you every kindness ever deal kindly with you.

When the reading of the Torah is concluded, the Reader recites:

Glorified and sanctified be God's great name throughout the world which he has created according to his will. May he establish his kingdom in your lifetime and during your days, and within the life of the entire house of Israel, speedily and soon; and say, Amen.

May his great name be blessed forever and to all eternity.

Blessed and praised, glorified and exalted, extolled and honored, adored and lauded be the name of the Holy One, blessed be he, beyond all the blessings and hymns, praises and consolations that are ever spoken in the world; and say, Amen.

---

where it is said that four classes of men should offer thanks: 1) those who have made a voyage by sea, 2) or a journey through the desert, 3) or have recovered from a severe illness, 4) or have been released from prison.

When the Torah is raised, the Congregation recites:

וְזֹאת הַתּוֹרָה אֲשֶׁר שָׂם מֹשֶׁה לִפְנֵי בְּנֵי יִשְׂרָאֵל, עַל פִּי יְיָ בְּיַד מֹשֶׁה.

עֵץ חַיִּים הִיא לַמַּחֲזִיקִים בָּהּ, וְתֹמְכֶיהָ מְאֻשָּׁר. דְּרָכֶיהָ דַרְכֵי נֹעַם, וְכָל נְתִיבוֹתֶיהָ שָׁלוֹם. אֹרֶךְ יָמִים בִּימִינָהּ, בִּשְׂמֹאלָהּ עֹשֶׁר וְכָבוֹד. יְיָ חָפֵץ לְמַעַן צִדְקוֹ, יַגְדִּיל תּוֹרָה וְיַאְדִּיר.

On Mondays and Thursdays (if *Taḥanun* has been said), before returning the Torah to the ark, the Reader recites:

יְהִי רָצוֹן מִלִּפְנֵי אָבִינוּ שֶׁבַּשָּׁמַיִם לְכוֹנֵן אֶת בֵּית חַיֵּינוּ, וּלְהָשִׁיב אֶת שְׁכִינָתוֹ בְּתוֹכֵנוּ בִּמְהֵרָה בְיָמֵינוּ, וְנֹאמַר אָמֵן.

יְהִי רָצוֹן מִלִּפְנֵי אָבִינוּ שֶׁבַּשָּׁמַיִם לְרַחֵם עָלֵינוּ וְעַל פְּלֵיטָתֵנוּ, וְלִמְנֹעַ מַשְׁחִית וּמַגֵּפָה מֵעָלֵינוּ וּמֵעַל כָּל עַמּוֹ בֵּית יִשְׂרָאֵל, וְנֹאמַר אָמֵן.

יְהִי רָצוֹן מִלִּפְנֵי אָבִינוּ שֶׁבַּשָּׁמַיִם לְקַיֵּם־בָּנוּ חַכְמֵי יִשְׂרָאֵל, הֵם וּנְשֵׁיהֶם וּבְנֵיהֶם וּבְנוֹתֵיהֶם, וְתַלְמִידֵיהֶם וְתַלְמִידֵי תַלְמִידֵיהֶם, בְּכָל מְקוֹמוֹת מוֹשְׁבוֹתֵיהֶם, וְנֹאמַר אָמֵן.

יְהִי רָצוֹן מִלִּפְנֵי אָבִינוּ שֶׁבַּשָּׁמַיִם שֶׁנִּשְׁמַע וְנִתְבַּשֵּׂר בְּשׂוֹרוֹת טוֹבוֹת, יְשׁוּעוֹת וְנֶחָמוֹת; וִיקַבֵּץ נִדָּחֵינוּ מֵאַרְבַּע כַּנְפוֹת הָאָרֶץ, וְנֹאמַר אָמֵן.

אַחֵינוּ כָּל בֵּית יִשְׂרָאֵל, הַנְּתוּנִים בְּצָרָה וּבְשִׁבְיָה, הָעוֹמְדִים בֵּין בַּיָּם וּבֵין בַּיַּבָּשָׁה, הַמָּקוֹם יְרַחֵם עֲלֵיהֶם וְיוֹצִיאֵם מִצָּרָה לִרְוָחָה, וּמֵאֲפֵלָה לְאוֹרָה, וּמִשִּׁעְבּוּד לִגְאֻלָּה, הַשְׁתָּא בַּעֲגָלָא וּבִזְמַן קָרִיב, וְנֹאמַר אָמֵן.

The Reader takes the Torah and says:

יְהַלְלוּ אֶת שֵׁם יְיָ, כִּי נִשְׂגָּב שְׁמוֹ לְבַדּוֹ—

When the Torah is raised, the Congregation recites:

This is the Torah which Moses placed before the children of Israel. It is in accordance with the Lord's command through Moses.[1]

It is a tree of life to those who take hold of it, and happy are those who support it. Its ways are pleasant ways, and all its paths are peace. Long life is in its right hand, and in its left hand are riches and honor. The Lord was pleased, because of his righteousness, to render the Torah great and glorious.[2]

On Mondays and Thursdays (if Taḥanun has been said), before returning the Torah to the ark, the Reader recites:

May it be the will of our Father who is in heaven to establish our Temple, and to restore his divine presence in our midst, speedily in our days; and let us say, Amen.

May it be the will of our Father who is in heaven to have mercy on us and on our remnant, and to ward off destruction and pestilence from us and from all his people, the house of Israel; and let us say, Amen.

May it be the will of our Father who is in heaven to preserve everywhere among us the wise men of Israel and their wives, their sons and daughters, their disciples and the disciples of their disciples; and let us say, Amen.

May it be the will of our Father who is in heaven that we receive good tidings of deliverance and comfort; may he gather our dispersed from the four corners of the earth; and let us say, Amen.

As for our brethren, the whole house of Israel, who are handed over to distress and captivity, on sea or on land, may God have mercy on them and grant them relief, bringing them from darkness to light, from servitude to liberty, speedily and very soon; and let us say, Amen.

The Reader takes the Torah and says:

Let them praise the name of the Lord, for his name alone is exalted—

---

[1] *Deuteronomy* 4:44; *Numbers* 9:23.   [2] *Proverbs* 3:18, 17, 16; *Isaiah* 42:21.

Congregation:

הוֹדוּ עַל אֶרֶץ וְשָׁמָיִם. וַיָּרֶם קֶרֶן לְעַמּוֹ, תְּהִלָּה לְכָל חֲסִידָיו, לִבְנֵי יִשְׂרָאֵל עַם קְרוֹבוֹ; הַלְלוּיָהּ.

תהלים כד

לְדָוִד מִזְמוֹר. לַיָי הָאָרֶץ וּמְלוֹאָהּ, תֵּבֵל וְיֹשְׁבֵי בָהּ. כִּי הוּא עַל יַמִּים יְסָדָהּ, וְעַל נְהָרוֹת יְכוֹנְנֶהָ. מִי יַעֲלֶה בְּהַר יְיָ, וּמִי יָקוּם בִּמְקוֹם קָדְשׁוֹ. נְקִי כַפַּיִם וּבַר לֵבָב, אֲשֶׁר לֹא נָשָׂא לַשָּׁוְא נַפְשִׁי, וְלֹא נִשְׁבַּע לְמִרְמָה. יִשָּׂא בְרָכָה מֵאֵת יְיָ, וּצְדָקָה מֵאֱלֹהֵי יִשְׁעוֹ. זֶה דּוֹר דֹּרְשָׁיו, מְבַקְשֵׁי פָנֶיךָ יַעֲקֹב, סֶלָה. שְׂאוּ שְׁעָרִים רָאשֵׁיכֶם, וְהִנָּשְׂאוּ פִּתְחֵי עוֹלָם, וְיָבוֹא מֶלֶךְ הַכָּבוֹד. מִי זֶה מֶלֶךְ הַכָּבוֹד, יְיָ עִזּוּז וְגִבּוֹר, יְיָ גִּבּוֹר מִלְחָמָה. שְׂאוּ שְׁעָרִים רָאשֵׁיכֶם, וּשְׂאוּ פִּתְחֵי עוֹלָם, וְיָבֹא מֶלֶךְ הַכָּבוֹד. מִי הוּא זֶה מֶלֶךְ הַכָּבוֹד, יְיָ צְבָאוֹת הוּא מֶלֶךְ הַכָּבוֹד, סֶלָה.

While the Torah is being placed in the ark:

וּבְנֻחֹה יֹאמַר: שׁוּבָה, יְיָ, רִבְבוֹת אַלְפֵי יִשְׂרָאֵל. קוּמָה יְיָ לִמְנוּחָתֶךָ, אַתָּה וַאֲרוֹן עֻזֶּךָ. כֹּהֲנֶיךָ יִלְבְּשׁוּ צֶדֶק, וַחֲסִידֶיךָ יְרַנֵּנוּ. בַּעֲבוּר דָּוִד עַבְדֶּךָ, אַל תָּשֵׁב פְּנֵי מְשִׁיחֶךָ. כִּי לֶקַח טוֹב נָתַתִּי לָכֶם, תּוֹרָתִי אַל תַּעֲזֹבוּ. עֵץ חַיִּים הִיא לַמַּחֲזִיקִים בָּהּ, וְתֹמְכֶיהָ מְאֻשָּׁר. דְּרָכֶיהָ דַרְכֵי נֹעַם, וְכָל נְתִיבוֹתֶיהָ שָׁלוֹם. הֲשִׁיבֵנוּ יְיָ אֵלֶיךָ, וְנָשׁוּבָה; חַדֵּשׁ יָמֵינוּ כְּקֶדֶם.

The ark is closed The morning service continues.

אַשְׁרֵי יוֹשְׁבֵי בֵיתֶךָ; עוֹד יְהַלְלוּךָ סֶּלָה.
אַשְׁרֵי הָעָם שֶׁכָּכָה לּוֹ; אַשְׁרֵי הָעָם שֶׁיְיָ אֱלֹהָיו.

תהלים קמה

תְּהִלָּה לְדָוִד
אֲרוֹמִמְךָ, אֱלוֹהַי הַמֶּלֶךְ, וַאֲבָרְכָה שִׁמְךָ לְעוֹלָם וָעֶד.

His majesty is above earth and heaven. He has raised the honor of his people, the glory of his faithful followers, the children of Israel, the people near to him. Praise the Lord![1]

Psalm 24

A psalm of David. The earth and its entire contents belong to the Lord, the world and its inhabitants. For it is he who has founded it upon the seas, and established it on the floods. Who may ascend the Lord's mountain? Who may stand within his holy place? He who has clean hands and a pure heart; he who strives not after vanity and swears not deceitfully. He will receive a blessing from the Lord, and justice from his saving God. Such is the generation of those who are in quest of him, who seek the presence of the God of Jacob. Raise your heads, O gates, raise yourselves, you ancient doors, that the glorious King may come in. Who, then, is the glorious King? The Lord strong and mighty, the Lord strong in battle. Raise your heads, O gates, raise yourselves, you ancient doors, that the glorious King may come in. Who, then. is the glorious King? The Lord of hosts, he is the glorious King.

While the Torah is being placed in the ark:

When the ark rested, Moses would say: "Return, O Lord, to the myriads of Israel's families." Arise, O Lord, for thy resting place, thou and thy glorious ark. May thy priests be clothed with righteousness; may thy faithful followers shout for joy. For the sake of thy servant David, reject not thy anointed. I give you good instruction; forsake not my Torah. It is a tree of life to those who take hold of it, and happy are those who support it. Its ways are ways of pleasantness, and all its paths are peace. Turn us to thee, O Lord, and let us return; renew our days as of old.[2]

The ark is closed. The morning service continues.

Happy are those who dwell in thy house; they are ever praising thee. Happy the people that is so situated; happy the people whose God is the Lord.[3]

Psalm 145

A hymn of praise by David
I extol thee, my God the King,
And bless thy name forever and ever.

---

[1] *Psalm* 148:13–14.   [2] *Numbers* 10:36; *Psalm* 132:8–10; *Proverbs* 4:2; 3:18, 17: *Lamentations* 5:21.   [3] *Psalms* 84:5; 144:15.

בְּכָל יוֹם אֲבָרְכֶךָ, וַאֲהַלְלָה שִׁמְךָ לְעוֹלָם וָעֶד.

גָּדוֹל יְיָ וּמְהֻלָּל מְאֹד, וְלִגְדֻלָּתוֹ אֵין חֵקֶר.

דּוֹר לְדוֹר יְשַׁבַּח מַעֲשֶׂיךָ, וּגְבוּרֹתֶיךָ יַגִּידוּ.

הֲדַר כְּבוֹד הוֹדֶךָ, וְדִבְרֵי נִפְלְאֹתֶיךָ אָשִׂיחָה.

וֶעֱזוּז נוֹרְאֹתֶיךָ יֹאמֵרוּ, וּגְדֻלָּתְךָ אֲסַפְּרֶנָּה.

זֵכֶר רַב טוּבְךָ יַבִּיעוּ, וְצִדְקָתְךָ יְרַנֵּנוּ.

חַנּוּן וְרַחוּם יְיָ, אֶרֶךְ אַפַּיִם וּגְדָל־חָסֶד.

טוֹב יְיָ לַכֹּל, וְרַחֲמָיו עַל כָּל מַעֲשָׂיו.

יוֹדוּךָ יְיָ כָּל מַעֲשֶׂיךָ, וַחֲסִידֶיךָ יְבָרְכוּכָה.

כְּבוֹד מַלְכוּתְךָ יֹאמֵרוּ, וּגְבוּרָתְךָ יְדַבֵּרוּ.

לְהוֹדִיעַ לִבְנֵי הָאָדָם גְּבוּרֹתָיו, וּכְבוֹד הֲדַר מַלְכוּתוֹ.

מַלְכוּתְךָ מַלְכוּת כָּל עֹלָמִים, וּמֶמְשַׁלְתְּךָ בְּכָל דּוֹר וָדֹר.

סוֹמֵךְ יְיָ לְכָל הַנֹּפְלִים, וְזוֹקֵף לְכָל הַכְּפוּפִים.

עֵינֵי כֹל אֵלֶיךָ יְשַׂבֵּרוּ, וְאַתָּה נוֹתֵן לָהֶם אֶת אָכְלָם בְּעִתּוֹ.

פּוֹתֵחַ אֶת יָדֶךָ, וּמַשְׂבִּיעַ לְכָל חַי רָצוֹן.

צַדִּיק יְיָ בְּכָל דְּרָכָיו, וְחָסִיד בְּכָל מַעֲשָׂיו.

קָרוֹב יְיָ לְכָל קֹרְאָיו, לְכֹל אֲשֶׁר יִקְרָאֻהוּ בֶאֱמֶת.

רְצוֹן יְרֵאָיו יַעֲשֶׂה, וְאֶת שַׁוְעָתָם יִשְׁמַע וְיוֹשִׁיעֵם.

שׁוֹמֵר יְיָ אֶת כָּל אֹהֲבָיו, וְאֵת כָּל הָרְשָׁעִים יַשְׁמִיד.

תְּהִלַּת יְיָ יְדַבֶּר־פִּי; וִיבָרֵךְ כָּל בָּשָׂר שֵׁם קָדְשׁוֹ לְעוֹלָם וָעֶד.

Reader וַאֲנַחְנוּ נְבָרֵךְ יָהּ מֵעַתָּה וְעַד עוֹלָם; הַלְלוּיָהּ.

Every day I bless thee,
And praise thy name forever and ever.
Great is the Lord and most worthy of praise;
His greatness is unsearchable.
One generation to another praises thy works;
They recount thy mighty acts.
On the splendor of thy glorious majesty
And on thy wondrous deeds I meditate.
They speak of thy awe-inspiring might,
And I tell of thy greatness.
They spread the fame of thy great goodness,
And sing of thy righteousness.
Gracious and merciful is the Lord,
Slow to anger and of great kindness.
The Lord is good to all,
And his mercy is over all his works.
All thy works praise thee, O Lord,
And thy faithful followers bless thee.
They speak of thy glorious kingdom,
And talk of thy might,
To let men know thy mighty deeds,
And the glorious splendor of thy kingdom.
Thy kingdom is a kingdom of all ages,
And thy dominion is for all generations.
The Lord upholds all who fall,
And raises all who are bowed down.
The eyes of all look hopefully to thee,
And thou givest them their food in due season.
Thou openest thy hand,
And satisfiest every living thing with favor.
The Lord is righteous in all his ways,
And gracious in all his deeds.
The Lord is near to all who call upon him,
To all who call upon him sincerely.
He fulfills the desire of those who revere him;
He hears their cry and saves them.
The Lord preserves all who love him,
But all the wicked he destroys.
My mouth speaks the praise of the Lord;
Let all creatures bless his holy name forever and ever.
  [1]We will bless the Lord henceforth and forever.
    Praise the Lord!

---

[1] *Psalm* 115:18.

The following psalm is omitted on *Rosh Ḥodesh, Ḥanukkah, Ḥol ha-Mo'ed,*
the 14th and 15th of *Adar* and *Adar Sheni,* the 9th of *Av, Erev Pesaḥ*
and *Erev Yom Kippur.*

תהלים כ

לַמְנַצֵּחַ, מִזְמוֹר לְדָוִד. יַעַנְךָ יְיָ בְּיוֹם צָרָה; יְשַׂגֶּבְךָ שֵׁם אֱלֹהֵי
יַעֲקֹב. יִשְׁלַח עֶזְרְךָ מִקֹּדֶשׁ, וּמִצִּיּוֹן יִסְעָדֶךָּ. יִזְכֹּר כָּל מִנְחֹתֶיךָ,
וְעוֹלָתְךָ יְדַשְּׁנֶה סֶלָה. יִתֶּן לְךָ כִלְבָבֶךָ, וְכָל עֲצָתְךָ יְמַלֵּא.
נְרַנְּנָה בִּישׁוּעָתֶךָ, וּבְשֵׁם אֱלֹהֵינוּ נִדְגֹּל; יְמַלֵּא יְיָ כָּל מִשְׁאֲלוֹתֶיךָ.
עַתָּה יָדַעְתִּי, כִּי הוֹשִׁיעַ יְיָ מְשִׁיחוֹ, יַעֲנֵהוּ מִשְּׁמֵי קָדְשׁוֹ,
בִּגְבוּרוֹת יֵשַׁע יְמִינוֹ. אֵלֶּה בָרֶכֶב וְאֵלֶּה בַסּוּסִים, וַאֲנַחְנוּ בְּשֵׁם
יְיָ אֱלֹהֵינוּ נַזְכִּיר. הֵמָּה כָּרְעוּ וְנָפָלוּ, וַאֲנַחְנוּ קַמְנוּ וַנִּתְעוֹדָד.
Reader יְיָ, הוֹשִׁיעָה; הַמֶּלֶךְ יַעֲנֵנוּ בְיוֹם קָרְאֵנוּ.

וּבָא לְצִיּוֹן גּוֹאֵל, וּלְשָׁבֵי פֶשַׁע בְּיַעֲקֹב, נְאֻם יְיָ. וַאֲנִי, זֹאת
בְּרִיתִי אֹתָם, אָמַר יְיָ: רוּחִי אֲשֶׁר עָלֶיךָ, וּדְבָרַי אֲשֶׁר שַׂמְתִּי
בְּפִיךָ לֹא יָמוּשׁוּ מִפִּיךָ וּמִפִּי זַרְעֲךָ, וּמִפִּי זֶרַע זַרְעֲךָ, אָמַר יְיָ,
מֵעַתָּה וְעַד עוֹלָם. וְאַתָּה קָדוֹשׁ, יוֹשֵׁב תְּהִלּוֹת יִשְׂרָאֵל. וְקָרָא
זֶה אֶל זֶה וְאָמַר: קָדוֹשׁ, קָדוֹשׁ, קָדוֹשׁ יְיָ צְבָאוֹת, מְלֹא כָל
הָאָרֶץ כְּבוֹדוֹ. וּמְקַבְּלִין דֵּין מִן דֵּין וְאָמְרִין: קַדִּישׁ בִּשְׁמֵי מְרוֹמָא
עִלָּאָה, בֵּית שְׁכִינְתֵּהּ; קַדִּישׁ עַל אַרְעָא, עוֹבַד גְּבוּרְתֵּהּ; קַדִּישׁ
לְעָלַם וּלְעָלְמֵי עָלְמַיָּא יְיָ צְבָאוֹת; מַלְיָא כָל אַרְעָא זִיו יְקָרֵהּ.
וַתִּשָּׂאֵנִי רוּחַ, וָאֶשְׁמַע אַחֲרַי קוֹל רַעַשׁ גָּדוֹל: בָּרוּךְ כְּבוֹד יְיָ
מִמְּקוֹמוֹ. וּנְטָלַתְנִי רוּחָא, וְשִׁמְעֵת בַּתְרַי קָל זִיעַ סַגִּיא דִי
מְשַׁבְּחִין וְאָמְרִין: בְּרִיךְ יְקָרָא דַיְיָ מֵאֲתַר בֵּית שְׁכִינְתֵּהּ. יְיָ

וּבָא לציון, which consists of biblical passages accompanied by the paraphrase of the Targum, was designed to enable every Jew to have a daily share
in the study of the Torah (Rashi, Sotah 49a). On Sabbaths and festivals,
when the Torah and the Prophets are read at great length, the recitation of
this collection of Scriptural passages is postponed till the afternoon service.

The following psalm is omitted on Rosh Ḥodesh, Ḥanukkah, Ḥol ha-Moʻed, the 14th and 15th of Adar and Adar Sheni, the 9th of Av, Erev Pesaḥ and Erev Yom Kippur.

Psalm 20

For the Choirmaster; a psalm of David. May the Lord answer you in the day of trouble; may the name of Jacob's God protect you. May he send you help from the sanctuary, and give you support from Zion. May he remember all of your offerings, and be pleased with all your sacrifices. May he grant you your heart's desire, and fulfill all your plans. We will exult over your victory, and raise our banners in the name of God; may he fulfill all your requests. Now I know that the Lord has saved his anointed, answering him from his holy heavens with the mighty acts of his saving power. Some trust in chariots, and some in horses, but we call upon the name of the Lord our God. They bend and fall; we rise and stand upright. O Lord, save us; may the King answer us when we call.

A redeemer shall come to Zion and to those in Jacob who turn from transgression, says the Lord. As for me, this is my covenant with them, says the Lord: My spirit it is which shall be upon you; and my words which I have put in your mouth shall not depart from your mouth, nor from the mouth of your children, nor from the mouth of your children's children, says the Lord, henceforth and forever.[1]

Thou, holy God, art enthroned amidst the praises of Israel.[2] They keep calling to one another: "Holy, holy, holy is the Lord of hosts; the whole earth is full of his glory."[3] *They receive it from one another, and say: "Holy in the highest heavens, his divine abode; holy upon earth, his work of might; holy forever and to all eternity is the Lord of hosts; the whole earth is full of his radiant glory."* Then a wind lifted me up, and I heard behind me a mighty sound: "Blessed be the glory of the Lord from his abode."[4] *Then a wind lifted me up and I heard behind me a great moving sound of those who uttered praises, saying: "Blessed be the glory of the Lord from the*

---

* The words in italics are the Targum paraphrase of the preceding verse.

[1] *Isaiah* 59:20–21. [2] *Psalm* 22:4. [3] *Isaiah* 6:3. [4] *Ezekiel* 3:12.

יִמְלֹךְ לְעֹלָם וָעֶד. יְיָ מַלְכוּתֵהּ (קָאֵם) לְעָלַם וּלְעָלְמֵי עָלְמַיָּא.

יְיָ אֱלֹהֵי אַבְרָהָם יִצְחָק וְיִשְׂרָאֵל אֲבוֹתֵינוּ, שָׁמְרָה־זֹּאת לְעוֹלָם,

לְיֵצֶר מַחְשְׁבוֹת לְבַב עַמֶּךָ, וְהָכֵן לְבָבָם אֵלֶיךָ. וְהוּא רַחוּם,

יְכַפֵּר עָוֹן וְלֹא יַשְׁחִית, וְהִרְבָּה לְהָשִׁיב אַפּוֹ, וְלֹא יָעִיר כָּל

חֲמָתוֹ. כִּי אַתָּה, אֲדֹנָי, טוֹב וְסַלָּח וְרַב חֶסֶד לְכָל קֹרְאֶיךָ.

צִדְקָתְךָ צֶדֶק לְעוֹלָם, וְתוֹרָתְךָ אֱמֶת. תִּתֵּן אֱמֶת לְיַעֲקֹב, חֶסֶד

לְאַבְרָהָם, אֲשֶׁר נִשְׁבַּעְתָּ לַאֲבוֹתֵינוּ מִימֵי קֶדֶם. בָּרוּךְ יְיָ, יוֹם יוֹם

יַעֲמָס־לָנוּ; הָאֵל יְשׁוּעָתֵנוּ, סֶלָה. יְיָ צְבָאוֹת עִמָּנוּ, מִשְׂגָּב לָנוּ

אֱלֹהֵי יַעֲקֹב, סֶלָה. יְיָ צְבָאוֹת, אַשְׁרֵי אָדָם בֹּטֵחַ בָּךְ. יְיָ,

הוֹשִׁיעָה; הַמֶּלֶךְ יַעֲנֵנוּ בְיוֹם קָרְאֵנוּ. בָּרוּךְ הוּא אֱלֹהֵינוּ שֶׁבְּרָאָנוּ

לִכְבוֹדוֹ, וְהִבְדִּילָנוּ מִן הַתּוֹעִים, וְנָתַן לָנוּ תּוֹרַת אֱמֶת, וְחַיֵּי

עוֹלָם נָטַע בְּתוֹכֵנוּ; הוּא יִפְתַּח לִבֵּנוּ בְּתוֹרָתוֹ, וְיָשֵׂם בְּלִבֵּנוּ

אַהֲבָתוֹ וְיִרְאָתוֹ, לַעֲשׂוֹת רְצוֹנוֹ וּלְעָבְדוֹ בְּלֵבָב שָׁלֵם, לְמַעַן

לֹא נִיגַע לָרִיק, וְלֹא נֵלֵד לַבֶּהָלָה. יְהִי רָצוֹן מִלְּפָנֶיךָ, יְיָ

אֱלֹהֵינוּ וֵאלֹהֵי אֲבוֹתֵינוּ, שֶׁנִּשְׁמוֹר חֻקֶּיךָ בָּעוֹלָם הַזֶּה, וְנִזְכֶּה

וְנִחְיֶה וְנִרְאֶה, וְנִירַשׁ טוֹבָה וּבְרָכָה, לִשְׁנֵי יְמוֹת הַמָּשִׁיחַ וּלְחַיֵּי

הָעוֹלָם הַבָּא. לְמַעַן יְזַמֶּרְךָ כָבוֹד וְלֹא יִדֹּם; יְיָ אֱלֹהַי, לְעוֹלָם

אוֹדֶךָ. בָּרוּךְ הַגֶּבֶר אֲשֶׁר יִבְטַח בַּיְיָ, וְהָיָה יְיָ מִבְטַחוֹ. בִּטְחוּ

בַיְיָ עֲדֵי עַד, כִּי בְּיָהּ יְיָ צוּר עוֹלָמִים. Reader וְיִבְטְחוּ בְךָ יוֹדְעֵי

שְׁמֶךָ, כִּי לֹא עָזַבְתָּ דֹרְשֶׁיךָ, יְיָ. יְיָ חָפֵץ לְמַעַן צִדְקוֹ, יַגְדִּיל

תּוֹרָה וְיַאְדִּיר.

Musaf for *Rosh Ḥodesh*, page 575; for *Ḥol ha-Mo'ed*, page 609.

Reader:

יִתְגַּדַּל וְיִתְקַדַּשׁ שְׁמֵהּ רַבָּא בְּעָלְמָא דִי בְרָא כִרְעוּתֵהּ;

וְיַמְלִיךְ מַלְכוּתֵהּ בְּחַיֵּיכוֹן וּבְיוֹמֵיכוֹן, וּבְחַיֵּי דְכָל בֵּית יִשְׂרָאֵל,

בַּעֲגָלָא וּבִזְמַן קָרִיב, וְאִמְרוּ אָמֵן.

place of his divine abode." The Lord shall reign forever and ever.[1]
The Lord's kingship is established forever and to all eternity.

Lord God of Abraham, Isaac and Israel our fathers, keep the mind and purpose of thy people ever in this spirit, and direct their heart to thyself.[2] He, being merciful, forgives iniquity, and does not destroy; frequently he turns his anger away, and does not stir up all his wrath. For thou, O Lord, art good and forgiving, and exceedingly kind to all who call upon thee. Thy righteousness is eternal, and thy Torah is truth.[3] Thou wilt show grace to Jacob, love to Abraham, as thou hast sworn to our fathers from days of old.[4] Blessed be the Lord who day by day bears our burden; God is ever our salvation. The Lord of hosts is with us; the God of Jacob is our stronghold. Lord of hosts, happy is the man who trusts in thee. O Lord, save us; may the King answer us when we call.[5]

Blessed be our God who has created us for his glory, and has separated us from those who go astray; who has given us the Torah of truth and planted eternal life in our midst. May he open our heart to his Torah; may he set in our heart love and reverence for him to do his will and serve him with a perfect heart, so that we shall not labor in vain, nor rear children for disaster. May it be thy will, Lord our God and God of our fathers, that we keep thy laws in this world, and thus be worthy to live to see and share the happiness and blessing in the Messianic days and in the life of the world to come. So that my soul may sing praise to thee, and not be silent; Lord my God, I will thank thee forever.[6] Blessed is the man who trusts in the Lord; the Lord will be his protection. Trust in the Lord forever and ever, for the Lord God is an everlasting stronghold. Those who know thy name put their trust in thee, for thou hast not forsaken those who seek thee, O Lord.[7]

The Lord was pleased, because of his righteousness, to render the Torah great and glorious.[8]

Musaf for Rosh Ḥodesh, page 576; for Ḥol ha-Mo'ed, page 610.

Reader:

Glorified and sanctified be God's great name throughout the world which he has created according to his will. May he establish his kingdom in your lifetime and during your days, and within the life of the entire house of Israel, speedily and soon; and say, Amen.

---

[1] *Exodus* 15:18. [2] *I Chronicles* 29:18. [3] *Psalms* 78:38; 86:5; 119:142. [4] *Micah* 7:20. [5] *Psalms* 68:20; 46:8; 84:13; 20:10. [6] *Psalm* 30:13. [7] *Jeremiah* 17:7; *Isaiah* 26:4; *Psalm* 9:11. [8] *Isaiah* 42:21.

יְהֵא שְׁמֵהּ רַבָּא מְבָרַךְ לְעָלַם וּלְעָלְמֵי עָלְמַיָּא.

יִתְבָּרַךְ וְיִשְׁתַּבַּח, וְיִתְפָּאַר וְיִתְרוֹמַם, וְיִתְנַשֵּׂא וְיִתְהַדָּר, וְיִתְעַלֶּה וְיִתְהַלָּל שְׁמֵהּ דְּקֻדְשָׁא, בְּרִיךְ הוּא, לְעֵלָּא (לְעֵלָּא) מִן כָּל בִּרְכָתָא וְשִׁירָתָא, תֻּשְׁבְּחָתָא וְנֶחֱמָתָא, דַּאֲמִירָן בְּעָלְמָא, וְאִמְרוּ אָמֵן.

תִּתְקַבַּל צְלוֹתְהוֹן וּבָעוּתְהוֹן דְּכָל בֵּית יִשְׂרָאֵל קֳדָם אֲבוּהוֹן דִּי בִשְׁמַיָּא, וְאִמְרוּ אָמֵן.

יְהֵא שְׁלָמָא רַבָּא מִן שְׁמַיָּא, וְחַיִּים, עָלֵינוּ וְעַל כָּל יִשְׂרָאֵל, וְאִמְרוּ אָמֵן.

עֹשֶׂה שָׁלוֹם בִּמְרוֹמָיו, הוּא יַעֲשֶׂה שָׁלוֹם עָלֵינוּ וְעַל כָּל יִשְׂרָאֵל, וְאִמְרוּ אָמֵן.

עָלֵינוּ לְשַׁבֵּחַ לַאֲדוֹן הַכֹּל, לָתֵת גְּדֻלָּה לְיוֹצֵר בְּרֵאשִׁית, שֶׁלֹּא עָשָׂנוּ כְּגוֹיֵי הָאֲרָצוֹת, וְלֹא שָׂמָנוּ כְּמִשְׁפְּחוֹת הָאֲדָמָה; שֶׁלֹּא שָׂם חֶלְקֵנוּ כָּהֶם, וְגֹרָלֵנוּ כְּכָל הֲמוֹנָם. וַאֲנַחְנוּ כּוֹרְעִים וּמִשְׁתַּחֲוִים וּמוֹדִים לִפְנֵי מֶלֶךְ מַלְכֵי הַמְּלָכִים, הַקָּדוֹשׁ בָּרוּךְ הוּא, שֶׁהוּא נוֹטֶה שָׁמַיִם וְיוֹסֵד אָרֶץ, וּמוֹשַׁב יְקָרוֹ בַּשָּׁמַיִם מִמַּעַל, וּשְׁכִינַת עֻזּוֹ בְּגָבְהֵי מְרוֹמִים. הוּא אֱלֹהֵינוּ, אֵין עוֹד; אֱמֶת מַלְכֵּנוּ, אֶפֶס זוּלָתוֹ, כַּכָּתוּב בְּתוֹרָתוֹ: וְיָדַעְתָּ הַיּוֹם וַהֲשֵׁבֹתָ אֶל לְבָבֶךָ, כִּי יְיָ הוּא הָאֱלֹהִים בַּשָּׁמַיִם מִמַּעַל וְעַל הָאָרֶץ מִתָּחַת, אֵין עוֹד.

עַל כֵּן נְקַוֶּה לְךָ, יְיָ אֱלֹהֵינוּ, לִרְאוֹת מְהֵרָה בְּתִפְאֶרֶת עֻזֶּךָ, לְהַעֲבִיר גִּלּוּלִים מִן הָאָרֶץ, וְהָאֱלִילִים כָּרוֹת יִכָּרֵתוּן; לְתַקֵּן עוֹלָם בְּמַלְכוּת שַׁדַּי, וְכָל בְּנֵי בָשָׂר יִקְרְאוּ בִשְׁמֶךָ, לְהַפְנוֹת

עלינו is the proclamation of God as King over a united humanity. An old tradition claims Joshua as its author. Taken from the *Musaf* service of *Rosh*

May his great name be blessed forever and to all eternity.

Blessed and praised, glorified and exalted, extolled and honored, adored and lauded be the name of the Holy One, blessed be he, beyond all the blessings and hymns, praises and consolations that are ever spoken in the world; and say, Amen.

May the prayers and supplications of the whole house of Israel be accepted by their Father who is in heaven; and say, Amen.

May there be abundant peace from heaven, and life, for us and for all Israel; and say, Amen.

He who creates peace in his celestial heights, may he create peace for us and for all Israel; and say, Amen.

ALENU

It is our duty to praise the Master of all, to exalt the Creator of the universe, who has not made us like the nations of the world and has not placed us like the families of the earth; who has not designed our destiny to be like theirs, nor our lot like that of all their multitude. We bend the knee and bow and acknowledge before the supreme King of kings, the Holy One, blessed be he, that it is he who stretched forth the heavens and founded the earth. His seat of glory is in the heavens above; his abode of majesty is in the lofty heights. He is our God, there is none else; truly, he is our King, there is none besides him, as it is written in his Torah: "You shall know this day, and reflect in your heart, that it is the Lord who is God in the heavens above and on the earth beneath, there is none else."[1]

We hope therefore, Lord our God, soon to behold thy majestic glory, when the abominations shall be removed from the earth, and the false gods exterminated; when the world shall be perfected under the reign of the Almighty, and all mankind will call upon

---

Hashanah, Alenu has been used as the closing prayer of the daily services since the thirteenth century. It is reported that it was the death-song of Jewish martyrs in the Middle Ages. *Alenu* has been the occasion of repeated attacks on account of the passage: "They bow to vanity and emptiness and pray to a god that cannot save" (שהם משתחוים להבל וריק ומתפללים אל אל לא יושיע). Through fear of the official censors, the passage in question has been excluded from the prayer.

[1] *Deuteronomy* 4:39.

אֵלֶיךָ כָּל רִשְׁעֵי אֶרֶץ. יַכִּירוּ וְיֵדְעוּ כָּל יוֹשְׁבֵי תֵבֵל, כִּי לְךָ
תִּכְרַע כָּל בֶּרֶךְ, תִּשָּׁבַע כָּל לָשׁוֹן. לְפָנֶיךָ, יְיָ אֱלֹהֵינוּ, יִכְרְעוּ
וְיִפְּלוּ, וְלִכְבוֹד שִׁמְךָ יְקָר יִתֵּנוּ, וִיקַבְּלוּ כֻלָּם אֶת עֹל מַלְכוּתֶךָ,
וְתִמְלֹךְ עֲלֵיהֶם מְהֵרָה לְעוֹלָם וָעֶד; כִּי הַמַּלְכוּת שֶׁלְּךָ הִיא,
וּלְעוֹלְמֵי עַד תִּמְלוֹךְ בְּכָבוֹד, כַּכָּתוּב בְּתוֹרָתֶךָ: יְיָ יִמְלֹךְ
לְעֹלָם וָעֶד. Reader וְנֶאֱמַר: וְהָיָה יְיָ לְמֶלֶךְ עַל כָּל הָאָרֶץ;
בַּיּוֹם הַהוּא יִהְיֶה יְיָ אֶחָד וּשְׁמוֹ אֶחָד.

MOURNERS' KADDISH

יִתְגַּדַּל וְיִתְקַדַּשׁ שְׁמֵהּ רַבָּא בְּעָלְמָא דִי בְרָא כִרְעוּתֵהּ;
וְיַמְלִיךְ מַלְכוּתֵהּ בְּחַיֵּיכוֹן וּבְיוֹמֵיכוֹן, וּבְחַיֵּי דְכָל בֵּית יִשְׂרָאֵל,
בַּעֲגָלָא וּבִזְמַן קָרִיב, וְאִמְרוּ אָמֵן.

יְהֵא שְׁמֵהּ רַבָּא מְבָרַךְ לְעָלַם וּלְעָלְמֵי עָלְמַיָּא.

יִתְבָּרַךְ וְיִשְׁתַּבַּח, וְיִתְפָּאַר וְיִתְרוֹמַם, וְיִתְנַשֵּׂא וְיִתְהַדָּר,
וְיִתְעַלֶּה וְיִתְהַלַּל שְׁמֵהּ דְּקֻדְשָׁא, בְּרִיךְ הוּא, לְעֵלָּא (לְעֵלָּא)
מִן כָּל בִּרְכָתָא וְשִׁירָתָא, תֻּשְׁבְּחָתָא וְנֶחֱמָתָא, דַּאֲמִירָן בְּעָלְמָא,
וְאִמְרוּ אָמֵן.

יְהֵא שְׁלָמָא רַבָּא מִן שְׁמַיָּא, וְחַיִּים, עָלֵינוּ וְעַל כָּל יִשְׂרָאֵל,
וְאִמְרוּ אָמֵן.

עֹשֶׂה שָׁלוֹם בִּמְרוֹמָיו, הוּא יַעֲשֶׂה שָׁלוֹם עָלֵינוּ וְעַל כָּל
יִשְׂרָאֵל, וְאִמְרוּ אָמֵן.

אַל תִּירָא מִפַּחַד פִּתְאֹם, וּמִשֹּׁאַת רְשָׁעִים כִּי תָבֹא. עֻצוּ
עֵצָה וְתֻפָר, דַּבְּרוּ דָבָר וְלֹא יָקוּם, כִּי עִמָּנוּ אֵל. וְעַד זִקְנָה
אֲנִי הוּא, וְעַד שֵׂיבָה אֲנִי אֶסְבֹּל; אֲנִי עָשִׂיתִי וַאֲנִי אֶשָּׂא, וַאֲנִי
אֶסְבֹּל וַאֲמַלֵּט.

thy name, and all the wicked of the earth will be turned to thee. May all the inhabitants of the world realize and know that to thee every knee must bend, every tongue must vow allegiance. May they bend the knee and prostrate themselves before thee, Lord our God, and give honor to thy glorious name; may they all accept the yoke of thy kingdom, and do thou reign over them speedily forever and ever. For the kingdom is thine, and to all eternity thou wilt reign in glory, as it is written in thy Torah: "The Lord shall be King forever and ever."[1] And it is said: "The Lord shall be King over all the earth; on that day the Lord shall be One, and his name One."[2]

MOURNERS' KADDISH

Glorified and sanctified be God's great name throughout the world which he has created according to his will. May he establish his kingdom in your lifetime and during your days, and within the life of the entire house of Israel, speedily and soon; and say, Amen.

May his great name be blessed forever and to all eternity.

Blessed and praised, glorified and exalted, extolled and honored, adored˜and lauded be the name of the Holy One, blessed be he, beyond all the blessings and hymns, praises and consolations that are ever spoken in the world; and say, Amen.

May there be abundant peace from heaven, and life, for us and for all Israel; and say, Amen.

He who creates peace in his celestial heights, may he create peace for us and for all Israel; and say, Amen.

Be not afraid of sudden terror, nor of the storm that strikes the wicked. Form your plot—it shall fail; lay your plan—it shall not prevail! For God is with us. Even to your old age I will be the same; when you are gray-headed, still I will sustain you; I have made you, and I will bear you; I will sustain you and save you.[3]

---

[1] *Exodus* 15:18. [2] *Zechariah* 14:9. [3] *Proverbs* 3:25; *Isaiah* 8:10, 46:4.

שִׁיר שֶׁל יוֹם

The following six psalms are recited on the respective days of the week.

On Sundays:

הַיּוֹם יוֹם רִאשׁוֹן בַּשַּׁבָּת, שֶׁבּוֹ הָיוּ הַלְוִיִּם אוֹמְרִים
בְּבֵית הַמִּקְדָּשׁ:

תהלים כד

לְדָוִד מִזְמוֹר . לַיָי הָאָרֶץ וּמְלוֹאָהּ, תֵּבֵל וְיֹשְׁבֵי בָהּ. כִּי הוּא
עַל יַמִּים יְסָדָהּ, וְעַל נְהָרוֹת יְכוֹנְנֶהָ. מִי יַעֲלֶה בְהַר יְיָ, וּמִי
יָקוּם בִּמְקוֹם קָדְשׁוֹ. נְקִי כַפַּיִם וּבַר לֵבָב, אֲשֶׁר לֹא נָשָׂא לַשָּׁוְא
נַפְשִׁי, וְלֹא נִשְׁבַּע לְמִרְמָה. יִשָּׂא בְרָכָה מֵאֵת יְיָ, וּצְדָקָה מֵאֱלֹהֵי
יִשְׁעוֹ. זֶה דּוֹר דֹּרְשָׁיו, מְבַקְשֵׁי פָנֶיךָ יַעֲקֹב, סֶלָה. שְׂאוּ שְׁעָרִים
רָאשֵׁיכֶם, וְהִנָּשְׂאוּ פִּתְחֵי עוֹלָם, וְיָבוֹא מֶלֶךְ הַכָּבוֹד. מִי זֶה
מֶלֶךְ הַכָּבוֹד, יְיָ עִזּוּז וְגִבּוֹר, יְיָ גִּבּוֹר מִלְחָמָה. שְׂאוּ שְׁעָרִים
רָאשֵׁיכֶם, וּשְׂאוּ פִּתְחֵי עוֹלָם, וְיָבֹא מֶלֶךְ הַכָּבוֹד. Reader מִי
הוּא זֶה מֶלֶךְ הַכָּבוֹד, יְיָ צְבָאוֹת הוּא מֶלֶךְ הַכָּבוֹד, סֶלָה.

Mourners' Kaddish.

On Mondays:

הַיּוֹם יוֹם שֵׁנִי בַּשַּׁבָּת, שֶׁבּוֹ הָיוּ הַלְוִיִּם אוֹמְרִים
בְּבֵית הַמִּקְדָּשׁ:

תהלים מח

שִׁיר מִזְמוֹר לִבְנֵי קֹרַח. גָּדוֹל יְיָ וּמְהֻלָּל מְאֹד, בְּעִיר אֱלֹהֵינוּ,
הַר קָדְשׁוֹ. יְפֵה נוֹף, מְשׂוֹשׂ כָּל הָאָרֶץ הַר צִיּוֹן, יַרְכְּתֵי צָפוֹן,
קִרְיַת מֶלֶךְ רָב. אֱלֹהִים בְּאַרְמְנוֹתֶיהָ נוֹדַע לְמִשְׂגָּב. כִּי הִנֵּה

שיר של יום, the Psalm of the Day, was chanted by the Levites each day
during the Temple service (Mishnah Tamid 7:4). According to the Talmud,
the daily psalms were intended to recall the incidents of the six days of creation (Rosh Hashanah 31a).

PSALM OF THE DAY

The following six psalms are recited on the respective days of the week.

On Sundays:

This is the first day of the week, on which the Levites in the Temple used to recite:

Psalm 24

A psalm of David. The earth and its entire contents belong to the Lord, the world and its inhabitants. For it is he who has founded it upon the seas, and established it on the floods. Who may ascend the Lord's mountain? Who may stand within his holy place? He who has clean hands and a pure heart; he who strives not after vanity and swears not deceitfully. He will receive a blessing from the Lord, and justice from his saving God. Such is the generation of those who are in quest of him, who seek the presence of the God of Jacob. Raise your heads, O gates, raise yourselves, you ancient doors, that the glorious King may come in. Who, then, is the glorious King? The Lord strong and mighty, the Lord strong in battle. Raise your heads, O gates, raise yourselves, you ancient doors, that the glorious King may come in. Who, then, is the glorious King? The Lord of hosts, he is the glorious King.

Mourners' Kaddish.

On Mondays:

This is the second day of the week, on which the Levites in the Temple used to recite:

Psalm 48

A song, a psalm of the Korahites. Great is the Lord, and highly to be praised, in the city of our God, his holy mountain. Beautiful in elevation, the joy of the whole earth, on the northern slope, is Mount Zion, the city of the great King. God in her palaces has made himself known as a stronghold. For lo, the kings assembled

---

מזמור a poem sung to the accompaniment of musical instruments in the Temple service.

שאו שערים ראשיכם The ancient gates of Zion are poetically commanded to raise their heads, in token of reverence to God whose entrance is an act of condescension. Different parts of this psalm were sung by different choirs of singers at the time when David brought the ark to Mount Zion.

בני קרח descendants of Korah, a division of Levites who sang in the Temple.

הַמְּלָכִים נוֹעֲדוּ, עָבְרוּ יַחְדָּו. הֵמָּה רָאוּ, כֵּן תָּמָהוּ, נִבְהֲלוּ נֶחְפָּזוּ. רְעָדָה אֲחָזָתַם שָׁם, חִיל כַּיּוֹלֵדָה. בְּרוּחַ קָדִים תְּשַׁבֵּר אֳנִיּוֹת תַּרְשִׁישׁ. כַּאֲשֶׁר שָׁמַעְנוּ, כֵּן רָאִינוּ בְּעִיר יְיָ צְבָאוֹת, בְּעִיר אֱלֹהֵינוּ; אֱלֹהִים יְכוֹנְנֶהָ עַד עוֹלָם, סֶלָה. דִּמִּינוּ אֱלֹהִים חַסְדֶּךָ, בְּקֶרֶב הֵיכָלֶךָ. כְּשִׁמְךָ אֱלֹהִים, כֵּן תְּהִלָּתְךָ עַל קַצְוֵי אֶרֶץ; צֶדֶק מָלְאָה יְמִינֶךָ. יִשְׂמַח הַר צִיּוֹן, תָּגֵלְנָה בְּנוֹת יְהוּדָה, לְמַעַן מִשְׁפָּטֶיךָ. סֹבּוּ צִיּוֹן וְהַקִּיפוּהָ, סִפְרוּ מִגְדָּלֶיהָ. שִׁיתוּ לִבְּכֶם לְחֵילָה, פַּסְּגוּ אַרְמְנוֹתֶיהָ, לְמַעַן תְּסַפְּרוּ לְדוֹר אַחֲרוֹן. Reader כִּי זֶה אֱלֹהִים אֱלֹהֵינוּ עוֹלָם וָעֶד; הוּא יְנַהֲגֵנוּ עַל מוּת.

Mourners' Kaddish.

On Tuesdays:

הַיּוֹם יוֹם שְׁלִישִׁי בַּשַּׁבָּת, שֶׁבּוֹ הָיוּ הַלְוִיִּם אוֹמְרִים בְּבֵית הַמִּקְדָּשׁ:

תהלים פב

מִזְמוֹר לְאָסָף. אֱלֹהִים נִצָּב בַּעֲדַת אֵל, בְּקֶרֶב אֱלֹהִים יִשְׁפֹּט. עַד מָתַי תִּשְׁפְּטוּ עָוֶל, וּפְנֵי רְשָׁעִים תִּשְׂאוּ סֶלָה. שִׁפְטוּ דָל וְיָתוֹם, עָנִי וָרָשׁ הַצְדִּיקוּ. פַּלְּטוּ דַל וְאֶבְיוֹן, מִיַּד רְשָׁעִים הַצִּילוּ. לֹא יָדְעוּ וְלֹא יָבִינוּ, בַּחֲשֵׁכָה יִתְהַלָּכוּ; יִמּוֹטוּ כָּל מוֹסְדֵי אָרֶץ. אֲנִי אָמַרְתִּי אֱלֹהִים אַתֶּם, וּבְנֵי עֶלְיוֹן כֻּלְּכֶם. אָכֵן כְּאָדָם תְּמוּתוּן, וּכְאַחַד הַשָּׂרִים תִּפֹּלוּ. Reader קוּמָה אֱלֹהִים, שָׁפְטָה הָאָרֶץ; כִּי אַתָּה תִנְחַל בְּכָל הַגּוֹיִם.

Mourners' Kaddish.

המה ראו they saw the impregnable might of Zion and were terrified.

אניות תרשיש the great seagoing vessels that made the long voyage to Tarshish, a seacoast city in Spain (or Carthage).

כאשר שמענו כן ראינו that is, history has repeated itself. We have now experienced events similar to those which occurred in the past. This psalm celebrates the escape of Jerusalem from a threatened invasion by the armies of various confederate kings.

themselves, they invaded together. They saw [her defense] and were amazed; they were terrified, they fled in haste. Panic seized them, anguish as of a woman in travail. With the east wind thou breakest the ships of Tarshish. As we have heard, so have we seen now in the city of the Lord of hosts, in the city of our God; may God establish it forever. We meditate on thy kindness, O God, within thy temple. Like thy name, O God, thy fame shall extend to the ends of the earth; thy right hand is full of justice. Let Mount Zion be glad, let the towns of Judah rejoice, because of thy judgments. Walk about Zion, go round her, count her towers, mark well her ramparts, go through her palaces, that you may tell a later generation that such is God, our God, forever and ever. He will guide us eternally.

Mourners' Kaddish.

On Tuesdays:

This is the third day of the week, on which the Levites in the Temple used to recite:

Psalm 82

A psalm of Asaph. God stands in the divine assembly; in the midst of the judges he gives judgment. "How long will you judge unjustly, and show partiality toward the wicked? Do justice to the poor and fatherless; deal righteously with the afflicted and destitute. Rescue the poor and needy; save them from the hand of the wicked." But they neither know nor understand; they walk about in darkness; all the foundations of the earth are shaken. I thought you were angels, that you were all sons of the Most High. Yet you shall die as men do, and fall like any prince. Arise, O God, rule the earth, for thou hast dominion over all the nations.

Mourners' Kaddish.

... סובו ציון that is, after the miraculous deliverance of Zion, its inhabitants can now freely walk around and contemplate the safety of the walls and towers and palaces so lately menaced with destruction.

... נצב בעדת אל God takes his stand in the assembly summoned by him, and denounces the wickedness and partiality of judges. He reminds them of their duties, and declares that because they are ignorant and corrupt human society is undermined.

... אני אמרתי I appointed you as judges and thus invested you with authority of administering divine justice; however, your high title will not exempt you from punishment. You shall die like common men, and fall like any other prince.

קומה The psalmist pleads that God should act as judge over all peoples, since the human judges have failed so miserably.

On Wednesdays:

הַיּוֹם יוֹם רְבִיעִי בַּשַּׁבָּת, שֶׁבּוֹ הָיוּ הַלְוִיִּם אוֹמְרִים
בְּבֵית הַמִּקְדָּשׁ:

תהלים צד; צה, א–ג

אֵל נְקָמוֹת, יְיָ, אֵל נְקָמוֹת, הוֹפִיעַ. הִנָּשֵׂא, שֹׁפֵט הָאָרֶץ,
הָשֵׁב גְּמוּל עַל גֵּאִים. עַד מָתַי רְשָׁעִים, יְיָ, עַד מָתַי רְשָׁעִים
יַעֲלֹזוּ. יַבִּיעוּ יְדַבְּרוּ עָתָק, יִתְאַמְּרוּ כָּל פֹּעֲלֵי אָוֶן. עַמְּךָ יְיָ
יְדַכְּאוּ, וְנַחֲלָתְךָ יְעַנּוּ. אַלְמָנָה וְגֵר יַהֲרֹגוּ, וִיתוֹמִים יְרַצֵּחוּ.
וַיֹּאמְרוּ לֹא יִרְאֶה יָּהּ, וְלֹא יָבִין אֱלֹהֵי יַעֲקֹב. בִּינוּ בֹּעֲרִים
בָּעָם, וּכְסִילִים מָתַי תַּשְׂכִּילוּ. הֲנֹטַע אֹזֶן הֲלֹא יִשְׁמָע, אִם
יֹצֵר עַיִן הֲלֹא יַבִּיט. הֲיֹסֵר גּוֹיִם הֲלֹא יוֹכִיחַ, הַמְלַמֵּד אָדָם
דָּעַת. יְיָ יֹדֵעַ מַחְשְׁבוֹת אָדָם, כִּי הֵמָּה הָבֶל. אַשְׁרֵי הַגֶּבֶר
אֲשֶׁר תְּיַסְּרֶנּוּ יָּהּ, וּמִתּוֹרָתְךָ תְלַמְּדֶנּוּ. לְהַשְׁקִיט לוֹ מִימֵי רָע,
עַד יִכָּרֶה לָרָשָׁע שָׁחַת. כִּי לֹא יִטֹּשׁ יְיָ עַמּוֹ, וְנַחֲלָתוֹ לֹא יַעֲזֹב.
כִּי עַד צֶדֶק יָשׁוּב מִשְׁפָּט, וְאַחֲרָיו כָּל יִשְׁרֵי לֵב. מִי יָקוּם לִי
עִם מְרֵעִים, מִי יִתְיַצֵּב לִי עִם פֹּעֲלֵי אָוֶן. לוּלֵי יְיָ עֶזְרָתָה לִּי,
כִּמְעַט, שָׁכְנָה דוּמָה נַפְשִׁי. אִם אָמַרְתִּי מָטָה רַגְלִי, חַסְדְּךָ יְיָ
יִסְעָדֵנִי. בְּרֹב שַׂרְעַפַּי בְּקִרְבִּי, תַּנְחוּמֶיךָ יְשַׁעַשְׁעוּ נַפְשִׁי.
הַיְחָבְרְךָ כִּסֵּא הַוּוֹת, יֹצֵר עָמָל עֲלֵי חֹק. יָגוֹדּוּ עַל נֶפֶשׁ צַדִּיק,
וְדָם נָקִי יַרְשִׁיעוּ. וַיְהִי יְיָ לִי לְמִשְׂגָּב, וֵאלֹהַי לְצוּר מַחְסִי. וַיָּשֶׁב
עֲלֵיהֶם אֶת אוֹנָם, וּבְרָעָתָם יַצְמִיתֵם; יַצְמִיתֵם יְיָ אֱלֹהֵינוּ.
לְכוּ נְרַנְּנָה לַיְיָ, נָרִיעָה לְצוּר יִשְׁעֵנוּ. נְקַדְּמָה פָנָיו בְּתוֹדָה,

---

אל נקמות is repeated for emphasis. The psalmist appeals to God to punish
the arrogant who contemptuously declare that God is indifferent to the sufferings of his people. He then turns to argue with those who foolishly agree
with their oppressors and think that God will not defend them. He who gave
others the power to hear and see can surely himself hear and see. God knows

On Wednesdays:

This is the fourth day of the week, on which the Levites in the Temple used to recite:

Psalms 94; 95:1-3

God of retribution, Lord God of retribution, appear! Arise, thou judge of the earth, render to the arrogant what they deserve. How long shall the wicked, O Lord, how long shall the wicked exult? They bluster, they speak arrogantly; all the evildoers act boastfully. They crush thy people, O Lord, and afflict thy heritage. The widow and the stranger they slay, and the fatherless they murder. And they think the Lord does not see, the God of Jacob does not observe. Consider, you most stupid of the people; you fools, when will you understand? He who sets the ear, does he not hear? He who forms the eye, does he not see? He who punishes nations, shall he not punish you? He who teaches man knowledge? The Lord knows the inner thoughts of men; indeed, they are futile. Happy is the man whom thou dost instruct, O Lord, and teachest him out of thy Torah, granting him relief in days of adversity, till a pit is dug for the wicked. Indeed, the Lord will not abandon his people, nor forsake his heritage. For judgment shall again conform with justice, and all the upright in heart will follow it. Who rises up for me against the ungodly? Who stands up for me against the wrongdoers? If the Lord had not been my help, I would have soon dwelt in the silent grave. When I think my foot is slipping, thy goodness, O Lord, holds me up. When my cares are many within me, thy comforts cheer me. Can one in the seat of wickedness have fellowship with thee—one who frames evil by law? They band themselves against the life of the righteous, and condemn innocent blood. But the Lord is my stronghold; my God is the rock of my safety. He will requite them for their crime, and destroy them for their wickedness; the Lord our God will destroy them.

Come, let us sing to the Lord; let us acclaim our saving Stronghold. Let us approach him with thanksgiving; let us acclaim him

---

the evil thoughts of the wicked, and eventually the righteous will be vindicated when the day of retribution comes. It is unthinkable that God would abandon his people to the ravages of lawless judges and tyrannical rulers.

בְּזִמְרוֹת נָרִיעַ לוֹ. Reader כִּי אֵל גָּדוֹל יְיָ, וּמֶלֶךְ גָּדוֹל עַל כָּל אֱלֹהִים.

Mourners' Kaddish.

On Thursdays:

הַיּוֹם יוֹם חֲמִישִׁי בַּשַּׁבָּת, שֶׁבּוֹ הָיוּ הַלְוִיִּם אוֹמְרִים בְּבֵית הַמִּקְדָּשׁ:

תהלים פא

לַמְנַצֵּחַ עַל הַגִּתִּית לְאָסָף. הַרְנִינוּ לֵאלֹהִים עוּזֵּנוּ, הָרִיעוּ לֵאלֹהֵי יַעֲקֹב. שְׂאוּ זִמְרָה וּתְנוּ תֹף, כִּנּוֹר נָעִים עִם נָבֶל. תִּקְעוּ בַחֹדֶשׁ שׁוֹפָר, בַּכֶּסֶה לְיוֹם חַגֵּנוּ. כִּי חֹק לְיִשְׂרָאֵל הוּא, מִשְׁפָּט לֵאלֹהֵי יַעֲקֹב. עֵדוּת בִּיהוֹסֵף שָׂמוֹ, בְּצֵאתוֹ עַל אֶרֶץ מִצְרָיִם; שְׂפַת לֹא יָדַעְתִּי אֶשְׁמָע. הֲסִירוֹתִי מִסֵּבֶל שִׁכְמוֹ, כַּפָּיו מִדּוּד תַּעֲבֹרְנָה. בַּצָּרָה קָרָאתָ וָאֲחַלְּצֶךָ, אֶעֶנְךָ בְּסֵתֶר רָעַם; אֶבְחָנְךָ עַל מֵי מְרִיבָה, סֶלָה. שְׁמַע עַמִּי, וְאָעִידָה בָּךְ, יִשְׂרָאֵל אִם תִּשְׁמַע לִי. לֹא יִהְיֶה בְךָ אֵל זָר, וְלֹא תִשְׁתַּחֲוֶה לְאֵל נֵכָר. אָנֹכִי יְיָ אֱלֹהֶיךָ, הַמַּעַלְךָ מֵאֶרֶץ מִצְרָיִם; הַרְחֶב־פִּיךָ וַאֲמַלְאֵהוּ. וְלֹא שָׁמַע עַמִּי לְקוֹלִי, וְיִשְׂרָאֵל לֹא אָבָה לִי. וָאֲשַׁלְּחֵהוּ בִּשְׁרִירוּת לִבָּם, יֵלְכוּ בְּמוֹעֲצוֹתֵיהֶם. לוּ עַמִּי שֹׁמֵעַ לִי, יִשְׂרָאֵל בִּדְרָכַי יְהַלֵּכוּ. כִּמְעַט אוֹיְבֵיהֶם אַכְנִיעַ, וְעַל צָרֵיהֶם אָשִׁיב יָדִי. מְשַׂנְאֵי יְיָ יְכַחֲשׁוּ לוֹ, וִיהִי עִתָּם לְעוֹלָם. Reader וַיַּאֲכִילֵהוּ מֵחֵלֶב חִטָּה, וּמִצּוּר דְּבַשׁ אַשְׂבִּיעֶךָ.

Mourners' Kaddish.

למנצח occurs in the titles of fifty-five psalms, and refers to the use of the psalm in the Temple services. The word means the conductor of the Temple choir, who trained the choir and led the music.

על הגתית occurs in the titles of three psalms. According to the Targum, *Gittith* was a harp used by the Philistines of Gath. Since the Hebrew word *gath* means "a winepress," *Gittith* may mean a melody sung at vintage festivals.

בחדש is rendered by the Targum and the Talmud: *Rosh Ḥodesh Tishri,* that is *Rosh Hashanah*. Metal trumpets, and not a *shofar*, were used on all other occasions of *Rosh Ḥodesh*.

with songs of praise. For the Lord is a great God, a King supreme above all powers. *Mourners' Kaddish.*

On Thursdays:

This is the fifth day of the week, on which the Levites in the Temple used to recite: *Psalm 81*

For the Choirmaster, upon the *Gittith;* a psalm of Asaph.

Sing aloud to God our strength; shout for joy to the God of Jacob. Raise the chorus, sound the drum, the sweet harp and the lute. Blow the trumpet on the new moon, at the full moon for our feast day. This is a statute for Israel, an ordinance of the God of Jacob. He made it a law in Joseph, when he went forth against the land of Egypt. I heard an unfamiliar speech: 'I have removed the burden from your shoulder; your hands are relieved from the heavy basket. In trouble you called, and I saved you; I answered you from the thunder cloud; I tested you at the waters of Meribah. Hear, my people, while I warn you; O Israel, if you would only listen to me! You shall have no strange god; you shall worship no foreign god. I am the Lord your God, who brought you up from the land of Egypt; open your mouth, and I will fill it. But my people did not listen to my voice; Israel would have none of me. So I left them to their own stubbornness, that they might follow their own devices. If only my people would listen to me, if Israel would only walk in my ways! I would soon subdue their foes, and turn my hand against their oppressors. Those who hate the Lord would cringe before them, and their time would be forever. I would feed them with the finest of wheat, and with honey from the rock would I satisfy them.

Mourners' Kaddish.

בכסה ליום חגנו that is, the *Sukkoth* festival which begins on the fifteenth of *Tishri* when the moon is full.

יהוסף is a synonym for Israel, so called from the favored son of Israel. In Psalm 77:16, Jacob and Joseph are named as the fathers of the entire people of Israel.

שפת לא ידעתי ... The psalmist represents Israel as quoting the following words of God, heard for the first time after the exodus from Egypt.

מי מריבה refers to Exodus 17:7; Numbers 20:13.

הרחב פיך ... God will abundantly supply your needs as long as you are faithful to him.

משנאי ה' ... God's enemies are the enemies of his people, and he would compel them to pay homage to Israel. Israel's national existence and prosperity would know no end.

On Fridays:

הַיּוֹם יוֹם שִׁשִּׁי בַּשַּׁבָּת, שֶׁבּוֹ הָיוּ הַלְוִיִּם אוֹמְרִים בְּבֵית הַמִּקְדָּשׁ:

תהלים צג

יְיָ מָלָךְ, גֵּאוּת לָבֵשׁ; לָבֵשׁ יְיָ, עֹז הִתְאַזָּר; אַף תִּכּוֹן תֵּבֵל, בַּל תִּמּוֹט. נָכוֹן כִּסְאֲךָ מֵאָז, מֵעוֹלָם אָתָּה. נָשְׂאוּ נְהָרוֹת, יְיָ, נָשְׂאוּ נְהָרוֹת קוֹלָם, יִשְׂאוּ נְהָרוֹת דָּכְיָם. מִקֹּלוֹת מַיִם רַבִּים, אַדִּירִים מִשְׁבְּרֵי יָם, אַדִּיר בַּמָּרוֹם יְיָ. Reader עֵדֹתֶיךָ נֶאֶמְנוּ מְאֹד; לְבֵיתְךָ נַאֲוָה קֹּדֶשׁ, יְיָ, לְאֹרֶךְ יָמִים.

Mourners' Kaddish.

The following is recited daily from *Rosh Ḥodesh Elul* until *Simḥath Torah.*

תהלים כז

לְדָוִד. יְיָ אוֹרִי וְיִשְׁעִי, מִמִּי אִירָא; יְיָ מָעוֹז חַיַּי, מִמִּי אֶפְחָד. בִּקְרֹב עָלַי מְרֵעִים לֶאֱכֹל אֶת בְּשָׂרִי, צָרַי וְאֹיְבַי לִי, הֵמָּה כָּשְׁלוּ וְנָפָלוּ. אִם תַּחֲנֶה עָלַי מַחֲנֶה, לֹא יִירָא לִבִּי; אִם תָּקוּם עָלַי מִלְחָמָה, בְּזֹאת אֲנִי בוֹטֵחַ. אַחַת שָׁאַלְתִּי מֵאֵת יְיָ, אוֹתָהּ אֲבַקֵּשׁ: שִׁבְתִּי בְּבֵית יְיָ כָּל יְמֵי חַיַּי, לַחֲזוֹת בְּנֹעַם יְיָ, וּלְבַקֵּר בְּהֵיכָלוֹ. כִּי יִצְפְּנֵנִי בְּסֻכֹּה בְּיוֹם רָעָה, יַסְתִּרֵנִי בְּסֵתֶר אָהֳלוֹ; בְּצוּר יְרוֹמְמֵנִי. וְעַתָּה יָרוּם רֹאשִׁי עַל אֹיְבַי סְבִיבוֹתַי, וְאֶזְבְּחָה בְאָהֳלוֹ זִבְחֵי תְרוּעָה; אָשִׁירָה וַאֲזַמְּרָה לַיְיָ. שְׁמַע יְיָ קוֹלִי אֶקְרָא, וְחָנֵּנִי וַעֲנֵנִי. לְךָ אָמַר לִבִּי, בַּקְּשׁוּ פָנָי; אֶת פָּנֶיךָ יְיָ

נאות לבש ... The psalmist speaks of God's attributes as a glorious garment wrapped about him. God's rule reestablishes the moral order of the world. Rashi and others interpret this psalm in connection with the Messianic era.

נשאו נהרות ... God's control of the violent forces of nature is used here to represent his power over the mighty enemies of his people.

עדותיך ... God's moral laws are firmly established and unchangeable. Zion, his house, shall no longer be desecrated by heathen invaders.

ה' אורי וישעי The first part of this psalm expresses fearless confidence in the face of hostile armies, while the second part is a prayer of one in deep distress and beset by false accusers.

On Fridays:

This is the sixth day of the week, on which the Levites in the Temple used to recite: *Psalm* 93

The Lord is King; he is robed in majesty; the Lord is robed, he has girded himself with strength; thus the world is set firm and cannot be shaken. Thy throne stands firm from of old, thou art from all eternity. The floods have lifted up, O Lord, the floods have lifted up their voice; the floods lift up their mighty waves. But above the sound of many waters, mighty breakers of the sea, the Lord on high stands supreme. Thy testimonies are very sure; holiness befits thy house, O Lord, for all time.

Mourners' Kaddish.

The following is recited daily from Rosh Ḥodesh Elul until Simḥath Torah.

Psalm 27

A psalm of David. The Lord is my light and aid; whom shall I fear? The Lord is the stronghold of my life; of whom shall I be afraid? When evildoers press against me to eat up my flesh—my enemies and my foes—it is they who stumble and fall. Even though an army were arrayed against me, my heart would not fear; though war should arise against me, still would I be confident. One thing I ask from the Lord, one thing I desire—that I may dwell in the house of the Lord all the days of my life, to behold the pleasantness of the Lord, and to meditate in his sanctuary. Surely, he will hide me within his own tabernacle in the day of distress; he will conceal me in the shelter of his tent; he will set me safe upon a rock. Thus my head shall be high above all my foes around me; I will offer sacrifices within his tabernacle to the sound of trumpets; I will sing and chant praises to the Lord. Hear, O Lord, my voice when I call; be gracious to me and answer me. In thy behalf my heart has said: "Seek you my presence";

לאכל את בשרי to eat my flesh, like wild beasts of prey.

שבתי בבית ה' . . . that is, living securely under God's protection and enjoying his hospitality.

לך אמר לבי . . . The psalmist, in his heart, quotes God's command to the effect that all must seek access to his presence.

אֲבַקֵּשׁ. אַל תַּסְתֵּר פָּנֶיךָ מִמֶּנִּי, אַל תַּט בְּאַף עַבְדֶּךָ, עֶזְרָתִי
הָיִיתָ; אַל תִּטְּשֵׁנִי וְאַל תַּעַזְבֵנִי, אֱלֹהֵי יִשְׁעִי. כִּי אָבִי וְאִמִּי
עֲזָבוּנִי, וַיְיָ יַאַסְפֵנִי. הוֹרֵנִי יְיָ דַּרְכֶּךָ, וּנְחֵנִי בְּאֹרַח מִישׁוֹר, לְמַעַן
שׁוֹרְרָי. אַל תִּתְּנֵנִי בְּנֶפֶשׁ צָרָי; כִּי קָמוּ בִי עֵדֵי שֶׁקֶר וִיפֵחַ חָמָס.
לוּלֵא הֶאֱמַנְתִּי לִרְאוֹת בְּטוּב יְיָ בְּאֶרֶץ חַיִּים. Reader קַוֵּה אֶל
יְיָ, חֲזַק וְיַאֲמֵץ לִבֶּךָ, וְקַוֵּה אֶל יְיָ.

Mourners' Kaddish.

The following is recited in the house of a mourner during the week of mourning.

תהלים מט

לַמְנַצֵּחַ, לִבְנֵי קֹרַח מִזְמוֹר. שִׁמְעוּ זֹאת, כָּל הָעַמִּים; הַאֲזִינוּ,
כָּל יֹשְׁבֵי חָלֶד. גַּם בְּנֵי אָדָם, גַּם בְּנֵי אִישׁ, יַחַד עָשִׁיר וְאֶבְיוֹן.
פִּי יְדַבֵּר חָכְמוֹת, וְהָגוּת לִבִּי תְבוּנוֹת. אַטֶּה לְמָשָׁל אָזְנִי, אֶפְתַּח
בְּכִנּוֹר חִידָתִי. לָמָּה אִירָא בִּימֵי רָע, עֲוֹן עֲקֵבַי יְסוּבֵּנִי.
הַבֹּטְחִים עַל חֵילָם, וּבְרֹב עָשְׁרָם יִתְהַלָּלוּ. אָח לֹא פָדֹה יִפְדֶּה
אִישׁ, לֹא יִתֵּן לֵאלֹהִים כָּפְרוֹ. וְיֵקַר פִּדְיוֹן נַפְשָׁם, וְחָדַל
לְעוֹלָם. וִיחִי עוֹד לָנֶצַח, לֹא יִרְאֶה הַשָּׁחַת. כִּי יִרְאֶה חֲכָמִים
יָמוּתוּ, יַחַד כְּסִיל וָבַעַר יֹאבֵדוּ, וְעָזְבוּ לַאֲחֵרִים חֵילָם. קִרְבָּם
בָּתֵּימוֹ לְעוֹלָם, מִשְׁכְּנֹתָם לְדֹר וָדֹר; קָרְאוּ בִשְׁמוֹתָם עֲלֵי
אֲדָמוֹת. וְאָדָם בִּיקָר בַּל יָלִין; נִמְשַׁל כַּבְּהֵמוֹת נִדְמוּ. זֶה דַרְכָּם
כֵּסֶל לָמוֹ, וְאַחֲרֵיהֶם בְּפִיהֶם יִרְצוּ, סֶלָה. כַּצֹּאן לִשְׁאוֹל שַׁתּוּ,
מָוֶת יִרְעֵם; וַיִּרְדּוּ בָם יְשָׁרִים לַבֹּקֶר, וְצוּרָם לְבַלּוֹת שְׁאוֹל

... אבי ואמי עזבוני Though I am orphaned, friendless and deserted, God
will be father to me and protect me.

... לולא האמנתי The remainder of the sentence is left to the imagination:
"What would my condition be, if I had not believed!"

... שמעו זאת The psalmist addresses all the inhabitants of the world and
summons them to hear his parable which concerns all humanity.

חכמות moral philosophy. The rich man cannot deliver his friends or him-

thy presence, O Lord, I do seek. Hide not thy face from me; turn not thy servant away in anger; thou hast been my help; do not abandon me, forsake me not, O God my Savior. Though my father and mother have forsaken me, the Lord will take care of me. Teach me thy way, O Lord, and guide me in a straight path, in spite of my enemies. Deliver me not to the will of my adversaries; for false witnesses have risen up against me, such as breathe forth violence. I do believe I shall yet see the goodness of the Lord in the land of the living. Hope in the Lord; be strong, and let your heart be brave; yes, hope in the Lord.

Mourners' Kaddish.

The following is recited in the house of a mourner during the week of mourning.

Psalm 49

For the Choirmaster; a psalm of the Korahites. Hear this, all you peoples; listen, all you inhabitants of the world, both low and high, rich and poor alike. My mouth speaks wisdom, and my heart's meditation is deep insight. I incline my ear to a parable; I unfold my profound problem to the accompaniment of a harp.

Why should I be afraid in days of evil, when the iniquity of my foes surrounds me, those who trust in their wealth, and boast of their great riches? No man can redeem his brother [from death], nor give to God a ransom for him—for too costly is the ransom of one's soul and can never be—that he should go on living forever, that he should not see the grave. Surely, one must see that wise men die, that the stupid and senseless perish alike, and leave their wealth to others. Their inward consolation is that their houses shall continue forever, and their homes throughout all generations; they name estates after themselves. But man abides not in his splendor; he is like the beasts that perish. Such is the fate of those who trust in themselves, and the end of those who are pleased with their own mouthing. Like sheep they are destined to die; death shall shepherd them; the upright shall triumph over them in the morning; their form is to decay in the nether-world,

---

self from death, and his prosperity need cause no dismay to those who are less fortunate.

קרבם ... They delude themselves with the thought that their names will be perpetuated in the names of their estates.

מות ירעם ... death will take control of them; and in the morning, when the dark night of suffering is over, the victims of lawlessness will be triumphant over their fallen oppressors.

מִזְבֵּל לוֹ. אַךְ אֱלֹהִים יִפְדֶּה נַפְשִׁי מִיַּד שְׁאוֹל, כִּי יִקָּחֵנִי סֶלָה.

אַל תִּירָא כִּי יַעֲשִׁר אִישׁ, כִּי יִרְבֶּה כְּבוֹד בֵּיתוֹ. כִּי לֹא בְמוֹתוֹ

יִקַּח הַכֹּל, לֹא יֵרֵד אַחֲרָיו כְּבוֹדוֹ. כִּי נַפְשׁוֹ בְּחַיָּיו יְבָרֵךְ; וְיוֹדֻךָ

כִּי תֵיטִיב לָךְ. תָּבֹא עַד דּוֹר אֲבוֹתָיו, עַד נֵצַח לֹא יִרְאוּ אוֹר.

Reader אָדָם בִּיקָר וְלֹא יָבִין, נִמְשַׁל כַּבְּהֵמוֹת נִדְמוּ.

Mourners' Kaddish.

עֲשֶׂרֶת הַדִּבְּרוֹת

שמות כ, א–יז

וַיְדַבֵּר אֱלֹהִים אֵת כָּל הַדְּבָרִים הָאֵלֶּה, לֵאמֹר:

א. אָנֹכִי יְהֹוָה אֱלֹהֶיךָ, אֲשֶׁר הוֹצֵאתִיךָ מֵאֶרֶץ מִצְרַיִם, מִבֵּית עֲבָדִים.

ב. לֹא יִהְיֶה לְךָ אֱלֹהִים אֲחֵרִים עַל פָּנָי. לֹא תַעֲשֶׂה לְךָ פֶסֶל וְכָל תְּמוּנָה אֲשֶׁר בַּשָּׁמַיִם מִמַּעַל, וַאֲשֶׁר בָּאָרֶץ מִתָּחַת, וַאֲשֶׁר בַּמַּיִם מִתַּחַת לָאָרֶץ. לֹא תִשְׁתַּחֲוֶה לָהֶם וְלֹא תָעָבְדֵם, כִּי אָנֹכִי יְהֹוָה אֱלֹהֶיךָ אֵל קַנָּא, פֹּקֵד עֲוֹן אָבֹת עַל בָּנִים, עַל שִׁלֵּשִׁים וְעַל רִבֵּעִים, לְשֹׂנְאָי. וְעֹשֶׂה חֶסֶד לַאֲלָפִים, לְאֹהֲבַי וּלְשֹׁמְרֵי מִצְוֹתָי.

ג. לֹא תִשָּׂא אֶת שֵׁם יְהֹוָה אֱלֹהֶיךָ לַשָּׁוְא, כִּי לֹא יְנַקֶּה יְהֹוָה אֵת אֲשֶׁר יִשָּׂא אֶת שְׁמוֹ לַשָּׁוְא.

ד. זָכוֹר אֶת יוֹם הַשַּׁבָּת לְקַדְּשׁוֹ. שֵׁשֶׁת יָמִים תַּעֲבֹד וְעָשִׂיתָ כָּל מְלַאכְתֶּךָ. וְיוֹם הַשְּׁבִיעִי שַׁבָּת לַיהֹוָה אֱלֹהֶיךָ; לֹא תַעֲשֶׂה כָל מְלָאכָה, אַתָּה וּבִנְךָ וּבִתֶּךָ, עַבְדְּךָ וַאֲמָתְךָ וּבְהֶמְתֶּךָ, וְגֵרְךָ

אך ... יפדה נפשי The psalmist is confident that God will deliver him from the premature death of the wicked and will receive him under his divine protection.

עשרת הדברות, the Ten Commandments, were recited in the Temple daily

its habitation. However, God will release me from the grasp of death, for he will receive me. So fear not when a man grows rich, when the splendor of his house increases; for he will take nothing with him when he dies; his wealth will not follow him below. Though while he lives he flatters himself [saying]: "Men acclaim you when you do well for yourself," he will join the generation of his fathers, who will never see the light. The man who lives in splendor and understands not is like the beasts that perish.

Mourners' Kaddish.

THE TEN COMMANDMENTS

Exodus 20:1–17

God spoke all these words, saying:

1.   I am the Lord your God, who brought you out of the land of Egypt, out of the house of slavery.

2.   You shall have no other gods beside me. You shall not make for yourself any idols in the shape of anything that is in heaven above, or that is on the earth below, or that is in the water under the earth. You shall not bow down to them nor worship them; for I, the Lord your God, am a zealous God, punishing children for the sins of their fathers, down to the third or fourth generation of those who hate me, but showing kindness to the thousandth generation of those who love me and keep my commandments.

3.   You shall not utter the name of the Lord your God in vain; for the Lord will not hold guiltless anyone who utters his name in vain.

4.   Remember the Sabbath day to keep it holy. Six days you shall labor and do all your work; but on the seventh day, which is a day of rest in honor of the Lord your God, you shall not do any work, neither you, nor your son, nor your daughter, nor your male or female servant, nor your cattle, nor the stranger who is

---

before the *Shema*. On account of the heretics, however, who asserted that only the Ten Commandments were divinely given, this custom was abolished outside Palestine (Berakhoth 12a).

... לשנאי The penalty of man's sins will be shared by his immediate descendants only if they too hate the ways of God; but the benefits of a man's good deeds will extend indefinitely.

אֲשֶׁר בִּשְׁעָרֶיךָ. כִּי שֵׁשֶׁת יָמִים עָשָׂה יְהֹוָה אֶת הַשָּׁמַיִם וְאֶת
הָאָרֶץ, אֶת הַיָּם, וְאֶת כָּל אֲשֶׁר בָּם, וַיָּנַח בַּיּוֹם הַשְּׁבִיעִי; עַל
כֵּן בֵּרַךְ יְהֹוָה אֶת יוֹם הַשַּׁבָּת וַיְקַדְּשֵׁהוּ.

ה. כַּבֵּד אֶת אָבִיךָ וְאֶת אִמֶּךָ, לְמַעַן יַאֲרִכוּן יָמֶיךָ עַל
הָאֲדָמָה אֲשֶׁר יְהֹוָה אֱלֹהֶיךָ נֹתֵן לָךְ.

ו. לֹא תִּרְצָח.

ז. לֹא תִּנְאָף.

ח. לֹא תִּגְנֹב.

ט. לֹא תַעֲנֶה בְרֵעֲךָ עֵד שָׁקֶר.

י. לֹא תַחְמֹד בֵּית רֵעֶךָ; לֹא תַחְמֹד אֵשֶׁת רֵעֶךָ, וְעַבְדּוֹ
וַאֲמָתוֹ וְשׁוֹרוֹ וַחֲמֹרוֹ, וְכֹל אֲשֶׁר לְרֵעֶךָ.

שְׁלֹשָׁה עָשָׂר עִקָּרִים

א. אֲנִי מַאֲמִין בֶּאֱמוּנָה שְׁלֵמָה שֶׁהַבּוֹרֵא, יִתְבָּרַךְ שְׁמוֹ, הוּא
בּוֹרֵא וּמַנְהִיג לְכָל הַבְּרוּאִים, וְהוּא לְבַדּוֹ עָשָׂה וְעוֹשֶׂה וְיַעֲשֶׂה
לְכָל הַמַּעֲשִׂים.

ב. אֲנִי מַאֲמִין בֶּאֱמוּנָה שְׁלֵמָה שֶׁהַבּוֹרֵא, יִתְבָּרַךְ שְׁמוֹ, הוּא
יָחִיד, וְאֵין יְחִידוּת כָּמוֹהוּ בְּשׁוּם פָּנִים, וְהוּא לְבַדּוֹ אֱלֹהֵינוּ,
הָיָה, הֹוֶה, וְיִהְיֶה.

ג. אֲנִי מַאֲמִין בֶּאֱמוּנָה שְׁלֵמָה שֶׁהַבּוֹרֵא, יִתְבָּרַךְ שְׁמוֹ, אֵינוֹ
גוּף, וְלֹא יַשִּׂיגוּהוּ מַשִּׂיגֵי הַגּוּף, וְאֵין לוֹ שׁוּם דִּמְיוֹן כְּלָל.

ד. אֲנִי מַאֲמִין בֶּאֱמוּנָה שְׁלֵמָה שֶׁהַבּוֹרֵא, יִתְבָּרַךְ שְׁמוֹ, הוּא
רִאשׁוֹן וְהוּא אַחֲרוֹן.

כבד ... The last six commandments are intended to safeguard a man's
life, domestic relations, property, and reputation.

within your gates; for in six days the Lord made the heavens, the earth, the sea, and all that they contain, and rested on the seventh day; therefore the Lord blessed the Sabbath day and hallowed it.

5. Honor your father and your mother, that you may live long in the land which the Lord your God is giving you.

6. You shall not murder.

7. You shall not commit adultery.

8. You shall not steal.

9. You shall not testify falsely against your neighbor.

10. You shall not covet your neighbor's house; you shall not covet your neighbor's wife, nor his servant, male or female, nor his ox, nor his ass, nor anything that belongs to your neighbor.

THIRTEEN PRINCIPLES OF FAITH

1. I firmly believe that the Creator, blessed be his name, is the Creator and Ruler of all created beings, and that he alone has made, does make, and ever will make all things.

2. I firmly believe that the Creator, blessed be his name, is One; that there is no oneness in any form like his; and that he alone was, is, and ever will be our God.

3. I firmly believe that the Creator, blessed be his name, is not corporeal; that no bodily accidents apply to him; and that there exists nothing whatever that resembles him.

4. I firmly believe that the Creator, blessed be his name, was the first and will be the last.

אני מאמין, like the poem *Yigdal*, is based on the Thirteen Principles in which Moses Maimonides (1135–1204) sums up his Jewish philosophy, namely: 1) There is a Creator. 2) He is One. 3) He is incorporeal. 4) He is eternal. 5) He alone must be worshiped. 6) The prophets are true. 7) Moses was the greatest of all prophets. 8) The entire Torah was divinely given to Moses. 9) The Torah is immutable. 10) God knows all the acts and thoughts of man. 11) He rewards and punishes. 12) Messiah will come. 13) There will be resurrection.

ה. אֲנִי מַאֲמִין בֶּאֱמוּנָה שְׁלֵמָה שֶׁהַבּוֹרֵא, יִתְבָּרַךְ שְׁמוֹ, לוֹ
לְבַדּוֹ רָאוּי לְהִתְפַּלֵּל, וְאֵין רָאוּי לְהִתְפַּלֵּל לְזוּלָתוֹ.

ו. אֲנִי מַאֲמִין בֶּאֱמוּנָה שְׁלֵמָה שֶׁכָּל דִּבְרֵי נְבִיאִים אֱמֶת.

ז. אֲנִי מַאֲמִין בֶּאֱמוּנָה שְׁלֵמָה שֶׁנְּבוּאַת מֹשֶׁה רַבֵּנוּ, עָלָיו
הַשָּׁלוֹם, הָיְתָה אֲמִתִּית, וְשֶׁהוּא הָיָה אָב לַנְּבִיאִים, לַקּוֹדְמִים
לְפָנָיו וְלַבָּאִים אַחֲרָיו.

ח. אֲנִי מַאֲמִין בֶּאֱמוּנָה שְׁלֵמָה שֶׁכָּל הַתּוֹרָה הַמְּצוּיָה עַתָּה
בְּיָדֵינוּ, הִיא הַנְּתוּנָה לְמֹשֶׁה רַבֵּנוּ, עָלָיו הַשָּׁלוֹם.

ט. אֲנִי מַאֲמִין בֶּאֱמוּנָה שְׁלֵמָה שֶׁזֹּאת הַתּוֹרָה לֹא תְהִי
מֻחֲלֶפֶת, וְלֹא תְהִי תּוֹרָה אַחֶרֶת מֵאֵת הַבּוֹרֵא, יִתְבָּרַךְ שְׁמוֹ.

י. אֲנִי מַאֲמִין בֶּאֱמוּנָה שְׁלֵמָה שֶׁהַבּוֹרֵא, יִתְבָּרַךְ שְׁמוֹ, יוֹדֵעַ
כָּל מַעֲשֵׂה בְנֵי אָדָם וְכָל מַחְשְׁבוֹתָם, שֶׁנֶּאֱמַר: הַיֹּצֵר יַחַד לִבָּם,
הַמֵּבִין אֶל כָּל מַעֲשֵׂיהֶם.

יא. אֲנִי מַאֲמִין בֶּאֱמוּנָה שְׁלֵמָה שֶׁהַבּוֹרֵא, יִתְבָּרַךְ שְׁמוֹ,
גּוֹמֵל טוֹב לְשׁוֹמְרֵי מִצְוֹתָיו, וּמַעֲנִישׁ לְעוֹבְרֵי מִצְוֹתָיו.

יב. אֲנִי מַאֲמִין בֶּאֱמוּנָה שְׁלֵמָה בְּבִיאַת הַמָּשִׁיחַ; וְאַף עַל פִּי
שֶׁיִּתְמַהְמֵהַּ, עִם כָּל זֶה אֲחַכֶּה לוֹ בְּכָל יוֹם שֶׁיָּבֹא.

יג. אֲנִי מַאֲמִין בֶּאֱמוּנָה שְׁלֵמָה שֶׁתִּהְיֶה תְּחִיַּת הַמֵּתִים בְּעֵת
שֶׁיַּעֲלֶה רָצוֹן מֵאֵת הַבּוֹרֵא, יִתְבָּרַךְ שְׁמוֹ וְיִתְעַלֶּה זִכְרוֹ לָעַד
וּלְנֵצַח נְצָחִים.

לִישׁוּעָתְךָ קִוִּיתִי, יְיָ. קִוִּיתִי, יְיָ, לִישׁוּעָתְךָ. יְיָ, לִישׁוּעָתְךָ
קִוִּיתִי.

לְפֻרְקָנָךְ סַבְּרִית, יְיָ. סַבְּרִית, יְיָ, לְפֻרְקָנָךְ. יְיָ, לְפֻרְקָנָךְ
סַבְּרִית.

5. I firmly believe that the Creator, blessed be his name, is the only one to whom it is proper to address our prayers, and that we must not pray to anyone else.

6. I firmly believe that all the words of the Prophets are true.

7. I firmly believe that the prophecy of Moses our teacher, may he rest in peace, was true; and that he was the chief of the prophets, both of those who preceded and of those that followed him.

8. I firmly believe that the whole Torah which we now possess is the same which was given to Moses our teacher, may he rest in peace.

9. I firmly believe that this Torah will not be changed, and that there will be no other Torah given by the Creator, blessed be his name.

10. I firmly believe that the Creator, blessed be his name, knows all the actions and thoughts of human beings, as it is said: "It is he who fashions the hearts of them all, he who notes all their deeds."[1]

11. I firmly believe that the Creator, blessed be his name, rewards those who keep his commands, and punishes those who transgress his commands.

12. I firmly believe in the coming of Messiah; and although he may tarry, I daily wait for his coming.

13. I firmly believe that there will be a revival of the dead at a time which will please the Creator, blessed and exalted be his name forever and ever.

For thy salvation I hope, O Lord.[2] I hope, O Lord, for thy salvation. O Lord, for thy salvation I hope.

לפרקנך סברית is the Targum paraphrase of the preceding verse.

[1] *Psalm* 33:15.   [2] *Genesis* 49:18.

תְּפִלַּת מִנְחָה

אַשְׁרֵי יוֹשְׁבֵי בֵיתֶךָ; עוֹד יְהַלְלוּךָ סֶּלָה.

אַשְׁרֵי הָעָם שֶׁכָּכָה לּוֹ; אַשְׁרֵי הָעָם שֶׁיְיָ אֱלֹהָיו.

תהלים קמה

תְּהִלָּה לְדָוִד

אֲרוֹמִמְךָ, אֱלֹהַי הַמֶּלֶךְ, וַאֲבָרְכָה שִׁמְךָ לְעוֹלָם וָעֶד.

בְּכָל יוֹם אֲבָרְכֶךָ, וַאֲהַלְלָה שִׁמְךָ לְעוֹלָם וָעֶד.

גָּדוֹל יְיָ וּמְהֻלָּל מְאֹד, וְלִגְדֻלָּתוֹ אֵין חֵקֶר.

דּוֹר לְדוֹר יְשַׁבַּח מַעֲשֶׂיךָ, וּגְבוּרֹתֶיךָ יַגִּידוּ.

הֲדַר כְּבוֹד הוֹדֶךָ וְדִבְרֵי נִפְלְאֹתֶיךָ אָשִׂיחָה.

וֶעֱזוּז נוֹרְאֹתֶיךָ יֹאמֵרוּ, וּגְדֻלָּתְךָ אֲסַפְּרֶנָּה.

זֵכֶר רַב טוּבְךָ יַבִּיעוּ, וְצִדְקָתְךָ יְרַנֵּנוּ.

חַנּוּן וְרַחוּם יְיָ, אֶרֶךְ אַפַּיִם וּגְדָל־חָסֶד.

טוֹב יְיָ לַכֹּל, וְרַחֲמָיו עַל כָּל מַעֲשָׂיו.

יוֹדוּךָ יְיָ כָּל מַעֲשֶׂיךָ, וַחֲסִידֶיךָ יְבָרְכוּכָה.

כְּבוֹד מַלְכוּתְךָ יֹאמֵרוּ, וּגְבוּרָתְךָ יְדַבֵּרוּ.

לְהוֹדִיעַ לִבְנֵי הָאָדָם גְּבוּרֹתָיו, וּכְבוֹד הֲדַר מַלְכוּתוֹ.

מַלְכוּתְךָ מַלְכוּת כָּל עֹלָמִים, וּמֶמְשַׁלְתְּךָ בְּכָל דּוֹר וָדֹר.

מנחה occurs in the Bible frequently in the sense of "gift" and "meal-offering." It is only in talmudic literature that *Minḥah* denotes afternoon service. *Minḥah* is one of the three daily services mentioned in Daniel 6:11 ("and three times a day he kneeled upon his knees, praying and giving thanks before his God"). According to tradition, the patriarchs Abraham, Isaac and Jacob were the authors of the three daily services. Both *Shaḥarith* and *Minḥah* correspond to the daily sacrifice (*Tamid*) which was offered in the Temple in the morning and in the afternoon. Since the recital of the *Shema* is obligatory only "when you lie down and when you rise up," it is not included in the

AFTERNOON SERVICE

Happy are those who dwell in thy house; they are ever praising thee. Happy the people that is so situated; happy the people whose God is the Lord.[1] *Psalm 145*

A hymn of praise by David.
I extol thee, my God the King,
And bless thy name forever and ever.
Every day I bless thee,
And praise thy name forever and ever.
Great is the Lord and most worthy of praise;
His greatness is unsearchable.
One generation to another praises thy works;
They recount thy mighty acts.
On the splendor of thy glorious majesty
And on thy wondrous deeds I meditate.
They speak of thy awe-inspiring might,
And I tell of thy greatness.
They spread the fame of thy great goodness,
And sing of thy righteousness.
Gracious and merciful is the Lord,
Slow to anger and of great kindness.
The Lord is good to all,
And his mercy is over all his works.
All thy works praise thee, O Lord,
And thy faithful followers bless thee.
They speak of thy glorious kingdom,
And talk of thy might,
To let men know thy mighty deeds,
And the glorious splendor of thy kingdom.
Thy kingdom is a kingdom of all ages,
And thy dominion is for all generations.

---

afternoon service. *Minḥah* may be recited at any time from noon (12:30) to sunset. The *Minḥah* service was postponed in the nineteenth century to very near sunset for the sake of convenience, so that *Minḥah* might be followed by *Ma'ariv* after a short interval.

On אשרי, see pages 57–59.

[1] *Psalms* 84:5; 144:15.

158

סוֹמֵךְ יְיָ לְכָל הַנֹּפְלִים, וְזוֹקֵף לְכָל הַכְּפוּפִים.

עֵינֵי כֹל אֵלֶיךָ יְשַׂבֵּרוּ, וְאַתָּה נוֹתֵן לָהֶם אֶת אָכְלָם בְּעִתּוֹ.

פּוֹתֵחַ אֶת יָדֶךָ, וּמַשְׂבִּיעַ לְכָל חַי רָצוֹן.

צַדִּיק יְיָ בְּכָל דְּרָכָיו, וְחָסִיד בְּכָל מַעֲשָׂיו.

קָרוֹב יְיָ לְכָל קֹרְאָיו, לְכֹל אֲשֶׁר יִקְרָאֻהוּ בֶאֱמֶת.

רְצוֹן יְרֵאָיו יַעֲשֶׂה, וְאֶת שַׁוְעָתָם יִשְׁמַע וְיוֹשִׁיעֵם.

שׁוֹמֵר יְיָ אֶת כָּל אֹהֲבָיו, וְאֵת כָּל הָרְשָׁעִים יַשְׁמִיד.

תְּהִלַּת יְיָ יְדַבֶּר־פִּי; וִיבָרֵךְ כָּל בָּשָׂר שֵׁם קָדְשׁוֹ לְעוֹלָם וָעֶד.

Reader וַאֲנַחְנוּ נְבָרֵךְ יָהּ מֵעַתָּה וְעַד עוֹלָם; הַלְלוּיָהּ.

Reader:

יִתְגַּדַּל וְיִתְקַדַּשׁ שְׁמֵהּ רַבָּא בְּעָלְמָא דִי בְרָא כִרְעוּתֵהּ;
וְיַמְלִיךְ מַלְכוּתֵהּ בְּחַיֵּיכוֹן וּבְיוֹמֵיכוֹן, וּבְחַיֵּי דְכָל בֵּית יִשְׂרָאֵל,
בַּעֲגָלָא וּבִזְמַן קָרִיב, וְאִמְרוּ אָמֵן.

יְהֵא שְׁמֵהּ רַבָּא מְבָרַךְ לְעָלַם וּלְעָלְמֵי עָלְמַיָּא.

יִתְבָּרַךְ וְיִשְׁתַּבַּח, וְיִתְפָּאַר וְיִתְרוֹמַם, וְיִתְנַשֵּׂא וְיִתְהַדָּר,
וְיִתְעַלֶּה וְיִתְהַלָּל שְׁמֵהּ דְּקֻדְשָׁא, בְּרִיךְ הוּא, לְעֵלָּא (לְעֵלָּא)
מִן כָּל בִּרְכָתָא וְשִׁירָתָא, תֻּשְׁבְּחָתָא וְנֶחֱמָתָא, דַּאֲמִירָן בְּעָלְמָא,
וְאִמְרוּ אָמֵן.

The *Shemoneh Esreh* is recited in silent devotion while standing, facing east.
The Reader repeats the *Shemoneh Esreh* aloud when a *minyan* holds service.

כִּי שֵׁם יְיָ אֶקְרָא, הָבוּ גֹדֶל לֵאלֹהֵינוּ.

אֲדֹנָי, שְׂפָתַי תִּפְתָּח, וּפִי יַגִּיד תְּהִלָּתֶךָ.

בָּרוּךְ אַתָּה, יְיָ אֱלֹהֵינוּ וֵאלֹהֵי אֲבוֹתֵינוּ, אֱלֹהֵי אַבְרָהָם,

On fast days the Torah is taken out before the *Shemoneh Esreh* is recited, and Exodus 32:11–14 and 34:1–10 is read (if ten people fasting are
present). The Torah reading is followed by the *Haftarah* taken from Isaiah
55:6–56:8.

The Lord upholds all who fall,
And raises all who are bowed down.
The eyes of all look hopefully to thee,
And thou givest them their food in due season.
Thou openest thy hand,
And satisfiest every living thing with favor.
The Lord is righteous in all his ways,
And gracious in all his deeds.
The Lord is near to all who call upon him,
To all who call upon him sincerely.
He fulfills the desire of those who revere him;
He hears their cry and saves them.
The Lord preserves all who love him,
But all the wicked he destroys.
My mouth speaks the praise of the Lord;
Let all creatures bless his holy name forever and ever.
¹We will bless the Lord henceforth and forever.
Praise the Lord!

Reader:

Glorified and sanctified be God's great name throughout the world which he has created according to his will. May he establish his kingdom in your lifetime and during your days, and within the life of the entire house of Israel, speedily and soon; and say, Amen.

May his great name be blessed forever and to all eternity.

Blessed and praised, glorified and exalted, extolled and honored, adored and lauded be the name of the Holy One, blessed be he, beyond all the blessings and hymns, praises and consolations that are ever spoken in the world; and say, Amen.

SHEMONEH ESREH

The Shemoneh Esreh is recited in silent devotion while standing, facing east.
The Reader repeats the Shemoneh Esreh aloud when a minyan holds service.

When I proclaim the name of the Lord, give glory to our God!²
O Lord, open thou my lips, that my mouth may declare thy praise.³

Blessed art thou, Lord our God and God of our fathers, God

כי שם precedes the *Amidahs* of *Musaf* and *Minḥah* only. In *Shaḥarith* and *Ma'ariv* this verse is omitted, because there it would interrupt the connection between the benediction גאל ישראל and the *Amidah*.

---

¹*Psalm* 115:18.   ²*Deuteronomy* 32:3.   ³*Psalm* 51:17.

אֱלֹהֵי יִצְחָק, וֵאלֹהֵי יַעֲקֹב, הָאֵל הַגָּדוֹל הַגִּבּוֹר וְהַנּוֹרָא, אֵל
עֶלְיוֹן, גּוֹמֵל חֲסָדִים טוֹבִים, וְקוֹנֵה הַכֹּל, וְזוֹכֵר חַסְדֵי אָבוֹת,
וּמֵבִיא גוֹאֵל לִבְנֵי בְנֵיהֶם לְמַעַן שְׁמוֹ בְּאַהֲבָה.

Between *Rosh Hashanah* and *Yom Kippur* add:

(זָכְרֵנוּ לְחַיִּים, מֶלֶךְ חָפֵץ בַּחַיִּים,
וְכָתְבֵנוּ בְּסֵפֶר הַחַיִּים, לְמַעַנְךָ אֱלֹהִים חַיִּים.)

מֶלֶךְ עוֹזֵר וּמוֹשִׁיעַ וּמָגֵן. בָּרוּךְ אַתָּה, יְיָ, מָגֵן אַבְרָהָם.

אַתָּה גִבּוֹר לְעוֹלָם, אֲדֹנָי; מְחַיֵּה מֵתִים אַתָּה, רַב לְהוֹשִׁיעַ.

Between *Sukkoth* and *Pesaḥ* add:

(מַשִּׁיב הָרוּחַ וּמוֹרִיד הַגֶּשֶׁם.)

מְכַלְכֵּל חַיִּים בְּחֶסֶד, מְחַיֵּה מֵתִים בְּרַחֲמִים רַבִּים, סוֹמֵךְ
נוֹפְלִים, וְרוֹפֵא חוֹלִים, וּמַתִּיר אֲסוּרִים, וּמְקַיֵּם אֱמוּנָתוֹ לִישֵׁנֵי
עָפָר. מִי כָמוֹךָ, בַּעַל גְּבוּרוֹת, וּמִי דוֹמֶה לָךְ, מֶלֶךְ מֵמִית
וּמְחַיֶּה וּמַצְמִיחַ יְשׁוּעָה.

Between *Rosh Hashanah* and *Yom Kippur* add:

(מִי כָמוֹךָ, אַב הָרַחֲמִים,
זוֹכֵר יְצוּרָיו לְחַיִּים בְּרַחֲמִים.)

וְנֶאֱמָן אַתָּה לְהַחֲיוֹת מֵתִים. בָּרוּךְ אַתָּה, יְיָ, מְחַיֵּה הַמֵּתִים.

When the Reader repeats the *Shemoneh Esreh,* the following *Kedushah* is said.

נְקַדֵּשׁ אֶת שִׁמְךָ בָּעוֹלָם כְּשֵׁם שֶׁמַּקְדִּישִׁים אוֹתוֹ בִּשְׁמֵי מָרוֹם,
כַּכָּתוּב עַל יַד נְבִיאֶךָ: וְקָרָא זֶה אֶל זֶה וְאָמַר:
קָדוֹשׁ, קָדוֹשׁ, קָדוֹשׁ יְיָ צְבָאוֹת; מְלֹא כָל הָאָרֶץ כְּבוֹדוֹ.
Reader —לְעֻמָּתָם בָּרוּךְ יֹאמֵרוּ
בָּרוּךְ כְּבוֹד יְיָ מִמְּקוֹמוֹ.
Reader וּבְדִבְרֵי קָדְשְׁךָ כָּתוּב לֵאמֹר:
יִמְלֹךְ יְיָ לְעוֹלָם, אֱלֹהַיִךְ צִיּוֹן לְדֹר וָדֹר; הַלְלוּיָהּ.

of Abraham, God of Isaac and God of Jacob; great, mighty and revered God, sublime God, who bestowest lovingkindness, and art Master of all things; who rememberest the good deeds of our fathers, and who wilt graciously bring a redeemer to their children's children for the sake of thy name.

Between Rosh Hashanah and Yom Kippur add:

(Remember us to life, O King who delightest in life; inscribe us in the book of life for thy sake, O living God.)

O King, Supporter, Savior and Shield. Blessed art thou, O Lord, Shield of Abraham.

Thou, O Lord, art mighty forever; thou revivest the dead; thou art powerful to save.

Between Sukkoth and Pesaḥ add:

(Thou causest the wind to blow and the rain to fall.)

Thou sustainest the living with kindness, and revivest the dead with great mercy; thou supportest all who fall, and healest the sick; thou settest the captives free, and keepest faith with those who sleep in the dust. Who is like thee, Lord of power? Who resembles thee, O King? Thou bringest death and restorest life, and causest salvation to flourish.

Between Rosh Hashanah and Yom Kippur add:

(Who is like thee, merciful Father? In mercy thou rememberest thy creatures to life.)

Thou art faithful to revive the dead. Blessed art thou, O Lord, who revivest the dead.

KEDUSHAH

When the Reader repeats the Shemoneh Esreh, the following Kedushah is said.

We sanctify thy name in this world even as they sanctify it in the highest heavens, as it is written by thy prophet: "They keep calling to one another:

> Holy, holy, holy is the Lord of hosts;
> The whole earth is full of his glory."[1]

Those opposite them say: Blessed—
Blessed be the glory of the Lord from his abode.[2]
And in thy holy Scriptures it is written:

> The Lord shall reign forever,
> Your God, O Zion, for all generations.
> Praise the Lord![3]

---

[1] *Isaiah* 6:3.   [2] *Ezekiel* 3:12.   [3] *Psalm* 146:10.

Reader לְדוֹר וָדוֹר נַגִּיד גָּדְלֶךָ, וּלְנֵצַח נְצָחִים קְדֻשָּׁתְךָ
נַקְדִּישׁ, וְשִׁבְחֲךָ אֱלֹהֵינוּ מִפִּינוּ לֹא יָמוּשׁ לְעוֹלָם וָעֶד, כִּי אֵל
מֶלֶךְ גָּדוֹל וְקָדוֹשׁ אָתָּה. * בָּרוּךְ אַתָּה, יְיָ, הָאֵל הַקָּדוֹשׁ.

*Between *Rosh Hashanah* and *Yom Kippur* substitute:

(בָּרוּךְ אַתָּה, יְיָ, הַמֶּלֶךְ הַקָּדוֹשׁ.)

───────

אַתָּה קָדוֹשׁ וְשִׁמְךָ קָדוֹשׁ, וּקְדוֹשִׁים בְּכָל יוֹם יְהַלְלוּךָ סֶּלָה.
*בָּרוּךְ אַתָּה, יְיָ, הָאֵל הַקָּדוֹשׁ.

*Between *Rosh Hashanah* and *Yom Kippur* substitute:

(בָּרוּךְ אַתָּה, יְיָ, הַמֶּלֶךְ הַקָּדוֹשׁ.)

אַתָּה חוֹנֵן לְאָדָם דַּעַת, וּמְלַמֵּד לֶאֱנוֹשׁ בִּינָה. חָנֵּנוּ מֵאִתְּךָ
דֵּעָה, בִּינָה וְהַשְׂכֵּל. בָּרוּךְ אַתָּה, יְיָ, חוֹנֵן הַדָּעַת.

הֲשִׁיבֵנוּ אָבִינוּ לְתוֹרָתֶךָ, וְקָרְבֵנוּ מַלְכֵּנוּ לַעֲבוֹדָתֶךָ;
וְהַחֲזִירֵנוּ בִּתְשׁוּבָה שְׁלֵמָה לְפָנֶיךָ. בָּרוּךְ אַתָּה, יְיָ, הָרוֹצֶה
בִּתְשׁוּבָה.

סְלַח לָנוּ אָבִינוּ כִּי חָטָאנוּ, מְחַל לָנוּ מַלְכֵּנוּ כִּי פָשָׁעְנוּ,
כִּי מוֹחֵל וְסוֹלֵחַ אָתָּה. בָּרוּךְ אַתָּה, יְיָ, חַנּוּן הַמַּרְבֶּה לִסְלֹחַ.
רְאֵה נָא בְעָנְיֵנוּ וְרִיבָה רִיבֵנוּ, וּגְאָלֵנוּ מְהֵרָה לְמַעַן שְׁמֶךָ,
כִּי גוֹאֵל חָזָק אָתָּה. בָּרוּךְ אַתָּה, יְיָ, גּוֹאֵל יִשְׂרָאֵל.

On fast days the Reader adds here:

(עֲנֵנוּ, יְיָ, עֲנֵנוּ בְּיוֹם צוֹם תַּעֲנִיתֵנוּ, כִּי בְצָרָה גְדוֹלָה אֲנָחְנוּ. אַל תֵּפֶן אֶל רִשְׁעֵנוּ,
וְאַל תַּסְתֵּר פָּנֶיךָ מִמֶּנּוּ, וְאַל תִּתְעַלַּם מִתְּחִנָּתֵנוּ. הֱיֵה נָא קָרוֹב לְשַׁוְעָתֵנוּ, יְהִי נָא
חַסְדְּךָ לְנַחֲמֵנוּ; טֶרֶם נִקְרָא אֵלֶיךָ עֲנֵנוּ, כַּדָּבָר שֶׁנֶּאֱמַר: וְהָיָה טֶרֶם יִקְרָאוּ, וַאֲנִי
אֶעֱנֶה; עוֹד הֵם מְדַבְּרִים, וַאֲנִי אֶשְׁמָע. כִּי אַתָּה, יְיָ, הָעוֹנֶה בְּעֵת צָרָה, פּוֹדֶה וּמַצִּיל
בְּכָל עֵת צָרָה וְצוּקָה. בָּרוּךְ אַתָּה, יְיָ, הָעוֹנֶה בְּעֵת צָרָה.)

רְפָאֵנוּ יְיָ וְנֵרָפֵא, הוֹשִׁיעֵנוּ וְנִוָּשֵׁעָה, כִּי תְהִלָּתֵנוּ אָתָּה;
וְהַעֲלֵה רְפוּאָה שְׁלֵמָה לְכָל מַכּוֹתֵינוּ, כִּי אֵל מֶלֶךְ רוֹפֵא

Reader:

Through all generations we will declare thy greatness; to all eternity we will proclaim thy holiness; thy praise, our God, shall never depart from our mouth, for thou art a great and holy God and King. * Blessed art thou, O Lord, holy God.

Between Rosh Hashanah and Yom Kippur substitute:
(Blessed art thou, O Lord, holy King.)

Thou art holy and thy name is holy, and holy beings praise thee daily. * Blessed art thou, O Lord, holy God.

Between Rosh Hashanah and Yom Kippur substitute:
(Blessed art thou, O Lord, holy King.)

Thou favorest man with knowledge, and teachest mortals understanding. O grant us knowledge, understanding and insight. Blessed art thou, O Lord, gracious Giver of knowledge.

Restore us, our Father, to thy Torah; draw us near, our King, to thy service; cause us to return to thee in perfect repentance. Blessed art thou, O Lord, who art pleased with repentance.

Forgive us, our Father, for we have sinned; pardon us, our King, for we have transgressed; for thou dost pardon and forgive. Blessed art thou, O Lord, who art gracious and ever forgiving.

Look upon our affliction and champion our cause; redeem us speedily for thy name's sake, for thou art a mighty Redeemer. Blessed art thou, O Lord, Redeemer of Israel.

On fast days the Reader adds here:

(Answer us, O Lord, answer us on the day of our fast, for we are in great distress. Regard not our wickedness; conceal not thy presence from us, and hide not thyself from our supplication. Be near to our cry, and let thy kindness comfort us; even before we call to thee answer us, as it is said: "Before they call, I will answer; while they are yet speaking, I will hear."[1] For thou, O Lord, art he who answers in time of trouble, who redeems and delivers in all times of woe and stress. Blessed art thou, O Lord, who answerest in time of distress.)

Heal us, O Lord, and we shall be healed; save us and we shall be saved; for thou art our praise. Grant a perfect healing to all our wounds; for thou art a faithful and merciful God, King and

---

[1] *Isaiah* 65:24.

נֶאֱמָן וְרַחֲמָן אָתָּה. בָּרוּךְ אַתָּה, יְיָ, רוֹפֵא חוֹלֵי עַמּוֹ יִשְׂרָאֵל.

בָּרֵךְ עָלֵינוּ, יְיָ אֱלֹהֵינוּ, אֶת הַשָּׁנָה הַזֹּאת וְאֶת כָּל מִינֵי תְבוּאָתָהּ לְטוֹבָה,

From December 4th till *Pesaḥ* say:	From *Pesaḥ* till December 4th say:
וְתֵן טַל וּמָטָר לִבְרָכָה	וְתֵן בְּרָכָה

עַל פְּנֵי הָאֲדָמָה, וְשַׂבְּעֵנוּ מִטּוּבֶךָ, וּבָרֵךְ שְׁנָתֵנוּ כַּשָּׁנִים הַטּוֹבוֹת. בָּרוּךְ אַתָּה, יְיָ, מְבָרֵךְ הַשָּׁנִים.

תְּקַע בְּשׁוֹפָר גָּדוֹל לְחֵרוּתֵנוּ, וְשָׂא נֵס לְקַבֵּץ גָּלֻיּוֹתֵינוּ, וְקַבְּצֵנוּ יַחַד מֵאַרְבַּע כַּנְפוֹת הָאָרֶץ. בָּרוּךְ אַתָּה, יְיָ, מְקַבֵּץ נִדְחֵי עַמּוֹ יִשְׂרָאֵל.

הָשִׁיבָה שׁוֹפְטֵינוּ כְּבָרִאשׁוֹנָה, וְיוֹעֲצֵינוּ כְּבַתְּחִלָּה; וְהָסֵר מִמֶּנּוּ יָגוֹן וַאֲנָחָה; וּמְלוֹךְ עָלֵינוּ, אַתָּה יְיָ לְבַדְּךָ, בְּחֶסֶד וּבְרַחֲמִים, וְצַדְּקֵנוּ בַּמִּשְׁפָּט. * בָּרוּךְ אַתָּה, יְיָ, מֶלֶךְ אוֹהֵב צְדָקָה וּמִשְׁפָּט.

*Between *Rosh Hashanah* and *Yom Kippur* substitute:
(בָּרוּךְ אַתָּה, יְיָ, הַמֶּלֶךְ הַמִּשְׁפָּט.)

וְלַמַּלְשִׁינִים אַל תְּהִי תִקְוָה, וְכָל הָרִשְׁעָה כְּרֶגַע תֹּאבֵד, וְכָל אֹיְבֶיךָ מְהֵרָה יִכָּרֵתוּ; וְהַזֵּדִים מְהֵרָה תְעַקֵּר וּתְשַׁבֵּר וּתְמַגֵּר וְתַכְנִיעַ בִּמְהֵרָה בְיָמֵינוּ. בָּרוּךְ אַתָּה, יְיָ, שׁוֹבֵר אֹיְבִים וּמַכְנִיעַ זֵדִים.

עַל הַצַּדִּיקִים וְעַל הַחֲסִידִים, וְעַל זִקְנֵי עַמְּךָ בֵּית יִשְׂרָאֵל וְעַל פְּלֵיטַת סוֹפְרֵיהֶם, וְעַל גֵּרֵי הַצֶּדֶק וְעָלֵינוּ, יֶהֱמוּ נָא רַחֲמֶיךָ, יְיָ אֱלֹהֵינוּ; וְתֵן שָׂכָר טוֹב לְכָל הַבּוֹטְחִים בְּשִׁמְךָ בֶּאֱמֶת, וְשִׂים חֶלְקֵנוּ עִמָּהֶם, וּלְעוֹלָם לֹא נֵבוֹשׁ, כִּי בְךָ בָּטָחְנוּ. בָּרוּךְ אַתָּה, יְיָ, מִשְׁעָן וּמִבְטָח לַצַּדִּיקִים.

Healer. Blessed art thou, O Lord, who healest the sick among thy people Israel.

Bless for us, Lord our God, this year and all kinds of its produce for the best.

From Pesaḥ till Dec. 4th say:	*From Dec. 4th till Pesaḥ say:*
Bestow a blessing	Bestow dew and rain for a blessing

upon the face of the earth. Satisfy us with thy goodness, and bless our year like the other good years. Blessed art thou, O Lord, who blessest the years.

Sound the great Shofar for our freedom; lift up the banner to bring our exiles together, and assemble us from the four corners of the earth. Blessed art thou, O Lord, who gatherest the dispersed of thy people Israel.

Restore our judges as at first, and our counselors as at the beginning; remove from us sorrow and sighing; reign thou alone over us, O Lord, in kindness and mercy, and clear us in judgment.
* Blessed art thou, O Lord, King who lovest righteousness and justice.

* Between Rosh Hashanah and Yom Kippur substitute:
(Blessed art thou, O Lord, King of Justice.)

May the slanderers have no hope; may all wickedness perish instantly; may all thy enemies be soon cut down. Do thou speedily uproot and crush the arrogant; cast them down and humble them speedily in our days. Blessed art thou, O Lord, who breakest the enemies and humblest the arrogant.

May thy compassion, Lord our God, be aroused over the righteous and over the godly; over the leaders of thy people, the house of Israel, and over the remnant of their sages; over the true proselytes and over us. Grant a good reward to all who truly trust in thy name, and place our lot among them; may we never come to shame, for in thee we trust. Blessed art thou, O Lord, who art the stay and trust of the righteous.

וְלִירוּשָׁלַיִם עִירְךָ בְּרַחֲמִים תָּשׁוּב, וְתִשְׁכּוֹן בְּתוֹכָהּ כַּאֲשֶׁר דִּבַּרְתָּ; וּבְנֵה אוֹתָהּ בְּקָרוֹב בְּיָמֵינוּ בִּנְיַן עוֹלָם; וְכִסֵּא דָוִד מְהֵרָה לְתוֹכָהּ תָּכִין. * בָּרוּךְ אַתָּה, יְיָ, בּוֹנֵה יְרוּשָׁלָיִם.

*On Tish'ah b'Av say:

(נַחֵם, יְיָ אֱלֹהֵינוּ, אֶת אֲבֵלֵי צִיּוֹן וְאֶת אֲבֵלֵי יְרוּשָׁלַיִם, וְאֶת הָעִיר הָאֲבֵלָה וְהַחֲרֵבָה, וְהַבְּזוּיָה וְהַשּׁוֹמֵמָה: הָאֲבֵלָה מִבְּלִי בָנֶיהָ, וְהַחֲרֵבָה מִמְּעוֹנוֹתֶיהָ, וְהַבְּזוּיָה מִכְּבוֹדָהּ, וְהַשּׁוֹמֵמָה מֵאֵין יוֹשֵׁב. וְהִיא יוֹשֶׁבֶת וְרֹאשָׁהּ חָפוּי, כְּאִשָּׁה עֲקָרָה שֶׁלֹּא יָלָדָה; וַיְבַלְּעוּהָ לִגְיוֹנוֹת, וַיִּירָשׁוּהָ עוֹבְדֵי פְסִילִים, וַיַּטִּילוּ אֶת עַמְּךָ יִשְׂרָאֵל לֶחָרֶב, וַיַּהַרְגוּ בְזָדוֹן חֲסִידֵי עֶלְיוֹן. עַל כֵּן צִיּוֹן בְּמַר תִּבְכֶּה, וִירוּשָׁלַיִם תִּתֵּן קוֹלָהּ. לִבִּי לִבִּי עַל חַלְלֵיהֶם, מֵעַי מֵעַי עַל חַלְלֵיהֶם. כִּי אַתָּה, יְיָ, בָּאֵשׁ הִצַּתָּהּ, וּבָאֵשׁ אַתָּה עָתִיד לִבְנוֹתָהּ, כָּאָמוּר: וַאֲנִי אֶהְיֶה לָּהּ, נְאֻם יְיָ, חוֹמַת אֵשׁ סָבִיב, וּלְכָבוֹד אֶהְיֶה בְתוֹכָהּ. בָּרוּךְ אַתָּה, יְיָ, מְנַחֵם צִיּוֹן וּבוֹנֵה יְרוּשָׁלָיִם.)

אֶת צֶמַח דָּוִד עַבְדְּךָ מְהֵרָה תַצְמִיחַ, וְקַרְנוֹ תָּרוּם בִּישׁוּעָתֶךָ, כִּי לִישׁוּעָתְךָ קִוִּינוּ כָּל הַיּוֹם. בָּרוּךְ אַתָּה, יְיָ, מַצְמִיחַ קֶרֶן יְשׁוּעָה.

שְׁמַע קוֹלֵנוּ, יְיָ אֱלֹהֵינוּ; חוּס וְרַחֵם עָלֵינוּ, וְקַבֵּל בְּרַחֲמִים וּבְרָצוֹן אֶת תְּפִלָּתֵנוּ, כִּי אֵל שׁוֹמֵעַ תְּפִלּוֹת וְתַחֲנוּנִים אָתָּה; וּמִלְּפָנֶיךָ מַלְכֵּנוּ רֵיקָם אַל תְּשִׁיבֵנוּ, * כִּי אַתָּה שׁוֹמֵעַ תְּפִלַּת עַמְּךָ יִשְׂרָאֵל בְּרַחֲמִים. בָּרוּךְ אַתָּה, יְיָ, שׁוֹמֵעַ תְּפִלָּה.

*On fast days, the Congregation recites here:

(עֲנֵנוּ, יְיָ, עֲנֵנוּ בְּיוֹם צוֹם תַּעֲנִיתֵנוּ, כִּי בְצָרָה גְדוֹלָה אֲנָחְנוּ. אַל תֵּפֶן אֶל רִשְׁעֵנוּ, וְאַל תַּסְתֵּר פָּנֶיךָ מִמֶּנּוּ, וְאַל תִּתְעַלַּם

Return in mercy to thy city Jerusalem and dwell in it, as thou hast promised; rebuild it soon, in our days, as an everlasting structure, and speedily establish in it the throne of David. * Blessed art thou, O Lord, Builder of Jerusalem.

* On Tish'ah b'Av say:

(Comfort, Lord our God, the mourners of Zion, the mourners of Jerusalem, and the city that is in mourning, laid waste, despised and desolate. She is in mourning because she is without her children; she is laid waste as to her homes; she is despised in the downfall of her glory; she is desolate through the loss of her inhabitants. She sits with her head covered like a barren, childless woman. Legions devoured her; idolaters took possession of her; they put thy people Israel to the sword, and killed wantonly the faithful followers of the Most High. Because of that, Zion weeps bitterly; Jerusalem raises her voice. How my heart grieves for the slain! How my heart yearns for the slain! Thou, O Lord, didst consume her with fire, and with fire thou wilt in future rebuild her, as it is said: "I will be to her, says the Lord, a wall of fire round about; and for glory—I will be in the midst of her."[1] Blessed art thou, O Lord, Comforter of Zion and Builder of Jerusalem.)

Speedily cause the offspring of thy servant David to flourish, and let his glory be exalted by thy help, for we hope for thy deliverance all day. Blessed art thou, O Lord, who causest salvation to flourish.

Hear our voice, Lord our God; spare us and have pity on us; accept our prayer in mercy and favor, for thou art God who hearest prayers and supplications; from thy presence, our King, dismiss us not empty-handed, * for thou hearest in mercy the prayer of thy people Israel. Blessed art thou, O Lord, who hearest prayer.

*On fast days, the Congregation recites here:

(Answer us, O Lord, answer us on the day of our fast, for we are in great distress. Regard not our wickedness; conceal not thy

---

[1] *Zechariah 2:9.*

מִתְחַנְּנֵנוּ. הֱיֵה נָא קָרוֹב לְשַׁוְעָתֵנוּ, יְהִי נָא חַסְדְּךָ לְנַחֲמֵנוּ; טֶרֶם
נִקְרָא אֵלֶיךָ עֲנֵנוּ, כַּדָּבָר שֶׁנֶּאֱמַר: וְהָיָה טֶרֶם יִקְרָאוּ, וַאֲנִי
אֶעֱנֶה; עוֹד הֵם מְדַבְּרִים, וַאֲנִי אֶשְׁמָע. כִּי אַתָּה, יְיָ, הָעוֹנֶה
בְּעֵת צָרָה, פּוֹדֶה וּמַצִּיל בְּכָל עֵת צָרָה וְצוּקָה. כִּי אַתָּה
שׁוֹמֵעַ תְּפִלַּת עַמְּךָ יִשְׂרָאֵל בְּרַחֲמִים. בָּרוּךְ אַתָּה, יְיָ, שׁוֹמֵעַ
תְּפִלָּה.)

רְצֵה, יְיָ אֱלֹהֵינוּ, בְּעַמְּךָ יִשְׂרָאֵל וּבִתְפִלָּתָם; וְהָשֵׁב אֶת
הָעֲבוֹדָה לִדְבִיר בֵּיתֶךָ, וְאִשֵּׁי יִשְׂרָאֵל וּתְפִלָּתָם בְּאַהֲבָה
תְקַבֵּל בְּרָצוֹן, וּתְהִי לְרָצוֹן תָּמִיד עֲבוֹדַת יִשְׂרָאֵל עַמֶּךָ.

On Rosh Ḥodesh and Ḥol ha-Mo'ed add:

(אֱלֹהֵינוּ וֵאלֹהֵי אֲבוֹתֵינוּ, יַעֲלֶה וְיָבֹא, וְיַגִּיעַ וְיֵרָאֶה, וְיֵרָצֶה
וְיִשָּׁמַע, וְיִפָּקֵד וְיִזָּכֵר זִכְרוֹנֵנוּ וּפִקְדוֹנֵנוּ, וְזִכְרוֹן אֲבוֹתֵינוּ,
וְזִכְרוֹן מָשִׁיחַ בֶּן דָּוִד עַבְדֶּךָ, וְזִכְרוֹן יְרוּשָׁלַיִם עִיר קָדְשֶׁךָ,
וְזִכְרוֹן כָּל עַמְּךָ בֵּית יִשְׂרָאֵל לְפָנֶיךָ, לִפְלֵיטָה וּלְטוֹבָה, לְחֵן
וּלְחֶסֶד וּלְרַחֲמִים, לְחַיִּים וּלְשָׁלוֹם, בְּיוֹם

Sukkoth	Pesaḥ	Rosh Ḥodesh
חַג הַסֻּכּוֹת	חַג הַמַּצּוֹת	רֹאשׁ הַחֹדֶשׁ

הַזֶּה. זָכְרֵנוּ, יְיָ אֱלֹהֵינוּ, בּוֹ לְטוֹבָה, וּפָקְדֵנוּ בוֹ לִבְרָכָה,
וְהוֹשִׁיעֵנוּ בוֹ לְחַיִּים; וּבִדְבַר יְשׁוּעָה וְרַחֲמִים חוּס וְחָנֵּנוּ, וְרַחֵם
עָלֵינוּ וְהוֹשִׁיעֵנוּ, כִּי אֵלֶיךָ עֵינֵינוּ, כִּי אֵל מֶלֶךְ חַנּוּן וְרַחוּם
אָתָּה.)

וְתֶחֱזֶינָה עֵינֵינוּ בְּשׁוּבְךָ לְצִיּוֹן בְּרַחֲמִים. בָּרוּךְ אַתָּה, יְיָ,
הַמַּחֲזִיר שְׁכִינָתוֹ לְצִיּוֹן.

presence from us, and hide not thyself from our supplication. Be near to our cry, and let thy kindness comfort us; even before we call to thee answer us, as it is said: "Before they call, I will answer; while they are yet speaking, I will hear."[1] For thou, O Lord, art he who answers in time of trouble, who redeems and delivers in all times of woe and stress. For thou hearest in mercy the prayer of thy people Israel. Blessed art thou, O Lord, who hearest prayer.)

Be pleased, Lord our God, with thy people Israel and with their prayer; restore the worship to thy most holy sanctuary; accept Israel's offerings and prayer with gracious love. May the worship of thy people Israel be ever pleasing to thee.

On Rosh Ḥodesh and Ḥol ha-Mo'ed add:

(Our God and God of our fathers, may the remembrance of us, of our fathers, of Messiah the son of David thy servant, of Jerusalem thy holy city, and of all thy people the house of Israel, ascend and come and be accepted before thee for deliverance and happiness, for grace, kindness and mercy, for life and peace, on this day of

Rosh Ḥodesh	*Pesaḥ*	*Sukkoth*
the New Moon.	the Feast of Unleavened Bread.	the Feast of Tabernacles.

Remember us this day, Lord our God, for happiness; be mindful of us for blessing; save us to enjoy life. With a promise of salvation and mercy spare us and be gracious to us; have pity on us and save us, for we look to thee, for thou art a gracious and merciful God and King.)

May our eyes behold thy return in mercy to Zion. Blessed art thou, O Lord, who restorest thy divine presence to Zion.

---

[1] *Isaiah* 65:24.

מוֹדִים אֲנַחְנוּ לָךְ, שָׁאַתָּה הוּא
יְיָ אֱלֹהֵינוּ וֵאלֹהֵי אֲבוֹתֵינוּ
לְעוֹלָם וָעֶד. צוּר חַיֵּינוּ, מָגֵן
יִשְׁעֵנוּ אַתָּה הוּא. לְדוֹר וָדוֹר
נוֹדֶה לְּךָ, וּנְסַפֵּר תְּהִלָּתֶךָ, עַל
חַיֵּינוּ הַמְּסוּרִים בְּיָדֶךָ, וְעַל
נִשְׁמוֹתֵינוּ הַפְּקוּדוֹת לָךְ, וְעַל
נִסֶּיךָ שֶׁבְּכָל יוֹם עִמָּנוּ, וְעַל
נִפְלְאוֹתֶיךָ וְטוֹבוֹתֶיךָ שֶׁבְּכָל
עֵת, עֶרֶב וָבֹקֶר וְצָהֳרָיִם.
הַטּוֹב כִּי לֹא כָלוּ רַחֲמֶיךָ,
וְהַמְרַחֵם כִּי לֹא תַמּוּ חֲסָדֶיךָ,
מֵעוֹלָם קִוִּינוּ לָךְ.

When the Reader repeats the *Shemoneh Esreh*, the Congregation responds here by saying:

(מוֹדִים אֲנַחְנוּ לָךְ, שָׁאַתָּה
הוּא יְיָ אֱלֹהֵינוּ וֵאלֹהֵי
אֲבוֹתֵינוּ. אֱלֹהֵי כָל בָּשָׂר,
יוֹצְרֵנוּ, יוֹצֵר בְּרֵאשִׁית,
בְּרָכוֹת וְהוֹדָאוֹת לְשִׁמְךָ
הַגָּדוֹל וְהַקָּדוֹשׁ עַל שֶׁהֶחֱיִיתָנוּ
וְקִיַּמְתָּנוּ. כֵּן תְּחַיֵּנוּ וּתְקַיְּמֵנוּ,
וְתֶאֱסוֹף גָּלֻיוֹתֵינוּ לְחַצְרוֹת
קָדְשֶׁךָ לִשְׁמוֹר חֻקֶּיךָ וְלַעֲשׂוֹת
רְצוֹנֶךָ, וּלְעָבְדְּךָ בְּלֵבָב
שָׁלֵם, עַל שֶׁאֲנַחְנוּ מוֹדִים לָךְ.
בָּרוּךְ אֵל הַהוֹדָאוֹת.)

On Ḥanukkah add:

(עַל הַנִּסִּים וְעַל הַפֻּרְקָן, וְעַל הַגְּבוּרוֹת וְעַל הַתְּשׁוּעוֹת, וְעַל
הַמִּלְחָמוֹת, שֶׁעָשִׂיתָ לַאֲבוֹתֵינוּ בַּיָּמִים הָהֵם בַּזְּמַן הַזֶּה—

בִּימֵי מַתִּתְיָהוּ בֶּן יוֹחָנָן כֹּהֵן גָּדוֹל, חַשְׁמוֹנַי וּבָנָיו, כְּשֶׁעָמְדָה
מַלְכוּת יָוָן הָרְשָׁעָה עַל עַמְּךָ יִשְׂרָאֵל לְהַשְׁכִּיחָם תּוֹרָתֶךָ,
וּלְהַעֲבִירָם מֵחֻקֵּי רְצוֹנֶךָ. וְאַתָּה בְּרַחֲמֶיךָ הָרַבִּים עָמַדְתָּ לָהֶם
בְּעֵת צָרָתָם, רַבְתָּ אֶת רִיבָם, דַּנְתָּ אֶת דִּינָם, נָקַמְתָּ אֶת נִקְמָתָם;
מָסַרְתָּ גִבּוֹרִים בְּיַד חַלָּשִׁים, וְרַבִּים בְּיַד מְעַטִּים, וּטְמֵאִים בְּיַד
טְהוֹרִים, וּרְשָׁעִים בְּיַד צַדִּיקִים, וְזֵדִים בְּיַד עוֹסְקֵי תוֹרָתֶךָ.
וּלְךָ עָשִׂיתָ שֵׁם גָּדוֹל וְקָדוֹשׁ בְּעוֹלָמֶךָ, וּלְעַמְּךָ יִשְׂרָאֵל עָשִׂיתָ
תְּשׁוּעָה גְדוֹלָה וּפֻרְקָן כְּהַיּוֹם הַזֶּה. וְאַחַר כֵּן בָּאוּ בָנֶיךָ לִדְבִיר
בֵּיתֶךָ, וּפִנּוּ אֶת הֵיכָלֶךָ, וְטִהֲרוּ אֶת מִקְדָּשֶׁךָ, וְהִדְלִיקוּ נֵרוֹת

We ever thank thee, who art the Lord our God and the God of our fathers. Thou art the strength of our life and our saving shield. In every generation we will thank thee and recount thy praise—for our lives which are in thy charge, for our souls which are in thy care, for thy miracles which are daily with us, and for thy continual wonders and favors—evening, morning and noon. Beneficent One, whose mercies never fail, Merciful One, whose kindnesses never cease, thou hast always been our hope.

When the Reader repeats the Shemoneh Esreh, the Congregation responds here by saying:

(We thank thee, who art the Lord our God and the God of our fathers. God of all mankind, our Creator and Creator of the universe, blessings and thanks are due to thy great and holy name, because thou hast kept us alive and sustained us; mayest thou ever grant us life and sustenance. O gather our exiles to thy holy courts to observe thy laws, to do thy will, and to serve thee with a perfect heart. For this we thank thee. Blessed be God to whom all thanks are due.)

On Ḥanukkah add:

(We thank thee for the miracles, for the redemption, for the mighty deeds and triumphs, and for the battles which thou didst perform for our fathers in those days, at this season—

In the days of the Hasmonean, Mattathias ben Yoḥanan, the High Priest, and his sons, when a wicked Hellenic government rose up against thy people Israel to make them forget thy Torah and transgress the laws of thy will. Thou in thy great mercy didst stand by them in the time of their distress. Thou didst champion their cause, defend their rights and avenge their wrong; thou didst deliver the strong into the hands of the weak, the many into the hands of the few, the impure into the hands of the pure, the wicked into the hands of the righteous, and the arrogant into the hands of the students of thy Torah. Thou didst make a great and holy name for thyself in thy world, and for thy people Israel thou didst perform a great deliverance unto this day. Thereupon thy children entered the shrine of thy house, cleansed thy Temple, purified thy

בְּחַצְרוֹת קָדְשֶׁךָ, וְקָבְעוּ שְׁמוֹנַת יְמֵי חֲנֻכָּה אֵלּוּ לְהוֹדוֹת וּלְהַלֵּל לְשִׁמְךָ הַגָּדוֹל.)

On *Purim* add:

(עַל הַנִּסִּים וְעַל הַפֻּרְקָן, וְעַל הַגְּבוּרוֹת וְעַל הַתְּשׁוּעוֹת, וְעַל הַמִּלְחָמוֹת, שֶׁעָשִׂיתָ לַאֲבוֹתֵינוּ בַּיָּמִים הָהֵם בַּזְּמַן הַזֶּה—

בִּימֵי מָרְדְּכַי וְאֶסְתֵּר בְּשׁוּשַׁן הַבִּירָה, כְּשֶׁעָמַד עֲלֵיהֶם הָמָן הָרָשָׁע. בִּקֵּשׁ לְהַשְׁמִיד לַהֲרֹג וּלְאַבֵּד אֶת כָּל הַיְּהוּדִים, מִנַּעַר וְעַד זָקֵן, טַף וְנָשִׁים, בְּיוֹם אֶחָד, בִּשְׁלוֹשָׁה עָשָׂר לְחֹדֶשׁ שְׁנֵים עָשָׂר, הוּא חֹדֶשׁ אֲדָר, וּשְׁלָלָם לָבוֹז. וְאַתָּה בְּרַחֲמֶיךָ הָרַבִּים הֵפַרְתָּ אֶת עֲצָתוֹ, וְקִלְקַלְתָּ אֶת מַחֲשַׁבְתּוֹ, וַהֲשֵׁבוֹתָ גְּמוּלוֹ בְּרֹאשׁוֹ, וְתָלוּ אוֹתוֹ וְאֶת בָּנָיו עַל הָעֵץ.)

וְעַל כֻּלָּם יִתְבָּרַךְ וְיִתְרוֹמַם שִׁמְךָ, מַלְכֵּנוּ, תָּמִיד לְעוֹלָם וָעֶד.

Between *Rosh Hashanah* and *Yom Kippur* add:

(וּכְתוֹב לְחַיִּים טוֹבִים כָּל בְּנֵי בְרִיתֶךָ.)

וְכֹל הַחַיִּים יוֹדוּךָ סֶּלָה, וִיהַלְלוּ אֶת שִׁמְךָ בֶּאֱמֶת, הָאֵל, יְשׁוּעָתֵנוּ וְעֶזְרָתֵנוּ סֶלָה. בָּרוּךְ אַתָּה, יְיָ, הַטּוֹב שִׁמְךָ, וּלְךָ נָאֶה לְהוֹדוֹת.

On fast days, the Reader recites here the priestly blessing (page 93) and instead of the following paragraph, שים שלום is said (page 95).

שָׁלוֹם רָב עַל יִשְׂרָאֵל עַמְּךָ תָּשִׂים לְעוֹלָם, כִּי אַתָּה הוּא מֶלֶךְ אָדוֹן לְכָל הַשָּׁלוֹם, וְטוֹב בְּעֵינֶיךָ לְבָרֵךְ אֶת עַמְּךָ יִשְׂרָאֵל בְּכָל עֵת וּבְכָל שָׁעָה בִּשְׁלוֹמֶךָ. * בָּרוּךְ אַתָּה, יְיָ, הַמְבָרֵךְ אֶת עַמּוֹ יִשְׂרָאֵל בַּשָּׁלוֹם.

* Between *Rosh Hashanah* and *Yom Kippur* say:

(בְּסֵפֶר חַיִּים, בְּרָכָה וְשָׁלוֹם וּפַרְנָסָה טוֹבָה, נִזָּכֵר וְנִכָּתֵב לְפָנֶיךָ, אֲנַחְנוּ וְכָל עַמְּךָ בֵּית יִשְׂרָאֵל, לְחַיִּים טוֹבִים וּלְשָׁלוֹם. בָּרוּךְ אַתָּה, יְיָ, עוֹשֵׂה הַשָּׁלוֹם.)

sanctuary, kindled lights in thy holy courts, and designated these eight days of Ḥanukkah for giving thanks and praise to thy great name.)

On Purim add:

(We thank thee for the miracles, for the redemption, for the mighty deeds and triumphs, and for the battles which thou didst perform for our fathers in those days, at this season—

In the days of Mordecai and Esther, in Shushan the capital [of Persia], when the wicked Haman rose up against them and sought to destroy, slay and wipe out all the Jews, young and old, infants and women, in one day, on the thirteenth of the twelfth month Adar, and to plunder their wealth. Thou in thy great mercy didst frustrate his counsel and upset his plan; thou didst cause his mischief to recoil on his own head, so that he and his sons were hanged upon the gallows.)

For all these acts, may thy name, our King, be blessed and exalted forever and ever.

Between Rosh Hashanah and Yom Kippur add:

(Inscribe all thy people of the covenant for a happy life.)

All the living shall ever thank thee and sincerely praise thy name, O God, who art always our salvation and help. Blessed art thou, O Lord, Beneficent One, to whom it is fitting to give thanks.

On fast days, the Reader recites here the priestly blessing (page 94) and instead of the following paragraph, "O grant peace..." is said (page 96).

O grant abundant peace to Israel thy people forever, for thou art the King and Lord of all peace. May it please thee to bless thy people Israel with peace at all times and at all hours. *Blessed art thou, O Lord, who blessest thy people Israel with peace.

* Between Rosh Hashanah and Yom Kippur say:

(May we and all Israel thy people be remembered and inscribed before thee in the book of life and blessing, peace and prosperity, for a happy life and for peace. Blessed art thou, O Lord, Author of peace.)

After the *Shemoneh Esreh* add the following meditation:

אֱלֹהַי, נְצֹר לְשׁוֹנִי מֵרָע, וּשְׂפָתַי מִדַּבֵּר מִרְמָה; וְלִמְקַלְלַי
נַפְשִׁי תִדּוֹם, וְנַפְשִׁי כֶּעָפָר לַכֹּל תִּהְיֶה. פְּתַח לִבִּי בְּתוֹרָתֶךָ,
וּבְמִצְוֹתֶיךָ תִּרְדּוֹף נַפְשִׁי; וְכָל הַחוֹשְׁבִים עָלַי רָעָה, מְהֵרָה
הָפֵר עֲצָתָם וְקַלְקֵל מַחֲשַׁבְתָּם. עֲשֵׂה לְמַעַן שְׁמֶךָ, עֲשֵׂה לְמַעַן
יְמִינֶךָ, עֲשֵׂה לְמַעַן קְדֻשָּׁתֶךָ, עֲשֵׂה לְמַעַן תּוֹרָתֶךָ. לְמַעַן יֵחָלְצוּן
יְדִידֶיךָ, הוֹשִׁיעָה יְמִינְךָ וַעֲנֵנִי. יִהְיוּ לְרָצוֹן אִמְרֵי פִי וְהֶגְיוֹן לִבִּי
לְפָנֶיךָ, יְיָ, צוּרִי וְגוֹאֲלִי. עֹשֶׂה שָׁלוֹם בִּמְרוֹמָיו, הוּא יַעֲשֶׂה
שָׁלוֹם עָלֵינוּ וְעַל כָּל יִשְׂרָאֵל, וְאִמְרוּ אָמֵן.

יְהִי רָצוֹן מִלְּפָנֶיךָ, יְיָ אֱלֹהֵינוּ וֵאלֹהֵי אֲבוֹתֵינוּ, שֶׁיִּבָּנֶה בֵּית
הַמִּקְדָּשׁ בִּמְהֵרָה בְיָמֵינוּ, וְתֵן חֶלְקֵנוּ בְּתוֹרָתֶךָ. וְשָׁם נַעֲבָדְךָ
בְּיִרְאָה, כִּימֵי עוֹלָם וּכְשָׁנִים קַדְמוֹנִיּוֹת. וְעָרְבָה לַיְיָ מִנְחַת
יְהוּדָה וִירוּשָׁלָיִם, כִּימֵי עוֹלָם וּכְשָׁנִים קַדְמוֹנִיּוֹת.

Between *Rosh Hashanah* and *Yom Kippur* and on fast days:

אָבִינוּ מַלְכֵּנוּ, חָטָאנוּ לְפָנֶיךָ.
אָבִינוּ מַלְכֵּנוּ, אֵין לָנוּ מֶלֶךְ אֶלָּא אָתָּה.
אָבִינוּ מַלְכֵּנוּ, עֲשֵׂה עִמָּנוּ לְמַעַן שְׁמֶךָ.

On fast days:	From *Rosh Hashanah* to *Yom Kippur*:
אָבִינוּ מַלְכֵּנוּ,	אָבִינוּ מַלְכֵּנוּ,
בָּרֵךְ עָלֵינוּ שָׁנָה טוֹבָה.	חַדֵּשׁ עָלֵינוּ שָׁנָה טוֹבָה.

אָבִינוּ מַלְכֵּנוּ, בַּטֵּל מֵעָלֵינוּ כָּל גְּזֵרוֹת קָשׁוֹת.
אָבִינוּ מַלְכֵּנוּ, בַּטֵּל מַחְשְׁבוֹת שׂוֹנְאֵינוּ.
אָבִינוּ מַלְכֵּנוּ, הָפֵר עֲצַת אוֹיְבֵינוּ.

After the Shemoneh Esreh add the following meditation:

My God, guard my tongue from evil, and my lips from speaking falsehood. May my soul be silent to those who insult me; be my soul lowly to all as the dust. Open my heart to thy Torah, that my soul may follow thy commands. Speedily defeat the counsel of all those who plan evil against me, and upset their design. Do it for the glory of thy name; do it for the sake of thy power; do it for the sake of thy holiness; do it for the sake of thy Torah. That thy beloved may be rescued, save with thy right hand and answer me. May the words of my mouth and the meditation of my heart be pleasing before thee, O Lord, my Stronghold and my Redeemer.[1] May he who creates peace in his high heavens create peace for us and for all Israel. Amen.

May it be thy will, Lord our God and God of our fathers, that the Temple be speedily rebuilt in our days, and grant us a share in thy Torah. There we will serve thee with reverence, as in the days of old and as in former years. Then the offering of Judah and Jerusalem will be pleasing to the Lord, as in the days of old and as in former years.[2]

Between Rosh Hashanah and Yom Kippur and on fast days:

Our Father, our King, we have sinned before thee.

Our Father, our King, we have no King except thee.

Our Father, our King, deal with us kindly for the sake of thy name.

From Rosh Hashanah to Yom Kippur:	*On fast days:*
Our Father, our King, renew for us a good year.	Our Father, our King, bestow on us a good year.

Our Father, our King, abolish all evil decrees against us.

Our Father, our King, annul the plans of our enemies.

Our Father, our King, frustrate the counsel of our foes.

---

[1] *Psalms* 60:7; 19:15.   [2] *Malachi* 3:4.

אָבִינוּ מַלְכֵּנוּ, כַּלֵּה כָּל צַר וּמַשְׂטִין מֵעָלֵינוּ.

אָבִינוּ מַלְכֵּנוּ, סְתוֹם פִּיּוֹת מַשְׂטִינֵינוּ וּמְקַטְרִגֵינוּ.

אָבִינוּ מַלְכֵּנוּ, כַּלֵּה דֶבֶר וְחֶרֶב וְרָעָב, וּשְׁבִי וּמַשְׁחִית וְעָוֹן וּשְׁמַד, מִבְּנֵי בְרִיתֶךָ.

אָבִינוּ מַלְכֵּנוּ, מְנַע מַגֵּפָה מִנַּחֲלָתֶךָ.

אָבִינוּ מַלְכֵּנוּ, סְלַח וּמְחַל לְכָל עֲוֹנוֹתֵינוּ.

אָבִינוּ מַלְכֵּנוּ, מְחֵה וְהַעֲבֵר פְּשָׁעֵינוּ וְחַטֹּאתֵינוּ מִנֶּגֶד עֵינֶיךָ.

אָבִינוּ מַלְכֵּנוּ, מְחוֹק בְּרַחֲמֶיךָ הָרַבִּים כָּל שִׁטְרֵי חוֹבוֹתֵינוּ.

אָבִינוּ מַלְכֵּנוּ, הַחֲזִירֵנוּ בִּתְשׁוּבָה שְׁלֵמָה לְפָנֶיךָ.

אָבִינוּ מַלְכֵּנוּ, שְׁלַח רְפוּאָה שְׁלֵמָה לְחוֹלֵי עַמֶּךָ.

אָבִינוּ מַלְכֵּנוּ, קְרַע רֹעַ גְּזַר דִּינֵנוּ.

אָבִינוּ מַלְכֵּנוּ, זָכְרֵנוּ בְּזִכָּרוֹן טוֹב לְפָנֶיךָ.

On fast days:	From *Rosh Hashanah* to *Yom Kippur*:
אָבִינוּ מַלְכֵּנוּ, זָכְרֵנוּ לְחַיִּים טוֹבִים.	אָבִינוּ מַלְכֵּנוּ, כָּתְבֵנוּ בְּסֵפֶר חַיִּים טוֹבִים.
אָבִינוּ מַלְכֵּנוּ, זָכְרֵנוּ לִגְאֻלָּה וִישׁוּעָה.	אָבִינוּ מַלְכֵּנוּ, כָּתְבֵנוּ בְּסֵפֶר גְּאֻלָּה וִישׁוּעָה.
אָבִינוּ מַלְכֵּנוּ, זָכְרֵנוּ לְפַרְנָסָה וְכַלְכָּלָה.	אָבִינוּ מַלְכֵּנוּ, כָּתְבֵנוּ בְּסֵפֶר פַּרְנָסָה וְכַלְכָּלָה.
אָבִינוּ מַלְכֵּנוּ, זָכְרֵנוּ לִזְכֻיּוֹת.	אָבִינוּ מַלְכֵּנוּ, כָּתְבֵנוּ בְּסֵפֶר זְכֻיּוֹת.
אָבִינוּ מַלְכֵּנוּ, זָכְרֵנוּ לִסְלִיחָה וּמְחִילָה.	אָבִינוּ מַלְכֵּנוּ, כָּתְבֵנוּ בְּסֵפֶר סְלִיחָה וּמְחִילָה.

אָבִינוּ מַלְכֵּנוּ, הַצְמַח לָנוּ יְשׁוּעָה בְּקָרוֹב.

אָבִינוּ מַלְכֵּנוּ, הָרֵם קֶרֶן יִשְׂרָאֵל עַמֶּךָ.

Our Father, our King, rid us of every oppressor and adversary.

Our Father, our King, close the mouths of our adversaries and accusers.

Our Father, our King, remove pestilence, sword, famine, captivity, destruction, iniquity and persecution from thy people of the covenant.

Our Father, our King, keep the plague back from thy heritage.

Our Father, our King, forgive and pardon all our sins.

Our Father, our King, blot out and remove our transgressions and sins from thy sight.

Our Father, our King, cancel in thy abundant mercy all the records of our sins.

Our Father, our King, bring us back in perfect repentance to thee.

Our Father, our King, send a perfect healing to the sick among thy people.

Our Father, our King, tear up the evil sentence decreed against us.

Our Father, our King, remember us favorably.

Our Father, our King, * inscribe us in the book of happy life.

Our Father, our King, * inscribe us in the book of redemption and salvation.

Our Father, our King, * inscribe us in the book of maintenance and sustenance.

Our Father, our King, * inscribe us in the book of merit.

Our Father, our King, * inscribe us in the book of pardon and forgiveness.

Our Father, our King, cause our salvation soon to flourish.

Our Father, our King, raise the strength of Israel thy people.

* On fast days, instead of "inscribe us" the phrase "remember us" is used.

אָבִינוּ מַלְכֵּנוּ, הָרֵם קֶרֶן מְשִׁיחֶךָ.

אָבִינוּ מַלְכֵּנוּ, מַלֵּא יָדֵינוּ מִבִּרְכוֹתֶיךָ.

אָבִינוּ מַלְכֵּנוּ, מַלֵּא אֲסָמֵינוּ שָׂבָע.

אָבִינוּ מַלְכֵּנוּ, שְׁמַע קוֹלֵנוּ, חוּס וְרַחֵם עָלֵינוּ.

אָבִינוּ מַלְכֵּנוּ, קַבֵּל בְּרַחֲמִים וּבְרָצוֹן אֶת תְּפִלָּתֵנוּ.

אָבִינוּ מַלְכֵּנוּ, פְּתַח שַׁעֲרֵי שָׁמַיִם לִתְפִלָּתֵנוּ.

אָבִינוּ מַלְכֵּנוּ, נָא אַל תְּשִׁיבֵנוּ רֵיקָם מִלְּפָנֶיךָ.

אָבִינוּ מַלְכֵּנוּ, זְכוֹר כִּי עָפָר אֲנָחְנוּ.

אָבִינוּ מַלְכֵּנוּ, תְּהֵא הַשָּׁעָה הַזֹּאת שְׁעַת רַחֲמִים וְעֵת רָצוֹן מִלְּפָנֶיךָ.

אָבִינוּ מַלְכֵּנוּ, חֲמוֹל עָלֵינוּ וְעַל עוֹלָלֵינוּ וְטַפֵּנוּ.

אָבִינוּ מַלְכֵּנוּ, עֲשֵׂה לְמַעַן הֲרוּגִים עַל שֵׁם קָדְשֶׁךָ.

אָבִינוּ מַלְכֵּנוּ, עֲשֵׂה לְמַעַן טְבוּחִים עַל יִחוּדֶךָ.

אָבִינוּ מַלְכֵּנוּ, עֲשֵׂה לְמַעַן בָּאֵי בָאֵשׁ וּבַמַּיִם עַל קִדּוּשׁ שְׁמֶךָ.

אָבִינוּ מַלְכֵּנוּ, נְקוֹם נִקְמַת דַּם עֲבָדֶיךָ הַשָּׁפוּךְ.

אָבִינוּ מַלְכֵּנוּ, עֲשֵׂה לְמַעַנְךָ אִם לֹא לְמַעֲנֵנוּ.

אָבִינוּ מַלְכֵּנוּ, עֲשֵׂה לְמַעַנְךָ וְהוֹשִׁיעֵנוּ.

אָבִינוּ מַלְכֵּנוּ, עֲשֵׂה לְמַעַן רַחֲמֶיךָ הָרַבִּים.

אָבִינוּ מַלְכֵּנוּ, עֲשֵׂה לְמַעַן שִׁמְךָ הַגָּדוֹל הַגִּבּוֹר וְהַנּוֹרָא שֶׁנִּקְרָא עָלֵינוּ.

אָבִינוּ מַלְכֵּנוּ, חָנֵּנוּ וַעֲנֵנוּ, כִּי אֵין בָּנוּ מַעֲשִׂים; עֲשֵׂה עִמָּנוּ צְדָקָה וָחֶסֶד וְהוֹשִׁיעֵנוּ.

Our Father, our King, raise the strength of thy anointed one.

Our Father, our King, fill our hands with thy blessings.

Our Father, our King, fill our storehouses with plenty.

Our Father, our King, hear our voice, spare us and have mercy on us.

Our Father, our King, receive our prayer with mercy and favor.

Our Father, our King, open the gates of heaven to our prayer.

Our Father, our King, dismiss us not empty-handed from thy presence.

Our Father, our King, remember that we are but dust.

Our Father, our King, may this hour be an hour of mercy and a time of grace with thee.

Our Father, our King, have compassion on us, on our children and our infants.

Our Father, our King, act for the sake of those who were slain for thy holy name.

Our Father, our King, act for the sake of those who were slaughtered for proclaiming thy Oneness.

Our Father, our King, act for the sake of those who went through fire and water for the sanctification of thy name.

Our Father, our King, avenge the spilt blood of thy servants.

Our Father, our King, do it for thy sake, if not for ours.

Our Father, our King, do it for thy sake and save us.

Our Father, our King, do it for the sake of thy abundant mercy.

Our Father, our King, do it for the sake of thy great, mighty and revered name by which we are called.

Our Father, our King, be gracious to us and answer us, though we have no merits; deal charitably and kindly with us and save us.

תַּחֲנוּן

Taḥanun is recited on weekday afternoons, except on Fridays and the following occasions: *Erev Rosh Ḥodesh* and *Rosh Ḥodesh*, the entire month of *Nisan*, the day preceding *Lag b'Omer* and *Lag b'Omer*, the first eight days of *Sivan*, the 8th, 9th, 14th and 15th of *Av*, from *Erev Yom Kippur* until the second day after *Sukkoth*, from the 24th of *Kislev* until after *Ḥanukkah*, the 14th and 15th of *Shevat*, the 13th, 14th and 15th of *Adar* and *Adar Sheni*. *Taḥanun* is also omitted in the house of a mourner during the week of mourning, and on the occasion of a *Brith Milah*.

וַיֹּאמֶר דָּוִד אֶל גָּד: צַר לִי מְאֹד; נִפְּלָה נָּא בְיַד יְיָ, כִּי רַבִּים רַחֲמָיו, וּבְיַד אָדָם אַל אֶפֹּלָה.

רַחוּם וְחַנּוּן, חָטָאתִי לְפָנֶיךָ; יְיָ מָלֵא רַחֲמִים, רַחֵם עָלַי וְקַבֵּל תַּחֲנוּנָי.

תהלים ו

יְיָ, אַל בְּאַפְּךָ תוֹכִיחֵנִי, וְאַל בַּחֲמָתְךָ תְיַסְּרֵנִי. חָנֵּנִי, יְיָ, כִּי אֻמְלַל אָנִי; רְפָאֵנִי, יְיָ, כִּי נִבְהֲלוּ עֲצָמָי. וְנַפְשִׁי נִבְהֲלָה מְאֹד; וְאַתָּה יְיָ, עַד מָתָי. שׁוּבָה, יְיָ, חַלְּצָה נַפְשִׁי; הוֹשִׁיעֵנִי לְמַעַן חַסְדֶּךָ. כִּי אֵין בַּמָּוֶת זִכְרֶךָ; בִּשְׁאוֹל מִי יוֹדֶה לָּךְ. יָגַעְתִּי בְּאַנְחָתִי, אַשְׂחֶה בְכָל לַיְלָה מִטָּתִי: בְּדִמְעָתִי עַרְשִׂי אַמְסֶה. עָשְׁשָׁה מִכַּעַס עֵינִי; עָתְקָה בְּכָל צוֹרְרָי. סוּרוּ מִמֶּנִּי, כָּל פֹּעֲלֵי אָוֶן, כִּי שָׁמַע יְיָ קוֹל בִּכְיִי. שָׁמַע יְיָ תְּחִנָּתִי; יְיָ תְּפִלָּתִי יִקָּח. יֵבֹשׁוּ וְיִבָּהֲלוּ מְאֹד כָּל אֹיְבָי; יָשֻׁבוּ יֵבֹשׁוּ רָגַע.

שׁוֹמֵר יִשְׂרָאֵל, שְׁמוֹר שְׁאֵרִית יִשְׂרָאֵל, וְאַל יֹאבַד יִשְׂרָאֵל, הָאוֹמְרִים שְׁמַע יִשְׂרָאֵל.

שׁוֹמֵר גּוֹי אֶחָד, שְׁמוֹר שְׁאֵרִית עַם אֶחָד, וְאַל יֹאבַד גּוֹי אֶחָד, הַמְיַחֲדִים שְׁמֶךָ, יְיָ אֱלֹהֵינוּ, יְיָ אֶחָד.

שׁוֹמֵר גּוֹי קָדוֹשׁ, שְׁמוֹר שְׁאֵרִית עַם קָדוֹשׁ, וְאַל יֹאבַד גּוֹי קָדוֹשׁ, הַמְשַׁלְּשִׁים בְּשָׁלֹשׁ קְדֻשּׁוֹת לְקָדוֹשׁ.

TAHANUN

Tahanun is recited on weekday afternoons, except on Fridays and the following occasions: Erev Rosh Hodesh and Rosh Hodesh, the entire month of Nisan, the day preceding Lag b'Omer and Lag b'Omer, the first eight days of Sivan, the 8th, 9th, 14th and 15th of Av, from Erev Yom Kippur until the second day after Sukkoth, from the 24th of Kislev until after Hanukkah, the 14th and 15th of Shevat, the 13th, 14th and 15th of Adar and Adar Sheni. Tahanun is also omitted in the house of a mourner during the week of mourning, and on the occasion of a Brith Milah.

And David said to Gad: "I am deeply distressed; let us fall into the hand of the Lord, for his mercy is great, but let me not fall into the hand of man."[1]

Merciful and gracious God, I have sinned before thee; O Lord, who art full of compassion, have mercy on me and accept my supplications.

Psalm 6

O Lord, punish me not in thy anger; chastise me not in thy wrath. Have pity on me, O Lord, for I languish away; heal me, O Lord, for my health is shaken. My soul is severely troubled; and thou, O Lord, how long? O Lord, deliver my life once again; save me because of thy grace. For in death there is no thought of thee; in the grave who gives thanks to thee? I am worn out with my groaning; every night I flood my bed with tears; I cause my couch to melt with my weeping. My eye is dimmed from grief; it grows old because of all my foes. Depart from me, all you evildoers, for the Lord has heard the sound of my weeping. The Lord has heard my supplication; the Lord receives my prayer. All my foes shall be utterly ashamed and terrified; they shall turn back; they shall be suddenly ashamed.

Guardian of Israel, preserve the remnant of Israel; let not Israel perish, who say: "Hear, O Israel."

Guardian of a unique people, preserve the remnant of a unique people; let not a unique people perish, who proclaim thy Oneness, saying: "The Lord is our God, the Lord is One."

Guardian of a holy people, preserve the remnant of a holy people; let not a holy people perish, who repeat the threefold sanctification to the Holy One.

On נפילת אפים, the posture assumed during the recital of *Tahanun*, see page 103.

[1] *II Samuel* 24:14

מִתְרַצֶּה בְּרַחֲמִים וּמִתְפַּיֵּס בְּתַחֲנוּנִים, הִתְרַצֶּה וְהִתְפַּיֵּס לְדוֹר עָנִי, כִּי אֵין עוֹזֵר. אָבִינוּ מַלְכֵּנוּ, חָנֵּנוּ וַעֲנֵנוּ, כִּי אֵין בָּנוּ מַעֲשִׂים; עֲשֵׂה עִמָּנוּ צְדָקָה וָחֶסֶד וְהוֹשִׁיעֵנוּ.

וַאֲנַחְנוּ לֹא נֵדַע מַה נַּעֲשֶׂה, כִּי עָלֶיךָ עֵינֵינוּ. זְכֹר רַחֲמֶיךָ יְיָ, וַחֲסָדֶיךָ, כִּי מֵעוֹלָם הֵמָּה. יְהִי חַסְדְּךָ יְיָ עָלֵינוּ, כַּאֲשֶׁר יִחַלְנוּ לָךְ. אַל תִּזְכָּר־לָנוּ עֲוֹנוֹת רִאשֹׁנִים; מַהֵר יְקַדְּמוּנוּ רַחֲמֶיךָ, כִּי דַלּוֹנוּ מְאֹד. חָנֵּנוּ יְיָ חָנֵּנוּ, כִּי רַב שָׂבַעְנוּ בוּז. בְּרֹגֶז רַחֵם תִּזְכּוֹר. כִּי הוּא יָדַע יִצְרֵנוּ, זָכוּר כִּי עָפָר אֲנָחְנוּ. Reader עָזְרֵנוּ, אֱלֹהֵי יִשְׁעֵנוּ, עַל דְּבַר כְּבוֹד שְׁמֶךָ, וְהַצִּילֵנוּ וְכַפֵּר עַל חַטֹּאתֵינוּ לְמַעַן שְׁמֶךָ.

Reader:

יִתְגַּדַּל וְיִתְקַדַּשׁ שְׁמֵהּ רַבָּא בְּעָלְמָא דִּי בְרָא כִרְעוּתֵהּ; וְיַמְלִיךְ מַלְכוּתֵהּ בְּחַיֵּיכוֹן וּבְיוֹמֵיכוֹן, וּבְחַיֵּי דְכָל בֵּית יִשְׂרָאֵל, בַּעֲגָלָא וּבִזְמַן קָרִיב, וְאִמְרוּ אָמֵן.

יְהֵא שְׁמֵהּ רַבָּא מְבָרַךְ לְעָלַם וּלְעָלְמֵי עָלְמַיָּא.

יִתְבָּרַךְ וְיִשְׁתַּבַּח, וְיִתְפָּאַר וְיִתְרוֹמַם, וְיִתְנַשֵּׂא וְיִתְהַדָּר, וְיִתְעַלֶּה וְיִתְהַלָּל שְׁמֵהּ דְּקֻדְשָׁא, בְּרִיךְ הוּא, לְעֵלָּא (לְעֵלָּא) מִן כָּל בִּרְכָתָא וְשִׁירָתָא, תֻּשְׁבְּחָתָא וְנֶחֱמָתָא, דַּאֲמִירָן בְּעָלְמָא, וְאִמְרוּ אָמֵן.

תִּתְקַבֵּל צְלוֹתְהוֹן וּבָעוּתְהוֹן דְּכָל בֵּית יִשְׂרָאֵל קֳדָם אֲבוּהוֹן דִּי בִשְׁמַיָּא, וְאִמְרוּ אָמֵן.

יְהֵא שְׁלָמָא רַבָּא מִן שְׁמַיָּא, וְחַיִּים, עָלֵינוּ וְעַל כָּל יִשְׂרָאֵל, וְאִמְרוּ אָמֵן.

עֹשֶׂה שָׁלוֹם בִּמְרוֹמָיו, הוּא יַעֲשֶׂה שָׁלוֹם עָלֵינוּ וְעַל כָּל יִשְׂרָאֵל, וְאִמְרוּ אָמֵן.

O thou who art reconciled by prayers and conciliated by supplications, be thou reconciled and conciliated to an afflicted generation, for there is none to help.

Our Father, our King, be gracious to us and answer us, for we have no merits; deal charitably and kindly with us and save us.

We know not what to do, but our eyes are upon thee. Remember thy mercy and thy kindness, O Lord, for they are eternal. May thy kindness rest on us, O Lord, as our hope rests on thee. O mind not our former iniquities; may thy compassion hasten to our aid, for we are brought very low. Take pity on us, O Lord, take pity on us, for we are exceedingly sated with contempt. When in wrath, remember to be merciful. He knows what we are made of, remembering that we are but dust. Help us, our saving God, for the sake of thy glorious name; rescue us and pardon our sins for thy name's sake.[1]

Reader:

Glorified and sanctified be God's great name throughout the world which he has created according to his will. May he establish his kingdom in your lifetime and during your days, and within the life of the entire house of Israel, speedily and soon; and say, Amen.

May his great name be blessed forever and to all eternity.

Blessed and praised, glorified and exalted, extolled and honored, adored and lauded be the name of the Holy One, blessed be he, beyond all the blessings and hymns, praises and consolations that are ever spoken in the world; and say, Amen.

May the prayers and supplications of the whole house of Israel be accepted by their Father who is in heaven; and say, Amen.

May there be abundant peace from heaven, and life, for us and for all Israel; and say, Amen.

He who creates peace in his celestial heights, may he create peace for us and for all Israel; and say, Amen.

---

[1] *II Chronicles* 20:12; *Psalms* 25:6; 33:22; 79:8; 123:3; *Habakkuk* **3:2;** *Psalms* 103:14; **79:9.**

עָלֵינוּ לְשַׁבֵּחַ לַאֲדוֹן הַכֹּל, לָתֵת גְּדֻלָּה לְיוֹצֵר בְּרֵאשִׁית,
שֶׁלֹא עָשָׂנוּ כְּגוֹיֵי הָאֲרָצוֹת, וְלֹא שָׂמָנוּ כְּמִשְׁפְּחוֹת הָאֲדָמָה;
שֶׁלֹא שָׂם חֶלְקֵנוּ כָּהֶם, וְגוֹרָלֵנוּ כְּכָל הֲמוֹנָם. וַאֲנַחְנוּ כּוֹרְעִים
וּמִשְׁתַּחֲוִים וּמוֹדִים לִפְנֵי מֶלֶךְ מַלְכֵי הַמְּלָכִים, הַקָּדוֹשׁ בָּרוּךְ
הוּא. שֶׁהוּא נוֹטֶה שָׁמַיִם וְיוֹסֵד אָרֶץ, וּמוֹשַׁב יְקָרוֹ בַּשָּׁמַיִם
מִמַּעַל, וּשְׁכִינַת עֻזּוֹ בְּגָבְהֵי מְרוֹמִים. הוּא אֱלֹהֵינוּ, אֵין עוֹד;
אֱמֶת מַלְכֵּנוּ, אֶפֶס זוּלָתוֹ, כַּכָּתוּב בְּתוֹרָתוֹ: וְיָדַעְתָּ הַיּוֹם
וַהֲשֵׁבֹתָ אֶל לְבָבֶךָ, כִּי יְיָ הוּא הָאֱלֹהִים בַּשָּׁמַיִם מִמַּעַל וְעַל
הָאָרֶץ מִתָּחַת, אֵין עוֹד.

עַל כֵּן נְקַוֶּה לְּךָ, יְיָ אֱלֹהֵינוּ, לִרְאוֹת מְהֵרָה בְּתִפְאֶרֶת עֻזֶּךָ,
לְהַעֲבִיר גִּלּוּלִים מִן הָאָרֶץ, וְהָאֱלִילִים כָּרוֹת יִכָּרֵתוּן; לְתַקֵּן
עוֹלָם בְּמַלְכוּת שַׁדַּי, וְכָל בְּנֵי בָשָׂר יִקְרְאוּ בִשְׁמֶךָ, לְהַפְנוֹת
אֵלֶיךָ כָּל רִשְׁעֵי אָרֶץ. יַכִּירוּ וְיֵדְעוּ כָּל יוֹשְׁבֵי תֵבֵל, כִּי לְךָ
תִּכְרַע כָּל בֶּרֶךְ, תִּשָּׁבַע כָּל לָשׁוֹן. לְפָנֶיךָ, יְיָ אֱלֹהֵינוּ, יִכְרְעוּ
וְיִפֹּלוּ, וְלִכְבוֹד שִׁמְךָ יְקָר יִתֵּנוּ, וִיקַבְּלוּ כֻלָּם אֶת עֹל מַלְכוּתֶךָ,
וְתִמְלוֹךְ עֲלֵיהֶם מְהֵרָה לְעוֹלָם וָעֶד; כִּי הַמַּלְכוּת שֶׁלְּךָ הִיא,
וּלְעוֹלְמֵי עַד תִּמְלוֹךְ בְּכָבוֹד, כַּכָּתוּב בְּתוֹרָתֶךָ: יְיָ יִמְלֹךְ
לְעֹלָם וָעֶד. Reader וְנֶאֱמַר: וְהָיָה יְיָ לְמֶלֶךְ עַל כָּל הָאָרֶץ;
בַּיּוֹם הַהוּא יִהְיֶה יְיָ אֶחָד וּשְׁמוֹ אֶחָד.

MOURNERS' KADDISH

יִתְגַּדַּל וְיִתְקַדַּשׁ שְׁמֵהּ רַבָּא בְּעָלְמָא דִּי בְרָא כִרְעוּתֵהּ;
וְיַמְלִיךְ מַלְכוּתֵהּ בְּחַיֵּיכוֹן וּבְיוֹמֵיכוֹן, וּבְחַיֵּי דְכָל בֵּית יִשְׂרָאֵל,
בַּעֲגָלָא וּבִזְמַן קָרִיב, וְאִמְרוּ אָמֵן.

יְהֵא שְׁמֵהּ רַבָּא מְבָרַךְ לְעָלַם וּלְעָלְמֵי עָלְמַיָּא.

On עלינו, see page 135.

ALENU

It is our duty to praise the Master of all, to exalt the Creator of the universe, who has not made us like the nations of the world and has not placed us like the families of the earth; who has not designed our destiny to be like theirs, nor our lot like that of all their multitude. We bend the knee and bow and acknowledge before the supreme King of kings, the Holy One, blessed be he, that it is he who stretched forth the heavens and founded the earth. His seat of glory is in the heavens above; his abode of majesty is in the lofty heights. He is our God, there is none else; truly, he is our King, there is none besides him, as it is written in his Torah: "You shall know this day, and reflect in your heart, that it is the Lord who is God in the heavens above and on the earth beneath, there is none else."[1]

We hope therefore, Lord our God, soon to behold thy majestic glory, when the abominations shall be removed from the earth, and the false gods exterminated; when the world shall be perfected under the reign of the Almighty, and all mankind will call upon thy name, and all the wicked of the earth will be turned to thee. May all the inhabitants of the world realize and know that to thee every knee must bend, every tongue must vow allegiance. May they bend the knee and prostrate themselves before thee, Lord our God, and give honor to thy glorious name; may they all accept the yoke of thy kingdom, and do thou reign over them speedily forever and ever. For the kingdom is thine, and to all eternity thou wilt reign in glory, as it is written in thy Torah: "The Lord shall be King forever and ever."[2] And it is said: "The Lord shall be King over all the earth; on that day the Lord shall be One, and his name One."[3]

MOURNERS' KADDISH

Glorified and sanctified be God's great name throughout the world which he has created according to his will. May he establish his kingdom in your lifetime and during your days, and within the life of the entire house of Israel, speedily and soon; and say, Amen.

May his great name be blessed forever and to all eternity.

---

[1] *Deuteronomy* 4:39.   [2] *Exodus* 15:18.   [3] *Zechariah* 14.9.

יִתְבָּרַךְ וְיִשְׁתַּבַּח, וְיִתְפָּאַר וְיִתְרוֹמַם, וְיִתְנַשֵּׂא וְיִתְהַדָּר,
וְיִתְעַלֶּה וְיִתְהַלָּל שְׁמֵהּ דְּקֻדְשָׁא, בְּרִיךְ הוּא, לְעֵלָּא (לְעֵלָּא)
מִן כָּל בִּרְכָתָא וְשִׁירָתָא, תֻּשְׁבְּחָתָא וְנֶחֱמָתָא, דַּאֲמִירָן בְּעָלְמָא,
וְאִמְרוּ אָמֵן.

יְהֵא שְׁלָמָא רַבָּא מִן שְׁמַיָּא, וְחַיִּים, עָלֵינוּ וְעַל כָּל יִשְׂרָאֵל,
וְאִמְרוּ אָמֵן.

עֹשֶׂה שָׁלוֹם בִּמְרוֹמָיו, הוּא יַעֲשֶׂה שָׁלוֹם עָלֵינוּ וְעַל כָּל
יִשְׂרָאֵל, וְאִמְרוּ אָמֵן.

אַל תִּירָא מִפַּחַד פִּתְאֹם, וּמִשֹּׁאַת רְשָׁעִים כִּי תָבֹא. עֻצוּ
עֵצָה וְתֻפָר, דַּבְּרוּ דָבָר וְלֹא יָקוּם, כִּי עִמָּנוּ אֵל. וְעַד זִקְנָה אֲנִי
הוּא, וְעַד שֵׂיבָה אֲנִי אֶסְבֹּל; אֲנִי עָשִׂיתִי וַאֲנִי אֶשָּׂא, וַאֲנִי אֶסְבֹּל
וַאֲמַלֵּט.

THE KADDISH

The essential part of the Kaddish consists of the congregational response: "May his great name be blessed forever and ever." Around this response, which is found almost verbatim in Daniel 2:20, the whole Kaddish developed. Originally, it was recited at the close of sermons delivered in Aramaic, the language spoken by the Jews for about a thousand years after the Babylonian captivity. Hence the Kaddish was composed in Aramaic, the language in which the religious discourses were held. At a later period the Kaddish was introduced into the liturgy to mark the conclusion of sections of the service or of the reading of the biblical and talmudic passages.

The Kaddish contains no reference to the dead. The earliest allusion to the Kaddish as a mourners' prayer is found in Maḥzor Vitry, dated 1208, where it is said plainly: "The lad rises and recites Kaddish." One may safely assume that since the Kaddish has as its underlying thought the hope for the redemption and ultimate healing of suffering mankind, the power of redeeming the dead from the sufferings of *Gehinnom* came to be ascribed in the course of time to the recitation of this sublime doxology. Formerly the Kaddish was recited the whole year of mourning, so as to rescue the soul of one's parents from the torture of *Gehinnom* where the wicked are said to spend no less than twelve months. In order not to count one's own parents among the wicked, the period for reciting the Kaddish was later reduced to eleven months.

Blessed and praised, glorified and exalted, extolled and honored, adored and lauded be the name of the Holy One, blessed be he, beyond all the blessings and hymns, praises and consolations that are ever spoken in the world; and say, Amen.

May there be abundant peace from heaven, and life, for us and for all Israel; and say, Amen.

He who creates peace in his celestial heights, may he create peace for us and for all Israel; and say, Amen.

Be not afraid of sudden terror, nor of the storm that strikes the wicked. Form your plot—it shall fail; lay your plan—it shall not prevail! For God is with us. Even to your old age I will be the same; when you are gray-headed, still I will sustain you; I have made you, and I will bear you; I will sustain you and save you.[1]

The observance of the anniversary of parents' death, the Jahrzeit, originated in Germany, as the term itself well indicates. Rabbi Isaac Luria, the celebrated Kabbalist of the sixteenth century, explains that "while the orphan's Kaddish within the eleven months helps the soul to pass from *Gehinnom* to *Gan-Eden,* the Jahrzeit Kaddish elevates the soul every year to a higher sphere in Paradise." The Kaddish has thus become a great pillar of Judaism. No matter how far a Jew may have drifted away from Jewish life, the Kaddish restores him to his people and to the Jewish way of living.

לעלא מן כל... ושירתא תשבחתא refers to the hymns of praise contained in the Psalms of David; compare the expression על כל דברי שירות ותשבחות דוד.

לעלא לעלא is said between *Rosh Hashanah* and *Yom Kippur*; otherwise only לעלא is said. In the Italian ritual לעלא is repeated throughout the year. לעלא לעלא is the Targum's rendering of מעלה מעלה (Deuteronomy 28:43).

נחמתא ("consolations"), occurring in the Kaddish as a synonym of praise, probably refers to prophetic works such as the Book of Isaiah, called Books of Consolation, which contain hymns of praise as well as Messianic prophecies.

עושה שלום, which repeats in Hebrew the thought expressed in the preceding Aramaic paragraph, seems to have been added from the meditation recited at the end of the *Shemoneh Esreh.* The same sentence is also added at the end of the grace recited after meals. The three steps backwards, which formed the respectful manner of retiring from a superior, were likewise transferred from the concluding sentence of the *Shemoneh Esreh.* On the other hand, the phrase "and say Amen", added at the end of the silent meditation after the *Shemoneh Esreh,* must have been borrowed from the Kaddish which is always recited in the hearing of no fewer than ten men.

---

[1] *Proverbs* 3:25; *Isaiah* 8:10; 46:4.

תְּפִלַּת עַרְבִית

On Saturday night, *Ma'ariv* is preceded by Psalms 144 and 67 (page 535).
On weekdays, if *Ma'ariv* is not recited immediately after *Minḥah,*
the evening service begins on this page.

תהלים קלד

שִׁיר הַמַּעֲלוֹת. הִנֵּה בָּרְכוּ אֶת יְיָ כָּל עַבְדֵי יְיָ, הָעֹמְדִים
בְּבֵית יְיָ בַּלֵּילוֹת. שְׂאוּ יְדֵכֶם קֹדֶשׁ, וּבָרְכוּ אֶת יְיָ. יְבָרֶכְךָ יְיָ
מִצִּיּוֹן, עֹשֵׂה שָׁמַיִם וָאָרֶץ.

יְיָ צְבָאוֹת עִמָּנוּ, מִשְׂגַּב־לָנוּ אֱלֹהֵי יַעֲקֹב, סֶלָה.
יְיָ צְבָאוֹת, אַשְׁרֵי אָדָם בֹּטֵחַ בָּךְ.
יְיָ, הוֹשִׁיעָה; הַמֶּלֶךְ יַעֲנֵנוּ בְיוֹם קָרְאֵנוּ.

Reader:

יִתְגַּדַּל וְיִתְקַדַּשׁ שְׁמֵהּ רַבָּא בְּעָלְמָא דִּי בְרָא כִרְעוּתֵהּ;
וְיַמְלִיךְ מַלְכוּתֵהּ בְּחַיֵּיכוֹן וּבְיוֹמֵיכוֹן, וּבְחַיֵּי דְכָל בֵּית יִשְׂרָאֵל,
בַּעֲגָלָא וּבִזְמַן קָרִיב, וְאִמְרוּ אָמֵן.

יְהֵא שְׁמֵהּ רַבָּא מְבָרַךְ לְעָלַם וּלְעָלְמֵי עָלְמַיָּא.

יִתְבָּרַךְ וְיִשְׁתַּבַּח, וְיִתְפָּאַר וְיִתְרוֹמַם, וְיִתְנַשֵּׂא וְיִתְהַדָּר,
וְיִתְעַלֶּה וְיִתְהַלָּל שְׁמֵהּ דְּקֻדְשָׁא, בְּרִיךְ הוּא, לְעֵלָּא (לְעֵלָּא)
מִן כָּל בִּרְכָתָא וְשִׁירָתָא, תֻּשְׁבְּחָתָא וְנֶחֱמָתָא, דַּאֲמִירָן בְּעָלְמָא,
וְאִמְרוּ אָמֵן.

תפלת ערבית, the evening service, does not correspond to any sacrifice in
the Temple since the offering of sacrifices occurred only twice a day, morning
and afternoon. Hence in talmudic times and in a greater part of the geonic
period the *Shemoneh Esreh* was omitted from the *Ma'ariv* service. To replace
the Eighteen Benedictions, eighteen scattered biblical verses, each mentioning
the name of God, were introduced at the end of the *Ma'ariv* service. This
passage, beginning with **ברוך ה' לעולם**, was arranged by "the heads of the

189

EVENING SERVICE

*On Saturday night, Ma'ariv is preceded by Psalms 144 and 67 (page 536).
On weekdays, if Ma'ariv is not recited immediately after Minḥah,
the evening service begins on this page.*

Psalm 134

A Pilgrim Song. Come, bless the Lord, all you servants of the Lord, who nightly stand in the house of the Lord. Lift your hands in holiness, and bless the Lord. May the Lord, who made heaven and earth, bless you from Zion.

The Lord of hosts is with us; the God of Jacob is our fortress. Lord of hosts, happy is the man who trusts in thee. Save us, O Lord; may the King answer us when we call.[1]

Reader:

Glorified and sanctified be God's great name throughout the world which he has created according to his will. May he establish his kingdom in your lifetime and during your days, and within the life of the entire house of Israel, speedily and soon; and say, Amen.

May his great name be blessed forever and to all eternity.

Blessed and praised, glorified and exalted, extolled and honored, adored and lauded be the name of the Holy One, blessed be he, beyond all the blessings and hymns, praises and consolations that are ever spoken in the world; and say, Amen.

Babylonian academies" (Maḥzor Vitry, page 78). It is followed by half-Kaddish probably because at one time it marked the end of the evening service, as may be seen from the *Siddur* of Amram Gaon (ninth century). Maimonides asserts that since the Jews everywhere consented to say the evening prayer regularly, it is equivalent to an obligation (Tefillah 1:6). The controversy in the Talmud as to whether the evening prayer is optional or obligatory refers to the *Shemoneh Esreh* and not to the *Shema*, which it is obligatory to recite morning and evening. Since the *Ma'ariv* prayer was considered by some talmudic rabbis to be optional, the *Shemoneh Esreh* is not repeated by the Reader and the *Kedushah* is not recited.

[1] *Psalms* 46:8; 84:13; 20:10.

190

The *Ma'ariv* service properly begins here.

וְהוּא רַחוּם, יְכַפֵּר עָוֹן וְלֹא יַשְׁחִית; וְהִרְבָּה לְהָשִׁיב אַפּוֹ,
וְלֹא יָעִיר כָּל חֲמָתוֹ. יְיָ, הוֹשִׁיעָה; הַמֶּלֶךְ יַעֲנֵנוּ בְיוֹם קָרְאֵנוּ.

Silent meditation:

Reader:

בָּרְכוּ אֶת יְיָ הַמְבֹרָךְ.

Congregation and Reader:

יִתְבָּרַךְ וְיִשְׁתַּבַּח, וְיִתְפָּאַר וְיִתְרוֹמַם
וְיִתְנַשֵּׂא שְׁמוֹ שֶׁל מֶלֶךְ מַלְכֵי הַמְּלָכִים,
הַקָּדוֹשׁ בָּרוּךְ הוּא, שֶׁהוּא רִאשׁוֹן וְהוּא
אַחֲרוֹן, וּמִבַּלְעָדָיו אֵין אֱלֹהִים. סֹלוּ

בָּרוּךְ יְיָ הַמְבֹרָךְ לְעוֹלָם וָעֶד.

לָרֹכֵב בָּעֲרָבוֹת, בְּיָהּ שְׁמוֹ, וְעִלְזוּ לְפָנָיו. וּשְׁמוֹ מְרוֹמָם עַל כָּל בְּרָכָה וּתְהִלָּה. בָּרוּךְ
שֵׁם כְּבוֹד מַלְכוּתוֹ לְעוֹלָם וָעֶד. יְהִי שֵׁם יְיָ מְבֹרָךְ מֵעַתָּה וְעַד עוֹלָם.

בָּרוּךְ אַתָּה, יְיָ אֱלֹהֵינוּ, מֶלֶךְ הָעוֹלָם, אֲשֶׁר בִּדְבָרוֹ מַעֲרִיב
עֲרָבִים. בְּחָכְמָה פּוֹתֵחַ שְׁעָרִים, וּבִתְבוּנָה מְשַׁנֶּה עִתִּים,
וּמַחֲלִיף אֶת הַזְּמַנִּים, וּמְסַדֵּר אֶת הַכּוֹכָבִים בְּמִשְׁמְרוֹתֵיהֶם
בָּרָקִיעַ כִּרְצוֹנוֹ. בּוֹרֵא יוֹם וָלָיְלָה, גּוֹלֵל אוֹר מִפְּנֵי חֹשֶׁךְ וְחֹשֶׁךְ
מִפְּנֵי אוֹר, וּמַעֲבִיר יוֹם וּמֵבִיא לָיְלָה, וּמַבְדִּיל בֵּין יוֹם וּבֵין
לָיְלָה, יְיָ צְבָאוֹת שְׁמוֹ. Reader אֵל חַי וְקַיָּם, תָּמִיד יִמְלוֹךְ עָלֵינוּ,
לְעוֹלָם וָעֶד. בָּרוּךְ אַתָּה, יְיָ, הַמַּעֲרִיב עֲרָבִים.

אַהֲבַת עוֹלָם בֵּית יִשְׂרָאֵל עַמְּךָ אָהָבְתָּ; תּוֹרָה וּמִצְוֹת,
חֻקִּים וּמִשְׁפָּטִים, אוֹתָנוּ לִמַּדְתָּ. עַל כֵּן, יְיָ אֱלֹהֵינוּ, בְּשָׁכְבֵנוּ
וּבְקוּמֵנוּ נָשִׂיחַ בְּחֻקֶּיךָ, וְנִשְׂמַח בְּדִבְרֵי תוֹרָתֶךָ וּבְמִצְוֹתֶיךָ
לְעוֹלָם וָעֶד. כִּי הֵם חַיֵּינוּ וְאֹרֶךְ יָמֵינוּ, וּבָהֶם נֶהְגֶּה יוֹמָם וָלָיְלָה.
וְאַהֲבָתְךָ אַל תָּסִיר מִמֶּנּוּ לְעוֹלָמִים. Reader בָּרוּךְ אַתָּה, יְיָ,
אוֹהֵב עַמּוֹ יִשְׂרָאֵל.

The verse וְהוּא רַחוּם, consisting of thirteen words, was held by some to
recall the thirteen attributes of divine mercy (Exodus 34:6–7). "As the evening
approaches, man is conscious of having sinned during the day, and thus begins
his prayer with this appeal to the divine mercy" (Maḥzor Vitry, page 77).

The Ma'ariv service properly begins here.

He, being merciful, forgives iniquity, and does not destroy;
frequently he turns his anger away, and does not stir up all his
wrath. O Lord, save us; may the King answer us when we call.[1]

Reader:	*Silent meditation:*
Bless the Lord who is blessed.	Blessed, praised, glorified, ex-

Congregation and Reader:

Blessed be the Lord who is blessed
forever and ever.

tolled and exalted be the name
of the supreme King of kings,
the Holy One, blessed be he,
who is the first and the last, and
besides him there is no God. Extol him who is in the heavens—Lord is his
name, and rejoice before him. His name is exalted above all blessing and
praise. Blessed be the name of his glorious majesty forever and ever. Let the
name of the Lord be blessed henceforth and forever.

Blessed art thou, Lord our God, King of the universe, who
at thy word bringest on the evenings. With wisdom thou openest
the gates of heaven, and with understanding thou changest the
times and causest the seasons to alternate. Thou arrangest the
stars in their courses in the sky according to thy will. Thou createst day and night; thou rollest away light before darkness, and
darkness before light; thou causest the day to pass and the night
to come, and makest the distinction between day and night—Lord
of hosts is thy name. Eternal God, mayest thou reign over us
forever and ever. Blessed art thou, O Lord, who bringest on the
evenings.

Thou hast loved the house of Israel thy people with everlasting
love; thou hast taught us Torah and precepts, laws and judgments.
Therefore, Lord our God, when we lie down and when we rise up
we will speak of thy laws, and rejoice in the words of thy Torah
and in thy precepts for evermore. Indeed, they are our life and the
length of our days; we will meditate on them day and night.
Mayest thou never take away thy love from us. Blessed art thou,
O Lord, who lovest thy people Israel.

---

[1] *Psalms* 78:38; 20:10.

(אֵל מֶלֶךְ נֶאֱמָן :When praying in private, add)

דברים ו, ד-ט

שְׁמַע יִשְׂרָאֵל, יְיָ אֱלֹהֵינוּ, יְיָ אֶחָד.

בָּרוּךְ שֵׁם כְּבוֹד מַלְכוּתוֹ לְעוֹלָם וָעֶד.

וְאָהַבְתָּ אֵת יְיָ אֱלֹהֶיךָ בְּכָל לְבָבְךָ וּבְכָל נַפְשְׁךָ וּבְכָל מְאֹדֶךָ. וְהָיוּ הַדְּבָרִים הָאֵלֶּה, אֲשֶׁר אָנֹכִי מְצַוְּךָ הַיּוֹם, עַל לְבָבֶךָ. וְשִׁנַּנְתָּם לְבָנֶיךָ, וְדִבַּרְתָּ בָּם בְּשִׁבְתְּךָ בְּבֵיתֶךָ, וּבְלֶכְתְּךָ בַדֶּרֶךְ, וּבְשָׁכְבְּךָ וּבְקוּמֶךָ. וּקְשַׁרְתָּם לְאוֹת עַל יָדֶךָ, וְהָיוּ לְטֹטָפֹת בֵּין עֵינֶיךָ. וּכְתַבְתָּם עַל מְזֻזוֹת בֵּיתֶךָ וּבִשְׁעָרֶיךָ.

דברים יא, יג-כא

וְהָיָה אִם שָׁמֹעַ תִּשְׁמְעוּ אֶל מִצְוֹתַי, אֲשֶׁר אָנֹכִי מְצַוֶּה אֶתְכֶם הַיּוֹם, לְאַהֲבָה אֶת יְיָ אֱלֹהֵיכֶם, וּלְעָבְדוֹ בְּכָל לְבַבְכֶם וּבְכָל נַפְשְׁכֶם. וְנָתַתִּי מְטַר אַרְצְכֶם בְּעִתּוֹ, יוֹרֶה וּמַלְקוֹשׁ, וְאָסַפְתָּ דְגָנֶךָ, וְתִירֹשְׁךָ וְיִצְהָרֶךָ. וְנָתַתִּי עֵשֶׂב בְּשָׂדְךָ לִבְהֶמְתֶּךָ, וְאָכַלְתָּ וְשָׂבָעְתָּ. הִשָּׁמְרוּ לָכֶם פֶּן יִפְתֶּה לְבַבְכֶם, וְסַרְתֶּם וַעֲבַדְתֶּם אֱלֹהִים אֲחֵרִים, וְהִשְׁתַּחֲוִיתֶם לָהֶם. וְחָרָה אַף יְיָ בָּכֶם, וְעָצַר אֶת הַשָּׁמַיִם וְלֹא יִהְיֶה מָטָר, וְהָאֲדָמָה לֹא תִתֵּן אֶת יְבוּלָהּ; וַאֲבַדְתֶּם מְהֵרָה מֵעַל הָאָרֶץ הַטֹּבָה אֲשֶׁר יְיָ נֹתֵן לָכֶם. וְשַׂמְתֶּם אֶת דְּבָרַי אֵלֶּה עַל לְבַבְכֶם וְעַל נַפְשְׁכֶם; וּקְשַׁרְתֶּם אֹתָם לְאוֹת עַל יֶדְכֶם, וְהָיוּ לְטוֹטָפֹת בֵּין עֵינֵיכֶם. וְלִמַּדְתֶּם אֹתָם אֶת בְּנֵיכֶם לְדַבֵּר בָּם, בְּשִׁבְתְּךָ בְּבֵיתֶךָ, וּבְלֶכְתְּךָ בַדֶּרֶךְ, וּבְשָׁכְבְּךָ וּבְקוּמֶךָ. וּכְתַבְתָּם עַל מְזוּזוֹת בֵּיתֶךָ וּבִשְׁעָרֶיךָ.

לְמַעַן יִרְבּוּ יְמֵיכֶם וִימֵי בְנֵיכֶם, עַל הָאֲדָמָה אֲשֶׁר נִשְׁבַּע יְיָ לַאֲבֹתֵיכֶם לָתֵת לָהֶם, כִּימֵי הַשָּׁמַיִם עַל הָאָרֶץ.

במדבר טו, לז-מא

וַיֹּאמֶר יְיָ אֶל מֹשֶׁה לֵּאמֹר: דַּבֵּר אֶל בְּנֵי יִשְׂרָאֵל וְאָמַרְתָּ

SHEMA

(When praying in private, add: God is a faithful King.)

Deuteronomy 6:4–9

Hear, O Israel, the Lord is our God, the Lord is One.

Blessed be the name of his glorious majesty forever and ever.

You shall love the Lord your God with all your heart and with all your soul and with all your might. And these words which I command you today shall be in your heart. You shall teach them diligently to your children, and you shall speak of them when you are sitting at home and when you go on a journey, when you lie down and when you rise up. You shall bind them for a sign on your hand, and they shall be for frontlets between your eyes. You shall inscribe them on the doorposts of your house and on your gates.

Deuteronomy 11:13–21

And if you will carefully obey my commands which I give you today, to love the Lord your God and to serve him with all your heart and with all your soul, I will give rain for your land at the right season, the autumn rains and the spring rains, that you may gather in your grain, your wine and your oil. And I will produce grass in your fields for your cattle, and you will eat and be satisfied. Beware lest your heart be deceived, and you turn and serve other gods and worship them; for then the Lord's anger will blaze against you, and he will shut up the skies so that there will be no rain, and the land will yield no produce, and you will quickly perish from the good land which the Lord gives you. So you shall place these words of mine in your heart and in your soul, and you shall bind them for a sign on your hand, and they shall be for frontlets between your eyes. You shall teach them to your children, speaking of them when you are sitting at home and when you go on a journey, when you lie down and when you rise up. You shall inscribe them on the doorposts of your house and on your gates— that your life and the life of your children may be prolonged in the land, which the Lord promised he would give to your fathers, for as long as the sky remains over the earth.

Numbers 15:37–41

The Lord spoke to Moses, saying: Speak to the children of

אֱלֵהֶם, וְעָשׂוּ לָהֶם צִיצִת עַל כַּנְפֵי בִגְדֵיהֶם לְדֹרֹתָם; וְנָתְנוּ עַל
צִיצִת הַכָּנָף פְּתִיל תְּכֵלֶת. וְהָיָה לָכֶם לְצִיצִת, וּרְאִיתֶם אֹתוֹ
וּזְכַרְתֶּם אֶת כָּל מִצְוֹת יְיָ, וַעֲשִׂיתֶם אֹתָם; וְלֹא תָתוּרוּ אַחֲרֵי
לְבַבְכֶם וְאַחֲרֵי עֵינֵיכֶם, אֲשֶׁר אַתֶּם זֹנִים אַחֲרֵיהֶם. לְמַעַן
תִּזְכְּרוּ וַעֲשִׂיתֶם אֶת כָּל מִצְוֹתָי, וִהְיִיתֶם קְדֹשִׁים לֵאלֹהֵיכֶם.
אֲנִי יְיָ אֱלֹהֵיכֶם, אֲשֶׁר הוֹצֵאתִי אֶתְכֶם מֵאֶרֶץ מִצְרַיִם לִהְיוֹת
לָכֶם לֵאלֹהִים; אֲנִי Reader יְיָ אֱלֹהֵיכֶם—

אֱמֶת וֶאֱמוּנָה כָּל זֹאת, וְקַיָּם עָלֵינוּ כִּי הוּא יְיָ אֱלֹהֵינוּ וְאֵין
זוּלָתוֹ, וַאֲנַחְנוּ יִשְׂרָאֵל עַמּוֹ. הַפּוֹדֵנוּ מִיַּד מְלָכִים, מַלְכֵּנוּ
הַגּוֹאֲלֵנוּ מִכַּף כָּל הֶעָרִיצִים; הָאֵל הַנִּפְרָע לָנוּ מִצָּרֵינוּ,
וְהַמְשַׁלֵּם גְּמוּל לְכָל אֹיְבֵי נַפְשֵׁנוּ; הָעֹשֶׂה גְדֹלוֹת עַד אֵין חֵקֶר,
וְנִפְלָאוֹת עַד אֵין מִסְפָּר; הַשָּׂם נַפְשֵׁנוּ בַּחַיִּים, וְלֹא נָתַן לַמּוֹט
רַגְלֵנוּ; הַמַּדְרִיכֵנוּ עַל בָּמוֹת אוֹיְבֵינוּ, וַיָּרֶם קַרְנֵנוּ עַל כָּל שׂנְאֵינוּ;
הָעֹשֶׂה לָּנוּ נִסִּים וּנְקָמָה בְּפַרְעֹה, אוֹתוֹת וּמוֹפְתִים בְּאַדְמַת
בְּנֵי חָם; הַמַּכֶּה בְעֶבְרָתוֹ כָּל בְּכוֹרֵי מִצְרָיִם, וַיּוֹצֵא אֶת עַמּוֹ
יִשְׂרָאֵל מִתּוֹכָם לְחֵרוּת עוֹלָם. הַמַּעֲבִיר בָּנָיו בֵּין גִּזְרֵי יַם סוּף;
אֶת רוֹדְפֵיהֶם וְאֶת שׂוֹנְאֵיהֶם בִּתְהוֹמוֹת טִבַּע. וְרָאוּ בָנָיו גְּבוּרָתוֹ;
שִׁבְּחוּ וְהוֹדוּ לִשְׁמוֹ, וּמַלְכוּתוֹ בְּרָצוֹן קִבְּלוּ עֲלֵיהֶם.

מֹשֶׁה וּבְנֵי יִשְׂרָאֵל לְךָ עָנוּ שִׁירָה בְּשִׂמְחָה רַבָּה, וְאָמְרוּ כֻלָּם:
מִי כָמֹכָה בָּאֵלִם, יְיָ; מִי כָּמֹכָה נֶאְדָּר בַּקֹּדֶשׁ, נוֹרָא תְהִלֹּת,
עֹשֵׂה פֶלֶא.

מַלְכוּתְךָ רָאוּ בָנֶיךָ, בּוֹקֵעַ יָם לִפְנֵי מֹשֶׁה; זֶה אֵלִי עָנוּ
וְאָמְרוּ:
יְיָ יִמְלֹךְ לְעֹלָם וָעֶד.

וְנֶאֱמַר: כִּי פָדָה יְיָ אֶת יַעֲקֹב, וּגְאָלוֹ מִיַּד חָזָק מִמֶּנּוּ. בָּרוּךְ
אַתָּה, יְיָ, גָּאַל יִשְׂרָאֵל.

Israel and tell them to make for themselves fringes on the corners
of their garments throughout their generations, and to put on the
fringe of each corner a blue thread. You shall have it as a fringe,
so that when you look upon it you will remember to do all the
commands of the Lord, and you will not follow the desires of
your heart and your eyes which lead you astray. It is for you to
remember and do all my commands and be holy for your God. I
am the Lord your God who brought you out of the land of Egypt
to be your God; I am the Lord your God.

True and trustworthy is all this. We are certain that he is the
Lord our God, and no one else, and that we Israel are his people.
It is he, our King, who redeemed us from the power of despots,
delivered us from the grasp of all the tyrants, avenged us upon
our oppressors, and requited all our mortal enemies. He did great,
incomprehensible acts and countless wonders; he kept us alive,
and did not let us slip.[1] He made us tread upon the high places
of our enemies, and raised our strength over all our foes. He
performed for us miracles and vengeance upon Pharaoh, signs
and wonders in the land of the Hamites; he smote in his wrath
all the first-born of Egypt, and brought his people Israel from
their midst to enduring freedom. He made his children pass between the divided parts of the Red Sea, and engulfed their pursuers
and their enemies in the depths. His children beheld his might;
they gave praise and thanks to his name, and willingly accepted
his sovereignty.

Moses and the children of Israel sang a song to thee with
great rejoicing; all of them said:

"Who is like thee, O Lord, among the mighty? Who is like
thee, glorious in holiness, awe-inspiring in renown, doing wonders?"[2]

Thy children saw thy majesty as thou didst part the sea before
Moses. "This is my God!" they shouted, and they said:

"The Lord shall reign forever and ever."[3]

And it is said: "Indeed, the Lord has delivered Jacob, and
rescued him from a stronger power."[4] Blessed art thou, O Lord,
who hast redeemed Israel.

---

[1] *Job* 9:10; *Psalm* 66:9. [2] *Exodus* 15:11. [3] *Exodus* 15:18. [4] *Jeremiah* 31:10

הַשְׁכִּיבֵנוּ, יְיָ אֱלֹהֵינוּ, לְשָׁלוֹם, וְהַעֲמִידֵנוּ, מַלְכֵּנוּ, לְחַיִּים;
וּפְרוֹשׁ עָלֵינוּ סֻכַּת שְׁלוֹמֶךָ, וְתַקְּנֵנוּ בְּעֵצָה טוֹבָה מִלְּפָנֶיךָ,
וְהוֹשִׁיעֵנוּ לְמַעַן שְׁמֶךָ; וְהָגֵן בַּעֲדֵנוּ, וְהָסֵר מֵעָלֵינוּ אוֹיֵב, דֶּבֶר
וְחֶרֶב וְרָעָב וְיָגוֹן; וְהָסֵר שָׂטָן מִלְּפָנֵינוּ וּמֵאַחֲרֵינוּ, וּבְצֵל כְּנָפֶיךָ
תַּסְתִּירֵנוּ; כִּי אֵל שׁוֹמְרֵנוּ וּמַצִּילֵנוּ אָתָּה, כִּי אֵל מֶלֶךְ חַנּוּן
וְרַחוּם אָתָּה. Reader וּשְׁמוֹר צֵאתֵנוּ וּבוֹאֵנוּ לְחַיִּים וּלְשָׁלוֹם,
מֵעַתָּה וְעַד עוֹלָם. בָּרוּךְ אַתָּה, יְיָ, שׁוֹמֵר עַמּוֹ יִשְׂרָאֵל לָעַד.

בָּרוּךְ יְיָ לְעוֹלָם, אָמֵן וְאָמֵן. בָּרוּךְ יְיָ מִצִּיּוֹן, שֹׁכֵן יְרוּשָׁלָיִם;
הַלְלוּיָהּ. בָּרוּךְ יְיָ אֱלֹהִים, אֱלֹהֵי יִשְׂרָאֵל, עֹשֵׂה נִפְלָאוֹת לְבַדּוֹ.
וּבָרוּךְ שֵׁם כְּבוֹדוֹ לְעוֹלָם, וְיִמָּלֵא כְבוֹדוֹ אֶת כָּל הָאָרֶץ, אָמֵן
וְאָמֵן. יְהִי כְבוֹד יְיָ לְעוֹלָם; יִשְׂמַח יְיָ בְּמַעֲשָׂיו. יְהִי שֵׁם יְיָ
מְבֹרָךְ, מֵעַתָּה וְעַד עוֹלָם. כִּי לֹא יִטֹּשׁ יְיָ אֶת עַמּוֹ בַּעֲבוּר שְׁמוֹ
הַגָּדוֹל; כִּי הוֹאִיל יְיָ לַעֲשׂוֹת אֶתְכֶם לוֹ לְעָם. וַיַּרְא כָּל הָעָם
וַיִּפְּלוּ עַל פְּנֵיהֶם, וַיֹּאמְרוּ: יְיָ הוּא הָאֱלֹהִים, יְיָ הוּא הָאֱלֹהִים.
וְהָיָה יְיָ לְמֶלֶךְ עַל כָּל הָאָרֶץ; בַּיּוֹם הַהוּא יִהְיֶה יְיָ אֶחָד וּשְׁמוֹ
אֶחָד. יְהִי חַסְדְּךָ יְיָ עָלֵינוּ, כַּאֲשֶׁר יִחַלְנוּ לָךְ. הוֹשִׁיעֵנוּ, יְיָ
אֱלֹהֵינוּ, וְקַבְּצֵנוּ מִן הַגּוֹיִם, לְהֹדוֹת לְשֵׁם קָדְשֶׁךָ, לְהִשְׁתַּבֵּחַ
בִּתְהִלָּתֶךָ. כָּל גּוֹיִם אֲשֶׁר עָשִׂיתָ יָבֹאוּ וְיִשְׁתַּחֲווּ לְפָנֶיךָ, אֲדֹנָי,
וִיכַבְּדוּ לִשְׁמֶךָ. כִּי גָדוֹל אַתָּה וְעֹשֵׂה נִפְלָאוֹת; אַתָּה אֱלֹהִים
לְבַדֶּךָ. וַאֲנַחְנוּ, עַמְּךָ וְצֹאן מַרְעִיתֶךָ, נוֹדֶה לְּךָ לְעוֹלָם, לְדוֹר
וָדוֹר נְסַפֵּר תְּהִלָּתֶךָ.

בָּרוּךְ יְיָ בַּיּוֹם, בָּרוּךְ יְיָ בַּלָּיְלָה; בָּרוּךְ יְיָ בְּשָׁכְבֵּנוּ, בָּרוּךְ
יְיָ בְּקוּמֵנוּ; כִּי בְיָדְךָ נַפְשׁוֹת הַחַיִּים וְהַמֵּתִים. אֲשֶׁר בְּיָדוֹ נֶפֶשׁ
כָּל חָי, וְרוּחַ כָּל בְּשַׂר אִישׁ. בְּיָדְךָ אַפְקִיד רוּחִי; פָּדִיתָה אוֹתִי,

Grant, Lord our God, that we lie down in peace, and that we rise again, O our King, to life. Spread over us thy shelter of peace, and direct us with good counsel of thy own. Save us for thy name's sake; shield us, and remove from us every enemy and pestilence, sword and famine and grief; remove the adversary from before us and from behind us; shelter us in the shadow of thy wings; for thou art our protecting and saving God; thou art indeed a gracious and merciful God and King. Guard thou our going out and our coming in, for life and peace, henceforth and forever. Blessed art thou, O Lord, who guardest thy people Israel forever.

Blessed be the Lord forever—Amen, Amen. Blessed from Zion be the Lord who dwells in Jerusalem. Praise the Lord! Blessed be the Lord God, the God of Israel, who alone does wonders. Blessed be his glorious name forever, and may the whole earth be filled with his glory—Amen, Amen. May the glory of the Lord be forever; may the Lord rejoice in his works. Blessed be the name of the Lord henceforth and forever. Surely, the Lord will not forsake his people by virtue of his great name, for the Lord has determined to make you into a people of his own. When all the people saw it, they fell on their faces and exclaimed: "The Lord is God! The Lord is God!" The Lord shall reign over all the earth; on that day the Lord shall be One, and his name One. May thy kindness, O Lord, rest on us, as our hope rests in thee. Lord our God, save us; gather us from the nations, that we may give thanks to thy holy name, and triumph in thy praise. All the nations whom thou hast made shall come and bow down before thee, O Lord, and shall honor thy name; for thou art great and doest wonders; thou alone art God. We thy people, the flock of thy pasture, will ever praise thee; throughout all generations we will recount thy praise.[1]

Blessed be the Lord by day; blessed be the Lord by night; blessed be the Lord when we lie down; blessed be the Lord when we rise up. In thy hand are the souls of the living and the dead, *as it is written:* "In his hand is the soul of every living thing, and the spirit of every human being."[2] Into thy hand I commit my

[1] *Psalms* 89:53; 135:21; 72:18–19; 104:31; 113:2; *I Samuel* 12:22; *I Kings* 18:39; *Zechariah* 14:9; *Psalms* 33:22; 106.47; 86:9–10; 79:13. [2] *Job* 12:10.

יְיָ, אֵל אֱמֶת. אֱלֹהֵינוּ שֶׁבַּשָּׁמַיִם, יַחֵד שִׁמְךָ וְקַיֵּם מַלְכוּתְךָ
תָּמִיד, וּמְלוֹךְ עָלֵינוּ לְעוֹלָם וָעֶד.

יִרְאוּ עֵינֵינוּ וְיִשְׂמַח לִבֵּנוּ, וְתָגֵל נַפְשֵׁנוּ בִּישׁוּעָתְךָ בֶּאֱמֶת,
בֶּאֱמֹר לְצִיּוֹן מָלַךְ אֱלֹהָיִךְ. יְיָ מֶלֶךְ, יְיָ מָלָךְ, יְיָ יִמְלֹךְ לְעוֹלָם
וָעֶד. Reader כִּי הַמַּלְכוּת שֶׁלְּךָ הִיא, וּלְעוֹלְמֵי עַד תִּמְלֹךְ
בְּכָבוֹד, כִּי אֵין לָנוּ מֶלֶךְ אֶלָּא אָתָּה. בָּרוּךְ אַתָּה, יְיָ, הַמֶּלֶךְ
בִּכְבוֹדוֹ תָּמִיד יִמְלֹךְ עָלֵינוּ, לְעוֹלָם וָעֶד, וְעַל כָּל מַעֲשָׂיו.

Reader:

יִתְגַּדַּל וְיִתְקַדַּשׁ שְׁמֵהּ רַבָּא בְּעָלְמָא דִּי בְרָא כִרְעוּתֵהּ,
וְיַמְלִיךְ מַלְכוּתֵהּ בְּחַיֵּיכוֹן וּבְיוֹמֵיכוֹן, וּבְחַיֵּי דְכָל בֵּית יִשְׂרָאֵל,
בַּעֲגָלָא וּבִזְמַן קָרִיב, וְאִמְרוּ אָמֵן.

יְהֵא שְׁמֵהּ רַבָּא מְבָרַךְ לְעָלַם וּלְעָלְמֵי עָלְמַיָּא.

יִתְבָּרַךְ וְיִשְׁתַּבַּח, וְיִתְפָּאַר וְיִתְרוֹמַם, וְיִתְנַשֵּׂא וְיִתְהַדָּר,
וְיִתְעַלֶּה וְיִתְהַלַּל שְׁמֵהּ דְּקֻדְשָׁא, בְּרִיךְ הוּא, לְעֵלָּא (לְעֵלָּא)
מִן כָּל בִּרְכָתָא וְשִׁירָתָא, תֻּשְׁבְּחָתָא וְנֶחֱמָתָא, דַּאֲמִירָן בְּעָלְמָא,
וְאִמְרוּ אָמֵן.

The *Shemoneh Esreh* is recited in silent devotion while standing, facing east.

אֲדֹנָי, שְׂפָתַי תִּפְתָּח, וּפִי יַגִּיד תְּהִלָּתֶךָ.

בָּרוּךְ אַתָּה, יְיָ אֱלֹהֵינוּ וֵאלֹהֵי אֲבוֹתֵינוּ, אֱלֹהֵי אַבְרָהָם,
אֱלֹהֵי יִצְחָק, וֵאלֹהֵי יַעֲקֹב, הָאֵל הַגָּדוֹל הַגִּבּוֹר וְהַנּוֹרָא, אֵל
עֶלְיוֹן, גּוֹמֵל חֲסָדִים טוֹבִים, וְקוֹנֵה הַכֹּל, וְזוֹכֵר חַסְדֵי אָבוֹת,
וּמֵבִיא גוֹאֵל לִבְנֵי בְנֵיהֶם לְמַעַן שְׁמוֹ בְּאַהֲבָה.

Between *Rosh Hashanah* and *Yom Kippur* add:

(זָכְרֵנוּ לְחַיִּים, מֶלֶךְ חָפֵץ בַּחַיִּים,
וְכָתְבֵנוּ בְּסֵפֶר הַחַיִּים, לְמַעַנְךָ אֱלֹהִים חַיִּים.)

spirit; O Lord, faithful God, thou savest me.[1] Our God who art
in heaven, reveal thy Oneness and establish thy kingdom forever;
do thou reign over us forever and ever.

May our eyes behold, our heart rejoice, and our soul exult in
thy true salvation, when it will be said to Zion: "Your God is
King." The Lord is King, the Lord was King, the Lord will be
King forever and ever. For the kingdom is thine, and to all eternity
thou wilt reign in glory; we have no King except thee. Blessed art
thou, O Lord, glorious King, who wilt reign over us and over thy
entire creation forever and ever.

Reader:

Glorified and sanctified be God's great name throughout the
world which he has created according to his will. May he establish
his kingdom in your lifetime and during your days, and within the
life of the entire house of Israel, speedily and soon; and say, Amen.

May his great name be blessed forever and to all eternity.

Blessed and praised, glorified and exalted, extolled and honored,
adored and lauded be the name of the Holy One, blessed be he,
beyond all the blessings and hymns, praises and consolations that
are ever spoken in the world; and say, Amen.

SHEMONEH ESREH

The Shemoneh Esreh is recited in silent devotion while standing, facing east.

O Lord, open thou my lips, that my mouth may declare thy
praise.[2]

Blessed art thou, Lord our God and God of our fathers, God
of Abraham, God of Isaac and God of Jacob; great, mighty and
revered God, sublime God, who bestowest lovingkindness, and
art Master of all things; who rememberest the good deeds of our
fathers, and who wilt graciously bring a redeemer to their children's children for the sake of thy name.

Between Rosh Hashanah and Yom Kippur add:

(Remember us to life, O King who delightest in life; inscribe us
in the book of life for thy sake, O living God.)

On שמונה עשרה, see pages 81-92.

[1] *Psalm* 31:6.   [2] *Psalm* 51:17.

מֶלֶךְ עוֹזֵר וּמוֹשִׁיעַ וּמָגֵן. בָּרוּךְ אַתָּה, יְיָ, מָגֵן אַבְרָהָם.

אַתָּה גִּבּוֹר לְעוֹלָם, אֲדֹנָי; מְחַיֵּה מֵתִים אַתָּה, רַב לְהוֹשִׁיעַ.

Between *Sukkoth* and *Pesaḥ* add:

(מַשִּׁיב הָרוּחַ וּמוֹרִיד הַגָּשֶׁם.)

מְכַלְכֵּל חַיִּים בְּחֶסֶד, מְחַיֵּה מֵתִים בְּרַחֲמִים רַבִּים, סוֹמֵךְ
נוֹפְלִים, וְרוֹפֵא חוֹלִים, וּמַתִּיר אֲסוּרִים, וּמְקַיֵּם אֱמוּנָתוֹ לִישֵׁנֵי
עָפָר. מִי כָמֽוֹךָ, בַּעַל גְּבוּרוֹת, וּמִי דּֽוֹמֶה לָּךְ, מֶלֶךְ מֵמִית
וּמְחַיֶּה וּמַצְמִיחַ יְשׁוּעָה.

Between *Rosh Hashanah* and *Yom Kippur* add:

(מִי כָמֽוֹךָ, אַב הָרַחֲמִים,

זוֹכֵר יְצוּרָיו לְחַיִּים בְּרַחֲמִים.)

וְנֶאֱמָן אַתָּה לְהַחֲיוֹת מֵתִים. בָּרוּךְ אַתָּה, יְיָ, מְחַיֵּה הַמֵּתִים.

אַתָּה קָדוֹשׁ וְשִׁמְךָ קָדוֹשׁ, וּקְדוֹשִׁים בְּכָל יוֹם יְהַלְלֽוּךָ סֶּלָה.
* בָּרוּךְ אַתָּה, יְיָ, הָאֵל הַקָּדוֹשׁ.

*Between *Rosh Hashanah* and *Yom Kippur* substitute:

(בָּרוּךְ אַתָּה, יְיָ, הַמֶּלֶךְ הַקָּדוֹשׁ.)

אַתָּה חוֹנֵן לְאָדָם דַּעַת, וּמְלַמֵּד לֶאֱנוֹשׁ בִּינָה.

On the night following the Sabbath or any other holy day, add:

(אַתָּה חוֹנַנְתָּנוּ מַדַּע תּוֹרָתֶךָ, וַתְּלַמְּדֵנוּ לַעֲשׂוֹת חֻקֵּי רְצוֹנֶךָ;
וַתַּבְדֵּל, יְיָ אֱלֹהֵינוּ, בֵּין קֹדֶשׁ לְחֹל, בֵּין אוֹר לְחֹשֶׁךְ, בֵּין
יִשְׂרָאֵל לָעַמִּים, בֵּין יוֹם הַשְּׁבִיעִי לְשֵׁשֶׁת יְמֵי הַמַּעֲשֶׂה. אָבִינוּ
מַלְכֵּנוּ, הָחֵל עָלֵינוּ הַיָּמִים הַבָּאִים לִקְרָאתֵנוּ לְשָׁלוֹם, חֲשׂוּכִים
מִכָּל חֵטְא, וּמְנֻקִּים מִכָּל עָוֹן, וּמְדֻבָּקִים בְּיִרְאָתֶךָ.)

(וְ)חָנֵּנוּ מֵאִתְּךָ דֵּעָה, בִּינָה וְהַשְׂכֵּל. בָּרוּךְ אַתָּה, יְיָ, חוֹנֵן
הַדָּעַת.

O King, Supporter, Savior and Shield. Blessed art thou, O Lord, Shield of Abraham.

Thou, O Lord, art mighty forever; thou revivest the dead; thou art powerful to save.

Between Sukkoth and Pesaḥ add:

(Thou causest the wind to blow and the rain to fall.)

Thou sustainest the living with kindness, and revivest the dead with great mercy; thou supportest all who fall, and healest the sick; thou settest the captives free, and keepest faith with those who sleep in the dust. Who is like thee, Lord of power? Who resembles thee, O King? Thou bringest death and restorest life, and causest salvation to flourish.

Between Rosh Hashanah and Yom Kippur add:

(Who is like thee, merciful Father? In mercy thou rememberest thy creatures to life.)

Thou art faithful to revive the dead. Blessed art thou, O Lord, who revivest the dead.

Thou art holy and thy name is holy, and holy beings praise thee daily. * Blessed art thou, O Lord, holy God.

*Between Rosh Hashanah and Yom Kippur substitute:

(Blessed art thou, O Lord, holy King.)

Thou favorest man with knowledge, and teachest mortals understanding.

On the night following the Sabbath or any other holy day, add:

(Thou hast favored us with a knowledge of thy Torah, and taught us to perform the laws of thy will. Thou hast made a distinction, Lord our God, between the holy and the profane, between light and darkness, between Israel and the nations, between the seventh day and the six days of work. Our Father, our King, grant that the approaching days may begin for us in peace; may we be withheld from all sin, cleansed from all iniquity, and devoted to the veneration of thee.)

O grant us knowledge, understanding and insight. Blessed art thou, O Lord, gracious Giver of knowledge.

הֲשִׁיבֵנוּ אָבִינוּ לְתוֹרָתֶךָ, וְקָרְבֵנוּ מַלְכֵּנוּ לַעֲבוֹדָתֶךָ; וְהַחֲזִירֵנוּ בִּתְשׁוּבָה שְׁלֵמָה לְפָנֶיךָ. בָּרוּךְ אַתָּה, יְיָ, הָרוֹצֶה בִּתְשׁוּבָה.

סְלַח לָנוּ אָבִינוּ כִּי חָטָאנוּ, מְחַל לָנוּ מַלְכֵּנוּ כִּי פָשָׁעְנוּ, כִּי מוֹחֵל וְסוֹלֵחַ אָתָּה. בָּרוּךְ אַתָּה, יְיָ, חַנּוּן הַמַּרְבֶּה לִסְלֹחַ.

רְאֵה נָא בְעָנְיֵנוּ וְרִיבָה רִיבֵנוּ, וּגְאָלֵנוּ מְהֵרָה לְמַעַן שְׁמֶךָ, כִּי גוֹאֵל חָזָק אָתָּה. בָּרוּךְ אַתָּה, יְיָ, גּוֹאֵל יִשְׂרָאֵל.

רְפָאֵנוּ יְיָ וְנֵרָפֵא, הוֹשִׁיעֵנוּ וְנִוָּשֵׁעָה, כִּי תְהִלָּתֵנוּ אָתָּה; וְהַעֲלֵה רְפוּאָה שְׁלֵמָה לְכָל מַכּוֹתֵינוּ, כִּי אֵל מֶלֶךְ רוֹפֵא נֶאֱמָן וְרַחֲמָן אָתָּה. בָּרוּךְ אַתָּה, יְיָ, רוֹפֵא חוֹלֵי עַמּוֹ יִשְׂרָאֵל.

בָּרֵךְ עָלֵינוּ, יְיָ אֱלֹהֵינוּ, אֶת הַשָּׁנָה הַזֹּאת וְאֶת כָּל מִינֵי תְבוּאָתָהּ לְטוֹבָה,

<table>
<tr><td>From December 4th till Pesaḥ say:</td><td>From Pesaḥ till December 4th say:</td></tr>
<tr><td>וְתֵן בְּרָכָה</td><td>וְתֵן טַל וּמָטָר לִבְרָכָה</td></tr>
</table>

עַל פְּנֵי הָאֲדָמָה, וְשַׂבְּעֵנוּ מִטּוּבֶךָ, וּבָרֵךְ שְׁנָתֵנוּ כַּשָּׁנִים הַטּוֹבוֹת. בָּרוּךְ אַתָּה, יְיָ, מְבָרֵךְ הַשָּׁנִים.

תְּקַע בְּשׁוֹפָר גָּדוֹל לְחֵרוּתֵנוּ, וְשָׂא נֵס לְקַבֵּץ גָּלְיוֹתֵינוּ, וְקַבְּצֵנוּ יַחַד מֵאַרְבַּע כַּנְפוֹת הָאָרֶץ. בָּרוּךְ אַתָּה, יְיָ, מְקַבֵּץ נִדְחֵי עַמּוֹ יִשְׂרָאֵל.

הָשִׁיבָה שׁוֹפְטֵינוּ כְּבָרִאשׁוֹנָה, וְיוֹעֲצֵינוּ כְּבַתְּחִלָּה; וְהָסֵר מִמֶּנּוּ יָגוֹן וַאֲנָחָה; וּמְלוֹךְ עָלֵינוּ, אַתָּה יְיָ לְבַדְּךָ, בְּחֶסֶד וּבְרַחֲמִים, וְצַדְּקֵנוּ בַּמִּשְׁפָּט. * בָּרוּךְ אַתָּה, יְיָ, מֶלֶךְ אוֹהֵב צְדָקָה וּמִשְׁפָּט.

*Between Rosh Hashanah and Yom Kippur substitute:

(בָּרוּךְ אַתָּה, יְיָ, הַמֶּלֶךְ הַמִּשְׁפָּט.)

Restore us, our Father, to thy Torah; draw us near, our King, to thy service; cause us to return to thee in perfect repentance. Blessed art thou, O Lord, who art pleased with repentance.

Forgive us, our Father, for we have sinned; pardon us, our King, for we have transgressed; for thou dost pardon and forgive. Blessed art thou, O Lord, who art gracious and ever forgiving.

Look upon our affliction and champion our cause; redeem us speedily for thy name's sake, for thou art a mighty Redeemer. Blessed art thou, O Lord, Redeemer of Israel.

Heal us, O Lord, and we shall be healed; save us and we shall be saved; for thou art our praise. Grant a perfect healing to all our wounds; for thou art a faithful and merciful God, King and Healer. Blessed art thou, O Lord, who healest the sick among thy people Israel.

Bless for us, Lord our God, this year and all kinds of its produce for the best.

From Pesaḥ till December 4th say: *From December 4th till Pesaḥ say:*

Bestow a blessing   Bestow dew and rain for a blessing upon the face of the earth. Satisfy us with thy goodness, and bless our year like other good years. Blessed art thou, O Lord, who blessest the years.

Sound the great Shofar for our freedom; lift up the banner to bring our exiles together, and assemble us from the four corners of the earth. Blessed art thou, O Lord, who gatherest the dispersed of thy people Israel.

Restore our judges as at first, and our counselors as at the beginning; remove from us sorrow and sighing; reign thou alone over us, O Lord, in kindness and mercy, and clear us in judgment. * Blessed art thou, O Lord, King who lovest righteousness and justice.

> ** Between Rosh Hashanah and Yom Kippur substitute:*
> (Blessed art thou, O Lord, King of Justice.)

This century, טל ומטר is inserted from December 5. In some years it is December 6.

וְלַמַּלְשִׁינִים אַל תְּהִי תִקְוָה, וְכָל הָרִשְׁעָה כְּרֶגַע תֹּאבֵד,
וְכָל אֹיְבֶיךָ מְהֵרָה יִכָּרֵתוּ; וְהַזֵּדִים מְהֵרָה תְעַקֵּר וּתְשַׁבֵּר
וּתְמַגֵּר וְתַכְנִיעַ בִּמְהֵרָה בְיָמֵינוּ. בָּרוּךְ אַתָּה, יְיָ, שׁוֹבֵר אֹיְבִים
וּמַכְנִיעַ זֵדִים.

עַל הַצַּדִּיקִים וְעַל הַחֲסִידִים, וְעַל זִקְנֵי עַמְּךָ בֵּית יִשְׂרָאֵל
וְעַל פְּלֵיטַת סוֹפְרֵיהֶם, וְעַל גֵּרֵי הַצֶּדֶק וְעָלֵינוּ, יֶהֱמוּ נָא
רַחֲמֶיךָ, יְיָ אֱלֹהֵינוּ; וְתֵן שָׂכָר טוֹב לְכָל הַבּוֹטְחִים בְּשִׁמְךָ
בֶּאֱמֶת, וְשִׂים חֶלְקֵנוּ עִמָּהֶם, וּלְעוֹלָם לֹא נֵבוֹשׁ, כִּי בְךָ בָּטָחְנוּ.
בָּרוּךְ אַתָּה, יְיָ, מִשְׁעָן וּמִבְטָח לַצַּדִּיקִים.

וְלִירוּשָׁלַיִם עִירְךָ בְּרַחֲמִים תָּשׁוּב, וְתִשְׁכּוֹן בְּתוֹכָהּ כַּאֲשֶׁר
דִּבַּרְתָּ; וּבְנֵה אוֹתָהּ בְּקָרוֹב בְּיָמֵינוּ בִּנְיַן עוֹלָם; וְכִסֵּא דָוִד
מְהֵרָה לְתוֹכָהּ תָּכִין. בָּרוּךְ אַתָּה, יְיָ, בּוֹנֵה יְרוּשָׁלָיִם.

אֶת צֶמַח דָּוִד עַבְדְּךָ מְהֵרָה תַצְמִיחַ, וְקַרְנוֹ תָּרוּם
בִּישׁוּעָתֶךָ, כִּי לִישׁוּעָתְךָ קִוִּינוּ כָּל הַיּוֹם. בָּרוּךְ אַתָּה, יְיָ,
מַצְמִיחַ קֶרֶן יְשׁוּעָה.

שְׁמַע קוֹלֵנוּ, יְיָ אֱלֹהֵינוּ; חוּס וְרַחֵם עָלֵינוּ, וְקַבֵּל בְּרַחֲמִים
וּבְרָצוֹן אֶת תְּפִלָּתֵנוּ, כִּי אֵל שׁוֹמֵעַ תְּפִלּוֹת וְתַחֲנוּנִים אָתָּה;
וּמִלְּפָנֶיךָ מַלְכֵּנוּ רֵיקָם אַל תְּשִׁיבֵנוּ, כִּי אַתָּה שׁוֹמֵעַ תְּפִלַּת
עַמְּךָ יִשְׂרָאֵל בְּרַחֲמִים. בָּרוּךְ אַתָּה, יְיָ, שׁוֹמֵעַ תְּפִלָּה.

רְצֵה, יְיָ אֱלֹהֵינוּ, בְּעַמְּךָ יִשְׂרָאֵל וּבִתְפִלָּתָם; וְהָשֵׁב אֶת
הָעֲבוֹדָה לִדְבִיר בֵּיתֶךָ, וְאִשֵּׁי יִשְׂרָאֵל וּתְפִלָּתָם בְּאַהֲבָה
תְקַבֵּל בְּרָצוֹן, וּתְהִי לְרָצוֹן תָּמִיד עֲבוֹדַת יִשְׂרָאֵל עַמֶּךָ.

On *Rosh Ḥodesh* and *Ḥol ha-Moʻed* add:

(אֱלֹהֵינוּ וֵאלֹהֵי אֲבוֹתֵינוּ, יַעֲלֶה וְיָבֹא, וְיַגִּיעַ וְיֵרָאֶה, וְיֵרָצֶה
וְיִשָּׁמַע, וְיִפָּקֵד וְיִזָּכֵר זִכְרוֹנֵנוּ וּפִקְדוֹנֵנוּ, וְזִכְרוֹן אֲבוֹתֵינוּ,

May the slanderers have no hope; may all wickedness perish instantly; may all thy enemies be soon cut down. Do thou speedily uproot and crush the arrogant; cast them down and humble them speedily in our days. Blessed art thou, O Lord, who breakest the enemies and humblest the arrogant.

May thy compassion, Lord our God, be aroused over the righteous and over the godly; over the leaders of thy people, the house of Israel, and over the remnant of their sages; over the true proselytes and over us. Grant a good reward to all who truly trust in thy name, and place our lot among them; may we never come to shame, for in thee we trust. Blessed art thou, O Lord, who art the stay and trust of the righteous.

Return in mercy to thy city Jerusalem and dwell in it, as thou hast promised; rebuild it soon, in our days, as an everlasting structure, and speedily establish in it the throne of David. Blessed art thou, O Lord, Builder of Jerusalem.

Speedily cause the offspring of thy servant David to flourish, and let his glory be exalted by thy help, for we hope for thy deliverance all day. Blessed art thou, O Lord, who causest salvation to flourish.

Hear our voice, Lord our God; spare us and have pity on us; accept our prayer in mercy and favor, for thou art God who hearest prayers and supplications; from thy presence, our King, dismiss us not empty-handed, for thou hearest in mercy the prayer of thy people Israel. Blessed art thou, O Lord, who hearest prayer.

Be pleased, Lord our God, with thy people Israel and with their prayer; restore the worship to thy most holy sanctuary; accept Israel's offerings and prayer with gracious love. May the worship of thy people Israel be ever pleasing to thee.

On Rosh Ḥodesh and Ḥol ha-Mo'ed add:

(Our God and God of our fathers, may the remembrance of us, of our fathers. of Messiah the son of David thy servant, of

וְזִכְרוֹן מָשִׁיחַ בֶּן דָּוִד עַבְדֶּךָ, וְזִכְרוֹן יְרוּשָׁלַיִם עִיר קָדְשֶׁךָ, וְזִכְרוֹן כָּל עַמְּךָ בֵּית יִשְׂרָאֵל לְפָנֶיךָ, לִפְלֵיטָה וּלְטוֹבָה, לְחֵן וּלְחֶסֶד וּלְרַחֲמִים, לְחַיִּים וּלְשָׁלוֹם, בְּיוֹם

Sukkoth	*Pesaḥ*	*Rosh Ḥodesh*
חַג הַסֻּכּוֹת	חַג הַמַּצּוֹת	רֹאשׁ הַחֹדֶשׁ

הַזֶּה. זָכְרֵנוּ, יְיָ אֱלֹהֵינוּ, בּוֹ לְטוֹבָה, וּפָקְדֵנוּ בוֹ לִבְרָכָה, וְהוֹשִׁיעֵנוּ בוֹ לְחַיִּים; וּבִדְבַר יְשׁוּעָה וְרַחֲמִים חוּס וְחָנֵּנוּ, וְרַחֵם עָלֵינוּ וְהוֹשִׁיעֵנוּ, כִּי אֵלֶיךָ עֵינֵינוּ, כִּי אֵל מֶלֶךְ חַנּוּן וְרַחוּם אָתָּה.)

וְתֶחֱזֶינָה עֵינֵינוּ בְּשׁוּבְךָ לְצִיּוֹן בְּרַחֲמִים. בָּרוּךְ אַתָּה, יְיָ, הַמַּחֲזִיר שְׁכִינָתוֹ לְצִיּוֹן.

מוֹדִים אֲנַחְנוּ לָךְ, שָׁאַתָּה הוּא יְיָ אֱלֹהֵינוּ וֵאלֹהֵי אֲבוֹתֵינוּ לְעוֹלָם וָעֶד. צוּר חַיֵּינוּ, מָגֵן יִשְׁעֵנוּ אַתָּה הוּא. לְדוֹר וָדוֹר נוֹדֶה לָּךְ, וּנְסַפֵּר תְּהִלָּתֶךָ, עַל חַיֵּינוּ הַמְּסוּרִים בְּיָדֶךָ, וְעַל נִשְׁמוֹתֵינוּ הַפְּקוּדוֹת לָךְ, וְעַל נִסֶּיךָ שֶׁבְּכָל יוֹם עִמָּנוּ, וְעַל נִפְלְאוֹתֶיךָ וְטוֹבוֹתֶיךָ שֶׁבְּכָל עֵת, עֶרֶב וָבֹקֶר וְצָהֳרָיִם. הַטּוֹב כִּי לֹא כָלוּ רַחֲמֶיךָ, וְהַמְרַחֵם כִּי לֹא תַמּוּ חֲסָדֶיךָ, מֵעוֹלָם קִוִּינוּ לָךְ.

On Ḥanukkah add:

(עַל הַנִּסִּים וְעַל הַפֻּרְקָן, וְעַל הַגְּבוּרוֹת וְעַל הַתְּשׁוּעוֹת, וְעַל הַמִּלְחָמוֹת, שֶׁעָשִׂיתָ לַאֲבוֹתֵינוּ בַּיָּמִים הָהֵם בַּזְּמַן הַזֶּה–

בִּימֵי מַתִּתְיָהוּ בֶּן יוֹחָנָן כֹּהֵן גָּדוֹל, חַשְׁמוֹנַי וּבָנָיו, כְּשֶׁעָמְדָה מַלְכוּת יָוָן הָרְשָׁעָה עַל עַמְּךָ יִשְׂרָאֵל לְהַשְׁכִּיחָם תּוֹרָתֶךָ, וּלְהַעֲבִירָם מֵחֻקֵּי רְצוֹנֶךָ. וְאַתָּה בְּרַחֲמֶיךָ הָרַבִּים עָמַדְתָּ לָהֶם בְּעֵת צָרָתָם, רַבְתָּ אֶת רִיבָם, דַּנְתָּ אֶת דִּינָם, נָקַמְתָּ אֶת נִקְמָתָם; מָסַרְתָּ גִבּוֹרִים בְּיַד חַלָּשִׁים, וְרַבִּים בְּיַד מְעַטִּים, וּטְמֵאִים בְּיַד

Jerusalem thy holy city, and of all thy people the house of Israel, ascend and come and be accepted before thee for deliverance and happiness, for grace, kindness and mercy, for life and peace, on this day of

Rosh Ḥodesh	*Pesaḥ*	*Sukkoth*
the New Moon.	the Feast of Un-leavened Bread.	the Feast of Tabernacles.

Remember us this day, Lord our God, for happiness; be mindful of us for blessing; save us to enjoy life. With a promise of salvation and mercy spare us and be gracious to us; have pity on us and save us, for we look to thee, for thou art a gracious and merciful God and King.)

May our eyes behold thy return in mercy to Zion. Blessed art thou, O Lord, who restorest thy divine presence to Zion.

We ever thank thee, who art the Lord our God and the God of our fathers. Thou art the strength of our life and our saving shield. In every generation we will thank thee and recount thy praise—for our lives which are in thy charge, for our souls which are in thy care, for thy miracles which are daily with us, and for thy continual wonders and favors—evening, morning and noon. Beneficent One, whose mercies never fail, Merciful One, whose kindnesses never cease, thou hast always been our hope.

On Ḥanukkah add:

(We thank thee for the miracles, for the redemption, for the mighty deeds and triumphs, and for the battles which thou didst perform for our fathers in those days, at this season—

In the days of the Hasmonean, Mattathias ben Yoḥanan, the High Priest, and his sons, when a wicked Hellenic government rose up against thy people Israel to make them forget thy Torah and transgress the laws of thy will. Thou in thy great mercy didst stand by them in the time of their distress. Thou didst champion their cause, defend their rights and avenge their wrong; thou didst deliver the strong into the hands of the weak, the many into the hands of the few, the impure into the hands of the pure, the wicked

טְהוֹרִים, וּרְשָׁעִים בְּיַד צַדִּיקִים, וְזֵדִים בְּיַד עוֹסְקֵי תוֹרָתֶךָ.
וּלְךָ עָשִׂיתָ שֵׁם גָּדוֹל וְקָדוֹשׁ בְּעוֹלָמֶךָ, וּלְעַמְּךָ יִשְׂרָאֵל עָשִׂיתָ
תְּשׁוּעָה גְדוֹלָה וּפֻרְקָן כְּהַיּוֹם הַזֶּה. וְאַחַר כֵּן בָּאוּ בָנֶיךָ לִדְבִיר
בֵּיתֶךָ, וּפִנּוּ אֶת הֵיכָלֶךָ, וְטִהֲרוּ אֶת מִקְדָּשֶׁךָ, וְהִדְלִיקוּ נֵרוֹת
בְּחַצְרוֹת קָדְשֶׁךָ, וְקָבְעוּ שְׁמוֹנַת יְמֵי חֲנֻכָּה אֵלּוּ לְהוֹדוֹת וּלְהַלֵּל
לְשִׁמְךָ הַגָּדוֹל.)

On Purim add:

(עַל הַנִּסִּים וְעַל הַפֻּרְקָן, וְעַל הַגְּבוּרוֹת וְעַל הַתְּשׁוּעוֹת, וְעַל
הַמִּלְחָמוֹת, שֶׁעָשִׂיתָ לַאֲבוֹתֵינוּ בַּיָּמִים הָהֵם בַּזְּמַן הַזֶּה–

בִּימֵי מָרְדְּכַי וְאֶסְתֵּר בְּשׁוּשַׁן הַבִּירָה, כְּשֶׁעָמַד עֲלֵיהֶם הָמָן
הָרָשָׁע. בִּקֵּשׁ לְהַשְׁמִיד לַהֲרוֹג וּלְאַבֵּד אֶת כָּל הַיְּהוּדִים, מִנַּעַר
וְעַד זָקֵן, טַף וְנָשִׁים, בְּיוֹם אֶחָד, בִּשְׁלוֹשָׁה עָשָׂר לְחֹדֶשׁ שְׁנֵים
עָשָׂר, הוּא חֹדֶשׁ אֲדָר, וּשְׁלָלָם לָבוֹז. וְאַתָּה בְּרַחֲמֶיךָ הָרַבִּים
הֵפַרְתָּ אֶת עֲצָתוֹ, וְקִלְקַלְתָּ אֶת מַחֲשַׁבְתּוֹ, וַהֲשֵׁבוֹתָ גְּמוּלוֹ
בְּרֹאשׁוֹ, וְתָלוּ אוֹתוֹ וְאֶת בָּנָיו עַל הָעֵץ.)

וְעַל כֻּלָּם יִתְבָּרַךְ וְיִתְרוֹמַם שִׁמְךָ, מַלְכֵּנוּ, תָּמִיד לְעוֹלָם וָעֶד.

Between Rosh Hashanah and Yom Kippur add:

(וּכְתוֹב לְחַיִּים טוֹבִים כָּל בְּנֵי בְרִיתֶךָ.)

וְכֹל הַחַיִּים יוֹדוּךָ סֶּלָה, וִיהַלְלוּ אֶת שִׁמְךָ בֶּאֱמֶת, הָאֵל,
יְשׁוּעָתֵנוּ וְעֶזְרָתֵנוּ סֶלָה. בָּרוּךְ אַתָּה, יְיָ, הַטּוֹב שִׁמְךָ, וּלְךָ נָאֶה
לְהוֹדוֹת.

שָׁלוֹם רָב עַל יִשְׂרָאֵל עַמְּךָ תָּשִׂים לְעוֹלָם, כִּי אַתָּה הוּא
מֶלֶךְ אָדוֹן לְכָל הַשָּׁלוֹם, וְטוֹב בְּעֵינֶיךָ לְבָרֵךְ אֶת עַמְּךָ יִשְׂרָאֵל
בְּכָל עֵת וּבְכָל שָׁעָה בִּשְׁלוֹמֶךָ. * בָּרוּךְ אַתָּה, יְיָ, הַמְבָרֵךְ אֶת
עַמּוֹ יִשְׂרָאֵל בַּשָּׁלוֹם.

*Between Rosh Hashanah and Yom Kippur say:

(בְּסֵפֶר חַיִּים, בְּרָכָה וְשָׁלוֹם וּפַרְנָסָה טוֹבָה, נִזָּכֵר וְנִכָּתֵב

into the hands of the righteous, and the arrogant into the hands of the students of thy Torah. Thou didst make a great and holy name for thyself in thy world, and for thy people Israel thou didst perform a great deliverance unto this day. Thereupon thy children entered the shrine of thy house, cleansed thy Temple, purified thy sanctuary, kindled lights in thy holy courts, and designated these eight days of Ḥanukkah for giving thanks and praise to thy great name.)

On Purim add:

(We thank thee for the miracles, for the redemption, for the mighty deeds and triumphs, and for the battles which thou didst perform for our fathers in those days, at this season—

In the days of Mordecai and Esther, in Shushan the capital [of Persia], when the wicked Haman rose up against them and sought to destroy, slay and wipe out all the Jews, young and old, infants and women, in one day, on the thirteenth of the twelfth month Adar, and to plunder their wealth. Thou in thy great mercy didst frustrate his counsel and upset his plan; thou didst cause his mischief to recoil on his own head, so that he and his sons were hanged upon the gallows.)

For all these acts, may thy name, our King, be blessed and exalted forever and ever.

Between Rosh Hashanah and Yom Kippur add:

(Inscribe all thy people of the covenant for a happy life.)

All the living shall ever thank thee and sincerely praise thy name, O God, who art always our salvation and help. Blessed art thou, O Lord, Beneficent One, to whom it is fitting to give thanks.

O grant abundant peace to Israel thy people forever, for thou art the King and Lord of all peace. May it please thee to bless thy people Israel with peace at all times and at all hours. *Blessed art thou, O Lord, who blessest thy people Israel with peace.

* Between Rosh Hashanah and Yom Kippur say:

(May we and all Israel thy people be remembered and inscribed before thee in the book of life and blessing, peace and prosperity,

לְפָנֶיךָ, אֲנַחְנוּ וְכָל עַמְּךָ בֵּית יִשְׂרָאֵל, לְחַיִּים טוֹבִים וּלְשָׁלוֹם. בָּרוּךְ אַתָּה, יְיָ, עוֹשֵׂה הַשָּׁלוֹם.)

After the *Shemoneh Esreh* add the following meditation:

אֱלֹהַי, נְצֹר לְשׁוֹנִי מֵרָע, וּשְׂפָתַי מִדַּבֵּר מִרְמָה; וְלִמְקַלְלַי נַפְשִׁי תִדּוֹם, וְנַפְשִׁי כֶּעָפָר לַכֹּל תִּהְיֶה. פְּתַח לִבִּי בְּתוֹרָתֶךָ, וּבְמִצְוֹתֶיךָ תִּרְדּוֹף נַפְשִׁי; וְכָל הַחוֹשְׁבִים עָלַי רָעָה, מְהֵרָה הָפֵר עֲצָתָם וְקַלְקֵל מַחֲשַׁבְתָּם. עֲשֵׂה לְמַעַן שְׁמֶךָ, עֲשֵׂה לְמַעַן יְמִינֶךָ, עֲשֵׂה לְמַעַן קְדֻשָּׁתֶךָ, עֲשֵׂה לְמַעַן תּוֹרָתֶךָ. לְמַעַן יֵחָלְצוּן יְדִידֶיךָ, הוֹשִׁיעָה יְמִינְךָ וַעֲנֵנִי. יִהְיוּ לְרָצוֹן אִמְרֵי פִי וְהֶגְיוֹן לִבִּי לְפָנֶיךָ, יְיָ, צוּרִי וְגוֹאֲלִי. עֹשֶׂה שָׁלוֹם בִּמְרוֹמָיו, הוּא יַעֲשֶׂה שָׁלוֹם עָלֵינוּ וְעַל כָּל יִשְׂרָאֵל, וְאִמְרוּ אָמֵן.

יְהִי רָצוֹן מִלְּפָנֶיךָ, יְיָ אֱלֹהֵינוּ וֵאלֹהֵי אֲבוֹתֵינוּ, שֶׁיִּבָּנֶה בֵּית הַמִּקְדָּשׁ בִּמְהֵרָה בְיָמֵינוּ, וְתֵן חֶלְקֵנוּ בְּתוֹרָתֶךָ. וְשָׁם נַעֲבָדְךָ בְּיִרְאָה, כִּימֵי עוֹלָם וּכְשָׁנִים קַדְמוֹנִיּוֹת. וְעָרְבָה לַייָ מִנְחַת יְהוּדָה וִירוּשָׁלָיִם, כִּימֵי עוֹלָם וּכְשָׁנִים קַדְמוֹנִיּוֹת.

On Saturday night, after the recital of half-Kaddish, *Ma'ariv* is continued on page 537.

Reader:

יִתְגַּדַּל וְיִתְקַדַּשׁ שְׁמֵהּ רַבָּא בְּעָלְמָא דִּי בְרָא כִרְעוּתֵהּ; וְיַמְלִיךְ מַלְכוּתֵהּ בְּחַיֵּיכוֹן וּבְיוֹמֵיכוֹן, וּבְחַיֵּי דְכָל בֵּית יִשְׂרָאֵל, בַּעֲגָלָא וּבִזְמַן קָרִיב, וְאִמְרוּ אָמֵן.

יְהֵא שְׁמֵהּ רַבָּא מְבָרַךְ לְעָלַם וּלְעָלְמֵי עָלְמַיָּא.

יִתְבָּרַךְ וְיִשְׁתַּבַּח, וְיִתְפָּאַר וְיִתְרוֹמַם, וְיִתְנַשֵּׂא וְיִתְהַדָּר, וְיִתְעַלֶּה וְיִתְהַלָּל שְׁמֵהּ דְּקֻדְשָׁא, בְּרִיךְ הוּא, לְעֵלָּא (לְעֵלָּא) מִן כָּל בִּרְכָתָא וְשִׁירָתָא, תֻּשְׁבְּחָתָא וְנֶחֱמָתָא, דַּאֲמִירָן בְּעָלְמָא, וְאִמְרוּ אָמֵן.

for a happy life and for peace. Blessed art thou, O Lord, Author of peace.)

After the Shemoneh Esreh add the following meditation:

My God, guard my tongue from evil, and my lips from speaking falsehood. May my soul be silent to those who insult me; be my soul lowly to all as the dust. Open my heart to thy Torah, that my soul may follow thy commands. Speedily defeat the counsel of all those who plan evil against me, and upset their design. Do it for the glory of thy name; do it for the sake of thy power; do it for the sake of thy holiness; do it for the sake of thy Torah. That thy beloved may be rescued, save with thy right hand and answer me. May the words of my mouth and the meditation of my heart be pleasing before thee, O Lord, my Stronghold and my Redeemer.[1] May he who creates peace in his high heavens create peace for us and for all Israel. Amen.

May it be thy will, Lord our God and God of our fathers, that the Temple be speedily rebuilt in our days, and grant us a share in thy Torah. There we will serve thee with reverence, as in the days of old and as in former years. Then the offering of Judah and Jerusalem will be pleasing to the Lord, as in the days of old and as in former years.[2]

On Saturday night, after the recital of half-Kaddish, Ma'ariv is continued on page 538.

Reader:

Glorified and sanctified be God's great name throughout the world which he has created according to his will. May he establish his kingdom in your lifetime and during your days, and within the life of the entire house of Israel, speedily and soon; and say, Amen.

May his great name be blessed forever and to all eternity.

Blessed and praised, glorified and exalted, extolled and honored, adored and lauded be the name of the Holy One, blessed be he, beyond all the blessings and hymns, praises and consolations that are ever spoken in the world; and say, Amen.

[1] *Psalms* 60:7; 19:15.   [2] *Malachi* 3:4.

תִּתְקַבֵּל צְלוֹתְהוֹן וּבָעוּתְהוֹן דְּכָל בֵּית יִשְׂרָאֵל קֳדָם אֲבוּהוֹן
דִּי בִשְׁמַיָּא, וְאִמְרוּ אָמֵן.

יְהֵא שְׁלָמָא רַבָּא מִן שְׁמַיָּא, וְחַיִּים, עָלֵינוּ וְעַל כָּל יִשְׂרָאֵל,
וְאִמְרוּ אָמֵן.

עוֹשֶׂה שָׁלוֹם בִּמְרוֹמָיו, הוּא יַעֲשֶׂה שָׁלוֹם עָלֵינוּ וְעַל כָּל
יִשְׂרָאֵל, וְאִמְרוּ אָמֵן.

The counting of the עומר between *Pesaḥ* and *Shavuoth* is on page 637.

עָלֵינוּ לְשַׁבֵּחַ לַאֲדוֹן הַכֹּל, לָתֵת גְּדֻלָּה לְיוֹצֵר בְּרֵאשִׁית,
שֶׁלֹּא עָשָׂנוּ כְּגוֹיֵי הָאֲרָצוֹת, וְלֹא שָׂמָנוּ כְּמִשְׁפְּחוֹת הָאֲדָמָה;
שֶׁלֹּא שָׂם חֶלְקֵנוּ כָּהֶם, וְגֹרָלֵנוּ כְּכָל הֲמוֹנָם. וַאֲנַחְנוּ כּוֹרְעִים
וּמִשְׁתַּחֲוִים וּמוֹדִים לִפְנֵי מֶלֶךְ מַלְכֵי הַמְּלָכִים, הַקָּדוֹשׁ בָּרוּךְ
הוּא, שֶׁהוּא נוֹטֶה שָׁמַיִם וְיוֹסֵד אָרֶץ, וּמוֹשַׁב יְקָרוֹ בַּשָּׁמַיִם
מִמַּעַל, וּשְׁכִינַת עֻזּוֹ בְּגָבְהֵי מְרוֹמִים. הוּא אֱלֹהֵינוּ, אֵין עוֹד;
אֱמֶת מַלְכֵּנוּ, אֶפֶס זוּלָתוֹ, כַּכָּתוּב בְּתוֹרָתוֹ: וְיָדַעְתָּ הַיּוֹם
וַהֲשֵׁבֹתָ אֶל לְבָבֶךָ, כִּי יְיָ הוּא הָאֱלֹהִים בַּשָּׁמַיִם מִמַּעַל וְעַל
הָאָרֶץ מִתָּחַת, אֵין עוֹד.

עַל כֵּן נְקַוֶּה לְךָ, יְיָ אֱלֹהֵינוּ, לִרְאוֹת מְהֵרָה בְּתִפְאֶרֶת עֻזֶּךָ,
לְהַעֲבִיר גִּלּוּלִים מִן הָאָרֶץ, וְהָאֱלִילִים כָּרוֹת יִכָּרֵתוּן; לְתַקֵּן
עוֹלָם בְּמַלְכוּת שַׁדַּי, וְכָל בְּנֵי בָשָׂר יִקְרְאוּ בִשְׁמֶךָ, לְהַפְנוֹת
אֵלֶיךָ כָּל רִשְׁעֵי אָרֶץ. יַכִּירוּ וְיֵדְעוּ כָּל יוֹשְׁבֵי תֵבֵל, כִּי לְךָ
תִּכְרַע כָּל בֶּרֶךְ, תִּשָּׁבַע כָּל לָשׁוֹן. לְפָנֶיךָ, יְיָ אֱלֹהֵינוּ, יִכְרְעוּ
וְיִפֹּלוּ, וְלִכְבוֹד שִׁמְךָ יְקָר יִתֵּנוּ, וִיקַבְּלוּ כֻלָּם אֶת עֹל מַלְכוּתֶךָ,
וְתִמְלוֹךְ עֲלֵיהֶם מְהֵרָה לְעוֹלָם וָעֶד. כִּי הַמַּלְכוּת שֶׁלְּךָ הִיא,
וּלְעוֹלְמֵי עַד תִּמְלוֹךְ בְּכָבוֹד, כַּכָּתוּב בְּתוֹרָתֶךָ: יְיָ יִמְלֹךְ

May the prayers and supplications of the whole house of Israel be accepted by their Father who is in heaven; and say, Amen.

May there be abundant peace from heaven, and life, for us and for all Israel; and say, Amen.

He who creates peace in his celestial heights, may he create peace for us and for all Israel; and say, Amen.

The counting of the omer between Pesaḥ and Shavuoth is on page 638.

ALENU

It is our duty to praise the Master of all, to exalt the Creator of the universe, who has not made us like the nations of the world and has not placed us like the families of the earth; who has not designed our destiny to be like theirs, nor our lot like that of all their multitude. We bend the knee and bow and acknowledge before the supreme King of kings, the Holy One, blessed be he, that it is he who stretched forth the heavens and founded the earth. His seat of glory is in the heavens above; his abode of majesty is in the lofty heights. He is our God, there is none else; truly, he is our King, there is none besides him, as it is written in his Torah: "You shall know this day, and reflect in your heart, that it is the Lord who is God in the heavens above and on the earth beneath, there is none else."[1]

We hope therefore, Lord our God, soon to behold thy majestic glory, when the abominations shall be removed from the earth, and the false gods exterminated; when the world shall be perfected under the reign of the Almighty, and all mankind will call upon thy name, and all the wicked of the earth will be turned to thee. May all the inhabitants of the world realize and know that to thee every knee must bend, every tongue must vow allegiance. May they bend the knee and prostrate themselves before thee, Lord our God, and give honor to thy glorious name; may they all accept the yoke of thy kingdom, and do thou reign over them speedily forever and ever. For the kingdom is thine, and to all eternity thou wilt reign in glory, as it is written in thy Torah:

---

[1] *Deuteronomy* 4:39

לְעוֹלָם וָעֶד. Reader וְנֶאֱמַר: וְהָיָה יְיָ לְמֶלֶךְ עַל כָּל הָאָרֶץ;
בַּיּוֹם הַהוּא יִהְיֶה יְיָ אֶחָד וּשְׁמוֹ אֶחָד.

MOURNERS' KADDISH

יִתְגַּדַּל וְיִתְקַדַּשׁ שְׁמֵהּ רַבָּא בְּעָלְמָא דִי בְרָא כִרְעוּתֵהּ;
וְיַמְלִיךְ מַלְכוּתֵהּ בְּחַיֵּיכוֹן וּבְיוֹמֵיכוֹן, וּבְחַיֵּי דְכָל בֵּית יִשְׂרָאֵל,
בַּעֲגָלָא וּבִזְמַן קָרִיב, וְאִמְרוּ אָמֵן.

יְהֵא שְׁמֵהּ רַבָּא מְבָרַךְ לְעָלַם וּלְעָלְמֵי עָלְמַיָּא.

יִתְבָּרַךְ וְיִשְׁתַּבַּח, וְיִתְפָּאַר וְיִתְרוֹמַם, וְיִתְנַשֵּׂא וְיִתְהַדָּר,
וְיִתְעַלֶּה וְיִתְהַלָּל שְׁמֵהּ דְּקֻדְשָׁא, בְּרִיךְ הוּא, לְעֵלָּא (לְעֵלָּא)
מִן כָּל בִּרְכָתָא וְשִׁירָתָא, תֻּשְׁבְּחָתָא וְנֶחֱמָתָא, דַּאֲמִירָן בְּעָלְמָא,
וְאִמְרוּ אָמֵן.

יְהֵא שְׁלָמָא רַבָּא מִן שְׁמַיָּא, וְחַיִּים, עָלֵינוּ וְעַל כָּל יִשְׂרָאֵל,
וְאִמְרוּ אָמֵן.

עֹשֶׂה שָׁלוֹם בִּמְרוֹמָיו, הוּא יַעֲשֶׂה שָׁלוֹם עָלֵינוּ וְעַל כָּל
יִשְׂרָאֵל, וְאִמְרוּ אָמֵן.

אַל תִּירָא מִפַּחַד פִּתְאֹם, וּמִשֹּׁאַת רְשָׁעִים כִּי תָבֹא. עֻצוּ
עֵצָה וְתֻפָר, דַּבְּרוּ דָבָר וְלֹא יָקוּם, כִּי עִמָּנוּ אֵל. וְעַד זִקְנָה
אֲנִי הוּא, וְעַד שֵׂיבָה אֲנִי אֶסְבֹּל; אֲנִי עָשִׂיתִי וַאֲנִי אֶשָּׂא, וַאֲנִי
אֶסְבֹּל וַאֲמַלֵּט.

The following is recited daily from *Rosh Ḥodesh Elul* until *Simḥath Torah*.

תהלים כז

לְדָוִד. יְיָ אוֹרִי וְיִשְׁעִי, מִמִּי אִירָא; יְיָ מָעוֹז חַיַּי, מִמִּי אֶפְחָד.
בִּקְרֹב עָלַי מְרֵעִים לֶאֱכֹל אֶת בְּשָׂרִי, צָרַי וְאֹיְבַי לִי, הֵמָּה
כָשְׁלוּ וְנָפָלוּ. אִם תַּחֲנֶה עָלַי מַחֲנֶה, לֹא יִירָא לִבִּי; אִם תָּקוּם

On Psalm 27, see pages 147–149.

"The Lord shall be King forever and ever."[1] And it is said: "The Lord shall be King over all the earth; on that day the Lord shall be One, and his name One."[2]

MOURNERS' KADDISH

Glorified and sanctified be God's great name throughout the world which he has created according to his will. May he establish his kingdom in your lifetime and during your days, and within the life of the entire house of Israel, speedily and soon; and say, Amen.

May his great name be blessed forever and to all eternity.

Blessed and praised, glorified and exalted, extolled and honored, adored and lauded be the name of the Holy One, blessed be he, beyond all the blessings and hymns, praises and consolations that are ever spoken in the world; and say, Amen.

May there be abundant peace from heaven, and life, for us and for all Israel; and say, Amen.

He who creates peace in his celestial heights, may he create peace for us and for all Israel; and say, Amen.

Be not afraid of sudden terror, nor of the storm that strikes the wicked. Form your plot—it shall fail; lay your plan—it shall not prevail! For God is with us. Even to your old age I will be the same; when you are gray-headed, still I will sustain you; I have made you, and I will bear you; I will sustain you and save you.[3]

The following is recited daily from Rosh Ḥodesh Elul until Simḥath Torah.

Psalm 27

A psalm of David. The Lord is my light and aid; whom shall I fear? The Lord is the stronghold of my life; of whom shall I be afraid? When evildoers press against me to eat up my flesh—my enemies and my foes—it is they who stumble and fall. Even though an army were arrayed against me, my heart would not fear; though

---

[1] *Exodus* 15:18. [2] *Zechariah* 14:9. [3] *Proverbs* 3:25; *Isaiah* 8:10; 46:4.

עָלַי מִלְחָמָה, בְּזֹאת אֲנִי בוֹטֵחַ. אַחַת שָׁאַלְתִּי מֵאֵת יְיָ, אוֹתָהּ
אֲבַקֵּשׁ: שִׁבְתִּי בְּבֵית יְיָ כָּל יְמֵי חַיַּי, לַחֲזוֹת בְּנְעַם יְיָ, וּלְבַקֵּר
בְּהֵיכָלוֹ. כִּי יִצְפְּנֵנִי בְּסֻכֹּה בְּיוֹם רָעָה, יַסְתִּירֵנִי בְּסֵתֶר אָהֳלוֹ;
בְּצוּר יְרוֹמְמֵנִי. וְעַתָּה יָרוּם רֹאשִׁי עַל אֹיְבַי סְבִיבוֹתַי, וְאֶזְבְּחָה
בְּאָהֳלוֹ זִבְחֵי תְרוּעָה; אָשִׁירָה וַאֲזַמְּרָה לַיְיָ. שְׁמַע יְיָ קוֹלִי
אֶקְרָא, וְחָנֵּנִי וַעֲנֵנִי. לְךָ אָמַר לִבִּי, בַּקְּשׁוּ פָנָי; אֶת פָּנֶיךָ יְיָ
אֲבַקֵּשׁ. אַל תַּסְתֵּר פָּנֶיךָ מִמֶּנִּי, אַל תַּט בְּאַף עַבְדֶּךָ, עֶזְרָתִי
הָיִיתָ; אַל תִּטְּשֵׁנִי וְאַל תַּעַזְבֵנִי, אֱלֹהֵי יִשְׁעִי. כִּי אָבִי וְאִמִּי
עֲזָבוּנִי, וַיְיָ יַאַסְפֵנִי. הוֹרֵנִי יְיָ דַּרְכֶּךָ, וּנְחֵנִי בְּאֹרַח מִישׁוֹר, לְמַעַן
שׁוֹרְרָי. אַל תִּתְּנֵנִי בְּנֶפֶשׁ צָרָי, כִּי קָמוּ בִי עֵדֵי שֶׁקֶר וִיפֵחַ חָמָס.
לוּלֵא הֶאֱמַנְתִּי לִרְאוֹת בְּטוּב יְיָ בְּאֶרֶץ חַיִּים. Reader קַוֵּה אֶל יְיָ,
חֲזַק וְיַאֲמֵץ לִבֶּךָ, וְקַוֵּה אֶל יְיָ.

Mourners' Kaddish.

The following is recited in the house of a mourner
during the week of mourning.

תהלים מט

לַמְנַצֵּחַ, לִבְנֵי קֹרַח מִזְמוֹר. שִׁמְעוּ זֹאת, כָּל הָעַמִּים; הַאֲזִינוּ,
כָּל יֹשְׁבֵי חָלֶד. גַּם בְּנֵי אָדָם, גַּם בְּנֵי אִישׁ, יַחַד עָשִׁיר וְאֶבְיוֹן.
פִּי יְדַבֵּר חָכְמוֹת, וְהָגוּת לִבִּי תְבוּנוֹת. אַטֶּה לְמָשָׁל אָזְנִי, אֶפְתַּח
בְּכִנּוֹר חִידָתִי. לָמָּה אִירָא בִּימֵי רָע, עֲוֹן עֲקֵבַי יְסוּבֵּנִי.
הַבֹּטְחִים עַל חֵילָם, וּבְרֹב עָשְׁרָם יִתְהַלָּלוּ. אָח לֹא פָדֹה יִפְדֶּה
אִישׁ, לֹא יִתֵּן לֵאלֹהִים כָּפְרוֹ. וְיֵקַר פִּדְיוֹן נַפְשָׁם, וְחָדַל
לְעוֹלָם. וִיחִי עוֹד לָנֶצַח, לֹא יִרְאֶה הַשָּׁחַת. כִּי יִרְאֶה חֲכָמִים
יָמוּתוּ, יַחַד כְּסִיל וָבַעַר יֹאבֵדוּ, וְעָזְבוּ לַאֲחֵרִים חֵילָם. קִרְבָּם
בָּתֵּימוֹ לְעוֹלָם, מִשְׁכְּנוֹתָם לְדֹר וָדֹר; קָרְאוּ בִשְׁמוֹתָם עֲלֵי

On Psalm 49, see pages 149–151.

war should arise against me, still would I be confident. One thing I ask from the Lord, one thing do I desire—that I may dwell in the house of the Lord all the days of my life, to behold the pleasantness of the Lord, and to meditate in his sanctuary. Surely, he will hide me within his own tabernacle in the days of distress; he will conceal me in the shelter of his tent; he will set me safe upon a rock. Thus my head shall be high above all my foes around me; I will offer sacrifices within his tabernacle to the sound of trumpets; I will sing and chant praises to the Lord. Hear, O Lord, my voice when I call; be gracious to me and answer me. In thy behalf my heart has said: "Seek you my presence"; thy presence, O Lord, I do seek. Hide not thy face from me; turn not thy servant away in anger; thou hast been my help; do not abandon me, forsake me not, O God my Savior. Though my father and mother have forsaken me, the Lord will take care of me. Teach me thy way, O Lord, and guide me in a straight path, in spite of my enemies. Deliver me not to the will of my adversaries; for false witnesses have risen up against me, such as breathe forth violence. I do believe I shall yet see the goodness of the Lord in the land of the living. Hope in the Lord; be strong, and let your heart be brave; yes, hope in the Lord.

Mourners' Kaddish.

The following is recited in the house of a mourner during the week of mourning.

Psalm 49

For the Choirmaster; a psalm for the Korahites. Hear this, all you peoples; listen, all you inhabitants of the world, both low and high, rich and poor alike. My mouth speaks wisdom, and my heart's meditation is deep insight. I incline my ear to a parable; I unfold my profound problem to the accompaniment of the harp.

Why should I be afraid in days of evil, when the iniquity of my foes surrounds me, those who trust in their wealth, and boast of their great riches? No man can redeem his brother [from death], nor give to God a ransom for him—for too costly is the ransom of one's soul and can never be—that he should go on living forever, that he should not see the grave. Surely, one must see that wise men die, that the stupid and senseless perish alike, and leave their wealth to others. Their inward consolation is that their houses shall continue forever, and their homes throughout all

אֲדָמוֹת. וְאָדָם בִּיקָר בַּל יָלִין; נִמְשַׁל כַּבְּהֵמוֹת נִדְמוּ. זֶה דַרְכָּם
כֶּסֶל לָמוֹ, וְאַחֲרֵיהֶם בְּפִיהֶם יִרְצוּ, סֶלָה. כַּצֹּאן לִשְׁאוֹל שַׁתּוּ,
מָוֶת יִרְעֵם; וַיִּרְדּוּ בָם יְשָׁרִים לַבֹּקֶר, וְצוּרָם לְבַלּוֹת שְׁאוֹל
מִזְּבֻל לוֹ. אַךְ אֱלֹהִים יִפְדֶּה נַפְשִׁי מִיַּד שְׁאוֹל, כִּי יִקָּחֵנִי סֶלָה.
אַל תִּירָא כִּי יַעֲשִׁר אִישׁ, כִּי יִרְבֶּה כְּבוֹד בֵּיתוֹ. כִּי לֹא בְמוֹתוֹ
יִקַּח הַכֹּל, לֹא יֵרֵד אַחֲרָיו כְּבוֹדוֹ. כִּי נַפְשׁוֹ בְּחַיָּיו יְבָרֵךְ; וְיוֹדֻךָ
כִּי תֵיטִיב לָךְ. תָּבוֹא עַד דּוֹר אֲבוֹתָיו, עַד נֵצַח לֹא יִרְאוּ אוֹר.
Reader אָדָם בִּיקָר וְלֹא יָבִין, נִמְשַׁל כַּבְּהֵמוֹת נִדְמוּ.

MOURNERS' KADDISH

יִתְגַּדַּל וְיִתְקַדַּשׁ שְׁמֵהּ רַבָּא בְּעָלְמָא דִּי בְרָא כִרְעוּתֵהּ;
וְיַמְלִיךְ מַלְכוּתֵהּ בְּחַיֵּיכוֹן וּבְיוֹמֵיכוֹן וּבְחַיֵּי דְכָל בֵּית יִשְׂרָאֵל,
בַּעֲגָלָא וּבִזְמַן קָרִיב, וְאִמְרוּ אָמֵן.

יְהֵא שְׁמֵהּ רַבָּא מְבָרַךְ לְעָלַם וּלְעָלְמֵי עָלְמַיָּא.

יִתְבָּרַךְ וְיִשְׁתַּבַּח, וְיִתְפָּאַר וְיִתְרוֹמַם, וְיִתְנַשֵּׂא וְיִתְהַדָּר,
וְיִתְעַלֶּה וְיִתְהַלַּל שְׁמֵהּ דְּקֻדְשָׁא, בְּרִיךְ הוּא, לְעֵלָּא מִן כָּל
בִּרְכָתָא וְשִׁירָתָא, תֻּשְׁבְּחָתָא וְנֶחֱמָתָא, דַּאֲמִירָן בְּעָלְמָא,
וְאִמְרוּ אָמֵן.

יְהֵא שְׁלָמָא רַבָּא מִן שְׁמַיָּא, וְחַיִּים, עָלֵינוּ וְעַל כָּל יִשְׂרָאֵל,
וְאִמְרוּ אָמֵן.

עֹשֶׂה שָׁלוֹם בִּמְרוֹמָיו, הוּא יַעֲשֶׂה שָׁלוֹם עָלֵינוּ וְעַל כָּל
יִשְׂרָאֵל, וְאִמְרוּ אָמֵן.

מות ירעם ... death will take control of them; and in the morning, when the dark night of suffering is over, the victims of lawlessness will be triumphant over their fallen oppressors.

generations; they name estates after themselves. But man abides not in his splendor; he is like the beasts that perish. Such is the fate of those who trust in themselves, and the end of those who are pleased with their own mouthing. Like sheep they are destined to die; death shall shepherd them; the upright shall triumph over them in the morning; their form is to decay in the nether-world, its habitation. However, God will release me from the grasp of death, for he will receive me. So fear not when a man grows rich, when the splendor of his house increases; for he will take nothing with him when he dies; his wealth will not follow him below. Though while he lives he flatters himself [saying]: "Men acclaim you when you do well for yourself," he will join the generation of his fathers, who will never see the light. The man who lives in splendor and understands not is like the beasts that perish.

MOURNERS' KADDISH

Glorified and sanctified be God's great name throughout the world which he has created according to his will. May he establish his kingdom in your lifetime and during your days, and within the life of the entire house of Israel, speedily and soon; and say, Amen.

May his great name be blessed forever and to all eternity.

Blessed and praised, glorified and exalted, extolled and honored, adored and lauded be the name of the Holy One, blessed be he, beyond all the blessings and hymns, praises and consolations that are ever spoken in the world; and say, Amen.

May there be abundant peace from heaven, and life, for us and for all Israel; and say, Amen.

He who creates peace in his celestial heights, may he create peace for us and for all Israel; and say, Amen.

אך ... יפדה נפשי The psalmist is confident that God will deliver him from the premature death of the wicked and will receive him under his divine protection.

הַדְלָקַת נֵר שֶׁל שַׁבָּת

Upon lighting the Sabbath lights:

בָּרוּךְ אַתָּה, יְיָ אֱלֹהֵינוּ, מֶלֶךְ הָעוֹלָם, אֲשֶׁר קִדְּשָׁנוּ בְּמִצְוֹתָיו וְצִוָּנוּ לְהַדְלִיק נֵר שֶׁל שַׁבָּת.

בִּרְכַּת הוֹרִים

For daughters:

יְשִׂמֵךְ אֱלֹהִים כְּשָׂרָה, רִבְקָה, רָחֵל וְלֵאָה.

For sons:

יְשִׂמְךָ אֱלֹהִים כְּאֶפְרַיִם וְכִמְנַשֶּׁה.

יְבָרֶכְךָ יְיָ וְיִשְׁמְרֶךָ. יָאֵר יְיָ פָּנָיו אֵלֶיךָ וִיחֻנֶּךָּ. יִשָּׂא יְיָ פָּנָיו אֵלֶיךָ, וְיָשֵׂם לְךָ שָׁלוֹם.

שִׁיר הַשִּׁירִים

Chanted shortly before the *Kabbalath Shabbath* service.

[א]

שִׁיר הַשִּׁירִים אֲשֶׁר לִשְׁלֹמֹה. יִשָּׁקֵנִי מִנְּשִׁיקוֹת פִּיהוּ, כִּי טוֹבִים דֹּדֶיךָ מִיָּיִן. לְרֵיחַ שְׁמָנֶיךָ טוֹבִים, שֶׁמֶן תּוּרַק שְׁמֶךָ; עַל כֵּן עֲלָמוֹת אֲהֵבוּךָ. מָשְׁכֵנִי אַחֲרֶיךָ נָּרוּצָה; הֱבִיאַנִי הַמֶּלֶךְ

ברכת הנר, the blessing pronounced at the lighting of the Sabbath light, is not cited in the Talmud but is found in the ninth century *Siddur* of Amram Gaon. The custom of lighting two lights is in keeping with the two terms "Remember" and "Observe" which introduce the Sabbath Commandment in Exodus 20:8 and Deuteronomy 5:12, respectively. The lights are symbolical of the cheerfulness and serenity which distinguish the holy days.

ברכת הורים, the blessing of children by their parents on all important occasions, notably on the eve of Sabbaths and festivals, is one of the most beautiful customs. The *Brantspiegel*, a treatise on morals published in 1602, mentions this in the following terms: "Before the children can walk they

221

LIGHTING OF THE SABBATH LIGHTS

Blessed art thou, Lord our God, King of the universe, who hast sanctified us with thy commandments, and commanded us to light the Sabbath lights.

PARENTAL BLESSING

For sons:

May God make you like Ephraim and like Manasseh.

For daughters:

May God make you like Sarah and Rebekah, Rachel and Leah.

May the Lord bless you and protect you; may the Lord countenance you and be gracious to you; may the Lord favor you and grant you peace.[1]

THE SONG OF SONGS

Chanted shortly before the Kabbalath Shabbath service.

I

The Song of Songs by Solomon.

O that he would kiss me with his lips! Indeed, your caresses are better than wine. Sweet is the fragrance of your perfumes; your very self is a precious perfume; therefore do the maidens love you. Take me with you; let us hasten! The king brings me

should be carried on Sabbaths and festivals to the father and mother to be blessed; after they are able to walk they shall go of their own accord with bowed body and shall incline their heads and receive the blessing." This custom has linked the generations together in mutual loyalty and affection.

שיר השירים is recited every Friday evening because of the religious idealism attached to it by tradition. The poem has been accepted throughout the ages as an allegory of the relations between God and his people. Some nineteen centuries ago, Rabbi Akiba declared: "All the *Kethubim* are holy, but the Song of Songs is the holiest of all." According to the paraphrase of the Targum, the poem portrays the history of Israel till the times of the Messiah. It has been regarded also as a representation of the affection of Israel for the Sabbath. The author of the poem לכה דודי, "one of the finest pieces of

[1] *Numbers* 6:24–26.

222

חֲדָרָיו, נָגִילָה וְנִשְׂמְחָה בָּךְ; נַזְכִּירָה דֹדֶיךָ מִיַּיִן, מֵישָׁרִים
אֲהֵבוּךָ. שְׁחוֹרָה אֲנִי וְנָאוָה, בְּנוֹת יְרוּשָׁלָם; כְּאָהֳלֵי קֵדָר,
כִּירִיעוֹת שְׁלֹמֹה. אַל תִּרְאֻנִי שֶׁאֲנִי שְׁחַרְחֹרֶת, שֶׁשְּׁזָפַתְנִי הַשָּׁמֶשׁ;
בְּנֵי אִמִּי נִחֲרוּ בִי, שָׂמֻנִי נֹטֵרָה אֶת הַכְּרָמִים; כַּרְמִי שֶׁלִּי לֹא
נָטָרְתִּי. הַגִּידָה לִּי, שֶׁאָהֲבָה נַפְשִׁי, אֵיכָה תִרְעֶה, אֵיכָה תַּרְבִּיץ
בַּצָּהֳרָיִם; שַׁלָּמָה אֶהְיֶה כְּעֹטְיָה עַל עֶדְרֵי חֲבֵרֶיךָ. אִם לֹא
תֵדְעִי לָךְ, הַיָּפָה בַּנָּשִׁים, צְאִי לָךְ בְּעִקְבֵי הַצֹּאן, וּרְעִי אֶת
גְּדִיֹּתַיִךְ עַל מִשְׁכְּנוֹת הָרֹעִים. לְסֻסָתִי בְּרִכְבֵי פַרְעֹה דִּמִּיתִיךְ,
רַעְיָתִי. נָאווּ לְחָיַיִךְ בַּתֹּרִים, צַוָּארֵךְ בַּחֲרוּזִים. תּוֹרֵי זָהָב
נַעֲשֶׂה לָּךְ, עִם נְקֻדּוֹת הַכָּסֶף. עַד שֶׁהַמֶּלֶךְ בִּמְסִבּוֹ, נִרְדִּי נָתַן
רֵיחוֹ. צְרוֹר הַמֹּר דּוֹדִי לִי, בֵּין שָׁדַי יָלִין. אֶשְׁכֹּל הַכֹּפֶר דּוֹדִי
לִי, בְּכַרְמֵי עֵין גֶּדִי. הִנָּךְ יָפָה, רַעְיָתִי, הִנָּךְ יָפָה, עֵינַיִךְ יוֹנִים.
הִנְּךָ יָפֶה, דוֹדִי, אַף נָעִים; אַף עַרְשֵׂנוּ רַעֲנָנָה. קֹרוֹת בָּתֵּינוּ
אֲרָזִים, רַהִיטֵנוּ בְּרוֹתִים.

[ב]

אֲנִי חֲבַצֶּלֶת הַשָּׁרוֹן, שׁוֹשַׁנַּת הָעֲמָקִים. כְּשׁוֹשַׁנָּה בֵּין
הַחוֹחִים, כֵּן רַעְיָתִי בֵּין הַבָּנוֹת. כְּתַפּוּחַ בַּעֲצֵי הַיַּעַר, כֵּן דּוֹדִי
בֵּין הַבָּנִים; בְּצִלּוֹ חִמַּדְתִּי וְיָשַׁבְתִּי, וּפִרְיוֹ מָתוֹק לְחִכִּי. הֱבִיאַנִי
אֶל בֵּית הַיַּיִן, וְדִגְלוֹ עָלַי אַהֲבָה. סַמְּכוּנִי בָּאֲשִׁישׁוֹת, רַפְּדוּנִי
בַּתַּפּוּחִים, כִּי חוֹלַת אַהֲבָה אָנִי. שְׂמֹאלוֹ תַּחַת לְרֹאשִׁי, וִימִינוֹ

religious poetry in existence," used the theme of the Sabbath bride and borrowed the title of his famous hymn from the Song of Songs (7:12). Although
its meaning has been extended by various methods of interpretation, one cannot miss the beauty of the poem in its literal interpretation. Its author takes us
along with him into the open air, to the vineyards, the villages, the mountains.
He awakens us at daybreak to catch the scent of the forest trees, to gather the
apples and the pomegranates. His verse is fragrant with the breath of spring.
קדר a tribe of nomads who wandered in the Arabian desert.

into his chambers. We will thrill with delight over you; we will celebrate your caresses more than wine! Rightly do they love you.

I am dark yet comely, maidens of Jerusalem: dark as the tents of Kedar, comely as the curtains of Solomon. Do not stare at me because I am dark, for the sun has tanned me; my mother's sons were angry with me, they made me keeper of the vineyards; I did not look after my own vineyard.

Tell me, you whom my soul loves, where you feed the flocks, where you make them rest at noon; why should I wander among the flocks of your companions?

If you do not know, fairest of women, follow the sheep-tracks, and pasture your kids beside the tents of the shepherds. I compare you, my love, to a mare in Pharaoh's chariots. Beautiful are your cheeks with circlets, your neck with strings of beads! Circlets of gold will we make for you, with studs of silver.

While the king sits at his table, my nard gives forth its fragrance. My beloved is my bunch of myrrh that lies between my breasts. My beloved is my cluster of henna-blossom from the gardens of Engedi.

You are beautiful, my love, you are beautiful; your eyes are dove-like.

You are handsome, my beloved, and pleasant; and our couch is leafy. The beams of our houses are cedars, and our rafters are firs.

II

I am a rose of Sharon, a lily of the valleys.

Like a lily among thorns, so is my loved one among the maidens.

Like an apple tree among the trees of the forest, so is my beloved among the youths; in his shadow I long to sit, and his fruit is sweet to my taste. He brings me to the house of wine, and looks at me with love. Sustain me with raisins, refresh me with apples, for I am love-sick. O that his left hand were under my

---

כרמי שלי that is, my personal beauty. The phrase is often used in the sense of neglecting one's family while being engrossed in public duties.

לססתי The point of comparison is the rich ornamentation of the bride.

רהיטנו our rafters, panelled ceilings. The cedar trees and fir trees form the roof over their heads as they sit in the green grass.

חבצלת השרון She modestly compares herself to the wild flowers of Sharon.

תְּחַבְּקֵנִי. הִשְׁבַּעְתִּי אֶתְכֶם, בְּנוֹת יְרוּשָׁלַ͏ִם, בִּצְבָאוֹת אוֹ
בְּאַיְלוֹת הַשָּׂדֶה, אִם תָּעִירוּ וְאִם תְּעוֹרְרוּ אֶת הָאַהֲבָה עַד
שֶׁתֶּחְפָּץ. קוֹל דּוֹדִי הִנֵּה־זֶה בָּא, מְדַלֵּג עַל הֶהָרִים, מְקַפֵּץ
עַל הַגְּבָעוֹת. דּוֹמֶה דוֹדִי לִצְבִי, אוֹ לְעֹפֶר הָאַיָּלִים; הִנֵּה־זֶה
עוֹמֵד אַחַר כָּתְלֵנוּ, מַשְׁגִּיחַ מִן הַחַלֹּנוֹת, מֵצִיץ מִן הַחֲרַכִּים.
עָנָה דוֹדִי וְאָמַר לִי: קוּמִי לָךְ, רַעְיָתִי, יָפָתִי, וּלְכִי לָךְ. כִּי
הִנֵּה הַסְּתָו עָבָר; הַגֶּשֶׁם חָלַף הָלַךְ לוֹ. הַנִּצָּנִים נִרְאוּ בָאָרֶץ,
עֵת הַזָּמִיר הִגִּיעַ; וְקוֹל הַתּוֹר נִשְׁמַע בְּאַרְצֵנוּ. הַתְּאֵנָה חָנְטָה
פַגֶּיהָ, וְהַגְּפָנִים סְמָדַר נָתְנוּ רֵיחַ; קוּמִי לָךְ, רַעְיָתִי, יָפָתִי, וּלְכִי
לָךְ. יוֹנָתִי, בְּחַגְוֵי הַסֶּלַע, בְּסֵתֶר הַמַּדְרֵגָה, הַרְאִינִי אֶת מַרְאַיִךְ,
הַשְׁמִיעִנִי אֶת קוֹלֵךְ; כִּי קוֹלֵךְ עָרֵב, וּמַרְאֵיךְ נָאוֶה. אֶחֱזוּ לָנוּ
שֻׁעָלִים, שֻׁעָלִים קְטַנִּים, מְחַבְּלִים כְּרָמִים; וּכְרָמֵינוּ סְמָדַר.
דּוֹדִי לִי, וַאֲנִי לוֹ, הָרֹעֶה בַּשּׁוֹשַׁנִּים. עַד שֶׁיָּפוּחַ הַיּוֹם, וְנָסוּ
הַצְּלָלִים, סֹב דְּמֵה לְךָ, דוֹדִי, לִצְבִי אוֹ לְעֹפֶר הָאַיָּלִים, עַל
הָרֵי בָתֶר.

[ג]

עַל מִשְׁכָּבִי בַּלֵּילוֹת בִּקַּשְׁתִּי אֵת שֶׁאָהֲבָה נַפְשִׁי; בִּקַּשְׁתִּיו
וְלֹא מְצָאתִיו. אָקוּמָה נָּא וַאֲסוֹבְבָה בָעִיר, בַּשְּׁוָקִים וּבָרְחֹבוֹת,
אֲבַקְשָׁה אֵת שֶׁאָהֲבָה נַפְשִׁי; בִּקַּשְׁתִּיו וְלֹא מְצָאתִיו. מְצָאוּנִי
הַשֹּׁמְרִים הַסֹּבְבִים בָּעִיר; אֵת שֶׁאָהֲבָה נַפְשִׁי רְאִיתֶם. כִּמְעַט
שֶׁעָבַרְתִּי מֵהֶם, עַד שֶׁמָּצָאתִי אֵת שֶׁאָהֲבָה נַפְשִׁי; אֲחַזְתִּיו וְלֹא
אַרְפֶּנּוּ, עַד שֶׁהֲבֵיאתִיו אֶל בֵּית אִמִּי, וְאֶל חֶדֶר הוֹרָתִי.

צבאות, אילות are symbolic of shyness and timidity as well as of beauty.

עד שתחפץ that is, it should be allowed to awake of itself. A true love is
spontaneous.

אחזו לנו שעלים is a couplet of a vineyard song which she sings in response
to his request to let him hear her voice.

head, and his right hand were embracing me! I adjure you, maidens
of Jerusalem, by the gazelles, or by the deer of the field, do not
stir up, do not rouse love, until it please.

The voice of my beloved! Here he comes, leaping across the
mountains, bounding over the hills! My beloved is like a gazelle,
like a young deer; here he stands, behind our wall, gazing through
the windows, peering through the lattice.

My beloved called and said to me: "Rise, my love, my beauty,
come away. For, lo, the winter is over, the rain is past and gone;
the flowers appear on the earth, the time of song has come;
and the call of the turtle-dove is heard in our land; the fig-tree
is ripening its early figs, and the vines in blossom give forth
their fragrance. Rise, my love, my beauty, come away. O my dove,
in the clefts of the rock, in the covert of the cliff, let me see your
form, let me hear your voice; for sweet is your voice, and your
form is comely."

Seize us the foxes, the little foxes, that spoil the vineyards; for
our vineyards are in blossom.

My beloved is mine, and I am his; he feeds his flock among
the lilies. When the day grows cool, and the shadows flee, return,
my beloved, and be like a gazelle, or like a young deer, on the
mountains of Bether.

III

On my bed at night I sought him whom my soul loves; I
sought him, but I did not find him. "I will rise [I said] and go
about the city, in the streets and in the squares—I will seek him
whom my soul loves." I sought him, but I did not find him. The
watchmen who go about the city found me: "Have you seen him
whom my soul loves?" Scarcely had I left them, when I found him
whom my soul loves. I held him and would not let him go, until I
brought him into my mother's house, into the chamber of her who
conceived me.

ונסו הצללים the shadows of rocks and trees disappear when the sun sets.
על משכבי ... is a dream she narrates to her friends.

הִשְׁבַּעְתִּי אֶתְכֶם, בְּנוֹת יְרוּשָׁלַָם, בִּצְבָאוֹת אוֹ בְּאַיְלוֹת הַשָּׂדֶה,
אִם תָּעִירוּ וְאִם תְּעוֹרְרוּ אֶת הָאַהֲבָה עַד שֶׁתֶּחְפָּץ. מִי זֹאת
עֹלָה מִן הַמִּדְבָּר, כְּתִימְרוֹת עָשָׁן, מְקֻטֶּרֶת מֹר וּלְבוֹנָה, מִכֹּל
אַבְקַת רוֹכֵל. הִנֵּה מִטָּתוֹ שֶׁלִּשְׁלֹמֹה, שִׁשִּׁים גִּבֹּרִים סָבִיב לָהּ,
מִגִּבֹּרֵי יִשְׂרָאֵל. כֻּלָּם אֲחֻזֵי חֶרֶב, מְלֻמְּדֵי מִלְחָמָה, אִישׁ חַרְבּוֹ
עַל יְרֵכוֹ, מִפַּחַד בַּלֵּילוֹת. אַפִּרְיוֹן עָשָׂה לוֹ הַמֶּלֶךְ שְׁלֹמֹה
מֵעֲצֵי הַלְּבָנוֹן. עַמּוּדָיו עָשָׂה כֶסֶף, רְפִידָתוֹ זָהָב, מֶרְכָּבוֹ
אַרְגָּמָן; תּוֹכוֹ רָצוּף אַהֲבָה מִבְּנוֹת יְרוּשָׁלָם. צְאֶינָה וּרְאֶינָה,
בְּנוֹת צִיּוֹן, בַּמֶּלֶךְ שְׁלֹמֹה, בָּעֲטָרָה שֶׁעִטְּרָה לּוֹ אִמּוֹ בְּיוֹם
חֲתֻנָּתוֹ, וּבְיוֹם שִׂמְחַת לִבּוֹ.

[ד]

הִנָּךְ יָפָה, רַעְיָתִי, הִנָּךְ יָפָה, עֵינַיִךְ יוֹנִים, מִבַּעַד לְצַמָּתֵךְ;
שַׂעְרֵךְ כְּעֵדֶר הָעִזִּים, שֶׁגָּלְשׁוּ מֵהַר גִּלְעָד. שִׁנַּיִךְ כְּעֵדֶר
הַקְּצוּבוֹת שֶׁעָלוּ מִן הָרַחְצָה; שֶׁכֻּלָּם מַתְאִימוֹת, וְשַׁכֻּלָה אֵין
בָּהֶם. כְּחוּט הַשָּׁנִי שִׂפְתוֹתַיִךְ, וּמִדְבָּרֵךְ נָאוֶה; כְּפֶלַח הָרִמּוֹן
רַקָּתֵךְ, מִבַּעַד לְצַמָּתֵךְ. כְּמִגְדַּל דָּוִיד צַוָּארֵךְ, בָּנוּי לְתַלְפִּיּוֹת;
אֶלֶף הַמָּגֵן תָּלוּי עָלָיו, כֹּל שִׁלְטֵי הַגִּבֹּרִים. שְׁנֵי שָׁדַיִךְ כִּשְׁנֵי
עֳפָרִים, תְּאוֹמֵי צְבִיָּה, הָרֹעִים, בַּשּׁוֹשַׁנִּים. עַד שֶׁיָּפוּחַ הַיּוֹם,
וְנָסוּ הַצְּלָלִים, אֵלֶךְ לִי אֶל הַר הַמּוֹר, וְאֶל גִּבְעַת הַלְּבוֹנָה.
כֻּלָּךְ יָפָה, רַעְיָתִי, וּמוּם אֵין בָּךְ. אִתִּי מִלְּבָנוֹן, כַּלָּה, אִתִּי
מִלְּבָנוֹן תָּבוֹאִי; תָּשׁוּרִי מֵרֹאשׁ אֲמָנָה, מֵרֹאשׁ שְׂנִיר וְחֶרְמוֹן,
מִמְּעֹנוֹת אֲרָיוֹת, מֵהַרְרֵי נְמֵרִים. לִבַּבְתִּנִי, אֲחֹתִי כַלָּה;

תמרות עשן the pillars of smoke are caused by the burning of incense.
שערך . . . The bride's dark hair, hanging down in tresses over her shoulders,
is compared to a herd of black goats couching on the slopes of the hill.
מתאימות symmetrical, running accurately in pairs, the upper teeth corresponding to the lower.

I adjure you, maidens of Jerusalem, by the gazelles, or by the deer of the field, do not stir up, do not rouse love, until it please. What is this coming up from the wilderness, like columns of smoke, perfumed with myrrh and frankincense, with all aromatic powders of the merchant? It is Solomon's palanquin; sixty heroes are around it, heroes of Israel. All of them are armed with swords, and are trained in war; each has his sword on his hip, because of danger at night. King Solomon made himself a palanquin of the wood of Lebanon. He made its columns of silver, its top of gold, its seat of purple, its interior inlaid with love, from the maidens of Jerusalem. Go forth, maidens of Zion, and gaze upon King Solomon, wearing a crown with which his mother crowned him on the day of his marriage, on the day of his profound joy.

IV

You are beautiful, my love, you are beautiful! Your eyes are dove-like behind your veil; your hair is like a flock of goats, trailing down from Mount Gilead. Your teeth are like a flock of sheep all shaped alike, which have come up from the washing; all of them are paired, and not one of them is missing. Your lips are like a thread of scarlet, and your mouth is comely; your temples, behind your veil, are like a slice of pomegranate. Your neck is like the tower of David built for trophies; a thousand shields hang on it, all armor of heroes. Your two breasts are like two fawns, twins of a gazelle, pasturing among the lilies. When the day grows cool, and the shadows flee, I will betake myself to the mountain of myrrh, and to the hill of frankincense. You are altogether beautiful, my love; there is no blemish in you.

Come with me from Lebanon, bride of mine, with me from Lebanon come; depart from the top of Amana, from the peaks of Senir and Hermon, from the dens of lions, from the mountains of leopards. You have ravished my heart, my sister, my bride; you

---

כפלח הרמון like the rounded form and ruddy color of a pomegranate.

בנוי לתלפיות is an allusion to the bride's necklace. On shields used as adornments on the outside of towers, see Ezekiel 27:10–11.

אתי מלבנון ... is a warning to flee from Lebanon being full of dangers.

תשורי מ ... depart; compare ותשורי (Isaiah 57:9) "you journeyed."

אחותי is used here in the sense of "my own."

לִבַּבְתִּנִי בְּאַחַת מֵעֵינַיִךְ, בְּאַחַד עֲנָק מִצַּוְּרֹנָיִךְ. מַה יָּפוּ דֹדַיִךְ,
אֲחֹתִי כַלָּה; מַה טֹּבוּ דֹדַיִךְ מִיַּיִן, וְרֵיחַ שְׁמָנַיִךְ מִכָּל בְּשָׂמִים.
נֹפֶת תִּטֹּפְנָה שִׂפְתוֹתַיִךְ, כַּלָּה; דְּבַשׁ וְחָלָב תַּחַת לְשׁוֹנֵךְ, וְרֵיחַ
שַׂלְמֹתַיִךְ כְּרֵיחַ לְבָנוֹן. גַּן נָעוּל אֲחֹתִי כַלָּה, גַּל נָעוּל, מַעְיָן
חָתוּם. שְׁלָחַיִךְ פַּרְדֵּס רִמּוֹנִים, עִם פְּרִי מְגָדִים, כְּפָרִים עִם
נְרָדִים. נֵרְדְּ וְכַרְכֹּם, קָנֶה וְקִנָּמוֹן, עִם כָּל עֲצֵי לְבוֹנָה; מֹר
וַאֲהָלוֹת, עִם כָּל רָאשֵׁי בְשָׂמִים. מַעְיַן גַּנִּים, בְּאֵר מַיִם חַיִּים,
וְנֹזְלִים מִן לְבָנוֹן. עוּרִי צָפוֹן, וּבוֹאִי תֵימָן, הָפִיחִי גַנִּי, יִזְּלוּ
בְשָׂמָיו; יָבֹא דוֹדִי לְגַנּוֹ, וְיֹאכַל פְּרִי מְגָדָיו.

[ה]

בָּאתִי לְגַנִּי, אֲחֹתִי כַלָּה, אָרִיתִי מוֹרִי עִם בְּשָׂמִי, אָכַלְתִּי
יַעְרִי עִם דִּבְשִׁי, שָׁתִיתִי יֵינִי עִם חֲלָבִי; אִכְלוּ רֵעִים, שְׁתוּ
וְשִׁכְרוּ דּוֹדִים. אֲנִי יְשֵׁנָה וְלִבִּי עֵר; קוֹל דּוֹדִי דוֹפֵק: פִּתְחִי
לִי, אֲחֹתִי, רַעְיָתִי, יוֹנָתִי, תַמָּתִי, שֶׁרֹּאשִׁי נִמְלָא טָל, קְוֻצּוֹתַי
רְסִיסֵי לָיְלָה. פָּשַׁטְתִּי אֶת כֻּתָּנְתִּי, אֵיכָכָה אֶלְבָּשֶׁנָּה; רָחַצְתִּי
אֶת רַגְלַי, אֵיכָכָה אֲטַנְּפֵם. דּוֹדִי שָׁלַח יָדוֹ מִן הַחוֹר, וּמֵעַי הָמוּ
עָלָיו. קַמְתִּי אֲנִי לִפְתֹּחַ לְדוֹדִי, וְיָדַי נָטְפוּ מוֹר, וְאֶצְבְּעֹתַי
מוֹר עֹבֵר, עַל כַּפּוֹת הַמַּנְעוּל. פָּתַחְתִּי אֲנִי לְדוֹדִי, וְדוֹדִי חָמַק
עָבָר; נַפְשִׁי יָצְאָה בְדַבְּרוֹ; בִּקַּשְׁתִּיהוּ וְלֹא מְצָאתִיהוּ, קְרָאתִיו
וְלֹא עָנָנִי. מְצָאֻנִי הַשֹּׁמְרִים הַסֹּבְבִים בָּעִיר, הִכּוּנִי פְצָעוּנִי;
נָשְׂאוּ אֶת רְדִידִי מֵעָלַי שֹׁמְרֵי הַחֹמוֹת. הִשְׁבַּעְתִּי אֶתְכֶם, בְּנוֹת
יְרוּשָׁלָיִם, אִם תִּמְצְאוּ אֶת דּוֹדִי, מַה תַּגִּידוּ לוֹ שֶׁחוֹלַת אַהֲבָה

נפת honey that drips from the honeycomb. The reference is to loving words.
צפון, תימן The north wind clears the air in Palestine; the south wind warms
and ripens. The east and west winds are stormy.

מה is here used in the sense of "not." Compare below מה תעירו ומה תעררו
את האהבה (8:4); מה לנו חלק בדוד ולא נחלה בבן-ישי (I Kings 12:16).

have ravished my heart with one glance of your eyes, with one bead of your necklace. How lovely are your caresses, my sister, my bride! How much better than wine are your caresses, and the fragrance of your ointments than all kinds of perfume! Your lips, my bride, drip honey; honey and milk are under your tongue; the fragrance of your garments is like the fragrance of Lebanon. A garden inclosed is my sister, my bride, a spring inclosed, a fountain sealed. Your plants are an orchard of pomegranates, with precious fruits, henna with nard, nard and saffron, calamus and cinnamon, with all trees of frankincense, myrrh and aloes, together with all the finest perfumes. You are a fountain of gardens, a well of fresh water, and flowing streams from Lebanon.

Awake, northwind, and come, southwind! Blow upon my garden, that its perfume may waft out. Let my beloved come into his garden, and eat its precious fruits.

V

I have come into my garden, my sister, my bride; I have gathered my myrrh and my spice; I have eaten my honeycomb with my honey; I have drunk my wine and my milk. Eat, friends; drink, drink abundantly, beloved friends!

I was asleep, but my heart was awake; hark, my beloved is knocking: "Open to me, my sister, my love, my dove, my innocent one; for my head is drenched with dew, my locks with the drops of the night." But I have taken off my robe; how shall I put it on again? I have washed my feet; how shall I soil them? My beloved put his hand through the doorway, and my heart yearned for him. I rose to open to my beloved, and my hands dripped with myrrh, and my fingers with the finest myrrh, upon the handles of the bar. I opened to my beloved; but my beloved had turned away, had gone; my soul failed when he spoke. I sought him, but I could not find him; I called him, but he did not answer me. The watchmen who go about the city found me; they struck me, they wounded me; the guardians of the walls stripped me of my mantle. I adjure you, maidens of Jerusalem, if you find my beloved, do not tell him that I am love-sick.

אָנִי. מַה דּוֹדֵךְ מִדּוֹד, הַיָּפָה בַּנָּשִׁים; מַה דּוֹדֵךְ מִדּוֹד, שֶׁכָּכָה
הִשְׁבַּעְתָּנוּ. דּוֹדִי צַח וְאָדוֹם, דָּגוּל מֵרְבָבָה. רֹאשׁוֹ כֶּתֶם פָּז;
קְוֻצּוֹתָיו תַּלְתַּלִּים, שְׁחֹרוֹת כָּעוֹרֵב. עֵינָיו כְּיוֹנִים עַל אֲפִיקֵי
מָיִם; רֹחֲצוֹת בֶּחָלָב, יֹשְׁבוֹת עַל מִלֵּאת. לְחָיָו כַּעֲרוּגַת הַבֹּשֶׂם,
מִגְדְּלוֹת מֶרְקָחִים; שִׂפְתוֹתָיו שׁוֹשַׁנִּים, נֹטְפוֹת מוֹר עֹבֵר. יָדָיו
גְּלִילֵי זָהָב, מְמֻלָּאִים בַּתַּרְשִׁישׁ; מֵעָיו עֶשֶׁת שֵׁן, מְעֻלֶּפֶת
סַפִּירִים. שׁוֹקָיו עַמּוּדֵי שֵׁשׁ, מְיֻסָּדִים עַל אַדְנֵי פָז; מַרְאֵהוּ
כַּלְּבָנוֹן, בָּחוּר כָּאֲרָזִים. חִכּוֹ מַמְתַקִּים, וְכֻלּוֹ מַחֲמַדִּים; זֶה
דוֹדִי וְזֶה רֵעִי, בְּנוֹת יְרוּשָׁלָם.

[ו]

אָנָה הָלַךְ דּוֹדֵךְ, הַיָּפָה בַּנָּשִׁים; אָנָה פָּנָה דוֹדֵךְ, וּנְבַקְשֶׁנּוּ
עִמָּךְ. דּוֹדִי יָרַד לְגַנּוֹ, לַעֲרוּגוֹת הַבֹּשֶׂם, לִרְעוֹת בַּגַּנִּים וְלִלְקֹט
שׁוֹשַׁנִּים. אֲנִי לְדוֹדִי, וְדוֹדִי לִי, הָרוֹעֶה בַּשּׁוֹשַׁנִּים. יָפָה אַתְּ
רַעְיָתִי כְּתִרְצָה, נָאוָה כִּירוּשָׁלָם, אֲיֻמָּה כַּנִּדְגָּלוֹת. הָסֵבִּי עֵינַיִךְ
מִנֶּגְדִּי, שֶׁהֵם הִרְהִיבֻנִי; שַׂעְרֵךְ כְּעֵדֶר הָעִזִּים, שֶׁגָּלְשׁוּ מִן
הַגִּלְעָד. שִׁנַּיִךְ כְּעֵדֶר הָרְחֵלִים, שֶׁעָלוּ מִן הָרַחְצָה; שֶׁכֻּלָּם
מַתְאִימוֹת, וְשַׁכֻּלָה אֵין בָּהֶם. כְּפֶלַח הָרִמּוֹן רַקָּתֵךְ, מִבַּעַד
לְצַמָּתֵךְ. שִׁשִּׁים הֵמָּה מְלָכוֹת, וּשְׁמֹנִים פִּילַגְשִׁים, וַעֲלָמוֹת אֵין
מִסְפָּר. אַחַת הִיא יוֹנָתִי תַמָּתִי, אַחַת הִיא לְאִמָּהּ, בָּרָה הִיא
לְיוֹלַדְתָּהּ; רָאוּהָ בָנוֹת וַיְאַשְּׁרוּהָ, מְלָכוֹת וּפִילַגְשִׁים, וַיְהַלְלוּהָ.
מִי זֹאת הַנִּשְׁקָפָה כְּמוֹ שָׁחַר; יָפָה כַלְּבָנָה, בָּרָה כַּחַמָּה, אֲיֻמָּה
כַּנִּדְגָּלוֹת. אֶל גִּנַּת אֱגוֹז יָרַדְתִּי לִרְאוֹת בְּאִבֵּי הַנָּחַל; לִרְאוֹת

... ידיו his fingers are delicately rounded, and his nails are as transparent
as topaz. ספירים the bright blue veins showing through the lighter skin.

תרצה ("delight") was an ancient city famed for its attractiveness. It is
mentioned in Joshua 12:24; I Kings 14:17.

What is your beloved more than another lover, O fairest of women? What is your beloved more than another lover, that you adjure us thus?

Dazzling and ruddy is my beloved, distinguished among ten thousand. His head is fine gold, his locks are curled, and as black as a raven. His eyes are like doves beside the water-brooks, bathing in milk, and fitly set. His cheeks are beds of balsam-flower, producing sweet perfumes; his lips are [red] lilies, breathing the finest myrrh. His hands are rods of gold, studded with topaz pink; his body is polished ivory, inlaid with sapphires. His legs are pillars of marble, set on bases of fine gold; his form is like Lebanon, excellent as the cedars. His mouth is most sweet, and he is altogether lovely. Such is my beloved, and such is my lover, O maidens of Jerusalem.

VI

Where has your beloved gone, O fairest of women? Where has your beloved turned, that we may seek him with you?

My beloved has gone down to his garden, to the flower-beds of balsam, to pasture in the gardens, and to gather lilies. I am my beloved's, and my beloved is mine, who pastures among the lilies.

You are as beautiful as Tirzah, my love, as comely as Jerusalem, as overawing as the most distinguished. Turn your eyes away from me, for they dazzle me. Your hair is like a flock of goats, trailing down from Mount Gilead. Your teeth are like a flock of sheep, which have come up from the washing; all of them are paired, and not one of them is missing. Your temples are like a slice of pomegranate, behind your veil. There are sixty queens, eighty concubines, and maidens without number; but one alone is my dove, my innocent one; she is the only one of her mother; she is her mother's own darling. The maidens look upon her, and bless her; the queens and the concubines praise her. Who is she that appears like the dawn, as beautiful as the moon, as bright as the sun, as overawing as the most distinguished?

I went down to the nut garden, to look at the green plants of

הָפָרְחָה הַגֶּפֶן, הֵנֵצוּ הָרִמּוֹנִים. לֹא יָדַעְתִּי, נַפְשִׁי שָׂמַתְנִי מַרְכְּבוֹת עַמִּי נָדִיב.

[ז]

שׁוּבִי שׁוּבִי, הַשּׁוּלַמִּית, שׁוּבִי שׁוּבִי וְנֶחֱזֶה בָּךְ; מַה תֶּחֱזוּ בַּשּׁוּלַמִּית, כִּמְחֹלַת הַמַּחֲנָיִם. מַה יָּפוּ פְעָמַיִךְ בַּנְּעָלִים, בַּת נָדִיב; חַמּוּקֵי יְרֵכַיִךְ כְּמוֹ חֲלָאִים, מַעֲשֵׂה יְדֵי אָמָּן. שָׁרְרֵךְ אַגַּן הַסַּהַר, אַל יֶחְסַר הַמָּזֶג; בִּטְנֵךְ עֲרֵמַת חִטִּים, סוּגָה בַּשּׁוֹשַׁנִּים. שְׁנֵי שָׁדַיִךְ כִּשְׁנֵי עֳפָרִים, תָּאֳמֵי צְבִיָּה. צַוָּארֵךְ כְּמִגְדַּל הַשֵּׁן; עֵינַיִךְ בְּרֵכוֹת בְּחֶשְׁבּוֹן, עַל שַׁעַר בַּת רַבִּים; אַפֵּךְ כְּמִגְדַּל הַלְּבָנוֹן, צוֹפֶה פְּנֵי דַמָּשֶׂק. רֹאשֵׁךְ עָלַיִךְ כַּכַּרְמֶל, וְדַלַּת רֹאשֵׁךְ כָּאַרְגָּמָן; מֶלֶךְ אָסוּר בָּרְהָטִים. מַה יָּפִית וּמַה נָּעַמְתְּ, אַהֲבָה בַּתַּעֲנוּגִים. זֹאת קוֹמָתֵךְ דָּמְתָה לְתָמָר, וְשָׁדַיִךְ לְאַשְׁכֹּלוֹת. אָמַרְתִּי, אֶעֱלֶה בְתָמָר, אֹחֲזָה בְּסַנְסִנָּיו; וְיִהְיוּ נָא שָׁדַיִךְ כְּאֶשְׁכְּלוֹת הַגֶּפֶן, וְרֵיחַ אַפֵּךְ כַּתַּפּוּחִים. וְחִכֵּךְ כְּיֵין הַטּוֹב, הוֹלֵךְ לְדוֹדִי לְמֵישָׁרִים, דּוֹבֵב שִׂפְתֵי יְשֵׁנִים. אֲנִי לְדוֹדִי, וְעָלַי תְּשׁוּקָתוֹ. לְכָה דוֹדִי, נֵצֵא הַשָּׂדֶה, נָלִינָה בַּכְּפָרִים. נַשְׁכִּימָה לַכְּרָמִים, נִרְאֶה אִם פָּרְחָה הַגֶּפֶן, פִּתַּח הַסְּמָדַר, הֵנֵצוּ הָרִמּוֹנִים; שָׁם אֶתֵּן אֶת דֹּדַי לָךְ. הַדּוּדָאִים נָתְנוּ רֵיחַ, וְעַל פְּתָחֵינוּ כָּל מְגָדִים, חֲדָשִׁים גַּם יְשָׁנִים, דּוֹדִי, צָפַנְתִּי לָךְ.

[ח]

מִי יִתֶּנְךָ כְּאָח לִי, יוֹנֵק שְׁדֵי אִמִּי; אֶמְצָאֲךָ בַחוּץ אֶשָּׁקְךָ, גַּם לֹא יָבֻזוּ לִי. אֶנְהָגְךָ, אֲבִיאֲךָ אֶל בֵּית אִמִּי, תְּלַמְּדֵנִי; אַשְׁקְךָ

<hr>

מה תחזו בשולמית are the words of the Shulammite, who asks why they would stare at her as at a public spectacle.

בטנך "your body," like נפשי ובטני ("my soul and my body") in Psalm 31:10.

צוארך כמגדל השן white, straight and slender.

ברכות בחשבון refers to the soft shimmer of her eyes.

the dale, to see if the grapevine was a-budding, whether the pomegranates were in flower. Before I was aware, my fancy set me among the chariots of my noble people.

VII

Return, return, O Shulammite; return, return, that we may gaze at you.

Why should you gaze at the Shulammite as upon the dance of Mahanaim?

How beautiful are your steps in sandals, O princess; the curves of your thighs are like ornaments made by an artist. Your chest is like a round goblet ever filled with wine; your body is like a heap of wheat set about with lilies. Your two breasts are like two fawns, twins of a gazelle. Your neck is like a tower of ivory; your eyes are like the pools of Heshbon, at the gate of Bathrabim; your nose is like a tower of Lebanon, overlooking Damascus. Your head is on you like Carmel, and the hair of your head is like purple; the king is held captive in its tresses. How beautiful, how sweet you are, O love's delight! This stature of yours is like a palm tree, and your breasts like clusters. I say: I will climb the palm tree, I will take hold of its branches; let your breasts be like clusters of the vine, and the fragrance of your breath like that of apples, and your soft speech like the best wine—flowing smoothly for my beloved, gliding over the lips of those about to sleep.

I am my beloved's, and his longing is for me. Come, my beloved, let us go into the field, let us stay in the villages; let us go early to the vineyards, to see whether the grapevine has budded, whether the vine blossoms have opened, if the pomegranates are in flower. There I will give my love to you. The love-plants yield their fragrance, and at our doors are all kinds of precious fruits, both new and old, which I have kept for you, my beloved.

VIII

O that you were my brother. who had been nursed by my mother! I would meet you in the street and kiss you, and none would despise me. I would lead you and bring you into my mother's

---

אפך כמגדל הלבנן straight and symmetrical. The tower of Lebanon was probably some watch-tower in the direction of Damascus.

כרמל an emblem of stateliness and beauty. The point of comparison is a head proudly held.

מִנְיַן הָרֶקַח, מֵעֲסִיס רִמֹּנִי. שְׂמֹאלוֹ תַּחַת רֹאשִׁי, וִימִינוֹ תְּחַבְּקֵנִי. הִשְׁבַּעְתִּי אֶתְכֶם, בְּנוֹת יְרוּשָׁלָם, מַה תָּעִירוּ וּמַה תְּעֹרְרוּ אֶת הָאַהֲבָה עַד שֶׁתֶּחְפָּץ. מִי זֹאת עֹלָה מִן הַמִּדְבָּר, מִתְרַפֶּקֶת עַל דּוֹדָהּ; תַּחַת הַתַּפּוּחַ עוֹרַרְתִּיךָ, שָׁמָּה חִבְּלַתְךָ אִמֶּךָ, שָׁמָּה חִבְּלָה יְלָדַתְךָ. שִׂימֵנִי כַחוֹתָם עַל לִבֶּךָ, כַּחוֹתָם עַל זְרוֹעֶךָ; כִּי עַזָּה כַמָּוֶת אַהֲבָה, קָשָׁה כִשְׁאוֹל קִנְאָה; רְשָׁפֶיהָ רִשְׁפֵּי אֵשׁ, שַׁלְהֶבֶתְיָה. מַיִם רַבִּים לֹא יוּכְלוּ לְכַבּוֹת אֶת הָאַהֲבָה, וּנְהָרוֹת לֹא יִשְׁטְפוּהָ; אִם יִתֵּן אִישׁ אֶת כָּל הוֹן בֵּיתוֹ בָּאַהֲבָה, בּוֹז יָבוּזוּ לוֹ. אָחוֹת לָנוּ קְטַנָּה, וְשָׁדַיִם אֵין לָהּ; מַה נַּעֲשֶׂה לַאֲחוֹתֵנוּ בַּיּוֹם שֶׁיְּדֻבַּר בָּהּ. אִם חוֹמָה הִיא, נִבְנֶה עָלֶיהָ טִירַת כָּסֶף; וְאִם דֶּלֶת הִיא, נָצוּר עָלֶיהָ לוּחַ אָרֶז. אֲנִי חוֹמָה, וְשָׁדַי כַּמִּגְדָּלוֹת; אָז הָיִיתִי בְעֵינָיו כְּמוֹצְאֵת שָׁלוֹם. כֶּרֶם הָיָה לִשְׁלֹמֹה בְּבַעַל הָמוֹן; נָתַן אֶת הַכֶּרֶם לַנֹּטְרִים; אִישׁ יָבָא בְּפִרְיוֹ אֶלֶף כָּסֶף. כַּרְמִי שֶׁלִּי לְפָנָי; הָאֶלֶף לְךָ שְׁלֹמֹה, וּמָאתַיִם לְנֹטְרִים אֶת פִּרְיוֹ. הַיּוֹשֶׁבֶת בַּגַּנִּים, חֲבֵרִים מַקְשִׁיבִים לְקוֹלֵךְ, הַשְׁמִיעִנִי. בְּרַח דּוֹדִי, וּדְמֵה לְךָ לִצְבִי, אוֹ לְעֹפֶר הָאַיָּלִים, עַל הָרֵי בְשָׂמִים.

מִי זֹאת עֹלָה ... She points out incidents and places that are memorable to both of them.

חוֹתַם signet ring, engraved with the owner's name or some design. The seal, affixed as signature to letters and documents, was worn on the finger or was strung on a cord and hung around the neck. She wishes to be united in the closest way with her beloved.

שַׁלְהֶבֶתְיָה a flame of supernatural, stupendous power.

אָחוֹת לָנוּ קְטַנָּה was the speech of her brothers in the past, when she was still too young to marry. She recalls having heard them say that they would reward her modesty with adornments and provide strong protection in the case of any sign of moral weakness.

אִם חוֹמָה הִיא ... that is, if she preserves her innocence, we will reward her.

house, that you might instruct me; I would give you some spiced wine to drink, some of my pomegranate juice.

O that his left hand were under my head, and his right hand were embracing me! I adjure you, maidens of Jerusalem, do not stir up, do not rouse love, until it please.

Who is this coming up from the wilderness, leaning upon her beloved?

I woke you under the apple tree, where your mother had been in travail with you, where she had brought you forth. Place me like a seal upon your heart, like a seal upon your arm. Indeed, love is strong as death itself, ardent love is severe as the grave; its flashes are flashes of fire, a flame of the Lord. Floods cannot quench love, rivers cannot drown it; if a man offered all the wealth of his house for love, he would be laughed aside.

We have a young sister, and she has no breasts yet; but what shall we do with our sister when she will be asked in marriage? If she is a wall, we will build a silver turret on her; but if she is a door, we will inclose her with cedar boards.

Now I am a wall, and my breasts like towers, then I should win his favor.

Solomon had a vineyard at Baalhamon; he gave over the vineyard to caretakers; each would bring in a thousand silver pieces for its fruits. I keep my vineyard to myself; you, Solomon, are welcome to the thousand shekels, and the caretakers of the fruit to the two hundred shekels.

O you who sit in the gardens, the companions are listening to your voice; let me hear it too!

Make haste, my beloved, be like a gazelle, or like a young deer, on the mountains of spices.

כרם היה that is, his possession is prized more than Solomon's highly-cultivated vineyard with all its rich revenues.

ברח דודי is a repetition of her song in 2:17. Allegorically, it is a prayer addressed to God: Mayest thou hasten to reappear on Mount Moriah.

קַבָּלַת שַׁבָּת

The following *Kabbalath Shabbath* service is omitted on festivals which coincide with the Sabbath. The *Ma'ariv* service for festivals begins on page 257.

תהלים צה

לְכוּ נְרַנְּנָה לַיָי, נָרִיעָה לְצוּר יִשְׁעֵנוּ. נְקַדְּמָה פָנָיו בְּתוֹדָה,
בִּזְמִרוֹת נָרִיעַ לוֹ. כִּי אֵל גָּדוֹל יְיָ, וּמֶלֶךְ גָּדוֹל עַל כָּל אֱלֹהִים.
אֲשֶׁר בְּיָדוֹ מֶחְקְרֵי אָרֶץ, וְתוֹעֲפוֹת הָרִים לוֹ. אֲשֶׁר לוֹ הַיָּם,
וְהוּא עָשָׂהוּ; וְיַבֶּשֶׁת יָדָיו יָצָרוּ. בֹּאוּ נִשְׁתַּחֲוֶה וְנִכְרָעָה, נִבְרְכָה
לִפְנֵי יְיָ עֹשֵׂנוּ. כִּי הוּא אֱלֹהֵינוּ, וַאֲנַחְנוּ עַם מַרְעִיתוֹ וְצֹאן יָדוֹ;
הַיּוֹם אִם בְּקֹלוֹ תִשְׁמָעוּ. אַל תַּקְשׁוּ לְבַבְכֶם כִּמְרִיבָה, כְּיוֹם
מַסָּה בַּמִּדְבָּר. אֲשֶׁר נִסּוּנִי אֲבוֹתֵיכֶם; בְּחָנוּנִי, גַּם רָאוּ פָעֳלִי.
Reader אַרְבָּעִים שָׁנָה אָקוּט בְּדוֹר, וָאֹמַר עַם תֹּעֵי לֵבָב הֵם,
וְהֵם לֹא יָדְעוּ דְרָכָי. אֲשֶׁר נִשְׁבַּעְתִּי בְאַפִּי, אִם יְבֹאוּן אֶל
מְנוּחָתִי.

תהלים צו

שִׁירוּ לַיָי שִׁיר חָדָשׁ, שִׁירוּ לַיָי כָּל הָאָרֶץ. שִׁירוּ לַיָי, בָּרֲכוּ
שְׁמוֹ, בַּשְּׂרוּ מִיּוֹם לְיוֹם יְשׁוּעָתוֹ. סַפְּרוּ בַגּוֹיִם כְּבוֹדוֹ, בְּכָל
הָעַמִּים נִפְלְאוֹתָיו. כִּי גָדוֹל יְיָ וּמְהֻלָּל מְאֹד, נוֹרָא הוּא עַל כָּל
אֱלֹהִים. כִּי כָּל אֱלֹהֵי הָעַמִּים אֱלִילִים, וַיָי שָׁמַיִם עָשָׂה. הוֹד

קבלת שבת, the opening service on Friday evening, was introduced by the Kabbalists of the sixteenth century in Safed, Palestine. The six psalms, symbolizing the six working days of the week, were selected by Rabbi Moses Cordovero, whose brother-in-law Rabbi Solomon Alkabets composed the hymn welcoming the Sabbath bride (לכה דודי). The initial letters of the six psalms (ל, ש, מ, י, מ) have the numerical value of 430 which equals that of נפש ("soul"). מזמור לדוד (Psalm 29) contains the name of God eighteen times, a number corresponding to the eighteen blessings of the *Shemoneh Esreh*.

Psalm 95 is a call to worship the Creator of the world and Guardian of

WELCOMING THE SABBATH

The following Kabbalath Shabbath Service is omitted on festivals which coincide with the Sabbath. The Ma'ariv service for festivals begins on page 258.

Psalm 95

Come, let us sing to the Lord; let us acclaim our saving Stronghold.

Let us approach him with thanksgiving; let us acclaim him with songs of praise.

For the Lord is a great God, a King supreme above all gods.

In his hand are the depths of the earth; the mountain-peaks are his.

His is the sea, for he made it; his hands formed the dry land.

Come, let us worship and bow down; let us bend the knee before the Lord who made us.

For he is our God, and we are the people he sustains, the flock under his charge; if this day you would only obey his voice!

Harden not your heart as at Meribah, as in the day of Massah in the wilderness, when your fathers tried me.

They tested me, although they had seen my work.

For forty years I loathed that generation, and said: "They are a senseless people, who know not my ways."

So I vowed in my anger that they should never enter my land.

Psalm 96

Sing a new song to the Lord; sing to the Lord, all the earth.

Sing to the Lord, bless his name; announce his salvation from day to day.

Recount his glory among the nations, his wonders—among the peoples.

For great is the Lord and highly to be praised; he is to be revered above all gods.

For all the gods of the peoples are idols, but the Lord made the heavens.

---

his people. It contains a warning against disobedience, and alludes to the fate of the rebellious Israelites in the wilderness (Exodus 17:7; Numbers 20:13).

Psalm 96 contrasts God's power and glory with the worthlessness of the heathen idols, and appeals to the nations to acknowledge God and to rejoice in the prospect of his righteous rule on earth.

וְהָדָר לְפָנָיו, עֹז וְתִפְאֶרֶת בְּמִקְדָּשׁוֹ. הָבוּ לַיָי, מִשְׁפְּחוֹת עַמִּים,
הָבוּ לַיָי כָּבוֹד וָעֹז. הָבוּ לַיָי כְּבוֹד שְׁמוֹ, שְׂאוּ מִנְחָה וּבְאוּ
לְחַצְרוֹתָיו. הִשְׁתַּחֲווּ לַיָי בְּהַדְרַת קֹדֶשׁ; חִילוּ מִפָּנָיו, כָּל
הָאָרֶץ. אִמְרוּ בַגּוֹיִם יְיָ מָלָךְ, אַף תִּכּוֹן תֵּבֵל בַּל תִּמּוֹט; יָדִין
עַמִּים בְּמֵישָׁרִים. יִשְׂמְחוּ הַשָּׁמַיִם וְתָגֵל הָאָרֶץ; יִרְעַם הַיָּם
וּמְלֹאוֹ. יַעֲלֹז שָׂדַי וְכָל אֲשֶׁר בּוֹ; אָז יְרַנְּנוּ כָּל עֲצֵי יָעַר.
Reader לִפְנֵי יְיָ כִּי בָא, כִּי בָא לִשְׁפֹּט הָאָרֶץ; יִשְׁפֹּט תֵּבֵל
בְּצֶדֶק, וְעַמִּים בֶּאֱמוּנָתוֹ.

תהלים צז

יְיָ מָלָךְ, תָּגֵל הָאָרֶץ; יִשְׂמְחוּ אִיִּים רַבִּים. עָנָן וַעֲרָפֶל
סְבִיבָיו, צֶדֶק וּמִשְׁפָּט מְכוֹן כִּסְאוֹ. אֵשׁ לְפָנָיו תֵּלֵךְ, וּתְלַהֵט
סָבִיב צָרָיו. הֵאִירוּ בְרָקָיו תֵּבֵל, רָאֲתָה וַתָּחֵל הָאָרֶץ. הָרִים
כַּדּוֹנַג נָמַסּוּ מִלִּפְנֵי יְיָ, מִלִּפְנֵי אֲדוֹן כָּל הָאָרֶץ. הִגִּידוּ הַשָּׁמַיִם
צִדְקוֹ, וְרָאוּ כָל הָעַמִּים כְּבוֹדוֹ. יֵבֹשׁוּ כָּל עֹבְדֵי פֶסֶל,
הַמִּתְהַלְלִים בָּאֱלִילִים; הִשְׁתַּחֲווּ לוֹ כָּל אֱלֹהִים. שָׁמְעָה
וַתִּשְׂמַח צִיּוֹן, וַתָּגֵלְנָה בְּנוֹת יְהוּדָה, לְמַעַן מִשְׁפָּטֶיךָ יְיָ. כִּי
אַתָּה, יְיָ, עֶלְיוֹן עַל כָּל הָאָרֶץ; מְאֹד נַעֲלֵיתָ עַל כָּל אֱלֹהִים.
אֹהֲבֵי יְיָ, שִׂנְאוּ רָע; שֹׁמֵר נַפְשׁוֹת חֲסִידָיו, מִיַּד רְשָׁעִים יַצִּילֵם.
Reader אוֹר זָרֻעַ לַצַּדִּיק, וּלְיִשְׁרֵי לֵב שִׂמְחָה. שִׂמְחוּ צַדִּיקִים
בַּיְיָ, וְהוֹדוּ לְזֵכֶר קָדְשׁוֹ.

Psalm 97 is a mosaic of phrases borrowed from various Scriptural passages.
It celebrates God's manifestation of his sovereignty and calls his people to
hate evil. All, even the gods existing in the minds of their worshipers, must
do homage to the only true God. The Septuagint renders אור זרוע לצדיק in the
sense of אור לישרים ... זרח (Psalm 112:4): "Light dawns on the upright."

Grandeur and majesty are before him; glory and beauty are in his sanctuary.

Ascribe to the Lord, O families of peoples, ascribe to the Lord glory and majesty.

Ascribe to the Lord the glory due to his name; bring an offering and come into his courts.

Worship the Lord in holy array; tremble before him, all the earth.

Say among the nations: "The Lord is King!"

The world is so established that it cannot be shaken; he rules the peoples justly.

Let the heavens rejoice, let the earth be glad, let the sea and all its fulness roar praise.

Let the field exult and all that is therein; let all the trees of the forest sing before the Lord who comes, who comes to rule the earth.

He will rule the world with righteousness, and the peoples—with his truth.

Psalm 97

The Lord is King; let the earth rejoice; let many islands be glad.

Clouds and darkness are around him; righteousness and justice are the foundation of his throne.

Fire goes before him, and burns his foes round about.

His lightnings illuminate the world; the earth beholds and trembles.

The mountains melt like wax before the Lord, before the Lord of all the earth.

The heavens proclaim his righteousness, and all the peoples witness his glory.

Ashamed be those who serve images, those who take pride in idols; bow down to him, all you gods!

Zion hears and is glad, and the towns of Judah rejoice, because of thy judgments, O Lord.

Thou, O Lord, art indeed supreme over all the earth; thou art exalted high above all gods.

You who love the Lord, hate evil! He preserves the lives of his faithful followers; he rescues them from the hand of the wicked.

Light is sown for the righteous, and joy for the upright in heart.

Rejoice in the Lord, you righteous, and give thanks to his holy name.

תהלים צח

מִזְמוֹר. שִׁירוּ לַיָי שִׁיר חָדָשׁ, כִּי נִפְלָאוֹת עָשָׂה. הוֹשִׁיעָה לּוֹ
יְמִינוֹ וּזְרוֹעַ קָדְשׁוֹ. הוֹדִיעַ יְיָ יְשׁוּעָתוֹ, לְעֵינֵי הַגּוֹיִם גִּלָּה צִדְקָתוֹ.
זָכַר חַסְדּוֹ וֶאֱמוּנָתוֹ לְבֵית יִשְׂרָאֵל; רָאוּ כָל אַפְסֵי אֶרֶץ אֵת
יְשׁוּעַת אֱלֹהֵינוּ. הָרִיעוּ לַיָי, כָּל הָאָרֶץ, פִּצְחוּ וְרַנְּנוּ וְזַמֵּרוּ.
זַמְּרוּ לַיָי בְּכִנּוֹר, בְּכִנּוֹר וְקוֹל זִמְרָה. בַּחֲצֹצְרוֹת וְקוֹל שׁוֹפָר,
הָרִיעוּ לִפְנֵי הַמֶּלֶךְ יְיָ. יִרְעַם הַיָּם וּמְלֹאוֹ, תֵּבֵל וְיֹשְׁבֵי בָהּ.
נְהָרוֹת יִמְחֲאוּ כָף, יַחַד הָרִים יְרַנֵּנוּ. Reader לִפְנֵי יְיָ כִּי בָא
לִשְׁפֹּט הָאָרֶץ; יִשְׁפֹּט תֵּבֵל בְּצֶדֶק, וְעַמִּים בְּמֵישָׁרִים.

תהלים צט

יְיָ מָלָךְ, יִרְגְּזוּ עַמִּים; יֹשֵׁב כְּרוּבִים, תָּנוּט הָאָרֶץ. יְיָ בְּצִיּוֹן
גָּדוֹל, וְרָם הוּא עַל כָּל הָעַמִּים. יוֹדוּ שִׁמְךָ, גָּדוֹל וְנוֹרָא; קָדוֹשׁ
הוּא. וְעֹז מֶלֶךְ מִשְׁפָּט אָהֵב, אַתָּה כּוֹנַנְתָּ מֵישָׁרִים; מִשְׁפָּט
וּצְדָקָה בְּיַעֲקֹב אַתָּה עָשִׂיתָ. רוֹמְמוּ יְיָ אֱלֹהֵינוּ, וְהִשְׁתַּחֲווּ לַהֲדֹם
רַגְלָיו, קָדוֹשׁ הוּא. מֹשֶׁה וְאַהֲרֹן בְּכֹהֲנָיו, וּשְׁמוּאֵל בְּקֹרְאֵי שְׁמוֹ,
קֹרְאִים אֶל יְיָ, וְהוּא יַעֲנֵם. בְּעַמּוּד עָנָן יְדַבֵּר אֲלֵיהֶם; שָׁמְרוּ
עֵדֹתָיו וְחֹק נָתַן לָמוֹ. Reader יְיָ אֱלֹהֵינוּ, אַתָּה עֲנִיתָם; אֵל נֹשֵׂא
הָיִיתָ לָהֶם, וְנֹקֵם עַל עֲלִילוֹתָם. רוֹמְמוּ יְיָ אֱלֹהֵינוּ, וְהִשְׁתַּחֲווּ
לְהַר קָדְשׁוֹ, כִּי קָדוֹשׁ יְיָ אֱלֹהֵינוּ.

תהלים כט

מִזְמוֹר לְדָוִד. הָבוּ לַיָי, בְּנֵי אֵלִים, הָבוּ לַיָי כָּבוֹד וָעֹז;

Psalm 98 is largely made up of quotations, yet it is a stirring song of
joyous praise. ירעם הים ומלאו, and the whole description of nature rejoicing at
God's coming to rule the world, is identical with Psalm 96:11–13. נהרות ימחאו
כף is descriptive of the crashing of the waves.

Psalm 99 celebrates God's universal sovereignty. His righteousness and
faithfulness are manifested in the history of Israel. הדום רגליו refers to the ark
(I Chronicles 28:2).

Psalm 98

Sing a new song to the Lord, for he has done wonders; his right hand, his holy arm, has brought him triumph.

The Lord has made known his saving power; he has let the nations see his justice.

He has remembered his kindness and faithfulness to the house of Israel; all the ends of the earth have seen the saving power of our God.

Shout praise to the Lord, all the earth; break into music, be jubilant and sing.

Praise the Lord with the harp, with the harp and the voice of song.

With trumpets and the sound of the horn, shout praise before the King, the Lord.

Let the sea and all its fulness thunder praise, the world and those living in it.

Let the rivers applaud, let the mountains sing in chorus, before the Lord who comes to rule the earth!

He will rule the world with righteousness, and the peoples with justice.

Psalm 99

The Lord is King; let the peoples tremble. He is enthroned upon the cherubim; let the earth quake.

The Lord is great in Zion; high is he above all the peoples.

Let them praise thy great and revered name; holy it is!

Thou, glorious King who lovest justice, hast established equity; thou hast wrought justice and righteousness in Jacob.

Exalt the Lord our God, and worship at his footstool; holy is he.

Moses and Aaron among his priests, and Samuel among those invoking his name, called upon the Lord, and he answered them.

Out of a pillar of cloud he spoke to them; they observed his precepts and the law which he gave them.

Lord our God, thou didst answer them; thou wast a forgiving God to them, though punishing them for their misdeeds.

Exalt the Lord our God, and worship at his holy mountain, for the Lord our God is holy.

Psalm 29

A Psalm of David. Give to the Lord, O heavenly beings, give to the Lord honor and glory.

Psalm 29 describes the manifestation of God's power in the thunderstorm and the flood, and ends with an assurance of his favor to his people.

הָבוּ לַיָי כְּבוֹד שְׁמוֹ, הִשְׁתַּחֲווּ לַיָי בְּהַדְרַת קֹדֶשׁ. קוֹל יָי עַל
הַמָּיִם, אֵל הַכָּבוֹד הִרְעִים, יָי עַל מַיִם רַבִּים. קוֹל יָי בַּכְּחַ,
קוֹל יָי בֶּהָדָר. קוֹל יָי שֹׁבֵר אֲרָזִים, וַיְשַׁבֵּר יָי אֶת אַרְזֵי הַלְּבָנוֹן.
וַיַּרְקִידֵם כְּמוֹ עֵגֶל, לְבָנוֹן וְשִׂרְיוֹן כְּמוֹ בֶן־רְאֵמִים. קוֹל יָי חֹצֵב
לַהֲבוֹת אֵשׁ. קוֹל יָי יָחִיל מִדְבָּר, יָחִיל יָי מִדְבַּר קָדֵשׁ. קוֹל יָי
יְחוֹלֵל אַיָּלוֹת, וַיֶּחֱשֹׂף יְעָרוֹת, וּבְהֵיכָלוֹ כֻּלּוֹ אֹמֵר כָּבוֹד.
יָי לַמַּבּוּל יָשָׁב, וַיֵּשֶׁב יָי מֶלֶךְ לְעוֹלָם. **Reader** יָי עֹז לְעַמּוֹ יִתֵּן;
יָי יְבָרֵךְ אֶת עַמּוֹ בַשָּׁלוֹם.

אָנָּא, בְּכֹחַ גְּדֻלַּת יְמִינְךָ תַּתִּיר צְרוּרָה.

קַבֵּל רִנַּת עַמְּךָ, שַׂגְּבֵנוּ, טַהֲרֵנוּ, נוֹרָא.

נָא, גִבּוֹר, דּוֹרְשֵׁי יִחוּדְךָ כְּבָבַת שָׁמְרֵם.

בָּרְכֵם, טַהֲרֵם, רַחֲמֵם, צִדְקָתְךָ תָּמִיד גָּמְלֵם.

חֲסִין קָדוֹשׁ, בְּרֹב טוּבְךָ נַהֵל עֲדָתֶךָ.

יָחִיד גֵּאֶה, לְעַמְּךָ פְּנֵה, זוֹכְרֵי קְדֻשָּׁתֶךָ.

שַׁוְעָתֵנוּ קַבֵּל, וּשְׁמַע צַעֲקָתֵנוּ, יוֹדֵעַ תַּעֲלֻמוֹת.

בָּרוּךְ שֵׁם כְּבוֹד מַלְכוּתוֹ לְעוֹלָם וָעֶד.

Reader and Congregation:

לְכָה דוֹדִי לִקְרַאת כַּלָּה, פְּנֵי שַׁבָּת נְקַבְּלָה.
לְכָה דוֹדִי לִקְרַאת כַּלָּה, פְּנֵי שַׁבָּת נְקַבְּלָה.

אנא בכח a mystical meditation attributed to Rabbi Neḥunyah ben ha-Kanah, *tanna* of the second century.

לכה דודי was written by Rabbi Solomon Alkabets about the middle of the sixteenth century. The name of the author, שלמה הלוי, is signed in the form of an acrostic at the beginning of the stanzas. This poem, "perhaps one of the finest pieces of religious poetry in existence," became a favorite text of synagogal composers; a great number of melodies were set to it. Each stanza consists of four parts, three of which have the same rhyme, while the fourth part ends in the common rhyme לה throughout the poem. There is scarcely a

Give to the Lord the glory due to his name; worship the Lord in holy array.

The voice of the Lord peals across the waters; it is the God of glory thundering! The Lord is over the vast waters.

The voice of the Lord is mighty; the voice of the Lord is majestic.

The voice of the Lord breaks the cedars; the Lord shatters the cedars of Lebanon.

He makes Lebanon and Sirion leap like a calf, like a wild ox.

The voice of the Lord strikes flames of fire; the voice of the Lord causes the desert to tremble; the Lord causes the desert of Kadesh to tremble.

The voice of the Lord whirls the oaks, and strips the woods bare; in his palace everything says: "Glory."

The Lord sat enthroned at the flood; the Lord remains King forever.

The Lord will give strength to his people; the Lord will bless his people with peace.

By the great power of thy right hand, O set the captive free.

Revered God, accept thy people's prayer; strengthen us, cleanse us.

Almighty God, guard as the apple of the eye those who seek thee.

Bless them, cleanse them, pity them; ever grant them thy truth.

Mighty, holy God, in thy abundant grace, guide thy people.

Exalted God, turn to thy people who proclaim thy holiness.

Accept our prayer, hear our cry, thou who knowest secret thoughts.

Blessed be the name of his glorious majesty forever and ever.

Reader and Congregation:

Come, my friend, to meet the bride; let us welcome the Sabbath.

---

phrase in the poem which is not borrowed from the Bible. Combining the language of the Bible into a rare mosaic, the poet utilized phrases from Isaiah 52:2; 51:17; 60:1; Judges 5:12; Isaiah 60:1; 54:4; Psalm 42:12; Isaiah 14:32; Jeremiah 30:18, 16; Isaiah 49:19; 62:5; 54:3; 25:9. The Sabbath is personified here and compared to a bride, in the same sense as Israel is likened to a bride (Jeremiah 2:2). The poem gives expression to the hope of Israel in vivid figures of speech.

Each of the following stanzas is recited first by the Congregation and then by the Reader.

שָׁמוֹר וְזָכוֹר בְּדִבּוּר אֶחָד הִשְׁמִיעָנוּ אֵל הַמְּיֻחָד;
יְיָ אֶחָד וּשְׁמוֹ אֶחָד לְשֵׁם וּלְתִפְאֶרֶת וְלִתְהִלָּה.

לְכָה דוֹדִי לִקְרַאת כַּלָּה, פְּנֵי שַׁבָּת נְקַבְּלָה.

לִקְרַאת שַׁבָּת לְכוּ וְנֵלְכָה כִּי הִיא מְקוֹר הַבְּרָכָה;
מֵרֹאשׁ מִקֶּדֶם נְסוּכָה סוֹף מַעֲשֶׂה בְּמַחֲשָׁבָה תְּחִלָּה.

לְכָה דוֹדִי לִקְרַאת כַּלָּה, פְּנֵי שַׁבָּת נְקַבְּלָה.

מִקְדַּשׁ מֶלֶךְ עִיר מְלוּכָה קוּמִי צְאִי מִתּוֹךְ הַהֲפֵכָה;
רַב לָךְ שֶׁבֶת בְּעֵמֶק הַבָּכָא וְהוּא יַחֲמֹל עָלַיִךְ חֶמְלָה.

לְכָה דוֹדִי לִקְרַאת כַּלָּה, פְּנֵי שַׁבָּת נְקַבְּלָה.

הִתְנַעֲרִי מֵעָפָר קוּמִי לִבְשִׁי בִּגְדֵי תִפְאַרְתֵּךְ עַמִּי;
עַל יַד בֶּן יִשַׁי בֵּית הַלַּחְמִי קָרְבָה אֶל נַפְשִׁי גְאָלָהּ.

לְכָה דוֹדִי לִקְרַאת כַּלָּה, פְּנֵי שַׁבָּת נְקַבְּלָה.

הִתְעוֹרְרִי הִתְעוֹרְרִי כִּי בָא אוֹרֵךְ קוּמִי אוֹרִי;
עוּרִי עוּרִי שִׁיר דַּבֵּרִי כְּבוֹד יְיָ עָלַיִךְ נִגְלָה.

לְכָה דוֹדִי לִקְרַאת כַּלָּה, פְּנֵי שַׁבָּת נְקַבְּלָה.

לֹא תֵבשִׁי וְלֹא תִכָּלְמִי מַה תִּשְׁתּוֹחֲחִי וּמַה תֶּהֱמִי;
בָּךְ יֶחֱסוּ עֲנִיֵּי עַמִּי וְנִבְנְתָה עִיר עַל תִּלָּהּ.

לְכָה דוֹדִי לִקְרַאת כַּלָּה, פְּנֵי שַׁבָּת נְקַבְּלָה.

וְהָיוּ לִמְשִׁסָּה שֹׁאסָיִךְ וְרָחֲקוּ כָּל מְבַלְּעָיִךְ;
יָשִׂישׂ עָלַיִךְ אֱלֹהָיִךְ כִּמְשׂושׂ חָתָן עַל כַּלָּה.

לְכָה דוֹדִי לִקְרַאת כַּלָּה, פְּנֵי שַׁבָּת נְקַבְּלָה.

Each of the following stanzas is recited first by the Congregation and then by the Reader:

"Observe" and "Remember," in a single command, the One God announced to us. The Lord is One, and his name is One, for fame, for glory and for praise.

Come, my friend, to meet the bride; let us welcome the Sabbath.

Come, let us go to meet the Sabbath, for it is a source of blessing. From the very beginning it was ordained; last in creation, first in God's plan.

Come, my friend, to meet the bride; let us welcome the Sabbath.

Shrine of the King, royal city, arise! Come forth from thy ruins. Long enough have you dwelt in the vale of tears! He will show you abundant mercy.

Come, my friend, to meet the bride; let us welcome the Sabbath.

Shake off your dust, arise! Put on your glorious garments, my people, and pray: "Be near to my soul, and redeem it through the son of Jesse, the Bethlehemite."

Come, my friend, to meet the bride; let us welcome the Sabbath.

Bestir yourself, bestir yourself, for your light has come; arise and shine! Awake, awake, utter a song; the Lord's glory is revealed upon you.

Come, my friend, to meet the bride; let us welcome the Sabbath.

Be not ashamed nor confounded. Why are you downcast? Why do you moan? The afflicted of my people will be sheltered within you; the city shall be rebuilt on its ancient site.

Come, my friend, to meet the bride; let us welcome the Sabbath.

Those who despoiled you shall become a spoil, and all who would devour you shall be far away. Your God will rejoice over you as a bridegroom rejoices over his bride.

Come, my friend, to meet the bride; let us welcome the Sabbath.

שמור וזכור refers to the talmudic explanation of the discrepancy between the two versions of the fourth commandment. In Exodus 20:8 the text reads: "Remember the Sabbath day," and in Deuteronomy 5:12: "Observe the Sabbath day." According to the Talmud (Shebuoth 20b), both words, זכור and שמור, were miraculously pronounced by God simultaneously.

יָמִין וּשְׂמֹאל תִּפְרוֹצִי   וְאֶת יְיָ תַּעֲרִיצִי;

עַל יַד אִישׁ בֶּן פַּרְצִי   וְנִשְׂמְחָה וְנָגִילָה.

לְכָה דוֹדִי לִקְרַאת כַּלָּה, פְּנֵי שַׁבָּת נְקַבְּלָה.

Congregation rises and turns toward the door, as if to welcome a guest.

בּוֹאִי בְשָׁלוֹם עֲטֶרֶת בַּעְלָהּ   גַּם בְּשִׂמְחָה וּבְצָהֳלָה;

תּוֹךְ אֱמוּנֵי עַם סְגֻלָּה   בּוֹאִי כַלָּה, בּוֹאִי כַלָּה.

לְכָה דוֹדִי לִקְרַאת כַּלָּה, פְּנֵי שַׁבָּת נְקַבְּלָה.

There is a custom that mourners, in the first week of their mourning, remain at the entrance of the synagogue until one of the congregation says to them:

הַמָּקוֹם יְנַחֵם אֶתְכֶם בְּתוֹךְ שְׁאָר אֲבֵלֵי צִיּוֹן וִירוּשָׁלָיִם.

If a festival occurs on Friday, the evening service begins here.

תהלים צב

מִזְמוֹר שִׁיר לְיוֹם הַשַּׁבָּת. טוֹב לְהֹדוֹת לַיְיָ, וּלְזַמֵּר לְשִׁמְךָ עֶלְיוֹן. לְהַגִּיד בַּבֹּקֶר חַסְדֶּךָ, וֶאֱמוּנָתְךָ בַּלֵּילוֹת. עֲלֵי עָשׂוֹר וַעֲלֵי נָבֶל, עֲלֵי הִגָּיוֹן בְּכִנּוֹר. כִּי שִׂמַּחְתַּנִי יְיָ בְּפָעֳלֶךָ; בְּמַעֲשֵׂי יָדֶיךָ אֲרַנֵּן. מַה גָּדְלוּ מַעֲשֶׂיךָ, יְיָ; מְאֹד עָמְקוּ מַחְשְׁבֹתֶיךָ. אִישׁ בַּעַר לֹא יֵדָע, וּכְסִיל לֹא יָבִין אֶת זֹאת. בִּפְרֹחַ רְשָׁעִים כְּמוֹ עֵשֶׂב, וַיָּצִיצוּ כָּל פֹּעֲלֵי אָוֶן, לְהִשָּׁמְדָם עֲדֵי עַד. וְאַתָּה מָרוֹם לְעֹלָם, יְיָ. כִּי הִנֵּה אֹיְבֶיךָ, יְיָ, כִּי הִנֵּה אֹיְבֶיךָ יֹאבֵדוּ, יִתְפָּרְדוּ כָּל פֹּעֲלֵי אָוֶן. וַתָּרֶם כִּרְאֵים קַרְנִי; בַּלֹּתִי בְּשֶׁמֶן רַעֲנָן. וַתַּבֵּט עֵינִי בְּשׁוּרָי, בַּקָּמִים עָלַי מְרֵעִים תִּשְׁמַעְנָה אָזְנָי. צַדִּיק כַּתָּמָר יִפְרָח, כְּאֶרֶז בַּלְּבָנוֹן יִשְׂגֶּה. שְׁתוּלִים בְּבֵית יְיָ, בְּחַצְרוֹת אֱלֹהֵינוּ יַפְרִיחוּ. Reader עוֹד יְנוּבוּן בְּשֵׂיבָה, דְּשֵׁנִים וְרַעֲנַנִּים יִהְיוּ. לְהַגִּיד כִּי יָשָׁר יְיָ; צוּרִי, וְלֹא עַוְלָתָה בּוֹ.

Psalm 92 was sung by the Levites in the Temple during the Sabbath offering. The psalmist reflects on the meaning of God's works, a meaning which

You shall extend to the right and to the left, and you shall re-vere the Lord. Through the advent of a descendant of Perez we shall rejoice and exult.

Come, my friend, to meet the bride; let us welcome the Sabbath.

Congregation rises and turns toward the door, as if to welcome a guest.

Come in peace, crown of God, come with joy and cheerfulness; amidst the faithful of the chosen people come O bride; come, O bride.

Come, my friend, to meet the bride; let us welcome the Sabbath.

There is a custom that mourners, in the first week of their mourning, remain at the entrance of the synagogue until one of the congregation says to them:

May God console you among the other mourners for Zion and Jerusalem.

If a festival occurs on Friday, the evening service begins here.

Psalm 92

A psalm, a song for the Sabbath day. It is good to give thanks to the Lord, and to sing praises to thy name, O Most High; to proclaim thy goodness in the morning, and thy faithfulness at night, with a ten-stringed lyre and a flute, to the sound of a harp. For thou, O Lord, hast made me glad through thy work; I sing for joy at all that thou hast done. How great are thy works, O Lord! How very deep are thy designs! A stupid man cannot know, a fool cannot understand this. When the wicked thrive like grass, and all evildoers flourish, it is that they may be destroyed forever. But thou, O Lord, art supreme for evermore. For lo, thy enemies, O Lord, for lo, thy enemies shall perish; all evildoers shall be dispersed. But thou hast exalted my power like that of the wild ox; I am anointed with fresh oil. My eye has gazed on my foes; my ears have heard my enemies' doom. The righteous will flourish like the palm tree; they will grow like a cedar in Lebanon. Planted in the house of the Lord, they shall flourish in the courts of our God. They shall yield fruit even in old age; vigorous and fresh they shall be, to proclaim that the Lord is just! He is my Stronghold, and there is no wrong in him.

---

the foolish fail to perceive. The wicked seem to flourish only that they may be destroyed. The palm and cedar are long-lived and flourish during all seasons. They represent the enduring happiness of the faithful in contrast with the short-lived prosperity of the wicked.

תהלים צג

יְיָ מָלָךְ, גֵּאוּת לָבֵשׁ; לָבֵשׁ יְיָ, עֹז הִתְאַזָּר; אַף תִּכּוֹן תֵּבֵל,
בַּל תִּמּוֹט. נָכוֹן כִּסְאֲךָ מֵאָז, מֵעוֹלָם אָתָּה. נָשְׂאוּ נְהָרוֹת, יְיָ,
נָשְׂאוּ נְהָרוֹת קוֹלָם, יִשְׂאוּ נְהָרוֹת דָּכְיָם. מִקֹּלוֹת מַיִם רַבִּים,
אַדִּירִים מִשְׁבְּרֵי יָם, אַדִּיר בַּמָּרוֹם יְיָ. Reader עֵדֹתֶיךָ נֶאֶמְנוּ
מְאֹד, לְבֵיתְךָ נַאֲוָה קֹּדֶשׁ, יְיָ, לְאֹרֶךְ יָמִים.

MOURNERS' KADDISH

יִתְגַּדַּל וְיִתְקַדַּשׁ שְׁמֵהּ רַבָּא בְּעָלְמָא דִּי בְרָא כִרְעוּתֵהּ;
וְיַמְלִיךְ מַלְכוּתֵהּ בְּחַיֵּיכוֹן וּבְיוֹמֵיכוֹן, וּבְחַיֵּי דְכָל בֵּית יִשְׂרָאֵל,
בַּעֲגָלָא וּבִזְמַן קָרִיב, וְאִמְרוּ אָמֵן.

יְהֵא שְׁמֵהּ רַבָּא מְבָרַךְ לְעָלַם וּלְעָלְמֵי עָלְמַיָּא.

יִתְבָּרַךְ וְיִשְׁתַּבַּח, וְיִתְפָּאַר וְיִתְרוֹמַם, וְיִתְנַשֵּׂא וְיִתְהַדַּר,
וְיִתְעַלֶּה וְיִתְהַלַּל שְׁמֵהּ דְּקֻדְשָׁא, בְּרִיךְ הוּא, לְעֵלָּא (לְעֵלָּא)
מִן כָּל בִּרְכָתָא וְשִׁירָתָא, תֻּשְׁבְּחָתָא וְנֶחֱמָתָא, דַּאֲמִירָן בְּעָלְמָא,
וְאִמְרוּ אָמֵן.

יְהֵא שְׁלָמָא רַבָּא מִן שְׁמַיָּא, וְחַיִּים, עָלֵינוּ וְעַל כָּל יִשְׂרָאֵל,
וְאִמְרוּ אָמֵן.

עֹשֶׂה שָׁלוֹם בִּמְרוֹמָיו, הוּא יַעֲשֶׂה שָׁלוֹם עָלֵינוּ וְעַל כָּל
יִשְׂרָאֵל, וְאִמְרוּ אָמֵן.

Psalm 93 speaks of God's majesty and power. His control of the violent forces of nature represents his power over the mightiest enemies of Israel. God's rule is the security of all moral order in the world.

Psalm 93

The Lord is King; he is robed in majesty; the Lord is robed, he has girded himself with strength; thus the world is set firm and cannot be shaken. Thy throne stands firm from of old; thou art from all eternity. The floods have lifted up, O Lord, the floods have lifted up their voice; the floods lift up their mighty waves. But above the sound of many waters, mighty breakers of the sea, the Lord on high stands supreme. Thy testimonies are very sure; holiness befits thy house, O Lord, for all time.

MOURNERS' KADDISH

Glorified and sanctified be God's great name throughout the world which he has created according to his will. May he establish his kingdom in your lifetime and during your days, and within the life of the entire house of Israel, speedily and soon; and say, Amen.

May his great name be blessed forever and to all eternity.

Blessed and praised, glorified and exalted, extolled and honored, adored and lauded be the name of the Holy One, blessed be he, beyond all the blessings and hymns, praises and consolations that are ever spoken in the world; and say, Amen.

May there be abundant peace from heaven, and life, for us and for all Israel; and say, Amen.

He who creates peace in his celestial heights, may he create peace for us and for all Israel; and say, Amen.

... נאות לבש The psalmist speaks of God's attributes as a glorious garment wrapped about him. God's rule reestablishes the moral order of the world. Rashi and others interpret this psalm in connection with the Messianic era.

... נשאו נהרות God's control of the violent forces of nature is used here to represent his power over the mighty enemies of his people.

עדותיך נאמנו God's moral laws are firmly established and unchangeable. Zion, his house, shall no longer be desecrated by heathen invaders. Rashi and others interpret this psalm in connection with the Messianic era.

The following chapter is omitted on festivals.

משנה שבת, פרק ב

א. בַּמֶּה מַדְלִיקִין וּבַמָּה אֵין מַדְלִיקִין. אֵין מַדְלִיקִין לֹא בְלֶכֶשׁ וְלֹא בְחֹסֶן וְלֹא בְכַלָּךְ, וְלֹא בִּפְתִילַת הָאִידָן וְלֹא בִּפְתִילַת הַמִּדְבָּר וְלֹא בִּירוֹקָה שֶׁעַל פְּנֵי הַמָּיִם; וְלֹא בְזֶפֶת וְלֹא בְשַׁעֲוָה וְלֹא בְשֶׁמֶן קִיק, וְלֹא בְשֶׁמֶן שְׂרֵפָה וְלֹא בְאַלְיָה וְלֹא בְחֵלֶב. נַחוּם הַמָּדִי אוֹמֵר: מַדְלִיקִין בְּחֵלֶב מְבֻשָּׁל. וַחֲכָמִים אוֹמְרִים: אֶחָד מְבֻשָּׁל וְאֶחָד שֶׁאֵינוֹ מְבֻשָּׁל אֵין מַדְלִיקִין בּוֹ.

ב. אֵין מַדְלִיקִין בְּשֶׁמֶן שְׂרֵפָה בְּיוֹם טוֹב. רַבִּי יִשְׁמָעֵאל אוֹמֵר: אֵין מַדְלִיקִין בְּעִטְרָן מִפְּנֵי כְּבוֹד הַשַּׁבָּת. וַחֲכָמִים מַתִּירִין בְּכָל הַשְּׁמָנִים: בְּשֶׁמֶן שֻׁמְשְׁמִין, בְּשֶׁמֶן אֱגוֹזִים, בְּשֶׁמֶן צְנוֹנוֹת, בְּשֶׁמֶן דָּגִים, בְּשֶׁמֶן פַּקֻּעוֹת, בְּעִטְרָן, וּבְנֵפְטְ. רַבִּי טַרְפוֹן אוֹמֵר: אֵין מַדְלִיקִין אֶלָּא בְשֶׁמֶן זַיִת בִּלְבָד.

ג. כָּל הַיּוֹצֵא מִן הָעֵץ אֵין מַדְלִיקִין בּוֹ אֶלָּא פִשְׁתָּן. וְכָל הַיּוֹצֵא מִן הָעֵץ אֵינוֹ מִטַּמֵּא טֻמְאַת אֹהָלִים אֶלָּא פִשְׁתָּן. פְּתִילַת הַבֶּגֶד שֶׁקִּפְּלָהּ וְלֹא הִבְהֲבָהּ, רַבִּי אֱלִיעֶזֶר אוֹמֵר: טְמֵאָה הִיא, וְאֵין מַדְלִיקִין בָּהּ. רַבִּי עֲקִיבָא אוֹמֵר: טְהוֹרָה הִיא, וּמַדְלִיקִין בָּהּ.

ד. לֹא יִקֹּב אָדָם שְׁפוֹפֶרֶת שֶׁל בֵּיצָה וִימַלְאֶנָּה שֶׁמֶן וְיִתְּנֶנָּה

במה מדליקין was inserted during the geonic period. Various reasons are given for the recital of this chapter from the Mishnah, which deals with the oils and wicks appropriate for the Sabbath lights. Rashi in his *Siddur* (page 243) says that this chapter is recited *after* the Sabbath eve service so as to enable the late-comers to complete their prayers and leave the synagogue together with the rest of the congregation. Accordingly, this chapter is omitted on festival occasions when late-coming is not likely to happen. Rabbi Isaiah Horowitz and Rabbi Jacob Emden, in their respective editions of the *Siddur*, are of the opinion that *Bammeh Madlikin* is to be recited before *Kabbalath Shabbath.*

The following chapter is omitted on festivals.

Mishnah Shabbath, Chapter 2

1. With what may we light the Sabbath lamp, and with what may we not light it? We may not light it with a wick made of cedar-bast, uncombed flax, floss-silk, or with a wick of willow-fiber, desert weed, or duck-weed [since such wicks burn unevenly]. It may not be lighted with pitch, liquid wax, castor oil, nor with oil that must be burned and destroyed, nor with tail fat, nor with tallow. Naḥum of Media says: We may use melted tallow. The sages, however, say: It is immaterial whether or not it is melted, it must not be used for the Sabbath lamp.

2. Oil that must be burned and destroyed may not be used for lighting on a festival. Rabbi Ishmael says: One must not, out of respect for the Sabbath, use [ill-smelling] resin. The sages allow all kinds of oil: sesame-oil, nut-oil, radish-oil, fish-oil, gourd-oil, resin, and naphtha. Rabbi Tarfon says: We may use only olive-oil for lighting the Sabbath lamp.

3. Nothing that comes from a tree may be used as a wick for the Sabbath lamp except flax; nor can any part of a tree contract uncleanness by overshadowing a dead body except flax. A wick made of a piece of cloth which one has twisted but not yet singed, Rabbi Eliezer says that [it is still considered a part of a garment and] it is subject to the law of uncleanness; it must not be used for lighting the Sabbath lamp. Rabbi Akiba declares that it remains clean and may be used for lighting [for as soon as it was twisted it no longer was part of a garment subject to the law of pollution].

4. One may not pierce an eggshell, fill it with oil, and place

---

כלך, חסן, לכש and the other unfamiliar terms are discussed and explained in the *Gemara* (Shabbath 20b).

שמן שרפה oil of consecrated *terumah* that has been defiled. It is called "oil for burning" because of one's duty to burn and destroy defiled *terumah*. שמן שרפה must not be used for the Sabbath lights, for fear that one may tilt the lamp to accelerate the burning of the oil.

פשתן is classed among trees in Joshua 2:6 (פשתי העץ). It contracts ritual uncleanness, though the other materials originating from trees do not.

לא יקוב ... for fear that one may draw oil from the eggshell and thus cause the light to go out sooner. The same rule applies even to a shell made of clay, though the oil it contains becomes loathsome and useless as food.

עַל פִּי הַנֵּר, בִּשְׁבִיל שֶׁתְּהֵא מְנַטֶּפֶת, וַאֲפִילוּ הִיא שֶׁל חֶרֶס;
וְרַבִּי יְהוּדָה מַתִּיר. אֲבָל אִם חִבְּרָהּ הַיּוֹצֵר מִתְּחִלָּה, מֻתָּר,
מִפְּנֵי שֶׁהוּא כְלִי אֶחָד. לֹא יְמַלֵּא אָדָם קְעָרָה שֶׁמֶן, וְיִתְּנֶנָּה
בְּצַד הַנֵּר, וְיִתֵּן רֹאשׁ הַפְּתִילָה בְּתוֹכָהּ בִּשְׁבִיל שֶׁתְּהֵא שׁוֹאֶבֶת;
וְרַבִּי יְהוּדָה מַתִּיר.

ה. הַמְכַבֶּה אֶת הַנֵּר מִפְּנֵי שֶׁהוּא מִתְיָרֵא מִפְּנֵי גוֹיִם, מִפְּנֵי
לִסְטִים, מִפְּנֵי רוּחַ רָעָה, אוֹ בִּשְׁבִיל הַחוֹלֶה שֶׁיִּישָׁן, פָּטוּר;
כְּחָס עַל הַנֵּר, כְּחָס עַל הַשֶּׁמֶן, כְּחָס עַל הַפְּתִילָה, חַיָּב. רַבִּי
יוֹסֵי פּוֹטֵר בְּכֻלָּן, חוּץ מִן הַפְּתִילָה, מִפְּנֵי שֶׁהוּא עוֹשָׂהּ פֶּחָם.

ו. עַל שָׁלֹשׁ עֲבֵרוֹת נָשִׁים מֵתוֹת בִּשְׁעַת לֵדָתָן: עַל שֶׁאֵינָן
זְהִירוֹת בְּנִדָּה, בְּחַלָּה, וּבְהַדְלָקַת הַנֵּר.

ז. שְׁלֹשָׁה דְבָרִים צָרִיךְ אָדָם לוֹמַר בְּתוֹךְ בֵּיתוֹ עֶרֶב שַׁבָּת
עִם חֲשֵׁכָה: עִשַּׂרְתֶּם, עֵרַבְתֶּם, הַדְלִיקוּ אֶת הַנֵּר. סָפֵק חֲשֵׁכָה,
סָפֵק אֵינָהּ חֲשֵׁכָה, אֵין מְעַשְּׂרִין אֶת הַוַּדַּאי, וְאֵין מַטְבִּילִין אֶת
הַכֵּלִים, וְאֵין מַדְלִיקִין אֶת הַנֵּרוֹת; אֲבָל מְעַשְּׂרִין אֶת הַדְּמַאי,
וּמְעָרְבִין, וְטוֹמְנִין אֶת הַחַמִּין.

מסכת ברכות סד, א

אָמַר רַבִּי אֶלְעָזָר אָמַר רַבִּי חֲנִינָא: תַּלְמִידֵי חֲכָמִים מַרְבִּים
שָׁלוֹם בָּעוֹלָם, שֶׁנֶּאֱמַר: וְכָל בָּנַיִךְ לִמּוּדֵי יְיָ, וְרַב שְׁלוֹם בָּנָיִךְ.

גוים refers to idolaters, like the Persians, who permitted no lights to burn
on certain nights except in their temples (Rashi).

פטור is used here in the sense of מותר, that is, one is allowed to do so.

ערוב, which renders permissible the carrying of objects on the Sabbath
from one household to another, consists of food placed in a room accessible
to all inhabitants of a court or a town. Since each of the householders con-
tributes his share to it, the eruv ("mixture") symbolically turns all of them
into one household.

טבילת כלים, the act of purifying utensils from their defilement, renders
them fit for use; hence it is forbidden work on Friday at twilight.

דמאי, produce concerning which there is a doubt as to whether the rules

it so that the oil will drip from it into the opening of the Sabbath lamp; it is forbidden even if it was made of earthenware; but Rabbi Judah permits it. If, however, the potter had originally joined it with the lamp, it is allowed, because it is one utensil. A person may not fill a dish with oil, place it beside a Sabbath lamp, and put the end of the wick into it so that it may draw the oil to the flame; but Rabbi Judah permits it.

5. If one puts out a light on the Sabbath because he is afraid of heathen, robbers, or an evil spirit, or for the sake of enabling a sick person to sleep, he is not guilty of violating the Sabbath law; but if he did it with the intention of sparing the lamp or the oil or the wick, he is guilty. Rabbi Yosé exempts him in every case, except in that of sparing the wick, since he thereby forms charcoal [and prepares a wick with a singed end for easier lighting].

6. For three transgressions do women die in childbirth: for being careless in the observance of the laws of menstruation, for not separating *ḥallah*, and for not lighting the Sabbath lamp.

7. One is required to say three things in his house on the eve of Sabbath just before it gets dark: "Have you separated the tithe [of the food we are to eat on the Sabbath]? Have you prepared the *eruv?* Light the lamp!" If it is doubtful whether or not it is already dark, we may not tithe grain which is untithed, or immerse utensils for cleansing, or light the Sabbath lamps; but we may still tithe that concerning which there is doubt whether or not it has been tithed, and prepare an *eruv*, and store away hot food [for the Sabbath].

Talmud Berakhoth 64a

Rabbi Elazar said in the name of Rabbi Ḥanina: Scholars increase peace throughout the world, for it is said: "All your children shall be taught of the Lord, and great shall be the peace of your children."[1] Read not here *banayikh* [your children], but

---

relating to the priestly and Levitical dues were strictly observed, may be tithed at twilight, because the probability is that the tithes have already been set apart, so that this tithing does not really make it fit for use.

אל תקרא is not intended to indicate a variant in the text. בוניך=בניך is a mere play on words, designed to attract the attention to the great significance of peace.

[1] *Isaiah* 54:13.

אַל תִּקְרָא בָּנֶיִךְ, אֶלָּא בֹּנָיִךְ. שָׁלוֹם רָב לְאֹהֲבֵי תוֹרָתֶךָ,
וְאֵין לָמוֹ מִכְשׁוֹל. יְהִי שָׁלוֹם בְּחֵילֵךְ, שַׁלְוָה בְּאַרְמְנוֹתָיִךְ.
Reader לְמַעַן אַחַי וְרֵעָי, אֲדַבְּרָה נָּא שָׁלוֹם בָּךְ. לְמַעַן בֵּית יְיָ
אֱלֹהֵינוּ, אֲבַקְשָׁה טוֹב לָךְ. יְיָ עֹז לְעַמּוֹ יִתֵּן, יְיָ יְבָרֵךְ אֶת עַמּוֹ
בַשָּׁלוֹם.

קַדִּישׁ דְּרַבָּנָן

Mourners:

יִתְגַּדַּל וְיִתְקַדַּשׁ שְׁמֵהּ רַבָּא בְּעָלְמָא דִי בְרָא כִרְעוּתֵהּ;
וְיַמְלִיךְ מַלְכוּתֵהּ בְּחַיֵּיכוֹן וּבְיוֹמֵיכוֹן, וּבְחַיֵּי דְכָל בֵּית יִשְׂרָאֵל,
בַּעֲגָלָא וּבִזְמַן קָרִיב, וְאִמְרוּ אָמֵן.

יְהֵא שְׁמֵהּ רַבָּא מְבָרַךְ לְעָלַם וּלְעָלְמֵי עָלְמַיָּא.

יִתְבָּרַךְ וְיִשְׁתַּבַּח וְיִתְפָּאַר וְיִתְרוֹמַם, וְיִתְנַשֵּׂא וְיִתְהַדָּר,
וְיִתְעַלֶּה וְיִתְהַלָּל שְׁמֵהּ דְּקֻדְשָׁא, בְּרִיךְ הוּא, לְעֵלָּא (לְעֵלָּא)
מִן כָּל בִּרְכָתָא וְשִׁירָתָא, תֻּשְׁבְּחָתָא וְנֶחֱמָתָא, דַּאֲמִירָן בְּעָלְמָא,
וְאִמְרוּ אָמֵן.

עַל יִשְׂרָאֵל וְעַל רַבָּנָן, וְעַל תַּלְמִידֵיהוֹן וְעַל כָּל תַּלְמִידֵי
תַלְמִידֵיהוֹן, וְעַל כָּל מָן דְּעָסְקִין בְּאוֹרַיְתָא, דִּי בְּאַתְרָא הָדֵן
וְדִי בְכָל אֲתַר וַאֲתַר, יְהֵא לְהוֹן וּלְכוֹן שְׁלָמָא רַבָּא, חִנָּא
וְחִסְדָּא וְרַחֲמִין, וְחַיִּין אֲרִיכִין, וּמְזוֹנֵי רְוִיחֵי, וּפֻרְקָנָא מִן קֳדָם
אֲבוּהוֹן דְּבִשְׁמַיָּא וְאַרְעָא, וְאִמְרוּ אָמֵן.

יְהֵא שְׁלָמָא רַבָּא מִן שְׁמַיָּא, וְחַיִּים טוֹבִים, עָלֵינוּ וְעַל כָּל
יִשְׂרָאֵל, וְאִמְרוּ אָמֵן.

עֹשֶׂה שָׁלוֹם בִּמְרוֹמָיו, הוּא בְּרַחֲמָיו יַעֲשֶׂה שָׁלוֹם עָלֵינוּ וְעַל
כָּל יִשְׂרָאֵל, וְאִמְרוּ אָמֵן.

bonayikh [your builders—scholars are the true builders of the ideal of peace].

Abundant peace have they who love thy Torah, and there is no stumbling for them. Peace be within your walls, and security within your palaces. In behalf of my brethren and friends, let me pronounce peace for you. For the sake of the house of the Lord our God, I will seek your good. The Lord will give strength to his people; the Lord will bless his people with peace.[1]

KADDISH D'RABBANAN

Mourners:

Glorified and sanctified be God's great name throughout the world which he has created according to his will. May he establish his kingdom in your lifetime and during your days, and within the life of the entire house of Israel, speedily and soon; and say, Amen.

May his great name be blessed forever and to all eternity.

Blessed and praised, glorified and exalted, extolled and honored, adored and lauded be the name of the Holy One, blessed be he, beyond all the blessings and hymns, praises and consolations that are ever spoken in the world; and say, Amen.

[We pray] for Israel, for our teachers and their disciples and the disciples of their disciples, and for all who study the Torah, here and everywhere. May they have abundant peace, loving-kindness, ample sustenance and salvation from their Father who is in heaven; and say, Amen.

May there be abundant peace from heaven, and a happy life, for us and for all Israel; and say, Amen.

He who creates peace in his celestial heights, may he in his mercy create peace for us and for all Israel; and say, Amen.

---

[1] *Psalms* 119:165; 122:7–9; 29:11

Silent meditation: | Reader:

בָּרְכוּ אֶת יְיָ הַמְבֹרָךְ.

יִתְבָּרַךְ וְיִשְׁתַּבַּח, וְיִתְפָּאַר וְיִתְרוֹמַם
וְיִתְנַשֵּׂא שְׁמוֹ שֶׁל מֶלֶךְ מַלְכֵי הַמְּלָכִים,

Congregation and Reader:

בָּרוּךְ יְיָ הַמְבֹרָךְ לְעוֹלָם וָעֶד.

הַקָּדוֹשׁ בָּרוּךְ הוּא, שֶׁהוּא רִאשׁוֹן וְהוּא
אַחֲרוֹן, וּמִבַּלְעָדָיו אֵין אֱלֹהִים. סֹלּוּ
לָרֹכֵב בָּעֲרָבוֹת, בְּיָהּ שְׁמוֹ, וְעִלְזוּ לְפָנָיו; וּשְׁמוֹ מְרוֹמָם עַל כָּל בְּרָכָה וּתְהִלָּה. בָּרוּךְ
שֵׁם כְּבוֹד מַלְכוּתוֹ לְעוֹלָם וָעֶד. יְהִי שֵׁם יְיָ מְבֹרָךְ מֵעַתָּה וְעַד עוֹלָם.

בָּרוּךְ אַתָּה, יְיָ אֱלֹהֵינוּ, מֶלֶךְ הָעוֹלָם, אֲשֶׁר בִּדְבָרוֹ מַעֲרִיב
עֲרָבִים; בְּחָכְמָה פּוֹתֵחַ שְׁעָרִים, וּבִתְבוּנָה מְשַׁנֶּה עִתִּים;
וּמַחֲלִיף אֶת הַזְּמַנִּים, וּמְסַדֵּר אֶת הַכּוֹכָבִים בְּמִשְׁמְרוֹתֵיהֶם
בָּרָקִיעַ כִּרְצוֹנוֹ. בּוֹרֵא יוֹם וָלָיְלָה, גּוֹלֵל אוֹר מִפְּנֵי חֹשֶׁךְ וְחֹשֶׁךְ
מִפְּנֵי אוֹר, וּמַעֲבִיר יוֹם וּמֵבִיא לָיְלָה, וּמַבְדִּיל בֵּין יוֹם וּבֵין
לָיְלָה, יְיָ צְבָאוֹת שְׁמוֹ. Reader אֵל חַי וְקַיָּם, תָּמִיד יִמְלוֹךְ עָלֵינוּ,
לְעוֹלָם וָעֶד. בָּרוּךְ אַתָּה, יְיָ, הַמַּעֲרִיב עֲרָבִים.

אַהֲבַת עוֹלָם בֵּית יִשְׂרָאֵל עַמְּךָ אָהָבְתָּ; תּוֹרָה וּמִצְוֹת,
חֻקִּים וּמִשְׁפָּטִים, אוֹתָנוּ לִמַּדְתָּ; עַל כֵּן, יְיָ אֱלֹהֵינוּ, בְּשָׁכְבֵּנוּ
וּבְקוּמֵנוּ נָשִׂיחַ בְּחֻקֶּיךָ, וְנִשְׂמַח בְּדִבְרֵי תוֹרָתֶךָ וּבְמִצְוֹתֶיךָ
לְעוֹלָם וָעֶד. כִּי הֵם חַיֵּינוּ וְאֹרֶךְ יָמֵינוּ, וּבָהֶם נֶהְגֶּה יוֹמָם וָלָיְלָה;
Reader וְאַהֲבָתְךָ אַל תָּסִיר מִמֶּנּוּ לְעוֹלָמִים. בָּרוּךְ אַתָּה, יְיָ,
אוֹהֵב עַמּוֹ יִשְׂרָאֵל.

(When praying in private, add: אֵל מֶלֶךְ נֶאֱמָן)

דברים ו, ד–ט

שְׁמַע יִשְׂרָאֵל, יְיָ אֱלֹהֵינוּ, יְיָ אֶחָד.

בָּרוּךְ שֵׁם כְּבוֹד מַלְכוּתוֹ לְעוֹלָם וָעֶד.

וְאָהַבְתָּ אֵת יְיָ אֱלֹהֶיךָ בְּכָל לְבָבְךָ וּבְכָל נַפְשְׁךָ וּבְכָל
מְאֹדֶךָ. וְהָיוּ הַדְּבָרִים הָאֵלֶּה, אֲשֶׁר אָנֹכִי מְצַוְּךָ הַיּוֹם, עַל

Reader:	*Silent meditation:*
Bless the Lord who is blessed.	Blessed, praised, glorified, ex-
Congregation and Reader:	tolled and exalted be the name
Blessed be the Lord who is blessed	of the supreme King of kings, the Holy One, blessed be he,
forever and ever.	who is the first and the last, and

besides him there is no God. Extol him who is in the heavens—Lord is his name, and rejoice before him. His name is exalted above all blessing and praise. Blessed be the name of his glorious majesty forever and ever. Let the name of the Lord be blessed henceforth and forever.

Blessed art thou, Lord our God, King of the universe, who at thy word bringest on the evenings. With wisdom thou openest the gates of heaven, and with understanding thou changest the times and causest the seasons to alternate. Thou arrangest the stars in their courses in the sky according to thy will. Thou createst day and night; thou rollest away light before darkness, and darkness before light; thou causest the day to pass and the night to come, and makest the distinction between day and night— Lord of hosts is thy name. Eternal God, mayest thou reign over us forever and ever. Blessed art thou, O Lord, who bringest on the evenings.

Thou hast loved the house of Israel with everlasting love; thou hast taught us Torah and precepts, laws and judgments. Therefore, Lord our God, when we lie down and when we rise up we will speak of thy laws, and rejoice in the words of thy Torah and in thy precepts for evermore. Indeed, they are our life and the length of our days; we will meditate on them day and night. Mayest thou never take away thy love from us. Blessed art thou, O Lord, who lovest thy people Israel.

SHEMA

(When praying in private, add: God is a faithful King).

Deuteronomy 6:4-9

Hear, O Israel, the Lord is our God, the Lord is One.

Blessed be the name of his glorious majesty forever and ever.

You shall love the Lord your God with all your heart, and with all your soul, and with all your might. And these words which I command you today shall be in your heart. You shall

לְבָבֶךָ. וְשִׁנַּנְתָּם לְבָנֶיךָ, וְדִבַּרְתָּ בָּם בְּשִׁבְתְּךָ בְּבֵיתֶךָ, וּבְלֶכְתְּךָ
בַדֶּרֶךְ, וּבְשָׁכְבְּךָ וּבְקוּמֶךָ. וּקְשַׁרְתָּם לְאוֹת עַל יָדֶךָ, וְהָיוּ
לְטֹטָפֹת בֵּין עֵינֶיךָ. וּכְתַבְתָּם עַל מְזֻזוֹת בֵּיתֶךָ וּבִשְׁעָרֶיךָ.

דברים יא, יג–כא

וְהָיָה אִם שָׁמֹעַ תִּשְׁמְעוּ אֶל מִצְוֹתַי, אֲשֶׁר אָנֹכִי מְצַוֶּה אֶתְכֶם
הַיּוֹם, לְאַהֲבָה אֶת יְיָ אֱלֹהֵיכֶם, וּלְעָבְדוֹ בְּכָל לְבַבְכֶם וּבְכָל
נַפְשְׁכֶם. וְנָתַתִּי מְטַר אַרְצְכֶם בְּעִתּוֹ, יוֹרֶה וּמַלְקוֹשׁ, וְאָסַפְתָּ
דְגָנֶךָ, וְתִירֹשְׁךָ וְיִצְהָרֶךָ. וְנָתַתִּי עֵשֶׂב בְּשָׂדְךָ לִבְהֶמְתֶּךָ, וְאָכַלְתָּ
וְשָׂבָעְתָּ. הִשָּׁמְרוּ לָכֶם פֶּן יִפְתֶּה לְבַבְכֶם, וְסַרְתֶּם וַעֲבַדְתֶּם
אֱלֹהִים אֲחֵרִים, וְהִשְׁתַּחֲוִיתֶם לָהֶם. וְחָרָה אַף יְיָ בָּכֶם, וְעָצַר
אֶת הַשָּׁמַיִם וְלֹא יִהְיֶה מָטָר, וְהָאֲדָמָה לֹא תִתֵּן אֶת יְבוּלָהּ;
וַאֲבַדְתֶּם מְהֵרָה מֵעַל הָאָרֶץ הַטֹּבָה אֲשֶׁר יְיָ נֹתֵן לָכֶם. וְשַׂמְתֶּם
אֶת דְּבָרַי אֵלֶּה עַל לְבַבְכֶם וְעַל נַפְשְׁכֶם; וּקְשַׁרְתֶּם אֹתָם לְאוֹת
עַל יֶדְכֶם, וְהָיוּ לְטוֹטָפֹת בֵּין עֵינֵיכֶם. וְלִמַּדְתֶּם אֹתָם אֶת
בְּנֵיכֶם לְדַבֵּר בָּם, בְּשִׁבְתְּךָ בְּבֵיתֶךָ, וּבְלֶכְתְּךָ בַדֶּרֶךְ, וּבְשָׁכְבְּךָ
וּבְקוּמֶךָ. וּכְתַבְתָּם עַל מְזוּזוֹת בֵּיתֶךָ וּבִשְׁעָרֶיךָ.

לְמַעַן יִרְבּוּ יְמֵיכֶם וִימֵי בְנֵיכֶם, עַל הָאֲדָמָה אֲשֶׁר נִשְׁבַּע
יְיָ לַאֲבֹתֵיכֶם לָתֵת לָהֶם, כִּימֵי הַשָּׁמַיִם עַל הָאָרֶץ.

במדבר טו, לז–מא

וַיֹּאמֶר יְיָ אֶל מֹשֶׁה לֵּאמֹר: דַּבֵּר אֶל בְּנֵי יִשְׂרָאֵל וְאָמַרְתָּ
אֲלֵהֶם, וְעָשׂוּ לָהֶם צִיצִת עַל כַּנְפֵי בִגְדֵיהֶם לְדֹרֹתָם, וְנָתְנוּ עַל
צִיצִת הַכָּנָף פְּתִיל תְּכֵלֶת. וְהָיָה לָכֶם לְצִיצִת, וּרְאִיתֶם אֹתוֹ
וּזְכַרְתֶּם אֶת כָּל מִצְוֹת יְיָ, וַעֲשִׂיתֶם אֹתָם; וְלֹא תָתוּרוּ אַחֲרֵי
לְבַבְכֶם וְאַחֲרֵי עֵינֵיכֶם, אֲשֶׁר אַתֶּם זֹנִים אַחֲרֵיהֶם. לְמַעַן
תִּזְכְּרוּ וַעֲשִׂיתֶם אֶת כָּל מִצְוֹתָי, וִהְיִיתֶם קְדֹשִׁים לֵאלֹהֵיכֶם.

teach them diligently to your children, and you shall speak of them when you are sitting at home and when you go on a journey, when you lie down and when you rise up. You shall bind them for a sign on your hand, and they shall be for frontlets between your eyes. You shall inscribe them on the doorposts of your house and on your gates.

Deuteronomy 11:13-21

And if you will carefully obey my commands which I give you today, to love the Lord your God and to serve him with all your heart and with all your soul, I will give rain for your land at the right season, the autumn rains and the spring rains, that you may gather in your grain, your wine and your oil. And I will produce grass in your fields for your cattle, and you will eat and be satisfied. Beware lest your heart be deceived, and you turn and serve other gods and worship them; for then the Lord's anger will blaze against you, and he will shut up the skies so that there will be no rain, and the land will yield no produce, and you will quickly perish from the good land which the Lord gives you. So you shall place these words of mine in your heart and in your soul, and you shall bind them for a sign on your hand, and they shall be for frontlets between your eyes. You shall teach them to your children, speaking of them when you are sitting at home and when you go on a journey, when you lie down and when you rise up. You shall inscribe them on the doorposts of your house and on your gates— that your life and the life of your children may be prolonged in the land, which the Lord promised he would give to your fathers, for as long as the sky remains over the earth.

Numbers 15:37-41

The Lord spoke to Moses, saying: Speak to the children of Israel and tell them to make for themselves fringes on the corners of their garments throughout their generations, and to put on the fringe of each corner a blue thread. You shall have it as a fringe, so that when you look upon it you will remember to do all the commands of the Lord, and you will not follow the desires of your heart and your eyes which lead you astray. It is for you to remember and do all my commands and be holy for your God. 1

אֲנִי יְיָ אֱלֹהֵיכֶם, אֲשֶׁר הוֹצֵאתִי אֶתְכֶם מֵאֶרֶץ מִצְרַיִם לִהְיוֹת
לָכֶם לֵאלֹהִים; אֲנִי יְיָ אֱלֹהֵיכֶם— Reader

אֱמֶת וֶאֱמוּנָה כָּל זֹאת, וְקַיָּם עָלֵינוּ כִּי הוּא יְיָ אֱלֹהֵינוּ וְאֵין
זוּלָתוֹ, וַאֲנַחְנוּ יִשְׂרָאֵל עַמּוֹ. הַפּוֹדֵנוּ מִיַּד מְלָכִים, מַלְכֵּנוּ
הַגּוֹאֲלֵנוּ מִכַּף כָּל הֶעָרִיצִים; הָאֵל הַנִּפְרָע לָנוּ מִצָּרֵינוּ,
וְהַמְשַׁלֵּם גְּמוּל לְכָל אֹיְבֵי נַפְשֵׁנוּ; הָעֹשֶׂה גְדֹלוֹת עַד אֵין חֵקֶר,
וְנִפְלָאוֹת עַד אֵין מִסְפָּר; הַשָּׂם נַפְשֵׁנוּ בַּחַיִּים, וְלֹא נָתַן לַמּוֹט
רַגְלֵנוּ; הַמַּדְרִיכֵנוּ עַל בָּמוֹת אוֹיְבֵינוּ, וַיָּרֶם קַרְנֵנוּ עַל כָּל שֹׂנְאֵינוּ;
הָעֹשֶׂה לָנוּ נִסִּים וּנְקָמָה בְּפַרְעֹה, אוֹתוֹת וּמוֹפְתִים בְּאַדְמַת
בְּנֵי חָם; הַמַּכֶּה בְעֶבְרָתוֹ כָּל בְּכוֹרֵי מִצְרָיִם, וַיּוֹצֵא אֶת עַמּוֹ
יִשְׂרָאֵל מִתּוֹכָם לְחֵרוּת עוֹלָם. הַמַּעֲבִיר בָּנָיו בֵּין גִּזְרֵי יַם סוּף;
אֶת רוֹדְפֵיהֶם וְאֶת שׂוֹנְאֵיהֶם בִּתְהוֹמוֹת טִבַּע. וְרָאוּ בָנָיו
גְּבוּרָתוֹ; שִׁבְּחוּ וְהוֹדוּ לִשְׁמוֹ, וּמַלְכוּתוֹ בְּרָצוֹן קִבְּלוּ עֲלֵיהֶם.

מֹשֶׁה וּבְנֵי יִשְׂרָאֵל לְךָ עָנוּ שִׁירָה בְּשִׂמְחָה רַבָּה, וְאָמְרוּ
כֻלָּם:

מִי כָמֹכָה בָּאֵלִם, יְיָ; מִי כָּמֹכָה נֶאְדָּר בַּקֹּדֶשׁ, נוֹרָא תְהִלֹּת,
עֹשֵׂה פֶלֶא.

מַלְכוּתְךָ רָאוּ בָנֶיךָ, בּוֹקֵעַ יָם לִפְנֵי מֹשֶׁה; זֶה אֵלִי עָנוּ
וְאָמְרוּ: יְיָ יִמְלֹךְ לְעֹלָם וָעֶד.

וְנֶאֱמַר: כִּי פָדָה יְיָ אֶת יַעֲקֹב, וּגְאָלוֹ מִיַּד חָזָק מִמֶּנּוּ. בָּרוּךְ
אַתָּה, יְיָ, גָּאַל יִשְׂרָאֵל.

הַשְׁכִּיבֵנוּ, יְיָ אֱלֹהֵינוּ, לְשָׁלוֹם; וְהַעֲמִידֵנוּ, מַלְכֵּנוּ, לְחַיִּים;
וּפְרֹשׂ עָלֵינוּ סֻכַּת שְׁלוֹמֶךָ, וְתַקְּנֵנוּ בְּעֵצָה טוֹבָה מִלְּפָנֶיךָ,
וְהוֹשִׁיעֵנוּ לְמַעַן שְׁמֶךָ; וְהָגֵן בַּעֲדֵנוּ, וְהָסֵר מֵעָלֵינוּ אוֹיֵב, דֶּבֶר
וְחֶרֶב וְרָעָב וְיָגוֹן; וְהָסֵר שָׂטָן מִלְּפָנֵינוּ וּמֵאַחֲרֵינוּ, וּבְצֵל כְּנָפֶיךָ

am the Lord your God who brought you out of the land of Egypt to be your God; I am the Lord your God.

True and trustworthy is all this. We are certain that he is the Lord our God, and no one else, and that we Israel are his people. It is he, our King, who redeemed us from the power of despots, delivered us from the grasp of all the tyrants, avenged us upon our oppressors, and requited all our mortal enemies. He did great, incomprehensible acts and countless wonders; he kept us alive, and did not let us slip.[1] He made us tread upon the high places of our enemies, and raised our strength over all our foes. He performed for us miracles and vengeance upon Pharaoh, signs and wonders in the land of the Hamites; he smote in his wrath all the first-born of Egypt, and brought his people Israel from their midst to enduring freedom. He made his children pass between the divided parts of the Red Sea, and engulfed their pursuers and their enemies in the depths. His children beheld his might; they gave praise and thanks to his name, and willingly accepted his sovereignty.

Moses and the children of Israel sang a song to thee with great rejoicing; all of them said:

"Who is like thee, O Lord, among the mighty? Who is like thee, glorious in holiness, awe-inspiring in renown, doing wonders?"[2]

Thy children saw thy majesty as thou didst part the sea before Moses. "This is my God!" they shouted, and they said:

"The Lord shall reign forever and ever."[3]

And it is said: "Indeed, the Lord has delivered Jacob, and rescued him from a stronger power."[4] Blessed art thou, O Lord, who hast redeemed Israel.

Grant, Lord our God, that we lie down in peace, and that we rise again, O our King, to life. Spread over us thy shelter of peace, and direct us with good counsel of thy own. Save us for thy name's sake; shield us, and remove from us every enemy and pestilence, sword and famine and grief; remove the adversary from before us and from behind us; shelter us in the shadow of thy wings;

---

[1] *Job* 9:10; *Psalm* 66:9.   [2] *Exodus* 15:11.   [3] *Exodus* 15:18.   [4] *Jeremiah* 31:11.

תַּסְתִּירֵנוּ; כִּי אֵל שׁוֹמְרֵנוּ וּמַצִּילֵנוּ אָתָּה, כִּי אֵל מֶלֶךְ חַנּוּן
וְרַחוּם אָתָּה. וּשְׁמֹר צֵאתֵנוּ וּבוֹאֵנוּ לְחַיִּים וּלְשָׁלוֹם, מֵעַתָּה
וְעַד עוֹלָם, Reader וּפְרוֹשׂ עָלֵינוּ סֻכַּת שְׁלוֹמֶךָ. בָּרוּךְ אַתָּה, יְיָ,
הַפּוֹרֵשׂ סֻכַּת שָׁלוֹם עָלֵינוּ, וְעַל כָּל עַמּוֹ יִשְׂרָאֵל, וְעַל יְרוּשָׁלָיִם.

Congregation and Reader:

וְשָׁמְרוּ בְנֵי יִשְׂרָאֵל אֶת הַשַּׁבָּת, לַעֲשׂוֹת אֶת הַשַּׁבָּת לְדֹרֹתָם
בְּרִית עוֹלָם. בֵּינִי וּבֵין בְּנֵי יִשְׂרָאֵל אוֹת הִיא לְעֹלָם, כִּי שֵׁשֶׁת
יָמִים עָשָׂה יְיָ אֶת הַשָּׁמַיִם וְאֶת הָאָרֶץ, וּבַיּוֹם הַשְּׁבִיעִי שָׁבַת
וַיִּנָּפַשׁ.

On Pesah, Shavuoth and Sukkoth:

(וַיְדַבֵּר מֹשֶׁה אֶת מֹעֲדֵי יְיָ אֶל בְּנֵי יִשְׂרָאֵל.)

On Rosh Hashanah:

(תִּקְעוּ בַחֹדֶשׁ שׁוֹפָר, בַּכֶּסֶה לְיוֹם חַגֵּנוּ. כִּי חֹק לְיִשְׂרָאֵל
הוּא, מִשְׁפָּט לֵאלֹהֵי יַעֲקֹב.)

Reader:

יִתְגַּדַּל וְיִתְקַדַּשׁ שְׁמֵהּ רַבָּא בְּעָלְמָא דִּי בְרָא כִרְעוּתֵהּ;
וְיַמְלִיךְ מַלְכוּתֵהּ בְּחַיֵּיכוֹן וּבְיוֹמֵיכוֹן, וּבְחַיֵּי דְכָל בֵּית יִשְׂרָאֵל,
בַּעֲגָלָא וּבִזְמַן קָרִיב, וְאִמְרוּ אָמֵן.

יְהֵא שְׁמֵהּ רַבָּא מְבָרַךְ לְעָלַם וּלְעָלְמֵי עָלְמַיָּא.

יִתְבָּרַךְ וְיִשְׁתַּבַּח, וְיִתְפָּאַר וְיִתְרוֹמַם, וְיִתְנַשֵּׂא וְיִתְהַדָּר,
וְיִתְעַלֶּה וְיִתְהַלָּל שְׁמֵהּ דְּקֻדְשָׁא, בְּרִיךְ הוּא, לְעֵלָּא (לְעֵלָּא)
מִן כָּל בִּרְכָתָא וְשִׁירָתָא, תֻּשְׁבְּחָתָא וְנֶחֱמָתָא, דַּאֲמִירָן בְּעָלְמָא,
וְאִמְרוּ אָמֵן.

The Amidah for festivals begins on page 585.

הַפּוֹרֵשׂ סֻכַּת שָׁלוֹם, instead of the weekday ending שׁוֹמֵר עַמּוֹ יִשְׂרָאֵל, is used to
express the idea of peace which fills the Jewish home on Friday evening.

for thou art our protecting and saving God; thou art indeed a gracious and merciful God and King. Guard thou our going out and our coming in, for life and peace, henceforth and forever. Do thou spread over us thy shelter of peace. Blessed art thou, O Lord, who spreadest the shelter of peace over us and over all thy people Israel and over Jerusalem.

Congregation and Reader:

The children of Israel shall keep the Sabbath, observing the Sabbath throughout their generations as an everlasting covenant. It is a sign between me and the children of Israel forever, that in six days the Lord made the heavens and the earth, and on the seventh day he ceased from work and rested.[1]

On Pesaḥ, Shavuoth and Sukkoth:

(Moses announced the festivals of the Lord to the children of Israel.[2])

On Rosh Hashanah:

(Sound the Shofar at the new moon, at full moon for our feast-day. This is a statute for Israel, an ordinance of the God of Jacob.[3])

Reader:

Glorified and sanctified be God's great name throughout the world which he has created according to his will. May he establish his kingdom in your lifetime and during your days, and within the life of the entire house of Israel, speedily and soon; and say, Amen.

May his great name be blessed forever and to all eternity.

Blessed and praised, glorified and exalted, extolled and honored, adored and lauded be the name of the Holy One, blessed be he, beyond all the blessings and hymns, praises and consolations that are ever spoken in the world; and say, Amen.

The Amidah for festivals begins on page 586.

---

[1] *Exodus* 31:16–17.   [2] *Leviticus* 23:44.   [3] *Psalm* 81:4–5.

The *Amidah* is recited in silent devotion while standing, facing east.

אֲדֹנָי, שְׂפָתַי תִּפְתָּח, וּפִי יַגִּיד תְּהִלָּתֶךָ.

בָּרוּךְ אַתָּה, יְיָ אֱלֹהֵינוּ וֵאלֹהֵי אֲבוֹתֵינוּ, אֱלֹהֵי אַבְרָהָם,
אֱלֹהֵי יִצְחָק, וֵאלֹהֵי יַעֲקֹב, הָאֵל הַגָּדוֹל הַגִּבּוֹר וְהַנּוֹרָא, אֵל
עֶלְיוֹן, גּוֹמֵל חֲסָדִים טוֹבִים, וְקוֹנֵה הַכֹּל, וְזוֹכֵר חַסְדֵי אָבוֹת,
וּמֵבִיא גוֹאֵל לִבְנֵי בְנֵיהֶם לְמַעַן שְׁמוֹ בְּאַהֲבָה.

Between *Rosh Hashanah* and *Yom Kippur* add:

(זָכְרֵנוּ לְחַיִּים, מֶלֶךְ חָפֵץ בַּחַיִּים,
וְכָתְבֵנוּ בְּסֵפֶר הַחַיִּים, לְמַעַנְךָ אֱלֹהִים חַיִּים.)

מֶלֶךְ עוֹזֵר וּמוֹשִׁיעַ וּמָגֵן. בָּרוּךְ אַתָּה, יְיָ, מָגֵן אַבְרָהָם.

אַתָּה גִבּוֹר לְעוֹלָם, אֲדֹנָי, מְחַיֵּה מֵתִים אַתָּה, רַב לְהוֹשִׁיעַ.

Between *Sukkoth* and *Pesaḥ* add:

(מַשִּׁיב הָרוּחַ וּמוֹרִיד הַגָּשֶׁם.)

מְכַלְכֵּל חַיִּים בְּחֶסֶד, מְחַיֵּה מֵתִים בְּרַחֲמִים רַבִּים, סוֹמֵךְ
נוֹפְלִים, וְרוֹפֵא חוֹלִים, וּמַתִּיר אֲסוּרִים, וּמְקַיֵּם אֱמוּנָתוֹ לִישֵׁנֵי
עָפָר. מִי כָמוֹךָ, בַּעַל גְּבוּרוֹת, וּמִי דּוֹמֶה לָּךְ, מֶלֶךְ מֵמִית
וּמְחַיֶּה וּמַצְמִיחַ יְשׁוּעָה.

Between *Rosh Hashanah* and *Yom Kippur* add:

(מִי כָמוֹךָ, אַב הָרַחֲמִים,
זוֹכֵר יְצוּרָיו לְחַיִּים בְּרַחֲמִים.)

וְנֶאֱמָן אַתָּה לְהַחֲיוֹת מֵתִים. בָּרוּךְ אַתָּה, יְיָ, מְחַיֵּה הַמֵּתִים.

תפלת שבע is the name of the Sabbath *Amidah*, because it contains only
seven blessings. The first three and the last three are the same in all forms of
the *Amidah*, whereas the intermediary blessing varies in all four services of
the Sabbath. The thirteen petitions of the weekday *Shemoneh Esreh* are elimi-
nated on the ground that no personal requests may be made during Sabbaths
and festivals. When one recites these petitions, he is reminded of his failings
and troubles, and on the days of rest one ought not to be sad but cheerful.

AMIDAH

The Amidah is recited in silent devotion while standing, facing east.

O Lord, open thou my lips, that my mouth may declare thy praise.[1]

Blessed art thou, Lord our God and God of our fathers, God of Abraham, God of Isaac and God of Jacob; great, mighty and revered God, sublime God, who bestowest lovingkindness, and art Master of all things; who rememberest the good deeds of our fathers, and who wilt graciously bring a redeemer to their children's children for the sake of thy name.

Between Rosh Hashanah and Yom Kippur add:

(Remember us to life, O King who delightest in life; inscribe us in the book of life for thy sake, O living God.)

O King, Supporter, Savior and Shield. Blessed art thou, O Lord, Shield of Abraham.

Thou, O Lord, art mighty forever; thou revivest the dead; thou art powerful to save.

Between Sukkoth and Pesah add:

(Thou causest the wind to blow and the rain to fall.)

Thou sustainest the living with kindness, and revivest the dead with great mercy; thou supportest all who fall, and healest the sick; thou settest the captives free, and keepest faith with those who sleep in the dust. Who is like thee, Lord of power? Who resembles thee, O King? Thou bringest death and restorest life, and causest salvation to flourish.

Between Rosh Hashanah and Yom Kippur add:

(Who is like thee, merciful Father? In mercy thou rememberest thy creatures to life.)

Thou art faithful to revive the dead. Blessed art thou, O Lord, who revivest the dead.

---

[1] *Psalm* 51:17.

אַתָּה קָדוֹשׁ וְשִׁמְךָ קָדוֹשׁ, וּקְדוֹשִׁים בְּכָל יוֹם יְהַלְלוּךָ סֶּלָה.
*בָּרוּךְ אַתָּה יְיָ, הָאֵל הַקָּדוֹשׁ.

*Between *Rosh Hashanah* and *Yom Kippur* substitute:

(בָּרוּךְ אַתָּה, יְיָ, הַמֶּלֶךְ הַקָּדוֹשׁ.)

אַתָּה קִדַּשְׁתָּ אֶת יוֹם הַשְּׁבִיעִי לִשְׁמֶךָ, תַּכְלִית מַעֲשֵׂה שָׁמַיִם
וָאָרֶץ, וּבֵרַכְתּוֹ מִכָּל הַיָּמִים וְקִדַּשְׁתּוֹ מִכָּל הַזְּמַנִּים, וְכֵן כָּתוּב
בְּתוֹרָתֶךָ:

וַיְכֻלּוּ הַשָּׁמַיִם וְהָאָרֶץ וְכָל צְבָאָם. וַיְכַל אֱלֹהִים בַּיּוֹם
הַשְּׁבִיעִי מְלַאכְתּוֹ אֲשֶׁר עָשָׂה, וַיִּשְׁבֹּת בַּיּוֹם הַשְּׁבִיעִי מִכָּל
מְלַאכְתּוֹ אֲשֶׁר עָשָׂה. וַיְבָרֶךְ אֱלֹהִים אֶת יוֹם הַשְּׁבִיעִי וַיְקַדֵּשׁ
אֹתוֹ, כִּי בוֹ שָׁבַת מִכָּל מְלַאכְתּוֹ אֲשֶׁר בָּרָא אֱלֹהִים לַעֲשׂוֹת.

אֱלֹהֵינוּ וֵאלֹהֵי אֲבוֹתֵינוּ, רְצֵה בִמְנוּחָתֵנוּ. קַדְּשֵׁנוּ בְּמִצְוֹתֶיךָ,
וְתֵן חֶלְקֵנוּ בְּתוֹרָתֶךָ; שַׂבְּעֵנוּ מִטּוּבֶךָ, וְשַׂמְּחֵנוּ בִּישׁוּעָתֶךָ; וְטַהֵר
לִבֵּנוּ לְעָבְדְּךָ בֶּאֱמֶת; וְהַנְחִילֵנוּ, יְיָ אֱלֹהֵינוּ, בְּאַהֲבָה וּבְרָצוֹן
שַׁבַּת קָדְשֶׁךָ, וְיָנוּחוּ בָה יִשְׂרָאֵל מְקַדְּשֵׁי שְׁמֶךָ. בָּרוּךְ אַתָּה, יְיָ,
מְקַדֵּשׁ הַשַּׁבָּת.

רְצֵה, יְיָ אֱלֹהֵינוּ, בְּעַמְּךָ יִשְׂרָאֵל וּבִתְפִלָּתָם; וְהָשֵׁב אֶת
הָעֲבוֹדָה לִדְבִיר בֵּיתֶךָ, וְאִשֵּׁי יִשְׂרָאֵל וּתְפִלָּתָם בְּאַהֲבָה תְקַבֵּל
בְּרָצוֹן, וּתְהִי לְרָצוֹן תָּמִיד עֲבוֹדַת יִשְׂרָאֵל עַמֶּךָ.

On *Rosh Ḥodesh* and *Ḥol ha-Mo'ed* add:

(אֱלֹהֵינוּ וֵאלֹהֵי אֲבוֹתֵינוּ, יַעֲלֶה וְיָבֹא, וְיַגִּיעַ וְיֵרָאֶה, וְיֵרָצֶה
וְיִשָּׁמַע, וְיִפָּקֵד וְיִזָּכֵר, זִכְרוֹנֵנוּ וּפִקְדוֹנֵנוּ, וְזִכְרוֹן אֲבוֹתֵינוּ,
וְזִכְרוֹן מָשִׁיחַ בֶּן דָּוִד עַבְדֶּךָ, וְזִכְרוֹן יְרוּשָׁלַיִם עִיר קָדְשֶׁךָ,

אתה קדשת appears in the ninth century *Siddur* of Amram Gaon and in Maimonides' text with slight variations.

Thou art holy and thy name is holy, and holy beings praise thee daily. * Blessed art thou, O Lord, holy God.

*Between Rosh Hashanah and Yom Kippur substitute:
(Blessed art thou, O Lord, holy King.)

Thou hast sanctified to thyself the seventh day, marking the end of the creation of heaven and earth; thou hast blessed it above all days, and hallowed it above all festivals, as it is written in thy Torah:

Thus the heavens and the earth were finished, and all their host. By the seventh day God had completed his work which he had made, and he rested on the seventh day from all his work in which he had been engaged. Then God blessed the seventh day and hallowed it, because on it he rested from all his work which he had created.[1]

Our God and God of our fathers, be pleased with our rest. Sanctify us with thy commandments and grant us a share in thy Torah; satisfy us with thy goodness and gladden us with thy help; purify our heart to serve thee sincerely. In thy gracious love, Lord our God, grant that we keep thy holy Sabbath as a heritage; may Israel who sanctifies thy name rest on it. Blessed art thou, O Lord, who hallowest the Sabbath.

Be pleased, Lord our God, with thy people Israel and with their prayer; restore the worship to thy most holy sanctuary; accept Israel's offerings and prayer with gracious love. May the worship of thy people Israel be ever pleasing to thee.

On Rosh Ḥodesh and Ḥol ha-Mo'ed add:

(Our God and God of our fathers, may the remembrance of us, of our fathers, of Messiah the son of David thy servant, of Jerusalem thy holy city, and of all thy people the house of Israel,

---

רצה במנוחתנו, like the *Kiddush*, ends with מקדש השבת; on festivals, however, Israel is included in the formula מקדש ישראל והזמנים. According to the Talmud (Pesaḥim 117b), Israel is mentioned in the phrase used on festivals because through Israel the festivals are sanctified, since the length of each month is fixed by Jewish authorities who thereby fix the dates of the festivals. The Sabbath, on the other hand, is permanently fixed and depends entirely on God.

[1] *Genesis* 2:1–3.

וְזִכְרוֹן כָּל עַמְּךָ בֵּית יִשְׂרָאֵל לְפָנֶיךָ, לִפְלֵיטָה וּלְטוֹבָה, לְחֵן
וּלְחֶסֶד וּלְרַחֲמִים, לְחַיִּים וּלְשָׁלוֹם, בְּיוֹם

Sukkoth	Pesaḥ	Rosh Ḥodesh
חַג הַסֻּכּוֹת	חַג הַמַּצּוֹת	רֹאשׁ הַחֹדֶשׁ

הַזֶּה. זָכְרֵנוּ, יְיָ אֱלֹהֵינוּ, בּוֹ לְטוֹבָה, וּפָקְדֵנוּ בוֹ לִבְרָכָה,
וְהוֹשִׁיעֵנוּ בוֹ לְחַיִּים. וּבִדְבַר יְשׁוּעָה וְרַחֲמִים חוּס וְחָנֵּנוּ, וְרַחֵם
עָלֵינוּ וְהוֹשִׁיעֵנוּ, כִּי אֵלֶיךָ עֵינֵינוּ, כִּי אֵל מֶלֶךְ חַנּוּן וְרַחוּם
אָתָּה.)

וְתֶחֱזֶינָה עֵינֵינוּ בְּשׁוּבְךָ לְצִיּוֹן בְּרַחֲמִים. בָּרוּךְ אַתָּה, יְיָ,
הַמַּחֲזִיר שְׁכִינָתוֹ לְצִיּוֹן.

מוֹדִים אֲנַחְנוּ לָךְ, שָׁאַתָּה הוּא יְיָ אֱלֹהֵינוּ וֵאלֹהֵי אֲבוֹתֵינוּ
לְעוֹלָם וָעֶד. צוּר חַיֵּינוּ, מָגֵן יִשְׁעֵנוּ אַתָּה הוּא. לְדוֹר וָדוֹר
נוֹדֶה לְּךָ, וּנְסַפֵּר תְּהִלָּתֶךָ, עַל חַיֵּינוּ הַמְּסוּרִים בְּיָדֶךָ, וְעַל
נִשְׁמוֹתֵינוּ הַפְּקוּדוֹת לָךְ, וְעַל נִסֶּיךָ שֶׁבְּכָל יוֹם עִמָּנוּ, וְעַל
נִפְלְאוֹתֶיךָ וְטוֹבוֹתֶיךָ שֶׁבְּכָל עֵת, עֶרֶב וָבֹקֶר וְצָהֳרָיִם. הַטּוֹב
כִּי לֹא כָלוּ רַחֲמֶיךָ, וְהַמְרַחֵם כִּי לֹא תַמּוּ חֲסָדֶיךָ, מֵעוֹלָם
קִוִּינוּ לָךְ.

On Ḥanukkah add:

(עַל הַנִּסִּים וְעַל הַפֻּרְקָן, וְעַל הַגְּבוּרוֹת וְעַל הַתְּשׁוּעוֹת, וְעַל
הַמִּלְחָמוֹת, שֶׁעָשִׂיתָ לַאֲבוֹתֵינוּ בַּיָּמִים הָהֵם בַּזְּמַן הַזֶּה—

בִּימֵי מַתִּתְיָהוּ בֶּן יוֹחָנָן כֹּהֵן גָּדוֹל, חַשְׁמוֹנַי וּבָנָיו, כְּשֶׁעָמְדָה
מַלְכוּת יָוָן הָרְשָׁעָה עַל עַמְּךָ יִשְׂרָאֵל לְהַשְׁכִּיחָם תּוֹרָתֶךָ,
וּלְהַעֲבִירָם מֵחֻקֵּי רְצוֹנֶךָ. וְאַתָּה בְּרַחֲמֶיךָ הָרַבִּים עָמַדְתָּ לָהֶם
בְּעֵת צָרָתָם, רַבְתָּ אֶת רִיבָם, דַּנְתָּ אֶת דִּינָם, נָקַמְתָּ אֶת נִקְמָתָם;
מָסַרְתָּ גִבּוֹרִים בְּיַד חַלָּשִׁים, וְרַבִּים בְּיַד מְעַטִּים, וּטְמֵאִים בְּיַד
טְהוֹרִים, וּרְשָׁעִים בְּיַד צַדִּיקִים, וְזֵדִים בְּיַד עוֹסְקֵי תוֹרָתֶךָ.

ascend and come and be accepted before thee for deliverance and happiness, for grace, kindness and mercy, for life and peace, on this day of

Rosh Ḥodesh	*Pesaḥ*	*Sukkoth*
the New Moon.'	the Feast of Unleavened Bread.	the Feast of Tabernacles.

Remember us this day, Lord our God, for happiness; be mindful of us for blessing; save us to enjoy life. With a promise of salvation and mercy spare us and be gracious to us; have pity on us and save us, for we look to thee, for thou art a gracious and merciful God and King.)

May our eyes behold thy return in mercy to Zion. Blessed art thou, O Lord, who restorest thy divine presence to Zion.

We ever thank thee, who art the Lord our God and the God of our fathers. Thou art the strength of our life and our saving shield. In every generation we will thank thee and recount thy praise—for our lives which are in thy charge, for our souls which are in thy care, for thy miracles which are daily with us, and for thy continual wonders and favors—evening, morning and noon. Beneficent One, whose mercies never fail, Merciful One, whose kindnesses never cease, thou hast always been our hope.

On Ḥanukkah add:

(We thank thee for the miracles, for the redemption, for the mighty deeds and triumphs, and for the battles which thou didst perform for our fathers in those days, at this season—

In the days of the Hasmonean, Mattathias ben Yoḥanan, the High Priest, and his sons, when a wicked Hellenic government rose up against thy people Israel to make them forget thy Torah and transgress the laws of thy will. Thou in thy great mercy didst stand by them in the time of their distress. Thou didst champion their cause, defend their rights and avenge their wrong; thou didst deliver the strong into the hands of the weak, the many into the hands of the few, the impure into the hands of the pure, the wicked into the hands of the righteous, and the arrogant into the hands

וּלְךָ עָשִׂיתָ שֵׁם גָּדוֹל וְקָדוֹשׁ בְּעוֹלָמֶךָ, וּלְעַמְּךָ יִשְׂרָאֵל עָשִׂיתָ
תְּשׁוּעָה גְדוֹלָה וּפֻרְקָן כְּהַיּוֹם הַזֶּה. וְאַחַר כֵּן בָּאוּ בָנֶיךָ לִדְבִיר
בֵּיתֶךָ, וּפִנּוּ אֶת הֵיכָלֶךָ, וְטִהֲרוּ אֶת מִקְדָּשֶׁךָ, וְהִדְלִיקוּ נֵרוֹת
בְּחַצְרוֹת קָדְשֶׁךָ, וְקָבְעוּ שְׁמוֹנַת יְמֵי חֲנֻכָּה אֵלּוּ לְהוֹדוֹת וּלְהַלֵּל
לְשִׁמְךָ הַגָּדוֹל.)

וְעַל כֻּלָּם יִתְבָּרַךְ וְיִתְרוֹמַם שִׁמְךָ, מַלְכֵּנוּ, תָּמִיד לְעוֹלָם
וָעֶד.

Between *Rosh Hashanah* and *Yom Kippur* add:

(וּכְתוֹב לְחַיִּים טוֹבִים כָּל בְּנֵי בְרִיתֶךָ.)

וְכֹל הַחַיִּים יוֹדוּךָ סֶּלָה, וִיהַלְלוּ אֶת שִׁמְךָ בֶּאֱמֶת, הָאֵל,
יְשׁוּעָתֵנוּ וְעֶזְרָתֵנוּ סֶלָה. בָּרוּךְ אַתָּה, יְיָ, הַטּוֹב שִׁמְךָ, וּלְךָ נָאֶה
לְהוֹדוֹת.

שָׁלוֹם רָב עַל יִשְׂרָאֵל עַמְּךָ תָּשִׂים לְעוֹלָם, כִּי אַתָּה הוּא
מֶלֶךְ אָדוֹן לְכָל הַשָּׁלוֹם, וְטוֹב בְּעֵינֶיךָ לְבָרֵךְ אֶת עַמְּךָ יִשְׂרָאֵל
בְּכָל עֵת וּבְכָל שָׁעָה בִּשְׁלוֹמֶךָ. * בָּרוּךְ אַתָּה, יְיָ, הַמְבָרֵךְ אֶת
עַמּוֹ יִשְׂרָאֵל בַּשָּׁלוֹם.

*Between *Rosh Hashanah* and *Yom Kippur* say:

(בְּסֵפֶר חַיִּים, בְּרָכָה וְשָׁלוֹם וּפַרְנָסָה טוֹבָה, נִזָּכֵר וְנִכָּתֵב
לְפָנֶיךָ, אֲנַחְנוּ וְכָל עַמְּךָ בֵּית יִשְׂרָאֵל, לְחַיִּים טוֹבִים וּלְשָׁלוֹם.
בָּרוּךְ אַתָּה, יְיָ, עוֹשֵׂה הַשָּׁלוֹם.)

After the *Amidah* add the following meditation:

אֱלֹהַי, נְצֹר לְשׁוֹנִי מֵרָע, וּשְׂפָתַי מִדַּבֵּר מִרְמָה; וְלִמְקַלְלַי
נַפְשִׁי תִדּוֹם, וְנַפְשִׁי כֶּעָפָר לַכֹּל תִּהְיֶה. פְּתַח לִבִּי בְּתוֹרָתֶךָ,
וּבְמִצְוֹתֶיךָ תִּרְדּוֹף נַפְשִׁי; וְכָל הַחוֹשְׁבִים עָלַי רָעָה, מְהֵרָה
הָפֵר עֲצָתָם וְקַלְקֵל מַחֲשַׁבְתָּם. עֲשֵׂה לְמַעַן שְׁמֶךָ, עֲשֵׂה לְמַעַן
יְמִינֶךָ, עֲשֵׂה לְמַעַן קְדֻשָּׁתֶךָ, עֲשֵׂה לְמַעַן תּוֹרָתֶךָ. לְמַעַן יֵחָלְצוּן

of the students of thy Torah. Thou didst make a great and holy
name for thyself in thy world, and for thy people Israel thou didst
perform a great deliverance unto this day. Thereupon thy children
entered the shrine of thy house, cleansed thy Temple, purified thy
sanctuary, kindled lights in thy holy courts, and designated these
eight days of Ḥanukkah for giving thanks and praise to thy great
name.)

For all these acts may thy name, our King, be blessed and
exalted forever and ever.

Between Rosh Hashanah and Yom Kippur add:

(Inscribe all thy people of the covenant for a happy life.)

All the living shall ever thank thee and sincerely praise thy
name, O God, who art always our salvation and help. Blessed art
thou, O God, Beneficent One, to whom it is fitting to give thanks.

O grant abundant peace to Israel thy people forever, for thou
art the King and Lord of all peace. May it please thee to bless
thy people Israel with peace at all times and at all hours. * Blessed
art thou, O Lord, who blessest thy people Israel with peace.

*Between Rosh Hashanah and Yom Kippur say:

(May we and all Israel thy people be remembered and inscribed
before thee in the book of life and blessing, peace and prosperity,
for a happy life and for peace. Blessed art thou, O Lord, Author
of peace.)

After the Amidah add the following meditation:

My God, guard my tongue from evil, and my lips from speaking falsehood. May my soul be silent to those who insult me; be
my soul lowly to all as the dust. Open my heart to thy Torah,
that my soul may follow thy commands. Speedily defeat the
counsel of all those who plan evil against me and upset their design. Do it for the glory of thy name; do it for the sake of thy
power; do it for the sake of thy holiness; do it for the sake of thy
Torah. That thy beloved may be rescued, save with thy right hand

יְדִידֶיךָ, הוֹשִׁיעָה יְמִינְךָ וַעֲנֵנִי. יִהְיוּ לְרָצוֹן אִמְרֵי פִי וְהֶגְיוֹן לִבִּי
לְפָנֶיךָ, יְיָ, צוּרִי וְגוֹאֲלִי. עֹשֶׂה שָׁלוֹם בִּמְרוֹמָיו, הוּא יַעֲשֶׂה
שָׁלוֹם עָלֵינוּ וְעַל כָּל יִשְׂרָאֵל, וְאִמְרוּ אָמֵן.

יְהִי רָצוֹן מִלְּפָנֶיךָ, יְיָ אֱלֹהֵינוּ וֵאלֹהֵי אֲבוֹתֵינוּ, שֶׁיִּבָּנֶה בֵּית
הַמִּקְדָּשׁ בִּמְהֵרָה בְיָמֵינוּ, וְתֵן חֶלְקֵנוּ בְּתוֹרָתֶךָ. וְשָׁם נַעֲבָדְךָ
בְּיִרְאָה, כִּימֵי עוֹלָם וּכְשָׁנִים קַדְמוֹנִיּוֹת. וְעָרְבָה לַיְיָ מִנְחַת
יְהוּדָה וִירוּשָׁלָיִם, כִּימֵי עוֹלָם וּכְשָׁנִים קַדְמוֹנִיּוֹת.

Reader and Congregation:

וַיְכֻלּוּ הַשָּׁמַיִם וְהָאָרֶץ וְכָל צְבָאָם. וַיְכַל אֱלֹהִים בַּיּוֹם
הַשְּׁבִיעִי מְלַאכְתּוֹ אֲשֶׁר עָשָׂה, וַיִּשְׁבֹּת בַּיּוֹם הַשְּׁבִיעִי מִכָּל
מְלַאכְתּוֹ אֲשֶׁר עָשָׂה. וַיְבָרֶךְ אֱלֹהִים אֶת יוֹם הַשְּׁבִיעִי וַיְקַדֵּשׁ
אֹתוֹ, כִּי בוֹ שָׁבַת מִכָּל מְלַאכְתּוֹ אֲשֶׁר בָּרָא אֱלֹהִים לַעֲשׂוֹת.

Reader:

בָּרוּךְ אַתָּה, יְיָ אֱלֹהֵינוּ וֵאלֹהֵי אֲבוֹתֵינוּ, אֱלֹהֵי אַבְרָהָם,
אֱלֹהֵי יִצְחָק, וֵאלֹהֵי יַעֲקֹב, הָאֵל הַגָּדוֹל הַגִּבּוֹר וְהַנּוֹרָא, אֵל
עֶלְיוֹן, קוֹנֵה שָׁמַיִם וָאָרֶץ.

Congregation:

מָגֵן אָבוֹת בִּדְבָרוֹ, מְחַיֵּה מֵתִים בְּמַאֲמָרוֹ, הָאֵל (*הַמֶּלֶךְ)
הַקָּדוֹשׁ שֶׁאֵין כָּמוֹהוּ, הַמֵּנִיחַ לְעַמּוֹ בְּיוֹם שַׁבַּת קָדְשׁוֹ, כִּי בָם
רָצָה לְהָנִיחַ לָהֶם; לְפָנָיו נַעֲבֹד בְּיִרְאָה וָפַחַד, וְנוֹדֶה לִשְׁמוֹ
* Between *Rosh Hashanah* and *Yom Kippur* substitute הַמֶּלֶךְ for הָאֵל.

וִיכֻלּוּ, considered an essential part of the service (Shabbath 119b), is re-
peated after the *Amidah* because the *Amidah* of festivals occurring on the
Sabbath does not include this passage. Since וִיכֻלּוּ has to be recited after the
Amidah when a festival occurs on the Sabbath, it has become the rule for all
Sabbaths (Tosafoth, Pesaḥim 106a).

מָגֵן אָבוֹת is termed מֵעֵין שֶׁבַע because it contains the substance of the seven
blessings of the *Amidah*. This abridged form of the *Amidah* was originally

and answer me. May the words of my mouth and the meditation of my heart be pleasing before thee, O Lord, my Stronghold and my Redeemer.[1] May he who creates peace in his high heavens create peace for us and for all Israel. Amen.

May it be thy will, Lord our God and God of our fathers, that the Temple be speedily rebuilt in our days, and grant us a share in thy Torah. There we will serve thee with reverence, as in the days of old and as in former years. Then the offering of Judah and Jerusalem will be pleasing to the Lord, as in the days of old and as in former years.[2]

Reader and Congregation:

Thus the heavens and the earth were finished, and all their host. By the seventh day God had completed his work which he had made, and he rested on the seventh day from all his work in which he had been engaged. Then God blessed the seventh day and hallowed it, because on it he rested from all his work which he had created.[3]

Reader:

Blessed art thou, Lord our God and God of our fathers, God of Abraham, God of Isaac and God of Jacob; great, mighty and revered God, supreme God, Master of heaven and earth.

Congregation:

He with his word was a shield to our fathers, and by his bidding he will revive the dead. He is the holy God,* like whom there is none. He gives rest to his people on his holy Sabbath day, for he is pleased to grant them rest. Him we will serve with reverence and

*Between Rosh Hashanah and Yom Kippur substitute: "holy King."

---

added in order to prolong the service for the convenience of late-comers. The synagogues were often located outside the precincts of the city (since the rulers did not tolerate Jewish worship within the confines of their municipalities), and it was dangerous to walk home alone at night. By prolonging the Sabbath-eve service, which was far better attended than weekday services, the late-comers were given an opportunity to finish their prayers with the rest of the congregation (Rashi, Shabbath 24b; compare note on במה מדליקין, page 251).

[1] *Psalms* 60:7; 19:15.   [2] *Malachi* 3:4.   [3] *Genesis* 2:1-3.

בְּכָל יוֹם תָּמִיד מֵעֵין הַבְּרָכוֹת. Reader אֵל הַהוֹדָאוֹת, אֲדוֹן
הַשָּׁלוֹם, מְקַדֵּשׁ הַשַּׁבָּת וּמְבָרֵךְ שְׁבִיעִי, וּמֵנִיחַ בִּקְדֻשָּׁה לְעַם
מְדֻשְּׁנֵי עֹנֶג, זֵכֶר לְמַעֲשֵׂה בְרֵאשִׁית.

Reader:

אֱלֹהֵינוּ וֵאלֹהֵי אֲבוֹתֵינוּ, רְצֵה בִמְנוּחָתֵנוּ; קַדְּשֵׁנוּ בְּמִצְוֹתֶיךָ,
וְתֵן חֶלְקֵנוּ בְּתוֹרָתֶךָ; שַׂבְּעֵנוּ מִטּוּבֶךָ, וְשַׂמְּחֵנוּ בִּישׁוּעָתֶךָ; וְטַהֵר
לִבֵּנוּ לְעָבְדְּךָ בֶּאֱמֶת; וְהַנְחִילֵנוּ, יְיָ אֱלֹהֵינוּ, בְּאַהֲבָה וּבְרָצוֹן
שַׁבַּת קָדְשֶׁךָ, וְיָנוּחוּ בָהּ יִשְׂרָאֵל מְקַדְּשֵׁי שְׁמֶךָ. בָּרוּךְ אַתָּה, יְיָ,
מְקַדֵּשׁ הַשַּׁבָּת.

יִתְגַּדַּל וְיִתְקַדַּשׁ שְׁמֵהּ רַבָּא בְּעָלְמָא דִי בְרָא כִרְעוּתֵהּ;
וְיַמְלִיךְ מַלְכוּתֵהּ בְּחַיֵּיכוֹן וּבְיוֹמֵיכוֹן, וּבְחַיֵּי דְכָל בֵּית יִשְׂרָאֵל,
בַּעֲגָלָא וּבִזְמַן קָרִיב, וְאִמְרוּ אָמֵן.

יְהֵא שְׁמֵהּ רַבָּא מְבָרַךְ לְעָלַם וּלְעָלְמֵי עָלְמַיָּא.

יִתְבָּרַךְ וְיִשְׁתַּבַּח, וְיִתְפָּאַר וְיִתְרוֹמַם, וְיִתְנַשֵּׂא וְיִתְהַדָּר,
וְיִתְעַלֶּה וְיִתְהַלָּל שְׁמֵהּ דְּקֻדְשָׁא, בְּרִיךְ הוּא, לְעֵלָּא* (לְעֵלָּא)
מִן כָּל בִּרְכָתָא וְשִׁירָתָא, תֻּשְׁבְּחָתָא וְנֶחֱמָתָא, דַּאֲמִירָן בְּעָלְמָא,
וְאִמְרוּ אָמֵן.

תִּתְקַבֵּל צְלוֹתְהוֹן וּבָעוּתְהוֹן דְּכָל בֵּית יִשְׂרָאֵל קֳדָם אֲבוּהוֹן
דִּי בִשְׁמַיָּא, וְאִמְרוּ אָמֵן.

יְהֵא שְׁלָמָא רַבָּא מִן שְׁמַיָּא, וְחַיִּים, עָלֵינוּ וְעַל כָּל יִשְׂרָאֵל,
וְאִמְרוּ אָמֵן.

עֹשֶׂה שָׁלוֹם בִּמְרוֹמָיו, הוּא יַעֲשֶׂה שָׁלוֹם עָלֵינוּ וְעַל כָּל
יִשְׂרָאֵל, וְאִמְרוּ אָמֵן.

---

*לְעֵלָּא לְעֵלָּא is said between *Rosh Hashanah* and *Yom Kippur*.

awe, and to his name we will give thanks every day, constantly, in the fitting form of blessings. He is the God to whom thanks are due, the Lord of peace, who hallows the Sabbath and blesses the seventh day, who gives sanctified rest to a joyful people—in remembrance of the creation.

Reader:

Our God and God of our fathers, be pleased with our rest. Sanctify us with thy commandments and grant us a share in thy Torah; satisfy us with thy goodness and gladden us with thy deliverance; purify our heart to serve thee in truth; and, in thy gracious love, Lord our God, grant that we keep thy holy Sabbath as a heritage, and that Israel, who hallow thy name, may rest on it. Blessed art thou, O Lord, who hallowest the Sabbath.

Glorified and sanctified be God's great name throughout the world which he has created according to his will. May he establish his kingdom in your lifetime and during your days, and within the life of the entire house of Israel, speedily and soon; and say, Amen.

May his great name be blessed forever and to all eternity.

Blessed and praised, glorified and exalted, extolled and honored, adored and lauded be the name of the Holy One, blessed be he, beyond all the blessings and hymns, praises and consolations that are ever spoken in the world; and say, Amen.

May the prayers and supplications of the whole household of Israel be accepted by their Father who is in heaven; and say, Amen.

May there be abundant peace from heaven, and life, for us and for all Israel; and say, Amen.

He who creates peace in his celestial heights, may he create peace for us and for all Israel; and say, Amen.

The Reader recites the following *Kiddush* over wine.

סָבְרִי מָרָנָן וְרַבּוֹתַי.

בָּרוּךְ אַתָּה, יְיָ אֱלֹהֵינוּ, מֶלֶךְ הָעוֹלָם, בּוֹרֵא פְּרִי הַגָּפֶן.

בָּרוּךְ אַתָּה, יְיָ אֱלֹהֵינוּ, מֶלֶךְ הָעוֹלָם, אֲשֶׁר קִדְּשָׁנוּ בְּמִצְוֹתָיו
וְרָצָה בָנוּ, וְשַׁבַּת קָדְשׁוֹ בְּאַהֲבָה וּבְרָצוֹן הִנְחִילָנוּ, זִכָּרוֹן
לְמַעֲשֵׂה בְרֵאשִׁית; כִּי הוּא יוֹם תְּחִלָּה לְמִקְרָאֵי קֹדֶשׁ, זֵכֶר
לִיצִיאַת מִצְרָיִם. כִּי בָנוּ בָחַרְתָּ וְאוֹתָנוּ קִדַּשְׁתָּ מִכָּל הָעַמִּים,
וְשַׁבַּת קָדְשְׁךָ בְּאַהֲבָה וּבְרָצוֹן הִנְחַלְתָּנוּ. בָּרוּךְ אַתָּה, יְיָ,
מְקַדֵּשׁ הַשַּׁבָּת.

עָלֵינוּ לְשַׁבֵּחַ לַאֲדוֹן הַכֹּל, לָתֵת גְּדֻלָּה לְיוֹצֵר בְּרֵאשִׁית,
שֶׁלֹּא עָשָׂנוּ כְּגוֹיֵי הָאֲרָצוֹת, וְלֹא שָׂמָנוּ כְּמִשְׁפְּחוֹת הָאֲדָמָה;
שֶׁלֹּא שָׂם חֶלְקֵנוּ כָּהֶם, וְגוֹרָלֵנוּ כְּכָל הֲמוֹנָם. וַאֲנַחְנוּ כּוֹרְעִים
וּמִשְׁתַּחֲוִים וּמוֹדִים לִפְנֵי מֶלֶךְ מַלְכֵי הַמְּלָכִים, הַקָּדוֹשׁ בָּרוּךְ
הוּא, שֶׁהוּא נוֹטֶה שָׁמַיִם וְיוֹסֵד אָרֶץ, וּמוֹשַׁב יְקָרוֹ בַּשָּׁמַיִם
מִמַּעַל, וּשְׁכִינַת עֻזּוֹ בְּגָבְהֵי מְרוֹמִים. הוּא אֱלֹהֵינוּ, אֵין עוֹד;
אֱמֶת מַלְכֵּנוּ, אֶפֶס זוּלָתוֹ, כַּכָּתוּב בְּתוֹרָתוֹ: וְיָדַעְתָּ הַיּוֹם
וַהֲשֵׁבֹתָ אֶל לְבָבֶךָ, כִּי יְיָ הוּא הָאֱלֹהִים בַּשָּׁמַיִם מִמַּעַל וְעַל
הָאָרֶץ מִתָּחַת, אֵין עוֹד.

עַל כֵּן נְקַוֶּה לְךָ, יְיָ אֱלֹהֵינוּ, לִרְאוֹת מְהֵרָה בְּתִפְאֶרֶת עֻזֶּךָ,
לְהַעֲבִיר גִּלּוּלִים מִן הָאָרֶץ, וְהָאֱלִילִים כָּרוֹת יִכָּרֵתוּן; לְתַקֵּן
עוֹלָם בְּמַלְכוּת שַׁדַּי, וְכָל בְּנֵי בָשָׂר יִקְרְאוּ בִשְׁמֶךָ, לְהַפְנוֹת

קידוש recited by the Reader in the synagogue has its origin in the period
when strangers were given their Sabbath meal in a room adjoining the Synagogue. Abudarham, writing in Spain early in the fourteenth century, says:
"As our predecessors have set up the rule, though for a reason which no longer
exists, the rule remains unshaken."

278 *Evening Service for Sabbaths*

The Reader recites the following Kiddush over wine.

Blessed art thou, Lord our God, King of the universe, who createst the fruit of the vine.

Blessed art thou, Lord our God, King of the universe, who hast sanctified us with thy commandments and hast been pleased with us; thou hast graciously given us thy holy Sabbath as a heritage, in remembrance of the creation. The Sabbath is the first among the holy festivals which recall the exodus from Egypt. Indeed, thou hast chosen us and hallowed us above all nations, and hast graciously given us thy holy Sabbath as a heritage. Blessed art thou, O Lord, who hallowest the Sabbath.

ALENU

It is our duty to praise the Master of all, to exalt the Creator of the universe, who has not made us like the nations of the world and has not placed us like the families of the earth; who has not designed our destiny to be like theirs, nor our lot like that of all their multitude. We bend the knee and bow and acknowledge before the supreme King of kings, the Holy One, blessed be he, that it is he who stretched forth the heavens and founded the earth. His seat of glory is in the heavens above; his abode of majesty is in the lofty heights. He is our God, there is none else; truly, he is our King, there is none besides him, as it is written in his Torah: "You shall know this day, and reflect in your heart, that it is the Lord who is God in the heavens above and on the earth beneath, there is none else."[1]

We hope therefore, Lord our God, soon to behold thy majestic glory, when the abominations shall be removed from the earth, and the false gods exterminated; when the world shall be perfected under the reign of the Almighty, and all mankind will call upon

---

סברי מרנן is used here in the sense of "Gentlemen, attention!" It is intended to call attention to the blessing which is about to be pronounced over the wine, so that those present may answer Amen. According to a midrashic source (Tanḥuma, *Pekudé*), this phrase was originally used in the form of a question, namely: "Gentlemen, what is your opinion?" Is it safe to drink of this wine? The response was לחיים!

[1] *Deuteronomy* 4:39.

אֵלֶיךָ כָּל רִשְׁעֵי אָרֶץ. יַכִּירוּ וְיֵדְעוּ כָּל יוֹשְׁבֵי תֵבֵל, כִּי לְךָ
תִּכְרַע כָּל בֶּרֶךְ, תִּשָּׁבַע כָּל לָשׁוֹן. לְפָנֶיךָ, יְיָ אֱלֹהֵינוּ, יִכְרְעוּ
וְיִפֹּלוּ, וְלִכְבוֹד שִׁמְךָ יְקָר יִתֵּנוּ, וִיקַבְּלוּ כֻלָּם אֶת עֹל מַלְכוּתֶךָ,
וְתִמְלוֹךְ עֲלֵיהֶם מְהֵרָה לְעוֹלָם וָעֶד; כִּי הַמַּלְכוּת שֶׁלְּךָ הִיא,
וּלְעוֹלְמֵי עַד תִּמְלוֹךְ בְּכָבוֹד, כַּכָּתוּב בְּתוֹרָתֶךָ: יְיָ יִמְלֹךְ
לְעֹלָם וָעֶד. Reader וְנֶאֱמַר: וְהָיָה יְיָ לְמֶלֶךְ עַל כָּל הָאָרֶץ;
בַּיּוֹם הַהוּא יִהְיֶה יְיָ אֶחָד וּשְׁמוֹ אֶחָד.

MOURNERS' KADDISH

יִתְגַּדַּל וְיִתְקַדַּשׁ שְׁמֵהּ רַבָּא בְּעָלְמָא דִּי בְרָא כִרְעוּתֵהּ;
וְיַמְלִיךְ מַלְכוּתֵהּ בְּחַיֵּיכוֹן וּבְיוֹמֵיכוֹן, וּבְחַיֵּי דְכָל בֵּית יִשְׂרָאֵל,
בַּעֲגָלָא וּבִזְמַן קָרִיב, וְאִמְרוּ אָמֵן.

יְהֵא שְׁמֵהּ רַבָּא מְבָרַךְ לְעָלַם וּלְעָלְמֵי עָלְמַיָּא.

יִתְבָּרַךְ וְיִשְׁתַּבַּח, וְיִתְפָּאַר וְיִתְרוֹמַם, וְיִתְנַשֵּׂא וְיִתְהַדָּר,
וְיִתְעַלֶּה וְיִתְהַלָּל שְׁמֵהּ דְּקֻדְשָׁא, בְּרִיךְ הוּא, לְעֵלָּא* (לְעֵלָּא)
מִן כָּל בִּרְכָתָא וְשִׁירָתָא, תֻּשְׁבְּחָתָא וְנֶחֱמָתָא, דַּאֲמִירָן בְּעָלְמָא,
וְאִמְרוּ אָמֵן.

יְהֵא שְׁלָמָא רַבָּא מִן שְׁמַיָּא, וְחַיִּים, עָלֵינוּ וְעַל כָּל יִשְׂרָאֵל,
וְאִמְרוּ אָמֵן.

עֹשֶׂה שָׁלוֹם בִּמְרוֹמָיו, הוּא יַעֲשֶׂה שָׁלוֹם עָלֵינוּ וְעַל כָּל
יִשְׂרָאֵל, וְאִמְרוּ אָמֵן.

אַל תִּירָא מִפַּחַד פִּתְאֹם, וּמִשֹּׁאַת רְשָׁעִים כִּי תָבֹא. עֻצוּ
עֵצָה וְתֻפָר, דַּבְּרוּ דָבָר וְלֹא יָקוּם, כִּי עִמָּנוּ אֵל. וְעַד זִקְנָה
אֲנִי הוּא, וְעַד שֵׂיבָה אֲנִי אֶסְבֹּל; אֲנִי עָשִׂיתִי וַאֲנִי אֶשָּׂא, וַאֲנִי
אֶסְבֹּל וַאֲמַלֵּט.

---

*לְעֵלָּא לְעֵלָּא is said between *Rosh Hashanah* and *Yom Kippur*.

thy name, and all the wicked of the earth will be turned to thee. May all the inhabitants of the world realize and know that to thee every knee must bend, every tongue must vow allegiance. May they bend the knee and prostrate themselves before thee, Lord our God, and give honor to thy glorious name; may they all accept the yoke of thy kingdom, and do thou reign over them speedily forever and ever. For the kingdom is thine, and to all eternity thou wilt reign in glory, as it is written in thy Torah: "The Lord shall be King forever and ever."[1] And it is said: "The Lord shall be King over all the earth; on that day the Lord shall be One, and his name One."[2]

MOURNERS' KADDISH

Glorified and sanctified be God's great name throughout the world which he has created according to his will. May he establish his kingdom in your lifetime and during your days, and within the life of the entire house of Israel, speedily and soon; and say, Amen.

May his great name be blessed forever and to all eternity.

Blessed and praised, glorified and exalted, extolled and honored, adored and lauded be the name of the Holy One, blessed be he, beyond all the blessings and hymns, praises and consolations that are ever spoken in the world; and say, Amen.

May there be abundant peace from heaven, and life, for us and for all Israel; and say, Amen.

He who creates peace in his celestial heights, may he create peace for us and for all Israel; and say, Amen.

Be not afraid of sudden terror, nor of the storm that strikes the wicked. Form your plot—it shall fail; lay your plan—it shall not prevail! For God is with us. Even to your old age I will be the same; when you are gray-headed, still I will sustain you; I have made you, and I will bear you; I will sustain you and save you.[3]

---

[1] *Exodus* 15:18.   [2] *Zechariah* 14:9.   [3] *Proverbs* 3:25; *Isaiah* 8:10; 4b:4.

The following is recited from *Rosh Ḥodesh Elul* until *Simḥath Torah.*

תהלים כז

לְדָוִד. יְיָ אוֹרִי וְיִשְׁעִי, מִמִּי אִירָא; יְיָ מָעוֹז חַיַּי, מִמִּי אֶפְחָד.
בִּקְרֹב עָלַי מְרֵעִים לֶאֱכֹל אֶת בְּשָׂרִי, צָרַי וְאֹיְבַי לִי, הֵמָּה
כָשְׁלוּ וְנָפָלוּ. אִם תַּחֲנֶה עָלַי מַחֲנֶה, לֹא יִירָא לִבִּי; אִם תָּקוּם
עָלַי מִלְחָמָה, בְּזֹאת אֲנִי בוֹטֵחַ. אַחַת שָׁאַלְתִּי מֵאֵת יְיָ, אוֹתָהּ
אֲבַקֵּשׁ: שִׁבְתִּי בְּבֵית יְיָ כָּל יְמֵי חַיַּי, לַחֲזוֹת בְּנֹעַם יְיָ, וּלְבַקֵּר
בְּהֵיכָלוֹ. כִּי יִצְפְּנֵנִי בְּסֻכֹּה בְּיוֹם רָעָה, יַסְתִּרֵנִי בְּסֵתֶר אָהֳלוֹ;
בְּצוּר יְרוֹמְמֵנִי. וְעַתָּה יָרוּם רֹאשִׁי עַל אֹיְבַי סְבִיבוֹתַי, וְאֶזְבְּחָה
בְאָהֳלוֹ זִבְחֵי תְרוּעָה; אָשִׁירָה וַאֲזַמְּרָה לַיְיָ. שְׁמַע, יְיָ, קוֹלִי
אֶקְרָא, וְחָנֵּנִי וַעֲנֵנִי. לְךָ אָמַר לִבִּי, בַּקְּשׁוּ פָנָי; אֶת פָּנֶיךָ, יְיָ,
אֲבַקֵּשׁ. אַל תַּסְתֵּר פָּנֶיךָ מִמֶּנִּי, אַל תַּט בְּאַף עַבְדֶּךָ, עֶזְרָתִי
הָיִיתָ; אַל תִּטְּשֵׁנִי וְאַל תַּעַזְבֵנִי, אֱלֹהֵי יִשְׁעִי. כִּי אָבִי וְאִמִּי
עֲזָבוּנִי, וַיְיָ יַאַסְפֵנִי. הוֹרֵנִי יְיָ דַּרְכֶּךָ, וּנְחֵנִי בְּאֹרַח מִישׁוֹר, לְמַעַן
שׁוֹרְרָי. אַל תִּתְּנֵנִי בְּנֶפֶשׁ צָרָי, כִּי קָמוּ בִי עֵדֵי שֶׁקֶר וִיפֵחַ חָמָס.
לוּלֵא הֶאֱמַנְתִּי לִרְאוֹת בְּטוּב יְיָ בְּאֶרֶץ חַיִּים. Reader. קַוֵּה אֶל יְיָ,
חֲזַק וְיַאֲמֵץ לִבֶּךָ, וְקַוֵּה אֶל יְיָ.

Mourners' Kaddish.

אֲדוֹן עוֹלָם

בְּטֶרֶם כָּל יְצִיר נִבְרָא.	אֲדוֹן עוֹלָם אֲשֶׁר מָלַךְ
אֲזַי מֶלֶךְ שְׁמוֹ נִקְרָא,	לְעֵת נַעֲשָׂה בְחֶפְצוֹ כֹּל
לְבַדּוֹ יִמְלוֹךְ נוֹרָא.	וְאַחֲרֵי כִּכְלוֹת הַכֹּל
וְהוּא יִהְיֶה בְּתִפְאָרָה.	וְהוּא הָיָה וְהוּא הֹוֶה
לְהַמְשִׁיל לוֹ לְהַחְבִּירָה.	וְהוּא אֶחָד וְאֵין שֵׁנִי
וְלוֹ הָעֹז וְהַמִּשְׂרָה.	בְּלִי רֵאשִׁית בְּלִי תַכְלִית

The following is recited from Rosh Ḥodesh Elul until Simḥath Torah

Psalm 27

A psalm of David. The Lord is my light and aid; whom shall I fear? The Lord is the stronghold of my life; of whom shall I be afraid? When evildoers press against me to eat up my flesh—my enemies and my foes—it is they who stumble and fall. Even though an army were arrayed against me, my heart would not fear; though war should arise against me, still would I be confident. One thing I ask from the Lord, one thing I desire—that I may dwell in the house of the Lord all the days of my life, to behold the pleasantness of the Lord, and to meditate in his sanctuary. Surely, he will hide me within his own tabernacle in the day of distress; he will conceal me in the shelter of his tent; he will set me safe upon a rock. Thus my head shall be high above all my foes around me; I will offer sacrifices within his tabernacle to the sound of trumpets; I will sing and chant praises to the Lord. Hear, O Lord, my voice when I call; be gracious to me and answer me. In thy behalf my heart has said: "Seek you my presence"; thy presence, O Lord, I do seek. Hide not thy face from me; turn not thy servant away in anger; thou hast been my help; do not abandon me, forsake me not, O God my savior. Though my father and mother have forsaken me, the Lord will take care of me. Teach me thy way, O Lord, and guide me in a straight path, in spite of my enemies. Deliver me not to the will of my adversaries; for false witnesses have risen up against me, such as breathe forth violence. I do believe I shall yet see the goodness of the Lord in the land of the living. Hope in the Lord; be strong, and let your heart be brave; yes, hope in the Lord.

Mourners' Kaddish.

ADON OLAM

He is the eternal Lord who reigned
Before any being was created.
At the time when all was made by his will,
He was at once acknowledged as King.
And at the end, when all shall cease to be,
The revered God alone shall still be King.
He was, he is, and he shall be
In glorious eternity.
He is One, and there is no other
To compare to him, to place beside him.
He is without beginning, without end;
Power and dominion belong to him.

וְהוּא אֵלִי וְחַי גּוֹאֲלִי וְצוּר חֶבְלִי בְּעֵת צָרָה׃

וְהוּא נִסִּי וּמָנוֹס לִי מְנָת כּוֹסִי בְּיוֹם אֶקְרָא׃

בְּיָדוֹ אַפְקִיד רוּחִי בְּעֵת אִישָׁן וְאָעִירָה׃

וְעִם רוּחִי גְּוִיָּתִי יְיָ לִי וְלֹא אִירָא׃

Upon returning from synagogue:

שָׁלוֹם עֲלֵיכֶם, מַלְאֲכֵי הַשָּׁרֵת, מַלְאֲכֵי עֶלְיוֹן, מִמֶּלֶךְ מַלְכֵי הַמְּלָכִים, הַקָּדוֹשׁ בָּרוּךְ הוּא.

בּוֹאֲכֶם לְשָׁלוֹם, מַלְאֲכֵי הַשָּׁלוֹם, מַלְאֲכֵי עֶלְיוֹן, מִמֶּלֶךְ מַלְכֵי הַמְּלָכִים, הַקָּדוֹשׁ בָּרוּךְ הוּא.

בָּרְכוּנִי לְשָׁלוֹם, מַלְאֲכֵי הַשָּׁלוֹם, מַלְאֲכֵי עֶלְיוֹן, מִמֶּלֶךְ מַלְכֵי הַמְּלָכִים, הַקָּדוֹשׁ בָּרוּךְ הוּא.

צֵאתְכֶם לְשָׁלוֹם, מַלְאֲכֵי הַשָּׁלוֹם, מַלְאֲכֵי עֶלְיוֹן, מִמֶּלֶךְ מַלְכֵי הַמְּלָכִים, הַקָּדוֹשׁ בָּרוּךְ הוּא.

כִּי מַלְאָכָיו יְצַוֶּה לָּךְ, לִשְׁמָרְךָ בְּכָל דְּרָכֶיךָ. יְיָ יִשְׁמָר־צֵאתְךָ וּבוֹאֶךָ, מֵעַתָּה וְעַד עוֹלָם.

רִבּוֹן כָּל הָעוֹלָמִים, אֲדוֹן כָּל הַנְּשָׁמוֹת, אֲדוֹן הַשָּׁלוֹם, מֶלֶךְ אַבִּיר, מֶלֶךְ בָּרוּךְ, מֶלֶךְ גָּדוֹל, מֶלֶךְ דּוֹבֵר שָׁלוֹם, מֶלֶךְ הָדוּר, מֶלֶךְ וָתִיק, מֶלֶךְ זַךְ, מֶלֶךְ חֵי הָעוֹלָמִים, מֶלֶךְ טוֹב וּמֵטִיב, מֶלֶךְ יָחִיד וּמְיֻחָד, מֶלֶךְ כַּבִּיר, מֶלֶךְ לוֹבֵשׁ רַחֲמִים, מֶלֶךְ מַלְכֵי הַמְּלָכִים, מֶלֶךְ נִשְׂגָּב, מֶלֶךְ סוֹמֵךְ נוֹפְלִים, מֶלֶךְ עוֹשֶׂה מַעֲשֵׂה בְרֵאשִׁית, מֶלֶךְ פּוֹדֶה וּמַצִּיל, מֶלֶךְ צַח וְאָדוֹם, מֶלֶךְ קָדוֹשׁ, מֶלֶךְ רָם וְנִשָּׂא, מֶלֶךְ שׁוֹמֵעַ תְּפִלָּה, מֶלֶךְ תָּמִים דַּרְכּוֹ.

שלום עליכם was introduced by the Kabbalists some three hundred years ago. This song of peace is based on the talmudic passage concerning a good angel and an evil angel accompanying every man home from the synagogue

He is my God, my living Redeemer,
My stronghold in times of distress.
He is my guide and my refuge,
My share of bliss the day I call.
To him I entrust my spirit
When I sleep and when I wake.
As long as my soul is with my body
The Lord is with me; I am not afraid.

Upon returning from synagogue:

Peace be with you, ministering angels, angels of the Most High, the supreme King of kings, the Holy One, blessed be he.

May your coming be in peace, messengers of peace, angels of the Most High, the supreme King of kings, the Holy One, blessed be he.

Bless me with peace, messengers of peace, angels of the Most High, the supreme King of kings, the Holy One, blessed be he.

May your departure be in peace, messengers of peace, angels of the Most High, the supreme King of kings, the Holy One, blessed be he.

He will give his angels charge over you, to guard you in all your ways. The Lord will guard you as you come and go, henceforth and forever.[1]

Meditation

Sovereign of all worlds, Master of all souls, Lord of peace, thou art the life of the universe, the Only One, the beneficent and merciful King of kings, who supportest all who fall; thou art the Creator, the holy and most exalted King, who hearest prayer, redeemest and deliverest; thou art the King whose way is perfect.

---

on Friday evening. If they find the house in good order, the good angel says: "May the next Sabbath be as this one." If, on the other hand, they find the house neglected, the evil angel says: "May the next Sabbath be as this one." The reading מלך, instead of ממלך, is preferred by Rabbi Jacob Emden and others.

רבון כל העולמים is attributed to Rabbi Joseph of Rashkow, Posen, who lived towards the end of the eighteenth century. The adjectives in the first paragraph are in alphabetic order.

---

[1] *Psalms* 91:11; 121:8.

מוֹדֶה אֲנִי לְפָנֶיךָ, יְיָ אֱלֹהַי וֵאלֹהֵי אֲבוֹתַי, עַל כָּל הַחֶסֶד
אֲשֶׁר עָשִׂיתָ עִמָּדִי, וַאֲשֶׁר אַתָּה עָתִיד לַעֲשׂוֹת עִמִּי וְעִם כָּל בְּנֵי
בֵיתִי וְעִם כָּל בְּרִיּוֹתֶיךָ, בְּנֵי בְרִיתִי, וּבְרוּכִים הֵם מַלְאָכֶיךָ
הַקְּדוֹשִׁים וְהַטְּהוֹרִים שֶׁעוֹשִׂים רְצוֹנֶךָ. אֲדוֹן הַשָּׁלוֹם, מֶלֶךְ
שֶׁהַשָּׁלוֹם שֶׁלּוֹ, בָּרְכֵנִי בַשָּׁלוֹם, וְתִפְקֹד אוֹתִי וְאֶת כָּל בְּנֵי בֵיתִי,
וְכָל עַמְּךָ בֵּית יִשְׂרָאֵל, לְחַיִּים טוֹבִים וּלְשָׁלוֹם. מֶלֶךְ עֶלְיוֹן
עַל כָּל צְבָא מָרוֹם, יוֹצְרֵנוּ, יוֹצֵר בְּרֵאשִׁית, אֲחַלֶּה פָנֶיךָ
הַמְּאִירִים, שֶׁתְּזַכֶּה אוֹתִי וְאֶת כָּל בְּנֵי בֵיתִי לִמְצֹא חֵן וְשֵׂכֶל
טוֹב בְּעֵינֶיךָ וּבְעֵינֵי כָל בְּנֵי אָדָם, וּבְעֵינֵי כָל רוֹאֵינוּ,
לַעֲבוֹדָתֶךָ. וְזַכֵּנוּ לְקַבֵּל שַׁבָּתוֹת מִתּוֹךְ רֹב שִׂמְחָה, וּמִתּוֹךְ עֹשֶׁר
וְכָבוֹד, וּמִתּוֹךְ מִעוּט עֲוֹנוֹת; וְהָסֵר מִמֶּנִּי וּמִכָּל בְּנֵי בֵיתִי, וּמִכָּל
עַמְּךָ בֵּית יִשְׂרָאֵל, כָּל מִינֵי חֹלִי וְכָל מִינֵי מַדְוֶה, וְכָל מִינֵי
דַלּוּת וַעֲנִיּוּת וְאֶבְיוֹנוּת; וְתֶן־בָּנוּ יֵצֶר טוֹב לְעָבְדְךָ בֶּאֱמֶת
וּבְיִרְאָה וּבְאַהֲבָה. וְנִהְיֶה מְכֻבָּדִים בְּעֵינֶיךָ וּבְעֵינֵי כָל רוֹאֵינוּ,
כִּי אַתָּה הוּא מֶלֶךְ הַכָּבוֹד, כִּי לְךָ נָאֶה, כִּי לְךָ יָאֶה. אָנָּא,
מֶלֶךְ מַלְכֵי הַמְּלָכִים, צַוֵּה לְמַלְאָכֶיךָ, מַלְאֲכֵי הַשָּׁרֵת, מְשָׁרְתֵי
עֶלְיוֹן, שֶׁיִּפְקְדוּנִי בְּרַחֲמִים, וִיבָרְכוּנִי בְּבוֹאָם לְבֵיתִי בְּיוֹם
קָדְשֵׁנוּ; כִּי הִדְלַקְתִּי נֵרוֹתַי, וְהִצַּעְתִּי מִטָּתִי, וְהֶחֱלַפְתִּי שִׂמְלוֹתַי
לִכְבוֹד יוֹם הַשַּׁבָּת, וּבָאתִי לְבֵיתְךָ לְהַפִּיל תְּחִנָּתִי לְפָנֶיךָ
שֶׁתַּעֲבִיר אַנְחָתִי, וָאָעִיד אֲשֶׁר בָּרֵאתָ בְּשִׁשָּׁה יָמִים כָּל הַיְצוּר;
וָאֶשְׁנֶה וַאֲשַׁלֵּשׁ עוֹד לְהָעִיד עַל כּוֹסִי בְּתוֹךְ שִׂמְחָתִי, כַּאֲשֶׁר
צִוִּיתַנִי לְזָכְרוֹ וּלְהִתְעַנֵּג בְּיֶתֶר נִשְׁמָתִי אֲשֶׁר נָתַתָּ בִּי. בּוֹ אֶשְׁבֹּת
כַּאֲשֶׁר צִוִּיתַנִי לְשָׁרְתֶךָ, וְכֵן אַגִּיד גְּדֻלָּתְךָ בְרִנָּה. וְשִׁוִּיתִי יְיָ
לְקִרְאָתִי, שֶׁתְּרַחֲמֵנִי עוֹד בְּגָלוּתִי לְגָאֳלֵנִי וּלְעוֹרֵר לִבִּי

I render thanks to thee, Lord my God and God of my fathers, for all the kindness that thou hast shown me and art ready to show me and my family and my friends, thy creatures. Blessed be thy holy angels who perform thy will. Lord of peace, bless me with peace. Remember me and my family, and all thy people the house of Israel, for a happy and peaceful life. Supreme King, our Creator and Creator of the universe, grant that I and my family find favor in thy sight and in the sight of the people we meet. Enable us to welcome the Sabbaths amid wealth, honor and sinlessness. O remove all sickness and suffering and poverty from me and my family and all thy people, the house of Israel. Inspire us to serve thee sincerely, reverently and eagerly. May we be distinguished in thy sight and in the sight of the people we meet. Thou art indeed the King of glory, for all glory is thine.

Supreme King of kings, command the heavenly angels to visit my house in mercy and to bless me on our holy day. I kindled my lights, arranged my bed and changed my garments in honor of the Sabbath, and I entered thy house to petition thee to remove my sighing. I affirmed that thou didst create the universe in six days; twice again will I affirm this over my cup while I celebrate, as thou didst command me to remember the Sabbath and to enjoy it with all my soul, which thou hast placed within me. I will rest on the Sabbath, as thou didst command me, and I will sing thy greatness. I am mindful of thy presence, O Lord; have mercy on me while I am still in captivity; set me free, and stir my heart to

לְאַהֲבָתֶךָ, וְאָז אֶשְׁמֹר פִּקּוּדֶיךָ וְחֻקֶּיךָ בְּלִי עֶצֶב, וְאֶתְפַּלֵּל כַּדָּת, כָּרָאוּי וּכְנָכוֹן. מַלְאֲכֵי הַשָּׁלוֹם, בּוֹאֲכֶם לְשָׁלוֹם, בָּרְכוּנִי לְשָׁלוֹם, וְאִמְרוּ בָּרוּךְ לְשֻׁלְחָנִי הֶעָרוּךְ, וְצֵאתְכֶם לְשָׁלוֹם, מֵעַתָּה וְעַד עוֹלָם, אָמֵן סֶלָה.

משלי לא, י–לא

אֵשֶׁת חַיִל מִי יִמְצָא	וְרָחֹק מִפְּנִינִים מִכְרָהּ.
בָּטַח בָּהּ לֵב בַּעְלָהּ	וְשָׁלָל לֹא יֶחְסָר.
גְּמָלַתְהוּ טוֹב וְלֹא רָע	כֹּל יְמֵי חַיֶּיהָ.
דָּרְשָׁה צֶמֶר וּפִשְׁתִּים	וַתַּעַשׂ בְּחֵפֶץ כַּפֶּיהָ.
הָיְתָה כָּאֳנִיּוֹת סוֹחֵר	מִמֶּרְחָק תָּבִיא לַחְמָהּ.
וַתָּקָם בְּעוֹד לַיְלָה	וַתִּתֵּן טֶרֶף לְבֵיתָהּ
וְחֹק לְנַעֲרֹתֶיהָ.	
זָמְמָה שָׂדֶה וַתִּקָּחֵהוּ	מִפְּרִי כַפֶּיהָ נָטְעָה כָּרֶם.
חָגְרָה בְעוֹז מָתְנֶיהָ	וַתְּאַמֵּץ זְרוֹעֹתֶיהָ.
טָעֲמָה כִּי טוֹב סַחְרָהּ	לֹא יִכְבֶּה בַלַּיְלָה נֵרָהּ.
יָדֶיהָ שִׁלְּחָה בַכִּישׁוֹר	וְכַפֶּיהָ תָּמְכוּ פָלֶךְ.
כַּפָּהּ פָּרְשָׂה לֶעָנִי	וְיָדֶיהָ שִׁלְּחָה לָאֶבְיוֹן.
לֹא תִירָא לְבֵיתָהּ מִשָּׁלֶג	כִּי כָל בֵּיתָהּ לָבֻשׁ שָׁנִים.
מַרְבַדִּים עָשְׂתָה לָּהּ	שֵׁשׁ וְאַרְגָּמָן לְבוּשָׁהּ.
נוֹדָע בַּשְּׁעָרִים בַּעְלָהּ	בְּשִׁבְתּוֹ עִם זִקְנֵי אָרֶץ.
סָדִין עָשְׂתָה וַתִּמְכֹּר	וַחֲגוֹר נָתְנָה לַכְּנַעֲנִי.
עֹז וְהָדָר לְבוּשָׁהּ	וַתִּשְׂחַק לְיוֹם אַחֲרוֹן.

אשת חיל is an acrostic poem in which the verses begin with the letters of the alphabeth in regular order. It describes the perfect housewife, trusted by her husband, obeyed by her servants, and admired by the people. She is kind to the poor and gentle to all; she is self-respecting and dignified. Husband and children praise her as the source of their happiness.

love thee. Without discomfort will I then keep thy ordinances and thy laws, and worship thee properly and correctly.

Angels of peace, may your coming be in peace; bless me with peace, and bless my prepared table. May your departure be in peace, henceforth and forever. Amen.

Proverbs 31:10–31

A good wife who can find?
She is worth far more than rubies.
Her husband trusts in her,
And he never lacks gain.
She brings him good and not harm,
All the days of her life.
She seeks out wool and flax,
And works with her willing hands.
She is like the merchant ships—
She brings her food from afar.
She rises while it is yet night,
And gives food to her household,
And rations to her maids.
She considers a field and buys it;
With her earnings she plants a vineyard.
She girds herself with strength,
And braces her arms for work.
She finds that her trade is profitable;
Her lamp goes not out at night.
She sets her hands to the distaff;
Her fingers hold the spindle.
She stretches out her hand to the poor;
She reaches out her arms to the needy.
She is not afraid of the snow for her household,
For all her household is clad in scarlet wool.
She makes her own tapestries;
Her clothing is fine linen and purple.
Her husband is known at the gates,
As he sits among the elders of the land.
She makes linen cloth and sells it;
She supplies the merchants with girdles.
Dignity and honor are her garb;
She smiles looking at the future.

וְתוֹרַת חֶסֶד עַל לְשׁוֹנָהּ.	פִּיהָ פָּתְחָה בְחָכְמָה
וְלֶחֶם עַצְלוּת לֹא תֹאכֵל.	צוֹפִיָּה הֲלִיכוֹת בֵּיתָהּ
בַּעְלָהּ וַיְהַלְלָהּ.	קָמוּ בָנֶיהָ וַיְאַשְּׁרוּהָ
וְאַתְּ עָלִית עַל כֻּלָּנָה.	רַבּוֹת בָּנוֹת עָשׂוּ חָיִל
אִשָּׁה יִרְאַת יְיָ הִיא תִתְהַלָּל.	שֶׁקֶר הַחֵן וְהֶבֶל הַיֹּפִי
וִיהַלְלוּהָ בַשְּׁעָרִים מַעֲשֶׂיהָ.	תְּנוּ לָהּ מִפְּרִי יָדֶיהָ

קִדּוּשׁ

Recited before the Sabbath meal

וַיְהִי עֶרֶב וַיְהִי בֹקֶר

יוֹם הַשִּׁשִּׁי. וַיְכֻלּוּ הַשָּׁמַיִם וְהָאָרֶץ וְכָל צְבָאָם. וַיְכַל אֱלֹהִים
בַּיּוֹם הַשְּׁבִיעִי מְלַאכְתּוֹ אֲשֶׁר עָשָׂה, וַיִּשְׁבֹּת בַּיּוֹם הַשְּׁבִיעִי מִכָּל
מְלַאכְתּוֹ אֲשֶׁר עָשָׂה. וַיְבָרֶךְ אֱלֹהִים אֶת יוֹם הַשְּׁבִיעִי וַיְקַדֵּשׁ
אֹתוֹ, כִּי בוֹ שָׁבַת מִכָּל מְלַאכְתּוֹ אֲשֶׁר בָּרָא אֱלֹהִים לַעֲשׂוֹת.

סַבְרִי מָרָנָן וְרַבּוֹתַי.

בָּרוּךְ אַתָּה, יְיָ אֱלֹהֵינוּ, מֶלֶךְ הָעוֹלָם, בּוֹרֵא פְּרִי הַגָּפֶן.

בָּרוּךְ אַתָּה, יְיָ אֱלֹהֵינוּ, מֶלֶךְ הָעוֹלָם, אֲשֶׁר קִדְּשָׁנוּ בְּמִצְוֹתָיו
וְרָצָה בָנוּ, וְשַׁבַּת קָדְשׁוֹ בְּאַהֲבָה וּבְרָצוֹן הִנְחִילָנוּ, זִכָּרוֹן
לְמַעֲשֵׂה בְרֵאשִׁית. כִּי הוּא יוֹם תְּחִלָּה לְמִקְרָאֵי קֹדֶשׁ, זֵכֶר
לִיצִיאַת מִצְרָיִם. כִּי בָנוּ בָחַרְתָּ וְאוֹתָנוּ קִדַּשְׁתָּ מִכָּל הָעַמִּים,
וְשַׁבַּת קָדְשְׁךָ בְּאַהֲבָה וּבְרָצוֹן הִנְחַלְתָּנוּ. בָּרוּךְ אַתָּה, יְיָ,
מְקַדֵּשׁ הַשַּׁבָּת.

קידוש recited at home over wine, the symbol of joy, is attributed to the
men of the Great Assembly who flourished during the early period of the
Second Temple. It is referred to as **קידוש היום**, "the sanctification of the day"

She opens her mouth with wisdom,
And kindly counsel is on her tongue.
She looks after her household;
She never eats the bread of idleness.
Her children rise and bless her,
And her husband praises her, saying:
"Many women do worthily,
But you excel them all."
Charm is deceptive, and beauty is vain;
Only a God-fearing woman shall be praised.
Give her due credit for her achievement;
Let her own works praise her at the gates.

KIDDUSH

Recited before the Sabbath meal.

There was evening and there was morning—
The sixth day. Thus the heavens and the earth were finished,
and all their host. By the seventh day God had completed his
work which he had made, and he rested on the seventh day from
all his work in which he had been engaged. Then God blessed the
seventh day and hallowed it, because on it he rested from all his
work which he had created.[1]

Blessed art thou, Lord our God, King of the universe, who
createst the fruit of the vine.

Blessed art thou, Lord our God, King of the universe, who
hast sanctified us with thy commandments and hast been pleased
with us; thou hast graciously given us thy holy Sabbath as a heritage, in remembrance of the creation. The Sabbath is the first
among the holy festivals which recall the exodus from Egypt. Indeed, thou hast chosen us and hallowed us above all nations, and
hast graciously given us thy holy Sabbath as a heritage. Blessed
art thou, O Lord, who hallowest the Sabbath.

(Pesaḥim 105a). When wine is not available, the *Kiddush* is pronounced over
two loaves of bread which are in memory of the double portion of manna that
was gathered on Fridays.

---

[1] *Genesis* 1:31; 2:1–3.

זְמִירוֹת לְלֵיל שַׁבָּת

Chanted at the table

כָּל מְקַדֵּשׁ שְׁבִיעִי כָּרָאוּי לוֹ, כָּל שׁוֹמֵר שַׁבָּת כַּדָּת מֵחַלְּלוֹ, שְׂכָרוֹ הַרְבֵּה מְאֹד עַל פִּי פָעֳלוֹ, אִישׁ עַל מַחֲנֵהוּ וְאִישׁ עַל דִּגְלוֹ.

אֹהֲבֵי יְיָ הַמְחַכִּים לְבִנְיַן אֲרִיאֵל, בְּיוֹם הַשַּׁבָּת שִׂישׂוּ וְשִׂמְחוּ כִּמְקַבְּלֵי מַתַּן נַחֲלִיאֵל, גַּם שְׂאוּ יְדֵכֶם קֹדֶשׁ וְאִמְרוּ לָאֵל, בָּרוּךְ יְיָ אֲשֶׁר נָתַן מְנוּחָה לְעַמּוֹ יִשְׂרָאֵל.

דּוֹרְשֵׁי יְיָ זֶרַע אַבְרָהָם אוֹהֲבוֹ, הַמְאַחֲרִים לָצֵאת מִן הַשַּׁבָּת וּמְמַהֲרִים לָבֹא, וּשְׂמֵחִים לְשָׁמְרוֹ וּלְעָרֵב עֵרוּבוֹ, זֶה הַיּוֹם עָשָׂה יְיָ נָגִילָה וְנִשְׂמְחָה בוֹ.

זִכְרוּ תּוֹרַת מֹשֶׁה בְּמִצְוַת שַׁבָּת גְּרוּסָה, חֲרוּתָה לַיּוֹם הַשְּׁבִיעִי כְּכַלָּה בֵּין רֵעוֹתֶיהָ מְשֻׁבָּצָה, טְהוֹרִים יִירָשׁוּהָ וִיקַדְּשׁוּהוּ בְּמַאֲמַר כָּל אֲשֶׁר עָשָׂה, וַיְכַל אֱלֹהִים בַּיּוֹם הַשְּׁבִיעִי מְלַאכְתּוֹ אֲשֶׁר עָשָׂה.

יוֹם קָדוֹשׁ הוּא מִבּוֹאוֹ וְעַד צֵאתוֹ, כָּל זֶרַע יַעֲקֹב יְכַבְּדוּהוּ כִּדְבַר הַמֶּלֶךְ וְדָתוֹ, לָנוּחַ בּוֹ וְלִשְׂמוֹחַ בְּתַעֲנוּג אָכוֹל וְשָׁתוֹ, כָּל עֲדַת יִשְׂרָאֵל יַעֲשׂוּ אוֹתוֹ.

זמירות became particularly popular during the sixteenth century through kabbalistic influence. These songs, composed at a much earlier date, are not a mere glorification of food and drink, but an appreciation of God's continual vigilance. They sum up the very essence of holy joyousness which has been the keynote of Judaism. The love for song gave rise to many Hebrew poets, whose hymns were frequently collected and published by various congre-

SABBATH EVE HYMNS
Chanted at the table

Whoever duly observes the Sabbath,
Whoever keeps the Sabbath unprofaned,
Shall be greatly rewarded for his deed,
Each in his own camp, each in his own home.

Friends of the Lord, you who yearn for the Temple,
Enjoy the Sabbath, welcome the Torah's gift;
Lift up your hands to the shrine and praise God,
Who has granted rest to his people Israel.

You who seek the Lord, children of Abraham,
Late to end Sabbath, early to welcome it,
Glad to protect it and form its *eruv*,
This is the Lord's day, let us rejoice in it!

Heed the Sabbath law in Moses' Torah,
Arrayed like a bride amid her maids;
The pure keep it holy while proclaiming:
On the seventh day God finished his work.

A holy day from sunset to sunset,
Let all Jacob's seed honor God's command
By resting and feasting on the Sabbath;
All the people of Israel must keep it!

---

gations. Only a small number of the hundreds of *Zemiroth* by many medieval poets may be found in the current editions of the *Siddur*.

כל מקדש was probably composed by Rabbi Moses ben Kalonymus who lived in Mayence towards the end of the tenth century. His name משה is given as an acrostic in the first stanza, and is formed from the initial letters of the words שמר, מקדש and הרבה. Each stanza of the poem כל מקדש consists of four verses, the last of which being a quotation from the Bible. The quotations are taken from Numbers 1:52; I Kings 8:56; Psalm 118:24; Genesis 2:2; Exodus 12:47; Psalm 36:9; I Samuel 14:41. Beginning with the second stanza, the poem is alphabetically arranged. The last stanza, which completes the

מְשׁוֹךְ חַסְדְּךָ לְיוֹדְעֶיךָ אֵל קַנּוֹא וְנוֹקֵם, נוֹטְרֵי יוֹם הַשְּׁבִיעִי זָכוֹר וְשָׁמוֹר לְהָקֵם, שַׂמְּחֵם בְּבִנְיַן שָׁלֵם וּבְאוֹר פָּנֶיךָ תַּבְהִיקֵם, יִרְוְיֻן מִדֶּשֶׁן בֵּיתֶךָ וְנַחַל עֲדָנֶיךָ תַשְׁקֵם.

עֲזוֹר לַשּׁוֹבְתִים בַּשְּׁבִיעִי בֶּחָרִישׁ וּבַקָּצִיר לְעוֹלָמִים, פּוֹסְעִים בּוֹ פְּסִיעָה קְטַנָּה סוֹעֲדִים בּוֹ לְבָרֵךְ שָׁלֹשׁ פְּעָמִים, צִדְקָתָם תַּצְהִיר כְּאוֹר שִׁבְעַת הַיָּמִים, יְיָ אֱלֹהֵי יִשְׂרָאֵל הָבָה תָמִים.

מְנוּחָה וְשִׂמְחָה אוֹר לַיְּהוּדִים, יוֹם שַׁבָּתוֹן יוֹם מַחֲמַדִּים, שׁוֹמְרָיו וְזוֹכְרָיו הֵמָּה מְעִידִים, כִּי לְשִׁשָּׁה כֹּל בְּרוּאִים וְעוֹמְדִים.

שְׁמֵי שָׁמַיִם אֶרֶץ וְיַמִּים, כָּל צְבָא מָרוֹם גְּבוֹהִים וְרָמִים, תַּנִּין וְאָדָם וְחַיַּת רְאֵמִים, כִּי בְּיָהּ יְיָ צוּר עוֹלָמִים.

הוּא אֲשֶׁר דִּבֶּר לְעַם סְגֻלָּתוֹ, שָׁמוֹר לְקַדְּשׁוֹ מִבֹּא וְעַד צֵאתוֹ, שַׁבַּת קֹדֶשׁ יוֹם חֶמְדָּתוֹ, כִּי בוֹ שָׁבַת מִכָּל מְלַאכְתּוֹ.

בְּמִצְוַת שַׁבָּת אֵל יַחֲלִיצָךְ, קוּם קְרָא אֵלָיו יָחוּשׁ לְאַמְּצָךְ, נִשְׁמַת כָּל חַי וְגַם נַעֲרִיצָךְ, אֱכֹל בְּשִׂמְחָה כִּי כְבָר רָצָךְ.

בְּמִשְׁנֶה לֶחֶם וְקִדּוּשׁ רַבָּה, בְּרֹב מַטְעַמִּים וְרוּחַ נְדִיבָה, יִזְכּוּ לְרַב טוּב מִתְעַנְּגִים בָּהּ, בְּבִיאַת גּוֹאֵל לְעוֹלָם הַבָּא.

------

alphabet, may be supplied from Maḥzor Vitry (page 147) where the entire poem is cited. The last stanza, according to Maḥzor Vitry, reads:

קַדְּשֵׁם בְּמִצְוֹתֶיךָ וְטַהֲרֵם כְּעֶצֶם הַשָּׁמַיִם לָטֹהַר
רוּחֲךָ תְּנִיחֵמוֹ כַּבְּהֵמָה תֵּרֵד בַּבִּקְעָה מִן הָהָר (Isaiah 63:14)
שַׁבָּתָם תְּשַׁכְּנֵם בְּנַחֲלַת הַסַּהַר
כִּנְחָלִים נִטָּיוּ עֲלֵי נָהָר (Numbers 24:6).

מנוחה ושמחה is an acrostic, the initial letters of the first three stanzas form-ing the author's name, משה. The unidentified poet speaks of the Sabbath as a

Grant thy love to those who know thee, O God,
Those who keep the laws of the seventh day;
Cheer them, show them thy grace, rebuild Zion,
Let them eat and drink of thy land's delights.

Ever help those who rest on the Sabbath,
Taking small strides and saying grace thrice;
May their goodliness shine sevenfold strong!
O Lord, God of Israel, declare the right.

Repose and gladness, a light to the Jews,
The day of Sabbath is a day of bliss;
Those who observe it give testimony
That in six days all things were created:

The highest heavens, the land and the seas,
All the celestial hosts, lofty and great,
Sea-monster as well as man and wild beast;
Indeed, God is Creator of all worlds.

He it is who bade his chosen people:
Keep it holy from sunset to sunset;
The holy Sabbath is his beloved day,
For on it he rested from all his work.

By the Sabbath command God makes you strong;
Arise, call upon him; soon will he strengthen you;
Read the prayers, *Nishmath* and *Kedushah*,
Then eat with joy, for he is pleased with you.

Recite the day's *Kiddush* over twin loaves;
Be generous with abundant dainties;
All who enjoy the Sabbath shall merit
The future world when the redeemer comes.

------

day of rest and joy to those who recite the *Kiddush*, proclaiming that God
created the universe in six days. He concludes with a wish for a speedy deliverance of those who observe the Sabbath properly.

יָהּ רִבּוֹן עָלַם וְעָלְמַיָּא, אַנְתְּ הוּא מַלְכָּא מֶלֶךְ מַלְכַיָּא, עוֹבַד
גְּבוּרְתֵּךְ וְתִמְהַיָּא, שְׁפַר קָדְמַי לְהַחֲוָיָה.

יָהּ רִבּוֹן עָלַם וְעָלְמַיָּא, אַנְתְּ הוּא מַלְכָּא מֶלֶךְ מַלְכַיָּא.

שְׁבָחִין אֲסַדֵּר צַפְרָא וְרַמְשָׁא, לָךְ אֱלָהָא קַדִּישָׁא דִּי בְרָא כָל
נַפְשָׁא, עִירִין קַדִּישִׁין וּבְנֵי אֱנָשָׁא, חֵיוַת בָּרָא וְעוֹפֵי שְׁמַיָּא.

יָהּ רִבּוֹן עָלַם וְעָלְמַיָּא, אַנְתְּ הוּא מַלְכָּא מֶלֶךְ מַלְכַיָּא.

רַבְרְבִין עוֹבְדָיךְ וְתַקִּיפִין, מָכֵךְ רָמַיָּא וְזָקֵף כְּפִיפִין, לוּ יְחְיֵא
גְבַר שְׁנִין אַלְפִין, לָא יֵעַל גְּבוּרְתֵּךְ בְּחֻשְׁבְּנַיָּא.

יָהּ רִבּוֹן עָלַם וְעָלְמַיָּא, אַנְתְּ הוּא מַלְכָּא מֶלֶךְ מַלְכַיָּא.

אֱלָהָא דִּי לֵהּ יְקַר וּרְבוּתָא, פְּרֹק יָת עָנָךְ מִפֻּם אַרְיְוָתָא, וְאַפֵּק
יָת עַמָּךְ מִגּוֹ גָלוּתָא, עַמָּךְ דִּי בְחַרְתְּ מִכָּל אֻמַּיָּא.

יָהּ רִבּוֹן עָלַם וְעָלְמַיָּא, אַנְתְּ הוּא מַלְכָּא מֶלֶךְ מַלְכַיָּא.

לְמִקְדָּשָׁךְ תּוּב וּלְקֹדֶשׁ קֻדְשִׁין, אֲתַר דִּי בֵהּ יֶחֱדוּן רוּחִין וְנַפְשִׁין,
וִיזַמְּרוּן לָךְ שִׁירִין וְרַחֲשִׁין, בִּירוּשְׁלֵם קַרְתָּא דְשֻׁפְרַיָּא.

יָהּ רִבּוֹן עָלַם וְעָלְמַיָּא, אַנְתְּ הוּא מַלְכָּא מֶלֶךְ מַלְכַיָּא.

יה רבון was written in Aramaic by Rabbi Israel Najara, one of the most prolific Hebrew writers of the sixteenth century. His signature is seen in the initials of the five stanzas of this beautiful poem. At the end of the six-teenth century, he published a second and enlarged edition of his *Zemiroth Yisrael*, comprising three hundred and forty-six poems, which soon became the most popular songbook among the Jewish communities in the Orient. He was familiar with several languages, and was inspired by the kabbalistic school of Rabbi Isaac Luria at Safed, Palestine. His song *Yah Ribbon*, which

Lord, eternal Master of worlds,
Thou art the supreme King of kings.
Thy mighty acts and wondrous deeds
It is my pleasure to declare.

Lord, eternal Master. . .

Morning and evening I praise thee,
Holy God, who didst form all life:
Sacred spirits, human beings,
Beasts of the field, birds of the sky.

Lord, eternal Master. . .

Great and mighty are thy deeds,
Humbling the proud, raising the meek;
Were man to live a thousand years,
Yet he could not recount thy might.

Lord, eternal Master. . .

O God of glory and greatness,
Save thy flock from the lions' jaws;
Free thy people from captivity,
Thy people chosen from all nations.

Lord, eternal Master. . .

Return to thy most holy shrine,
The place where all souls will rejoice
And sing melodic hymns of praise—
Jerusalem, city of beauty.

Lord, eternal Master. . .

---

contains no allusion to the Sabbath, is chanted on Friday evenings all over the
world. After describing the wonders of God's creation, the poet concludes
with a prayer that God may redeem Israel and restore Jerusalem, the city
of beauty. The phrase שפר קדמי להחויה is borrowed from Daniel 3:32.

צוּר מִשֶּׁלּוֹ אָכַלְנוּ בָּרְכוּ אֱמוּנַי, שָׂבַעְנוּ וְהוֹתַרְנוּ כִּדְבַר יְיָ.

הַזָּן אֶת עוֹלָמוֹ, רוֹעֵנוּ אָבִינוּ, אָכַלְנוּ אֶת לַחְמוֹ, וְיֵינוֹ שָׁתִינוּ,
עַל כֵּן נוֹדֶה לִשְׁמוֹ, וּנְהַלְלוֹ בְּפִינוּ, אָמַרְנוּ וְעָנִינוּ, אֵין קָדוֹשׁ כַּיְיָ.

צוּר מִשֶּׁלּוֹ אָכַלְנוּ בָּרְכוּ אֱמוּנַי, שָׂבַעְנוּ וְהוֹתַרְנוּ כִּדְבַר יְיָ.

בְּשִׁיר וְקוֹל תּוֹדָה, נְבָרֵךְ לֵאלֹהֵינוּ, עַל אֶרֶץ חֶמְדָּה,
שֶׁהִנְחִיל לַאֲבוֹתֵינוּ, מָזוֹן וְצֵדָה הִשְׂבִּיעַ לְנַפְשֵׁנוּ, חַסְדּוֹ גָּבַר
עָלֵינוּ, וֶאֱמֶת יְיָ.

צוּר מִשֶּׁלּוֹ אָכַלְנוּ בָּרְכוּ אֱמוּנַי, שָׂבַעְנוּ וְהוֹתַרְנוּ כִּדְבַר יְיָ.

רַחֵם בְּחַסְדֶּךָ, עַל עַמְּךָ צוּרֵנוּ, עַל צִיּוֹן מִשְׁכַּן כְּבוֹדֶךָ,
זְבוּל בֵּית תִּפְאַרְתֵּנוּ בֶּן דָּוִד עַבְדֶּךָ, יָבֹא וְיִגְאָלֵנוּ, רוּחַ אַפֵּינוּ,
מְשִׁיחַ יְיָ.

צוּר מִשֶּׁלּוֹ אָכַלְנוּ בָּרְכוּ אֱמוּנַי, שָׂבַעְנוּ וְהוֹתַרְנוּ כִּדְבַר יְיָ.

יִבָּנֶה הַמִּקְדָּשׁ, עִיר צִיּוֹן תְּמַלֵּא, וְשָׁם נָשִׁיר שִׁיר חָדָשׁ,
וּבִרְנָנָה נַעֲלֶה, הָרַחֲמָן הַנִּקְדָּשׁ, יִתְבָּרַךְ וְיִתְעַלֶּה, עַל כּוֹס יַיִן
מָלֵא, כְּבִרְכַּת יְיָ.

צוּר מִשֶּׁלּוֹ אָכַלְנוּ בָּרְכוּ אֱמוּנַי, שָׂבַעְנוּ וְהוֹתַרְנוּ כִּדְבַר יְיָ.

צור משלו is of unknown authorship. This poem is an introduction to the grace recited after the meal. Its four stanzas contain the substance of that prayer. The first stanza is based on the first paragraph of the grace; the second stanza relates to the second paragraph of the grace (עודה); the third stanza corresponds to the third paragraph of the grace (רחם... על ישראל...ועל ירושלים); and the fourth stanza has reference to the grace recited over a cup of wine. This poem, though it has no bearing on the Sabbath, is not used on the busy weekdays.

My comrades, bless the Lord whose food we ate!
We ate and have some left, as God has said.

He feeds his world—our Shepherd, our Father;
His was the bread we ate, his the wine we drank;
Hence, let us thank and praise him with our lips,
Chanting: There is none holy like the Lord!

> *My comrades, bless the Lord . . .*

We praise our God with song and thanksgiving
For the good land he gave to our fathers
And for the ample sustenance he grants us;
Great is his love to us; the Lord is true.

> *My comrades, bless the Lord . . .*

Our God, O have mercy on thy people,
On Zion thy shrine and our splendid home;
May David's scion come to redeem us,
The Lord's anointed, the breath of our life.

> *My comrades, bless the Lord . . .*

Let the shrine be restored, Zion refilled,
That we may come up singing a new song;
Blessed be the Merciful, Holy One,
Over the brimful cup of wine, God's gift.

> *My comrades, bless the Lord . . .*

ברכו אמוני corresponds to the introductory phrase רבותי נברך, inviting the
table companions to recite the grace. אמוני my faithful friends. כדבר ה'
refers to II Kings 4:43 (אכול והותר 'כה אמר ה). Other biblical references are:
I Samuel 2:2; Jeremiah 3:19; 33:15; Lamentations 4:20; Isaiah 63:15; 33:5.
גבר עלינו חסדו,ואמת ה' לעולם is Psalm 117:2 transposed, which reads: חסדו גבר עלינו.

שַׁחֲרִית לְשַׁבָּת וְיוֹם טוֹב

The Preliminary Morning Service (pages 11–48) is read as on weekdays.

תהלים ל

מִזְמוֹר שִׁיר חֲנֻכַּת הַבַּיִת לְדָוִד. אֲרוֹמִמְךָ, יְיָ, כִּי דִלִּיתָנִי,
וְלֹא שִׂמַּחְתָּ אֹיְבַי לִי. יְיָ אֱלֹהָי, שִׁוַּעְתִּי אֵלֶיךָ וַתִּרְפָּאֵנִי. יְיָ,
הֶעֱלִיתָ מִן שְׁאוֹל נַפְשִׁי, חִיִּיתַנִי מִיָּרְדִי בוֹר. זַמְּרוּ לַיְיָ חֲסִידָיו,
וְהוֹדוּ לְזֵכֶר קָדְשׁוֹ. כִּי רֶגַע בְּאַפּוֹ, חַיִּים בִּרְצוֹנוֹ; בָּעֶרֶב יָלִין
בֶּכִי, וְלַבֹּקֶר רִנָּה. וַאֲנִי אָמַרְתִּי בְשַׁלְוִי, בַּל אֶמּוֹט לְעוֹלָם. יְיָ,
בִּרְצוֹנְךָ הֶעֱמַדְתָּה לְהַרְרִי עֹז; הִסְתַּרְתָּ פָנֶיךָ, הָיִיתִי נִבְהָל.
אֵלֶיךָ יְיָ אֶקְרָא, וְאֶל אֲדֹנָי אֶתְחַנָּן. מַה בֶּצַע בְּדָמִי, בְּרִדְתִּי
אֶל שָׁחַת; הֲיוֹדְךָ עָפָר, הֲיַגִּיד אֲמִתֶּךָ. שְׁמַע יְיָ וְחָנֵּנִי; יְיָ, הֱיֵה
עֹזֵר לִי. הָפַכְתָּ מִסְפְּדִי לְמָחוֹל לִי; פִּתַּחְתָּ שַׂקִּי וַתְּאַזְּרֵנִי
שִׂמְחָה. לְמַעַן יְזַמֶּרְךָ כָבוֹד, וְלֹא יִדֹּם; יְיָ אֱלֹהָי, לְעוֹלָם אוֹדֶךָּ.

MOURNERS' KADDISH

יִתְגַּדַּל וְיִתְקַדַּשׁ שְׁמֵהּ רַבָּא בְּעָלְמָא דִי בְרָא כִרְעוּתֵהּ;
וְיַמְלִיךְ מַלְכוּתֵהּ בְּחַיֵּיכוֹן וּבְיוֹמֵיכוֹן, וּבְחַיֵּי דְכָל בֵּית יִשְׂרָאֵל,
בַּעֲגָלָא וּבִזְמַן קָרִיב, וְאִמְרוּ אָמֵן.

יְהֵא שְׁמֵהּ רַבָּא מְבָרַךְ לְעָלַם וּלְעָלְמֵי עָלְמַיָּא.

יִתְבָּרַךְ וְיִשְׁתַּבַּח, וְיִתְפָּאַר וְיִתְרוֹמַם, וְיִתְנַשֵּׂא וְיִתְהַדָּר,
וְיִתְעַלֶּה וְיִתְהַלָּל שְׁמֵהּ דְּקֻדְשָׁא, בְּרִיךְ הוּא, לְעֵלָּא* (לְעֵלָּא)
מִן כָּל בִּרְכָתָא וְשִׁירָתָא, תֻּשְׁבְּחָתָא וְנֶחֱמָתָא, דַּאֲמִירָן בְּעָלְמָא,
וְאִמְרוּ אָמֵן.

---

*לְעֵלָּא לְעֵלָּא is said between *Rosh Hashanah* and *Yom Kippur*.

MORNING SERVICE FOR SABBATHS
AND FESTIVALS

The Preliminary Morning Service (pages 11–48) is read as on weekdays.

Psalm 30

A psalm, a song for the dedication of the house; by David.

I extol thee, O Lord, for thou hast lifted me, and hast not let my foes rejoice over me. Lord my God, I cried to thee, and thou didst heal me. O Lord, thou hast lifted me up from the grave; thou hast let me live, that I should not go down to the pit. Sing to the Lord, you who are godly, and give thanks to his holy name. For his anger only lasts a moment, but his favor lasts a lifetime; weeping may lodge with us at evening, but in the morning there are shouts of joy. I thought in my security I never would be shaken. O Lord, by thy favor thou hadst established my mountain as a stronghold; but when thy favor was withdrawn, I was dismayed. To thee, O Lord, I called; I appealed to my God: "What profit would my blood be, if I went down to the grave? Will the dust praise thee? Will it declare thy faithfulness? Hear, O Lord, and be gracious to me; Lord, be thou my helper." Thou hast changed my mourning into dancing; thou hast put off my sackcloth and girded me with joy; so that my soul may praise thee, and not be silent. Lord my God, I will thank thee forever.

MOURNERS' KADDISH

Glorified and sanctified be God's great name throughout the world which he has created according to his will. May he establish his kingdom in your lifetime and during your days, and within the life of the entire house of Israel, speedily and soon; and say, Amen.

May his great name be blessed forever and to all eternity.

Blessed and praised, glorified and exalted, extolled and honored, adored and lauded be the name of the Holy One, blessed be he, beyond all the blessings and hymns, praises and consolations that are ever spoken in the world; and say, Amen.

יְהֵא שְׁלָמָא רַבָּא מִן שְׁמַיָּא, וְחַיִּים, עָלֵינוּ וְעַל כָּל יִשְׂרָאֵל,
וְאִמְרוּ אָמֵן.

עֹשֶׂה שָׁלוֹם בִּמְרוֹמָיו, הוּא יַעֲשֶׂה שָׁלוֹם עָלֵינוּ וְעַל כָּל
יִשְׂרָאֵל, וְאִמְרוּ אָמֵן.

הֲרֵינִי מְזַמֵּן אֶת פִּי לְהוֹדוֹת וּלְהַלֵּל וּלְשַׁבֵּחַ אֶת בּוֹרְאִי.

בָּרוּךְ שֶׁאָמַר וְהָיָה הָעוֹלָם, בָּרוּךְ הוּא. בָּרוּךְ עֹשֶׂה
בְרֵאשִׁית, בָּרוּךְ אוֹמֵר וְעֹשֶׂה, בָּרוּךְ גּוֹזֵר וּמְקַיֵּם, בָּרוּךְ מְרַחֵם
עַל הָאָרֶץ, בָּרוּךְ מְרַחֵם עַל הַבְּרִיּוֹת, בָּרוּךְ מְשַׁלֵּם שָׂכָר טוֹב
לִירֵאָיו, בָּרוּךְ חַי לָעַד וְקַיָּם לָנֶצַח, בָּרוּךְ פּוֹדֶה וּמַצִּיל, בָּרוּךְ
שְׁמוֹ. בָּרוּךְ אַתָּה, יְיָ אֱלֹהֵינוּ, מֶלֶךְ הָעוֹלָם, הָאֵל, הָאָב
הָרַחֲמָן, הַמְהֻלָּל בְּפִי עַמּוֹ, מְשֻׁבָּח וּמְפֹאָר בִּלְשׁוֹן חֲסִידָיו
וַעֲבָדָיו. וּבְשִׁירֵי דָוִד עַבְדֶּךָ נְהַלֶּלְךָ, יְיָ אֱלֹהֵינוּ; בִּשְׁבָחוֹת
וּבִזְמִרוֹת נְגַדֶּלְךָ, וּנְשַׁבֵּחֲךָ וּנְפָאֶרְךָ וְנַזְכִּיר שִׁמְךָ וְנַמְלִיכְךָ,
מַלְכֵּנוּ אֱלֹהֵינוּ. Reader יָחִיד, חֵי הָעוֹלָמִים, מֶלֶךְ, מְשֻׁבָּח
וּמְפֹאָר עֲדֵי עַד שְׁמוֹ הַגָּדוֹל. בָּרוּךְ אַתָּה, יְיָ, מֶלֶךְ מְהֻלָּל
בַּתִּשְׁבָּחוֹת.

דברי הימים א טז, ח–לו

הוֹדוּ לַיְיָ, קִרְאוּ בִשְׁמוֹ, הוֹדִיעוּ בָעַמִּים עֲלִילוֹתָיו. שִׁירוּ לוֹ,
זַמְּרוּ לוֹ, שִׂיחוּ בְּכָל נִפְלְאוֹתָיו. הִתְהַלְלוּ בְּשֵׁם קָדְשׁוֹ; יִשְׂמַח
לֵב מְבַקְשֵׁי יְיָ. דִּרְשׁוּ יְיָ וְעֻזּוֹ, בַּקְּשׁוּ פָנָיו תָּמִיד. זִכְרוּ נִפְלְאֹתָיו
אֲשֶׁר עָשָׂה, מֹפְתָיו וּמִשְׁפְּטֵי פִּיהוּ. זֶרַע יִשְׂרָאֵל עַבְדּוֹ, בְּנֵי
יַעֲקֹב בְּחִירָיו. הוּא יְיָ אֱלֹהֵינוּ, בְּכָל הָאָרֶץ מִשְׁפָּטָיו. זִכְרוּ
לְעוֹלָם בְּרִיתוֹ, דָּבָר צִוָּה לְאֶלֶף דּוֹר. אֲשֶׁר כָּרַת אֶת אַבְרָהָם,
וּשְׁבוּעָתוֹ לְיִצְחָק. וַיַּעֲמִידֶהָ לְיַעֲקֹב לְחֹק, לְיִשְׂרָאֵל בְּרִית
עוֹלָם. לֵאמֹר, לְךָ אֶתֵּן אֶרֶץ כְּנָעַן, חֶבֶל נַחֲלַתְכֶם. בִּהְיוֹתְכֶם

May there be abundant peace from heaven, and life, for us and for all Israel; and say, Amen.

He who creates peace in his celestial heights, may he create peace for us and for all Israel; and say, Amen.

Blessed be he who spoke, and the world came into being; blessed be he. Blessed be he who created the universe. Blessed be he who says and performs. Blessed be he who decrees and fulfills. Blessed be he who has mercy on the world. Blessed be he who has mercy on all creatures. Blessed be he who grants a fair reward to those who revere him. Blessed be he who lives forever and exists eternally. Blessed be he who redeems and saves; blessed be his name. Blessed art thou, Lord our God, King of the universe, O God, merciful Father, who art praised by the mouth of thy people, lauded and glorified by the tongue of thy faithful servants. With the songs of thy servant David will we praise thee, Lord our God; with his hymns and psalms will we exalt, extol and glorify thee. We will call upon thy name and proclaim thee King, our King, our God. Thou who art One, the life of the universe, O King, praised and glorified be thy great name forever and ever. Blessed art thou, O Lord, King extolled with hymns of praise.

I Chronicles 16:8–36

Give thanks to the Lord, call upon his name; make known his deeds among the peoples. Sing to him, sing praises to him; speak of all his wonders. Take pride in his holy name; let the heart of those who seek the Lord rejoice. Inquire of the Lord and his might; seek his presence continually. Remember the wonders he has done, his marvels, and the judgments of his mouth, O descendants of Israel his servant, children of Jacob, his chosen. He is the Lord our God; his judgments are over all the earth. Remember his covenant forever, the word which he pledged for a thousand generations, the covenant he made with Abraham, and his oath to Isaac. He confirmed the same to Jacob as a statute, to Israel as an everlasting covenant, saying: "To you I give the land of Canaan as the portion of your possession." While they were but a few men,

מְתֵי מִסְפָּר, כִּמְעַט וְגָרִים בָּהּ. וַיִּתְהַלְּכוּ מִגּוֹי אֶל גּוֹי, וּמִמַּמְלָכָה אֶל עַם אַחֵר. לֹא הִנִּיחַ לְאִישׁ לְעָשְׁקָם, וַיּוֹכַח עֲלֵיהֶם מְלָכִים. אַל תִּגְּעוּ בִּמְשִׁיחָי, וּבִנְבִיאַי אַל תָּרֵעוּ. שִׁירוּ לַיְיָ כָּל הָאָרֶץ, בַּשְּׂרוּ מִיּוֹם אֶל יוֹם יְשׁוּעָתוֹ. סַפְּרוּ בַגּוֹיִם אֶת כְּבוֹדוֹ, בְּכָל הָעַמִּים נִפְלְאוֹתָיו. כִּי גָדוֹל יְיָ וּמְהֻלָּל מְאֹד, וְנוֹרָא הוּא עַל כָּל אֱלֹהִים. כִּי כָּל אֱלֹהֵי הָעַמִּים אֱלִילִים, וַיְיָ שָׁמַיִם עָשָׂה. הוֹד וְהָדָר לְפָנָיו, עֹז וְחֶדְוָה בִּמְקוֹמוֹ. הָבוּ לַיְיָ מִשְׁפְּחוֹת עַמִּים, הָבוּ לַיְיָ כָּבוֹד וָעֹז. הָבוּ לַיְיָ כְּבוֹד שְׁמוֹ, שְׂאוּ מִנְחָה וּבֹאוּ לְפָנָיו, הִשְׁתַּחֲווּ לַיְיָ בְּהַדְרַת קֹדֶשׁ. חִילוּ מִלְּפָנָיו כָּל הָאָרֶץ, אַף תִּכּוֹן תֵּבֵל בַּל תִּמּוֹט. יִשְׂמְחוּ הַשָּׁמַיִם וְתָגֵל הָאָרֶץ, וְיֹאמְרוּ בַגּוֹיִם יְיָ מָלָךְ. יִרְעַם הַיָּם וּמְלֹאוֹ, יַעֲלֹץ הַשָּׂדֶה וְכָל אֲשֶׁר בּוֹ. אָז יְרַנְּנוּ עֲצֵי הַיָּעַר, מִלִּפְנֵי יְיָ, כִּי בָא לִשְׁפּוֹט אֶת הָאָרֶץ. הוֹדוּ לַיְיָ כִּי טוֹב, כִּי לְעוֹלָם חַסְדּוֹ. וְאִמְרוּ, הוֹשִׁיעֵנוּ אֱלֹהֵי יִשְׁעֵנוּ, וְקַבְּצֵנוּ וְהַצִּילֵנוּ מִן הַגּוֹיִם, לְהוֹדוֹת לְשֵׁם קָדְשֶׁךָ, לְהִשְׁתַּבֵּחַ בִּתְהִלָּתֶךָ. בָּרוּךְ יְיָ אֱלֹהֵי יִשְׂרָאֵל מִן הָעוֹלָם וְעַד הָעֹלָם; וַיֹּאמְרוּ כָל הָעָם אָמֵן וְהַלֵּל לַיְיָ.

רוֹמְמוּ יְיָ אֱלֹהֵינוּ, וְהִשְׁתַּחֲווּ לַהֲדֹם רַגְלָיו, קָדוֹשׁ הוּא. רוֹמְמוּ יְיָ אֱלֹהֵינוּ, וְהִשְׁתַּחֲווּ לְהַר קָדְשׁוֹ, כִּי קָדוֹשׁ יְיָ אֱלֹהֵינוּ.

וְהוּא רַחוּם, יְכַפֵּר עָוֹן וְלֹא יַשְׁחִית, וְהִרְבָּה לְהָשִׁיב אַפּוֹ, וְלֹא יָעִיר כָּל חֲמָתוֹ. אַתָּה, יְיָ, לֹא תִכְלָא רַחֲמֶיךָ מִמֶּנִּי, חַסְדְּךָ וַאֲמִתְּךָ תָּמִיד יִצְּרוּנִי. זְכֹר רַחֲמֶיךָ יְיָ, וַחֲסָדֶיךָ, כִּי מֵעוֹלָם הֵמָּה. תְּנוּ עֹז לֵאלֹהִים, עַל יִשְׂרָאֵל גַּאֲוָתוֹ, וְעֻזּוֹ בַּשְּׁחָקִים. נוֹרָא אֱלֹהִים מִמִּקְדָּשֶׁיךָ; אֵל יִשְׂרָאֵל, הוּא נֹתֵן עֹז וְתַעֲצֻמוֹת לָעָם; בָּרוּךְ אֱלֹהִים. אֵל נְקָמוֹת, יְיָ, אֵל נְקָמוֹת, הוֹפִיעַ. הִנָּשֵׂא, שֹׁפֵט הָאָרֶץ, הָשֵׁב גְּמוּל עַל גֵּאִים. לַיְיָ הַיְשׁוּעָה, עַל עַמְּךָ בִרְכָתֶךָ

very few, and strangers in it; when they went about from nation to nation and from realm to realm, he permitted no man to oppress them, and warned kings concerning them: "Touch not my anointed, and do my prophets no harm!" Sing to the Lord, all the earth; proclaim his salvation day after day. Recount his glory among the nations, and his wonders among all the peoples. For great is the Lord and most worthy of praise; he is to be feared above all gods. For all the gods of the peoples are mere idols, but the Lord made the heavens. Majesty and beauty are in his presence; strength and joy are in his sanctuary. Ascribe to the Lord, O families of peoples, ascribe to the Lord glory and strength. Give to the Lord the honor due to his name; bring an offering and come before him; worship the Lord in holy array. Tremble before him, all the earth; indeed, the world is firm that it cannot be shaken. Let the heavens rejoice, let the earth exult, and let them say among the nations: "The Lord is King!" Let the sea and its fulness roar; let the field and all that is therein rejoice. Then let the trees of the forest sing before the Lord, who comes to rule the world. Praise the Lord, for he is good; for his kindness endures forever. And say: "Save us, O God of our salvation, gather us and deliver us from the nations, to give thanks to thy holy name, to glory in thy praise." Blessed be the Lord, the God of Israel, from eternity to eternity. Then all the people said "Amen" and praised the Lord.

Exalt the Lord our God, and worship at his footstool—holy is he. Exalt the Lord our God, and worship at his holy mountain, for holy is the Lord our God. He, being merciful, forgives iniquity, and does not destroy; frequently he turns his anger away, and does not stir up all his wrath. Thou, O Lord, wilt not hold back thy mercy from me; thy kindness and thy faithfulness will always protect me. Remember thy mercy, O Lord, and thy kindness, for they have been since eternity. Give honor to God, whose majesty is over Israel, whose glory is in the skies. Feared art thou, O Lord, from thy sanctuary; the God of Israel gives strength and power to his people. Blessed be God! God of vengeance, O Lord, God of vengeance, appear! Arise, O Ruler of the world, and render to the arrogant what they deserve. Salvation belongs to the Lord; thy blessing be upon thy people. The Lord of hosts is with us; the

סֶֽלָה. יְיָ צְבָאוֹת עִמָּֽנוּ, מִשְׂגָּב לָֽנוּ אֱלֹהֵי יַעֲקֹב סֶֽלָה. יְיָ צְבָאוֹת,
אַשְׁרֵי אָדָם בֹּטֵֽחַ בָּךְ. יְיָ, הוֹשִֽׁיעָה; הַמֶּֽלֶךְ יַעֲנֵֽנוּ בְיוֹם קָרְאֵֽנוּ.
הוֹשִֽׁיעָה אֶת עַמֶּֽךָ, וּבָרֵךְ אֶת נַחֲלָתֶֽךָ, וּרְעֵם וְנַשְּׂאֵם עַד
הָעוֹלָם. נַפְשֵֽׁנוּ חִכְּתָה לַיְיָ, עֶזְרֵֽנוּ וּמָגִנֵּֽנוּ הוּא. כִּי בוֹ יִשְׂמַח
לִבֵּֽנוּ, כִּי בְשֵׁם קָדְשׁוֹ בָטָֽחְנוּ. יְהִי חַסְדְּךָ יְיָ עָלֵֽינוּ, כַּאֲשֶׁר יִחַֽלְנוּ
לָךְ. הַרְאֵֽנוּ יְיָ חַסְדֶּֽךָ, וְיֶשְׁעֲךָ תִּתֶּן־לָֽנוּ. קוּמָה עֶזְרָֽתָה לָּֽנוּ,
וּפְדֵֽנוּ לְמַֽעַן חַסְדֶּֽךָ. אָנֹכִי יְיָ אֱלֹהֶֽיךָ הַמַּעַלְךָ מֵאֶֽרֶץ מִצְרָֽיִם,
הַרְחֶב־פִּֽיךָ וַאֲמַלְאֵֽהוּ. אַשְׁרֵי הָעָם שֶׁכָּֽכָה לּוֹ, אַשְׁרֵי הָעָם שֶׁיְיָ
אֱלֹהָיו. **Reader** וַאֲנִי בְּחַסְדְּךָ בָטַֽחְתִּי, יָגֵל לִבִּי בִּישׁוּעָתֶֽךָ;
אָשִֽׁירָה לַיְיָ, כִּי גָמַל עָלָי.

תהלים יט

לַמְנַצֵּֽחַ, מִזְמוֹר לְדָוִד. הַשָּׁמַֽיִם מְסַפְּרִים כְּבוֹד אֵל, וּמַעֲשֵׂה
יָדָיו מַגִּיד הָרָקִֽיעַ. יוֹם לְיוֹם יַבִּֽיעַ אֹֽמֶר, וְלַֽיְלָה לְּלַֽיְלָה יְחַוֶּה
דָּֽעַת. אֵין אֹֽמֶר וְאֵין דְּבָרִים, בְּלִי נִשְׁמָע קוֹלָם. בְּכָל הָאָֽרֶץ
יָצָא קַוָּם, וּבִקְצֵה תֵבֵל מִלֵּיהֶם; לַשֶּֽׁמֶשׁ שָׂם אֹֽהֶל בָּהֶם. וְהוּא
כְּחָתָן יֹצֵא מֵחֻפָּתוֹ, יָשִׂישׂ כְּגִבּוֹר לָרוּץ אֹֽרַח. מִקְצֵה הַשָּׁמַֽיִם
מוֹצָאוֹ, וּתְקוּפָתוֹ עַל קְצוֹתָם, וְאֵין נִסְתָּר מֵחַמָּתוֹ. תּוֹרַת יְיָ
תְּמִימָה, מְשִֽׁיבַת נָֽפֶשׁ; עֵדוּת יְיָ נֶאֱמָנָה, מַחְכִּֽימַת פֶּֽתִי. פִּקּוּדֵי
יְיָ יְשָׁרִים, מְשַׂמְּחֵי לֵב; מִצְוַת יְיָ בָּרָה, מְאִירַת עֵינָֽיִם. יִרְאַת יְיָ
טְהוֹרָה, עוֹמֶֽדֶת לָעַד; מִשְׁפְּטֵי יְיָ אֱמֶת, צָדְקוּ יַחְדָּו. הַנֶּחֱמָדִים
מִזָּהָב וּמִפַּז רָב, וּמְתוּקִים מִדְּבַשׁ וְנֹֽפֶת צוּפִים. גַּם עַבְדְּךָ נִזְהָר
בָּהֶם, בְּשָׁמְרָם עֵֽקֶב רָב. שְׁגִיאוֹת מִי יָבִין; מִנִּסְתָּרוֹת נַקֵּֽנִי. גַּם
מִזֵּדִים חֲשֹׂךְ עַבְדֶּֽךָ, אַל יִמְשְׁלוּ בִי; אָז אֵיתָם, וְנִקֵּֽיתִי מִפֶּֽשַׁע
רָב. **Reader** יִהְיוּ לְרָצוֹן אִמְרֵי פִי וְהֶגְיוֹן לִבִּי לְפָנֶֽיךָ, יְיָ, צוּרִי
וְגוֹאֲלִי.

God of Jacob is our Stronghold. O Lord of hosts, happy is the man who trusts in thee. O Lord, save us; may the King answer us when we call. Save thy people and bless thy heritage; tend them and sustain them forever. Our soul waits for the Lord; he is our help and our shield. Indeed, our heart rejoices in him, for in his holy name we trust. May thy kindness, O Lord, rest on us, as our hope rests in thee. Show us thy kindness, O Lord, and grant us thy salvation. Arise for our help, and set us free for thy goodness' sake. I am the Lord your God, who brought you up from the land of Egypt; open your mouth and I will fill it. Happy the people that is so situated; happy the people whose God is the Lord. I have trusted in thy kindness; may my heart rejoice in thy salvation. I will sing to the Lord, because he has treated me kindly.[1]

Psalm 19

For the Choirmaster; a psalm of David. The heavens proclaim the glory of God; the sky declares his handiwork. Day unto day pours forth speech, and night unto night reveals knowledge. There is no speech, there are no words; unheard is their voice. Yet their message extends through all the earth, and their words reach the end of the world. In the heavens he has pitched a tent for the sun, which is like a bridegroom coming out of his chamber, like an athlete rejoicing to run the course. It sets out from one end of the heaven, and round it passes to the other end, and there is nothing hidden from its heat. The Lord's Torah is perfect, refreshing the soul; the Lord's testimony is trustworthy, teaching the simple man wisdom. The Lord's precepts are right, gladdening the heart; the Lord's commandment is clear, enlightening the eyes. The Lord's faith is pure, enduring forever; the Lord's judgments are true, they are altogether just. They are more desirable than gold, than much rare gold; sweeter are they than honey, than honey from the honeycomb. Thy servant is indeed careful with them; in keeping them there is great reward. Yet who discerns his own errors? Of unconscious faults hold me guiltless. Restrain thy servant also from wilful sins; let them not have dominion over me; then shall I be blameless, and I shall be clear of great transgression. May the words of my mouth and the meditation of my heart be pleasing before thee, O Lord, my Stronghold and my Redeemer.

Psalm 19 has been summed up in the saying: "The starry sky above me and the moral law within me are two things which fill the soul with ever new and increasing admiration and reverence."

[1] *Psalms* 99:5, 9; 78:38; 40:12; 25:6; 68:35–36; 94:1–2; 3:9; 46:8; 84:13; 20:10; 28:9; 33:20–22; 85:8; 44:27; 81:11; 144:15; 13:6.

תהלים לד

לְדָוִד, בְּשַׁנּוֹתוֹ אֶת טַעְמוֹ לִפְנֵי אֲבִימֶלֶךְ, וַיְגָרְשֵׁהוּ וַיֵּלַךְ׃

אֲבָרְכָה אֶת יְיָ בְּכָל עֵת; תָּמִיד תְּהִלָּתוֹ בְּפִי׃

בַּיְיָ תִּתְהַלֵּל נַפְשִׁי; יִשְׁמְעוּ עֲנָוִים וְיִשְׂמָחוּ׃

גַּדְּלוּ לַיְיָ אִתִּי, וּנְרוֹמְמָה שְׁמוֹ יַחְדָּו׃

דָּרַשְׁתִּי אֶת יְיָ וְעָנָנִי, וּמִכָּל מְגוּרוֹתַי הִצִּילָנִי׃

הִבִּיטוּ אֵלָיו וְנָהָרוּ, וּפְנֵיהֶם אַל יֶחְפָּרוּ׃

זֶה עָנִי קָרָא וַיְיָ שָׁמֵעַ, וּמִכָּל צָרוֹתָיו הוֹשִׁיעוֹ׃

חֹנֶה מַלְאַךְ יְיָ סָבִיב לִירֵאָיו וַיְחַלְּצֵם׃

טַעֲמוּ וּרְאוּ כִּי טוֹב יְיָ; אַשְׁרֵי הַגֶּבֶר יֶחֱסֶה בּוֹ׃

יְראוּ אֶת יְיָ, קְדֹשָׁיו, כִּי אֵין מַחְסוֹר לִירֵאָיו׃

כְּפִירִים רָשׁוּ וְרָעֵבוּ, וְדֹרְשֵׁי יְיָ לֹא יַחְסְרוּ כָל טוֹב׃

לְכוּ בָנִים, שִׁמְעוּ לִי, יִרְאַת יְיָ אֲלַמֶּדְכֶם׃

מִי הָאִישׁ הֶחָפֵץ חַיִּים, אֹהֵב יָמִים לִרְאוֹת טוֹב׃

נְצֹר לְשׁוֹנְךָ מֵרָע, וּשְׂפָתֶיךָ מִדַּבֵּר מִרְמָה׃

סוּר מֵרָע וַעֲשֵׂה טוֹב, בַּקֵּשׁ שָׁלוֹם וְרָדְפֵהוּ׃

עֵינֵי יְיָ אֶל צַדִּיקִים, וְאָזְנָיו אֶל שַׁוְעָתָם׃

פְּנֵי יְיָ בְּעֹשֵׂי רָע, לְהַכְרִית מֵאֶרֶץ זִכְרָם׃

צָעֲקוּ וַיְיָ שָׁמֵעַ, וּמִכָּל צָרוֹתָם הִצִּילָם׃

קָרוֹב יְיָ לְנִשְׁבְּרֵי לֵב, וְאֶת דַּכְּאֵי רוּחַ יוֹשִׁיעַ׃

רַבּוֹת רָעוֹת צַדִּיק, וּמִכֻּלָּם יַצִּילֶנּוּ יְיָ׃

בשנותו את טעמו (Psalm 34) refers to the incident related in I Samuel 21:11–
16 where the Philistine king, to whom David fled for refuge, is called Achish.
Finding himself recognized as the slayer of Goliath, David feigned madness,
and so escaped vengeance. The psalm is arranged alphabetically, except that
the verse beginning with the letter ו is omitted and there is an additional
verse at the end. **יְראוּ** is pronounced **יְרוּ**.

Psalm 34

A song of David, when he feigned madness before Abimelech,
who drove him out and he departed.
I bless the Lord at all times;
His praise is ever in my mouth.
My soul glories in the Lord;
The humble hear it and are glad.
Exalt the Lord with me,
And let us extol his name together.
I sought the Lord and he answered me,
And delivered me from all my fears.
Those who look to him are jubilant,
And they are never abashed.
This poor man cried, and the Lord heard him;
He saved him from all his troubles.
The angel of the Lord encamps
Around those who revere him, and rescues them.
Consider and see that the Lord is good;
Happy is the man who takes shelter with him.
Revere the Lord, you his holy people;
For those who revere him suffer no want.
Young lions may suffer want and hunger,
But those who seek the Lord shall lack nothing.
Come, children, listen to me;
I will teach you how to revere the Lord.
Who is the man that desires life,
And loves a long life of happiness?
Keep your tongue from evil,
And your lips from speaking falsehood.
Shun evil and do good;
Seek peace and pursue it.
The eyes of the Lord are toward the righteous,
And his ears are open to their cry.
The Lord's anger is set against evildoers,
To cut off their name from the earth.
When they cry, the Lord listens,
And delivers them from all their troubles.
The Lord is near to the broken-hearted,
And saves those who are crushed in spirit.
A good man may have many ills,
But the Lord delivers him from them all.

שׁוֹמֵר כָּל עַצְמוֹתָיו, אַחַת מֵהֵנָּה לֹא נִשְׁבָּרָה.

תְּמוֹתֵת רָשָׁע רָעָה, וְשֹׂנְאֵי צַדִּיק יֶאְשָׁמוּ.

Reader פּוֹדֶה יְיָ נֶפֶשׁ עֲבָדָיו, וְלֹא יֶאְשְׁמוּ כָּל הַחֹסִים בּוֹ.

תהלים צ

תְּפִלָּה לְמֹשֶׁה, אִישׁ הָאֱלֹהִים. אֲדֹנָי, מָעוֹן אַתָּה הָיִיתָ לָנוּ בְּדֹר וָדֹר. בְּטֶרֶם הָרִים יֻלָּדוּ, וַתְּחוֹלֵל אֶרֶץ וְתֵבֵל, וּמֵעוֹלָם עַד עוֹלָם אַתָּה אֵל. תָּשֵׁב אֱנוֹשׁ עַד דַּכָּא, וַתֹּאמֶר שׁוּבוּ בְנֵי אָדָם. כִּי אֶלֶף שָׁנִים בְּעֵינֶיךָ כְּיוֹם אֶתְמוֹל כִּי יַעֲבֹר, וְאַשְׁמוּרָה בַלָּיְלָה. זְרַמְתָּם, שֵׁנָה יִהְיוּ; בַּבֹּקֶר כֶּחָצִיר יַחֲלֹף. בַּבֹּקֶר יָצִיץ וְחָלָף, לָעֶרֶב יְמוֹלֵל וְיָבֵשׁ. כִּי כָלִינוּ בְאַפֶּךָ, וּבַחֲמָתְךָ נִבְהָלְנוּ. שַׁתָּ עֲוֹנֹתֵינוּ לְנֶגְדֶּךָ, עֲלֻמֵנוּ לִמְאוֹר פָּנֶיךָ. כִּי כָל יָמֵינוּ פָּנוּ בְעֶבְרָתֶךָ, כִּלִּינוּ שָׁנֵינוּ כְמוֹ הֶגֶה. יְמֵי שְׁנוֹתֵינוּ בָהֶם שִׁבְעִים שָׁנָה, וְאִם בִּגְבוּרֹת שְׁמוֹנִים שָׁנָה, וְרָהְבָּם עָמָל וָאָוֶן, כִּי גָז חִישׁ וַנָּעֻפָה. מִי יוֹדֵעַ עֹז אַפֶּךָ, וּכְיִרְאָתְךָ עֶבְרָתֶךָ. לִמְנוֹת יָמֵינוּ כֵּן הוֹדַע, וְנָבִא לְבַב חָכְמָה. שׁוּבָה יְיָ, עַד מָתָי, וְהִנָּחֵם עַל עֲבָדֶיךָ. שַׂבְּעֵנוּ בַבֹּקֶר חַסְדֶּךָ, וּנְרַנְּנָה וְנִשְׂמְחָה בְּכָל יָמֵינוּ. שַׂמְּחֵנוּ כִּימוֹת עִנִּיתָנוּ, שְׁנוֹת רָאִינוּ רָעָה. **Reader** יֵרָאֶה אֶל עֲבָדֶיךָ פָעֳלֶךָ, וַהֲדָרְךָ עַל בְּנֵיהֶם. וִיהִי נֹעַם אֲדֹנָי אֱלֹהֵינוּ עָלֵינוּ, וּמַעֲשֵׂה יָדֵינוּ כּוֹנְנָה עָלֵינוּ, וּמַעֲשֵׂה יָדֵינוּ כּוֹנְנֵהוּ.

תהלים צא

יֹשֵׁב בְּסֵתֶר עֶלְיוֹן, בְּצֵל שַׁדַּי יִתְלוֹנָן. אֹמַר לַיְיָ, מַחְסִי וּמְצוּדָתִי, אֱלֹהַי אֶבְטַח בּוֹ. כִּי הוּא יַצִּילְךָ מִפַּח יָקוּשׁ, מִדֶּבֶר

Psalm 90 contrasts the eternity of God with the brevity of human life, and ends with a prayer for God's forgiveness and favor.

He protects all his limbs,
So that not one of them is broken.
Evil destroys the wicked,
And those who hate the righteous are doomed.
The Lord saves the life of his servants;
All who take shelter with him are never desolate.

Psalm 90

A prayer of Moses, the man of God. O Lord, thou hast been our shelter in every generation. Before the mountains were brought forth, before earth and world were formed—from eternity to eternity thou art God. Thou turnest man back to dust, and sayest: "Return, you children of man." Indeed, a thousand years in thy sight are like a day that passes, like a watch in the night. Thou sweepest men away and they sleep; they are like grass that grows in the morning. It flourishes and grows in the morning; in the evening it fades and withers. For we are consumed by thy anger; by thy wrath we are hurried away. Thou settest our iniquities before thee, and our guilty secrets are exposed in the light of thy presence. Indeed, all our days decline under thy displeasure; we spend our years like a fleeting sound. The length of our life is seventy years, or, by reason of strength, eighty years; their pride is only toil and futility, for it is speedily gone, and we fly away. Who knows the power of thy anger, to fear thee in proportion to thy displeasure? Teach us how to number our days, that we may attain a heart of wisdom. Relent, O Lord; how long? Relent as to thy servants. Satisfy us in the morning with thy kindness, that we may sing and rejoice throughout our days. Gladden us in proportion to the days wherein thou hast afflicted us, the years wherein we have seen evil. Let thy work be revealed to thy servants, and thy glory upon their children. May thy favor, Lord our God, rest on us; establish for us the work of our hands; the work of our hands establish thou.

Psalm 91

He who dwells in the shelter of the Most High abides under the protection of the Almighty. I say of the Lord: "He is my refuge and my fortress, my God, in whom I trust." Indeed, he will save you from the snare of the fowler, and from the destructive

---

Psalm 91 is termed שיר של פגעים, "a song against evil occurrences" (Shebuoth 15b). It describes the safety of those who trust in God amid the perils of their journey through life. ארך ימים is repeated so that the number of verses of this psalm reach a total of seventeen, the numerical value of טוב.

הַוּוֹת. בְּאֶבְרָתוֹ יָסֶךְ לָךְ, וְתַחַת כְּנָפָיו תֶּחְסֶה; צִנָּה וְסֹחֵרָה
אֲמִתּוֹ. לֹא תִירָא מִפַּחַד לָיְלָה, מֵחֵץ יָעוּף יוֹמָם. מִדֶּבֶר בָּאֹפֶל
יַהֲלֹךְ, מִקֶּטֶב יָשׁוּד צָהֳרָיִם. יִפֹּל מִצִּדְּךָ אֶלֶף, וּרְבָבָה מִימִינֶךָ;
אֵלֶיךָ לֹא יִגָּשׁ. רַק בְּעֵינֶיךָ תַבִּיט, וְשִׁלֻּמַת רְשָׁעִים תִּרְאֶה. כִּי
אַתָּה, יְיָ, מַחְסִי; עֶלְיוֹן שַׂמְתָּ מְעוֹנֶךָ. לֹא תְאֻנֶּה אֵלֶיךָ רָעָה,
וְנֶגַע לֹא יִקְרַב בְּאָהֳלֶךָ. כִּי מַלְאָכָיו יְצַוֶּה לָּךְ, לִשְׁמָרְךָ בְּכָל
דְּרָכֶיךָ. עַל כַּפַּיִם יִשָּׂאוּנְךָ, פֶּן תִּגֹּף בָּאֶבֶן רַגְלֶךָ. עַל שַׁחַל
וָפֶתֶן תִּדְרֹךְ, תִּרְמֹס כְּפִיר וְתַנִּין. כִּי בִי חָשַׁק וַאֲפַלְּטֵהוּ;
אֲשַׂגְּבֵהוּ כִּי יָדַע שְׁמִי. Reader יִקְרָאֵנִי וְאֶעֱנֵהוּ, עִמּוֹ אָנֹכִי
בְצָרָה, אֲחַלְּצֵהוּ וַאֲכַבְּדֵהוּ. אֹרֶךְ יָמִים אַשְׂבִּיעֵהוּ, וְאַרְאֵהוּ
בִּישׁוּעָתִי. אֹרֶךְ יָמִים אַשְׂבִּיעֵהוּ, וְאַרְאֵהוּ בִּישׁוּעָתִי.

תהלים קלה

הַלְלוּיָהּ, הַלְלוּ אֶת שֵׁם יְיָ; הַלְלוּ, עַבְדֵי יְיָ. שֶׁעֹמְדִים
בְּבֵית יְיָ, בְּחַצְרוֹת בֵּית אֱלֹהֵינוּ. הַלְלוּיָהּ, כִּי טוֹב יְיָ; זַמְּרוּ
לִשְׁמוֹ, כִּי נָעִים. כִּי יַעֲקֹב בָּחַר לוֹ יָהּ, יִשְׂרָאֵל לִסְגֻלָּתוֹ. כִּי
אֲנִי יָדַעְתִּי כִּי גָדוֹל יְיָ, וַאֲדֹנֵינוּ מִכָּל אֱלֹהִים. כֹּל אֲשֶׁר חָפֵץ
יְיָ עָשָׂה, בַּשָּׁמַיִם וּבָאָרֶץ, בַּיַּמִּים וְכָל תְּהֹמוֹת. מַעֲלֶה נְשִׂאִים
מִקְצֵה הָאָרֶץ, בְּרָקִים לַמָּטָר עָשָׂה; מוֹצֵא רוּחַ מֵאוֹצְרוֹתָיו.
שֶׁהִכָּה בְּכוֹרֵי מִצְרָיִם, מֵאָדָם עַד בְּהֵמָה. שָׁלַח אוֹתֹת וּמֹפְתִים
בְּתוֹכֵכִי מִצְרָיִם, בְּפַרְעֹה וּבְכָל עֲבָדָיו. שֶׁהִכָּה גּוֹיִם רַבִּים,
וְהָרַג מְלָכִים עֲצוּמִים. לְסִיחוֹן מֶלֶךְ הָאֱמֹרִי, וּלְעוֹג מֶלֶךְ
הַבָּשָׁן, וּלְכֹל מַמְלְכוֹת כְּנָעַן. וְנָתַן אַרְצָם נַחֲלָה, נַחֲלָה
לְיִשְׂרָאֵל עַמּוֹ. יְיָ, שִׁמְךָ לְעוֹלָם; יְיָ, זִכְרְךָ לְדֹר וָדֹר. כִּי יָדִין
יְיָ עַמּוֹ, וְעַל עֲבָדָיו יִתְנֶחָם. עֲצַבֵּי הַגּוֹיִם כֶּסֶף וְזָהָב, מַעֲשֵׂה
יְדֵי אָדָם. פֶּה לָהֶם וְלֹא יְדַבֵּרוּ, עֵינַיִם לָהֶם וְלֹא יִרְאוּ. אָזְנַיִם

pestilence. With his pinions he will cover you, and under his wings you will find refuge; his faithfulness is a shield and buckler. Fear not the terror of the night, nor the arrow that flies by day, nor the pestilence that stalks in darkness, nor the destruction that ravages at noon. Though a thousand fall at your side, and a myriad at your right hand, it shall not come near you. Only with your eyes will you gaze, and see the reward oi' evil men. Thou, O Lord art my refuge! When you have made the Most High your shelter, no disaster shall befall you, no calamity shall come near your tent. For he will give his angels charge over you, to guard you in all your ways. They will bear you upon their hands, lest you strike your foot against a stone. You can tread on lion and asp; you can trample young lion and serpent. "He clings to me, so I deliver him; I set him safe, because he loves me. When he calls upon me, I will answer him; I will be with him in trouble; I will rescue him and bring him to honor. With long life will I satisfy him, and let him see my saving power."

Psalm 135

Praise the Lord! Praise the name of the Lord; give praise, you servants of the Lord, who stand in the house of the Lord, in the courts of the house of our God. Praise the Lord, for the Lord is good; sing praise to his name, for it is pleasant. Surely, the Lord has chosen Jacob to be his, and Israel as his prized possession. I know that the Lord is great; our Lord is above all gods. The Lord does whatever he pleases, in heaven and earth, in the seas and all the depths. He makes clouds rise from the ends of the earth; he makes lightning for the rain, and brings forth the wind from his storehouses. It was he who smote the first-born of Egypt, both of man and beast. He sent signs and wonders into the midst of Egypt, on Pharaoh and on all his servants. It was he who struck down many nations, and slew mighty kings: Sihon, the king of the Amorites, Og, the king of Bashan, and all the kingdoms of Canaan. He gave their land as a heritage, a possession of his people Israel. O Lord, thy name is forever; O Lord, thy fame is for all generations. The Lord will do justice for his people; he will have compassion on his servants. Pagan gods are mere silver and gold, the work of men's hands. They have a mouth, but cannot speak; eyes have they, but cannot see; they have ears, but cannot

---

Psalm 135 is a hymn of praise particularly suitable for public worship, for it begins and ends with the liturgical *Halleluyah*. It is a mosaic of fragments from various biblical passages illustrating God's greatness. The first verse, for example, is identical with Psalm 113:1, except that the clauses are transposed.

לָהֶם וְלֹא יַאֲזִינוּ, אַף אֵין־יֶשׁ־רוּחַ בְּפִיהֶם. כְּמוֹהֶם יִהְיוּ
עֹשֵׂיהֶם, כֹּל אֲשֶׁר בֹּטֵחַ בָּהֶם. Reader בֵּית יִשְׂרָאֵל, בָּרְכוּ אֶת
יְיָ; בֵּית אַהֲרֹן, בָּרְכוּ אֶת יְיָ. בֵּית הַלֵּוִי, בָּרְכוּ אֶת יְיָ; יִרְאֵי יְיָ,
בָּרְכוּ אֶת יְיָ. בָּרוּךְ יְיָ מִצִּיּוֹן, שֹׁכֵן יְרוּשָׁלָםִ; הַלְלוּיָהּ.

תהלים קלו

כִּי לְעוֹלָם חַסְדּוֹ.	הוֹדוּ לַייָ כִּי טוֹב
כִּי לְעוֹלָם חַסְדּוֹ.	הוֹדוּ לֵאלֹהֵי הָאֱלֹהִים
כִּי לְעוֹלָם חַסְדּוֹ.	הוֹדוּ לַאֲדֹנֵי הָאֲדֹנִים
כִּי לְעוֹלָם חַסְדּוֹ.	לְעֹשֵׂה נִפְלָאוֹת גְּדֹלוֹת לְבַדּוֹ
כִּי לְעוֹלָם חַסְדּוֹ.	לְעֹשֵׂה הַשָּׁמַיִם בִּתְבוּנָה
כִּי לְעוֹלָם חַסְדּוֹ.	לְרוֹקַע הָאָרֶץ עַל הַמָּיִם
כִּי לְעוֹלָם חַסְדּוֹ.	לְעֹשֵׂה אוֹרִים גְּדֹלִים
כִּי לְעוֹלָם חַסְדּוֹ.	אֶת הַשֶּׁמֶשׁ לְמֶמְשֶׁלֶת בַּיּוֹם
כִּי לְעוֹלָם חַסְדּוֹ.	אֶת הַיָּרֵחַ וְכוֹכָבִים לְמֶמְשְׁלוֹת בַּלָּיְלָה
כִּי לְעוֹלָם חַסְדּוֹ.	לְמַכֵּה מִצְרַיִם בִּבְכוֹרֵיהֶם
כִּי לְעוֹלָם חַסְדּוֹ.	וַיּוֹצֵא יִשְׂרָאֵל מִתּוֹכָם
כִּי לְעוֹלָם חַסְדּוֹ.	בְּיָד חֲזָקָה וּבִזְרוֹעַ נְטוּיָה
כִּי לְעוֹלָם חַסְדּוֹ.	לְגֹזֵר יַם סוּף לִגְזָרִים
כִּי לְעוֹלָם חַסְדּוֹ.	וְהֶעֱבִיר יִשְׂרָאֵל בְּתוֹכוֹ
כִּי לְעוֹלָם חַסְדּוֹ.	וְנִעֵר פַּרְעֹה וְחֵילוֹ בְיַם סוּף
כִּי לְעוֹלָם חַסְדּוֹ.	לְמוֹלִיךְ עַמּוֹ בַּמִּדְבָּר
כִּי לְעוֹלָם חַסְדּוֹ.	לְמַכֵּה מְלָכִים גְּדֹלִים

Psalm 136 is called in the Talmud *Hallel ha-Gadol*, "the Great Hallel" (Pesaḥim 118a) to distinguish it from the "Egyptian Hallel" (Psalms 113–118) sung on festivals. It differs from all other psalms in that each verse closes with a refrain, probably designed to be sung in full chorus by the people.

hear; neither, indeed, is there any breath in their mouth. Those who make them will become like them—everyone who trusts in them. House of Israel, bless the Lord; house of Aaron, bless the the Lord; house of Levi, bless the Lord; you who revere the Lord, bless the Lord. Blessed from Zion be the Lord, who dwells in Jerusalem. Praise the Lord!

Psalm 136

Give thanks to the Lord, for he is good,
    His mercy endures forever;
Give thanks to the supreme God,
    His mercy endures forever;
Give thanks to the Lord of lords,
    His mercy endures forever;
To him who alone does great wonders,
    His mercy endures forever;
To him who made the heavens with wisdom,
    His mercy endures forever;
To him who spread the earth over the waters,
    His mercy endures forever;
To him who made the great lights,
    His mercy endures forever;
The sun to rule by day,
    His mercy endures forever;
The moon and stars to rule by night,
    His mercy endures forever;
To him who smote Egypt's first-born,
    His mercy endures forever;
And brought out Israel from among them,
    His mercy endures forever;
With strong hand and with outstretched arm,
    His mercy endures forever;
To him who divided the Red Sea,
    His mercy endures forever;
And brought Israel through it,
    His mercy endures forever;
And drowned Pharaoh and his host in the Red Sea,
    His mercy endures forever;
To him who led his people through the wilderness,
    His mercy endures forever;
To him who struck down great kings,
    His mercy endures forever;

כִּי לְעוֹלָם חַסְדּוֹ.	וַיַּהֲרֹג מְלָכִים אַדִּירִים
כִּי לְעוֹלָם חַסְדּוֹ.	לְסִיחוֹן מֶלֶךְ הָאֱמֹרִי
כִּי לְעוֹלָם חַסְדּוֹ.	וּלְעוֹג מֶלֶךְ הַבָּשָׁן
כִּי לְעוֹלָם חַסְדּוֹ.	וְנָתַן אַרְצָם לְנַחֲלָה
כִּי לְעוֹלָם חַסְדּוֹ.	נַחֲלָה לְיִשְׂרָאֵל עַבְדּוֹ
כִּי לְעוֹלָם חַסְדּוֹ.	שֶׁבְּשִׁפְלֵנוּ זָכַר לָנוּ
כִּי לְעוֹלָם חַסְדּוֹ.	וַיִּפְרְקֵנוּ מִצָּרֵינוּ
כִּי לְעוֹלָם חַסְדּוֹ.	נֹתֵן לֶחֶם לְכָל בָּשָׂר
כִּי לְעוֹלָם חַסְדּוֹ.	הוֹדוּ לְאֵל הַשָּׁמָיִם

תהלים לג

רַנְּנוּ צַדִּיקִים בַּיְיָ, לַיְשָׁרִים נָאוָה תְהִלָּה. הוֹדוּ לַיְיָ בְּכִנּוֹר,
בְּנֵבֶל עָשׂוֹר זַמְּרוּ לוֹ. שִׁירוּ לוֹ שִׁיר חָדָשׁ, הֵיטִיבוּ נַגֵּן בִּתְרוּעָה.
כִּי יָשָׁר דְּבַר יְיָ, וְכָל מַעֲשֵׂהוּ בֶּאֱמוּנָה. אֹהֵב צְדָקָה וּמִשְׁפָּט,
חֶסֶד יְיָ מָלְאָה הָאָרֶץ. בִּדְבַר יְיָ שָׁמַיִם נַעֲשׂוּ, וּבְרוּחַ פִּיו כָּל
צְבָאָם. כֹּנֵס כַּנֵּד מֵי הַיָּם, נֹתֵן בְּאוֹצָרוֹת תְּהוֹמוֹת. יִירְאוּ מֵיְיָ
כָּל הָאָרֶץ, מִמֶּנּוּ יָגוּרוּ כָּל יֹשְׁבֵי תֵבֵל. כִּי הוּא אָמַר וַיֶּהִי, הוּא
צִוָּה וַיַּעֲמֹד. יְיָ הֵפִיר עֲצַת גּוֹיִם, הֵנִיא מַחְשְׁבוֹת עַמִּים. עֲצַת
יְיָ לְעוֹלָם תַּעֲמֹד, מַחְשְׁבוֹת לִבּוֹ לְדֹר וָדֹר. אַשְׁרֵי הַגּוֹי אֲשֶׁר
יְיָ אֱלֹהָיו, הָעָם בָּחַר לְנַחֲלָה לוֹ. מִשָּׁמַיִם הִבִּיט יְיָ, רָאָה אֶת
כָּל בְּנֵי הָאָדָם. מִמְּכוֹן שִׁבְתּוֹ הִשְׁגִּיחַ, אֶל כָּל יֹשְׁבֵי הָאָרֶץ.
הַיֹּצֵר יַחַד לִבָּם, הַמֵּבִין אֶל כָּל מַעֲשֵׂיהֶם. אֵין הַמֶּלֶךְ נוֹשָׁע
בְּרָב־חָיִל, גִּבּוֹר לֹא יִנָּצֵל בְּרָב־כֹּחַ. שֶׁקֶר הַסּוּס לִתְשׁוּעָה,

---

Psalm 33 is a hymn of praise called forth by some national deliverance.
The opening call to praise is followed by a description of God's righteous rule
and creative omnipotence. He is to be praised for his choice and care of Israel,
whose protection does not depend on military power but on God.

And slew mighty kings,
 His mercy endures forever;
Sihon, king of the Amorites,
 His mercy endures forever;
And Og, king of Bashan,
 His mercy endures forever;
And gave their land as a heritage,
 His mercy endures forever;
A heritage to Israel his servant,
 His mercy endures forever;
Who remembered us when we were downcast,
 His mercy endures forever;
And delivered us from our foes,
 His mercy endures forever;
Who gives food to all creatures,
 His mercy endures forever;
Give thanks to the God of heaven,
 His mercy endures forever.

Psalm 33

Rejoice in the Lord, you righteous; it is fitting for the upright to give praise. Give thanks to the Lord with the harp; sing to him with the ten-stringed lute. Sing a new song to him; play skillfully amid shouts of joy. The word of the Lord is right; all his work is done with faithfulness. He loves righteousness and justice; the earth is full of the Lord's kindness. By the word of the Lord the heavens were made, and all their host by the breath of his mouth. He gathers the waters of the sea as a heap; he places the deeps in storehouses. Let all the earth revere the Lord; let all the inhabitants of the world stand in awe of him. For he spoke, and the world came into being; he commanded, and it stood firm. The Lord annuls the counsel of nations; he foils the plans of peoples. But the Lord's purpose stands forever; his plans are through all generations. Happy is the nation whose God is the Lord, the people he has chosen for his possession. From heaven the Lord looks down; he sees all of mankind. From his abode he looks carefully on all the inhabitants of the earth. It is he who fashions the hearts of them all, he who notes all their deeds. A king is not saved by the size of an army; a warrior is not rescued by sheer strength. Vain is the horse for victory; nor does it afford escape by its great strength.

וּבְרֹב חֵילוֹ לֹא יִמָּלֵט. הִנֵּה עֵין יְיָ אֶל יְרֵאָיו, לַמְיַחֲלִים לְחַסְדּוֹ. לְהַצִּיל מִמָּוֶת נַפְשָׁם, וּלְחַיּוֹתָם בָּרָעָב. נַפְשֵׁנוּ חִכְּתָה לַיְיָ, עֶזְרֵנוּ וּמָגִנֵּנוּ הוּא. Reader כִּי בוֹ יִשְׂמַח לִבֵּנוּ, כִּי בְשֵׁם קָדְשׁוֹ בָטָחְנוּ. יְהִי חַסְדְּךָ יְיָ עָלֵינוּ, כַּאֲשֶׁר יִחַלְנוּ לָךְ.

מִזְמוֹר שִׁיר לְיוֹם הַשַּׁבָּת. טוֹב לְהֹדוֹת לַיְיָ, וּלְזַמֵּר לְשִׁמְךָ עֶלְיוֹן. לְהַגִּיד בַּבֹּקֶר חַסְדֶּךָ, וֶאֱמוּנָתְךָ בַּלֵּילוֹת. עֲלֵי עָשׂוֹר וַעֲלֵי נָבֶל, עֲלֵי הִגָּיוֹן בְּכִנּוֹר. כִּי שִׂמַּחְתַּנִי יְיָ בְּפָעֳלֶךָ, בְּמַעֲשֵׂי יָדֶיךָ אֲרַנֵּן. מַה גָּדְלוּ מַעֲשֶׂיךָ, יְיָ, מְאֹד עָמְקוּ מַחְשְׁבֹתֶיךָ. אִישׁ בַּעַר לֹא יֵדַע, וּכְסִיל לֹא יָבִין אֶת זֹאת. בִּפְרֹחַ רְשָׁעִים כְּמוֹ עֵשֶׂב, וַיָּצִיצוּ כָּל פֹּעֲלֵי אָוֶן, לְהִשָּׁמְדָם עֲדֵי עַד. וְאַתָּה מָרוֹם לְעֹלָם, יְיָ. כִּי הִנֵּה אֹיְבֶיךָ, יְיָ, כִּי הִנֵּה אֹיְבֶיךָ יֹאבֵדוּ, יִתְפָּרְדוּ כָּל פֹּעֲלֵי אָוֶן. וַתָּרֶם כִּרְאֵים קַרְנִי, בַּלֹּתִי בְּשֶׁמֶן רַעֲנָן. וַתַּבֵּט עֵינִי בְּשׁוּרָי, בַּקָּמִים עָלַי מְרֵעִים תִּשְׁמַעְנָה אָזְנָי. צַדִּיק כַּתָּמָר יִפְרָח, כְּאֶרֶז בַּלְּבָנוֹן יִשְׂגֶּה. שְׁתוּלִים בְּבֵית יְיָ, בְּחַצְרוֹת אֱלֹהֵינוּ יַפְרִיחוּ. Reader עוֹד יְנוּבוּן בְּשֵׂיבָה, דְּשֵׁנִים וְרַעֲנַנִּים יִהְיוּ. לְהַגִּיד כִּי יָשָׁר יְיָ, צוּרִי, וְלֹא עַוְלָתָה בּוֹ.

יְיָ מָלָךְ, גֵּאוּת לָבֵשׁ; לָבֵשׁ יְיָ, עֹז הִתְאַזָּר; אַף תִּכּוֹן תֵּבֵל, בַּל תִּמּוֹט. נָכוֹן כִּסְאֲךָ מֵאָז, מֵעוֹלָם אָתָּה. נָשְׂאוּ נְהָרוֹת, יְיָ, נָשְׂאוּ נְהָרוֹת קוֹלָם, יִשְׂאוּ נְהָרוֹת דָּכְיָם. מִקֹּלוֹת מַיִם רַבִּים, אַדִּירִים מִשְׁבְּרֵי יָם, אַדִּיר בַּמָּרוֹם יְיָ. Reader עֵדֹתֶיךָ נֶאֶמְנוּ מְאֹד, לְבֵיתְךָ נַאֲוָה קֹדֶשׁ, יְיָ, לְאֹרֶךְ יָמִים.

The eye of the Lord rests on those who revere him, those who hope for his kindness, to save them from death and to keep them alive in famine. Our soul waits for the Lord; he is our help and our shield. In him our heart rejoices; in his holy name we trust. May thy kindness, O Lord, rest on us, even as our hope rests in thee.

Psalm 92

A psalm, a song for the Sabbath day. It is good to give thanks to the Lord, and to sing praises to thy name, O Most High; to proclaim thy goodness in the morning, and thy faithfulness at night, with a ten-stringed lyre and a flute, to the sound of a harp. For thou, O Lord, hast made me glad through thy work; I sing for joy at all that thou hast done. How great are thy works, O Lord! How very deep are thy designs! A stupid man cannot know, a fool cannot understand this. When the wicked thrive like grass, and all evildoers flourish, it is that they may be destroyed forever. But thou, O Lord, art supreme for evermore. For lo, thy enemies, O Lord, for lo, thy enemies shall perish; all evildoers shall be dispersed. But thou hast exalted my power like that of the wild ox; I am anointed with fresh oil. My eye has gazed on my foes; my ears have heard my enemies' doom. The righteous will flourish like the palm tree; they will grow like a cedar in Lebanon. Planted in the house of the Lord, they shall flourish in the courts of our God. They shall yield fruit even in old age; vigorous and fresh they shall be, to proclaim that the Lord is just! He is my Stronghold, and there is no wrong in him.

Psalm 93

The Lord is King; he is robed in majesty; the Lord is robed, he has girded himself with strength; thus the world is set firm and cannot be shaken. Thy throne stands firm from of old, thou art from all eternity. The floods have lifted up, O Lord, the floods have lifted up their voice; the floods lift up their mighty waves. But above the sound of many waters, mighty breakers of the sea, the Lord on high stands supreme. Thy testimonies are very sure; holiness befits thy house, O Lord, for all time.

יְהִי כְבוֹד יְיָ לְעוֹלָם; יִשְׂמַח יְיָ בְּמַעֲשָׂיו. יְהִי שֵׁם יְיָ מְבֹרָךְ, מֵעַתָּה וְעַד עוֹלָם. מִמִּזְרַח שֶׁמֶשׁ עַד מְבוֹאוֹ, מְהֻלָּל שֵׁם יְיָ. רָם עַל כָּל גּוֹיִם יְיָ, עַל הַשָּׁמַיִם כְּבוֹדוֹ. יְיָ, שִׁמְךָ לְעוֹלָם; יְיָ, זִכְרְךָ לְדֹר וָדֹר. יְיָ בַּשָּׁמַיִם הֵכִין כִּסְאוֹ, וּמַלְכוּתוֹ בַּכֹּל מָשָׁלָה. יִשְׂמְחוּ הַשָּׁמַיִם וְתָגֵל הָאָרֶץ, וְיֹאמְרוּ בַגּוֹיִם יְיָ מָלָךְ. יְיָ מֶלֶךְ, יְיָ מָלָךְ, יְיָ יִמְלֹךְ לְעֹלָם וָעֶד. יְיָ מֶלֶךְ עוֹלָם וָעֶד, אָבְדוּ גוֹיִם מֵאַרְצוֹ. יְיָ הֵפִיר עֲצַת גּוֹיִם, הֵנִיא מַחְשְׁבוֹת עַמִּים. רַבּוֹת מַחֲשָׁבוֹת בְּלֶב־אִישׁ, וַעֲצַת יְיָ הִיא תָקוּם. עֲצַת יְיָ לְעוֹלָם תַּעֲמֹד, מַחְשְׁבוֹת לִבּוֹ לְדֹר וָדֹר. כִּי הוּא אָמַר וַיֶּהִי, הוּא צִוָּה וַיַּעֲמֹד. כִּי בָחַר יְיָ בְּצִיּוֹן, אִוָּהּ לְמוֹשָׁב לוֹ. כִּי יַעֲקֹב בָּחַר לוֹ יָהּ, יִשְׂרָאֵל לִסְגֻלָּתוֹ. כִּי לֹא יִטֹּשׁ יְיָ עַמּוֹ, וְנַחֲלָתוֹ לֹא יַעֲזֹב. Reader וְהוּא רַחוּם, יְכַפֵּר עָוֹן וְלֹא יַשְׁחִית, וְהִרְבָּה לְהָשִׁיב אַפּוֹ, וְלֹא יָעִיר כָּל חֲמָתוֹ. יְיָ, הוֹשִׁיעָה; הַמֶּלֶךְ יַעֲנֵנוּ בְיוֹם קָרְאֵנוּ.

אַשְׁרֵי יוֹשְׁבֵי בֵיתֶךָ; עוֹד יְהַלְלוּךָ סֶּלָה.

אַשְׁרֵי הָעָם שֶׁכָּכָה לּוֹ; אַשְׁרֵי הָעָם שֶׁיְיָ אֱלֹהָיו.

תהלים קמה

תְּהִלָּה לְדָוִד

אֲרוֹמִמְךָ, אֱלוֹהַי הַמֶּלֶךְ, וַאֲבָרְכָה שִׁמְךָ לְעוֹלָם וָעֶד.

בְּכָל יוֹם אֲבָרְכֶךָּ, וַאֲהַלְלָה שִׁמְךָ לְעוֹלָם וָעֶד.

גָּדוֹל יְיָ וּמְהֻלָּל מְאֹד, וְלִגְדֻלָּתוֹ אֵין חֵקֶר.

דּוֹר לְדוֹר יְשַׁבַּח מַעֲשֶׂיךָ, וּגְבוּרֹתֶיךָ יַגִּידוּ.

הֲדַר כְּבוֹד הוֹדֶךָ, וְדִבְרֵי נִפְלְאֹתֶיךָ אָשִׂיחָה.

וֶעֱזוּז נוֹרְאֹתֶיךָ יֹאמֵרוּ, וּגְדֻלָּתְךָ אֲסַפְּרֶנָּה.

May the glory of the Lord be forever; may the Lord rejoice in his works. Blessed be the name of the Lord henceforth and forever. From the rising of the sun to its setting let the Lord's name be praised. High above all nations is the Lord; above the heavens is his glory. O Lord, thy name is forever; O Lord, thy fame is through all generations. The Lord has set up his throne in the heavens, and his kingdom rules over all. Let the heavens rejoice, let the earth exult, and let them say among the nations, "The Lord is King!" The Lord is King, the Lord was King, the Lord shall be King forever and ever. The Lord is King for evermore; the heathen have vanished from his land. The Lord annuls the counsel of nations; he foils the plans of peoples. Many are the plans in a man's heart, but it is the Lord's purpose that shall stand. The Lord's purpose stands forever; his plans are through all generations. For he spoke, and the world came into being; he commanded, and it stood firm. Surely, the Lord has chosen Zion; he has desired it for his habitation. Surely, the Lord has chosen Jacob to be his, and Israel as his prized possession. Surely, the Lord will not abandon his people, nor forsake his heritage. He, being merciful, forgives iniquity, and does not destroy; frequently he turns his anger away, and does not stir up all his wrath. O Lord, save us; may the King answer us when we call.[1]

Happy are those who dwell in thy house; they are ever praising thee. Happy the people that is so situated; happy the people whose God is the Lord.[2]

Psalm 145

A hymn of praise by David

I extol thee, my God the King,
And bless thy name forever and ever.
Every day I bless thee,
And praise thy name forever and ever.
Great is the Lord and most worthy of praise;
His greatness is unsearchable.
One generation to another praises thy works;
They recount thy mighty acts.
On the splendor of thy glorious majesty
And on thy wondrous deeds I meditate.
They speak of thy awe-inspiring might,
And I tell of thy greatness.

---

[1] *Psalms* 104:31; 113:2–4; 135:13; 103:19; *I Chronicles* 16:31; *Psalms* 10:16; 33:10; *Proverbs* 19:21; *Psalms* 33:11, 9; 132:13; 135:4; 94:14; 78:38; 20:10.   [2] *Psalms* 84:5; 144:15.

זֵכֶר רַב טוּבְךָ יַבִּיעוּ, וְצִדְקָתְךָ יְרַנֵּנוּ.

חַנּוּן וְרַחוּם יְיָ, אֶרֶךְ אַפַּיִם וּגְדָל־חָסֶד.

טוֹב יְיָ לַכֹּל, וְרַחֲמָיו עַל כָּל מַעֲשָׂיו.

יוֹדוּךָ יְיָ כָּל מַעֲשֶׂיךָ, וַחֲסִידֶיךָ יְבָרְכוּכָה.

כְּבוֹד מַלְכוּתְךָ יֹאמֵרוּ, וּגְבוּרָתְךָ יְדַבֵּרוּ.

לְהוֹדִיעַ לִבְנֵי הָאָדָם גְּבוּרֹתָיו, וּכְבוֹד הֲדַר מַלְכוּתוֹ.

מַלְכוּתְךָ מַלְכוּת כָּל עֹלָמִים, וּמֶמְשַׁלְתְּךָ בְּכָל דּוֹר וָדֹר.

סוֹמֵךְ יְיָ לְכָל הַנֹּפְלִים, וְזוֹקֵף לְכָל הַכְּפוּפִים.

עֵינֵי כֹל אֵלֶיךָ יְשַׂבֵּרוּ, וְאַתָּה נוֹתֵן לָהֶם אֶת אָכְלָם בְּעִתּוֹ.

פּוֹתֵחַ אֶת יָדֶךָ, וּמַשְׂבִּיעַ לְכָל חַי רָצוֹן.

צַדִּיק יְיָ בְּכָל דְּרָכָיו, וְחָסִיד בְּכָל מַעֲשָׂיו.

קָרוֹב יְיָ לְכָל קֹרְאָיו, לְכֹל אֲשֶׁר יִקְרָאֻהוּ בֶאֱמֶת.

רְצוֹן יְרֵאָיו יַעֲשֶׂה, וְאֶת שַׁוְעָתָם יִשְׁמַע וְיוֹשִׁיעֵם.

שׁוֹמֵר יְיָ אֶת כָּל אֹהֲבָיו, וְאֵת כָּל הָרְשָׁעִים יַשְׁמִיד.

תְּהִלַּת יְיָ יְדַבֶּר־פִּי; וִיבָרֵךְ כָּל בָּשָׂר שֵׁם קָדְשׁוֹ לְעוֹלָם וָעֶד.

Reader וַאֲנַחְנוּ נְבָרֵךְ יָהּ מֵעַתָּה וְעַד עוֹלָם; הַלְלוּיָהּ.

תהלים קמו

הַלְלוּיָהּ; הַלְלִי נַפְשִׁי אֶת יְיָ. אֲהַלְלָה יְיָ בְּחַיָּי, אֲזַמְּרָה לֵאלֹהַי בְּעוֹדִי. אַל תִּבְטְחוּ בִנְדִיבִים, בְּבֶן־אָדָם שֶׁאֵין לוֹ תְשׁוּעָה. תֵּצֵא רוּחוֹ יָשֻׁב לְאַדְמָתוֹ, בַּיּוֹם הַהוּא אָבְדוּ עֶשְׁתֹּנֹתָיו. אַשְׁרֵי שֶׁאֵל יַעֲקֹב בְּעֶזְרוֹ, שִׂבְרוֹ עַל יְיָ אֱלֹהָיו. עֹשֶׂה שָׁמַיִם וָאָרֶץ, אֶת הַיָּם, וְאֶת כָּל אֲשֶׁר בָּם; הַשֹּׁמֵר אֱמֶת לְעוֹלָם. עֹשֶׂה מִשְׁפָּט לַעֲשׁוּקִים, נֹתֵן לֶחֶם לָרְעֵבִים; יְיָ מַתִּיר אֲסוּרִים. יְיָ

They spread the fame of thy great goodness,
And sing of thy righteousness.
Gracious and merciful is the Lord,
Slow to anger and of great kindness.
The Lord is good to all,
And his mercy is over all his works.
All thy works praise thee, O Lord,
And thy faithful followers bless thee.
They speak of thy glorious kingdom,
And talk of thy might,
To let men know thy mighty deeds,
And the glorious splendor of thy kingdom.
Thy kingdom is a kingdom of all ages,
And thy dominion is for all generations.
The Lord upholds all who fall,
And raises all who are bowed down.
The eyes of all look hopefully to thee,
And thou givest them their food in due season.
Thou openest thy hand,
And satisfiest every living thing with favor.
The Lord is righteous in all his ways,
And gracious in all his deeds.
The Lord is near to all who call upon him,
To all who call upon him sincerely.
He fulfills the desire of those who revere him;
He hears their cry and saves them.
The Lord preserves all who love him,
But all the wicked he destroys.
My mouth speaks the praise of the Lord;
Let all creatures bless his holy name forever and ever.
[1]We will bless the Lord henceforth and forever.
Praise the Lord!

Psalm 146

Praise the Lord! Praise the Lord, O my soul! I will praise the Lord as long as I live; I will sing to my God as long as I exist. Put no trust in princes, in mortal man who can give no help. When his breath goes, he returns to the dust, and on that very day his designs perish. Happy is he who has the God of Jacob as his help, whose hope rests upon the Lord his God, Maker of heaven and earth and sea and all that is therein; who keeps faith forever, renders justice to the oppressed, and feeds those who are hungry. The Lord sets the captives free. The Lord opens the eyes of the

---

[1] *Psalm* 115:18.

פֹּקֵחַ עִוְרִים, יְיָ זֹקֵף כְּפוּפִים, יְיָ אֹהֵב צַדִּיקִים. יְיָ שֹׁמֵר אֶת
גֵּרִים; יָתוֹם וְאַלְמָנָה יְעוֹדֵד, וְדֶרֶךְ רְשָׁעִים יְעַוֵּת. Reader יִמְלֹךְ
יְיָ לְעוֹלָם, אֱלֹהַיִךְ צִיּוֹן לְדֹר וָדֹר; הַלְלוּיָהּ.

תהלים קמז

הַלְלוּיָהּ; כִּי טוֹב זַמְּרָה אֱלֹהֵינוּ, כִּי נָעִים, נָאוָה תְהִלָּה.
בּוֹנֵה יְרוּשָׁלַיִם יְיָ; נִדְחֵי יִשְׂרָאֵל יְכַנֵּס. הָרוֹפֵא לִשְׁבוּרֵי לֵב,
וּמְחַבֵּשׁ לְעַצְּבוֹתָם. מוֹנֶה מִסְפָּר לַכּוֹכָבִים, לְכֻלָּם שֵׁמוֹת
יִקְרָא. גָּדוֹל אֲדוֹנֵינוּ וְרַב כֹּחַ, לִתְבוּנָתוֹ אֵין מִסְפָּר. מְעוֹדֵד
עֲנָוִים יְיָ, מַשְׁפִּיל רְשָׁעִים עֲדֵי אָרֶץ. עֱנוּ לַייָ בְּתוֹדָה, זַמְּרוּ
לֵאלֹהֵינוּ בְכִנּוֹר. הַמְכַסֶּה שָׁמַיִם בְּעָבִים, הַמֵּכִין לָאָרֶץ מָטָר,
הַמַּצְמִיחַ הָרִים חָצִיר. נוֹתֵן לִבְהֵמָה לַחְמָהּ, לִבְנֵי עֹרֵב אֲשֶׁר
יִקְרָאוּ. לֹא בִגְבוּרַת הַסּוּס יֶחְפָּץ, לֹא בְשׁוֹקֵי הָאִישׁ יִרְצֶה.
רוֹצֶה יְיָ אֶת יְרֵאָיו, אֶת הַמְיַחֲלִים לְחַסְדּוֹ. שַׁבְּחִי, יְרוּשָׁלַיִם,
אֶת יְיָ; הַלְלִי אֱלֹהַיִךְ, צִיּוֹן. כִּי חִזַּק בְּרִיחֵי שְׁעָרָיִךְ, בֵּרַךְ בָּנַיִךְ
בְּקִרְבֵּךְ. הַשָּׂם גְּבוּלֵךְ שָׁלוֹם, חֵלֶב חִטִּים יַשְׂבִּיעֵךְ. הַשֹּׁלֵחַ
אִמְרָתוֹ אָרֶץ, עַד מְהֵרָה יָרוּץ דְּבָרוֹ. הַנֹּתֵן שֶׁלֶג כַּצָּמֶר; כְּפוֹר
כָּאֵפֶר יְפַזֵּר. מַשְׁלִיךְ קַרְחוֹ כְפִתִּים; לִפְנֵי קָרָתוֹ מִי יַעֲמֹד.
יִשְׁלַח דְּבָרוֹ וְיַמְסֵם; יַשֵּׁב רוּחוֹ, יִזְּלוּ מָיִם. מַגִּיד דְּבָרָיו לְיַעֲקֹב,
חֻקָּיו וּמִשְׁפָּטָיו לְיִשְׂרָאֵל. Reader לֹא עָשָׂה כֵן לְכָל גּוֹי,
וּמִשְׁפָּטִים בַּל יְדָעוּם; הַלְלוּיָהּ.

תהלים קמח

הַלְלוּיָהּ; הַלְלוּ אֶת יְיָ מִן הַשָּׁמַיִם, הַלְלוּהוּ בַּמְּרוֹמִים.
הַלְלוּהוּ כָל מַלְאָכָיו, הַלְלוּהוּ כָּל צְבָאָיו. הַלְלוּהוּ שֶׁמֶשׁ
וְיָרֵחַ, הַלְלוּהוּ כָּל כּוֹכְבֵי אוֹר. הַלְלוּהוּ שְׁמֵי הַשָּׁמַיִם, וְהַמַּיִם
אֲשֶׁר מֵעַל הַשָּׁמָיִם. יְהַלְלוּ אֶת שֵׁם יְיָ; כִּי הוּא צִוָּה וְנִבְרָאוּ.

blind, raises those who are bowed down, and loves the righteous. The Lord protects the strangers, and upholds the fatherless and the widow; but the way of the wicked he thwarts. The Lord shall reign forever; your God, O Zion, for all generations. Praise the Lord!

Psalm 147

Praise the Lord! It is good to sing to our God, it is pleasant; praise is comely. The Lord rebuilds Jerusalem; he gathers together the dispersed people of Israel. He heals the broken-hearted, and binds up their wounds. He counts the number of the stars, and gives a name to each. Great is our Lord and abundant in power; his wisdom is infinite. The Lord raises the humble; he casts the wicked down to the ground. Sing thanks to the Lord; make melody upon the harp to our God, who covers the sky with clouds, provides rain for the earth, and causes grass to grow upon the hills. He gives food to the cattle, and to the crying young ravens. He cares not for [those who rely on] the strength of the horse; he delights not in [those who rely on] a warrior's legs. The Lord is pleased with those who revere him, those who yearn for his kindness. Praise the Lord, O Jerusalem! Praise your God, O Zion! He has indeed fortified your gates; he has blessed your children within. He establishes peace within your territory, and fills you with the finest of wheat. He sends forth his command to the earth; his word runs very swiftly. He gives snow like wool; he scatters hoarfrost like ashes. He casts forth his ice like crumbs; who can stand before his cold? He sends forth his word and melts them; he causes his wind to blow, and the waters flow. He declares his word to Jacob, his statutes and ordinances to Israel. He has not dealt so with heathen nations; his ordinances they do not know. Praise the Lord!

Psalm 148

Praise the Lord! Praise the Lord from the heavens; praise him in the heights. Praise him, all his angels; praise him, all his hosts. Praise him, sun and moon; praise him, all you stars of light. Praise him, highest heavens and waters that are above the heavens. Let them praise the name of the Lord; for he commanded and they were created. He fixed them fast forever and ever; he gave

וַיַּעֲמִידֵם לָעַד לְעוֹלָם, חָק־נָתַן וְלֹא יַעֲבוֹר. הַלְלוּ אֶת יְיָ מִן
הָאָרֶץ, תַּנִּינִים וְכָל תְּהֹמוֹת. אֵשׁ וּבָרָד, שֶׁלֶג וְקִיטוֹר, רֽוּחַ
סְעָרָה עֹשָׂה דְבָרוֹ. הֶהָרִים וְכָל גְּבָעוֹת, עֵץ פְּרִי וְכָל אֲרָזִים.
הַחַיָּה וְכָל בְּהֵמָה, רֶמֶשׂ וְצִפּוֹר כָּנָף. מַלְכֵי אֶרֶץ וְכָל לְאֻמִּים,
שָׂרִים וְכָל שֹׁפְטֵי אָרֶץ. בַּחוּרִים וְגַם בְּתוּלוֹת, זְקֵנִים עִם
נְעָרִים. יְהַלְלוּ אֶת שֵׁם יְיָ, כִּי נִשְׂגָּב שְׁמוֹ לְבַדּוֹ; הוֹדוֹ עַל אֶרֶץ
וְשָׁמָיִם. Reader וַיָּרֶם קֶרֶן לְעַמּוֹ, תְּהִלָּה לְכָל חֲסִידָיו, לִבְנֵי
יִשְׂרָאֵל עַם קְרֹבוֹ; הַלְלוּיָהּ.

תהלים קמט

הַלְלוּיָהּ; שִׁירוּ לַייָ שִׁיר חָדָשׁ, תְּהִלָּתוֹ בִּקְהַל חֲסִידִים.
יִשְׂמַח יִשְׂרָאֵל בְּעֹשָׂיו, בְּנֵי צִיּוֹן יָגִילוּ בְמַלְכָּם. יְהַלְלוּ שְׁמוֹ
בְמָחוֹל, בְּתֹף וְכִנּוֹר יְזַמְּרוּ לוֹ. כִּי רוֹצֶה יְיָ בְּעַמּוֹ, יְפָאֵר עֲנָוִים
בִּישׁוּעָה. יַעְלְזוּ חֲסִידִים בְּכָבוֹד, יְרַנְּנוּ עַל מִשְׁכְּבוֹתָם. רוֹמְמוֹת
אֵל בִּגְרוֹנָם, וְחֶרֶב פִּיפִיּוֹת בְּיָדָם. לַעֲשׂוֹת נְקָמָה בַּגּוֹיִם,
תּוֹכֵחוֹת בַּלְאֻמִּים. Reader לֶאְסֹר מַלְכֵיהֶם בְּזִקִּים, וְנִכְבְּדֵיהֶם
בְּכַבְלֵי בַרְזֶל. לַעֲשׂוֹת בָּהֶם מִשְׁפָּט כָּתוּב; הָדָר הוּא לְכָל
חֲסִידָיו; הַלְלוּיָהּ.

תהלים קנ

הַלְלוּיָהּ; הַלְלוּ אֵל בְּקָדְשׁוֹ, הַלְלוּהוּ בִּרְקִיעַ עֻזּוֹ. הַלְלוּהוּ
בִּגְבוּרֹתָיו, הַלְלוּהוּ כְּרֹב גֻּדְלוֹ. הַלְלוּהוּ בְּתֵקַע שׁוֹפָר, הַלְלוּהוּ
בְּנֵבֶל וְכִנּוֹר. הַלְלוּהוּ בְּתֹף וּמָחוֹל, הַלְלוּהוּ בְּמִנִּים וְעֻגָב.
הַלְלוּהוּ בְּצִלְצְלֵי שָׁמַע, הַלְלוּהוּ בְּצִלְצְלֵי תְרוּעָה. Reader כֹּל
הַנְּשָׁמָה תְּהַלֵּל יָהּ; הַלְלוּיָהּ. כֹּל הַנְּשָׁמָה תְּהַלֵּל יָהּ; הַלְלוּיָהּ.

a law which none transgresses. Praise the Lord from the earth, you sea-monsters and all depths; fire and hail, snow and vapor, stormy wind, fulfilling his word; mountains and all hills, fruit-trees and all cedars; wild animals and all cattle, crawling things and winged fowl; kings of the earth and all nations, princes and all earthly rulers; young men and maidens, old men and children; let them praise the name of the Lord, for his name alone is exalted; his majesty is above earth and heaven. He has raised the honor of his people, the glory of his faithful followers, the children of Israel, the people near to him. Praise the Lord!

Psalm 149

Praise the Lord! Sing a new song to the Lord; praise him in the assembly of the faithful. Let Israel rejoice in his Maker; let the children of Zion exult in their King. Let them praise his name with dancing; let them make music to him with drum and harp. For the Lord is pleased with his people; he adorns the meek with triumph. Let the faithful exult in glory; let them sing upon their beds. Let the praises of God be in their mouth, and a double-edged sword in their hand, to execute vengeance upon the nations, punishment upon the peoples; to bind their kings with chains, and their nobles with fetters of iron; to execute upon them the written judgment. He is the glory of all his faithful. Praise the Lord!

Psalm 150

Praise the Lord! Praise God in his sanctuary; praise him in his glorious heaven. Praise him for his mighty deeds; praise him for his abundant greatness. Praise him with the blast of the horn; praise him with the harp and the lyre. Praise him with the drum and dance; praise him with strings and flute. Praise him with re-sounding cymbals; praise him with clanging cymbals. Let everything that has breath praise the Lord. Praise the Lord!

בָּרוּךְ יְיָ לְעוֹלָם, אָמֵן וְאָמֵן. בָּרוּךְ יְיָ מִצִּיּוֹן, שֹׁכֵן יְרוּשָׁלָיִם; הַלְלוּיָהּ. בָּרוּךְ יְיָ אֱלֹהִים, אֱלֹהֵי יִשְׂרָאֵל, עֹשֵׂה נִפְלָאוֹת לְבַדּוֹ. Reader וּבָרוּךְ שֵׁם כְּבוֹדוֹ לְעוֹלָם; וְיִמָּלֵא כְבוֹדוֹ אֶת כָּל הָאָרֶץ, אָמֵן וְאָמֵן.

דברי הימים א כט, י—יג

וַיְבָרֶךְ דָּוִיד אֶת יְיָ לְעֵינֵי כָּל הַקָּהָל, וַיֹּאמֶר דָּוִיד: בָּרוּךְ אַתָּה יְיָ, אֱלֹהֵי יִשְׂרָאֵל אָבִינוּ, מֵעוֹלָם וְעַד עוֹלָם. לְךָ יְיָ הַגְּדֻלָּה וְהַגְּבוּרָה וְהַתִּפְאֶרֶת וְהַנֵּצַח וְהַהוֹד, כִּי כֹל בַּשָּׁמַיִם וּבָאָרֶץ; לְךָ יְיָ הַמַּמְלָכָה, וְהַמִּתְנַשֵּׂא לְכֹל לְרֹאשׁ. וְהָעֹשֶׁר וְהַכָּבוֹד מִלְּפָנֶיךָ, וְאַתָּה מוֹשֵׁל בַּכֹּל, וּבְיָדְךָ כֹּחַ וּגְבוּרָה, וּבְיָדְךָ לְגַדֵּל וּלְחַזֵּק לַכֹּל. וְעַתָּה אֱלֹהֵינוּ, מוֹדִים אֲנַחְנוּ לָךְ, וּמְהַלְלִים לְשֵׁם תִּפְאַרְתֶּךָ.

נחמיה ט, ו—יא

אַתָּה הוּא יְיָ לְבַדֶּךָ, אַתָּה עָשִׂיתָ אֶת הַשָּׁמַיִם, שְׁמֵי הַשָּׁמַיִם וְכָל צְבָאָם, הָאָרֶץ וְכָל אֲשֶׁר עָלֶיהָ, הַיַּמִּים וְכָל אֲשֶׁר בָּהֶם, וְאַתָּה מְחַיֶּה אֶת כֻּלָּם, וּצְבָא הַשָּׁמַיִם לְךָ מִשְׁתַּחֲוִים. Reader אַתָּה הוּא יְיָ הָאֱלֹהִים, אֲשֶׁר בָּחַרְתָּ בְּאַבְרָם וְהוֹצֵאתוֹ מֵאוּר כַּשְׂדִּים וְשַׂמְתָּ שְּׁמוֹ אַבְרָהָם. וּמָצָאתָ אֶת לְבָבוֹ נֶאֱמָן לְפָנֶיךָ—

וְכָרוֹת עִמּוֹ הַבְּרִית לָתֵת אֶת אֶרֶץ הַכְּנַעֲנִי, הַחִתִּי, הָאֱמֹרִי, וְהַפְּרִזִּי וְהַיְבוּסִי וְהַגִּרְגָּשִׁי, לָתֵת לְזַרְעוֹ; וַתָּקֶם אֶת דְּבָרֶיךָ, כִּי צַדִּיק אָתָּה. וַתֵּרֶא אֶת עֳנִי אֲבֹתֵינוּ בְּמִצְרָיִם, וְאֶת זַעֲקָתָם שָׁמַעְתָּ עַל יַם סוּף. וַתִּתֵּן אֹתֹת וּמֹפְתִים בְּפַרְעֹה וּבְכָל עֲבָדָיו וּבְכָל עַם אַרְצוֹ, כִּי יָדַעְתָּ כִּי הֵזִידוּ עֲלֵיהֶם; וַתַּעַשׂ לְךָ שֵׁם כְּהַיּוֹם הַזֶּה. Reader וְהַיָּם בָּקַעְתָּ לִפְנֵיהֶם, וַיַּעַבְרוּ בְתוֹךְ הַיָּם בַּיַּבָּשָׁה; וְאֶת רֹדְפֵיהֶם הִשְׁלַכְתָּ בִמְצוֹלֹת, כְּמוֹ אֶבֶן בְּמַיִם עַזִּים.

Blessed be the Lord forever. Amen, Amen. Blessed out of Zion be the Lord who dwells in Jerusalem. Praise the Lord! Blessed be the Lord God, the God of Israel, who alone works wonders; blessed be his glorious name forever. May the whole earth be filled with his glory. Amen, Amen.[1]

I Chronicles 29:10–13

David blessed the Lord before all the assembly, and David said: Blessed art thou, O Lord, God of Israel our Father, forever and ever. Thine, O Lord, is the greatness and the power, the glory and the victory and the majesty, for all that is in heaven and on earth is thine; thine, O Lord, is the kingdom, and thou art supreme over all. Riches and honor come from thee; thou rulest over all; in thy hand are power and might, and it is in thy power to make all great and strong. Hence, our God, we ever thank thee and praise thy glorious name.

Nehemiah 9:6–11

Thou art the Lord, thou alone. Thou hast made the heavens and the heaven of heavens with all their host, the earth and all the things upon it, the seas and all that is in them, and thou preservest them all; the host of the heavens worships thee. Thou art the Lord God, who didst choose Abram, and didst bring him out of Ur of the Chaldeans, and gavest him the name of Abraham. Thou didst find his heart faithful before thee, and didst make a covenant with him to give the land of the Canaanite, the Hittite, the Amorite, the Perizzite, the Jebusite, and the Girgashite—to give it to his descendants, and hast fulfilled thy words, for thou art righteous. Thou didst see the distress of our fathers in Egypt and hear their cry by the Red Sea; thou didst show signs and wonders on Pharaoh and all his servants and all the people of his land, for thou knewest that they dealt viciously against them; and so hast thou made a name for thyself to this day. The sea thou didst divide before them, so that they went through the middle of the sea on dry ground; and their pursuers thou didst cast into the depths, like a stone into the mighty waters.

---

[1] *Psalms* 89:53; 135:21; 72:18–19.

שמות יד, ל–לא

וַיּוֹשַׁע יְיָ בַּיּוֹם הַהוּא אֶת יִשְׂרָאֵל מִיַּד מִצְרָיִם; וַיַּרְא יִשְׂרָאֵל אֶת מִצְרַיִם מֵת עַל שְׂפַת הַיָּם. Reader וַיַּרְא יִשְׂרָאֵל אֶת הַיָּד הַגְּדֹלָה אֲשֶׁר עָשָׂה יְיָ בְּמִצְרַיִם, וַיִּירְאוּ הָעָם אֶת יְיָ, וַיַּאֲמִינוּ בַּייָ וּבְמשֶׁה עַבְדּוֹ.

שמות טו, א–יח

אָז יָשִׁיר משֶׁה וּבְנֵי יִשְׂרָאֵל אֶת הַשִּׁירָה הַזֹּאת לַייָ, וַיֹּאמְרוּ לֵאמֹר: אָשִׁירָה לַייָ כִּי גָאֹה גָּאָה, סוּס וְרֹכְבוֹ רָמָה בַיָּם. עָזִּי וְזִמְרָת יָהּ, וַיְהִי לִי לִישׁוּעָה; זֶה אֵלִי וְאַנְוֵהוּ, אֱלֹהֵי אָבִי וַאֲרֹמְמֶנְהוּ. יְיָ אִישׁ מִלְחָמָה, יְיָ שְׁמוֹ. מַרְכְּבֹת פַּרְעֹה וְחֵילוֹ יָרָה בַיָּם, וּמִבְחַר שָׁלִשָׁיו טֻבְּעוּ בְיַם סוּף. תְּהֹמֹת יְכַסְיֻמוּ, יָרְדוּ בִמְצוֹלֹת כְּמוֹ אָבֶן. יְמִינְךָ יְיָ נֶאְדָּרִי בַּכֹּחַ, יְמִינְךָ יְיָ תִּרְעַץ אוֹיֵב. וּבְרֹב גְּאוֹנְךָ תַּהֲרֹס קָמֶיךָ; תְּשַׁלַּח חֲרֹנְךָ, יֹאכְלֵמוֹ כַּקַּשׁ. וּבְרוּחַ אַפֶּיךָ נֶעֶרְמוּ מַיִם, נִצְּבוּ כְמוֹ נֵד נֹזְלִים, קָפְאוּ תְהֹמֹת בְּלֶב־יָם. אָמַר אוֹיֵב: אֶרְדֹּף אַשִּׂיג, אֲחַלֵּק שָׁלָל, תִּמְלָאֵמוֹ נַפְשִׁי, אָרִיק חַרְבִּי, תּוֹרִישֵׁמוֹ יָדִי. נָשַׁפְתָּ בְרוּחֲךָ, כִּסָּמוֹ יָם; צָלֲלוּ כַּעוֹפֶרֶת בְּמַיִם אַדִּירִים. מִי כָמֹכָה בָּאֵלִם יְיָ, מִי כָּמֹכָה נֶאְדָּר בַּקֹּדֶשׁ, נוֹרָא תְהִלֹּת, עֹשֵׂה פֶלֶא. נָטִיתָ יְמִינְךָ, תִּבְלָעֵמוֹ אָרֶץ. נָחִיתָ בְחַסְדְּךָ עַם־זוּ גָּאָלְתָּ; נֵהַלְתָּ בְעָזְּךָ אֶל נְוֵה קָדְשֶׁךָ. שָׁמְעוּ עַמִּים, יִרְגָּזוּן; חִיל אָחַז יֹשְׁבֵי פְּלָשֶׁת. אָז נִבְהֲלוּ אַלּוּפֵי אֱדוֹם, אֵילֵי מוֹאָב יֹאחֲזֵמוֹ רָעַד; נָמֹגוּ כֹּל יֹשְׁבֵי כְנָעַן. תִּפֹּל עֲלֵיהֶם אֵימָתָה וָפַחַד; בִּגְדֹל זְרוֹעֲךָ יִדְּמוּ כָּאָבֶן; עַד יַעֲבֹר עַמְּךָ יְיָ, עַד יַעֲבֹר עַם־זוּ קָנִיתָ. תְּבִאֵמוֹ וְתִטָּעֵמוֹ בְּהַר נַחֲלָתְךָ, מָכוֹן לְשִׁבְתְּךָ פָּעַלְתָּ, יְיָ; מִקְּדָשׁ, אֲדֹנָי, כּוֹנְנוּ יָדֶיךָ. יְיָ יִמְלֹךְ לְעֹלָם וָעֶד. יְיָ יִמְלֹךְ לְעֹלָם וָעֶד.

Exodus 14:30-31

Thus did the Lord save Israel that day from the power of the Egyptians; and Israel saw the Egyptians dead on the seashore. Israel saw the mighty act which the Lord had performed against the Egyptians, and the people revered the Lord: they believed in the Lord and in his servant Moses.

Exodus 15:1-18

Then Moses and the children of Israel sang this song to the Lord; they said: I will sing to the Lord, for he has completely triumphed; the horse and its rider he has hurled into the sea. The Lord is my strength and song, for he has come to my aid. This is my God, and I will glorify him; my father's God, and I will extol him. The Lord is a warrior—Lord is his name. Pharaoh's chariots and his army he has cast into the sea, and his picked captains are engulfed in the Red Sea. The depths cover them; they went down into the depths like a stone. Thy right hand, O Lord, glorious in power, thy right hand, O Lord, crushes the enemy. By thy great majesty thou destroyest thy opponents. Thou sendest forth thy wrath—it consumes them like stubble. By the blast of thy nostrils the waters piled up—the floods stood upright like a wall; the depths were congealed in the heart of the sea. The enemy said: "I will pursue them, I will overtake them, I will divide the spoil, my lust shall be glutted with them; I will draw my sword, my hand shall destroy them." Thou didst blow with thy wind—the sea covered them; they sank like lead in the mighty waters. Who is there like thee among the mighty, O Lord? Who is like thee, glorious in holiness, awe-inspiring in renown, doing marvels? Thou didst stretch out thy right hand—the earth swallowed them. In thy grace thou hast led the people whom thou hast redeemed; by thy power thou hast guided them to thy holy habitation. The peoples have heard of it and trembled; pangs have seized the inhabitants of Philistia. Then were the chieftains of Edom in agony; trembling seized the lords of Moab; all the inhabitants of Canaan melted away. Terror and dread fell on them. Under the great sweep of thy arm they are as still as a stone, till thy people pass over, O Lord, till the people thou hast acquired pass over. Thou wilt bring them in and plant them in the highlands of thy own, the place which thou, O Lord, hast made for thy dwelling, the sanctuary, O Lord, which thy hands have established. The Lord shall reign forever and ever. The Lord shall reign forever and ever.

כִּי לַיְיָ הַמְּלוּכָה, וּמוֹשֵׁל בַּגּוֹיִם. Reader וְעָלוּ מוֹשִׁיעִים בְּהַר
צִיּוֹן לִשְׁפֹּט אֶת הַר עֵשָׂו, וְהָיְתָה לַיְיָ הַמְּלוּכָה. וְהָיָה יְיָ לְמֶלֶךְ
עַל כָּל הָאָרֶץ; בַּיּוֹם הַהוּא יִהְיֶה יְיָ אֶחָד וּשְׁמוֹ אֶחָד.

נִשְׁמַת כָּל חַי תְּבָרֵךְ אֶת שִׁמְךָ, יְיָ אֱלֹהֵינוּ, וְרוּחַ כָּל בָּשָׂר
תְּפָאֵר וּתְרוֹמֵם זִכְרְךָ, מַלְכֵּנוּ, תָּמִיד. מִן הָעוֹלָם וְעַד הָעוֹלָם
אַתָּה אֵל, וּמִבַּלְעָדֶיךָ אֵין לָנוּ מֶלֶךְ גּוֹאֵל וּמוֹשִׁיעַ, פּוֹדֶה
וּמַצִּיל וּמְפַרְנֵס, וּמְרַחֵם בְּכָל עֵת צָרָה וְצוּקָה; אֵין לָנוּ מֶלֶךְ
אֶלָּא אָתָּה. אֱלֹהֵי הָרִאשׁוֹנִים וְהָאַחֲרוֹנִים, אֱלוֹהַּ כָּל בְּרִיּוֹת,
אֲדוֹן כָּל תּוֹלָדוֹת, הַמְהֻלָּל בְּרֹב הַתִּשְׁבָּחוֹת, הַמְנַהֵג עוֹלָמוֹ
בְּחֶסֶד וּבְרִיּוֹתָיו בְּרַחֲמִים. וַיְיָ לֹא יָנוּם וְלֹא יִישָׁן, הַמְעוֹרֵר
יְשֵׁנִים, וְהַמֵּקִיץ נִרְדָּמִים, וְהַמֵּשִׂיחַ אִלְּמִים, וְהַמַּתִּיר אֲסוּרִים,
וְהַסּוֹמֵךְ נוֹפְלִים, וְהַזּוֹקֵף כְּפוּפִים. לְךָ לְבַדְּךָ אֲנַחְנוּ מוֹדִים.

אִלּוּ פִינוּ מָלֵא שִׁירָה כַיָּם, וּלְשׁוֹנֵנוּ רִנָּה כַּהֲמוֹן גַּלָּיו,
וְשִׂפְתוֹתֵינוּ שֶׁבַח כְּמֶרְחֲבֵי רָקִיעַ, וְעֵינֵינוּ מְאִירוֹת כַּשֶּׁמֶשׁ
וְכַיָּרֵחַ, וְיָדֵינוּ פְרוּשׂוֹת כְּנִשְׁרֵי שָׁמָיִם, וְרַגְלֵינוּ קַלּוֹת כָּאַיָּלוֹת,
אֵין אֲנַחְנוּ מַסְפִּיקִים לְהוֹדוֹת לְךָ, יְיָ אֱלֹהֵינוּ וֵאלֹהֵי אֲבוֹתֵינוּ,
וּלְבָרֵךְ אֶת שְׁמֶךָ עַל אַחַת מֵאֶלֶף, אֶלֶף אַלְפֵי אֲלָפִים וְרִבֵּי
רְבָבוֹת פְּעָמִים הַטּוֹבוֹת שֶׁעָשִׂיתָ עִם אֲבוֹתֵינוּ וְעִמָּנוּ. מִמִּצְרַיִם
גְּאַלְתָּנוּ, יְיָ אֱלֹהֵינוּ, וּמִבֵּית עֲבָדִים פְּדִיתָנוּ; בְּרָעָב זַנְתָּנוּ
וּבְשָׂבָע כִּלְכַּלְתָּנוּ; מֵחֶרֶב הִצַּלְתָּנוּ וּמִדֶּבֶר מִלַּטְתָּנוּ, וּמֵחֳלָיִם
רָעִים וְנֶאֱמָנִים דִּלִּיתָנוּ. עַד הֵנָּה עֲזָרוּנוּ רַחֲמֶיךָ וְלֹא עֲזָבוּנוּ
חֲסָדֶיךָ; וְאַל תִּטְּשֵׁנוּ, יְיָ אֱלֹהֵינוּ, לָנֶצַח. עַל כֵּן, אֵבָרִים שֶׁפִּלַּגְתָּ

נשמת was well known in the talmudic period. A portion of this poem is
quoted as part of the prayer for rain (Berakhoth 59b; Ta'anith 6b). The
phrase "countless millions of favors" probably refers to the drops of rain,
each drop being a separate favor; indeed, the Talmud suggests that thanks

For sovereignty is the Lord's, and he governs the nations. Deliverers shall go up to Mount Zion to rule the hill country of Esau, and dominion shall be the Lord's. The Lord shall be King over all the earth; on that day shall the Lord be One and his name One.[1]

NISHMATH

The soul of every living being shall bless thy name, Lord our God; the spirit of all mortals shall ever glorify and extol thy fame, our King. From eternity to eternity thou art God. Besides thee we have no king who redeems and saves, ransoms and rescues, sustains and shows mercy in all times of woe and stress. We have no King but thee.

God of the first and of the last, God of all creatures, Lord of all generations, endlessly praised be he who guides his world with kindness and his creatures with mercy. The Lord neither slumbers nor sleeps; he rouses those who sleep and awakens those who slumber; he enables the speechless to speak and sets the captives free; he supports all who fall and raises all who are bowed down. To thee alone we give thanks.

Were our mouth filled with song as the sea [is with water], and our tongue with ringing praise as the roaring waves; were our lips full of adoration as the wide expanse of heaven, and our eyes sparkling like the sun or the moon; were our hands spread out in prayer as the eagles of the sky, and our feet as swift as the deer— we should still be unable to thank thee and bless thy name, Lord our God and God of our fathers, for one thousandth of the countless millions of favors which thou hast conferred on our fathers and on us. Thou hast delivered us from Egypt, Lord our God, and redeemed us from slavery. Thou hast nourished us in famine and provided us with plenty. Thou hast rescued us from the sword, made us escape the plague, and freed us from severe and lasting diseases. Until now thy mercy has helped us, and thy kindness has not abandoned us; mayest thou, Lord our God, never forsake us.

---

should be given for every drop of rain. *Nishmath* is identified in the Talmud (Pesaḥim 118a) with ברכת השיר, recommended by the Mishnah for the closing of the *Haggadah* service on Passover.

---

[1] *Psalm* 22:29; *Obadiah* 1:21; *Zechariah* 14:9.

בָּנוּ, וְרוּחַ וּנְשָׁמָה שֶׁנָּפַחְתָּ בְּאַפֵּינוּ, וְלָשׁוֹן אֲשֶׁר שַׂמְתָּ בְּפִינוּ, הֵן הֵם יוֹדוּ וִיבָרְכוּ, וִישַׁבְּחוּ וִיפָאֲרוּ, וִירוֹמְמוּ וְיַעֲרִיצוּ, וְיַקְדִּישׁוּ וְיַמְלִיכוּ אֶת שִׁמְךָ, מַלְכֵּנוּ. כִּי כָל פֶּה לְךָ יוֹדֶה, וְכָל לָשׁוֹן לְךָ תִשָּׁבַע, וְכָל בֶּרֶךְ לְךָ תִכְרַע, וְכָל קוֹמָה לְפָנֶיךָ תִשְׁתַּחֲוֶה, וְכָל לְבָבוֹת יִירָאוּךָ, וְכָל קֶרֶב וּכְלָיוֹת יְזַמְּרוּ לִשְׁמֶךָ, כַּדָּבָר שֶׁכָּתוּב: כָּל עַצְמוֹתַי תֹּאמַרְנָה, יְיָ מִי כָמְוֹךָ, מַצִּיל עָנִי מֵחָזָק מִמֶּנּוּ, וְעָנִי וְאֶבְיוֹן מִגֹּזְלוֹ. מִי יִדְמֶה לָּךְ, וּמִי יִשְׁוֶה לָּךְ, וּמִי יַעֲרָךְ־לָךְ, הָאֵל הַגָּדוֹל, הַגִּבּוֹר וְהַנּוֹרָא, אֵל עֶלְיוֹן, קֹנֵה שָׁמַיִם וָאָרֶץ. Reader • נְהַלֶּלְךָ וּנְשַׁבֵּחֲךָ וּנְפָאֶרְךָ, וּנְבָרֵךְ אֶת שֵׁם קָדְשֶׁךָ, כָּאָמוּר: לְדָוִד, בָּרְכִי נַפְשִׁי אֶת יְיָ, וְכָל קְרָבַי אֶת שֵׁם קָדְשׁוֹ.

On festivals the Reader begins here:

הָאֵל בְּתַעֲצֻמוֹת עֻזֶּךָ, הַגָּדוֹל בִּכְבוֹד שְׁמֶךָ, הַגִּבּוֹר לָנֶצַח וְהַנּוֹרָא בְּנוֹרְאוֹתֶיךָ, הַמֶּלֶךְ הַיּוֹשֵׁב עַל כִּסֵּא רָם וְנִשָּׂא.

On Sabbaths the Reader begins here:

שׁוֹכֵן עַד, מָרוֹם וְקָדוֹשׁ שְׁמוֹ, וְכָתוּב: רַנְּנוּ צַדִּיקִים בַּיְיָ, לַיְשָׁרִים נָאוָה תְהִלָּה.

בְּפִי יְשָׁרִים תִּתְהַלָּל,

וּבְדִבְרֵי צַדִּיקִים תִּתְבָּרַךְ,

וּבִלְשׁוֹן חֲסִידִים תִּתְרוֹמָם,

וּבְקֶרֶב קְדוֹשִׁים תִּתְקַדָּשׁ.

וּבְמַקְהֲלוֹת רִבְבוֹת עַמְּךָ בֵּית יִשְׂרָאֵל בְּרִנָּה יִתְפָּאַר שִׁמְךָ, מַלְכֵּנוּ, בְּכָל דּוֹר וָדוֹר; שֶׁכֵּן חוֹבַת כָּל הַיְצוּרִים לְפָנֶיךָ, יְיָ

שׁוכן עד is borrowed from Isaiah 57:15. The initials of the four synonyms for "righteous" in בפי ישרים happen to form the acrostic יצחק; by re-arranging

Therefore, the limbs which thou hast apportioned in us, the spirit and soul which thou hast breathed into our nostrils, and the tongue which thou hast placed in our mouth, shall all thank and bless, praise and glorify, extol and revere, hallow and do homage to thy name, our King. Indeed, every mouth shall praise thee; every tongue shall vow allegiance to thee; every knee shall bend to thee, and every person shall bow before thee. All hearts shall revere thee, and men's inmost being shall sing to thy name, as it is written: "All my being shall say: O Lord, who is like thee? Thou savest the poor man from one that is stronger, the poor and needy from one who would rob him."[1] Who is like thee, who is equal to thee, who can be compared to thee, O great, mighty and revered God, supreme God, Master of heaven and earth? We will praise, laud and glorify thee and bless thy holy name, as it is said by David: "Bless the Lord, O my soul, and let my whole being bless his holy name."[2]

On festivals the Reader begins here:

Thou art God in thy tremendous power, great in thy glorious name, mighty forever and revered for thy awe-inspiring acts; thou, O King, art seated upon a high and lofty throne.

On Sabbaths the Reader begins here:

Thou who abidest forever, exalted and holy is thy name. It is written: "Rejoice in the Lord, you righteous; it is fitting for the upright to give praise."[3]

By the mouth of the upright thou art praised;
By the speech of the righteous thou art blessed;
By the tongue of the faithful thou art extolled;
Inside the holy thou art sanctified.

In the assemblies of the tens of thousands of thy people, the house of Israel, with ringing song shall thy name, our King, be glorified in every generation; for this is the duty of all creatures

---

the verbs תתרומם, תתברך, תתקדש, תתהלל, the third letters spell רבקה. Such re-arrangement is found in the Sephardic *Siddur*.

---

[1] *Psalm* 35:10.   [2] *Psalm* 103:1.   [3] *Psalm* 33:1.

אֱלֹהֵינוּ וֵאלֹהֵי אֲבוֹתֵינוּ, Reader לְהוֹדוֹת, לְהַלֵּל, לְשַׁבֵּחַ, לְפָאֵר, לְרוֹמֵם, לְהַדֵּר, לְבָרֵךְ, לְעַלֵּה וּלְקַלֵּס עַל כָּל דִּבְרֵי שִׁירוֹת וְתִשְׁבְּחוֹת דָּוִד בֶּן־יִשַׁי עַבְדְּךָ מְשִׁיחֶךָ.

יִשְׁתַּבַּח שִׁמְךָ לָעַד, מַלְכֵּנוּ, הָאֵל הַמֶּלֶךְ הַגָּדוֹל וְהַקָּדוֹשׁ, בַּשָּׁמַיִם וּבָאָרֶץ. כִּי לְךָ נָאֶה, יְיָ אֱלֹהֵינוּ וֵאלֹהֵי אֲבוֹתֵינוּ, שִׁיר וּשְׁבָחָה, הַלֵּל וְזִמְרָה, עֹז וּמֶמְשָׁלָה, נֶצַח, גְּדֻלָּה וּגְבוּרָה, תְּהִלָּה וְתִפְאֶרֶת, קְדֻשָּׁה וּמַלְכוּת, Reader בְּרָכוֹת וְהוֹדָאוֹת, מֵעַתָּה וְעַד עוֹלָם. בָּרוּךְ אַתָּה, יְיָ, אֵל מֶלֶךְ גָּדוֹל בַּתִּשְׁבָּחוֹת, אֵל הַהוֹדָאוֹת, אֲדוֹן הַנִּפְלָאוֹת, הַבּוֹחֵר בְּשִׁירֵי זִמְרָה, מֶלֶךְ, אֵל, חֵי הָעוֹלָמִים.

Reader:

יִתְגַּדַּל וְיִתְקַדַּשׁ שְׁמֵהּ רַבָּא בְּעָלְמָא דִּי בְרָא כִרְעוּתֵהּ; וְיַמְלִיךְ מַלְכוּתֵהּ בְּחַיֵּיכוֹן וּבְיוֹמֵיכוֹן, וּבְחַיֵּי דְכָל בֵּית יִשְׂרָאֵל, בַּעֲגָלָא וּבִזְמַן קָרִיב, וְאִמְרוּ אָמֵן.

יְהֵא שְׁמֵהּ רַבָּא מְבָרַךְ לְעָלַם וּלְעָלְמֵי עָלְמַיָּא.

יִתְבָּרַךְ וְיִשְׁתַּבַּח, וְיִתְפָּאַר וְיִתְרוֹמַם, וְיִתְנַשֵּׂא וְיִתְהַדָּר, וְיִתְעַלֶּה וְיִתְהַלָּל שְׁמֵהּ דְּקֻדְשָׁא, בְּרִיךְ הוּא, לְעֵלָּא (לְעֵלָּא) מִן כָּל בִּרְכָתָא וְשִׁירָתָא, תֻּשְׁבְּחָתָא וְנֶחֱמָתָא, דַּאֲמִירָן בְּעָלְמָא, וְאִמְרוּ אָמֵן.

Silent meditation:	Reader:

Reader:
בָּרְכוּ אֶת יְיָ הַמְבֹרָךְ.

Congregation and Reader:
בָּרוּךְ יְיָ הַמְבֹרָךְ לְעוֹלָם וָעֶד.

Silent meditation:
יִתְבָּרַךְ וְיִשְׁתַּבַּח, וְיִתְפָּאַר וְיִתְרוֹמַם וְיִתְנַשֵּׂא שְׁמוֹ שֶׁל מֶלֶךְ מַלְכֵי הַמְּלָכִים, הַקָּדוֹשׁ בָּרוּךְ הוּא, שֶׁהוּא רִאשׁוֹן וְהוּא אַחֲרוֹן, וּמִבַּלְעָדָיו אֵין אֱלֹהִים. סֹלוּ לָרֹכֵב בָּעֲרָבוֹת, בְּיָהּ שְׁמוֹ, וְעִלְזוּ לְפָנָיו; וּשְׁמוֹ מְרוֹמָם עַל כָּל בְּרָכָה וּתְהִלָּה. בָּרוּךְ שֵׁם כְּבוֹד מַלְכוּתוֹ לְעוֹלָם וָעֶד. יְהִי שֵׁם יְיָ מְבֹרָךְ מֵעַתָּה וְעַד עוֹלָם.

towards thee, Lord our God and God of our fathers, to thank and praise, laud and glorify, extol and honor, bless and exalt and acclaim thee, even beyond all the songs of praise by David, son of Jesse, thy anointed servant.

Praised be thy name forever, our King, great and holy God and King, in heaven and on earth; for to thee, Lord our God and God of our fathers, pertain song and praise, hymn and psalm, power and dominion, victory, greatness and might, renown and glory, holiness and kingship, blessings and thanks, henceforth and forever. Blessed art thou, O Lord, most exalted God and King, Lord of wonders, who art pleased with hymns, thou God and King, the life of the universe.

Reader:

Glorified and sanctified be God's great name throughout the world which he has created according to his will. May he establish his kingdom in your lifetime and during your days, and within the life of the entire house of Israel, speedily and soon; and say, Amen.

May his great name be blessed forever and to all eternity.

Blessed and praised, glorified and exalted, extolled and honored, adored and lauded be the name of the Holy One, blessed be he, beyond all the blessings and hymns, praises and consolations that are ever spoken in the world; and say, Amen.

Reader:	*Silent meditation:*
Bless the Lord who is blessed.	Blessed, praised, glorified, extolled and exalted be the name
Congregation and Reader:	of the supreme King of kings,
Blessed be the Lord who is blessed forever and ever.	the Holy One, blessed be he, who is the first and the last, and

besides him there is no God. Extol him who is in the heavens—Lord is his name, and rejoice before him. His name is exalted above all blessing and praise. Blessed be the name of his glorious majesty forever and ever. Let the name of the Lord be blessed henceforth and forever.

בָּרוּךְ אַתָּה, יְיָ אֱלֹהֵינוּ, מֶלֶךְ הָעוֹלָם, יוֹצֵר אוֹר וּבוֹרֵא
חֹשֶׁךְ, עֹשֶׂה שָׁלוֹם, וּבוֹרֵא אֶת הַכֹּל.

On festivals occurring on weekdays say:

(הַמֵּאִיר לָאָרֶץ וְלַדָּרִים עָלֶיהָ בְּרַחֲמִים, וּבְטוּבוֹ מְחַדֵּשׁ
בְּכָל יוֹם תָּמִיד מַעֲשֵׂה בְרֵאשִׁית. מָה רַבּוּ מַעֲשֶׂיךָ, יְיָ; כֻּלָּם
בְּחָכְמָה עָשִׂיתָ, מָלְאָה הָאָרֶץ קִנְיָנֶךָ. הַמֶּלֶךְ הַמְּרוֹמָם לְבַדּוֹ
מֵאָז, הַמְשֻׁבָּח וְהַמְפֹאָר וְהַמִּתְנַשֵּׂא מִימוֹת עוֹלָם. אֱלֹהֵי עוֹלָם,
בְּרַחֲמֶיךָ הָרַבִּים רַחֵם עָלֵינוּ, אֲדוֹן עֻזֵּנוּ, צוּר מִשְׂגַּבֵּנוּ, מָגֵן
יִשְׁעֵנוּ, מִשְׂגָּב בַּעֲדֵנוּ.

אֵל בָּרוּךְ גְּדוֹל דֵּעָה, הֵכִין וּפָעַל זָהֳרֵי חַמָּה, טוֹב יָצַר
כָּבוֹד לִשְׁמוֹ, מְאוֹרוֹת נָתַן סְבִיבוֹת עֻזּוֹ, פִּנּוֹת צְבָאָיו קְדוֹשִׁים,
רוֹמְמֵי שַׁדַּי, תָּמִיד מְסַפְּרִים כְּבוֹד אֵל וּקְדֻשָּׁתוֹ. תִּתְבָּרַךְ, יְיָ
אֱלֹהֵינוּ, עַל שֶׁבַח מַעֲשֵׂה יָדֶיךָ, וְעַל מְאוֹרֵי אוֹר שֶׁעָשִׂיתָ;
יְפָאֲרוּךָ סֶּלָה.) Continue תִּתְבָּרַךְ on page 341.

On Sabbaths say:

הַכֹּל יוֹדוּךָ וְהַכֹּל יְשַׁבְּחוּךָ, וְהַכֹּל יֹאמְרוּ אֵין קָדוֹשׁ כַּיְיָ.
הַכֹּל יְרוֹמְמוּךָ סֶּלָה, יוֹצֵר הַכֹּל, הָאֵל הַפּוֹתֵחַ בְּכָל יוֹם
דַּלְתוֹת שַׁעֲרֵי מִזְרָח, וּבוֹקֵעַ חַלּוֹנֵי רָקִיעַ, מוֹצִיא חַמָּה
מִמְּקוֹמָהּ, וּלְבָנָה מִמְּכוֹן שִׁבְתָּהּ, וּמֵאִיר לָעוֹלָם כֻּלּוֹ וּלְיוֹשְׁבָיו
שֶׁבָּרָא בְּמִדַּת רַחֲמִים. הַמֵּאִיר לָאָרֶץ וְלַדָּרִים עָלֶיהָ בְּרַחֲמִים,
וּבְטוּבוֹ מְחַדֵּשׁ בְּכָל יוֹם תָּמִיד מַעֲשֵׂה בְרֵאשִׁית. הַמֶּלֶךְ
הַמְּרוֹמָם לְבַדּוֹ מֵאָז, הַמְשֻׁבָּח וְהַמְפֹאָר וְהַמִּתְנַשֵּׂא מִימוֹת
עוֹלָם. אֱלֹהֵי עוֹלָם, בְּרַחֲמֶיךָ הָרַבִּים רַחֵם עָלֵינוּ, אֲדוֹן עֻזֵּנוּ,
צוּר מִשְׂגַּבֵּנוּ, מָגֵן יִשְׁעֵנוּ, מִשְׂגָּב בַּעֲדֵנוּ. אֵין כְּעֶרְכְּךָ וְאֵין
זוּלָתֶךָ; אֶפֶס בִּלְתֶּךָ, וּמִי דוֹמֶה לָּךְ. Reader אֵין כְּעֶרְכְּךָ, יְיָ

אֵל בָּרוּךְ גְּדוֹל דֵּעָה is an alphabetic acrostic ending with תָּמִיד.

Blessed art thou, Lord our God, King of the universe, who formest light and createst darkness, who makest peace and createst all things.

On festivals occurring on weekdays say:

(In mercy thou givest light to the earth and to those who dwell on it; in thy goodness thou renewest the work of creation every day, constantly. How great are thy works, O Lord! In wisdom hast thou made them all; the earth is full of thy creations. Thou alone, O King, art ever exalted! Thou art lauded, glorified and extolled from days of old. Eternal God, show us thy great mercy! Lord of our strength, thou art our secure Stronghold, our saving Shield, our Refuge.

The blessed God, great in knowledge, designed and made the brilliant sun. The Beneficent One created glory for his name. He placed luminaries round about his majesty. His chief hosts are holy beings that extol the Almighty. They constantly recount God's glory and holiness. Be thou blessed, Lord our God, for thy excellent handiwork and for the luminaries which thou hast made; they ever render thee glory.)

Continue "Be thou blessed" on page 342.

On Sabbaths say:

All shall thank thee; all shall praise thee; all shall declare: There is none holy like the Lord! All shall forever extol thee, Creator of all. Thou, O God, openest daily the gates of the east, and cleavest the windows of the sky; thou bringest forth the sun from its place, and the moon from its abode, and givest light to the whole world and to its inhabitants whom thou hast created in thy mercy.

In mercy thou givest light to the earth and to those who dwell on it; in thy goodness thou renewest the work of creation every day, constantly. Thou alone, O King, art ever exalted! Thou art lauded, glorified and extolled from days of old. Eternal God, show us thy great mercy! Lord of our strength, thou art our secure Stronghold, our saving Shield, our Refuge.

There is none to be compared to thee, and there is none besides thee; there is none but thee. Who is like thee? *There is none to be compared to thee.* Lord our God, in this world, *and there is none*

אֱלֹהֵינוּ, בָּעוֹלָם הַזֶּה; וְאֵין זוּלָתֶךָ, מַלְכֵּנוּ, לְחַיֵּי הָעוֹלָם הַבָּא.
אֶפֶס בִּלְתֶּךָ, גּוֹאֲלֵנוּ, לִימוֹת הַמָּשִׁיחַ; וְאֵין דּוֹמֶה לְךָ, מוֹשִׁיעֵנוּ,
לִתְחִיַּת הַמֵּתִים.

בָּרוּךְ וּמְבֹרָךְ בְּפִי כָּל נְשָׁמָה;	אֵל אָדוֹן עַל כָּל הַמַּעֲשִׂים
דַּעַת וּתְבוּנָה סוֹבְבִים אֹתוֹ.	גָּדְלוֹ וְטוּבוֹ מָלֵא עוֹלָם
וְנֶהְדָּר בְּכָבוֹד עַל הַמֶּרְכָּבָה;	הַמִּתְגָּאֶה עַל חַיּוֹת הַקֹּדֶשׁ
חֶסֶד וְרַחֲמִים לִפְנֵי כְבוֹדוֹ.	זְכוּת וּמִישׁוֹר לִפְנֵי כִסְאוֹ
יְצָרָם בְּדַעַת בְּבִינָה וּבְהַשְׂכֵּל;	טוֹבִים מְאוֹרוֹת שֶׁבָּרָא אֱלֹהֵינוּ
לִהְיוֹת מוֹשְׁלִים בְּקֶרֶב תֵּבֵל.	כֹּחַ וּגְבוּרָה נָתַן בָּהֶם
נָאֶה זִיוָם בְּכָל הָעוֹלָם;	מְלֵאִים זִיו וּמְפִיקִים נֹגַהּ
עוֹשִׂים בְּאֵימָה רְצוֹן קוֹנָם.	שְׂמֵחִים בְּצֵאתָם וְשָׂשִׂים בְּבוֹאָם
צָהֳלָה וְרִנָּה לְזֵכֶר מַלְכוּתוֹ;	פְּאֵר וְכָבוֹד נוֹתְנִים לִשְׁמוֹ
רָאָה וְהִתְקִין צוּרַת הַלְּבָנָה.	קָרָא לַשֶּׁמֶשׁ וַיִּזְרַח אוֹר

שֶׁבַח נוֹתְנִים לוֹ כָּל צְבָא מָרוֹם, תִּפְאֶרֶת וּגְדֻלָּה,
שְׂרָפִים וְאוֹפַנִּים וְחַיּוֹת הַקֹּדֶשׁ—

לָאֵל אֲשֶׁר שָׁבַת מִכָּל הַמַּעֲשִׂים בַּיּוֹם הַשְּׁבִיעִי; הִתְעַלָּה
וְיָשַׁב עַל כִּסֵּא כְבוֹדוֹ; תִּפְאֶרֶת עָטָה לְיוֹם הַמְּנוּחָה, עֹנֶג קָרָא
לְיוֹם הַשַּׁבָּת. זֶה שֶׁבַח שֶׁל יוֹם הַשְּׁבִיעִי, שֶׁבּוֹ שָׁבַת אֵל מִכָּל

אל אדון is an alphabetical hymn, generally attributed to the *Yorde Mer-kavah*, mystics of the eighth century, who applied their minds to theosophy. The *Tur* mentions a variant reading, והקטין instead of והתקין, according to which the clause concerning the moon refers to the talmudic tradition that God diminished the original size of the moon (Ḥullin 60b). *El Adon* is a praise of God who created the seven seemingly "wandering" celestial bodies (כוכבי לכת). Having spoken of the sun and the moon, the poet alludes to the five

besides thee, our King, in the life of the world to come; *there is none but thee,* our Redeemer, in the days of the Messiah; *and there is none like thee,* our Deliverer, in the revival of the dead.

God is the Lord of all creation;
Blessed and praised is he by every soul.
His greatness and goodness fill the universe;
Knowledge and wisdom surround him.

He is exalted above the celestial beings,
And adorned in glory above the chariot.
Purity and justice stand before his throne;
Kindness and mercy are in his glorious presence.

Good are the luminaries which our God has created,
He made them with knowledge, wisdom and insight;
He placed in them energy and power
To have dominion over the world.

Full of splendor, they radiate brightness;
Beautiful is their brilliance throughout the world.
They rejoice in their rising and exult in their setting,
Performing with reverence the will of their Creator.

Glory and honor do they give to his name,
And joyous song to his majestic fame.
He called forth the sun, and it shone;
He saw to regulate the form of the moon.

All the hosts of heaven give him praise;
All the celestial beings attribute glory and grandeur—

To God who rested from all the work of creation on the seventh day, and ascended to sit upon his throne of glory. He vested the day of rest with beauty, and called the Sabbath a delight. Such is the distinction of the seventh day, on which God rested from

---

planets Saturn (שבתאי), Venus (נוגה), Mercury (כוכב), Jupiter (צדק), and Mars (מאדים), by means of the initials of the words שבח נותנים כל צבא מרום.

⌐ ¬ לאל אשר שבת is found in the geonic liturgy. Like the other Sabbath additions to the *Yotser* benediction, it probably belongs to the talmudic period. According to the Midrash, Adam and the Sabbath sang in unison: "It is good to give thanks to the Lord"; hence ויום השביעי משבח ואומר.

מְלַאכְתּוֹ. וְיוֹם הַשְּׁבִיעִי מְשַׁבֵּחַ וְאוֹמֵר: מִזְמוֹר שִׁיר לְיוֹם
הַשַּׁבָּת, טוֹב לְהוֹדוֹת לַיְיָ. לְפִיכָךְ יְפָאֲרוּ וִיבָרְכוּ לְאֵל כָּל
יְצוּרָיו; שֶׁבַח, יְקָר וּגְדֻלָּה יִתְּנוּ לְאֵל מֶלֶךְ, יוֹצֵר כֹּל, הַמַּנְחִיל
מְנוּחָה לְעַמּוֹ יִשְׂרָאֵל בִּקְדֻשָּׁתוֹ בְּיוֹם שַׁבַּת קֹדֶשׁ. שִׁמְךָ יְיָ
אֱלֹהֵינוּ יִתְקַדַּשׁ, וְזִכְרְךָ מַלְכֵּנוּ יִתְפָּאַר, בַּשָּׁמַיִם מִמַּעַל וְעַל
הָאָרֶץ מִתָּחַת. תִּתְבָּרַךְ, מוֹשִׁיעֵנוּ, עַל שֶׁבַח מַעֲשֵׂה יָדֶיךָ, וְעַל
מְאוֹרֵי אוֹר שֶׁעָשִׂיתָ; יְפָאֲרוּךָ סֶּלָה.

תִּתְבָּרַךְ צוּרֵנוּ, מַלְכֵּנוּ וְגוֹאֲלֵנוּ, בּוֹרֵא קְדוֹשִׁים; יִשְׁתַּבַּח
שִׁמְךָ לָעַד מַלְכֵּנוּ, יוֹצֵר מְשָׁרְתִים, וַאֲשֶׁר מְשָׁרְתָיו כֻּלָּם
עוֹמְדִים בְּרוּם עוֹלָם, וּמַשְׁמִיעִים בְּיִרְאָה, יַחַד בְּקוֹל, דִּבְרֵי
אֱלֹהִים חַיִּים וּמֶלֶךְ עוֹלָם. כֻּלָּם אֲהוּבִים, כֻּלָּם בְּרוּרִים, כֻּלָּם
גִּבּוֹרִים, וְכֻלָּם עֹשִׂים בְּאֵימָה וּבְיִרְאָה רְצוֹן קוֹנָם. Reader וְכֻלָּם
פּוֹתְחִים אֶת פִּיהֶם בִּקְדֻשָּׁה וּבְטָהֳרָה, בְּשִׁירָה וּבְזִמְרָה,
וּמְבָרְכִים וּמְשַׁבְּחִים, וּמְפָאֲרִים וּמַעֲרִיצִים, וּמַקְדִּישִׁים
וּמַמְלִיכִים—

אֶת שֵׁם הָאֵל הַמֶּלֶךְ הַגָּדוֹל, הַגִּבּוֹר וְהַנּוֹרָא, קָדוֹשׁ הוּא.
וְכֻלָּם מְקַבְּלִים עֲלֵיהֶם עֹל מַלְכוּת שָׁמַיִם זֶה מִזֶּה, וְנוֹתְנִים
רְשׁוּת זֶה לָזֶה Reader לְהַקְדִּישׁ לְיוֹצְרָם. בְּנַחַת רוּחַ, בְּשָׂפָה
בְרוּרָה וּבִנְעִימָה קְדֻשָׁה, כֻּלָּם כְּאֶחָד עוֹנִים וְאוֹמְרִים בְּיִרְאָה:
קָדוֹשׁ, קָדוֹשׁ, קָדוֹשׁ יְיָ צְבָאוֹת; מְלֹא כָל הָאָרֶץ כְּבוֹדוֹ.
וְהָאוֹפַנִּים וְחַיּוֹת הַקֹּדֶשׁ, בְּרַעַשׁ גָּדוֹל מִתְנַשְּׂאִים לְעֻמַּת
שְׂרָפִים. Reader לְעֻמָּתָם מְשַׁבְּחִים וְאוֹמְרִים:
בָּרוּךְ כְּבוֹד יְיָ מִמְּקוֹמוֹ.

לְאֵל בָּרוּךְ נְעִימוֹת יִתֵּנוּ; לַמֶּלֶךְ, אֵל חַי וְקַיָּם, זְמִרוֹת
יֹאמֵרוּ, וְתִשְׁבָּחוֹת יַשְׁמִיעוּ; כִּי הוּא לְבַדּוֹ פּוֹעֵל גְּבוּרוֹת, עֹשֶׂה

all his work. The seventh day itself utters praise, saying: "A song of the Sabbath day—It is good to give thanks to the Lord." Therefore, let all God's creatures glorify and bless him; let them attribute excellence, glory and grandeur to God, the King and Creator of all, who in his holiness bestows rest upon his people Israel on the holy Sabbath day. Thy name, Lord our God, shall be hallowed; thy fame, our King, shall be glorified in heaven above and on earth beneath. Be thou blessed, our Deliverer, for thy excellent handiwork, and for the bright luminaries which thou hast made; they ever render thee glory.

Be thou blessed, our Stronghold, our King and Redeemer, Creator of holy beings; praised be thy name forever, our King, Creator of ministering angels, all of whom stand in the heights of the universe and reverently proclaim in unison, aloud, the words of the living God and everlasting King. All of them are beloved, all of them are pure, all of them are mighty; they all perform with awe and reverence the will of their Creator; they all open their mouth with holiness and purity, with song and melody, while they bless and praise, glorify and reverence, sanctify and acclaim—

The name of the great, mighty and revered God and King, holy is he. They all accept the rule of the kingdom of heaven, one from the other, granting permission to one another to hallow their Creator. In serene spirit, with pure speech and sacred melody, they all exclaim in unison and with reverence:

Holy, holy, holy is the Lord of hosts;
The whole earth is full of his glory.[1]

Then the celestial ofannim and the holy beings, rising with a loud sound toward the seraphim, respond with praise and say:

Blessed be the glory of the Lord from his abode.[2]

To the blessed God they offer melodies; to the King, the living and eternal God, they utter hymns and praises. Truly, he alone performs mighty acts and creates new things; he is a warrior who

---

[1] *Isaiah* 6:3. [2] *Ezekiel* 3:12.

חֲדָשׁוֹת, בַּעַל מִלְחָמוֹת, זוֹרֵעַ צְדָקוֹת, מַצְמִיחַ יְשׁוּעוֹת, בּוֹרֵא
רְפוּאוֹת, נוֹרָא תְהִלּוֹת, אֲדוֹן הַנִּפְלָאוֹת, הַמְחַדֵּשׁ בְּטוּבוֹ בְּכָל
יוֹם תָּמִיד מַעֲשֵׂה בְרֵאשִׁית, כָּאָמוּר: לְעֹשֵׂה אוֹרִים גְּדֹלִים, כִּי
לְעוֹלָם חַסְדּוֹ. Reader אוֹר חָדָשׁ עַל צִיּוֹן תָּאִיר, וְנִזְכֶּה כֻלָּנוּ
מְהֵרָה לְאוֹרוֹ. בָּרוּךְ אַתָּה, יְיָ, יוֹצֵר הַמְּאוֹרוֹת.

אַהֲבָה רַבָּה אֲהַבְתָּנוּ, יְיָ אֱלֹהֵינוּ; חֶמְלָה גְדוֹלָה וִיתֵרָה
חָמַלְתָּ עָלֵינוּ. אָבִינוּ מַלְכֵּנוּ, בַּעֲבוּר אֲבוֹתֵינוּ שֶׁבָּטְחוּ בְךָ,
וַתְּלַמְּדֵם חֻקֵּי חַיִּים, כֵּן תְּחָנֵּנוּ וּתְלַמְּדֵנוּ. אָבִינוּ הָאָב הָרַחֲמָן,
הַמְרַחֵם, רַחֵם עָלֵינוּ וְתֵן בְּלִבֵּנוּ לְהָבִין וּלְהַשְׂכִּיל, לִשְׁמֹעַ
לִלְמֹד וּלְלַמֵּד, לִשְׁמֹר וְלַעֲשׂוֹת וּלְקַיֵּם אֶת כָּל דִּבְרֵי תַלְמוּד
תוֹרָתֶךָ, בְּאַהֲבָה. וְהָאֵר עֵינֵינוּ בְּתוֹרָתֶךָ, וְדַבֵּק לִבֵּנוּ בְּמִצְוֹתֶיךָ,
וְיַחֵד לְבָבֵנוּ לְאַהֲבָה וּלְיִרְאָה אֶת שְׁמֶךָ, וְלֹא נֵבוֹשׁ לְעוֹלָם
וָעֶד. כִּי בְשֵׁם קָדְשְׁךָ הַגָּדוֹל וְהַנּוֹרָא בָּטָחְנוּ, נָגִילָה וְנִשְׂמְחָה
בִּישׁוּעָתֶךָ. Reader וַהֲבִיאֵנוּ לְשָׁלוֹם מֵאַרְבַּע כַּנְפוֹת הָאָרֶץ,
וְתוֹלִיכֵנוּ קוֹמְמִיּוּת לְאַרְצֵנוּ, כִּי אֵל פּוֹעֵל יְשׁוּעוֹת אָתָּה, וּבָנוּ
בָחַרְתָּ מִכָּל עַם וְלָשׁוֹן, וְקֵרַבְתָּנוּ לְשִׁמְךָ הַגָּדוֹל סֶלָה בֶּאֱמֶת,
לְהוֹדוֹת לְךָ וּלְיַחֶדְךָ בְּאַהֲבָה. בָּרוּךְ אַתָּה, יְיָ, הַבּוֹחֵר בְּעַמּוֹ
יִשְׂרָאֵל בְּאַהֲבָה.

(אֵל מֶלֶךְ נֶאֱמָן :When praying in private, add)

דברים ו, ד—ט

שְׁמַע יִשְׂרָאֵל, יְיָ אֱלֹהֵינוּ, יְיָ אֶחָד.

בָּרוּךְ שֵׁם כְּבוֹד מַלְכוּתוֹ לְעוֹלָם וָעֶד.

וְאָהַבְתָּ אֵת יְיָ אֱלֹהֶיךָ בְּכָל לְבָבְךָ וּבְכָל נַפְשְׁךָ וּבְכָל
מְאֹדֶךָ. וְהָיוּ הַדְּבָרִים הָאֵלֶּה, אֲשֶׁר אָנֹכִי מְצַוְּךָ הַיּוֹם, עַל
לְבָבֶךָ. וְשִׁנַּנְתָּם לְבָנֶיךָ, וְדִבַּרְתָּ בָּם בְּשִׁבְתְּךָ בְּבֵיתֶךָ, וּבְלֶכְתְּךָ

sows justice, produces triumphs, and creates healing. Revered in renown, Lord of wonders, in his goodness he renews the creation every day, constantly, as it is said: "He makes the great lights; truly, his mercy endures forever."[1] O cause a new light to shine upon Zion, and may we all be worthy soon to enjoy its brightness. Blessed art thou, O Lord, Creator of the lights.

With great love hast thou loved us, Lord our God; great and abundant mercy hast thou bestowed upon us. Our Father, our King, for the sake of our forefathers who trusted in thee, whom thou didst teach laws of life, be gracious to us and teach us likewise. Our Father, merciful Father, thou who art ever compassionate, have pity on us and inspire us to understand and discern, to perceive, learn and teach, to observe, do, and fulfill gladly all the teachings of thy Torah. Enlighten our eyes in thy Torah; attach our heart to thy commandments; unite our heart to love and reverence thy name, so that we may never be put to shame. In thy holy, great and revered name we trust—may we thrill with joy over thy salvation. O bring us home in peace from the four corners of the earth, and make us walk upright to our land, for thou art the God who performs triumphs. Thou hast chosen us from all peoples and nations, and hast truly brought us near to thy great name forever, that we may eagerly praise thee and acclaim thy Oneness. Blessed art thou, O Lord, who hast graciously chosen thy people Israel.

SHEMA

(When praying in private, add: God is a faithful King.*)*

Deuteronomy 6:4-9

Hear, O Israel, the Lord is our God, the Lord is One.

Blessed be the name of his glorious majesty forever and ever.

You shall love the Lord your God with all your heart, and with all your soul, and with all your might. And these words which I command you today shall be in your heart. You shall teach them diligently to your children, and you shall speak of them when you are sitting at home and when you go on a journey,

---

ברוך שם כבוד was regularly used in the Temple. It is attributed to Jacob.

[1] *Psalm* 136:7.

בַדֶּרֶךְ, וּבְשָׁכְבְּךָ וּבְקוּמֶךָ, וּקְשַׁרְתָּם לְאוֹת עַל יָדֶךָ, וְהָיוּ
לְטֹטָפֹת בֵּין עֵינֶיךָ. וּכְתַבְתָּם עַל מְזֻזוֹת בֵּיתֶךָ וּבִשְׁעָרֶיךָ.

דברים יא, יג—כא

וְהָיָה אִם שָׁמֹעַ תִּשְׁמְעוּ אֶל מִצְוֹתַי, אֲשֶׁר אָנֹכִי מְצַוֶּה אֶתְכֶם
הַיּוֹם, לְאַהֲבָה אֶת יְיָ אֱלֹהֵיכֶם, וּלְעָבְדוֹ בְּכָל לְבַבְכֶם וּבְכָל
נַפְשְׁכֶם. וְנָתַתִּי מְטַר אַרְצְכֶם בְּעִתּוֹ, יוֹרֶה וּמַלְקוֹשׁ; וְאָסַפְתָּ
דְגָנֶךָ, וְתִירֹשְׁךָ וְיִצְהָרֶךָ. וְנָתַתִּי עֵשֶׂב בְּשָׂדְךָ לִבְהֶמְתֶּךָ; וְאָכַלְתָּ
וְשָׂבָעְתָּ. הִשָּׁמְרוּ לָכֶם פֶּן יִפְתֶּה לְבַבְכֶם, וְסַרְתֶּם וַעֲבַדְתֶּם
אֱלֹהִים אֲחֵרִים, וְהִשְׁתַּחֲוִיתֶם לָהֶם. וְחָרָה אַף יְיָ בָּכֶם, וְעָצַר
אֶת הַשָּׁמַיִם וְלֹא יִהְיֶה מָטָר, וְהָאֲדָמָה לֹא תִתֵּן אֶת יְבוּלָהּ;
וַאֲבַדְתֶּם מְהֵרָה מֵעַל הָאָרֶץ הַטֹּבָה אֲשֶׁר יְיָ נֹתֵן לָכֶם. וְשַׂמְתֶּם
אֶת דְּבָרַי אֵלֶּה עַל לְבַבְכֶם וְעַל נַפְשְׁכֶם; וּקְשַׁרְתֶּם אֹתָם
לְאוֹת עַל יֶדְכֶם, וְהָיוּ לְטוֹטָפֹת בֵּין עֵינֵיכֶם. וְלִמַּדְתֶּם אֹתָם
אֶת בְּנֵיכֶם לְדַבֵּר בָּם, בְּשִׁבְתְּךָ בְּבֵיתֶךָ, וּבְלֶכְתְּךָ בַדֶּרֶךְ,
וּבְשָׁכְבְּךָ וּבְקוּמֶךָ. וּכְתַבְתָּם עַל מְזוּזוֹת בֵּיתֶךָ וּבִשְׁעָרֶיךָ.
לְמַעַן יִרְבּוּ יְמֵיכֶם וִימֵי בְנֵיכֶם, עַל הָאֲדָמָה אֲשֶׁר נִשְׁבַּע
יְיָ לַאֲבֹתֵיכֶם לָתֵת לָהֶם, כִּימֵי הַשָּׁמַיִם עַל הָאָרֶץ.

במדבר טו, לז—מא

וַיֹּאמֶר יְיָ אֶל מֹשֶׁה לֵּאמֹר: דַּבֵּר אֶל בְּנֵי יִשְׂרָאֵל וְאָמַרְתָּ
אֲלֵהֶם, וְעָשׂוּ לָהֶם צִיצִת עַל כַּנְפֵי בִגְדֵיהֶם לְדֹרֹתָם; וְנָתְנוּ עַל
צִיצִת הַכָּנָף פְּתִיל תְּכֵלֶת. וְהָיָה לָכֶם לְצִיצִת, וּרְאִיתֶם אֹתוֹ
וּזְכַרְתֶּם אֶת כָּל מִצְוֹת יְיָ, וַעֲשִׂיתֶם אֹתָם. וְלֹא תָתוּרוּ אַחֲרֵי
לְבַבְכֶם וְאַחֲרֵי עֵינֵיכֶם, אֲשֶׁר אַתֶּם זֹנִים אַחֲרֵיהֶם. לְמַעַן
תִּזְכְּרוּ וַעֲשִׂיתֶם אֶת כָּל מִצְוֹתָי, וִהְיִיתֶם קְדֹשִׁים לֵאלֹהֵיכֶם.
אֲנִי יְיָ אֱלֹהֵיכֶם, אֲשֶׁר הוֹצֵאתִי אֶתְכֶם מֵאֶרֶץ מִצְרַיִם לִהְיוֹת
לָכֶם לֵאלֹהִים; Reader אֲנִי יְיָ אֱלֹהֵיכֶם—

when you lie down and when you rise up. You shall bind them for a sign on your hand, and they shall be for frontlets between your eyes. You shall inscribe them on the doorposts of your house and on your gates.

Deuteronomy 11:13–21

And if you will carefully obey my commands which I give you today, to love the Lord your God and to serve him with all your heart and with all your soul, I will give rain for your land at the right season, the autumn rains and the spring rains, that you may gather in your grain, your wine and your oil. And I will produce grass in your fields for your cattle, and you will eat and be satisfied. Beware lest your heart be deceived, and you turn and serve other gods and worship them; for then the Lord's anger will blaze against you, and he will shut up the skies so that there will be no rain, and the land will yield no produce, and you will quickly perish from the good land which the Lord gives you. So you shall place these words of mine in your heart and in your soul, and you shall bind them for a sign on your hand, and they shall be for frontlets between your eyes. You shall teach them to your children, speaking of them when you are sitting at home and when you go on a journey, when you lie down and when you rise up. You shall inscribe them on the doorposts of your house and on your gates— that your life and the life of your children may be prolonged in the land, which the Lord promised he would give to your fathers, for as long as the sky remains over the earth.

Numbers 15:37–41

The Lord spoke to Moses, saying: Speak to the children of Israel and tell them to make for themselves fringes on the corners of their garments throughout their generations, and to put on the fringe of each corner a blue thread. You shall have it as a fringe, so that when you look upon it you will remember to do all the commands of the Lord, and you will not follow the desires of your heart and your eyes which lead you astray. It is for you to remember and do all my commands and be holy to your God. I am the Lord your God who brought you out of the land of Egypt to be your God; I am the Lord your God.

אֱמֶת וְיַצִּיב, וְנָכוֹן וְקַיָּם, וְיָשָׁר וְנֶאֱמָן, וְאָהוּב וְחָבִיב, וְנֶחְמָד
וְנָעִים, וְנוֹרָא וְאַדִּיר, וּמְתֻקָּן וּמְקֻבָּל, וְטוֹב וְיָפֶה הַדָּבָר הַזֶּה
עָלֵינוּ לְעוֹלָם וָעֶד. אֱמֶת, אֱלֹהֵי עוֹלָם מַלְכֵּנוּ, צוּר יַעֲקֹב מָגֵן
יִשְׁעֵנוּ. Reader לְדֹר וָדֹר הוּא קַיָּם, וּשְׁמוֹ קַיָּם, וְכִסְאוֹ נָכוֹן,
וּמַלְכוּתוֹ וֶאֱמוּנָתוֹ לָעַד קַיָּמֶת. וּדְבָרָיו חָיִים וְקַיָּמִים, נֶאֱמָנִים
וְנֶחֱמָדִים, לָעַד וּלְעוֹלְמֵי עוֹלָמִים, עַל אֲבוֹתֵינוּ וְעָלֵינוּ, עַל
בָּנֵינוּ וְעַל דּוֹרוֹתֵינוּ, וְעַל כָּל דּוֹרוֹת זֶרַע יִשְׂרָאֵל עֲבָדֶיךָ.

עַל הָרִאשׁוֹנִים וְעַל הָאַחֲרוֹנִים דָּבָר טוֹב וְקַיָּם לְעוֹלָם
וָעֶד, אֱמֶת וֶאֱמוּנָה, חֹק וְלֹא יַעֲבֹר. Reader אֱמֶת, שָׁאַתָּה הוּא
יְיָ אֱלֹהֵינוּ וֵאלֹהֵי אֲבוֹתֵינוּ, מַלְכֵּנוּ מֶלֶךְ אֲבוֹתֵינוּ, גֹּאֲלֵנוּ גֹּאֵל
אֲבוֹתֵינוּ, יוֹצְרֵנוּ צוּר יְשׁוּעָתֵנוּ, פּוֹדֵנוּ וּמַצִּילֵנוּ; מֵעוֹלָם שְׁמֶךָ,
אֵין אֱלֹהִים זוּלָתֶךָ.

עֶזְרַת אֲבוֹתֵינוּ אַתָּה הוּא מֵעוֹלָם, מָגֵן וּמוֹשִׁיעַ לִבְנֵיהֶם
אַחֲרֵיהֶם בְּכָל דּוֹר וָדוֹר. בְּרוּם עוֹלָם מוֹשָׁבֶךָ, וּמִשְׁפָּטֶיךָ
וְצִדְקָתְךָ עַד אַפְסֵי אָרֶץ. אַשְׁרֵי אִישׁ שֶׁיִּשְׁמַע לְמִצְוֹתֶיךָ,
וְתוֹרָתְךָ וּדְבָרְךָ יָשִׂים עַל לִבּוֹ. אֱמֶת, אַתָּה הוּא אָדוֹן לְעַמֶּךָ,
וּמֶלֶךְ גִּבּוֹר לָרִיב רִיבָם. אֱמֶת, אַתָּה הוּא רִאשׁוֹן וְאַתָּה הוּא
אַחֲרוֹן, וּמִבַּלְעָדֶיךָ אֵין לָנוּ מֶלֶךְ גּוֹאֵל וּמוֹשִׁיעַ. מִמִּצְרַיִם
גְּאַלְתָּנוּ, יְיָ אֱלֹהֵינוּ, וּמִבֵּית עֲבָדִים פְּדִיתָנוּ. כָּל בְּכוֹרֵיהֶם
הָרָגְתָּ, וּבְכוֹרְךָ גָּאָלְתָּ, וְיַם סוּף בָּקַעְתָּ, וְזֵדִים טִבַּעְתָּ, וִידִידִים
הֶעֱבַרְתָּ, וַיְכַסּוּ מַיִם צָרֵיהֶם, אֶחָד מֵהֶם לֹא נוֹתָר. עַל זֹאת
שִׁבְּחוּ אֲהוּבִים וְרוֹמְמוּ אֵל, וְנָתְנוּ יְדִידִים זְמִירוֹת, שִׁירוֹת
וְתִשְׁבָּחוֹת, בְּרָכוֹת וְהוֹדָאוֹת לַמֶּלֶךְ, אֵל חַי וְקַיָּם. רָם וְנִשָּׂא,
גָּדוֹל וְנוֹרָא, מַשְׁפִּיל גֵּאִים וּמַגְבִּיהַּ שְׁפָלִים, מוֹצִיא אֲסִירִים

True and certain, established and enduring, right and steadfast, beloved and precious, pleasant and sweet, revered and glorious, correct and acceptable, good and beautiful is this faith to us forever and ever. True it is that the eternal God is our King, the Stronghold of Jacob and our saving Shield. He exists throughout all generations; his name endures; his throne is firm; his kingship and his truth are forever established. His words are living and enduring, faithful and precious, forever and to all eternity, as for our fathers so also for us, for our children and future generations, and for all generations of the seed of Israel his servants.

Alike for the first and the last generations this faith is good and valid forever and ever; it is true and trustworthy, a law that will not pass away. True it is that thou art the Lord our God and the God of our fathers, our King and the King of our fathers, our Redeemer and the Redeemer of our fathers, our Maker and saving Stronghold, our Deliverer and Rescuer. Thou art eternal; there is no God besides thee.

Thou wast the help of our fathers from of old, and hast been a Shield and Savior to their children after them in every generation. In the heights of the universe is thy habitation, and thy justice and righteousness reach to the furthest ends of the earth. Happy is the man who obeys thy commands and takes thy Torah and thy word to heart. True it is that thou art the Lord of thy people, and a mighty King to champion their cause. True it is that thou art the first and thou art the last, and besides thee we have no King who redeems and saves. From Egypt thou didst redeem us, Lord our God, and from the house of slavery thou didst deliver us; all their first-born thou didst slay, but thy first-born thou didst redeem; thou didst divide the Red Sea and drown the arrogant, but thy beloved people thou didst take across; the water covered their enemies, not one of them was left.

For this, the beloved people praised and extolled God; they offered hymns, blessings and thanksgivings to the King, the living and eternal God. He is high and exalted, great and revered; he brings low the arrogant, and raises up the lowly; he frees the captives, and delivers the afflicted; he helps the poor, and answers

וּפוֹדֶה עֲנָוִים, וְעוֹזֵר דַּלִּים, וְעוֹנֶה לְעַמּוֹ בְּעֵת שַׁוְּעָם אֵלָיו.
תְּהִלּוֹת לְאֵל עֶלְיוֹן, בָּרוּךְ הוּא וּמְבֹרָךְ.

מֹשֶׁה וּבְנֵי יִשְׂרָאֵל לְךָ עָנוּ שִׁירָה בְּשִׂמְחָה רַבָּה, וְאָמְרוּ כֻלָּם:
מִי כָמֹכָה בָּאֵלִם, יְיָ, מִי כָּמֹכָה נֶאְדָּר בַּקֹּדֶשׁ, נוֹרָא תְהִלֹּת,
עֹשֵׂה פֶלֶא.

שִׁירָה חֲדָשָׁה שִׁבְּחוּ גְאוּלִים לְשִׁמְךָ עַל שְׂפַת הַיָּם; יַחַד
כֻּלָּם הוֹדוּ וְהִמְלִיכוּ וְאָמְרוּ:

יְיָ יִמְלֹךְ לְעוֹלָם וָעֶד.

צוּר יִשְׂרָאֵל, קוּמָה בְּעֶזְרַת יִשְׂרָאֵל, וּפְדֵה כִנְאֻמְךָ יְהוּדָה
וְיִשְׂרָאֵל. Reader גֹּאֲלֵנוּ יְיָ צְבָאוֹת שְׁמוֹ, קְדוֹשׁ יִשְׂרָאֵל. בָּרוּךְ
אַתָּה, יְיָ, גָּאַל יִשְׂרָאֵל.

The *Amidah* for festivals begins on page 585.

The *Amidah* is recited in silent devotion while standing, facing east.
The Reader repeats the *Amidah* aloud when a *minyan* holds service.

אֲדֹנָי, שְׂפָתַי תִּפְתָּח, וּפִי יַגִּיד תְּהִלָּתֶךָ.

בָּרוּךְ אַתָּה, יְיָ אֱלֹהֵינוּ וֵאלֹהֵי אֲבוֹתֵינוּ, אֱלֹהֵי אַבְרָהָם,
אֱלֹהֵי יִצְחָק, וֵאלֹהֵי יַעֲקֹב, הָאֵל הַגָּדוֹל הַגִּבּוֹר וְהַנּוֹרָא, אֵל
עֶלְיוֹן, גּוֹמֵל חֲסָדִים טוֹבִים, וְקוֹנֵה הַכֹּל, וְזוֹכֵר חַסְדֵי אָבוֹת,
וּמֵבִיא גוֹאֵל לִבְנֵי בְנֵיהֶם לְמַעַן שְׁמוֹ בְּאַהֲבָה.

Between *Rosh Hashanah* and *Yom Kippur* add:

(זָכְרֵנוּ לְחַיִּים, מֶלֶךְ חָפֵץ בַּחַיִּים,
וְכָתְבֵנוּ בְּסֵפֶר הַחַיִּים, לְמַעַנְךָ אֱלֹהִים חַיִּים.)

מֶלֶךְ עוֹזֵר וּמוֹשִׁיעַ וּמָגֵן. בָּרוּךְ אַתָּה, יְיָ, מָגֵן אַבְרָהָם.

אַתָּה גִבּוֹר לְעוֹלָם, אֲדֹנָי, מְחַיֵּה מֵתִים אַתָּה, רַב לְהוֹשִׁיעַ.

Between *Sukkoth* and *Pesaḥ* add:

(מַשִּׁיב הָרוּחַ וּמוֹרִיד הַגָּשֶׁם.)

his people whenever they cry to him. Praised be the supreme God; be he ever blessed.

Moses and the children of Israel sang a song to thee with great joy; all of them said:

"Who is like thee, O Lord, among the mighty?
Who is like thee, glorious in holiness,
Awe-inspiring in renown, doing wonders?"[1]

The redeemed people sang a new song of praise to thy name at the seashore; they all, in unison, gave thanks and proclaimed thy sovereignty, and said:

"The Lord shall reign forever and ever."[2]

Stronghold of Israel, arise to the help of Israel; deliver Judah and Israel, as thou hast promised. Our Redeemer, thou art the Lord of hosts, the Holy One of Israel. Blessed art thou, O Lord, who hast redeemed Israel.

The Amidah for festivals begins on page 586.

AMIDAH

The Amidah is recited in silent devotion while standing, facing east.
The Reader repeats the Amidah aloud when a minyan holds service.

O Lord, open thou my lips, that my mouth may declare thy praise.[3]

Blessed art thou, Lord our God and God of our fathers, God of Abraham, God of Isaac and God of Jacob; great, mighty and revered God, sublime God, who bestowest lovingkindness, and art Master of all things; who rememberest the good deeds of our fathers, and who wilt graciously bring a redeemer to their children's children for the sake of thy name.

Between Rosh Hashanah and Yom Kippur add:

(Remember us to life, O King who delightest in life; inscribe us in the book of life for thy sake, O living God.)

O King, Supporter, Savior and Shield! Blessed art thou, O Lord, Shield of Abraham.

Thou, O Lord, art mighty forever; thou revivest the dead; thou art powerful to save.

Between Sukkoth and Pesaḥ add:

(Thou causest the wind to blow and the rain to fall.)

---

[1] *Exodus* 15:11.   [2] *Exodus* 15:18.   [3] *Psalm* 51:17.

מְכַלְכֵּל חַיִּים בְּחֶסֶד, מְחַיֵּה מֵתִים בְּרַחֲמִים רַבִּים, סוֹמֵךְ
נוֹפְלִים, וְרוֹפֵא חוֹלִים, וּמַתִּיר אֲסוּרִים, וּמְקַיֵּם אֱמוּנָתוֹ לִישֵׁנֵי
עָפָר. מִי כָמוֹךָ, בַּעַל גְּבוּרוֹת, וּמִי דוֹמֶה לָּךְ, מֶלֶךְ מֵמִית
וּמְחַיֶּה וּמַצְמִיחַ יְשׁוּעָה.

Between *Rosh Hashanah* and *Yom Kippur* add:

(מִי כָמוֹךָ, אַב הָרַחֲמִים, זוֹכֵר יְצוּרָיו לְחַיִּים בְּרַחֲמִים.)
וְנֶאֱמָן אַתָּה לְהַחֲיוֹת מֵתִים. בָּרוּךְ אַתָּה, יְיָ, מְחַיֵּה הַמֵּתִים.

When the Reader repeats the *Amidah*, the following *Kedushah* is said.

נְקַדֵּשׁ אֶת שִׁמְךָ בָּעוֹלָם כְּשֵׁם שֶׁמַּקְדִּישִׁים אוֹתוֹ בִּשְׁמֵי
מָרוֹם, כַּכָּתוּב עַל יַד נְבִיאֶךָ: וְקָרָא זֶה אֶל זֶה וְאָמַר:

קָדוֹשׁ, קָדוֹשׁ, קָדוֹשׁ יְיָ צְבָאוֹת; מְלֹא כָל הָאָרֶץ כְּבוֹדוֹ.

אָז בְּקוֹל רַעַשׁ גָּדוֹל, אַדִּיר וְחָזָק, מַשְׁמִיעִים קוֹל, מִתְנַשְּׂאִים
לְעֻמַּת שְׂרָפִים, לְעֻמָּתָם בָּרוּךְ יֹאמֵרוּ—

בָּרוּךְ כְּבוֹד יְיָ מִמְּקוֹמוֹ.

מִמְּקוֹמְךָ מַלְכֵּנוּ תוֹפִיעַ וְתִמְלֹךְ עָלֵינוּ, כִּי מְחַכִּים אֲנַחְנוּ
לָךְ. מָתַי תִּמְלֹךְ בְּצִיּוֹן, בְּקָרוֹב בְּיָמֵינוּ לְעוֹלָם וָעֶד תִּשְׁכּוֹן.
תִּתְגַּדַּל וְתִתְקַדַּשׁ בְּתוֹךְ יְרוּשָׁלַיִם עִירְךָ לְדוֹר וָדוֹר וּלְנֵצַח
נְצָחִים. וְעֵינֵינוּ תִרְאֶינָה מַלְכוּתֶךָ, כַּדָּבָר הָאָמוּר בְּשִׁירֵי עֻזֶּךָ,
עַל יְדֵי דָוִד מְשִׁיחַ צִדְקֶךָ:

יִמְלֹךְ יְיָ לְעוֹלָם, אֱלֹהַיִךְ צִיּוֹן לְדֹר וָדֹר; הַלְלוּיָהּ.

Reader:

לְדוֹר וָדוֹר נַגִּיד גָּדְלֶךָ, וּלְנֵצַח נְצָחִים קְדֻשָּׁתְךָ נַקְדִּישׁ,
וְשִׁבְחֲךָ אֱלֹהֵינוּ מִפִּינוּ לֹא יָמוּשׁ לְעוֹלָם וָעֶד, כִּי אֵל מֶלֶךְ גָּדוֹל
וְקָדוֹשׁ אָתָּה. בָּרוּךְ אַתָּה, יְיָ, הָאֵל * (הַמֶּלֶךְ) הַקָּדוֹשׁ.

*Between *Rosh Hashanah* and *Yom Kippur* say הַמֶּלֶךְ הַקָּדוֹשׁ.

Thou sustainest the living with kindness, and revivest the dead with great mercy; thou supportest all who fall, and healest the sick; thou settest the captives free, and keepest faith with those who sleep in the dust. Who is like thee, Lord of power? Who resembles thee, O King? Thou bringest death and restorest life, and causest salvation to flourish.

Between Rosh Hashanah and Yom Kippur add:

(Who is like thee, merciful Father? In mercy thou rememberest thy creatures to life.)

Thou art faithful to revive the dead. Blessed art thou, O Lord, who revivest the dead.

KEDUSHAH

When the Reader repeats the Amidah, the following Kedushah is said:

We sanctify thy name in the world even as they sanctify it in the highest heavens, as it is written by thy prophet: "They keep calling to one another:

Holy, holy, holy is the Lord of hosts;
The whole earth is full of his glory."[1]

Then with a loud sound, mighty and strong, they make their voice heard; upraising themselves toward the Seraphim, they respond by exclaiming: Blessed—

Blessed be the glory of the Lord from his abode.[2]

From thy abode, our King, appear and reign over us, for we wait for thee. O when wilt thou reign in Zion? Speedily, in our days, do thou dwell there forever. Mayest thou be exalted and sanctified in Jerusalem thy city throughout all generations and to all eternity. May our eyes behold thy kingdom, as it is said in thy glorious Psalms by thy truly anointed David:

The Lord shall reign forever,
Your God, O Zion, for all generations.
Praise the Lord![3]

Reader:

Through all generations we will declare thy greatness; to all eternity we will proclaim thy holiness; thy praise, our God, shall never depart from our mouth, for thou art a great and holy God and King. Blessed art thou, O Lord, * holy God.

*Between Rosh Hashanah and Yom Kippur say "holy King".

ממקומך מלכנו is included in the weekday *Kedushah* in the *Siddur* of Amram Gaon with some variations: ... בקרוב בימינו ובחיינו תשכן ... תופיע ותושיענו.

[1] *Isaiah 6:3.* [2] *Ezekiel 3:12.* [3] *Psalm 146:10.*

אַתָּה קָדוֹשׁ וְשִׁמְךָ קָדוֹשׁ, וּקְדוֹשִׁים בְּכָל יוֹם יְהַלְלוּךָ סֶּלָה. בָּרוּךְ אַתָּה, יְיָ, הָאֵל (הַמֶּלֶךְ) הַקָּדוֹשׁ.

יִשְׂמַח מֹשֶׁה בְּמַתְּנַת חֶלְקוֹ, כִּי עֶבֶד נֶאֱמָן קָרָאתָ לּוֹ; כְּלִיל תִּפְאֶרֶת בְּרֹאשׁוֹ נָתַתָּ, בְּעָמְדוֹ לְפָנֶיךָ עַל הַר סִינָי. וּשְׁנֵי לוּחוֹת אֲבָנִים הוֹרִיד בְּיָדוֹ, וְכָתוּב בָּהֶם שְׁמִירַת שַׁבָּת, וְכֵן כָּתוּב בְּתוֹרָתֶךָ:

וְשָׁמְרוּ בְנֵי יִשְׂרָאֵל אֶת הַשַּׁבָּת, לַעֲשׂוֹת אֶת הַשַּׁבָּת לְדֹרֹתָם בְּרִית עוֹלָם. בֵּינִי וּבֵין בְּנֵי יִשְׂרָאֵל אוֹת הִיא לְעוֹלָם, כִּי שֵׁשֶׁת יָמִים עָשָׂה יְיָ אֶת הַשָּׁמַיִם וְאֶת הָאָרֶץ, וּבַיּוֹם הַשְּׁבִיעִי שָׁבַת וַיִּנָּפַשׁ.

וְלֹא נְתַתּוֹ, יְיָ אֱלֹהֵינוּ, לְגוֹיֵי הָאֲרָצוֹת; וְלֹא הִנְחַלְתּוֹ, מַלְכֵּנוּ, לְעוֹבְדֵי פְסִילִים; וְגַם בִּמְנוּחָתוֹ לֹא יִשְׁכְּנוּ עֲרֵלִים; כִּי לְיִשְׂרָאֵל עַמְּךָ נְתַתּוֹ בְּאַהֲבָה, לְזֶרַע יַעֲקֹב אֲשֶׁר בָּם בָּחָרְתָּ. עַם מְקַדְּשֵׁי שְׁבִיעִי, כֻּלָּם יִשְׂבְּעוּ וְיִתְעַנְּגוּ מִטּוּבֶךָ. וְהַשְּׁבִיעִי רָצִיתָ בּוֹ וְקִדַּשְׁתּוֹ, חֶמְדַּת יָמִים אוֹתוֹ קָרָאתָ, זֵכֶר לְמַעֲשֵׂה בְרֵאשִׁית.

אֱלֹהֵינוּ וֵאלֹהֵי אֲבוֹתֵינוּ, רְצֵה בִמְנוּחָתֵנוּ; קַדְּשֵׁנוּ בְּמִצְוֹתֶיךָ, וְתֵן חֶלְקֵנוּ בְּתוֹרָתֶךָ; שַׂבְּעֵנוּ מִטּוּבֶךָ, וְשַׂמְּחֵנוּ בִּישׁוּעָתֶךָ; וְטַהֵר לִבֵּנוּ לְעָבְדְּךָ בֶּאֱמֶת; וְהַנְחִילֵנוּ, יְיָ אֱלֹהֵינוּ, בְּאַהֲבָה וּבְרָצוֹן שַׁבַּת קָדְשֶׁךָ, וְיָנוּחוּ בָהּ יִשְׂרָאֵל מְקַדְּשֵׁי שְׁמֶךָ. בָּרוּךְ אַתָּה, יְיָ, מְקַדֵּשׁ הַשַּׁבָּת.

רְצֵה, יְיָ אֱלֹהֵינוּ, בְּעַמְּךָ יִשְׂרָאֵל וּבִתְפִלָּתָם; וְהָשֵׁב אֶת הָעֲבוֹדָה לִדְבִיר בֵּיתֶךָ, וְאִשֵּׁי יִשְׂרָאֵל וּתְפִלָּתָם בְּאַהֲבָה תְקַבֵּל בְּרָצוֹן, וּתְהִי לְרָצוֹן תָּמִיד עֲבוֹדַת יִשְׂרָאֵל עַמֶּךָ.

On *Rosh Ḥodesh* and *Ḥol ha-Mo'ed* add:

(אֱלֹהֵינוּ וֵאלֹהֵי אֲבוֹתֵינוּ, יַעֲלֶה וְיָבֹא, וְיַגִּיעַ וְיֵרָאֶה, וְיֵרָצֶה וְיִשָּׁמַע, וְיִפָּקֵד וְיִזָּכֵר, זִכְרוֹנֵנוּ וּפִקְדוֹנֵנוּ, וְזִכְרוֹן אֲבוֹתֵינוּ,

Thou art holy and thy name is holy, and holy beings praise thee daily. Blessed art thou, O Lord, holy God

Moses was pleased with the gift bestowed on him, for thou didst call him a faithful servant. A glorious crown didst thou place on his head as he stood before thee on Mount Sinai. He brought down in his hand the two tablets of stone upon which was engraved the command to observe the Sabbath, as it is written in thy Torah:

The children of Israel shall keep the Sabbath, observing the Sabbath throughout their generations as an everlasting covenant. It is a sign between me and the children of Israel forever, that in six days the Lord made the heavens and the earth, and on the seventh day he ceased from work and rested.[1]

Thou, Lord our God, hast not given the Sabbath day to the nations of the world; thou, our King, hast not given it as a heritage to those who worship idols; heathen do not enjoy its rest. But thou hast graciously given it to Israel thy people, the descendants of Jacob whom thou hast chosen. May all the people who sanctify the seventh day be satisfied and delighted with thy goodness. Thou wast pleased with the seventh day and didst hallow it— the most desirable of days didst thou call it—in remembrance of the creation.

Our God and God of our fathers, be pleased with our rest. Sanctify us with thy commandments and grant us a share in thy Torah; satisfy us with thy goodness and gladden us with thy help; purify our heart to serve thee sincerely. In gracious love, Lord our God, grant that we keep thy holy Sabbath as a heritage; may Israel who sanctifies thy name rest on it. Blessed art thou, O Lord, who hallowest the Sabbath.

Be pleased, Lord our God, with thy people Israel and with their prayer; restore the worship to thy most holy sanctuary; accept Israel's offerings and prayer with gracious love. May the worship of thy people Israel be ever pleasing to thee.

On Rosh Ḥodesh and Ḥol ha-Moʻed add:

(Our God and God of our fathers, may the remembrance of us, of our fathers, of Messiah the son of David thy servant, of Je-

---

ישמח משה alludes to the talmudic statement that God said to Moses: "I have a precious gift in my treasure house, called the Sabbath, and I desire to give it to Israel" (Shabbath 10b).

עבד נאמן קראת לו refers to Numbers 12:7 ("Moses my servant, so faithful in all my household").

---

[1] *Exodus* 31:16–17

וְזִכְרוֹן מָשִׁיחַ בֶּן־דָּוִד עַבְדֶּךָ, וְזִכְרוֹן יְרוּשָׁלַיִם עִיר קָדְשֶׁךָ, וְזִכְרוֹן כָּל עַמְּךָ בֵּית יִשְׂרָאֵל לְפָנֶיךָ, לִפְלֵיטָה וּלְטוֹבָה, לְחֵן וּלְחֶסֶד וּלְרַחֲמִים, לְחַיִּים וּלְשָׁלוֹם, בְּיוֹם

Sukkoth	*Pesah*	*Rosh Ḥodesh*
חַג הַסֻּכּוֹת	חַג הַמַּצּוֹת	רֹאשׁ הַחֹדֶשׁ

הַזֶּה. זָכְרֵנוּ, יְיָ אֱלֹהֵינוּ, בּוֹ לְטוֹבָה, וּפָקְדֵנוּ בוֹ לִבְרָכָה, וְהוֹשִׁיעֵנוּ בוֹ לְחַיִּים. וּבִדְבַר יְשׁוּעָה וְרַחֲמִים חוּס וְחָנֵּנוּ, וְרַחֵם עָלֵינוּ וְהוֹשִׁיעֵנוּ, כִּי אֵלֶיךָ עֵינֵינוּ, כִּי אֵל מֶלֶךְ חַנּוּן וְרַחוּם אָתָּה.)

וְתֶחֱזֶינָה עֵינֵינוּ בְּשׁוּבְךָ לְצִיּוֹן בְּרַחֲמִים. בָּרוּךְ אַתָּה, יְיָ, הַמַּחֲזִיר שְׁכִינָתוֹ לְצִיּוֹן.

מוֹדִים אֲנַחְנוּ לָךְ, שָׁאַתָּה הוּא יְיָ אֱלֹהֵינוּ וֵאלֹהֵי אֲבוֹתֵינוּ לְעוֹלָם וָעֶד. צוּר חַיֵּינוּ, מָגֵן יִשְׁעֵנוּ אַתָּה הוּא. לְדוֹר וָדוֹר נוֹדֶה לְּךָ, וּנְסַפֵּר תְּהִלָּתֶךָ, עַל חַיֵּינוּ הַמְּסוּרִים בְּיָדֶךָ, וְעַל נִשְׁמוֹתֵינוּ הַפְּקוּדוֹת לָךְ, וְעַל נִסֶּיךָ שֶׁבְּכָל יוֹם עִמָּנוּ, וְעַל נִפְלְאוֹתֶיךָ וְטוֹבוֹתֶיךָ שֶׁבְּכָל עֵת, עֶרֶב וָבֹקֶר וְצָהֳרָיִם. הַטּוֹב כִּי לֹא כָלוּ רַחֲמֶיךָ, וְהַמְרַחֵם כִּי לֹא תַמּוּ חֲסָדֶיךָ, מֵעוֹלָם קִוִּינוּ לָךְ.

When the Reader repeats the *Amidah*, the Congregation responds here by saying:

(מוֹדִים אֲנַחְנוּ לָךְ, שָׁאַתָּה הוּא יְיָ אֱלֹהֵינוּ וֵאלֹהֵי אֲבוֹתֵינוּ. אֱלֹהֵי כָל בָּשָׂר, יוֹצְרֵנוּ, יוֹצֵר בְּרֵאשִׁית, בְּרָכוֹת וְהוֹדָאוֹת לְשִׁמְךָ הַגָּדוֹל וְהַקָּדוֹשׁ עַל שֶׁהֶחֱיִיתָנוּ וְקִיַּמְתָּנוּ. כֵּן תְּחַיֵּנוּ וּתְקַיְּמֵנוּ, וְתֶאֱסוֹף גָּלֻיּוֹתֵינוּ לְחַצְרוֹת קָדְשֶׁךָ לִשְׁמוֹר חֻקֶּיךָ וְלַעֲשׂוֹת רְצוֹנֶךָ, וּלְעָבְדְּךָ בְּלֵבָב שָׁלֵם, עַל שֶׁאֲנַחְנוּ מוֹדִים לָךְ. בָּרוּךְ אֵל הַהוֹדָאוֹת.)

rusalem thy holy city, and of all thy people the house of Israel,
ascend and come and be accepted before thee for deliverance and
happiness, for grace, kindness and mercy, for life and peace, on
this day of

Rosh Ḥodesh	*Pesaḥ*	*Sukkoth*
the New Moon.	the Feast of Un-leavened Bread	the Feast of Tabernacles.

Remember us this day, Lord our God, for happiness; be mindful of us for blessing; save us to enjoy life. With a promise of salvation and mercy spare us and be gracious to us; have pity on us
and save us, for we look to thee, for thou art a gracious and merciful God and King.)

May our eyes behold thy return in mercy to Zion. Blessed art
thou, O Lord, who restorest thy divine presence to Zion.

We ever thank thee, who art
the Lord our God and the God
of our fathers. Thou art the
strength of our life and our
saving shield. In every generation we will thank thee and
recount thy praise—for our
lives which are in thy charge,
for our souls which are in thy
care, for thy miracles which are
daily with us, and for thy continual wonders and favors—
evening, morning and noon.
Beneficent One, whose mercies
never fail, Merciful One, whose
kindnesses never cease, thou
hast always been our hope.

*When the Reader repeats the Ami-
dah, the Congregation responds
here by saying:*

(We thank thee, who art the
Lord our God and the God of
our fathers. God of all mankind,
our Creator and Creator of the
universe, blessings and thanks
are due to thy great and holy
name, because thou hast kept us
alive and sustained us; mayest
thou ever grant us life and sustenance. O gather our exiles to thy
holy courts to observe thy laws,
to do thy will, and to serve thee
with a perfect heart. For this we
thank thee. Blessed be God to
whom all thanks are due.)

On *Ḥanukkah* add:

(עַל הַנִּסִּים וְעַל הַפֻּרְקָן, וְעַל הַגְּבוּרוֹת וְעַל הַתְּשׁוּעוֹת, וְעַל
הַמִּלְחָמוֹת, שֶׁעָשִׂיתָ לַאֲבוֹתֵינוּ בַּיָּמִים הָהֵם בַּזְּמַן הַזֶּה—

בִּימֵי מַתִּתְיָהוּ בֶּן יוֹחָנָן כֹּהֵן גָּדוֹל, חַשְׁמוֹנַי וּבָנָיו, כְּשֶׁעָמְדָה
מַלְכוּת יָוָן הָרְשָׁעָה עַל עַמְּךָ יִשְׂרָאֵל לְהַשְׁכִּיחָם תּוֹרָתֶךָ,
וּלְהַעֲבִירָם מֵחֻקֵּי רְצוֹנֶךָ. וְאַתָּה בְּרַחֲמֶיךָ הָרַבִּים עָמַדְתָּ לָהֶם
בְּעֵת צָרָתָם, רַבְתָּ אֶת רִיבָם, דַּנְתָּ אֶת דִּינָם, נָקַמְתָּ אֶת נִקְמָתָם;
מָסַרְתָּ גִבּוֹרִים בְּיַד חַלָּשִׁים, וְרַבִּים בְּיַד מְעַטִּים, וּטְמֵאִים בְּיַד
טְהוֹרִים, וּרְשָׁעִים בְּיַד צַדִּיקִים, וְזֵדִים בְּיַד עוֹסְקֵי תוֹרָתֶךָ.
וּלְךָ עָשִׂיתָ שֵׁם גָּדוֹל וְקָדוֹשׁ בְּעוֹלָמֶךָ, וּלְעַמְּךָ יִשְׂרָאֵל עָשִׂיתָ
תְּשׁוּעָה גְדוֹלָה וּפֻרְקָן כְּהַיּוֹם הַזֶּה. וְאַחַר כֵּן בָּאוּ בָנֶיךָ לִדְבִיר
בֵּיתֶךָ, וּפִנּוּ אֶת הֵיכָלֶךָ, וְטִהֲרוּ אֶת מִקְדָּשֶׁךָ, וְהִדְלִיקוּ נֵרוֹת
בְּחַצְרוֹת קָדְשֶׁךָ, וְקָבְעוּ שְׁמוֹנַת יְמֵי חֲנֻכָּה אֵלּוּ לְהוֹדוֹת וּלְהַלֵּל
לְשִׁמְךָ הַגָּדוֹל.)

וְעַל כֻּלָּם יִתְבָּרַךְ וְיִתְרוֹמַם שִׁמְךָ, מַלְכֵּנוּ, תָּמִיד לְעוֹלָם
וָעֶד

Between *Rosh Hashanah* and *Yom Kippur* add:

(וּכְתוֹב לְחַיִּים טוֹבִים כָּל בְּנֵי בְרִיתֶךָ.)

וְכֹל הַחַיִּים יוֹדוּךָ סֶּלָה, וִיהַלְלוּ אֶת שִׁמְךָ בֶּאֱמֶת, הָאֵל,
יְשׁוּעָתֵנוּ וְעֶזְרָתֵנוּ סֶלָה. בָּרוּךְ אַתָּה, יְיָ, הַטּוֹב שִׁמְךָ, וּלְךָ נָאֶה
לְהוֹדוֹת.

Priestly blessing recited by the Reader:

אֱלֹהֵינוּ וֵאלֹהֵי אֲבוֹתֵינוּ, בָּרְכֵנוּ בַבְּרָכָה הַמְשֻׁלֶּשֶׁת בַּתּוֹרָה
הַכְּתוּבָה עַל יְדֵי מֹשֶׁה עַבְדֶּךָ, הָאֲמוּרָה מִפִּי אַהֲרֹן וּבָנָיו,
כֹּהֲנִים עַם קְדוֹשֶׁךָ, כָּאָמוּר: יְבָרֶכְךָ יְיָ וְיִשְׁמְרֶךָ. יָאֵר יְיָ פָּנָיו
אֵלֶיךָ וִיחֻנֶּךָּ. יִשָּׂא יְיָ פָּנָיו אֵלֶיךָ, וְיָשֵׂם לְךָ שָׁלוֹם

On Ḥanukkah add:

(We thank thee for the miracles, for the redemption, for the mighty deeds and triumphs, and for the battles which thou didst perform for our fathers in those days, at this season—

In the days of the Hasmonean, Mattathias ben Yoḥanan, the High Priest, and his sons, when a wicked Hellenic government rose up against thy people Israel to make them forget thy Torah and transgress the laws of thy will. Thou in thy great mercy didst stand by them in the time of their distress. Thou didst champion their cause, defend their rights and avenge their wrong; thou didst deliver the strong into the hands of the weak, the many into the hands of the few, the impure into the hands of the pure, the wicked into the hands of the righteous, and the arrogant into the hands of the students of thy Torah. Thou didst make a great and holy name for thyself in the world, and for thy people Israel thou didst perform a great deliverance unto this day. Thereupon thy children entered the shrine of thy house, cleansed thy Temple, purified thy sanctuary, kindled lights in thy holy courts, and designated these eight days of Ḥanukkah for giving thanks and praise to thy great name.)

For all these acts may thy name, our King, be blessed and exalted forever and ever.

Between Rosh Hashanah and Yom Kippur add:

(Inscribe all thy people of the covenant for a happy life.)

All the living shall ever thank thee and sincerely praise thy name, O God, who art always our salvation and help. Blessed art thou, O Lord, Beneficent One, to whom it is fitting to give thanks.

Priestly blessing recited by the Reader:

Our God and God of our fathers, bless us with the threefold blessing written in thy Torah by thy servant Moses and spoken by Aaron and his sons the priests, thy holy people, as it is said: "May the Lord bless you and protect you; may the Lord countenance you and be gracious to you; may the Lord favor you and grant you peace "[1]

---

[1] *Numbers* 6:24–26.

שִׂים שָׁלוֹם, טוֹבָה וּבְרָכָה, חֵן וָחֶסֶד וְרַחֲמִים, עָלֵינוּ וְעַל
כָּל יִשְׂרָאֵל עַמֶּךָ· בָּרְכֵנוּ אָבִינוּ, כֻּלָּנוּ כְּאֶחָד, בְּאוֹר פָּנֶיךָ;
כִּי בְאוֹר פָּנֶיךָ נָתַתָּ לָּנוּ, יְיָ אֱלֹהֵינוּ, תּוֹרַת חַיִּים וְאַהֲבַת חֶסֶד,
וּצְדָקָה וּבְרָכָה וְרַחֲמִים, וְחַיִּים וְשָׁלוֹם. וְטוֹב בְּעֵינֶיךָ לְבָרֵךְ
אֶת עַמְּךָ יִשְׂרָאֵל בְּכָל עֵת וּבְכָל שָׁעָה בִּשְׁלוֹמֶךָ. * בָּרוּךְ
אַתָּה, יְיָ, הַמְבָרֵךְ אֶת עַמּוֹ יִשְׂרָאֵל בַּשָּׁלוֹם.

*Between *Rosh Hashanah* and *Yom Kippur* say:

בְּסֵפֶר חַיִּים, בְּרָכָה וְשָׁלוֹם וּפַרְנָסָה טוֹבָה, נִזָּכֵר וְנִכָּתֵב
לְפָנֶיךָ, אֲנַחְנוּ וְכָל עַמְּךָ בֵּית יִשְׂרָאֵל, לְחַיִּים טוֹבִים וּלְשָׁלוֹם.
בָּרוּךְ אַתָּה, יְיָ, עוֹשֵׂה הַשָּׁלוֹם.

After the *Amidah* add the following meditation:

אֱלֹהַי, נְצֹר לְשׁוֹנִי מֵרָע, וּשְׂפָתַי מִדַּבֵּר מִרְמָה; וְלִמְקַלְלַי
נַפְשִׁי תִדּוֹם, וְנַפְשִׁי כֶּעָפָר לַכֹּל תִּהְיֶה. פְּתַח לִבִּי בְּתוֹרָתֶךָ,
וּבְמִצְוֹתֶיךָ תִּרְדּוֹף נַפְשִׁי; וְכֹל הַחוֹשְׁבִים עָלַי רָעָה, מְהֵרָה
הָפֵר עֲצָתָם וְקַלְקֵל מַחֲשַׁבְתָּם. עֲשֵׂה לְמַעַן שְׁמֶךָ, עֲשֵׂה לְמַעַן
יְמִינֶךָ, עֲשֵׂה לְמַעַן קְדֻשָּׁתֶךָ, עֲשֵׂה לְמַעַן תּוֹרָתֶךָ. לְמַעַן יֵחָלְצוּן
יְדִידֶיךָ, הוֹשִׁיעָה יְמִינְךָ וַעֲנֵנִי· יִהְיוּ לְרָצוֹן אִמְרֵי פִי וְהֶגְיוֹן לִבִּי
לְפָנֶיךָ, יְיָ, צוּרִי וְגוֹאֲלִי. עֹשֶׂה שָׁלוֹם בִּמְרוֹמָיו, הוּא יַעֲשֶׂה
שָׁלוֹם עָלֵינוּ וְעַל כָּל יִשְׂרָאֵל, וְאִמְרוּ אָמֵן.

יְהִי רָצוֹן מִלְּפָנֶיךָ, יְיָ אֱלֹהֵינוּ וֵאלֹהֵי אֲבוֹתֵינוּ, שֶׁיִּבָּנֶה בֵּית
הַמִּקְדָּשׁ בִּמְהֵרָה בְיָמֵינוּ, וְתֵן חֶלְקֵנוּ בְּתוֹרָתֶךָ. וְשָׁם נַעֲבָדְךָ
בְּיִרְאָה, כִּימֵי עוֹלָם וּכְשָׁנִים קַדְמוֹנִיּוֹת. וְעָרְבָה לַיָי מִנְחַת
יְהוּדָה וִירוּשָׁלָיִם, כִּימֵי עוֹלָם וּכְשָׁנִים קַדְמוֹנִיּוֹת.

Hallel (page 565) is recited here on *Rosh Ḥodesh, Ḥol ha-Mo'ed* and *Ḥanukkah*.

O grant peace, happiness, blessing, grace, kindness and mercy to us and to all Israel thy people. Bless us all alike, our Father, with the light of thy countenance; indeed, by the light of thy countenance thou hast given us, Lord our God, a Torah of life, lovingkindness, charity, blessing, mercy, life and peace. May it please thee to bless thy people Israel with peace at all times and hours. * Blessed art thou, O Lord, who blessest thy people Israel with peace.

*Between Rosh Hashanah and Yom Kippur say:

(May we and all Israel thy people be remembered and inscribed before thee in the book of life and blessing, peace and prosperity, for a happy life and for peace. Blessed art thou, O Lord, Author of peace.)

After the Amidah add the following meditation:

My God, guard my tongue from evil, and my lips from speaking falsehood. May my soul be silent to those who insult me; be my soul lowly to all as the dust. Open my heart to thy Torah, that my soul may follow thy commands. Speedily defeat the counsel of all those who plan evil against me, and upset their design. Do it for the glory of thy name; do it for the sake of thy power; do it for the sake of thy holiness; do it for the sake of thy Torah. That thy beloved may be rescued, save with thy right hand and answer me. May the words of my mouth and the meditation of my heart be pleasing before thee, O Lord, my Stronghold and my Redeemer.[1] May he who creates peace in his high heavens create peace for us and for all Israel, Amen.

May it be thy will, Lord our God and God of our fathers,that the Temple be speedily rebuilt in our days, and grant us a share in thy Torah. There we will serve thee with reverence, as in the days of old and as in former years. Then the offering of Judah and Jerusalem will be pleasing to the Lord, as in the days of old and as in former years.[2]

Hallel (page 566) is recited here on Rosh Ḥodesh, Ḥol ha-Moʻed and Ḥanukkah.

---

[1] *Psalms* 60:7; 19:15.   [2] *Malachi* 3:4.

Reader:

יִתְגַּדַּל וְיִתְקַדַּשׁ שְׁמֵהּ רַבָּא בְּעָלְמָא דִי בְרָא כִרְעוּתֵהּ;
וְיַמְלִיךְ מַלְכוּתֵהּ בְּחַיֵּיכוֹן וּבְיוֹמֵיכוֹן, וּבְחַיֵּי דְכָל בֵּית יִשְׂרָאֵל,
בַּעֲגָלָא וּבִזְמַן קָרִיב, וְאִמְרוּ אָמֵן.

יְהֵא שְׁמֵהּ רַבָּא מְבָרַךְ לְעָלַם וּלְעָלְמֵי עָלְמַיָּא.

יִתְבָּרַךְ וְיִשְׁתַּבַּח, וְיִתְפָּאַר וְיִתְרוֹמַם, וְיִתְנַשֵּׂא וְיִתְהַדָּר,
וְיִתְעַלֶּה וְיִתְהַלָּל שְׁמֵהּ דְּקֻדְשָׁא, בְּרִיךְ הוּא, לְעֵלָּא (לְעֵלָּא)
מִן כָּל בִּרְכָתָא וְשִׁירָתָא, תֻּשְׁבְּחָתָא וְנֶחֱמָתָא, דַּאֲמִירָן בְּעָלְמָא,
וְאִמְרוּ אָמֵן.

תִּתְקַבַּל צְלוֹתְהוֹן וּבָעוּתְהוֹן דְּכָל בֵּית יִשְׂרָאֵל קֳדָם אֲבוּהוֹן
דִּי בִשְׁמַיָּא, וְאִמְרוּ אָמֵן.

יְהֵא שְׁלָמָא רַבָּא מִן שְׁמַיָּא, וְחַיִּים, עָלֵינוּ וְעַל כָּל יִשְׂרָאֵל,
וְאִמְרוּ אָמֵן.

עֹשֶׂה שָׁלוֹם בִּמְרוֹמָיו, הוּא יַעֲשֶׂה שָׁלוֹם עָלֵינוּ וְעַל כָּל
יִשְׂרָאֵל, וְאִמְרוּ אָמֵן.

קְרִיאַת הַתּוֹרָה

Congregation and Reader:

אֵין כָּמוֹךָ בָאֱלֹהִים, אֲדֹנָי, וְאֵין כְּמַעֲשֶׂיךָ. מַלְכוּתְךָ מַלְכוּת
כָּל עֹלָמִים, וּמֶמְשַׁלְתְּךָ בְּכָל דֹּר וָדֹר. יְיָ מֶלֶךְ, יְיָ מָלָךְ, יְיָ
יִמְלֹךְ לְעֹלָם וָעֶד. יְיָ עֹז לְעַמּוֹ יִתֵּן, יְיָ יְבָרֵךְ אֶת עַמּוֹ בַשָּׁלוֹם.

קריאת התורה, the public reading from the Torah at the synagogue, has
been one of the most powerful factors of education. Formerly, the reading
was accompanied by interpretation so that the Torah became the property of
all Israel. Josephus, writing in the first century, says that Moses "showed the
Torah to be the best and the most necessary means of instruction by en-
joining the people to assemble not once or twice or frequently, but every
week while abstaining from all other work, in order to hear the Torah and
learn it in a thorough manner—a thing which all other lawgivers seem to have.

Reader:

Glorified and sanctified be God's great name throughout the world which he has created according to his will. May he establish his kingdom in your lifetime and during your days, and within the life of the entire house of Israel, speedily and soon; and say, Amen.

May his great name be blessed forever and to all eternity.

Blessed and praised, glorified and exalted, extolled and honored, adored and lauded be the name of the Holy One, blessed be he, beyond all the blessings and hymns, praises and consolations that are ever spoken in the world; and say, Amen.

May the prayers and supplications of the whole household of Israel be accepted by their Father who is in heaven; and say, Amen.

May there be abundant peace from heaven, and life, for us and for all Israel; and say, Amen.

He who creates peace in his celestial heights, may he create peace for us and for all Israel; and say, Amen.

READING OF THE TORAH

Congregation and Reader:

There is no God like thee, O Lord, and there are no deeds like thine. Thy kingdom is an everlasting kingdom; thy dominion endures through all generations. The Lord is King; the Lord was King; the Lord shall be King forever and ever. The Lord will give strength to his people; the Lord will bless his people with peace.[1]

---

neglected." The custom of reading from the Torah on Sabbath afternoon, when people have leisure, and on Mondays and Thursdays, the market days in early times, is attributed to Ezra the Scribe who organized Jewish life in Palestine after Israel's return from the Babylonian Captivity.

At one time it was the practice in Palestine to read the Torah in triennial cycles; the Torah was thus divided into about one hundred and seventy-five weekly portions. The universal custom today is to complete the reading of the Torah each year and to divide the Torah into fifty-four larger portions. Since, however, the ordinary year does not contain fifty-four Sabbaths it was found necessary, in order to complete the annual cycle, to have two portions read on some Sabbaths. Festivals frequently coincide with Sabbaths, in which case not the portion of the week but one which has some bearing on the festival is read.

[1] *Psalms* 86:8; 145:13; 29:11.

אָב הָרַחֲמִים, הֵיטִיבָה בִרְצוֹנְךָ אֶת צִיּוֹן, תִּבְנֶה חוֹמוֹת
יְרוּשָׁלָיִם. כִּי בְךָ לְבַד בָּטָחְנוּ, מֶלֶךְ אֵל רָם וְנִשָּׂא, אֲדוֹן
עוֹלָמִים.

The ark is opened.

Reader and Congregation:

וַיְהִי בִּנְסְעַ הָאָרֹן וַיֹּאמֶר מֹשֶׁה: קוּמָה יְיָ, וְיָפֻצוּ אֹיְבֶיךָ,
וְיָנֻסוּ מְשַׂנְאֶיךָ מִפָּנֶיךָ. כִּי מִצִּיּוֹן תֵּצֵא תוֹרָה, וּדְבַר יְיָ
מִירוּשָׁלָיִם. בָּרוּךְ שֶׁנָּתַן תּוֹרָה לְעַמּוֹ יִשְׂרָאֵל בִּקְדֻשָּׁתוֹ.

On festivals occurring on weekdays add:

(יְיָ, יְיָ אֵל רַחוּם וְחַנּוּן, אֶרֶךְ אַפַּיִם, וְרַב חֶסֶד וֶאֱמֶת; נֹצֵר
חֶסֶד לָאֲלָפִים, נֹשֵׂא עָוֹן וָפֶשַׁע וְחַטָּאָה, וְנַקֵּה.

רִבּוֹנוֹ שֶׁל עוֹלָם, מַלֵּא מִשְׁאֲלוֹת לִבִּי לְטוֹבָה, וְהָפֵק רְצוֹנִי
וְתֵן שְׁאֵלָתִי, לִי עַבְדְּךָ בֶּן אֲמָתֶךָ, וְזַכֵּנִי (וְאֶת אִשְׁתִּי וּבָנַי וּבְנוֹתַי)
לַעֲשׂוֹת רְצוֹנְךָ בְּלֵבָב שָׁלֵם. וּמַלְּטֵנוּ מִיֵּצֶר הָרָע, וְתֵן חֶלְקֵנוּ
בְּתוֹרָתֶךָ, וְזַכֵּנוּ שֶׁתִּשְׁרֶה שְׁכִינָתְךָ עָלֵינוּ, וְהוֹפַע עָלֵינוּ רוּחַ
חָכְמָה וּבִינָה, רוּחַ עֵצָה וּגְבוּרָה, רוּחַ דַּעַת וְיִרְאַת יְיָ. וְכֵן יְהִי
רָצוֹן מִלְּפָנֶיךָ, יְיָ אֱלֹהֵינוּ וֵאלֹהֵי אֲבוֹתֵינוּ, שֶׁתְּזַכֵּנוּ לַעֲשׂוֹת
מַעֲשִׂים טוֹבִים בְּעֵינֶיךָ וְלָלֶכֶת בְּדַרְכֵי יְשָׁרִים לְפָנֶיךָ. וְקַדְּשֵׁנוּ
בְּמִצְוֹתֶיךָ, כְּדֵי שֶׁנִּזְכֶּה לְחַיִּים טוֹבִים וַאֲרֻכִּים וּלְחַיֵּי הָעוֹלָם
הַבָּא; וְתִשְׁמְרֵנוּ מִמַּעֲשִׂים רָעִים וּמִשָּׁעוֹת רָעוֹת הַמִּתְרַגְּשׁוֹת
לָבֹא לָעוֹלָם. וְהַבּוֹטֵחַ בַּיְיָ חֶסֶד יְסוֹבְבֶנּוּ. אָמֵן.

יִהְיוּ לְרָצוֹן אִמְרֵי פִי וְהֶגְיוֹן לִבִּי לְפָנֶיךָ, יְיָ, צוּרִי וְגוֹאֲלִי.
וַאֲנִי תְפִלָּתִי לְךָ, יְיָ, עֵת רָצוֹן; אֱלֹהִים, בְּרָב־חַסְדֶּךָ, עֲנֵנִי
בֶּאֱמֶת יִשְׁעֶךָ.)

רבונו של עולם appeared for the first time in שערי ציון, a collection of prayers
and customs by Rabbi Nathan Hannover of the seventeenth century.

Merciful Father, may it be thy will to favor Zion with thy goodness; mayest thou rebuild the walls of Jerusalem. Truly, in thee alone we trust, high and exalted King and God, eternal Lord.

The ark is opened.

Reader and Congregation:

And it came to pass, whenever the ark started, Moses would say: "Arise, O Lord, and let thy enemies be scattered; let those who hate thee flee before thee."[1] Truly, out of Zion shall come forth Torah, and the word of the Lord out of Jerusalem.[2]

Blessed be he who in holiness gave the Torah to his people Israel.   *On festivals occurring on weekdays add:*

(The Lord, the Lord is a merciful and gracious God, slow to anger and abounding in kindness and truth. He keeps kindness to the thousandth generation, forgiving iniquity and transgression and sin, and acquitting the penitent.[3]

Lord of the universe, fulfill the prayers of my heart for happiness; grant my petition and my request; enable me to do thy will with a perfect heart; deliver me from the evil impulse. Grant us a share in thy Torah; make us worthy of thy divine presence; bestow on us the spirit of wisdom and understanding, the spirit of counsel and courage, the spirit of knowledge and piety. May it be thy will, Lord our God and God of our fathers, to enable me to perform deeds that please thee, and to walk before thee in the paths of the upright. Sanctify us with thy commandments, that we may merit the long and blessed life of the world to come; guard us from evil deeds, and from evil times which assail the world.

May kindness surround him who trusts in the Lord. Amen.

May the words of my mouth and the meditation of my heart be pleasing before thee, O Lord, my Stronghold and my Redeemer.

I offer my prayer to thee, O Lord, at a time of grace. O God, in thy abundant kindness, answer me with thy saving truth.)[4]

---

[1] *Numbers* 10:35.   [2] *Isaiah* 2:3.   [3] *Exodus* 34:6–7.   [4] *Psalms* 32:10; 19:15; 69:14.

זוהר, ויקהל

בְּרִיךְ שְׁמֵהּ דְּמָרֵא עָלְמָא, בְּרִיךְ כִּתְרָךְ וְאַתְרָךְ. יְהֵא
רְעוּתָךְ עִם עַמָּךְ יִשְׂרָאֵל לְעָלַם, וּפֻרְקַן יְמִינָךְ אַחֲזֵי לְעַמָּךְ
בְּבֵית מַקְדְּשָׁךְ; וּלְאַמְטוּיֵא לָנָא מִטּוּב נְהוֹרָךְ, וּלְקַבֵּל צְלוֹתָנָא
בְּרַחֲמִין. יְהֵא רַעֲוָא קָדָמָךְ, דְּתוֹרִיךְ לָן חַיִּין בְּטִיבוּתָא;
וְלֶהֱוֵא אֲנָא פְקִידָא בְּגוֹ צַדִּיקַיָּא, לְמִרְחַם עֲלַי וּלְמִנְטַר יָתִי
וְיָת כָּל דִּי לִי וְדִי לְעַמָּךְ יִשְׂרָאֵל. אַנְתְּ הוּא זָן לְכֹלָּא וּמְפַרְנֵס
לְכֹלָּא; אַנְתְּ הוּא שַׁלִּיט עַל כֹּלָּא; אַנְתְּ הוּא דְּשַׁלִּיט עַל
מַלְכַיָּא, וּמַלְכוּתָא דִּילָךְ הִיא. אֲנָא עַבְדָּא דְּקֻדְשָׁא בְּרִיךְ
הוּא, דְּסָגִדְנָא קַמֵּהּ וּמִקַּמָּא דִּיקַר אוֹרַיְתֵהּ בְּכָל עִדָּן וְעִדָּן.
לָא עַל אֱנָשׁ רָחִצְנָא, וְלָא עַל בַּר אֱלָהִין סָמִכְנָא, אֶלָּא
בֵּאלָהָא דִּשְׁמַיָּא, דְּהוּא אֱלָהָא קְשׁוֹט, וְאוֹרַיְתֵהּ קְשׁוֹט,
וּנְבִיאוֹהִי קְשׁוֹט, וּמַסְגֵּא לְמֶעְבַּד טַבְוָן וּקְשׁוֹט. בֵּהּ אֲנָא רָחִץ,
וְלִשְׁמֵהּ קַדִּישָׁא יַקִּירָא אֲנָא אָמַר תֻּשְׁבְּחָן. יְהֵא רַעֲוָא קָדָמָךְ,
דְּתִפְתַּח לִבָּאִי בְּאוֹרַיְתָא, Reader וְתַשְׁלֵם מִשְׁאֲלִין דְּלִבָּאִי,
וְלִבָּא דְכָל עַמָּךְ יִשְׂרָאֵל, לְטָב וּלְחַיִּין וְלִשְׁלָם.

The Reader takes the Torah.

Reader and Congregation:

שְׁמַע יִשְׂרָאֵל, יְיָ אֱלֹהֵינוּ, יְיָ אֶחָד.

Reader and Congregation:

אֶחָד אֱלֹהֵינוּ, גָּדוֹל אֲדוֹנֵינוּ, קָדוֹשׁ שְׁמוֹ.

Reader:

גַּדְּלוּ לַיְיָ אִתִּי, וּנְרוֹמְמָה שְׁמוֹ יַחְדָּו.

Congregation:

לְךָ יְיָ הַגְּדֻלָּה וְהַגְּבוּרָה וְהַתִּפְאֶרֶת וְהַנֵּצַח וְהַהוֹד, כִּי כֹל
בַּשָּׁמַיִם וּבָאָרֶץ; לְךָ, יְיָ, הַמַּמְלָכָה וְהַמִּתְנַשֵּׂא לְכֹל לְרֹאשׁ.

Zohar, Wayyakhel

Blessed be the name of the Lord of the universe! Blessed be thy crown and thy dominion. May thy good will ever abide with thy people Israel. Reveal thy saving power to thy people in thy sanctuary; bestow on us the good gift of thy light, and accept our prayer in mercy. May it be thy will to prolong our life in happiness.

Let me also be counted among the righteous, so that thou mayest have compassion on me and shelter me and mine and all that belong to thy people Israel. Thou art he who nourishes and sustains all; thou art he who rules over all; thou art he who rules over kings, for dominion is thine. I am the servant of the Holy One, blessed be he, before whom and before whose glorious Torah I bow at all times. Not in man do I put my trust, nor do I rely on any angel, but only in the God of heaven who is the God of truth, whose Torah is truth and whose Prophets are truth, and who performs many deeds of goodness and truth. In him I put my trust, and to his holy and glorious name I utter praises. May it be thy will to open my heart to thy Torah, and to fulfill the wishes of my heart and of the heart of all thy people Israel for happiness, life and peace.

The Reader takes the Torah.

Reader and Congregation:

Hear, O Israel, the Lord is our God, the Lord is One.[1]

Reader and Congregation:

One is our God; Great is our Lord; Holy is his name.

Reader:

Exalt the Lord with me, and let us extol his name together.[2]

Congregation

Thine, O Lord, is the greatness and the power, the glory and the victory and the majesty; for all that is in heaven and on earth is thine; thine, O Lord, is the kingdom, and thou art supreme

---

[1] *Deuteronomy* 6:4.　[2] *Psalm* 34:4.

רוֹמְמוּ יְיָ אֱלֹהֵינוּ, וְהִשְׁתַּחֲווּ לַהֲדֹם רַגְלָיו, קָדוֹשׁ הוּא. רוֹמְמוּ יְיָ אֱלֹהֵינוּ, וְהִשְׁתַּחֲווּ לְהַר קָדְשׁוֹ, כִּי קָדוֹשׁ יְיָ אֱלֹהֵינוּ.

עַל הַכֹּל יִתְגַּדַּל וְיִתְקַדַּשׁ, וְיִשְׁתַּבַּח וְיִתְפָּאַר, וְיִתְרוֹמַם וְיִתְנַשֵּׂא שְׁמוֹ שֶׁל מֶלֶךְ מַלְכֵי הַמְּלָכִים, הַקָּדוֹשׁ בָּרוּךְ הוּא, בָּעוֹלָמוֹת שֶׁבָּרָא, הָעוֹלָם הַזֶּה וְהָעוֹלָם הַבָּא, כִּרְצוֹנוֹ וְכִרְצוֹן יְרֵאָיו, וְכִרְצוֹן כָּל בֵּית יִשְׂרָאֵל. צוּר הָעוֹלָמִים, אֲדוֹן כָּל הַבְּרִיּוֹת, אֱלוֹהַּ כָּל הַנְּפָשׁוֹת, הַיּוֹשֵׁב בְּמֶרְחֲבֵי מָרוֹם, הַשּׁוֹכֵן בִּשְׁמֵי שְׁמֵי קֶדֶם; קְדֻשָּׁתוֹ עַל הַחַיּוֹת, וּקְדֻשָּׁתוֹ עַל כִּסֵּא הַכָּבוֹד. וּבְכֵן יִתְקַדַּשׁ שִׁמְךָ בָּנוּ, יְיָ אֱלֹהֵינוּ, לְעֵינֵי כָּל חָי. וְנֹאמַר לְפָנָיו שִׁיר חָדָשׁ, כַּכָּתוּב: שִׁירוּ לֵאלֹהִים, זַמְּרוּ שְׁמוֹ, סֹלּוּ לָרֹכֵב בָּעֲרָבוֹת, בְּיָהּ שְׁמוֹ, וְעִלְזוּ לְפָנָיו. וְנִרְאֵהוּ עַיִן בְּעַיִן בְּשׁוּבוֹ אֶל נָוֵהוּ, כַּכָּתוּב: כִּי עַיִן בְּעַיִן יִרְאוּ בְּשׁוּב יְיָ צִיּוֹן. וְנֶאֱמַר: וְנִגְלָה כְּבוֹד יְיָ, וְרָאוּ כָל בָּשָׂר יַחְדָּו, כִּי פִּי יְיָ דִּבֵּר.

Reader:

אַב הָרַחֲמִים, הוּא יְרַחֵם עַם עֲמוּסִים, וְיִזְכֹּר בְּרִית אֵיתָנִים, וְיַצִּיל נַפְשׁוֹתֵינוּ מִן הַשָּׁעוֹת הָרָעוֹת, וְיִגְעַר בְּיֵצֶר הָרָע מִן הַנְּשׂוּאִים, וְיָחֹן אוֹתָנוּ לִפְלֵיטַת עוֹלָמִים, וִימַלֵּא מִשְׁאֲלוֹתֵינוּ בְּמִדָּה טוֹבָה, יְשׁוּעָה וְרַחֲמִים.

The Torah is placed on the desk. The Reader unrolls it and says:

וְיַעֲזֹר וְיָגֵן וְיוֹשִׁיעַ לְכָל הַחוֹסִים בּוֹ, וְנֹאמַר אָמֵן. הַכֹּל הָבוּ גֹדֶל לֵאלֹהֵינוּ, וּתְנוּ כָבוֹד לַתּוֹרָה. כֹּהֵן, קְרָב; יַעֲמֹד (פְּלוֹנִי בֶּן פְּלוֹנִי) הַכֹּהֵן. בָּרוּךְ שֶׁנָּתַן תּוֹרָה לְעַמּוֹ יִשְׂרָאֵל בִּקְדֻשָּׁתוֹ.

על הכל, quoted in Sofrim 14:12, is omitted on the busy weekdays.

over all.[1] Exalt the Lord our God, and worship at his footstool;
holy is he. Exalt the Lord our God, and worship at his holy mountain, for holy is the Lord our God.[2]

Magnified and hallowed, praised and glorified, exalted and extolled above all be the name of the supreme King of kings, the
Holy One, blessed be he, in the worlds which he has created—
this world and the world to come—in accordance with his desire
and the desire of those who revere him, and of all the house of
Israel. He is the eternal Stronghold, the Lord of all creatures, the
God of all souls, who dwells in the wide extended heights, who
inhabits the ancient high heavens; whose holiness is above the
celestial beings and above the throne of glory. Now, thy name,
Lord our God, shall be sanctified among us in the sight of all the
living. Let us sing a new song before him, as it is written: "Sing
to God, praise his name; extol him who is above the heavens,
whose name is Lord, and exult before him."[3] May we see him eye
to eye when he returns to his abode, as it is written: "For they
shall see eye to eye when the Lord returns to Zion."[4] And it is
said: "Then the glory of the Lord shall be revealed, and all shall
see it together; for thus has the Lord promised."[5]

Reader:

May the merciful Father have compassion on the people who
have been upheld by him, and remember the covenant with the
patriarchs; may he deliver us from evil times, and check the evil
impulse in those who have been tended by him; may he graciously
grant us everlasting deliverance, and in his goodness fulfill our
petitions for salvation and mercy.

The Torah is placed on the desk. The Reader unrolls it and says:

May he help, shield and save all who trust in him; and let us
say, Amen. Let us all ascribe greatness to our God, and give honor
to the Torah. Let the *Kohen* come forward (*the Reader names the
first person called to the Torah*). Blessed be he who in his holiness
gave the Torah to his people Israel.

---

[1] *I Chronicles* 29:11.   [2] *Psalm* 99:5, 9.   [3] *Psalm* 68:5.   [4] *Isaiah* 52:8.
[5] *Isaiah* 40:5.

Congregation and Reader:

וְאַתֶּם הַדְּבֵקִים בַּיָי אֱלֹהֵיכֶם, חַיִּים כֻּלְּכֶם הַיּוֹם.

The person called to the Torah recites:

בָּרְכוּ אֶת יְיָ הַמְבֹרָךְ.

Congregation responds:

בָּרוּךְ יְיָ הַמְבֹרָךְ לְעוֹלָם וָעֶד.

He repeats the response and continues:

בָּרוּךְ אַתָּה, יְיָ אֱלֹהֵינוּ, מֶלֶךְ הָעוֹלָם, אֲשֶׁר בָּחַר בָּנוּ מִכָּל הָעַמִּים, וְנָתַן לָנוּ אֶת תּוֹרָתוֹ. בָּרוּךְ אַתָּה, יְיָ, נוֹתֵן הַתּוֹרָה.

The Torah is read; then he recites:

בָּרוּךְ אַתָּה, יְיָ אֱלֹהֵינוּ, מֶלֶךְ הָעוֹלָם, אֲשֶׁר נָתַן לָנוּ תּוֹרַת אֱמֶת, וְחַיֵּי עוֹלָם נָטַע בְּתוֹכֵנוּ. בָּרוּךְ אַתָּה, יְיָ, נוֹתֵן הַתּוֹרָה.

בִּרְכַּת הַגּוֹמֵל

One who has come safely through a dangerous experience recites:

בָּרוּךְ אַתָּה, יְיָ אֱלֹהֵינוּ, מֶלֶךְ הָעוֹלָם, הַגּוֹמֵל לְחַיָּבִים טוֹבוֹת, שֶׁגְּמָלַנִי כָּל טוֹב.

Congregation responds:

מִי שֶׁגְּמָלְךָ כָּל טוֹב, הוּא יִגְמָלְךָ כָּל טוֹב סֶלָה.

The father of a *Bar-Mitzvah* pronounces the following blessing:

בָּרוּךְ שֶׁפְּטָרַנִי מֵעָנְשׁוֹ שֶׁל זֶה.

ברכות התורה, the two blessings pronounced over the Torah, contain forty words which are said to allude to the forty days spent by Moses on Mount Sinai. These benedictions are quoted in the Talmud (Berakhoth 11b; 49b).

ברכת הגומל is based on a talmudic statement to the effect that all who escape serious danger arising from illness, imprisonment or a perilous voyage, must offer thanks to God (Berakhoth 54b). This is derived from Psalm 107, where thanksgiving is offered on occasions such as these.

Congregation and Reader:

And you who cling to the Lord your God are all alive today.[1]

The person called to the Torah recites:

Bless the Lord who is blessed.

Congregation responds:

Blessed be the Lord who is blessed forever and ever.

He repeats the response and continues:

Blessed art thou, Lord our God, King of the universe, who hast chosen us from all peoples, and hast given us thy Torah. Blessed art thou, O Lord, Giver of the Torah.

The Torah is read; then he recites:

Blessed art thou, Lord our God, King of the universe, who hast given us the Torah of truth, and hast planted everlasting life in our midst. Blessed art thou, O Lord, Giver of the Torah.

THANKSGIVING

One who has come safely through a dangerous experience recites:

Blessed art thou, Lord our God, King of the universe, who bestowest favors on the undeserving, and hast shown me every kindness.

Congregation responds:

May he who has shown you every kindness ever deal kindly with you.

The father of a Bar-Mitzvah pronounces the following blessing:

Blessed be he who has relieved me of the responsibility for this boy.

בר מצוה, "man of duty," is applied in the Talmud (Baba Metsia 96a) to every adult Israelite. Since the fourteenth century the term *Bar-Mitzvah* has been applied to a boy attaining the age of thirteen, at which time he enters manhood and becomes personally responsible for his religious behavior. Henceforth the boy is regarded as an adult, being counted as one of the ten men necessary for a *minyan*.

---

[1] *Deuteronomy* 4:4.

On behalf of each person called to the Torah:

מִי שֶׁבֵּרַךְ אֲבוֹתֵינוּ, אַבְרָהָם יִצְחָק וְיַעֲקֹב, הוּא יְבָרֵךְ
אֶת...* שֶׁעָלָה לִכְבוֹד הַמָּקוֹם וְלִכְבוֹד הַתּוֹרָה (on festivals
וְלִכְבוֹד הָרֶגֶל). הַקָּדוֹשׁ בָּרוּךְ הוּא יִשְׁמְרֵהוּ וְיַצִּילֵהוּ
מִכָּל צָרָה וְצוּקָה וּמִכָּל נֶגַע וּמַחֲלָה, וְיִשְׁלַח בְּרָכָה
וְהַצְלָחָה בְּכָל מַעֲשֵׂה יָדָיו (וְיִזְכֶּה לַעֲלוֹת לָרֶגֶל festivals on)
עִם כָּל יִשְׂרָאֵל אֶחָיו; וְנֹאמַר אָמֵן.

On the occasion of naming a new-born daughter:

מִי שֶׁבֵּרַךְ אֲבוֹתֵינוּ, אַבְרָהָם יִצְחָק וְיַעֲקֹב, מֹשֶׁה וְאַהֲרֹן,
דָּוִד וּשְׁלֹמֹה, הוּא יְבָרֵךְ אֶת הָאִשָּׁה הַיּוֹלֶדֶת...* וְאֶת בִּתָּהּ
שֶׁנּוֹלְדָה לָהּ; וְיִקָּרֵא שְׁמָהּ בְּיִשְׂרָאֵל...* וְיִזְכּוּ לְגַדְּלָהּ
לְחֻפָּה וּלְמַעֲשִׂים טוֹבִים; וְנֹאמַר אָמֵן.

On behalf of a sick man:

מִי שֶׁבֵּרַךְ אֲבוֹתֵינוּ אַבְרָהָם יִצְחָק וְיַעֲקֹב, מֹשֶׁה
וְאַהֲרֹן, דָּוִד וּשְׁלֹמֹה, הוּא יְרַפֵּא אֶת הַחוֹלֶה...* הַקָּדוֹשׁ
בָּרוּךְ הוּא יִמָּלֵא רַחֲמִים עָלָיו לְהַחֲלִימוֹ וּלְרַפֹּאתוֹ,
לְהַחֲזִיקוֹ וּלְהַחֲיוֹתוֹ, וְיִשְׁלַח לוֹ מְהֵרָה רְפוּאָה שְׁלֵמָה,
רְפוּאַת הַנֶּפֶשׁ וּרְפוּאַת הַגּוּף; וְנֹאמַר אָמֵן.

On behalf of a sick woman:

מִי שֶׁבֵּרַךְ אֲבוֹתֵינוּ, אַבְרָהָם יִצְחָק וְיַעֲקֹב, מֹשֶׁה
וְאַהֲרֹן, דָּוִד וּשְׁלֹמֹה, הוּא יְרַפֵּא אֶת הַחוֹלָה...* הַקָּדוֹשׁ
בָּרוּךְ הוּא יִמָּלֵא רַחֲמִים עָלֶיהָ לְהַחֲלִימָהּ וּלְרַפֹּאתָהּ,
לְהַחֲזִיקָהּ וּלְהַחֲיוֹתָהּ, וְיִשְׁלַח לָהּ מְהֵרָה רְפוּאָה שְׁלֵמָה,
רְפוּאַת הַנֶּפֶשׁ וּרְפוּאַת הַגּוּף; וְנֹאמַר אָמֵן.

* The name is given.

On behalf of each person called to the Torah:

He who blessed our fathers Abraham, Isaac and Jacob, may he bless . . .* who has come up to honor God and the Torah. May the Holy One, blessed be he, protect and deliver him from all distress and illness, and bless all his efforts with success (*on festivals:* may he live to celebrate festivals in Jerusalem) among all Israel his brethren; and let us say, Amen.

On the occasion of naming a new-born daughter:

He who blessed our fathers Abraham, Isaac and Jacob, Moses and Aaron, David and Solomon, may he bless the mother . . .* and her new-born daughter, whose name in Israel shall be . . .* May they raise her for the marriage canopy and for a life of good deeds; and let us say, Amen.

On behalf of a sick man:

He who blessed our fathers Abraham, Isaac and Jacob, Moses and Aaron, David and Solomon, may he heal . . .* who is ill. May the Holy One, blessed be he, have mercy and speedily restore him to perfect health, both spiritual and physical; and let us say, Amen.

On behalf of a sick woman:

He who blessed our fathers Abraham, Isaac and Jacob, Moses and Aaron, David and Solomon, may he heal . . .* who is ill. May the Holy One, blessed be he, have mercy and speedily restore her to perfect health, both spiritual and physical; and let us say, Amen.

* *The name is given.*

After the reading of the Torah, the Reader recites:

יִתְגַּדַּל וְיִתְקַדַּשׁ שְׁמֵהּ רַבָּא בְּעָלְמָא דִי בְרָא כִרְעוּתֵהּ,
וְיַמְלִיךְ מַלְכוּתֵהּ בְּחַיֵּיכוֹן וּבְיוֹמֵיכוֹן, וּבְחַיֵּי דְכָל בֵּית יִשְׂרָאֵל,
בַּעֲגָלָא וּבִזְמַן קָרִיב, וְאִמְרוּ אָמֵן.

יְהֵא שְׁמֵהּ רַבָּא מְבָרַךְ לְעָלַם וּלְעָלְמֵי עָלְמַיָּא.

יִתְבָּרַךְ וְיִשְׁתַּבַּח, וְיִתְפָּאַר וְיִתְרוֹמַם, וְיִתְנַשֵּׂא וְיִתְהַדָּר,
וְיִתְעַלֶּה וְיִתְהַלָּל שְׁמֵהּ דְּקֻדְשָׁא, בְּרִיךְ הוּא, לְעֵלָּא (לְעֵלָּא)
מִן כָּל בִּרְכָתָא וְשִׁירָתָא, תֻּשְׁבְּחָתָא וְנֶחֱמָתָא, דַּאֲמִירָן בְּעָלְמָא,
וְאִמְרוּ אָמֵן.

The *Torah* is raised, and the Congregation recites:

וְזֹאת הַתּוֹרָה אֲשֶׁר שָׂם מֹשֶׁה לִפְנֵי בְּנֵי יִשְׂרָאֵל, עַל פִּי יְיָ
בְּיַד מֹשֶׁה.

עֵץ חַיִּים הִיא לַמַּחֲזִיקִים בָּהּ, וְתֹמְכֶיהָ מְאֻשָּׁר. דְּרָכֶיהָ
דַרְכֵי נֹעַם, וְכָל נְתִיבוֹתֶיהָ שָׁלוֹם. אֹרֶךְ יָמִים בִּימִינָהּ,
בִּשְׂמֹאלָהּ עֹשֶׁר וְכָבוֹד. יְיָ חָפֵץ לְמַעַן צִדְקוֹ, יַגְדִּיל תּוֹרָה
וְיַאְדִּיר.

Before reading the *Haftarah*, the *Maftir* chants:

בָּרוּךְ אַתָּה יְיָ אֱלֹהֵינוּ מֶלֶךְ הָעוֹלָם אֲשֶׁר בָּחַר בִּנְבִיאִים
טוֹבִים וְרָצָה בְדִבְרֵיהֶם הַנֶּאֱמָרִים בֶּאֱמֶת בָּרוּךְ אַתָּה יְיָ
הַבּוֹחֵר בַּתּוֹרָה וּבְמֹשֶׁה עַבְדּוֹ וּבְיִשְׂרָאֵל עַמּוֹ וּבִנְבִיאֵי הָאֱמֶת
וָצֶדֶק.

הפטרה, signifying completion, includes those portions of the Prophets recited immediately after the reading of the Torah. Usually, though not always, the *Haftarah* passage contains some reference to an occasion described in the section read from the Torah. On the three Sabbaths preceding *Tish'ah b'Av*, passages of rebuke are recited; on the seven Sabbaths after *Tish'ah*

After the reading of the Torah, the Reader recites:

Glorified and sanctified be God's great name throughout the world which he has created according to his will. May he establish his kingdom in your lifetime and during your days, and within the life of the entire house of Israel, speedily and soon; and say, Amen.

May his great name be blessed forever and to all eternity.

Blessed and praised, glorified and exalted, extolled and honored, adored and lauded be the name of the Holy One, blessed be he, beyond all the blessings and hymns, praises and consolations that are ever spoken in the world; and say, Amen.

The Torah is raised, and the Congregation recites:

This is the Torah which Moses placed before the children of Israel. It is in accordance with the Lord's command through Moses.[1]

It is a tree of life to those who take hold of it, and happy are those who support it. Its ways are pleasant ways, and all its paths are peace. Long life is in its right hand, and in its left hand are riches and honor. The Lord was pleased, for the sake of his righteousness, to render the Torah great and glorious.[2]

Before reading the Haftarah, the Maftir chants:

Blessed art thou, Lord our God, King of the universe, who hast chosen good prophets, and hast been pleased with their words which were truthfully spoken. Blessed art thou, O Lord, who hast chosen the Torah and thy servant Moses, thy people Israel and the true and righteous prophets.

---

b'Av prophetic consolations are read. Abudarham (fourteenth century) traces the *Haftarah* back to the period of persecution preceding the Maccabean revolt, when the reading from the Torah was prohibited and sections from the Prophets were substituted. At any rate, the custom of concluding the Torah reading by a supplementary portion from the Prophets is very old. *Haftarah* is mentioned in the Mishnah and the Tosefta. At least three verses from the end of the weekly portion are repeated when the *Maftir*, reader of the *Haftarah*, is called to the Torah. The blessings before and after the *Haftarah* are from the tractate *Sofrim* (seventh century).

---

[1] *Deuteronomy* 4:44; *Numbers* 9:23.   [2] *Proverbs* 3:18, 17, 16; *Isaiah* 42:21.

After reading the *Haftarah*, the *Maftir* recites:

בָּרוּךְ אַתָּה, יְיָ אֱלֹהֵינוּ, מֶלֶךְ הָעוֹלָם, צוּר כָּל הָעוֹלָמִים,
צַדִּיק בְּכָל הַדּוֹרוֹת, הָאֵל הַנֶּאֱמָן, הָאוֹמֵר וְעוֹשֶׂה, הַמְדַבֵּר
וּמְקַיֵּם, שֶׁכָּל דְּבָרָיו אֱמֶת וָצֶדֶק.

נֶאֱמָן אַתָּה הוּא, יְיָ אֱלֹהֵינוּ, וְנֶאֱמָנִים דְּבָרֶיךָ, וְדָבָר אֶחָד
מִדְּבָרֶיךָ אָחוֹר לֹא יָשׁוּב רֵיקָם, כִּי אֵל מֶלֶךְ נֶאֱמָן וְרַחֲמָן
אָתָּה. בָּרוּךְ אַתָּה, יְיָ, הָאֵל הַנֶּאֱמָן בְּכָל דְּבָרָיו.

רַחֵם עַל צִיּוֹן, כִּי הִיא בֵּית חַיֵּינוּ, וְלַעֲלוּבַת נֶפֶשׁ תּוֹשִׁיעַ
בִּמְהֵרָה בְיָמֵינוּ. בָּרוּךְ אַתָּה, יְיָ, מְשַׂמֵּחַ צִיּוֹן בְּבָנֶיהָ.

שַׂמְּחֵנוּ, יְיָ אֱלֹהֵינוּ, בְּאֵלִיָּהוּ הַנָּבִיא עַבְדֶּךָ, וּבְמַלְכוּת בֵּית
דָּוִד מְשִׁיחֶךָ. בִּמְהֵרָה יָבֹא, וְיָגֵל לִבֵּנוּ; עַל כִּסְאוֹ לֹא יֵשֶׁב זָר,
וְלֹא יִנְחֲלוּ עוֹד אֲחֵרִים אֶת כְּבוֹדוֹ, כִּי בְשֵׁם קָדְשְׁךָ נִשְׁבַּעְתָּ
לּוֹ, שֶׁלֹּא יִכְבֶּה נֵרוֹ לְעוֹלָם וָעֶד. בָּרוּךְ אַתָּה, יְיָ, מָגֵן דָּוִד.

On Sabbaths:

עַל הַתּוֹרָה, וְעַל הָעֲבוֹדָה, וְעַל הַנְּבִיאִים, וְעַל יוֹם הַשַּׁבָּת
הַזֶּה, שֶׁנָּתַתָּ לָּנוּ, יְיָ אֱלֹהֵינוּ, לִקְדֻשָּׁה וְלִמְנוּחָה, לְכָבוֹד
וּלְתִפְאָרֶת.

עַל הַכֹּל, יְיָ אֱלֹהֵינוּ, אֲנַחְנוּ מוֹדִים לָךְ, וּמְבָרְכִים אוֹתָךְ;
יִתְבָּרַךְ שִׁמְךָ בְּפִי כָּל חַי תָּמִיד לְעוֹלָם וָעֶד. בָּרוּךְ אַתָּה, יְיָ,
מְקַדֵּשׁ הַשַּׁבָּת.

On festivals:

(עַל הַתּוֹרָה וְעַל הָעֲבוֹדָה וְעַל הַנְּבִיאִים [וְעַל יוֹם הַשַּׁבָּת
הַזֶּה] וְעַל יוֹם

Shemini Atsereth	*Sukkoth*	*Shavuoth*	*Pesah*
חַג הַשְּׁמִינִי חַג הָעֲצֶרֶת	חַג הַסֻּכּוֹת	חַג הַשָּׁבֻעוֹת	חַג הַמַּצּוֹת

הַזֶּה, שֶׁנָּתַתָּ לָּנוּ, יְיָ אֱלֹהֵינוּ, [לִקְדֻשָּׁה וְלִמְנוּחָה], לְשָׂשׂוֹן
וּלְשִׂמְחָה, לְכָבוֹד וּלְתִפְאָרֶת.

After reading the Haftarah, the Maftir recites:

Blessed art thou, Lord our God, King of the universe, Creator of all the worlds, righteous in all generations, faithful God, who sayest and performest, who speakest and fulfillest, for all thy words are true and just.

Faithful art thou, Lord our God, and faithful are thy words; no word of thine returns unfulfilled, for thou art a faithful and merciful God and King. Blessed art thou, O Lord God, who art faithful in all thy words.

Have compassion on Zion, for it is the source of our life; save the humbled soul speedily in our days. Blessed art thou, O Lord, who makest Zion rejoice in her children.

Gladden us, Lord our God, with the appearance of thy servant Elijah the prophet, and with the rule of the house of David thy anointed. May he soon come and bring joy to our heart. Let no stranger occupy David's throne; let others no longer possess themselves of his glory, for thou didst promise him by thy holy name that his light would never go out. Blessed art thou, O Lord, Shield of David.

On Sabbaths:

We thank thee for the Torah, for the worship, for the Prophets and for this Sabbath day, which thou hast given us, Lord our God, for holiness and rest, for glory and beauty.

We thank and bless thee, Lord our God, for all things; be thy name ever blessed by every living being. Blessed art thou, O Lord, who hallowest the Sabbath.

On festivals:

(We thank thee for the Torah, for the worship, for the Prophets [for this Sabbath day] and for this day of

Pesaḥ	*Shavuoth*	*Sukkoth*	*Shemini Atsereth*
the Feast of Un-leavened Bread,	the Feast of Weeks,	the Feast of Tabernacles,	the Eighth-Day Feast,

which thou hast given us, Lord our God, [for holiness and rest], for joy and gladness, for glory and beauty.

עַל הַכֹּל, יְיָ אֱלֹהֵינוּ, אֲנַחְנוּ מוֹדִים לָךְ, וּמְבָרְכִים אוֹתָךְ;
יִתְבָּרַךְ שִׁמְךָ בְּפִי כָל חַי תָּמִיד, לְעוֹלָם וָעֶד. בָּרוּךְ אַתָּה, יְיָ,
מְקַדֵּשׁ [הַשַּׁבָּת וְ]יִשְׂרָאֵל וְהַזְּמַנִּים.)

The following three paragraphs are recited on Sabbaths only.

יְקוּם פֻּרְקָן מִן שְׁמַיָּא, חִנָּא וְחִסְדָּא וְרַחֲמֵי, וְחַיֵּי אֲרִיכֵי
וּמְזוֹנֵי רְוִיחֵי וְסַיַּעְתָּא דִשְׁמַיָּא, וּבַרְיוּת גּוּפָא וּנְהוֹרָא מַעַלְיָא,
זַרְעָא חַיָּא וְקַיָּמָא, זַרְעָא דִי לָא יִפְסֻק וְדִי לָא יִבְטֵל מִפִּתְגָּמֵי
אוֹרַיְתָא, לְמָרָנָן וְרַבָּנָן, חֲבוּרָתָא קַדִּישָׁתָא דִי בְּאַרְעָא
דְיִשְׂרָאֵל וְדִי בְּבָבֶל; לְרֵישֵׁי כַלֵּי וּלְרֵישֵׁי גַלְוָתָא, וּלְרֵישֵׁי
מְתִיבָתָא וּלְדַיָּנֵי דִי בָבָא; לְכָל תַּלְמִידֵיהוֹן וּלְכָל תַּלְמִידֵי
תַלְמִידֵיהוֹן, וּלְכָל מָן דְּעָסְקִין בְּאוֹרַיְתָא. מַלְכָּא דְעָלְמָא
יְבָרֵךְ יַתְהוֹן, יַפִּישׁ חַיֵּיהוֹן וְיַסְגֵּא יוֹמֵיהוֹן וְיִתֵּן אַרְכָה לִשְׁנֵיהוֹן,
וְיִתְפָּרְקוּן וְיִשְׁתֵּיזְבוּן מִן כָּל עָקָא וּמִן כָּל מַרְעִין בִּישִׁין. מָרָן
דִּי בִשְׁמַיָּא יְהֵא בְּסַעֲדְהוֹן כָּל זְמַן וְעִדָּן, וְנֹאמַר אָמֵן.

When praying in private, omit the following two paragraphs.

יְקוּם פֻּרְקָן מִן שְׁמַיָּא, חִנָּא וְחִסְדָּא וְרַחֲמֵי, וְחַיֵּי אֲרִיכֵי
וּמְזוֹנֵי רְוִיחֵי וְסַיַּעְתָּא דִשְׁמַיָּא, וּבַרְיוּת גּוּפָא וּנְהוֹרָא מַעַלְיָא,
זַרְעָא חַיָּא וְקַיָּמָא, זַרְעָא דִי לָא יִפְסֻק וְדִי לָא יִבְטֵל מִפִּתְגָּמֵי
אוֹרַיְתָא, לְכָל קְהָלָא קַדִּישָׁא הָדֵן, רַבְרְבַיָּא עִם זְעֵרַיָּא,
טַפְלָא וּנְשַׁיָּא. מַלְכָּא דְעָלְמָא יְבָרֵךְ יַתְכוֹן, יַפִּישׁ חַיֵּיכוֹן וְיַסְגֵּא
יוֹמֵיכוֹן וְיִתֵּן אַרְכָה לִשְׁנֵיכוֹן, וְתִתְפָּרְקוּן וְתִשְׁתֵּיזְבוּן מִן כָּל
עָקָא וּמִן כָּל מַרְעִין בִּישִׁין. מָרָן דִּי בִשְׁמַיָּא יְהֵא בְּסַעֲדְכוֹן
כָּל זְמַן וְעִדָּן, וְנֹאמַר אָמֵן.

יקום פרקן, the prayer in Aramaic, was composed in Babylonia where
Aramaic remained the daily language of the Jews for more than a thousand
years, until the ninth century when Arabic became the popular language.
The first *Yekum Purkan*, recited in behalf of Babylonian and Palestinian

We thank and bless thee, Lord our God, for all things; be thy name ever blessed by every living being. Blessed art thou, O Lord, who hallowest [the Sabbath] and Israel and the festivals.)

The following three paragraphs are recited on Sabbaths only.

May salvation arise from heaven. May grace, kindness and mercy—long life, ample sustenance and divine aid; physical health, perfect vision, and healthy children who will never neglect the study of the Torah—be granted to our scholars and teachers, to the holy societies that are in the land of Israel and in the land of Babylon, to the heads of the academies and the chiefs of the captivity, to the presidents of the colleges and the judges of the towns, to their disciples and the disciples of their disciples, and to all who study the Torah. May the King of the universe bless them, prolong their lives, increase their days and add to their years; may they be saved and delivered from all distress and disease. May our Lord who is in heaven be their help at all times; and let us say, Amen.

When praying in private, omit the following two paragraphs.

May salvation arise from heaven. May grace, kindness and mercy—long life, ample sustenance and divine aid; physical health, perfect vision and healthy children who will never neglect the study of the Torah—be granted to this entire congregation, great and small, women and children. May the King of the universe bless you, prolong your lives, increase your days and add to your years; may you be saved and delivered from all distress and disease. May our Lord who is in heaven be your help at all times; and let us say, Amen.

---

scholars and leaders, was of late amplified by the addition of וּדִי בכל ארעת גלותנא ("and that are in all the lands of our diaspora") in order to make the whole passage applicable to our own times (Baer's edition, page 229). Curiously enough, *Yekum Purkan* is not included in the Babylonian *Siddurim* of Amram Gaon and Saadyah Gaon, but is mentioned in Maḥzor Vitry which has come down to us from France. רישי כלה refers to the heads of the semiannual conventions of the Babylonian scholars which were held during the months of *Adar* and *Elul*. The second *Yekum Purkan*, phrased like the first, is a prayer for the congregation, similar in content to the Hebrew paragraph מִי שברך, which singles out those who contribute toward the maintenance of the synagogue as well as to charity.

מִי שֶׁבֵּרַךְ אֲבוֹתֵינוּ אַבְרָהָם יִצְחָק וְיַעֲקֹב, הוּא יְבָרֵךְ אֶת
כָּל הַקָּהָל הַקָּדוֹשׁ הַזֶּה עִם כָּל קְהִלּוֹת הַקֹּדֶשׁ, הֵם וּנְשֵׁיהֶם
וּבְנֵיהֶם וּבְנוֹתֵיהֶם וְכֹל אֲשֶׁר לָהֶם, וּמִי שֶׁמְּיַחֲדִים בָּתֵּי כְנֵסִיּוֹת
לִתְפִלָּה, וּמִי שֶׁבָּאִים בְּתוֹכָם לְהִתְפַּלֵּל, וּמִי שֶׁנּוֹתְנִים נֵר
לַמָּאוֹר, וְיַיִן לְקִדּוּשׁ וּלְהַבְדָּלָה, וּפַת לָאוֹרְחִים וּצְדָקָה לָעֲנִיִּים,
Reader וְכָל מִי שֶׁעוֹסְקִים בְּצָרְכֵי צִבּוּר בֶּאֱמוּנָה. הַקָּדוֹשׁ בָּרוּךְ
הוּא יְשַׁלֵּם שְׂכָרָם, וְיָסִיר מֵהֶם כָּל מַחֲלָה, וְיִרְפָּא לְכָל גּוּפָם,
וְיִסְלַח לְכָל עֲוֺנָם, וְיִשְׁלַח בְּרָכָה וְהַצְלָחָה בְּכָל מַעֲשֵׂה
יְדֵיהֶם, עִם כָּל יִשְׂרָאֵל אֲחֵיהֶם, וְנֹאמַר אָמֵן.

תְּפִלָּה בִּשְׁלוֹמָה שֶׁל מַלְכוּת

The Reader takes the Torah and recites:

הַנּוֹתֵן תְּשׁוּעָה לַמְּלָכִים וּמֶמְשָׁלָה לַנְּסִיכִים, מַלְכוּתוֹ
מַלְכוּת כָּל עוֹלָמִים; הַפּוֹצֶה אֶת דָּוִד עַבְדּוֹ מֵחֶרֶב רָעָה,
הַנּוֹתֵן בַּיָּם דָּרֶךְ, וּבְמַיִם עַזִּים נְתִיבָה, הוּא יְבָרֵךְ וְיִשְׁמוֹר וְיִנְצוֹר
וְיַעֲזוֹר וִירוֹמֵם וִיגַדֵּל וִינַשֵּׂא לְמַעְלָה

אֶת הַנָּשִׂיא וְאֶת מִשְׁנֵהוּ

וְאֶת כָּל שָׂרֵי הָאָרֶץ הַזֹּאת.

מֶלֶךְ מַלְכֵי הַמְּלָכִים בְּרַחֲמָיו יְחַיֵּם וְיִשְׁמְרֵם, וּמִכָּל צָרָה
וְיָגוֹן וָנֶזֶק יַצִּילֵם. מֶלֶךְ מַלְכֵי הַמְּלָכִים בְּרַחֲמָיו יִתֵּן בְּלִבָּם
וּבְלֵב כָּל יוֹעֲצֵיהֶם וְשָׂרֵיהֶם לַעֲשׂוֹת טוֹבָה עִמָּנוּ וְעִם כָּל
יִשְׂרָאֵל. בִּימֵיהֶם וּבְיָמֵינוּ תִּוָּשַׁע יְהוּדָה, וְיִשְׂרָאֵל יִשְׁכּוֹן
לָבֶטַח, וּבָא לְצִיּוֹן גּוֹאֵל. וְכֵן יְהִי רָצוֹן, וְנֹאמַר אָמֵן.

הנותן תשועה has undergone some verbal variations in the course of time.
The custom to pray for the welfare of the government is based on Jeremiah
29:7 ("Seek the welfare of the country where I have sent you into exile; pray

May he who blessed our fathers, Abraham, Isaac and Jacob, bless this entire congregation and all other congregations—their wives, their sons and daughters, and all that belongs to them. May he bless those who dedicate synagogues for worship and those who enter therein to pray, those who provide lamps for lighting and wine for Kiddush and Havdalah and those who give food to the transient guests and charity to the poor, as well as all those who faithfully occupy themselves with the needs of the community. May the Holy One, blessed be he, grant them their reward, remove from them all sickness, preserve them in good health, and forgive all their sins; may he bless and prosper their work and the work of all Israel their brethren; and let us say, Amen.

PRAYER FOR THE GOVERNMENT

The Reader takes the Torah and recites:

He who granted victory to kings and dominion to princes, his kingdom is a kingdom of all ages; he who delivered his servant David from the evil sword, he who opened a road through the sea, a path amid the mighty waters—may he bless and protect, help and exalt

THE PRESIDENT AND THE VICE-PRESIDENT
AND ALL THE OFFICERS OF THIS COUNTRY.

May the supreme King of kings, in his mercy, sustain them and deliver them from all distress and misfortune. May the supreme King of kings, in his mercy, inspire them and all their counselors and aides to deal kindly with us and with all Israel. In their days and in our days Judah shall be saved, Israel shall dwell in security, and a redeemer shall come to Zion. May this be the will of God; and let us say, Amen.

---

to the Lord for it, for your welfare depends on its welfare"). This prayer is composed of excerpts from Psalms 145:13; 144:10; Isaiah 43:16; Jeremiah 23:6; Isaiah 59:20. Abudarham wrote in the fourteenth century: "It is the custom to bless the king and to pray to God that he may give him victory."

בִּרְכַּת הַחֹדֶשׁ

Recited on the Sabbath preceding *Rosh Hodesh.*

יְהִי רָצוֹן מִלְּפָנֶיךָ, יְיָ אֱלֹהֵינוּ וֵאלֹהֵי אֲבוֹתֵינוּ, שֶׁתְּחַדֵּשׁ
עָלֵינוּ אֶת הַחֹדֶשׁ הַזֶּה לְטוֹבָה וְלִבְרָכָה; וְתִתֶּן־לָנוּ חַיִּים
אֲרֻכִּים, חַיִּים שֶׁל שָׁלוֹם, חַיִּים שֶׁל טוֹבָה, חַיִּים שֶׁל בְּרָכָה,
חַיִּים שֶׁל פַּרְנָסָה, חַיִּים שֶׁל חִלּוּץ עֲצָמוֹת, חַיִּים שֶׁיֵּשׁ בָּהֶם
יִרְאַת שָׁמַיִם וְיִרְאַת חֵטְא, חַיִּים שֶׁאֵין בָּהֶם בּוּשָׁה וּכְלִמָּה,
חַיִּים שֶׁל עֹשֶׁר וְכָבוֹד, חַיִּים שֶׁתְּהֵי בָנוּ אַהֲבַת תּוֹרָה וְיִרְאַת
שָׁמַיִם, חַיִּים שֶׁיִּמָּלְאוּ מִשְׁאֲלוֹת לִבֵּנוּ לְטוֹבָה, אָמֵן סֶלָה.

The Reader takes the Torah and recites:

מִי שֶׁעָשָׂה נִסִּים לַאֲבוֹתֵינוּ וְגָאַל אוֹתָם מֵעַבְדוּת לְחֵרוּת,
הוּא יִגְאַל אוֹתָנוּ בְּקָרוֹב, וִיקַבֵּץ נִדָּחֵינוּ מֵאַרְבַּע כַּנְפוֹת הָאָרֶץ,
חֲבֵרִים כָּל יִשְׂרָאֵל, וְנֹאמַר אָמֵן.

Announcing the day of *Rosh Hodesh.*

רֹאשׁ חֹדֶשׁ . . . יִהְיֶה בְּיוֹם . . .
הַבָּא עָלֵינוּ וְעַל כָּל יִשְׂרָאֵל לְטוֹבָה.

Congregation and Reader:

יְחַדְּשֵׁהוּ הַקָּדוֹשׁ בָּרוּךְ הוּא עָלֵינוּ וְעַל כָּל עַמּוֹ, בֵּית
יִשְׂרָאֵל, לְחַיִּים וּלְשָׁלוֹם, לְשָׂשׂוֹן וּלְשִׂמְחָה, לִישׁוּעָה וּלְנֶחָמָה,
וְנֹאמַר אָמֵן.

ברכת החודש is reminiscent of the Temple period when the arrival of a new
month was solemnly announced by the Sanhedrin after examining the witnesses who had noticed the appearance of the new moon. The thirtieth day of
the expiring month was proclaimed as the first day of the new month if the
statement of the witnesses was found to be correct. The proclamation of the
new month was signaled from mountain top to mountain top throughout
Palestine by lighting flares. In the middle of the fourth century, Hillel II
published scientific rules for the computation of the calendar, making the
months to alternate between 30 and 29 days. *Nisan, Sivan, Av, Tishri, Kislev*

BLESSING OF THE NEW MONTH

Recited on the Sabbath preceding Rosh Ḥodesh

May it be thy will, Lord our God and God of our fathers, to grant us this new month for happiness and blessedness. O grant us long life, a life of peace and well-being, a life of blessing and sustenance, a life of physical health, a life of piety and dread of sin, a life free from shame and disgrace, a life of wealth and honor, a life marked by our love for Torah and our fear of Heaven, a life in which the wishes of our heart shall be fulfilled for happiness. Amen.

The Reader takes the Torah and recites:

May he who performed miracles for our fathers, and freed them from slavery, speedily redeem us and gather our dispersed people from the four corners of the earth so that all Israel be knit together; and let us say, Amen.

Announcing the day of Rosh Ḥodesh:

The new month of . . . will begin on . . . . May it come to us and to all Israel for happiness.

Congregation and Reader:

May the Holy One, blessed be he, grant that the new month bring to us and to all his people, the house of Israel, life and peace, joy and gladness, salvation and comfort; and let us say, Amen.

---

and *Shevat* have each 30 days; the other six months have 29 days each. In leap year, the first *Adar* has 30 days, the second 29. *Ḥeshvan* is occasionally lengthened to 30 days. When the preceding month has 30 days, its last day is celebrated as the first day of *Rosh Ḥodesh*, while the second day of *Rosh Ḥodesh* marks the first day of the new month.

יהי רצון is cited in the Talmud (Berakhoth 16b) as the daily private prayer of Rav, the founder of the Babylonian academy of Sura (third century). It was adopted in the eighteenth century as a prayer for the coming of a happy month by adding the words שתחדש עלינו את החדש הזה לטובה ולברכה. The phrase יראת שמים is not repeated in the talmudic source of this prayer.

ויקבץ... is similar to the biblical expression ויאסף כל איש חברים כל ישראל ישראל... כאיש אחד חברים (Judges 20:11), which is rendered "all the men of Israel were knit together as one man"; see Ezekiel 37:16-22; Ḥagigah 26a.

הַזְכָּרַת נִשְׁמוֹת הַקְּדוֹשִׁים

Omitted on festivals, on Sabbath-*Rosh Ḥodesh*, and on all distinguished
Sabbaths such as *Parashath Shekalim*.

אַב הָרַחֲמִים, שׁוֹכֵן מְרוֹמִים, בְּרַחֲמָיו הָעֲצוּמִים, הוּא
יִפְקֹד בְּרַחֲמִים הַחֲסִידִים וְהַיְשָׁרִים וְהַתְּמִימִים, קְהִלּוֹת הַקְּדֶשׁ
שֶׁמָּסְרוּ נַפְשָׁם עַל קְדָשַׁת הַשֵּׁם, הַנֶּאֱהָבִים וְהַנְּעִימִים בְּחַיֵּיהֶם,
וּבְמוֹתָם לֹא נִפְרָדוּ. מִנְּשָׁרִים קַלּוּ, וּמֵאֲרָיוֹת גָּבֵרוּ, לַעֲשׂוֹת
רְצוֹן קוֹנָם וְחֵפֶץ צוּרָם. יִזְכְּרֵם אֱלֹהֵינוּ לְטוֹבָה עִם שְׁאָר
צַדִּיקֵי עוֹלָם, וְיִנְקֹם נִקְמַת דַּם עֲבָדָיו הַשָּׁפוּךְ, כַּכָּתוּב בְּתוֹרַת
מֹשֶׁה אִישׁ הָאֱלֹהִים: הַרְנִינוּ, גוֹיִם, עַמּוֹ, כִּי דַם עֲבָדָיו יִקּוֹם,
וְנָקָם יָשִׁיב לְצָרָיו, וְכִפֶּר אַדְמָתוֹ עַמּוֹ. וְעַל יְדֵי עֲבָדֶיךָ
הַנְּבִיאִים כָּתוּב לֵאמֹר: וְנִקֵּיתִי דָמָם, לֹא נִקֵּיתִי, וַיְיָ שֹׁכֵן בְּצִיּוֹן.
וּבְכִתְבֵי הַקְּדֶשׁ נֶאֱמַר: לָמָּה יֹאמְרוּ הַגּוֹיִם אַיֵּה אֱלֹהֵיהֶם, יִוָּדַע
בַּגּוֹיִם לְעֵינֵינוּ נִקְמַת דַּם עֲבָדֶיךָ הַשָּׁפוּךְ. Reader וְאוֹמֵר: כִּי
דֹרֵשׁ דָּמִים אוֹתָם זָכָר, לֹא שָׁכַח צַעֲקַת עֲנָוִים. וְאוֹמֵר: יָדִין
בַּגּוֹיִם, מָלֵא גְוִיּוֹת, מָחַץ רֹאשׁ עַל אֶרֶץ רַבָּה, מִנַּחַל בַּדֶּרֶךְ
יִשְׁתֶּה, עַל כֵּן יָרִים רֹאשׁ.

אַשְׁרֵי יוֹשְׁבֵי בֵיתֶךָ; עוֹד יְהַלְלוּךָ סֶּלָה.
אַשְׁרֵי הָעָם שֶׁכָּכָה לּוֹ; אַשְׁרֵי הָעָם שֶׁיְיָ אֱלֹהָיו.

אב הרחמים was probably composed during the first Crusade in 1096, when
many Jewish communities were destroyed. Speaking of the Hebrew elegies
occasioned by the medieval persecutions, Zunz writes: "If there are ranks in
suffering, Israel takes precedence of all the nations . . . if a literature is called
rich in the possession of a few classic tragedies, what shall we say to a national
tragedy . . . in which the poets and the actors were also the heroes?"

COMMEMORATION OF MARTYRS

Omitted on festivals, on Sabbath-Rosh Ḥodesh, and on all distinguished Sabbaths such as Parashath Shekalim.

May the merciful Father who dwells on high, in his infinite mercy, remember those saintly, upright and blameless souls, the holy communities who offered their lives for the sanctification of the divine name. They were lovely and amiable in their life, and were not parted in their death. They were swifter than eagles and stronger than lions to do the will of their Master and the desire of their Stronghold. May our God remember them favorably among the other righteous of the world; may he avenge the blood of his servants which has been shed, as it is written in the Torah of Moses, the man of God: "O nations, make his people joyful! He avenges the blood of his servants, renders retribution to his foes, and provides atonement for his land and his people."[1] And by thy servants, the prophets, it is written: "I will avenge their blood which I have not yet avenged; the Lord dwells in Zion."[2] And in the holy writings it is said: "Why should the nations say, 'Where then is their God?' Let the vengeance for thy servants' blood that is shed be made known among the nations in our sight." And it is said: "The avenger of bloodshed remembers them; he does not forget the cry of the humble." And it is further said: "He will execute judgment upon the nations and fill [the battle-field] with corpses; he will shatter the [enemy's] head over all the wide earth. From the brook by the wayside he will drink; then he will lift up his head triumphantly."[3]

Happy are those who dwell in thy house; they are ever praising thee. Happy the people that is so situated; happy the people whose God is the Lord.[4]

מנחל בדרך ישתה describes the victor in hot pursuit of the enemy. Wearied from the toil of battle, he halts for a moment to drink from the brook which he crosses. Refreshed, he presses forward to complete his victory.

---

[1] *Deuteronomy* 32:43.   [2] *Joel* 4:21.   [3] *Psalms* 79:10; 9:13; 110:6–7.
[4] *Psalms* 84:5; 144:15.

תהלים קמה

תְּהִלָּה לְדָוִד

אֲרוֹמִמְךָ, אֱלוֹהַי הַמֶּלֶךְ, וַאֲבָרְכָה שִׁמְךָ לְעוֹלָם וָעֶד.

בְּכָל יוֹם אֲבָרְכֶךָ, וַאֲהַלְלָה שִׁמְךָ לְעוֹלָם וָעֶד.

גָּדוֹל יְיָ וּמְהֻלָּל מְאֹד, וְלִגְדֻלָּתוֹ אֵין חֵקֶר.

דּוֹר לְדוֹר יְשַׁבַּח מַעֲשֶׂיךָ, וּגְבוּרֹתֶיךָ יַגִּידוּ.

הֲדַר כְּבוֹד הוֹדֶךָ וְדִבְרֵי נִפְלְאֹתֶיךָ אָשִׂיחָה.

וֶעֱזוּז נוֹרְאוֹתֶיךָ יֹאמֵרוּ, וּגְדֻלָּתְךָ אֲסַפְּרֶנָּה.

זֵכֶר רַב טוּבְךָ יַבִּיעוּ, וְצִדְקָתְךָ יְרַנֵּנוּ.

חַנּוּן וְרַחוּם יְיָ, אֶרֶךְ אַפַּיִם וּגְדָל־חָסֶד.

טוֹב יְיָ לַכֹּל, וְרַחֲמָיו עַל כָּל מַעֲשָׂיו.

יוֹדוּךָ יְיָ כָּל מַעֲשֶׂיךָ, וַחֲסִידֶיךָ יְבָרְכוּכָה.

כְּבוֹד מַלְכוּתְךָ יֹאמֵרוּ, וּגְבוּרָתְךָ יְדַבֵּרוּ.

לְהוֹדִיעַ לִבְנֵי הָאָדָם גְּבוּרֹתָיו, וּכְבוֹד הֲדַר מַלְכוּתוֹ.

מַלְכוּתְךָ מַלְכוּת כָּל עֹלָמִים, וּמֶמְשַׁלְתְּךָ בְּכָל דּוֹר וָדֹר.

סוֹמֵךְ יְיָ לְכָל הַנֹּפְלִים, וְזוֹקֵף לְכָל הַכְּפוּפִים.

עֵינֵי כֹל אֵלֶיךָ יְשַׂבֵּרוּ, וְאַתָּה נוֹתֵן לָהֶם אֶת אָכְלָם בְּעִתּוֹ.

פּוֹתֵחַ אֶת יָדֶךָ, וּמַשְׂבִּיעַ לְכָל חַי רָצוֹן.

צַדִּיק יְיָ בְּכָל דְּרָכָיו, וְחָסִיד בְּכָל מַעֲשָׂיו.

קָרוֹב יְיָ לְכָל קֹרְאָיו, לְכֹל אֲשֶׁר יִקְרָאֻהוּ בֶאֱמֶת.

רְצוֹן יְרֵאָיו יַעֲשֶׂה, וְאֶת שַׁוְעָתָם יִשְׁמַע וְיוֹשִׁיעֵם.

שׁוֹמֵר יְיָ אֶת כָּל אֹהֲבָיו, וְאֵת כָּל הָרְשָׁעִים יַשְׁמִיד.

Psalm 145

A hymn of praise by David.

I extol thee, my God the King,
And bless thy name forever and ever.
Every day I bless thee,
And praise thy name forever and ever.
Great is the Lord and most worthy of praise;
His greatness is unsearchable.
One generation to another praises thy works;
They recount thy mighty acts.
On the splendor of thy glorious majesty
And on thy wondrous deeds I meditate.
They speak of thy awe-inspiring might,
And I tell of thy greatness.
They spread the fame of thy great goodness,
And sing of thy righteousness.
Gracious and merciful is the Lord,
Slow to anger and of great kindness.
The Lord is good to all,
And his compassion is over all his works.
All thy works praise thee, O Lord,
And thy faithful followers bless thee.
They speak of thy glorious kingdom,
And talk of thy might,
To let men know thy mighty deeds,
And the glorious splendor of thy kingdom.
Thy kingdom is a kingdom of all ages,
And thy dominion is for all generations.
The Lord upholds all who fall,
And raises all who are bowed down.
The eyes of all look hopefully to thee,
And thou givest them their food in due season.
Thou openest thy hand,
And satisfiest every living thing with favor.
The Lord is righteous in all his ways,
And gracious in all his deeds.
The Lord is near to all who call upon him,
To all who call upon him sincerely.
He fulfills the desire of those who revere him:
He hears their cry and saves them.
The Lord preserves all who love him,
But all the wicked he destroys.

תְּהִלַּת יְיָ יְדַבֶּר־פִּי; וִיבָרֵךְ כָּל בָּשָׂר שֵׁם קָדְשׁוֹ לְעוֹלָם וָעֶד.
וַאֲנַחְנוּ נְבָרֵךְ יָהּ מֵעַתָּה וְעַד עוֹלָם; הַלְלוּיָהּ.

The Reader takes the Torah and says:

יְהַלְלוּ אֶת שֵׁם יְיָ, כִּי נִשְׂגָּב שְׁמוֹ לְבַדּוֹ—

Congregation:

הוֹדוֹ עַל אֶרֶץ וְשָׁמָיִם. וַיָּרֶם קֶרֶן לְעַמּוֹ, תְּהִלָּה לְכָל
חֲסִידָיו, לִבְנֵי יִשְׂרָאֵל עַם קְרֹבוֹ; הַלְלוּיָהּ.

On Sabbaths:

תהלים כט

מִזְמוֹר לְדָוִד. הָבוּ לַיְיָ, בְּנֵי אֵלִים, הָבוּ לַיְיָ כָּבוֹד וָעֹז.
הָבוּ לַיְיָ כְּבוֹד שְׁמוֹ, הִשְׁתַּחֲווּ לַיְיָ בְּהַדְרַת קֹדֶשׁ. קוֹל יְיָ עַל
הַמָּיִם, אֵל הַכָּבוֹד הִרְעִים, יְיָ עַל מַיִם רַבִּים. קוֹל יְיָ בַּכֹּחַ,
קוֹל יְיָ בֶּהָדָר, קוֹל יְיָ שֹׁבֵר אֲרָזִים, וַיְשַׁבֵּר יְיָ אֶת אַרְזֵי הַלְּבָנוֹן.
וַיַּרְקִידֵם כְּמוֹ עֵגֶל, לְבָנוֹן וְשִׂרְיוֹן כְּמוֹ בֶן־רְאֵמִים. קוֹל יְיָ חֹצֵב
לַהֲבוֹת אֵשׁ. קוֹל יְיָ יָחִיל מִדְבָּר, יָחִיל יְיָ מִדְבַּר קָדֵשׁ. קוֹל יְיָ
יְחוֹלֵל אַיָּלוֹת, וַיֶּחֱשֹׂף יְעָרוֹת, וּבְהֵיכָלוֹ כֻּלּוֹ אֹמֵר כָּבוֹד. יְיָ
לַמַּבּוּל יָשָׁב, וַיֵּשֶׁב יְיָ מֶלֶךְ לְעוֹלָם. יְיָ עֹז לְעַמּוֹ יִתֵּן, יְיָ יְבָרֵךְ
אֶת עַמּוֹ בַשָּׁלוֹם.

On festivals occurring on weekdays:

תהלים כד

(לְדָוִד מִזְמוֹר. לַיְיָ הָאָרֶץ וּמְלוֹאָהּ, תֵּבֵל וְיֹשְׁבֵי בָהּ. כִּי הוּא
עַל יַמִּים יְסָדָהּ, וְעַל נְהָרוֹת יְכוֹנְנֶהָ. מִי יַעֲלֶה בְהַר יְיָ, וּמִי
יָקוּם בִּמְקוֹם קָדְשׁוֹ. נְקִי כַפַּיִם וּבַר לֵבָב, אֲשֶׁר לֹא נָשָׂא לַשָּׁוְא
נַפְשִׁי, וְלֹא נִשְׁבַּע לְמִרְמָה. יִשָּׂא בְרָכָה מֵאֵת יְיָ, וּצְדָקָה מֵאֱלֹהֵי
יִשְׁעוֹ. זֶה דּוֹר דֹּרְשָׁיו, מְבַקְשֵׁי פָנֶיךָ, יַעֲקֹב, סֶלָה. שְׂאוּ שְׁעָרִים

My mouth speaks the praise of the Lord;
Let all creatures bless his holy name forever and ever.
[1]We will bless the Lord henceforth and forever.
Praise the Lord!

The Reader takes the Torah and says:

Let them praise the name of the Lord, for his name alone is exalted—

Congregation:

His majesty is above earth and heaven. He has raised the honor of his people, the glory of his faithful followers, the people near to him. Praise the Lord![2]

On Sabbaths:

Psalm 29

A psalm of David. Give to the Lord, heavenly beings, give to the Lord honor and glory. Give to the Lord the glory due to his name; worship the Lord in holy array. The voice of the Lord peals across the waters; it is the God of glory thundering! The Lord is over the vast waters. The voice of the Lord is mighty; the voice of the Lord is majestic. The voice of the Lord breaks the cedars; the Lord shatters the cedars of Lebanon. He makes Lebanon and Sirion leap like a calf, like a wild ox. The voice of the Lord strikes flames of fire; the voice of the Lord causes the desert to tremble; the Lord causes the desert of Kadesh to tremble. The voice of the Lord whirls the oaks, and strips the woods bare; in his palace everything says: "Glory." The Lord sat enthroned at the flood; the Lord remains King forever. The Lord will give strength to his people; the Lord will bless his people with peace.

On festivals occurring on weekdays:

Psalm 24

(A psalm of David. The earth and its entire contents belong to the Lord, the world and its inhabitants. For it is he who has founded it upon the seas, and established it on the floods. Who may ascend the Lord's mountain? Who may stand within his holy place? He who has clean hands and a pure heart; he who strives not after vanity and swears not deceitfully. He will receive a blessing from the Lord, and justice from his saving God. Such is the generation of those who are in quest of him, who seek the presence of the God of Jacob. Raise your heads, O gates, raise yourselves,

---

[1] *Psalm* 115:18.   [2] *Psalm* 148:13–14.

רָאשֵׁיכֶם, וְהִנָּשְׂאוּ פִּתְחֵי עוֹלָם, וְיָבוֹא מֶלֶךְ הַכָּבוֹד. מִי זֶה
מֶלֶךְ הַכָּבוֹד, יְיָ עִזּוּז וְגִבּוֹר, יְיָ גִבּוֹר מִלְחָמָה. שְׂאוּ שְׁעָרִים
רָאשֵׁיכֶם, וּשְׂאוּ פִּתְחֵי עוֹלָם, וְיָבֹא מֶלֶךְ הַכָּבוֹד. מִי הוּא זֶה
מֶלֶךְ הַכָּבוֹד, יְיָ צְבָאוֹת הוּא מֶלֶךְ הַכָּבוֹד, סֶלָה.)

While the *Torah* is being placed in the ark:

וּבְנֻחֹה יֹאמַר: שׁוּבָה, יְיָ, רִבְבוֹת אַלְפֵי יִשְׂרָאֵל. קוּמָה יְיָ
לִמְנוּחָתֶךָ, אַתָּה וַאֲרוֹן עֻזֶּךָ. כֹּהֲנֶיךָ יִלְבְּשׁוּ צֶדֶק, וַחֲסִידֶיךָ
יְרַנֵּנוּ. בַּעֲבוּר דָּוִד עַבְדֶּךָ, אַל תָּשֵׁב פְּנֵי מְשִׁיחֶךָ. כִּי לֶקַח טוֹב
נָתַתִּי לָכֶם, תּוֹרָתִי אַל תַּעֲזֹבוּ. עֵץ חַיִּים הִיא לַמַּחֲזִיקִים בָּהּ,
וְתֹמְכֶיהָ מְאֻשָּׁר. דְּרָכֶיהָ דַרְכֵי נֹעַם, וְכָל נְתִיבוֹתֶיהָ שָׁלוֹם.
הֲשִׁיבֵנוּ יְיָ אֵלֶיךָ, וְנָשׁוּבָה; חַדֵּשׁ יָמֵינוּ כְּקֶדֶם.

Reader:

יִתְגַּדַּל וְיִתְקַדַּשׁ שְׁמֵהּ רַבָּא בְּעָלְמָא דִּי בְרָא כִרְעוּתֵהּ;
וְיַמְלִיךְ מַלְכוּתֵהּ בְּחַיֵּיכוֹן וּבְיוֹמֵיכוֹן, וּבְחַיֵּי דְכָל בֵּית יִשְׂרָאֵל,
בַּעֲגָלָא וּבִזְמַן קָרִיב, וְאִמְרוּ אָמֵן.

יְהֵא שְׁמֵהּ רַבָּא מְבָרַךְ לְעָלַם וּלְעָלְמֵי עָלְמַיָּא.

יִתְבָּרַךְ וְיִשְׁתַּבַּח, וְיִתְפָּאַר וְיִתְרוֹמַם, וְיִתְנַשֵּׂא וְיִתְהַדָּר,
וְיִתְעַלֶּה וְיִתְהַלָּל שְׁמֵהּ דְּקֻדְשָׁא, בְּרִיךְ הוּא, לְעֵלָּא (לְעֵלָּא)
מִן כָּל בִּרְכָתָא וְשִׁירָתָא, תֻּשְׁבְּחָתָא וְנֶחֱמָתָא, דַּאֲמִירָן בְּעָלְמָא,
וְאִמְרוּ אָמֵן.

The *Musaf* service for festivals begins on page 609

שָׂאוּ שְׁעָרִים רָאשֵׁיכֶם The ancient gates of Zion are poetically called on to
raise their heads, in token of reverence to God. Different parts of this psalm
were sung by different choirs at the time when David brought the ark to
Mount Zion.

סֶלָה marks a pause or a transition between one thought and another. It
calls forth changes in the orchestral music corresponding to the ideas, and

you ancient doors, that the glorious King may come in. Who, then, is the glorious King? The Lord strong and mighty, the Lord strong in battle. Raise your heads, O gates, raise yourselves, ancient doors, that the glorious King may come in. Who, then, is the glorious King? The Lord of hosts, he is the glorious King.)

While the Torah is being placed in the ark:

When the ark rested, Moses would say: "Return, O Lord, to the myriads of Israel's families." Arise, O Lord, for thy resting place, thou and thy glorious ark. May thy priests be clothed in righteousness; may thy faithful followers shout for joy. For the sake of thy servant David, reject not thy anointed. I give you good instruction; forsake not my Torah. It is a tree of life to those who take hold of it, and happy are those who support it. Its ways are ways of pleasantness, and all its paths are peace. Turn us to thee, O Lord, and let us return; renew our days as of old.[1]

Reader:

Glorified and sanctified be God's great name throughout the world which he has created according to his will. May he establish his kingdom in your lifetime and during your days, and within the life of the entire house of Israel, speedily and soon; and say, Amen.

May his great name be blessed forever and to all eternity.

Blessed and praised, glorified and exalted, extolled and honored, adored and lauded be the name of the Holy One, blessed be he, beyond all the blessings and hymns, praises and consolations that are ever spoken in the world; and say, Amen.

The Musaf service for festivals begins on page 610

---

cessation of music or hushed music. The last four verses of Psalm 24 describe the holy ark, "which is called by the name of the Lord," as standing outside the gates. The gatekeepers are summoned to open the gates high and wide in order that the holy ark, the symbol of God's majesty, may enter.

---

[1] *Numbers* 10:36; *Psalm* 132:8-10; *Proverbs* 4:2; 3:18, 17; *Lamentations* 5:21.

מוּסָף לְשַׁבָּת

The *Amidah* is recited in silent devotion while standing, facing east.
The Reader repeats the *Amidah* aloud when a *minyan* holds service.

כִּי שֵׁם יְיָ אֶקְרָא, הָבוּ גֹּדֶל לֵאלֹהֵינוּ.

אֲדֹנָי, שְׂפָתַי תִּפְתָּח, וּפִי יַגִּיד תְּהִלָּתֶךָ.

בָּרוּךְ אַתָּה, יְיָ אֱלֹהֵינוּ וֵאלֹהֵי אֲבוֹתֵינוּ, אֱלֹהֵי אַבְרָהָם,
אֱלֹהֵי יִצְחָק, וֵאלֹהֵי יַעֲקֹב, הָאֵל הַגָּדוֹל הַגִּבּוֹר וְהַנּוֹרָא, אֵל
עֶלְיוֹן, גּוֹמֵל חֲסָדִים טוֹבִים, וְקוֹנֵה הַכֹּל, וְזוֹכֵר חַסְדֵי אָבוֹת,
וּמֵבִיא גוֹאֵל לִבְנֵי בְנֵיהֶם לְמַעַן שְׁמוֹ בְּאַהֲבָה.

Between *Rosh Hashanah* and *Yom Kippur* add:

(זָכְרֵנוּ לְחַיִּים, מֶלֶךְ חָפֵץ בַּחַיִּים,

וְכָתְבֵנוּ בְּסֵפֶר הַחַיִּים, לְמַעַנְךָ אֱלֹהִים חַיִּים.)

מֶלֶךְ עוֹזֵר וּמוֹשִׁיעַ וּמָגֵן. בָּרוּךְ אַתָּה, יְיָ, מָגֵן אַבְרָהָם.
אַתָּה גִּבּוֹר לְעוֹלָם, אֲדֹנָי, מְחַיֵּה מֵתִים אַתָּה, רַב לְהוֹשִׁיעַ.

Between *Sukkoth* and *Pesah* add:

(מַשִּׁיב הָרוּחַ וּמוֹרִיד הַגֶּשֶׁם.)

מְכַלְכֵּל חַיִּים בְּחֶסֶד, מְחַיֵּה מֵתִים בְּרַחֲמִים רַבִּים, סוֹמֵךְ
נוֹפְלִים, וְרוֹפֵא חוֹלִים, וּמַתִּיר אֲסוּרִים, וּמְקַיֵּם אֱמוּנָתוֹ לִישֵׁנֵי
עָפָר. מִי כָמוֹךָ, בַּעַל גְּבוּרוֹת, וּמִי דּוֹמֶה לָּךְ, מֶלֶךְ מֵמִית
וּמְחַיֶּה וּמַצְמִיחַ יְשׁוּעָה.

Between *Rosh Hashanah* and *Yom Kippur* add:

(מִי כָמוֹךָ, אַב הָרַחֲמִים, זוֹכֵר יְצוּרָיו לְחַיִּים בְּרַחֲמִים.)

מוסף, the prayer added after *Shaharith*, corresponds to the additional
sacrifices on Sabbaths and festive days over and above the regular daily *tamid*
offered in the Temple.

The Amidah is recited in silent devotion while standing, facing east.
The Reader repeats the Amidah aloud when a minyan holds service.

When I proclaim the name of the Lord, give glory to our God![1]
O Lord, open thou my lips, that my mouth may declare thy praise.[2]

Blessed art thou, Lord our God and God of our fathers, God of Abraham, God of Isaac and God of Jacob; great, mighty and revered God, sublime God, who bestowest lovingkindness, and art Master of all things; who rememberest the good deeds of our fathers, and who wilt graciously bring a redeemer to their children's children for the sake of thy name.

Between Rosh Hashanah and Yom Kippur add:

(Remember us to life, O King who delightest in life; inscribe us in the book of life for thy sake, O living God.)

O King, Supporter, Savior and Shield! Blessed art thou, O Lord, Shield of Abraham.

Thou, O Lord, art mighty forever; thou revivest the dead; thou art powerful to save.

Between Sukkoth and Pesaḥ add:

(Thou causest the wind to blow and the rain to fall.)

Thou sustainest the living with kindness, and revivest the dead with great mercy; thou supportest all who fall, and healest the sick; thou settest the captives free, and keepest faith with those who sleep in the dust. Who is like thee, Lord of power? Who resembles thee, O King? Thou bringest death and restorest life, and causest salvation to flourish.

Between Rosh Hashanah and Yom Kippur add:

(Who is like thee, merciful Father? In mercy thou rememberest thy creatures to life.)

כי שם precedes the *Amidahs* of *Musaf* and *Minḥah* only. In *Shaḥarith* and *Ma'ariv* this verse is omitted, because there it would interrupt the connection between the benediction גאל ישראל and the *Amidah.*

---

[1] *Deuteronomy* 32:3.   [2] *Psalm* 51:17.

וְנֶאֱמָן אַתָּה לְהַחֲיוֹת מֵתִים. בָּרוּךְ אַתָּה, יְיָ, מְחַיֵּה הַמֵּתִים.

When the Reader repeats the *Amidah*, the following *Kedushah* is said.

נַעֲרִיצְךָ וְנַקְדִּישְׁךָ כְּסוֹד שִׂיחַ שַׂרְפֵי קֹדֶשׁ הַמַּקְדִּישִׁים שִׁמְךָ
בַּקֹּדֶשׁ, כַּכָּתוּב עַל יַד נְבִיאֶךָ: וְקָרָא זֶה אֶל זֶה וְאָמַר:

קָדוֹשׁ, קָדוֹשׁ, קָדוֹשׁ יְיָ צְבָאוֹת; מְלֹא כָל הָאָרֶץ כְּבוֹדוֹ.
כְּבוֹדוֹ מָלֵא עוֹלָם; מְשָׁרְתָיו שׁוֹאֲלִים זֶה לָזֶה אַיֵּה מְקוֹם
כְּבוֹדוֹ; לְעֻמָּתָם בָּרוּךְ יֹאמֵרוּ—

בָּרוּךְ כְּבוֹד יְיָ מִמְּקוֹמוֹ.

מִמְּקוֹמוֹ הוּא יִפֶן בְּרַחֲמִים, וְיָחֹן עַם הַמְיַחֲדִים שְׁמוֹ; עֶרֶב
וָבֹקֶר, בְּכָל יוֹם תָּמִיד, פַּעֲמַיִם בְּאַהֲבָה שְׁמַע אוֹמְרִים—

שְׁמַע, יִשְׂרָאֵל, יְיָ אֱלֹהֵינוּ, יְיָ אֶחָד.

הוּא אֱלֹהֵינוּ, הוּא אָבִינוּ, הוּא מַלְכֵּנוּ, הוּא מוֹשִׁיעֵנוּ, וְהוּא
יַשְׁמִיעֵנוּ בְּרַחֲמָיו שֵׁנִית לְעֵינֵי כָּל חָי: לִהְיוֹת לָכֶם לֵאלֹהִים—
אֲנִי יְיָ אֱלֹהֵיכֶם.

וּבְדִבְרֵי קָדְשְׁךָ כָּתוּב לֵאמֹר:

יִמְלֹךְ יְיָ לְעוֹלָם, אֱלֹהַיִךְ צִיּוֹן לְדֹר וָדֹר; הַלְלוּיָהּ.

Reader:

לְדוֹר וָדוֹר נַגִּיד גָּדְלֶךָ, וּלְנֵצַח נְצָחִים קְדֻשָּׁתְךָ נַקְדִּישׁ,
וְשִׁבְחֲךָ אֱלֹהֵינוּ מִפִּינוּ לֹא יָמוּשׁ לְעוֹלָם וָעֶד, כִּי אֵל מֶלֶךְ
גָּדוֹל וְקָדוֹשׁ אָתָּה. בָּרוּךְ אַתָּה, יְיָ, הָאֵל * (הַמֶּלֶךְ) הַקָּדוֹשׁ.

———

אַתָּה קָדוֹשׁ וְשִׁמְךָ קָדוֹשׁ, וּקְדוֹשִׁים בְּכָל יוֹם יְהַלְלוּךָ סֶּלָה.
בָּרוּךְ אַתָּה, יְיָ, הָאֵל * (הַמֶּלֶךְ) הַקָּדוֹשׁ.

* Between *Rosh Hashanah* and *Yom Kippur* say הַמֶּלֶךְ הַקָּדוֹשׁ.

———

שִׂיחַ סוֹד שַׂרְפֵי קֹדֶשׁ equals שִׂיחַ סוֹד שַׂרְפֵי קוֹדֶשׁ; compare שִׂיחַ סוֹד in the Sephardic *Siddur*.
נַעֲרִיצְךָ כְּסוֹד is based on אֵל נַעֲרָץ בְּסוֹד קְדֹשִׁים (Psalm 89:8) where the meaning is: "God is revered in the council of the holy ones."

Thou art faithful to revive the dead. Blessed art thou, O Lord, who revivest the dead.

KEDUSHAH

When the Reader repeats the Amidah, the following Kedushah is said.

We revere and sanctify thee in the words of the assembly of holy seraphim who hallow thy name in the sanctuary, as it is written by thy prophet: "They keep calling to one another:

Holy, holy, holy is the Lord of hosts;
The whole earth is full of his glory."[1]

His glory fills the universe; his ministering angels ask one another: "Where is his glorious place?" They say to one another: "Blessed—

Blessed be the glory of the Lord from his abode."[2]

From his abode may he turn with compassion and be gracious to the people who acclaim his Oneness evening and morning, twice every day, and with tender affection recite the Shema—

"Hear, O Israel, the Lord is our God, the Lord is One."[3]

He is our God; he is our Father; he is our King; he is our Deliverer. He will again in his mercy proclaim to us in the presence of all the living:". . . to be your God—

I am the Lord your God."[4]

And in the holy Scriptures it is written:
The Lord shall reign forever,
Your God, O Zion, for all generations.
Praise the Lord![5]

Reader:

Through all generations we will declare thy greatness; to all eternity we will proclaim thy holiness; thy praise, our God, shall never depart from our mouth, for thou art a great and holy God and King. Blessed art thou, O Lord, * holy God.

Thou art holy and thy name is holy, and holy beings praise thee daily. Blessed art thou, O Lord, * holy God.

*Between Rosh Hashanah and Yom Kippur say, "holy King."

שמע ישראל and the concluding words of the *Shema* were inserted here in the fifth century, when special government officials were posted in the synagogues to prevent the congregational proclamation of God's Oneness. Toward the end of the service, when the spies had left, the *Shema* was thus recited in an abridged form.

[1] *Isaiah* 6:3. [2] *Ezekiel* 3:12. [3] *Deuteronomy* 6:4. [4] *Numbers* 15:41.
[5] *Psalm* 146:10.

On regular Sabbaths:

תִּכַּנְתָּ שַׁבָּת, רָצִיתָ קָרְבְּנוֹתֶיהָ. צִוִּיתָ פֵּרוּשֶׁיהָ עִם סִדּוּרֵי
נְסָכֶיהָ. מְעַנְּגֶיהָ לְעוֹלָם כָּבוֹד יִנְחָלוּ; טוֹעֲמֶיהָ חַיִּים זָכוּ; וְגַם
הָאוֹהֲבִים דְּבָרֶיהָ גְּדֻלָּה בָחָרוּ. אָז מִסִּינַי נִצְטַוּוּ עָלֶיהָ. וַתְּצַוֵּנוּ,
יְיָ אֱלֹהֵינוּ, לְהַקְרִיב בָּהּ קָרְבַּן מוּסַף שַׁבָּת כָּרָאוּי. יְהִי רָצוֹן
מִלְּפָנֶיהָ, יְיָ אֱלֹהֵינוּ וֵאלֹהֵי אֲבוֹתֵינוּ, שֶׁתַּעֲלֵנוּ בְשִׂמְחָה לְאַרְצֵנוּ,
וְתִטָּעֵנוּ בִּגְבוּלֵנוּ; וְשָׁם נַעֲשֶׂה לְפָנֶיהָ אֶת קָרְבְּנוֹת חוֹבוֹתֵינוּ,
תְּמִידִים כְּסִדְרָם וּמוּסָפִים כְּהִלְכָתָם. וְאֶת מוּסַף יוֹם הַשַּׁבָּת
הַזֶּה נַעֲשֶׂה וְנַקְרִיב לְפָנֶיהָ בְּאַהֲבָה, כְּמִצְוַת רְצוֹנֶהָ, כְּמוֹ
שֶׁכָּתַבְתָּ עָלֵינוּ בְּתוֹרָתֶהָ, עַל יְדֵי מֹשֶׁה עַבְדֶּהָ, מִפִּי כְבוֹדֶהָ,
כָּאָמוּר:

וּבְיוֹם הַשַּׁבָּת, שְׁנֵי כְבָשִׂים בְּנֵי שָׁנָה תְּמִימִם; וּשְׁנֵי עֶשְׂרֹנִים
סֹלֶת, מִנְחָה בְּלוּלָה בַשֶּׁמֶן, וְנִסְכּוֹ. עֹלַת שַׁבַּת בְּשַׁבַּתּוֹ, עַל
עֹלַת הַתָּמִיד וְנִסְכָּהּ.

יִשְׂמְחוּ בְמַלְכוּתְהָ שׁוֹמְרֵי שַׁבָּת וְקוֹרְאֵי עֹנֶג, עַם מְקַדְּשֵׁי
שְׁבִיעִי, כֻּלָּם יִשְׂבְּעוּ וְיִתְעַנְּגוּ מִטּוּבֶהָ; וְהַשְּׁבִיעִי רָצִיתָ בּוֹ
וְקִדַּשְׁתּוֹ, חֶמְדַּת יָמִים אוֹתוֹ קָרֵאתָ, זֵכֶר לְמַעֲשֵׂה בְרֵאשִׁית.

אֱלֹהֵינוּ וֵאלֹהֵי אֲבוֹתֵינוּ, רְצֵה בִמְנוּחָתֵנוּ. קַדְּשֵׁנוּ בְּמִצְוֹתֶיהָ,
וְתֵן חֶלְקֵנוּ בְּתוֹרָתֶהָ; שַׂבְּעֵנוּ מִטּוּבֶהָ, וְשַׂמְּחֵנוּ בִּישׁוּעָתֶהָ; וְטַהֵר
לִבֵּנוּ לְעָבְדְּהָ בֶּאֱמֶת; וְהַנְחִילֵנוּ, יְיָ אֱלֹהֵינוּ, בְּאַהֲבָה וּבְרָצוֹן
שַׁבַּת קָדְשֶׁהָ, וְיָנוּחוּ בָהּ יִשְׂרָאֵל מְקַדְּשֵׁי שְׁמֶהָ. בָּרוּךְ אַתָּה, יְיָ,
מְקַדֵּשׁ הַשַּׁבָּת. (page 399) רְצֵה Continue

תכנת שבת, the first twenty-two words of which run in a reversed alphabetic acrostic, is found in Maḥzor Vitry and was known to Amram Gaon
(ninth century). The passage begins with ת, the last letter of the alphabet,
and ends with א, the first letter.

On regular Sabbaths:

Thou hast instituted the Sabbath and favorably accepted its offerings; thou hast prescribed its special duties and the order of its libations. Those who observe it with joy will forever possess glory; those who enjoy its happiness merit eternal life; those who love its laws have chosen greatness. Of yore, at Sinai they were commanded concerning it. Thou, Lord our God, didst command us to offer the additional Sabbath offering in due form. May it be thy will, Lord our God and God of our fathers, to bring us in joy back to our land and to plant us within our borders. There we will prepare in thy honor our obligatory offerings, the regular daily offerings and the additional offerings, according to rule. The additional offering of this Sabbath day we will prepare and present to thee with love according to the command of thy will, as thou hast prescribed for us in thy Torah through thy servant Moses, as it is said:

On the Sabbath day, two perfect yearling male lambs and two-tenths of an *ephah* of fine flour mixed with oil as a meal offering, and the libation. This is the burnt-offering of each Sabbath, in addition to the daily burnt-offering and its libation.[1]

Those who keep the Sabbath and call it a delight shall rejoice in thy kingdom; all the people who hallow the seventh day shall fully enjoy thy goodness. Thou wast pleased with the seventh day and didst hallow it; the most desirable of days didst thou call it—in remembrance of the creation.

Our God and God of our fathers, be pleased with our rest. Sanctify us with thy commandments and grant us a share in thy Torah; satisfy us with thy goodness and gladden us with thy help; purify our heart to serve thee sincerely. In thy gracious love, Lord our God, grant that we keep thy holy Sabbath as a heritage; may Israel who sanctifies thy name rest on it. Blessed art thou, O Lord, who hallowest the Sabbath.

Continue "Be pleased..." (page 400)

---

[1] *Numbers* 28:9–10.

On Sabbath-*Rosh Ḥodesh*:

(אַתָּה יָצַרְתָּ עוֹלָמְךָ מִקֶּדֶם; כָּלִיתָ מְלַאכְתְּךָ בַּיּוֹם הַשְּׁבִיעִי.
אָהַבְתָּ אוֹתָנוּ וְרָצִיתָ בָּנוּ, וְרוֹמַמְתָּנוּ מִכָּל הַלְּשׁוֹנוֹת, וְקִדַּשְׁתָּנוּ
בְּמִצְוֹתֶיךָ, וְקֵרַבְתָּנוּ מַלְכֵּנוּ לַעֲבוֹדָתֶךָ, וְשִׁמְךָ הַגָּדוֹל וְהַקָּדוֹשׁ
עָלֵינוּ קָרָאתָ; וַתִּתֶּן־לָנוּ, יְיָ אֱלֹהֵינוּ, בְּאַהֲבָה, שַׁבָּתוֹת לִמְנוּחָה
וְרָאשֵׁי חֳדָשִׁים לְכַפָּרָה. וּלְפִי שֶׁחָטָאנוּ לְפָנֶיךָ, אֲנַחְנוּ וַאֲבוֹתֵינוּ,
חָרְבָה עִירֵנוּ, וְשָׁמֵם בֵּית מִקְדָּשֵׁנוּ, וְגָלָה יְקָרֵנוּ, וְנֻטַּל כְּבוֹד
מִבֵּית חַיֵּינוּ, וְאֵין אֲנַחְנוּ יְכוֹלִים לַעֲשׂוֹת חוֹבוֹתֵינוּ בְּבֵית
בְּחִירָתֶךָ, בַּבַּיִת הַגָּדוֹל וְהַקָּדוֹשׁ שֶׁנִּקְרָא שִׁמְךָ עָלָיו, מִפְּנֵי
הַיָּד שֶׁנִּשְׁתַּלְּחָה בְּמִקְדָּשֶׁךָ. יְהִי רָצוֹן מִלְּפָנֶיךָ, יְיָ אֱלֹהֵינוּ
וֵאלֹהֵי אֲבוֹתֵינוּ, שֶׁתַּעֲלֵנוּ בְשִׂמְחָה לְאַרְצֵנוּ, וְתִטָּעֵנוּ בִּגְבוּלֵנוּ;
וְשָׁם נַעֲשֶׂה לְפָנֶיךָ אֶת קָרְבְּנוֹת חוֹבוֹתֵינוּ, תְּמִידִים כְּסִדְרָם
וּמוּסָפִים כְּהִלְכָתָם. וְאֶת מוּסְפֵי יוֹם הַשַּׁבָּת הַזֶּה וְיוֹם רֹאשׁ
הַחֹדֶשׁ הַזֶּה נַעֲשֶׂה וְנַקְרִיב לְפָנֶיךָ בְּאַהֲבָה, כְּמִצְוַת רְצוֹנֶךָ, כְּמוֹ
שֶׁכָּתַבְתָּ עָלֵינוּ בְּתוֹרָתֶךָ, עַל יְדֵי מֹשֶׁה עַבְדֶּךָ, מִפִּי כְבוֹדֶךָ,
כָּאָמוּר:

וּבְיוֹם הַשַּׁבָּת, שְׁנֵי כְבָשִׂים בְּנֵי שָׁנָה תְּמִימִם; וּשְׁנֵי עֶשְׂרֹנִים
סֹלֶת, מִנְחָה בְּלוּלָה בַשֶּׁמֶן, וְנִסְכּוֹ. עֹלַת שַׁבַּת בְּשַׁבַּתּוֹ עַל עֹלַת
הַתָּמִיד וְנִסְכָּהּ.

וּבְרָאשֵׁי חָדְשֵׁיכֶם תַּקְרִיבוּ עֹלָה לַיְיָ: פָּרִים בְּנֵי בָקָר שְׁנַיִם,
וְאַיִל אֶחָד, כְּבָשִׂים בְּנֵי שָׁנָה שִׁבְעָה, תְּמִימִם.

וּמִנְחָתָם וְנִסְכֵּיהֶם, כִּמְדֻבָּר: שְׁלֹשָׁה עֶשְׂרֹנִים לַפָּר, וּשְׁנֵי
עֶשְׂרֹנִים לָאַיִל, וְעִשָּׂרוֹן לַכֶּבֶשׂ, וְיַיִן כְּנִסְכּוֹ, וְשָׂעִיר לְכַפֵּר,
וּשְׁנֵי תְמִידִים כְּהִלְכָתָם.

On Sabbath-Rosh Ḥodesh:

Thou didst form thy world long ago, completing thy work on the seventh day. Thou hast loved, favored and exalted us above all nations, and sanctified us with thy commandments. Thou, our King, hast brought us near to thy service, and called us by thy great and holy name. Thou, Lord our God, hast graciously given us Sabbaths for rest, and new moon festivals for atonement. But since we and our fathers sinned against thee, our city is destroyed, our sanctuary is laid waste, our glory is departed, and removed is the glory from the source of our life. We cannot perform our duties in thy chosen House, the great and holy Temple which was called by thy name, on account of the destruction that has come upon thy sanctuary. May it be thy will, Lord our God and God of our fathers, to bring us in joy back to our land and to plant us within our borders. There we will prepare in thy honor our obligatory offerings, the regular daily offerings and the additional offerings, according to rule. The additional offerings of this Sabbath day and of this new moon festival we will prepare and present to thee with love according to the command of thy will, as thou hast prescribed for us in thy Torah through thy servant Moses, as it is said:

On the Sabbath day, two perfect yearling male lambs and two-tenths of an *ephah* of fine flour mixed with oil as a meal-offering, and the libation. This is the burnt-offering of each Sabbath, in addition to the daily burnt-offering and its libation.

And on your new moon festivals you shall offer as a burnt-offering to the Lord two young bullocks, one ram and seven yearling male lambs without blemish.[1]

Their meal-offering and their libations were as specified: three-tenths of an *ephah* [of fine flour] for each bullock, two-tenths for the ram, one tenth for each lamb; wine according to their requisite libations. Moreover, a he-goat was offered to make atonement in addition to the two regular daily offerings.

---

[1] *Numbers* 28:9-11.

יִשְׂמְחוּ בְמַלְכוּתְךָ שׁוֹמְרֵי שַׁבָּת וְקוֹרְאֵי עֹנֶג, עַם מְקַדְּשֵׁי שְׁבִיעִי, כֻּלָּם יִשְׂבְּעוּ וְיִתְעַנְּגוּ מִטּוּבֶךָ; וְהַשְּׁבִיעִי רָצִיתָ בּוֹ וְקִדַּשְׁתּוֹ, חֶמְדַּת יָמִים אוֹתוֹ קָרָאתָ, זֵכֶר לְמַעֲשֵׂה בְרֵאשִׁית.

אֱלֹהֵינוּ וֵאלֹהֵי אֲבוֹתֵינוּ, רְצֵה בִמְנוּחָתֵנוּ, וְחַדֵּשׁ עָלֵינוּ בְּיוֹם הַשַּׁבָּת הַזֶּה אֶת הַחֹדֶשׁ הַזֶּה לְטוֹבָה וְלִבְרָכָה, לְשָׂשׂוֹן וּלְשִׂמְחָה, לִישׁוּעָה וּלְנֶחָמָה, לְפַרְנָסָה וּלְכַלְכָּלָה, לְחַיִּים וּלְשָׁלוֹם, לִמְחִילַת חֵטְא וְלִסְלִיחַת עָוֹן (וּלְכַפָּרַת פֶּשַׁע during leap year:).

כִּי בְעַמְּךָ יִשְׂרָאֵל בָּחַרְתָּ מִכָּל הָאֻמּוֹת, וְשַׁבַּת קָדְשְׁךָ לָהֶם הוֹדָעְתָּ, וְחֻקֵּי רָאשֵׁי חֳדָשִׁים לָהֶם קָבָעְתָּ. בָּרוּךְ אַתָּה, יְיָ, מְקַדֵּשׁ הַשַּׁבָּת וְיִשְׂרָאֵל וְרָאשֵׁי חֳדָשִׁים.)

Continued from page 395

רְצֵה, יְיָ אֱלֹהֵינוּ, בְּעַמְּךָ יִשְׂרָאֵל וּבִתְפִלָּתָם; וְהָשֵׁב אֶת הָעֲבוֹדָה לִדְבִיר בֵּיתֶךָ, וְאִשֵּׁי יִשְׂרָאֵל וּתְפִלָּתָם בְּאַהֲבָה תְקַבֵּל בְּרָצוֹן, וּתְהִי לְרָצוֹן תָּמִיד עֲבוֹדַת יִשְׂרָאֵל עַמֶּךָ.

וְתֶחֱזֶינָה עֵינֵינוּ בְּשׁוּבְךָ לְצִיּוֹן בְּרַחֲמִים. בָּרוּךְ אַתָּה, יְיָ, הַמַּחֲזִיר שְׁכִינָתוֹ לְצִיּוֹן.

מוֹדִים אֲנַחְנוּ לָךְ, שָׁאַתָּה	When the Reader repeats the *Ami-dah*, the Congregation responds here by saying:
הוּא יְיָ אֱלֹהֵינוּ וֵאלֹהֵי אֲבוֹתֵינוּ	(מוֹדִים אֲנַחְנוּ לָךְ, שָׁאַתָּה
לְעוֹלָם וָעֶד. צוּר חַיֵּינוּ, מָגֵן	הוּא יְיָ אֱלֹהֵינוּ וֵאלֹהֵי
יִשְׁעֵנוּ אַתָּה הוּא. לְדוֹר וָדוֹר	אֲבוֹתֵינוּ. אֱלֹהֵי כָל בָּשָׂר,
נוֹדֶה לְךָ, וּנְסַפֵּר תְּהִלָּתֶךָ, עַל	יוֹצְרֵנוּ, יוֹצֵר בְּרֵאשִׁית,
חַיֵּינוּ הַמְּסוּרִים בְּיָדֶךָ, וְעַל	בְּרָכוֹת וְהוֹדָאוֹת לְשִׁמְךָ
נִשְׁמוֹתֵינוּ הַפְּקוּדוֹת לָךְ, וְעַל	הַגָּדוֹל וְהַקָּדוֹשׁ עַל שֶׁהֶחֱיִיתָנוּ
נִסֶּיךָ שֶׁבְּכָל יוֹם עִמָּנוּ, וְעַל	וְקִיַּמְתָּנוּ. כֵּן תְּחַיֵּנוּ וּתְקַיְּמֵנוּ,

Those who keep the Sabbath and call it a delight shall rejoice in thy kingdom; all the people who hallow the seventh day shall fully enjoy thy goodness. Thou wast pleased with the seventh day and didst hallow it; the most desirable of days didst thou call it—in remembrance of the creation.

Our God and God of our fathers, be pleased with our rest. On this Sabbath day give us this new month for happiness and blessing, joy and gladness, deliverance and consolation, maintenance and sustenance, life and peace, pardon of sin and forgiveness of iniquity (*during leap year:* and atonement of transgression). Truly thou hast chosen thy people Israel from all nations; thou hast made the holy Sabbath known to them, and hast instituted for them the rules relating to the new moon festivals. Blessed art thou, O Lord, who sanctifiest the Sabbath, Israel and the new moon festivals.)

Continued from page 396

Be pleased, Lord our God, with thy people Israel and with their prayer; restore the worship to thy most holy sanctuary; accept Israel's offerings and prayer with gracious love. May the worship of thy people Israel be ever pleasing to thee.

May our eyes behold thy return in mercy to Zion. Blessed art thou, O Lord, who restorest thy divine presence to Zion.

We ever thank thee, who art the Lord our God and the God of our fathers. Thou art the strength of our life and our saving shield. In every generation we will thank thee and recount thy praise—for our lives which are in thy charge, for our souls which are in thy care, for thy miracles which are daily with us, and for thy continual wonders and favors—

When the Reader repeats the Amidah, the Congregation responds here by saying:

(We thank thee, who art the Lord our God and the God of our fathers. God of all mankind, our Creator and Creator of the universe, blessings and thanks are due to thy great and holy name, because thou hast kept us alive and sustained us; mayest thou ever grant us life and sustenance. O gather our exiles to thy

וְתֶאֱסוֹף גָּלֻיּוֹתֵינוּ לְחַצְרוֹת | נִפְלְאוֹתֶיךָ וְטוֹבוֹתֶיךָ שֶׁבְּכָל
קָדְשֶׁךָ לִשְׁמוֹר חֻקֶּיךָ וְלַעֲשׂוֹת | עֵת, עֶרֶב וָבֹקֶר וְצָהֳרָיִם.
רְצוֹנֶךָ, וּלְעָבְדְּךָ בְּלֵבָב | הַטּוֹב כִּי לֹא כָלוּ רַחֲמֶיךָ,
שָׁלֵם, עַל שֶׁאֲנַחְנוּ מוֹדִים לָךְ. | וְהַמְרַחֵם כִּי לֹא תַמּוּ חֲסָדֶיךָ,
בָּרוּךְ אֵל הַהוֹדָאוֹת.) | מֵעוֹלָם קִוִּינוּ לָךְ.

On *Ḥanukkah* add:

(עַל הַנִּסִּים וְעַל הַפֻּרְקָן, וְעַל הַגְּבוּרוֹת וְעַל הַתְּשׁוּעוֹת, וְעַל
הַמִּלְחָמוֹת, שֶׁעָשִׂיתָ לַאֲבוֹתֵינוּ בַּיָּמִים הָהֵם בַּזְּמַן הַזֶּה־

בִּימֵי מַתִּתְיָהוּ בֶן יוֹחָנָן כֹּהֵן גָּדוֹל, חַשְׁמוֹנַי וּבָנָיו, כְּשֶׁעָמְדָה
מַלְכוּת יָוָן הָרְשָׁעָה עַל עַמְּךָ יִשְׂרָאֵל לְהַשְׁכִּיחָם תּוֹרָתֶךָ,
וּלְהַעֲבִירָם מֵחֻקֵּי רְצוֹנֶךָ. וְאַתָּה בְּרַחֲמֶיךָ הָרַבִּים עָמַדְתָּ לָהֶם
בְּעֵת צָרָתָם, רַבְתָּ אֶת רִיבָם, דַּנְתָּ אֶת דִּינָם, נָקַמְתָּ אֶת נִקְמָתָם;
מָסַרְתָּ גִבּוֹרִים בְּיַד חַלָּשִׁים, וְרַבִּים בְּיַד מְעַטִּים, וּטְמֵאִים בְּיַד
טְהוֹרִים, וּרְשָׁעִים בְּיַד צַדִּיקִים, וְזֵדִים בְּיַד עוֹסְקֵי תוֹרָתֶךָ.
וּלְךָ עָשִׂיתָ שֵׁם גָּדוֹל וְקָדוֹשׁ בְּעוֹלָמֶךָ, וּלְעַמְּךָ יִשְׂרָאֵל עָשִׂיתָ
תְּשׁוּעָה גְדוֹלָה וּפֻרְקָן כְּהַיּוֹם הַזֶּה. וְאַחַר כֵּן בָּאוּ בָנֶיךָ לִדְבִיר
בֵּיתֶךָ, וּפִנּוּ אֶת הֵיכָלֶךָ, וְטִהֲרוּ אֶת מִקְדָּשֶׁךָ, וְהִדְלִיקוּ נֵרוֹת
בְּחַצְרוֹת קָדְשֶׁךָ, וְקָבְעוּ שְׁמוֹנַת יְמֵי חֲנֻכָּה אֵלוּ לְהוֹדוֹת וּלְהַלֵּל
לְשִׁמְךָ הַגָּדוֹל.)

וְעַל כֻּלָּם יִתְבָּרַךְ וְיִתְרוֹמַם שִׁמְךָ, מַלְכֵּנוּ, תָּמִיד לְעוֹלָם
וָעֶד.

Between *Rosh Hashanah* and *Yom Kippur* add:

(וּכְתוֹב לְחַיִּים טוֹבִים כָּל בְּנֵי בְרִיתֶךָ.)

וְכֹל הַחַיִּים יוֹדוּךָ סֶּלָה, וִיהַלְלוּ אֶת שִׁמְךָ בֶּאֱמֶת, הָאֵל,
יְשׁוּעָתֵנוּ וְעֶזְרָתֵנוּ סֶלָה. בָּרוּךְ אַתָּה, יְיָ, הַטּוֹב שִׁמְךָ, וּלְךָ נָאֶה
לְהוֹדוֹת.

evening, morning and noon. Beneficent One, whose mercies never fail, Merciful One, whose kindnesses never cease, thou hast always been our hope.

holy courts to observe thy laws, to do thy will, and to serve thee with a perfect heart. For this we thank thee. Blessed be God to whom all thanks are due.)

On Ḥanukkah add:

(We thank thee for the miracles, for the redemption, for the mighty deeds and triumphs, and for the battles which thou didst perform for our fathers in those days, at this season—

In the days of the Hasmonean, Mattathias ben Yoḥanan, the High Priest, and his sons, when a wicked Hellenic government rose up against thy people Israel to make them forget thy Torah and transgress the laws of thy will. Thou in thy great mercy didst stand by them in the time of their distress. Thou didst champion their cause, defend their rights and avenge their wrong; thou didst deliver the strong into the hands of the weak, the many into the hands of the few, the impure into the hands of the pure, the wicked into the hands of the righteous, and the arrogant into the hands of the students of thy Torah. Thou didst make a great and holy name for thyself in thy world, and for thy people Israel thou didst perform a great deliverance unto this day. Thereupon thy children entered the shrine of thy house, cleansed thy Temple, purified thy sanctuary, kindled lights in thy holy courts, and designated these eight days of Ḥanukkah for giving thanks and praise to thy great name.)

For all these acts may thy name, our King, be blessed and exalted forever and ever.

Between Rosh Hashanah and Yom Kippur add:

(Inscribe all thy people of the covenant for a happy life.)

All the living shall ever thank thee and sincerely praise thy name, O God, who art always our salvation and help. Blessed art thou, O Lord, Beneficent One, to whom it is fitting to give thanks.

Priestly blessing recited by Reader:

אֱלֹהֵינוּ וֵאלֹהֵי אֲבוֹתֵינוּ, בָּרְכֵנוּ בַבְּרָכָה הַמְשֻׁלֶּשֶׁת בַּתּוֹרָה הַכְּתוּבָה עַל יְדֵי מֹשֶׁה עַבְדֶּךָ, הָאֲמוּרָה מִפִּי אַהֲרֹן וּבָנָיו, כֹּהֲנִים עַם קְדוֹשֶׁךָ, כָּאָמוּר: יְבָרֶכְךָ יְיָ וְיִשְׁמְרֶךָ. יָאֵר יְיָ פָּנָיו אֵלֶיךָ וִיחֻנֶּךָּ. יִשָּׂא יְיָ פָּנָיו אֵלֶיךָ, וְיָשֵׂם לְךָ שָׁלוֹם.

שִׂים שָׁלוֹם, טוֹבָה וּבְרָכָה, חֵן וָחֶסֶד וְרַחֲמִים, עָלֵינוּ וְעַל כָּל יִשְׂרָאֵל עַמֶּךָ. בָּרְכֵנוּ אָבִינוּ, כֻּלָּנוּ כְּאֶחָד, בְּאוֹר פָּנֶיךָ; כִּי בְאוֹר פָּנֶיךָ נָתַתָּ לָּנוּ, יְיָ אֱלֹהֵינוּ, תּוֹרַת חַיִּים וְאַהֲבַת חֶסֶד, וּצְדָקָה וּבְרָכָה וְרַחֲמִים, וְחַיִּים וְשָׁלוֹם. וְטוֹב בְּעֵינֶיךָ לְבָרֵךְ אֶת עַמְּךָ יִשְׂרָאֵל בְּכָל עֵת וּבְכָל שָׁעָה בִּשְׁלוֹמֶךָ. ✻ בָּרוּךְ אַתָּה, יְיָ, הַמְבָרֵךְ אֶת עַמּוֹ יִשְׂרָאֵל בַּשָּׁלוֹם.

✻ Between *Rosh Hashanah* and *Yom Kippur* say:

(בְּסֵפֶר חַיִּים, בְּרָכָה וְשָׁלוֹם וּפַרְנָסָה טוֹבָה, נִזָּכֵר וְנִכָּתֵב לְפָנֶיךָ, אֲנַחְנוּ וְכָל עַמְּךָ בֵּית יִשְׂרָאֵל, לְחַיִּים טוֹבִים וּלְשָׁלוֹם. בָּרוּךְ אַתָּה, יְיָ, עוֹשֵׂה הַשָּׁלוֹם.)

After the *Amidah* add the following meditation:

אֱלֹהַי, נְצֹר לְשׁוֹנִי מֵרָע, וּשְׂפָתַי מִדַּבֵּר מִרְמָה; וְלִמְקַלְלַי נַפְשִׁי תִדּוֹם, וְנַפְשִׁי כֶּעָפָר לַכֹּל תִּהְיֶה. פְּתַח לִבִּי בְּתוֹרָתֶךָ, וּבְמִצְוֹתֶךָ תִּרְדּוֹף נַפְשִׁי; וְכָל הַחוֹשְׁבִים עָלַי רָעָה, מְהֵרָה הָפֵר עֲצָתָם וְקַלְקֵל מַחֲשַׁבְתָּם. עֲשֵׂה לְמַעַן שְׁמֶךָ, עֲשֵׂה לְמַעַן יְמִינֶךָ, עֲשֵׂה לְמַעַן קְדֻשָּׁתֶךָ, עֲשֵׂה לְמַעַן תּוֹרָתֶךָ. לְמַעַן יֵחָלְצוּן יְדִידֶיךָ, הוֹשִׁיעָה יְמִינְךָ וַעֲנֵנִי. יִהְיוּ לְרָצוֹן אִמְרֵי פִי וְהֶגְיוֹן לִבִּי לְפָנֶיךָ, יְיָ, צוּרִי וְגוֹאֲלִי. עֹשֶׂה שָׁלוֹם בִּמְרוֹמָיו, הוּא יַעֲשֶׂה שָׁלוֹם עָלֵינוּ וְעַל כָּל יִשְׂרָאֵל, וְאִמְרוּ אָמֵן.

Priestly blessing recited by Reader:

Our God and God of our fathers, bless us with the threefold blessing written in thy Torah by thy servant Moses and spoken by Aaron and his sons the priests, thy holy people, as it is said: "May the Lord bless you and protect you; may the Lord countenance you and be gracious to you; may the Lord favor you and grant you peace."[1]

O grant peace, happiness, blessing, grace, kindness and mercy to us and to all Israel thy people. Bless us all alike, our Father, with the light of thy countenance; indeed, by the light of thy countenance thou hast given us, Lord our God, a Torah of life, lovingkindness, charity, blessing, mercy, life and peace. May it please thee to bless thy people Israel with peace at all times and hours. * Blessed art thou, O Lord, who blessest thy people Israel with peace.

*Between Rosh Hashanah and Yom Kippur say:

(May we and all Israel thy people be remembered and inscribed before thee in the book of life and blessing, peace and prosperity, for a happy life and for peace. Blessed art thou, O Lord, Author of peace.)

After the Amidah add the following meditation:

My God, guard my tongue from evil, and my lips from speaking falsehood. May my soul be silent to those who insult me; be my soul lowly to all as the dust. Open my heart to thy Torah, that my soul may follow thy commands. Speedily defeat the counsel of all those who plan evil against me, and upset their design. Do it for the glory of thy name; do it for the sake of thy power; do it for the sake of thy holiness; do it for the sake of thy Torah. That thy beloved may be rescued, save with thy right hand and answer me. May the words of my mouth and the meditation of my heart be pleasing before thee, O Lord, my Stronghold and my Redeemer.[2] May he who creates peace in his high heavens create peace for us and for all Israel. Amen.

---

[1] *Numbers* 6:24-26.   [2] *Psalms* 60:7; 19:15.

יְהִי רָצוֹן מִלְּפָנֶיךָ, יְיָ אֱלֹהֵינוּ וֵאלֹהֵי אֲבוֹתֵינוּ, שֶׁיִּבָּנֶה בֵּית
הַמִּקְדָּשׁ בִּמְהֵרָה בְיָמֵינוּ, וְתֵן חֶלְקֵנוּ בְּתוֹרָתֶךָ. וְשָׁם נַעֲבָדְךָ
בְּיִרְאָה, כִּימֵי עוֹלָם וּכְשָׁנִים קַדְמוֹנִיּוֹת. וְעָרְבָה לַיְיָ מִנְחַת
יְהוּדָה וִירוּשָׁלָיִם, כִּימֵי עוֹלָם וּכְשָׁנִים קַדְמוֹנִיּוֹת.

Reader:

יִתְגַּדַּל וְיִתְקַדַּשׁ שְׁמֵהּ רַבָּא בְּעָלְמָא דִּי בְרָא כִרְעוּתֵהּ;
וְיַמְלִיךְ מַלְכוּתֵהּ בְּחַיֵּיכוֹן וּבְיוֹמֵיכוֹן, וּבְחַיֵּי דְכָל בֵּית יִשְׂרָאֵל,
בַּעֲגָלָא וּבִזְמַן קָרִיב, וְאִמְרוּ אָמֵן.

יְהֵא שְׁמֵהּ רַבָּא מְבָרַךְ לְעָלַם וּלְעָלְמֵי עָלְמַיָּא.

יִתְבָּרַךְ וְיִשְׁתַּבַּח, וְיִתְפָּאַר וְיִתְרוֹמַם, וְיִתְנַשֵּׂא וְיִתְהַדָּר,
וְיִתְעַלֶּה וְיִתְהַלָּל שְׁמֵהּ דְּקֻדְשָׁא, בְּרִיךְ הוּא, לְעֵלָּא (לְעֵלָּא)
מִן כָּל בִּרְכָתָא וְשִׁירָתָא, תֻּשְׁבְּחָתָא וְנֶחֱמָתָא, דַּאֲמִירָן בְּעָלְמָא,
וְאִמְרוּ אָמֵן.

תִּתְקַבַּל צְלוֹתְהוֹן וּבָעוּתְהוֹן דְּכָל בֵּית יִשְׂרָאֵל קֳדָם אֲבוּהוֹן
דִּי בִשְׁמַיָּא, וְאִמְרוּ אָמֵן.

יְהֵא שְׁלָמָא רַבָּא מִן שְׁמַיָּא, וְחַיִּים, עָלֵינוּ וְעַל כָּל יִשְׂרָאֵל,
וְאִמְרוּ אָמֵן.

עֹשֶׂה שָׁלוֹם בִּמְרוֹמָיו, הוּא יַעֲשֶׂה שָׁלוֹם עָלֵינוּ וְעַל כָּל
יִשְׂרָאֵל, וְאִמְרוּ אָמֵן.

קַוֵּה אֶל יְיָ, חֲזַק וְיַאֲמֵץ לִבֶּךָ, וְקַוֵּה אֶל יְיָ. אֵין קָדוֹשׁ כַּיְיָ,
כִּי אֵין בִּלְתֶּךָ, וְאֵין צוּר כֵּאלֹהֵינוּ. כִּי מִי אֱלוֹהַּ מִבַּלְעֲדֵי יְיָ,
וּמִי צוּר זוּלָתִי אֱלֹהֵינוּ.

לְעֵלָּא לְעֵלָּא is said between *Rosh Hashanah* and *Yom Kippur;* otherwise
only לְעֵלָּא is said. In some rituals לְעֵלָּא is repeated throughout the year.
לְעֵלָּא לְעֵלָּא is the Targum's rendering of מַעֲלָה מָּעְלָה (Deuteronomy 28:43).

May it be thy will, Lord our God and God of our fathers, that the Temple be speedily rebuilt in our days, and grant us a share in thy Torah. There we will serve thee with reverence, as in the days of old and as in former years. Then the offering of Judah and Jerusalem will be pleasing to the Lord, as in the days of old and as in former years.[1]

Reader:

Glorified and sanctified be God's great name throughout the world which he has created according to his will. May he establish his kingdom in your lifetime and during your days, and within the life of the entire house of Israel, speedily and soon; and say, Amen.

May his great name be blessed forever and to all eternity.

Blessed and praised, glorified and exalted, extolled and honored, adored and lauded be the name of the Holy One, blessed be he, beyond all the blessings and hymns, praises and consolations that are ever spoken in the world; and say, Amen.

May the prayers and supplications of the whole household of Israel be accepted by their Father who is in heaven; and say, Amen.

May there be abundant peace from heaven, and life, for us and for all Israel; and say, Amen.

He who creates peace in his celestial heights, may he create peace for us and for all Israel; and say, Amen.

Hope in the Lord; be strong and brave, and hope in the Lord. None is holy like the Lord; there is none but thee; no stronghold is steadfast like our God. For who is God but the Lord? Who is a stronghold but our God?[2]

נחמתא ("consolations"), occurring in the Kaddish as a synonym of praise, probably refers to prophetic works such as the Book of Isaiah, called Books of Consolation, which contain hymns of praise as well as Messianic prophecies.

[1] *Malachi* 3:4.　　[2] *Psalm* 27:14; *I Samuel* 2:2; *Psalm* 18:32.

אֵין כֵּאלֹהֵינוּ, אֵין כַּאדוֹנֵינוּ, אֵין כְּמַלְכֵּנוּ, אֵין כְּמוֹשִׁיעֵנוּ.

מִי כֵאלֹהֵינוּ, מִי כַאדוֹנֵינוּ, מִי כְמַלְכֵּנוּ, מִי כְמוֹשִׁיעֵנוּ.

נוֹדֶה לֵאלֹהֵינוּ, נוֹדֶה לַאדוֹנֵינוּ, נוֹדֶה לְמַלְכֵּנוּ, נוֹדֶה לְמוֹשִׁיעֵנוּ.

בָּרוּךְ אֱלֹהֵינוּ, בָּרוּךְ אֲדוֹנֵינוּ, בָּרוּךְ מַלְכֵּנוּ, בָּרוּךְ מוֹשִׁיעֵנוּ.

אַתָּה הוּא אֱלֹהֵינוּ, אַתָּה הוּא אֲדוֹנֵינוּ, אַתָּה הוּא מַלְכֵּנוּ, אַתָּה
הוּא מוֹשִׁיעֵנוּ.

אַתָּה הוּא שֶׁהִקְטִירוּ אֲבוֹתֵינוּ לְפָנֶיךָ אֶת קְטֹרֶת הַסַּמִּים.

מסכת כריתות ו, א

פִּטּוּם הַקְּטֹרֶת: הַצֳּרִי, וְהַצִּפֹּרֶן, הַחֶלְבְּנָה וְהַלְּבוֹנָה, מִשְׁקַל
שִׁבְעִים שִׁבְעִים מָנֶה; מֹר וּקְצִיעָה, שִׁבֹּלֶת נֵרְדְּ וְכַרְכֹּם, מִשְׁקַל
שִׁשָּׁה עָשָׂר שִׁשָּׁה עָשָׂר מָנֶה; הַקֹּשְׁטְ שְׁנֵים עָשָׂר, וְקִלּוּפָה שְׁלֹשָׁה,
וְקִנָּמוֹן תִּשְׁעָה, בֹּרִית כַּרְשִׁינָה תִּשְׁעָה קַבִּין; יֵין קַפְרִיסִין סְאִין
תְּלָתָא וְקַבִּין תְּלָתָא; וְאִם אֵין לוֹ יֵין קַפְרִיסִין, מֵבִיא חֲמַר
חִוַּרְיָן עַתִּיק; מֶלַח סְדוֹמִית רֹבַע הַקָּב; מַעֲלֶה עָשָׁן כָּל שֶׁהוּא.
רַבִּי נָתָן אוֹמֵר: אַף כִּפַּת הַיַּרְדֵּן כָּל שֶׁהוּא. וְאִם נָתַן בָּהּ דְּבַשׁ,
פְּסָלָהּ; וְאִם חִסַּר אַחַת מִכָּל סַמָּנֶיהָ, חַיָּב מִיתָה. רַבָּן שִׁמְעוֹן
בֶּן גַּמְלִיאֵל אוֹמֵר: הַצֳּרִי אֵינוֹ אֶלָּא שְׂרָף הַנּוֹטֵף מֵעֲצֵי הַקְּטָף.
בֹּרִית כַּרְשִׁינָה, שֶׁשָּׁפִין בָּהּ אֶת הַצִּפֹּרֶן כְּדֵי שֶׁתְּהֵא נָאָה; יֵין
קַפְרִיסִין, שֶׁשּׁוֹרִין בּוֹ אֶת הַצִּפֹּרֶן כְּדֵי שֶׁתְּהֵא עַזָּה. וַהֲלֹא מֵי
רַגְלַיִם יָפִין לָהּ, אֶלָּא שֶׁאֵין מַכְנִיסִין מֵי רַגְלַיִם בָּעֲזָרָה מִפְּנֵי
הַכָּבוֹד.

ברוך אתה, אמן ,אין כאלהינו forms the acrostic. Each of the three letters of
אמן is repeated four times, totalling twelve. Rashi, in his *Siddur*, points out
that אין כאלהינו is recited on Sabbaths and festivals, when the *Amidah* prayer

EN KELOHENU

There is none like our God; there is none like our Lord; there is none like our King; there is none like our Deliverer.

Who is like our God? Who is like our Lord? Who is like our King? Who is like our Deliverer?

Let us give thanks to our God; let us give thanks to our Lord; let us give thanks to our King; let us give thanks to our Deliverer.

Blessed be our God; blessed be our Lord; blessed be our King; blessed be our Deliverer.

Thou art our God; thou art our Lord; thou art our King; thou art our Deliverer.

Thou art he to whom our fathers offered the fragrant incense.

Talmud Kerithoth 6a

The incense was composed of balm, onycha, galbanum, and frankincense, seventy minas' weight of each; myrrh, cassia, spikenard, and saffron, sixteen minas' weight of each; twelve minas of costus; three minas of an aromatic bark; nine minas of cinnamon; nine *kabs* of Karsina lye; three *seahs* and three *kabs* of Cyprus wine—if Cyprus wine could not be obtained, strong white wine might be substituted for it—a fourth of a *kab* of Sodom salt, and a minute quantity of *ma'aleh ashan* [a smoke-producing ingredient]. Rabbi Nathan says: A minute quantity of Jordan amber was also required. If one added honey to the mixture, he rendered the incense unfit for sacred use; and if he left out one of its required ingredients, he was subject to the penalty of death.

Rabban Simeon ben Gamaliel says: The balm required for the incense is a resin exuding from the balsam trees. The Karsina lye was rubbed over the onycha to refine it; the Cyprus wine was used to steep the onycha in it so as to make it more pungent. Though *mei raglayim* might have been good for that purpose, it was not decent to bring it into the Temple.

---

is limited to seven benedictions instead of the nineteen benedictions contained in the regular *Shemoneh Esreh*, in order to bring the blessings to a total of nineteen. *En Kelohenu* was composed during the period of the Geonim.

משנה תמיד ז, ד

הַשִּׁיר שֶׁהָיוּ הַלְוִיִּם אוֹמְרִים בְּבֵית הַמִּקְדָּשׁ.

בַּיּוֹם הָרִאשׁוֹן הָיוּ אוֹמְרִים: לַיְיָ הָאָרֶץ וּמְלוֹאָהּ, תֵּבֵל וְיֹשְׁבֵי בָהּ.

בַּשֵּׁנִי הָיוּ אוֹמְרִים: גָּדוֹל יְיָ וּמְהֻלָּל מְאֹד, בְּעִיר אֱלֹהֵינוּ, הַר קָדְשׁוֹ.

בַּשְּׁלִישִׁי הָיוּ אוֹמְרִים: אֱלֹהִים נִצָּב בַּעֲדַת אֵל, בְּקֶרֶב אֱלֹהִים יִשְׁפֹּט.

בָּרְבִיעִי הָיוּ אוֹמְרִים: אֵל נְקָמוֹת יְיָ, אֵל נְקָמוֹת הוֹפִיעַ.

בַּחֲמִישִׁי הָיוּ אוֹמְרִים: הַרְנִינוּ לֵאלֹהִים עוּזֵּנוּ, הָרִיעוּ לֵאלֹהֵי יַעֲקֹב.

בַּשִּׁשִּׁי הָיוּ אוֹמְרִים: יְיָ מָלָךְ, גֵּאוּת לָבֵשׁ; לָבֵשׁ יְיָ, עֹז הִתְאַזָּר; אַף תִּכּוֹן תֵּבֵל, בַּל תִּמּוֹט.

בַּשַּׁבָּת הָיוּ אוֹמְרִים: מִזְמוֹר שִׁיר לְיוֹם הַשַּׁבָּת. מִזְמוֹר שִׁיר לֶעָתִיד לָבֹא, לְיוֹם שֶׁכֻּלּוֹ שַׁבָּת וּמְנוּחָה, לְחַיֵּי הָעוֹלָמִים.

מסכת מגילה כח, ב

תָּנָא דְבֵי אֵלִיָּהוּ: כָּל הַשּׁוֹנֶה הֲלָכוֹת בְּכָל יוֹם, מֻבְטָח לוֹ שֶׁהוּא בֶן עוֹלָם הַבָּא, שֶׁנֶּאֱמַר: הֲלִיכוֹת עוֹלָם לוֹ. אַל תִּקְרָא הֲלִיכוֹת, אֶלָּא הֲלָכוֹת.

מסכת ברכות סד, א

אָמַר רַבִּי אֶלְעָזָר, אָמַר רַבִּי חֲנִינָא: תַּלְמִידֵי חֲכָמִים מַרְבִּים שָׁלוֹם בָּעוֹלָם, שֶׁנֶּאֱמַר: וְכָל בָּנַיִךְ לִמּוּדֵי יְיָ, וְרַב שְׁלוֹם

יום שכלו שבת, "the great Sabbath," a symbolic description of the world to come, a foretaste of which is offered by the weekly Sabbath.

תנא דבי אליהו, a midrashic collection of mysterious authorship, consists of two parts: *Seder Eliyyahu Rabba* (thirty-one chapters) and *Seder Eliyyahu Zuta* (twenty-five chapters). According to the Talmud (Kethuboth 106a), Elijah

Mishnah Tamid 7:4

Following are the psalms which the Levites used to recite in the Temple.

On Sunday they used to recite: "The earth and its entire contents belong to the Lord, the world and its inhabitants."[1]

On Monday they used to recite: "Great is the Lord, and highly to be praised, in the city of our God, his holy mountain."[2]

On Tuesday they used to recite: "God stands in the divine assembly; in the midst of the judges he gives judgment."[3]

On Wednesday they used to recite: "God of retribution, Lord God of retribution, appear!"[4]

On Thursday they used to recite: "Sing aloud to God our strength; shout for joy to the God of Jacob."[5]

On Friday they used to recite: "The Lord is King; he is robed in majesty; the Lord is robed, he has girded himself with strength; thus the world is set firm and cannot be shaken."[6]

On the Sabbath they used to recite: "A song for the Sabbath day."[7] It is a song for the hereafter, for the day which will be all Sabbath and rest in life everlasting.

Talmud Megillah 28b

It was taught in the school of Elijah: Whoever studies traditional laws every day is assured of life in the world to come, for it is said: "His ways are eternal."[8] Read not here *halikhoth* [ways] but *halakhoth* [traditional laws].

Talmud Berakhoth 64a

Rabbi Elazar said in the name of Rabbi Ḥanina: Scholars increase peace throughout the world, for it is said: "All your children shall be taught of the Lord, and great shall be the peace

---

frequently visited Rabbi Anan (third century) and taught him *Seder Eliyyahu.* This work, which has been named "the jewel of aggadic literature," repeatedly emphasizes the importance of diligence in the study of the Torah.

[1] *Psalm 24.*　[2] *Psalm 48.*　[3] *Psalm 82.*　[4] *Psalm 94.*　[5] *Psalm 81.*　[6] *Psalm 93.*　[7] *Psalm 92.*　[8] *Habakkuk 3:6.*

בָּנָיִךְ. אַל תִּקְרָא בָּנָיִךְ, אֶלָּא בּוֹנָיִךְ. שָׁלוֹם רָב לְאֹהֲבֵי תוֹרָתֶךָ,
וְאֵין לָמוֹ מִכְשׁוֹל. יְהִי שָׁלוֹם בְּחֵילֵךְ, שַׁלְוָה בְּאַרְמְנוֹתָיִךְ.
Reader לְמַעַן אַחַי וְרֵעָי, אֲדַבְּרָה נָּא שָׁלוֹם בָּךְ. לְמַעַן בֵּית יְיָ
אֱלֹהֵינוּ, אֲבַקְשָׁה טוֹב לָךְ. יְיָ עֹז לְעַמּוֹ יִתֵּן, יְיָ יְבָרֵךְ אֶת עַמּוֹ
בַשָּׁלוֹם.

<h1 style="text-align:center">קַדִּישׁ דְּרַבָּנָן</h1>

Mourners:

יִתְגַּדַּל וְיִתְקַדַּשׁ שְׁמֵהּ רַבָּא בְּעָלְמָא דִי בְרָא כִרְעוּתֵהּ;
וְיַמְלִיךְ מַלְכוּתֵהּ בְּחַיֵּיכוֹן וּבְיוֹמֵיכוֹן, וּבְחַיֵּי דְכָל בֵּית יִשְׂרָאֵל,
בַּעֲגָלָא וּבִזְמַן קָרִיב, וְאִמְרוּ אָמֵן.

יְהֵא שְׁמֵהּ רַבָּא מְבָרַךְ לְעָלַם וּלְעָלְמֵי עָלְמַיָּא.

יִתְבָּרַךְ וְיִשְׁתַּבַּח, וְיִתְפָּאַר וְיִתְרוֹמַם, וְיִתְנַשֵּׂא וְיִתְהַדָּר,
וְיִתְעַלֶּה וְיִתְהַלַּל שְׁמֵהּ דְּקֻדְשָׁא, בְּרִיךְ הוּא, לְעֵלָּא (לְעֵלָּא)
מִן כָּל בִּרְכָתָא וְשִׁירָתָא, תֻּשְׁבְּחָתָא וְנֶחֱמָתָא, דַּאֲמִירָן בְּעָלְמָא,
וְאִמְרוּ אָמֵן.

עַל יִשְׂרָאֵל וְעַל רַבָּנָן, וְעַל תַּלְמִידֵיהוֹן וְעַל כָּל תַּלְמִידֵי
תַלְמִידֵיהוֹן, וְעַל כָּל מָן דְּעָסְקִין בְּאוֹרַיְתָא, דִּי בְּאַתְרָא הָדֵן
וְדִי בְּכָל אֲתַר וַאֲתַר, יְהֵא לְהוֹן וּלְכוֹן שְׁלָמָא רַבָּא, חִנָּא
וְחִסְדָּא וְרַחֲמִין, וְחַיִּין אֲרִיכִין, וּמְזוֹנֵי רְוִיחֵי, וּפֻרְקָנָא מִן קֳדָם
אֲבוּהוֹן דִּבִשְׁמַיָּא וְאַרְעָא, וְאִמְרוּ אָמֵן.

יְהֵא שְׁלָמָא רַבָּא מִן שְׁמַיָּא, וְחַיִּים טוֹבִים, עָלֵינוּ וְעַל כָּל
יִשְׂרָאֵל, וְאִמְרוּ אָמֵן.

עֹשֶׂה שָׁלוֹם בִּמְרוֹמָיו, הוּא בְּרַחֲמָיו יַעֲשֶׂה שָׁלוֹם עָלֵינוּ וְעַל
כָּל יִשְׂרָאֵל, וְאִמְרוּ אָמֵן.

אל תקרא introduces a play on words, and is not intended as an emendation
of the biblical text.

of your children.''[1] Read not here *banayikh* [your children], but *bonayikh* [your builders—scholars are the true builders of peace].

Abundant peace have they who love thy Torah, and there is no stumbling for them. Peace be within your walls, and security within your palaces. In behalf of my brethren and friends, let me pronounce peace for you. For the sake of the house of the Lord our God, I will seek your good. The Lord will give strength to his people; the Lord will bless his people with peace.[2]

KADDISH D'RABBANAN
Mourners:

Glorified and sanctified be God's great name throughout the world which he has created according to his will. May he establish his kingdom in your lifetime and during your days, and within the life of the entire house of Israel, speedily and soon; and say, Amen.

May his great name be blessed forever and to all eternity.

Blessed and praised, glorified and exalted, extolled and honored, adored and lauded be the name of the Holy One, blessed be he, beyond all the blessings and hymns, praises and consolations that are ever spoken in the world; and say, Amen.

[We pray] for Israel, for our teachers and their disciples and the disciples of their disciples, and for all who study the Torah, here and everywhere. May they have abundant peace, loving-kindness, ample sustenance and salvation from their Father who is in heaven; and say, Amen.

May there be abundant peace from heaven, and a happy life, for us and for all Israel; and say, Amen.

He who creates peace in his celestial heights, may he in his mercy create peace for us and for all Israel; and say, Amen.

---

[1] *Isaiah* 54:13.   [2] *Psalms* 119:165; 122:7–9; 29:11.

עָלֵינוּ לְשַׁבֵּחַ לַאֲדוֹן הַכֹּל, לָתֵת גְּדֻלָּה לְיוֹצֵר בְּרֵאשִׁית,
שֶׁלֹּא עָשָׂנוּ כְּגוֹיֵי הָאֲרָצוֹת, וְלֹא שָׂמָנוּ כְּמִשְׁפְּחוֹת הָאֲדָמָה;
שֶׁלֹּא שָׂם חֶלְקֵנוּ כָּהֶם, וְגֹרָלֵנוּ כְּכָל הֲמוֹנָם. וַאֲנַחְנוּ כּוֹרְעִים
וּמִשְׁתַּחֲוִים וּמוֹדִים לִפְנֵי מֶלֶךְ מַלְכֵי הַמְּלָכִים, הַקָּדוֹשׁ בָּרוּךְ
הוּא, שֶׁהוּא נוֹטֶה שָׁמַיִם וְיוֹסֵד אָרֶץ, וּמוֹשַׁב יְקָרוֹ בַּשָּׁמַיִם
מִמַּעַל, וּשְׁכִינַת עֻזּוֹ בְּגָבְהֵי מְרוֹמִים. הוּא אֱלֹהֵינוּ, אֵין עוֹד;
אֱמֶת מַלְכֵּנוּ, אֶפֶס זוּלָתוֹ, כַּכָּתוּב בְּתוֹרָתוֹ: וְיָדַעְתָּ הַיּוֹם
וַהֲשֵׁבֹתָ אֶל לְבָבֶךָ, כִּי יְיָ הוּא הָאֱלֹהִים בַּשָּׁמַיִם מִמַּעַל וְעַל
הָאָרֶץ מִתָּחַת, אֵין עוֹד.

עַל כֵּן נְקַוֶּה לְךָ, יְיָ אֱלֹהֵינוּ, לִרְאוֹת מְהֵרָה בְּתִפְאֶרֶת עֻזֶּךָ,
לְהַעֲבִיר גִּלּוּלִים מִן הָאָרֶץ, וְהָאֱלִילִים כָּרוֹת יִכָּרֵתוּן; לְתַקֵּן
עוֹלָם בְּמַלְכוּת שַׁדַּי, וְכָל בְּנֵי בָשָׂר יִקְרְאוּ בִשְׁמֶךָ, לְהַפְנוֹת
אֵלֶיךָ כָּל רִשְׁעֵי אָרֶץ. יַכִּירוּ וְיֵדְעוּ כָּל יוֹשְׁבֵי תֵבֵל, כִּי לְךָ
תִּכְרַע כָּל בֶּרֶךְ, תִּשָּׁבַע כָּל לָשׁוֹן. לְפָנֶיךָ, יְיָ אֱלֹהֵינוּ, יִכְרְעוּ
וְיִפֹּלוּ, וְלִכְבוֹד שִׁמְךָ יְקָר יִתֵּנוּ, וִיקַבְּלוּ כֻלָּם אֶת עֹל מַלְכוּתֶךָ,
וְתִמְלוֹךְ עֲלֵיהֶם מְהֵרָה לְעוֹלָם וָעֶד. כִּי הַמַּלְכוּת שֶׁלְּךָ הִיא,
וּלְעוֹלְמֵי עַד תִּמְלוֹךְ בְּכָבוֹד, כַּכָּתוּב בְּתוֹרָתֶךָ: יְיָ יִמְלֹךְ
לְעֹלָם וָעֶד. Reader וְנֶאֱמַר: וְהָיָה יְיָ לְמֶלֶךְ עַל כָּל הָאָרֶץ;
בַּיּוֹם הַהוּא יִהְיֶה יְיָ אֶחָד וּשְׁמוֹ אֶחָד.

MOURNERS' KADDISH

יִתְגַּדַּל וְיִתְקַדַּשׁ שְׁמֵהּ רַבָּא בְּעָלְמָא דִי בְרָא כִרְעוּתֵהּ;
וְיַמְלִיךְ מַלְכוּתֵהּ בְּחַיֵּיכוֹן וּבְיוֹמֵיכוֹן, וּבְחַיֵּי דְכָל בֵּית יִשְׂרָאֵל,
בַּעֲגָלָא וּבִזְמַן קָרִיב, וְאִמְרוּ אָמֵן.
יְהֵא שְׁמֵהּ רַבָּא מְבָרַךְ לְעָלַם וּלְעָלְמֵי עָלְמַיָּא.

ALENU

It is our duty to praise the Master of all, to exalt the Creator of the universe, who has not made us like the nations of the world and has not placed us like the families of the earth; who has not designed our destiny to be like theirs, nor our lot like that of all their multitude. We bend the knee and bow and acknowledge before the supreme King of kings, the Holy One, blessed be he, that it is he who stretched forth the heavens and founded the earth. His seat of glory is in the heavens above; his abode of majesty is in the lofty heights. He is our God, there is none else; truly, he is our King, there is none besides him, as it is written in his Torah: "You shall know this day, and reflect in your heart, that it is the Lord who is God in the heavens above and on the earth beneath, there is none else."[1]

We hope therefore, Lord our God, soon to behold thy majestic glory, when the abominations shall be removed from the earth, and the false gods exterminated; when the world shall be perfected under the reign of the Almighty, and all mankind will call upon thy name, and all the wicked of the earth will be turned to thee. May all the inhabitants of the world realize and know that to thee every knee must bend, every tongue must vow allegiance. May they bend the knee and prostrate themselves before thee, Lord our God, and give honor to thy glorious name; may they all accept the yoke of thy kingdom, and do thou reign over them speedily forever and ever. For the kingdom is thine, and to all eternity thou wilt reign in glory, as it is written in thy Torah: "The Lord shall be King forever and ever."[2] And it is said: "The Lord shall be King over all the earth; on that day the Lord shall be One, and his name One."[3]

MOURNERS' KADDISH

Glorified and sanctified be God's great name throughout the world which he has created according to his will. May he establish his kingdom in your lifetime and during your days, and within the life of the entire house of Israel, speedily and soon; and say, Amen.

May his great name be blessed forever and to all eternity.

---

[1] *Deuteronomy* 4:39.   [2] *Exodus* 15:18.   [3] *Zechariah* 14:9

יִתְבָּרַךְ וְיִשְׁתַּבַּח, וְיִתְפָּאַר וְיִתְרוֹמַם, וְיִתְנַשֵּׂא וְיִתְהַדָּר, וְיִתְעַלֶּה וְיִתְהַלָּל שְׁמֵהּ דְּקֻדְשָׁא, בְּרִיךְ הוּא, לְעֵלָּא (לְעֵלָּא) מִן כָּל בִּרְכָתָא וְשִׁירָתָא, תֻּשְׁבְּחָתָא וְנֶחֱמָתָא, דַּאֲמִירָן בְּעָלְמָא, וְאִמְרוּ אָמֵן.

יְהֵא שְׁלָמָא רַבָּא מִן שְׁמַיָּא, וְחַיִּים, עָלֵינוּ וְעַל כָּל יִשְׂרָאֵל. וְאִמְרוּ אָמֵן.

עֹשֶׂה שָׁלוֹם בִּמְרוֹמָיו, הוּא יַעֲשֶׂה שָׁלוֹם עָלֵינוּ וְעַל כָּל יִשְׂרָאֵל, וְאִמְרוּ אָמֵן.

אַל תִּירָא מִפַּחַד פִּתְאֹם, וּמִשֹּׁאַת רְשָׁעִים כִּי תָבֹא. עֻצוּ עֵצָה וְתֻפָר, דַּבְּרוּ דָבָר וְלֹא יָקוּם, כִּי עִמָּנוּ אֵל. וְעַד זִקְנָה אֲנִי הוּא, וְעַד שֵׂיבָה אֲנִי אֶסְבֹּל; אֲנִי עָשִׂיתִי וַאֲנִי אֶשָּׂא, וַאֲנִי אֶסְבֹּל וַאֲמַלֵּט.

שִׁיר הַכָּבוֹד

Recited in responsive form

The ark is opened.

אַנְעִים זְמִירוֹת וְשִׁירִים אֶאֱרֹג, כִּי אֵלֶיךָ נַפְשִׁי תַעֲרֹג.

נַפְשִׁי חִמְּדָה בְּצֵל יָדֶךָ, לָדַעַת כָּל רָז סוֹדֶךָ.

מִדֵּי דַבְּרִי בִּכְבוֹדֶךָ, הוֹמֶה לִבִּי אֶל דּוֹדֶיךָ.

עַל כֵּן אֲדַבֵּר בְּךָ נִכְבָּדוֹת, וְשִׁמְךָ אֲכַבֵּד בְּשִׁירֵי יְדִידוֹת.

אֲסַפְּרָה כְבוֹדְךָ וְלֹא רְאִיתִיךָ, אֲדַמְּךָ אֲכַנְּךָ וְלֹא יְדַעְתִּיךָ.

בְּיַד נְבִיאֶיךָ בְּסוֹד עֲבָדֶיךָ, דִּמִּיתָ הֲדַר כְּבוֹד הוֹדֶךָ.

(ר' יהודה החסיד) אנעים זמירות is attributed to Rabbi Judah of Regensburg who was a philosopher and poet, saint and mystic. He died in 1217. Each stanza in this poem contains sixteen syllables.

Blessed and praised, glorified and exalted, extolled and honored, adored and lauded be the name of the Holy One, blessed be he, beyond all the blessings and hymns, praises and consolations that are ever spoken in the world; and say, Amen.

May there be abundant peace from heaven, and life, for us and for all Israel; and say, Amen.

He who creates peace in his celestial heights, may he create peace for us and for all Israel; and say, Amen.

Be not afraid of sudden terror, nor of the storm that strikes the wicked. Form your plot—it shall fail; lay your plan—it shall not prevail! For God is with us. Even to your old age I will be the same; when you are gray-headed, still will I sustain you; I have made you, and I will bear you; I will sustain you and save you.[1]

HYMN OF GLORY

Recited in responsive form
The ark is opened.

I sing hymns and compose songs
Because my soul longs for thee.

> My soul desires thy shelter,
> To know all thy mystery.

When I speak of thy glory,
My heart yearns after thy love.

> Hence I utter thy glories,
> And offer thee songs of love.

I tell thy praise, though I have not seen thee;
I describe thee, though I have not known thee.

> Through thy prophets amidst thy worshipers
> Didst thou show forth thy majestic splendor.

בסוד עבדיך has been mistranslated: "in the mystic utterance of thy servants." However, the poet uses בסוד עבדיך in the sense of בסוד קדושים (Psalm 89:8) which is rendered "in the council of the holy ones." See page 393.

---

[1] *Proverbs* 3:25; *Isaiah* 8:10; 46:4.

גְּדֻלָּתְךָ וּגְבוּרָתֶךָ, כִּנּוּ לְתֹקֶף פְּעֻלָּתֶךָ.

דִּמּוּ אוֹתְךָ וְלֹא כְּפִי יֶשְׁךָ, וַיְשַׁוּוּךָ לְפִי מַעֲשֶׂיךָ.

הִמְשִׁילוּךָ בְּרֹב חֶזְיוֹנוֹת, הִנְּךָ אֶחָד בְּכָל דִּמְיוֹנוֹת.

וַיֶּחֱזוּ בְךָ זִקְנָה וּבַחֲרוּת, וּשְׂעַר רֹאשְׁךָ בְּשֵׂיבָה וְשַׁחֲרוּת.

זִקְנָה בְּיוֹם דִּין וּבַחֲרוּת בְּיוֹם קְרָב, כְּאִישׁ מִלְחָמוֹת יָדָיו לוֹ רָב.

חָבַשׁ כּוֹבַע יְשׁוּעָה בְּרֹאשׁוֹ, הוֹשִׁיעָה לּוֹ יְמִינוֹ וּזְרוֹעַ קָדְשׁוֹ.

טַלְלֵי אוֹרוֹת רֹאשׁוֹ נִמְלָא, וּקְוֻצּוֹתָיו רְסִיסֵי לָיְלָה.

יִתְפָּאֵר בִּי כִּי חָפֵץ בִּי, וְהוּא יִהְיֶה לִי לַעֲטֶרֶת צְבִי.

כֶּתֶם טָהוֹר פָּז דְּמוּת רֹאשׁוֹ, וְחַק עַל מֵצַח כְּבוֹד שֵׁם קָדְשׁוֹ.

לְחֵן וּלְכָבוֹד צְבִי תִפְאָרָה, אֻמָּתוֹ לוֹ עִטְּרָה עֲטָרָה.

מַחְלְפוֹת רֹאשׁוֹ כְּבִימֵי בְחֻרוֹת, קְוֻצּוֹתָיו תַּלְתַּלִּים שְׁחוֹרוֹת.

נְוֵה הַצֶּדֶק צְבִי תִפְאַרְתּוֹ, יַעֲלֶה נָּא עַל רֹאשׁ שִׂמְחָתוֹ.

סְגֻלָּתוֹ תְּהִי בְיָדוֹ עֲטֶרֶת, וּצְנִיף מְלוּכָה צְבִי תִפְאֶרֶת.

עֲמוּסִים נְשָׂאָם עֲטֶרֶת עִנְּדָם, מֵאֲשֶׁר יָקְרוּ בְעֵינָיו כִּבְּדָם.

פְּאֵרוֹ עָלַי וּפְאֵרִי עָלָיו, וְקָרוֹב אֵלַי בְּקָרְאִי אֵלָיו.

צַח וְאָדוֹם לִלְבוּשׁוֹ אָדֹם, פּוּרָה בְּדָרְכוֹ בְּבוֹאוֹ מֵאֱדוֹם.

קֶשֶׁר תְּפִלִּין הֶרְאָה לֶעָנָו, תְּמוּנַת יְיָ לְנֶגֶד עֵינָיו.

רוֹצֶה בְעַמּוֹ עֲנָוִים יְפָאֵר, יוֹשֵׁב תְּהִלּוֹת בָּם לְהִתְפָּאֵר.

לפי מעשיך that is, the human intellect cannot conceive the essence of God, but only his acts.

... ויחזו בך alludes to Daniel 7:9; Song of Songs 5:11; Exodus 15:3; Deuteronomy 33:7; Psalm 98:1; Isaiah 26:19; 28:5; Song of Songs 5:2, 11.

על מצח the plate on Aaron's forehead, upon which was engraved: "Holy to the Lord" (Exodus 28:36). עטרה hymns of praise. נוה הצדק Jerusalem.

פארו עלי the *tefillin* containing the words ה' אחד, "the Lord is One".

פארי עליו God's *tefillin* containing the words מי כעמך ... גוי אחד.

... צבי תפארת Isaiah 62:3; 46:3; 43:4; Song of Songs 5:10; Isaiah 63:1-3.

קשר תפלין refers to the talmudic statement that Moses saw God's *tefillin*.

Thy greatness and thy power
They traced in thy mighty work.

> They imaged thee, not as thou art really;
> They described thee by thy acts only.

They depicted thee in countless visions;
Despite all comparisons thou art One.

> They saw in thee both old age and young age,
> With the hair of thy head now grey, now black:

Age in judgment day, youth in time of war,
As a warrior whose hands fight for him,

> A helmet of triumph tied on his head,
> His holy right arm bringing victory;

As though his head is drenched with dew of light,
And his locks are filled with drops of the night.

> He glories in me, he delights in me;
> My crown of beauty he shall ever be.

His head is like pure gold; on the forehead
He engraved his glorious holy name.

> For grace and glory, beauty and splendor,
> His own people has made a crown for him.

The locks of his head are such as in youth;
His curls, forming countless ringlets, are black.

> May his splendid Temple of righteousness
> Be prized by him above his highest joy.

May his people be a crown in his hand,
A royal diadem of great beauty.

> Borne by him, he uplifted and crowned them;
> Being precious to him, he honored them.

His glory rests on me, and mine on him:
He is near to me when I call to him.

> Dazzling he is and ruddy, his clothes red,
> When from treading Edom's winepress he comes.

Meek Moses was shown symbolic tefillin
When the Lord's image was before his eyes.

> Pleased with his people, he glorifies them;
> Enthroned in glories, he glories in them.

רֹאשׁ דְּבָרְךָ אֱמֶת, קוֹרֵא מֵרֹאשׁ דּוֹר וָדוֹר, עַם דּוֹרְשֶׁךָ דְּרוֹשׁ.

שִׁית הֲמוֹן שִׁירֵי נָא עָלֶיךָ, וְרִנָּתִי תִּקְרַב אֵלֶיךָ.

תְּהִלָּתִי תְּהִי לְרֹאשְׁךָ עֲטֶרֶת, וּתְפִלָּתִי תִּכּוֹן קְטֹרֶת.

תִּיקַר שִׁירַת רָשׁ בְּעֵינֶיךָ, כַּשִּׁיר יוּשַׁר עַל קָרְבָּנֶיךָ.

בִּרְכָתִי תַעֲלֶה לְרֹאשׁ מַשְׁבִּיר, מְחוֹלֵל וּמוֹלִיד צַדִּיק כַּבִּיר.

וּבְבִרְכָתִי תְנַעֲנַע לִי רֹאשׁ, וְאוֹתָהּ קַח לְךָ כִּבְשָׂמִים רֹאשׁ.

יֶעֱרַב נָא שִׂיחִי עָלֶיךָ, כִּי נַפְשִׁי תַעֲרֹג אֵלֶיךָ.

לְךָ, יְיָ, הַגְּדֻלָּה וְהַגְּבוּרָה וְהַתִּפְאֶרֶת וְהַנֵּצַח וְהַהוֹד, כִּי כֹל בַּשָּׁמַיִם וּבָאָרֶץ. לְךָ, יְיָ, הַמַּמְלָכָה וְהַמִּתְנַשֵּׂא לְכֹל לְרֹאשׁ. מִי יְמַלֵּל גְּבוּרוֹת יְיָ, יַשְׁמִיעַ כָּל תְּהִלָּתוֹ.

Mourners' Kaddish.

הַיּוֹם שַׁבַּת קֹדֶשׁ, שֶׁבּוֹ הָיוּ הַלְוִיִּם אוֹמְרִים בְּבֵית הַמִּקְדָּשׁ:

תהלים צב

מִזְמוֹר שִׁיר לְיוֹם הַשַּׁבָּת. טוֹב לְהֹדוֹת לַיְיָ, וּלְזַמֵּר לְשִׁמְךָ עֶלְיוֹן. לְהַגִּיד בַּבֹּקֶר חַסְדֶּךָ, וֶאֱמוּנָתְךָ בַּלֵּילוֹת. עֲלֵי עָשׂוֹר וַעֲלֵי נָבֶל, עֲלֵי הִגָּיוֹן בְּכִנּוֹר. כִּי שִׂמַּחְתַּנִי יְיָ בְּפָעֳלֶךָ; בְּמַעֲשֵׂי יָדֶיךָ אֲרַנֵּן. מַה גָּדְלוּ מַעֲשֶׂיךָ, יְיָ; מְאֹד עָמְקוּ מַחְשְׁבֹתֶיךָ. אִישׁ בַּעַר לֹא יֵדָע, וּכְסִיל לֹא יָבִין אֶת זֹאת. בִּפְרֹחַ רְשָׁעִים כְּמוֹ עֵשֶׂב, וַיָּצִיצוּ כָּל פֹּעֲלֵי אָוֶן, לְהִשָּׁמְדָם עֲדֵי עַד. וְאַתָּה מָרוֹם לְעֹלָם, יְיָ. כִּי הִנֵּה אֹיְבֶיךָ, יְיָ, כִּי הִנֵּה אֹיְבֶיךָ יֹאבֵדוּ, יִתְפָּרְדוּ כָּל פֹּעֲלֵי אָוֶן. וַתָּרֶם כִּרְאֵים קַרְנִי; בַּלֹּתִי בְּשֶׁמֶן רַעֲנָן. וַתַּבֵּט

רֹאשׁ דְּבָרְךָ אֱמֶת alludes to בְּרֵאשִׁית בָּרָא אֱלֹהִים, the first three words of the Torah, whose final letters spell אֱמֶת.

Thy chief word is truth, Creator of all;
Care for thy people who seek thee forever.

O set my abundant songs before thee;
May my ringing cry come near to thee.

May my praise be deemed a crown for thy head;
Let my prayer rise like incense before thee.

Let a poor man's song be precious to thee
As the song that was sung at the offerings.

May my blessings rise to God who sustains,
Creates and brings forth, the Just, the Mighty.

As for my prayer, nod thy approval,
And accept it as the choicest incense.

May my meditation be sweet to thee,
For all my being is yearning for thee.

Thine, O Lord, is the greatness and the power, the glory and the victory and the majesty; for all that is in heaven and on earth is thine; thine, O Lord, is the kingdom, and thou art supreme over all. Who can describe the mighty deeds of the Lord, or utter all his praise?[1]

Mourners' Kaddish.

This is the holy Sabbath day, on which the Levites in the Temple used to recite:

Psalm 92

A psalm, a song for the Sabbath day. It is good to give thanks to the Lord, and to sing praises to thy name, O Most High; to proclaim thy goodness in the morning, and thy faithfulness at night, with a ten-stringed lyre and a flute, to the sound of a harp. For thou, O Lord, hast made me glad through thy work; I sing for joy at all that thou hast done. How great are thy works, O Lord! How very deep are thy designs! A stupid man cannot know, a fool cannot understand this. When the wicked thrive like grass, and all evildoers flourish, it is that they may be destroyed forever. But thou, O Lord, art supreme for evermore. For lo, thy enemies, O Lord, for lo, thy enemies shall perish; all evildoers shall be dispersed. But thou hast exalted my power like that of the wild ox; I am anointed with fresh oil. My eye has gazed on my foes; my

---

[1] *I Chronicles* 29:11; *Psalm* 106:2

עֵינֵי בְּשׁוּרָי, בַּקָּמִים עָלַי מְרֵעִים תִּשְׁמַעְנָה אָזְנָי. צַדִּיק כַּתָּמָר
יִפְרָח, כְּאֶרֶז בַּלְּבָנוֹן יִשְׂגֶּה. שְׁתוּלִים בְּבֵית יְיָ, בְּחַצְרוֹת אֱלֹהֵינוּ
יַפְרִיחוּ. Reader עוֹד יְנוּבוּן בְּשֵׂיבָה, דְּשֵׁנִים וְרַעֲנַנִּים יִהְיוּ.
לְהַגִּיד כִּי יָשָׁר יְיָ; צוּרִי, וְלֹא עַוְלָתָה בּוֹ.

Mourners' Kaddish.

The following is recited from Rosh Ḥodesh Elul until Simḥath Torah.

תהלים כז

לְדָוִד. יְיָ אוֹרִי וְיִשְׁעִי, מִמִּי אִירָא; יְיָ מָעוֹז חַיַּי, מִמִּי אֶפְחָד.
בִּקְרֹב עָלַי מְרֵעִים לֶאֱכֹל אֶת בְּשָׂרִי, צָרַי וְאֹיְבַי לִי, הֵמָּה
כָּשְׁלוּ וְנָפָלוּ. אִם תַּחֲנֶה עָלַי מַחֲנֶה, לֹא יִירָא לִבִּי; אִם תָּקוּם
עָלַי מִלְחָמָה, בְּזֹאת אֲנִי בוֹטֵחַ. אַחַת שָׁאַלְתִּי מֵאֵת יְיָ, אוֹתָהּ
אֲבַקֵּשׁ: שִׁבְתִּי בְּבֵית יְיָ כָּל יְמֵי חַיַּי, לַחֲזוֹת בְּנֹעַם יְיָ, וּלְבַקֵּר
בְּהֵיכָלוֹ. כִּי יִצְפְּנֵנִי בְּסֻכֹּה בְּיוֹם רָעָה, יַסְתִּרֵנִי בְּסֵתֶר אָהֳלוֹ;
בְּצוּר יְרוֹמְמֵנִי. וְעַתָּה יָרוּם רֹאשִׁי עַל אֹיְבַי סְבִיבוֹתַי, וְאֶזְבְּחָה
בְּאָהֳלוֹ זִבְחֵי תְרוּעָה; אָשִׁירָה וַאֲזַמְּרָה לַיְיָ. שְׁמַע יְיָ קוֹלִי
אֶקְרָא, וְחָנֵּנִי וַעֲנֵנִי. לְךָ אָמַר לִבִּי, בַּקְּשׁוּ פָנָי; אֶת פָּנֶיךָ, יְיָ,
אֲבַקֵּשׁ. אַל תַּסְתֵּר פָּנֶיךָ מִמֶּנִּי, אַל תַּט בְּאַף עַבְדֶּךָ, עֶזְרָתִי
הָיִיתָ; אַל תִּטְּשֵׁנִי וְאַל תַּעַזְבֵנִי, אֱלֹהֵי יִשְׁעִי. כִּי אָבִי וְאִמִּי
עֲזָבוּנִי, וַיְיָ יַאַסְפֵנִי. הוֹרֵנִי יְיָ דַּרְכֶּךָ, וּנְחֵנִי בְּאֹרַח מִישׁוֹר, לְמַעַן
שֹׁרְרָי. אַל תִּתְּנֵנִי בְּנֶפֶשׁ צָרָי; כִּי קָמוּ בִי עֵדֵי שֶׁקֶר וִיפֵחַ חָמָס.
לוּלֵא הֶאֱמַנְתִּי לִרְאוֹת בְּטוּב יְיָ בְּאֶרֶץ חַיִּים. Reader קַוֵּה אֶל יְיָ,
חֲזַק וְיַאֲמֵץ לִבֶּךָ, וְקַוֵּה אֶל יְיָ.

Mourners' Kaddish.

אבי ואמי עזבוני ... Though I am orphaned, friendless and deserted, God
will be father to me and protect me.

לולא האמנתי ... The remainder of the sentence is left to the imagination:
"What would my condition be, if I had not believed!" The word **לולא** is
marked with dots in the Massoretic text.

ears have heard my enemies' doom. The righteous will flourish like the palm tree; they will grow like a cedar in Lebanon. Planted in the house of the Lord, they shall flourish in the courts of our God. They shall yield fruit even in old age; vigorous and fresh they shall be, to proclaim that the Lord is just! He is my Stronghold, and there is no wrong in him.

Mourners' Kaddish.

The following is recited from Rosh Ḥodesh Elul until Simḥath Torah.

Psalm 27

A psalm of David. The Lord is my light and aid; whom shall I fear? The Lord is the stronghold of my life; of whom shall I be afraid? When evildoers press against me to eat up my flesh—my enemies and my foes—it is they who stumble and fall. Even though an army were arrayed against me, my heart would not fear; though war should arise against me, still would I be confident. One thing I ask from the Lord, one thing I desire—that I may dwell in the house of the Lord all the days of my life, to behold the pleasantness of the Lord, and to meditate in his sanctuary. Surely, he will hide me within his own tabernacle in the day of distress; he will conceal me in the shelter of his tent; he will set me safe upon a rock. Thus my head shall be high above all my foes around me; I will offer sacrifices within his tabernacle to the sound of trumpets; I will sing and chant praises to the Lord. Hear, O Lord, my voice when I call; be gracious to me and answer me. In thy behalf my heart has said: "Seek you my presence"; thy presence, O Lord, I do seek. Hide not thy face from me; turn not thy servant away in anger; thou hast been my help; do not abandon me, forsake me not, O God my Savior. Though my father and mother have forsaken me, the Lord will take care of me. Teach me thy way, O Lord, and guide me in a straight path, in spite of my enemies. Deliver me not to the will of my adversaries; for false witnesses have risen up against me, such as breathe forth violence. I do believe I shall yet see the goodness of the Lord in the land of the living. Hope in the Lord; be strong, and let your heart be brave; yes, hope in the Lord.

Mourners' Kaddish.

אֲדוֹן עוֹלָם אֲשֶׁר מָלַךְ בְּטֶרֶם כָּל יְצִיר נִבְרָא.
לְעֵת נַעֲשָׂה בְחֶפְצוֹ כֹּל אֲזַי מֶלֶךְ שְׁמוֹ נִקְרָא.
וְאַחֲרֵי כִּכְלוֹת הַכֹּל לְבַדּוֹ יִמְלוֹךְ נוֹרָא.
וְהוּא הָיָה וְהוּא הֹוֶה וְהוּא יִהְיֶה בְּתִפְאָרָה.
וְהוּא אֶחָד וְאֵין שֵׁנִי לְהַמְשִׁיל לוֹ לְהַחְבִּירָה.
בְּלִי רֵאשִׁית בְּלִי תַכְלִית וְלוֹ הָעֹז וְהַמִּשְׂרָה.
וְהוּא אֵלִי וְחַי גֹּאֲלִי וְצוּר חֶבְלִי בְּעֵת צָרָה.
וְהוּא נִסִּי וּמָנוֹס לִי מְנָת כּוֹסִי בְּיוֹם אֶקְרָא.
בְּיָדוֹ אַפְקִיד רוּחִי בְּעֵת אִישַׁן וְאָעִירָה.
וְעִם רוּחִי גְּוִיָּתִי יְיָ לִי וְלֹא אִירָא.

קִדּוּשׁ לְיוֹם הַשַּׁבָּת

שמות לא, טז–יז

וְשָׁמְרוּ בְנֵי יִשְׂרָאֵל אֶת הַשַּׁבָּת, לַעֲשׂוֹת אֶת הַשַּׁבָּת לְדֹרֹתָם בְּרִית עוֹלָם. בֵּינִי וּבֵין בְּנֵי יִשְׂרָאֵל אוֹת הִיא לְעוֹלָם, כִּי שֵׁשֶׁת יָמִים עָשָׂה יְיָ אֶת הַשָּׁמַיִם וְאֶת הָאָרֶץ, וּבַיּוֹם הַשְּׁבִיעִי שָׁבַת וַיִּנָּפַשׁ.

שמות כ, ח–יא

זָכוֹר אֶת יוֹם הַשַּׁבָּת לְקַדְּשׁוֹ. שֵׁשֶׁת יָמִים תַּעֲבֹד וְעָשִׂיתָ כָּל מְלַאכְתֶּךָ. וְיוֹם הַשְּׁבִיעִי שַׁבָּת לַיְיָ אֱלֹהֶיךָ; לֹא תַעֲשֶׂה כָל מְלָאכָה, אַתָּה וּבִנְךָ וּבִתֶּךָ, עַבְדְּךָ וַאֲמָתְךָ וּבְהֶמְתֶּךָ, וְגֵרְךָ אֲשֶׁר בִּשְׁעָרֶיךָ. כִּי שֵׁשֶׁת יָמִים עָשָׂה יְיָ אֶת הַשָּׁמַיִם וְאֶת הָאָרֶץ, אֶת הַיָּם, וְאֶת כָּל אֲשֶׁר בָּם, וַיָּנַח בַּיּוֹם הַשְּׁבִיעִי; עַל כֵּן בֵּרַךְ יְיָ אֶת יוֹם הַשַּׁבָּת וַיְקַדְּשֵׁהוּ.

בָּרוּךְ אַתָּה, יְיָ אֱלֹהֵינוּ, מֶלֶךְ הָעוֹלָם, בּוֹרֵא פְּרִי הַגָּפֶן.

ADON OLAM

He is the eternal Lord who reigned
Before any being was created.
At the time when all was made by his will,
He was at once acknowledged as King.
And at the end, when all shall cease to be,
The revered God alone shall still be King.
He was, he is, and he shall be
In glorious eternity.
He is One, and there is no other
To compare to him, to place beside him.
He is without beginning, without end;
Power and dominion belong to him.
He is my God, my living Redeemer,
My stronghold in times of distress.
He is my guide and my refuge,
My share of bliss the day I call.
To him I entrust my spirit
When I sleep and when I wake.
As long as my soul is with my body
The Lord is with me; I am not afraid.

KIDDUSH FOR SABBATH MORNING

Exodus 31:16–17

The children of Israel shall keep the Sabbath, observing the
Sabbath throughout their generations as an everlasting covenant.
It is a sign between me and the children of Israel forever that in
six days the Lord made the heavens and the earth, and on the
seventh day he ceased from work and rested.

Exodus 20:8–11

Remember the Sabbath day, to keep it holy. Six days you shall
labor and do all your work; but on the seventh day, which is a
a day of rest in honor of the Lord your God, you shall not do any
work, neither you, nor your son, nor your daughter, nor your male
or female servant, nor your cattle, nor the stranger who is within your gates; for in six days the Lord made the heavens, the earth,
the sea, and all that they contain. and rested on the seventh day;
therefore the Lord blessed the Sabbath day and hallowed it.

Blessed art thou, Lord our God, King of the universe, who
createst the fruit of the vine.

קדושא רבא, the great Kiddush, so called by way of inversion, since it is of
later origin and of less importance than the Kiddush recited in the evening.

זְמִירוֹת לְשַׁבָּת

Chanted at the table

בָּרוּךְ אֲדֹנָי יוֹם יוֹם, יַעֲמָס־לָנוּ יֶשַׁע וּפִדְיוֹם, וּבִשְׁמוֹ נָגִיל כָּל
הַיּוֹם, וּבִישׁוּעָתוֹ נָרִים רֹאשׁ עֶלְיוֹן, כִּי הוּא מָעוֹז לַדָּל וּמַחְסֶה
לָאֶבְיוֹן.

שִׁבְטֵי יָהּ לְיִשְׂרָאֵל עֵדוּת, בְּצָרָתָם לוֹ צָר בְּסִבְלוֹת וּבְעַבְדוּת,
בְּלִבְנַת הַסַּפִּיר הֶרְאָם עֹז יְדִידוּת, וְנִגְלָה לְהַעֲלוֹתָם מֵעָמְק
בּוֹר וָדוּת, כִּי עִם יְיָ הַחֶסֶד וְהַרְבֵּה עִמּוֹ פְדוּת.

מַה יָּקָר חַסְדּוֹ בְּצִלּוֹ לְגוֹנְנְמוֹ, בְּגָלוּת בָּבֶלָה שֻׁלַּח לְמַעֲנֵמוֹ,
לְהוֹרִיד בָּרִיחִים נִמְנָה בֵינֵימוֹ, וַיִּתְּנֵם לְרַחֲמִים לִפְנֵי שׁוֹבֵימוֹ,
כִּי לֹא יִטּשׁ יְיָ אֶת עַמּוֹ, בַּעֲבוּר הַגָּדוֹל שְׁמוֹ.

עֵילָם שָׁת כִּסְאוֹ לְהַצִּיל יְדִידָיו, לְהַעֲבִיר מִשָּׁם מָעֻזְנֵי מוֹרְדָיו,
מֵעֲבֹר בְּשֶׁלַח פָּדָה אֶת עֲבָדָיו, קֶרֶן לְעַמּוֹ יָרִים תְּהִלָּה לְכָל
חֲסִידָיו, כִּי אִם הוֹגָה וְרִחַם כְּרַחֲמָיו וּכְרֹב חֲסָדָיו.

וּצְפִיר הָעִזִּים הִגְדִּיל עֲצוּמָיו, וְגַם חָזוּת אַרְבַּע עָלוּ לִמְרוֹמָיו,
וּבְלִבָּם דִּמּוּ לְהַשְׁחִית אֶת רְחוּמָיו, עַל יְדֵי כֹהֲנָיו מִגֵּר
מִתְקוֹמְמָיו, חַסְדֵי יְיָ כִּי לֹא תָמְנוּ כִּי לֹא כָלוּ רַחֲמָיו.

ברוך ה׳ יום יום was composed by Rabbi Simeon bar Isaac bar Abun, a
native of Mayence, who was one of the most important liturgical writers and
scholars of the eleventh century. The name of the author (שמעון בר יצחק)
forms the acrostic of the stanzas, each of which consists of five rhymed verses.
The part beginning with ברוך הוא אלהינו seems to be a later addition.

The poem bears no reference to the Sabbath, but deals with the persecutions endured by our people in *Galuth*. Each stanza ends with a biblical
verse as a chorus. The poet utilized the following biblical verses: Psalm 68:20;
Isaiah 25:4; 63:9; Exodus 24:10; Psalm 130:7; Isaiah 43:14; Psalm 106:46;

SABBATH HYMNS

Chanted at the table

Blessed be the Lord day by day!
He brings us help and redemption;
In his name we rejoice all day;
By his aid we raise our head high;
He is the poor man's strength and shield.

"God's tribes" proves Israel's merit;
He feels their stress while in slavery;
By the sapphire he showed them strong **love;**
He came to lift them out of the depths;
The Lord is kind and great to save.

How precious is his protecting love!
He went to Babylon for their sake;
He was with them in their exile;
He made their captors pity them;
The great Lord forsakes not his people.

In Persia he saved his loved ones,
And destroyed his rebels' strongholds;
He saved his servants from the sword,
Raising the honor of his people;
Though he wounds, he shows great mercy.

The Hellenic power waxed strong;
Four horns pointed against his heights;
They meant to destroy his loved ones;
He cast his foes down by his priests,
For the Lord's mercies never fail.

I Samuel 12:22; Jeremiah 49:38; Job 33:18; Psalm 148:14; Lamentations 3:32; Daniel 8:8,21; Lamentations 3:23; Jeremiah 60:34; Job 38:6; Lamentations 3:31; Isaiah 63:1; 34:6; Psalm 76:13; Isaiah 27:8; Deuteronomy 4:43; Psalms 31:24; 42:9; Ezekiel 37:9; 17:23; 20:40; 34:14; Deuteronomy 30:3-4; Isaiah 63:7; 43:7; Psalm 117:2; Isaiah 9:5.

נִסְגַּרְתִּי לֶאֱדוֹם בְּיַד רֵעַי מְדָנַי, שֶׁבְּכָל יוֹם מְמַלְאִים כְּרֵסָם
מֵעֲדָנַי, עֶזְרָתוֹ עִמִּי לִסְמֹךְ אֶת אֲדָנַי, וְלֹא נְטַשְׁתַּנִי כָּל יְמֵי
עִדָנַי, כִּי לֹא יִזְנַח לְעוֹלָם אֲדֹנָי.

בְּבוֹאוֹ מֵאֱדוֹם חֲמוּץ בְּגָדִים, זֶבַח לוֹ בְּבָצְרָה וְטֶבַח לוֹ
בְּבוֹגְדִים, וְיֵז נִצְחָם מַלְבּוּשָׁיו לְהַאְדִים, בְּכֹחוֹ הַגָּדוֹל יִבְצֹר
רוּחַ נְגִידִים, הָגָה בְּרוּחוֹ הַקָּשָׁה בְּיוֹם קָדִים.

רְאוֹתוֹ כִּי כֵן אֲדוֹמִי הָעוֹצֵר, יַחְשָׁב־לוֹ בְּבָצְרָה תִּקְלוֹט כְּבֶצֶר,
וּמַלְאָךְ כְּאָדָם בְּתוֹכָהּ יָנְצֵר, וּמֵזִיד כַּשּׁוֹגֵג בְּמִקְלָט יֵעָצֵר,
אֶהֱבוּ אֶת יְיָ כָּל חֲסִידָיו אֱמוּנִים נוֹצֵר.

יְצַוֶּה צוּר חַסְדּוֹ קְהִלּוֹתָיו לְקַבֵּץ, מֵאַרְבַּע רוּחוֹת עָדָיו
לְהִקָּבֵץ, וּבְהַר מְרוֹם הָרִים אוֹתָנוּ לְהַרְבֵּץ, וְאִתָּנוּ יָשׁוּב
נִדָּחִים קוֹבֵץ, יָשִׁיב לֹא נֶאֱמַר כִּי אִם וְשָׁב וְקִבֵּץ.

בָּרוּךְ הוּא אֱלֹהֵינוּ אֲשֶׁר טוֹב גְּמָלָנוּ, כְּרַחֲמָיו וּכְרֹב חֲסָדָיו
הִגְדִּיל לָנוּ, אֵלֶּה וְכָאֵלֶּה יוֹסֵף עִמָּנוּ, לְהַגְדִּיל שְׁמוֹ הַגָּדוֹל
הַגִּבּוֹר וְהַנּוֹרָא שֶׁנִּקְרָא עָלֵינוּ. בָּרוּךְ הוּא אֱלֹהֵינוּ שֶׁבְּרָאָנוּ
לִכְבוֹדוֹ, לְהַלְלוֹ וּלְשַׁבְּחוֹ וּלְסַפֵּר הוֹדוֹ, מִכָּל אֹם גָּבַר עָלֵינוּ
חַסְדּוֹ, לָכֵן בְּכָל לֵב וּבְכָל נֶפֶשׁ וּבְכָל מְאֹד נַמְלִיכוֹ וּנְיַחֲדוֹ.
שֶׁהַשָּׁלוֹם שֶׁלּוֹ יָשִׂים עָלֵינוּ בְּרָכָה וְשָׁלוֹם; מִשְּׂמֹאל וּמִיָּמִין עַל
יִשְׂרָאֵל שָׁלוֹם; הָרַחֲמָן הוּא יְבָרֵךְ אֶת עַמּוֹ בַשָּׁלוֹם; וְיִזְכּוּ
לִרְאוֹת בָּנִים וּבְנֵי בָנִים עוֹסְקִים בַּתּוֹרָה וּבְמִצְוֹת; עַל יִשְׂרָאֵל
שָׁלוֹם; יוֹעֵץ אֵל גִּבּוֹר אֲבִי־עַד שַׂר־שָׁלוֹם.

ראותו... אדומי העוצר refers to a statement in the Talmud (Makkoth 12a) that the guardian angel of Edom will commit three errors in fleeing to Bozrah. He will think that Bozrah is a city of refuge, confusing it with Bezer; he will think that the cities of refuge afford protection to wilful murderers; he will be ignorant of the fact that only human beings may seek refuge in these cities.

I was sold to Rome by my foes,
Who daily gorge themselves with my wealth;
God's help supports my foundations;
Throughout my life he deserts me not,
For the Lord never abandons.

Coming from Edom all crimsoned,
Having slain the traitors in Bozrah,
Whose lifeblood splashed and stained his robes—
He cut off the breath of princes,
Sweeping them away by his rough blast.

Edom's guardian lord, on seeing this,
Will think that Bozrah is a refuge,
Like Bezer, for both angel and man,
And that it protects wilful crimes.
Love the Lord who guards the faithful!

May God grant his love to his people
And gather them from all ends to him,
To make them rest on the lofty Mount;
May he return among those gathered,
For it is written: "He will come back..."

Praised be our God who deals well with us,
And graciously does great things for us;
May he manifold these things for us,
To magnify his great name which we bear.

Praised be our God who created us
For his glory, to recount his praise;
His love to us is greatest of all,
Let us acclaim him with all our might.

May the Author of peace grant us peace;
Peace be to Israel north and south!
May the Lord bless his people with peace;
May they live to see sons and grandsons
Occupied with Torah and good deeds.
O God, Author and Champion of peace!

בָּרוּךְ אֵל עֶלְיוֹן אֲשֶׁר נָתַן מְנוּחָה, לְנַפְשֵׁנוּ פִּדְיוֹן מִשֵּׁאת וַאֲנָחָה,
וְהוּא יִדְרוֹשׁ לְצִיּוֹן עִיר הַנִּדָּחָה, עַד אָנָה תּוּגְיוֹן נֶפֶשׁ נֶאֱנָחָה.
הַשּׁוֹמֵר שַׁבָּת הַבֵּן עִם הַבַּת, לָאֵל יֵרָצוּ כְּמִנְחָה עַל מַחֲבַת.

רוֹכֵב בָּעֲרָבוֹת מֶלֶךְ עוֹלָמִים, אֶת עַמּוֹ לִשְׁבֹּת אִזֵּן בַּנְּעִימִים,
בְּמַאֲכָלוֹת עֲרֵבוֹת בְּמִינֵי מַטְעַמִּים, בְּמַלְבּוּשֵׁי כָבוֹד זֶבַח
מִשְׁפָּחָה.
הַשּׁוֹמֵר שַׁבָּת הַבֵּן עִם הַבַּת, לָאֵל יֵרָצוּ כְּמִנְחָה עַל מַחֲבַת.

וְאַשְׁרֵי כָּל חוֹכֶה לְתַשְׁלוּמֵי כֵפֶל, מֵאֵת כֹּל סוֹכֶה שׁוֹכֵן
בָּעֲרָפֶל, נַחֲלָה לוֹ יִזְכֶּה בָּהָר וּבַשָּׁפֶל, נַחֲלָה וּמְנוּחָה כַּשֶּׁמֶשׁ
לוֹ זָרְחָה.
הַשּׁוֹמֵר שַׁבָּת הַבֵּן עִם הַבַּת, לָאֵל יֵרָצוּ כְּמִנְחָה עַל מַחֲבַת.

כָּל שׁוֹמֵר שַׁבָּת כַּדָּת מֵחַלְּלוֹ, הֵן הַכְשֵׁר חִבַּת קֹדֶשׁ גּוֹרָלוֹ,
וְאִם יֵצֵא חוֹבַת הַיּוֹם אַשְׁרֵי לוֹ, לָאֵל אָדוֹן מְחוֹלְלוֹ מִנְחָה
הִיא שְׁלוּחָה.
הַשּׁוֹמֵר שַׁבָּת הַבֵּן עִם הַבַּת, לָאֵל יֵרָצוּ כְּמִנְחָה עַל מַחֲבַת.

חֶמְדַּת הַיָּמִים קְרָאוֹ אֵלִי צוּר, וְאַשְׁרֵי לִתְמִימִים אִם יִהְיֶה
נָצוּר, כֶּתֶר הִלּוּמִים עַל רֹאשָׁם יָצוּר, צוּר הָעוֹלָמִים רוּחוֹ
בָּם נָחָה.
הַשּׁוֹמֵר שַׁבָּת הַבֵּן עִם הַבַּת, לָאֵל יֵרָצוּ כְּמִנְחָה עַל מַחֲבַת.

ברוך אל עליון is a poem by Rabbi Baruch ben Samuel of Mayence, one of
the most eminent German rabbis of the thirteenth century. The stanzas,
consisting of four verses each with a cross rhyme and a refrain, bear the
acrostic ברוך, חזק. Each of the seven stanzas, including the refrain, has a total
of sixty syllables. The refrain הבן עם הבת is an allusion to the fourth commandment: "You shall not do any work, neither you, nor your son, nor your
daughter . . ." מנחה על מחבת, the offering baked on a griddle, is ordained in
Leviticus 2:5. The expression עד אנה תוגיון נפש is borrowed from Job 19:2.

Blessed be God Most High who gives repose,
To our soul relief from dismay and woe;
He cares for Zion, the forlorn city:
"How long will you oppress a moaning soul?"
All sons and daughters who keep the Sabbath—
Most pleasing to God is their offering.

God in heaven, King of the universe,
Bade his people keep Sabbath with delight—
Savory food and all kinds of dainties,
Distinguished clothes and a family feast.
All sons and daughters who keep the Sabbath. . .

Happy is he who awaits double reward
From God who sees all and is invisible;
He will merit land on hill and in vale,
A sunlit heritage and a serene mind.
All sons and daughters who keep the Sabbath. . .

Whoever keeps the Sabbath unprofaned
Is qualified to love what is holy;
Happy he who fulfills the day's precept,
As an offering to his Creator.
All sons and daughters who keep the Sabbath. . .

My God has proclaimed it the choicest day;
Happy are the faithful who keep it holy;
God will place a fitting crown on their head,
His divine spirit resting in their midst.
All sons and daughters who keep the Sabbath. . .

The biblical verses utilized in this poem are: Genesis 14:20; I Kings 8:56; Lamentations 3:47; Jeremiah 30:17; Job 19:2 (Stanza I). Psalm 68:5; Ecclesiastes 12:9; I Samuel 20:29 (Stanza II). Isaiah 30:18; I Kings 8:12; Deuteronomy 1:7; Malachi 3:20, or Genesis 32:32 (Stanza III). Isaiah 56:6; Genesis 32:19 (Stanza IV). Psalm 119:1; Isaiah 26:4; 11:2 (Stanza V). Numbers 6:7; Proverbs 29:17; Exodus 29:29 (Stanza VI). Exodus 35:2; Ezekiel 44:30; Exodus 35:3; 20:10 (Stanza VII).

תשלומי כפל, the twofold reward for Sabbath observance, is in keeping with the opening words of the fourth commandment, זכור and שמור, in Exodus 20:8 and Deuteronomy 5:12, respectively.

זָכוֹר אֶת יוֹם הַשַּׁבָּת לְקַדְּשׁוֹ, קַרְנוֹ כִּי גָבְהָה נֵזֶר עַל רֹאשׁוֹ,
עַל כֵּן יִתֵּן הָאָדָם לְנַפְשׁוֹ עֹנֶג וְגַם שִׂמְחָה, בָּהֶם לוֹ לְמָשְׁחָה.
הַשּׁוֹמֵר שַׁבָּת הַבֵּן עִם הַבַּת, לָאֵל יֵרָצוּ כְּמִנְחָה עַל מַחֲבַת.

קֹדֶשׁ הִיא לָכֶם שַׁבָּת הַמַּלְכָּה, אֶל תּוֹךְ בָּתֵּיכֶם לְהָנִיחַ בְּרָכָה,
בְּכָל מוֹשְׁבוֹתֵיכֶם לֹא תַעֲשׂוּ מְלָאכָה, בְּנֵיכֶם וּבְנוֹתֵיכֶם עֶבֶד
וְגַם שִׁפְחָה.
הַשּׁוֹמֵר שַׁבָּת הַבֵּן עִם הַבַּת, לָאֵל יֵרָצוּ כְּמִנְחָה עַל מַחֲבַת.

יוֹם זֶה מְכֻבָּד מִכָּל יָמִים, כִּי בוֹ שָׁבַת צוּר עוֹלָמִים.

שֵׁשֶׁת יָמִים עֲשֵׂה מְלַאכְתֶּךָ, וְיוֹם הַשְּׁבִיעִי לֵאלֹהֶיךָ,
שַׁבָּת לֹא תַעֲשֶׂה בוֹ מְלָאכָה, כִּי כֹל עָשָׂה שֵׁשֶׁת יָמִים.
יוֹם זֶה מְכֻבָּד מִכָּל יָמִים, כִּי בוֹ שָׁבַת צוּר עוֹלָמִים.

רִאשׁוֹן הוּא לְמִקְרָאֵי קֹדֶשׁ, יוֹם שַׁבָּתוֹן שַׁבַּת קֹדֶשׁ,
עַל כֵּן כָּל אִישׁ בְּיֵינוֹ יְקַדֵּשׁ, עַל שְׁתֵּי לֶחֶם יִבְצְעוּ תְמִימִים.
יוֹם זֶה מְכֻבָּד מִכָּל יָמִים, כִּי בוֹ שָׁבַת צוּר עוֹלָמִים.

אֱכֹל מַשְׁמַנִּים שְׁתֵה מַמְתַּקִּים, כִּי אֵל יִתֵּן לְכֹל בּוֹ דְבֵקִים,
בֶּגֶד לִלְבּוֹשׁ לֶחֶם חֻקִּים, בָּשָׂר וְדָגִים וְכָל מַטְעַמִּים.
יוֹם זֶה מְכֻבָּד מִכָּל יָמִים, כִּי בוֹ שָׁבַת צוּר עוֹלָמִים.

יום זה מכובד **is by an unidentified poet, Rabbi Israel, whose name appears
in the acrostic, which adds** הגר **("the proselyte") in the last stanza. Each verse
contains 8 syllables. The biblical verses utilized in this poem are: Isaiah
58:13; Genesis 2:3; Exodus 20:9–11; 12:2; 16:23; Nehemiah 8:10; Deuteronomy 4:4; Genesis 28:20; Proverbs 30:8; Deuteronomy 8:9–10; 7:14; 15:6;
Psalms 19:2; 33:5; Isaiah 66:2; Deuteronomy 32:4.**

Remember to keep the Sabbath holy;
High its glory, a crown rests on its head;
Hence, let man give himself pleasure and joy,
And let him feel exalted like a prince.
    All sons and daughters who keep the Sabbath. . :

Let Queen Sabbath be holy unto you,
That she may place a blessing in your house;
You shall do no work in all your dwellings,
Nor your sons and daughters, nor your servants.
    All sons and daughters who keep the Sabbath. . .

———

This day is the most precious of all days,
Because on it the Eternal ceased from work.

Six days you are to perform all your work,
But the seventh day is your God's Sabbath;
On it you must not do any labor,
For in six days he accomplished all things.
    This day is the most precious of all days. . .

It is foremost among the holy feasts,
The day of rest, the holy Sabbath day;
Hence, let each recite *Kiddush* over wine,
Let the faithful say grace over the twin loaves.
    This day is the most precious of all days. . .

Come, enjoy the dainties and drink the sweet,
For God provides for all who cling to him
Clothes to wear and portions of nourishment,
Meat and fish and all luxurious foods.
    This day is the most precious of all days. . .

...אכל משמנים is based on the talmudic statement that the best food should be prepared for the Sabbath, for "he who delights in the Sabbath is granted his heart's desires" (Shabbath 118a-b). The emphasis on the Sabbath as a day of eating and drinking was meant, according to some, to counteract the ascetic tendencies of the Essenes.

לֹא תֶחְסַר כֹּל בּוֹ וְאָכַלְתָּ וְשָׂבַעְתָּ וּבֵרַכְתָּ
אֶת יְיָ אֱלֹהֶיךָ אֲשֶׁר אָהַבְתָּ, כִּי בֵרַכְךָ מִכָּל עַמִּים.
יוֹם זֶה מְכֻבָּד מִכָּל יָמִים, כִּי בוֹ שָׁבַת צוּר עוֹלָמִים.

הַשָּׁמַיִם מְסַפְּרִים כְּבוֹדוֹ, וְגַם הָאָרֶץ מָלְאָה חַסְדּוֹ,
רְאוּ כָל אֵלֶּה עָשְׂתָה יָדוֹ, כִּי הוּא הַצּוּר פָּעֳלוֹ תָמִים.
יוֹם זֶה מְכֻבָּד מִכָּל יָמִים, כִּי בוֹ. שָׁבַת צוּר עוֹלָמִים.

יָהּ רִבּוֹן עָלַם וְעָלְמַיָּא, אַנְתְּ הוּא מַלְכָּא מֶלֶךְ מַלְכַיָּא, עוֹבַד
גְּבוּרְתֵּךְ וְתִמְהַיָּא, שְׁפַר קֳדָמֵי לְהַחֲוָיֵהּ.
יָהּ רִבּוֹן עָלַם וְעָלְמַיָּא, אַנְתְּ הוּא מַלְכָּא מֶלֶךְ מַלְכַיָּא.

שְׁבָחִין אֲסַדֵּר צַפְרָא וְרַמְשָׁא, לָךְ אֱלָהָא קַדִּישָׁא דִּי בְרָא כָל
נַפְשָׁא, עִירִין קַדִּישִׁין וּבְנֵי אֱנָשָׁא, חֵיוַת בָּרָא וְעוֹפֵי שְׁמַיָּא.
יָהּ רִבּוֹן עָלַם וְעָלְמַיָּא, אַנְתְּ הוּא מַלְכָּא מֶלֶךְ מַלְכַיָּא.

רַבְרְבִין עוֹבְדָיךְ וְתַקִּיפִין, מָכֵךְ רָמַיָּא וְזָקֵף כְּפִיפִין, לוּ יֶחֱיֵא
גְבַר שְׁנִין אַלְפִין, לָא יֵעַל גְּבוּרְתֵּךְ בְּחֻשְׁבְּנַיָּא.
יָהּ רִבּוֹן עָלַם וְעָלְמַיָּא, אַנְתְּ הוּא מַלְכָּא מֶלֶךְ מַלְכַיָּא.

אֱלָהָא דִּי לֵהּ יְקַר וּרְבוּתָא, פְּרֹק יָת עָנָךְ מִפֻּם אַרְיְוָתָא, וְאַפֵּק
יָת עַמָּךְ מִגּוֹ גָלוּתָא, עַמָּךְ דִּי בְחַרְתְּ מִכָּל אֻמַּיָּא.
יָהּ רִבּוֹן עָלַם וְעָלְמַיָּא, אַנְתְּ הוּא מַלְכָּא מֶלֶךְ מַלְכַיָּא.

יה רבון was written in Aramaic by Rabbi Israel Najara, one of the most prolific Hebrew writers of the sixteenth century. His signature is seen in the initials of the five stanzas of this beautiful poem. At the end of the sixteenth century, he published a second and enlarged edition of his *Zemiroth Yisrael*, comprising three hundred and forty-six poems, which soon became the most popular songbook among the Jewish communities in the Orient. He was familiar with several languages, and was inspired by the kabbalistic school of Rabbi Isaac Luria at Safed, Palestine. His song *Yah Ribbon*, which

You shall not be in want of anything;
When you have eaten and are satisfied,
You shall bless the Lord your God whom you **love,**
For he has blessed you above all people.
This day is the most precious of all days. . .

The heavens declare his glory,
The earth is full of his kindness;
Lo, his hand has made all these things!
He is God, whose work is perfect!
This day is the most precious of all days. . .

Lord, eternal Master of worlds,
Thou art the Supreme King of kings.
Thy mighty acts and wondrous deeds
It is my pleasure to declare.
Lord, eternal Master. . .

Morning and evening I praise thee,
Holy God, who didst form all life:
Sacred spirits, human beings,
Beasts of the field, birds of the sky.
Lord, eternal Master. . .

Great and mighty are thy deeds,
Humbling the proud, raising the meek;
Were man to live a thousand years,
Yet he could not recount thy might.
Lord, eternal Master. . .

O God of glory and greatness,
Save thy flock from the lion's jaws;
Free thy people from captivity,
Thy people chosen from all nations.
Lord, eternal Master. . .

---

contains no allusion to the Sabbath, is chanted on Friday evenings all over the
world. After describing the wonders of God's creation, the poet concludes
with a prayer that God may redeem Israel and restore Jerusalem, the citv
of beauty. The phrase שפר קדמי להחויה is borrowed from Daniel 3:32.

לְמִקְדָּשָׁךְ תּוּב וּלְקֹדֶשׁ קֻדְשִׁין, אֲתַר דִּי בֵהּ יֶחֱדוּן רוּחִין וְנַפְשִׁין,

וִיזַמְּרוּן לָךְ שִׁירִין וְרַחֲשִׁין, בִּירוּשְׁלֵם קַרְתָּא דְשֻׁפְרַיָּא.

יָהּ רִבּוֹן עָלַם וְעָלְמַיָּא, אַנְתְּ הוּא מַלְכָּא מֶלֶךְ מַלְכַיָּא.

צוּר מִשֶּׁלּוֹ אָכַלְנוּ בָּרְכוּ אֱמוּנַי, שָׂבַעְנוּ וְהוֹתַרְנוּ כִּדְבַר יְיָ.

הַזָּן אֶת עוֹלָמוֹ, רוֹעֵנוּ אָבִינוּ, אָכַלְנוּ אֶת לַחְמוֹ, וְיֵינוֹ שָׁתִינוּ,

עַל כֵּן נוֹדֶה לִשְׁמוֹ, וּנְהַלְלוֹ בְּפִינוּ, אָמַרְנוּ וְעָנִינוּ, אֵין קָדוֹשׁ כַּיְיָ.

צוּר מִשֶּׁלּוֹ אָכַלְנוּ בָּרְכוּ אֱמוּנַי, שָׂבַעְנוּ וְהוֹתַרְנוּ כִּדְבַר יְיָ.

בְּשִׁיר וְקוֹל תּוֹדָה, נְבָרֵךְ לֵאלֹהֵינוּ, עַל אֶרֶץ חֶמְדָּה, שֶׁהִנְחִיל לַאֲבוֹתֵינוּ, מָזוֹן וְצֵדָה הִשְׂבִּיעַ לְנַפְשֵׁנוּ, חַסְדּוֹ גָּבַר עָלֵינוּ, וֶאֱמֶת יְיָ.

צוּר מִשֶּׁלּוֹ אָכַלְנוּ בָּרְכוּ אֱמוּנַי, שָׂבַעְנוּ וְהוֹתַרְנוּ כִּדְבַר יְיָ.

רַחֵם בְּחַסְדֶּךָ, עַל עַמְּךָ צוּרֵנוּ, עַל צִיּוֹן מִשְׁכַּן כְּבוֹדֶךָ, זְבוּל בֵּית תִּפְאַרְתֵּנוּ, בֶּן דָּוִד עַבְדֶּךָ, יָבֹא וְיִגְאָלֵנוּ, רוּחַ אַפֵּינוּ, מְשִׁיחַ יְיָ.

צוּר מִשֶּׁלּוֹ אָכַלְנוּ בָּרְכוּ אֱמוּנַי, שָׂבַעְנוּ וְהוֹתַרְנוּ כִּדְבַר יְיָ.

יִבָּנֶה הַמִּקְדָּשׁ, עִיר צִיּוֹן תִּמָּלֵא, וְשָׁם נָשִׁיר שִׁיר חָדָשׁ, וּבִרְנָנָה נַעֲלֶה, הָרַחֲמָן הַנִּקְדָּשׁ, יִתְבָּרַךְ וְיִתְעַלֶּה, עַל כּוֹס יַיִן מָלֵא, כְּבִרְכַּת יְיָ.

צוּר מִשֶּׁלּוֹ אָכַלְנוּ בָּרְכוּ אֱמוּנַי, שָׂבַעְנוּ וְהוֹתַרְנוּ כִּדְבַר יְיָ.

צור משלו is of unknown authorship. This poem is an introduction to the grace recited after the meal. Its four stanzas contain the substance of that prayer. The first stanza is based on the first paragraph of the grace; the second stanza relates to the second paragraph of the grace (עודה); the third stanza corresponds to the third paragraph of the grace (רחם... על ישראל...ועל ירושלים); and the fourth stanza has reference to the grace recited over a cup of wine. This poem, though it has no bearing on the Sabbath, is not used on the busy weekdays.

Return to thy most holy shrine,
The place where all souls will rejoice
And sing melodic hymns of praise—
Jerusalem, city of beauty.
  Lord, eternal Master. . .

———

My comrades, bless the Lord whose food we ate!
We ate and have some left, as God has said.

He feeds his world—our Shepherd, our Father;
His was the bread we ate, his the wine we drank;
Hence, let us thank and praise him with our lips,
Chanting: There is none holy like the Lord!
  My comrades, bless the Lord . . .

We praise our God with song and thanksgiving
For the good land he gave to our fathers
And for the ample sustenance he grants us;
Great is his love to us; the Lord is true.
  My comrades, bless the Lord . . .

Our God, O have mercy on thy people,
On Zion thy shrine and our splendid home;
May David's scion come to redeem us,
The Lord's anointed, the breath of our life.
  My comrades, bless the Lord . . .

Let the shrine be restored, Zion refilled,
That we may come up singing a new song;
Blessed be the Merciful, Holy One,
Over the brimful cup of wine, God's gift.
  My comrades, bless the Lord . . .

ברכו אמוני corresponds to the introductory phrase רבותי נברך, inviting the table companions to recite the grace. אמוני my faithful friends. כדבר ה' refers to II Kings 4:43 (כה אמר ה' אכול והותר). Other biblical references are: I Samuel 2:2; Jeremiah 3:19; 33:15; Lamentations 4:20; Isaiah 63:15; 33:5. גבר עלינו חסדו is Psalm 117:2 transposed, which reads: ואמת ה' לעולם, גבר עלינו חסדו.

מִנְחָה לְשַׁבָּת וְיוֹם טוֹב

אַשְׁרֵי יוֹשְׁבֵי בֵיתֶךָ; עוֹד יְהַלְלוּךָ סֶּלָה.

אַשְׁרֵי הָעָם שֶׁכָּכָה לּוֹ; אַשְׁרֵי הָעָם שֶׁיְיָ אֱלֹהָיו.

תְּהִלָּה לְדָוִד

אֲרוֹמִמְךָ, אֱלוֹהַי הַמֶּלֶךְ, וַאֲבָרְכָה שִׁמְךָ לְעוֹלָם וָעֶד.

בְּכָל יוֹם אֲבָרְכֶךָ, וַאֲהַלְלָה שִׁמְךָ לְעוֹלָם וָעֶד.

גָּדוֹל יְיָ וּמְהֻלָּל מְאֹד, וְלִגְדֻלָּתוֹ אֵין חֵקֶר.

דּוֹר לְדוֹר יְשַׁבַּח מַעֲשֶׂיךָ, וּגְבוּרֹתֶיךָ יַגִּידוּ.

הֲדַר כְּבוֹד הוֹדֶךָ, וְדִבְרֵי נִפְלְאֹתֶיךָ אָשִׂיחָה.

וֶעֱזוּז נוֹרְאוֹתֶיךָ יֹאמֵרוּ, וּגְדֻלָּתְךָ אֲסַפְּרֶנָּה.

זֵכֶר רַב טוּבְךָ יַבִּיעוּ, וְצִדְקָתְךָ יְרַנֵּנוּ.

חַנּוּן וְרַחוּם יְיָ, אֶרֶךְ אַפַּיִם וּגְדָל־חָסֶד.

טוֹב יְיָ לַכֹּל, וְרַחֲמָיו עַל כָּל מַעֲשָׂיו.

יוֹדוּךָ יְיָ כָּל מַעֲשֶׂיךָ, וַחֲסִידֶיךָ יְבָרְכוּכָה.

כְּבוֹד מַלְכוּתְךָ יֹאמֵרוּ, וּגְבוּרָתְךָ יְדַבֵּרוּ.

לְהוֹדִיעַ לִבְנֵי הָאָדָם גְּבוּרֹתָיו, וּכְבוֹד הֲדַר מַלְכוּתוֹ.

מַלְכוּתְךָ מַלְכוּת כָּל עֹלָמִים, וּמֶמְשַׁלְתְּךָ בְּכָל דּוֹר וָדֹר.

סוֹמֵךְ יְיָ לְכָל הַנֹּפְלִים, וְזוֹקֵף לְכָל הַכְּפוּפִים.

עֵינֵי כֹל אֵלֶיךָ יְשַׂבֵּרוּ, וְאַתָּה נוֹתֵן לָהֶם אֶת אָכְלָם בְּעִתּוֹ.

Happy are those who dwell in thy house; they are ever praising thee. Happy the people that is so situated; happy the people whose God is the Lord.[1]

Psalm 145

A hymn of praise by David.

I extol thee, my God the King,
And bless thy name forever and ever.

Every day I bless thee,
And praise thy name forever and ever.

Great is the Lord and most worthy of praise;
His greatness is unsearchable.

One generation to another praises thy works;
They recount thy mighty acts.

On the splendor of thy glorious majesty
And on thy wondrous deeds I meditate.

They speak of thy awe-inspiring might,
And I tell of thy greatness.

They spread the fame of thy great goodness,
And sing of thy righteousness.

Gracious and merciful is the Lord,
Slow to anger and of great kindness.

The Lord is good to all,
And his mercy is over all his works.

All thy works praise thee, O Lord,
And thy faithful followers bless thee.

They speak of thy glorious kingdom,
And talk of thy might,

To let men know thy mighty deeds,
And the glorious splendor of thy kingdom.

Thy kingdom is a kingdom of all ages,
And thy dominion is for all generations.

The Lord upholds all who fall,
And raises all who are bowed down.

The eyes of all look hopefully to thee,
And thou givest them their food in due season.

---

[1] *Psalms* 84:5; 144:15.

פּוֹתֵחַ אֶת יָדֶךָ, וּמַשְׂבִּיעַ לְכָל חַי רָצוֹן.

צַדִּיק יְיָ בְּכָל דְּרָכָיו, וְחָסִיד בְּכָל מַעֲשָׂיו.

קָרוֹב יְיָ לְכָל קֹרְאָיו, לְכֹל אֲשֶׁר יִקְרָאֻהוּ בֶאֱמֶת.

רְצוֹן יְרֵאָיו יַעֲשֶׂה, וְאֶת שַׁוְעָתָם יִשְׁמַע וְיוֹשִׁיעֵם.

שׁוֹמֵר יְיָ אֶת כָּל אֹהֲבָיו, וְאֵת כָּל הָרְשָׁעִים יַשְׁמִיד.

תְּהִלַּת יְיָ יְדַבֶּר־פִּי, וִיבָרֵךְ כָּל בָּשָׂר שֵׁם קָדְשׁוֹ לְעוֹלָם וָעֶד.

Reader וַאֲנַחְנוּ נְבָרֵךְ יָהּ מֵעַתָּה וְעַד עוֹלָם, הַלְלוּיָהּ.

וּבָא לְצִיּוֹן גּוֹאֵל, וּלְשָׁבֵי פֶשַׁע בְּיַעֲקֹב, נְאֻם יְיָ. וַאֲנִי, זֹאת בְּרִיתִי אוֹתָם, אָמַר יְיָ: רוּחִי אֲשֶׁר עָלֶיךָ, וּדְבָרַי אֲשֶׁר שַׂמְתִּי בְּפִיךָ לֹא יָמוּשׁוּ מִפִּיךָ וּמִפִּי זַרְעֲךָ, וּמִפִּי זֶרַע זַרְעֲךָ, אָמַר יְיָ, מֵעַתָּה וְעַד עוֹלָם. וְאַתָּה קָדוֹשׁ, יוֹשֵׁב תְּהִלּוֹת יִשְׂרָאֵל. וְקָרָא זֶה אֶל זֶה וְאָמַר: קָדוֹשׁ, קָדוֹשׁ, קָדוֹשׁ יְיָ צְבָאוֹת, מְלֹא כָל הָאָרֶץ כְּבוֹדוֹ. וּמְקַבְּלִין דֵּין מִן דֵּין וְאָמְרִין: קַדִּישׁ בִּשְׁמֵי מְרוֹמָא עִלָּאָה, בֵּית שְׁכִינְתֵּהּ; קַדִּישׁ עַל אַרְעָא, עוֹבַד גְּבוּרְתֵּהּ; קַדִּישׁ לְעָלַם וּלְעָלְמֵי עָלְמַיָּא יְיָ צְבָאוֹת; מַלְיָא כָל אַרְעָא זִיו יְקָרֵהּ. וַתִּשָּׂאֵנִי רוּחַ, וָאֶשְׁמַע אַחֲרַי קוֹל רַעַשׁ גָּדוֹל: בָּרוּךְ כְּבוֹד יְיָ מִמְּקוֹמוֹ. וּנְטָלַתְנִי רוּחָא, וְשִׁמְעֵת בַּתְרַי קָל זִיעַ סַגִּיא דִי מְשַׁבְּחִין וְאָמְרִין: בְּרִיךְ יְקָרָא דַיְיָ מֵאֲתַר בֵּית שְׁכִינְתֵּהּ. יְיָ יִמְלֹךְ לְעֹלָם וָעֶד. יְיָ מַלְכוּתֵהּ (קָאֵם) לְעָלַם וּלְעָלְמֵי עָלְמַיָּא. יְיָ אֱלֹהֵי אַבְרָהָם יִצְחָק וְיִשְׂרָאֵל אֲבוֹתֵינוּ, שָׁמְרָה זֹאת לְעוֹלָם, לְיֵצֶר מַחְשְׁבוֹת לְבַב עַמֶּךָ, וְהָכֵן לְבָבָם אֵלֶיךָ. וְהוּא רַחוּם, יְכַפֵּר עָוֹן וְלֹא יַשְׁחִית, וְהִרְבָּה לְהָשִׁיב אַפּוֹ, וְלֹא יָעִיר כָּל חֲמָתוֹ. כִּי אַתָּה, אֲדֹנָי, טוֹב וְסַלָּח וְרַב חֶסֶד לְכָל קֹרְאֶיךָ.

ובא לציון is postponed till *Minḥah* on Sabbaths and festivals. The reason is explained on page 131.

Thou openest thy hand
And satisfiest every living thing with favor.
The Lord is righteous in all his ways,
And gracious in all his deeds.
The Lord is near to all who call upon him,
To all who call upon him sincerely.
He fulfills the desire of those who revere him;
He hears their cry and saves them.
The Lord preserves all who love him;
But all the wicked he destroys.
My mouth speaks the praise of the Lord;
Let all creatures bless his holy name forever and ever.
[1]We will bless the Lord henceforth and forever.
Praise the Lord!

A redeemer shall come to Zion and to those in Jacob who turn from transgression, says the Lord. As for me, this is my covenant with them, says the Lord: My spirit it is which shall be upon you; and my words which I have put in your mouth shall not depart from your mouth, nor from the mouth of your children, nor from the mouth of your children's children, says the Lord, henceforth and forever.[2]

Thou, holy God, art enthroned amidst the praises of Israel.[3] They keep calling to one another: "Holy, holy, holy is the Lord of hosts; the whole earth is full of his glory."[4] *They receive it from one another, and say: "Holy in the highest heavens, his divine abode; holy upon earth, his work of might; holy forever and to all eternity is the Lord of hosts; the whole earth is full of his radiant glory."* Then a wind lifted me up, and I heard behind me a mighty sound: "Blessed be the glory of the Lord from his abode."[5] *Then a wind lifted me up and I heard behind me a great moving sound of those who uttered praises, saying: "Blessed be the glory of the Lord from the place of his divine abode."* The Lord shall reign forever and ever.[6] *The Lord's kingship is established forever and to all eternity.*

Lord God of Abraham, Isaac and Israel our fathers, keep the mind and purpose of thy people ever in this spirit, and direct their heart to thyself.[7] He, being merciful, forgives iniquity, and does not destroy; frequently he turns his anger away, and does not stir up all his wrath. For thou, O Lord, art good and forgiving, and exceedingly kind to all who call upon thee. Thy righteousness

*The words in italics are the Targum paraphrase of the preceding verse.

---

[1] *Psalm* 115:18. [2] *Isaiah* 59:20-21. [3] *Psalm* 22:4. [4] *Isaiah* 6:3. [5] *Ezekiel* 3:12. [6] *Exodus* 15:18. [7] *I Chronicles* 29:18.

צִדְקָתְךָ צֶדֶק לְעוֹלָם, וְתוֹרָתְךָ אֱמֶת. תִּתֵּן אֱמֶת לְיַעֲקֹב, חֶסֶד
לְאַבְרָהָם, אֲשֶׁר נִשְׁבַּעְתָּ לַאֲבֹתֵינוּ מִימֵי קֶדֶם. בָּרוּךְ יְיָ, יוֹם יוֹם
יַעֲמָס-לָנוּ, הָאֵל יְשׁוּעָתֵנוּ, סֶלָה. יְיָ צְבָאוֹת עִמָּנוּ, מִשְׂגָּב לָנוּ
אֱלֹהֵי יַעֲקֹב, סֶלָה. יְיָ צְבָאוֹת, אַשְׁרֵי אָדָם בֹּטֵחַ בָּךְ. יְיָ,
הוֹשִׁיעָה; הַמֶּלֶךְ יַעֲנֵנוּ בְיוֹם קָרְאֵנוּ. בָּרוּךְ הוּא אֱלֹהֵינוּ שֶׁבְּרָאָנוּ
לִכְבוֹדוֹ, וְהִבְדִּילָנוּ מִן הַתּוֹעִים, וְנָתַן לָנוּ תּוֹרַת אֱמֶת, וְחַיֵּי
עוֹלָם נָטַע בְּתוֹכֵנוּ; הוּא יִפְתַּח לִבֵּנוּ בְּתוֹרָתוֹ, וְיָשֵׂם בְּלִבֵּנוּ
אַהֲבָתוֹ וְיִרְאָתוֹ, לַעֲשׂוֹת רְצוֹנוֹ וּלְעָבְדוֹ בְּלֵבָב שָׁלֵם. לְמַעַן
לֹא נִיגַע לָרִיק, וְלֹא נֵלֵד לַבֶּהָלָה. יְהִי רָצוֹן מִלְּפָנֶיךָ, יְיָ
אֱלֹהֵינוּ וֵאלֹהֵי אֲבוֹתֵינוּ, שֶׁנִּשְׁמֹר חֻקֶּיךָ בָּעוֹלָם הַזֶּה, וְנִזְכֶּה
וְנִחְיֶה וְנִרְאֶה, וְנִירַשׁ טוֹבָה וּבְרָכָה, לִשְׁנֵי יְמוֹת הַמָּשִׁיחַ וּלְחַיֵּי
הָעוֹלָם הַבָּא. לְמַעַן יְזַמֶּרְךָ כָבוֹד וְלֹא יִדֹּם; יְיָ אֱלֹהַי, לְעוֹלָם
אוֹדֶךָ. בָּרוּךְ הַגֶּבֶר אֲשֶׁר יִבְטַח בַּיְיָ, וְהָיָה יְיָ מִבְטַחוֹ. בִּטְחוּ
בַיְיָ עֲדֵי עַד, כִּי בְּיָהּ יְיָ צוּר עוֹלָמִים. Reader וְיִבְטְחוּ בְךָ יוֹדְעֵי
שְׁמֶךָ, כִּי לֹא עָזַבְתָּ דֹרְשֶׁיךָ, יְיָ. יְיָ חָפֵץ לְמַעַן צִדְקוֹ, יַגְדִּיל
תּוֹרָה וְיַאְדִּיר.

Reader:

יִתְגַּדַּל וְיִתְקַדַּשׁ שְׁמֵהּ רַבָּא בְּעָלְמָא דִּי בְרָא כִרְעוּתֵהּ;
וְיַמְלִיךְ מַלְכוּתֵהּ בְּחַיֵּיכוֹן וּבְיוֹמֵיכוֹן, וּבְחַיֵּי דְכָל בֵּית יִשְׂרָאֵל,
בַּעֲגָלָא וּבִזְמַן קָרִיב, וְאִמְרוּ אָמֵן.

יְהֵא שְׁמֵהּ רַבָּא מְבָרַךְ לְעָלַם וּלְעָלְמֵי עָלְמַיָּא.

יִתְבָּרַךְ וְיִשְׁתַּבַּח, וְיִתְפָּאַר וְיִתְרוֹמַם, וְיִתְנַשֵּׂא וְיִתְהַדָּר,
וְיִתְעַלֶּה וְיִתְהַלָּל שְׁמֵהּ דְּקֻדְשָׁא, בְּרִיךְ הוּא, לְעֵלָּא (לְעֵלָּא)
מִן כָּל בִּרְכָתָא וְשִׁירָתָא, תֻּשְׁבְּחָתָא וְנֶחֱמָתָא, דַּאֲמִירָן בְּעָלְמָא,
וְאִמְרוּ אָמֵן.

---

is eternal, and thy Torah is truth.[1] Thou wilt show grace to Jacob, love to Abraham, as thou hast sworn to our fathers from days of old.[2] Blessed be the Lord who day by day bears our burden; God is ever our salvation. The Lord of hosts is with us; the God of Jacob is our stronghold. Lord of hosts, happy is the man who trusts in thee. O Lord, save us; may the King answer us when we call.[3]

Blessed be our God who has created us for his glory, and has separated us from those who go astray; who has given us the Torah of truth and planted eternal life in our midst. May he open our heart to his Torah; may he set in our heart love and reverence for him to do his will and serve him with a perfect heart, so that we shall not labor in vain, nor rear children for disaster. May it be thy will, Lord our God and God of our fathers, that we keep thy laws in this world, and thus be worthy to live to see and share the happiness and blessing in the Messianic days and in the life of the world to come. So that my soul may sing praise to thee, and not be silent; Lord my God, I will praise thee forever.[4] Blessed is the man who trusts in the Lord; the Lord will be his protection. Trust in the Lord forever and ever, for the Lord God is an everlasting stronghold. Those who know thy name put their trust in thee, for thou hast not forsaken those who seek thee, O Lord.[5]

The Lord was pleased, because of his righteousness, to render the Torah great and glorious.[6]

Reader:

Glorified and sanctified be God's great name throughout the world which he has created according to his will. May he establish his kingdom in your lifetime and during your days, and within the life of the entire house of Israel, speedily and soon; and say, Amen.

May his great name be blessed forever and to all eternity.

Blessed and praised, glorified and exalted, extolled and honored, adored and lauded be the name of the Holy One, blessed be he, beyond all the blessings and hymns, praises and consolations that are ever spoken in the world; and say, Amen.

---

[1] *Psalms* 78:38; 86:5; 119:142. [2] *Micah* 7:20. [3] *Psalms* 68:20; 46:8; 84:13; 20:10. [4] *Psalm* 30:13. [5] *Jeremiah* 17:7; *Isaiah* 26:4; *Psalm* 9:11. [6] *Isaiah* 42:21.

On festivals the *Minḥah* service is continued on page 585.

וַאֲנִי תְפִלָּתִי לְךָ, יְיָ, עֵת רָצוֹן; אֱלֹהִים, בְּרָב־חַסְדֶּךָ, עֲנֵנִי בֶּאֱמֶת יִשְׁעֶךָ.

קְרִיאַת הַתּוֹרָה

The ark is opened.

Reader and Congregation:

וַיְהִי בִּנְסֹעַ הָאָרֹן וַיֹּאמֶר מֹשֶׁה: קוּמָה יְיָ, וְיָפֻצוּ אֹיְבֶיךָ, וְיָנֻסוּ מְשַׂנְאֶיךָ מִפָּנֶיךָ. כִּי מִצִּיּוֹן תֵּצֵא תוֹרָה, וּדְבַר יְיָ מִירוּשָׁלָיִם. בָּרוּךְ שֶׁנָּתַן תּוֹרָה לְעַמּוֹ יִשְׂרָאֵל בִּקְדֻשָּׁתוֹ.

זוהר, ויקהל

בְּרִיךְ שְׁמֵהּ דְּמָרֵא עָלְמָא, בְּרִיךְ כִּתְרָךְ וְאַתְרָךְ. יְהֵא רְעוּתָךְ עִם עַמָּךְ יִשְׂרָאֵל לְעָלַם, וּפֻרְקַן יְמִינָךְ אַחֲזִי לְעַמָּךְ בְּבֵית מִקְדְּשָׁךְ; וּלְאַמְטוּיֵא לָנָא מִטּוּב נְהוֹרָךְ, וּלְקַבֵּל צְלוֹתָנָא בְּרַחֲמִין. יְהֵא רַעֲוָא קֳדָמָךְ, דְּתוֹרִיךְ לָן חַיִּין בְּטִיבוּתָא; וְלֶהֱוֵא אֲנָא פְּקִידָא בְּגוֹ צַדִּיקַיָּא, לְמִרְחַם עֲלַי וּלְמִנְטַר יָתִי וְיָת כָּל דִּי לִי וְדִי לְעַמָּךְ יִשְׂרָאֵל. אַנְתְּ הוּא זָן לְכֹלָּא וּמְפַרְנֵס לְכֹלָּא, אַנְתְּ הוּא שַׁלִּיט עַל כֹּלָּא. אַנְתְּ הוּא דְּשַׁלִּיט עַל מַלְכַיָּא, וּמַלְכוּתָא דִּילָךְ הִיא. אֲנָא עַבְדָּא דְּקֻדְשָׁא בְּרִיךְ הוּא, דְּסָגֵדְנָא קַמֵּהּ וּמִקַּמָּא דִּיקַר אוֹרַיְתֵהּ בְּכָל עִדָּן וְעִדָּן. לָא עַל אֱנָשׁ רָחִצְנָא, וְלָא עַל בַּר אֱלֹהִין סָמִכְנָא, אֶלָּא בֶּאֱלָהָא דִשְׁמַיָּא, דְּהוּא אֱלָהָא קְשׁוֹט, וְאוֹרַיְתֵהּ קְשׁוֹט, וּנְבִיאוֹהִי קְשׁוֹט, וּמַסְגֵּא לְמֶעְבַּד טַבְוָן וּקְשׁוֹט. בֵּהּ אֲנָא רָחֵץ, וְלִשְׁמֵהּ קַדִּישָׁא יַקִּירָא אֲנָא אֲמַר תֻּשְׁבְּחָן. יְהֵא רַעֲוָא קֳדָמָךְ, דְּתִפְתַּח לִבָּאִי בְּאוֹרַיְתָא, Reader וְתַשְׁלֵם מִשְׁאֲלִין דְּלִבָּאִי וְלִבָּא דְכָל עַמָּךְ יִשְׂרָאֵל, לְטָב וּלְחַיִּין וְלִשְׁלָם.

On festivals the Minḥah service is continued on page 586.

I offer my prayer to thee, O Lord, at a time of grace. O God, in thy abundant kindness, answer me with thy saving truth.[1]

READING OF THE TORAH

The ark is opened.

Reader and Congregation:

And it came to pass, whenever the ark started, Moses would say: "Arise, O Lord, and let thy enemies be scattered; let those who hate thee flee before thee."[2] Truly, out of Zion shall come forth Torah, and the word of the Lord out of Jerusalem.[3]

Blessed be he who in his holiness gave the Torah to his people Israel.

Zohar, Wayyakhel

Blessed be the name of the Lord of the universe! Blessed be thy crown and thy dominion. May thy good will ever abide with thy people Israel. Reveal thy saving power to thy people in thy sanctuary; bestow on us the good gift of thy light, and accept our prayer in mercy. May it be thy will to prolong our life in happiness.

Let me also be counted among the righteous, so that thou mayest have compassion on me and shelter me and mine and all that belong to thy people Israel. Thou art he who nourishes and sustains all; thou art he who rules over all; thou art he who rules over kings, for dominion is thine. I am the servant of the Holy One, blessed be he, before whom and before whose glorious Torah I bow at all times. Not in man do I put my trust, nor do I rely on any angel, but only in the God of heaven who is the God of truth, whose Torah is truth and whose Prophets are truth, and who performs many deeds of goodness and truth. In him I put my trust, and to his holy and glorious name I utter praises. May it be thy will to open my heart to thy Torah, and to fulfill the wishes of my heart and of the heart of all thy people Israel for happiness, life and peace.

---

[1] *Psalm* 69:14.   [2] *Numbers* 10:35.   [3] *Isaiah* 2:3.

The Reader takes the Torah and says:

גַּדְּלוּ לַיָי אִתִּי, וּנְרוֹמְמָה שְׁמוֹ יַחְדָּו.

Congregation:

לְךָ יְיָ הַגְּדֻלָּה וְהַגְּבוּרָה וְהַתִּפְאֶרֶת וְהַנֵּצַח וְהַהוֹד, כִּי כֹל
בַּשָּׁמַיִם וּבָאָרֶץ. לְךָ, יְיָ, הַמַּמְלָכָה וְהַמִּתְנַשֵּׂא לְכֹל לְרֹאשׁ.
רוֹמְמוּ יְיָ אֱלֹהֵינוּ, וְהִשְׁתַּחֲווּ לַהֲדֹם רַגְלָיו, קָדוֹשׁ הוּא. רוֹמְמוּ
יְיָ אֱלֹהֵינוּ, וְהִשְׁתַּחֲווּ לְהַר קָדְשׁוֹ, כִּי קָדוֹשׁ יְיָ אֱלֹהֵינוּ.

Reader:

אַב הָרַחֲמִים, הוּא יְרַחֵם עַם עֲמוּסִים, וְיִזְכּוֹר בְּרִית
אֵיתָנִים, וְיַצִּיל נַפְשׁוֹתֵינוּ מִן הַשָּׁעוֹת הָרָעוֹת, וְיִגְעַר בְּיֵצֶר הָרָע
מִן הַנְּשׂוּאִים, וְיָחֹן אוֹתָנוּ לִפְלֵיטַת עוֹלָמִים, וִימַלֵּא מִשְׁאֲלוֹתֵינוּ
בְּמִדָּה טוֹבָה, יְשׁוּעָה וְרַחֲמִים.

The Torah is placed on the desk. The Reader unrolls it and says:

וְתִגָּלֶה וְתֵרָאֶה מַלְכוּתוֹ עָלֵינוּ בִּזְמַן קָרוֹב, וְיָחֹן פְּלֵיטָתֵנוּ
וּפְלֵיטַת עַמּוֹ בֵּית יִשְׂרָאֵל לְחֵן וּלְחֶסֶד, לְרַחֲמִים וּלְרָצוֹן,
וְנֹאמַר אָמֵן. הַכֹּל הָבוּ גֹדֶל לֵאלֹהֵינוּ וּתְנוּ כָבוֹד לַתּוֹרָה; כֹּהֵן,
קְרָב; יַעֲמֹד (פלוני בן פלוני) הַכֹּהֵן. בָּרוּךְ שֶׁנָּתַן תּוֹרָה לְעַמּוֹ
יִשְׂרָאֵל בִּקְדֻשָּׁתוֹ.

Congregation and Reader:

וְאַתֶּם הַדְּבֵקִים בַּיְיָ אֱלֹהֵיכֶם, חַיִּים כֻּלְּכֶם הַיּוֹם.

The person called to the Torah recites:

בָּרְכוּ אֶת יְיָ הַמְבֹרָךְ.

Congregation responds:

בָּרוּךְ יְיָ הַמְבֹרָךְ לְעוֹלָם וָעֶד.

He repeats the response and continues:

בָּרוּךְ אַתָּה, יְיָ אֱלֹהֵינוּ, מֶלֶךְ הָעוֹלָם, אֲשֶׁר בָּחַר בָּנוּ מִכָּל
הָעַמִּים, וְנָתַן לָנוּ אֶת תּוֹרָתוֹ. בָּרוּךְ אַתָּה, יְיָ, נוֹתֵן הַתּוֹרָה.

The Reader takes the Torah and says:

Exalt the Lord with me, and let us extol his name together.[1]

Congregation:

Thine, O Lord, is the greatness and the power, the glory and
the victory and the majesty; for all that is in heaven and on earth
is thine; thine, O Lord, is the kingdom, and thou art supreme
over all.[2] Exalt the Lord our God, and worship at his footstool;
holy is he. Exalt the Lord our God, and worship at his holy
mountain, for holy is the Lord our God.[3]

Reader:

May the merciful Father have compassion on the people who
have been upheld by him, and remember the covenant with the
patriarchs; may he deliver us from evil times, and check the evil
impulse in those who have been tended by him; may he graciously
grant us everlasting deliverance, and in his goodness fulfill our
petitions for salvation and mercy.

The Torah is placed on the desk. The Reader unrolls it and says:

May his kingdom soon be revealed and made visible to us;
may he be gracious to our remnant, the remnant of his people,
the house of Israel, granting them grace and kindness, mercy and
favor; and let us say, Amen. Let us all ascribe greatness to our
God, and give honor to the Torah. Let the *Kohen* come forward
[*the Reader names the first person called to the Torah*]. Blessed be
he who in his holiness gave the Torah to his people Israel.

Congregation and Reader:

And you who cling to the Lord your God are all alive today.[4]

The person called to the Torah recites:

Bless the Lord who is blessed.

Congregation responds:

Blessed be the Lord who is blessed forever and ever.

He repeats the response and continues:

Blessed art thou, Lord our God, King of the universe, who
hast chosen us from all peoples, and hast given us thy Torah.
Blessed art thou, O Lord, Giver of the Torah.

---

[1] *Psalm* 34:4.   [2] *I Chronicles* 29:11.   [3] *Psalm* 99:5, 9.   [4] *Deuteronomy* 4:4.

The Torah is read; then he recites:

בָּרוּךְ אַתָּה, יְיָ אֱלֹהֵינוּ, מֶלֶךְ הָעוֹלָם, אֲשֶׁר נָתַן לָנוּ תּוֹרַת
אֱמֶת, וְחַיֵּי עוֹלָם נָטַע בְּתוֹכֵנוּ. בָּרוּךְ אַתָּה, יְיָ, נוֹתֵן הַתּוֹרָה.

When the Torah is raised, the Congregation recites:

וְזֹאת הַתּוֹרָה אֲשֶׁר שָׂם מֹשֶׁה לִפְנֵי בְּנֵי יִשְׂרָאֵל, עַל פִּי יְיָ
בְּיַד מֹשֶׁה.

עֵץ חַיִּים הִיא לַמַּחֲזִיקִים בָּהּ, וְתֹמְכֶיהָ מְאֻשָּׁר. דְּרָכֶיהָ
דַרְכֵי נֹעַם, וְכָל נְתִיבוֹתֶיהָ שָׁלוֹם. אֹרֶךְ יָמִים בִּימִינָהּ;
בִּשְׂמֹאלָהּ עֹשֶׁר וְכָבוֹד. יְיָ חָפֵץ לְמַעַן צִדְקוֹ, יַגְדִּיל תּוֹרָה
וְיַאְדִּיר.

The Reader takes the Torah and says:

יְהַלְלוּ אֶת שֵׁם יְיָ, כִּי נִשְׂגָּב שְׁמוֹ לְבַדּוֹ—

Congregation:

הוֹדוֹ עַל אֶרֶץ וְשָׁמָיִם. וַיָּרֶם קֶרֶן לְעַמּוֹ, תְּהִלָּה לְכָל
חֲסִידָיו, לִבְנֵי יִשְׂרָאֵל עַם קְרֹבוֹ; הַלְלוּיָהּ.

תהלים כד

לְדָוִד מִזְמוֹר. לַיְיָ הָאָרֶץ וּמְלוֹאָהּ, תֵּבֵל וְיֹשְׁבֵי בָהּ. כִּי הוּא
עַל יַמִּים יְסָדָהּ, וְעַל נְהָרוֹת יְכוֹנְנֶהָ. מִי יַעֲלֶה בְהַר יְיָ, וּמִי
יָקוּם בִּמְקוֹם קָדְשׁוֹ. נְקִי כַפַּיִם וּבַר לֵבָב, אֲשֶׁר לֹא נָשָׂא לַשָּׁוְא
נַפְשִׁי וְלֹא נִשְׁבַּע לְמִרְמָה. יִשָּׂא בְרָכָה מֵאֵת יְיָ, וּצְדָקָה מֵאֱלֹהֵי
יִשְׁעוֹ. זֶה דּוֹר דֹּרְשָׁיו, מְבַקְשֵׁי פָנֶיךָ, יַעֲקֹב, סֶלָה. שְׂאוּ שְׁעָרִים
רָאשֵׁיכֶם, וְהִנָּשְׂאוּ פִּתְחֵי עוֹלָם, וְיָבוֹא מֶלֶךְ הַכָּבוֹד. מִי זֶה
מֶלֶךְ הַכָּבוֹד, יְיָ עִזּוּז וְגִבּוֹר, יְיָ גִּבּוֹר מִלְחָמָה. שְׂאוּ שְׁעָרִים
רָאשֵׁיכֶם, וּשְׂאוּ פִּתְחֵי עוֹלָם, וְיָבֹא מֶלֶךְ הַכָּבוֹד. מִי הוּא זֶה
מֶלֶךְ הַכָּבוֹד, יְיָ צְבָאוֹת הוּא מֶלֶךְ הַכָּבוֹד, סֶלָה.

The Torah is read; then he recites:

Blessed art thou, Lord our God, King of the universe, who hast given us the Torah of truth, and hast planted everlasting life in our midst. Blessed art thou, O Lord, Giver of the Torah.

When the Torah is raised, the Congregation recites:

This is the Torah which Moses placed before the children of Israel. It is in accordance with the Lord's command through Moses.[1]

It is a tree of life to those who take hold of it, and happy are those who support it. Its ways are pleasant ways, and all its paths are peace. Long life is in its right hand, and in its left hand are riches and honor. The Lord is pleased, for the sake of his righteousness, to render the Torah great and glorious.[2]

The Reader takes the Torah and says:

Let them praise the name of the Lord, for his name alone is exalted—   *Congregation:*

His majesty is above earth and heaven. He has raised the honor of his people, the glory of his faithful followers, the children of Israel, the people near to him. Praise the Lord![3]

Psalm 24

A psalm of David. The earth and its entire contents belong to the Lord, the world and its inhabitants. For it is he who has founded it upon the seas, and established it on the floods. Who may ascend the Lord's mountain? Who may stand within his holy place? He who has clean hands and a pure heart; he who strives not after vanity and swears not deceitfully. He will receive a blessing from the Lord, and justice from his saving God. Such is the generation of those who are in quest of him, who seek the presence of the God of Jacob. Raise your heads, O gates, raise yourselves, you ancient doors, that the glorious King may come in. Who, then, is the glorious King? The Lord strong and mighty, the Lord strong in battle. Raise your heads, O gates, raise yourselves, you ancient doors, that the glorious King may come in. Who, then, is the glorious King? The Lord of hosts, he is the glorious King.

---

[1] *Deuteronomy* 4:44; *Numbers* 9:23.   [2] *Proverbs* 3:18, 17, 16; *Isaiah* 42:21.
[3] *Psalm* 148:13–14.

While the Torah is being placed in the ark:

וּבְנֻחֹה יֹאמַר: שׁוּבָה, יְיָ, רִבְבוֹת אַלְפֵי יִשְׂרָאֵל. קוּמָה יְיָ
לִמְנוּחָתֶךָ, אַתָּה וַאֲרוֹן עֻזֶּךָ. כֹּהֲנֶיךָ יִלְבְּשׁוּ צֶדֶק, וַחֲסִידֶיךָ
יְרַנֵּנוּ. בַּעֲבוּר דָּוִד עַבְדֶּךָ, אַל תָּשֵׁב פְּנֵי מְשִׁיחֶךָ. כִּי לֶקַח טוֹב
נָתַתִּי לָכֶם, תּוֹרָתִי אַל תַּעֲזֹבוּ. עֵץ חַיִּים הִיא לַמַּחֲזִיקִים בָּהּ,
וְתֹמְכֶיהָ מְאֻשָּׁר. דְּרָכֶיהָ דַרְכֵי נֹעַם, וְכָל נְתִיבוֹתֶיהָ שָׁלוֹם.
הֲשִׁיבֵנוּ יְיָ אֵלֶיךָ, וְנָשׁוּבָה; חַדֵּשׁ יָמֵינוּ כְּקֶדֶם.

Reader:

יִתְגַּדַּל וְיִתְקַדַּשׁ שְׁמֵהּ רַבָּא בְּעָלְמָא דִי בְרָא כִרְעוּתֵהּ;
וְיַמְלִיךְ מַלְכוּתֵהּ בְּחַיֵּיכוֹן וּבְיוֹמֵיכוֹן, וּבְחַיֵּי דְכָל בֵּית יִשְׂרָאֵל,
בַּעֲגָלָא וּבִזְמַן קָרִיב, וְאִמְרוּ אָמֵן.

יְהֵא שְׁמֵהּ רַבָּא מְבָרַךְ לְעָלַם וּלְעָלְמֵי עָלְמַיָּא.

יִתְבָּרַךְ וְיִשְׁתַּבַּח, וְיִתְפָּאַר וְיִתְרוֹמַם, וְיִתְנַשֵּׂא וְיִתְהַדָּר,
וְיִתְעַלֶּה וְיִתְהַלָּל שְׁמֵהּ דְּקֻדְשָׁא, בְּרִיךְ הוּא, לְעֵלָּא (לְעֵלָּא)
מִן כָּל בִּרְכָתָא וְשִׁירָתָא, תֻּשְׁבְּחָתָא וְנֶחֱמָתָא, דַּאֲמִירָן בְּעָלְמָא,
וְאִמְרוּ אָמֵן.

The *Amidah* is recited in silent devotion while standing, facing east.
The Reader repeats the *Amidah* aloud when a *minyan* holds service.

כִּי שֵׁם יְיָ אֶקְרָא, הָבוּ גֹדֶל לֵאלֹהֵינוּ.

אֲדֹנָי, שְׂפָתַי תִּפְתָּח, וּפִי יַגִּיד תְּהִלָּתֶךָ.

בָּרוּךְ אַתָּה, יְיָ אֱלֹהֵינוּ וֵאלֹהֵי אֲבוֹתֵינוּ, אֱלֹהֵי אַבְרָהָם,
אֱלֹהֵי יִצְחָק, וֵאלֹהֵי יַעֲקֹב, הָאֵל הַגָּדוֹל הַגִּבּוֹר וְהַנּוֹרָא, אֵל
עֶלְיוֹן, גּוֹמֵל חֲסָדִים טוֹבִים, וְקוֹנֵה הַכֹּל, וְזוֹכֵר חַסְדֵי אָבוֹת,
וּמֵבִיא גוֹאֵל לִבְנֵי בְנֵיהֶם לְמַעַן שְׁמוֹ בְּאַהֲבָה.

While the Torah is being placed in the ark:

When the ark rested, Moses would say: "Return, O Lord, to the myriads of Israel's families." Arise, O Lord, for thy resting place, thou and thy glorious ark. May thy priests be clothed in righteousness; may thy faithful followers shout for joy. For the sake of thy servant David, reject not thy anointed. I give you good instruction; forsake not my Torah. It is a tree of life to those who take hold of it, and happy are those who support it. Its ways are ways of pleasantness, and all its paths are peace. Turn us to thee, O Lord, and let us return; renew our days as of old.[1]

Reader:

Glorified and sanctified be God's great name throughout the world which he has created according to his will. May he establish his kingdom in your lifetime and during your days, and within the life of the entire house of Israel, speedily and soon; and say, Amen.

May his great name be blessed forever and to all eternity.

Blessed and praised, glorified and exalted, extolled and honored, adored and lauded be the name of the Holy One, blessed be he, beyond all the blessings and hymns, praises and consolations that are ever spoken in the world; and say, Amen.

AMIDAH

The Amidah is recited in silent devotion while standing, facing east.
The Reader repeats the Amidah aloud when a minyan holds service.

When I proclaim the name of the Lord, give glory to our God![2]

O Lord, open thou my lips, that my mouth may declare thy praise.[3]

Blessed art thou, Lora our God and God of our fathers, God of Abraham, God of Isaac and God of Jacob; great, mighty and revered God, sublime God, who bestowest lovingkindness, and art Master of all things; who rememberest the good deeds of our fathers, and who wilt graciously bring a redeemer to their children's children for the sake of thy name.

[1] *Numbers* 10:36; *Psalm* 132:8–10; *Proverbs* 4:2; 3:18, 17; *Lamentations* 5:21.   [2] *Deuteronomy* 32:3.   [3] *Psalm* 51:17.

Between *Rosh Hashanah* and *Yom Kippur* add:

(זָכְרֵנוּ לְחַיִּים, מֶלֶךְ חָפֵץ בַּחַיִּים,

וְכָתְבֵנוּ בְּסֵפֶר הַחַיִּים, לְמַעַנְךָ אֱלֹהִים חַיִּים.)

מֶלֶךְ עוֹזֵר וּמוֹשִׁיעַ וּמָגֵן. בָּרוּךְ אַתָּה, יְיָ, מָגֵן אַבְרָהָם.

אַתָּה גִבּוֹר לְעוֹלָם, אֲדֹנָי; מְחַיֵּה מֵתִים אַתָּה, רַב לְהוֹשִׁיעַ.

Between *Sukkoth* and *Pesaḥ* add:

(מַשִּׁיב הָרוּחַ וּמוֹרִיד הַגָּשֶׁם.)

מְכַלְכֵּל חַיִּים בְּחֶסֶד, מְחַיֵּה מֵתִים בְּרַחֲמִים רַבִּים, סוֹמֵךְ

נוֹפְלִים, וְרוֹפֵא חוֹלִים, וּמַתִּיר אֲסוּרִים, וּמְקַיֵּם אֱמוּנָתוֹ לִישֵׁנֵי

עָפָר. מִי כָמוֹךָ, בַּעַל גְּבוּרוֹת, וּמִי דּוֹמֶה לָּךְ, מֶלֶךְ מֵמִית

וּמְחַיֶּה וּמַצְמִיחַ יְשׁוּעָה.

Between *Rosh Hashanah* and *Yom Kippur* add:

(מִי כָמוֹךָ, אַב הָרַחֲמִים,

זוֹכֵר יְצוּרָיו לְחַיִּים בְּרַחֲמִים.)

וְנֶאֱמָן אַתָּה לְהַחֲיוֹת מֵתִים. בָּרוּךְ אַתָּה, יְיָ, מְחַיֵּה הַמֵּתִים.

When the Reader repeats the *Amidah,* the following *Kedushah* is said.

נְקַדֵּשׁ אֶת שִׁמְךָ בָּעוֹלָם כְּשֵׁם שֶׁמַּקְדִּישִׁים אוֹתוֹ בִּשְׁמֵי מָרוֹם.

כַּכָּתוּב עַל יַד נְבִיאֶךָ: וְקָרָא זֶה אֶל זֶה וְאָמַר:

קָדוֹשׁ, קָדוֹשׁ, קָדוֹשׁ יְיָ צְבָאוֹת; מְלֹא כָל הָאָרֶץ כְּבוֹדוֹ.

לְעֻמָּתָם בָּרוּךְ יֹאמֵרוּ—

בָּרוּךְ כְּבוֹד יְיָ מִמְּקוֹמוֹ.

וּבְדִבְרֵי קָדְשְׁךָ כָּתוּב לֵאמֹר:

יִמְלֹךְ יְיָ לְעוֹלָם, אֱלֹהַיִךְ צִיּוֹן לְדֹר וָדֹר; הַלְלוּיָהּ.

Between Rosh Hashanah and Yom Kippur add:

(Remember us to life, O King who delightest in life; inscribe us in the book of life for thy sake, O living God.)

O King, Supporter, Savior and Shield! Blessed art thou, O Lord, Shield of Abraham.

Thou, O Lord, art mighty forever; thou revivest the dead; thou art powerful to save.

Between Sukkoth and Pesaḥ add:

(Thou causest the wind to blow and the rain to fall.)

Thou sustainest the living with kindness, and revivest the dead with great mercy; thou supportest all who fall, and healest the sick; thou settest the captives free, and keepest faith with those who sleep in the dust. Who is like thee, Lord of power? Who resembles thee, O King? Thou bringest death and restorest life, and causest salvation to flourish.

Between Rosh Hashanah and Yom Kippur add:

(Who is like thee, merciful Father? In mercy thou rememberest thy creatures to life.)

Thou art faithful to revive the dead. Blessed art thou, O Lord, who revivest the dead.

When the Reader repeats the Amidah, the following Kedushah is said:

We sanctify thy name in this world even as they sanctify it in the highest heavens, as it is written by thy prophet: "They keep calling to one another:

> Holy, holy, holy is the Lord of hosts;
> The whole earth is full of his glory."[1]

Those opposite them say: Blessed—

Blessed be the glory of the Lord from his abode.[2]

And in thy holy Scriptures it is written:

> The Lord shall reign forever,
> Your God, O Zion, for all generations.
> Praise the Lord.[3]

---

[1] *Isaiah* 6:3   [2] *Ezekiel* 3:12.   [3] *Psalm* 146:10.

Reader:

לְדוֹר וָדוֹר נַגִּיד גָּדְלֶךָ, וּלְנֵצַח נְצָחִים קְדֻשָּׁתְךָ נַקְדִּישׁ,
וְשִׁבְחֲךָ אֱלֹהֵינוּ מִפִּינוּ לֹא יָמוּשׁ לְעוֹלָם וָעֶד, כִּי אֵל מֶלֶךְ
גָּדוֹל וְקָדוֹשׁ אָתָּה. בָּרוּךְ אַתָּה, יְיָ, הָאֵל * (הַמֶּלֶךְ) הַקָּדוֹשׁ.

אַתָּה קָדוֹשׁ וְשִׁמְךָ קָדוֹשׁ, וּקְדוֹשִׁים בְּכָל יוֹם יְהַלְלוּךָ סֶּלָה.
בָּרוּךְ אַתָּה, יְיָ, הָאֵל * (הַמֶּלֶךְ) הַקָּדוֹשׁ.

* Between *Rosh Hashanah* and *Yom Kippur* say הַמֶּלֶךְ הַקָּדוֹשׁ.

אַתָּה אֶחָד וְשִׁמְךָ אֶחָד, וּמִי כְּעַמְּךָ יִשְׂרָאֵל גּוֹי אֶחָד בָּאָרֶץ.
תִּפְאֶרֶת גְּדֻלָּה, וַעֲטֶרֶת יְשׁוּעָה, יוֹם מְנוּחָה וּקְדֻשָּׁה לְעַמְּךָ
נָתָתָּ. אַבְרָהָם יָגֵל, יִצְחָק יְרַנֵּן, יַעֲקֹב וּבָנָיו יָנוּחוּ בוֹ. מְנוּחַת
אַהֲבָה וּנְדָבָה, מְנוּחַת אֱמֶת וֶאֱמוּנָה, מְנוּחַת שָׁלוֹם וְשַׁלְוָה
וְהַשְׁקֵט וָבֶטַח, מְנוּחָה שְׁלֵמָה שָׁאַתָּה רוֹצֶה בָּהּ; יַכִּירוּ בָנֶיךָ
וְיֵדְעוּ, כִּי מֵאִתְּךָ הִיא מְנוּחָתָם, וְעַל מְנוּחָתָם יַקְדִּישׁוּ אֶת שְׁמֶךָ.

אֱלֹהֵינוּ וֵאלֹהֵי אֲבוֹתֵינוּ, רְצֵה בִמְנוּחָתֵנוּ. קַדְּשֵׁנוּ בְּמִצְוֹתֶיךָ,
וְתֵן חֶלְקֵנוּ בְּתוֹרָתֶךָ; שַׂבְּעֵנוּ מִטּוּבֶךָ, וְשַׂמְּחֵנוּ בִּישׁוּעָתֶךָ; וְטַהֵר
לִבֵּנוּ לְעָבְדְּךָ בֶּאֱמֶת; וְהַנְחִילֵנוּ, יְיָ אֱלֹהֵינוּ, בְּאַהֲבָה וּבְרָצוֹן
שַׁבַּת קָדְשֶׁךָ, וְיָנוּחוּ בָהּ יִשְׂרָאֵל מְקַדְּשֵׁי שְׁמֶךָ. בָּרוּךְ אַתָּה, יְיָ,
מְקַדֵּשׁ הַשַּׁבָּת.

רְצֵה, יְיָ אֱלֹהֵינוּ, בְּעַמְּךָ יִשְׂרָאֵל וּבִתְפִלָּתָם; וְהָשֵׁב אֶת
הָעֲבוֹדָה לִדְבִיר בֵּיתֶךָ, וְאִשֵּׁי יִשְׂרָאֵל וּתְפִלָּתָם בְּאַהֲבָה תְקַבֵּל
בְּרָצוֹן, וּתְהִי לְרָצוֹן תָּמִיד עֲבוֹדַת יִשְׂרָאֵל עַמֶּךָ.

On *Rosh Ḥodesh* and *Ḥol ha-Mo'ed* add:

(אֱלֹהֵינוּ וֵאלֹהֵי אֲבוֹתֵינוּ, יַעֲלֶה וְיָבֹא, וְיַגִּיעַ וְיֵרָאֶה, וְיֵרָצֶה

אתה אחד ... בארץ is based on Zechariah 14:9; I Chronicles 17:21. The
Siddur of Amram Gaon records the following variant in use during the ninth
century: הנח לנו ה' אלהינו כי אתה אבינו... ואל תהי צרה ויגון ביום מנוחתנו, מנוחת אהבה
ונדבה, מנוחת אמת ואמונה.

Reader:

Through all generations we will declare thy greatness; to all eternity we will proclaim thy holiness; thy praise, our God, shall never depart from our mouth, for thou art a great and holy God and King. * Blessed art thou, O Lord, holy God.

Thou art holy and thy name is holy, and holy beings praise thee daily. Blessed art thou, O Lord, * holy God.

*Between Rosh Hashanah and Yom Kippur say, "holy King".

Thou art One and thy name is One; and who is like thy people Israel unique on earth? Thou gavest thy people a crown of distinction, a crown of triumph—a day of rest and holiness. Abraham and Isaac rejoiced on the Sabbath; Jacob and his children found rest in it. It is a rest granted in gracious love, a true and genuine rest, a rest that yields peace and tranquillity, serenity and confidence, a perfect rest with which thou art pleased. May thy children realize and know that their rest comes from thee, and by keeping the Sabbath they hallow thy name.

Our God and God of our fathers, be pleased with our rest. Sanctify us with thy commandments and grant us a share in thy Torah; satisfy us with thy goodness and gladden us with thy help; purify our heart to serve thee sincerely. In thy gracious love, Lord our God, grant that we keep thy holy Sabbath as a heritage; may Israel who sanctifies thy name rest on it. Blessed art thou, O Lord, who hallowest the Sabbath.

Be pleased, Lord our God, with thy people Israel and with their prayer; restore the worship to thy most holy sanctuary; accept Israel's offerings and prayer with gracious love. May the worship of thy people Israel be ever pleasing to thee.

On Rosh Ḥodesh and Ḥol ha-Mo'ed add:

(Our God and God of our fathers, may the remembrance of us,

יעקב ובניו ינוחו According to midrashic literature, the patriarchs observed the Sabbath and fulfilled all the commands that were revealed later. The children of Abraham and of Isaac are not mentioned because Ishmael and Esau are not credited with the observance of the Sabbath.

וְיִשָּׁמַע, וְיִפָּקֵד וְיִזָּכֵר, זִכְרוֹנֵנוּ וּפִקְדוֹנֵנוּ, וְזִכְרוֹן אֲבוֹתֵינוּ, וְזִכְרוֹן מָשִׁיחַ בֶּן דָּוִד עַבְדֶּךָ, וְזִכְרוֹן יְרוּשָׁלַיִם עִיר קָדְשֶׁךָ, וְזִכְרוֹן כָּל עַמְּךָ בֵּית יִשְׂרָאֵל לְפָנֶיךָ, לִפְלֵיטָה וּלְטוֹבָה, לְחֵן וּלְחֶסֶד וּלְרַחֲמִים, לְחַיִּים וּלְשָׁלוֹם, בְּיוֹם

| *Sukkoth* | *Pesah* | *Rosh Ḥodesh* |
| חַג הַסֻּכּוֹת | חַג הַמַּצּוֹת | רֹאשׁ הַחֹדֶשׁ |

הַזֶּה. זָכְרֵנוּ, יְיָ אֱלֹהֵינוּ, בּוֹ לְטוֹבָה, וּפָקְדֵנוּ בוֹ לִבְרָכָה, וְהוֹשִׁיעֵנוּ בוֹ לְחַיִּים. וּבִדְבַר יְשׁוּעָה וְרַחֲמִים חוּס וְחָנֵּנוּ, וְרַחֵם עָלֵינוּ וְהוֹשִׁיעֵנוּ, כִּי אֵלֶיךָ עֵינֵינוּ, כִּי אֵל מֶלֶךְ חַנּוּן וְרַחוּם אָתָּה.)

וְתֶחֱזֶינָה עֵינֵינוּ בְּשׁוּבְךָ לְצִיּוֹן בְּרַחֲמִים. בָּרוּךְ אַתָּה, יְיָ, הַמַּחֲזִיר שְׁכִינָתוֹ לְצִיּוֹן.

מוֹדִים אֲנַחְנוּ לָךְ, שָׁאַתָּה הוּא יְיָ אֱלֹהֵינוּ וֵאלֹהֵי אֲבוֹתֵינוּ לְעוֹלָם וָעֶד. צוּר חַיֵּינוּ, מָגֵן יִשְׁעֵנוּ אַתָּה הוּא. לְדוֹר וָדוֹר נוֹדֶה לְּךָ, וּנְסַפֵּר תְּהִלָּתֶךָ, עַל חַיֵּינוּ הַמְּסוּרִים בְּיָדֶךָ, וְעַל נִשְׁמוֹתֵינוּ הַפְּקוּדוֹת לָךְ, וְעַל נִסֶּיךָ שֶׁבְּכָל יוֹם עִמָּנוּ, וְעַל נִפְלְאוֹתֶיךָ וְטוֹבוֹתֶיךָ שֶׁבְּכָל עֵת, עֶרֶב וָבֹקֶר וְצָהֳרָיִם. הַטּוֹב כִּי לֹא כָלוּ רַחֲמֶיךָ, וְהַמְרַחֵם כִּי לֹא תַמּוּ חֲסָדֶיךָ, מֵעוֹלָם קִוִּינוּ לָךְ.

When the Reader repeats the *Amidah*, the Congregation responds here by saying:

(מוֹדִים אֲנַחְנוּ לָךְ, שָׁאַתָּה הוּא יְיָ אֱלֹהֵינוּ וֵאלֹהֵי אֲבוֹתֵינוּ. אֱלֹהֵי כָל בָּשָׂר, יוֹצְרֵנוּ, יוֹצֵר בְּרֵאשִׁית, בְּרָכוֹת וְהוֹדָאוֹת לְשִׁמְךָ הַגָּדוֹל וְהַקָּדוֹשׁ עַל שֶׁהֶחֱיִיתָנוּ וְקִיַּמְתָּנוּ. כֵּן תְּחַיֵּנוּ וּתְקַיְּמֵנוּ, וְתֶאֱסוֹף גָּלֻיּוֹתֵינוּ לְחַצְרוֹת קָדְשֶׁךָ לִשְׁמוֹר חֻקֶּיךָ וְלַעֲשׂוֹת רְצוֹנֶךָ, וּלְעָבְדְּךָ בְּלֵבָב שָׁלֵם, עַל שֶׁאֲנַחְנוּ מוֹדִים לָךְ. בָּרוּךְ אֵל הַהוֹדָאוֹת.)

of our fathers, of Messiah the son of David thy servant, of Jerusalem thy holy city, and of all thy people the house of Israel, ascend and come and be accepted before thee for deliverance and happiness, for grace, kindness and mercy, for life and peace, on this day of

Rosh Ḥodesh	*Pesaḥ*	*Sukkoth*
the New Moon.	the Feast of Unleavened Bread.	the Feast of Tabernacles.

Remember us this day, Lord our God, for happiness; be mindful of us for blessing; save us to enjoy life. With a promise of salvation and mercy spare us and be gracious to us; have pity on us and save us, for we look to thee, for thou art a gracious and merciful God and King.)

May our eyes behold thy return in mercy to Zion. Blessed art thou, O Lord, who restorest thy divine presence to Zion.

We ever thank thee, who art the Lord our God and the God of our fathers. Thou art the strength of our life and our saving shield. In every generation we will thank thee and recount thy praise—for our lives which are in thy charge, for our souls which are in thy care, for thy miracles which are daily with us, and for thy continual wonders and favors—evening, morning and noon. Beneficent One, whose mercies never fail, Merciful One, whose kindnesses never cease, thou hast always been our hope.

When the Reader repeats the Amidah, the Congregation responds here by saying:

(We thank thee, who art the Lord our God and the God of our fathers. God of all mankind, our Creator and Creator of the universe, blessings and thanks are due to thy great and holy name, because thou hast kept us alive and sustained us; mayest thou ever grant us life and sustenance. O gather our exiles to thy holy courts to observe thy laws, to do thy will, and to serve thee with a perfect heart. For this we thank thee. Blessed be God to whom all thanks are due.)

מודים is based on Psalms 79:13 and 55:18, namely: נודה לך לעולם, לדור ודור נספר תהלתך and ערב ובקר וצהרים אשיחה.

מודים דרבנן is a composite of variants suggested by several rabbis of the Talmud (Sotah 40a).

On Ḥanukkah add:

(עַל הַנִּסִּים וְעַל הַפֻּרְקָן, וְעַל הַגְּבוּרוֹת וְעַל הַתְּשׁוּעוֹת, וְעַל
הַמִּלְחָמוֹת, שֶׁעָשִׂיתָ לַאֲבוֹתֵינוּ בַּיָּמִים הָהֵם בַּזְּמַן הַזֶּה–

בִּימֵי מַתִּתְיָהוּ בֶּן יוֹחָנָן כֹּהֵן גָּדוֹל, חַשְׁמוֹנַי וּבָנָיו, כְּשֶׁעָמְדָה
מַלְכוּת יָוָן הָרְשָׁעָה עַל עַמְּךָ יִשְׂרָאֵל לְהַשְׁכִּיחָם תּוֹרָתֶךָ,
וּלְהַעֲבִירָם מֵחֻקֵּי רְצוֹנֶךָ. וְאַתָּה בְּרַחֲמֶיךָ הָרַבִּים עָמַדְתָּ לָהֶם
בְּעֵת צָרָתָם, רַבְתָּ אֶת רִיבָם, דַּנְתָּ אֶת דִּינָם, נָקַמְתָּ אֶת נִקְמָתָם;
מָסַרְתָּ גִבּוֹרִים בְּיַד חַלָּשִׁים, וְרַבִּים בְּיַד מְעַטִּים, וּטְמֵאִים בְּיַד
טְהוֹרִים, וּרְשָׁעִים בְּיַד צַדִּיקִים, וְזֵדִים בְּיַד עוֹסְקֵי תוֹרָתֶךָ.
וּלְךָ עָשִׂיתָ שֵׁם גָּדוֹל וְקָדוֹשׁ בְּעוֹלָמֶךָ, וּלְעַמְּךָ יִשְׂרָאֵל עָשִׂיתָ
תְּשׁוּעָה גְדוֹלָה וּפֻרְקָן כְּהַיּוֹם הַזֶּה. וְאַחַר כֵּן בָּאוּ בָנֶיךָ לִדְבִיר
בֵּיתֶךָ, וּפִנּוּ אֶת הֵיכָלֶךָ, וְטִהֲרוּ אֶת מִקְדָּשֶׁךָ, וְהִדְלִיקוּ נֵרוֹת
בְּחַצְרוֹת קָדְשֶׁךָ, וְקָבְעוּ שְׁמוֹנַת יְמֵי חֲנֻכָּה אֵלּוּ לְהוֹדוֹת וּלְהַלֵּל
לְשִׁמְךָ הַגָּדוֹל.)

וְעַל כֻּלָּם יִתְבָּרַךְ וְיִתְרוֹמַם שִׁמְךָ, מַלְכֵּנוּ, תָּמִיד לְעוֹלָם
וָעֶד.

Between *Rosh Hashanah* and *Yom Kippur* add:

וּכְתוֹב לְחַיִּים טוֹבִים כָּל בְּנֵי בְרִיתֶךָ.

וְכֹל הַחַיִּים יוֹדוּךָ סֶּלָה, וִיהַלְלוּ אֶת שִׁמְךָ בֶּאֱמֶת, הָאֵל,
יְשׁוּעָתֵנוּ וְעֶזְרָתֵנוּ סֶלָה. בָּרוּךְ אַתָּה, יְיָ, הַטּוֹב שִׁמְךָ, וּלְךָ נָאֶה
לְהוֹדוֹת.

שָׁלוֹם רָב עַל יִשְׂרָאֵל עַמְּךָ תָּשִׂים לְעוֹלָם, כִּי אַתָּה הוּא
מֶלֶךְ אָדוֹן לְכָל הַשָּׁלוֹם, וְטוֹב בְּעֵינֶיךָ לְבָרֵךְ אֶת עַמְּךָ יִשְׂרָאֵל
בְּכָל עֵת וּבְכָל שָׁעָה בִּשְׁלוֹמֶךָ. בָּרוּךְ אַתָּה, יְיָ, הַמְבָרֵךְ אֶת
עַמּוֹ יִשְׂרָאֵל בַּשָּׁלוֹם.

On Ḥanukkah add:

(We thank thee for the miracles, for the redemption, for the mighty deeds and triumphs, and for the battles which thou didst perform for our fathers in those days, at this season—

In the days of the Hasmonean, Mattathias ben Yoḥanan, the High Priest, and his sons, when a wicked Hellenic government rose up against thy people Israel to make them forget thy Torah and transgress the laws of thy will. Thou in thy great mercy didst stand by them in the time of their distress. Thou didst champion their cause, defend their rights and avenge their wrong; thou didst deliver the strong into the hands of the weak, the many into the hands of the few, the impure into the hands of the pure, the wicked into the hands of the righteous, and the arrogant into the hands of the students of thy Torah. Thou didst make a great and holy name for thyself in thy world, and for thy people Israel thou didst perform a great deliverance unto this day. Thereupon thy children entered the shrine of thy house, cleansed thy Temple, purified thy sanctuary, kindled lights in thy holy courts, and designated these eight days of Ḥanukkah for giving thanks and praise to thy great name.)

For all these acts may thy name, our King, be blessed and exalted forever and ever.

Between Rosh Hashanah and Yom Kippur add:

(Inscribe all thy people of the covenant for a happy life.)

All the living shall ever thank thee and sincerely praise thy name, O God, who art always our salvation and help. Blessed art thou, O Lord, Beneficent One, to whom it is fitting to give thanks.

O grant abundant peace to Israel thy people forever, for thou art the King and Lord of all peace. May it please thee to bless thy people Israel with peace at all times and at all hours. Blessed art thou, O Lord, who blessest thy people Israel with peace.

מתתיהו, the leader of the Maccabean revolt against the Syrians, was the father of Simeon who became High Priest in 141 before the common era. Hence, it is suggested that the epithet כהן גדול refers to that fact. According to Sofrim 20:8, מתתיהו and חשמונאי were two different persons. There the reading is: בימי מתתיהו... וחשמונאי ובניו.

Between *Rosh Hashanah* and *Yom Kippur* say:

(בְּסֵפֶר חַיִּים, בְּרָכָה וְשָׁלוֹם וּפַרְנָסָה טוֹבָה, נִזָּכֵר וְנִכָּתֵב
לְפָנֶיךָ, אֲנַחְנוּ וְכָל עַמְּךָ בֵּית יִשְׂרָאֵל, לְחַיִּים טוֹבִים וּלְשָׁלוֹם.
בָּרוּךְ אַתָּה, יְיָ, עוֹשֵׂה הַשָּׁלוֹם.)

After the *Amidah* add the following meditation:

אֱלֹהַי, נְצֹר לְשׁוֹנִי מֵרָע, וּשְׂפָתַי מִדַּבֵּר מִרְמָה; וְלִמְקַלְלַי
נַפְשִׁי תִדּוֹם, וְנַפְשִׁי כֶּעָפָר לַכֹּל תִּהְיֶה. פְּתַח לִבִּי בְּתוֹרָתֶךָ,
וּבְמִצְוֹתֶיךָ תִּרְדּוֹף נַפְשִׁי; וְכָל הַחוֹשְׁבִים עָלַי רָעָה, מְהֵרָה
הָפֵר עֲצָתָם וְקַלְקֵל מַחֲשַׁבְתָּם. עֲשֵׂה לְמַעַן שְׁמֶךָ, עֲשֵׂה לְמַעַן
יְמִינֶךָ, עֲשֵׂה לְמַעַן קְדֻשָּׁתֶךָ, עֲשֵׂה לְמַעַן תּוֹרָתֶךָ. לְמַעַן יֵחָלְצוּן
יְדִידֶיךָ, הוֹשִׁיעָה יְמִינְךָ וַעֲנֵנִי. יִהְיוּ לְרָצוֹן אִמְרֵי פִי וְהֶגְיוֹן לִבִּי
לְפָנֶיךָ, יְיָ, צוּרִי וְגוֹאֲלִי. עֹשֶׂה שָׁלוֹם בִּמְרוֹמָיו, הוּא יַעֲשֶׂה
שָׁלוֹם עָלֵינוּ וְעַל כָּל יִשְׂרָאֵל, וְאִמְרוּ אָמֵן.

יְהִי רָצוֹן מִלְּפָנֶיךָ, יְיָ אֱלֹהֵינוּ וֵאלֹהֵי אֲבוֹתֵינוּ, שֶׁיִּבָּנֶה בֵּית
הַמִּקְדָּשׁ בִּמְהֵרָה בְיָמֵינוּ; וְתֵן חֶלְקֵנוּ בְּתוֹרָתֶךָ. וְשָׁם נַעֲבָדְךָ
בְּיִרְאָה, כִּימֵי עוֹלָם וּכְשָׁנִים קַדְמוֹנִיּוֹת. וְעָרְבָה לַיְיָ מִנְחַת
יְהוּדָה וִירוּשָׁלָיִם, כִּימֵי עוֹלָם וּכְשָׁנִים קַדְמוֹנִיּוֹת.

The following paragraph is omitted on occasions when the *Taḥanun*
(page 103) is omitted on weekdays.

צִדְקָתְךָ צֶדֶק לְעוֹלָם, וְתוֹרָתְךָ אֱמֶת. וְצִדְקָתְךָ אֱלֹהִים עַד
מָרוֹם, אֲשֶׁר עָשִׂיתָ גְדֹלוֹת; אֱלֹהִים, מִי כָמוֹךָ. צִדְקָתְךָ כְּהַרְרֵי
אֵל, מִשְׁפָּטֶיךָ תְּהוֹם רַבָּה; אָדָם וּבְהֵמָה תוֹשִׁיעַ, יְיָ.

צדק צדקתך is regarded as a form of **הדין צדוק** said on the occasion of a
death. According to tradition, Moses died on Sabbath afternoon. These three
verses, containing the words **אמת אלהים 'ה**, are arranged in a reverse order in
the Sephardic *Siddur*. **צדק צדקתך** is presumably a substitute for the *Taḥanun*
of the *Minḥah* for weekdays.

Between Rosh Hashanah and Yom Kippur say:

(May we and all Israel thy people be remembered and inscribed before thee in the book of life and blessing, peace and prosperity, for a happy life and for peace. Blessed art thou, O Lord, Author of peace.)

After the Amidah add the following meditation:

My God, guard my tongue from evil, and my lips from speaking falsehood. May my soul be silent to those who insult me; be my soul lowly to all as the dust. Open my heart to thy Torah, that my soul may follow thy commands. Speedily defeat the counsel of all those who plan evil against me, and upset their design. Do it for the glory of thy name; do it for the sake of thy power; do it for the sake of thy holiness; do it for the sake of thy Torah. That thy beloved may be rescued, save with thy right hand and answer me. May the words of my mouth and the meditation of my heart be pleasing before thee, O Lord, my Stronghold and my Redeemer.[1] May he who creates peace in his high heavens create peace for us and for all Israel. Amen.

May it be thy will, Lord our God and God of our fathers, that the Temple be speedily rebuilt in our days, and grant us a share in thy Torah. There we will serve thee with reverence, as in the days of old and as in former years. Then the offering of Judah and Jerusalem will be pleasing to the Lord, as in the days of old and as in former years.[2]

The following paragraph is omitted on occasions when the Taḥanun (page 104) is omitted on weekdays.

Thy righteousness is an everlasting righteousness, and thy Torah is truth. Thy righteousness, O God, is most high; thou who hast done great things, O God, who is like thee? Thy righteousness is like the mighty mountains; thy judgments are like the vast sea; man and beast dost thou save, O Lord.[3]

---

[1] *Psalms* 60:7; 19:15.   [2] *Malachi* 3:4.   [3] *Psalms* 119:142, 71:19; 36:7.

Reader:

יִתְגַּדַּל וְיִתְקַדַּשׁ שְׁמֵהּ רַבָּא בְּעָלְמָא דִּי בְרָא כִרְעוּתֵהּ;
וְיַמְלִיךְ מַלְכוּתֵהּ בְּחַיֵּיכוֹן וּבְיוֹמֵיכוֹן, וּבְחַיֵּי דְכָל בֵּית יִשְׂרָאֵל,
בַּעֲגָלָא וּבִזְמַן קָרִיב, וְאִמְרוּ אָמֵן.

יְהֵא שְׁמֵהּ רַבָּא מְבָרַךְ לְעָלַם וּלְעָלְמֵי עָלְמַיָּא.

יִתְבָּרַךְ וְיִשְׁתַּבַּח, וְיִתְפָּאַר וְיִתְרוֹמַם, וְיִתְנַשֵּׂא וְיִתְהַדָּר,
וְיִתְעַלֶּה וְיִתְהַלָּל שְׁמֵהּ דְּקֻדְשָׁא, בְּרִיךְ הוּא, לְעֵלָּא ⟨לְעֵלָּא⟩
מִן כָּל בִּרְכָתָא וְשִׁירָתָא, תֻּשְׁבְּחָתָא וְנֶחֱמָתָא, דַּאֲמִירָן בְּעָלְמָא,
וְאִמְרוּ אָמֵן.

תִּתְקַבַּל צְלוֹתְהוֹן וּבָעוּתְהוֹן דְּכָל בֵּית יִשְׂרָאֵל קֳדָם אֲבוּהוֹן
דִּי בִשְׁמַיָּא, וְאִמְרוּ אָמֵן.

יְהֵא שְׁלָמָא רַבָּא מִן שְׁמַיָּא, וְחַיִּים, עָלֵינוּ וְעַל כָּל יִשְׂרָאֵל,
וְאִמְרוּ אָמֵן.

עֹשֶׂה שָׁלוֹם בִּמְרוֹמָיו, הוּא יַעֲשֶׂה שָׁלוֹם עָלֵינוּ וְעַל כָּל
יִשְׂרָאֵל, וְאִמְרוּ אָמֵן.

עָלֵינוּ לְשַׁבֵּחַ לַאֲדוֹן הַכֹּל, לָתֵת גְּדֻלָּה לְיוֹצֵר בְּרֵאשִׁית,
שֶׁלֹּא עָשָׂנוּ כְּגוֹיֵי הָאֲרָצוֹת, וְלֹא שָׂמָנוּ כְּמִשְׁפְּחוֹת הָאֲדָמָה;
שֶׁלֹּא שָׂם חֶלְקֵנוּ כָּהֶם, וְגֹרָלֵנוּ כְּכָל הֲמוֹנָם. וַאֲנַחְנוּ כּוֹרְעִים
וּמִשְׁתַּחֲוִים וּמוֹדִים לִפְנֵי מֶלֶךְ מַלְכֵי הַמְּלָכִים, הַקָּדוֹשׁ בָּרוּךְ
הוּא, שֶׁהוּא נוֹטֶה שָׁמַיִם וְיוֹסֵד אָרֶץ, וּמוֹשַׁב יְקָרוֹ בַּשָּׁמַיִם
מִמַּעַל, וּשְׁכִינַת עֻזּוֹ בְּגָבְהֵי מְרוֹמִים. הוּא אֱלֹהֵינוּ, אֵין עוֹד;
אֱמֶת מַלְכֵּנוּ, אֶפֶס זוּלָתוֹ, כַּכָּתוּב בְּתוֹרָתוֹ: וְיָדַעְתָּ הַיּוֹם
וַהֲשֵׁבֹתָ אֶל לְבָבֶךָ, כִּי יְיָ הוּא הָאֱלֹהִים בַּשָּׁמַיִם מִמַּעַל וְעַל
הָאָרֶץ מִתָּחַת, אֵין עוֹד.

Reader:

Glorified and sanctified be God's great name throughout the world which he has created according to his will. May he establish his kingdom in your lifetime and during your days, and within the life of the entire house of Israel, speedily and soon; and say, Amen.

May his great name be blessed forever and to all eternity.

Blessed and praised, glorified and exalted, extolled and honored, adored and lauded be the name of the Holy One, blessed be he, beyond all the blessings and hymns, praises and consolations that are ever spoken in the world; and say, Amen.

May the prayers and supplications of the whole household of Israel be accepted by their Father who is in heaven; and say, Amen.

May there be abundant peace from heaven, and life, for us and for all Israel; and say, Amen.

He who creates peace in his celestial heights, may he create peace for us and for all Israel; and say, Amen.

ALENU

It is our duty to praise the Master of all, to exalt the Creator of the universe, who has not made us like the nations of the world and has not placed us like the families of the earth; who has not designed our destiny to be like theirs, nor our lot like that of all their multitude. We bend the knee and bow and acknowledge before the supreme King of kings, the Holy One, blessed be he, that it is he who stretched forth the heavens and founded the earth. His seat of glory is in the heavens above; his abode of majesty is in the lofty heights. He is our God, there is none else; truly, he is our King, there is none besides him, as it is written in his Torah: "You shall know this day, and reflect in your heart, that it is the Lord who is God in the heavens above and on the earth beneath, there is none else."[1]

---

[1] *Deuteronomy* 4:39.

עַל כֵּן נְקַוֶּה לְּךָ, יְיָ אֱלֹהֵינוּ, לִרְאוֹת מְהֵרָה בְּתִפְאֶרֶת עֻזֶּךָ, לְהַעֲבִיר גִּלּוּלִים מִן הָאָרֶץ, וְהָאֱלִילִים כָּרוֹת יִכָּרֵתוּן; לְתַקֵּן עוֹלָם בְּמַלְכוּת שַׁדַּי, וְכָל בְּנֵי בָשָׂר יִקְרְאוּ בִשְׁמֶךָ, לְהַפְנוֹת אֵלֶיךָ כָּל רִשְׁעֵי אָרֶץ. יַכִּירוּ וְיֵדְעוּ כָּל יוֹשְׁבֵי תֵבֵל, כִּי לְךָ תִּכְרַע כָּל בֶּרֶךְ, תִּשָּׁבַע כָּל לָשׁוֹן. לְפָנֶיךָ, יְיָ אֱלֹהֵינוּ, יִכְרְעוּ וְיִפֹּלוּ, וְלִכְבוֹד שִׁמְךָ יְקָר יִתֵּנוּ, וִיקַבְּלוּ כֻלָּם אֶת עֹל מַלְכוּתֶךָ, וְתִמְלוֹךְ עֲלֵיהֶם מְהֵרָה לְעוֹלָם וָעֶד. כִּי הַמַּלְכוּת שֶׁלְּךָ הִיא, וּלְעוֹלְמֵי עַד תִּמְלוֹךְ בְּכָבוֹד, כַּכָּתוּב בְּתוֹרָתֶךָ: יְיָ יִמְלֹךְ לְעֹלָם וָעֶד. Reader · וְנֶאֱמַר: וְהָיָה יְיָ לְמֶלֶךְ עַל כָּל הָאָרֶץ; בַּיּוֹם הַהוּא יִהְיֶה יְיָ אֶחָד וּשְׁמוֹ אֶחָד.

MOURNERS' KADDISH

יִתְגַּדַּל וְיִתְקַדַּשׁ שְׁמֵהּ רַבָּא בְּעָלְמָא דִּי בְרָא כִרְעוּתֵהּ; וְיַמְלִיךְ מַלְכוּתֵהּ בְּחַיֵּיכוֹן וּבְיוֹמֵיכוֹן וּבְחַיֵּי דְכָל בֵּית יִשְׂרָאֵל, בַּעֲגָלָא וּבִזְמַן קָרִיב, וְאִמְרוּ אָמֵן.

יְהֵא שְׁמֵהּ רַבָּא מְבָרַךְ לְעָלַם וּלְעָלְמֵי עָלְמַיָּא.

יִתְבָּרַךְ וְיִשְׁתַּבַּח, וְיִתְפָּאַר וְיִתְרוֹמַם, וְיִתְנַשֵּׂא וְיִתְהַדָּר, וְיִתְעַלֶּה וְיִתְהַלָּל שְׁמֵהּ דְּקֻדְשָׁא, בְּרִיךְ הוּא, לְעֵלָּא (לְעֵלָּא) מִן כָּל בִּרְכָתָא וְשִׁירָתָא, תֻּשְׁבְּחָתָא וְנֶחֱמָתָא, דַּאֲמִירָן בְּעָלְמָא, וְאִמְרוּ אָמֵן.

יְהֵא שְׁלָמָא רַבָּא מִן שְׁמַיָּא, וְחַיִּים, עָלֵינוּ וְעַל כָּל יִשְׂרָאֵל, וְאִמְרוּ אָמֵן.

עֹשֶׂה שָׁלוֹם בִּמְרוֹמָיו, הוּא יַעֲשֶׂה שָׁלוֹם עָלֵינוּ וְעַל כָּל יִשְׂרָאֵל, וְאִמְרוּ אָמֵן.

אַל תִּירָא מִפַּחַד פִּתְאֹם, וּמִשֹּׁאַת רְשָׁעִים כִּי תָבֹא. עֻצוּ עֵצָה וְתֻפָר, דַּבְּרוּ דָבָר וְלֹא יָקוּם, כִּי עִמָּנוּ אֵל. וְעַד זִקְנָה

We hope therefore, Lord our God, soon to behold thy majestic glory, when the abominations shall be removed from the earth, and the false gods exterminated; when the world shall be perfected under the reign of the Almighty, and all mankind will call upon thy name, and all the wicked of the earth will be turned to thee. May all the inhabitants of the world realize and know that to thee every knee must bend, every tongue must vow allegiance. May they bend the knee and prostrate themselves before thee, Lord our God, and give honor to thy glorious name; may they all accept the yoke of thy kingdom, and do thou reign over them speedily forever and ever. For the kingdom is thine, and to all eternity thou wilt reign in glory, as it is written in thy Torah: "The Lord shall be King forever and ever."[1] And it is said: "The Lord shall be King over all the earth; on that day the Lord shall be One, and his name One."[2]

MOURNERS' KADDISH

Glorified and sanctified be God's great name throughout the world which he has created according to his will. May he establish his kingdom in your lifetime and during your days, and within the life of the entire house of Israel, speedily and soon; and say, Amen.

May his great name be blessed forever and to all eternity.

Blessed and praised, glorified and exalted, extolled and honored, adored and lauded be the name of the Holy One, blessed be he, beyond all the blessings and hymns, praises and consolations that are ever spoken in the world; and say, Amen.

May there be abundant peace from heaven, and life, for us and for all Israel; and say, Amen.

He who creates peace in his celestial heights, may he create peace for us and for all Israel; and say, Amen.

Be not afraid of sudden terror, nor of the storm that strikes the wicked. Form your plot—it shall fail; lay your plan—it shall not prevail! For God is with us. Even to your old age I will be the

[1] *Exodus* 15:18.   [2] *Zechariah* 14:9.

אֲנִי הוּא, וְעַד שֵׂיבָה אֲנִי אֶסְבֹּל; אֲנִי עָשִׂיתִי וַאֲנִי אֶשָּׂא, וַאֲנִי
אֶסְבֹּל וַאֲמַלֵּט.

The following psalms are recited on the Sabbaths between *Sukkoth* and *Pesaḥ*.

תהלים קד

בָּרְכִי נַפְשִׁי אֶת יְיָ; יְיָ אֱלֹהַי, גָּדַלְתָּ מְאֹד; הוֹד וְהָדָר
לָבָשְׁתָּ. עֹטֶה אוֹר כַּשַּׂלְמָה, נוֹטֶה שָׁמַיִם כַּיְרִיעָה. הַמְקָרֶה
בַמַּיִם עֲלִיּוֹתָיו, הַשָּׂם עָבִים רְכוּבוֹ, הַמְהַלֵּךְ עַל כַּנְפֵי רוּחַ.
עֹשֶׂה מַלְאָכָיו רוּחוֹת, מְשָׁרְתָיו אֵשׁ לֹהֵט. יָסַד אֶרֶץ עַל
מְכוֹנֶיהָ, בַּל תִּמּוֹט עוֹלָם וָעֶד. תְּהוֹם כַּלְּבוּשׁ כִּסִּיתוֹ; עַל הָרִים
יַעַמְדוּ מָיִם. מִן גַּעֲרָתְךָ יְנוּסוּן, מִן קוֹל רַעַמְךָ יֵחָפֵזוּן. יַעֲלוּ
הָרִים, יֵרְדוּ בְקָעוֹת, אֶל מְקוֹם זֶה יָסַדְתָּ לָהֶם. גְּבוּל שַׂמְתָּ
בַּל יַעֲבֹרוּן, בַּל יְשׁוּבוּן לְכַסּוֹת הָאָרֶץ. הַמְשַׁלֵּחַ מַעְיָנִים
בַּנְּחָלִים; בֵּין הָרִים יְהַלֵּכוּן. יַשְׁקוּ כָּל חַיְתוֹ שָׂדָי; יִשְׁבְּרוּ
פְרָאִים צְמָאָם. עֲלֵיהֶם עוֹף הַשָּׁמַיִם יִשְׁכּוֹן; מִבֵּין עֳפָאיִם יִתְּנוּ
קוֹל. מַשְׁקֶה הָרִים מֵעֲלִיּוֹתָיו; מִפְּרִי מַעֲשֶׂיךָ תִּשְׂבַּע הָאָרֶץ.
מַצְמִיחַ חָצִיר לַבְּהֵמָה, וְעֵשֶׂב לַעֲבֹדַת הָאָדָם, לְהוֹצִיא לֶחֶם
מִן הָאָרֶץ. וְיַיִן יְשַׂמַּח לְבַב אֱנוֹשׁ, לְהַצְהִיל פָּנִים מִשָּׁמֶן; וְלֶחֶם
לְבַב אֱנוֹשׁ יִסְעָד. יִשְׂבְּעוּ עֲצֵי יְיָ, אַרְזֵי לְבָנוֹן אֲשֶׁר נָטָע. אֲשֶׁר
שָׁם צִפֳּרִים יְקַנֵּנוּ; חֲסִידָה, בְּרוֹשִׁים בֵּיתָהּ. הָרִים הַגְּבֹהִים
לַיְּעֵלִים, סְלָעִים מַחְסֶה לַשְׁפַנִּים. עָשָׂה יָרֵחַ לְמוֹעֲדִים; שֶׁמֶשׁ
יָדַע מְבוֹאוֹ. תָּשֶׁת חֹשֶׁךְ וִיהִי לָיְלָה; בּוֹ תִרְמֹשׂ כָּל חַיְתוֹ יָעַר.
הַכְּפִירִים שֹׁאֲגִים לַטָּרֶף, וּלְבַקֵּשׁ מֵאֵל אָכְלָם. תִּזְרַח הַשֶּׁמֶשׁ
יֵאָסֵפוּן, וְאֶל מְעוֹנֹתָם יִרְבָּצוּן. יֵצֵא אָדָם לְפָעֳלוֹ, וְלַעֲבֹדָתוֹ

ברכי נפשי (Psalm 104) is closely similar to the story of creation in Genesis. The psalmist celebrates God's glory as seen in the forces of nature. It has been declared that it is worthwhile studying the Hebrew language for ten years in order to read Psalm 104 in the original.

same; when you are gray-headed, still I will sustain you; I have made you, and I will bear you; I will sustain you and save you.[1]

The following psalms are recited on the Sabbaths between Sukkoth and Pesaḥ.

Psalm 104

Bless the Lord, my soul! Lord my God, thou art very great; thou art robed in glory and majesty. Thou wrappest thyself in light as in a garment; thou spreadest the heavens like a curtain. Thou buildest thy upper chambers on the waters; thou makest clouds thy chariot, and ridest on the wings of the wind. Thou makest winds thy messengers, the flaming fire thy servant.

Thou didst establish the earth upon its pillars, that it might never be shaken. Thou hadst covered it with the deep as with a garment; the waters stood above the mountains. At thy rebuke they fled; at the sound of thy thunder they hastened away. The mountains rose, the valleys sank down, to the place which thou hadst founded for them. Thou didst set a limit which they should not cross over, so that they should not again cover the earth.

Thou sendest forth streams into the valleys; they run between the mountains. They furnish drink for all the beasts of the field; the wild asses quench their thirst there. Beside them the birds of the sky dwell; from among the branches they sing. Thou waterest the mountains from thy upper chambers; the earth is full of the fruit of thy works.

Thou makest grass grow for the cattle, and fodder for the working animals of man, to bring forth bread from the earth, and wine that cheers man's heart, making his face brighter than oil, and bread that stays man's heart. The trees of the Lord drink their fill, the cedars of Lebanon which he has planted, wherein the birds make their nests, the stork with her home in the cypress. The high mountains are for the wild goats; the rocks are a refuge for the rabbits.

Thou hast made the moon for marking the seasons; the sun knows its time of setting. Thou makest darkness and it is night, wherein all the beasts of the forest creep forth. The young lions roar after their prey, and seek their food from God. When the sun rises, they slink away and couch in their dens. Man goes forth to his work, to his labor until evening.

---

[1] *Proverbs* 3:25; *Isaiah* 8:10; 46:4.

עֲרֵי עָרֶב. מָה רַבּוּ מַעֲשֶׂיךָ, יְיָ; כֻּלָּם בְּחָכְמָה עָשִׂיתָ; מָלְאָה
הָאָרֶץ קִנְיָנֶךָ. זֶה הַיָּם גָּדוֹל וּרְחַב יָדָיִם, שָׁם רֶמֶשׂ וְאֵין מִסְפָּר,
חַיּוֹת קְטַנּוֹת עִם גְּדֹלוֹת. שָׁם אֳנִיּוֹת יְהַלֵּכוּן, לִוְיָתָן זֶה יָצַרְתָּ
לְשַׂחֶק־בּוֹ. כֻּלָּם אֵלֶיךָ יְשַׂבֵּרוּן, לָתֵת אָכְלָם בְּעִתּוֹ. תִּתֵּן לָהֶם
יִלְקֹטוּן, תִּפְתַּח יָדְךָ יִשְׂבְּעוּן טוֹב. תַּסְתִּיר פָּנֶיךָ יִבָּהֵלוּן, תֹּסֵף
רוּחָם יִגְוָעוּן, וְאֶל עֲפָרָם יְשׁוּבוּן. תְּשַׁלַּח רוּחֲךָ יִבָּרֵאוּן, וּתְחַדֵּשׁ
פְּנֵי אֲדָמָה. יְהִי כְבוֹד יְיָ לְעוֹלָם; יִשְׂמַח יְיָ בְּמַעֲשָׂיו. הַמַּבִּיט
לָאָרֶץ וַתִּרְעָד, יִגַּע בֶּהָרִים וְיֶעֱשָׁנוּ. אָשִׁירָה לַיְיָ בְּחַיָּי, אֲזַמְּרָה
לֵאלֹהַי בְּעוֹדִי. יֶעֱרַב עָלָיו שִׂיחִי; אָנֹכִי אֶשְׂמַח בַּיְיָ. יִתַּמּוּ
חַטָּאִים מִן הָאָרֶץ, וּרְשָׁעִים עוֹד אֵינָם; בָּרְכִי נַפְשִׁי אֶת יְיָ;
הַלְלוּיָהּ.

תהלים קכ

שִׁיר הַמַּעֲלוֹת. אֶל יְיָ, בַּצָּרָתָה לִּי, קָרָאתִי וַיַּעֲנֵנִי. יְיָ,
הַצִּילָה נַפְשִׁי מִשְּׂפַת שֶׁקֶר, מִלָּשׁוֹן רְמִיָּה. מַה יִּתֵּן לְךָ, וּמַה
יֹּסִיף לָךְ, לָשׁוֹן רְמִיָּה. חִצֵּי גִבּוֹר שְׁנוּנִים, עִם גַּחֲלֵי רְתָמִים.
אוֹיָה־לִי, כִּי גַרְתִּי מֶשֶׁךְ; שָׁכַנְתִּי עִם אָהֳלֵי קֵדָר. רַבַּת שָׁכְנָה
לָּהּ נַפְשִׁי עִם שׂוֹנֵא שָׁלוֹם. אֲנִי שָׁלוֹם, וְכִי אֲדַבֵּר, הֵמָּה
לַמִּלְחָמָה.

תהלים קכא

שִׁיר לַמַּעֲלוֹת. אֶשָּׂא עֵינַי אֶל הֶהָרִים, מֵאַיִן יָבוֹא עֶזְרִי.
עֶזְרִי מֵעִם יְיָ, עֹשֵׂה שָׁמַיִם וָאָרֶץ. אַל יִתֵּן לַמּוֹט רַגְלֶךָ, אַל יָנוּם

שיר המעלות, the title prefixed to the following fifteen psalms, is now generally understood to mean a psalm sung by the pilgrims as they went up to
Jerusalem to celebrate the three pilgrim festivals in the center of national and
religious life.

Psalm 120 is directed against slanderers. They are doomed to severe
punishment. They shall be pierced with sharp arrows and burned with the hot
charcoal of the broom bush. משך and קדר, wild tribes, symbolize barbarian
enemies.

How manifold are thy works, O Lord! In wisdom hast thou made them all; the earth is full of thy creations. There is the sea, vast and broad, wherein are creeping things innumerable, creatures small and great. There go the ships; there is the leviathan, which thou hast created to frolic therein. All of them wait for thee to give them their food at the right time. What thou givest them, they gather up; when thou openest thy hand, they are satisfied with good things. When thou hidest thy face, they vanish; when thou takest away their breath, they die and turn again to dust. When thou sendest forth thy spirit they are created, and thou renewest the face of the earth.

May the glory of the Lord be forever; may the Lord rejoice in his works! He looks on the earth, and it trembles; he touches the mountains, and they smoke. I will sing to the Lord as long as I live; I will sing praise to my God while I exist. May my meditation please him; I will rejoice in the Lord. Sinners shall vanish from the earth, and the wicked shall be no more. Bless the Lord, my soul! Praise the Lord!

Psalm 120

A Pilgrim Song. In my distress I called to the Lord, and he answered me. O Lord, save me from lying lips, from a deceitful tongue. What will a deceitful tongue give you, what will it profit you? Sharp arrows of a warrior with burning coals of broom! Woe is me that I dwell in Meshek, that I reside amid the tents of Kedar Too long have I been living where men hate peace. I am all for peace; but when I speak, they are for war.

Psalm 121

A Pilgrim Song. I lift my eyes to the hills; whence will my help come? My help comes from the Lord who made heaven and earth. He will not let your foot slip; he who guards you will not slumber.

Psalm 121 is a perfect expression of trust in God, and has been on the lips of countless people when they felt the need of help beyond that which, mortals can offer.

שֹׁמְרֶךָ. הִנֵּה לֹא יָנוּם וְלֹא יִישָׁן, שׁוֹמֵר יִשְׂרָאֵל. יְיָ שֹׁמְרֶךָ, יְיָ צִלְּךָ, עַל יַד יְמִינֶךָ. יוֹמָם הַשֶּׁמֶשׁ לֹא יַכֶּכָּה, וְיָרֵחַ בַּלָּיְלָה. יְיָ יִשְׁמָרְךָ מִכָּל רָע, יִשְׁמֹר אֶת נַפְשֶׁךָ. יְיָ יִשְׁמָר־צֵאתְךָ וּבוֹאֶךָ, מֵעַתָּה וְעַד עוֹלָם.

תהלים קכב

שִׁיר הַמַּעֲלוֹת לְדָוִד. שָׂמַחְתִּי בְּאֹמְרִים לִי, בֵּית יְיָ נֵלֵךְ. עֹמְדוֹת הָיוּ רַגְלֵינוּ בִּשְׁעָרַיִךְ, יְרוּשָׁלָיִם. יְרוּשָׁלַיִם הַבְּנוּיָה כְּעִיר שֶׁחֻבְּרָה־לָּהּ יַחְדָּו. שֶׁשָּׁם עָלוּ שְׁבָטִים, שִׁבְטֵי יָהּ, עֵדוּת לְיִשְׂרָאֵל, לְהֹדוֹת לְשֵׁם יְיָ. כִּי שָׁמָּה יָשְׁבוּ כִסְאוֹת לְמִשְׁפָּט, כִּסְאוֹת לְבֵית דָּוִד. שַׁאֲלוּ שְׁלוֹם יְרוּשָׁלָיִם; יִשְׁלָיוּ אֹהֲבָיִךְ. יְהִי שָׁלוֹם בְּחֵילֵךְ, שַׁלְוָה בְּאַרְמְנוֹתָיִךְ. לְמַעַן אַחַי וְרֵעָי, אֲדַבְּרָה נָּא שָׁלוֹם בָּךְ. לְמַעַן בֵּית יְיָ אֱלֹהֵינוּ, אֲבַקְשָׁה טוֹב לָךְ.

תהלים קכג

שִׁיר הַמַּעֲלוֹת. אֵלֶיךָ נָשָׂאתִי אֶת עֵינַי, הַיֹּשְׁבִי בַּשָּׁמָיִם. הִנֵּה כְעֵינֵי עֲבָדִים אֶל יַד אֲדוֹנֵיהֶם, כְּעֵינֵי שִׁפְחָה אֶל יַד גְּבִרְתָּהּ, כֵּן עֵינֵינוּ אֶל יְיָ אֱלֹהֵינוּ, עַד שֶׁיְּחָנֵּנוּ. חָנֵּנוּ יְיָ חָנֵּנוּ, כִּי רַב שָׂבַעְנוּ בוּז. רַבַּת שָׂבְעָה לָּהּ נַפְשֵׁנוּ הַלַּעַג הַשַּׁאֲנַנִּים, הַבּוּז לִגְאֵי־יוֹנִים.

תהלים קכד

שִׁיר הַמַּעֲלוֹת לְדָוִד. לוּלֵי יְיָ שֶׁהָיָה לָנוּ, יֹאמַר נָא יִשְׂרָאֵל. לוּלֵי יְיָ שֶׁהָיָה לָנוּ, בְּקוּם עָלֵינוּ אָדָם. אֲזַי חַיִּים בְּלָעוּנוּ, בַּחֲרוֹת אַפָּם בָּנוּ. אֲזַי הַמַּיִם שְׁטָפוּנוּ, נַחְלָה עָבַר עַל נַפְשֵׁנוּ. אֲזַי עָבַר עַל נַפְשֵׁנוּ הַמַּיִם הַזֵּידוֹנִים. בָּרוּךְ יְיָ, שֶׁלֹּא נְתָנָנוּ טֶרֶף לְשִׁנֵּיהֶם. נַפְשֵׁנוּ כְּצִפּוֹר נִמְלְטָה מִפַּח יוֹקְשִׁים; הַפַּח נִשְׁבָּר, וַאֲנַחְנוּ נִמְלָטְנוּ. עֶזְרֵנוּ בְּשֵׁם יְיָ, עֹשֵׂה שָׁמַיִם וָאָרֶץ.

Psalm 122 is a pilgrim's recollection of a visit to Jerusalem and the many sacred memories associated with that magnificent city.

Psalm 123 begins in the singular and continues in the plural. It is a hymn of faith composed in a time of distress, contemptuous scorn and mockery.

Behold, the guardian of Israel neither slumbers nor sleeps. The Lord is your guardian; the Lord is your shelter upon your right hand. The sun shall never hurt you in the day, nor the moon by night. The Lord will guard you from all evil; the Lord will guard your life. The Lord will guard you as you come and go, henceforth and forever.

Psalm 122

A Pilgrim Song by David. I was glad when they said to me: "Let us go to the house of the Lord." Our feet are standing within your gates, O Jerusalem; Jerusalem that is rebuilt like a city that is compact altogether; whither the tribes went on pilgrimage, the tribes of the Lord, as a testimony of Israel, to offer praise to the name of the Lord. There, indeed, were set the seats of justice, the thrones of the house of David. Pray for the welfare of Jerusalem; they will prosper who love you. May all go well within your walls, within your palaces. For the sake of my brethren and friends I pray: "May all be well with you!" For the sake of the house of the Lord our God I seek your good.

Psalm 123

A Pilgrim Song. To thee I lift my eyes, O thou who dwellest in heaven. Lo, as the eyes of servants look to the hand of their master, and as a maid's eyes to the hand of her mistress, so our eyes look to the Lord our God, till he take pity on us. Have pity on us, O Lord, have pity on us, for we are full sated with contempt. We are full sated with the sneering of those who live at ease, with the contempt of the arrogant.

Psalm 124

A Pilgrim Song by David. "Had not the Lord been on our side," let Israel say, "had not the Lord been on our side when men rose up against us, they would have swallowed us alive when their anger blazed forth against us; the floods would have swept us away, the torrent would have surged over us, the impetuous waters would have gone over us." Blessed be the Lord, who did not give us as a prey to their teeth. We are like a bird escaped from a fowler's snare; the snare is broken and we have escaped. Our help is in the name of the Lord, who made heaven and earth.

Psalm 124 commemorates an escape from some imminent danger.

תהלים קכה

שִׁיר הַמַּעֲלוֹת. הַבֹּטְחִים בַּיְיָ, כְּהַר צִיּוֹן לֹא יִמּוֹט, לְעוֹלָם יֵשֵׁב. יְרוּשָׁלַם הָרִים סָבִיב לָהּ, וַיְיָ סָבִיב לְעַמּוֹ, מֵעַתָּה וְעַד עוֹלָם. כִּי לֹא יָנוּחַ שֵׁבֶט הָרֶשַׁע עַל גּוֹרַל הַצַּדִּיקִים, לְמַעַן לֹא יִשְׁלְחוּ הַצַּדִּיקִים בְּעַוְלָתָה יְדֵיהֶם. הֵיטִיבָה, יְיָ, לַטּוֹבִים, וְלִישָׁרִים בְּלִבּוֹתָם. וְהַמַּטִּים עֲקַלְקַלּוֹתָם, יוֹלִיכֵם יְיָ אֶת פֹּעֲלֵי הָאָוֶן; שָׁלוֹם עַל יִשְׂרָאֵל.

תהלים קכו

שִׁיר הַמַּעֲלוֹת. בְּשׁוּב יְיָ אֶת שִׁיבַת צִיּוֹן הָיִינוּ כְּחֹלְמִים. אָז יִמָּלֵא שְׂחוֹק פִּינוּ, וּלְשׁוֹנֵנוּ רִנָּה; אָז יֹאמְרוּ בַגּוֹיִם, הִגְדִּיל יְיָ לַעֲשׂוֹת עִם אֵלֶּה. הִגְדִּיל יְיָ לַעֲשׂוֹת עִמָּנוּ, הָיִינוּ שְׂמֵחִים. שׁוּבָה יְיָ אֶת שְׁבִיתֵנוּ, כַּאֲפִיקִים בַּנֶּגֶב. הַזֹּרְעִים בְּדִמְעָה, בְּרִנָּה יִקְצֹרוּ. הָלוֹךְ יֵלֵךְ וּבָכֹה נֹשֵׂא מֶשֶׁךְ הַזָּרַע; בֹּא יָבֹא בְרִנָּה נֹשֵׂא אֲלֻמֹּתָיו.

תהלים קכז

שִׁיר הַמַּעֲלוֹת לִשְׁלֹמֹה. אִם יְיָ לֹא יִבְנֶה בַיִת, שָׁוְא עָמְלוּ בוֹנָיו בּוֹ; אִם יְיָ לֹא יִשְׁמָר־עִיר, שָׁוְא שָׁקַד שׁוֹמֵר. שָׁוְא לָכֶם, מַשְׁכִּימֵי קוּם, מְאַחֲרֵי שֶׁבֶת, אֹכְלֵי לֶחֶם הָעֲצָבִים; כֵּן יִתֵּן לִידִידוֹ שֵׁנָא. הִנֵּה נַחֲלַת יְיָ בָּנִים, שָׂכָר פְּרִי הַבָּטֶן. כְּחִצִּים בְּיַד גִּבּוֹר, כֵּן בְּנֵי הַנְּעוּרִים. אַשְׁרֵי הַגֶּבֶר אֲשֶׁר מִלֵּא אֶת אַשְׁפָּתוֹ מֵהֶם: לֹא יֵבֹשׁוּ כִּי יְדַבְּרוּ אֶת אוֹיְבִים בַּשָּׁעַר.

תהלים קכח

שִׁיר הַמַּעֲלוֹת. אַשְׁרֵי כָּל יְרֵא יְיָ, הַהֹלֵךְ בִּדְרָכָיו. יְגִיעַ כַּפֶּיךָ כִּי תֹאכֵל, אַשְׁרֶיךָ וְטוֹב לָךְ. אֶשְׁתְּךָ כְּגֶפֶן פֹּרִיָּה בְּיַרְכְּתֵי

Psalm 125 expresses the unshakable confidence of Israel in God, and the assurance that the evildoers shall perish.

Psalm 126 is a song of those who have been redeemed from exile, and a hopeful prayer for those who have not yet returned. כאפיקים בנגב like the hill

Psalm 125

A Pilgrim Song. Those who trust in the Lord are like Mount Zion which cannot be shaken, but abides forever. The mountains are round about Jerusalem, and the Lord is round about his people, henceforth and forever. Verily, the wicked scepter shall not stay in the land of the righteous, or else the righteous themselves might take to evil. Do good, O Lord, to those who are good, to those who are upright in heart. But as for those who turn to their crooked ways, may the Lord lead them [to destruction] together with the evildoers. Peace be on Israel!

Psalm 126

A Pilgrim Song. When the Lord brought the exiles back to Zion, we were like those who dream. Our mouth was filled with laughter, and our tongue with ringing song; then it was said among the nations: "The Lord has done great things for them." The Lord had done great things for us, and we rejoiced. Restore our fortunes O Lord, like streams in the Negev. Those who are sowing in tears shall reap in joy. Sadly the farmer bears the bag of seed to the field; he shall come home with joy, bearing his sheaves.

Psalm 127

A Pilgrim Song by Solomon. Unless the Lord builds a house, its builders toil on it in vain; unless the Lord guards a city, the watchman wakes in vain. It is vain for you to rise early and sit up late, gaining your bread with anxious toil! God's gifts come to his loved ones during sleep. Lo, children are a gift of the Lord; offspring is a reward from him. Like arrows in the hand of a warrior, so are the children of one's youth. Happy is the man whose quiver is filled with them! They will not be put to shame when they speak with their enemies in the gate.

Psalm 128

A Pilgrim Song. Happy is everyone who reveres the Lord, who walks in his ways. When you eat the toil of your hands, you shall be happy and at ease. Your wife shall be like a fruitful vine

---

streams of the Negev, dry in summer but becoming suddenly swollen torrents in the rains of the autumn.

Psalm 127 is a warning against over-anxiety in any work. Man's labor is in vain without God's help. A numerous family is one of God's special blessings; it secures for the parents influence and respect.

Psalm 128 contains a picture of an ideal homelife. The welfare of the state depends upon virtuous family life.

בֵּיתֶךָ, בָּנֶיךָ כִּשְׁתִילֵי זֵיתִים סָבִיב לְשֻׁלְחָנֶךָ. הִנֵּה כִי כֵן יְבֹרַךְ
גָּבֶר, יְרֵא יְיָ. יְבָרֶכְךָ יְיָ מִצִּיוֹן, וּרְאֵה בְּטוּב יְרוּשָׁלָםִ, כֹּל יְמֵי
חַיֶּיךָ. וּרְאֵה בָנִים לְבָנֶיךָ; שָׁלוֹם עַל יִשְׂרָאֵל.

תהלים קכט

שִׁיר הַמַּעֲלוֹת. רַבַּת צְרָרוּנִי מִנְּעוּרַי, יֹאמַר נָא יִשְׂרָאֵל.
רַבַּת צְרָרוּנִי מִנְּעוּרָי, גַּם לֹא יָכְלוּ לִי. עַל גַּבִּי חָרְשׁוּ חֹרְשִׁים,
הֶאֱרִיכוּ לְמַעֲנִיתָם. יְיָ צַדִּיק, קִצֵּץ עֲבוֹת רְשָׁעִים. יֵבֹשׁוּ וְיִסֹּגוּ
אָחוֹר כֹּל שֹׂנְאֵי צִיּוֹן. יִהְיוּ כַּחֲצִיר גַּגּוֹת, שֶׁקַּדְמַת שָׁלַף יָבֵשׁ.
שֶׁלֹּא מִלֵּא כַפּוֹ קוֹצֵר, וְחִצְנוֹ מְעַמֵּר. וְלֹא אָמְרוּ הָעֹבְרִים
בִּרְכַּת יְיָ אֲלֵיכֶם, בֵּרַכְנוּ אֶתְכֶם בְּשֵׁם יְיָ.

תהלים קל

שִׁיר הַמַּעֲלוֹת. מִמַּעֲמַקִּים קְרָאתִיךָ, יְיָ, אֲדֹנָי, שִׁמְעָה
בְקוֹלִי, תִּהְיֶינָה אָזְנֶיךָ קַשֻּׁבוֹת לְקוֹל תַּחֲנוּנָי. אִם עֲוֹנוֹת תִּשְׁמָר־
יָהּ, אֲדֹנָי, מִי יַעֲמֹד. כִּי עִמְּךָ הַסְּלִיחָה, לְמַעַן תִּוָּרֵא. קִוִּיתִי
יְיָ, קִוְּתָה נַפְשִׁי, וְלִדְבָרוֹ הוֹחָלְתִּי. נַפְשִׁי לַאדֹנָי מִשֹּׁמְרִים
לַבֹּקֶר, שֹׁמְרִים לַבֹּקֶר. יַחֵל יִשְׂרָאֵל אֶל יְיָ, כִּי עִם יְיָ הַחֶסֶד,
וְהַרְבֵּה עִמּוֹ פְדוּת. וְהוּא יִפְדֶּה אֶת יִשְׂרָאֵל מִכֹּל עֲוֹנוֹתָיו.

תהלים קלא

שִׁיר הַמַּעֲלוֹת לְדָוִד. יְיָ, לֹא גָבַהּ לִבִּי, וְלֹא רָמוּ עֵינַי, וְלֹא
הִלַּכְתִּי בִּגְדֹלוֹת וּבְנִפְלָאוֹת מִמֶּנִּי. אִם לֹא שִׁוִּיתִי וְדוֹמַמְתִּי,
נַפְשִׁי כְּגָמֻל עֲלֵי אִמּוֹ, כַּגָּמֻל עָלַי נַפְשִׁי. יַחֵל יִשְׂרָאֵל אֶל יְיָ,
מֵעַתָּה וְעַד עוֹלָם.

Psalm 129 is a song of deliverance and the overthrow of the wicked. On
the flat roofs of oriental houses grass often springs up in the rainy season
but quickly withers, yielding nothing useful. So the enemies of Zion shall be
destroyed before their malicious schemes can mature.

Psalm 130 is an expression of remorse for sin and a plea for forgiveness.
Since God reveals himself as a forgiving God, Israel can hope and trust.

in the interior of your house; your children like olive plants. around your table. Behold, thus indeed shall the man be blessed who reveres the Lord. The Lord bless you from Zion; may you see the welfare of Jerusalem all the days of your life; may you live to see your children's children. Peace be upon Israel!

Psalm 129

A Pilgrim Song. "Much have they afflicted me from my youth up," let Israel say, "much have they afflicted me from my youth up, but they have never overcome me. The plowers plowed upon my back; they made their furrows long. The Lord is righteous; he has cut the cords of the wicked." May all who hate Zion be shamed and routed. Let them be like the grass on the roofs, that fades ere ever it flourishes, with which the reaper does not fill his hands, nor the binder of sheaves his bosom. Those passing by will not say: "The blessing of the Lord be upon you; we bless you in the name of the Lord!"

Psalm 130

A Pilgrim Song. Out of the depths I call to thee, O Lord. O Lord, hear my voice; let thy ears be attentive to my supplicating voice. If thou, O Lord, shouldst keep strict account of iniquities, O Lord, who could live on? But with thee there is forgiveness, that thou mayest be revered. I look for the Lord, my whole being hopes; I wait for his word. My soul waits for the Lord more eagerly than watchmen for the dawn, than watchmen for the dawn. O Israel, put your hope in the Lord, for with the Lord there is kindness; with him there is great saving power. It is he who will redeem Israel from all its iniquities.

Psalm 131

A Pilgrim Song by David. O Lord, my heart is not haughty, nor are my eyes lofty; neither do I concern myself with matters too great and too wonderful for me. Surely I have soothed and stilled my soul, like a weaned child with its mother; my soul is with me like a weaned child. O Israel, put your hope in the Lord, henceforth and forever.

Psalm 131 is a song of child-like humility. As the child that has gone through the troublesome process of weaning can lie happily in its mother's arms, so the psalmist's soul has found contentment and happiness through the discipline of humility.

תהלים קלב

שִׁיר הַמַּעֲלוֹת. זְכוֹר יְיָ לְדָוִד אֵת כָּל עֻנּוֹתוֹ. אֲשֶׁר נִשְׁבַּע
לַיְיָ, נָדַר לַאֲבִיר יַעֲקֹב. אִם אָבֹא בְּאֹהֶל בֵּיתִי, אִם אֶעֱלֶה עַל
עֶרֶשׂ יְצוּעָי. אִם אֶתֵּן שְׁנַת לְעֵינָי, לְעַפְעַפַּי תְּנוּמָה. עַד אֶמְצָא
מָקוֹם לַיְיָ, מִשְׁכָּנוֹת לַאֲבִיר יַעֲקֹב. הִנֵּה שְׁמַעֲנוּהָ בְאֶפְרָתָה,
מְצָאנוּהָ בִּשְׂדֵי יָעַר. נָבוֹאָה לְמִשְׁכְּנוֹתָיו, נִשְׁתַּחֲוֶה לַהֲדֹם רַגְלָיו.
קוּמָה יְיָ לִמְנוּחָתֶךָ, אַתָּה וַאֲרוֹן עֻזֶּךָ. כֹּהֲנֶיךָ יִלְבְּשׁוּ צֶדֶק,
וַחֲסִידֶיךָ יְרַנֵּנוּ. בַּעֲבוּר דָּוִד עַבְדֶּךָ, אַל תָּשֵׁב פְּנֵי מְשִׁיחֶךָ.
נִשְׁבַּע יְיָ לְדָוִד, אֱמֶת לֹא יָשׁוּב מִמֶּנָּה: מִפְּרִי בִטְנְךָ אָשִׁית
לְכִסֵּא לָךְ. אִם יִשְׁמְרוּ בָנֶיךָ בְּרִיתִי, וְעֵדֹתִי זוֹ אֲלַמְּדֵם, גַּם
בְּנֵיהֶם עֲדֵי עַד יֵשְׁבוּ לְכִסֵּא לָךְ. כִּי בָחַר יְיָ בְּצִיּוֹן, אִוָּהּ
לְמוֹשָׁב לוֹ. זֹאת מְנוּחָתִי עֲדֵי עַד, פֹּה אֵשֵׁב, כִּי אִוִּתִיהָ. צֵידָהּ
בָּרֵךְ אֲבָרֵךְ, אֶבְיוֹנֶיהָ אַשְׂבִּיעַ לָחֶם. וְכֹהֲנֶיהָ אַלְבִּישׁ יֶשַׁע,
וַחֲסִידֶיהָ רַנֵּן יְרַנֵּנוּ. שָׁם אַצְמִיחַ קֶרֶן לְדָוִד, עָרַכְתִּי נֵר
לִמְשִׁיחִי. אוֹיְבָיו אַלְבִּישׁ בֹּשֶׁת, וְעָלָיו יָצִיץ נִזְרוֹ.

תהלים קלג

שִׁיר הַמַּעֲלוֹת לְדָוִד. הִנֵּה מַה טּוֹב וּמַה נָּעִים שֶׁבֶת אַחִים
גַּם יָחַד. כַּשֶּׁמֶן הַטּוֹב עַל הָרֹאשׁ, יֹרֵד עַל הַזָּקָן, זְקַן אַהֲרֹן,
שֶׁיֹּרֵד עַל פִּי מִדּוֹתָיו. כְּטַל חֶרְמוֹן שֶׁיֹּרֵד עַל הַרְרֵי צִיּוֹן: כִּי
שָׁם צִוָּה יְיָ אֶת הַבְּרָכָה, חַיִּים עַד הָעוֹלָם.

תהלים קלד

שִׁיר הַמַּעֲלוֹת. הִנֵּה בָּרְכוּ אֶת יְיָ, כָּל עַבְדֵי יְיָ, הָעֹמְדִים
בְּבֵית יְיָ בַּלֵּילוֹת. שְׂאוּ יְדֵכֶם קֹדֶשׁ, וּבָרְכוּ אֶת יְיָ. יְבָרֶכְךָ יְיָ
מִצִּיּוֹן, עֹשֵׂה שָׁמַיִם וָאָרֶץ.

Psalm 132 contains the prayer that David's efforts in establishing a
sanctuary in Jerusalem should be well remembered and rewarded by God.

Psalm 132

A Pilgrim Song. O Lord, remember David and all his affliction; how he swore to the Lord, and vowed to the Mighty One of Jacob: "I will not enter my house, I will not lie on my bed, I will not give sleep to my eyes, nor slumber to my eyelids, until I find a place for the Lord, a residence for the Mighty One of Jacob." We heard of the ark in Ephrath; we found it in the fields of Yaar. Let us enter his dwelling; let us worship at his footstool. Arise, O Lord, to thy resting-place, thou and thy glorious ark. May thy priests be clothed in righteousness, and let my faithful followers sing for joy. For the sake of thy servant David, reject not thy own anointed. The Lord swore an oath to David, from which he will not swerve: "I will set one of your offspring on your throne. If your children will keep my covenant and the laws which I teach them, their children also shall sit on your throne forever." For the Lord has chosen Zion; he has desired it for his habitation. "This is my resting-place forever; here will I dwell, for I have desired it. I will richly bless its food supply; its needy I will satisfy with bread. Its priests will I clothe with triumph, and its godly shall sing for joy. There will I make David's dynasty flourish; there have I prepared a lamp for my anointed. His foes I will clothe with shame, but his own crown shall shine."

Psalm 133

A Pilgrim Song by David. Behold, how good and pleasant it is for brethren to dwell together in unity! It is like the precious oil upon the head, flowing down the beard, Aaron's beard, that comes down upon the edge of his robes. It is like the dew of Mount Hermon, that comes down upon the hills of Zion; for there the Lord commanded the blessing, life for evermore.

Psalm 134

A Pilgrim Song. Come bless the Lord, all you servants of the Lord, who nightly stand in the house of the Lord. Lift up your hands in holiness, and bless the Lord. May the Lord, who made heaven and earth, bless you from Zion.

Psalm 133 describes the blessing of unity and brotherly love. כשמן הטוב as the fragrant oil with which Aaron was anointed diffused its fragrance all around, so the spirit of amity and mutual friendship is spread throughout the environment.

Psalm 134 is a night-salutation addressed to the priests and Levites in the Temple, and their reply.

פִּרְקֵי אָבוֹת

Recited on the Sabbaths between *Pesaḥ* and *Rosh Hashanah*

כָּל יִשְׂרָאֵל יֵשׁ לָהֶם חֵלֶק לָעוֹלָם הַבָּא, שֶׁנֶּאֱמַר: וְעַמֵּךְ כֻּלָּם צַדִּיקִים, לְעוֹלָם יִירְשׁוּ אָרֶץ; נֵצֶר מַטָּעַי, מַעֲשֵׂה יָדַי לְהִתְפָּאֵר.

פֶּרֶק רִאשׁוֹן

א. מֹשֶׁה קִבֵּל תּוֹרָה מִסִּינַי, וּמְסָרָהּ לִיהוֹשֻׁעַ, וִיהוֹשֻׁעַ לִזְקֵנִים, וּזְקֵנִים לִנְבִיאִים, וּנְבִיאִים מְסָרוּהָ לְאַנְשֵׁי כְנֶסֶת הַגְּדוֹלָה. הֵם אָמְרוּ שְׁלֹשָׁה דְבָרִים: הֱווּ מְתוּנִים בַּדִּין, וְהַעֲמִידוּ תַלְמִידִים הַרְבֵּה, וַעֲשׂוּ סְיָג לַתּוֹרָה.

ב. שִׁמְעוֹן הַצַּדִּיק הָיָה מִשְּׁיָרֵי כְנֶסֶת הַגְּדוֹלָה. הוּא הָיָה אוֹמֵר: עַל שְׁלֹשָׁה דְבָרִים הָעוֹלָם עוֹמֵד: עַל הַתּוֹרָה, וְעַל הָעֲבוֹדָה, וְעַל גְּמִילוּת חֲסָדִים.

ג. אַנְטִיגְנוֹס אִישׁ שׂוֹכוֹ קִבֵּל מִשִּׁמְעוֹן הַצַּדִּיק. הוּא הָיָה אוֹמֵר: אַל תִּהְיוּ כַּעֲבָדִים הַמְשַׁמְּשִׁים אֶת הָרַב עַל מְנָת לְקַבֵּל פְּרָס, אֶלָּא הֱווּ כַּעֲבָדִים הַמְשַׁמְּשִׁים אֶת הָרַב שֶׁלֹּא עַל מְנָת לְקַבֵּל פְּרָס, וִיהִי מוֹרָא שָׁמַיִם עֲלֵיכֶם.

אבות, one of the sixty-three tractates of the Mishnah, deals with the ethical principles given by the fathers of Jewish tradition who flourished over a period of nearly five centuries, from the time of the last prophet to the end of the second century. Having achieved a place in the Prayerbook, *Avoth* became the most popular of all the books of the Mishnah and its contents exercised a most salutary influence on the Jewish people. The custom of reading *Pirke Avoth* ("Chapters of the Fathers") on Sabbath afternoons was originally limited, it seems, to the period between *Pesaḥ* and *Shavuoth*. A sixth chapter, derived from a source other than the Mishnah, was added to the five chapters of *Avoth* in order to provide a separate chapter for each of the six Sabbaths between the two festivals. The sixth chapter, called *Kinyan*

477

ETHICS OF THE FATHERS

Recited on the Sabbaths between Pesaḥ and Rosh Hashanah

All Israel have a share in the world to come, as it is said: "Your people shall all be righteous; they shall possess the land forever; they are a plant of my own, the work of my hands, wherein I may glory."[1]

CHAPTER ONE

1. Moses received the Torah at Sinai and handed it down to Joshua; Joshua to the elders; the elders to the prophets; and the prophets handed it down to the men of the Great Assembly. The latter said three things: Be patient in the administration of justice; develop many students; and make a fence for the Torah.

2. Simeon the Just was one of the last survivors of the Great Assembly. He used to say: The world is based on three principles: Torah, worship, and kindliness.

3. Antigonus of Sokho received the oral tradition from Simeon the Just. He used to say: Be not like servants who serve the master for the sake of receiving a reward, but be like servants who serve the master without the expectation of receiving a reward; and let the fear of Heaven be upon you.

Torah ("The Acquisition of Torah"), was chosen to be read on the Sabbath preceding *Shavuoth*, the anniversary of the giving of the Torah, because its subject-matter is almost exclusively in praise of the Torah. The liturgical use of *Avoth* on Sabbath afternoons is mentioned in the *Siddur* of Amram Gaon (ninth century).

כל ישראל introduces each chapter of *Avoth* in the Prayerbook. It is an excerpt from Mishnah Sanhedrin 11:1.

תורה consists of two parts: the written law and the oral law. The written law is contained in the Five Books of Moses, and the oral law consists of the traditional interpretations and amplifications handed down by word of mouth from generation to generation until finally embodied in the talmudic literature.

כנסת הגדולה a legislative body of 120 men said to have functioned during and after the Persian period in Jewish history, about 500-300 before the common era.

סיג לתורה additional regulations, designed to preserve the biblical laws.

אנטיגנוס a Greek name. מורא שמים reverence for God.

[1] *Isaiah* 60:21.

478

ד. יוֹסֵי בֶּן יוֹעֶזֶר, אִישׁ צְרֵדָה, וְיוֹסֵי בֶּן יוֹחָנָן, אִישׁ
יְרוּשָׁלַיִם, קִבְּלוּ מֵהֶם. יוֹסֵי בֶּן יוֹעֶזֶר, אִישׁ צְרֵדָה, אוֹמֵר: יְהִי
בֵיתְךָ בֵּית וָעַד לַחֲכָמִים, וֶהֱוֵי מִתְאַבֵּק בַּעֲפַר רַגְלֵיהֶם, וֶהֱוֵי
שׁוֹתֶה בַצָּמָא אֶת דִּבְרֵיהֶם.

ה. יוֹסֵי בֶּן יוֹחָנָן, אִישׁ יְרוּשָׁלַיִם, אוֹמֵר: יְהִי בֵיתְךָ פָּתוּחַ
לָרְוָחָה, וְיִהְיוּ עֲנִיִּים בְּנֵי בֵיתֶךָ, וְאַל תַּרְבֶּה שִׂיחָה עִם הָאִשָּׁה.
בְּאִשְׁתּוֹ אָמְרוּ, קַל וָחֹמֶר בְּאֵשֶׁת חֲבֵרוֹ. מִכָּאן אָמְרוּ חֲכָמִים:
כָּל הַמַּרְבֶּה שִׂיחָה עִם הָאִשָּׁה גּוֹרֵם רָעָה לְעַצְמוֹ, וּבוֹטֵל
מִדִּבְרֵי תוֹרָה, וְסוֹפוֹ יוֹרֵשׁ גֵּיהִנֹּם.

ו. יְהוֹשֻׁעַ בֶּן פְּרַחְיָה וְנִתַּי הָאַרְבֵּלִי קִבְּלוּ מֵהֶם. יְהוֹשֻׁעַ בֶּן
פְּרַחְיָה אוֹמֵר: עֲשֵׂה לְךָ רַב, וּקְנֵה לְךָ חָבֵר, וֶהֱוֵי דָן אֶת כָּל
הָאָדָם לְכַף זְכוּת.

ז. נִתַּי הָאַרְבֵּלִי אוֹמֵר: הַרְחֵק מִשָּׁכֵן רָע, וְאַל תִּתְחַבֵּר
לְרָשָׁע, וְאַל תִּתְיָאֵשׁ מִן הַפֻּרְעָנוּת.

ח. יְהוּדָה בֶּן טַבַּאי וְשִׁמְעוֹן בֶּן שָׁטַח קִבְּלוּ מֵהֶם. יְהוּדָה בֶּן
טַבַּאי אוֹמֵר: אַל תַּעַשׂ עַצְמְךָ כְּעוֹרְכֵי הַדַּיָּנִים, וּכְשֶׁיִּהְיוּ בַּעֲלֵי
הַדִּין עוֹמְדִים לְפָנֶיךָ, יִהְיוּ בְעֵינֶיךָ כִּרְשָׁעִים, וּכְשֶׁנִּפְטָרִים
מִלְּפָנֶיךָ, יִהְיוּ בְעֵינֶיךָ כְּזַכָּאִים, כְּשֶׁקִּבְּלוּ עֲלֵיהֶם אֶת הַדִּין.

ט. שִׁמְעוֹן בֶּן שָׁטַח אוֹמֵר: הֱוֵי מַרְבֶּה לַחֲקֹר אֶת הָעֵדִים,
וֶהֱוֵי זָהִיר בִּדְבָרֶיךָ, שֶׁמָּא מִתּוֹכָם יִלְמְדוּ לְשַׁקֵּר.

י. שְׁמַעְיָה וְאַבְטַלְיוֹן קִבְּלוּ מֵהֶם. שְׁמַעְיָה אוֹמֵר: אֱהַב אֶת
הַמְּלָאכָה, וּשְׂנָא אֶת הָרַבָּנוּת, וְאַל תִּתְוַדַּע לָרָשׁוּת.

יוֹסֵי ... יוֹסֵי In this and the following four paragraphs are given the names of the five *Zugoth*, "pairs" of leading scholars, who were president and vice-president of the Sanhedrin in the course of 150 years, the period preceding the *Tannaim*.

4. Yosé ben Yo'ezer of Zeredah and Yosé ben Yoḥanan of Jerusalem received the oral tradition from the preceding. Yosé ben Yo'ezer of Zeredah said: Let your house be a meeting-place for scholars; sit at their feet in the dust, and drink in their words thirstingly.

5. Yosé ben Yoḥanan of Jerusalem said: Let your house be wide open [to strangers]; treat the poor as members of your own family; and do not gossip with women. This has been said even with regard to one's own wife, how much more does it apply to another man's wife. Hence the sages say: Whoever gossips with women brings harm to himself, for he neglects the study of the Torah and will in the end inherit *Gehinnom*.

6. Joshua ben Peraḥyah and Nittai of Arbel received the oral tradition from the preceding. Joshua ben Peraḥyah said: Provide yourself with a teacher; get yourself a companion; and judge all men favorably.

7. Nittai of Arbel said: Keep aloof from a bad neighbor; do not associate with an evil man; and do not give up the belief in retribution [wickedness will not succeed in the end].

8. Judah ben Tabbai and Simeon ben Shataḥ received the oral tradition from the preceding. Judah ben Tabbai said: Do not [as a judge] play the part of a counselor; when the parties in a lawsuit are standing before you, regard them both as guilty; but when they go away from you, after having submitted to the judgment, regard them both as innocent.

9. Simeon ben Shataḥ said: Examine the witnesses thoroughly; be careful with your words, lest through them they learn to tell lies.

10. Shemayah and Avtalyon received the oral tradition from the preceding. Shemayah said: Love work; hate the holding of public office; and do not be intimate with the ruling authorities.

גיהנם the place of punishment in the hereafter. גיא בן־הנם is mentioned in Jeremiah 32:35 as the valley of Ben-Hinnom, near Jerusalem, where idolaters used to sacrifice human lives. The valley of Hinnom became identified with woe and suffering as a result of the horrible crimes committed in it.

יהיו בעיניך כרשעים that is, the judge should be impartial; he must not look upon either litigant with favor, but should regard both sides with equal suspicion.

שמעון בן שטח, brother of queen Salome Alexandra, laid the foundations of an elementary school system among the Jews in the beginning of the first century before the common era.

שמעיה ואבטליון are said to have been descendants of proselytes.

יא. אַבְטַלְיוֹן אוֹמֵר: חֲכָמִים, הִזָּהֲרוּ בְדִבְרֵיכֶם, שֶׁמָּא תָחוּבוּ חוֹבַת גָּלוּת וְתִגְלוּ לִמְקוֹם מַיִם הָרָעִים, וְיִשְׁתּוּ הַתַּלְמִידִים הַבָּאִים אַחֲרֵיכֶם וְיָמוּתוּ, וְנִמְצָא שֵׁם שָׁמַיִם מִתְחַלֵּל.

יב. הִלֵּל וְשַׁמַּאי קִבְּלוּ מֵהֶם. הִלֵּל אוֹמֵר: הֱוֵי מִתַּלְמִידָיו שֶׁל אַהֲרֹן: אוֹהֵב שָׁלוֹם וְרוֹדֵף שָׁלוֹם, אוֹהֵב אֶת הַבְּרִיּוֹת וּמְקָרְבָן לַתּוֹרָה.

יג. הוּא הָיָה אוֹמֵר: נְגַד שְׁמָא אֲבַד שְׁמֵהּ, וּדְלָא מוֹסִיף יָסֵף, וּדְלָא יָלֵף קְטָלָא חַיָּב, וּדְאִשְׁתַּמַּשׁ בְּתָגָא חֲלָף.

יד. הוּא הָיָה אוֹמֵר: אִם אֵין אֲנִי לִי, מִי לִי; וּכְשֶׁאֲנִי לְעַצְמִי, מָה אֲנִי; וְאִם לֹא עַכְשָׁו, אֵימָתַי.

טו. שַׁמַּאי אוֹמֵר: עֲשֵׂה תוֹרָתְךָ קֶבַע, אֱמֹר מְעַט וַעֲשֵׂה הַרְבֵּה, וֶהֱוֵי מְקַבֵּל אֶת כָּל הָאָדָם בְּסֵבֶר פָּנִים יָפוֹת.

טז. רַבָּן גַּמְלִיאֵל אוֹמֵר: עֲשֵׂה לְךָ רַב, וְהִסְתַּלֵּק מִן הַסָּפֵק, וְאַל תַּרְבֶּה לְעַשֵּׂר אֲמָדוֹת.

יז. שִׁמְעוֹן בְּנוֹ אוֹמֵר: כָּל יָמַי גָּדַלְתִּי בֵּין הַחֲכָמִים וְלֹא מָצָאתִי לַגּוּף טוֹב מִשְּׁתִיקָה, וְלֹא הַמִּדְרָשׁ עִקָּר אֶלָּא הַמַּעֲשֶׂה, וְכָל הַמַּרְבֶּה דְבָרִים מֵבִיא חֵטְא.

יח. רַבָּן שִׁמְעוֹן בֶּן גַּמְלִיאֵל אוֹמֵר: עַל שְׁלֹשָׁה דְבָרִים הָעוֹלָם קַיָּם: עַל הָאֱמֶת, וְעַל הַדִּין, וְעַל הַשָּׁלוֹם, שֶׁנֶּאֱמַר: אֱמֶת וּמִשְׁפַּט שָׁלוֹם שִׁפְטוּ בְּשַׁעֲרֵיכֶם.

הזהרו בדבריכם Teachers are cautioned against their use of inexact language which might bring their students under the influence of heresy.

הלל ושמאי flourished in Jerusalem a few decades before the common era. The last of the five *Zugoth*, they are regarded as the first of the *Tannaim* whose interpretations of biblical law and oral tradition are recorded in the Mishnah, Tosefta, and other works. In contrast to Shammai, Hillel was

11. Avtalyon said: Scholars, be careful with your words! You may incur the penalty of exile and be banished to a place of evil waters [heretical teachings], and the disciples who follow you into exile are likely to drink of them and die [a spiritual death], with the result that the name of Heaven would be profaned.

12. Hillel and Shammai received the oral tradition from the preceding: Hillel said: Be of the disciples of Aaron, loving peace and pursuing peace; be one who loves his fellow men and draws them near to the Torah.

13. He used to say: He who seeks greater reputation loses his reputation; he who does not increase his knowledge decreases it; he who does not study deserves death; he who makes unworthy use of the crown [of learning] shall perish.

14. He used to say: If I am not for myself, who is for me? If I care only for myself, what am I? If not now, when?

15. Shammai said: Make your study of the Torah a regular habit; say little but do much; and receive all men cheerfully.

16. Rabban Gamaliel said: Provide yourself with a teacher and avoid doubt; and do not make a habit of giving tithes by guesswork.

17. Simeon his son said: All my life I have been brought up among the sages, and I have found nothing better for a person than silence; study is not the most important thing but practice; and whoever talks too much, brings about sin.

18. Rabban Simeon ben Gamaliel said: The world is established on three principles: truth, justice, and peace, as it is said: "You shall administer truth, justice and peace within your gates."[1]

---

famous for his meek and gentle disposition. They were the founders of the schools named after them: *Beth Hillel* and *Beth Shammai*.

אם אין אני לי ... that is, one must be self-reliant, but must not live for himself. אם לא עכשיו אימתי one must take swift advantage of opportunity.

רבן גמליאל was a grandson of Hillel. He was the first to be known by the title *Rabban* ("Master"), given to the heads of the Sanhedrin. Like Hillel, he is also known by the title *Zaken* ("Elder"). He lived shortly before the Second Temple was destroyed.

ואל תרבה לעשר אומדות that is, keep clear of all doubt. Even when you come to pay the tenth part of your annual income for charitable uses, let there be no doubt that what you pay represents really a tenth of your income.

---

[1] *Zechariah* 8:16.

רַבִּי חֲנַנְיָא בֶּן עֲקַשְׁיָא אוֹמֵר: רָצָה הַקָּדוֹשׁ בָּרוּךְ הוּא
לְזַכּוֹת אֶת יִשְׂרָאֵל, לְפִיכָךְ הִרְבָּה לָהֶם תּוֹרָה וּמִצְוֹת, שֶׁנֶּאֱמַר:
יְיָ חָפֵץ לְמַעַן צִדְקוֹ, יַגְדִּיל תּוֹרָה וְיַאְדִּיר.

פֶּרֶק שֵׁנִי

כָּל יִשְׂרָאֵל יֵשׁ לָהֶם חֵלֶק לָעוֹלָם הַבָּא, שֶׁנֶּאֱמַר: וְעַמֵּךְ
כֻּלָּם צַדִּיקִים, לְעוֹלָם יִירְשׁוּ אָרֶץ; נֵצֶר מַטָּעַי, מַעֲשֵׂה יָדַי
לְהִתְפָּאֵר.

א. רַבִּי אוֹמֵר: אֵיזוֹ הִיא דֶרֶךְ יְשָׁרָה שֶׁיָּבוֹר לוֹ הָאָדָם,
כָּל שֶׁהִיא תִפְאֶרֶת לְעוֹשֶׂהָ וְתִפְאֶרֶת לוֹ מִן הָאָדָם; וֶהֱוֵי זָהִיר
בְּמִצְוָה קַלָּה כְּבַחֲמוּרָה, שֶׁאֵין אַתָּה יוֹדֵעַ מַתַּן שְׂכָרָן שֶׁל
מִצְוֹת; וֶהֱוֵי מְחַשֵּׁב הֶפְסֵד מִצְוָה כְּנֶגֶד שְׂכָרָהּ, וּשְׂכַר עֲבֵרָה
כְּנֶגֶד הֶפְסֵדָהּ. הִסְתַּכֵּל בִּשְׁלֹשָׁה דְבָרִים וְאֵין אַתָּה בָא לִידֵי
עֲבֵרָה: דַּע מַה לְמַעְלָה מִמְּךָ, עַיִן רוֹאָה, וְאֹזֶן שׁוֹמַעַת, וְכָל
מַעֲשֶׂיךָ בַּסֵּפֶר נִכְתָּבִים.

ב. רַבָּן גַּמְלִיאֵל בְּנוֹ שֶׁל רַבִּי יְהוּדָה הַנָּשִׂיא אוֹמֵר: יָפֶה
תַלְמוּד תּוֹרָה עִם דֶּרֶךְ אָרֶץ, שֶׁיְּגִיעַת שְׁנֵיהֶם מַשְׁכַּחַת עָוֹן;
וְכָל תּוֹרָה שֶׁאֵין עִמָּהּ מְלָאכָה סוֹפָהּ בְּטֵלָה וְגוֹרֶרֶת עָוֹן; וְכָל
הָעוֹסְקִים עִם הַצִּבּוּר יִהְיוּ עוֹסְקִים עִמָּהֶם לְשֵׁם שָׁמַיִם, שֶׁזְּכוּת
אֲבוֹתָם מְסַיַּעְתָּם וְצִדְקָתָם עוֹמֶדֶת לָעַד. וְאַתֶּם, מַעֲלֶה אֲנִי
עֲלֵיכֶם שָׂכָר הַרְבֵּה כְּאִלּוּ עֲשִׂיתֶם.

רבי חנינא belonged to the third generation of the *Tannaim*, and flourished
in the middle of the second century. His dictum, which is added in the Prayerbook at the end of each chapter of *Avoth*, is an excerpt from Mishnah Makkoth 3:16.

רבי is sometimes called *Rabbenu ha-Kadosh* ("our saintly teacher"). All
the best qualities were combined in him. He is said to have been born in 135,
when Rabbi Akiba died. He lived to be 84 years old. Famous as the compiler

Rabbi Ḥananyah ben Akashyah said: The Holy One, blessed be he, desired to purify Israel; hence he gave them a Torah rich in rules of conduct, as it is said: "The Lord was pleased, for the sake of [Israel's] righteousness, to render the Torah great and glorious."[1]

Chapter Two

All Israel have a share in the world to come, as it is said: "Your people shall all be righteous; they shall possess the land forever; they are a plant of my own, the work of my hands, wherein I may glory."[2]

1. Rabbi [Judah ha-Nasi] said: Which is the right course that a man should choose for himself? One which is creditable to the person adopting it, and on account of which he gains respect from men. Be careful to perform a minor *mitzvah* just as well as a major one, for you do not know the reward for each *mitzvah*. Balance the loss sustained by the performance of a *mitzvah* against the reward secured by its observance, and the profit of a sin against its injury. Consider three things and you will not come into the grip of sin—know what is above you: a seeing eye, a hearing ear, and a book in which all your deeds are recorded.

2. Rabban Gamaliel, the son of Rabbi Judah ha-Nasi, said: It is well to combine Torah study with some worldly occupation, for the energy taken up by both of them keeps sin out of one's mind; all Torah study which is not combined with some trade must at length fail and occasion sin. Let all who work for the community do so from a spiritual motive, for then the merit of their fathers will sustain them, and their righteousness will endure forever. "I credit you with great reward [God says] as if you accomplished it all."

---

and editor of the Mishnah, he was without a rival among his contemporaries in learning. He said: "I learned much from my teachers, more from my colleagues, and most of all from my pupils" (Makkoth 10a). He possessed great wealth of which he gave freely to poor scholars. The greatest scholar of the period, he was designated simply *Rabbi* ("Master") par excellence. A descendant of Hillel in the seventh generation, he is also known as Judah ha-Nasi (head of the Sanhedrin).

רבן גמליאל the third, who belonged to the last generation of the *Tannaim*. He succeeded his father in the office of *Nasi* in the third century.

זוררת עון that is, one would be driven to dishonest means of obtaining a livelihood.

[1] *Isaiah* 42:21.   [2] *Isaiah* 60:21.

ג. הֱווּ זְהִירִין בָּרְשׁוּת, שֶׁאֵין מְקָרְבִין לוֹ לְאָדָם אֶלָּא לְצֹרֶךְ עַצְמָן; נִרְאִין כְּאוֹהֲבִין בִּשְׁעַת הֲנָאָתָן, וְאֵין עוֹמְדִין לוֹ לְאָדָם בִּשְׁעַת דָּחֳקוֹ.

ד. הוּא הָיָה אוֹמֵר: עֲשֵׂה רְצוֹנוֹ כִּרְצוֹנֶךָ, כְּדֵי שֶׁיַּעֲשֶׂה רְצוֹנְךָ כִּרְצוֹנוֹ; בַּטֵּל רְצוֹנְךָ מִפְּנֵי רְצוֹנוֹ, כְּדֵי שֶׁיְּבַטֵּל רְצוֹן אֲחֵרִים מִפְּנֵי רְצוֹנֶךָ.

ה. הִלֵּל אוֹמֵר: אַל תִּפְרוֹשׁ מִן הַצִּבּוּר; וְאַל תַּאֲמֵן בְּעַצְמְךָ עַד יוֹם מוֹתְךָ; וְאַל תָּדִין אֶת חֲבֵרְךָ עַד שֶׁתַּגִּיעַ לִמְקוֹמוֹ; וְאַל תֹּאמַר דָּבָר שֶׁאִי אֶפְשָׁר לִשְׁמֹעַ שֶׁסּוֹפוֹ לְהִשָּׁמֵעַ; וְאַל תֹּאמַר לִכְשֶׁאֶפָּנֶה אֶשְׁנֶה, שֶׁמָּא לֹא תִפָּנֶה.

ו. הוּא הָיָה אוֹמֵר: אֵין בּוּר יְרֵא חֵטְא, וְלֹא עַם הָאָרֶץ חָסִיד, וְלֹא הַבַּיְשָׁן לָמֵד, וְלֹא הַקַּפְּדָן מְלַמֵּד, וְלֹא כָל הַמַּרְבֶּה בִסְחוֹרָה מַחְכִּים; וּבַמָּקוֹם שֶׁאֵין אֲנָשִׁים הִשְׁתַּדֵּל לִהְיוֹת אִישׁ.

ז. אַף הוּא רָאָה גֻלְגֹּלֶת אַחַת שֶׁצָּפָה עַל פְּנֵי הַמָּיִם. אָמַר לָהּ: עַל דַּאֲטֵיפְתְּ אַטִיפוּךְ, וְסוֹף מְטַיְפַיִךְ יְטוּפוּן.

ח. הוּא הָיָה אוֹמֵר: מַרְבֶּה בָשָׂר, מַרְבֶּה רִמָּה; מַרְבֶּה נְכָסִים, מַרְבֶּה דְאָגָה; מַרְבֶּה נָשִׁים, מַרְבֶּה כְשָׁפִים; מַרְבֶּה שְׁפָחוֹת, מַרְבֶּה זִמָּה; מַרְבֶּה עֲבָדִים, מַרְבֶּה גָזֵל. מַרְבֶּה תוֹרָה, מַרְבֶּה חַיִּים; מַרְבֶּה יְשִׁיבָה, מַרְבֶּה חָכְמָה; מַרְבֶּה עֵצָה, מַרְבֶּה תְבוּנָה; מַרְבֶּה צְדָקָה, מַרְבֶּה שָׁלוֹם. קָנָה שֵׁם טוֹב, קָנָה לְעַצְמוֹ; קָנָה לוֹ דִבְרֵי תוֹרָה, קָנָה לוֹ חַיֵּי הָעוֹלָם הַבָּא.

שאי אפשר לשמוע is read by Rashi **שאפשר לשמוע** in the sense that one should take swift advantage of each opportunity to acquire knowledge.

3. Be cautious of the ruling authorities, for they befriend a man only for their own interests; they appear as friends when it is to their own advantage, but they do not stand by a man when he is in distress.

4. He used to say: Do God's will as you would do your own will, so that he may do your will as if it were his; sacrifice your will for the sake of his will, so that he may undo the will of others before yours.

5. Hillel said: Do not keep aloof from the community; be not sure of yourself till the day of your death; do not judge your fellow man until you have been in his position; do not say anything which cannot be understood at once, in the hope that ultimately it will be understood; and do not say: "When I shall have leisure I shall study," for you may never have leisure.

6. He used to say: An empty-headed man cannot be sin-fearing, nor can an ignorant person be pious; the bashful cannot learn, nor can the quick-tempered teach; nor can anyone who is engrossed in trade become a scholar; and in a place where there are no men, strive to be a man.

7. He saw a skull floating on the surface of the water. He said to it: Because you drowned others, others have drowned you; and those who have drowned you shall themselves be drowned [measure for measure].

8. He used to say: The more flesh, the more worms [in the grave]; the more property, the more anxiety; the more wives, the more witchcraft; the more female servants, the more lewdness; the more male servants, the more thievery; but the more Torah study, the more life; the more schooling, the more wisdom; the more counsel, the more understanding; the more righteousness, the more peace. One who has acquired a good name, has acquired it for himself; one who has acquired for himself Torah has acquired for himself the life of the world to come.

בור a man devoid of both knowledge and moral principles. This term originally signifies a piece of land completely uncultivated.

מרבה כשפים Rival wives often resorted to black magic in their efforts to retain their husband's affection.

ט. רַבָּן יוֹחָנָן בֶּן זַכַּי קִבֵּל מֵהִלֵּל וּמִשַּׁמַּי. הוּא הָיָה אוֹמֵר:
אִם לָמַדְתָּ תּוֹרָה הַרְבֵּה, אַל תַּחֲזִק טוֹבָה לְעַצְמֶךָ, כִּי לְכָךְ
נוֹצָרְתָּ.

י. חֲמִשָּׁה תַלְמִידִים הָיוּ לוֹ לְרַבָּן יוֹחָנָן בֶּן זַכַּי, וְאֵלּוּ הֵן:
רַבִּי אֱלִיעֶזֶר בֶּן הוֹרְקָנוֹס, רַבִּי יְהוֹשֻׁעַ בֶּן חֲנַנְיָא, רַבִּי יוֹסֵי
הַכֹּהֵן, רַבִּי שִׁמְעוֹן בֶּן נְתַנְאֵל, וְרַבִּי אֶלְעָזָר בֶּן עֲרָךְ.

יא. הוּא הָיָה מוֹנֶה שְׁבָחָם: רַבִּי אֱלִיעֶזֶר בֶּן הוֹרְקָנוֹס בּוֹר
סוּד, שֶׁאֵינוֹ מְאַבֵּד טִפָּה; רַבִּי יְהוֹשֻׁעַ בֶּן חֲנַנְיָא, אַשְׁרֵי יוֹלַדְתּוֹ;
רַבִּי יוֹסֵי הַכֹּהֵן חָסִיד; רַבִּי שִׁמְעוֹן בֶּן נְתַנְאֵל יְרֵא חֵטְא; רַבִּי
אֶלְעָזָר בֶּן עֲרָךְ כְּמַעְיָן הַמִּתְגַּבֵּר.

יב. הוּא הָיָה אוֹמֵר: אִם יִהְיוּ כָּל חַכְמֵי יִשְׂרָאֵל בְּכַף
מֹאזְנַיִם, וֶאֱלִיעֶזֶר בֶּן הוֹרְקָנוֹס בְּכַף שְׁנִיָּה, מַכְרִיעַ אֶת כֻּלָּם.
אַבָּא שָׁאוּל אוֹמֵר מִשְּׁמוֹ: אִם יִהְיוּ כָּל חַכְמֵי יִשְׂרָאֵל בְּכַף
מֹאזְנַיִם, וֶאֱלִיעֶזֶר בֶּן הוֹרְקָנוֹס אַף עִמָּהֶם, וְאֶלְעָזָר בֶּן עֲרָךְ
בְּכַף שְׁנִיָּה, מַכְרִיעַ אֶת כֻּלָּם.

יג. אָמַר לָהֶם: צְאוּ וּרְאוּ אֵיזוֹ הִיא דֶרֶךְ טוֹבָה שֶׁיִּדְבַּק
בָּהּ הָאָדָם. רַבִּי אֱלִיעֶזֶר אוֹמֵר: עַיִן טוֹבָה. רַבִּי יְהוֹשֻׁעַ אוֹמֵר:
חָבֵר טוֹב. רַבִּי יוֹסֵי אוֹמֵר: שָׁכֵן טוֹב. רַבִּי שִׁמְעוֹן אוֹמֵר:
הָרוֹאֶה אֶת הַנּוֹלָד. רַבִּי אֶלְעָזָר אוֹמֵר: לֵב טוֹב. אָמַר לָהֶם:
רוֹאֶה אֲנִי אֶת דִּבְרֵי אֶלְעָזָר בֶּן עֲרָךְ מִדִּבְרֵיכֶם, שֶׁבִּכְלַל
דְּבָרָיו דִּבְרֵיכֶם.

יוחנן בן זכאי saved the nation from disintegration after the destruction of
the Temple when he reorganized the Sanhedrin in Yavneh, south of Jaffa.
According to tradition, he died at the age of 120.

אליעזר בן הורקנוס is frequently quoted in the Mishnah. Against the wishes
of his father who threatened to disinherit him, he began to study late in life
and developed into the greatest scholar of the period. Though a brother-in-

9. Rabban Yoḥanan ben Zakkai received the oral tradition from Hillel and Shammai. He used to say: If you have learnt much Torah, do not claim credit for yourself, because you were created for this purpose.

10. Rabban Yoḥanan ben Zakkai had five pre-eminent disciples, namely: Rabbi Eliezer ben Hyrcanus, Rabbi Joshua ben Ḥananyah, Rabbi Yosé the Priest, Rabbi Simeon ben Nethanel, and Rabbi Elazar ben Arakh.

11. He used to sum up their merits: Eliezer ben Hyrcanus is a cemented cistern which loses not a drop [retentive memory]; Joshua ben Ḥananyah—happy is his mother; Yosé the Priest is most pious; Simeon ben Nethanel is one who fears sin; Elazar ben Arakh is like a spring that ever gathers force [creative mind].

12. He used to say: If all the sages of Israel were in one scale of the balance, and Eliezer ben Hyrcanus in the other, he would outweigh them all. Abba Saul, however, quoted him otherwise: If all the sages of Israel, including Eliezer ben Hyrcanus, were in one scale of the balance, and Elazar ben Arakh in the other, he would outweigh them all [originality surpasses retentiveness].

13. He [Yoḥanan ben Zakkai] said to them: Go and see which is the best quality to which a man should cling. Rabbi Eliezer said: A good eye [generosity]; Rabbi Joshua said: A good friend [friendliness]; Rabbi Yosé said: A good neighbor [goodwill]; Rabbi Simeon said: One who considers the probable consequences [foresight]; Rabbi Elazar said: A good heart [unselfishness]. Said he to them: I prefer what Elazar ben Arakh has said to what you have said, because in his words yours are included.

---

law of Gamaliel II, the president of the Sanhedrin, he was excommunicated by his colleagues because he refused to accept the decision of the majority on a point of law that arose for discussion. He is sometimes spoken of as "Rabbi Eliezer the Great."

אשרי ילדתו Great credit for his scholarship was due to his mother, who is said to have taken him as an infant to the academy of learning so that his ears might become attuned to the sound of Torah. Rabbi Joshua ben Ḥananyah successfully debated with Greek philosophers and was famous as the representative of Jewish wit and wisdom.

אבא ("father") is not part of this *Tanna's* name, but a title. Abba Saul lived during the second century.

יד. אָמַר לָהֶם: צְאוּ וּרְאוּ אִיזוֹ הִיא דֶרֶךְ רָעָה שֶׁיִתְרַחֵק
מִמֶּנָּה הָאָדָם. רַבִּי אֱלִיעֶזֶר אוֹמֵר: עַיִן רָעָה. רַבִּי יְהוֹשֻׁעַ
אוֹמֵר: חָבֵר רָע. רַבִּי יוֹסֵי אוֹמֵר: שָׁכֵן רָע. רַבִּי שִׁמְעוֹן אוֹמֵר:
הַלֹּוֶה וְאֵינוֹ מְשַׁלֵּם; אֶחָד הַלֹּוֶה מִן הָאָדָם כְּלֹוֶה מִן הַמָּקוֹם,
שֶׁנֶּאֱמַר: לֹוֶה רָשָׁע וְלֹא יְשַׁלֵּם, וְצַדִּיק חוֹנֵן וְנוֹתֵן. רַבִּי אֶלְעָזָר
אוֹמֵר: לֵב רָע. אָמַר לָהֶם: רוֹאֶה אֲנִי אֶת דִּבְרֵי אֶלְעָזָר בֶּן
עֲרָךְ מִדִּבְרֵיכֶם, שֶׁבִּכְלַל דְּבָרָיו דִּבְרֵיכֶם.

טו. הֵם אָמְרוּ שְׁלֹשָׁה דְבָרִים. רַבִּי אֱלִיעֶזֶר אוֹמֵר: יְהִי
כְבוֹד חֲבֵרְךָ חָבִיב עָלֶיךָ כְּשֶׁלָּךְ, וְאַל תְּהִי נוֹחַ לִכְעוֹס, וְשׁוּב
יוֹם אֶחָד לִפְנֵי מִיתָתְךָ. וֶהֱוֵי מִתְחַמֵּם כְּנֶגֶד אוּרָן שֶׁל חֲכָמִים,
וֶהֱוֵי זָהִיר בְּגַחַלְתָּן שֶׁלֹּא תִכָּוֶה, שֶׁנְּשִׁיכָתָן נְשִׁיכַת שׁוּעָל,
וַעֲקִיצָתָן עֲקִיצַת עַקְרָב, וּלְחִישָׁתָן לְחִישַׁת שָׂרָף, וְכָל דִּבְרֵיהֶם
כְּגַחֲלֵי אֵשׁ.

טז. רַבִּי יְהוֹשֻׁעַ אוֹמֵר: עַיִן הָרָע וְיֵצֶר הָרָע וְשִׂנְאַת הַבְּרִיּוֹת
מוֹצִיאִים אֶת הָאָדָם מִן הָעוֹלָם.

יז. רַבִּי יוֹסֵי אוֹמֵר: יְהִי מָמוֹן חֲבֵרְךָ חָבִיב עָלֶיךָ כְּשֶׁלָּךְ,
וְהַתְקֵן עַצְמְךָ לִלְמֹד תּוֹרָה שֶׁאֵינָה יְרֻשָּׁה לָךְ, וְכָל מַעֲשֶׂיךָ
יִהְיוּ לְשֵׁם שָׁמָיִם.

יח. רַבִּי שִׁמְעוֹן אוֹמֵר: הֱוֵי זָהִיר בִּקְרִיאַת שְׁמַע וּבִתְפִלָּה;
וּכְשֶׁאַתָּה מִתְפַּלֵּל, אַל תַּעַשׂ תְּפִלָּתְךָ קֶבַע אֶלָּא רַחֲמִים
וְתַחֲנוּנִים לִפְנֵי הַמָּקוֹם, שֶׁנֶּאֱמַר: כִּי חַנּוּן וְרַחוּם הוּא, אֶרֶךְ
אַפַּיִם וְרַב חֶסֶד וְנִחָם עַל הָרָעָה; וְאַל תְּהִי רָשָׁע בִּפְנֵי עַצְמְךָ.

כלוה מן המקום Since all wealth belongs to God, the borrower is considered as borrowing directly from God, the Righteous One, who will repay the benevolent lender what the debtor fails to repay.

14. He further said to them: Go and see which is the worst quality a man should shun. Rabbi Eliezer said: An evil eye [greed]; Rabbi Joshua said: A bad friend [hatred]; Rabbi Yosé said: A bad neighbor [discord]; Rabbi Simeon said: One who borrows and does not repay. It is the same whether one borrows from man or from God, as it is said: "The wicked borrows and repays not, but the righteous deals graciously and gives."[1] Rabbi Elazar said: An evil heart [selfishness]. Said he to them: I prefer what Elazar ben Arakh has said to what you have said, for in his words yours are included.

15. They each said three things. Rabbi Eliezer said: Let your friend's honor be as dear to you as your own; be not easily provoked to anger; repent one day before your death [every day, for you may die tomorrow]. He further said: Warm yourself by the fire of the scholars, but beware of their glowing coals [treat them respectfully], lest you burn yourself; for the bite of scholars is as hurtful as that of a fox, their sting is as deadly as that of a scorpion, their hiss is like that of a serpent, and all their words are like coals of fire [and should be heeded].

16. Rabbi Joshua said: The evil eye [greed], the evil impulse and hatred of mankind shorten a man's life.

17. Rabbi Yosé said: Let your friend's property be as precious to you as your own; give yourself to studying the Torah, for it does not come to you by inheritance; and let all your deeds be done in the name of Heaven.

18. Rabbi Simeon said: Be careful in reading the *Shema* and the *Shemoneh Esreh*; when you pray, do not regard your prayer as a perfunctory act, but as a plea for mercy and grace before God, as it is said: "For he is gracious and merciful, slow to anger, abounding in kindness, and relenting of evil."[2] Do not be wicked in your own esteem [lest you set yourself a low standard of conduct].

לשם שמים for the sake of God, that is, with pure purpose and good intentions. קריאת שמע and all regularly repeated prayers should never be recited in a mechanical manner, without understanding and a devotional frame of mind.

---

[1] *Psalm* 37:21.   [2] *Joel* 2:13.

יט. רַבִּי אֶלְעָזָר אוֹמֵר: הֱוֵי שָׁקוּד לִלְמֹד תּוֹרָה, וְדַע מַה שֶׁתָּשִׁיב לָאֶפִּיקוֹרוֹס, וְדַע לִפְנֵי מִי אַתָּה עָמֵל וּמִי הוּא בַּעַל מְלַאכְתְּךָ שֶׁיְּשַׁלֶּם־לָךְ שְׂכַר פְּעֻלָּתֶךָ.

כ. רַבִּי טַרְפוֹן אוֹמֵר: הַיּוֹם קָצָר, וְהַמְּלָאכָה מְרֻבָּה, וְהַפּוֹעֲלִים עֲצֵלִים, וְהַשָּׂכָר הַרְבֵּה, וּבַעַל הַבַּיִת דּוֹחֵק.

כא. הוּא הָיָה אוֹמֵר: לֹא עָלֶיךָ הַמְּלָאכָה לִגְמֹר, וְלֹא אַתָּה בֶן חוֹרִין לִהְבָּטֵל מִמֶּנָּה. אִם לָמַדְתָּ תּוֹרָה הַרְבֵּה, נוֹתְנִים לְךָ שָׂכָר הַרְבֵּה, וְנֶאֱמָן הוּא בַּעַל מְלַאכְתְּךָ שֶׁיְּשַׁלֶּם־לָךְ שְׂכַר פְּעֻלָּתֶךָ; וְדַע שֶׁמַּתַּן שְׂכָרָן שֶׁל צַדִּיקִים לֶעָתִיד לָבוֹא.

רַבִּי חֲנַנְיָא בֶּן עֲקַשְׁיָא אוֹמֵר: רָצָה הַקָּדוֹשׁ בָּרוּךְ הוּא לְזַכּוֹת אֶת יִשְׂרָאֵל, לְפִיכָךְ הִרְבָּה לָהֶם תּוֹרָה וּמִצְוֹת, שֶׁנֶּאֱמַר: יְיָ חָפֵץ לְמַעַן צִדְקוֹ, יַגְדִּיל תּוֹרָה וְיַאְדִּיר.

פֶּרֶק שְׁלִישִׁי

כָּל יִשְׂרָאֵל יֵשׁ לָהֶם חֵלֶק לָעוֹלָם הַבָּא, שֶׁנֶּאֱמַר: וְעַמֵּךְ כֻּלָּם צַדִּיקִים, לְעוֹלָם יִירְשׁוּ אָרֶץ: נֵצֶר מַטָּעַי, מַעֲשֵׂה יָדַי לְהִתְפָּאֵר.

א. עֲקַבְיָא בֶּן מַהֲלַלְאֵל אוֹמֵר: הִסְתַּכֵּל בִּשְׁלשָׁה דְבָרִים וְאֵין אַתָּה בָא לִידֵי עֲבֵרָה: דַּע מֵאַיִן בָּאתָ, וּלְאָן אַתָּה הוֹלֵךְ, וְלִפְנֵי מִי אַתָּה עָתִיד לִתֵּן דִּין וְחֶשְׁבּוֹן. מֵאַיִן בָּאתָ, מִטִּפָּה סְרוּחָה; וּלְאָן אַתָּה הוֹלֵךְ, לִמְקוֹם עָפָר, רִמָּה וְתוֹלֵעָה; וְלִפְנֵי מִי אַתָּה עָתִיד לִתֵּן דִּין וְחֶשְׁבּוֹן, לִפְנֵי מֶלֶךְ מַלְכֵי הַמְּלָכִים, הַקָּדוֹשׁ בָּרוּךְ הוּא.

רבי טרפון was a contemporary of Rabban Yoḥanan ben Zakkai and a colleague of Rabbi Akiba. He used his great wealth for charitable purposes.

19. Rabbi Elazar said: Be eager to study the Torah; know what to answer an unbeliever; know before whom you toil, who your Employer is, who will pay you the reward of your labor.

20. Rabbi Tarfon said: The day [life] is short; the task is great; the workmen [human beings] are lazy; the reward is great, and the Master is insistent.

21. He used to say: You are not called upon to complete the work [of Torah study], yet you are not free to evade it; if you have studied much Torah, much reward will be given you—your Employer can be trusted to pay you for your work; and know that the grant of reward to the righteous will be in the time to come.

Rabbi Ḥananyah ben Akashyah said: The Holy One, blessed be he, desired to purify Israel; hence he gave them a Torah rich in rules of conduct, as it is said: "The Lord was pleased, for the sake of [Israel's] righteousness, to render the Torah great and glorious."[1]

CHAPTER THREE

All Israel have a share in the world to come, as it is said: "Your people shall all be righteous; they shall possess the land forever; they are a plant of my own, the work of my hands, wherein I may glory."[2]

1. Akavyah ben Mahalalel said: Reflect on three things and you will not come into the grip of sin: know whence you came, whither you are going, and before whom you are destined to give a strict account. *Whence you came*—from a malodorous drop; *whither you are going*—to a place of dust, worms and moths; *and before whom you are destined to give a strict account*—before the supreme King of kings, the Holy One, blessed be he.

אפיקורוס a follower of Epicurus, the Greek philosopher who taught that "all parts of the universe . . . owe their origin to accident and chance" (Maimonides, *Guide*, III, 17). Because of the phonetic resemblance between אפיקורוס and פקר ("to be licentious") the term *epikurus* is used in talmudic literature to denote one who denies the authority of the Torah. There is a statement that he who insults a scholar is an *epikurus* (Sanhedrin 99b).

עקביא בן מהללאל was a contemporary of Hillel. On Shammai's death he was offered the position of vice-president of the Sanhedrin on condition that he first change his views on certain points of law, but he refused.

[1] *Isaiah* 42:21. [2] *Isaiah* 60:21.

ב. רַבִּי חֲנִינָא סְגַן הַכֹּהֲנִים אוֹמֵר: הֱוֵי מִתְפַּלֵּל בִּשְׁלוֹמָהּ
שֶׁל מַלְכוּת, שֶׁאִלְמָלֵא מוֹרָאָהּ אִישׁ אֶת רֵעֵהוּ חַיִּים בְּלָעוֹ.

ג. רַבִּי חֲנַנְיָא בֶּן תְּרַדְיוֹן אוֹמֵר: שְׁנַיִם שֶׁיּוֹשְׁבִים וְאֵין בֵּינֵיהֶם
דִּבְרֵי תוֹרָה, הֲרֵי זֶה מוֹשַׁב לֵצִים, שֶׁנֶּאֱמַר: וּבְמוֹשַׁב לֵצִים
לֹא יָשָׁב. אֲבָל שְׁנַיִם שֶׁיּוֹשְׁבִים וְיֵשׁ בֵּינֵיהֶם דִּבְרֵי תוֹרָה, שְׁכִינָה
שְׁרוּיָה בֵינֵיהֶם, שֶׁנֶּאֱמַר: אָז נִדְבְּרוּ יִרְאֵי יְיָ אִישׁ אֶל רֵעֵהוּ,
וַיַּקְשֵׁב יְיָ וַיִּשְׁמָע, וַיִּכָּתֵב סֵפֶר זִכָּרוֹן לְפָנָיו, לְיִרְאֵי יְיָ וּלְחֹשְׁבֵי
שְׁמוֹ. אֵין לִי אֶלָּא שְׁנַיִם, מִנַּיִן אֲפִילוּ אֶחָד שֶׁיּוֹשֵׁב וְעוֹסֵק
בַּתּוֹרָה, שֶׁהַקָּדוֹשׁ בָּרוּךְ הוּא קוֹבֵעַ לוֹ שָׂכָר, שֶׁנֶּאֱמַר: יֵשֵׁב
בָּדָד וְיִדֹּם כִּי נָטַל עָלָיו.

ד. רַבִּי שִׁמְעוֹן אוֹמֵר: שְׁלֹשָׁה שֶׁאָכְלוּ עַל שֻׁלְחָן אֶחָד וְלֹא
אָמְרוּ עָלָיו דִּבְרֵי תוֹרָה, כְּאִלּוּ אָכְלוּ מִזִּבְחֵי מֵתִים, שֶׁנֶּאֱמַר:
כִּי כָּל שֻׁלְחָנוֹת מָלְאוּ קִיא צוֹאָה בְּלִי מָקוֹם. אֲבָל שְׁלֹשָׁה
שֶׁאָכְלוּ עַל שֻׁלְחָן אֶחָד וְאָמְרוּ עָלָיו דִּבְרֵי תוֹרָה, כְּאִלּוּ אָכְלוּ
מִשֻּׁלְחָנוֹ שֶׁל מָקוֹם, שֶׁנֶּאֱמַר: וַיְדַבֵּר אֵלַי, זֶה הַשֻּׁלְחָן אֲשֶׁר
לִפְנֵי יְיָ.

ה. רַבִּי חֲנִינָא בֶּן חֲכִינַי אוֹמֵר: הַנֵּעוֹר בַּלַּיְלָה וְהַמְהַלֵּךְ
בַּדֶּרֶךְ יְחִידִי וּמְפַנֶּה לִבּוֹ לְבַטָּלָה, הֲרֵי זֶה מִתְחַיֵּב בְּנַפְשׁוֹ.

ו. רַבִּי נְחוּנְיָא בֶּן הַקָּנָה אוֹמֵר: כָּל הַמְקַבֵּל עָלָיו עֹל
תּוֹרָה, מַעֲבִירִים מִמֶּנּוּ עֹל מַלְכוּת וְעֹל דֶּרֶךְ אֶרֶץ; וְכָל
הַפּוֹרֵק מִמֶּנּוּ עֹל תּוֹרָה, נוֹתְנִים עָלָיו עֹל מַלְכוּת וְעֹל דֶּרֶךְ
אֶרֶץ.

רבי חנניא בן תרדיון was the father of Beruriah, famous wife of Rabbi Meir.
He was burned at the stake, after the defeat of Bar-Kokhba in 135, for his
refusal to obey the decrees of Hadrian.

שכינה ("habitation") denotes God's presence on earth. It is used as
one of God's names.

2. Rabbi Ḥanina, the deputy high-priest, said: Pray for the welfare of the government, since were it not for the fear of it men would swallow each other alive.

3. Rabbi Ḥananyah ben Teradyon said: If two sit together and no words of Torah are spoken between them, they are a session of scoffers, of whom it is said: "[A good man] does not sit in the company of scoffers."[1] But when two sit together and interchange words of the Torah, the *Shekhinah* abides between them, as it is said: "Then those who revered the Lord spoke to each other, and the Lord listened and heard, and in his presence a record was written of those who revere the Lord and respect his name."[2] Now, this verse refers to two persons; whence do we know that even if one person engages in the study of the Torah, the Holy One, blessed be he, determines his reward? It is said: "Though he sits alone in thoughtful meditation, yet he receives" [the reward].[3]

4. Rabbi Simeon said: If three have eaten at a table and have held no conversation on Torah, it is as though they had eaten of sacrifices offered to the dead [idols], as it is said: "For all their tables are full of filth without the presence of God."[4] But if three have eaten at a table and have conversed on Torah, they are as though they had eaten from the table of God, as it is said: "He said to me: This is the table which is in the presence of the Lord."[5]

5. Rabbi Ḥanina ben Ḥakinai said: He who is awake at night, or travels alone on the road, and turns his mind to idle thoughts, commits a deadly sin.

6. Rabbi Neḥunya ben ha-Kanah said: Whoever takes upon himself the yoke of the Torah will be relieved from the yoke of the government and the yoke of worldly affairs [struggle for existence]; whoever divests himself of the yoke of the Torah will be burdened with the yoke of the government and the yoke of worldly affairs.

רבי שמעון בן יוחאי, one of the most brilliant students of Rabbi Akiba. Strongly anti-Roman, he was forced for a long time to remain in hiding after the defeat of Bar-Kokhba. He is the supposed author of the *Zohar*, the mystical commentary on the Pentateuch. According to tradition, he died at Meron, northwest of Safed, on *Lag b'Omer*.

רבי חנינא בן חכיני was a disciple of Rabbi Akiba.

רבי נחוניא בן הקנה was a contemporary of Rabban Yoḥanan ben Zakkai. He attributed his attainment of great age to his forgiving nature, generosity in money matters and respect for the feelings of others (Megillah 28a).

---

[1] *Psaim* 1:1. [2] *Malachi* 3:16. [3] *Lamentations* 3:28. [4] *Isaiah* 28:8. [5] *Ezekiel* 41:22.

ז. רַבִּי חֲלַפְתָּא בֶּן דּוֹסָא, אִישׁ כְּפַר חֲנַנְיָא, אוֹמֵר: עֲשָׂרָה
שֶׁיּוֹשְׁבִים וְעוֹסְקִים בַּתּוֹרָה, שְׁכִינָה שְׁרוּיָה בֵינֵיהֶם, שֶׁנֶּאֱמַר:
אֱלֹהִים נִצָּב בַּעֲדַת אֵל. וּמִנַּיִן אֲפִילּוּ חֲמִשָּׁה, שֶׁנֶּאֱמַר: וַאֲגֻדָּתוֹ
עַל אֶרֶץ יְסָדָהּ. וּמִנַּיִן אֲפִילּוּ שְׁלֹשָׁה, שֶׁנֶּאֱמַר: בְּקֶרֶב אֱלֹהִים
יִשְׁפֹּט. וּמִנַּיִן אֲפִילּוּ שְׁנַיִם, שֶׁנֶּאֱמַר: אָז נִדְבְּרוּ יִרְאֵי יְיָ אִישׁ אֶל
רֵעֵהוּ, וַיַּקְשֵׁב יְיָ וַיִּשְׁמָע. וּמִנַּיִן אֲפִילּוּ אֶחָד, שֶׁנֶּאֱמַר: בְּכָל
הַמָּקוֹם אֲשֶׁר אַזְכִּיר אֶת שְׁמִי, אָבֹא אֵלֶיךָ וּבֵרַכְתִּיךָ.

ח. רַבִּי אֶלְעָזָר, אִישׁ בַּרְתּוֹתָא, אוֹמֵר: תֶּן־לוֹ מִשֶּׁלּוֹ,
שֶׁאַתָּה וְשֶׁלְּךָ שֶׁלּוֹ. וְכֵן בְּדָוִד הוּא אוֹמֵר: כִּי מִמְּךָ הַכֹּל, וּמִיָּדְךָ
נָתַנּוּ לָךְ.

ט. רַבִּי יַעֲקֹב אוֹמֵר: הַמְהַלֵּךְ בַּדֶּרֶךְ וְשׁוֹנֶה, וּמַפְסִיק
מִמִּשְׁנָתוֹ וְאוֹמֵר: מַה נָּאֶה אִילָן זֶה, מַה נָּאֶה נִיר זֶה, מַעֲלֶה
עָלָיו הַכָּתוּב כְּאִלּוּ מִתְחַיֵּב בְּנַפְשׁוֹ.

י. רַבִּי דּוֹסְתַּאי בַּר יַנַּאי, מִשּׁוּם רַבִּי מֵאִיר, אוֹמֵר: כָּל הַשּׁוֹכֵחַ
דָּבָר אֶחָד מִמִּשְׁנָתוֹ, מַעֲלֶה עָלָיו הַכָּתוּב כְּאִלּוּ מִתְחַיֵּב בְּנַפְשׁוֹ,
שֶׁנֶּאֱמַר: רַק הִשָּׁמֶר־לְךָ וּשְׁמֹר נַפְשְׁךָ מְאֹד, פֶּן תִּשְׁכַּח אֶת
הַדְּבָרִים אֲשֶׁר רָאוּ עֵינֶיךָ. יָכוֹל, אֲפִילּוּ תָּקְפָה עָלָיו מִשְׁנָתוֹ,
תַּלְמוּד לוֹמַר: וּפֶן יָסוּרוּ מִלְּבָבְךָ כֹּל יְמֵי חַיֶּיךָ; הָא, אֵינוֹ
מִתְחַיֵּב בְּנַפְשׁוֹ עַד שֶׁיֵּשֵׁב וִיסִירֵם מִלִּבּוֹ.

יא. רַבִּי חֲנִינָא בֶּן דּוֹסָא אוֹמֵר: כֹּל שֶׁיִּרְאַת חֶטְאוֹ קוֹדֶמֶת
לְחָכְמָתוֹ, חָכְמָתוֹ מִתְקַיֶּמֶת; וְכֹל שֶׁחָכְמָתוֹ קוֹדֶמֶת לְיִרְאַת
חֶטְאוֹ, אֵין חָכְמָתוֹ מִתְקַיֶּמֶת.

_____

רבי חלפתא was a disciple of Rabbi Meir. בן דוסא is omitted in some texts.
רבי אלעזר איש ברתותא was a contemporary of Rabbi Akiba.
רבי יעקב was one of the teachers of Rabbi Judah ha-Nasi.
רבי דוסתאי בר ינאי was an older contemporary of Rabbi Judah ha-Nasi.
רבי חנינא בן דוסא was a disciple of Rabban Yohanan ben Zakkai.

7.　Rabbi Ḥalafta ben Dosa of Kfar Ḥananya said: When ten people sit together and occupy themselves with the Torah, the *Shekhinah* abides among them, as it is said: "God stands in the godly congregation."[1] Whence do we know that the same applies even to five? It is said: "He has founded his band upon the earth."[2] Whence do we know that the same applies even to three? It is said: "In the midst of the judges he judges."[3] Whence do we know that the same applies even to two? It is said: "Then those who revered the Lord spoke to each other, and the Lord listened and heard."[4] Whence do we know that the same applies even to one? It is said: "In every place where I have my name mentioned I will come to you and bless you."[5]

8.　Rabbi Elazar of Bertotha said: Give to God of his own, for you and yours are his. The same thought was expressed by David, who said: "For all things come from thee, and we have given thee only what is thine."[6]

9.　Rabbi Jacob said: He who travels on the road while reviewing what he has learnt, and interrupts his study and says: "How fine is that tree, how fair is that field!" Scripture regards him as if he committed a grave sin [study is more important than the admiration of nature].

10.　Rabbi Dostai ben Yannai said in the name of Rabbi Meir: Whoever forgets anything of what he has learned, Scripture regards him as if he committed a grave sin, for it is said: "Only take care, and watch yourself well that you do not forget the things which your eyes saw.", Now, one might suppose that this applies even to a person who has forgotten because his study proved too hard for him; it is therefore explicitly added: "Lest they be removed from your heart all the days of your life."[7] Thus, he incurs a grave sin only when he deliberately removes the lessons from his heart.

11.　Rabbi Ḥanina ben Dosa said: Anyone whose fear of sin precedes his wisdom [whose moral conduct means more to him than his learning], his wisdom shall endure; anyone whose wisdom precedes his fear of sin, his wisdom shall not endure [not being subjected to the moral demands of wisdom, he will give up wisdom so that it might not trouble his conscience].

אין חכמתו מתקיימת Not being governed by the moral demands of wisdom, he will give up wisdom so that it might not trouble his conscience.

---

[1] *Psalm* 82:1.　[2] *Amos* 9:6.　[3] *Psalm* 82:1.　[4] *Malachi* 3:16.　[5] *Exodus* 20:24.
[6] I *Chronicles* 29:14.　[7] *Deuteronomy* 4:9.

יב. הוּא הָיָה אוֹמֵר: כֹּל שֶׁמַּעֲשָׂיו מְרֻבִּים מֵחָכְמָתוֹ, חָכְמָתוֹ מִתְקַיֶּמֶת; וְכֹל שֶׁחָכְמָתוֹ מְרֻבָּה מִמַּעֲשָׂיו, אֵין חָכְמָתוֹ מִתְקַיֶּמֶת.

יג. הוּא הָיָה אוֹמֵר: כֹּל שֶׁרוּחַ הַבְּרִיּוֹת נוֹחָה הֵימֶנּוּ, רוּחַ הַמָּקוֹם נוֹחָה הֵימֶנּוּ; וְכֹל שֶׁאֵין רוּחַ הַבְּרִיּוֹת נוֹחָה הֵימֶנּוּ, אֵין רוּחַ הַמָּקוֹם נוֹחָה הֵימֶנּוּ.

יד. רַבִּי דוֹסָא בֶּן הָרְכִּינַס אוֹמֵר: שֵׁנָה שֶׁל שַׁחֲרִית וְיַיִן שֶׁל צָהֳרַיִם, וְשִׂיחַת הַיְלָדִים וִישִׁיבַת בָּתֵּי כְנֵסִיּוֹת שֶׁל עַמֵּי הָאָרֶץ, מוֹצִיאִים אֶת הָאָדָם מִן הָעוֹלָם.

טו. רַבִּי אֶלְעָזָר הַמּוֹדָעִי אוֹמֵר: הַמְחַלֵּל אֶת הַקָּדָשִׁים, וְהַמְבַזֶּה אֶת הַמּוֹעֲדוֹת, וְהַמַּלְבִּין פְּנֵי חֲבֵרוֹ בָּרַבִּים, וְהַמֵּפֵר בְּרִיתוֹ שֶׁל אַבְרָהָם אָבִינוּ, וְהַמְגַלֶּה פָנִים בַּתּוֹרָה שֶׁלֹּא כַהֲלָכָה, אַף עַל פִּי שֶׁיֵּשׁ בְּיָדוֹ תּוֹרָה וּמַעֲשִׂים טוֹבִים, אֵין לוֹ חֵלֶק לָעוֹלָם הַבָּא.

טז. רַבִּי יִשְׁמָעֵאל אוֹמֵר: הֱוֵי קַל לְרֹאשׁ וְנוֹחַ לְתִשְׁחֹרֶת, וֶהֱוֵי מְקַבֵּל אֶת כָּל הָאָדָם בְּשִׂמְחָה.

יז. רַבִּי עֲקִיבָא אוֹמֵר: שְׂחוֹק וְקַלּוּת רֹאשׁ מַרְגִּילִים אֶת הָאָדָם לְעֶרְוָה. מַסֹּרֶת סְיָג לַתּוֹרָה, מַעַשְׂרוֹת סְיָג לָעֹשֶׁר, נְדָרִים סְיָג לַפְּרִישׁוּת; סְיָג לַחָכְמָה שְׁתִיקָה.

רבי דוסא בן הרכינס, a man of wealth, was a contemporary of Rabban Yoḥanan ben Zakkai.

רבי אלעזר המודעי was killed by Bar-Kokhba who suspected him of being in communication with the enemy during the siege of Bethar.

מגלה פנים בתורה... one who interprets the Torah in contrast to the authoritative rulings. It has been suggested that this phrase refers to the allegorizers who accepted only the symbolic sense of the commandments and rejected the traditional interpretation.

12. He used to say: Anyone whose deeds exceed his wisdom, his wisdom shall endure; anyone whose wisdom exceeds his deeds, his wisdom shall not endure.

13. He used to say: Anyone who is liked by his fellow men is liked by God; anyone who is not liked by his fellow men is not liked by God.

14. Rabbi Dosa ben Horkinas said: Morning sleep [late sleeping], wine drinking at noon, [frivolous] children's talk, and attending the meeting-places of the ignorant shorten a man's life.

15. Rabbi Elazar of Modin said: He who profanes sacred objects, slights the festivals, puts his fellow man to shame in public, breaks the covenant of our father Abraham, or misinterprets the Torah—even though he has Torah and good deeds to his credit—has no share in the world to come.

16. Rabbi Ishmael said: Be submissive to a superior and kindly to the young; and receive all men cheerfully.

17. Rabbi Akiba said: Jesting and light-headedness lead a man on to lewdness. The *Massorah* [the tradition as to the correct text of the Scriptures] is a fence to the Torah [and preserves its integrity]; tithes form a fence to wealth; vows are a fence [a help] to self-restraint; a fence to wisdom is silence.

רבי ישמעאל, when a boy, was taken prisoner to Rome after the fall of Jerusalem, and was ransomed by Rabbi Joshua ben Ḥananyah. He formulated the "thirteen rules" by which the Torah is to be interpreted. During the Hadrianic persecutions he died as a martyr.

תשחורת has been variously rendered. It is here rendered in the sense of "youth" on the basis of שחרות in Ecclesiastes 11:10.

רבי עקיבא, one of the most important interpreters of oral tradition, began his career as a student at the age of forty. He soon became one of the most prominent leaders of Palestine, and trained a vast number of students in his academy at Bné Brak, east of Jaffa. He is the hero of many stories which are tributes to his unselfishness, loyalty and devotion. One of the main supporters of Bar-Kokhba, he died as a martyr in 135.

מעשרות סיג לעושר that is, contributions to charity protect the donor from spending his fortune wastefully. This is generally illustrated by the proverbial saying: עשר בשביל שתתעשר "Give tithes so that you will become rich," a play on the words עשר תעשר (Deuteronomy 14:22).

יח. הוּא הָיָה אוֹמֵר: חָבִיב אָדָם, שֶׁנִּבְרָא בְּצֶלֶם; חִבָּה
יְתֵרָה נוֹדַעַת לוֹ שֶׁנִּבְרָא בְּצֶלֶם, שֶׁנֶּאֱמַר: כִּי בְּצֶלֶם אֱלֹהִים
עָשָׂה אֶת הָאָדָם. חֲבִיבִים יִשְׂרָאֵל, שֶׁנִּקְרְאוּ בָנִים לַמָּקוֹם;
חִבָּה יְתֵרָה נוֹדַעַת לָהֶם שֶׁנִּקְרְאוּ בָנִים לַמָּקוֹם, שֶׁנֶּאֱמַר: בָּנִים
אַתֶּם לַיָי אֱלֹהֵיכֶם. חֲבִיבִים יִשְׂרָאֵל, שֶׁנִּתַּן לָהֶם כְּלִי חֶמְדָּה;
חִבָּה יְתֵרָה נוֹדַעַת לָהֶם שֶׁנִּתַּן לָהֶם כְּלִי חֶמְדָּה, שֶׁבּוֹ נִבְרָא
הָעוֹלָם, שֶׁנֶּאֱמַר: כִּי לֶקַח טוֹב נָתַתִּי לָכֶם, תּוֹרָתִי אַל תַּעֲזֹבוּ.

יט. הַכֹּל צָפוּי, וְהָרְשׁוּת נְתוּנָה, וּבְטוֹב הָעוֹלָם נָדוֹן, וְהַכֹּל
לְפִי רֹב הַמַּעֲשֶׂה.

כ. הוּא הָיָה אוֹמֵר: הַכֹּל נָתוּן בָּעֵרָבוֹן, וּמְצוֹדָה פְרוּשָׂה
עַל כָּל הַחַיִּים. הֶחָנוּת פְּתוּחָה, וְהַחֶנְוָנִי מַקִּיף, וְהַפִּנְקָס פָּתוּחַ,
וְהַיָּד כּוֹתֶבֶת, וְכָל הָרוֹצֶה לִלְווֹת יָבֹא וְיִלְוֶה; וְהַגַּבָּאִים
מַחֲזִירִים תָּדִיר בְּכָל יוֹם וְנִפְרָעִים מִן הָאָדָם, מִדַּעְתּוֹ וְשֶׁלֹּא
מִדַּעְתּוֹ, וְיֵשׁ לָהֶם עַל מַה שֶׁיִּסְמֹכוּ. וְהַדִּין דִּין אֱמֶת, וְהַכֹּל
מְתֻקָּן לַסְּעֻדָּה.

כא. רַבִּי אֶלְעָזָר בֶּן עֲזַרְיָה אוֹמֵר: אִם אֵין תּוֹרָה, אֵין
דֶּרֶךְ אֶרֶץ; אִם אֵין דֶּרֶךְ אֶרֶץ, אֵין תּוֹרָה. אִם אֵין חָכְמָה, אֵין
יִרְאָה; אִם אֵין יִרְאָה, אֵין חָכְמָה. אִם אֵין דַּעַת, אֵין בִּינָה; אִם
אֵין בִּינָה, אֵין דָּעַת. אִם אֵין קֶמַח, אֵין תּוֹרָה; אִם אֵין תּוֹרָה,
אֵין קֶמַח.

הרשות נתונה that is, God's foreknowledge does not predetermine man's
actions, good or bad. In matters of ethical conduct man has the ability to
choose between alternative possibilities of action.

הכל לפי רוב המעשה Man's good deeds are set off against his evil deeds,
and he is condemned or acquitted according to the preponderance of his good
or bad deeds.

הכל נתון בערבון is a saying which employs the language of everyday business life to drive home the thought with greater force.

18. He used to say: Beloved is man, for he was created in the image of God; it is by special divine love that he is informed that he was created in the image of God, as it is said: "For God made man in his own image."[1] Beloved are Israel, for they were called the children of God; it is by special divine love that they are informed that they were called the children of God, as it is said: "You are the children of the Lord your God."[2] Beloved are Israel, for to them was given a precious instrument [the Torah]; it is by special divine love that they are informed that to them was given the precious instrument through which the world was created, as it is said: "For I give you good doctrine; forsake not my Torah."[3]

19. Everything is foreseen [by God], yet freewill is granted [to man]; the world is ruled with divine goodness, yet all is according to the amount of man's work.

20. He used to say: Everything is given on pledge, and a net is spread for all the living [none can escape divine justice]; the store is open, and the storekeeper [God] allows credit; the ledger is open, and the hand writes; whoever wishes to borrow may come and borrow, but the collectors go around regularly every day and exact payment from man, whether or not he realizes [that he is punished for his sins]; they have good authority on which they can rely, since the judgment is just; and all is prepared for the banquet [the reward of the righteous is assured].

21. Rabbi Elazar ben Azaryah said: Where there is no Torah, there is no proper conduct; where there is no proper conduct, there is no Torah. Where there is no wisdom, there is no reverence; where there is no reverence, there is no wisdom. Where there is no knowledge, there is no understanding; where there is no understanding, there is no knowledge. Where there is no bread, there is no Torah; where there is no Torah, there is no bread.

רבי אלעזר בן עזריה was elected president of the Sanhedrin when Rabban Gamaliel II was temporarily deposed. When Rabban Gamaliel was restored to his former position, Rabbi Elazar was retained as vice-president of the Sanhedrin. He used his great wealth for the welfare of his people during the Roman persecutions before the revolt of Bar-Kokhba.

---

[1] *Genesis* 9:6. [2] *Deuteronomy* 14:1. [3] *Proverbs* 4:2.

כב. הוּא הָיָה אוֹמֵר: כֹּל שֶׁחָכְמָתוֹ מְרֻבָּה מִמַּעֲשָׂיו, לְמָה הוּא דוֹמֶה, לְאִילָן שֶׁעֲנָפָיו מְרֻבִּים וְשָׁרָשָׁיו מְעָטִים, וְהָרוּחַ בָּאָה וְעוֹקַרְתּוֹ וְהוֹפַכְתּוֹ עַל פָּנָיו, שֶׁנֶּאֱמַר: וְהָיָה כְּעַרְעָר בָּעֲרָבָה, וְלֹא יִרְאֶה כִּי יָבוֹא טוֹב, וְשָׁכַן חֲרֵרִים בַּמִּדְבָּר, אֶרֶץ מְלֵחָה וְלֹא תֵשֵׁב. אֲבָל כָּל שֶׁמַּעֲשָׂיו מְרֻבִּים מֵחָכְמָתוֹ, לְמָה הוּא דוֹמֶה, לְאִילָן שֶׁעֲנָפָיו מְעָטִים וְשָׁרָשָׁיו מְרֻבִּים, שֶׁאֲפִילוּ כָּל הָרוּחוֹת שֶׁבָּעוֹלָם בָּאוֹת וְנוֹשְׁבוֹת בּוֹ, אֵין מְזִיזִים אוֹתוֹ מִמְּקוֹמוֹ, שֶׁנֶּאֱמַר: וְהָיָה כְּעֵץ שָׁתוּל עַל מַיִם, וְעַל יוּבַל יְשַׁלַּח שָׁרָשָׁיו, וְלֹא יִרְאֶה כִּי יָבֹא חֹם, וְהָיָה עָלֵהוּ רַעֲנָן, וּבִשְׁנַת בַּצֹּרֶת לֹא יִדְאָג, וְלֹא יָמִישׁ מֵעֲשׂוֹת פֶּרִי ׃

כג. רַבִּי אֶלְעָזָר בֶּן חִסְמָא אוֹמֵר: קִנִּין וּפִתְחֵי נִדָּה הֵן הֵן גּוּפֵי הֲלָכוֹת; תְּקוּפוֹת וְגִמַטְרִיָאוֹת פַּרְפְּרָאוֹת לַחָכְמָה ׃

רַבִּי חֲנַנְיָא בֶּן עֲקַשְׁיָא אוֹמֵר: רָצָה הַקָּדוֹשׁ בָּרוּךְ הוּא לְזַכּוֹת אֶת יִשְׂרָאֵל, לְפִיכָךְ הִרְבָּה לָהֶם תּוֹרָה וּמִצְוֹת, שֶׁנֶּאֱמַר: יְיָ חָפֵץ לְמַעַן צִדְקוֹ, יַגְדִּיל תּוֹרָה וְיַאְדִּיר ׃

פֶּרֶק רְבִיעִי

כָּל יִשְׂרָאֵל יֵשׁ לָהֶם חֵלֶק לָעוֹלָם הַבָּא, שֶׁנֶּאֱמַר: וְעַמֵּךְ כֻּלָּם צַדִּיקִים, לְעוֹלָם יִרְשׁוּ אָרֶץ; נֵצֶר מַטָּעַי, מַעֲשֵׂה יָדַי לְהִתְפָּאֵר ׃

כל שחכמתו מרובה.... is an elaboration of the maxim expressed above (3:12) by Rabbi Ḥanina ben Dosa. Moral goodness is more essential than speculative thought. Wisdom is valueless unless it improves a man's character. If he has more theoretical knowledge than good deeds, his life is ruined by his failure to live up to his ethical principles. On the other hand, a good life is possible even if it is not based on much learning.

22.   He used to say: One whose wisdom exceeds his deeds, to what is he like? To a tree that has many branches and few roots, so that when the wind comes, it plucks it up and turns it over, as it is said: "And he shall be like a lonely tree in the desert, and shall not see the coming of good; he shall inhabit the parched places in the wilderness, a salt land and uninhabited."[1] But one whose deeds exceed his wisdom, to what is he like? To a tree that has few branches and many roots, so that even if all the winds in the world come and blow upon it, they cannot move it out of its place, as it is said: "And he shall be like a tree planted by waters, that spreads out its roots beside a stream; it sees not the coming of heat, and its leaves are ever green; in a year of drought it is not troubled, and ceases not to bear fruit."[2]

23.   Rabbi Elazar Ḥisma said: The laws concerning the sacrifices of birds and the purification of women are essential precepts; astronomy and geometry are the auxiliaries of wisdom.

Rabbi Ḥananyah ben Akashyah said: The Holy One, blessed be he, desired to purify Israel; hence he gave them a Torah rich in rules of conduct, as it is said: "The Lord was pleased, for the sake of [Israel's] righteousness, to render the Torah great and glorious."[3]

CHAPTER FOUR

All Israel have a share in the world to come, as it is said; "Your people shall all be righteous; they shall possess the land forever; they are a plant of my own, the work of my hands, wherein I may glory."[4]

רבי אלעזר חסמא, a disciple of Rabbi Akiba, was famous for his knowledge of astronomy and physics. He means to say that though the laws concerning bird sacrifices do not apply when the Temple no longer exists, and though certain laws seem unattractive as a subject of study, they are nevertheless of highest importance, because they form the precepts of the Torah. The primary meaning of פרפרת is dessert, appetizer. Some derive this word from the Greek in the sense of periphery, outer circle, as opposed to the essence of the Torah. According to this view, Rabbi Elazar means to say that astronomy and geometry are of secondary importance to the study of the Torah.

---

[1] *Jeremiah* 17:6.   [2] *Jeremiah* 17:8.   [3] *Isaiah* 42:21.   [4] *Isaiah* 60:21.

א. בֶּן זוֹמָא אוֹמֵר: אֵיזֶהוּ חָכָם, הַלּוֹמֵד מִכָּל אָדָם,
שֶׁנֶּאֱמַר: מִכָּל מְלַמְּדַי הִשְׂכַּלְתִּי (כִּי עֵדְוֹתֶיךָ שִׂיחָה לִי). אֵיזֶהוּ
גִבּוֹר, הַכּוֹבֵשׁ אֶת יִצְרוֹ, שֶׁנֶּאֱמַר: טוֹב אֶרֶךְ אַפַּיִם מִגִּבּוֹר,
וּמוֹשֵׁל בְּרוּחוֹ מִלּוֹכֵד עִיר. אֵיזֶהוּ עָשִׁיר, הַשָּׂמֵחַ בְּחֶלְקוֹ,
שֶׁנֶּאֱמַר: יְגִיעַ כַּפֶּיךָ כִּי תֹאכֵל, אַשְׁרֶיךָ וְטוֹב לָךְ. אַשְׁרֶיךָ,
בָּעוֹלָם הַזֶּה; וְטוֹב לָךְ, לָעוֹלָם הַבָּא. אֵיזֶהוּ מְכֻבָּד, הַמְכַבֵּד
אֶת הַבְּרִיּוֹת, שֶׁנֶּאֱמַר: כִּי מְכַבְּדַי אֲכַבֵּד, וּבֹזַי יֵקָלּוּ.

ב. בֶּן עַזַּי אוֹמֵר: הֱוֵי רָץ לְמִצְוָה קַלָּה (כְּלַחֲמוּרָה) וּבוֹרֵחַ
מִן הָעֲבֵרָה, שֶׁמִּצְוָה גּוֹרֶרֶת מִצְוָה, וַעֲבֵרָה גּוֹרֶרֶת עֲבֵרָה;
שֶׁשְּׂכַר מִצְוָה מִצְוָה, וּשְׂכַר עֲבֵרָה עֲבֵרָה.

ג. הוּא הָיָה אוֹמֵר: אַל תְּהִי בָז לְכָל אָדָם, וְאַל תְּהִי מַפְלִיג
לְכָל דָּבָר, שֶׁאֵין לְךָ אָדָם שֶׁאֵין לוֹ שָׁעָה, וְאֵין לְךָ דָבָר שֶׁאֵין
לוֹ מָקוֹם.

ד. רַבִּי לְוִיטַס, אִישׁ יַבְנֶה, אוֹמֵר: מְאֹד מְאֹד הֱוֵי שְׁפַל
רוּחַ, שֶׁתִּקְוַת אֱנוֹשׁ רִמָּה.

ה. רַבִּי יוֹחָנָן בֶּן בְּרוֹקָא אוֹמֵר: כָּל הַמְחַלֵּל שֵׁם שָׁמַיִם
בַּסֵּתֶר, נִפְרָעִים מִמֶּנּוּ בַּגָּלוּי. אֶחָד שׁוֹגֵג וְאֶחָד מֵזִיד בְּחִלּוּל
הַשֵּׁם.

ו. רַבִּי יִשְׁמָעֵאל בְּנוֹ אוֹמֵר: הַלּוֹמֵד עַל מְנָת לְלַמֵּד,
מַסְפִּיקִים בְּיָדוֹ לִלְמֹד וּלְלַמֵּד; וְהַלּוֹמֵד עַל מְנָת לַעֲשׂוֹת,
מַסְפִּיקִים בְּיָדוֹ לִלְמֹד וּלְלַמֵּד, לִשְׁמֹר וְלַעֲשׂוֹת.

שמעון בן זומא, a younger contemporary of Rabbi Akiba, was a colleague of
שמעון בן עזי (quoted in the next paragraph). Their own names are omitted
because they both died at an early age, before they could be ordained. They
were deeply interested in mysticism and theosophy.

מצוה an act performed in the interests of religion or of fellow men.

שכר מצוה מצוה Habits are formed by the repetition of single acts.

1. Ben Zoma said: Who is wise? He who learns from every man, as it is said: "From all my teachers I gained wisdom."[1] Who is strong? He who subdues his [evil] impulse, as it is said: "He who is slow to anger is better than a strong man; he who rules his spirit is better than one who conquers a city."[2] Who is rich? He who is content with his lot, as it is said: "When you eat of the toil of your hands, happy shall you be, and it shall be well with you."[3] *Happy shall you be* in this world; *and it shall be well with you* in the world to come. Who is honored? He who honors his fellow-men, as it is said: "Those who honor me [by honoring man, created in the image of God] I will honor, and those who despise me shall be lightly esteemed."[4]

2. Ben Azzai said: Run to perform even a minor *mitzvah*, and flee from transgression; for one good deed draws [in its train] another good deed, and one transgression leads to another; for the reward of a good deed is a good deed, and the reward of sin is sin [virtue is its own reward, and sin its own penalty].

3. He used to say: Do not despise any man, and do not consider anything as impossible; for there is not a man who has not his hour, and there is not a thing that has not its place.

4. Rabbi Levitas of Yavneh said: Be exceedingly humble, since the end of man is worms.

5. Rabbi Yoḥanan ben Berokah said: Whoever profanes the name of God secretly is punished publicly, whether the profanation is committed intentionally or unintentionally.

6. Rabbi Ishmael said: He who learns in order to teach will be granted adequate means to learn and to teach; but he who learns in order to practise will be granted adequate means to learn and to teach, to observe and to practise.

רבי לויטס was a contemporary of Rabbi Akiba.

תקוה limit, end; compare הנותן תקוה לנזירותו, ("he who sets a limit to . . .") and the phrase אחריתנו רמה in the *nei'lah* service.

רבי יוחנן בן ברוקא was a disciple of Rabbi Joshua ben Ḥananyah (second century).

חלול השם ("defamation of God's name") is an act performed in defiance of religious or ethical principles.

רבי ישמעאל Some texts add בנו ("his son").

---

[1] *Psalm* 119:99.   [2] *Proverbs* 16:32.   [3] *Psalm* 128:2.   [4] *I Samuel* 2:30.

ז. רַבִּי צָדוֹק אוֹמֵר: אַל תִּפְרוֹשׁ מִן הַצִּבּוּר, וְאַל תַּעַשׂ עַצְמְךָ כְּעוֹרְכֵי הַדַּיָּנִים, וְאַל תַּעֲשֶׂהָ עֲטָרָה לְהִתְגַּדֶּל־בָּהּ, וְלֹא קַרְדֹּם לַחְפָּר־בָּהּ. וְכָךְ הָיָה הִלֵּל אוֹמֵר: וּדְאִשְׁתַּמַּשׁ בְּתָגָא חֲלָף. הָא לָמַדְתָּ, כָּל הַנֶּהֱנֶה מִדִּבְרֵי תוֹרָה נוֹטֵל חַיָּיו מִן הָעוֹלָם.

ח. רַבִּי יוֹסֵי אוֹמֵר: כָּל הַמְכַבֵּד אֶת הַתּוֹרָה, גּוּפוֹ מְכֻבָּד עַל הַבְּרִיּוֹת; וְכָל הַמְחַלֵּל אֶת הַתּוֹרָה, גּוּפוֹ מְחֻלָּל עַל הַבְּרִיּוֹת.

ט. רַבִּי יִשְׁמָעֵאל בְּנוֹ אוֹמֵר: הַחוֹשֵׂךְ עַצְמוֹ מִן הַדִּין, פּוֹרֵק מִמֶּנּוּ אֵיבָה וְגָזֵל וּשְׁבוּעַת שָׁוְא; וְהַגַּס לִבּוֹ בְהוֹרָאָה שׁוֹטֶה, רָשָׁע וְגַס רוּחַ.

י. הוּא הָיָה אוֹמֵר: אַל תְּהִי דָן יְחִידִי, שֶׁאֵין דָּן יְחִידִי אֶלָּא אֶחָד; וְאַל תֹּאמַר קַבְּלוּ דַעְתִּי, שֶׁהֵם רַשָּׁאִים וְלֹא אָתָּה.

יא. רַבִּי יוֹנָתָן אוֹמֵר: כָּל הַמְקַיֵּם אֶת הַתּוֹרָה מֵעֹנִי, סוֹפוֹ לְקַיְּמָהּ מֵעֹשֶׁר; וְכָל הַמְבַטֵּל אֶת הַתּוֹרָה מֵעֹשֶׁר, סוֹפוֹ לְבַטְּלָהּ מֵעֹנִי.

יב. רַבִּי מֵאִיר אוֹמֵר: הֱוֵי מְמַעֵט בְּעֵסֶק וַעֲסֹק בַּתּוֹרָה, וֶהֱוֵי שְׁפַל רוּחַ בִּפְנֵי כָל אָדָם. וְאִם בָּטַלְתָּ מִן הַתּוֹרָה, יֶשׁ־לְךָ בְטֵלִים הַרְבֵּה כְּנֶגְדֶּךָ; וְאִם עָמַלְתָּ בַתּוֹרָה, יֶשׁ־לוֹ שָׂכָר הַרְבֵּה לִתֶּן־לָךְ.

רבי צדוק was probably the one who is said to have fasted for forty years, praying that Jerusalem should not be destroyed.

יוסי בן חלפתא, one of the most distinguished disciples of Rabbi Akiba, compiled the chronological treatise *Seder Olam* ("Order of the World"), from the creation until the revolt of Bar-Kokhba.

רבי ישמעאל בנו Some texts omit בנו ("his son").

הגס לבו בהוראה one who is too sure of himself, not realizing that the judicial position is one that involves infinite pains in the sifting of evidence and in reaching a decision.

7. Rabbi Zadok said: Do not keep aloof from the community;
do not [as a judge] play the part of a counselor; do not make of the
Torah a crown wherewith to magnify yourself, nor a spade wherewith to dig. Hillel used to say: "He who makes unworthy use of
the crown [of the Torah] shall perish." Hence, whoever makes
selfish use of the Torah takes his own life.

8. Rabbi Yosé said: Whoever honors the Torah will himself
be honored by men; whoever dishonors the Torah will himself be
dishonored by men.

9. Rabbi Ishmael his son said: He who avoids entering into
litigation [and seeks a friendly settlement] rids himself of hatred,
robbery and perjury; he who proudly lays down decisions is
foolish, wicked and arrogant.

10. He used to say: Do not judge alone, for none may judge
alone except One [God]; do not say [to your co-judges]: "Accept my
view," for they [who are in the majority] are entitled to say that,
but not you.

11. Rabbi Jonathan said: Whoever fulfills the Torah despite
poverty shall in the end fulfill it in the midst of wealth; whoever
neglects the Torah in the midst of wealth shall in the end neglect
it on account of poverty.

12. Rabbi Meir said: Do rather less business and occupy
yourself with the Torah; be humble before all men; if you neglect
the Torah, you will have many disturbing causes in your way
but if you toil in the Torah, God has abundant reward to give you.

רבי יונתן was a disciple of Rabbi Akiba.

רבי מאיר, the greatest of Rabbi Akiba's disciples, was called *Meir* ("en-
lightener") on account of his pre-eminence as a teacher and lecturer. His wife,
Beruriah, was herself a scholar, whose wise utterances and legal views are
quoted in the Talmud. By profession a scribe, whose Bible copies were given
special notice, he denounced those who acquire learning but fail to impart it
to others. In order to obtain knowledge from all possible sources, he cultivated
the friendship of Elisha ben Abuyah (אחר), who had turned heretic. He departed from Palestine, and died in Asia Minor. His last wish was: "Bury me
by the seashore, that the waves which wash my fatherland may wash also
my bones." His name occurs some 800 times in tannaitic literature.

יג. רַבִּי אֱלִיעֶזֶר בֶּן יַעֲקֹב אוֹמֵר: הָעוֹשֶׂה מִצְוָה אַחַת קוֹנֶה
לוֹ פְּרַקְלִיט אֶחָד, וְהָעוֹבֵר עֲבֵרָה אַחַת קוֹנֶה לוֹ קַטֵּגוֹר אֶחָד.
תְּשׁוּבָה וּמַעֲשִׂים טוֹבִים כִּתְרִיס בִּפְנֵי הַפֻּרְעָנוּת.

יד. רַבִּי יוֹחָנָן הַסַּנְדְּלָר אוֹמֵר: כָּל כְּנֵסִיָּה שֶׁהִיא לְשֵׁם
שָׁמַיִם, סוֹפָהּ לְהִתְקַיֵּם; וְשֶׁאֵינָהּ לְשֵׁם שָׁמַיִם, אֵין סוֹפָהּ
לְהִתְקַיֵּם.

טו. רַבִּי אֶלְעָזָר בֶּן שַׁמּוּעַ אוֹמֵר: יְהִי כְבוֹד תַּלְמִידְךָ
חָבִיב עָלֶיךָ כְּשֶׁלָּךְ, וּכְבוֹד חֲבֵרְךָ כְּמוֹרָא רַבָּךְ, וּמוֹרָא רַבָּךְ
כְּמוֹרָא שָׁמָיִם.

טז. רַבִּי יְהוּדָה אוֹמֵר: הֱוֵי זָהִיר בְּתַלְמוּד, שֶׁשִּׁגְגַת תַּלְמוּד
עוֹלָה זָדוֹן.

יז. רַבִּי שִׁמְעוֹן אוֹמֵר: שְׁלֹשָׁה כְתָרִים הֵן: כֶּתֶר תּוֹרָה,
וְכֶתֶר כְּהֻנָּה, וְכֶתֶר מַלְכוּת; וְכֶתֶר שֵׁם טוֹב עוֹלֶה עַל גַּבֵּיהֶן.

יח. רַבִּי נְהוֹרַי אוֹמֵר: הֱוֵי גוֹלֶה לִמְקוֹם תּוֹרָה, וְאַל תֹּאמַר
שֶׁהִיא תָבוֹא אַחֲרֶיךָ, שֶׁחֲבֵרֶיךָ יְקַיְּמוּהָ בְיָדֶךָ, וְאֶל בִּינָתְךָ
אַל תִּשָּׁעֵן.

יט. רַבִּי יַנַּי אוֹמֵר: אֵין בְּיָדֵינוּ לֹא מִשַּׁלְוַת הָרְשָׁעִים, וְאַף
לֹא מִיִּסּוּרֵי הַצַּדִּיקִים.

כ. רַבִּי מַתִּתְיָה בֶּן חָרָשׁ אוֹמֵר: הֱוֵי מַקְדִּים בִּשְׁלוֹם כָּל
אָדָם, וֶהֱוֵי זָנָב לָאֲרָיוֹת וְאַל תְּהִי רֹאשׁ לַשֻּׁעָלִים.

רבי אליעזר בן יעקב, and the *Tannaim* who are quoted in paragraphs 13–18,
lived in the second century and studied under the guidance of Rabbi Akiba.

קונה לו פרקליט is to be compared with the midrashic statement: "If a man
performs one *mitzvah*, God gives him one angel to guard him. . . If he performs
two *mitzvoth*, God gives him two angels to guard him. . ." (*Shemoth Rabbah,*
32). Each good deed pleads for the man who stands in judgment before God.

תשובה ומעשים טובים is frequently emphasized in talmudic literature. One
of the rabbis was in the habit of saying: "The chief purpose of wisdom is

13.   Rabbi Eliezer ben Jacob said: He who performs one *mitzvah* gains for himself one advocate; he who commits one transgression acquires for himself one accuser. Repentance and good deeds are as a shield against punishment.

14.   Rabbi Yoḥanan ha-Sandlar said: Any assembly which is for the sake of Heaven [for the promotion of a noble purpose] will be of permanent value, but one which is not for the sake of Heaven will not be of permanent value.

15.   Rabbi Elazar ben Shammua said: Let the honor of your student be as dear to you as your own, and the honor of your colleague be like the reverence due to your teacher, and the reverence for your teacher be like the reverence for Heaven.

16.   Rabbi Judah said: Be careful in teaching, for an error in teaching amounts to intentional sin.

17.   Rabbi Simeon said: There are three crowns: the crown of Torah, the crown of priesthood, and the crown of royalty; but the crown of a good name excels them all.

18.   Rabbi Nehorai said: Go as a voluntary exile to a place of Torah, and do not say that the Torah will seek after you, for it is your fellow students who will make it your permanent possession; and do not rely on your own understanding.

19.   Rabbi Yannai said: It is not in our power to explain why the wicked are at ease, or why the righteous suffer.

20.   Rabbi Mattithyah ben Ḥeresh said: Meet every man with a friendly greeting; be the tail among lions rather than the head among foxes.

---

repentance and good deeds; let no man who engages in learning treat his parents with contempt. . ." (Berakhoth 17a).

רבי יוחנן הסנדלר was an Alexandrian. His surname is due either to his occupation as a sandal-maker, or to the fact that he was a native of Alexandria.

שגגת תלמוד עולה זדון if the error is due to carelessness.

רבי נהוראי is identified with Rabbi Elazar ben Arakh and Rabbi Meir.

חבריך יקיימוה בידך Torah knowledge is acquired by association with scholars.

אל בינתך אל תשען a quotation from Proverbs 3:5.

רבי ינאי is not mentioned elsewhere in tannaitic literature.

רבי מתתיה lived in Rome in the middle of the second century.

כא. רַבִּי יַעֲקֹב אוֹמֵר: הָעוֹלָם הַזֶּה דּוֹמֶה לִפְרוֹזְדוֹר בִּפְנֵי הָעוֹלָם הַבָּא; הַתְקֵן עַצְמְךָ בַּפְּרוֹזְדוֹר, כְּדֵי שֶׁתִּכָּנֵס לַטְּרַקְלִין.

כב. הוּא הָיָה אוֹמֵר: יָפָה שָׁעָה אַחַת בִּתְשׁוּבָה וּמַעֲשִׂים טוֹבִים בָּעוֹלָם הַזֶּה מִכָּל חַיֵּי הָעוֹלָם הַבָּא; וְיָפָה שָׁעָה אַחַת שֶׁל קָרַת רוּחַ בָּעוֹלָם הַבָּא מִכָּל חַיֵּי הָעוֹלָם הַזֶּה.

כג. רַבִּי שִׁמְעוֹן בֶּן אֶלְעָזָר אוֹמֵר: אַל תְּרַצֶּה אֶת חֲבֵרְךָ בִּשְׁעַת כַּעֲסוֹ, וְאַל תְּנַחֲמֵהוּ בְּשָׁעָה שֶׁמֵּתוֹ מֻטָּל לְפָנָיו, וְאַל תִּשְׁאַל לוֹ בִּשְׁעַת נִדְרוֹ, וְאַל תִּשְׁתַּדֵּל לִרְאוֹתוֹ בִּשְׁעַת קַלְקָלָתוֹ.

כד. שְׁמוּאֵל הַקָּטָן אוֹמֵר: בִּנְפֹל אֹיִבְךָ אַל תִּשְׂמָח, וּבִכָּשְׁלוֹ אַל יָגֵל לִבֶּךָ, פֶּן יִרְאֶה יְיָ וְרַע בְּעֵינָיו, וְהֵשִׁיב מֵעָלָיו אַפּוֹ.

כה. אֱלִישָׁע בֶּן אֲבוּיָה אוֹמֵר: הַלּוֹמֵד יֶלֶד, לְמָה הוּא דוֹמֶה, לִדְיוֹ כְּתוּבָה עַל נְיָר חָדָשׁ; וְהַלּוֹמֵד זָקֵן, לְמָה הוּא דוֹמֶה, לִדְיוֹ כְּתוּבָה עַל נְיָר מָחוּק.

כו. רַבִּי יוֹסֵי בַּר יְהוּדָה, אִישׁ כְּפַר הַבַּבְלִי, אוֹמֵר: הַלּוֹמֵד מִן הַקְּטַנִּים, לְמָה הוּא דוֹמֶה, לְאוֹכֵל עֲנָבִים קֵהוֹת וְשׁוֹתֶה יַיִן מִגִּתּוֹ; וְהַלּוֹמֵד מִן הַזְּקֵנִים, לְמָה הוּא דוֹמֶה, לְאוֹכֵל עֲנָבִים בְּשׁוּלוֹת וְשׁוֹתֶה יַיִן יָשָׁן.

כז. רַבִּי מֵאִיר אוֹמֵר: אַל תִּסְתַּכֵּל בַּקַּנְקַן אֶלָּא בְּמָה שֶׁיֶּשׁ בּוֹ: יֵשׁ קַנְקַן חָדָשׁ מָלֵא יָשָׁן, וְיָשָׁן שֶׁאֲפִילוּ חָדָשׁ אֵין בּוֹ.

רבי שמעון בן אלעזר was a disciple of Rabbi Meir and lived during the second century.

אל תרצה את חברך ... a warning against unintended provocation.

שמואל הקטן lived towards the end of the first century, and was famous for his humility; hence the surname "ha-Katan." The saying reported in his name is a quotation from Proverbs 24:17-18. It has been suggested that the phrase שהרי הכתוב אומר (=) שה"א is an amplification of the initials שמואל הקטן אומר

21. Rabbi Jacob said: This world is like a vestibule before the world to come; prepare yourself in the vestibule, so that you may enter the banquet hall.

22. He used to say: One hour spent in repentance and good deeds in this world is better [more exhilarating] than the whole life of the world to come; yet one hour of satisfaction in the world to come is better than a whole life of this world.

23. Rabbi Simeon ben Elazar said: Do not pacify your fellow in the hour of his anger; do not comfort him while his dead lies before him; do not question him at the time he makes a vow; and do not try to see him in the hour of his disgrace.

24. Samuel ha-Katan said: "Rejoice not when your enemy falls, and let not your heart exult when he stumbles; lest the Lord see it and be displeased, and he divert his wrath from him [to you]."[1]

25. Elisha ben Avuyah said: If one learns when he is young, to what is it like? To ink written on new [clean] paper. If one learns when he is old, to what is it like? To ink written on blotted paper.

26. Rabbi Yosé ben Judah of Kfar ha-Bavli said: He who learns from the young, to what is he like? To one who eats unripe grapes, or drinks [new] wine from his vat. He who learns from the old, to what is he like? To one who eats ripe grapes, or drinks old wine.

27. Rabbi Meir said: Do not look at the flask but at what it contains: a new flask may be filled with old wine and an old flask may be empty even of new wine [a man's age is not a reliable index to his learning].

---

introducing biblical support of the preceding statement that one must not try to see anyone in disgrace.

אלישע בן אבויה, known as *Aḥer* ("the other"), lived in the second century as one of the great scholars of the period, a colleague of Rabbi Akiba and teacher of Rabbi Meir, but turned heretic under the influence of Greek philosophy and theosophic speculations. Whether he completely broke away from Judaism is a matter of doubt.

רבי יוסי בר יהודה was an older contemporary of Rabbi Judah ha-Nasi (towards the end of the second century). *Kfar ha-Bavli* was a village in Galilee.

---

[1] *Proverbs* 24:17-18.

כח. רַבִּי אֶלְעָזָר הַקַּפָּר אוֹמֵר: הַקִּנְאָה וְהַתַּאֲוָה וְהַכָּבוֹד מוֹצִיאִים אֶת הָאָדָם מִן הָעוֹלָם.

כט. הוּא הָיָה אוֹמֵר: הַיִּלּוֹדִים לָמוּת, וְהַמֵּתִים לְהֵחָיוֹת, וְהַחַיִּים לִדּוֹן, לֵדַע וּלְהוֹדִיעַ וּלְהִוָּדַע שֶׁהוּא אֵל. הוּא הַיּוֹצֵר, הוּא הַבּוֹרֵא, הוּא הַמֵּבִין, הוּא הַדַּיָּן, הוּא הָעֵד, הוּא בַּעַל דִּין, הוּא עָתִיד לָדוּן. בָּרוּךְ הוּא, שֶׁאֵין לְפָנָיו לֹא עַוְלָה, וְלֹא שִׁכְחָה, וְלֹא מַשּׂוֹא פָנִים, וְלֹא מִקַּח שֹׁחַד. וְדַע שֶׁהַכֹּל לְפִי הַחֶשְׁבּוֹן. וְאַל יַבְטִיחֲךָ יִצְרְךָ שֶׁהַשְּׁאוֹל בֵּית מָנוֹס לָךְ, שֶׁעַל כָּרְחֲךָ אַתָּה נוֹצָר, וְעַל כָּרְחֲךָ אַתָּה נוֹלָד, וְעַל כָּרְחֲךָ אַתָּה חַי, וְעַל כָּרְחֲךָ אַתָּה מֵת, וְעַל כָּרְחֲךָ אַתָּה עָתִיד לִתֵּן דִּין וְחֶשְׁבּוֹן לִפְנֵי מֶלֶךְ מַלְכֵי הַמְּלָכִים, הַקָּדוֹשׁ בָּרוּךְ הוּא.

רַבִּי חֲנַנְיָא בֶּן עֲקַשְׁיָא אוֹמֵר: רָצָה הַקָּדוֹשׁ בָּרוּךְ הוּא לְזַכּוֹת אֶת יִשְׂרָאֵל, לְפִיכָךְ הִרְבָּה לָהֶם תּוֹרָה וּמִצְוֹת, שֶׁנֶּאֱמַר: יְיָ חָפֵץ לְמַעַן צִדְקוֹ, יַגְדִּיל תּוֹרָה וְיַאְדִּיר.

פֶּרֶק חֲמִישִׁי

כָּל יִשְׂרָאֵל יֵשׁ לָהֶם חֵלֶק לָעוֹלָם הַבָּא, שֶׁנֶּאֱמַר: וְעַמֵּךְ כֻּלָּם צַדִּיקִים, לְעוֹלָם יִירְשׁוּ אָרֶץ; נֵצֶר מַטָּעַי, מַעֲשֵׂה יָדַי לְהִתְפָּאֵר.

א. בַּעֲשָׂרָה מַאֲמָרוֹת נִבְרָא הָעוֹלָם. וּמַה תַּלְמוּד לוֹמַר, וַהֲלֹא בְּמַאֲמָר אֶחָד יָכוֹל לְהִבָּרְאוֹת, אֶלָּא לְהִפָּרַע מִן הָרְשָׁעִים, שֶׁמְּאַבְּדִים אֶת הָעוֹלָם שֶׁנִּבְרָא בַּעֲשָׂרָה מַאֲמָרוֹת, וְלִתֵּן שָׂכָר טוֹב לַצַּדִּיקִים, שֶׁמְּקַיְּמִים אֶת הָעוֹלָם שֶׁנִּבְרָא בַּעֲשָׂרָה מַאֲמָרוֹת.

רבי אלעזר הקפר, father of Bar Kappara, lived in the second century. **מקח שחד**. The Mishnah text has שהכל שלו after the words להחיות=**לחיות**.

28. Rabbi Elazar ha-Kappar said: Envy, lust and vainglory shorten a man's life.

29. He used to say: Those who are born are destined to die; those who are dead are destined to be brought to life again; and the living are destined to be judged. [It is for you] to know, proclaim and be sure that he is God. He is the Maker, he the Creator, he the Discerner, he the Judge, he the Witness, he the Complainant; it is he who will judge. Blessed be he in whose presence there is no wrongdoing, nor forgetting, nor partiality, nor taking of bribes. Know that all is according to reckoning, and let not your imagination persuade you that the grave is a place of refuge for you. Perforce you were formed and perforce you were born; perforce you live, perforce you shall die, and perforce you shall have to give a strict account before the supreme King of kings, the Holy One, blessed be he.

Rabbi Ḥananyah ben Akashyah said: The Holy One, blessed be he, desired to purify Israel; hence he gave them a Torah rich in rules of conduct, as it is said: "The Lord was pleased, for the sake of [Israel's] righteousness, to render the Torah great and glorious."[1]

CHAPTER FIVE

All Israel have a share in the world to come, as it is said: "Your people shall all be righteous; they shall possess the land forever; they are a plant of my own, the work of my hands, wherein I may glory."[2]

1. By ten divine utterances was the world created. Why does the Torah indicate this? Surely the world could have been created by one divine utterance. It means to emphasize that God will exact [severe] penalty from the wicked who destroy the world which was created by [no less than] ten utterances, and that he will grant a rich reward to the righteous who maintain the world which was created by ten utterances.

בעשרה מאמרות The several phases of creation are introduced by the phrase "and God said" nine times in Genesis 1:3–29 and once in 2:18.

The paragraphs in this chapter, arranged under several numerical headings, are of unknown authorship and folkloristic in nature.

---

[1] *Isaiah* 42:21.   [2] *Isaiah* 60:21.

ב. עֲשָׂרָה דוֹרוֹת מֵאָדָם וְעַד נֹחַ, לְהוֹדִיעַ כַּמָּה אֹרֶךְ אַפַּיִם לְפָנָיו, שֶׁכָּל הַדּוֹרוֹת הָיוּ מַכְעִיסִים לְפָנָיו, עַד שֶׁהֵבִיא עֲלֵיהֶם אֶת מֵי הַמַּבּוּל.

ג. עֲשָׂרָה דוֹרוֹת מִנֹּחַ וְעַד אַבְרָהָם, לְהוֹדִיעַ כַּמָּה אֹרֶךְ אַפַּיִם לְפָנָיו, שֶׁכָּל הַדּוֹרוֹת הָיוּ מַכְעִיסִים לְפָנָיו, עַד שֶׁבָּא אַבְרָהָם אָבִינוּ וְקִבֵּל שְׂכַר כֻּלָּם.

ד. עֲשָׂרָה נִסְיוֹנוֹת נִתְנַסָּה אַבְרָהָם אָבִינוּ וְעָמַד בְּכֻלָּם, לְהוֹדִיעַ כַּמָּה חִבָּתוֹ שֶׁל אַבְרָהָם אָבִינוּ.

ה. עֲשָׂרָה נִסִּים נַעֲשׂוּ לַאֲבוֹתֵינוּ בְּמִצְרַיִם, וַעֲשָׂרָה עַל הַיָּם. עֶשֶׂר מַכּוֹת הֵבִיא הַקָּדוֹשׁ בָּרוּךְ הוּא עַל הַמִּצְרִיִּים בְּמִצְרַיִם, וְעֶשֶׂר עַל הַיָּם.

ו. עֲשָׂרָה נִסְיוֹנוֹת נִסּוּ אֲבוֹתֵינוּ אֶת הַקָּדוֹשׁ בָּרוּךְ הוּא בַּמִּדְבָּר, שֶׁנֶּאֱמַר: וַיְנַסּוּ אֹתִי זֶה עֶשֶׂר פְּעָמִים, וְלֹא שָׁמְעוּ בְּקוֹלִי.

ז. עֲשָׂרָה נִסִּים נַעֲשׂוּ לַאֲבוֹתֵינוּ בְּבֵית הַמִּקְדָּשׁ: לֹא הִפִּילָה אִשָּׁה מֵרֵיחַ בְּשַׂר הַקֹּדֶשׁ, וְלֹא הִסְרִיחַ בְּשַׂר הַקֹּדֶשׁ מֵעוֹלָם, וְלֹא נִרְאָה זְבוּב בְּבֵית הַמִּטְבְּחַיִם, וְלֹא אֵרַע קֶרִי לְכֹהֵן גָּדוֹל בְּיוֹם הַכִּפּוּרִים, וְלֹא כִבּוּ הַגְּשָׁמִים אֵשׁ שֶׁל עֲצֵי הַמַּעֲרָכָה, וְלֹא נִצְּחָה הָרוּחַ אֶת עַמּוּד הֶעָשָׁן, וְלֹא נִמְצָא פְסוּל בָּעֹמֶר וּבִשְׁתֵּי הַלֶּחֶם וּבְלֶחֶם הַפָּנִים, עוֹמְדִים צְפוּפִים וּמִשְׁתַּחֲוִים רְוָחִים, וְלֹא הִזִּיק נָחָשׁ וְעַקְרָב בִּירוּשָׁלַיִם מֵעוֹלָם, וְלֹא אָמַר אָדָם לַחֲבֵרוֹ צַר לִי הַמָּקוֹם שֶׁאָלִין בִּירוּשָׁלָיִם.

לחם הפנים ("bread of presence"), the unleavened bread which the priests placed before the Lord in the sanctuary (Exodus 25:30). This consisted of twelve loaves, representing the twelve tribes of Israel, and was expressive of man's constant indebtedness to God who is the source of every material blessing. It had to be baked before the Sabbath; if there had been anything

2. The ten generations from Adam to Noah [are recorded in Genesis] to make known how great is God's patience; for all those generations continued provoking him, until he [finally] brought upon them the waters of the flood.

3. The ten generations from Noah to Abraham [are recorded] to make known how great is God's patience; for all those generations continued provoking him, until our father Abraham came and received the reward they should all have been given [had they not forfeited their share].

4. With ten trials was our father Abraham tried, and he stood firm in all of them; [this is recorded] to make known how great was the love of our father Abraham [towards God].

5. Ten miracles were performed for our fathers in Egypt, and ten at the Red Sea [the plagues did no harm to the Israelites]. Ten plagues did the Holy One, blessed be he, bring upon the Egyptians in Egypt, and ten at the Sea.

6. With ten trials did our fathers try the Holy One, blessed be he, in the wilderness, as it is said: "They have put me to the test ten times now, and have not obeyed my voice."

7. Ten miracles were done for our fathers in the Sanctuary: no woman miscarried from the scent of the sacrificial meat; the sacrificial meat never became putrid; no fly was seen in the slaughter-house; no unclean accident ever happened to the high priest on the Day of Atonement; the rain never extinguished the fire of the wood-pile [on the altar, which was under the open sky]; the wind did not prevail against the column of smoke [from the altar-fire, so that the smoke was not blown downward]; no disqualifying defect was ever found in the *Omer* [of new barley, offered on the second day of Passover], or in the two loaves [baked of the First Fruits of the wheat-harvest and offered up on Pentecost], or in the shewbread [which was changed weekly, on the Sabbath]; though the people stood closely pressed together, they found ample space to prostrate themselves; never did a serpent or scorpion do injury in Jerusalem; and no man ever said to his fellow: "I have not room to lodge overnight in Jerusalem."

---

wrong with it, they could not have changed the bread for another week. Similarly, if the עומר had been found defective, it would have been impossible to provide another supply in time for the offering. The baking of the two loaves of בכורים had to be done before the commencement of the *Shavuoth* festival; had they been defective, others could not have been prepared. The permission to bake on holy days is restricted to food required for those days.

ח. עֲשָׂרָה דְבָרִים נִבְרְאוּ בְּעֶרֶב שַׁבָּת בֵּין הַשְּׁמָשׁוֹת, וְאֵלּוּ
הֵן: פִּי הָאָרֶץ, פִּי הַבְּאֵר, פִּי הָאָתוֹן, הַקֶּשֶׁת, וְהַמָּן, וְהַמַּטֶּה,
וְהַשָּׁמִיר, הַכְּתָב, וְהַמִּכְתָּב, וְהַלּוּחוֹת. וְיֵשׁ אוֹמְרִים: אַף
הַמַּזִּיקִין, וּקְבוּרָתוֹ שֶׁל מֹשֶׁה, וְאֵילוֹ שֶׁל אַבְרָהָם אָבִינוּ. וְיֵשׁ
אוֹמְרִים: אַף צְבָת בִּצְבָת עֲשׂוּיָה.

ט. שִׁבְעָה דְבָרִים בְּגֹלֶם, וְשִׁבְעָה בְּחָכָם: חָכָם אֵינוֹ מְדַבֵּר
לִפְנֵי מִי שֶׁגָּדוֹל מִמֶּנּוּ בְּחָכְמָה (וּבְמִנְיָן), וְאֵינוֹ נִכְנָס לְתוֹךְ דִּבְרֵי
חֲבֵרוֹ, וְאֵינוֹ נִבְהָל לְהָשִׁיב, שׁוֹאֵל כָּעִנְיָן וּמֵשִׁיב כַּהֲלָכָה,
וְאוֹמֵר עַל רִאשׁוֹן רִאשׁוֹן וְעַל אַחֲרוֹן אַחֲרוֹן, וְעַל מַה שֶּׁלֹּא
שָׁמַע אוֹמֵר לֹא שָׁמַעְתִּי, וּמוֹדֶה עַל הָאֱמֶת; וְחִלּוּפֵיהֶם בְּגֹלֶם.

י. שִׁבְעָה מִינֵי פֻּרְעָנִיּוֹת בָּאִים לָעוֹלָם עַל שִׁבְעָה גוּפֵי
עֲבֵרָה: מִקְצָתָם מְעַשְּׂרִים וּמִקְצָתָם אֵינָם מְעַשְּׂרִים, רָעָב שֶׁל
בַּצֹּרֶת בָּא, מִקְצָתָם רְעֵבִים וּמִקְצָתָם שְׂבֵעִים. גָּמְרוּ שֶׁלֹּא
לְעַשֵּׂר, רָעָב שֶׁל מְהוּמָה וְשֶׁל בַּצֹּרֶת בָּא; וְשֶׁלֹּא לִטּוֹל אֶת
הַחַלָּה, רָעָב שֶׁל כְּלָיָה בָּא.

יא. דֶּבֶר בָּא לָעוֹלָם עַל מִיתוֹת הָאֲמוּרוֹת בַּתּוֹרָה שֶׁלֹּא
נִמְסְרוּ לְבֵית דִּין, וְעַל פֵּרוֹת שְׁבִיעִית. חֶרֶב בָּאָה לָעוֹלָם
עַל עִנּוּי הַדִּין, וְעַל עִוּוּת הַדִּין, וְעַל הַמּוֹרִים בַּתּוֹרָה שֶׁלֹּא
כַהֲלָכָה. חַיָּה רָעָה בָּאָה לָעוֹלָם עַל שְׁבוּעַת שָׁוְא וְעַל חִלּוּל
הַשֵּׁם. גָּלוּת בָּאָה לָעוֹלָם עַל עֲבוֹדַת כּוֹכָבִים, וְעַל גִּלּוּי
עֲרָיוֹת, וְעַל שְׁפִיכוּת דָּמִים, וְעַל שְׁמִטַּת הָאָרֶץ.

בין השמשות at the end of the six days of creation, prior to the first Sabbath.
שמיר in Jeremiah 17:1 means a hard flint used for engraving. In rab-
binic literature it denotes a tiny worm able to split the hardest stone. King
Solomon is said to have employed the *Shamir* in view of the command that
no iron tool be used at the building of an altar to God (Exodus 20:22), "for
iron was created to shorten man's life, whereas the altar was created to prolong man's life" (Middoth 3:4).

8. Ten things were created on the eve of Sabbath at twilight, namely: the mouth of the earth [which engulfed Korah]; the mouth of the well [which supplied the Israelites with water in the wilderness]; the mouth of the ass [which spoke to Balaam]; the rainbow [given as a sign after the flood]; the manna [dropped from heaven]; the rod [of Moses]; the *shamir* [employed for splitting stones at the building of the Temple]; the shape of the written characters; the engraving instrument; and the tablets of stone. Some include also the demons, the grave of Moses, and the ram of our father Abraham; others include also the original tongs, for tongs can [in human experience] be made only by means of tongs.

9. There are seven characteristics of a stupid person, and seven of a wise man. The wise man does not speak in the presence of one who is greater than he in wisdom; he does not interrupt the speech of his companion; he is not hasty to answer; he questions and answers properly, to the point; he speaks on the first point first, and on the last point last; regarding that which he has not learnt he says: "I have not learnt"; and he acknowledges the truth. The opposites of these traits are to be found in a stupid person.

10. Seven kinds of punishment come to the world for seven capital transgressions. When some people give tithes and others do not, there comes a famine from lack of rain; then some go hungry and others have plenty. If all have decided not to give tithes, there comes a famine from panic of war and drought; if they have further resolved not to set apart the dough-cake [for the priest], there comes a famine of extermination.

11. Pestilence comes to the world to inflict those death penalties mentioned in the Torah, the execution of which is not within the function of a human tribunal, and for making forbidden use of the harvest of the Sabbatical year. The sword comes to the world for the suppression [or delay] of justice, and for the perversion of justice, and on account of those who misinterpret the Torah. Wild beasts come to the world on account of perjury, and for the profanation of God's name. Exile comes to the world on account of idolatry, incest, bloodshed, and for not allowing the soil to rest in the Sabbatical year.

הכתב ... the writing on the tablets, the instrument with which it was written, and the tablets themselves.

צבת בצבת עשויה that is, all unexplained beginnings as well as everything supernatural resulted from the original Cause—God.

יב. בְּאַרְבָּעָה פְרָקִים הַדֶּבֶר מִתְרַבֶּה: בָּרְבִיעִית,
וּבַשְּׁבִיעִית, וּבְמוֹצָאֵי שְׁבִיעִית, וּבְמוֹצָאֵי הֶחָג שֶׁבְּכָל שָׁנָה וְשָׁנָה.
בָּרְבִיעִית, מִפְּנֵי מַעְשַׂר עָנִי שֶׁבַּשְּׁלִישִׁית; בַּשְּׁבִיעִית, מִפְּנֵי
מַעְשַׂר עָנִי שֶׁבַּשְּׁשִׁית; בְּמוֹצָאֵי שְׁבִיעִית, מִפְּנֵי פֵּרוֹת שְׁבִיעִית;
בְּמוֹצָאֵי הֶחָג שֶׁבְּכָל שָׁנָה וְשָׁנָה, מִפְּנֵי גֶּזֶל מַתְּנוֹת עֲנִיִּים.

יג. אַרְבַּע מִדּוֹת בָּאָדָם: הָאוֹמֵר שֶׁלִּי שֶׁלִּי וְשֶׁלְּךָ שֶׁלָּךְ, זוֹ
מִדָּה בֵּינוֹנִית, וְיֵשׁ אוֹמְרִים זוֹ מִדַּת סְדוֹם; שֶׁלִּי שֶׁלָּךְ וְשֶׁלְּךָ
שֶׁלִּי, עַם הָאָרֶץ; שֶׁלִּי שֶׁלָּךְ וְשֶׁלְּךָ שֶׁלָּךְ, חָסִיד; שֶׁלְּךָ שֶׁלִּי
וְשֶׁלִּי שֶׁלִּי, רָשָׁע.

יד. אַרְבַּע מִדּוֹת בַּדֵּעוֹת: נוֹחַ לִכְעֹס וְנוֹחַ לִרְצוֹת, יָצָא
הֶפְסֵדוֹ בִּשְׂכָרוֹ; קָשֶׁה לִכְעֹס וְקָשֶׁה לִרְצוֹת, יָצָא שְׂכָרוֹ
בְּהֶפְסֵדוֹ; קָשֶׁה לִכְעֹס וְנוֹחַ לִרְצוֹת, חָסִיד; נוֹחַ לִכְעֹס וְקָשֶׁה
לִרְצוֹת, רָשָׁע.

טו. אַרְבַּע מִדּוֹת בַּתַּלְמִידִים: מָהִיר לִשְׁמֹעַ וּמָהִיר לְאַבֵּד,
יָצָא שְׂכָרוֹ בְּהֶפְסֵדוֹ; קָשֶׁה לִשְׁמֹעַ וְקָשֶׁה לְאַבֵּד, יָצָא הֶפְסֵדוֹ
בִּשְׂכָרוֹ; מָהִיר לִשְׁמֹעַ וְקָשֶׁה לְאַבֵּד, זֶה חֵלֶק טוֹב; קָשֶׁה לִשְׁמֹעַ
וּמָהִיר לְאַבֵּד, זֶה חֵלֶק רָע.

מעשר עני, a tenth part of the third and sixth years' income, was given to
"the Levite, the stranger, the fatherless, and the widow" (Deuteronomy
14:28–29).

גזל מתנות עניים The right of proprietorship does not extend to the corners
of the field, the gleanings of the harvest, and the forgotten sheaf; these belong
to the poor people (Leviticus 19:9–10; 23:22).

מדות qualitative measures, standards by which a person may be judged.

האומר שלי שלי The man who neither gives nor takes is neither good nor
bad, but intermediate. Since, however, he is indifferent to the welfare of
others, there are some who regard him as a type of Sodom notorious for cor-
ruption and selfishness.

12. At four periods pestilence increases: in the fourth year, in the seventh [Sabbatical] year, in the year following the Sabbatical year, and at the conclusion of the Feast of Tabernacles in every year. In the fourth year, for having failed to give the tithe to the poor which was due in the third year; in the seventh year, for having failed to give the tithe to the poor which was due in the sixth year; in the year following the Sabbatical year, for having made forbidden use of the harvest of the Sabbatical year; at the conclusion of the Feast of Tabernacles in every year, for having robbed the gifts assigned to the poor [in the course of the whole agricultural year].

13. There are four characters among men: He who says: "What is mine is mine, and what is yours is yours" is the average type, though some say this is a Sodom-type; he who says: "What is mine is yours, and what is yours is mine" is ignorant; he who says: "What is mine is yours, and what is yours is yours" is godly; he who says: "What is yours is mine, and what is mine is mine" is wicked.

14. There are four kinds of dispositions: Easy to become angry and easy to be pacified, his loss is compensated by his gain; hard to become angry and hard to be pacified, his gain is offset by his loss; hard to become angry and easy to be pacified is godly; easy to become angry and hard to be pacified is wicked.

15. There are four types of students: Quick to learn and quick to forget, his gain is offset by his loss; slow to learn and slow to forget, his loss is compensated by his gain; quick to learn and slow to forget is the best quality; slow to learn and quick to forget is the worst quality.

עם הארץ who does not know that one must do good to others unconditionally, without a view to recompense.

ארבע מדות בתלמידים The types of students described by these similes are: the sponge, absorbing indiscriminately everything, the true and the false; the funnel, retaining none of the subjects learned; the strainer, retaining what is useless and forgetting what is useful; the sieve, retaining what is best.

טז. אַרְבַּע מִדּוֹת בְּנוֹתְנֵי צְדָקָה: הָרוֹצֶה שֶׁיִּתֵּן וְלֹא יִתְּנוּ
אֲחֵרִים, עֵינוֹ רָעָה בְּשֶׁל אֲחֵרִים; יִתְּנוּ אֲחֵרִים וְהוּא לֹא יִתֵּן,
עֵינוֹ רָעָה בְּשֶׁלּוֹ; יִתֵּן וְיִתְּנוּ אֲחֵרִים, חָסִיד; לֹא יִתֵּן וְלֹא יִתְּנוּ
אֲחֵרִים, רָשָׁע.

יז. אַרְבַּע מִדּוֹת בְּהוֹלְכֵי בֵית הַמִּדְרָשׁ: הוֹלֵךְ וְאֵינוֹ עוֹשֶׂה,
שְׂכַר הֲלִיכָה בְּיָדוֹ; עוֹשֶׂה וְאֵינוֹ הוֹלֵךְ, שְׂכַר מַעֲשֶׂה בְּיָדוֹ;
הוֹלֵךְ וְעוֹשֶׂה, חָסִיד; לֹא הוֹלֵךְ וְלֹא עוֹשֶׂה, רָשָׁע.

יח. אַרְבַּע מִדּוֹת בְּיוֹשְׁבִים לִפְנֵי חֲכָמִים: סְפוֹג, וּמַשְׁפֵּךְ,
מְשַׁמֶּרֶת, וְנָפָה. סְפוֹג, שֶׁהוּא סוֹפֵג אֶת הַכֹּל; וּמַשְׁפֵּךְ, שֶׁמַּכְנִיס
בְּזוֹ וּמוֹצִיא בְזוֹ; מְשַׁמֶּרֶת, שֶׁמּוֹצִיאָה אֶת הַיַּיִן וְקוֹלֶטֶת אֶת
הַשְּׁמָרִים; וְנָפָה, שֶׁמּוֹצִיאָה אֶת הַקֶּמַח וְקוֹלֶטֶת אֶת הַסֹּלֶת.

יט. כָּל אַהֲבָה שֶׁהִיא תְלוּיָה בְדָבָר, בָּטֵל דָּבָר בְּטֵלָה
אַהֲבָה; וְשֶׁאֵינָהּ תְּלוּיָה בְדָבָר, אֵינָהּ בְּטֵלָה לְעוֹלָם. אֵיזוֹ הִיא
אַהֲבָה שֶׁהִיא תְלוּיָה בְדָבָר, זוֹ אַהֲבַת אַמְנוֹן וְתָמָר; וְשֶׁאֵינָהּ
תְּלוּיָה בְדָבָר, זוֹ אַהֲבַת דָּוִד וִיהוֹנָתָן.

כ. כָּל מַחֲלֹקֶת שֶׁהִיא לְשֵׁם שָׁמַיִם, סוֹפָהּ לְהִתְקַיֵּם;
וְשֶׁאֵינָהּ לְשֵׁם שָׁמַיִם, אֵין סוֹפָהּ לְהִתְקַיֵּם. אֵיזוֹ הִיא מַחֲלֹקֶת
שֶׁהִיא לְשֵׁם שָׁמַיִם, זוֹ מַחֲלֹקֶת הִלֵּל וְשַׁמַּאי; וְשֶׁאֵינָהּ לְשֵׁם שָׁמַיִם,
זוֹ מַחֲלֹקֶת קֹרַח וְכָל עֲדָתוֹ.

כא. כָּל הַמְזַכֶּה אֶת הָרַבִּים, אֵין חֵטְא בָּא עַל יָדוֹ; וְכָל
הַמַּחֲטִיא אֶת הָרַבִּים, אֵין מַסְפִּיקִים בְּיָדוֹ לַעֲשׂוֹת תְּשׁוּבָה.
מֹשֶׁה זָכָה וְזִכָּה אֶת הָרַבִּים, זְכוּת הָרַבִּים תְּלוּיָה בּוֹ, שֶׁנֶּאֱמַר:
צִדְקַת יְיָ עָשָׂה, וּמִשְׁפָּטָיו עִם יִשְׂרָאֵל. יָרָבְעָם בֶּן נְבָט חָטָא
וְהֶחֱטִיא אֶת הָרַבִּים, חֵטְא הָרַבִּים תָּלוּי בּוֹ, שֶׁנֶּאֱמַר: עַל
חַטֹּאות יָרָבְעָם אֲשֶׁר חָטָא וַאֲשֶׁר הֶחֱטִיא אֶת יִשְׂרָאֵל.

קמח here denotes superfine dust of useless quality (Maimonides).

16.   There are four types of donors to charity: He who gives
and does not want others to give begrudges others; he who wants
others to give but will not give himself begrudges himself; he who
gives and wants others to give is saintly; he who will not give and
does not want others to give is wicked.

17.   There are four types of those who attend school: He who
attends and does not practise [the teachings of the school] secures
the reward for attending; he who practises [leading a good life] but
does not attend [to acquire knowledge] secures the reward for
practising; he who attends and practises is saintly; he who neither
attends nor practises is wicked.

18.   There are four types of those who sit in the presence of
sages: the sponge, the funnel, the strainer, and the sieve. The sponge
absorbs all; the funnel receives at one end and spills out at the
other; the strainer lets the wine through and retains the dregs; and
the sieve lets out the flour dust and retains the fine flour.

19.   All love which depends on sensual attraction will pass
away as soon as the sensual attraction disappears; but if it is not
dependent on sensual attraction, it will never pass away. Which
love was dependent on sensual attraction? The love of Amnon and
Tamar. And which depended on nothing selfish? The love of
David and Jonathan.

20.   Any controversy which is in the name of Heaven [from
sincere motive] is destined to result in something permanent; any
controversy which is not in the name of Heaven will never result
in anything permanent. Which controversy was in the name of
Heaven? The controversy between Hillel and Shammai. And which
was not in the name of Heaven? The controversy of Korah and
all his company.

21.   Whoever leads the people to righteousness, no sin shall
occur through him; whoever leads the people to sin shall not be
enabled to repent. Moses was righteous and led the people to
righteousness, hence the merit of the people is attributed to him,
as it is said: "He performed the justice of the Lord, and his ordinances with Israel."[1] Jeroboam, the son of Nebat, sinned and
caused others to sin, hence the sin of the people is attributed to
him, as it is said: "For the sins of Jeroboam which he sinned and
caused Israel to sin."[2]

---

[1] *Deuteronomy* 33:21.   [2] *I Kings* 15:30.

כב. כָּל מִי שֶׁיֶּשׁ־בּוֹ שְׁלשָׁה דְבָרִים הַלָּלוּ הוּא מִתַּלְמִידָיו
שֶׁל אַבְרָהָם אָבִינוּ, וּשְׁלשָׁה דְבָרִים אֲחֵרִים, הוּא מִתַּלְמִידָיו
שֶׁל בִּלְעָם הָרָשָׁע. עַיִן טוֹבָה, וְרוּחַ נְמוּכָה, וְנֶפֶשׁ שְׁפָלָה,
מִתַּלְמִידָיו שֶׁל אַבְרָהָם אָבִינוּ; עַיִן רָעָה, וְרוּחַ גְּבוֹהָה, וְנֶפֶשׁ
רְחָבָה, מִתַּלְמִידָיו שֶׁל בִּלְעָם הָרָשָׁע. מַה בֵּין תַּלְמִידָיו שֶׁל
אַבְרָהָם אָבִינוּ לְתַלְמִידָיו שֶׁל בִּלְעָם הָרָשָׁע, תַּלְמִידָיו שֶׁל
אַבְרָהָם אָבִינוּ אוֹכְלִים בָּעוֹלָם הַזֶּה וְנוֹחֲלִים הָעוֹלָם הַבָּא,
שֶׁנֶּאֱמַר: לְהַנְחִיל אֹהֲבַי יֵשׁ, וְאֹצְרֹתֵיהֶם אֲמַלֵּא. אֲבָל תַּלְמִידָיו
שֶׁל בִּלְעָם הָרָשָׁע יוֹרְשִׁים גֵּיהִנֹּם וְיוֹרְדִים לִבְאֵר שַׁחַת, שֶׁנֶּאֱמַר:
וְאַתָּה, אֱלֹהִים, תּוֹרִדֵם לִבְאֵר שַׁחַת, אַנְשֵׁי דָמִים וּמִרְמָה, לֹא
יֶחֱצוּ יְמֵיהֶם, וַאֲנִי אֶבְטַח בָּךְ.

כג. יְהוּדָה בֶן תֵּימָא אוֹמֵר: הֱוֵי עַז כַּנָּמֵר, וְקַל כַּנֶּשֶׁר, רָץ
כַּצְּבִי, וְגִבּוֹר כָּאֲרִי, לַעֲשׂוֹת רְצוֹן אָבִיךָ שֶׁבַּשָּׁמָיִם. הוּא הָיָה
אוֹמֵר: עַז פָּנִים לְגֵיהִנֹּם, וּבוֹשׁ פָּנִים לְגַן עֵדֶן.

יְהִי רָצוֹן מִלְּפָנֶיךָ, יְיָ אֱלֹהֵינוּ וֵאלֹהֵי אֲבוֹתֵינוּ, שֶׁיִּבָּנֶה
בֵּית הַמִּקְדָּשׁ בִּמְהֵרָה בְיָמֵינוּ, וְתֵן חֶלְקֵנוּ בְּתוֹרָתֶךָ.

כד. הוּא הָיָה אוֹמֵר: בֶּן חָמֵשׁ שָׁנִים לַמִּקְרָא, בֶּן עֶשֶׂר שָׁנִים
לַמִּשְׁנָה, בֶּן שְׁלשׁ עֶשְׂרֵה לַמִּצְוֹת, בֶּן חֲמֵשׁ עֶשְׂרֵה לַתַּלְמוּד, בֶּן
שְׁמֹנֶה עֶשְׂרֵה לַחֻפָּה, בֶּן עֶשְׂרִים לִרְדֹּף, בֶּן שְׁלשִׁים לַכֹּחַ, בֶּן
אַרְבָּעִים לַבִּינָה, בֶּן חֲמִשִּׁים לְעֵצָה, בֶּן שִׁשִּׁים לְזִקְנָה, בֶּן
שִׁבְעִים לְשֵׂיבָה, בֶּן שְׁמוֹנִים לִגְבוּרָה, בֶּן תִּשְׁעִים לָשׁוּחַ, בֶּן
מֵאָה כְּאִלּוּ מֵת וְעָבַר וּבָטֵל מִן הָעוֹלָם.

יֵשׁ ("substance") numerically equals 310. This word is here homiletically
represented as referring to the 310 worlds which are believed to be meant for
the righteous in the hereafter.

22. Whoever possesses the following three qualities is of the disciples of our father Abraham; whoever possesses the opposite three qualities is of the disciples of the wicked Balaam. Those who belong to the disciples of our father Abraham possess a good eye [generous nature], a humble spirit, and a modest desire. Those who belong to the disciples of the wicked Balaam possess an evil eye [grudging nature], a haughty spirit, and an excessive desire [for wealth]. What is the difference between the disciples of our father Abraham and the disciples of the wicked Balaam? The disciples of our father Abraham enjoy this world and inherit the world to come, as it is said: "Endowing my friends with wealth, I fill their treasures."[1] But the disciples of the wicked Balaam inherit *Gehinnom* and descend into the nethermost pit, as it is said: "Thou, O God, wilt bring them down into the nethermost pit; men of blood and fraud shall not live out half their days; as for me, I trust in thee."[2]

23. Judah ben Tema said: Be bold as a leopard, light as an eagle, swift as a deer, and strong as a lion, to do the will of your Father who is in heaven. He used to say: The impudent is destined for *Gehinnom*, but the shamefaced is destined for paradise.

May it be thy will, Lord our God and God of our fathers, that the Temple be rebuilt speedily in our days, and grant us a share in thy Torah.

24. He used to say: At five years the age is reached for the study of Bible, at ten for the study of Mishnah, at thirteen for the fulfillment of the commandments, at fifteen for the study of Talmud, at eighteen for marriage, at twenty for seeking a livelihood, at thirty for full strength, at forty for understanding, at fifty for giving counsel; at sixty a man attains old age, at seventy white old age, at eighty rare old age; at ninety he is bending over the grave; at a hundred he is as if he were already dead and had passed away from the world.

יהודה בן תימא probably lived towards the end of the second century, and belonged to the fifth and last generation of the *Tannaim*. His name occurs only once in the Mishnah.

יהי רצון should be at the end of the chapter, according to the Wilna Gaon. לשוח is rendered here in the combined sense of שוחה ("grave") and שחה ("to bend").

[1] *Proverbs* 8:21. [2] *Psalm* 55:24.

כה. בֶּן בַּג בַּג אוֹמֵר: הֲפָךְ־בַּהּ וַהֲפָךְ־בַּהּ דְּכֹלָּא בַהּ,
וּבַהּ תֶּחֱזֵי, וְסִיב וּבְלֵה בַהּ, וּמִנַּהּ לָא תָזוּעַ, שֶׁאֵין לָךְ מִדָּה
טוֹבָה הֵימֶנָּה.

כו. בֶּן הֵא הֵא אוֹמֵר: לְפֻם צַעֲרָא אַגְרָא.

רַבִּי חֲנַנְיָא בֶּן עֲקַשְׁיָא אוֹמֵר: רָצָה הַקָּדוֹשׁ בָּרוּךְ הוּא
לְזַכּוֹת אֶת יִשְׂרָאֵל, לְפִיכָךְ הִרְבָּה לָהֶם תּוֹרָה וּמִצְוֹת, שֶׁנֶּאֱמַר:
יְיָ חָפֵץ לְמַעַן צִדְקוֹ, יַגְדִּיל תּוֹרָה וְיַאְדִּיר.

פֶּרֶק שִׁשִּׁי

כָּל יִשְׂרָאֵל יֵשׁ לָהֶם חֵלֶק לָעוֹלָם הַבָּא, שֶׁנֶּאֱמַר: וְעַמֵּךְ
כֻּלָּם צַדִּיקִים, לְעוֹלָם יִירְשׁוּ אָרֶץ; נֵצֶר מַטָּעַי, מַעֲשֵׂה יָדַי
לְהִתְפָּאֵר.

שָׁנוּ חֲכָמִים בִּלְשׁוֹן הַמִּשְׁנָה; בָּרוּךְ שֶׁבָּחַר בָּהֶם וּבְמִשְׁנָתָם.

א. רַבִּי מֵאִיר אוֹמֵר: כָּל הָעוֹסֵק בַּתּוֹרָה לִשְׁמָהּ זוֹכֶה
לִדְבָרִים הַרְבֵּה; וְלֹא עוֹד, אֶלָּא שֶׁכָּל הָעוֹלָם כֻּלּוֹ כְּדַי הוּא
לוֹ: נִקְרָא רֵעַ, אָהוּב, אוֹהֵב אֶת הַמָּקוֹם, אוֹהֵב אֶת הַבְּרִיּוֹת,
מְשַׂמֵּחַ אֶת הַמָּקוֹם, מְשַׂמֵּחַ אֶת הַבְּרִיּוֹת. וּמַלְבַּשְׁתּוֹ עֲנָוָה
וְיִרְאָה, וּמַכְשַׁרְתּוֹ לִהְיוֹת צַדִּיק, חָסִיד, יָשָׁר וְנֶאֱמָן; וּמְרַחַקְתּוֹ
מִן הַחֵטְא, וּמְקָרַבְתּוֹ לִידֵי זְכוּת. וְנֶהֱנִים מִמֶּנּוּ עֵצָה וְתוּשִׁיָּה,
בִּינָה וּגְבוּרָה, שֶׁנֶּאֱמַר: לִי עֵצָה וְתוּשִׁיָּה, אֲנִי בִינָה, לִי גְבוּרָה.
וְנוֹתֶנֶת לוֹ מַלְכוּת וּמֶמְשָׁלָה, וְחִקּוּר דִּין. וּמְגַלִּים לוֹ רָזֵי

בֶּן בַּג בַּג and בֶּן הֵא הֵא are said to have been disciples of Hillel, and proselytes. There is a fanciful explanation to the effect that Ben Hé-Hé denotes
a spiritual son of Abraham and Sarah, whose names God altered by the in-
sertion of the letter ה (Abram's name was changed to Abraham, and that of
Sarai to Sarah). Since the numerical value of בַּג is equivalent to ה (five), it is
said that בֶּן בַּג בַּג is equivalent to בֶּן הֵא הֵא, and that both are epithets of proselytes (Tosafoth, Ḥagigah 9b).

25. Ben Bag-Bag said: Study the Torah again and again, for everything is contained in it; constantly examine it, grow old and gray over it, and swerve not from it, for there is nothing more excellent than it.

26. Ben Hé-Hé said: According to the effort is the reward.

Rabbi Ḥananyah ben Akashyah said: The Holy One, blessed be he, desired to purify Israel; hence he gave them a Torah rich in rules of conduct, as it is said: "The Lord was pleased, for the sake of [Israel's] righteousness, to render the Torah great and glorious."[1]

CHAPTER SIX

All Israel have a share in the world to come, as it is said: "Your people shall all be righteous; they shall possess the land forever; they are a plant of my own, the work of my hands, wherein I may glory."[2]

The sages taught [also the following] in the style of the Mishnah; blessed be he who was pleased with them and their teaching.

1. Rabbi Meir said: Whoever occupies himself with the study of the Torah for its own sake merits many things; nay more, the whole world is worthwhile for his sake. He is called friend, beloved; he loves God and he loves mankind; he pleases God and he pleases mankind. The Torah invests him with humility and reverence; it enables him to become righteous, godly, upright and faithful; it keeps him far from sin, and draws him near to virtue. Men are benefited by him with counsel and sound wisdom, understanding and strength, as it is said: "Mine are counsel and sound wisdom; mine are reason and might."[3] It gives him rule and dominion [personality that commands obedience] and judging ability. To him

---

לפום צערא אגרא and the preceding paragraph are given in Aramaic. In *Avoth d'Rabbi Nathan* 12:11 both sayings are ascribed to Hillel.

שנו חכמים is the Hebrew equivalent of the Aramaic תנו רבנן, used in the Talmud to introduce a *Baraitha*, a tannaitic teaching next in authority to the Mishnah. This chapter, which contains sayings of the Tannaim not included in the Mishnah, is known as *Kinyan Torah* because its subject–matter is in praise of the Torah. It is also known as *Baraitha d'Rabbi Meir* because it opens with the saying of Rabbi Meir.

---

[1] *Isaiah* 42:21. [2] *Isaiah* 60:21. [3] *Proverbs* 8:14.

תוֹרָה, וְנַעֲשֶׂה כְּמַעְיָן הַמִּתְגַּבֵּר וּכְנָהָר שֶׁאֵינוֹ פוֹסֵק. וְהֹוֶה
צָנֽוּעַ וְאֶֽרֶךְ רֽוּחַ, וּמוֹחֵל עַל עֶלְבּוֹנוֹ. וּמְגַדַּלְתּוֹ וּמְרוֹמַמְתּוֹ עַל
כָּל הַמַּעֲשִׂים.

ב. אָמַר רַבִּי יְהוֹשֻׁעַ בֶּן לֵוִי: בְּכָל יוֹם וָיוֹם בַּת קוֹל יוֹצֵאת
מֵהַר חוֹרֵב וּמַכְרֶֽזֶת וְאוֹמֶֽרֶת: אוֹי לָהֶם לַבְּרִיּוֹת מֵעֶלְבּוֹנָהּ שֶׁל
תּוֹרָה, שֶׁכָּל מִי שֶׁאֵינוֹ עוֹסֵק בַּתּוֹרָה נִקְרָא נָזוּף, שֶׁנֶּאֱמַר: נֶֽזֶם
זָהָב בְּאַף חֲזִיר, אִשָּׁה יָפָה וְסָֽרַת טָֽעַם. וְאוֹמֵר: וְהַלֻּחֹת מַעֲשֵׂה
אֱלֹהִים הֵֽמָּה, וְהַמִּכְתָּב מִכְתַּב אֱלֹהִים הוּא, חָרוּת עַל הַלֻּחֹת.
אַל תִּקְרָא חָרוּת אֶלָּא חֵרוּת, שֶׁאֵין לְךָ בֶּן־חוֹרִין אֶלָּא מִי
שֶׁעוֹסֵק בְּתַלְמוּד תּוֹרָה; וְכָל מִי שֶׁעוֹסֵק בְּתַלְמוּד תּוֹרָה הֲרֵי
זֶה מִתְעַלֶּה, שֶׁנֶּאֱמַר: וּמִמַּתָּנָה נַחֲלִיאֵל, וּמִנַּחֲלִיאֵל בָּמוֹת.

ג. הַלּוֹמֵד מֵחֲבֵרוֹ פֶּֽרֶק אֶחָד, אוֹ הֲלָכָה אַחַת, אוֹ פָּסוּק
אֶחָד, אוֹ דִּבּוּר אֶחָד, אוֹ אֲפִילוּ אוֹת אֶחָת, צָרִיךְ לִנְהָג־בּוֹ
כָּבוֹד; שֶׁכֵּן מָצִֽינוּ בְּדָוִד מֶֽלֶךְ יִשְׂרָאֵל, שֶׁלֹּא לָמַד מֵאֲחִיתֹֽפֶל
אֶלָּא שְׁנֵי דְבָרִים בִּלְבָד, קְרָאוֹ רַבּוֹ, אַלּוּפוֹ וּמְיֻדָּעוֹ, שֶׁנֶּאֱמַר:
וְאַתָּה אֱנוֹשׁ כְּעֶרְכִּי, אַלּוּפִי וּמְיֻדָּעִי. וַהֲלֹא דְבָרִים קַל וָחֹֽמֶר:
וּמַה דָּוִד מֶֽלֶךְ יִשְׂרָאֵל שֶׁלֹּא לָמַד מֵאֲחִיתֹֽפֶל אֶלָּא שְׁנֵי דְבָרִים

רבי יהושע בן לוי was one of the first generation of the *Amoraim*, whose
discussions of the mishnaic law are recorded in the Palestinian and Babylonian
Talmuds. He lived in Palestine during the middle of the third century and
became the subject of many legends.

נום זהב באף is interpreted by means of **נוטריקון** ("shorthand"). The initial
letters of **נום זהב** are combined with the last letter of **באף** to form **נוף.**

אשה יפה..., "a fair woman lacking in taste," refers here to one who has the
aptitude for Torah and makes no use of it.

אל תקרא introduces a play on words, and not an emendation of the text.

ממתנה נחליאל... The Hebrew place-names are here interpreted as if they
were common nouns.

the secrets of the Torah are revealed; he is made like a fountain, that ever gathers force, and like a never-failing stream. He becomes modest, patient, and forgiving of insults. The Torah makes him great and raises him above all creatures.

2.   Rabbi Joshua ben Levi said: Every day a heavenly voice resounds from Mount Horeb, proclaiming these words: "Woe to the people for their disregard of the Torah!" For whoever does not occupy himself with the Torah is considered rebuked, as it is said: "Like a golden ring in the snout of a swine is a fair woman lacking in taste:"[1] The Torah says: "The tablets were the work of God, and the writing was the writing of God, engraved upon the tablets."[2] Read not here *ḥaruth* [meaning 'engraved'] but *ḥeruth* [which means 'freedom'], for none can be considered free except those who occupy themselves with the study of the Torah. Anyone who occupies himself with the study of the Torah shall be exalted, as it is said: "Through the [Torah] gift one attains the heritage of God; by the heritage of God [one is raised] to high places."[3]

3.   He who learns from his fellow man a single section, a single rule, a single verse, a single expression, or even a single letter, ought to treat him with respect; for so we find with David, king of Israel, who learnt only two things from Ahitophel, and yet regarded him as his master, guide and intimate friend, as it is said: "You were my equal, my teacher and intimate friend."[4] This certainly presents an argument from minor to major: if David, king of Israel, who learnt only two things from Ahitophel, regarded him as his

---

הלכה a traditional opinion, a legal decision. פסוק a biblical passage. דבור a divine utterance, a biblical expression. אות refers to the correct spelling of words, whether to use א or ע for example (Kallah, chapter 8).

אחיתפל, who participated in Absalom's rebellion against David, was at first David's best friend. His wisdom was believed to be superhuman.

שני דברים בלבד two lessons only which were, according to a talmudic statement, to the effect that one should study in the company of a colleague and that it is proper to walk to the house of prayer eagerly and not leisurely (Kallah, chapter 8). It has been suggested that instead of שני דברים בלבד we should read שֶׁנִּדְבָּרִים בְּלָבָד, "who merely conversed."

---

[1] *Proverbs* 11:22.   [2] *Exodus* 32:16.   [3] *Numbers* 21:19.   [4] *Psalm* 55:14.

בִּלְבָד, קְרָאוֹ רַבּוֹ, אַלּוּפוֹ וּמְיֻדָּעוֹ, הַלּוֹמֵד מֵחֲבֵרוֹ פֶּרֶק אֶחָד, אוֹ הֲלָכָה אֶחָת, אוֹ פָּסוּק אֶחָד, אוֹ דִבּוּר אֶחָד, אוֹ אֲפִילוּ אוֹת אֶחָת, עַל אַחַת כַּמָּה וְכַמָּה שֶׁצָּרִיךְ לִנְהָג־בּוֹ כָּבוֹד. וְאֵין כָּבוֹד אֶלָּא תוֹרָה, שֶׁנֶּאֱמַר: כָּבוֹד חֲכָמִים יִנְחָלוּ, וּתְמִימִים יִנְחֲלוּ טוֹב. וְאֵין טוֹב אֶלָּא תוֹרָה, שֶׁנֶּאֱמַר: כִּי לֶקַח טוֹב נָתַתִּי לָכֶם, תּוֹרָתִי אַל תַּעֲזֹבוּ.

ד. כָּךְ הִיא דַרְכָּהּ שֶׁל תּוֹרָה: פַּת בְּמֶלַח תּאֹכֵל, וּמַיִם בִּמְשׂוּרָה תִּשְׁתֶּה, וְעַל הָאָרֶץ תִּישָׁן, וְחַיֵּי צַעַר תִּחְיֶה, וּבַתּוֹרָה אַתָּה עָמֵל. אִם אַתָּה עוֹשֶׂה כֵּן, אַשְׁרֶיךָ וְטוֹב לָךְ; אַשְׁרֶיךָ בָּעוֹלָם הַזֶּה, וְטוֹב לָךְ לָעוֹלָם הַבָּא.

ה. אַל תְּבַקֵּשׁ גְּדֻלָּה לְעַצְמֶךָ, וְאַל תַּחְמֹד כָּבוֹד. יוֹתֵר מִלִּמּוּדְךָ עֲשֵׂה, וְאַל תִּתְאַוֶּה לְשֻׁלְחָנָם שֶׁל מְלָכִים, שֶׁשֻּׁלְחָנְךָ גָּדוֹל מִשֻּׁלְחָנָם, וְכִתְרְךָ גָּדוֹל מִכִּתְרָם; וְנֶאֱמָן הוּא בַּעַל מְלַאכְתְּךָ, שֶׁיְשַׁלֶּם־לָךְ שְׂכַר פְּעֻלָּתֶךָ.

ו. גְּדוֹלָה תוֹרָה יוֹתֵר מִן הַכְּהֻנָּה וּמִן הַמַּלְכוּת, שֶׁהַמַּלְכוּת נִקְנֵית בִּשְׁלֹשִׁים מַעֲלוֹת, וְהַכְּהֻנָּה נִקְנֵית בְּעֶשְׂרִים וְאַרְבַּע, וְהַתּוֹרָה נִקְנֵית בְּאַרְבָּעִים וּשְׁמוֹנָה דְבָרִים, וְאֵלוּ הֵן: בְּתַלְמוּד, בִּשְׁמִיעַת הָאֹזֶן, בַּעֲרִיכַת שְׂפָתַיִם, בְּבִינַת הַלֵּב, בְּאֵימָה, בְּיִרְאָה, בַּעֲנָוָה, בְּשִׂמְחָה, בְּטָהֳרָה, בְּשִׁמּוּשׁ חֲכָמִים, בְּדִבּוּק חֲבֵרִים, בְּפִלְפּוּל הַתַּלְמִידִים, בְּיִשׁוּב בְּמִקְרָא וּבְמִשְׁנָה, בְּמִעוּט סְחוֹרָה, בְּמִעוּט דֶּרֶךְ אֶרֶץ, בְּמִעוּט תַּעֲנוּג, בְּמִעוּט שֵׁנָה, בְּמִעוּט שִׂיחָה, בְּמִעוּט שְׂחוֹק, בְּאֶרֶךְ אַפַּיִם, בְּלֵב טוֹב, בֶּאֱמוּנַת חֲכָמִים, בְּקַבָּלַת הַיִּסּוּרִים, הַמַּכִּיר אֶת מְקוֹמוֹ, וְהַשָּׂמֵחַ בְּחֶלְקוֹ, וְהָעוֹשֶׂה סְיָג לִדְבָרָיו, וְאֵינוֹ מַחֲזִיק טוֹבָה לְעַצְמוֹ, אָהוּב, אוֹהֵב אֶת הַמָּקוֹם, אוֹהֵב אֶת הַבְּרִיּוֹת, אוֹהֵב

master, guide and intimate friend, how much more ought one who learns from his companion a section, rule, verse, expression, or even a single letter, to treat him with respect. *Honor* implies Torah, as it is said: "The wise shall inherit honor; men of integrity shall attain good fortune."[1] *Good* implies Torah, as it is said: "I give you good doctrine; forsake not my Torah."[2]

4. This is the way of Torah study: eat bread with salt, drink water by measure, sleep on the bare ground, and live a life of hardship while you toil in the Torah [study of the Torah is expected even if one is extremely poor]. If you do this, "happy shall you be and it shall be well with you";[3] *happy shall you be* in this world, *and it shall be well with you* in the world to come.

5. Do not seek greatness for yourself and do not crave honor; let your deeds exceed your learning; do not desire the table of kings, for your table is greater than theirs, your crown is more glorious than theirs; your Employer can be trusted to pay you for your work.

6. The Torah is greater than priesthood or royalty; for royalty is acquired by virtue of thirty qualifications, and priesthood by twenty-four, while the Torah is acquired by forty-eight, namely: study, attentive listening, ordered speech [audible rehearsing], mental alertness, intuitive insight, awe [in the student's attitude towards his master], reverence [for God], humility, cheerfulness, attendance on scholars, close association with colleagues, discussion with students, sedateness, knowledge of Scriptures and Mishnah, moderation in business, moderation in worldly interests, moderation in pleasure, moderation in sleep, moderation in conversation, moderation in merriment, patience, a good heart [unselfishness], intellectual honesty, uncomplaining acceptance of chastisement, knowing one's place, being content with one's lot, setting a limit to one's words, claiming no credit for oneself, being beloved, loving God, loving mankind, loving righteousness, loving

---

[1] *Proverbs* 3:35;28:10.   [2] *Proverbs* 4:2.   [3] *Psalm* 128:2.

אֶת הַצְּדָקוֹת, אוֹהֵב אֶת הַמֵּישָׁרִים, אוֹהֵב אֶת הַתּוֹכָחוֹת,
וּמִתְרַחֵק מִן הַכָּבוֹד, וְלֹא מֵגִיס לִבּוֹ בְּתַלְמוּדוֹ, וְאֵינוֹ שָׂמֵחַ
בְּהוֹרָאָה, נוֹשֵׂא בְעֹל עִם חֲבֵרוֹ, וּמַכְרִיעוֹ לְכַף זְכוּת, וּמַעֲמִידוֹ
עַל הָאֱמֶת, וּמַעֲמִידוֹ עַל הַשָּׁלוֹם, וּמִתְיַשֵּׁב בְּתַלְמוּדוֹ, שׁוֹאֵל
וּמֵשִׁיב, שׁוֹמֵעַ וּמוֹסִיף, הַלּוֹמֵד עַל מְנָת לְלַמֵּד, וְהַלּוֹמֵד עַל
מְנָת לַעֲשׂוֹת, הַמַּחְכִּים אֶת רַבּוֹ, וְהַמְכַוֵּן אֶת שְׁמוּעָתוֹ, וְהָאוֹמֵר
דָּבָר בְּשֵׁם אוֹמְרוֹ. הָא לָמַדְתָּ, כָּל הָאוֹמֵר דָּבָר בְּשֵׁם אוֹמְרוֹ,
מֵבִיא גְאֻלָּה לָעוֹלָם, שֶׁנֶּאֱמַר: וַתֹּאמֶר אֶסְתֵּר לַמֶּלֶךְ בְּשֵׁם
מָרְדֳּכָי.

ז. גְּדוֹלָה תוֹרָה שֶׁהִיא נוֹתֶנֶת חַיִּים לְעוֹשֶׂיהָ בָּעוֹלָם הַזֶּה
וּבָעוֹלָם הַבָּא, שֶׁנֶּאֱמַר: כִּי חַיִּים הֵם לְמֹצְאֵיהֶם, וּלְכָל בְּשָׂרוֹ
מַרְפֵּא. וְאוֹמֵר: רִפְאוּת תְּהִי לְשָׁרֶּךָ, וְשִׁקּוּי לְעַצְמוֹתֶיךָ.
וְאוֹמֵר: עֵץ חַיִּים הִיא לַמַּחֲזִיקִים בָּהּ, וְתֹמְכֶיהָ מְאֻשָּׁר. וְאוֹמֵר:
כִּי לִוְיַת חֵן הֵם לְרֹאשֶׁךָ, וַעֲנָקִים לְגַרְגְּרֹתֶיךָ. וְאוֹמֵר: תִּתֵּן
לְרֹאשְׁךָ לִוְיַת חֵן, עֲטֶרֶת תִּפְאֶרֶת תְּמַגְּנֶךָּ. וְאוֹמֵר: כִּי בִי יִרְבּוּ
יָמֶיךָ, וְיוֹסִיפוּ לְךָ שְׁנוֹת חַיִּים. וְאוֹמֵר: אֹרֶךְ יָמִים בִּימִינָהּ,
בִּשְׂמֹאולָהּ עֹשֶׁר וְכָבוֹד. וְאוֹמֵר: כִּי אֹרֶךְ יָמִים וּשְׁנוֹת חַיִּים
וְשָׁלוֹם יוֹסִיפוּ לָךְ. וְאוֹמֵר: דְּרָכֶיהָ דַרְכֵי נֹעַם, וְכָל נְתִיבוֹתֶיהָ
שָׁלוֹם.

ח. רַבִּי שִׁמְעוֹן בֶּן יְהוּדָה, מִשּׁוּם רַבִּי שִׁמְעוֹן בֶּן יוֹחַי, אוֹמֵר:
הַנּוֹי, וְהַכֹּחַ, וְהָעֹשֶׁר, וְהַכָּבוֹד, וְהַחָכְמָה, הַזִּקְנָה וְהַשֵּׂיבָה,
וְהַבָּנִים, נָאֶה לַצַּדִּיקִים וְנָאֶה לָעוֹלָם, שֶׁנֶּאֱמַר: עֲטֶרֶת תִּפְאֶרֶת
שֵׂיבָה, בְּדֶרֶךְ צְדָקָה תִּמָּצֵא. וְאוֹמֵר: תִּפְאֶרֶת בַּחוּרִים כֹּחָם,

---

רבי שמעון בן יהודה belonged to the fourth generation of the *Tannaim* and
lived towards the end of the second century.

equity, loving reproof, shunning honors, taking no pride in one's learning, not delighting in dictating decisions, bearing the yoke with one's colleague, judging him favorably, directing him to truth and peace, being composed in one's study, asking and answering, listening and adding to one's knowledge, learning in order to teach, learning in order to practise, making his teacher wiser, noting with precision what one has learnt, and reporting a thing in the name of the person who said it. You may infer that whoever reports a thing in the name of the person who said it brings deliverance into the world, for it is said: "And Esther told the king in the name of Mordecai."[1]

7. Great is Torah, for it gives to those who fulfill it life in this world and in the world to come, as it is said: "For they are life to those who find them, health to all their flesh." "It shall be health to your body, marrow to your bones." "It is a tree of life to those who take hold of it; happy are those who support it." "They shall be a graceful garland for your head, a necklace around your neck." "It shall place on your head a graceful garland; a crown of glory shall it bestow on you." "By me your days shall be multiplied, the years of your life shall be increased." "Long life is in its right hand; in its left hand are riches and honor." "Length of days, years of life and peace, shall they add to you." "Its ways are ways of pleasantness, and all its paths are peace."[2]

8. Rabbi Simeon ben Judah said in the name of Rabbi Simeon ben Yoḥai: Beauty and strength, wealth and honor, wisdom and age, gray hair and children are comely to the righteous and comely to the world, as it is said: "Gray hair is a crown of glory, to be found in the path of righteousness." "The glory of the young

רבי שמעון בן יוחאי was one of the most brilliant disciples of Rabbi Akiba. A large number of students attended his lectures in Galilee. The Romans condemned him to death because he was accusing them of selfishness and immorality. He fled together with his son Rabbi Elazar and took refuge in a cave for thirteen years. His fame as a mystic became so great that the kabbalistic work *Zohar* has been attributed to him.

הנוי והכח והעשר are obviously good things and do not seem to require proof to that effect. It has therefore been suggested that the biblical texts are quoted here chiefly on behalf of old age and children, because these do not appear to be unmixed blessings.

[1] *Esther* 2:22.   [2] *Proverbs* 4:22; 3:8; 3:18; 1:9; 4:9; 9:11; 3:16; 3:2, 17.

וַהֲדַר זְקֵנִים שֵׂיבָה. וְאוֹמֵר: עֲטֶרֶת חֲכָמִים עָשְׁרָם. וְאוֹמֵר:
עֲטֶרֶת זְקֵנִים בְּנֵי בָנִים, וְתִפְאֶרֶת בָּנִים אֲבוֹתָם. וְאוֹמֵר: וְחָפְרָה
הַלְּבָנָה וּבוֹשָׁה הַחַמָּה, כִּי מָלַךְ יְיָ צְבָאוֹת בְּהַר צִיּוֹן וּבִירוּשָׁלַיִם,
וְנֶגֶד זְקֵנָיו כָּבוֹד. רַבִּי שִׁמְעוֹן בֶּן מְנַסְיָא אוֹמֵר: אֵלוּ שֶׁבַע
מִדּוֹת שֶׁמָּנוּ חֲכָמִים לַצַּדִּיקִים, כֻּלָּם נִתְקַיְּמוּ בְּרַבִּי וּבְבָנָיו.

ט. אָמַר רַבִּי יוֹסֵי בֶּן קִסְמָא: פַּעַם אַחַת הָיִיתִי מְהַלֵּךְ
בַּדֶּרֶךְ, וּפָגַע בִּי אָדָם אֶחָד וְנָתַן לִי שָׁלוֹם, וְהֶחֱזַרְתִּי לוֹ שָׁלוֹם.
אָמַר לִי: רַבִּי, מֵאֵיזֶה מָקוֹם אָתָּה. אָמַרְתִּי לוֹ: מֵעִיר גְּדוֹלָה
שֶׁל חֲכָמִים וְשֶׁל סוֹפְרִים אָנִי. אָמַר לִי: רַבִּי, רְצוֹנְךָ שֶׁתָּדוּר
עִמָּנוּ בִּמְקוֹמֵנוּ, וַאֲנִי אֶתֵּן לְךָ אֶלֶף אֲלָפִים דִּינְרֵי זָהָב וַאֲבָנִים
טוֹבוֹת וּמַרְגָּלִיּוֹת. אָמַרְתִּי לוֹ: אִם אַתָּה נוֹתֵן לִי כָּל כֶּסֶף וְזָהָב
וַאֲבָנִים טוֹבוֹת וּמַרְגָּלִיּוֹת שֶׁבָּעוֹלָם, אֵינִי דָר אֶלָּא בִּמְקוֹם
תּוֹרָה. וְכֵן כָּתוּב בְּסֵפֶר תְּהִלִּים עַל יְדֵי דָוִד מֶלֶךְ יִשְׂרָאֵל:
טוֹב לִי תוֹרַת פִּיךָ מֵאַלְפֵי זָהָב וָכָסֶף. וְלֹא עוֹד, אֶלָּא שֶׁבִּשְׁעַת
פְּטִירָתוֹ שֶׁל אָדָם אֵין מְלַוִּים לוֹ לְאָדָם לֹא כֶסֶף, וְלֹא זָהָב,
וְלֹא אֲבָנִים טוֹבוֹת וּמַרְגָּלִיּוֹת, אֶלָּא תּוֹרָה וּמַעֲשִׂים טוֹבִים
בִּלְבָד, שֶׁנֶּאֱמַר: בְּהִתְהַלֶּכְךָ תַּנְחֶה אֹתָךְ, בְּשָׁכְבְּךָ תִּשְׁמֹר
עָלֶיךָ, וַהֲקִיצוֹתָ הִיא תְשִׂיחֶךָ. בְּהִתְהַלֶּכְךָ תַּנְחֶה אֹתָךְ, בָּעוֹלָם
הַזֶּה; בְּשָׁכְבְּךָ תִּשְׁמֹר עָלֶיךָ, בַּקֶּבֶר; וַהֲקִיצוֹתָ הִיא תְשִׂיחֶךָ,
לָעוֹלָם הַבָּא. וְאוֹמֵר: לִי הַכֶּסֶף וְלִי הַזָּהָב, נְאֻם יְיָ צְבָאוֹת.

י. חֲמִשָּׁה קִנְיָנִים קָנָה הַקָּדוֹשׁ בָּרוּךְ הוּא בְּעוֹלָמוֹ, וְאֵלוּ
הֵן: תּוֹרָה קִנְיָן אֶחָד, שָׁמַיִם וָאָרֶץ קִנְיָן אֶחָד, אַבְרָהָם קִנְיָן
אֶחָד, יִשְׂרָאֵל קִנְיָן אֶחָד, בֵּית הַמִּקְדָּשׁ קִנְיָן אֶחָד. תּוֹרָה מִנַּיִן,

---

רבי שמעון בן מנסיא was a contemporary of Rabbi Judah ha-Nasi.
רבי יוסי בן קסמא lived at the beginning of the second century.

men is their strength, and the beauty of old men is gray hair."
"The crown of the wise is their riches." "Grandchildren are the
crown of old men, and fathers are the pride of their children."[1]
And it says: "The moon shall be confounded and the sun ashamed;
for the Lord of hosts will be King on Mount Zion and in Jerusalem,
and there shall be glory before the elders of his people."[2]

Rabbi Simeon ben Menasya said: These seven qualities, which
the sages have enumerated as becoming to the righteous, were all
realized in Rabbi Judah ha-Nasi and his sons.

9.　Rabbi Yosé ben Kisma said: I was once travelling on the
road when a man met me and greeted me, and I returned his
greeting. He said to me: "Rabbi, from what place are you?" I
said to him: "I come from a great city of sages and scholars." He
said to me: "Rabbi, are you willing to live with us in our place?
I will give you a million golden dinars, and precious stones and
pearls." I told him: "Were you to give me all the silver and gold
and precious stones and pearls in the world, I would not live anywhere except in a place of Torah." In a like manner, it is written
in the Book of Psalms by David, king of Israel: "Thy own teaching
means more to me than thousands in gold and silver."[3] Furthermore, when a man dies, neither silver nor gold nor precious stones
nor pearls accompany him, but Torah and good deeds alone, as it
is said: "When you walk, it shall guide you; when you lie down,
it shall watch over you; and when you awake, it shall talk with
you."[4] *When you walk, it shall guide you* in this world; *when you lie
down, it shall watch over you* in the grave; *and when you awake, it
shall talk with you* in the world to come. It says also: "Mine is the
silver and mine is the gold, says the Lord of hosts."[5]

10.　Five possessions has the Holy One, blessed be he, specifically declared his own in his world, namely: the Torah, heaven
and earth, Abraham, Israel, and the sanctuary. How do we know
this about the Torah? Because it is written: "The Lord possessed

---

[1] *Proverbs* 16:31; 20:29; 14:24; 17:6.　　[2] *Isaiah* 24:23.　　[3] *Psalm* 119:72.
[4] *Proverbs* 6:22.　　[5] *Haggai* 2:8.

דִּכְתִיב: יְיָ קָנָנִי רֵאשִׁית דַּרְכּוֹ, קֶדֶם מִפְעָלָיו מֵאָז. שָׁמַיִם וָאָרֶץ
מִנָּיִן, דִּכְתִיב: כֹּה אָמַר יְיָ, הַשָּׁמַיִם כִּסְאִי, וְהָאָרֶץ הֲדֹם רַגְלָי,
אֵי־זֶה בַיִת אֲשֶׁר תִּבְנוּ לִי, וְאֵי־זֶה מָקוֹם מְנוּחָתִי. וְאוֹמֵר: מָה
רַבּוּ מַעֲשֶׂיךָ, יְיָ, כֻּלָּם בְּחָכְמָה עָשִׂיתָ, מָלְאָה הָאָרֶץ קִנְיָנֶךָ.
אַבְרָהָם מִנָּיִן, דִּכְתִיב: וַיְבָרְכֵהוּ וַיֹּאמַר, בָּרוּךְ אַבְרָם לְאֵל
עֶלְיוֹן, קֹנֵה שָׁמַיִם וָאָרֶץ. יִשְׂרָאֵל מִנָּיִן, דִּכְתִיב: עַד יַעֲבֹר
עַמְּךָ, יְיָ, עַד יַעֲבֹר עַם זוּ קָנִיתָ; וְאוֹמֵר: לִקְדוֹשִׁים אֲשֶׁר בָּאָרֶץ
הֵמָּה, וְאַדִּירֵי כָּל חֶפְצִי בָם. בֵּית הַמִּקְדָּשׁ מִנָּיִן, דִּכְתִיב: מָכוֹן
לְשִׁבְתְּךָ פָּעַלְתָּ, יְיָ, מִקְּדָשׁ, אֲדֹנָי, כּוֹנְנוּ יָדֶיךָ; וְאוֹמֵר: וַיְבִיאֵם
אֶל גְּבוּל קָדְשׁוֹ, הַר זֶה קָנְתָה יְמִינוֹ.

יא. כֹּל מַה שֶּׁבָּרָא הַקָּדוֹשׁ בָּרוּךְ הוּא בְּעוֹלָמוֹ, לֹא בְּרָאוֹ
אֶלָּא לִכְבוֹדוֹ, שֶׁנֶּאֱמַר: כֹּל הַנִּקְרָא בִשְׁמִי, וְלִכְבוֹדִי בְּרָאתִיו,
יְצַרְתִּיו אַף עֲשִׂיתִיו. וְאוֹמֵר: יְיָ יִמְלֹךְ לְעֹלָם וָעֶד.

רַבִּי חֲנַנְיָא בֶּן עֲקַשְׁיָא אוֹמֵר: רָצָה הַקָּדוֹשׁ בָּרוּךְ הוּא
לְזַכּוֹת אֶת יִשְׂרָאֵל, לְפִיכָךְ הִרְבָּה לָהֶם תּוֹרָה וּמִצְוֹת, שֶׁנֶּאֱמַר:
יְיָ חָפֵץ לְמַעַן צִדְקוֹ, יַגְדִּיל תּוֹרָה וְיַאְדִּיר.

אברהם is entirely omitted in parallel passages enumerating these special
possessions. The biblical text, קונה שמים וארץ, refers directly to heaven and
earth as the possession of God, and does not seem to support the idea that
Abraham was called *kinyan*. According to the opinion of Rabbi Elijah, the
Wilna Gaon, this passage should be emended to include four possessions instead
of five.

קדושים is taken here to refer to Israel as the people sanctified by God's
commandments.

כל מה שברא amplifies the thought expressed in the preceding paragraph.
The whole creation bears witness that everything has come into being for a
noble and lofty purpose.

רבי חנניא בן עקשיא lived during the second century of the common era.
This paragraph, found at the close of the tractate Makkoth, is repeated at the
end of each of the six chapters of *Avoth* in order to emphasize the thought that

me first of his creation, first of all his works in days of old."[1] How do we know this about heaven and earth? Because it is written: "Thus says the Lord: The heaven is my throne, and the earth is my footstool; what manner of house would you build for me, what manner of place as my residence?"[2] It says also: "How manifold are thy works, O Lord! In wisdom hast thou made them all; the earth is full of thy possessions."[3] How do we know this about Abraham? Because it is written: "And he blessed him and said: Blessed be Abram of God Most High, Possessor of heaven and earth."[4] How do we know this about Israel? Because it is written: "Until thy people pass over, O Lord; until the people whom thou possessest pass over."[5] It says also: "As for the holy people who are on earth, they are the nobles in whom is all my delight."[6] How do we know this about the sanctuary? Because it is written: "The place of thy abode which thou, O Lord, hast made; the sanctuary, O Lord, which thy hands have established."[7] It says also: "And he brought them to the region of his sanctuary, to the mountain which his might had acquired."[8]

11. Whatever the Holy One, blessed be he, created in his world, he created only for his glory, as it is said: "Everything that is called by my name, it is for my glory that I have created it; I have formed it, I have made it."[9] It says also: "The Lord shall reign forever and ever."[10]

Rabbi Ḥananyah ben Akashyah said: The Holy One, blessed be he, desired to purify Israel; hence he gave them a Torah rich in rules of conduct, as it is said: "The Lord was pleased, for the sake of [Israel's] righteousness, to render the Torah great and glorious."[11]

---

the Torah was given as a mark of divine love and was designed to train Israel in holiness.

לזכות את ישראל to cause Israel to be צדיקים=וכאים ("righteous"). The Targum renders צדיק by וכאי (Genesis 6:9). למען צדק is here used homiletically in the sense that God meant to make Israel righteous, though literally the phrase refers to God's own righteousness.

---

[1]*Proverbs* 8:22. [2]*Isaiah* 66:1. [3]*Psalm* 104:24. [4]*Genesis* 14:19. [5]*Exodus* 15:16. [6]*Psalm* 16:3. [7]*Exodus* 15:17. [8]*Psalm* 78:54. [9]*Isaiah* 43:7. [10]*Exodus* 15:18. [11]*Isaiah* 42:21.

לְמוֹצָאֵי שַׁבָּת

On Saturday night, the following is recited before *Ma'ariv*, page 191.

לְדָוִד. בָּרוּךְ יְיָ צוּרִי, הַמְלַמֵּד יָדַי לַקְרָב, אֶצְבְּעוֹתַי
לַמִּלְחָמָה. חַסְדִּי וּמְצוּדָתִי, מִשְׂגַּבִּי וּמְפַלְטִי לִי, מָגִנִּי וּבוֹ
חָסִיתִי, הָרוֹדֵד עַמִּי תַחְתָּי. יְיָ, מָה אָדָם וַתֵּדָעֵהוּ, בֶּן־אֱנוֹשׁ
וַתְּחַשְּׁבֵהוּ. אָדָם לַהֶבֶל דָּמָה, יָמָיו כְּצֵל עוֹבֵר. יְיָ, הַט שָׁמֶיךָ
וְתֵרֵד, גַּע בֶּהָרִים וְיֶעֱשָׁנוּ. בְּרוֹק בָּרָק וּתְפִיצֵם, שְׁלַח חִצֶּיךָ
וּתְהֻמֵּם. שְׁלַח יָדֶיךָ מִמָּרוֹם, פְּצֵנִי וְהַצִּילֵנִי מִמַּיִם רַבִּים, מִיַּד
בְּנֵי נֵכָר. אֲשֶׁר פִּיהֶם דִּבֶּר־שָׁוְא, וִימִינָם יְמִין שָׁקֶר. אֱלֹהִים,
שִׁיר חָדָשׁ אָשִׁירָה לָּךְ; בְּנֵבֶל עָשׂוֹר אֲזַמְּרָה לָּךְ. הַנּוֹתֵן תְּשׁוּעָה
לַמְּלָכִים, הַפּוֹצֶה אֶת דָּוִד עַבְדּוֹ מֵחֶרֶב רָעָה. פְּצֵנִי וְהַצִּילֵנִי
מִיַּד בְּנֵי נֵכָר, אֲשֶׁר פִּיהֶם דִּבֶּר־שָׁוְא, וִימִינָם יְמִין שָׁקֶר. אֲשֶׁר
בָּנֵינוּ כִּנְטִעִים מְגֻדָּלִים בִּנְעוּרֵיהֶם, בְּנוֹתֵינוּ כְזָוִיֹּת, מְחֻטָּבוֹת
תַּבְנִית הֵיכָל. מְזָוֵינוּ מְלֵאִים, מְפִיקִים מִזַּן אֶל זַן; צֹאנֵנוּ
מַאֲלִיפוֹת, מְרֻבָּבוֹת, בְּחוּצוֹתֵינוּ. אַלּוּפֵינוּ מְסֻבָּלִים; אֵין פֶּרֶץ
וְאֵין יוֹצֵאת, וְאֵין צְוָחָה בִּרְחֹבֹתֵינוּ. אַשְׁרֵי הָעָם שֶׁכָּכָה לּוֹ;
אַשְׁרֵי הָעָם שֶׁיְיָ אֱלֹהָיו.

לַמְנַצֵּחַ בִּנְגִינֹת, מִזְמוֹר שִׁיר. אֱלֹהִים יְחָנֵּנוּ וִיבָרְכֵנוּ; יָאֵר
פָּנָיו אִתָּנוּ, סֶלָה. לָדַעַת בָּאָרֶץ דַּרְכֶּךָ, בְּכָל גּוֹיִם יְשׁוּעָתֶךָ.
יוֹדוּךָ עַמִּים, אֱלֹהִים; יוֹדוּךָ עַמִּים כֻּלָּם. יִשְׂמְחוּ וִירַנְּנוּ לְאֻמִּים,
כִּי תִשְׁפֹּט עַמִּים מִישֹׁר, וּלְאֻמִּים בָּאָרֶץ תַּנְחֵם, סֶלָה. יוֹדוּךָ
עַמִּים, אֱלֹהִים; יוֹדוּךָ עַמִּים כֻּלָּם. אֶרֶץ נָתְנָה יְבוּלָהּ; יְבָרְכֵנוּ
אֱלֹהִים, אֱלֹהֵינוּ. יְבָרְכֵנוּ אֱלֹהִים, וְיִירְאוּ אוֹתוֹ כָּל אַפְסֵי אָרֶץ.

535

FOR THE CONCLUSION OF SABBATH

On Saturday night, the following is recited before Ma'ariv, page 192.

Psalm 144

A psalm of David. Blessed be the Lord my stronghold, who trains my hands for war, my fingers for battle. He is my gracious God and my fortress, my refuge and my deliverer; he is my shield and I trust in him, who subdues peoples under me. O Lord, what is man that thou shouldst notice him; what is mortal man that thou shouldst consider him? Man is like a breath; his days are like a passing shadow. O Lord, bend thy heaven and come down; touch the mountains that they smoke. Flash lightning and scatter them [the foes]; send thy arrows and rout them. Stretch out thy hands from on high; rescue me, deliver me from the great floods, from the grip of the barbarians, who speak falsehood, whose oath is a false oath. O God, I will sing thee a new song; on a ten-stringed harp will I play to thee, who makest kings victorious, who savest thy servant David from the evil sword. Rescue me, deliver me from the grip of the barbarians, who speak falsehood, whose oath is a false oath. May our sons be like saplings, grown vigorous in their youth, and our daughters like corner-columns sculptured in palace-fashion. May our barns be full, affording all sorts of produce; may our sheep increase by thousands and tens of thousands in our fields. May our oxen be heavily laden [with produce]; may there be no riot, no surrender [to a foe], and no outcry in our streets. Happy the people that is so situated; happy the people whose God is the Lord.

Psalm 67

For the Choirmaster; with string-music; a psalm, a song. May God be gracious to us and bless us; may he cause his favor to shine among us. Then shall thy way be known on earth, thy saving power among all nations. The peoples shall praise thee, O God; all the peoples shall praise thee. Let the nations be glad and sing for joy, for thou rulest the peoples justly; thou guidest the nations on earth. The peoples shall praise thee, O Lord; all the peoples shall praise thee. The earth has yielded its produce; God, our own God, blesses us. God blesses us; all the ends of the earth shall revere him.

Psalm 144 is a prayer for protection in war and peace. The psalmist marvels at the thought that God who is so great should condescend to care for man who is so insignificant.

Unless a festival occurs during the same week, the following is recited after the *Shemoneh Esreh*. On *Tish'ah b'Av* the verse וִיהִי נֹעַם and יֹשֵׁב בְּסֵתֶר are omitted.

וִיהִי נֹעַם אֲדֹנָי אֱלֹהֵינוּ עָלֵינוּ, וּמַעֲשֵׂה יָדֵינוּ כּוֹנְנָה עָלֵינוּ,
וּמַעֲשֵׂה יָדֵינוּ כּוֹנְנֵהוּ.

תהלים צא

יֹשֵׁב בְּסֵתֶר עֶלְיוֹן, בְּצֵל שַׁדַּי יִתְלוֹנָן. אֹמַר לַייָ, מַחְסִי
וּמְצוּדָתִי; אֱלֹהַי אֶבְטַח בּוֹ. כִּי הוּא יַצִּילְךָ מִפַּח יָקוּשׁ, מִדֶּבֶר
הַוּוֹת. בְּאֶבְרָתוֹ יָסֶךְ לָךְ, וְתַחַת כְּנָפָיו תֶּחְסֶה; צִנָּה וְסֹחֵרָה
אֲמִתּוֹ. לֹא תִירָא מִפַּחַד לָיְלָה, מֵחֵץ יָעוּף יוֹמָם. מִדֶּבֶר בָּאֹפֶל
יַהֲלֹךְ, מִקֶּטֶב יָשׁוּד צָהֳרָיִם. יִפֹּל מִצִּדְּךָ אֶלֶף, וּרְבָבָה מִימִינֶךָ;
אֵלֶיךָ לֹא יִגָּשׁ. רַק בְּעֵינֶיךָ תַבִּיט, וְשִׁלֻּמַת רְשָׁעִים תִּרְאֶה. כִּי
אַתָּה, יְיָ, מַחְסִי; עֶלְיוֹן שַׂמְתָּ מְעוֹנֶךָ. לֹא תְאֻנֶּה אֵלֶיךָ רָעָה,
וְנֶגַע לֹא יִקְרַב בְּאָהֳלֶךָ. כִּי מַלְאָכָיו יְצַוֶּה לָּךְ, לִשְׁמָרְךָ בְּכָל
דְּרָכֶיךָ. עַל כַּפַּיִם יִשָּׂאוּנְךָ, פֶּן תִּגֹּף בָּאֶבֶן רַגְלֶךָ. עַל שַׁחַל
וָפֶתֶן תִּדְרֹךְ, תִּרְמֹס כְּפִיר וְתַנִּין. כִּי בִי חָשַׁק וַאֲפַלְּטֵהוּ,
אֲשַׂגְּבֵהוּ כִּי יָדַע שְׁמִי. יִקְרָאֵנִי וְאֶעֱנֵהוּ, עִמּוֹ אָנֹכִי בְצָרָה;
אֲחַלְּצֵהוּ וַאֲכַבְּדֵהוּ. אֹרֶךְ יָמִים אַשְׂבִּיעֵהוּ, וְאַרְאֵהוּ בִּישׁוּעָתִי.
אֹרֶךְ יָמִים אַשְׂבִּיעֵהוּ, וְאַרְאֵהוּ בִּישׁוּעָתִי.

וְאַתָּה קָדוֹשׁ, יוֹשֵׁב תְּהִלּוֹת יִשְׂרָאֵל. וְקָרָא זֶה אֶל זֶה וְאָמַר:
קָדוֹשׁ, קָדוֹשׁ, קָדוֹשׁ יְיָ צְבָאוֹת, מְלֹא כָל הָאָרֶץ כְּבוֹדוֹ.
וּמְקַבְּלִין דֵּן מִן דֵּן וְאָמְרִין: קַדִּישׁ בִּשְׁמֵי מְרוֹמָא עִלָּאָה, בֵּית
שְׁכִינְתֵּהּ; קַדִּישׁ עַל אַרְעָא, עוֹבַד גְּבוּרְתֵּהּ; קַדִּישׁ לְעָלַם
וּלְעָלְמֵי עָלְמַיָּא יְיָ צְבָאוֹת; מַלְיָא כָל אַרְעָא זִיו יְקָרֵהּ. וַתִּשָּׂאֵנִי
רוּחַ, וָאֶשְׁמַע אַחֲרַי קוֹל רַעַשׁ גָּדוֹל: בָּרוּךְ כְּבוֹד יְיָ מִמְּקוֹמוֹ.

וִיהִי נֹעַם is omitted on *Tish'ah b'Av*, which commemorates the destruction of the Temple, because "establish thou the work of our hands" was uttered by Moses when the sanctuary had been completed. The letter ז (=7) is not found in this psalm, which is omitted seven times each year when festivals occur.

Unless a festival occurs during the same week, the following is recited after the
Shemoneh Esreh. On Tish'ah b'Av, the first verse and Psalm 91 are omitted.

May the favor of the Lord our God rest on us. Establish thou
for us the work of our hands; the work of our hands establish
thou.[1]
                              Psalm 91

He who dwells in the shelter of the Most High abides under
the protection of the Almighty. I say of the Lord: "He is my
refuge and my fortress, my God in whom I trust." Indeed, he will
save you from the snare of the fowler, and from the destructive
pestilence. With his pinions he will cover you, and under his
wings you will find refuge; his faithfulness is a shield and buckler.
Fear not the terror of the night, nor the arrow that flies by day,
nor the pestilence that stalks in the darkness, nor the destruction
that ravages at noon. Though a thousand fall at your side, and a
myriad at your right hand, it shall not come near you. Only with
your eyes will you gaze, and see the reward of evil men. Thou, O
Lord, art my refuge! When you have made the Most High your
shelter, no disaster shall befall you, no calamity shall come near
your home. For he will give his angels charge over you, to guard
you in all your ways. They will bear you in their hands, lest you
strike your foot against a stone. You can tread on lion and asp;
you can trample young lion and serpent. "He clings to me, so I deliver him; I set him safe, because he loves my name. When he calls
upon me, I will answer him; I will be with him in trouble; I will
rescue him and bring him to honor. With long life will I satisfy him,
and let him see my saving power."

Thou, holy God, art enthroned amidst the praises of Israel.[2]
They keep calling to one another: "Holy, holy, holy is the Lord
of hosts; the whole earth is full of his glory."[3] *They receive it from
one another, and say: "Holy in the highest heavens, his divine abode;
holy upon earth, his work of might; holy forever and to all eternity is
the Lord of hosts; the whole earth is full of his radiant glory."* Then a
wind lifted me up, and I heard behind me a mighty sound: "Blessed be the glory of the Lord from his abode."[4] *Then a wind lifted*

* *The words in italics are the Targum paraphrase of the preceding verse.*

[1] *Psalm 90:17.*   [2] *Psalm 22:4.*   [3] *Isaiah 6:3.*   [4] *Ezekiel 3:12.*

וּנְטַלְתְּנִי רוּחָא, וְשִׁמְעֵת בַּתְרַי קָל זִיעַ סַגִּיא דִּי מְשַׁבְּחִין
וְאָמְרִין: בְּרִיךְ יְקָרָא דַיְיָ מֵאֲתַר בֵּית שְׁכִינְתֵּהּ. יְיָ יִמְלֹךְ לְעֹלָם
וָעֶד. יְיָ מַלְכוּתֵהּ (קָאֵם) לְעָלַם וּלְעָלְמֵי עָלְמַיָּא. יְיָ אֱלֹהֵי
אַבְרָהָם יִצְחָק וְיִשְׂרָאֵל אֲבוֹתֵינוּ, שָׁמְרָה זֹּאת לְעוֹלָם, לְיֵצֶר
מַחְשְׁבוֹת לְבַב עַמֶּךָ, וְהָכֵן לְבָבָם אֵלֶיךָ. וְהוּא רַחוּם, יְכַפֵּר
עָוֹן וְלֹא יַשְׁחִית, וְהִרְבָּה לְהָשִׁיב אַפּוֹ, וְלֹא יָעִיר כָּל חֲמָתוֹ. כִּי
אַתָּה, אֲדֹנָי, טוֹב וְסַלָּח וְרַב חֶסֶד לְכָל קֹרְאֶיךָ. צִדְקָתְךָ צֶדֶק
לְעוֹלָם, וְתוֹרָתְךָ אֱמֶת. תִּתֵּן אֱמֶת לְיַעֲקֹב, חֶסֶד לְאַבְרָהָם,
אֲשֶׁר נִשְׁבַּעְתָּ לַאֲבֹתֵינוּ מִימֵי קֶדֶם. בָּרוּךְ יְיָ, יוֹם יוֹם יַעֲמָס־לָנוּ
הָאֵל יְשׁוּעָתֵנוּ, סֶלָה. יְיָ צְבָאוֹת עִמָּנוּ, מִשְׂגָּב לָנוּ אֱלֹהֵי יַעֲקֹב,
סֶלָה. יְיָ צְבָאוֹת, אַשְׁרֵי אָדָם בֹּטֵחַ בָּךְ. יְיָ, הוֹשִׁיעָה; הַמֶּלֶךְ
יַעֲנֵנוּ בְיוֹם קָרְאֵנוּ. בָּרוּךְ הוּא אֱלֹהֵינוּ שֶׁבְּרָאָנוּ לִכְבוֹדוֹ,
וְהִבְדִּילָנוּ מִן הַתּוֹעִים, וְנָתַן לָנוּ תּוֹרַת אֱמֶת, וְחַיֵּי עוֹלָם נָטַע
בְּתוֹכֵנוּ. הוּא יִפְתַּח לִבֵּנוּ בְּתוֹרָתוֹ, וְיָשֵׂם בְּלִבֵּנוּ אַהֲבָתוֹ
וְיִרְאָתוֹ, לַעֲשׂוֹת רְצוֹנוֹ וּלְעָבְדוֹ בְּלֵבָב שָׁלֵם. לְמַעַן לֹא נִיגַע
לָרִיק, וְלֹא נֵלֵד לַבֶּהָלָה. יְהִי רָצוֹן מִלְּפָנֶיךָ, יְיָ אֱלֹהֵינוּ וֵאלֹהֵי
אֲבוֹתֵינוּ, שֶׁנִּשְׁמֹר חֻקֶּיךָ בָּעוֹלָם הַזֶּה, וְנִזְכֶּה וְנִחְיֶה וְנִרְאֶה,
וְנִירַשׁ טוֹבָה וּבְרָכָה, לִשְׁנֵי יְמוֹת הַמָּשִׁיחַ וּלְחַיֵּי הָעוֹלָם הַבָּא.
לְמַעַן יְזַמֶּרְךָ כָבוֹד וְלֹא יִדֹּם; יְיָ אֱלֹהַי, לְעוֹלָם אוֹדֶךָ. בָּרוּךְ
הַגֶּבֶר אֲשֶׁר יִבְטַח בַּיְיָ, וְהָיָה יְיָ מִבְטַחוֹ. בִּטְחוּ בַיְיָ עֲדֵי עַד,
כִּי בְּיָהּ יְיָ צוּר עוֹלָמִים. וְיִבְטְחוּ בְךָ יוֹדְעֵי שְׁמֶךָ, כִּי לֹא עָזַבְתָּ
דֹרְשֶׁיךָ, יְיָ. יְיָ חָפֵץ לְמַעַן צִדְקוֹ, יַגְדִּיל תּוֹרָה וְיַאְדִּיר.

לעשות רצונו is the correct reading found in the Sephardic editions of the
Siddur. Current Ashkenazic editions have here **ולעשות** ("and to do"), a
reading that interferes with the logical construction of the sentence. This is
presumably the result of an erroneous repetition of the letter ו in the immediately preceding **יראתו**.

me up and I heard behind me a great moving sound of those who uttered praises, saying: "Blessed be the glory of the Lord from the place of his divine abode." The Lord shall reign forever and ever.[1] *The Lord's kingship is established forever and to all eternity.*

Lord God of Abraham, Isaac and Israel our fathers, keep the mind and purpose of thy people ever in this spirit, and direct their heart to thyself.[2] He, being merciful, forgives iniquity, and does not destroy; frequently he turns his anger away, and does not stir up all his wrath. For thou, O Lord, art good and forgiving, and exceedingly kind to all who call upon thee. Thy righteousness is eternal, and thy Torah is truth.[3] Thou wilt show grace to Jacob, love to Abraham, as thou hast sworn to our fathers from days of old.[4] Blessed be the Lord who day by day bears our burden; God is ever our salvation. The Lord of hosts is with us; the God of Jacob is our stronghold. Lord of hosts, happy is the man who trusts in thee. O Lord, save us; may the King answer us when we call.[5]

Blessed be our God who has created us for his glory, and has separated us from those who go astray; who has given us the Torah of truth and planted eternal life in our midst. May he open our heart to his Torah; may he set in our heart love and reverence for him to do his will and serve him with a perfect heart, so that we shall not labor in vain, nor rear children for disaster. May it be thy will, Lord our God and God of our fathers, that we keep thy laws in this world, and thus be worthy to live to see and share the happiness and blessing in the Messianic days and in the life of the world to come. May my soul sing praise to thee, and not be silent; Lord my God, I will thank thee forever.[6] Blessed is the man who trusts in the Lord; the Lord will be his protection. Trust in the Lord forever and ever, for the Lord God is an everlasting stronghold. Those who know thy name put their trust in thee, for thou hast not forsaken those who seek thee, O Lord.[7]

The Lord was pleased, because of his righteousness, to make his Torah great and glorious.[8]

---

[1] *Exodus* 15:18.   [2] I *Chronicles* 29:18.   [3] *Psalms* 78:38; 86:5; 119:142.
[4] *Micah* 7:20.   [5] *Psalms* 68:20; 46:8; 84:13; 20:10.   [6] *Psalm* 30:13.   [7] *Jeremiah* 17:7; *Isaiah* 26:4; *Psalm* 9:11.   [8] *Isaiah* 42:21.

Reader:

יִתְגַּדַּל וְיִתְקַדַּשׁ שְׁמֵהּ רַבָּא בְּעָלְמָא דִי בְרָא כִרְעוּתֵהּ;
וְיַמְלִיךְ מַלְכוּתֵהּ בְּחַיֵּיכוֹן וּבְיוֹמֵיכוֹן, וּבְחַיֵּי דְכָל בֵּית יִשְׂרָאֵל,
בַּעֲגָלָא וּבִזְמַן קָרִיב, וְאִמְרוּ אָמֵן.

יְהֵא שְׁמֵהּ רַבָּא מְבָרַךְ לְעָלַם וּלְעָלְמֵי עָלְמַיָּא.

יִתְבָּרַךְ וְיִשְׁתַּבַּח, וְיִתְפָּאַר וְיִתְרוֹמַם, וְיִתְנַשֵּׂא וְיִתְהַדָּר,
וְיִתְעַלֶּה וְיִתְהַלָּל שְׁמֵהּ דְּקֻדְשָׁא, בְּרִיךְ הוּא, לְעֵלָּא (לְעֵלָּא)
מִן כָּל בִּרְכָתָא וְשִׁירָתָא, תֻּשְׁבְּחָתָא וְנֶחֱמָתָא, דַּאֲמִירָן בְּעָלְמָא,
וְאִמְרוּ אָמֵן.

תִּתְקַבֵּל צְלוֹתְהוֹן וּבָעוּתְהוֹן דְּכָל בֵּית יִשְׂרָאֵל קֳדָם אֲבוּהוֹן
דִּי בִשְׁמַיָּא, וְאִמְרוּ אָמֵן.

יְהֵא שְׁלָמָא רַבָּא מִן שְׁמַיָּא, וְחַיִּים, עָלֵינוּ וְעַל כָּל יִשְׂרָאֵל,
וְאִמְרוּ אָמֵן.

עֹשֶׂה שָׁלוֹם בִּמְרוֹמָיו, הוּא יַעֲשֶׂה שָׁלוֹם עָלֵינוּ וְעַל כָּל
יִשְׂרָאֵל, וְאִמְרוּ אָמֵן.

Between *Pesaḥ* and *Shavuoth*, the *Omer* is counted.
On *Ḥanukkah*, the Reader lights the *Ḥanukkah* lights.

וְיִתֶּן־לְךָ הָאֱלֹהִים מִטַּל הַשָּׁמַיִם וּמִשְׁמַנֵּי הָאָרֶץ, וְרֹב דָּגָן
וְתִירֹשׁ. יַעַבְדוּךָ עַמִּים, וְיִשְׁתַּחֲווּ לְךָ לְאֻמִּים; הֱוֵה גְבִיר
לְאַחֶיךָ, וְיִשְׁתַּחֲווּ לְךָ בְּנֵי אִמֶּךָ; אֹרְרֶיךָ אָרוּר, וּמְבָרְכֶיךָ
בָּרוּךְ. וְאֵל שַׁדַּי יְבָרֵךְ אֹתְךָ, וְיַפְרְךָ וְיַרְבֶּךָ, וְהָיִיתָ לִקְהַל
עַמִּים. וְיִתֶּן־לְךָ אֶת בִּרְכַּת אַבְרָהָם, לְךָ וּלְזַרְעֲךָ אִתָּךְ,
לְרִשְׁתְּךָ אֶת אֶרֶץ מְגֻרֶיךָ אֲשֶׁר נָתַן אֱלֹהִים לְאַבְרָהָם. מֵאֵל
אָבִיךָ וְיַעְזְרֶךָ, וְאֵת שַׁדַּי וִיבָרְכֶךָ, בִּרְכֹת שָׁמַיִם מֵעָל, בִּרְכֹת

ויתן לך is composed of scattered biblical verses containing the assurance
of deliverance, prosperity and peace. They are to serve as encouragement when
the new week of toil follows the Sabbath rest.

Reader:

Glorified and sanctified be God's great name throughout the world which he has created according to his will. May he establish his kingdom in your lifetime and during your days, and within the life of the entire house of Israel, speedily and soon; and say, Amen.

May his great name be blessed forever and to all eternity.

Blessed and praised, glorified and exalted, extolled and honored, adored and lauded be the name of the Holy One, blessed be he, beyond all the blessings and hymns, praises and consolations that are ever spoken in the world; and say, Amen.

May the prayers and supplications of the whole household of Israel be accepted by their Father who is in heaven; and say, Amen.

May there be abundant peace from heaven, and life, for us and for all Israel; and say, Amen.

He who creates peace in his celestial heights, may he create peace for us and for all Israel; and say, Amen.

Between Pesaḥ and Shavuoth, the Omer is counted.
On Ḥanukkah, the Reader lights the Ḥanukkah lights.

God grant you dew from heaven, rich soil, and plenty of grain and wine. May nations serve you, and peoples bow down to you; be master of your brothers, and let your mother's sons bow down to you; cursed be those who curse you, and blessed be those who bless you.[1]

God Almighty bless you and make you fruitful and multiply you, that you may become a multitude of families. May he bestow on you and on your descendants the blessing of Abraham that you may own the land where you dwell, which God gave to Abraham.[2]

[May you receive] from your father's God who will help you, from the Almighty who will bless you, blessings of heaven above,

---

[1] *Genesis* 27:28-29.   [2] *Genesis* 28:3-4.

תְּהוֹם רֹבֶצֶת תָּחַת, בִּרְכֹת שָׁדַיִם וָרָחַם. בִּרְכֹת אָבִיךָ גָּבְרוּ
עַל בִּרְכֹת הוֹרַי, עַד תַּאֲוַת גִּבְעֹת עוֹלָם, תִּהְיֶיןָ לְרֹאשׁ יוֹסֵף,
וּלְקָדְקֹד נְזִיר אֶחָיו. וַאֲהֵבְךָ וּבֵרַכְךָ וְהִרְבֶּךָ, וּבֵרַךְ פְּרִי בִטְנְךָ
וּפְרִי אַדְמָתֶךָ, דְּגָנְךָ וְתִירשְׁךָ וְיִצְהָרֶךָ, שְׁגַר אֲלָפֶיךָ וְעַשְׁתְּרֹת
צֹאנֶךָ, עַל הָאֲדָמָה אֲשֶׁר נִשְׁבַּע לַאֲבֹתֶיךָ לָתֶת־לָךְ. בָּרוּךְ
תִּהְיֶה מִכָּל הָעַמִּים; לֹא יִהְיֶה בְךָ עָקָר וַעֲקָרָה, וּבִבְהֶמְתֶּךָ.
וְהֵסִיר יְיָ מִמְּךָ כָּל חֹלִי; וְכָל מַדְוֵי מִצְרַיִם הָרָעִים, אֲשֶׁר
יָדַעְתָּ, לֹא יְשִׂימָם בָּךְ, וּנְתָנָם בְּכָל שׂנְאֶיךָ.

הַמַּלְאָךְ הַגֹּאֵל אֹתִי מִכָּל רָע יְבָרֵךְ אֶת הַנְּעָרִים, וְיִקָּרֵא
בָהֶם שְׁמִי, וְשֵׁם אֲבֹתַי אַבְרָהָם וְיִצְחָק, וְיִדְגּוּ לָרֹב בְּקֶרֶב
הָאָרֶץ. יְיָ אֱלֹהֵיכֶם הִרְבָּה אֶתְכֶם, וְהִנְּכֶם הַיּוֹם כְּכוֹכְבֵי
הַשָּׁמַיִם לָרֹב. יְיָ אֱלֹהֵי אֲבוֹתֵיכֶם יֹסֵף עֲלֵיכֶם כָּכֶם אֶלֶף
פְּעָמִים, וִיבָרֵךְ אֶתְכֶם כַּאֲשֶׁר דִּבֶּר־לָכֶם.

בָּרוּךְ אַתָּה בָּעִיר, וּבָרוּךְ אַתָּה בַּשָּׂדֶה. בָּרוּךְ אַתָּה בְּבֹאֶךָ,
וּבָרוּךְ אַתָּה בְּצֵאתֶךָ. בָּרוּךְ טַנְאֲךָ וּמִשְׁאַרְתֶּךָ. בָּרוּךְ פְּרִי
בִטְנְךָ וּפְרִי אַדְמָתְךָ וּפְרִי בְהֶמְתֶּךָ, שְׁגַר אֲלָפֶיךָ וְעַשְׁתְּרוֹת
צֹאנֶךָ. יְצַו יְיָ אִתְּךָ אֶת הַבְּרָכָה, בַּאֲסָמֶיךָ וּבְכֹל מִשְׁלַח יָדֶךָ;
וּבֵרַכְךָ בָּאָרֶץ אֲשֶׁר יְיָ אֱלֹהֶיךָ נֹתֵן לָךְ. יִפְתַּח יְיָ לְךָ אֶת אוֹצָרוֹ
הַטּוֹב, אֶת הַשָּׁמַיִם לָתֵת מְטַר אַרְצְךָ בְּעִתּוֹ, וּלְבָרֵךְ אֵת כָּל
מַעֲשֵׂה יָדֶךָ; וְהִלְוִיתָ גּוֹיִם רַבִּים, וְאַתָּה לֹא תִלְוֶה. כִּי יְיָ אֱלֹהֶיךָ
בֵּרַכְךָ, כַּאֲשֶׁר דִּבֶּר־לָךְ; וְהַעֲבַטְתָּ גּוֹיִם רַבִּים, וְאַתָּה לֹא
תַעֲבֹט; וּמָשַׁלְתָּ בְּגוֹיִם רַבִּים, וּבְךָ לֹא יִמְשֹׁלוּ. אַשְׁרֶיךָ יִשְׂרָאֵל,
מִי כָמוֹךָ, עַם נוֹשַׁע בַּיְיָ, מָגֵן עֶזְרֶךָ, וַאֲשֶׁר חֶרֶב גַּאֲוָתֶךָ; וְיִכָּחֲשׁוּ
אֹיְבֶיךָ לָךְ, וְאַתָּה עַל בָּמוֹתֵימוֹ תִדְרֹךְ.

blessings of the deep couching below, blessings of breast and of womb. The blessings of your father exceeded the blessings of my progenitors to the utmost limit of the eternal hills; may they rest on the head of Joseph, on the brow of him who is the prince of his brothers.[1]

He will love you, bless you, and multiply you; he will bless the fruit of your body and the fruit of your soil, your grain and wine and oil, the offspring of your cattle and the flocks of your sheep, in the land which he swore to your fathers that he would give to you. You shall be blessed above all peoples; not a male or female shall be barren among you or among your cattle. The Lord will also free you from all sickness; he will not inflict upon you any of Egypt's diseases which you know, but he will inflict them upon all who hate you.[2]

The angel who redeemed me from all evil bless the lads; may they carry on my name and the name of my fathers Abraham and Isaac; may they grow into a multitude on earth.[3]

The Lord your God has multiplied you, and you are today like the stars of heaven as to multitude. May the Lord God of your fathers multiply you still a thousand-fold, and bless you as he promised you.[4]

Blessed shall you be in the city, and blessed shall you be in the field. Blessed shall you be in your coming, and blessed shall you be in your going. Blessed shall be your basket and your kneading trough. Blessed shall be the fruit of your body and the fruit of your land, your cattle and your flocks of sheep. The Lord will command the blessing upon you in your barns and in every enterprise to which you put your hand, and will bless you in the land which the Lord your God gives you. The Lord will open his good treasure of heaven for you, to bestow rain in due season on your land, and to bless all your labor, so that you shall lend to many nations but never need to borrow from them.[5]

For the Lord your God blesses you as he promised you; you shall lend to many nations but never need to borrow; you shall rule over many nations, but they shall not rule over you.[6]

Happy are you, O Israel! Who is there like you, a people saved by the Lord, your shield of help, your sword of triumph; your foes shall come cringing to you, as you march across their heights.[7]

---

[1] *Genesis* 49:25-26. [2] *Deuteronomy* 7:13-15. [3] *Genesis* 48:16. [4] *Deuteronomy* 1:10-11. [5] *Deuteronomy* 28:3, 6, 5, 4, 8, 12. [6] *Deuteronomy* 15:6. [7] *Deuteronomy* 33:29.

מָחִיתִי כָעָב פְּשָׁעֶיךָ, וְכֶעָנָן חַטֹּאתֶיךָ; שׁוּבָה אֵלַי, כִּי
גְאַלְתִּיךָ. רָנּוּ שָׁמַיִם, כִּי עָשָׂה יְיָ, הָרִיעוּ תַּחְתִּיּוֹת אָרֶץ, פִּצְחוּ
הָרִים רִנָּה, יַעַר וְכָל עֵץ בּוֹ, כִּי גָאַל יְיָ יַעֲקֹב, וּבְיִשְׂרָאֵל
יִתְפָּאָר. וּגְאָלֵנוּ יְיָ צְבָאוֹת שְׁמוֹ, קְדוֹשׁ יִשְׂרָאֵל.

יִשְׂרָאֵל נוֹשַׁע בַּיְיָ תְּשׁוּעַת עוֹלָמִים; לֹא תֵבֹשׁוּ וְלֹא תִכָּלְמוּ
עַד עוֹלְמֵי עַד. וַאֲכַלְתֶּם אָכוֹל וְשָׂבוֹעַ, וְהִלַּלְתֶּם אֶת שֵׁם יְיָ
אֱלֹהֵיכֶם אֲשֶׁר עָשָׂה עִמָּכֶם לְהַפְלִיא, וְלֹא יֵבֹשׁוּ עַמִּי לְעוֹלָם.
וִידַעְתֶּם כִּי בְקֶרֶב יִשְׂרָאֵל אָנִי, וַאֲנִי יְיָ אֱלֹהֵיכֶם, וְאֵין עוֹד;
וְלֹא יֵבֹשׁוּ עַמִּי לְעוֹלָם. כִּי בְשִׂמְחָה תֵצֵאוּ, וּבְשָׁלוֹם תּוּבָלוּן;
הֶהָרִים וְהַגְּבָעוֹת יִפְצְחוּ לִפְנֵיכֶם רִנָּה, וְכָל עֲצֵי הַשָּׂדֶה יִמְחֲאוּ
כָף. הִנֵּה אֵל יְשׁוּעָתִי, אֶבְטַח וְלֹא אֶפְחָד; כִּי עָזִּי וְזִמְרָת יָהּ יְיָ,
וַיְהִי לִי לִישׁוּעָה. וּשְׁאַבְתֶּם מַיִם בְּשָׂשׂוֹן, מִמַּעַיְנֵי הַיְשׁוּעָה.
וַאֲמַרְתֶּם בַּיּוֹם הַהוּא: הוֹדוּ לַיְיָ, קִרְאוּ בִשְׁמוֹ, הוֹדִיעוּ בָעַמִּים
עֲלִילֹתָיו; הַזְכִּירוּ כִּי נִשְׂגָּב שְׁמוֹ. זַמְּרוּ יְיָ, כִּי גֵאוּת עָשָׂה;
מוּדַעַת זֹאת בְּכָל הָאָרֶץ. צַהֲלִי וָרֹנִּי, יוֹשֶׁבֶת צִיּוֹן, כִּי גָדוֹל
בְּקִרְבֵּךְ קְדוֹשׁ יִשְׂרָאֵל. וְאָמַר בַּיּוֹם הַהוּא, הִנֵּה אֱלֹהֵינוּ זֶה
קִוִּינוּ לוֹ וְיוֹשִׁיעֵנוּ; זֶה יְיָ קִוִּינוּ לוֹ, נָגִילָה וְנִשְׂמְחָה בִּישׁוּעָתוֹ.

בֵּית יַעֲקֹב, לְכוּ וְנֵלְכָה בְּאוֹר יְיָ. וְהָיָה אֱמוּנַת עִתֶּיךָ חֹסֶן
יְשׁוּעֹת, חָכְמַת וָדָעַת, יִרְאַת יְיָ הִיא אוֹצָרוֹ. וַיְהִי דָוִד לְכָל
דְּרָכָיו מַשְׂכִּיל, וַיְיָ עִמּוֹ. פָּדָה בְשָׁלוֹם נַפְשִׁי מִקְּרָב־לִי, כִּי
בְרַבִּים הָיוּ עִמָּדִי. וַיֹּאמֶר הָעָם אֶל שָׁאוּל: הֲיוֹנָתָן יָמוּת, אֲשֶׁר

ושאבתם מים בששון ("you shall draw water with joy") is a figurative expression indicating continuous divine protection. The term *water* is often used
symbolically. The Torah is frequently compared to water that purifies. In
Numbers 24:7, the constant flow of water is symbolic of numerous descendants.
In Temple times, the Water-Feast celebrated on the second night of *Sukkoth*
by a joyous procession to and from the well שמחת בית השואבה was a most
inspiring occasion.

I have swept aside your ill deeds like a mist, and your sins like a cloud; return to me, for I have redeemed you. Sing, O heavens, for the Lord has done it; shout, depths of the earth; burst into singing, you mountains, forests and all trees, for the Lord has redeemed Jacob, and will glory in Israel. Our Redeemer, Lord of hosts is his name, the Holy One of Israel.[1]

Israel is saved by the Lord in an everlasting triumph; you shall not be put to shame, you shall not be humilated, to all eternity. You shall eat and be satisfied, and praise the name of the Lord your God, who has dealt with you wondrously; never again shall my people be put to shame. You shall know that I am in the midst of Israel, that I am the Lord your God, and there is none else; never again shall my people be put to shame.[2]

With joy shall you go forth, and in peace shall be led; the mountains and the hills shall burst into song before you, and all the trees of the field shall applaud.[3]

Behold, God is my deliverance; I will trust, and will not be afraid; truly the Lord is my strength and my song; he has delivered me indeed. Joyfully shall you draw upon the fountains of deliverance, and say on that day: "Give thanks to the Lord; proclaim his name; tell the peoples all that he has done; record his exalted fame. Sing to the Lord, for he has done gloriously; let this be made known throughout the world. Rejoice and sing aloud, inhabitants of Zion, for great is the Holy One of Israel in the midst of you."[4]

On that day men shall say: "Here is our God, for whom we waited that he should save us; this is the Lord, for whom we waited; let us rejoice and be happy with his salvation."[5]

O house of Jacob, come, let us walk in the light of the Lord! A saving wealth of wisdom and knowledge shall be your steady experience; godliness is one's treasure.[6]

David prospered in all his ways, and the Lord was with him.[7]

He has saved my life in peace from the battle that was against me; those who were striving with me were many indeed.[8]

---

[1] *Isaiah* 44:22-23; 47:4. [2] *Isaiah* 45:17; *Joel* 2:26-27. [3] *Isaiah* 55:12. [4] *Isaiah* 12:2-6. [5] *Isaiah* 25:9. [6] *Isaiah* 2:5; 33:6. [7] *I Samuel* 18:14. [8] *Psalm* 55:19.

עָשָׂה הַיְשׁוּעָה הַגְּדוֹלָה הַזֹּאת בְּיִשְׂרָאֵל; חָלִילָה, חַי יְיָ אִם יִפֹּל
מִשַּׂעֲרַת רֹאשׁוֹ אָרְצָה, כִּי עִם אֱלֹהִים עָשָׂה הַיּוֹם הַזֶּה; וַיִּפְדּוּ
הָעָם אֶת יוֹנָתָן, וְלֹא מֵת. וּפְדוּיֵי יְיָ יְשֻׁבוּן, וּבָאוּ צִיּוֹן בְּרִנָּה,
וְשִׂמְחַת עוֹלָם עַל רֹאשָׁם; שָׂשׂוֹן וְשִׂמְחָה יַשִּׂיגוּ, וְנָסוּ יָגוֹן וַאֲנָחָה.
הָפַכְתָּ מִסְפְּדִי לְמָחוֹל לִי, פִּתַּחְתָּ שַׂקִּי וַתְּאַזְּרֵנִי שִׂמְחָה. וְלֹא
אָבָה יְיָ אֱלֹהֶיךָ לִשְׁמֹעַ אֶל בִּלְעָם, וַיַּהֲפֹךְ יְיָ אֱלֹהֶיךָ לְּךָ
אֶת הַקְּלָלָה לִבְרָכָה, כִּי אֲהֵבְךָ יְיָ אֱלֹהֶיךָ. אָז תִּשְׂמַח
בְּתוּלָה בְּמָחוֹל, וּבַחֻרִים וּזְקֵנִים יַחְדָּו; וְהָפַכְתִּי אֶבְלָם לְשָׂשׂוֹן,
וְנִחַמְתִּים וְשִׂמַּחְתִּים מִיגוֹנָם.

בּוֹרֵא נִיב שְׂפָתָיִם, שָׁלוֹם שָׁלוֹם לָרָחוֹק וְלַקָּרוֹב, אָמַר יְיָ,
וּרְפָאתִיו. וְרוּחַ לָבְשָׁה אֶת עֲמָשַׂי, רֹאשׁ הַשָּׁלִישִׁים; לְךָ דָוִיד,
וְעִמְּךָ בֶן־יִשַׁי, שָׁלוֹם שָׁלוֹם לְךָ, וְשָׁלוֹם לְעֹזְרֶךָ, כִּי עֲזָרְךָ
אֱלֹהֶיךָ; וַיְקַבְּלֵם דָּוִיד, וַיִּתְּנֵם בְּרָאשֵׁי הַגְּדוּד. וַאֲמַרְתֶּם כֹּה
לֶחָי, וְאַתָּה שָׁלוֹם, וּבֵיתְךָ שָׁלוֹם, וְכֹל אֲשֶׁר לְךָ שָׁלוֹם. יְיָ עֹז
לְעַמּוֹ יִתֵּן; יְיָ יְבָרֵךְ אֶת עַמּוֹ בַשָּׁלוֹם.

מסכת מגילה לא, א

אָמַר רַבִּי יוֹחָנָן: בְּכָל מָקוֹם שֶׁאַתָּה מוֹצֵא גְּדֻלָּתוֹ שֶׁל
הַקָּדוֹשׁ בָּרוּךְ הוּא, שָׁם אַתָּה מוֹצֵא עַנְוְתָנוּתוֹ. דָּבָר זֶה כָּתוּב
בַּתּוֹרָה, וְשָׁנוּי בַּנְּבִיאִים, וּמְשֻׁלָּשׁ בַּכְּתוּבִים. כָּתוּב בַּתּוֹרָה:
כִּי יְיָ אֱלֹהֵיכֶם הוּא אֱלֹהֵי הָאֱלֹהִים וַאֲדֹנֵי הָאֲדֹנִים, הָאֵל
הַגָּדֹל הַגִּבֹּר וְהַנּוֹרָא, אֲשֶׁר לֹא יִשָּׂא פָנִים וְלֹא יִקַּח שֹׁחַד.
וּכְתִיב בַּתְרֵהּ: עֹשֶׂה מִשְׁפַּט יָתוֹם וְאַלְמָנָה, וְאֹהֵב גֵּר לָתֶת־לוֹ

כה לחי is a salutation equivalent to "long life to you!" It was used in
David's message to Nabal when he solicited the latter's assistance. The word
לחי has been regarded by some as an abbreviation of לאחי ("to my
brethren").

ענותנותו is here used in the sense of forbearance, patience and kindness.

And the people said to Saul: Shall Jonathan die who has accomplished this great victory in Israel? God forbid! As the Lord lives, not a hair of his head shall fall to the ground, for with God's help has he performed on this day. So the people rescued Jonathan, and he did not die.[1]

The ransomed of the Lord shall return; they shall come to Zion in triumph, and everlasting joy shall crown their heads; joy and gladness shall they attain, and sorrow and sighing shall flee away.[2]

Thou hast changed my mourning into dancing; thou hast removed my sackcloth, and girded me with gladness.[3]

The Lord your God would not listen to Balaam; the Lord your God turned the curse into a blessing for you, because the Lord your God loved you.[4]

Then shall the maiden delight in dancing, and the young men and the old alike; I will change their mourning into joy; I will comfort them and cheer them after their sorrow.[5]

I will grant peace, peace to the far and the near, says the Lord who creates the speech of the lips, and I will heal him.[6]

The spirit came upon Amasai, the chief of the captains: "Yours are we, O David, on your side, son of Jesse; peace, peace be to you, and peace be to your helpers; truly your God helps you." Then David received them and made them chiefs of the band.[7]

And thus shall you say: "All hail! Peace be to you and your house and all that you have."[8]

The Lord will give strength to his people; the Lord will bless his people with peace.[9]

Talmud Megillah 31a

Rabbi Yoḥanan said: Wherever you find the Lord's greatness mentioned you find his gentleness indicated. This is so in the Torah, again in the Prophets, and a third time in the Psalms.

It is written in the Torah: "The Lord your God is the supreme God, the supreme Lord, the great God, mighty and revered, who is never partial and never takes a bribe"; and immediately afterwards it says: "He secures justice for the orphan and the widow, and loves the stranger, giving him food and clothing."[10] Again it is written

---

[1] *I Samuel* 14:45.   [2] *Isaiah* 35:10.   [3] *Psalm* 30:12.   [4] *Deuteronomy* 23:6.
[5] *Jeremiah* 31:12.   [6] *Isaiah* 57:19.   [7] *I Chronicles* 12:18.   [8] *I Samuel* 25:6.
[9] *Psalm* 29:11.   [10] *Deuteronomy* 10:17-18.

לֶחֶם וְשִׂמְלָה. שָׁנוּי בַּנְּבִיאִים, דִּכְתִיב: כִּי כֹה אָמַר רָם וְנִשָּׂא,
שֹׁכֵן עַד וְקָדוֹשׁ שְׁמוֹ, מָרוֹם וְקָדוֹשׁ אֶשְׁכּוֹן. וּכְתִיב בָּתְרֵהּ: וְאֶת
דַּכָּא וּשְׁפַל רוּחַ, לְהַחֲיוֹת רוּחַ שְׁפָלִים וּלְהַחֲיוֹת לֵב נִדְכָּאִים.
מְשֻׁלָּשׁ בַּכְּתוּבִים, דִּכְתִיב: שִׁירוּ לֵאלֹהִים, זַמְּרוּ שְׁמוֹ; סֹלוּ
לָרֹכֵב בָּעֲרָבוֹת, בְּיָהּ שְׁמוֹ, וְעִלְזוּ לְפָנָיו. וּכְתִיב בָּתְרֵהּ: אֲבִי
יְתוֹמִים וְדַיַּן אַלְמָנוֹת, אֱלֹהִים בִּמְעוֹן קָדְשׁוֹ.

יְהִי יְיָ אֱלֹהֵינוּ עִמָּנוּ כַּאֲשֶׁר הָיָה עִם אֲבוֹתֵינוּ, אַל יַעַזְבֵנוּ
וְאַל יִטְּשֵׁנוּ. וְאַתֶּם הַדְּבֵקִים בַּיְיָ אֱלֹהֵיכֶם, חַיִּים כֻּלְּכֶם הַיּוֹם.
כִּי נִחַם יְיָ צִיּוֹן, נִחַם כָּל חָרְבֹתֶיהָ, וַיָּשֶׂם מִדְבָּרָהּ כְּעֵדֶן,
וְעַרְבָתָהּ כְּגַן יְיָ; שָׂשׂוֹן וְשִׂמְחָה יִמָּצֵא בָהּ, תּוֹדָה וְקוֹל זִמְרָה.
יְיָ חָפֵץ לְמַעַן צִדְקוֹ, יַגְדִּיל תּוֹרָה וְיַאְדִּיר.

תהלים קכח

שִׁיר הַמַּעֲלוֹת. אַשְׁרֵי כָּל יְרֵא יְיָ, הַהֹלֵךְ בִּדְרָכָיו. יְגִיעַ
כַּפֶּיךָ כִּי תֹאכֵל, אַשְׁרֶיךָ וְטוֹב לָךְ. אֶשְׁתְּךָ כְּגֶפֶן פֹּרִיָּה בְּיַרְכְּתֵי
בֵיתֶךָ; בָּנֶיךָ כִּשְׁתִלֵי זֵיתִים סָבִיב לְשֻׁלְחָנֶךָ. הִנֵּה כִי כֵן יְבֹרַךְ
גָּבֶר, יְרֵא יְיָ. יְבָרֶכְךָ יְיָ מִצִּיּוֹן, וּרְאֵה בְּטוּב יְרוּשָׁלָיִם כֹּל יְמֵי
חַיֶּיךָ. וּרְאֵה בָנִים לְבָנֶיךָ; שָׁלוֹם עַל יִשְׂרָאֵל.

ה' חפץ למען צדקו... God graciously gave the great Torah for the improve-
ment of man. The biblical excerpts recited on Saturday night include the
blessings pronounced by Isaac, Jacob and Moses, along with the prophetic
promises addressed to Israel and various expressions laying stress upon the
ideal of peace.

Psalm 128 emphasizes the dignity of labor; hence it is recited at the
conclusion of the service which marks the beginning of the six working days
of the week. According to the Talmud, this psalm teaches that happiness in
this life and in the hereafter is the reward of one who enjoys what his own
hands have produced: "Greater is he who enjoys the fruit of his own labor
than he who is merely pious; for with regard to the pious it is written: 'Happy
is everyone who reveres the Lord,' but with regard to one who enjoys the
fruit of his labor it is written: 'When you eat of the toil of your hands, you

in the Prophets: "Thus says the High and Lofty One, who inhabits eternity, whose name is Holy: "I dwell in the high and holy place"; and immediately afterwards it says: "but with him also that is contrite and humble in spirit, to revive the spirit of the humble, and to revive the heart of the contrite."[1] And a third time it is written in the Psalms: "Sing to God, sing praises to his name; extol him who is in heaven—Lord is his name—and exult before him"; and immediately afterwards it says: "A father of orphans, a champion of widows, is God in his holy habitation."[2]

May the Lord our God be with us as he was with our fathers; may he never leave us nor forsake us.[3]

You who cling to the Lord your God are all alive this day.[4]

Truly the Lord shall comfort Zion, he shall comfort all her ruins; he shall make her wilderness like Eden, her desert like the garden of the Lord; joy and gladness shall be found in her, thanksgiving and song.[5]

The Lord was pleased, for the sake of his righteousness, to make the Torah great and glorious.[6]

Psalm 128

A Pilgrim Song. Happy is everyone who reveres the Lord, who walks in his ways. When you eat of the toil of your hands, you shall be happy and at ease. Your wife shall be like a fruitful vine in the interior of your house, your children like olive plants around your table. Behold, thus indeed shall the man be blessed who reveres the Lord. The Lord bless you from Zion; may you see the welfare of Jerusalem all the days of your life; may you live to see your children's children. Peace be upon Israel!

---

shall be happy and at ease'—*you shall be happy* in this world, *and at ease* in the future world" (Berakhoth 8a).

"Love work" (Avoth 1:10) is one of the essential principles in talmudic literature. "Even Adam did not taste food until he had done work, as it is said: 'The Lord God took the man and put him in the Garden of Eden to till it and look after it' "(Genesis 2:15). According to Rabban Gamaliel, "all Torah study that is not combined with some trade must at length fail and occasion sin" (Avoth 2:2). The rabbis of the Talmud practised what they preached. The majority of them were humble workmen.

[1]*Isaiah* 57:15.　[2]*Psalm* 68:5–6.　[3]*I Kings* 8:57.　[4]*Deuteronomy* 4:4.　[5]*Isaiah* 51:3.　[6]*Isaiah* 42:21.

הַבְדָלָה

Recited over a cup of wine and fragrant spices

הִנֵּה אֵל יְשׁוּעָתִי, אֶבְטַח וְלֹא אֶפְחָד, כִּי עָזִּי וְזִמְרָת יָהּ יְיָ,
וַיְהִי לִי לִישׁוּעָה. וּשְׁאַבְתֶּם מַיִם בְּשָׂשׂוֹן מִמַּעַיְנֵי הַיְשׁוּעָה. לַיְיָ
הַיְשׁוּעָה; עַל עַמְּךָ בִרְכָתֶךָ סֶּלָה. יְיָ צְבָאוֹת עִמָּנוּ, מִשְׂגָּב לָנוּ
אֱלֹהֵי יַעֲקֹב, סֶלָה. יְיָ צְבָאוֹת, אַשְׁרֵי אָדָם בֹּטֵחַ בָּךְ. יְיָ,
הוֹשִׁיעָה; הַמֶּלֶךְ יַעֲנֵנוּ בְיוֹם קָרְאֵנוּ. לַיְּהוּדִים הָיְתָה אוֹרָה
וְשִׂמְחָה, וְשָׂשׂוֹן וִיקָר. כֵּן תִּהְיֶה לָּנוּ. כּוֹס יְשׁוּעוֹת אֶשָּׂא, וּבְשֵׁם יְיָ
אֶקְרָא.

In the synagogue, the Reader begins here:

סָבְרִי מָרָנָן וְרַבּוֹתַי.

בָּרוּךְ אַתָּה, יְיָ אֱלֹהֵינוּ, מֶלֶךְ הָעוֹלָם, בּוֹרֵא פְּרִי הַגָּפֶן.

בָּרוּךְ אַתָּה, יְיָ אֱלֹהֵינוּ, מֶלֶךְ הָעוֹלָם, בּוֹרֵא מִינֵי בְשָׂמִים.

בָּרוּךְ אַתָּה, יְיָ אֱלֹהֵינוּ, מֶלֶךְ הָעוֹלָם, בּוֹרֵא מְאוֹרֵי הָאֵשׁ.

בָּרוּךְ אַתָּה, יְיָ אֱלֹהֵינוּ, מֶלֶךְ הָעוֹלָם, הַמַּבְדִּיל בֵּין קֹדֶשׁ
לְחֹל, בֵּין אוֹר לְחֹשֶׁךְ, בֵּין יִשְׂרָאֵל לָעַמִּים, בֵּין יוֹם הַשְּׁבִיעִי
לְשֵׁשֶׁת יְמֵי הַמַּעֲשֶׂה. בָּרוּךְ אַתָּה, יְיָ, הַמַּבְדִּיל בֵּין קֹדֶשׁ לְחֹל.

Ma'ariv is concluded on page 213.

הבדלה, marking the end of the Sabbath, is attributed to the men of the
Great Assembly (Berakhoth 33a). The introductory passage הנה אל ישועתי,
consisting of biblical verses, is of later origin. According to Maimonides, the
symbolic use of fragrant spices during the recital of the *Havdalah* is to cheer the
soul which is saddened at the departure of the Sabbath. When a festival follows immediately after the Sabbath the spices are omitted, because the soul
then rejoices with the incoming holiday. The wine for the *Havdalah* is allowed
to flow over as a symbol of the overflowing blessing expected in the coming
week. It is customary to cup the hands around the candle and to gaze at the
finger-nails. The reflection of the light on the finger-nails causes the shadow to

HAVDALAH

Recited over a cup of wine and fragrant spices

Behold, God is my deliverance; I will trust, and will not be afraid; truly the Lord is my strength and my song; he has delivered me indeed. Joyfully shall you draw upon the fountains of deliverance. It is for the Lord to bring help; my God, thy blessing be upon thy people. The Lord of hosts is with us; the God of Jacob is our Stronghold. Lord of hosts, happy is the man who trusts in thee. O Lord, save us; may the King answer us when we call. The Jews had light and joy, gladness and honor. So be it with us. I will take the cup of deliverance, and will call upon the name of the Lord.[1]

In the synagogue, the Reader begins here:

Blessed art thou, Lord our God, King of the universe, who createst the fruit of the vine.

Blessed art thou, Lord our God, King of the universe, who createst various kinds of spices.

Blessed art thou, Lord our God, King of the universe, who createst the lights of fire.

Blessed art thou, Lord our God, King of the universe, who hast made a distinction between the sacred and the profane, between light and darkness, between Israel and the other nations, between the seventh day and the six working days. Blessed art thou, O Lord, who hast made a distinction between the sacred and the profane.

Ma'ariv is concluded on page 214.

---

appear on the palm of the hand, thus indicating the distinction "between light and darkness" mentioned in the *Havdalah*. A twisted candle of several wicks is used since the phrase מאורי האש ("lights of fire") is in the plural. The custom of dipping the finger in the wine and passing it over the eyes alludes to Psalm 19:9 where God's commands are described as "enlightening the eyes."

[1] *Isaiah* 12:2-3; *Psalms* 3:9; 46:12; 84:13; 20:10; *Esther* 8:16; *Psalm* 116:13.

זְמִירוֹת

הַמַּבְדִּיל בֵּין קֹדֶשׁ לְחֹל   חַטֹּאתֵינוּ הוּא יִמְחֹל;

זַרְעֵנוּ וְכַסְפֵּנוּ יַרְבֶּה כַּחוֹל   וְכַכּוֹכָבִים בַּלָּיְלָה.

יוֹם פָּנָה כְּצֵל תֹּמֶר   אֶקְרָא לָאֵל עָלַי גֹּמֵר;

אָמַר שׁוֹמֵר   אָתָא בֹקֶר וְגַם לָיְלָה.

צִדְקָתְךָ כְּהַר תָּבוֹר   עַל חֲטָאַי עָבֹר תַּעֲבֹר;

כְּיוֹם אֶתְמוֹל כִּי יַעֲבֹר   וְאַשְׁמוּרָה בַלָּיְלָה.

חָלְפָה עוֹנַת מִנְחָתִי   מִי יִתֵּן מְנוּחָתִי;

יָגַעְתִּי בְאַנְחָתִי   אַשְׂחֶה בְכָל לָיְלָה.

קוֹלִי בַּל יֻטַּל   פְּתַח לִי שַׁעַר הַמְנֻטָּל;

שֶׁרֹּאשִׁי נִמְלָא טָל   קְוֻצּוֹתַי רְסִיסֵי לָיְלָה.

הֵעָתֵר נוֹרָא וְאָיוֹם   אֲשַׁוֵּעַ תְּנָה פִדְיוֹם;

בְּנֶשֶׁף בְּעֶרֶב יוֹם   בְּאִישׁוֹן לָיְלָה.

קְרָאתִיךָ יָהּ הוֹשִׁיעֵנִי   אֹרַח חַיִּים תּוֹדִיעֵנִי;

מִדַּלָּה תְבַצְּעֵנִי   מִיּוֹם עַד לָיְלָה.

טַהֵר טִנּוּף מַעֲשַׂי   פֶּן יֹאמְרוּ מַכְעִיסַי

אַיֵּה אֱלוֹהַּ עֹשָׂי   נֹתֵן זְמִרוֹת בַּלָּיְלָה.

נַחְנוּ בְיָדְךָ כַּחֹמֶר   סְלַח נָא עַל קַל וָחֹמֶר;

יוֹם לְיוֹם יַבִּיעַ אֹמֶר   וְלַיְלָה לְלָיְלָה.

המבדיל is attributed to Rabbi Isaac ibn Ghayyat, who lived in Spain during the eleventh century and was the teacher of Rabbi Isaac Alfasi (רי״ף), author of the famous compendium of the Talmud. יצחק הקטן is the acrostic of this hymn, said to have been originally composed for the Ne'ilah service of *Yom Kippur*. The biblical verses at the end of each stanza are: Genesis 15:5; Isaiah 21:12; Psalms 90:4; 6:7; Song of Songs 5:2; Proverbs 7:9; Isaiah 38:12; Job 35:10; Psalm 19:3.

HA-MAVDIL

He who marks the holy from the profane,
May he also pardon our transgressions;
May he multiply our seed as the sand,
And as the stars that appear in the night.

The day has declined like the shade of a palm;
I call upon God who fills all my needs;
The watchman-prophet has said: Morning comes,
Bright morning comes after a gloomy night.

Thy righteousness is like Mount Tabor high;
O condone and pardon my transgressions;
May they be like the flight of yesterday,
Or like the watch-hours passing in the night.

Gone is the time when I made offerings;
Oh, that again I had my place of rest!
I am worn out because of my moaning;
I flood my bed with tears every night.

Let not my supplication be repelled;
Open heaven's exalted gate for me,
Seeing that my head is drenched with the dew,
My locks are wet with the drops of the night.

Revered God, O respond to my prayer;
I call for thy help, O grant redemption,
In the twilight, the evening of the day,
And in the profound blackness of the night.

I call upon thee, O Lord, O save me;
Do thou reveal to me the path of life;
Do thou deliver me from privation,
Within the twilight, between day and night.

O cleanse the impurity of my deeds,
So that those who provoke me may not say:
"Where then is the God who created you,
He who inspires you to sing in the night?"

We are but like potter's clay in thy hand;
Pardon our transgressions, both light and grave;
Day after day proclaims the Lord's wonders,
His powers are revealed night after night.

בְּמוֹצָאֵי יוֹם מְנוּחָה   הַמְצֵא לְעַמְּךָ רְוָחָה:

שְׁלַח תִּשְׁבִּי לְנֶאֱנָחָה   וְנָס יָגוֹן וַאֲנָחָה.

יָאֶה הוּא לְךָ צוּרִי   לְקַבֵּץ עַם מְפֻזָּרִי

מִיַּד גּוֹי אַכְזָרִי   אֲשֶׁר כָּרָה לִי שׁוּחָה.

עֵת דּוֹדִים תְּעוֹרֵר אֵל   לְמַלֵּט עַם אֲשֶׁר שׁוֹאֵל

רְאוֹת טוּבְךָ בְּבוֹא גוֹאֵל   לְשֵׂה פְזוּרָה נִדָּחָה.

קָרָא יֶשַׁע לְעַם נִדְבָּה   אֶל דָּגוּל מֵרְבָבָה:

יְהִי הַשָּׁבוּעַ הַבָּא   לִישׁוּעָה וְלִרְוָחָה.

בַּת צִיּוֹן הַשְּׁכוּלָה   אֲשֶׁר הִיא הַיּוֹם גְּעוּלָה

מְהֵרָה תִהְיֶה בְעוּלָה   אֵם הַבָּנִים שְׂמֵחָה.

מַעְיָנוֹת אֲזַי יְזוּבוּן   וּפְדוּיֵי יְיָ יְשׁוּבוּן:

וּמֵי יֶשַׁע יִשְׁאֲבוּן   וְהַצָּרָה נִשְׁכָּחָה.

נְחֵה עַמְּךָ כְּאָב רַחֲמָן   יִצְפְּצְפוּ עִם לֹא אַלְמָן

דְּבַר יְיָ אֲשֶׁר נֶאֱמָן   בַּהֲקִימְךָ הַבְטָחָה.

וִידִידִים פְּלִיטֵי חֶרֶץ   נְגִינָתָם יִפְצְחוּ בְמֶרֶץ:

בְּלִי צְוָחָה וּבְלִי פֶרֶץ   וְאֵין יוֹצֵאת וְאֵין צְוָחָה.

יְהִי הַחֹדֶשׁ הַזֶּה   כִּנְבוּאַת אֲבִי חוֹזֶה:

וְיִשָּׁמַע בְּבַיִת זֶה   קוֹל שָׂשׂוֹן וְקוֹל שִׂמְחָה.

חֲזַק יְמַלֵּא מִשְׁאֲלוֹתֵינוּ   אַמִּיץ יַעֲשֶׂה בַּקָּשָׁתֵנוּ:

וְהוּא יִשְׁלַח בְּמַעֲשֵׂה יָדֵינוּ   בְּרָכָה וְהַצְלָחָה.

במוצאי יום מנוחה was composed by Rabbi Jacob Menuy who lived in the thirteenth century. The acrostic יעקב מנוי חזק begins with the second stanza. The theme of this hymn is a plea for deliverance through the appearance of Elijah as the forerunner of the Messiah.

At the close of the day of rest,
O grant relief to thy people;
Send Elijah to the distressed,
That grief and sighs may flee away.

It behooves thee, my Creator,
To gather my scattered people
From amidst a cruel nation
That is digging pitfalls for me.

O God, do thou arouse thy love,
To save a people that asks to see
Thy grace when a redeemer comes
To thy dispersed, unhappy flock.

Proclaim freedom to a noble people,
Thou who art worshiped by myriads;
May this coming week be given
To deliverance and relief.

The bereaved city of Zion,
Held today in utter contempt,
May she soon be populated—
A happy mother of children.

The fountains shall then be aflow;
Those freed by the Lord shall return;
They shall draw water that saves,
And trouble shall soon be forgotten.

Merciful Father, guide thy people;
Let a people, unbereft, say
That the word of God is faithful,
When thou wilt have kept thy promise.

Thy loved ones, escaping ruin,
Will break into vigorous song—
Without alarm, without havoc,
No surrender and no panic.

May the vision of the great seer,
Jeremiah, come to pass this month;
May in this household be heard
The sound of mirth and gladness.

May God fulfill our petitions,
The Almighty do what we ask;
May he prosper all our efforts,
And send us blessings and success.

בְּמוֹצָאֵי יוֹם גִּילָה   שִׁמְךָ נוֹרָא עֲלִילָה;

שָׁלַח תִּשְׁבִּי לְעַם סְגֻלָּה   רֶוַח שָׂשׂוֹן וַהֲנָחָה.

קוֹל צָהֳלָה וְרִנָּה   שְׂפָתֵינוּ אָז תְּרַנֵּנָה;

אָנָּא יְיָ הוֹשִׁיעָה נָּא   אָנָּא יְיָ הַצְלִיחָה נָּא.

אָמַר יְיָ לְיַעֲקֹב   אַל תִּירָא עַבְדִּי יַעֲקֹב.

בָּחַר יְיָ בְּיַעֲקֹב   אַל תִּירָא עַבְדִּי יַעֲקֹב.

גָּאַל יְיָ אֶת יַעֲקֹב   אַל תִּירָא עַבְדִּי יַעֲקֹב.

דָּרַךְ כּוֹכָב מִיַּעֲקֹב   אַל תִּירָא עַבְדִּי יַעֲקֹב.

הַבָּאִים יַשְׁרֵשׁ יַעֲקֹב   אַל תִּירָא עַבְדִּי יַעֲקֹב.

וְיֵרְדְּ מִיַּעֲקֹב   אַל תִּירָא עַבְדִּי יַעֲקֹב.

זָכֹר זֹאת לְיַעֲקֹב   אַל תִּירָא עַבְדִּי יַעֲקֹב.

חֶדְוַת יְשׁוּעוֹת יַעֲקֹב   אַל תִּירָא עַבְדִּי יַעֲקֹב.

טֹבוּ אֹהָלֶיךָ יַעֲקֹב   אַל תִּירָא עַבְדִּי יַעֲקֹב.

יוֹרוּ מִשְׁפָּטֶיךָ לְיַעֲקֹב   אַל תִּירָא עַבְדִּי יַעֲקֹב.

כִּי לֹא נַחַשׁ בְּיַעֲקֹב   אַל תִּירָא עַבְדִּי יַעֲקֹב.

לֹא הִבִּיט אָוֶן בְּיַעֲקֹב   אַל תִּירָא עַבְדִּי יַעֲקֹב.

מִי מָנָה עֲפַר יַעֲקֹב   אַל תִּירָא עַבְדִּי יַעֲקֹב.

נִשְׁבַּע יְיָ לְיַעֲקֹב   אַל תִּירָא עַבְדִּי יַעֲקֹב.

סְלַח נָא לַעֲוֹן יַעֲקֹב   אַל תִּירָא עַבְדִּי יַעֲקֹב.

עַתָּה הָשֵׁב שְׁבוּת יַעֲקֹב   אַל תִּירָא עַבְדִּי יַעֲקֹב.

אמר ה' ליעקב is of unknown authorship. It is a mosaic of biblical phrases in alphabetical order with the refrain: "Be not afraid, my servant Jacob" (Isaiah 44:2). The biblical verses utilized throughout the poem are: Isaiah 29:22; Psalm 135:4; Isaiah 44:23; Numbers 24:17; Isaiah 27:6; Numbers 24:19; Isaiah 44:21; Nehemiah 8:10; Isaiah 25:9; Numbers 24:5; Deuteronomy 33:10; Numbers 23:23; 23:21; 23:10; Amos 8:7; Numbers 14:19; Ezekiel 39:25; Jeremiah 31:11; Psalm 44:5; Genesis 27:22; Jeremiah 31:7; Nahum 2:3; Micah 7:20; Psalm 32:7; Isaiah 26:4; Psalm 29:11.

At the close of the joyous day,
Send Elijah to thy chosen people,
Thou whose deeds are awe-inspiring;
Send relief, mirth and a release.
Then shall our lips joyfully chant:
O Lord, save us; O Lord, prosper us.

The Lord said to Jacob:
  Fear not, my servant Jacob.
The Lord has chosen Jacob.
  Fear not, my servant Jacob.
The Lord has redeemed Jacob.
  Fear not, my servant Jacob.
A star has risen from Jacob.
  Fear not, my servant Jacob.
Then shall Jacob take root.
  Fear not, my servant Jacob.
Out of Jacob shall one rule.
  Fear not, my servant Jacob.
Remember this, O Jacob.
  Fear not, my servant Jacob.
Joyous triumph shall Jacob have.
  Fear not, my servant Jacob.
Goodly are your tents, O Jacob.
  Fear not, my servant Jacob.
Thy laws are taught to Jacob.
  Fear not, my servant Jacob.
There is no sorcery with Jacob.
  Fear not, my servant Jacob.
None has seen iniquity in Jacob.
  Fear not, my servant Jacob.
Who has counted Jacob's masses?
  Fear not, my servant Jacob.
The Lord has made promise to Jacob.
  Fear not, my servant Jacob.
O pardon the sins of Jacob.
  Fear not, my servant Jacob.
Bring now back the captivity of Jacob.
  Fear not, my servant Jacob.

פָּדָה יְיָ אֶת יַעֲקֹב.   אַל תִּירָא עַבְדִּי יַעֲקֹב.

צַוֵּה יְשׁוּעוֹת יַעֲקֹב   אַל תִּירָא עַבְדִּי יַעֲקֹב.

קוֹל קוֹל יַעֲקֹב   אַל תִּירָא עַבְדִּי יַעֲקֹב.

רָנּוּ שִׂמְחָה לְיַעֲקֹב   אַל תִּירָא עַבְדִּי יַעֲקֹב.

שָׁב יְיָ אֶת גְּאוֹן יַעֲקֹב   אַל תִּירָא עַבְדִּי יַעֲקֹב.

תִּתֵּן אֱמֶת לְיַעֲקֹב   אַל תִּירָא עַבְדִּי יַעֲקֹב.

רִבּוֹן הָעוֹלָמִים, אַב הָרַחֲמִים וְהַסְּלִיחוֹת, בְּסִמָּן טוֹב וּבְמַזָּל
טוֹב הָחֵל עָלֵינוּ אֶת (שֵׁשֶׁת) יְמֵי הַמַּעֲשֶׂה הַבָּאִים לִקְרָאתֵנוּ
לְשָׁלוֹם, חֲשׂוּכִים מִכָּל חֵטְא וָפֶשַׁע, וּמְנֻקִּים מִכָּל עָוֹן וְאַשְׁמָה
וָרֶשַׁע, וּמְדֻבָּקִים בְּתַלְמוּד תּוֹרָה וּבְמַעֲשִׂים טוֹבִים. וְחָנֵּנוּ דֵעָה
בִּינָה וְהַשְׂכֵּל מֵאִתָּךְ, וְתַשְׁמִיעֵנוּ בָהֶם שָׂשׂוֹן וְשִׂמְחָה; וְלֹא תַעֲלֶה
קִנְאָתֵנוּ עַל לֵב אָדָם, וְלֹא קִנְאַת אָדָם תַּעֲלֶה עַל לִבֵּנוּ.
מַלְכֵּנוּ אֱלֹהֵינוּ, הָאָב הָרַחֲמָן, שִׂים בְּרָכָה וּרְוָחָה וְהַצְלָחָה
בְּכָל מַעֲשֵׂה יָדֵינוּ; וְכָל הַיּוֹעֵץ עַל עַמְּךָ בֵּית יִשְׂרָאֵל עֵצָה
טוֹבָה וּמַחֲשָׁבָה טוֹבָה, אַמְּצוֹ וּבָרְכוֹ, גַּדְּלוֹ וְקַיְּמוֹ, קַיֵּם עֲצָתוֹ,
כַּדָּבָר שֶׁנֶּאֱמַר: יִתֶּן־לְךָ כִלְבָבֶךָ, וְכָל עֲצָתְךָ יְמַלֵּא. וְנֶאֱמַר:
וְתִגְזַר אֹמֶר וְיָקָם לָךְ, וְעַל דְּרָכֶיךָ נָגַהּ אוֹר. וְכָל הַיּוֹעֵץ עָלֵינוּ
וְעַל כָּל עַמְּךָ בֵּית יִשְׂרָאֵל עֵצָה שֶׁאֵינָה טוֹבָה, תּוֹפֵר עֲצָתוֹ,
כַּדָּבָר שֶׁנֶּאֱמַר: יְיָ הֵפִיר עֲצַת גּוֹיִם, הֵנִיא מַחְשְׁבוֹת עַמִּים.
וְנֶאֱמַר: עֻצוּ עֵצָה וְתֻפָר, דַּבְּרוּ דָבָר וְלֹא יָקוּם, כִּי עִמָּנוּ אֵל.

וּפְתַח לָנוּ, יְיָ אֱלֹהֵינוּ, אַב הָרַחֲמִים, אֲדוֹן הַסְּלִיחוֹת, בָּזֶה
הַשָּׁבוּעַ וּבְכָל שָׁבוּעַ, שַׁעֲרֵי אוֹרָה, שַׁעֲרֵי אֹרֶךְ יָמִים וְשָׁנִים,
שַׁעֲרֵי אֲרִיכַת אַפַּיִם, שַׁעֲרֵי בְרָכָה, שַׁעֲרֵי בִינָה, שַׁעֲרֵי גִילָה,
שַׁעֲרֵי גְדֻלָה, שַׁעֲרֵי גְאֻלָה, שַׁעֲרֵי גְבוּרָה, שַׁעֲרֵי דִיצָה, שַׁעֲרֵי

רבון העולמים is based upon the Palestinian Talmud, Berakhoth 5:1.
ופתח לנו contains an alphabetic list of synonyms for salvation and wisdom.

The Lord redeems Jacob.
    Fear not, my servant Jacob.
Command the salvation of Jacob.
    Fear not, my servant Jacob.
The voice is the voice of Jacob.
    Fear not, my servant Jacob.
Sing with gladness for Jacob.
    Fear not, my servant Jacob.
The Lord restores the pride of Jacob.
    Fear not, my servant Jacob.
Thou wilt grant kindness to Jacob.
    Fear not, my servant Jacob.

דֵעָה, שַׁעֲרֵי הוֹד, שַׁעֲרֵי הָדָר, שַׁעֲרֵי הַצְּלָחָה, שַׁעֲרֵי הָרְוָחָה,

שַׁעֲרֵי וָעַד טוֹב, שַׁעֲרֵי זְרִיזוּת, שַׁעֲרֵי זִמְרָה, שַׁעֲרֵי זְכֻיּוֹת,

שַׁעֲרֵי זִיו, שַׁעֲרֵי זְהַר תּוֹרָה, שַׁעֲרֵי זְהַר חָכְמָה, שַׁעֲרֵי זְהַר

בִּינָה, שַׁעֲרֵי זְהַר דַּעַת, שַׁעֲרֵי חֶדְוָה, שַׁעֲרֵי חֶמְלָה, שַׁעֲרֵי חֵן

וָחֶסֶד, שַׁעֲרֵי חַיִּים טוֹבִים, שַׁעֲרֵי חָכְמָה, שַׁעֲרֵי טוֹבָה, שַׁעֲרֵי

טֹהַר, שַׁעֲרֵי יְשׁוּעָה, שַׁעֲרֵי יְשֶׁר, שַׁעֲרֵי כַּפָּרָה, שַׁעֲרֵי כַלְכָּלָה,

שַׁעֲרֵי כָבוֹד, שַׁעֲרֵי לִמּוּד, שַׁעֲרֵי מָזוֹן, שַׁעֲרֵי מְנוּחוֹת, שַׁעֲרֵי

מְחִילוֹת, שַׁעֲרֵי מַדָּע, שַׁעֲרֵי נֶחָמָה, שַׁעֲרֵי נְקִיּוּת, שַׁעֲרֵי

סְלִיחָה, שַׁעֲרֵי סִיַּעְתָּא דִשְׁמַיָּא, שַׁעֲרֵי עֶזְרָה, שַׁעֲרֵי פְּדוּת,

שַׁעֲרֵי פַּרְנָסָה טוֹבָה, שַׁעֲרֵי צְדָקָה, שַׁעֲרֵי צָהֳלָה, שַׁעֲרֵי

קְדֻשָּׁה, שַׁעֲרֵי קוֹמְמִיּוּת, שַׁעֲרֵי רַחֲמִים, שַׁעֲרֵי רָצוֹן, שַׁעֲרֵי

רְפוּאָה שְׁלֵמָה, שַׁעֲרֵי שָׁלוֹם, שַׁעֲרֵי שִׂמְחָה, שַׁעֲרֵי שְׁמוּעוֹת

טוֹבוֹת, שַׁעֲרֵי שַׁלְוָה, שַׁעֲרֵי תוֹרָה, שַׁעֲרֵי תְפִלָּה, שַׁעֲרֵי

תְשׁוּבָה, שַׁעֲרֵי תְשׁוּעָה, כְּמוֹ שֶׁכָּתוּב: וּתְשׁוּעַת צַדִּיקִים מֵיְיָ,

מָעוּזָּם בְּעֵת צָרָה. וַיַּעְזְרֵם יְיָ וַיְפַלְּטֵם; יְפַלְּטֵם מֵרְשָׁעִים

וְיוֹשִׁיעֵם, כִּי חָסוּ בוֹ. וְנֶאֱמַר: חָשַׂף יְיָ אֶת זְרוֹעַ קָדְשׁוֹ לְעֵינֵי

כָּל הַגּוֹיִם, וְרָאוּ כָּל אַפְסֵי אָרֶץ אֵת יְשׁוּעַת אֱלֹהֵינוּ. וְנֶאֱמַר:

קוֹל צֹפַיִךְ נָשְׂאוּ קוֹל, יַחְדָּו יְרַנֵּנוּ; כִּי עַיִן בְּעַיִן יִרְאוּ בְּשׁוּב יְיָ

צִיּוֹן. וְקַיֶּם־לָנוּ, יְיָ אֱלֹהֵינוּ, מִקְרָא שֶׁכָּתוּב: מַה נָּאווּ עַל
הֶהָרִים רַגְלֵי מְבַשֵּׂר, מַשְׁמִיעַ שָׁלוֹם, מְבַשֵּׂר טוֹב, מַשְׁמִיעַ
יְשׁוּעָה, אֹמֵר לְצִיּוֹן מָלַךְ אֱלֹהָיִךְ. רִאשׁוֹן לְצִיּוֹן הִנֵּה הִנָּם;
וְלִירוּשָׁלַיִם מְבַשֵּׂר אֶתֵּן. אָמֵן סֶלָה.

בִּרְכַּת הַלְּבָנָה

Recited in the open air when the new moon is visible

תהלים קמח, א–ו

הַלְלוּיָהּ; הַלְלוּ אֶת יְיָ מִן הַשָּׁמַיִם, הַלְלוּהוּ בַּמְּרוֹמִים.
הַלְלוּהוּ כָל מַלְאָכָיו; הַלְלוּהוּ כָּל צְבָאָיו. הַלְלוּהוּ שֶׁמֶשׁ
וְיָרֵחַ; הַלְלוּהוּ כָּל כּוֹכְבֵי אוֹר. הַלְלוּהוּ שְׁמֵי הַשָּׁמָיִם, וְהַמַּיִם
אֲשֶׁר מֵעַל הַשָּׁמָיִם. יְהַלְלוּ אֶת שֵׁם יְיָ, כִּי הוּא צִוָּה וְנִבְרָאוּ.
וַיַּעֲמִידֵם לָעַד לְעוֹלָם; חָק־נָתַן וְלֹא יַעֲבוֹר.

מסכת סנהדרין מב, א

בָּרוּךְ אַתָּה, יְיָ אֱלֹהֵינוּ, מֶלֶךְ הָעוֹלָם, אֲשֶׁר בְּמַאֲמָרוֹ בָּרָא
שְׁחָקִים, וּבְרוּחַ פִּיו כָּל צְבָאָם. חֹק וּזְמַן נָתַן לָהֶם שֶׁלֹּא יְשַׁנּוּ
אֶת תַּפְקִידָם. שָׂשִׂים וּשְׂמֵחִים לַעֲשׂוֹת רְצוֹן קוֹנָם; פּוֹעֵל אֱמֶת
שֶׁפְּעֻלָּתוֹ אֱמֶת. וְלַלְּבָנָה אָמַר שֶׁתִּתְחַדֵּשׁ עֲטֶרֶת תִּפְאֶרֶת
לַעֲמוּסֵי בָטֶן, שֶׁהֵם עֲתִידִים לְהִתְחַדֵּשׁ כְּמוֹתָהּ, וּלְפָאֵר
לְיוֹצְרָם עַל שֵׁם כְּבוֹד מַלְכוּתוֹ. בָּרוּךְ אַתָּה, יְיָ, מְחַדֵּשׁ
חֳדָשִׁים.

בָּרוּךְ יוֹצְרֵךְ, בָּרוּךְ עוֹשֵׂךְ, בָּרוּךְ קוֹנֵךְ, בָּרוּךְ בּוֹרְאֵךְ.

כְּשֵׁם שֶׁאֲנִי רוֹקֵד כְּנֶגְדֵּךְ וְאֵינִי־יָכֹל לִנְגֹּעַ בָּךְ, כָּךְ לֹא יוּכְלוּ
כָּל אוֹיְבַי לִנְגֹּעַ בִּי לְרָעָה.

תִּפֹּל עֲלֵיהֶם אֵימָתָה וָפַחַד; בִּגְדֹל זְרוֹעֲךָ, יִדְּמוּ כָּאָבֶן.
כָּאֶבֶן יִדְּמוּ, זְרוֹעֲךָ בִּגְדֹל, וָפַחַד אֵימָתָה עֲלֵיהֶם תִּפֹּל.

NEW MOON BLESSING

Recited in the open air when the new moon is visible

Psalm 148:1-6

Praise the Lord! Praise the Lord from the heavens; praise him' in the heights. Praise him, all his angels; praise him, all his hosts. Praise him, sun and moon; praise him, all you stars of light. Praise him, highest heavens and waters that are above the heavens. Let them praise the name of the Lord; for he commanded and they were created. He fixed them fast forever and ever; he gave a law which none transgresses.

Talmud Sanhedrin 42a

Blessed art thou, Lord our God, King of the universe, who didst create the heavens by thy command, and all their host by thy mere word. Thou hast subjected them to fixed laws and time, so that they might not deviate from their set function. They are glad and happy to do the will of their Creator, the true Author, whose achievement is truth. He ordered the moon to renew itself as a glorious crown over those he sustained from birth, who likewise will be regenerated in the future, and will worship their Creator for his glorious majesty. Blessed art thou, O Lord, who renewest the months.

Blessed be your omnipotent Creator, O moon!

Even as one cannot touch the moon, so may my foes be unable to harm me.

May terror and dread fall on them; may they be motionless as a stone under the sweep of thy arm.[1]

ברכת הלבנה is discussed in the Talmud (Sanhedrin 42a). The moon, appearing every month in several phases, is symbolic of the Jewish people whose history has assumed a variety of phases. Like the moon, they reappear after being eclipsed. An allusion to the people of Israel is contained in the four synonyms יוצרך, עושך, קונך, בוראך whose initials spell the name יעקב.

---

[1] *Exodus* 15:16.

דָּוִד מֶלֶךְ יִשְׂרָאֵל חַי וְקַיָּם.

The worshipers exchange greetings:

שָׁלוֹם עֲלֵיכֶם. עֲלֵיכֶם שָׁלוֹם.

סִמָּן טוֹב וּמַזָּל טוֹב יְהֵא לָנוּ וּלְכָל יִשְׂרָאֵל, אָמֵן.

קוֹל דּוֹדִי הִנֵּה זֶה בָּא, מְדַלֵּג עַל הֶהָרִים, מְקַפֵּץ עַל
הַגְּבָעוֹת. דּוֹמֶה דוֹדִי לִצְבִי אוֹ לְעֹפֶר הָאַיָּלִים; הִנֵּה זֶה עוֹמֵד
אַחַר כָּתְלֵנוּ, מַשְׁגִּיחַ מִן הַחַלֹּנוֹת, מֵצִיץ מִן הַחֲרַכִּים.

תהלים קכא

שִׁיר לַמַּעֲלוֹת. אֶשָּׂא עֵינַי אֶל הֶהָרִים, מֵאַיִן יָבֹא עֶזְרִי.
עֶזְרִי מֵעִם יְיָ, עֹשֵׂה שָׁמַיִם וָאָרֶץ. אַל יִתֵּן לַמּוֹט רַגְלֶךָ, אַל יָנוּם
שֹׁמְרֶךָ. הִנֵּה לֹא יָנוּם וְלֹא יִישָׁן שׁוֹמֵר יִשְׂרָאֵל. יְיָ שֹׁמְרֶךָ, יְיָ
צִלְּךָ, עַל יַד יְמִינֶךָ. יוֹמָם הַשֶּׁמֶשׁ לֹא יַכֶּכָּה, וְיָרֵחַ בַּלָּיְלָה. יְיָ
יִשְׁמָרְךָ מִכָּל רָע, יִשְׁמֹר אֶת נַפְשֶׁךָ. יְיָ יִשְׁמָר־צֵאתְךָ וּבוֹאֶךָ,
מֵעַתָּה וְעַד עוֹלָם.

תהלים קנ

הַלְלוּיָהּ; הַלְלוּ אֵל בְּקָדְשׁוֹ, הַלְלוּהוּ בִּרְקִיעַ עֻזּוֹ. הַלְלוּהוּ
בִגְבוּרֹתָיו, הַלְלוּהוּ כְּרֹב גֻּדְלוֹ. הַלְלוּהוּ בְּתֵקַע שׁוֹפָר, הַלְלוּהוּ
בְּנֵבֶל וְכִנּוֹר. הַלְלוּהוּ בְּתֹף וּמָחוֹל, הַלְלוּהוּ בְּמִנִּים וְעֻגָב.
הַלְלוּהוּ בְּצִלְצְלֵי שָׁמַע, הַלְלוּהוּ בְּצִלְצְלֵי תְרוּעָה. כֹּל הַנְּשָׁמָה
תְּהַלֵּל יָהּ; הַלְלוּיָהּ.

מסכת סנהדרין מב, א

תָּנָא דְּבֵי רַבִּי יִשְׁמָעֵאל: אִלְמָלֵי לֹא זָכוּ יִשְׂרָאֵל אֶלָּא
לְהַקְבִּיל פְּנֵי אֲבִיהֶם שֶׁבַּשָּׁמַיִם פַּעַם אַחַת בַּחֹדֶשׁ, דַּיָּם. אָמַר
אַבַּיֵי: הִלְכָּךְ, צָרִיךְ לְמֵימְרָא מְעֻמָּד.

דוד מלך ישראל refers to Psalm 89:38, which says that David's dynasty shall
"like the moon be established forever." The numerical value of
דוד מלך ישראל (819) is equal to that of ראש חודש.

עליכם שלום, the response to שלום עליכם, differs from the greeting in order
to distinguish the saluter from the one saluted, so that one may not run the
risk of leaving a greeting unanswered.

Long live David, king of Israel!

The worshipers exchange greetings:

Shalom alekhem, peace be with you!

Alekhem shalom, peace be unto you!

May we and all Israel have a favorable omen and good fortune. Amen.

The voice of my beloved! Here he comes, leaping across the mountains, bounding over the hills! My beloved is like a gazelle, like a young deer; here he stands, behind our wall, gazing through the windows, peering through the lattice.[1]

Psalm 121

A Pilgrim Song. I lift my eyes to the hills; whence will my help come? My help comes from the Lord who made heaven and earth. He will not let your foot slip; he who guards you will not slumber. Behold, the guardian of Israel neither slumbers nor sleeps. The Lord is your guardian; the Lord is your shelter upon your right hand. The sun shall never hurt you in the day, nor the moon by night. The Lord will guard you from all evil; the Lord will guard your life. The Lord will guard you as you come and go, henceforth and forever.

Psalm 150

Praise the Lord! Praise God in his sanctuary; praise him in his glorious heaven. Praise him for his mighty deeds; praise him for his abundant greatness. Praise him with the blast of the horn; praise him with the harp and lyre. Praise him with the drum and dance; praise him with strings and flute. Praise him with resounding cymbals; praise him with clanging cymbals. Let everything that breathes praise the Lord! Praise the Lord!

Talmud Sanhedrin 42a.

In the school of Rabbi Ishmael it was taught: Had Israel merited no other privilege than greeting the presence of their heavenly Father once a month [by reciting the benediction over the new moon], they would be contented! Abbayé said: Therefore [since it is a greeting of God's presence], we must recite it standing.

קול דודי was inserted by Rabbi Judah of Regensberg (ר' יהודה החסיד) as an expression of Israel's hope for the speedy advent of the Messiah.

[1] *Song of Songs* 2:8-9.

מִי זֹאת עֹלָה מִן הַמִּדְבָּר, מִתְרַפֶּקֶת עַל דּוֹדָהּ.

וִיהִי רָצוֹן מִלְּפָנֶיךָ, יְיָ אֱלֹהַי וֵאלֹהֵי אֲבוֹתַי, לְמַלֹּאות פְּגִימַת הַלְּבָנָה, וְלֹא יִהְיֶה בָּהּ שׁוּם מִעוּט; וִיהִי אוֹר הַלְּבָנָה כְּאוֹר הַחַמָּה וּכְאוֹר שִׁבְעַת יְמֵי בְרֵאשִׁית, כְּמוֹ שֶׁהָיְתָה קֹדֶם מִעוּטָהּ, שֶׁנֶּאֱמַר: אֶת שְׁנֵי הַמְּאֹרֹת הַגְּדֹלִים. וְיִתְקַיֵּם בָּנוּ מִקְרָא שֶׁכָּתוּב: וּבִקְשׁוּ אֶת יְיָ אֱלֹהֵיהֶם וְאֵת דָּוִיד מַלְכָּם. אָמֵן.

תהלים סז

לַמְנַצֵּחַ בִּנְגִינֹת, מִזְמוֹר שִׁיר. אֱלֹהִים יְחָנֵּנוּ וִיבָרְכֵנוּ; יָאֵר פָּנָיו אִתָּנוּ, סֶלָה. לָדַעַת בָּאָרֶץ דַּרְכֶּךָ, בְּכָל גּוֹיִם יְשׁוּעָתֶךָ. יוֹדוּךָ עַמִּים, אֱלֹהִים; יוֹדוּךָ עַמִּים כֻּלָּם. יִשְׂמְחוּ וִירַנְּנוּ לְאֻמִּים, כִּי תִשְׁפֹּט עַמִּים מִישֹׁר, וּלְאֻמִּים בָּאָרֶץ תַּנְחֵם, סֶלָה. יוֹדוּךָ עַמִּים, אֱלֹהִים; יוֹדוּךָ עַמִּים כֻּלָּם. אֶרֶץ נָתְנָה יְבוּלָהּ; יְבָרְכֵנוּ אֱלֹהִים אֱלֹהֵינוּ. יְבָרְכֵנוּ אֱלֹהִים, וְיִירְאוּ אֹתוֹ כָּל אַפְסֵי אָרֶץ.

Mourners' Kaddish

הַלֵּל

Chanted after the Amidah of the morning service on Pesaḥ, Shavuoth,
Sukkoth, Ḥanukkah and Rosh Ḥodesh

בָּרוּךְ אַתָּה, יְיָ אֱלֹהֵינוּ, מֶלֶךְ הָעוֹלָם, אֲשֶׁר קִדְּשָׁנוּ בְּמִצְוֹתָיו וְצִוָּנוּ לִקְרֹא אֶת הַהַלֵּל.

תהלים קיג

הַלְלוּיָהּ; הַלְלוּ, עַבְדֵי יְיָ, הַלְלוּ אֶת שֵׁם יְיָ. יְהִי שֵׁם יְיָ מְבֹרָךְ, מֵעַתָּה וְעַד עוֹלָם. מִמִּזְרַח שֶׁמֶשׁ עַד מְבוֹאוֹ, מְהֻלָּל שֵׁם

הלל consists of Psalms 113–118. It is called הלל המצרי ("Egyptian *Hallel*") because Psalm 114 refers to the exodus from Egypt. On Purim, the reading of the *Megillah* takes the place of *Hallel*. On *Rosh Hashanah* and *Yom Kippur*, *Hallel* is omitted because the High Holydays are not intended for jubilation. Similarly, *Hallel* is not recited in the house of a mourner during *shiv'ah*. On *Rosh Ḥodesh*, a minor festival, *Hallel* is recited in abridged form,

Who is this coming up from the wilderness, leaning upon her beloved?[1]

May it be thy will, Lord my God and God of my fathers, to readjust the deficiency of the moon, so that it may no longer be reduced in size; may the light of the moon again be like the light of the sun, as it was during the first seven days of creation, before its size was reduced, for it is said: "The two great lights."[2] May the prophecy be realized in us, which says: "They will seek the Lord their God, and David their king."[3] Amen.

Psalm 67

For the Choirmaster; with string-music; a psalm, a song. May God be gracious to us and bless us; may he cause his favor to shine among us. Then shall thy way be known on earth, thy saving power among all nations. The peoples shall praise thee, O God; all the peoples shall praise thee. Let the nations be glad and sing for joy, for thou rulest the people justly; thou guidest the nations on earth. The peoples shall praise thee, O Lord; all the peoples shall praise thee. The earth has yielded its produce; God, our own God, blesses us. God blesses us; all the ends of the earth shall revere him.

Mourners' Kaddish

HALLEL

Chanted after the Amidah of the morning service on Pesaḥ, Shavuoth, Sukkoth, Ḥanukkah and Rosh Ḥodesh

Blessed art thou, Lord our God, King of the universe, who hast sanctified us with thy commandments and commanded us to recite the *Hallel*.

Psalm 113

Praise the Lord! Praise, you servants of the Lord, praise the name of the Lord. Blessed be the name of the Lord henceforth and forever. From the rising of the sun to its setting, the Lord's

---

the first eleven verses of Psalms 115 and 116 being omitted. This so-called "half-*Hallel*" is likewise used on the last six days of *Pesaḥ* by reason of the following tradition. When the Egyptians were drowning in the Red Sea on the seventh day of *Pesaḥ*, God restrained the angels from singing his praise, saying: "How can you sing hymns while my creatures are drowning in the sea?" (Megillah 10b). In order not to make *Ḥol ha-Mo'ed Pesaḥ* appear as more important than the seventh day of *Pesaḥ*, the *Hallel* is abridged throughout the last six days.

[1] *Song of Songs* 8:5.   [2] *Genesis* 1:16.   [3] *Hosea* 3:5.

יְיָ. רָם עַל כָּל גּוֹיִם יְיָ, עַל הַשָּׁמַיִם כְּבוֹדוֹ. מִי כַּיְיָ אֱלֹהֵינוּ,
הַמַּגְבִּיהִי לָשָׁבֶת. הַמַּשְׁפִּילִי לִרְאוֹת בַּשָּׁמַיִם וּבָאָרֶץ. מְקִימִי
מֵעָפָר דָּל, מֵאַשְׁפֹּת יָרִים אֶבְיוֹן. לְהוֹשִׁיבִי עִם נְדִיבִים, עִם
נְדִיבֵי עַמּוֹ. מוֹשִׁיבִי עֲקֶרֶת הַבַּיִת, אֵם הַבָּנִים שְׂמֵחָה; הַלְלוּיָהּ.

תהלים קי״ד

בְּצֵאת יִשְׂרָאֵל מִמִּצְרָיִם, בֵּית יַעֲקֹב מֵעַם לֹעֵז. הָיְתָה
יְהוּדָה לְקָדְשׁוֹ, יִשְׂרָאֵל מַמְשְׁלוֹתָיו. הַיָּם רָאָה וַיָּנֹס; הַיַּרְדֵּן
יִסֹּב לְאָחוֹר. הֶהָרִים רָקְדוּ כְאֵילִים, גְּבָעוֹת כִּבְנֵי צֹאן. מַה
לְּךָ הַיָּם כִּי תָנוּס; הַיַּרְדֵּן, תִּסֹּב לְאָחוֹר. הֶהָרִים, תִּרְקְדוּ
כְאֵילִים; גְּבָעוֹת, כִּבְנֵי צֹאן. מִלִּפְנֵי אָדוֹן חוּלִי אָרֶץ, מִלִּפְנֵי
אֱלֹוֹהַּ יַעֲקֹב. הַהֹפְכִי הַצּוּר אֲגַם מָיִם, חַלָּמִישׁ לְמַעְיְנוֹ־מָיִם.

On *Rosh Ḥodesh* and the last six days of *Pesaḥ* omit:

תהלים קט״ו, א-י״א

(לֹא לָנוּ, יְיָ, לֹא לָנוּ, כִּי לְשִׁמְךָ תֵּן כָּבוֹד, עַל חַסְדְּךָ, עַל
אֲמִתֶּךָ. לָמָה יֹאמְרוּ הַגּוֹיִם, אַיֵּה נָא אֱלֹהֵיהֶם. וֵאלֹהֵינוּ בַשָּׁמָיִם;
כֹּל אֲשֶׁר חָפֵץ עָשָׂה. עֲצַבֵּיהֶם כֶּסֶף וְזָהָב, מַעֲשֵׂה יְדֵי אָדָם.
פֶּה לָהֶם וְלֹא יְדַבֵּרוּ, עֵינַיִם לָהֶם וְלֹא יִרְאוּ. אָזְנַיִם לָהֶם וְלֹא
יִשְׁמָעוּ, אַף לָהֶם וְלֹא יְרִיחוּן. יְדֵיהֶם וְלֹא יְמִישׁוּן, רַגְלֵיהֶם
וְלֹא יְהַלֵּכוּ; לֹא יֶהְגּוּ בִּגְרוֹנָם. כְּמוֹהֶם יִהְיוּ עֹשֵׂיהֶם, כֹּל אֲשֶׁר
בֹּטֵחַ בָּהֶם. יִשְׂרָאֵל, בְּטַח בַּיְיָ; עֶזְרָם וּמָגִנָּם הוּא. בֵּית אַהֲרֹן,
בִּטְחוּ בַיְיָ; עֶזְרָם וּמָגִנָּם הוּא. יִרְאֵי יְיָ, בִּטְחוּ בַיְיָ; עֶזְרָם וּמָגִנָּם
הוּא.)

Psalm 114, one of the finest lyrics in literature, alludes to the dividing
of the Red Sea and the Jordan. The sea and the river are personified and
represented as awe-struck by the presence of the Lord. ההרים רקדו is a poetical description of the earthquake which accompanied the giving of the Torah.
הצור אגם מים alludes to the miraculous supply of water in the wilderness
(Exodus 17:6).

name is to be praised. High above all nations is the Lord; above the heavens is his glory. Who is like the Lord our God, enthroned on high, looking down upon heaven and earth? He raises the poor out of the dust, and lifts the needy out of the dunghill, to seat them with princes, with the princes of his people. He turns the barren housewife into a happy mother of children. Praise the Lord!

Psalm 114

When Israel went out of Egypt, Jacob's household from a people of strange speech, Judah became God's sanctuary, Israel his dominion. The sea beheld and fled; the Jordan turned backward; the mountains skipped like rams, and the hills like lambs. What ails you, O sea, that thus you flee? Why, O Jordan, do you turn backward? You mountains, why do you skip like rams? You hills, why do you leap like lambs? Tremble, O earth, at the Lord's presence, at the presence of the God of Jacob, who turns the rock into a pool of water, the flint into a flowing fountain.

On Rosh Ḥodesh and the last six days of Pesaḥ omit:

Psalm 115:1-11

(Not for our sake, O Lord, not for our sake, but for thy name's sake grant glory, because of thy kindness and thy truth. Why should the heathen say: "Where is their God?" Our God is in the heavens! He does whatever he pleases. Their idols are but silver and gold, the work of human hands. They have a mouth, but they cannot speak; they have eyes, but they cannot see; they have ears, but they cannot hear; they have a nose, but they cannot smell; they have hands, but they cannot feel; they have feet, but they cannot walk; nor can they make a sound with their throat. Those who make them shall become like them, whoever trusts in them. O Israel, trust in the Lord! He is your help and your shield. House of Aaron, trust in the Lord! He is your help and your shield. You who revere the Lord, trust in the Lord! He is your help and your shield.)

Psalm 115 appeals to God to raise his people from their degradation. Their restoration would vindicate the honor of his name. כמוהם יהיו עושיהם that is, men become like the objects of their worship. עזרם ומגנם הוא is the response of the choir.

תהלים קטו, יב–יח

יְיָ זְכָרֵנוּ יְבָרֵךְ; יְבָרֵךְ אֶת בֵּית יִשְׂרָאֵל, יְבָרֵךְ אֶת בֵּית
אַהֲרֹן. יְבָרֵךְ יִרְאֵי יְיָ, הַקְּטַנִּים עִם הַגְּדֹלִים. יֹסֵף יְיָ עֲלֵיכֶם,
עֲלֵיכֶם וְעַל בְּנֵיכֶם. בְּרוּכִים אַתֶּם לַיְיָ, עֹשֵׂה שָׁמַיִם וָאָרֶץ.
הַשָּׁמַיִם שָׁמַיִם לַיְיָ, וְהָאָרֶץ נָתַן לִבְנֵי אָדָם. לֹא הַמֵּתִים יְהַלְלוּ
יָהּ, וְלֹא כָּל יֹרְדֵי דוּמָה. וַאֲנַחְנוּ נְבָרֵךְ יָהּ מֵעַתָּה וְעַד עוֹלָם;
הַלְלוּיָהּ.

On *Rosh Ḥodesh* and the last six days of *Pesaḥ* omit:

תהלים קטז, א–יא

(אָהַבְתִּי כִּי יִשְׁמַע יְיָ אֶת קוֹלִי תַּחֲנוּנָי. כִּי הִטָּה אָזְנוֹ לִי,
וּבְיָמַי אֶקְרָא. אֲפָפוּנִי חֶבְלֵי מָוֶת, וּמְצָרֵי שְׁאוֹל מְצָאוּנִי; צָרָה
וְיָגוֹן אֶמְצָא. וּבְשֵׁם יְיָ אֶקְרָא, אָנָּה יְיָ, מַלְּטָה נַפְשִׁי. חַנּוּן יְיָ
וְצַדִּיק, וֵאלֹהֵינוּ מְרַחֵם. שֹׁמֵר פְּתָאִים יְיָ; דַּלּוֹתִי וְלִי יְהוֹשִׁיעַ.
שׁוּבִי נַפְשִׁי לִמְנוּחָיְכִי, כִּי יְיָ גָּמַל עָלָיְכִי. כִּי חִלַּצְתָּ נַפְשִׁי מִמָּוֶת,
אֶת עֵינִי מִן דִּמְעָה, אֶת רַגְלִי מִדֶּחִי. אֶתְהַלֵּךְ לִפְנֵי יְיָ, בְּאַרְצוֹת
הַחַיִּים. הֶאֱמַנְתִּי כִּי אֲדַבֵּר, אֲנִי עָנִיתִי מְאֹד. אֲנִי אָמַרְתִּי
בְחָפְזִי, כָּל הָאָדָם כֹּזֵב.)

תהלים קטז, יב–יט

מָה אָשִׁיב לַיְיָ כָּל תַּגְמוּלוֹהִי עָלָי. כּוֹס יְשׁוּעוֹת אֶשָּׂא, וּבְשֵׁם
יְיָ אֶקְרָא. נְדָרַי לַיְיָ אֲשַׁלֵּם, נֶגְדָה־נָּא לְכָל עַמּוֹ. יָקָר בְּעֵינֵי יְיָ
הַמָּוְתָה לַחֲסִידָיו. אָנָּה יְיָ, כִּי אֲנִי עַבְדֶּךָ, אֲנִי עַבְדְּךָ בֶּן אֲמָתֶךָ;
פִּתַּחְתָּ לְמוֹסֵרָי. לְךָ אֶזְבַּח זֶבַח תּוֹדָה, וּבְשֵׁם יְיָ אֶקְרָא. נְדָרַי
לַיְיָ אֲשַׁלֵּם, נֶגְדָה־נָּא לְכָל עַמּוֹ. בְּחַצְרוֹת בֵּית יְיָ, בְּתוֹכֵכִי
יְרוּשָׁלָיִם; הַלְלוּיָהּ.

Psalm 116 is a song of thanksgiving on being saved from imminent danger.
The psalmist's experiences pass through the stages of suffering, prayer, deliverance and public thanksgiving.

Psalm 115:12-18

The Lord who has remembered us will bless; he will bless the house of Israel; he will bless the house of Aaron; he will bless those who revere the Lord, small and great alike. May the Lord increase you, both you and your children. May you be blessed by the Lord, Creator of heaven and earth. The heaven is the Lord's heaven, but the earth he has given to mankind. The dead cannot praise the Lord, none of those who sink into silence. We will bless the Lord henceforth and forever. Praise the Lord!

On Rosh Ḥodesh and the last six days of Pesaḥ omit:

Psalm 116:1-11

(I love the Lord, for he hears my supplications. Because he has inclined his ear to me, I will call upon him as long as I live. The pangs of death encircled me; the agony of the grave seized me; I was in distress and sorrow. But I called upon the name of the Lord: "O Lord, save my life!" Gracious is the Lord, and righteous; our God is merciful. The Lord protects the simple; when I was brought low, he saved me. Be again at rest, O my soul, for the Lord has dealt kindly with you. Thou hast delivered my soul from death, my eyes from tears and my feet from stumbling. I shall walk before the Lord in the world of life. I trust even when I cry out: "I am greatly afflicted." [I have faith] even when I say in haste: "All men are deceitful.")

Psalm 116:12-19

What can I render to the Lord for all his kind acts toward me? I will take the cup of deliverance, and will call upon the name of the Lord. My vows to the Lord I will pay in the presence of all his people. Grievous in the sight of the Lord is the death of his faithful followers. O Lord, I am indeed thy servant; I am thy servant, the son of thy servant; thou hast removed my chains. To thee I offer thanksgiving, and call upon the name of the Lord. My vows to the Lord I will pay in the presence of all his people, in the courts of the Lord's house, in the midst of Jerusalem. Praise the Lord!

תהלים קיז

הַלְלוּ אֶת יְיָ, כָּל גּוֹיִם; שַׁבְּחוּהוּ, כָּל הָאֻמִּים. כִּי גָבַר עָלֵינוּ
חַסְדּוֹ, וֶאֱמֶת יְיָ לְעוֹלָם; הַלְלוּיָהּ.

Responsively

תהלים קיח

הוֹדוּ לַיְיָ כִּי טוֹב   כִּי לְעוֹלָם חַסְדּוֹ.
יֹאמַר נָא יִשְׂרָאֵל   כִּי לְעוֹלָם חַסְדּוֹ.
יֹאמְרוּ נָא בֵית אַהֲרֹן   כִּי לְעוֹלָם חַסְדּוֹ.
יֹאמְרוּ נָא יִרְאֵי יְיָ   כִּי לְעוֹלָם חַסְדּוֹ.

מִן הַמֵּצַר קָרָאתִי יָּהּ, עָנָנִי בַמֶּרְחָב יָהּ. יְיָ לִי, לֹא אִירָא;
מַה יַּעֲשֶׂה לִי אָדָם. יְיָ לִי בְּעֹזְרָי, וַאֲנִי אֶרְאֶה בְשֹׂנְאָי. טוֹב
לַחֲסוֹת בַּיְיָ מִבְּטֹחַ בָּאָדָם. טוֹב לַחֲסוֹת בַּיְיָ מִבְּטֹחַ בִּנְדִיבִים.
כָּל גּוֹיִם סְבָבוּנִי; בְּשֵׁם יְיָ, כִּי אֲמִילַם. סַבּוּנִי גַם סְבָבוּנִי; בְּשֵׁם
יְיָ, כִּי אֲמִילַם. סַבּוּנִי כִדְבֹרִים, דֹּעֲכוּ כְּאֵשׁ קוֹצִים; בְּשֵׁם יְיָ,
כִּי אֲמִילַם. דָּחֹה דְחִיתַנִי לִנְפֹּל, וַיְיָ עֲזָרָנִי. עָזִּי וְזִמְרָת יָהּ, וַיְהִי
לִי לִישׁוּעָה. קוֹל רִנָּה וִישׁוּעָה בְּאָהֳלֵי צַדִּיקִים; יְמִין יְיָ עֹשָׂה
חָיִל. יְמִין יְיָ רוֹמֵמָה, יְמִין יְיָ עֹשָׂה חָיִל. לֹא אָמוּת כִּי אֶחְיֶה,
וַאֲסַפֵּר מַעֲשֵׂי יָהּ. יַסֹּר יִסְּרַנִּי יָּהּ, וְלַמָּוֶת לֹא נְתָנָנִי. פִּתְחוּ לִי
שַׁעֲרֵי צֶדֶק; אָבֹא בָם, אוֹדֶה יָהּ. זֶה הַשַּׁעַר לַיְיָ, צַדִּיקִים
יָבֹאוּ בוֹ.

Psalm 117 is the shortest chapter in the Bible. Its two verses are an invitation to all nations to join in acknowledging God.

Psalm 118 is intended for alternating choirs. The last nine verses, from אודך to הודו לה׳, are spoken twice when the *Hallel* is recited, because they do not follow the arrangement of synonymous parallelism of the previous verses. Each of the last nine verses expresses a new thought.

Psalm 117

Praise the Lord, all you nations; laud him, all you peoples! For great is his kindness toward us; the Lord's truth endures forever.

Responsively

Psalm 118:1-4

Give thanks to the Lord, for he is good;
His mercy endures forever.
Let Israel say:
His mercy endures forever.
Let the house of Aaron say:
His mercy endures forever.
Let those who revere the Lord say:
His mercy endures forever.

Psalm 118:5-29

Out of distress I called upon the Lord; he answered me by setting me free. The Lord is with me; I have no fear. What can man do to me? The Lord is my helper; I shall see the defeat of my foes. It is better to seek refuge in the Lord than to trust in man. It is better to seek refuge in the Lord than to trust in princes. The heathen were all swarming round me; relying on the Lord, I routed them. Swarming round me, they beset me; relying on the Lord, I routed them. They swarmed like bees about me, but they were extinguished like a fire of thorns; relying on the Lord, I surely routed them. You did thrust at me that I might fall, but the Lord helped me. The Lord is my strength and my song; he has delivered me indeed. A joyful shout of triumph rings in the tents of the righteous: "The right hand of the Lord does valiantly. The Lord's right hand triumphs; the Lord's right hand does valiantly!" I shall not die, but live to recount the deeds of the Lord. The Lord has indeed punished me, but he has not left me to die. Open for me the gates of righteousness, that I may enter and praise the Lord. This is the gateway of the Lord; the righteous alone may enter.

Each verse is chanted twice:

אוֹדְךָ כִּי עֲנִיתָנִי, וַתְּהִי לִי לִישׁוּעָה.

אֶבֶן מָאֲסוּ הַבּוֹנִים, הָיְתָה לְרֹאשׁ פִּנָּה.

מֵאֵת יְיָ הָיְתָה זֹּאת; הִיא נִפְלָאת בְּעֵינֵינוּ.

זֶה הַיּוֹם עָשָׂה יְיָ, נָגִילָה וְנִשְׂמְחָה בוֹ.

Responsively

אָנָּא יְיָ, הוֹשִׁיעָה נָּא.

אָנָּא יְיָ, הוֹשִׁיעָה נָּא.

אָנָּא יְיָ, הַצְלִיחָה נָא.

אָנָּא יְיָ, הַצְלִיחָה נָא.

Each verse is chanted twice:

בָּרוּךְ הַבָּא בְּשֵׁם יְיָ; בֵּרַכְנוּכֶם מִבֵּית יְיָ.

אֵל יְיָ וַיָּאֶר לָנוּ, אִסְרוּ חַג בַּעֲבֹתִים, עַד קַרְנוֹת הַמִּזְבֵּחַ.

אֵלִי אַתָּה וְאוֹדֶךָּ, אֱלֹהַי אֲרוֹמְמֶךָּ.

הוֹדוּ לַיְיָ כִּי טוֹב, כִּי לְעוֹלָם חַסְדּוֹ.

יְהַלְלוּךָ, יְיָ אֱלֹהֵינוּ, כָּל מַעֲשֶׂיךָ; וַחֲסִידֶיךָ, צַדִּיקִים עוֹשֵׂי רְצוֹנֶךָ, וְכָל עַמְּךָ בֵּית יִשְׂרָאֵל, בְּרִנָּה יוֹדוּ וִיבָרְכוּ, וִישַׁבְּחוּ וִיפָאֲרוּ, וִירוֹמְמוּ וְיַעֲרִיצוּ, וְיַקְדִּישׁוּ וְיַמְלִיכוּ אֶת שִׁמְךָ, מַלְכֵּנוּ. Reader כִּי לְךָ טוֹב לְהוֹדוֹת, וּלְשִׁמְךָ נָאֶה לְזַמֵּר, כִּי מֵעוֹלָם עַד עוֹלָם אַתָּה אֵל. בָּרוּךְ אַתָּה, יְיָ, מֶלֶךְ מְהֻלָּל בַּתִּשְׁבָּחוֹת.

Full-*Kaddish* on *Rosh Ḥodesh* and festivals; half-*Kaddish* on *Ḥanukkah.*
Torah-reading on *Rosh Ḥodesh, Ḥanukkah* and *Ḥol ha-Moʻed*—page 119;
אַשְׁרֵי, וּבָא לְצִיּוֹן—page 127. Torah-reading on major festivals—page 361.

יהללוך, mentioned in Pesaḥim 118a, is similiar to ישתבח in its phraseology. Like ישתבח which follows the recital of *Pesuke d'Zimra,* יהללוך concludes the recital of the *Hallel* psalms.

Each verse is chanted twice:

I thank thee because thou hast answered me
And hast been my salvation.
The stone which the builders rejected
Has become the chief cornerstone.
This is the Lord's doing;
It is marvelous in our eyes.
This is the day which the Lord has made;
Let us be glad and rejoice on it.

Responsively

We implore thee, O Lord, save us!
We implore thee, O Lord, save us!
We implore thee, O Lord, prosper us!
We implore thee, O Lord, prosper us!

Each verse is chanted twice:

Blessed be he who comes in the name of the Lord;
We bless you from the house of the Lord.
The Lord is God, who has given us light;
Link the dance with boughs, up to the altar-horns.
Thou art my God, and I thank thee;
Thou art my God, and I extol thee.
Give thanks to the Lord, for he is good;
His mercy endures forever.

All thy works praise thee, Lord our God; thy righteous
followers who do thy will, and all thy people the house of Israel,
joyously thank and bless, praise and glorify, extol and revere,
sanctify and acclaim thy name, our King. It is good indeed to
render thanks to thee; it is pleasant to sing praises to thy name, for
thou art God from eternity to eternity. Blessed art thou, O Lord,
King extolled with praises.

Full-Kaddish on Rosh Ḥodesh and festivals; half-Kaddish on Ḥanukkah.
Torah-reading on Rosh Ḥodesh, Ḥanukkah and Ḥol ha-Moʻed—Page 120; Ashre,
Uva l'Zion—page 128. Torah-reading on major festivals—page 362.

מוּסָף לְרֹאשׁ חֹדֶשׁ

The *Amidah* is recited in silent devotion while standing, facing east.
The Reader repeats the *Amidah* aloud when a *minyan* holds service.

כִּי שֵׁם יְיָ אֶקְרָא, הָבוּ גֹדֶל לֵאלֹהֵינוּ.

אֲדֹנָי, שְׂפָתַי תִּפְתָּח, וּפִי יַגִּיד תְּהִלָּתֶךָ.

בָּרוּךְ אַתָּה, יְיָ אֱלֹהֵינוּ וֵאלֹהֵי אֲבוֹתֵינוּ, אֱלֹהֵי אַבְרָהָם,
אֱלֹהֵי יִצְחָק, וֵאלֹהֵי יַעֲקֹב, הָאֵל הַגָּדוֹל הַגִּבּוֹר וְהַנּוֹרָא, אֵל
עֶלְיוֹן, גּוֹמֵל חֲסָדִים טוֹבִים, וְקוֹנֶה הַכֹּל, וְזוֹכֵר חַסְדֵי אָבוֹת,
וּמֵבִיא גוֹאֵל לִבְנֵי בְנֵיהֶם לְמַעַן שְׁמוֹ בְּאַהֲבָה.

מֶלֶךְ עוֹזֵר וּמוֹשִׁיעַ וּמָגֵן. בָּרוּךְ אַתָּה, יְיָ, מָגֵן אַבְרָהָם.

אַתָּה גִּבּוֹר לְעוֹלָם, אֲדֹנָי; מְחַיֵּה מֵתִים אַתָּה, רַב לְהוֹשִׁיעַ.

Between Sukkoth and Pesaḥ add:

(מַשִּׁיב הָרוּחַ וּמוֹרִיד הַגָּשֶׁם.)

מְכַלְכֵּל חַיִּים בְּחֶסֶד, מְחַיֵּה מֵתִים בְּרַחֲמִים רַבִּים, סוֹמֵךְ
נוֹפְלִים, וְרוֹפֵא חוֹלִים, וּמַתִּיר אֲסוּרִים, וּמְקַיֵּם אֱמוּנָתוֹ לִישֵׁנֵי
עָפָר. מִי כָמוֹךָ, בַּעַל גְּבוּרוֹת, וּמִי דוֹמֶה לָּךְ, מֶלֶךְ מֵמִית
וּמְחַיֶּה וּמַצְמִיחַ יְשׁוּעָה.

וְנֶאֱמָן אַתָּה לְהַחֲיוֹת מֵתִים. בָּרוּךְ אַתָּה, יְיָ, מְחַיֵּה הַמֵּתִים.

When the Reader repeats the *Amidah*, the following *Kedushah* is said.

נְקַדֵּשׁ אֶת שִׁמְךָ בָּעוֹלָם כְּשֵׁם שֶׁמַּקְדִּישִׁים אוֹתוֹ בִּשְׁמֵי מָרוֹם,
כַּכָּתוּב עַל יַד נְבִיאֶךָ: וְקָרָא זֶה אֶל זֶה וְאָמַר:

קָדוֹשׁ, קָדוֹשׁ, קָדוֹשׁ יְיָ צְבָאוֹת; מְלֹא כָל הָאָרֶץ כְּבוֹדוֹ.

MUSAF FOR ROSH HODESH

The Amidah is recited in silent devotion while standing, facing east.
The Reader repeats the Amidah aloud when a minyan holds service.

When I proclaim the name of the Lord, give glory to our God![1]

O Lord, open thou my lips, that my mouth may declare thy praise.[2]

Blessed art thou, Lord our God and God of our fathers, God of Abraham, God of Isaac and God of Jacob; great, mighty and revered God, sublime God, who bestowest lovingkindness, and art Master of all things; who rememberest the good deeds of our fathers, and who wilt graciously bring a redeemer to their children's children for the sake of thy name.

O King, Supporter, Savior and Shield. Blessed art thou, O Lord, Shield of Abraham.

Thou, O Lord, art mighty forever; thou revivest the dead; thou art powerful to save.

Between Sukkoth and Pesah add:

(Thou causest the wind to blow and the rain to fall.)

Thou sustainest the living with kindness, and revivest the dead with great mercy; thou supportest all who fall, and healest the sick; thou settest the captives free, and keepest faith with those who sleep in the dust. Who is like thee, Lord of power? Who resembles thee, O King? Thou bringest death and restorest life, and causest salvation to flourish.

Thou art faithful to revive the dead. Blessed art thou, O Lord, who revivest the dead.

KEDUSHAH

When the Reader repeats the Amidah, the following Kedushah is said.

We sanctify thy name in this world even as they sanctify it in the highest heavens, as it is written by thy prophet: "They keep calling to one another:

> Holy, holy, holy is the Lord of hosts;
> The whole earth is full of his glory."[3]

---

[1] *Deuteronomy* 32:3.   [2] *Psalm* 51:17.   [3] *Isaiah* 6:3.

לְעֻמָּתָם בָּרוּךְ יֹאמֵרוּ—
בָּרוּךְ כְּבוֹד יְיָ מִמְּקוֹמוֹ.
וּבְדִבְרֵי קָדְשְׁךָ כָּתוּב לֵאמֹר:

יִמְלֹךְ יְיָ לְעוֹלָם, אֱלֹהַיִךְ צִיּוֹן לְדֹר וָדֹר; הַלְלוּיָהּ.

Reader:

לְדוֹר וָדוֹר נַגִּיד גָּדְלֶךָ, וּלְנֵצַח נְצָחִים קְדֻשָּׁתְךָ נַקְדִּישׁ,
וְשִׁבְחֲךָ אֱלֹהֵינוּ מִפִּינוּ לֹא יָמוּשׁ לְעוֹלָם וָעֶד, כִּי אֵל מֶלֶךְ
גָּדוֹל וְקָדוֹשׁ אָתָּה. בָּרוּךְ אַתָּה, יְיָ, הָאֵל הַקָּדוֹשׁ.

אַתָּה קָדוֹשׁ וְשִׁמְךָ קָדוֹשׁ, וּקְדוֹשִׁים בְּכָל יוֹם יְהַלְלוּךָ סֶּלָה.
בָּרוּךְ אַתָּה, יְיָ, הָאֵל הַקָּדוֹשׁ.

רָאשֵׁי חֳדָשִׁים לְעַמְּךָ נָתָתָּ, זְמַן כַּפָּרָה לְכָל תּוֹלְדוֹתָם.
בִּהְיוֹתָם מַקְרִיבִים לְפָנֶיךָ זִבְחֵי רָצוֹן וּשְׂעִירֵי חַטָּאת לְכַפֵּר
בַּעֲדָם, זִכָּרוֹן לְכֻלָּם יִהְיוּ, וּתְשׁוּעַת נַפְשָׁם מִיַּד שׂוֹנֵא. מִזְבֵּחַ
חָדָשׁ בְּצִיּוֹן תָּכִין, וְעוֹלַת רֹאשׁ חֹדֶשׁ נַעֲלֶה עָלָיו, וּשְׂעִירֵי עִזִּים
נַעֲשֶׂה בְרָצוֹן, וּבַעֲבוֹדַת בֵּית הַמִּקְדָּשׁ נִשְׂמַח כֻּלָּנוּ, וּבְשִׁירֵי
דָוִד עַבְדְּךָ הַנִּשְׁמָעִים בְּעִירֶךָ, הָאֲמוּרִים לִפְנֵי מִזְבְּחֶךָ. אַהֲבַת
עוֹלָם תָּבִיא לָהֶם, וּבְרִית אָבוֹת לַבָּנִים תִּזְכּוֹר. וַהֲבִיאֵנוּ לְצִיּוֹן
עִירְךָ בְּרִנָּה, וְלִירוּשָׁלַיִם בֵּית מִקְדָּשְׁךָ בְּשִׂמְחַת עוֹלָם; וְשָׁם
נַעֲשֶׂה לְפָנֶיךָ אֶת קָרְבְּנוֹת חוֹבוֹתֵינוּ, תְּמִידִים כְּסִדְרָם
וּמוּסָפִים כְּהִלְכָתָם. וְאֶת מוּסַף יוֹם רֹאשׁ הַחֹדֶשׁ הַזֶּה נַעֲשֶׂה
וְנַקְרִיב לְפָנֶיךָ בְּאַהֲבָה כְּמִצְוַת רְצוֹנֶךָ, כְּמוֹ שֶׁכָּתַבְתָּ עָלֵינוּ
בְּתוֹרָתֶךָ, עַל יְדֵי מֹשֶׁה עַבְדֶּךָ, מִפִּי כְבוֹדֶךָ, כָּאָמוּר:

ראשי חדשים is based on the tradition that the *Rosh Ḥodesh* offering
atoned for the sins committed during the previous month. The concluding
paragraph of the prayer for *Rosh Ḥodesh* contains twelve pleas for comfort and

Those opposite them say: Blessed—
Blessed be the glory of the Lord from his abode.[1]
And in thy holy Scriptures it is written:
>The Lord shall reign forever,
>Your God, O Zion, for all generations.
>Praise the Lord.[2]

Reader:

Through all generations we will declare thy greatness; to all eternity we will proclaim thy holiness; thy praise, our God, shall never depart from our mouth, for thou art a great and holy God and King. Blessed art thou, O Lord, holy God.

Thou art holy and thy name is holy, and holy beings praise thee daily. Blessed art thou, O Lord, holy God.

The new moon festivals thou didst assign to thy people as a season of atonement for all their offspring. The freewill offerings which they presented in thy honor, and the sin-offerings to atone for them, served as a reminder of them all, a deliverance of their soul from the power of the enemy. Thou wilt set up a new altar in Zion; upon it we will offer new moon offerings and acceptable sacrifices. All of us will rejoice in the service of the sanctuary and in the psalms of thy servant David, which will be heard in thy city and recited before thy altar. O grant us everlasting love; remember the covenant of the patriarchs in favor of their children. Bring us to Zion thy city with song, to Jerusalem thy sanctuary with everlasting joy. There we will prepare in thy honor our obligatory offerings, the regular daily offerings and the additional offerings according to rule. The additional offering of this new moon festival we will prepare and present to thee with love according to the command of thy will, as thou hast prescribed for us in thy Torah through thy servant Moses, as it is said:

---

forgiveness, corresponding to the twelve months of the year. The thirteenth plea, ולכפרת פשע, is inserted during the leap year which is composed of thirteen months.

---

[1] *Ezekiel* 3:12. [2] *Psalm* 146:10.

וּבְרָאשֵׁי חָדְשֵׁיכֶם תַּקְרִיבוּ עֹלָה לַיָי: פָּרִים בְּנֵי בָקָר שְׁנַיִם, וְאַיִל אֶחָד, כְּבָשִׂים בְּנֵי שָׁנָה שִׁבְעָה, תְּמִימִם.

וּמִנְחָתָם וְנִסְכֵּיהֶם כִּמְדֻבָּר: שְׁלשָׁה עֶשְׂרֹנִים לַפָּר, וּשְׁנֵי עֶשְׂרֹנִים לָאַיִל, וְעִשָּׂרוֹן לַכֶּבֶשׂ, וְיַיִן כְּנִסְכּוֹ, וְשָׂעִיר לְכַפֵּר, וּשְׁנֵי תְמִידִים כְּהִלְכָתָם.

אֱלֹהֵינוּ וֵאלֹהֵי אֲבוֹתֵינוּ, חַדֵּשׁ עָלֵינוּ אֶת הַחֹדֶשׁ הַזֶּה לְטוֹבָה וְלִבְרָכָה, לְשָׂשׂוֹן וּלְשִׂמְחָה, לִישׁוּעָה וּלְנֶחָמָה, לְפַרְנָסָה וּלְכַלְכָּלָה, לְחַיִּים וּלְשָׁלוֹם, לִמְחִילַת חֵטְא וְלִסְלִיחַת עָוֹן (during leap year: וּלְכַפָּרַת פָּשַׁע). כִּי בְעַמְּךָ יִשְׂרָאֵל בָּחַרְתָּ מִכָּל הָאֻמּוֹת, וְחֻקֵּי רָאשֵׁי חֳדָשִׁים לָהֶם קָבָעְתָּ. בָּרוּךְ אַתָּה, יְיָ, מְקַדֵּשׁ יִשְׂרָאֵל וְרָאשֵׁי חֳדָשִׁים.

רְצֵה, יְיָ אֱלֹהֵינוּ, בְּעַמְּךָ יִשְׂרָאֵל וּבִתְפִלָּתָם; וְהָשֵׁב אֶת הָעֲבוֹדָה לִדְבִיר בֵּיתֶךָ, וְאִשֵּׁי יִשְׂרָאֵל וּתְפִלָּתָם בְּאַהֲבָה תְקַבֵּל בְּרָצוֹן, וּתְהִי לְרָצוֹן תָּמִיד עֲבוֹדַת יִשְׂרָאֵל עַמֶּךָ.

וְתֶחֱזֶינָה עֵינֵינוּ בְּשׁוּבְךָ לְצִיּוֹן בְּרַחֲמִים. בָּרוּךְ אַתָּה, יְיָ, הַמַּחֲזִיר שְׁכִינָתוֹ לְצִיּוֹן.

מוֹדִים אֲנַחְנוּ לָךְ, שָׁאַתָּה הוּא יְיָ אֱלֹהֵינוּ וֵאלֹהֵי אֲבוֹתֵינוּ לְעוֹלָם וָעֶד. צוּר חַיֵּינוּ, מָגֵן יִשְׁעֵנוּ אַתָּה הוּא. לְדוֹר וָדוֹר נוֹדֶה לְּךָ, וּנְסַפֵּר תְּהִלָּתֶךָ, עַל חַיֵּינוּ הַמְּסוּרִים בְּיָדֶךָ, וְעַל נִשְׁמוֹתֵינוּ הַפְּקוּדוֹת לָךְ, וְעַל נִסֶּיךָ שֶׁבְּכָל יוֹם עִמָּנוּ, וְעַל

When the Reader repeats the *Amidah*, the Congregation responds here by saying:

(מוֹדִים אֲנַחְנוּ לָךְ, שָׁאַתָּה הוּא יְיָ אֱלֹהֵינוּ וֵאלֹהֵי אֲבוֹתֵינוּ. אֱלֹהֵי כָל בָּשָׂר, יוֹצְרֵנוּ, יוֹצֵר בְּרֵאשִׁית, בְּרָכוֹת וְהוֹדָאוֹת לְשִׁמְךָ הַגָּדוֹל וְהַקָּדוֹשׁ עַל שֶׁהֶחֱיִיתָנוּ וְקִיַּמְתָּנוּ. כֵּן תְּחַיֵּנוּ וּתְקַיְּמֵנוּ,

On your new moon festivals you shall offer as a burnt-offering
to the Lord two young bullocks, one ram and seven yearling male
lambs without blemish.[1]

Their meal-offering and their libations were as specified: three
tenths of an *ephah* [of fine flour] for each bullock, two-tenths for
the ram, one-tenth for each lamb; wine according to their requisite
libations. Moreover, a he-goat was offered to make atonement,
in addition to the two regular daily offerings.

Our God and God of our fathers, give us this new month for
happiness and blessing, joy and gladness, deliverance and consolation, maintenance and sustenance, life and peace, pardon of sin
and forgiveness of iniquity (*during leap year:* and atonement of
transgression). Truly thou hast chosen thy people Israel from all
nations, and hast instituted for them the rules relating to the new
moon festivals. Blessed art thou, O Lord, who sanctifiest Israel
and the new moon festivals.

Be pleased, Lord our God, with thy people Israel and with
their prayer; restore the worship to thy most holy sanctuary; accept Israel's offerings and prayer with gracious love. May the
worship of thy people Israel be ever pleasing to thee.

May our eyes behold thy return in mercy to Zion. Blessed art
thou, O Lord, who restorest thy divine presence to Zion.

We ever thank thee, who art
the Lord our God and the God
of our fathers. Thou art the
strength of our life and our
saving shield. In every generation we will thank thee and
recount thy praise—for our
lives which are in thy charge,
for our souls which are in thy
care, for thy miracles which are
daily with us, and for thy continual wonders and favors—

When the Reader repeats the Amidah,
the Congregation responds here by
saying:

(We thank thee, who art the
Lord our God and the God of
our fathers. God of all mankind,
our Creator and Creator of the
universe, blessings and thanks
are due to thy great and holy
name, because thou has kept us
alive and sustained us; mayest
thou ever grant us life and sustenance. O gather our exiles to thy

---

[1]*Numbers* 28:11.

נִפְלְאוֹתֶיךָ וְטוֹבוֹתֶיךָ שֶׁבְּכָל | וְתֶאֱסוֹף גָּלֻיּוֹתֵינוּ לְחַצְרוֹת
עֵת, עֶרֶב וָבֹקֶר וְצָהֳרָיִם. | קָדְשֶׁךָ לִשְׁמוֹר חֻקֶּיךָ וְלַעֲשׂוֹת
הַטּוֹב כִּי לֹא כָלוּ רַחֲמֶיךָ, | רְצוֹנֶךָ, וּלְעָבְדְּךָ בְּלֵבָב
וְהַמְרַחֵם כִּי לֹא תַמּוּ חֲסָדֶיךָ, | שָׁלֵם, עַל שֶׁאֲנַחְנוּ מוֹדִים לָךְ.
מֵעוֹלָם קִוִּינוּ לָךְ. | בָּרוּךְ אֵל הַהוֹדָאוֹת.)

On Ḥanukkah add:

(עַל הַנִּסִּים וְעַל הַפֻּרְקָן, וְעַל הַגְּבוּרוֹת וְעַל הַתְּשׁוּעוֹת, וְעַל
הַמִּלְחָמוֹת, שֶׁעָשִׂיתָ לַאֲבוֹתֵינוּ בַּיָּמִים הָהֵם בַּזְּמַן הַזֶּה—

בִּימֵי מַתִּתְיָהוּ בֶּן יוֹחָנָן כֹּהֵן גָּדוֹל, חַשְׁמוֹנַי וּבָנָיו, כְּשֶׁעָמְדָה
מַלְכוּת יָוָן הָרְשָׁעָה עַל עַמְּךָ יִשְׂרָאֵל לְהַשְׁכִּיחָם תּוֹרָתֶךָ,
וּלְהַעֲבִירָם מֵחֻקֵּי רְצוֹנֶךָ. וְאַתָּה בְּרַחֲמֶיךָ הָרַבִּים עָמַדְתָּ לָהֶם
בְּעֵת צָרָתָם, רַבְתָּ אֶת רִיבָם, דַּנְתָּ אֶת דִּינָם, נָקַמְתָּ אֶת נִקְמָתָם;
מָסַרְתָּ גִבּוֹרִים בְּיַד חַלָּשִׁים, וְרַבִּים בְּיַד מְעַטִּים, וּטְמֵאִים בְּיַד
טְהוֹרִים, וּרְשָׁעִים בְּיַד צַדִּיקִים, וְזֵדִים בְּיַד עוֹסְקֵי תוֹרָתֶךָ.
וּלְךָ עָשִׂיתָ שֵׁם גָּדוֹל וְקָדוֹשׁ בְּעוֹלָמֶךָ, וּלְעַמְּךָ יִשְׂרָאֵל עָשִׂיתָ
תְּשׁוּעָה גְדוֹלָה וּפֻרְקָן כְּהַיּוֹם הַזֶּה. וְאַחַר כֵּן בָּאוּ בָנֶיךָ לִדְבִיר
בֵּיתֶךָ, וּפִנּוּ אֶת הֵיכָלֶךָ, וְטִהֲרוּ אֶת מִקְדָּשֶׁךָ, וְהִדְלִיקוּ נֵרוֹת
בְּחַצְרוֹת קָדְשֶׁךָ, וְקָבְעוּ שְׁמוֹנַת יְמֵי חֲנֻכָּה אֵלּוּ לְהוֹדוֹת וּלְהַלֵּל
לְשִׁמְךָ הַגָּדוֹל.)

וְעַל כֻּלָּם יִתְבָּרַךְ וְיִתְרוֹמַם שִׁמְךָ, מַלְכֵּנוּ, תָּמִיד לְעוֹלָם
וָעֶד.

וְכֹל הַחַיִּים יוֹדוּךָ סֶּלָה, וִיהַלְלוּ אֶת שִׁמְךָ בֶּאֱמֶת, הָאֵל,
יְשׁוּעָתֵנוּ וְעֶזְרָתֵנוּ סֶלָה. בָּרוּךְ אַתָּה, יְיָ, הַטּוֹב שִׁמְךָ, וּלְךָ נָאֶה
לְהוֹדוֹת.

evening, morning and noon. Beneficent One, whose mercies never fail, Merciful One, whose kindnesses never cease, thou hast always been our hope. holy courts to observe thy laws to do thy will, and to serve thee with a perfect heart. For this we thank thee. Blessed be God to whom all thanks are due.)

On Ḥanukkah add:

(We thank thee for the miracles, for the redemption, for the mighty deeds and triumphs, and for the battles which thou didst perform for our fathers in those days, at this season—

In the days of the Hasmonean, Mattathias ben Yoḥanan, the High Priest, and his sons, when a wicked Hellenic government rose up against thy people Israel to make them forget thy Torah and transgress the laws of thy will. Thou in thy great mercy didst stand by them in the time of their distress. Thou didst champion their cause, defend their rights and avenge their wrong; thou didst deliver the strong into the hands of the weak, the many into the hands of the few, the impure into the hands of the pure, the wicked into the hands of the righteous, and the arrogant into the hands of the students of thy Torah. Thou didst make a great and holy name for thyself in thy world, and for thy people Israel thou didst perform a great deliverance unto this day. Thereupon thy children entered the shrine of thy house, cleansed thy temple, purified thy sanctuary, kindled lights in thy holy courts, and appointed these eight days of Ḥanukkah for giving thanks and praise to thy great name.)

For all these acts, may thy name, our King, be blessed and exalted forever and ever.

All the living shall ever thank thee and sincerely praise thy name, O God, who art always our salvation and help. Blessed art thou, O Lord, Beneficent One, to whom it is fitting to give thanks.

Priestly blessing recited by the Reader:

אֱלֹהֵינוּ וֵאלֹהֵי אֲבוֹתֵינוּ, בָּרְכֵנוּ בַבְּרָכָה הַמְשֻׁלֶּשֶׁת בַּתּוֹרָה הַכְּתוּבָה עַל יְדֵי מֹשֶׁה עַבְדֶּךָ, הָאֲמוּרָה מִפִּי אַהֲרֹן וּבָנָיו, כֹּהֲנִים עַם קְדוֹשֶׁךָ, כָּאָמוּר: יְבָרֶכְךָ יְיָ וְיִשְׁמְרֶךָ. יָאֵר יְיָ פָּנָיו אֵלֶיךָ וִיחֻנֶּךָּ. יִשָּׂא יְיָ פָּנָיו אֵלֶיךָ, וְיָשֵׂם לְךָ שָׁלוֹם.

שִׂים שָׁלוֹם, טוֹבָה וּבְרָכָה, חֵן וָחֶסֶד וְרַחֲמִים, עָלֵינוּ וְעַל כָּל יִשְׂרָאֵל עַמֶּךָ. בָּרְכֵנוּ אָבִינוּ, כֻּלָּנוּ כְּאֶחָד, בְּאוֹר פָּנֶיךָ; כִּי בְאוֹר פָּנֶיךָ נָתַתָּ לָּנוּ, יְיָ אֱלֹהֵינוּ, תּוֹרַת חַיִּים וְאַהֲבַת חֶסֶד, וּצְדָקָה וּבְרָכָה וְרַחֲמִים, וְחַיִּים וְשָׁלוֹם; וְטוֹב בְּעֵינֶיךָ לְבָרֵךְ אֶת עַמְּךָ יִשְׂרָאֵל בְּכָל עֵת וּבְכָל שָׁעָה בִּשְׁלוֹמֶךָ. בָּרוּךְ אַתָּה, יְיָ, הַמְבָרֵךְ אֶת עַמּוֹ יִשְׂרָאֵל בַּשָּׁלוֹם.

After the *Amidah* add the following meditation:

אֱלֹהַי, נְצֹר לְשׁוֹנִי מֵרָע, וּשְׂפָתַי מִדַּבֵּר מִרְמָה; וְלִמְקַלְלַי נַפְשִׁי תִדּוֹם, וְנַפְשִׁי כֶּעָפָר לַכֹּל תִּהְיֶה. פְּתַח לִבִּי בְּתוֹרָתֶךָ, וּבְמִצְוֹתֶיךָ תִּרְדּוֹף נַפְשִׁי; וְכָל הַחוֹשְׁבִים עָלַי רָעָה, מְהֵרָה הָפֵר עֲצָתָם וְקַלְקֵל מַחֲשַׁבְתָּם. עֲשֵׂה לְמַעַן שְׁמֶךָ, עֲשֵׂה לְמַעַן יְמִינֶךָ, עֲשֵׂה לְמַעַן קְדֻשָּׁתֶךָ, עֲשֵׂה לְמַעַן תּוֹרָתֶךָ. לְמַעַן יֵחָלְצוּן יְדִידֶיךָ, הוֹשִׁיעָה יְמִינְךָ וַעֲנֵנִי. יִהְיוּ לְרָצוֹן אִמְרֵי פִי וְהֶגְיוֹן לִבִּי לְפָנֶיךָ, יְיָ, צוּרִי וְגוֹאֲלִי. עֹשֶׂה שָׁלוֹם בִּמְרוֹמָיו, הוּא יַעֲשֶׂה שָׁלוֹם עָלֵינוּ וְעַל כָּל יִשְׂרָאֵל, וְאִמְרוּ אָמֵן.

יְהִי רָצוֹן מִלְּפָנֶיךָ, יְיָ אֱלֹהֵינוּ וֵאלֹהֵי אֲבוֹתֵינוּ, שֶׁיִּבָּנֶה בֵּית הַמִּקְדָּשׁ בִּמְהֵרָה בְיָמֵינוּ, וְתֵן חֶלְקֵנוּ בְּתוֹרָתֶךָ. וְשָׁם נַעֲבָדְךָ בְּיִרְאָה, כִּימֵי עוֹלָם וּכְשָׁנִים קַדְמוֹנִיּוֹת. וְעָרְבָה לַיְיָ מִנְחַת יְהוּדָה וִירוּשָׁלָיִם, כִּימֵי עוֹלָם וּכְשָׁנִים קַדְמוֹנִיּוֹת.

בָּרְכִי נַפְשִׁי page 465; עָלֵינוּ page 135

Priestly blessing recited by the Reader:

Our God and God of our fathers, bless us with the threefold blessing written in thy Torah by thy servant Moses and spoken by Aaron and his sons the priests, thy holy people, as it is said: "May the Lord bless you and protect you; may the Lord countenance you and be gracious to you; may the Lord favor you and grant you peace."[1]

O grant peace, happiness, blessing, grace, kindness and mercy to us and to all Israel thy people. Bless us all alike, our Father, with the light of thy countenance; indeed, by the light of thy countenance thou hast given us, Lord our God, a Torah of life, lovingkindness, charity, blessing, mercy, life and peace. May it please thee to bless thy people Israel with peace at all times and hours. Blessed art thou, O Lord, who blessest thy people Israel with peace.

After the Amidah add the following meditation:

My God, guard my tongue from evil, and my lips from speaking falsehood. May my soul be silent to those who insult me; be my soul lowly to all as the dust. Open my heart to thy Torah, that my soul may follow thy commands. Speedily defeat the counsel of all those who plan evil against me and upset their design. Do it for the glory of thy name; do it for the sake of thy power; do it for the sake of thy holiness; do it for the sake of thy Torah. That thy beloved may be rescued, save with thy right hand and answer me. May the words of my mouth and the meditation of my heart be pleasing before thee, O Lord, my Stronghold and my Redeemer.[2] May he who creates peace in his high heavens create peace for us and for all Israel. Amen.

May it be thy will, Lord our God and God of our fathers, that the Temple be speedily rebuilt in our days, and grant us a share in thy Torah. There we will serve thee with reverence, as in the days of old and as in former years. Then the offering of Judah and Jerusalem will be pleasing to the Lord, as in the days of old and as in former years.[3]

Psalm 104, *page* 466; *Alenu, page* 136

[1]*Numbers* 6:24-26. [2]*Psalms* 60:7; 19:15. [3]*Malachi* **3:4.**

עֵרוּב תַּבְשִׁילִין

Recited over food on the eve of a festival that is followed by a Sabbath

בָּרוּךְ אַתָּה, יְיָ אֱלֹהֵינוּ, מֶלֶךְ הָעוֹלָם, אֲשֶׁר קִדְּשָׁנוּ בְּמִצְוֹתָיו וְצִוָּנוּ עַל מִצְוַת עֵרוּב.

בְּדֵן עֵרוּבָא יְהֵא שָׁרֵא לָנָא לְמֵיפָא וּלְבַשָּׁלָא וּלְאַטְמָנָא, וּלְאַדְלָקָא שְׁרָגָא, וּלְמֶעְבַּד כָּל צָרְכָּנָא מִיּוֹמָא טָבָא לְשַׁבְּתָא, לָנוּ וּלְכָל הַדָּרִים בָּעִיר הַזֹּאת.

הַדְלָקַת נֵר שֶׁל יוֹם טוֹב

בָּרוּךְ אַתָּה, יְיָ אֱלֹהֵינוּ, מֶלֶךְ הָעוֹלָם, אֲשֶׁר קִדְּשָׁנוּ בְּמִצְוֹתָיו וְצִוָּנוּ לְהַדְלִיק נֵר שֶׁל (שַׁבָּת וְשֶׁל) יוֹם טוֹב.

On the last two nights of *Pesaḥ* omit:

בָּרוּךְ אַתָּה, יְיָ אֱלֹהֵינוּ, מֶלֶךְ הָעוֹלָם, שֶׁהֶחֱיָנוּ וְקִיְּמָנוּ וְהִגִּיעָנוּ לַזְּמַן הַזֶּה.

עֲמִידָה לְשָׁלֹשׁ רְגָלִים

The *Amidah* is recited in silent devotion while standing, facing east.

(כִּי שֵׁם יְיָ אֶקְרָא, הָבוּ גֹדֶל לֵאלֹהֵינוּ.)

אֲדֹנָי, שְׂפָתַי תִּפְתָּח, וּפִי יַגִּיד תְּהִלָּתֶךָ.

בָּרוּךְ אַתָּה, יְיָ אֱלֹהֵינוּ וֵאלֹהֵי אֲבוֹתֵינוּ, אֱלֹהֵי אַבְרָהָם, אֱלֹהֵי יִצְחָק, וֵאלֹהֵי יַעֲקֹב, הָאֵל הַגָּדוֹל הַגִּבּוֹר וְהַנּוֹרָא, אֵל עֶלְיוֹן, גּוֹמֵל חֲסָדִים טוֹבִים, וְקוֹנֵה הַכֹּל, וְזוֹכֵר חַסְדֵי אָבוֹת, וּמֵבִיא גוֹאֵל לִבְנֵי בְנֵיהֶם לְמַעַן שְׁמוֹ בְּאַהֲבָה.

עֵרוּב תַּבְשִׁילִין (''mixture of dishes'') renders it permissible to prepare food on a holy day for use on the Sabbath which immediately follows it. The permission to prepare food on holy days is restricted to food required for those

ERUV TAVSHILIN

Recited over food on the eve of a festival that is followed by a Sabbath

Blessed art thou, Lord our God, King of the universe, who hast sanctified us with thy commandments, and commanded us concerning the observance of *eruv.*

By means of this *eruv* may we be permitted to bake, cook, keep dishes warm, light Sabbath lights, and prepare during the festival all we need for the Sabbath—we and all Israelites that live in this town.

LIGHTING THE FESTIVAL LIGHTS

Blessed art thou, Lord our God, King of the universe, who hast sanctified us with thy commandments, and commanded us to light (the Sabbath and) the festival lights.

On the last two nights of Pesaḥ omit:

Blessed art thou, Lord our God, King of the universe, who hast granted us life and sustenance and permitted us to reach this season.

AMIDAH FOR FESTIVALS

The Amidah is recited in silent devotion while standing, facing east.

(When I proclaim the name of the Lord, give glory to our God!)

O Lord, open thou my lips, that my mouth may declare thy praise.

Blessed art thou, Lord our God and God of our fathers, God of Abraham, God of Isaac and God of Jacob; great, mighty and revered God, sublime God, who bestowest lovingkindness, and art Master of all things; who rememberest the good deeds of our fathers, and who wilt graciously bring a redeemer to their children's children for the sake of thy name.

---

days; but if the preparation was begun before the holy day, it may be continued on the holy day itself. This is accomplished by symbolically singling out food for the Sabbath on the eve of the festival.

מֶלֶךְ עוֹזֵר וּמוֹשִׁיעַ וּמָגֵן. בָּרוּךְ אַתָּה, יְיָ, מָגֵן אַבְרָהָם.

אַתָּה גִבּוֹר לְעוֹלָם, אֲדֹנָי; מְחַיֵּה מֵתִים אַתָּה, רַב לְהוֹשִׁיעַ.

From *Musaf* of *Shemini Atsereth* till *Musaf* of the first day of *Pesaḥ:*

(מַשִּׁיב הָרוּחַ וּמוֹרִיד הַגֶּשֶׁם.)

מְכַלְכֵּל חַיִּים בְּחֶסֶד, מְחַיֵּה מֵתִים בְּרַחֲמִים רַבִּים, סוֹמֵךְ

נוֹפְלִים, וְרוֹפֵא חוֹלִים, וּמַתִּיר אֲסוּרִים, וּמְקַיֵּם אֱמוּנָתוֹ לִישֵׁנֵי

עָפָר. מִי כָמוֹךָ, בַּעַל גְּבוּרוֹת, וּמִי דוֹמֶה לָּךְ, מֶלֶךְ מֵמִית

וּמְחַיֶּה וּמַצְמִיחַ יְשׁוּעָה.

וְנֶאֱמָן אַתָּה לְהַחֲיוֹת מֵתִים. בָּרוּךְ אַתָּה, יְיָ, מְחַיֵּה הַמֵּתִים.

KEDUSHAH FOR SHAḤARITH

נְקַדֵּשׁ אֶת שִׁמְךָ בָּעוֹלָם כְּשֵׁם שֶׁמַּקְדִּישִׁים אוֹתוֹ בִּשְׁמֵי

מָרוֹם, כַּכָּתוּב עַל יַד נְבִיאֶךָ: וְקָרָא זֶה אֶל זֶה וְאָמַר:

קָדוֹשׁ, קָדוֹשׁ, קָדוֹשׁ יְיָ צְבָאוֹת; מְלֹא כָל הָאָרֶץ כְּבוֹדוֹ.

אָז בְּקוֹל רַעַשׁ גָּדוֹל, אַדִּיר וְחָזָק, מַשְׁמִיעִים קוֹל, מִתְנַשְּׂאִים

לְעֻמַּת שְׂרָפִים; לְעֻמָּתָם בָּרוּךְ יֹאמֵרוּ—

בָּרוּךְ כְּבוֹד יְיָ מִמְּקוֹמוֹ.

מִמְּקוֹמְךָ מַלְכֵּנוּ תוֹפִיעַ וְתִמְלֹךְ עָלֵינוּ, כִּי מְחַכִּים אֲנַחְנוּ

לָּךְ. מָתַי תִּמְלֹךְ בְּצִיּוֹן, בְּקָרוֹב בְּיָמֵינוּ לְעוֹלָם וָעֶד תִּשְׁכּוֹן.

תִּתְגַּדַּל וְתִתְקַדַּשׁ בְּתוֹךְ יְרוּשָׁלַיִם עִירְךָ לְדוֹר וָדוֹר וּלְנֵצַח

נְצָחִים. וְעֵינֵינוּ תִרְאֶינָה מַלְכוּתֶךָ, כַּדָּבָר הָאָמוּר בְּשִׁירֵי עֻזֶּךָ

עַל יְדֵי דָוִד מְשִׁיחַ צִדְקֶךָ:

יִמְלֹךְ יְיָ לְעוֹלָם, אֱלֹהַיִךְ צִיּוֹן לְדֹר וָדֹר; הַלְלוּיָהּ.

O King, Supporter, Savior and Shield! Blessed art thou, O Lord, Shield of Abraham.

Thou, O Lord, art mighty forever; thou revivest the dead; thou art powerful to save.

From Musaf of Shemini Atsereth till Musaf of the first day of Pesaḥ:

(Thou causest the wind to blow and the rain to fall.)

Thou sustainest the living with kindness, and revivest the dead with great mercy; thou supportest all who fall, and healest the sick; thou settest the captives free, and keepest faith with those who sleep in the dust. Who is like thee, Lord of power? Who resembles thee, O King? Thou bringest death and restorest life, and causest salvation to flourish.

Thou art faithful to revive the dead. Blessed art thou, O Lord, who revivest the dead.

KEDUSHAH FOR SHAḤARITH

We sanctify thy name in the world even as they sanctify it in the highest heavens, as it is written by thy prophet: "They keep calling to one another:

> Holy, holy, holy is the Lord of hosts;
> The whole earth is full of his glory."

Then with a loud sound, mighty and strong, they make their voice heard; upraising themselves toward the Seraphim, they respond by exclaiming: Blessed—

Blessed be the glory of the Lord from his abode.

From thy abode, our King, appear and reign over us, for we wait for thee. O when wilt thou reign in Zion? Speedily, in our days, do thou dwell there forever. Mayest thou be exalted and sanctified in Jerusalem thy city throughout all generations and to all eternity. May our eyes behold thy kingdom, as it is said in thy glorious Psalms by thy truly anointed David:

> The Lord shall reign forever,
> Your God, O Zion, for all generations.
> Praise the Lord!

KEDUSHAH FOR MINḤAH

נְקַדֵּשׁ אֶת שִׁמְךָ בָּעוֹלָם כְּשֵׁם שֶׁמַּקְדִּישִׁים אוֹתוֹ בִּשְׁמֵי מָרוֹם,

כַּכָּתוּב עַל יַד נְבִיאֶךָ: וְקָרָא זֶה אֶל זֶה וְאָמַר:

קָדוֹשׁ, קָדוֹשׁ, קָדוֹשׁ יְיָ צְבָאוֹת; מְלֹא כָל הָאָרֶץ כְּבוֹדוֹ.

לְעֻמָּתָם בָּרוּךְ יֹאמֵרוּ־

בָּרוּךְ כְּבוֹד יְיָ מִמְּקוֹמוֹ.

וּבְדִבְרֵי קָדְשְׁךָ כָּתוּב לֵאמֹר:

יִמְלֹךְ יְיָ לְעוֹלָם, אֱלֹהַיִךְ צִיּוֹן לְדֹר וָדֹר; הַלְלוּיָהּ.

Reader:

לְדוֹר וָדוֹר נַגִּיד גָּדְלֶךָ, וּלְנֵצַח נְצָחִים קְדֻשָּׁתְךָ נַקְדִּישׁ, וְשִׁבְחֲךָ אֱלֹהֵינוּ מִפִּינוּ לֹא יָמוּשׁ לְעוֹלָם וָעֶד, כִּי אֵל מֶלֶךְ גָּדוֹל וְקָדוֹשׁ אָתָּה. בָּרוּךְ אַתָּה, יְיָ, הָאֵל הַקָּדוֹשׁ.

אַתָּה קָדוֹשׁ וְשִׁמְךָ קָדוֹשׁ, וּקְדוֹשִׁים בְּכָל יוֹם יְהַלְלוּךָ סֶּלָה. בָּרוּךְ אַתָּה, יְיָ, הָאֵל הַקָּדוֹשׁ.

אַתָּה בְחַרְתָּנוּ מִכָּל הָעַמִּים, אָהַבְתָּ אוֹתָנוּ וְרָצִיתָ בָּנוּ, וְרוֹמַמְתָּנוּ מִכָּל הַלְּשׁוֹנוֹת, וְקִדַּשְׁתָּנוּ בְּמִצְוֹתֶיךָ, וְקֵרַבְתָּנוּ מַלְכֵּנוּ לַעֲבוֹדָתֶךָ, וְשִׁמְךָ הַגָּדוֹל וְהַקָּדוֹשׁ עָלֵינוּ קָרָאתָ.

On Saturday night:

(וַתּוֹדִיעֵנוּ, יְיָ אֱלֹהֵינוּ, אֶת מִשְׁפְּטֵי צִדְקֶךָ, וַתְּלַמְּדֵנוּ לַעֲשׂוֹת חֻקֵּי רְצוֹנֶךָ. וַתִּתֶּן־לָנוּ, יְיָ אֱלֹהֵינוּ, מִשְׁפָּטִים יְשָׁרִים וְתוֹרוֹת אֱמֶת, חֻקִּים וּמִצְוֹת טוֹבִים; וַתַּנְחִילֵנוּ זְמַנֵּי שָׂשׂוֹן וּמוֹעֲדֵי קֹדֶשׁ וְחַגֵּי נְדָבָה, וַתּוֹרִישֵׁנוּ קְדֻשַּׁת שַׁבָּת וּכְבוֹד מוֹעֵד וַחֲגִיגַת הָרֶגֶל; וַתַּבְדֵּל, יְיָ אֱלֹהֵינוּ, בֵּין קֹדֶשׁ לְחֹל, בֵּין אוֹר לְחֹשֶׁךְ, בֵּין

אתה בחרתנו, mentioned in Yoma 87b, is based on Deuteronomy 10:15 and 14:2; Psalm 149:4; Jeremiah 14:9.

KEDUSHAH FOR MINḤAH

We sanctify thy name in the world even as they sanctify it in the highest heavens, as it is written by thy prophet: "They keep calling to one another:

> Holy, holy, holy is the Lord of hosts;
> The whole earth is full of his glory."

Those opposite them say: Blessed—
Blessed be the glory of the Lord from his abode.
And in thy holy Scriptures it is written:

> The Lord shall reign forever,
> Your God, O Zion, for all generations.
> Praise the Lord.

Reader:

Through all generations we will declare thy greatness; to all eternity we will proclaim thy holiness; thy praise, our God, shall never depart from our mouth, for thou art a great and holy God and King. Blessed art thou, O Lord, holy God.

Thou art holy and thy name is holy, and holy beings praise thee daily. Blessed art thou, O Lord, holy God.

Thou didst choose us from among all peoples; thou didst love and favor us; thou didst exalt us above all tongues and sanctify us with thy commandments. Thou, our King, didst draw us near to thy service and call us by thy great and holy name.

On Saturday night:

(Thou, Lord our God, hast made known to us thy righteous judgments and taught us to perform thy pleasing statutes. Thou, Lord our God, hast given us right ordinances, true precepts and good laws. Thou hast granted us joyous holidays, holy festivals and feasts for freewill offerings; thou hast vouchsafed to us the holiness of the Sabbath, the glory of the festival and the pilgrimage of the festive season. Thou, Lord our God, hast made a distinction between the holy and the profane, between light and darkness, be-

---

ותודיענו is quoted in Berakhoth 33b as a precious pearl (מרגניתא) and is attributed to Rav and Samuel, the founders of talmudic learning in Babylonia during the third century.

יִשְׂרָאֵל לָעַמִּים, בֵּין יוֹם הַשְּׁבִיעִי לְשֵׁשֶׁת יְמֵי הַמַּעֲשֶׂה. בֵּין
קְדֻשַּׁת שַׁבָּת לִקְדֻשַּׁת יוֹם טוֹב הִבְדַּלְתָּ, וְאֶת יוֹם הַשְּׁבִיעִי
מִשֵּׁשֶׁת יְמֵי הַמַּעֲשֶׂה קִדַּשְׁתָּ; הִבְדַּלְתָּ וְקִדַּשְׁתָּ אֶת עַמְּךָ יִשְׂרָאֵל
בִּקְדֻשָּׁתֶךָ.)

וַתִּתֶּן־לָנוּ, יְיָ אֱלֹהֵינוּ, בְּאַהֲבָה (שַׁבָּתוֹת לִמְנוּחָה וּ)מוֹעֲדִים
לְשִׂמְחָה, חַגִּים וּזְמַנִּים לְשָׂשׂוֹן, אֶת יוֹם (הַשַּׁבָּת הַזֶּה וְאֶת יוֹם)

Shemini Atsereth and Simḥath Torah	*Sukkoth*	*Shavuoth*	*Pesaḥ*
הַשְּׁמִינִי, חַג	חַג הַסֻּכּוֹת	חַג הַשָּׁבֻעוֹת	חַג הַמַּצּוֹת
הָעֲצֶרֶת הַזֶּה,	הַזֶּה, זְמַן	הַזֶּה, זְמַן	הַזֶּה, זְמַן
זְמַן שִׂמְחָתֵנוּ,	שִׂמְחָתֵנוּ,	מַתַּן תּוֹרָתֵנוּ,	חֵרוּתֵנוּ,

(בְּאַהֲבָה) מִקְרָא קֹדֶשׁ, זֵכֶר לִיצִיאַת מִצְרָיִם.

אֱלֹהֵינוּ וֵאלֹהֵי אֲבוֹתֵינוּ, יַעֲלֶה וְיָבֹא, וְיַגִּיעַ וְיֵרָאֶה, וְיֵרָצֶה
וְיִשָּׁמַע, וְיִפָּקֵד וְיִזָּכֵר, זִכְרוֹנֵנוּ וּפִקְדוֹנֵנוּ, וְזִכְרוֹן אֲבוֹתֵינוּ,
וְזִכְרוֹן מָשִׁיחַ בֶּן דָּוִד עַבְדֶּךָ, וְזִכְרוֹן יְרוּשָׁלַיִם עִיר קָדְשֶׁךָ,
וְזִכְרוֹן כָּל עַמְּךָ בֵּית יִשְׂרָאֵל לְפָנֶיךָ, לִפְלֵיטָה וּלְטוֹבָה, לְחֵן
וּלְחֶסֶד וּלְרַחֲמִים, לְחַיִּים וּלְשָׁלוֹם, בְּיוֹם

Shemini Atsereth and Simḥath Torah	*Sukkoth*	*Shavuoth*	*Pesaḥ*
הַשְּׁמִינִי, חַג	חַג הַסֻּכּוֹת	חַג הַשָּׁבֻעוֹת	חַג הַמַּצּוֹת
הָעֲצֶרֶת הַזֶּה.	הַזֶּה.	הַזֶּה.	הַזֶּה.

זָכְרֵנוּ, יְיָ אֱלֹהֵינוּ, בּוֹ לְטוֹבָה, וּפָקְדֵנוּ בוֹ לִבְרָכָה, וְהוֹשִׁיעֵנוּ
בוֹ לְחַיִּים; וּבִדְבַר יְשׁוּעָה וְרַחֲמִים חוּס וְחָנֵּנוּ, וְרַחֵם עָלֵינוּ
וְהוֹשִׁיעֵנוּ, כִּי אֵלֶיךָ עֵינֵינוּ, כִּי אֵל מֶלֶךְ חַנּוּן וְרַחוּם אָתָּה.

וְהַשִּׂיאֵנוּ, יְיָ אֱלֹהֵינוּ, אֶת בִּרְכַּת מוֹעֲדֶיךָ לְחַיִּים וּלְשָׁלוֹם,
לְשִׂמְחָה וּלְשָׂשׂוֹן, כַּאֲשֶׁר רָצִיתָ וְאָמַרְתָּ לְבָרְכֵנוּ. אֱלֹהֵינוּ
וֵאלֹהֵי אֲבוֹתֵינוּ, (רְצֵה בִמְנוּחָתֵנוּ) קַדְּשֵׁנוּ בְּמִצְוֹתֶיךָ וְתֵן חֶלְקֵנוּ

tween Israel and the nations, between the seventh day and the six working days. Thou hast made a distinction between the holiness of the Sabbath and the holiness of the festival, and hast hallowed the seventh day above the six working days; thou hast distinguished and sanctified thy people Israel with thy holiness.)

Thou, Lord our God, hast graciously given us (Sabbaths for rest,) holidays for gladness and festive seasons for joy: (this Sabbath day and) this

Pesaḥ

Feast of Unleavened Bread, our Festival of Freedom,

Shavuoth

Feast of Weeks, our Festival of the Giving of the Torah,

Sukkoth

Feast of Tabernacles, our Festival of Rejoicing,

Shemini Atsereth and Simḥath Torah

Eighth Day Feast, our Festival of Rejoicing,

a holy convocation in remembrance of the exodus from Egypt.

Our God and God of our fathers, may the remembrance of us, of our fathers, of Messiah the son of David thy servant, of Jerusalem thy holy city, and of all thy people the house of Israel, ascend and come and be accepted before thee for deliverance and happiness, for grace, kindness and mercy, for life and peace, on this day of

Pesaḥ	*Shavuoth*	*Sukkoth*
the Feast of Un-	the Feast of Weeks.	the Feast of
leavened Bread.		Tabernacles.

Shemini Atsereth and Simḥath Torah

the Eighth Day Feast.

Remember us this day, Lord our God, for happiness; be mindful of us for blessing; save us to enjoy life. With a promise of salvation and mercy spare us and be gracious to us; have pity on us and save us, for we look to thee, for thou art a gracious and merciful God and King.

Bestow on us, Lord our God, the blessings of thy festivals for life and peace, for joy and gladness, as thou didst promise to bless us. Our God and God of our Fathers, (be pleased with our rest)

באהבה, repeated on Sabbaths, has been variously explained. According to some authorities, the second באהבה should be omitted even on Sabbaths because it is a case of dittography; see אוצר התפלות, page 926.

בְּתוֹרָתֶךָ, שַׂבְּעֵנוּ מִטּוּבֶךָ וְשַׂמְּחֵנוּ בִּישׁוּעָתֶךָ, וְטַהֵר לִבֵּנוּ
לְעָבְדְּךָ בֶּאֱמֶת, וְהַנְחִילֵנוּ, יְיָ אֱלֹהֵינוּ, (בְּאַהֲבָה וּבְרָצוֹן)
בְּשִׂמְחָה וּבְשָׂשׂוֹן (שַׁבָּת וּ)מוֹעֲדֵי קָדְשֶׁךָ, וְיִשְׂמְחוּ בְךָ יִשְׂרָאֵל
מְקַדְּשֵׁי שְׁמֶךָ. בָּרוּךְ אַתָּה, יְיָ, מְקַדֵּשׁ (הַשַּׁבָּת וְ)יִשְׂרָאֵל
וְהַזְּמַנִּים.

רְצֵה, יְיָ אֱלֹהֵינוּ, בְּעַמְּךָ יִשְׂרָאֵל וּבִתְפִלָּתָם; וְהָשֵׁב אֶת
הָעֲבוֹדָה לִדְבִיר בֵּיתֶךָ, וְאִשֵּׁי יִשְׂרָאֵל וּתְפִלָּתָם בְּאַהֲבָה
תְקַבֵּל בְּרָצוֹן, וּתְהִי לְרָצוֹן תָּמִיד עֲבוֹדַת יִשְׂרָאֵל עַמֶּךָ.

וְתֶחֱזֶינָה עֵינֵינוּ בְּשׁוּבְךָ לְצִיּוֹן בְּרַחֲמִים. בָּרוּךְ אַתָּה, יְיָ,
הַמַּחֲזִיר שְׁכִינָתוֹ לְצִיּוֹן.

When the Reader repeats the *Amidah*,
the Congregation responds here by
saying:

(מוֹדִים אֲנַחְנוּ לָךְ, שָׁאַתָּה
הוּא יְיָ אֱלֹהֵינוּ וֵאלֹהֵי
אֲבוֹתֵינוּ. אֱלֹהֵי כָל בָּשָׂר,
יוֹצְרֵנוּ, יוֹצֵר בְּרֵאשִׁית,
בְּרָכוֹת וְהוֹדָאוֹת לְשִׁמְךָ
הַגָּדוֹל וְהַקָּדוֹשׁ עַל שֶׁהֶחֱיִיתָנוּ
וְקִיַּמְתָּנוּ. כֵּן תְּחַיֵּנוּ וּתְקַיְּמֵנוּ.
וְתֶאֱסֹף גָּלֻיּוֹתֵינוּ לְחַצְרוֹת
קָדְשֶׁךָ לִשְׁמוֹר חֻקֶּיךָ וְלַעֲשׂוֹת
רְצוֹנֶךָ, וּלְעָבְדְּךָ בְּלֵבָב
שָׁלֵם, עַל שֶׁאֲנַחְנוּ מוֹדִים לָךְ.
בָּרוּךְ אֵל הַהוֹדָאוֹת.)

מוֹדִים אֲנַחְנוּ לָךְ, שָׁאַתָּה
הוּא יְיָ אֱלֹהֵינוּ וֵאלֹהֵי אֲבוֹתֵינוּ
לְעוֹלָם וָעֶד. צוּר חַיֵּינוּ, מָגֵן
יִשְׁעֵנוּ אַתָּה הוּא. לְדוֹר וָדוֹר
נוֹדֶה לְּךָ, וּנְסַפֵּר תְּהִלָּתֶךָ, עַל
חַיֵּינוּ הַמְּסוּרִים בְּיָדֶךָ, וְעַל
נִשְׁמוֹתֵינוּ הַפְּקוּדוֹת לָךְ, וְעַל
נִסֶּיךָ שֶׁבְּכָל יוֹם עִמָּנוּ, וְעַל
נִפְלְאוֹתֶיךָ וְטוֹבוֹתֶיךָ שֶׁבְּכָל
עֵת, עֶרֶב וָבֹקֶר וְצָהֳרָיִם.
הַטּוֹב כִּי לֹא כָלוּ רַחֲמֶיךָ,
וְהַמְרַחֵם כִּי לֹא תַמּוּ חֲסָדֶיךָ,
מֵעוֹלָם קִוִּינוּ לָךְ.

וְעַל כֻּלָּם יִתְבָּרַךְ וְיִתְרוֹמַם שִׁמְךָ, מַלְכֵּנוּ, תָּמִיד לְעוֹלָם וָעֶד.

sanctify us with thy commandments and grant us a share in thy Torah; satisfy us with thy goodness and gladden us with thy help; purify our heart to serve thee sincerely. In thy gracious love, Lord our God, grant us thy holy (Sabbath and) festivals for gladness and joy; may Israel who sanctifies thy name rejoice in thee. Blessed art thou, O Lord, who hallowest (the Sabbath and) Israel and the festivals.

Be pleased, Lord our God, with thy people Israel and with their prayer; restore the worship to thy most holy sanctuary; accept Israel's offerings and prayer with gracious love. May the worship of thy people Israel be ever pleasing to thee.

May our eyes behold thy return in mercy to Zion. Blessed art thou, O Lord, who restorest thy divine presence to Zion.

We ever thank thee, who art the Lord our God and the God of our fathers. Thou art the strength of our life and our saving shield. In every generation we will thank thee and recount thy praise—for our lives which are in thy charge, for our souls which are in thy care, for thy miracles which are daily with us, and for thy continual wonders and favors—evening, morning and noon. Beneficent One, whose mercies never fail, Merciful One, whose kindnesses never cease, thou hast always been our hope.

When the Reader repeats the Amidah, the Congregation responds here by saying:

(We thank thee, who art the Lord our God and the God of our fathers. God of all mankind, our Creator and Creator of the universe, blessings and thanks are due to thy great and holy name, because thou hast kept us alive and sustained us; mayest thou ever grant us life and sustenance. O gather our exiles to thy holy courts to observe thy laws, to do thy will, and to serve thee with a perfect heart. For this we thank thee. Blessed be God to whom all thanks are due.)

For all these acts may thy name, our King, be blessed and exalted forever and ever.

וְכָל הַחַיִּים יוֹדוּךָ סֶּלָה, וִיהַלְלוּ אֶת שִׁמְךָ בֶּאֱמֶת, הָאֵל,
יְשׁוּעָתֵנוּ וְעֶזְרָתֵנוּ סֶלָה. בָּרוּךְ אַתָּה, יְיָ, הַטּוֹב שִׁמְךָ, וּלְךָ נָאֶה
לְהוֹדוֹת.

Priestly blessing recited by the Reader:

אֱלֹהֵינוּ וֵאלֹהֵי אֲבוֹתֵינוּ, בָּרְכֵנוּ בַבְּרָכָה הַמְשֻׁלֶּשֶׁת בַּתּוֹרָה
הַכְּתוּבָה עַל יְדֵי מֹשֶׁה עַבְדֶּךָ, הָאֲמוּרָה מִפִּי אַהֲרֹן וּבָנָיו,
כֹּהֲנִים עַם קְדוֹשֶׁךָ, כָּאָמוּר: יְבָרֶכְךָ יְיָ וְיִשְׁמְרֶךָ. יָאֵר יְיָ פָּנָיו
אֵלֶיךָ וִיחֻנֶּךָּ. יִשָּׂא יְיָ פָּנָיו אֵלֶיךָ, וְיָשֵׂם לְךָ שָׁלוֹם.

For Shaḥarith:

שִׂים שָׁלוֹם, טוֹבָה וּבְרָכָה, חֵן וָחֶסֶד וְרַחֲמִים, עָלֵינוּ וְעַל
כָּל יִשְׂרָאֵל עַמֶּךָ. בָּרְכֵנוּ אָבִינוּ, כֻּלָּנוּ כְּאֶחָד, בְּאוֹר פָּנֶיךָ;
כִּי בְאוֹר פָּנֶיךָ נָתַתָּ לָּנוּ, יְיָ אֱלֹהֵינוּ, תּוֹרַת חַיִּים וְאַהֲבַת חֶסֶד,
וּצְדָקָה וּבְרָכָה וְרַחֲמִים, וְחַיִּים וְשָׁלוֹם, וְטוֹב בְּעֵינֶיךָ לְבָרֵךְ
אֶת עַמְּךָ יִשְׂרָאֵל בְּכָל עֵת וּבְכָל שָׁעָה בִּשְׁלוֹמֶךָ. בָּרוּךְ אַתָּה,
יְיָ, הַמְבָרֵךְ אֶת עַמּוֹ יִשְׂרָאֵל בַּשָּׁלוֹם.

For *Minḥah* and *Ma‘ariv:*

שָׁלוֹם רָב עַל יִשְׂרָאֵל עַמְּךָ תָּשִׂים לְעוֹלָם, כִּי אַתָּה הוּא
מֶלֶךְ אָדוֹן לְכָל הַשָּׁלוֹם, וְטוֹב בְּעֵינֶיךָ לְבָרֵךְ אֶת עַמְּךָ
יִשְׂרָאֵל בְּכָל עֵת וּבְכָל שָׁעָה בִּשְׁלוֹמֶךָ. בָּרוּךְ אַתָּה, יְיָ, הַמְבָרֵךְ
אֶת עַמּוֹ יִשְׂרָאֵל בַּשָּׁלוֹם.

After the *Amidah* add the following meditation:

אֱלֹהַי, נְצֹר לְשׁוֹנִי מֵרָע, וּשְׂפָתַי מִדַּבֵּר מִרְמָה; וְלִמְקַלְלַי
נַפְשִׁי תִדּוֹם, וְנַפְשִׁי כֶּעָפָר לַכֹּל תִּהְיֶה. פְּתַח לִבִּי בְּתוֹרָתֶךָ,
וּבְמִצְוֹתֶיךָ תִּרְדּוֹף נַפְשִׁי; וְכָל הַחוֹשְׁבִים עָלַי רָעָה, מְהֵרָה
הָפֵר עֲצָתָם וְקַלְקֵל מַחֲשַׁבְתָּם. עֲשֵׂה לְמַעַן שְׁמֶךָ, עֲשֵׂה לְמַעַן
יְמִינֶךָ, עֲשֵׂה לְמַעַן קְדֻשָּׁתֶךָ, עֲשֵׂה לְמַעַן תּוֹרָתֶךָ. לְמַעַן יֵחָלְצוּן

All the living shall ever thank thee and sincerely praise thy name, O God, who art always our salvation and help. Blessed art thou, O Lord, Beneficent One, to whom it is fitting to give thanks.

Priestly blessing recited by the Reader:

Our God and God of our fathers, bless us with the threefold blessing written in thy Torah by thy servant Moses and spoken by Aaron and his sons the priests, thy holy people, as it is said: "May the Lord bless you and protect you; may the Lord countenance you and be gracious to you; may the Lord favor you and grant you peace."

For Shaḥarith:

O grant peace, happiness, blessing, grace, kindness and mercy to us and to all Israel thy people. Bless us all alike, our Father, with the light of thy countenance; indeed, by the light of thy countenance thou hast given us, Lord our God, a Torah of life, lovingkindness, charity, blessing, mercy, life and peace. May it please thee to bless thy people Israel with peace at all times and hours. Blessed art thou, O Lord, who blessest thy people Israel with peace.

For Minḥah and Maʻariv:

O grant abundant peace to Israel thy people forever, for thou art the King and Lord of all peace. May it please thee to bless thy people Israel with peace at all times and at all hours. Blessed art thou, O Lord, who blessest thy people Israel with peace.

After the Amidah add the following meditation:

My God, guard my tongue from evil, and my lips from speaking falsehood. May my soul be silent to those who insult me; be my soul lowly to all as the dust. Open my heart to thy Torah, that my soul may follow thy commands. Speedily defeat the counsel of all those who plan evil against me, and upset their design. Do it for the glory of thy name; do it for the sake of thy power; do it for the sake of thy holiness; do it for the sake of thy Torah. That thy beloved may be rescued, save with thy right hand

יְדִידֶיךָ, הוֹשִׁיעָה יְמִינְךָ וַעֲנֵנִי. יִהְיוּ לְרָצוֹן אִמְרֵי פִי וְהֶגְיוֹן לִבִּי
לְפָנֶיךָ, יְיָ, צוּרִי וְגוֹאֲלִי. עֹשֶׂה שָׁלוֹם בִּמְרוֹמָיו, הוּא יַעֲשֶׂה
שָׁלוֹם עָלֵינוּ וְעַל כָּל יִשְׂרָאֵל, וְאִמְרוּ אָמֵן.

יְהִי רָצוֹן מִלְּפָנֶיךָ, יְיָ אֱלֹהֵינוּ וֵאלֹהֵי אֲבוֹתֵינוּ, שֶׁיִּבָּנֶה בֵּית
הַמִּקְדָּשׁ בִּמְהֵרָה בְיָמֵינוּ, וְתֵן חֶלְקֵנוּ בְּתוֹרָתֶךָ. וְשָׁם נַעֲבָדְךָ
בְּיִרְאָה, כִּימֵי עוֹלָם וּכְשָׁנִים קַדְמוֹנִיּוֹת. וְעָרְבָה לַיְיָ מִנְחַת
יְהוּדָה וִירוּשָׁלָיִם, כִּימֵי עוֹלָם וּכְשָׁנִים קַדְמוֹנִיּוֹת.

קִדּוּשׁ לְשָׁלשׁ רְגָלִים

On Sabbath Eve:

(וַיְהִי עֶרֶב וַיְהִי בֹקֶר

יוֹם הַשִּׁשִּׁי. וַיְכֻלּוּ הַשָּׁמַיִם וְהָאָרֶץ וְכָל צְבָאָם. וַיְכַל אֱלֹהִים
בַּיּוֹם הַשְּׁבִיעִי מְלַאכְתּוֹ אֲשֶׁר עָשָׂה, וַיִּשְׁבֹּת בַּיּוֹם הַשְּׁבִיעִי מִכָּל
מְלַאכְתּוֹ אֲשֶׁר עָשָׂה. וַיְבָרֶךְ אֱלֹהִים אֶת יוֹם הַשְּׁבִיעִי וַיְקַדֵּשׁ
אֹתוֹ, כִּי בוֹ שָׁבַת מִכָּל מְלַאכְתּוֹ אֲשֶׁר בָּרָא אֱלֹהִים לַעֲשׂוֹת.)

סַבְרִי מָרָנָן וְרַבּוֹתַי.

בָּרוּךְ אַתָּה, יְיָ אֱלֹהֵינוּ, מֶלֶךְ הָעוֹלָם, בּוֹרֵא פְּרִי הַגָּפֶן.

בָּרוּךְ אַתָּה, יְיָ אֱלֹהֵינוּ, מֶלֶךְ הָעוֹלָם, אֲשֶׁר בָּחַר בָּנוּ מִכָּל
עָם, וְרוֹמְמָנוּ מִכָּל לָשׁוֹן, וְקִדְּשָׁנוּ בְּמִצְוֹתָיו. וַתִּתֶּן־לָנוּ, יְיָ
אֱלֹהֵינוּ, בְּאַהֲבָה (שַׁבָּתוֹת לִמְנוּחָה וּ)מוֹעֲדִים לְשִׂמְחָה, חַגִּים
וּזְמַנִּים לְשָׂשׂוֹן, אֶת יוֹם (הַשַּׁבָּת הַזֶּה, וְאֶת יוֹם)

סברי מרנן is used here in the sense of "Gentlemen, attention!" It is intended to call attention to the blessing which is about to be pronounced over

and answer me. May the words of my mouth and the meditation of my heart be pleasing before thee, O Lord, my Stronghold and my Redeemer. May he who creates peace in his high heavens create peace for us and for all Israel. Amen.

May it be thy will, Lord our God and God of our fathers, that the Temple be speedily rebuilt in our days, and grant us a share in thy Torah. There we will serve thee with reverence, as in the days of old and as in former years. Then the offering of Judah and Jerusalem will be pleasing to the Lord, as in the days of old and as in former years.

KIDDUSH FOR FESTIVALS

On Sabbath Eve:

(There was evening and there was morning—

The sixth day. Thus the heavens and the earth were finished, and all their host. By the seventh day God had completed his work which he had made, and he rested on the seventh day from all his work in which he had been engaged. Then God blessed the seventh day and hallowed it, because on it he rested from all his work which he had created.)

Blessed art thou, Lord our God, King of the universe, who createst the fruit of the vine.

Blessed art thou, Lord our God, King of the universe, who hast chosen and exalted us above all nations, and hast sanctified us with thy commandments. Thou, Lord our God, hast graciously given us (Sabbaths for rest,) holidays for gladness and festive seasons for joy: (this Sabbath day and) this

---

the wine, so that those present may answer Amen. According to a midrashic source (Tanḥuma, *Pekudé*), this phrase was originally used in the form of a question, namely: "Gentlemen, what is your opinion?" Is it safe to drink of this wine? The response was לחיים!

Shemini Atsereth and Simhath Torah	*Sukkoth*	*Shavuoth*	*Pesaḥ*
הַשְּׁמִינִי, חַג	חַג הַסֻּכּוֹת	חַג הַשָּׁבֻעוֹת	חַג הַמַצוֹת
הָעֲצֶרֶת הַזֶּה,	הַזֶּה, זְמַן	הַזֶּה, זְמַן	הַזֶּה, זְמַן
זְמַן שִׂמְחָתֵנוּ,	שִׂמְחָתֵנוּ,	מַתַּן תּוֹרָתֵנוּ,	חֵרוּתֵנוּ,

(בְּאַהֲבָה) מִקְרָא קֹדֶשׁ, זֵכֶר לִיצִיאַת מִצְרָיִם. כִּי בָנוּ בָחַרְתָּ,
וְאוֹתָנוּ קִדַּשְׁתָּ מִכָּל הָעַמִּים, (וְשַׁבָּת) וּמוֹעֲדֵי קָדְשֶׁךָ (בְּאַהֲבָה
וּבְרָצוֹן) בְּשִׂמְחָה וּבְשָׂשׂוֹן הִנְחַלְתָּנוּ. בָּרוּךְ אַתָּה, יְיָ, מְקַדֵּשׁ
(הַשַּׁבָּת וְ)יִשְׂרָאֵל וְהַזְּמַנִּים.

On Saturday night add:

בָּרוּךְ אַתָּה, יְיָ אֱלֹהֵינוּ, מֶלֶךְ הָעוֹלָם, בּוֹרֵא מְאוֹרֵי הָאֵשׁ.
בָּרוּךְ אַתָּה, יְיָ אֱלֹהֵינוּ, מֶלֶךְ הָעוֹלָם, הַמַּבְדִּיל בֵּין קֹדֶשׁ
לְחֹל, בֵּין אוֹר לְחֹשֶׁךְ, בֵּין יִשְׂרָאֵל לָעַמִּים, בֵּין יוֹם הַשְּׁבִיעִי
לְשֵׁשֶׁת יְמֵי הַמַּעֲשֶׂה. בֵּין קְדֻשַּׁת שַׁבָּת לִקְדֻשַּׁת יוֹם טוֹב
הִבְדַּלְתָּ, וְאֶת יוֹם הַשְּׁבִיעִי מִשֵּׁשֶׁת יְמֵי הַמַּעֲשֶׂה קִדַּשְׁתָּ; הִבְדַּלְתָּ
וְקִדַּשְׁתָּ אֶת עַמְּךָ יִשְׂרָאֵל בִּקְדֻשָּׁתֶךָ. בָּרוּךְ אַתָּה, יְיָ, הַמַּבְדִּיל
בֵּין קֹדֶשׁ לְקֹדֶשׁ.

On the last two nights of *Pesaḥ* omit:

בָּרוּךְ אַתָּה, יְיָ אֱלֹהֵינוּ, מֶלֶךְ הָעוֹלָם, שֶׁהֶחֱיָנוּ וְקִיְּמָנוּ
וְהִגִּיעָנוּ לַזְּמַן הַזֶּה.

In the *Sukkah:*

בָּרוּךְ אַתָּה, יְיָ אֱלֹהֵינוּ, מֶלֶךְ הָעוֹלָם, אֲשֶׁר קִדְּשָׁנוּ בְּמִצְוֹתָיו
וְצִוָּנוּ לֵישֵׁב בַּסֻּכָּה.

זכר ליציאת מצרים refers to *Pesaḥ*, *Shavuoth* and *Sukkoth*, directly connected
with the exodus from Egypt. The same phrase is elsewhere applied to the
Sabbath on the basis of Deuteronomy 5:15 ("Remember that you were once
a slave in the land of Egypt, and that the Lord your God brought you out
from there by a mighty hand and an outstretched arm; hence the Lord your
God has commanded you to observe the Sabbath day").

Pesaḥ

Feast of Unleavened Bread, our Festival of Freedom,

Shavuoth

Feast of Weeks, our Festival of the Giving of the Torah,

Sukkoth

Feast of Tabernacles, our Festival of Rejoicing,

Shemini Atsereth and Simḥath Torah

Eighth Day Feast, our Festival of Rejoicing,
a holy convocation in remembrance of the exodus from Egypt.
Thou didst choose and sanctify us above all peoples; in thy
gracious love, thou didst grant us thy holy (Sabbath and) festivals
for gladness and joy. Blessed art thou, O Lord, who hallowest (the
Sabbath,) Israel and the festivals.

On Saturday night add:

Blessed art thou, Lord our God, King of the universe, who
createst the light of the fire.

Blessed art thou, Lord our God, King of the universe, who
hast made a distinction between the sacred and the profane,
between light and darkness, between Israel and the nations,
between the seventh day and the six working days. Thou hast
made a distinction between the holiness of the Sabbath and the holiness of the festival, and hast hallowed the seventh day above the
six working days; thou hast distinguished and sanctified thy people
Israel with thy holiness. Blessed art thou, O Lord, who makest
a distinction between the greater holiness and the lesser holiness.

On the last two nights of Pesaḥ omit:

Blessed art thou, Lord our God, King of the universe, who
hast granted us life and sustenance and permitted us to reach this
season.   *In the Sukkah:*

Blessed art thou, Lord our God, King of the universe, who
hast sanctified us with thy commandments, and commanded us
to dwell in booths.

הַזְכָּרַת נְשָׁמוֹת

Conducted on *Yom Kippur* and *Shemini Atsereth*, on the last day of *Pesaḥ* and the second day of *Shavuoth*

Responsively

יְיָ, מָה אָדָם וַתֵּדָעֵהוּ, בֶּן־אֱנוֹשׁ וַתְּחַשְּׁבֵהוּ׃
אָדָם לַהֶבֶל דָּמָה, יָמָיו כְּצֵל עוֹבֵר׃
בַּבְּקֶר יָצִיץ וְחָלָף, לָעֶרֶב יְמוֹלֵל וְיָבֵשׁ׃
לִמְנוֹת יָמֵינוּ כֵּן הוֹדַע, וְנָבִא לְבַב חָכְמָה׃
שְׁמָר־תָּם וּרְאֵה יָשָׁר, כִּי אַחֲרִית לְאִישׁ שָׁלוֹם׃
אַךְ אֱלֹהִים יִפְדֶּה נַפְשִׁי מִיַּד שְׁאוֹל, כִּי יִקָּחֵנִי סֶלָה׃
כָּלָה שְׁאֵרִי וּלְבָבִי, צוּר לְבָבִי וְחֶלְקִי אֱלֹהִים לְעוֹלָם׃
וְיָשֹׁב הֶעָפָר עַל הָאָרֶץ כְּשֶׁהָיָה, וְהָרוּחַ תָּשׁוּב אֶל
הָאֱלֹהִים אֲשֶׁר נְתָנָהּ׃

תהלים צא

יֹשֵׁב בְּסֵתֶר עֶלְיוֹן, בְּצֵל שַׁדַּי יִתְלוֹנָן׃
אֹמַר לַיְיָ, מַחְסִי וּמְצוּדָתִי, אֱלֹהַי אֶבְטַח בּוֹ׃
כִּי הוּא יַצִּילְךָ מִפַּח יָקוּשׁ, מִדֶּבֶר הַוּוֹת׃
בְּאֶבְרָתוֹ יָסֶךְ לָךְ, וְתַחַת כְּנָפָיו תֶּחְסֶה; צִנָּה וְסֹחֵרָה אֲמִתּוֹ׃
לֹא תִירָא מִפַּחַד לָיְלָה, מֵחֵץ יָעוּף יוֹמָם׃
מִדֶּבֶר בָּאֹפֶל יַהֲלֹךְ, מִקֶּטֶב יָשׁוּד צָהֳרָיִם׃

הזכרת נשמות is an ancient custom mentioned in Midrash Tanḥuma (section *Ha'azinu*) and in Maḥzor Vitry, page 173.

Until the eighteenth century it was confined to *Yom Kippur*, since the Torah reading for the day begins with the words אחרי מות ("after the death"). In order not to disturb the participants in the memorial service, it is customary to send out those whose parents are still alive.

601

MEMORIAL SERVICE

*Conducted on Yom Kippur and Shemini Atsereth, on the last day of Pesah
and the second day of Shavuoth*

Responsively

O Lord, what is man that thou shouldst notice him?
What is mortal man that thou shouldst consider him?
Man is like a breath;
His days are like a passing shadow.

He flourishes and grows in the morning;
He fades and withers in the evening.

O teach us how to number our days,
That we may attain a heart of wisdom.

Mark the innocent, look upon the upright;
For there is a future for the man of peace.

Surely God will free me from the grave;
He will receive me indeed.

My flesh and my heart fail,
Yet God is my strength forever.

The dust returns to the earth as it was,
But the spirit returns to God who gave it.[1]

Psalm 91

He who dwells in the shelter of the Most High
Abides under the protection of the Almighty.
I call the Lord: "My refuge and my fortress,
My God in whom I trust."
He saves you from the fowler's snare
And from the destructive pestilence.

With his pinions he covers you,
And under his wings you find refuge;
His truth is a shield and armor.

Fear not the terror of the night,
Nor the arrow that flies by day.

Nor the pestilence that stalks in darkness,
Nor the destruction that ravages at noon.

---

[1] *Psalms* 144:3-4; 90:6,12; 37:37; 49:16; 73:26; *Ecclesiastes* 12:7.

יִפֹּל מִצִּדְּךָ אֶלֶף, וּרְבָבָה מִימִינֶךָ; אֵלֶיךָ לֹא יִגָּשׁ.

רַק בְּעֵינֶיךָ תַבִּיט, וְשִׁלֻּמַת רְשָׁעִים תִּרְאֶה.

כִּי אַתָּה, יְיָ, מַחְסִי; עֶלְיוֹן שַׂמְתָּ מְעוֹנֶךָ.

לֹא תְאֻנֶּה אֵלֶיךָ רָעָה, וְנֶגַע לֹא יִקְרַב בְּאָהֳלֶךָ.

כִּי מַלְאָכָיו יְצַוֶּה לָּךְ, לִשְׁמָרְךָ בְּכָל דְּרָכֶיךָ.

עַל כַּפַּיִם יִשָּׂאוּנְךָ, פֶּן תִּגֹּף בָּאֶבֶן רַגְלֶךָ.

עַל שַׁחַל וָפֶתֶן תִּדְרֹךְ, תִּרְמֹס כְּפִיר וְתַנִּין.

כִּי בִי חָשַׁק וַאֲפַלְּטֵהוּ; אֲשַׂגְּבֵהוּ כִּי יָדַע שְׁמִי.

יִקְרָאֵנִי וְאֶעֱנֵהוּ, עִמּוֹ אָנֹכִי בְצָרָה, אֲחַלְּצֵהוּ וַאֲכַבְּדֵהוּ.

אֹרֶךְ יָמִים אַשְׂבִּיעֵהוּ, וְאַרְאֵהוּ בִּישׁוּעָתִי.

In memory of a father:

יִזְכּוֹר אֱלֹהִים נִשְׁמַת אָבִי מוֹרִי . . .* שֶׁהָלַךְ לְעוֹלָמוֹ. בַּעֲבוּר

שֶׁאֲנִי נוֹדֵר צְדָקָה בַּעֲדוֹ, בִּשְׂכַר זֶה, תְּהֵא נַפְשׁוֹ צְרוּרָה

בִּצְרוֹר הַחַיִּים עִם נִשְׁמוֹת אַבְרָהָם יִצְחָק וְיַעֲקֹב, שָׂרָה

רִבְקָה רָחֵל וְלֵאָה, וְעִם שְׁאָר צַדִּיקִים וְצִדְקָנִיּוֹת שֶׁבְּגַן עֵדֶן.

אָמֵן.

In memory of a mother:

יִזְכּוֹר אֱלֹהִים נִשְׁמַת אִמִּי מוֹרָתִי . . .* שֶׁהָלְכָה לְעוֹלָמָהּ.

בַּעֲבוּר שֶׁאֲנִי נוֹדֵר צְדָקָה בַּעֲדָהּ, בִּשְׂכַר זֶה, תְּהֵא נַפְשָׁהּ

צְרוּרָה בִּצְרוֹר הַחַיִּים עִם נִשְׁמוֹת אַבְרָהָם יִצְחָק וְיַעֲקֹב,

שָׂרָה רִבְקָה רָחֵל וְלֵאָה, וְעִם שְׁאָר צַדִּיקִים וְצִדְקָנִיּוֹת שֶׁבְּגַן

עֵדֶן. אָמֵן.

* The name of the deceased is supplied.

Though a thousand fall at your side,
And a myriad at your right hand,
It shall not come to you.
You have only to look with your eyes
And see how evil men are punished.
Thou, O Lord, art my refuge!
When you have made the Most High your shelter,
No disaster shall befall you or come near your tent.
For he will give his angels charge over you,
To guard you in all your ways.
They will bear you upon their hands,
Lest you strike your foot against a stone.
You shall tread upon the lion and the asp;
You shall trample the young lion and the serpent.
"Because he clings to me, I deliver him;
I protect him because he loves me.
When he calls upon me, I answer him;
I am with him when he is in trouble;
I rescue him and bring him to honor.
I enrich him with a long life,
And I let him witness my deliverance."

In memory of a father:

May God remember the soul of my respected father . . .* who has passed to his eternal rest. I pledge charity in his behalf and pray that his soul be kept among the immortal souls of Abraham, Isaac, Jacob, Sarah, Rebekah, Rachel, Leah, and all the righteous men and women in paradise. Amen.

In memory of a mother:

May God remember the soul of my respected mother . . .* who has passed to her eternal rest. I pledge charity in her behalf and pray that her soul be kept among the immortal souls of Abraham, Isaac, Jacob, Sarah, Rebekah, Rachel, Leah, and all the righteous men and women in paradise. Amen.

*The name of the deceased is supplied.

In memory of a husband:

יִזְכּוֹר אֱלֹהִים נִשְׁמַת בַּעֲלִי הַיָּקָר . . . * שֶׁהָלַךְ לְעוֹלָמוֹ.
בַּעֲבוּר שֶׁאֲנִי נוֹדֶרֶת צְדָקָה בַּעֲדוֹ, בִּשְׂכַר זֶה, תְּהֵא נַפְשׁוֹ
צְרוּרָה בִּצְרוֹר הַחַיִּים עִם נִשְׁמוֹת אַבְרָהָם יִצְחָק וְיַעֲקֹב,
שָׂרָה רִבְקָה רָחֵל וְלֵאָה, וְעִם שְׁאָר צַדִּיקִים וְצִדְקָנִיּוֹת שֶׁבְּגַן
עֵדֶן. אָמֵן.

In memory of a wife:

יִזְכּוֹר אֱלֹהִים נִשְׁמַת אִשְׁתִּי הַיְקָרָה . . . * שֶׁהָלְכָה לְעוֹלָמָהּ.
בַּעֲבוּר שֶׁאֲנִי נוֹדֵר צְדָקָה בַּעֲדָהּ, בִּשְׂכַר זֶה, תְּהֵא נַפְשָׁהּ
צְרוּרָה בִּצְרוֹר הַחַיִּים עִם נִשְׁמוֹת אַבְרָהָם יִצְחָק וְיַעֲקֹב,
שָׂרָה רִבְקָה רָחֵל וְלֵאָה, וְעִם שְׁאָר צַדִּיקִים וְצִדְקָנִיּוֹת שֶׁבְּגַן
עֵדֶן. אָמֵן.

In memory of Jewish martyrs:

יִזְכּוֹר אֱלֹהִים נִשְׁמוֹת הַקְּדוֹשִׁים וְהַטְּהוֹרִים שֶׁנֶּהֶרְגוּ,
שֶׁנִּשְׁחֲטוּ וְשֶׁנִּשְׂרְפוּ, וְשֶׁנִּטְבְּעוּ וְשֶׁנֶּחְנְקוּ עַל קִדּוּשׁ הַשֵּׁם. בַּעֲבוּר
שֶׁנּוֹדְרִים צְדָקָה בְּעַד הַזְכָּרַת נִשְׁמוֹתֵיהֶם, בִּשְׂכַר זֶה, תִּהְיֶינָה
נַפְשׁוֹתֵיהֶם צְרוּרוֹת בִּצְרוֹר הַחַיִּים עִם נִשְׁמוֹת אַבְרָהָם יִצְחָק
וְיַעֲקֹב, שָׂרָה רִבְקָה רָחֵל וְלֵאָה, וְעִם שְׁאָר צַדִּיקִים
וְצִדְקָנִיּוֹת שֶׁבְּגַן עֵדֶן, וְנֹאמַר אָמֵן.

For a man:

אֵל מָלֵא רַחֲמִים, שׁוֹכֵן בַּמְּרוֹמִים, הַמְצֵא מְנוּחָה נְכוֹנָה
תַּחַת כַּנְפֵי הַשְּׁכִינָה, בְּמַעֲלוֹת קְדוֹשִׁים וּטְהוֹרִים כְּזֹהַר הָרָקִיעַ
מַזְהִירִים, אֶת נִשְׁמַת . . . * שֶׁהָלַךְ לְעוֹלָמוֹ. בַּעֲבוּר שֶׁנָּדְרוּ
צְדָקָה בְּעַד הַזְכָּרַת נִשְׁמָתוֹ, בְּגַן עֵדֶן תְּהֵא מְנוּחָתוֹ. לָכֵן בַּעַל
הָרַחֲמִים יַסְתִּירֵהוּ בְּסֵתֶר כְּנָפָיו לְעוֹלָמִים, וְיִצְרוֹר בִּצְרוֹר
הַחַיִּים אֶת נִשְׁמָתוֹ. יְיָ הוּא נַחֲלָתוֹ; וְיָנוּחַ עַל מִשְׁכָּבוֹ בְּשָׁלוֹם,
וְנֹאמַר אָמֵן.

* The name of the deceased is supplied.

In memory of a husband:

May God remember the soul of my beloved husband . . .* who has passed to his eternal rest. I pledge charity in his behalf and pray that his soul be kept among the immortal souls of Abraham, Isaac, Jacob, Sarah, Rebekah, Rachel, Leah, and all the righteous men and women in paradise. Amen.

In memory of a wife:

May God remember the soul of my beloved wife . . .* who has passed to her eternal rest. I pledge charity in her behalf and pray that her soul be kept among the immortal souls of Abraham, Isaac, Jacob, Sarah, Rebekah, Rachel, Leah, and all the righteous men and women in paradise. Amen.

In memory of Jewish martyrs:

May God remember the souls of the saintly martyrs who have been slaughtered, burned, drowned or strangled for their loyalty to God. We pledge charity in their memory and pray that their souls be kept among the immortal souls of Abraham, Isaac, Jacob, Sarah, Rebekah, Rachel, Leah, and all the righteous men and women in paradise; and let us say, Amen.

For a man:

Merciful God in heaven, grant perfect repose to the soul of . . . * who has passed to his eternal habitation; may he be under thy divine wings among the holy and pure who shine bright as the sky; may his place of rest be in paradise. Merciful One, O keep his soul forever alive under thy protective wings. The Lord being his heritage, may he rest in peace; and let us say, Amen.

* *The name of the deceased is supplied.*

אל מלא רחמים, the most soulful of the memorial prayers, is recited aloud.

בעד הזכרת נשמתו actually bears the same meaning as the word בעדו used in the preceding paragraphs. It seems that the phrase הזכרת נשמתו was originally intended as a direction to the effect that the name of the deceased must be mentioned after the word נשמת.

For a woman:

אֵל מָלֵא רַחֲמִים, שׁוֹכֵן בַּמְּרוֹמִים, הַמְצֵא מְנוּחָה נְכוֹנָה
תַּחַת כַּנְפֵי הַשְּׁכִינָה, בְּמַעֲלוֹת קְדוֹשִׁים וּטְהוֹרִים כְּזְהַר הָרָקִיעַ
מַזְהִירִים, אֶת נִשְׁמַת . . .* שֶׁהָלְכָה לְעוֹלָמָהּ. בַּעֲבוּר שֶׁנָּדְרוּ
צְדָקָה בְּעַד הַזְכָּרַת נִשְׁמָתָהּ, בְּגַן עֵדֶן תְּהֵא מְנוּחָתָהּ. לָכֵן בַּעַל
הָרַחֲמִים יַסְתִּירֶהָ בְּסֵתֶר כְּנָפָיו לְעוֹלָמִים, וְיִצְרוֹר בִּצְרוֹר
הַחַיִּים אֶת נִשְׁמָתָהּ. יְיָ הוּא נַחֲלָתָהּ; וְתָנוּחַ עַל מִשְׁכָּבָהּ בְּשָׁלוֹם,
וְנֹאמַר אָמֵן.

Congregation:

אַב הָרַחֲמִים, שׁוֹכֵן מְרוֹמִים, בְּרַחֲמָיו הָעֲצוּמִים, הוּא
יִפְקֹד בְּרַחֲמִים הַחֲסִידִים וְהַיְשָׁרִים וְהַתְּמִימִים, קְהִלּוֹת הַקֹּדֶשׁ
שֶׁמָּסְרוּ נַפְשָׁם עַל קְדֻשַּׁת הַשֵּׁם, הַנֶּאֱהָבִים וְהַנְּעִימִים בְּחַיֵּיהֶם,
וּבְמוֹתָם לֹא נִפְרָדוּ. מִנְּשָׁרִים קַלּוּ, וּמֵאֲרָיוֹת גָּבֵרוּ, לַעֲשׂוֹת
רְצוֹן קוֹנָם וְחֵפֶץ צוּרָם. יִזְכְּרֵם אֱלֹהֵינוּ לְטוֹבָה עִם שְׁאָר
צַדִּיקֵי עוֹלָם, וְיִנְקֹם נִקְמַת דַּם עֲבָדָיו הַשָּׁפוּךְ, כַּכָּתוּב בְּתוֹרַת
מֹשֶׁה אִישׁ הָאֱלֹהִים: הַרְנִינוּ, גוֹיִם, עַמּוֹ, כִּי דַם עֲבָדָיו יִקּוֹם,
וְנָקָם יָשִׁיב לְצָרָיו, וְכִפֶּר אַדְמָתוֹ עַמּוֹ. וְעַל יְדֵי עֲבָדֶיךָ
הַנְּבִיאִים כָּתוּב לֵאמֹר: וְנִקֵּיתִי דָמָם, לֹא נִקֵּיתִי, וַיְיָ שֹׁכֵן בְּצִיּוֹן.
וּבְכִתְבֵי הַקֹּדֶשׁ נֶאֱמַר: לָמָּה יֹאמְרוּ הַגּוֹיִם אַיֵּה אֱלֹהֵיהֶם, יִוָּדַע
בַּגּוֹיִם לְעֵינֵינוּ נִקְמַת דַּם עֲבָדֶיךָ הַשָּׁפוּךְ. Reader וְאוֹמֵר: כִּי
דֹרֵשׁ דָּמִים אוֹתָם זָכָר, לֹא שָׁכַח צַעֲקַת עֲנָוִים. וְאוֹמֵר: יָדִין
בַּגּוֹיִם, מָלֵא גְוִיּוֹת, מָחַץ רֹאשׁ עַל אֶרֶץ רַבָּה, מִנַּחַל בַּדֶּרֶךְ
יִשְׁתֶּה, עַל כֵּן יָרִים רֹאשׁ.

* The name of the deceased is supplied.

מנחל בדרך ישתה describes the victor in hot pursuit of the enemy. Wearied

For a woman:

Merciful God in heaven, grant perfect repose to the soul of . . . *
who has passed to her eternal habitation; may she be under thy
divine wings among the holy and pure who shine bright as the sky;
may her place of rest be in paradise. Merciful One, O keep her soul
forever alive under thy protective wings. The Lord being her heritage, may she rest in peace; and let us say, Amen.

Congregation:

May the merciful Father who dwells on high, in his infinite
mercy, remember those saintly, upright and blameless souls, the
holy communities who offered their lives for the sanctification of
the divine name. They were lovely and amiable in their life, and
were not parted in their death. They were swifter than eagles and
stronger than lions to do the will of their Master and the desire
of their Stronghold. May our God remember them favorably
among the other righteous of the world; may he avenge the blood
of his servants which has been shed, as it is written in the Torah
of Moses, the man of God: "O nations, make his people joyful!
He avenges the blood of his servants, renders retribution to his foes,
and provides atonement for his land and his people."[1] And by thy
servants, the prophets, it is written: "I will avenge their blood
which I have not yet avenged; the Lord dwells in Zion."[2] And in
the holy writings it is said: "Why should the nations say, 'Where
then is their God?' Let the vengeance for thy servants' blood that
is shed be made known among the nations in our sight." And it is
said: "The avenger of bloodshed remembers them; he does not
forget the cry of the humble." And it is further said: "He will
execute judgment upon the nations and fill [the battle-field] with
corpses; he will shatter the [enemy's] head over all the wide earth.
From the brook by the wayside he will drink; then he will lift up
his head triumphantly."[3]

* *The name of the deceased is supplied.*

from the toil of battle, he halts for a moment to drink from the brook which
he crosses. Refreshed, he presses forward to complete his victory.

[1] *Deuteronomy* 32:43. [2] *Joel* 4:21. [3] *Psalms* 79:10; 9:13; 110:6–7.

מוּסָף לְשָׁלֹשׁ רְגָלִים

The *Amidah* is recited in silent devotion while standing, facing east.

כִּי שֵׁם יְיָ אֶקְרָא, הָבוּ גֹדֶל לֵאלֹהֵינוּ.

אֲדֹנָי, שְׂפָתַי תִּפְתָּח, וּפִי יַגִּיד תְּהִלָּתֶךָ.

בָּרוּךְ אַתָּה, יְיָ אֱלֹהֵינוּ וֵאלֹהֵי אֲבוֹתֵינוּ, אֱלֹהֵי אַבְרָהָם,
אֱלֹהֵי יִצְחָק, וֵאלֹהֵי יַעֲקֹב, הָאֵל הַגָּדוֹל הַגִּבּוֹר וְהַנּוֹרָא, אֵל
עֶלְיוֹן, גּוֹמֵל חֲסָדִים טוֹבִים, וְקוֹנֵה הַכֹּל, וְזוֹכֵר חַסְדֵי אָבוֹת,
וּמֵבִיא גוֹאֵל לִבְנֵי בְנֵיהֶם לְמַעַן שְׁמוֹ בְּאַהֲבָה.

מֶלֶךְ עוֹזֵר וּמוֹשִׁיעַ וּמָגֵן. בָּרוּךְ אַתָּה, יְיָ, מָגֵן אַבְרָהָם.

אַתָּה גִבּוֹר לְעוֹלָם, אֲדֹנָי; מְחַיֵּה מֵתִים אַתָּה, רַב לְהוֹשִׁיעַ.

On *Shemini Atsereth* and *Simḥath Torah* add:

(מַשִּׁיב הָרוּחַ וּמוֹרִיד הַגָּשֶׁם.)

מְכַלְכֵּל חַיִּים בְּחֶסֶד, מְחַיֵּה מֵתִים בְּרַחֲמִים רַבִּים, סוֹמֵךְ
נוֹפְלִים, וְרוֹפֵא חוֹלִים, וּמַתִּיר אֲסוּרִים, וּמְקַיֵּם אֱמוּנָתוֹ לִישֵׁנֵי
עָפָר. מִי כָמוֹךָ, בַּעַל גְּבוּרוֹת, וּמִי דוֹמֶה לָּךְ, מֶלֶךְ מֵמִית
וּמְחַיֶּה וּמַצְמִיחַ יְשׁוּעָה.

וְנֶאֱמָן אַתָּה לְהַחֲיוֹת מֵתִים. בָּרוּךְ אַתָּה, יְיָ, מְחַיֵּה הַמֵּתִים.

KEDUSHAH FOR MAJOR FESTIVALS

נַעֲרִיצְךָ וְנַקְדִּישְׁךָ כְּסוֹד שִׂיחַ שַׂרְפֵי קֹדֶשׁ, הַמַּקְדִּישִׁים שִׁמְךָ
בַּקֹּדֶשׁ, כַּכָּתוּב עַל יַד נְבִיאֶךָ: וְקָרָא זֶה אֶל זֶה וְאָמַר:

מוּסָף לְשָׁלֹשׁ רְגָלִים corresponds to the additional sacrifices offered in the
Temple during the three pilgrim festivals, prescribed in Numbers 28:16-31;
29:12-39.

MUSAF FOR FESTIVALS

The Amidah is recited in silent devotion while standing, facing east.

When I proclaim the name of the Lord, give glory to our God![1]

O Lord, open thou my lips, that my mouth may declare thy praise.[2]

Blessed art thou, Lord our God and God of our fathers, God of Abraham, God of Isaac and God of Jacob; great, mighty and revered God, sublime God, who bestowest lovingkindness, and art Master of all things; who rememberest the good deeds of our fathers, and who wilt graciously bring a redeemer to their children's children for the sake of thy name.

O King, Supporter, Savior and Shield! Blessed art thou, O Lord, Shield of Abraham.

Thou, O Lord, art mighty forever; thou revivest the dead; thou art powerful to save.

On Shemini Atsereth and Simḥath Torah add:

(Thou causest the wind to blow and the rain to fall.)

Thou sustainest the living with kindness, and revivest the dead with great mercy; thou supportest all who fall, and healest the sick; thou settest the captives free, and keepest faith with those who sleep in the dust. Who is like thee, Lord of power? Who resembles thee, O King? Thou bringest death and restorest life, and causest salvation to flourish.

Thou art faithful to revive the dead. Blessed art thou, O Lord, who revivest the dead.

KEDUSHAH FOR MAJOR FESTIVALS

We revere and sanctify thee in the words of the assembly of holy seraphim who hallow thy name in the sanctuary, as it is written by thy prophet: "They keep calling to one another:

כי שם precedes the *Amidahs* of *Musaf* and *Minḥah* only. In *Shaḥarith* and *Ma'ariv* this verse is omitted, because there it would interrupt the connection between the benediction גאל ישראל and the *Amidah*.

---

[1] *Deuteronomy* 32:3.   [2] *Psalm* 51:17.

קָדוֹשׁ, קָדוֹשׁ, קָדוֹשׁ יְיָ צְבָאוֹת;
מְלֹא כָל הָאָרֶץ כְּבוֹדוֹ.

כְּבוֹדוֹ מָלֵא עוֹלָם, מְשָׁרְתָיו שׁוֹאֲלִים זֶה לָזֶה אַיֵּה מְקוֹם
כְּבוֹדוֹ, לְעֻמָּתָם בָּרוּךְ יֹאמֵרוּ־

בָּרוּךְ כְּבוֹד יְיָ מִמְּקוֹמוֹ.

מִמְּקוֹמוֹ הוּא יִפֶן בְּרַחֲמִים, וְיָחֹן עַם הַמְיַחֲדִים שְׁמוֹ עֶרֶב
וָבֹקֶר, בְּכָל יוֹם תָּמִיד, פַּעֲמַיִם בְּאַהֲבָה שְׁמַע אוֹמְרִים:

שְׁמַע יִשְׂרָאֵל, יְיָ אֱלֹהֵינוּ, יְיָ אֶחָד.

הוּא אֱלֹהֵינוּ, הוּא אָבִינוּ, הוּא מַלְכֵּנוּ, הוּא מוֹשִׁיעֵנוּ, וְהוּא
יַשְׁמִיעֵנוּ בְּרַחֲמָיו שֵׁנִית לְעֵינֵי כָּל חָי: לִהְיוֹת לָכֶם לֵאלֹהִים־
אֲנִי יְיָ אֱלֹהֵיכֶם.

Reader:

אַדִּיר אַדִּירֵנוּ, יְיָ אֲדֹנֵינוּ, מָה אַדִּיר שִׁמְךָ בְּכָל הָאָרֶץ.
וְהָיָה יְיָ לְמֶלֶךְ עַל כָּל הָאָרֶץ, בַּיּוֹם הַהוּא יִהְיֶה יְיָ אֶחָד וּשְׁמוֹ
אֶחָד.

וּבְדִבְרֵי קָדְשְׁךָ כָּתוּב לֵאמֹר:

יִמְלֹךְ יְיָ לְעוֹלָם, אֱלֹהַיִךְ צִיּוֹן לְדֹר וָדֹר; הַלְלוּיָהּ.

KEDUSHAH FOR ḤOL HA-MOʻED

נְקַדֵּשׁ אֶת שִׁמְךָ בָּעוֹלָם כְּשֵׁם שֶׁמַּקְדִּישִׁים אוֹתוֹ בִּשְׁמֵי מָרוֹם,
כַּכָּתוּב עַל יַד נְבִיאֶךָ: וְקָרָא זֶה אֶל זֶה וְאָמַר:

קָדוֹשׁ, קָדוֹשׁ, קָדוֹשׁ יְיָ צְבָאוֹת; מְלֹא כָל הָאָרֶץ כְּבוֹדוֹ.
לְעֻמָּתָם בָּרוּךְ יֹאמֵרוּ־

שמע ישראל and the concluding words of the *Shema* were inserted here in the
fifth century, when special government officials were posted in the synagogues
to prevent the congregational proclamation of God's Oneness. Toward the end
of the service, when the spies had left, the *Shema* was thus recited in an
abridged form.

Holy, holy, holy is the Lord of hosts;
The whole earth is full of his glory."[1]

His glory fills the universe; his ministering angels ask one another: "Where is his glorious place?" They say to one another: "Blessed—

Blessed be the glory of the Lord from his abode."[2]

From his abode may he turn with compassion and be gracious to the people who acclaim his Oneness evening and morning, twice every day, and with tender affection recite the Shema—

"Hear, O Israel, the Lord is our God, the Lord is One."[3]

He is our God; he is our Father; he is our King; he is our Deliverer. He will again in his mercy proclaim to us in the presence of all the living:". . . to be your God—

I am the Lord your God."[4]

Reader:

Our God Almighty, our Lord Eternal, how glorious is thy name over all the world! The Lord shall be King over all the earth; on that day the Lord shall be One, and his name One.[5]

And in thy holy Scriptures it is written:
The Lord shall reign forever,
Your God, O Zion, for all generations.
Praise the Lord![6]

KEDUSHAH FOR ḤOL HA-MO'ED

We sanctify thy name in the world even as they sanctify it in the highest heavens, as it is written by thy prophet: "They keep calling to one another:

Holy, holy, holy is the Lord of hosts;
The whole earth is full of his glory."

Those opposite them say: Blessed—

---

[1] *Isaiah* 6:3. [2] *Ezekiel* 3:12. [3] *Deuteronomy* 6:4. [4] *Numbers* 15:41. [5] *Psalm* 8:10; *Zechariah* 14:9. [6] *Psalm* 146:10.

בָּרוּךְ כְּבוֹד יְיָ מִמְּקוֹמוֹ.

וּבְדִבְרֵי קָדְשְׁךָ כָּתוּב לֵאמֹר:

יִמְלֹךְ יְיָ לְעוֹלָם, אֱלֹהַיִךְ צִיּוֹן לְדֹר וָדֹר; הַלְלוּיָהּ.

Reader לְדוֹר וָדוֹר נַגִּיד גָּדְלֶךָ, וּלְנֵצַח נְצָחִים קְדֻשָּׁתְךָ נַקְדִּישׁ, וְשִׁבְחֲךָ אֱלֹהֵינוּ מִפִּינוּ לֹא יָמוּשׁ לְעוֹלָם וָעֶד, כִּי אֵל מֶלֶךְ גָּדוֹל וְקָדוֹשׁ אָתָּה. בָּרוּךְ אַתָּה, יְיָ, הָאֵל הַקָּדוֹשׁ.

אַתָּה קָדוֹשׁ וְשִׁמְךָ קָדוֹשׁ, וּקְדוֹשִׁים בְּכָל יוֹם יְהַלְלוּךָ סֶּלָה. בָּרוּךְ אַתָּה, יְיָ, הָאֵל הַקָּדוֹשׁ.

אַתָּה בְחַרְתָּנוּ מִכָּל הָעַמִּים, אָהַבְתָּ אוֹתָנוּ וְרָצִיתָ בָּנוּ, וְרוֹמַמְתָּנוּ מִכָּל הַלְּשׁוֹנוֹת, וְקִדַּשְׁתָּנוּ בְּמִצְוֹתֶיךָ, וְקֵרַבְתָּנוּ מַלְכֵּנוּ לַעֲבוֹדָתֶךָ, וְשִׁמְךָ הַגָּדוֹל וְהַקָּדוֹשׁ עָלֵינוּ קָרָאתָ.

וַתִּתֶּן לָנוּ, יְיָ אֱלֹהֵינוּ, בְּאַהֲבָה, (שַׁבָּתוֹת לִמְנוּחָה וּ)מוֹעֲדִים לְשִׂמְחָה, חַגִּים וּזְמַנִּים לְשָׂשׂוֹן, אֶת יוֹם (הַשַּׁבָּת הַזֶּה וְאֶת יוֹם)

Pesah	Shavuoth	Sukkoth	Shemini Atsereth and Simhath Torah
חַג הַמַּצּוֹת	חַג הַשָּׁבֻעוֹת	חַג הַסֻּכּוֹת	הַשְּׁמִינִי, חַג
הַזֶּה, זְמַן	הַזֶּה, זְמַן	הַזֶּה, זְמַן	הָעֲצֶרֶת הַזֶּה,
חֵרוּתֵנוּ,	מַתַּן תּוֹרָתֵנוּ,	שִׂמְחָתֵנוּ,	זְמַן שִׂמְחָתֵנוּ,

(בְּאַהֲבָה) מִקְרָא קֹדֶשׁ, זֵכֶר לִיצִיאַת מִצְרָיִם.

וּמִפְּנֵי חֲטָאֵינוּ גָּלִינוּ מֵאַרְצֵנוּ וְנִתְרַחַקְנוּ מֵעַל אַדְמָתֵנוּ, וְאֵין אֲנַחְנוּ יְכוֹלִים לַעֲלוֹת וְלֵרָאוֹת וּלְהִשְׁתַּחֲוֹת לְפָנֶיךָ, וְלַעֲשׂוֹת חוֹבוֹתֵינוּ בְּבֵית בְּחִירָתֶךָ, בַּבַּיִת הַגָּדוֹל וְהַקָּדוֹשׁ שֶׁנִּקְרָא שִׁמְךָ עָלָיו, מִפְּנֵי הַיָּד שֶׁנִּשְׁתַּלְּחָה בְּמִקְדָּשֶׁךָ. יְהִי רָצוֹן מִלְּפָנֶיךָ, יְיָ אֱלֹהֵינוּ וֵאלֹהֵי אֲבוֹתֵינוּ, מֶלֶךְ רַחֲמָן, שֶׁתָּשׁוּב וּתְרַחֵם עָלֵינוּ

Blessed be the glory of the Lord from his abode.
And in thy holy Scriptures it is written:
The Lord shall reign forever,
Your God, O Zion, for all generations.
Praise the Lord!

Reader:

Through all generations we will declare thy greatness; to all eternity we will proclaim thy holiness; thy praise, our God, shall never depart from our mouth, for thou art a great and holy God and King. Blessed art thou, O Lord, holy God.

Thou art holy and thy name is holy, and holy beings praise thee daily. Blessed art thou, O Lord, holy God.

Thou didst choose us from among all peoples; thou didst love and favor us; thou didst exalt us above all tongues and sanctify us with thy commandments. Thou, our King, didst draw us near to thy service and call us by thy great and holy name.

Thou, Lord our God, hast graciously given us (Sabbaths for rest,) holidays for gladness and festive seasons for joy: (this Sabbath day and) this

Pesaḥ

Feast of Unleavened Bread, our Festival of Freedom,

Shavuoth

Feast of Weeks, our Festival of the Giving of the Torah,

Sukkoth

Feast of Tabernacles, our Festival of Rejoicing,

Shemini Atsereth and Simḥath Torah

Eighth Day Feast, our Festival of Rejoicing,
a holy convocation in remembrance of the exodus from Egypt.

Because of our sins we were exiled from our country and banished far from our land. We cannot go up as pilgrims to worship thee, to perform our duties in thy chosen House, the great and holy Temple which was called by thy name, on account of the hand that was let loose on thy sanctuary. May it be thy will, Lord our God and God of our fathers, merciful King, in thy abundant love

וְעַל מִקְדָּשְׁךָ בְּרַחֲמֶיךָ הָרַבִּים, וְתִבְנֵהוּ מְהֵרָה וּתְגַדֵּל כְּבוֹדוֹ.
אָבִינוּ מַלְכֵּנוּ, גַּלֵּה כְּבוֹד מַלְכוּתְךָ עָלֵינוּ מְהֵרָה, וְהוֹפַע
וְהִנָּשֵׂא עָלֵינוּ לְעֵינֵי כָּל חָי, וְקָרֵב פְּזוּרֵינוּ מִבֵּין הַגּוֹיִם,
וּנְפוּצוֹתֵינוּ כַּנֵּס מִיַּרְכְּתֵי אָרֶץ; וַהֲבִיאֵנוּ לְצִיּוֹן עִירְךָ בְּרִנָּה,
וְלִירוּשָׁלַיִם בֵּית מִקְדָּשְׁךָ בְּשִׂמְחַת עוֹלָם, וְשָׁם נַעֲשֶׂה לְפָנֶיךָ
אֶת קָרְבְּנוֹת חוֹבוֹתֵינוּ, תְּמִידִים כְּסִדְרָם וּמוּסָפִים כְּהִלְכָתָם.
(וְאֶת מוּסַף יוֹם הַשַּׁבָּת הַזֶּה) וְאֶת מוּסַף יוֹם

Pesaḥ	Shavuoth	Sukkoth	Shemini Atsereth and Simḥath Torah
חַג הַמַּצּוֹת	חַג הַשָּׁבוּעוֹת	חַג הַסֻּכּוֹת	הַשְּׁמִינִי, חַג
הַזֶּה,	הַזֶּה,	הַזֶּה,	הָעֲצֶרֶת הַזֶּה,

נַעֲשֶׂה וְנַקְרִיב לְפָנֶיךָ בְּאַהֲבָה בְּמִצְוַת רְצוֹנֶךָ, כְּמוֹ שֶׁכָּתַבְתָּ
עָלֵינוּ בְּתוֹרָתֶךָ עַל יְדֵי מֹשֶׁה עַבְדֶּךָ, מִפִּי כְבוֹדֶךָ, כָּאָמוּר:

On Sabbath:

(וּבְיוֹם הַשַּׁבָּת, שְׁנֵי כְבָשִׂים בְּנֵי שָׁנָה תְּמִימִם, וּשְׁנֵי עֶשְׂרֹנִים
סֹלֶת מִנְחָה בְּלוּלָה בַשֶּׁמֶן וְנִסְכּוֹ. עֹלַת שַׁבַּת בְּשַׁבַּתּוֹ, עַל עֹלַת
הַתָּמִיד וְנִסְכָּהּ.)

EACH OF THE FOLLOWING PASSAGES IS CONTINUED ON PAGE 619

On the first two days of Pesaḥ:

וּבַחֹדֶשׁ הָרִאשׁוֹן, בְּאַרְבָּעָה עָשָׂר יוֹם לַחֹדֶשׁ, פֶּסַח לַיָי.
וּבַחֲמִשָּׁה עָשָׂר יוֹם לַחֹדֶשׁ הַזֶּה חָג; שִׁבְעַת יָמִים מַצּוֹת יֵאָכֵל.
בַּיּוֹם הָרִאשׁוֹן מִקְרָא קֹדֶשׁ, כָּל מְלֶאכֶת עֲבוֹדָה לֹא תַעֲשׂוּ.

On all eight days of Pesaḥ:

וְהִקְרַבְתֶּם אִשֶּׁה, עֹלָה לַיָי: פָּרִים בְּנֵי בָקָר שְׁנַיִם, וְאַיִל
אֶחָד, וְשִׁבְעָה כְבָשִׂים בְּנֵי שָׁנָה, תְּמִימִם יִהְיוּ לָכֶם.

again to have mercy on us and on thy sanctuary; rebuild it speedily and magnify its glory.

Our Father, our King, speedily reveal thy glorious majesty to us; shine forth and be exalted over us in the sight of all the living. Unite our scattered people from among the nations; gather our dispersed from the far ends of the earth. Bring us to Zion thy city with ringing song, to Jerusalem thy sanctuary with everlasting joy. There we will prepare in thy honor our obligatory offerings, the regular daily offerings and the additional offerings, according to rule. The *Musaf* of (this Sabbath and that of) this

Pesaḥ	*Shavuoth*
Feast of Unleavened Bread	Feast of Weeks
Sukkoth	*Shemini Atsereth and Simḥath Torah*
Feast of Tabernacles	Eighth Day Feast

we will prepare and present in thy honor with love, according to thy command, as thou hast prescribed for us in thy Torah through thy servant Moses, as it is said:

On Sabbath:

(On the Sabbath day, two perfect yearling male lambs and two-tenths of an *ephah* of fine flour mixed with oil as a meal-offering, and the libation. This is the burnt-offering of each Sabbath, in addition to the daily burnt-offering and its libation.)[1]

Each Of The Following Passages Is Continued On Page 620

On the first two days of Pesaḥ:

On the fourteenth day of the first month is the Lord's Passover. On the fifteenth day of this month shall be a feast; for seven days shall unleavened bread be eaten. On the first day shall be a sacred assembly; you shall do no work.

On all eight days of Pesaḥ:

You shall present an offering made by fire, a burnt-offering to the Lord: two young bullocks, one ram, and seven yearling male lambs; you shall have them perfect.[2]

---

[1] *Numbers* 28:9-10.　　[2] *Numbers* 28:16-19.

On *Shavuoth*:

וּבְיוֹם הַבִּכּוּרִים, בְּהַקְרִיבְכֶם מִנְחָה חֲדָשָׁה לַיָּי,
בְּשָׁבֻעֹתֵיכֶם, מִקְרָא קֹדֶשׁ יִהְיֶה לָכֶם, כָּל מְלֶאכֶת עֲבֹדָה לֹא
תַעֲשׂוּ. וְהִקְרַבְתֶּם עֹלָה לְרֵיחַ נִיחֹחַ לַיָּי: פָּרִים בְּנֵי בָקָר שְׁנַיִם,
אַיִל אֶחָד, שִׁבְעָה כְבָשִׂים בְּנֵי שָׁנָה.

On the first two days of *Sukkoth*:

וּבַחֲמִשָּׁה עָשָׂר יוֹם לַחֹדֶשׁ הַשְּׁבִיעִי, מִקְרָא קֹדֶשׁ יִהְיֶה
לָכֶם, כָּל מְלֶאכֶת עֲבֹדָה לֹא תַעֲשׂוּ; וְחַגֹּתֶם חַג לַיָּי שִׁבְעַת
יָמִים. וְהִקְרַבְתֶּם עֹלָה, אִשֵּׁה רֵיחַ נִיחֹחַ לַיָּי: פָּרִים בְּנֵי בָקָר
שְׁלֹשָׁה עָשָׂר, אֵילִם שְׁנַיִם, כְּבָשִׂים בְּנֵי שָׁנָה אַרְבָּעָה עָשָׂר,
תְּמִימִם יִהְיוּ.

On the first day of *Ḥol ha-Mo'ed Sukkoth*:

וּבַיּוֹם הַשֵּׁנִי, פָּרִים בְּנֵי בָקָר שְׁנֵים עָשָׂר, אֵילִם שְׁנַיִם,
כְּבָשִׂים בְּנֵי שָׁנָה אַרְבָּעָה עָשָׂר, תְּמִימִם.

וּבַיּוֹם הַשְּׁלִישִׁי, פָּרִים עַשְׁתֵּי עָשָׂר, אֵילִם שְׁנַיִם, כְּבָשִׂים
בְּנֵי שָׁנָה אַרְבָּעָה עָשָׂר, תְּמִימִם.

On the second day of *Ḥol ha-Mo'ed Sukkoth*:

וּבַיּוֹם הַשְּׁלִישִׁי, פָּרִים עַשְׁתֵּי עָשָׂר, אֵילִם שְׁנַיִם, כְּבָשִׂים
בְּנֵי שָׁנָה אַרְבָּעָה עָשָׂר, תְּמִימִם.

וּבַיּוֹם הָרְבִיעִי, פָּרִים עֲשָׂרָה, אֵילִם שְׁנַיִם, כְּבָשִׂים בְּנֵי שָׁנָה
אַרְבָּעָה עָשָׂר, תְּמִימִם.

פרים... שׁלשה עשׂר The seventy bullocks that were offered during the seven days of *Sukkoth* corresponded to the seventy nations which were then supposed to inhabit the world. The single bullock that was offered on the eighth day of the festival was on behalf of Israel, the unique nation. According to the Talmud, the altar atoned for the nations when the Temple was in existence (Sukkah 55b).

On Shavuoth:

On the day of the first-fruits, when you bring a meal-offering from the new grain to the Lord, in your Feast of Weeks, you shall hold a sacred assembly; you shall do no work. You shall present a burnt-offering, as a soothing savor, to the Lord: two young bullocks, one ram, and seven yearling male lambs.[1]

On the first two days of Sukkoth:

On the fifteenth day of the seventh month you shall hold a sacred assembly; you shall do no work; you shall keep a feast unto the Lord for seven days. You shall present a burnt-offering, an offering made by fire, as a soothing savor, to the Lord: thirteen young bullocks, two rams, and fourteen yearling male lambs; they shall be without blemish.[2]

On the first day of Ḥol ha-Moʻed Sukkoth:

And on the second day you shall offer twelve young bullocks, two rams, fourteen yearling male lambs without blemish.

And on the third day you shall offer eleven bullocks, two rams, fourteen yearling male lambs without blemish.

On the second day of Ḥol ha-Moʻed Sukkoth:

And on the third day you shall offer eleven bullocks, two rams, fourteen yearling male lambs without blemish.

And on the fourth day you shall offer ten bullocks, two rams, fourteen yearling male lambs without blemish.

וביום השני refers to the second day of *Sukkoth*, observed as the first day of *Ḥol ha-Moʻed* in Eretz Yisrael. In the diaspora, however, the first day of *Ḥol ha-Moʻed* occurs on the third day of *Sukkoth*; hence, וביום השלישי is added to וביום השני anywhere outside of Palestine. The same applies to the remaining days of the festival.

---

[1] *Numbers* 28:26-27.   [2] *Numbers* 29:12-13.

On the third day of *Ḥol ha-Mo'ed Sukkoth*:

וּבַיּוֹם הָרְבִיעִי, פָּרִים עֲשָׂרָה, אֵילִם שְׁנָיִם, כְּבָשִׂים בְּנֵי שָׁנָה
אַרְבָּעָה עָשָׂר, תְּמִימִם.

וּבַיּוֹם הַחֲמִישִׁי, פָּרִים תִּשְׁעָה, אֵילִם שְׁנָיִם, כְּבָשִׂים בְּנֵי שָׁנָה
אַרְבָּעָה עָשָׂר, תְּמִימִם.

On the fourth day of *Ḥol ha-Mo'ed Sukkoth*:

וּבַיּוֹם הַחֲמִישִׁי, פָּרִים תִּשְׁעָה, אֵילִם שְׁנָיִם, כְּבָשִׂים בְּנֵי שָׁנָה
אַרְבָּעָה עָשָׂר, תְּמִימִם.

וּבַיּוֹם הַשִּׁשִּׁי, פָּרִים שְׁמֹנָה, אֵילִם שְׁנָיִם, כְּבָשִׂים בְּנֵי שָׁנָה
אַרְבָּעָה עָשָׂר, תְּמִימִם.

On *Hoshana Rabbah*:

וּבַיּוֹם הַשִּׁשִּׁי, פָּרִים שְׁמֹנָה, אֵילִם שְׁנָיִם, כְּבָשִׂים בְּנֵי שָׁנָה
אַרְבָּעָה עָשָׂר, תְּמִימִם.

וּבַיּוֹם הַשְּׁבִיעִי, פָּרִים שִׁבְעָה, אֵילִם שְׁנָיִם, כְּבָשִׂים בְּנֵי שָׁנָה
אַרְבָּעָה עָשָׂר, תְּמִימִם.

On *Shemini Atsereth* and *Simḥath Torah*:

בַּיּוֹם הַשְּׁמִינִי, עֲצֶרֶת תִּהְיֶה לָכֶם, כָּל מְלֶאכֶת עֲבֹדָה לֹא
תַעֲשׂוּ. וְהִקְרַבְתֶּם עֹלָה, אִשֵּׁה רֵיחַ נִיחֹחַ לַיְיָ: פַּר אֶחָד, אַיִל
אֶחָד, כְּבָשִׂים בְּנֵי שָׁנָה שִׁבְעָה, תְּמִימִם.

CONTINUED

וּמִנְחָתָם וְנִסְכֵּיהֶם כַּמְדֻבָּר: שְׁלֹשָׁה עֶשְׂרֹנִים לַפָּר, וּשְׁנֵי
עֶשְׂרֹנִים לָאַיִל, וְעִשָּׂרוֹן לַכֶּבֶשׂ, וְיַיִן כְּנִסְכּוֹ, וְשָׂעִיר לְכַפֵּר,
וּשְׁנֵי תְמִידִים כְּהִלְכָתָם.

ומנחתם... כמדובר refers to Numbers 29:41-61. Some read this passage twice, after וביום השני as well as after וביום השלישי, and so on each day of *Ḥol ha-Mo'ed Sukkoth*.

On the third day of Ḥol ha-Mo'ed Sukkoth:

And on the fourth day you shall offer ten bullocks, two rams, fourteen yearling male lambs without blemish.

And on the fifth day you shall offer nine bullocks, two rams, fourteen yearling male lambs without blemish.

On the fourth day of Ḥol ha-Mo'ed Sukkoth:

And on the fifth day you shall offer nine bullocks, two rams, fourteen yearling male lambs without blemish.

And on the sixth day you shall offer eight bullocks, two rams, fourteen yearling male lambs without blemish.

On Hoshana Rabbah:

And on the sixth day you shall offer eight bullocks, two rams, fourteen yearling male lambs without blemish.

And on the seventh day you shall offer seven bullocks, two rams, fourteen yearling male lambs without blemish.

On Shemini Atsereth and Simḥath Torah:

On the eighth day you shall hold a sacred assembly; you shall do no work. You shall present a burnt-offering, an offering made by fire, as a soothing savor, to the Lord: one bullock, one ram, seven yearling male lambs without blemish.[1]

CONTINUED

Their meal-offering and their libations were as specified: three tenths of an *ephah* [of fine flour] for each bullock, two-tenths for the ram, one-tenth for each lamb; wine according to their requisite libations. Moreover, a he-goat was offered to make atonement in addition to the two regular daily offerings.

---

[1] *Numbers* 29:17-36.

On Sabbath:

(יִשְׂמְחוּ בְמַלְכוּתְךָ שׁוֹמְרֵי שַׁבָּת וְקוֹרְאֵי עֹנֶג, עַם מְקַדְּשֵׁי שְׁבִיעִי, כֻּלָּם יִשְׂבְּעוּ וְיִתְעַנְּגוּ מִטּוּבֶךָ; וּבַשְּׁבִיעִי רָצִיתָ בּוֹ וְקִדַּשְׁתּוֹ, חֶמְדַּת יָמִים אוֹתוֹ קָרָאתָ, זֵכֶר לְמַעֲשֵׂה בְרֵאשִׁית.)

אֱלֹהֵינוּ וֵאלֹהֵי אֲבוֹתֵינוּ, מֶלֶךְ רַחֲמָן, רַחֵם עָלֵינוּ; טוֹב וּמֵטִיב, הִדָּרֶשׁ־לָנוּ; שׁוּבָה אֵלֵינוּ בַּהֲמוֹן רַחֲמֶיךָ בִּגְלַל אָבוֹת שֶׁעָשׂוּ רְצוֹנֶךָ; בְּנֵה בֵיתְךָ כְּבַתְּחִלָּה, וְכוֹנֵן מִקְדָּשְׁךָ עַל מְכוֹנוֹ, וְהַרְאֵנוּ בְּבִנְיָנוֹ וְשַׂמְּחֵנוּ בְּתִקּוּנוֹ, וְהָשֵׁב כֹּהֲנִים לַעֲבוֹדָתָם, וּלְוִיִּם לְשִׁירָם וּלְזִמְרָם, וְהָשֵׁב יִשְׂרָאֵל לִנְוֵיהֶם; וְשָׁם נַעֲלֶה וְנֵרָאֶה וְנִשְׁתַּחֲוֶה לְפָנֶיךָ בְּשָׁלֹשׁ פַּעֲמֵי רְגָלֵינוּ, כַּכָּתוּב בְּתוֹרָתֶךָ: שָׁלוֹשׁ פְּעָמִים בַּשָּׁנָה יֵרָאֶה כָל זְכוּרְךָ אֶת פְּנֵי יְיָ אֱלֹהֶיךָ בַּמָּקוֹם אֲשֶׁר יִבְחָר, בְּחַג הַמַּצּוֹת וּבְחַג הַשָּׁבֻעוֹת וּבְחַג הַסֻּכּוֹת; וְלֹא יֵרָאֶה אֶת פְּנֵי יְיָ רֵיקָם. אִישׁ כְּמַתְּנַת יָדוֹ, כְּבִרְכַּת יְיָ אֱלֹהֶיךָ אֲשֶׁר נָתַן לָךְ.

וְהַשִּׂיאֵנוּ, יְיָ אֱלֹהֵינוּ, אֶת בִּרְכַּת מוֹעֲדֶיךָ לְחַיִּים וּלְשָׁלוֹם, לְשִׂמְחָה וּלְשָׂשׂוֹן, כַּאֲשֶׁר רָצִיתָ וְאָמַרְתָּ לְבָרְכֵנוּ. אֱלֹהֵינוּ וֵאלֹהֵי אֲבוֹתֵינוּ, (רְצֵה בִמְנוּחָתֵנוּ) קַדְּשֵׁנוּ בְּמִצְוֹתֶיךָ וְתֵן חֶלְקֵנוּ בְּתוֹרָתֶךָ, שַׂבְּעֵנוּ מִטּוּבֶךָ, וְשַׂמְּחֵנוּ בִּישׁוּעָתֶךָ, וְטַהֵר לִבֵּנוּ לְעָבְדְּךָ בֶּאֱמֶת; וְהַנְחִילֵנוּ, יְיָ אֱלֹהֵינוּ (בְּאַהֲבָה וּבְרָצוֹן) בְּשִׂמְחָה וּבְשָׂשׂוֹן (שַׁבָּת וּ)מוֹעֲדֵי קָדְשֶׁךָ, וְיִשְׂמְחוּ בְךָ יִשְׂרָאֵל מְקַדְּשֵׁי שְׁמֶךָ. בָּרוּךְ אַתָּה, יְיָ, מְקַדֵּשׁ (הַשַּׁבָּת וְ)יִשְׂרָאֵל וְהַזְּמַנִּים.

רְצֵה, יְיָ אֱלֹהֵינוּ, בְּעַמְּךָ יִשְׂרָאֵל וּבִתְפִלָּתָם, וְהָשֵׁב אֶת הָעֲבוֹדָה לִדְבִיר בֵּיתֶךָ; וְאִשֵּׁי יִשְׂרָאֵל וּתְפִלָּתָם בְּאַהֲבָה תְקַבֵּל בְּרָצוֹן, וּתְהִי לְרָצוֹן תָּמִיד עֲבוֹדַת יִשְׂרָאֵל עַמֶּךָ.

On Sabbath:

(Those who keep the Sabbath and call it a delight shall rejoice in thy kingdom; all the people who hallow the seventh day shall fully enjoy thy goodness. Thou wast pleased with the seventh day and didst hallow it; the most desirable of days didst thou call it—in remembrance of the creation.)

Our God and God of our fathers, merciful King, have pity on us; thou art good and beneficent, answer our entreaty. In thy abundant mercy, return to us for the sake of our fathers who performed thy will. Rebuild thy Temple as of yore, and set up thy sanctuary on its site. Grant that we may see it rebuilt; gladden us by its restoration. Restore Kohanim to their service, Levites to their song and music, and Israelites to their homes. There we will go up to present ourselves and worship before thee at our three pilgrim seasons, as it is written in thy Torah: Three times a year shall all your males appear before the Lord your God in the place which he will choose: on the Feast of Unleavened Bread, on the Feast of Weeks, and on the Feast of Tabernacles; they shall not appear before the Lord empty-handed. Every man shall offer what he can afford, according as the Lord your God has blessed you.[1]

Bestow on us, Lord our God, the blessings of thy festivals for life and peace, for joy and gladness, as thou didst promise to bless us. Our God and God of our fathers, (be pleased with our rest) sanctify us with thy commandments and grant us a share in thy Torah; satisfy us with thy goodness and gladden us with thy help; purify our heart to serve thee sincerely. In thy gracious love, Lord our God, grant us thy holy (Sabbath and) festivals for gladness and joy; may Israel who sanctifies thy name rejoice in thee. Blessed art thou, O Lord, who hallowest (the Sabbath and) Israel and the festivals.

Be pleased, Lord our God, with thy people Israel and with their prayer; restore the worship to thy most holy sanctuary; accept Israel's offerings and prayer with gracious love. May the worship of thy people Israel be ever pleasing to thee.

---

[1] *Deuteronomy* 16:16-17.

Blessing of the *Kohanim* (page 625)

וְתֶחֱזֶינָה עֵינֵינוּ בְּשׁוּבְךָ לְצִיּוֹן בְּרַחֲמִים. בָּרוּךְ אַתָּה, יְיָ, הַמַּחֲזִיר שְׁכִינָתוֹ לְצִיּוֹן.

מוֹדִים אֲנַחְנוּ לָךְ, שָׁאַתָּה הוּא יְיָ אֱלֹהֵינוּ וֵאלֹהֵי אֲבוֹתֵינוּ לְעוֹלָם וָעֶד. צוּר חַיֵּינוּ, מָגֵן יִשְׁעֵנוּ, אַתָּה הוּא. לְדוֹר וָדוֹר נוֹדֶה לְּךָ, וּנְסַפֵּר תְּהִלָּתֶךָ, עַל חַיֵּינוּ הַמְּסוּרִים בְּיָדֶךָ, וְעַל נִשְׁמוֹתֵינוּ הַפְּקוּדוֹת לָךְ, וְעַל נִסֶּיךָ שֶׁבְּכָל יוֹם עִמָּנוּ, וְעַל נִפְלְאוֹתֶיךָ וְטוֹבוֹתֶיךָ שֶׁבְּכָל עֵת, עֶרֶב וָבֹקֶר וְצָהֳרָיִם. הַטּוֹב כִּי לֹא כָלוּ רַחֲמֶיךָ, וְהַמְרַחֵם כִּי לֹא תַמּוּ חֲסָדֶיךָ, מֵעוֹלָם קִוִּינוּ לָךְ.

When the Reader repeats the *Amidah*, the Congregation responds here by saying:

(מוֹדִים אֲנַחְנוּ לָךְ, שָׁאַתָּה הוּא יְיָ אֱלֹהֵינוּ וֵאלֹהֵי אֲבוֹתֵינוּ. אֱלֹהֵי כָל בָּשָׂר, יוֹצְרֵנוּ, יוֹצֵר בְּרֵאשִׁית, בְּרָכוֹת וְהוֹדָאוֹת לְשִׁמְךָ הַגָּדוֹל וְהַקָּדוֹשׁ עַל שֶׁהֶחֱיִיתָנוּ וְקִיַּמְתָּנוּ. כֵּן תְּחַיֵּנוּ וּתְקַיְּמֵנוּ, וְתֶאֱסוֹף גָּלֻיּוֹתֵינוּ לְחַצְרוֹת קָדְשֶׁךָ לִשְׁמוֹר חֻקֶּיךָ וְלַעֲשׂוֹת רְצוֹנֶךָ, וּלְעָבְדְּךָ בְּלֵבָב שָׁלֵם, עַל שֶׁאֲנַחְנוּ מוֹדִים לָךְ. בָּרוּךְ אֵל הַהוֹדָאוֹת.)

וְעַל כֻּלָּם יִתְבָּרַךְ וְיִתְרוֹמַם שִׁמְךָ, מַלְכֵּנוּ, תָּמִיד לְעוֹלָם וָעֶד.

וְכֹל הַחַיִּים יוֹדוּךָ סֶּלָה, וִיהַלְלוּ אֶת שִׁמְךָ בֶּאֱמֶת, הָאֵל, יְשׁוּעָתֵנוּ וְעֶזְרָתֵנוּ סֶלָה. בָּרוּךְ אַתָּה, יְיָ, הַטּוֹב שִׁמְךָ, וּלְךָ נָאֶה לְהוֹדוֹת.

Reader:

(אֱלֹהֵינוּ וֵאלֹהֵי אֲבוֹתֵינוּ, בָּרְכֵנוּ בַבְּרָכָה הַמְשֻׁלֶּשֶׁת בַּתּוֹרָה הַכְּתוּבָה עַל יְדֵי מֹשֶׁה עַבְדֶּךָ, הָאֲמוּרָה מִפִּי אַהֲרֹן וּבָנָיו, כֹּהֲנִים עַם קְדוֹשֶׁךָ, כָּאָמוּר: יְבָרֶכְךָ יְיָ וְיִשְׁמְרֶךָ. יָאֵר יְיָ פָּנָיו אֵלֶיךָ וִיחֻנֶּךָּ. יִשָּׂא יְיָ פָּנָיו אֵלֶיךָ, וְיָשֵׂם לְךָ שָׁלוֹם.)

Blessing of the Kohanim (page 626)

May our eyes behold thy return in mercy to Zion. Blessed art thou, O Lord, who restorest thy divine presence to Zion.

We ever thank thee, who art the Lord our God and the God of our fathers. Thou art the strength of our life and our saving shield. In every generation we will thank thee and recount thy praise—for our lives which are in thy charge, for our souls which are in thy care, for thy miracles which are daily with us, and for thy continual wonders and favors— evening, morning and noon. Beneficent One, whose mercies never fail, Merciful One, whose kindnesses never cease, thou hast always been our hope.

When the Reader repeats the Amidah, the Congregation responds here by saying:

(We thank thee, who art the Lord our God and the God of our fathers. God of all mankind, our Creator and Creator of the universe, blessings and thanks are due to thy great and holy name, because thou hast kept us alive and sustained us; mayest thou ever grant us life and sustenance. O gather our exiles to thy holy courts to observe thy laws, to do thy will, and to serve thee with a perfect heart. For this we thank thee. Blessed be God to whom all thanks are due.)

For all these acts may thy name, our King, be blessed and exalted forever and ever.

All the living shall ever thank thee and sincerely praise thy name, O God, who art always our salvation and help. Blessed art thou, O Lord, Beneficent One, to whom it is fitting to give thanks.

Reader:

(Our God and God of our fathers, bless us with the threefold blessing written in thy Torah by thy servant Moses and spoken by Aaron and his sons the priests, thy holy people, as it is said: "May the Lord bless you and protect you; may the Lord countenance you and be gracious to you; may the Lord favor you and give you peace.")[1]

---

[1] *Numbers* 6:24-26.

שִׂים שָׁלוֹם, טוֹבָה וּבְרָכָה, חֵן וָחֶסֶד וְרַחֲמִים, עָלֵינוּ וְעַל
כָּל יִשְׂרָאֵל עַמֶּךָ. בָּרְכֵנוּ אָבִינוּ, כֻּלָּנוּ כְּאֶחָד, בְּאוֹר פָּנֶיךָ;
כִּי בְאוֹר פָּנֶיךָ נָתַתָּ לָּנוּ, יְיָ אֱלֹהֵינוּ, תּוֹרַת חַיִּים וְאַהֲבַת חֶסֶד,
וּצְדָקָה וּבְרָכָה וְרַחֲמִים, וְחַיִּים וְשָׁלוֹם; וְטוֹב בְּעֵינֶיךָ לְבָרֵךְ
אֶת עַמְּךָ יִשְׂרָאֵל בְּכָל עֵת וּבְכָל שָׁעָה בִּשְׁלוֹמֶךָ. בָּרוּךְ אַתָּה,
יְיָ, הַמְבָרֵךְ אֶת עַמּוֹ יִשְׂרָאֵל בַּשָּׁלוֹם.

After the *Amidah* add the following meditation:

אֱלֹהַי, נְצֹר לְשׁוֹנִי מֵרָע, וּשְׂפָתַי מִדַּבֵּר מִרְמָה; וְלִמְקַלְלַי
נַפְשִׁי תִדּוֹם, וְנַפְשִׁי כֶּעָפָר לַכֹּל תִּהְיֶה. פְּתַח לִבִּי בְּתוֹרָתֶךָ,
וּבְמִצְוֹתֶיךָ תִּרְדּוֹף נַפְשִׁי; וְכָל הַחוֹשְׁבִים עָלַי רָעָה, מְהֵרָה
הָפֵר עֲצָתָם וְקַלְקֵל מַחֲשַׁבְתָּם. עֲשֵׂה לְמַעַן שְׁמֶךָ, עֲשֵׂה לְמַעַן
יְמִינֶךָ, עֲשֵׂה לְמַעַן קְדֻשָּׁתֶךָ, עֲשֵׂה לְמַעַן תּוֹרָתֶךָ. לְמַעַן יֵחָלְצוּן
יְדִידֶיךָ, הוֹשִׁיעָה יְמִינְךָ וַעֲנֵנִי. יִהְיוּ לְרָצוֹן אִמְרֵי פִי וְהֶגְיוֹן לִבִּי
לְפָנֶיךָ, יְיָ, צוּרִי וְגוֹאֲלִי. עֹשֶׂה שָׁלוֹם בִּמְרוֹמָיו, הוּא יַעֲשֶׂה
שָׁלוֹם עָלֵינוּ וְעַל כָּל יִשְׂרָאֵל, וְאִמְרוּ אָמֵן.

יְהִי רָצוֹן מִלְּפָנֶיךָ, יְיָ אֱלֹהֵינוּ וֵאלֹהֵי אֲבוֹתֵינוּ, שֶׁיִּבָּנֶה בֵּית
הַמִּקְדָּשׁ בִּמְהֵרָה בְיָמֵינוּ, וְתֵן חֶלְקֵנוּ בְּתוֹרָתֶךָ. וְשָׁם נַעֲבָדְךָ
בְּיִרְאָה, כִּימֵי עוֹלָם וּכְשָׁנִים קַדְמוֹנִיּוֹת. וְעָרְבָה לַיְיָ מִנְחַת
יְהוּדָה וִירוּשָׁלָיִם, כִּימֵי עוֹלָם וּכְשָׁנִים קַדְמוֹנִיּוֹת.

בִּרְכַּת כֹּהֲנִים

Congregation:

וְתֶעֱרַב עָלֶיךָ עֲתִירָתֵנוּ כְּעוֹלָה וּכְקָרְבָּן; אָנָּא, רַחוּם,
בְּרַחֲמֶיךָ הָרַבִּים הָשֵׁב שְׁכִינָתְךָ לְצִיּוֹן עִירֶךָ, וְסֵדֶר הָעֲבוֹדָה

ברכת כהנים, known as נשיאת כפים, was part of the daily service in the
Temple. Every morning and evening, before the thank-offering, the priests
raised their hands aloft and pronounced the priestly blessing from a special

O grant peace, happiness, blessing, grace, kindness and mercy
to us and to all Israel thy people. Bless us all alike, our Father,
with the light of thy countenance; indeed, by the light of thy
countenance thou hast given us, Lord our God, a Torah of life,
lovingkindness, charity, blessing, mercy, life and peace. May it
please thee to bless thy people Israel with peace at all times and
hours. Blessed art thou, O Lord, who blessest thy people Israel
with peace.

After the Amidah add the following meditation:

My God, guard my tongue from evil, and my lips from speaking falsehood. May my soul be silent to those who insult me; be
my soul lowly to all as the dust. Open my heart to thy Torah,
that my soul may follow thy commands. Speedily defeat the
counsel of all those who plan evil against me and upset their design. Do it for the glory of thy name; do it for the sake of thy
power; do it for the sake of thy holiness; do it for the sake of thy
Torah. That thy beloved may be rescued, save with thy right hand
and answer me. May the words of my mouth and the meditation
of my heart be pleasing before thee, O Lord, my Stronghold and
my Redeemer.[1] May he who creates peace in his high heavens
create peace for us and for all Israel, Amen.

May it be thy will, Lord our God and God of our fathers, that
the Temple be speedily rebuilt in our days, and grant us a share
in thy Torah. There we will serve thee with reverence, as in the
days of old and as in former years. Then the offering of Judah
and Jerusalem will be pleasing to the Lord, as in the days of old
and as in former years.[2]

THE PRIESTLY BLESSING

Congregation:

May our prayer please thee as burnt-offering and sacrifice.
Merciful God, in thy abundant love restore thy divine presence
to Zion, and the order of service to Jerusalem. May our eyes

---

platform (דוכן); hence the term "duchenen." The introductory prayer (יהי רצון),
and the concluding prayer recited by the *kohanim* are given in the Talmud
(Sotah 39b).

[1]*Psalms* 60:7; 19:15.   [2]*Malachi* 3:4.

לִירוּשָׁלָיִם. וְתֶחֱזֶינָה עֵינֵינוּ בְּשׁוּבְךָ לְצִיּוֹן בְּרַחֲמִים, וְשָׁם
נַעֲבָדְךָ בְּיִרְאָה כִּימֵי עוֹלָם וּכְשָׁנִים קַדְמוֹנִיּוֹת.

Reader:

בָּרוּךְ אַתָּה, יְיָ, שֶׁאוֹתְךָ לְבַדְּךָ בְּיִרְאָה נַעֲבוֹד.

לְהוֹדוֹת to מוֹדִים (page 623)

Congregation:

יְהִי רָצוֹן מִלְּפָנֶיךָ, יְיָ אֱלֹהֵינוּ וֵאלֹהֵי אֲבוֹתֵינוּ, שֶׁתְּהֵא
הַבְּרָכָה הַזֹּאת שֶׁצִּוִּיתָ לְבָרֵךְ אֶת עַמְּךָ יִשְׂרָאֵל, בְּרָכָה שְׁלֵמָה,
וְלֹא יִהְיֶה בָּהּ שׁוּם מִכְשׁוֹל וְעָוֹן מֵעַתָּה וְעַד עוֹלָם.

Reader:

אֱלֹהֵינוּ וֵאלֹהֵי אֲבוֹתֵינוּ, בָּרְכֵנוּ בַבְּרָכָה הַמְשֻׁלֶּשֶׁת בַּתּוֹרָה
הַכְּתוּבָה עַל יְדֵי מֹשֶׁה עַבְדֶּךָ, הָאֲמוּרָה מִפִּי אַהֲרֹן וּבָנָיו

כֹּהֲנִים

Congregation:

עַם קְדוֹשֶׁךָ, כָּאָמוּר.

Kohanim:

בָּרוּךְ אַתָּה, יְיָ אֱלֹהֵינוּ, מֶלֶךְ הָעוֹלָם, אֲשֶׁר קִדְּשָׁנוּ
בִּקְדֻשָּׁתוֹ שֶׁל אַהֲרֹן וְצִוָּנוּ לְבָרֵךְ אֶת עַמּוֹ יִשְׂרָאֵל בְּאַהֲבָה.

Congregation: Kohanim:

יָבֶרֶכְךָ   יְבָרֶכְךָ יְיָ מִצִּיּוֹן, עֹשֵׂה שָׁמַיִם וָאָרֶץ.

יְהֹוָה   יְיָ אֲדוֹנֵינוּ, מָה אַדִּיר שִׁמְךָ בְּכָל הָאָרֶץ.

וְיִשְׁמְרֶךָ.   שָׁמְרֵנִי, אֵל, כִּי חָסִיתִי בָךְ.

רִבּוֹנוֹ שֶׁל עוֹלָם, אֲנִי שֶׁלָּךְ וַחֲלוֹמוֹתַי שֶׁלָּךְ; חֲלוֹם חָלַמְתִּי
וְאֵינִי יוֹדֵעַ מַה הוּא. יְהִי רָצוֹן מִלְּפָנֶיךָ, יְיָ אֱלֹהַי וֵאלֹהֵי אֲבוֹתַי,
שֶׁיִּהְיוּ כָּל חֲלוֹמוֹתַי עָלַי וְעַל כָּל יִשְׂרָאֵל לְטוֹבָה, בֵּין שֶׁחָלַמְתִּי
עַל עַצְמִי וּבֵין שֶׁחָלַמְתִּי עַל אֲחֵרִים וּבֵין שֶׁחָלְמוּ אֲחֵרִים עָלָי;

רִבּוֹנוֹ שֶׁל עוֹלָם is derived from Berakhoth 55b.

behold thy return in mercy to Zion. There we will serve thee with reverence, as in the days of old and as in former years.

Reader:

Blessed art thou, O Lord, whom alone we serve with reverence.

"We ever thank thee"... (page 624)

Congregation:

May it be thy will, Lord our God and God of our fathers, that this blessing which thou hast commanded to pronounce upon thy people Israel may be a perfect blessing, forever free from stumbling and iniquity.

Reader:

Our God and God of our fathers, bless us with the threefold blessing written in thy Torah by thy servant Moses and spoken by Aaron and his sons THE PRIESTS—

Congregation:

THY HOLY PEOPLE.

Kohanim:

Blessed art thou, Lord our God, King of the universe, who hast sanctified us with the holiness of Aaron, and commanded us to bless thy people Israel with love.

Kohanim:	*Congregation:*
יְבָרֶכְךָ	May the Lord, who made heaven and earth, bless you from Zion.
יְיָ	Lord our God, how glorious is thy name over all the world!
וְיִשְׁמְרֶךָ	Protect me, O God, for I place my trust in thee.[1]

Lord of the universe, I am thine and my dreams are thine. I have dreamt a dream and I do not know what it is. May it be thy will, Lord my God and God of my fathers, to confirm all good dreams concerning myself and all the people of Israel for happiness; may they be fulfilled like the dreams of Joseph. But if they require

[1] *Psalms* 134:3; 8:10; 16:1.

אִם טוֹבִים הֵם, חַזְּקֵם וְאַמְּצֵם, וִיתְקַיְּמוּ בִי וּבָהֶם כַּחֲלוֹמוֹת
שֶׁל יוֹסֵף הַצַּדִּיק; וְאִם צְרִיכִים רְפוּאָה, רְפָאֵם כְּחִזְקִיָּהוּ מֶלֶךְ
יְהוּדָה מֵחָלְיוֹ, וּכְמִרְיָם הַנְּבִיאָה מִצָּרַעְתָּהּ, וּכְנַעֲמָן מִצָּרַעְתּוֹ,
וּכְמֵי מָרָה עַל יְדֵי מֹשֶׁה רַבֵּנוּ, וּכְמֵי יְרִיחוֹ עַל יְדֵי אֱלִישָׁע.
וּכְשֵׁם שֶׁהָפַכְתָּ אֶת קִלְלַת בִּלְעָם הָרָשָׁע מִקְּלָלָה לִבְרָכָה, כֵּן
תַּהֲפֹךְ כָּל חֲלוֹמוֹתַי עָלַי וְעַל כָּל יִשְׂרָאֵל לְטוֹבָה, וְתִשְׁמְרֵנִי
וּתְחָנֵּנִי וְתִרְצֵנִי. אָמֵן.

יָאֵר   אֱלֹהִים יְחָנֵּנוּ וִיבָרְכֵנוּ; יָאֵר פָּנָיו אִתָּנוּ סֶלָה.

יְהֹוָה   יְיָ יְיָ, אֵל רַחוּם וְחַנּוּן, אֶרֶךְ אַפַּיִם וְרַב חֶסֶד וֶאֱמֶת.

פָּנָיו   פְּנֵה אֵלַי וְחָנֵּנִי, כִּי יָחִיד וְעָנִי אָנִי.

אֵלֶיךָ   אֵלֶיךָ, יְיָ, נַפְשִׁי אֶשָּׂא.

וִיחֻנֶּךָ.   הִנֵּה כְעֵינֵי עֲבָדִים אֶל יַד אֲדוֹנֵיהֶם, כְּעֵינֵי שִׁפְחָה אֶל
יַד גְּבִרְתָּהּ, כֵּן עֵינֵינוּ אֶל יְיָ אֱלֹהֵינוּ עַד שֶׁיְּחָנֵּנוּ.

יִשָּׂא   יִשָּׂא בְרָכָה מֵאֵת יְיָ, וּצְדָקָה מֵאֱלֹהֵי יִשְׁעוֹ. וּמְצָא חֵן
וְשֵׂכֶל טוֹב בְּעֵינֵי אֱלֹהִים וְאָדָם.

יְהֹוָה   יְיָ, חָנֵּנוּ, לְךָ קִוִּינוּ, הֱיֵה זְרֹעָם לַבְּקָרִים, אַף יְשׁוּעָתֵנוּ
בְּעֵת צָרָה.

פָּנָיו   אַל תַּסְתֵּר פָּנֶיךָ מִמֶּנִּי בְּיוֹם צַר לִי; הַטֵּה אֵלַי אָזְנֶךָ,
בְּיוֹם אֶקְרָא מַהֵר עֲנֵנִי.

אֵלֶיךָ   אֵלֶיךָ נָשָׂאתִי אֶת עֵינַי, הַיֹּשְׁבִי בַּשָּׁמָיִם.

וְיָשֵׂם   וְשָׂמוּ אֶת שְׁמִי עַל בְּנֵי יִשְׂרָאֵל, וַאֲנִי אֲבָרְכֵם.

לְךָ   לְךָ, יְיָ, הַגְּדֻלָּה וְהַגְּבוּרָה וְהַתִּפְאֶרֶת וְהַנֵּצַח וְהַהוֹד,
כִּי כֹל בַּשָּׁמַיִם וּבָאָרֶץ; לְךָ, יְיָ, הַמַּמְלָכָה וְהַמִּתְנַשֵּׂא
לְכֹל לְרֹאשׁ.

שָׁלוֹם.   שָׁלוֹם שָׁלוֹם לָרָחוֹק וְלַקָּרוֹב, אָמַר יְיָ, וּרְפָאתִיו.

amending, heal them as thou didst heal Hezekiah king of Judah from his illness, Miriam the prophetess from her leprosy and Naaman from his leprosy. Sweeten them as the waters of Marah were sweetened by Moses, and the waters of Jericho by Elisha. Even as thou didst turn the curse of wicked Balaam into a blessing, mayest thou turn all my dreams into happiness for myself and for all Israel. Protect me; be gracious to me and favor me. Amen.

יָאֵר May God be gracious to us and bless us and countenance us.

יְיָ It is the Lord, the Lord, a God merciful and gracious, slow to anger, rich in kindness and faithfulness.

פְּנֵה Turn to me and be gracious to me, for I am lonely and afflicted.

אֵלֶיךָ Towards thee I direct my desire.

וִיחֻנֶּךָ As the eyes of servants look to the hand of their master, and as a maid's eyes to the hand of her mistress, so our eyes look to our God, till he take pity on us.[1]

יִשָּׂא He will receive a blessing from the Lord, and justice from God his Deliverer. You shall find favor and good will with God and man alike.

יְיָ O Lord, be gracious to us; we have waited for thee; be thou their strength every morning, our salvation in time of distress.

פָּנֶיךָ Hide not thy face from me in my day of trouble; incline thy ear to me; answer me speedily when I call.

אֵלֶיךָ To thee I raise my eyes, O thou who art enthroned in heaven.[2]

וְשָׂמוּ So shall they put my name upon the children of Israel, and I will bless them.

לְךָ Thine, O Lord, is the greatness, the power, the glory, the triumph, and the majesty; for all that is in heaven and on earth is thine; thine, O Lord, is the kingdom, and thou art supreme over all.

שָׁלוֹם "Peace, peace, to the far and the near," says the Lord, "I will heal him."[3]

---

[1]*Psalm* 67:2; *Exodus* 34:6; *Psalms* 25:16; 25:1; 123:2.
[2]*Psalm* 24:5; *Proverbs* 3:4; *Isaiah* 33:2; *Psalms* 102:3; 123:1.
[3]*Numbers* 6:27; *I Chronicles* 29:11; *Isaiah* 57:19.

Congregation:

אַדִּיר בַּמָּרוֹם, שׁוֹכֵן בִּגְבוּרָה, אַתָּה שָׁלוֹם וְשִׁמְךָ שָׁלוֹם; יְהִי
רָצוֹן שֶׁתָּשִׂים עָלֵינוּ וְעַל כָּל עַמְּךָ בֵּית יִשְׂרָאֵל חַיִּים וּבְרָכָה
לְמִשְׁמֶרֶת שָׁלוֹם.

Kohanim:

רִבּוֹנוֹ שֶׁל עוֹלָם, עָשִׂינוּ מַה שֶּׁגָּזַרְתָּ עָלֵינוּ; אַף אַתָּה עֲשֵׂה
עִמָּנוּ כְּמָה שֶׁהִבְטַחְתָּנוּ. הַשְׁקִיפָה מִמְּעוֹן קָדְשְׁךָ, מִן הַשָּׁמַיִם,
וּבָרֵךְ אֶת עַמְּךָ אֶת יִשְׂרָאֵל, וְאֵת הָאֲדָמָה אֲשֶׁר נָתַתָּה לָנוּ,
כַּאֲשֶׁר נִשְׁבַּעְתָּ לַאֲבוֹתֵינוּ, אֶרֶץ זָבַת חָלָב וּדְבָשׁ.

שִׂים שָׁלוֹם (page 625)

קִדוּשָׁא רַבָּה לְשָׁלֹשׁ רְגָלִים

On Sabbath:

(וְשָׁמְרוּ בְנֵי יִשְׂרָאֵל אֶת הַשַּׁבָּת, לַעֲשׂוֹת אֶת הַשַּׁבָּת לְדֹרֹתָם
בְּרִית עוֹלָם. בֵּינִי וּבֵין בְּנֵי יִשְׂרָאֵל אוֹת הִיא לְעוֹלָם, כִּי שֵׁשֶׁת
יָמִים עָשָׂה יְיָ אֶת הַשָּׁמַיִם וְאֶת הָאָרֶץ, וּבַיּוֹם הַשְּׁבִיעִי שָׁבַת
וַיִּנָּפַשׁ.   עַל כֵּן בֵּרַךְ יְיָ אֶת יוֹם הַשַּׁבָּת וַיְקַדְּשֵׁהוּ.)

אֵלֶּה מוֹעֲדֵי יְיָ, מִקְרָאֵי קֹדֶשׁ, אֲשֶׁר תִּקְרְאוּ אוֹתָם בְּמוֹעֲדָם.
וַיְדַבֵּר מֹשֶׁה אֶת מוֹעֲדֵי יְיָ אֶל בְּנֵי יִשְׂרָאֵל.

סַבְרִי מָרָנָן וְרַבּוֹתַי.

בָּרוּךְ אַתָּה, יְיָ אֱלֹהֵינוּ, מֶלֶךְ הָעוֹלָם, בּוֹרֵא פְּרִי הַגָּפֶן.

In the Sukkah:

בָּרוּךְ אַתָּה, יְיָ אֱלֹהֵינוּ, מֶלֶךְ הָעוֹלָם, אֲשֶׁר קִדְּשָׁנוּ בְּמִצְוֹתָיו
וְצִוָּנוּ לֵשֵׁב בַּסֻּכָּה.

אדיר במרום is quoted in Berakhoth 55b, רבונו של עולם in Sotah 39a.

Congregation:

Supreme and mighty art thou on high; thou art peace and thy name is Peace. May it be thy will to grant life and blessedness and enduring peace to us and to all thy people, the house of Israel.

Kohanim:

Lord of the universe, we have performed what thou hast decreed for us; do thou, too, fulfill what thou hast promised us. "Look down from heaven, thy holy habitation, and bless thy people Israel and the land thou hast given us—as thou didst promise to our fathers—a land abounding in milk and honey."[1]

The Reader continues "O grant peace" (page 626).

MORNING KIDDUSH FOR FESTIVALS

On Sabbath:

(The children of Israel shall keep the Sabbath, observing the Sabbath throughout their generations as an everlasting covenant. It is a sign between me and the children of Israel forever that in six days the Lord made the heavens and the earth, and on the seventh day he ceased from work and rested.

Therefore the Lord blessed the Sabbath day and hallowed it.)[2]

These are the Lord's festivals, holy convocations, which you shall proclaim in their proper season.

Moses announced the Lord's festivals to the children of Israel.[3]

Blessed art thou, Lord our God, King of the universe, who createst the fruit of the vine.

In the Sukkah:

Blessed art thou, Lord our God, King of the universe, who hast sanctified us with thy commandments, and commanded us to dwell in booths.

---

[1]*Deuteronomy* 26:15.　[2]*Exodus* 31:16-17; 20:11.　[3]*Leviticus* 23:4, 44.

תְּפִלַּת טַל

Chanted on the first day of *Pesaḥ* during *Musaf*

Reader:

בָּרוּךְ אַתָּה, יְיָ אֱלֹהֵינוּ וֵאלֹהֵי אֲבוֹתֵינוּ, אֱלֹהֵי אַבְרָהָם,
אֱלֹהֵי יִצְחָק, וֵאלֹהֵי יַעֲקֹב, הָאֵל הַגָּדוֹל הַגִּבּוֹר וְהַנּוֹרָא, אֵל
עֶלְיוֹן, גּוֹמֵל חֲסָדִים טוֹבִים, וְקוֹנֵה הַכֹּל, וְזוֹכֵר חַסְדֵי אָבוֹת,
וּמֵבִיא גוֹאֵל לִבְנֵי בְנֵיהֶם לְמַעַן שְׁמוֹ בְּאַהֲבָה. מֶלֶךְ עוֹזֵר
וּמוֹשִׁיעַ וּמָגֵן.

בְּדַעְתּוֹ אַבִּיעָה חִידוֹת, בְּעַם זוּ בְּזוּ בְּטַל לְהַחֲדוֹת, טַל גֵּיא
וּדְשָׁאֶיהָ לַחֲדוֹת, דָּצִים בְּצִלּוֹ לְהֵחָדוֹת, אוֹת יַלְדוּת טַל לְהָגֵן
לְתוֹלֵדוֹת.

בָּרוּךְ אַתָּה, יְיָ, מָגֵן אַבְרָהָם.

אַתָּה גִבּוֹר לְעוֹלָם, אֲדֹנָי; מְחַיֵּה מֵתִים אַתָּה, רַב לְהוֹשִׁיעַ.
תְּהוֹמוֹת הֲדוֹם לְרָסִיסוֹ כְּסוּפִים, וְכָל נְאוֹת דֶּשֶׁא לוֹ
נִכְסָפִים, טַל זִכְרוֹ גְּבוּרוֹת מוֹסִיפִים, חָקוּק בְּגִישַׁת מוּסָפִים,
טַל לְהַחֲיוֹת בּוֹ נְקוּקֵי סְעִיפִים.

אֱלֹהֵינוּ וֵאלֹהֵי אֲבוֹתֵינוּ,

טַל תֵּן לִרְצוֹת אַרְצֶךָ,
שִׁיתֵנוּ בְרָכָה בְּדִיצֶךָ,
רֹב דָּגָן וְתִירוֹשׁ בְּהַפְרִיצֶךָ,
קוֹמֵם עִיר בָּהּ חֶפְצֶךָ, בְּטַל.

תפלת טל is a prayer for the plants to be refreshed by the regular descent
of the dew during the warm season. The poems תהומת הדום and טל תן לרצות
are the creations of Rabbi Elazar ha-Kallir, who probably lived in Palestine
during the eighth century. The best known and most prolific of the *payyetanim*

633

PRAYER FOR DEW

Chanted on the first day of Pesaḥ during Musaf

Reader:

Blessed art thou, Lord our God and God of our fathers, God of Abraham, God of Isaac and God of Jacob; great, mighty and revered God, sublime God, who bestowest lovingkindness, and art Master of all things; who rememberest the good deeds of our fathers, and who wilt graciously bring a redeemer to their children's children for the sake of thy name. O King, Supporter, Savior and Shield!

With thy approval I utter deep thoughts,
To cheer thy people by this prayer for dew.
Dew refreshes the earth and its verdure,
Joyous to be under thy protection.
May dew—symbol of youth—shield our young.

Blessed art thou, O Lord, Shield of Abraham.

Thou, O Lord, art mighty forever; thou revivest the dead; thou art powerful to save.

Earth's depths are eager for the drops of dew;
All the green meadows long and pine for dew.
The prayer for dew speaks of God's powers;
Hence it forms part of the Musaf service.
Dew will revive those in the clefts of rocks.

Our God and God of our fathers,

Grant dew to favor thy land;
Make us blessed with rejoicing,
With plenty of grain and wine;
Restore thy beloved land—with dew.

---

or liturgical poets, he wrote at least two hundred *piyyutim*, many of which cannot be understood without a commentary. His prayer for dew is one of the most delightful of his poems. It conveys the hope for the fertilization of the earth and the restoration of Eretz Yisrael. טל תן is a reversed alphabetical acrostic. Each of the six stanzas begins and ends with טל.

טַל צַוֵּה שָׁנָה טוֹבָה וּמְעֻטֶּרֶת,

פְּרִי הָאָרֶץ לְגָאוֹן וּלְתִפְאֶרֶת,

עִיר כְּסֻכָּה נוֹתֶרֶת,

שִׂימָה בְּיָדְךָ עֲטֶרֶת, בְּטָל.

טַל נוֹפֵף עֲלֵי אֶרֶץ בְּרוּכָה,

מִמֶּגֶד שָׁמַיִם שַׂבְּעֵנוּ בְרָכָה,

לְהָאִיר מִתּוֹךְ חֲשֵׁכָה,

כַּנָּה אַחֲרֶיךָ מְשׁוּכָה, בְּטָל.

טַל יַעֲסִיס צוּף הָרִים,

טְעַם בִּמְאֹדֶיךָ מֻבְחָרִים,

חֲנוּנֶיךָ חַלֵּץ מִמַּסְגֵּרִים,

זִמְרָה נַנְעִים וְקוֹל נָרִים, בְּטָל.

טַל וְשֹׂבַע מַלֵּא אֲסָמֵינוּ,

הַכָּעֵת תְּחַדֵּשׁ יָמֵינוּ,

דּוֹד כְּעֶרְכְּךָ הַעֲמֵד שְׁמֵנוּ,

גַּן רָוֶה שִׂימֵנוּ, בְּטָל.

טַל בּוֹ תְבָרֵךְ מָזוֹן,

בְּמִשְׁמַנֵּינוּ אַל יְהִי רָזוֹן,

אֲיֻמָּה אֲשֶׁר הִסַּעְתָּ כַצֹּאן,

אָנָּא תָּפֵק לָהּ רָצוֹן, בְּטָל.

שָׁאַתָּה הוּא יְיָ אֱלֹהֵינוּ, מַשִּׁיב הָרוּחַ וּמוֹרִיד הַטָּל.

Congregation:	Congregation and Reader:
אָמֵן.	לִבְרָכָה וְלֹא לִקְלָלָה
אָמֵן.	לְחַיִּים וְלֹא לְמָוֶת
אָמֵן.	לְשֹׂבַע וְלֹא לְרָזוֹן

מְכַלְכֵּל חַיִּים (page 609)

Grant dew for a good year, crowned
With splendid fruit of the land;
Zion now left like a lone booth,
Take her in thy hand like a crown.

Let dew fall on the blessed land;
Bless us with the gift of heaven;
In the darkness let a light dawn
For Israel who follows thee.

Let dew sweeten the mountains;
Let thy chosen taste thy wealth:
Free thy people from exile,
That we may sing and exult.

Let our barns be filled with grain;
Renew our days as of old;
O God, uplift us by thy grace;
Make us like a watered garden.

Bless our sustenance with dew;
Let no ill befall our flocks;
Bestow thy favor on the people
Whom thou didst lead like a flock.

For thou art the Lord our God, who causest the wind to blow
and the dew to fall.

Congregation and Reader:	*Congregation:*
For a blessing and not for a curse.	Amen.
For life and not for death.	Amen.
For plenty and not for scarcity.	Amen.

"Thou sustainest the living" (*page* 610)

סְפִירַת הָעֹמֶר

After *Ma'ariv*–from the second night of *Pesaḥ* until the night before *Shavuoth*

הִנְנִי מוּכָן וּמְזֻמָּן לְקַיֵּם מִצְוַת עֲשֵׂה שֶׁל סְפִירַת הָעֹמֶר,
כְּמוֹ שֶׁכָּתוּב בַּתּוֹרָה: וּסְפַרְתֶּם לָכֶם מִמָּחֳרַת הַשַּׁבָּת, מִיּוֹם
הֲבִיאֲכֶם אֶת עֹמֶר הַתְּנוּפָה, שֶׁבַע שַׁבָּתוֹת תְּמִימֹת תִּהְיֶינָה;
עַד מִמָּחֳרַת הַשַּׁבָּת הַשְּׁבִיעִית תִּסְפְּרוּ חֲמִשִּׁים יוֹם.

בָּרוּךְ אַתָּה, יְיָ אֱלֹהֵינוּ, מֶלֶךְ הָעוֹלָם, אֲשֶׁר קִדְּשָׁנוּ בְּמִצְוֹתָיו
וְצִוָּנוּ עַל סְפִירַת הָעֹמֶר.

1	הַיּוֹם יוֹם אֶחָד לָעֹמֶר.
2	הַיּוֹם שְׁנֵי יָמִים לָעֹמֶר.
3	הַיּוֹם שְׁלֹשָׁה יָמִים לָעֹמֶר.
4	הַיּוֹם אַרְבָּעָה יָמִים לָעֹמֶר.
5	הַיּוֹם חֲמִשָּׁה יָמִים לָעֹמֶר.
6	הַיּוֹם שִׁשָּׁה יָמִים לָעֹמֶר.
7	הַיּוֹם שִׁבְעָה יָמִים, שֶׁהֵם שָׁבוּעַ אֶחָד לָעֹמֶר.
8	הַיּוֹם שְׁמֹנָה יָמִים, שֶׁהֵם שָׁבוּעַ אֶחָד וְיוֹם אֶחָד לָעֹמֶר.
9	הַיּוֹם תִּשְׁעָה יָמִים, שֶׁהֵם שָׁבוּעַ אֶחָד וּשְׁנֵי יָמִים לָעֹמֶר.
10	הַיּוֹם עֲשָׂרָה יָמִים, שֶׁהֵם שָׁבוּעַ אֶחָד וּשְׁלֹשָׁה יָמִים לָעֹמֶר.

ספירת העומר, the counting of seven weeks from the day on which the *omer*
was offered till *Shavuoth*, the Feast of Weeks, serves to connect the anniversary of the exodus from Egypt with the festival that commemorates the
giving of the Torah on Mount Sinai. According to tradition, it was announced
to the Israelites in Egypt that fifty days after the exodus the Torah would be
given to them. As soon as they were liberated, they were so eager for the
arrival of the promised day that they began to count the days, saying each

637

COUNTING OF THE OMER

After Ma'ariv—from the second night of Pesah until the night before Shavuoth

I am ready and prepared to perform the positive command concerning the counting of the *Omer*, as it is written in the Torah: "You shall count from the day following the day of rest, from the day you brought the sheaf of the wave-offering, seven full weeks shall be counted; you shall count fifty days to the day following the seventh week."[1]

Blessed art thou, Lord our God, King of the universe, who hast sanctified us with thy commandments, and commanded us concerning the counting of the *Omer*.

1. This is the first day of the *Omer*.

2. This is the second day of the *Omer*.

3. This is the third day of the *Omer*.

4. This is the fourth day of the *Omer*.

5. This is the fifth day of the *Omer*.

6. This is the sixth day of the *Omer*.

7. This is the seventh day, being one week of the *Omer*.

8. This is the eighth day, being one week and one day of the *Omer*.

9. This is the ninth day, being one week and two days of the *Omer*.

10. This is the tenth day, being one week and three days of the *Omer*.

---

time: "Now we have one day less to wait for the giving of the Torah." To commemorate this, the Torah prescribes that the days from *Pesah* to *Shavuoth* be counted.

---

[1] *Leviticus* 23:15-16.

11 הַיּוֹם אַחַד עָשָׂר יוֹם, שֶׁהֵם שָׁבוּעַ אֶחָד וְאַרְבָּעָה יָמִים לָעוֹמֶר.

12 הַיּוֹם שְׁנֵים עָשָׂר יוֹם, שֶׁהֵם שָׁבוּעַ אֶחָד וַחֲמִשָּׁה יָמִים לָעוֹמֶר.

13 הַיּוֹם שְׁלֹשָׁה עָשָׂר יוֹם, שֶׁהֵם שָׁבוּעַ אֶחָד וְשִׁשָּׁה יָמִים לָעוֹמֶר.

14 הַיּוֹם אַרְבָּעָה עָשָׂר יוֹם, שֶׁהֵם שְׁנֵי שָׁבוּעוֹת לָעוֹמֶר.

15 הַיּוֹם חֲמִשָּׁה עָשָׂר יוֹם, שֶׁהֵם שְׁנֵי שָׁבוּעוֹת וְיוֹם אֶחָד לָעוֹמֶר.

16 הַיּוֹם שִׁשָּׁה עָשָׂר יוֹם, שֶׁהֵם שְׁנֵי שָׁבוּעוֹת וּשְׁנֵי יָמִים לָעוֹמֶר.

17 הַיּוֹם שִׁבְעָה עָשָׂר יוֹם, שֶׁהֵם שְׁנֵי שָׁבוּעוֹת וּשְׁלֹשָׁה יָמִים לָעוֹמֶר.

18 הַיּוֹם שְׁמֹנָה עָשָׂר יוֹם, שֶׁהֵם שְׁנֵי שָׁבוּעוֹת וְאַרְבָּעָה יָמִים לָעוֹמֶר.

19 הַיּוֹם תִּשְׁעָה עָשָׂר יוֹם, שֶׁהֵם שְׁנֵי שָׁבוּעוֹת וַחֲמִשָּׁה יָמִים לָעוֹמֶר.

20 הַיּוֹם עֶשְׂרִים יוֹם, שֶׁהֵם שְׁנֵי שָׁבוּעוֹת וְשִׁשָּׁה יָמִים לָעוֹמֶר.

21 הַיּוֹם אֶחָד וְעֶשְׂרִים יוֹם, שֶׁהֵם שְׁלֹשָׁה שָׁבוּעוֹת לָעוֹמֶר.

22 הַיּוֹם שְׁנַיִם וְעֶשְׂרִים יוֹם, שֶׁהֵם שְׁלֹשָׁה שָׁבוּעוֹת וְיוֹם אֶחָד לָעוֹמֶר.

23 הַיּוֹם שְׁלֹשָׁה וְעֶשְׂרִים יוֹם, שֶׁהֵם שְׁלֹשָׁה שָׁבוּעוֹת וּשְׁנֵי יָמִים לָעוֹמֶר.

24 הַיּוֹם אַרְבָּעָה וְעֶשְׂרִים יוֹם, שֶׁהֵם שְׁלֹשָׁה שָׁבוּעוֹת וּשְׁלֹשָׁה יָמִים לָעוֹמֶר.

11. This is the eleventh day, being one week and four days of the *Omer*.

12. This is the twelfth day, being one week and five days of the *Omer*.

13. This is the thirteenth day, being one week and six days of the *Omer*.

14. This is the fourteenth day, being two weeks of the *Omer*.

15. This is the fifteenth day, being two weeks and one day of the *Omer*.

16. This is the sixteenth day, being two weeks and two days of the *Omer*.

17. This is the seventeenth day, being two weeks and three days of the *Omer*.

18. This is the eighteenth day, being two weeks and four days of the *Omer*.

19. This is the nineteenth day, being two weeks and five days of the *Omer*.

20. This is the twentieth day, being two weeks and six days of the *Omer*.

21. This is the twenty-first day, being three weeks of the *Omer*.

22. This is the twenty-second day, being three weeks and one day of the *Omer*.

23. This is the twenty-third day, being three weeks and two days of the *Omer*.

24. This is the twenty-fourth day, being three weeks and three days of the *Omer*.

25 הַיּוֹם חֲמִשָּׁה וְעֶשְׂרִים יוֹם, שֶׁהֵם שְׁלֹשָׁה שָׁבוּעוֹת וְאַרְבָּעָה יָמִים לָעֹמֶר.

26 הַיּוֹם שִׁשָּׁה וְעֶשְׂרִים יוֹם, שֶׁהֵם שְׁלֹשָׁה שָׁבוּעוֹת וַחֲמִשָּׁה יָמִים לָעֹמֶר.

27 הַיּוֹם שִׁבְעָה וְעֶשְׂרִים יוֹם, שֶׁהֵם שְׁלֹשָׁה שָׁבוּעוֹת וְשִׁשָּׁה יָמִים לָעֹמֶר.

28 הַיּוֹם שְׁמֹנָה וְעֶשְׂרִים יוֹם, שֶׁהֵם אַרְבָּעָה שָׁבוּעוֹת לָעֹמֶר.

29 הַיּוֹם תִּשְׁעָה וְעֶשְׂרִים יוֹם, שֶׁהֵם אַרְבָּעָה שָׁבוּעוֹת וְיוֹם אֶחָד לָעֹמֶר.

30 הַיּוֹם שְׁלֹשִׁים יוֹם, שֶׁהֵם אַרְבָּעָה שָׁבוּעוֹת וּשְׁנֵי יָמִים לָעֹמֶר.

31 הַיּוֹם אֶחָד וּשְׁלֹשִׁים יוֹם, שֶׁהֵם אַרְבָּעָה שָׁבוּעוֹת וּשְׁלֹשָׁה יָמִים לָעֹמֶר.

32 הַיּוֹם שְׁנַיִם וּשְׁלֹשִׁים יוֹם, שֶׁהֵם אַרְבָּעָה שָׁבוּעוֹת וְאַרְבָּעָה יָמִים לָעֹמֶר.

33 הַיּוֹם שְׁלֹשָׁה וּשְׁלֹשִׁים יוֹם, שֶׁהֵם אַרְבָּעָה שָׁבוּעוֹת וַחֲמִשָּׁה יָמִים לָעֹמֶר.

34 הַיּוֹם אַרְבָּעָה וּשְׁלֹשִׁים יוֹם, שֶׁהֵם אַרְבָּעָה שָׁבוּעוֹת וְשִׁשָּׁה יָמִים לָעֹמֶר.

35 הַיּוֹם חֲמִשָּׁה וּשְׁלֹשִׁים יוֹם, שֶׁהֵם חֲמִשָּׁה שָׁבוּעוֹת לָעֹמֶר.

36 הַיּוֹם שִׁשָּׁה וּשְׁלֹשִׁים יוֹם, שֶׁהֵם חֲמִשָּׁה שָׁבוּעוֹת וְיוֹם אֶחָד לָעֹמֶר.

37 הַיּוֹם שִׁבְעָה וּשְׁלֹשִׁים יוֹם, שֶׁהֵם חֲמִשָּׁה שָׁבוּעוֹת וּשְׁנֵי יָמִים לָעֹמֶר.

25. This is the twenty-fifth day, being three weeks and four days of the *Omer*.

26. This is the twenty-sixth day, being three weeks and five days of the *Omer*.

27. This is the twenty-seventh day, being three weeks and six days of the *Omer*.

28. This is the twenty-eighth day, being four weeks of the *Omer*.

29. This is the twenty-ninth day, being four weeks and one day of the *Omer*.

30. This is the thirtieth day, being four weeks and two days of the *Omer*.

31. This is the thirty-first day, being four weeks and three days of the *Omer*.

32. This is the thirty-second day, being four weeks and four days of the *Omer*.

33. This is the thirty-third day, being four weeks and five days of the *Omer*.

34. This is the thirty-fourth day, being four weeks and six days of the *Omer*.

35. This is the thirty-fifth day, being five weeks of the *Omer*.

36. This is the thirty-sixth day, being five weeks and one day of the *Omer*.

37. This is the thirty-seventh day, being five weeks and two days of the *Omer*.

38 הַיּוֹם שְׁמֹנָה וּשְׁלֹשִׁים יוֹם, שֶׁהֵם חֲמִשָּׁה שָׁבוּעוֹת וּשְׁלֹשָׁה יָמִים לָעֹמֶר.

39 הַיּוֹם תִּשְׁעָה וּשְׁלֹשִׁים יוֹם, שֶׁהֵם חֲמִשָּׁה שָׁבוּעוֹת וְאַרְבָּעָה יָמִים לָעֹמֶר.

40 הַיּוֹם אַרְבָּעִים יוֹם, שֶׁהֵם חֲמִשָּׁה שָׁבוּעוֹת וַחֲמִשָּׁה יָמִים לָעֹמֶר.

41 הַיּוֹם אֶחָד וְאַרְבָּעִים יוֹם, שֶׁהֵם חֲמִשָּׁה שָׁבוּעוֹת וְשִׁשָּׁה יָמִים לָעֹמֶר.

42 הַיּוֹם שְׁנַיִם וְאַרְבָּעִים יוֹם, שֶׁהֵם שִׁשָּׁה שָׁבוּעוֹת לָעֹמֶר.

43 הַיּוֹם שְׁלֹשָׁה וְאַרְבָּעִים יוֹם, שֶׁהֵם שִׁשָּׁה שָׁבוּעוֹת וְיוֹם אֶחָד לָעֹמֶר.

44 הַיּוֹם אַרְבָּעָה וְאַרְבָּעִים יוֹם, שֶׁהֵם שִׁשָּׁה שָׁבוּעוֹת וּשְׁנֵי יָמִים לָעֹמֶר.

45 הַיּוֹם חֲמִשָּׁה וְאַרְבָּעִים יוֹם, שֶׁהֵם שִׁשָּׁה שָׁבוּעוֹת וּשְׁלֹשָׁה יָמִים לָעֹמֶר.

46 הַיּוֹם שִׁשָּׁה וְאַרְבָּעִים יוֹם, שֶׁהֵם שִׁשָּׁה שָׁבוּעוֹת וְאַרְבָּעָה יָמִים לָעֹמֶר.

47 הַיּוֹם שִׁבְעָה וְאַרְבָּעִים יוֹם, שֶׁהֵם שִׁשָּׁה שָׁבוּעוֹת וַחֲמִשָּׁה יָמִים לָעֹמֶר.

48 הַיּוֹם שְׁמֹנָה וְאַרְבָּעִים יוֹם, שֶׁהֵם שִׁשָּׁה שָׁבוּעוֹת וְשִׁשָּׁה יָמִים לָעֹמֶר.

49 הַיּוֹם תִּשְׁעָה וְאַרְבָּעִים יוֹם, שֶׁהֵם שִׁבְעָה שָׁבוּעוֹת לָעֹמֶר.

After the counting:

הָרַחֲמָן, הוּא יַחֲזִיר לָנוּ עֲבוֹדַת בֵּית הַמִּקְדָּשׁ לִמְקוֹמָהּ בִּמְהֵרָה בְיָמֵינוּ. אָמֵן סֶלָה.

38. This is the thirty-eighth day, being five weeks and three days of the *Omer*.

39. This is the thirty-ninth day, being five weeks and four days of the *Omer*.

40. This is the fortieth day, being five weeks and five days of the *Omer*.

41. This is the forty-first day, being five weeks and six days of the *Omer*.

42. This is the forty-second day, being six weeks of the *Omer*.

43. This is the forty-third day, being six weeks and one day of the *Omer*.

44. This is the forty-fourth day, being six weeks and two days of the *Omer*.

45. This is the forty-fifth day, being six weeks and three days of the *Omer*.

46. This is the forty-sixth day, being six weeks and four days of the *Omer*.

47. This is the forty-seventh day, being six weeks and five days of the *Omer*.

48. This is the forty-eighth day, being six weeks and six days of the *Omer*.

49. This is the forty-ninth day, being seven weeks of the *Omer*.

After the counting:

May the Merciful One restore the Temple service to its place speedily in our days. Amen.

תהלים סז

לַמְנַצֵּחַ בִּנְגִינֹת מִזְמוֹר שִׁיר. אֱלֹהִים יְחָנֵּנוּ וִיבָרְכֵנוּ; יָאֵר פָּנָיו אִתָּנוּ, סֶלָה. לָדַעַת בָּאָרֶץ דַּרְכֶּךָ, בְּכָל גּוֹיִם יְשׁוּעָתֶךָ. יוֹדוּךָ עַמִּים, אֱלֹהִים; יוֹדוּךָ עַמִּים כֻּלָּם. יִשְׂמְחוּ וִירַנְּנוּ לְאֻמִּים, כִּי תִשְׁפֹּט עַמִּים מִישׁוֹר; וּלְאֻמִּים בָּאָרֶץ תַּנְחֵם, סֶלָה. יוֹדוּךָ עַמִּים, אֱלֹהִים; יוֹדוּךָ עַמִּים כֻּלָּם. אֶרֶץ נָתְנָה יְבוּלָהּ; יְבָרְכֵנוּ אֱלֹהִים אֱלֹהֵינוּ. יְבָרְכֵנוּ אֱלֹהִים, וְיִירְאוּ אוֹתוֹ כָּל אַפְסֵי אָרֶץ.

אָנָּא, בְּכֹחַ גְּדֻלַּת יְמִינְךָ תַּתִּיר צְרוּרָה.

קַבֵּל רִנַּת עַמְּךָ, שַׂגְּבֵנוּ, טַהֲרֵנוּ, נוֹרָא.

נָא, גִבּוֹר, דּוֹרְשֵׁי יִחוּדְךָ כְּבָבַת שָׁמְרֵם.

בָּרְכֵם, טַהֲרֵם, רַחֲמֵם, צִדְקָתְךָ תָּמִיד גָּמְלֵם.

חֲסִין קָדוֹשׁ, בְּרֹב טוּבְךָ נַהֵל עֲדָתֶךָ.

יָחִיד גֵּאֶה, לְעַמְּךָ פְּנֵה, זוֹכְרֵי קְדֻשָּׁתֶךָ.

שַׁוְעָתֵנוּ קַבֵּל וּשְׁמַע צַעֲקָתֵנוּ, יוֹדֵעַ תַּעֲלוּמוֹת.

בָּרוּךְ שֵׁם כְּבוֹד מַלְכוּתוֹ לְעוֹלָם וָעֶד.

רִבּוֹנוֹ שֶׁל עוֹלָם, אַתָּה צִוִּיתָנוּ עַל יְדֵי מֹשֶׁה עַבְדְּךָ לִסְפּוֹר סְפִירַת הָעֹמֶר, כְּדֵי לְטַהֲרֵנוּ מִקְּלִפּוֹתֵינוּ וּמִטֻּמְאוֹתֵינוּ, כְּמוֹ שֶׁכָּתַבְתָּ בְּתוֹרָתֶךָ: וּסְפַרְתֶּם לָכֶם מִמָּחֳרַת הַשַּׁבָּת, מִיּוֹם הֲבִיאֲכֶם אֶת עֹמֶר הַתְּנוּפָה, שֶׁבַע שַׁבָּתוֹת תְּמִימוֹת תִּהְיֶינָה; עַד מִמָּחֳרַת הַשַּׁבָּת הַשְּׁבִיעִית תִּסְפְּרוּ חֲמִשִּׁים יוֹם. כְּדֵי שֶׁיִּטַּהֲרוּ נַפְשׁוֹת עַמְּךָ יִשְׂרָאֵל מִזֻּהֲמָתָם. וּבְכֵן, יְהִי רָצוֹן מִלְּפָנֶיךָ, יְיָ אֱלֹהֵינוּ וֵאלֹהֵי אֲבוֹתֵינוּ, שֶׁבִּזְכוּת סְפִירַת הָעֹמֶר שֶׁסָּפַרְתִּי הַיּוֹם יְתֻקַּן מַה שֶּׁפָּגַמְתִּי בִּסְפִירָה, וְאֶטָּהֵר וְאֶתְקַדֵּשׁ בִּקְדֻשָּׁה שֶׁל מַעְלָה. אָמֵן סֶלָה.

למנצח, Psalm 67, consists of seven verses which total forty-nine words; suggesting the number of seven weeks or forty-nine days of the *Sefirah*.

Psalm 67

For the Choirmaster; with string-music; a psalm, a song. May God be gracious to us and bless us; may he cause his favor to shine among us. Then shall thy way be known on earth, and thy saving power among all nations. The peoples shall praise thee, O God; all the peoples shall praise thee! Let the nations be glad and sing for joy, for thou rulest the peoples justly; thou guidest the nations on earth. The peoples shall praise thee, O Lord; all the peoples shall praise thee! The earth has yielded its produce; God, our own God, blesses us. God blesses us; all the far ends of the earth shall revere him.

By the great power of thy right hand, O set the captive free.
Revered God, accept thy people's prayer; strengthen us, cleanse us.
Almighty God, guard as the apple of the eye those who seek thee.
Bless them, cleanse them, pity them; ever grant them thy truth.
Mighty, holy God, in thy abundant grace, guide thy people.
Exalted God, turn to thy people who proclaim thy holiness.
Accept our prayer, hear our cry, thou who knowest secret thoughts.
Blessed be the name of his glorious majesty forever and ever.

Lord of the universe, thou didst command us through Moses thy servant concerning the counting of the *Omer*, in order to cleanse us of our evil things and impurities; thou didst write in thy Torah: "You shall count from the day following the day of rest, from the day you brought the sheaf of the wave-offering; seven full weeks shall be counted; you shall count fifty days to the day following the seventh week."[1] May all thy people of Israel be purged from their impurities. May it be thy will, Lord our God and God of our fathers, that my counting the *Omer* today help set right again the errors I have committed; may I rise high in purity and holiness. Amen.

---

[1] *Leviticus* 23:15-16.

אַקְדָּמוּת

Chanted on the first day of *Shavuoth* before the reading of the Torah

אַקְדָּמוּת מִלִּין וְשָׁרָיוּת שׁוּתָא
אוֹלָא שָׁקֵלְנָא הַרְמָן וּרְשׁוּתָא.
בְּבָבֵי תְּרֵי וּתְלָת דְּאֶפְתַּח בְּנַקְשׁוּתָא
בְּבָרֵי דְּבָרֵי וְטָרֵי עֲדֵי לְקַשִׁשׁוּתָא.

גְּבוּרָן עָלְמִין לֵהּ וְלָא סְפֵק פְּרִישׁוּתָא
גְּוִיל אִלּוּ רְקִיעֵי קְנֵי כָּל חוּרְשָׁתָא.
דְּיוֹ אִלּוּ יַמֵּי וְכָל מֵי כְנִישׁוּתָא
דָּיְרֵי אַרְעָא סָפְרֵי וְרָשְׁמֵי רַשְׁוָתָא.
הֲדַר מָרֵא שְׁמַיָּא וְשַׁלִּיט בְּיַבֶּשְׁתָּא
הֲקֵם עָלְמָא יְחִידַאי וְכַבְּשֵׁהּ בְּכַבְּשׁוּתָא.
וּבְלָא לֵאוּ שַׁכְלְלֵהּ וּבְלָא תְשָׁשׁוּתָא
וּבְאָתָא קַלִּילָא דְּלֵית בַּהּ מְשָׁשׁוּתָא.
זַמֵּן כָּל עֲבִדְתֵּהּ בְּהַךְ יוֹמֵי שְׁתָּא
זָהוֹר יְקָרֵהּ עֲלֵי עֲלֵי כָרְסֵיהּ דְּאֶשָּׁתָא.
חַיָל אֶלֶף אַלְפִין וְרִבּוֹא לְשַׁמְּשׁוּתָא
חַדְתִּין נְבוֹט לְצַפְרִין סַגִּיאָה טְרָשׁוּתָא.
טְפֵי יְקִידִין שְׂרָפִין כְּלוֹל גַּפֵּי שִׁתָּא
טְעֵם עַד יִתְיְהֵב לְהוֹן שְׁתִיקִין בְּאַדִשְׁתָּא.

אקדמות was composed by Rabbi Meir ben Isaac of France, who lived in the eleventh century. The poem, written in Aramaic, consists of ninety verses alphabetically arranged. Its acrostic comprises, in addition to a twofold alphabet, the names of the author and his father as well as a short petition: מאיר ביר רבי יצחק, יגדל בתורה ובמעשים טובים אמן, וחזק ואמץ. There are ten syllables to each verse,

AKDAMUTH

Chanted on the first day of Shavuoth before the reading of the Torah

Before reciting the Ten Commandments,
I first ask permission and approval
To start with two or three stanzas in fear
Of God who creates and ever sustains.

He has endless might, not to be described
Were the skies parchment, were all the reeds quills,

Were the seas and all waters made of ink,
Were all the world's inhabitants made scribes.

The glorious Lord of heaven and earth,
Alone, formed the world, veiled in mystery.

Without exertion did he perfect it,
Only by a light sign, without substance.

He accomplished all his work in six days;
His glory ascended a throne of fire.

Millions of legions are at his service;
Fresh each morning they flourish with great faith.

More glowing are the six-winged seraphim,
Who keep silence till leave is given them.

---

and one rhyme (תא) runs through the entire hymn. Recited on the first day of *Shavuoth* when the *kohen* is called to the Torah, this mystical poem deals with the indescribable greatness of the Creator, the excellence of the Torah and the future hope of Israel.

עדי לקששותא is taken from Isaiah 46:4 (ועד זקנה... אני אסבל).

אתא קלילא refers to the mystic idea that the creation of the world was brought about by means of the Hebrew letter ה.

חדתין נבוט... a paraphrase of the verse חדשים לבקרים, רבה אמונתך (Lamentations 3:23). According to a midrashic statement, there are countless numbers of angels who come into being daily; they praise God and vanish immediately after the performance of their task.

648

יְקַבְּלוּן דֵּן מִן דֵּן שָׁוֵי דְּלָא בְשַׁשְׁתָּא

יְקַר מְלֵי כָל אַרְעָא לְתַלְוּתֵי קְדוּשְׁתָּא׃

בְּקָל מִן קֳדָם שַׁדַּי כְּקָל מֵי נְפִישׁוּתָא

בְּרוּבִין קֳבֵל גַּלְגַּלִּין מְרוֹמְמִין בְּאוּשָׁתָא׃

לְמֶחֱזֵי בְּאַנְפָּא עֵין כְּוָת גִּירֵי קַשְׁתָּא

לְכָל אֲתַר דְּמִשְׁתַּלְּחִין זְרִיזִין בְּאַשְׁוָתָא׃

מְבָרְכִין בְּרִיךְ יְקָרֵהּ בְּכָל לְשָׁן לְחִישׁוּתָא

מֵאֲתַר בֵּית שְׁכִינְתֵּהּ דְּלָא צְרִיךְ בְּחִישׁוּתָא׃

נְהִים כָּל חֵיל מְרוֹמָא מְקַלְּסִין בַּחֲשַׁשְׁתָּא

נְהִירָא מַלְכוּתֵהּ לְדָר וְדָר לְאַפְרַשְׁתָּא׃

סְדִירָא בְהוֹן קְדוּשְׁתָּא וְכַד חָלְפָא שַׁעֲתָא

סִיּוּמָא דִלְעָלַם וְאוֹף לָא לְשָׁבוּעֲתָא׃

עֲדַב יְקַר אַחֲסַנְתֵּהּ חֲבִיבִין דְּבִקְבַעְוָּתָא

עָבְדִין לֵהּ חַטִיבָא בִּדְנַח וּשְׁקַעְתָּא׃

פְּרִישָׁן לְמָנָתֵהּ לְמֶעֱבַּד לֵהּ רְעוּתָא

פְּרִישׁוּתֵהּ שְׁבָחֵהּ יְחַוּוּן בִּשְׁעוּתָא׃

צְבִי וְחַמֵּד וְרַגֵּג דְּיִלְאוּן בְּלָעוּתָא

צְלוֹתְהוֹן בְּכֵן מְקַבֵּל וְהַנְיָא בָעוּתָא׃

קְטִירָא לְחֵי עָלְמָא בְּתָגָא בִּשְׁבוּעֲתָא

קַבֵּל יְקַר טוֹטַפְתָּא יְתִיבָא בִּקְבִיעוּתָא׃

רְשִׁימָא הִיא גוּפָא בְּחָכְמְתָא וּבְדַעְתָּא

רְבוּתְהוֹן דְּיִשְׂרָאֵל קְרָאֵי בִּשְׁמַעְתָּא׃

שְׁבַח רִבּוֹן עָלְמָא אֲמִירָא דַכְוָתָא

שְׁפַר עֲלֵי לְחַוּוּיֵהּ בְּאַפֵּי מַלְכְּוָתָא׃

...יקר מלי contains the essential part of the *Kedushah*, derived from Isaiah 6:3.

Without delay they call to one another:
"God's majestic splendor fills the whole earth!"

Like a mighty thunder, like ocean's roar,
The cherubim and the spheres rise loudly

To gaze at the rainbowlike appearance.
Wherever sent, they hasten anxiously,

Whispering praise in each tongue: "Blessed be
His glory in his entire universe."

All the heavenly hosts shout praise in awe:
"His glory shines forever and ever!"

Their hymn is timed; when the hour is gone,
They shall at no period chant it again.

Dear to him are the people of Israel,
Acclaiming him each morning and evening.

They are dedicated to do his will;
His wonders, his praises, they declare hourly.

He desires them to toil in the Torah,
So that their prayer be well accepted,

Bound up in the crown of the Eternal,
Securely set near the precious frontlet.

His frontlet is most skilfully inscribed:
"Great is Israel who proclaims God's Oneness."

The praise of the world's Lord, in pure homage,
I am pleased to declare before the kings.

סיומא דלעלם that is, they are silent forever; they do not chant even after seven years. The reference is to the midrashic statement to the effect that whenever the daily angels do not chant their hymns at the exact moment, they disappear in the stream of fire known as *Dinur*.

עדב יקר אחסנתיה the lot of his precious heritage [Israel]. This refers to the talmudic passage (Ḥullin 91b) to the effect that Israel sings God's praises at all times, while the angels are limited in this respect.

קטירא לחי עלמא refers to the mystic idea that God's *tefillin* contain an inscription in praise of Israel.

תָּאִין וּמִתְכַּנְשִׁין כְּחֵזוּ אַדְוָתָא

תְּמֵהִין וְשָׁיְלִין לֵהּ בְּעֵסֶק אָחֲוָתָא.

מְנָן וּמָאן הוּא רְחִימָךְ שַׁפִּירָא בְּרֵוָתָא

אֲרוּם בְּגִינֵהּ סָפִית מְדוֹר אַרְיָוָתָא.

יְקָרָא וְיָאֵה אַתְּ אִין תְּעָרְבִי לְמַרְוָתָא

רְעוּתֵךְ נַעֲבֵד לִיךְ בְּכָל אַתְרְוָתָא.

בְּחָכְמְתָא מְתִיבְתָא לְהוֹן קְצָת לְהוֹדָעוּתָא

יְדַעְתּוּן חַכְּמִין לֵהּ בְּאִשְׁתְּמוֹדָעוּתָא.

רְבוּתְכוֹן מָה חֲשִׁיבָא קָבֵל הַהִיא שְׁבַחְתָּא

רְבוּתָא דְיַעְבֵד לִי כַּד מַטְיָא יְשׁוּעָתָא.

בְּמֵיתֵי לִי נְהוֹרָא וְתַחֲפֵי לְכוֹן בַּהֲתָא

יְקָרֵהּ כַּד אִתְגְּלֵי בְּתָקְפָּא וּבְגֵוָתָא.

יְשַׁלֵּם גְּמֻלַיָּא לְסָנְאֵי וְנַגְוָתָא

צִדְקָתָא לְעַם חֲבִיב וְסַגִּיא זַכְוָתָא.

חֲדוּ שְׁלֵמָא בְּמֵיתֵי וּמְנֵי דַכְיָתָא

קִרְיְתָא דִירוּשְׁלֵם כַּד יְכַנֵּשׁ גַּלְוָתָא.

יְקָרֵהּ מַטִּיל עֲלַהּ בְּיוֹמֵי וְלֵילָוָתָא

גְּנוּנֵהּ לְמֶעְבַּד בַּהּ בְּתוּשְׁבְּחָן כְּלִילָתָא.

דְּזָהוֹר עֲנָנַיָּא לְמִשְׁפַּר כִּילָתָא

לְפוּמֵהּ דַעֲבִידְתָּא עֲבִידָן מְטַלַלְתָּא.

בְּתַכְתְּקֵי דְהַב פִּזָּא וּשְׁבַע מַעֲלָתָא

תְּחִימִין צַדִּיקֵי קֳדָם רַב פָּעֲלָתָא.

וְרֵוֵיהוֹן דָּמֵה לְשַׁבְעָא חֶדְוָתָא

רְקִיעָא בְּזֵהוֹרֵהּ וְכוֹכְבֵי זִיוָתָא.

They come and gather like the surging waves,
Wondering and asking about the signs:

Whence and who is your beloved, O fair one?
For whom do you die in the lions' den?

Most precious are you; if you merge with us,
We will do your will in all the regions.

With wisdom I answer them concisely:
You must recognize and acknowledge him!

Of what value is your glory compared
With all that God will do for me in due time,

When light will come to me and shame to you,
When he will reveal himself in great might?

He will repay the foes in all the isles;
Triumph to the dear and upright people!

Perfect joy, pure delight, will come into
Jerusalem when he will gather the exiles.

His glory will shield Zion day and night,
While his tent for praise will be made in it

Under a splendid canopy of bright clouds.
For each godly man a booth will be made,

Furnished with a gold throne of seven steps.
The righteous will be arrayed before God,

Their sight resembling sevenfold delight,
The brilliant sky and the luminous stars—

תאין ומתכנשין alludes to the medieval public disputations on the relative merits of Judaism and other religions, with particular emphasis upon the Messianic idea.

וכן היו אומות תמהין ושילין and onwards is based upon the *Sifré*, section 143: העולם שאלים את ישראל ואומרים להם: "מה דודך מדוד" שכך אתם מומתים עליו, שכך אתם נהרגים עליו?... כולכם נאים, כולכם גבורים, בואו והתערבו עמנו. וישראל אומרים להם: נאמר לכם מקצת שבחו, ואתם מכירים אותו ...

הֲדָרָא דְלָא אֶפְשַׁר לְמִפְרַט בְּשִׂפְוָתָא
וְלָא אִשְׁתְּמַע וְחָמֵי נְבִיאָן חֲזַוָתָא.
בְּלָא שָׁלְטָא בֵהּ עֵין בְּגוֹ עֵדֶן גִּנְתָא
מְטַיְלֵי בֵּי חִנְגָּא לְבַחֲדֵי דִשְׁכִינְתָּא.
עֲלֵהּ רָמְזֵי דֵן הוּא בְּרַם בְּאָמְתָנוּתָא
שַׂבְּרָנָא לֵהּ בְּשִׁבְבִין תְּקוֹף הֵמְנוּתָא.
יַדְבַּר לָן עָלְמִין עֲלֵמִין מְדַמּוּתָא
מְנָת דִּילָן דְּמִלְּקַדְמִין פָּרֵשׁ בַּאֲרָמוּתָא.
טְלוּלֵהּ דְּלִוְיָתָן וְתוֹר טוּר רָמוּתָא
וְחַד בְּחַד כִּי סָבִיךְ וְעָבֵד קְרָבוּתָא.
בְּקַרְנוֹהִי מְנַגַּח בְּהֵמוֹת בְּרַבְרְבוּתָא
יְקַרְטַע נוּן לְקִבְלֵהּ בְּצִיצוֹי בִּגְבוּרְתָּא.
מְקָרֵב לֵהּ בָּרְיֵהּ בְּחַרְבֵּהּ רַבְרְבָתָא
אֲרִסְטוֹן לְצַדִּיקֵי יְתַקֵּן וְשֵׁרוּתָא.
מְסַחֲרִין עֲלֵי תַכֵּי דְּכַדְכֹּד וְגוּמַרְתָּא
נְגִידִין קַמֵּיהוֹן אֲפַרְסְמוֹן נַהֲרָתָא.
וּמִתְפַּנְּקִין וּרְווֹ בְּכַסֵּי רְוָיָתָא
חֲמַר מְרַת דְּמִבְּרֵאשִׁית נְטִיר בֵּי נַעֲוָתָא.
זַכָּאִין כַּד שְׁמַעְתּוּן שְׁבַח דָּא שִׁירָתָא
קְבִיעִין כֵּן תֶּהֱוֹון בְּהַנְהוּ חֲבוּרָתָא.
וְתִזְכּוּן דִּי תֵיתְבוּן בְּעֵלָּא דָרָתָא
אֲרֵי תְצִיתוּן לְמִלּוֹי דְּנָפְקִין בְּהַדְרָתָא.
מְרוֹמַם הוּא אֱלָהִין בְּקַדְמָא וּבַתְרַיְתָא
צְבִי בִי וְאִתְרְעִי בָן וּמְסַר לָן אוֹרַיְתָא.

A splendor that no language can describe,
That was not heard of nor viewed by prophets.

No eye has penetrated Paradise,
Where the righteous dance in presence of God,
Reverently pointing out: "This is he
For whom we looked in exile with firm faith!

He now gently guides us eternally,
Granting us the share long reserved for us."
Leviathan contends with Behemoth;
They are locked in combat with each other.

Behemoth gores mightily with its horns;
The sea-monster counters with potent fins.

The Creator slays them with his great sword,
And prepares a banquet for the righteous,

Who sit in rows at tables of precious stones,
While before them there flow streams of balsam,

And they indulge themselves and drink full cups
Of the precious old wine preserved in vats.

You upright, having heard this hymn of praise,
May you be in that blissful company!

You will merit to sit in the first row
If you will obey God's majestic words.

God, exalted from beginning to end,
Was pleased with us and gave us the Torah.

טלולה דליותן is a description of the contest between the legendary monsters, Leviathan and Behemoth, which ends with the destruction of both. In kabbalistic literature the Leviathan is identified with evil which will disappear in Messianic times. It has been suggested that the midrashic passages concerning the Messianic banquet convey the thought that this will be the last feast, after which there will be no bodily needs. There are some who conceive the Messianic banquet in a spiritual sense.

מקרב... בריה בחרביה a paraphrase of the verse העוש ימש חרבו (Job 40:19) in a description of Behemoth.

מִנְחָה וְעַרְבִית לְרֹאשׁ הַשָּׁנָה

The *Amidah* is recited in silent devotion while standing, facing east.

(כִּי שֵׁם יְיָ אֶקְרָא, הָבוּ גֹדֶל לֵאלֹהֵינוּ.)

אֲדֹנָי, שְׂפָתַי תִּפְתָּח, וּפִי יַגִּיד תְּהִלָּתֶךָ.

בָּרוּךְ אַתָּה, יְיָ אֱלֹהֵינוּ וֵאלֹהֵי אֲבוֹתֵינוּ, אֱלֹהֵי אַבְרָהָם,
אֱלֹהֵי יִצְחָק, וֵאלֹהֵי יַעֲקֹב, הָאֵל הַגָּדוֹל הַגִּבּוֹר וְהַנּוֹרָא, אֵל
עֶלְיוֹן, גּוֹמֵל חֲסָדִים טוֹבִים, וְקוֹנֵה הַכֹּל, וְזוֹכֵר חַסְדֵי אָבוֹת,
וּמֵבִיא גוֹאֵל לִבְנֵי בְנֵיהֶם לְמַעַן שְׁמוֹ בְּאַהֲבָה.

זָכְרֵנוּ לְחַיִּים, מֶלֶךְ חָפֵץ בַּחַיִּים, וְכָתְבֵנוּ בְּסֵפֶר הַחַיִּים,
לְמַעַנְךָ אֱלֹהִים חַיִּים.

מֶלֶךְ עוֹזֵר וּמוֹשִׁיעַ וּמָגֵן. בָּרוּךְ אַתָּה, יְיָ, מָגֵן אַבְרָהָם.

אַתָּה גִבּוֹר לְעוֹלָם, אֲדֹנָי; מְחַיֵּה מֵתִים אַתָּה, רַב לְהוֹשִׁיעַ.

מְכַלְכֵּל חַיִּים בְּחֶסֶד, מְחַיֵּה מֵתִים בְּרַחֲמִים רַבִּים, סוֹמֵךְ
נוֹפְלִים, וְרוֹפֵא חוֹלִים, וּמַתִּיר אֲסוּרִים, וּמְקַיֵּם אֱמוּנָתוֹ לִישֵׁנֵי
עָפָר. מִי כָמוֹךָ, בַּעַל גְּבוּרוֹת, וּמִי דוֹמֶה לָּךְ, מֶלֶךְ מֵמִית
וּמְחַיֶּה וּמַצְמִיחַ יְשׁוּעָה.

מִי כָמוֹךָ, אַב הָרַחֲמִים, זוֹכֵר יְצוּרָיו לְחַיִּים בְּרַחֲמִים.

וְנֶאֱמָן אַתָּה לְהַחֲיוֹת מֵתִים. בָּרוּךְ אַתָּה, יְיָ, מְחַיֵּה הַמֵּתִים.

When the Reader repeats the *Amidah*, the following *Kedushah* is said:

נְקַדֵּשׁ אֶת שִׁמְךָ בָּעוֹלָם כְּשֵׁם שֶׁמַּקְדִּישִׁים אוֹתוֹ בִּשְׁמֵי מָרוֹם,
כַּכָּתוּב עַל יַד נְבִיאֶךָ: וְקָרָא זֶה אֶל זֶה וְאָמַר:

ראש השנה is designated in the Mishnah (Rosh Hashanah 1:2) as a day
on which all mankind passes in judgment before God: hence, this festival is
known as יום הדין ("Day of Judgment"). Though the Bible speaks of but one
day's observance (Leviticus 23:24; Numbers 29:1), *Rosh Hashanah* has been

MINḤAH AND MA'ARIV FOR ROSH HASHANAH

The Amidah is recited in silent devotion while standing, facing east.

(When I proclaim the name of the Lord, give glory to our God!)[1]

O Lord, open thou my lips, that my mouth may declare thy praise.[2]

Blessed art thou, Lord our God and God of our fathers, God of Abraham, God of Isaac and God of Jacob; great, mighty and revered God, sublime God, who bestowest lovingkindness, and art master of all things; who rememberest the good deeds of our fathers, and who wilt graciously bring a redeemer to their children's children for the sake of thy name.

Remember us to life, O King who delightest in life; inscribe us in the book of life for thy sake, O living God.

O King, Supporter, Savior and Shield. Blessed art thou, O Lord, Shield of Abraham.

Thou, O Lord, art mighty forever; thou revivest the dead; thou art powerful to save.

Thou sustainest the living with kindness, and revivest the dead with great mercy; thou supportest all who fall, and healest the sick; thou settest the captives free, and keepest faith with those who sleep in the dust. Who is like thee, Lord of power? Who resembles thee, O King? Thou bringest death and restorest life, and causest salvation to flourish.

Who is like thee, merciful Father? In mercy thou rememberest thy creatures to life.

Thou art faithful to revive the dead. Blessed art thou, O Lord, who revivest the dead.

When the Reader repeats the Amidah, the following Kedushah is said:

We sanctify thy name in the world even as they sanctify it in the highest heavens, as it is written by thy prophet: "They keep calling to one another:

---

observed for two days even in Jerusalem, where all other holydays are kept only for one day. The reason is explained by Maimonides in his *Mishneh Torah* (*Kiddush ha-Ḥodesh* 5:7-8).

---

[1]*Deuteronomy* 32:3. [2]*Psalm* 51:17.

656

קָדוֹשׁ, קָדוֹשׁ, קָדוֹשׁ יְיָ צְבָאוֹת; מְלֹא כָל הָאָרֶץ כְּבוֹדוֹ.

לְעֻמָּתָם בָּרוּךְ יֹאמֵרוּ—

בָּרוּךְ כְּבוֹד יְיָ מִמְּקוֹמוֹ.

וּבְדִבְרֵי קָדְשְׁךָ כָּתוּב לֵאמֹר:

יִמְלֹךְ יְיָ לְעוֹלָם, אֱלֹהַיִךְ צִיּוֹן לְדֹר וָדֹר; הַלְלוּיָהּ.

Reader לְדוֹר וָדוֹר נַגִּיד גָּדְלֶךָ, וּלְנֵצַח נְצָחִים קְדֻשָּׁתְךָ
נַקְדִּישׁ, וְשִׁבְחֲךָ אֱלֹהֵינוּ מִפִּינוּ לֹא יָמוּשׁ לְעוֹלָם וָעֶד, רְ אֵל
מֶלֶךְ גָּדוֹל וְקָדוֹשׁ אָתָּה.

————

אַתָּה קָדוֹשׁ וְשִׁמְךָ קָדוֹשׁ, וּקְדוֹשִׁים בְּכָל יוֹם יְהַלְלוּךָ סֶּלָה.

וּבְכֵן תֵּן פַּחְדְּךָ, יְיָ אֱלֹהֵינוּ, עַל כָּל מַעֲשֶׂיךָ, וְאֵימָתְךָ עַל
כָּל מַה שֶּׁבָּרֵאתָ, וְיִירָאוּךָ כָּל הַמַּעֲשִׂים וְיִשְׁתַּחֲווּ לְפָנֶיךָ כָּל
הַבְּרוּאִים, וְיֵעָשׂוּ כֻלָּם אֲגֻדָּה אַחַת לַעֲשׂוֹת רְצוֹנְךָ בְּלֵבָב שָׁלֵם,
כְּמוֹ שֶׁיָּדַעְנוּ, יְיָ אֱלֹהֵינוּ, שֶׁהַשָּׁלְטָן לְפָנֶיךָ, עֹז בְּיָדְךָ וּגְבוּרָה
בִּימִינֶךָ, וְשִׁמְךָ נוֹרָא עַל כָּל מַה שֶּׁבָּרֵאתָ.

וּבְכֵן תֵּן כָּבוֹד, יְיָ, לְעַמֶּךָ, תְּהִלָּה לִירֵאֶיךָ וְתִקְוָה טוֹבָה
לְדוֹרְשֶׁיךָ, וּפִתְחוֹן פֶּה לַמְיַחֲלִים לָךְ, שִׂמְחָה לְאַרְצֶךָ וְשָׂשׂוֹן
לְעִירֶךָ, וּצְמִיחַת קֶרֶן לְדָוִד עַבְדֶּךָ, וַעֲרִיכַת נֵר לְבֶן־יִשַׁי
מְשִׁיחֶךָ, בִּמְהֵרָה בְיָמֵינוּ.

וּבְכֵן צַדִּיקִים יִרְאוּ וְיִשְׂמָחוּ, וִישָׁרִים יַעֲלֹזוּ, וַחֲסִידִים
בְּרִנָּה יָגִילוּ, וְעוֹלָתָה תִּקְפָּץ־פִּיהָ, וְכָל הָרִשְׁעָה כֻּלָּהּ כְּעָשָׁן
תִּכְלֶה, כִּי תַעֲבִיר מֶמְשֶׁלֶת זָדוֹן מִן הָאָרֶץ.

————————

וּבְכֵן תֵּן פחדך contains the vision of the time when God shall be acknowledged and worshiped by all peoples, when peace and righteousness shall reign
on the whole earth.

Holy, holy, holy is the Lord of hosts;
The whole earth is full of his glory."[1]
Those opposite them say: Blessed—
Blessed be the glory of the Lord from his abode.[2]
And in thy holy Scriptures it is written:
The Lord shall reign forever,
Your God, O Zion, for all generations.
Praise the Lord.[3]

Reader:

Through all generations we will declare thy greatness; to all eternity we will proclaim thy holiness; thy praise, our God, shall never depart from our mouth, for thou art a great and holy God and King.

Thou art holy and thy name is holy, and holy beings praise thee daily.

Now, Lord our God, put thy awe upon all whom thou hast made, thy dread upon all whom thou hast created; let thy works revere thee, let all thy creatures worship thee; may they all blend into one brotherhood to do thy will with a perfect heart. For we know, Lord our God, that thine is dominion, power and might; thou art revered above all that thou hast created.

Now, O Lord, grant honor to thy people, glory to those who revere thee, hope to those who seek thee, free speech to those who yearn for thee, joy to thy land and gladness to thy city, rising strength to David thy servant, a shining light to the son of Jesse, thy chosen one, speedily in our days.

May the righteous men see this and rejoice, the upright exult, and the godly thrill with delight. Iniquity shall shut its mouth, wickedness shall vanish like smoke, when thou wilt abolish the rule of tyranny on earth.

ובכן תן כבוד proclaims God's restoration of Israel in Palestine.

ובכן צדיקים announces the ultimate victory of righteousness when all evil and tyranny shall vanish.

---

[1] *Isaiah* 6:3.   [2] *Ezekiel* 3:12.   [3] *Psalm* 146:10.

וְתִמְלֹךְ, אַתָּה יְיָ, לְבַדֶּךָ עַל כָּל מַעֲשֶׂיךָ, בְּהַר צִיּוֹן מִשְׁכַּן כְּבוֹדֶךָ, וּבִירוּשָׁלַיִם עִיר קָדְשֶׁךָ, כַּכָּתוּב בְּדִבְרֵי קָדְשֶׁךָ: יִמְלֹךְ יְיָ לְעוֹלָם, אֱלֹהַיִךְ צִיּוֹן לְדֹר וָדֹר; הַלְלוּיָהּ.

קָדוֹשׁ אַתָּה וְנוֹרָא שְׁמֶךָ, וְאֵין אֱלוֹהַּ מִבַּלְעָדֶיךָ, כַּכָּתוּב: וַיִּגְבַּהּ יְיָ צְבָאוֹת בַּמִּשְׁפָּט, וְהָאֵל הַקָּדוֹשׁ נִקְדַּשׁ בִּצְדָקָה. בָּרוּךְ אַתָּה, יְיָ, הַמֶּלֶךְ הַקָּדוֹשׁ.

אַתָּה בְחַרְתָּנוּ מִכָּל הָעַמִּים, אָהַבְתָּ אוֹתָנוּ וְרָצִיתָ בָּנוּ, וְרוֹמַמְתָּנוּ מִכָּל הַלְּשׁוֹנוֹת, וְקִדַּשְׁתָּנוּ בְּמִצְוֹתֶיךָ, וְקֵרַבְתָּנוּ מַלְכֵּנוּ לַעֲבוֹדָתֶךָ, וְשִׁמְךָ הַגָּדוֹל וְהַקָּדוֹשׁ עָלֵינוּ קָרָאתָ.

On Saturday night add:

(וַתּוֹדִיעֵנוּ, יְיָ אֱלֹהֵינוּ, אֶת מִשְׁפְּטֵי צִדְקֶךָ, וַתְּלַמְּדֵנוּ לַעֲשׂוֹת חֻקֵּי רְצוֹנֶךָ; וַתִּתֶּן לָנוּ, יְיָ אֱלֹהֵינוּ, מִשְׁפָּטִים יְשָׁרִים וְתוֹרוֹת אֱמֶת, חֻקִּים וּמִצְוֹת טוֹבִים; וַתַּנְחִילֵנוּ זְמַנֵּי שָׂשׂוֹן וּמוֹעֲדֵי קֹדֶשׁ וְחַגֵּי נְדָבָה, וַתּוֹרִישֵׁנוּ קְדֻשַּׁת שַׁבָּת וּכְבוֹד מוֹעֵד וַחֲגִיגַת הָרֶגֶל; וַתַּבְדֵּל, יְיָ אֱלֹהֵינוּ, בֵּין קֹדֶשׁ לְחֹל, בֵּין אוֹר לְחֹשֶׁךְ, בֵּין יִשְׂרָאֵל לָעַמִּים, בֵּין יוֹם הַשְּׁבִיעִי לְשֵׁשֶׁת יְמֵי הַמַּעֲשֶׂה. בֵּין קְדֻשַּׁת שַׁבָּת לִקְדֻשַּׁת יוֹם טוֹב הִבְדַּלְתָּ, וְאֶת יוֹם הַשְּׁבִיעִי מִשֵּׁשֶׁת יְמֵי הַמַּעֲשֶׂה קִדַּשְׁתָּ; הִבְדַּלְתָּ וְקִדַּשְׁתָּ אֶת עַמְּךָ יִשְׂרָאֵל בִּקְדֻשָּׁתֶךָ.)

וַתִּתֶּן לָנוּ, יְיָ אֱלֹהֵינוּ, בְּאַהֲבָה אֶת יוֹם (הַשַּׁבָּת הַזֶּה וְאֶת יוֹם) הַזִּכָּרוֹן הַזֶּה, יוֹם (זִכְרוֹן) תְּרוּעָה (בְּאַהֲבָה) מִקְרָא קֹדֶשׁ, זֵכֶר לִיצִיאַת מִצְרָיִם.

Thou shalt reign over all whom thou hast made, thou alone, O Lord, on Mount Zion the abode of thy majesty, in Jerusalem thy holy city, as it is written in thy holy Scriptures: "The Lord shall reign forever, your God, O Zion, for all generations."[1]

Holy art thou, awe-inspiring is thy name, and there is no God but thee, as it is written: "The Lord of hosts is exalted through justice, the holy God is sanctified through righteousness."[2] Blessed art thou, O Lord, holy King.

Thou didst choose us from among all peoples; thou didst love and favor us; thou didst exalt us above all tongues and sanctify us with thy commandments. Thou, our King, didst draw us near to thy service and call us by thy great and holy name.

On Saturday night add:

(Thou, Lord our God, hast made known to us thy righteous judgments and taught us to perform thy pleasing statutes. Thou, Lord our God, hast given us right ordinances, true precepts and good laws. Thou hast granted us joyous holidays, holy festivals and feasts for freewill offerings; thou hast vouchsafed to us the holiness of the Sabbath, the glory of the festival and the pilgrimage of the festive season. Thou, Lord our God, hast made a distinction between the holy and the profane, between light and darkness, between Israel and the nations, between the seventh day and the six working days. Thou hast made a distinction between the holiness of the Sabbath and the holiness of the festival, and hast hallowed the seventh day above the six working days; thou hast distinguished and sanctified thy people Israel with thy holiness.)

Thou, Lord our God, hast graciously given us (this Sabbath day and) this Day of Remembrance, a day for the blowing of the *Shofar*, a holy festival in remembrance of the exodus from Egypt.

---

[1] *Psalm* 146:10.   [2] *Isaiah* 5:16.

אֱלֹהֵינוּ וֵאלֹהֵי אֲבוֹתֵינוּ, יַעֲלֶה וְיָבֹא, וְיַגִּיעַ וְיֵרָאֶה, וְיֵרָצֶה
וְיִשָּׁמַע, וְיִפָּקֵד וְיִזָּכֵר זִכְרוֹנֵנוּ וּפִקְדוֹנֵנוּ, וְזִכְרוֹן אֲבוֹתֵינוּ,
וְזִכְרוֹן מָשִׁיחַ בֶּן דָּוִד עַבְדֶּךָ, וְזִכְרוֹן יְרוּשָׁלַיִם עִיר קָדְשֶׁךָ,
וְזִכְרוֹן כָּל עַמְּךָ בֵּית יִשְׂרָאֵל לְפָנֶיךָ, לִפְלֵיטָה וּלְטוֹבָה, לְחֵן
וּלְחֶסֶד וּלְרַחֲמִים, לְחַיִּים וּלְשָׁלוֹם, בְּיוֹם הַזִּכָּרוֹן הַזֶּה. זָכְרֵנוּ,
יְיָ אֱלֹהֵינוּ, בּוֹ לְטוֹבָה, וּפָקְדֵנוּ בוֹ לִבְרָכָה, וְהוֹשִׁיעֵנוּ בוֹ
לְחַיִּים; וּבִדְבַר יְשׁוּעָה וְרַחֲמִים חוּס וְחָנֵּנוּ, וְרַחֵם עָלֵינוּ
וְהוֹשִׁיעֵנוּ, כִּי אֵלֶיךָ עֵינֵינוּ, כִּי אֵל מֶלֶךְ חַנּוּן וְרַחוּם אָתָּה.

אֱלֹהֵינוּ וֵאלֹהֵי אֲבוֹתֵינוּ, מְלוֹךְ עַל כָּל הָעוֹלָם כֻּלּוֹ
בִּכְבוֹדֶךָ, וְהִנָּשֵׂא עַל כָּל הָאָרֶץ בִּיקָרֶךָ, וְהוֹפַע בַּהֲדַר גְּאוֹן
עֻזֶּךָ, עַל כָּל יוֹשְׁבֵי תֵבֵל אַרְצֶךָ, וְיֵדַע כָּל פָּעוּל כִּי אַתָּה
פְעַלְתּוֹ, וְיָבִין כָּל יָצוּר כִּי אַתָּה יְצַרְתּוֹ, וְיֹאמַר כֹּל אֲשֶׁר נְשָׁמָה
בְּאַפּוֹ, יְיָ אֱלֹהֵי יִשְׂרָאֵל מֶלֶךְ, וּמַלְכוּתוֹ בַּכֹּל מָשָׁלָה. אֱלֹהֵינוּ
וֵאלֹהֵי אֲבוֹתֵינוּ (רְצֵה בִמְנוּחָתֵנוּ) קַדְּשֵׁנוּ בְּמִצְוֹתֶיךָ וְתֵן חֶלְקֵנוּ
בְּתוֹרָתֶךָ, שַׂבְּעֵנוּ מִטּוּבֶךָ וְשַׂמְּחֵנוּ בִּישׁוּעָתֶךָ (וְהַנְחִילֵנוּ, יְיָ
אֱלֹהֵינוּ, בְּאַהֲבָה וּבְרָצוֹן שַׁבַּת קָדְשֶׁךָ, וְיָנוּחוּ בָהּ יִשְׂרָאֵל
מְקַדְּשֵׁי שְׁמֶךָ) וְטַהֵר לִבֵּנוּ לְעָבְדְּךָ בֶּאֱמֶת, כִּי אַתָּה אֱלֹהִים
אֱמֶת, וּדְבָרְךָ אֱמֶת וְקַיָּם לָעַד. בָּרוּךְ אַתָּה, יְיָ, מֶלֶךְ עַל כָּל
הָאָרֶץ, מְקַדֵּשׁ (הַשַּׁבָּת וְ)יִשְׂרָאֵל וְיוֹם הַזִּכָּרוֹן.

רְצֵה, יְיָ אֱלֹהֵינוּ, בְּעַמְּךָ יִשְׂרָאֵל וּבִתְפִלָּתָם; וְהָשֵׁב אֶת
הָעֲבוֹדָה לִדְבִיר בֵּיתֶךָ, וְאִשֵּׁי יִשְׂרָאֵל וּתְפִלָּתָם בְּאַהֲבָה
תְקַבֵּל בְּרָצוֹן, וּתְהִי לְרָצוֹן תָּמִיד עֲבוֹדַת יִשְׂרָאֵל עַמֶּךָ.

וְתֶחֱזֶינָה עֵינֵינוּ בְּשׁוּבְךָ לְצִיּוֹן בְּרַחֲמִים. בָּרוּךְ אַתָּה, יְיָ,
הַמַּחֲזִיר שְׁכִינָתוֹ לְצִיּוֹן.

Our God and God of our fathers, may the remembrance of us, of our fathers, of Messiah the son of David thy servant, of Jerusalem thy holy city, and of all thy people the house of Israel, ascend and come and be accepted before thee for deliverance and happiness, for grace, kindness and mercy, for life and peace, on this Day of Remembrance. Remember us this day, Lord our God, for happiness; be mindful of us for blessing; save us to enjoy life. With a promise of salvation and mercy spare us and be gracious to us; have pity on us and save us, for we look to thee, for thou art a gracious and merciful God and King.

Our God and God of our fathers, reign over the whole universe in thy glory; be exalted over all the earth in thy grandeur; shine forth in thy splendid majesty over all the inhabitants of thy world. May every existing being know that thou hast made it; may every creature realize that thou hast created it; may every breathing thing proclaim: "The Lord God of Israel is King, and his kingdom rules over all."

Our God and God of our fathers, (be pleased with our rest,) sanctify us with thy commandments and grant us a share in thy Torah; satisfy us with thy goodness and gladden us with thy deliverance; (in thy gracious love, Lord our God, grant that we keep thy holy Sabbath as a heritage, and that Israel, who sanctifies thy name, may rest on it) purify our heart to serve thee in truth; for thou art the true God, and thy word is true and permanent forever. Blessed art thou, O Lord, King over all the earth, who sanctifiest (the Sabbath,) Israel and the Day of Remembrance.

Be pleased, Lord our God, with thy people Israel and with their prayer; restore the worship to thy most holy sanctuary; accept Israel's offerings and prayer with gracious love. May the worship of thy people Israel be ever pleasing to thee.

May our eyes behold thy return in mercy to Zion. Blessed art thou, O Lord, who restorest thy presence to Zion.

מוֹדִים אֲנַחְנוּ לָךְ, שָׁאַתָּה הוּא יְיָ אֱלֹהֵינוּ וֵאלֹהֵי אֲבוֹתֵינוּ לְעוֹלָם וָעֶד. צוּר חַיֵּינוּ, מָגֵן יִשְׁעֵנוּ אַתָּה הוּא. לְדוֹר וָדוֹר נוֹדֶה לְּךָ, וּנְסַפֵּר תְּהִלָּתֶךָ, עַל חַיֵּינוּ הַמְּסוּרִים בְּיָדֶךָ, וְעַל נִשְׁמוֹתֵינוּ הַפְּקוּדוֹת לָךְ, וְעַל נִסֶּיךָ שֶׁבְּכָל יוֹם עִמָּנוּ, וְעַל נִפְלְאוֹתֶיךָ וְטוֹבוֹתֶיךָ שֶׁבְּכָל עֵת, עֶרֶב וָבֹקֶר וְצָהֳרָיִם. הַטוֹב כִּי לֹא כָלוּ רַחֲמֶיךָ, וְהַמְרַחֵם כִּי לֹא תַמּוּ חֲסָדֶיךָ, מֵעוֹלָם קִוִּינוּ לָךְ.

When the Reader repeats the *Amidah*, the Congregation responds here by saying:

(מוֹדִים אֲנַחְנוּ לָךְ, שָׁאַתָּה הוּא יְיָ אֱלֹהֵינוּ וֵאלֹהֵי אֲבוֹתֵינוּ. אֱלֹהֵי כָל בָּשָׂר, יוֹצְרֵנוּ, יוֹצֵר בְּרֵאשִׁית, בְּרָכוֹת וְהוֹדָאוֹת לְשִׁמְךָ הַגָּדוֹל וְהַקָּדוֹשׁ עַל שֶׁהֶחֱיִיתָנוּ וְקִיַּמְתָּנוּ. כֵּן תְּחַיֵּנוּ וּתְקַיְּמֵנוּ, וְתֶאֱסוֹף גָּלֻיּוֹתֵינוּ לְחַצְרוֹת קָדְשֶׁךָ לִשְׁמוֹר חֻקֶּיךָ וְלַעֲשׂוֹת רְצוֹנֶךָ, וּלְעָבְדְּךָ בְּלֵבָב שָׁלֵם, עַל שֶׁאֲנַחְנוּ מוֹדִים לָךְ. בָּרוּךְ אֵל הַהוֹדָאוֹת.)

וְעַל כֻּלָּם יִתְבָּרַךְ וְיִתְרוֹמַם שִׁמְךָ, מַלְכֵּנוּ, תָּמִיד לְעוֹלָם וָעֶד.

וּכְתוֹב לְחַיִּים טוֹבִים כָּל בְּנֵי בְרִיתֶךָ.

וְכֹל הַחַיִּים יוֹדוּךָ סֶּלָה, וִיהַלְלוּ אֶת שִׁמְךָ בֶּאֱמֶת, הָאֵל, יְשׁוּעָתֵנוּ וְעֶזְרָתֵנוּ סֶלָה. בָּרוּךְ אַתָּה, יְיָ, הַטוֹב שִׁמְךָ, וּלְךָ נָאֶה לְהוֹדוֹת.

שָׁלוֹם רָב עַל יִשְׂרָאֵל עַמְּךָ תָּשִׂים לְעוֹלָם, כִּי אַתָּה הוּא מֶלֶךְ אָדוֹן לְכָל הַשָּׁלוֹם; וְטוֹב בְּעֵינֶיךָ לְבָרֵךְ אֶת עַמְּךָ יִשְׂרָאֵל בְּכָל עֵת וּבְכָל שָׁעָה בִּשְׁלוֹמֶךָ.

בְּסֵפֶר חַיִּים, בְּרָכָה וְשָׁלוֹם וּפַרְנָסָה טוֹבָה, נִזָּכֵר וְנִכָּתֵב לְפָנֶיךָ, אֲנַחְנוּ וְכָל עַמְּךָ בֵּית יִשְׂרָאֵל, לְחַיִּים טוֹבִים וּלְשָׁלוֹם. בָּרוּךְ אַתָּה, יְיָ, עוֹשֶׂה הַשָּׁלוֹם.

We ever thank thee, who art the Lord our God and the God of our fathers. Thou art the strength of our life and our saving shield. In every generation we will thank thee and recount thy praise—for our lives which are in thy charge, for our souls which are in thy care, for thy miracles which are daily with us, and for thy continual wonders and favors—evening, morning and noon. Beneficent One, whose mercies never fail, Merciful One, whose kindnesses never cease, thou hast always been our hope.

When the Reader repeats the Amidah, the Congregation responds here by saying:

(We thank thee, who art the Lord our God and the God of our fathers. God of all mankind, our Creator and Creator of the universe, blessings and thanks are due to thy great and holy name, because thou hast kept us alive and sustained us; mayest thou ever grant us life and sustenance. O gather our exiles to thy holy courts to observe thy laws, to do thy will, and to serve thee with a perfect heart. For this we thank thee. Blessed be God to whom all thanks are due.)

For all these acts may thy name, our King, be blessed and exalted forever and ever.

Inscribe all thy people of the covenant for a happy life.

All the living shall ever thank thee and sincerely praise thy name, O God, who art always our salvation and help. Blessed art thou, O Lord, Beneficent One, to whom it is fitting to give thanks.

O grant abundant peace to Israel thy people forever, for thou art the King and Lord of all peace. May it please thee to bless thy people Israel with peace at all times and at all hours.

May we and all Israel thy people be remembered and inscribed before thee in the book of life and blessing, peace and prosperity, for a happy life and for peace. Blessed art thou, O Lord, Author of peace.

בספר חיים can be rendered: "In the book of life... may we be remembered; may we and all Israel thy people be inscribed before thee for a happy life ..." The seeming redundancy of the passage would thus disappear. However, all worshipers are in the habit of joining the words נזכר ונכתב.

After the *Amidah* add the following meditation:

אֱלֹהַי, נְצֹר לְשׁוֹנִי מֵרָע, וּשְׂפָתַי מִדַּבֵּר מִרְמָה; וְלִמְקַלְלַי נַפְשִׁי תִדּוֹם, וְנַפְשִׁי כֶּעָפָר לַכֹּל תִּהְיֶה. פְּתַח לִבִּי בְּתוֹרָתֶךָ, וּבְמִצְוֹתֶיךָ תִּרְדּוֹף נַפְשִׁי; וְכָל הַחוֹשְׁבִים עָלַי רָעָה, מְהֵרָה הָפֵר עֲצָתָם וְקַלְקֵל מַחֲשַׁבְתָּם. עֲשֵׂה לְמַעַן שְׁמֶךָ, עֲשֵׂה לְמַעַן יְמִינֶךָ, עֲשֵׂה לְמַעַן קְדֻשָּׁתֶךָ, עֲשֵׂה לְמַעַן תּוֹרָתֶךָ. לְמַעַן יֵחָלְצוּן יְדִידֶיךָ, הוֹשִׁיעָה יְמִינְךָ וַעֲנֵנִי. יִהְיוּ לְרָצוֹן אִמְרֵי פִי וְהֶגְיוֹן לִבִּי לְפָנֶיךָ, יְיָ, צוּרִי וְגוֹאֲלִי. עֹשֶׂה שָׁלוֹם בִּמְרוֹמָיו, הוּא יַעֲשֶׂה שָׁלוֹם עָלֵינוּ וְעַל כָּל יִשְׂרָאֵל, וְאִמְרוּ אָמֵן.

יְהִי רָצוֹן מִלְּפָנֶיךָ, יְיָ אֱלֹהֵינוּ וֵאלֹהֵי אֲבוֹתֵינוּ, שֶׁיִּבָּנֶה בֵּית הַמִּקְדָּשׁ בִּמְהֵרָה בְיָמֵינוּ, וְתֵן חֶלְקֵנוּ בְּתוֹרָתֶךָ. וְשָׁם נַעֲבָדְךָ בְּיִרְאָה, כִּימֵי עוֹלָם וּכְשָׁנִים קַדְמוֹנִיּוֹת. וְעָרְבָה לַיְיָ מִנְחַת יְהוּדָה וִירוּשָׁלָיִם, כִּימֵי עוֹלָם וּכְשָׁנִים קַדְמוֹנִיּוֹת.

Rosh Hashanah Greeting:

Singular	Plural
לְשָׁנָה טוֹבָה תִּכָּתֵב וְתֵחָתֵם.	לְשָׁנָה טוֹבָה תִּכָּתֵבוּ וְתֵחָתֵמוּ.

קִדּוּשׁ לְרֹאשׁ הַשָּׁנָה

On Sabbath Eve:

(וַיְהִי עֶרֶב וַיְהִי בֹקֶר)

יוֹם הַשִּׁשִּׁי. וַיְכֻלּוּ הַשָּׁמַיִם וְהָאָרֶץ וְכָל צְבָאָם. וַיְכַל אֱלֹהִים בַּיּוֹם הַשְּׁבִיעִי מְלַאכְתּוֹ אֲשֶׁר עָשָׂה, וַיִּשְׁבֹּת בַּיּוֹם הַשְּׁבִיעִי מִכָּל מְלַאכְתּוֹ אֲשֶׁר עָשָׂה. וַיְבָרֶךְ אֱלֹהִים אֶת יוֹם הַשְּׁבִיעִי וַיְקַדֵּשׁ אֹתוֹ, כִּי בוֹ שָׁבַת מִכָּל מְלַאכְתּוֹ אֲשֶׁר בָּרָא אֱלֹהִים לַעֲשׂוֹת.)

לשנה טובה תכתב is a figurative expression, borrowed from the writing and signing of decrees by earthly rulers.

After the Amidah add the following meditation:

My God, guard my tongue from evil, and my lips from speaking falsehood. May my soul be silent to those who insult me; be my soul lowly to all as the dust. Open my heart to thy Torah, that my soul may follow thy commands. Speedily defeat the counsel of all those who plan evil against me and upset their design. Do it for the glory of thy name; do it for the sake of thy power; do it for the sake of thy holiness; do it for the sake of thy Torah. That thy beloved may be rescued, save with thy right hand and answer me. May the words of my mouth and the meditation of my heart be pleasing before thee, O Lord, my Stronghold and my Redeemer.[1] May he who creates peace in his high heavens create peace for us and for all Israel. Amen.

May it be thy will, Lord our God and God of our fathers, that the Temple be speedily rebuilt in our days, and grant us a share in thy Torah. There we will serve thee with reverence, as in the days of old and as in former years. Then the offering of Judah and Jerusalem will be pleasing to the Lord, as in the days of old and as in former years.[2]

Rosh Hashanah Greeting:

MAY YOU BE INSCRIBED FOR A HAPPY NEW YEAR.

KIDDUSH FOR ROSH HASHANAH

On Sabbath Eve:

(There was evening and there was morning— The sixth day. Thus the heavens and the earth were finished, and all their host. By the seventh day God had completed his his work which he had made, and he rested on the seventh day from all his work in which he had been engaged. Then God blessed the seventh day and hallowed it, because on it he rested from all his work which he had created.)[3]

---

[1] *Psalms* 60:7; 19:15. [2] *Malachi* 3:4. [3] *Genesis* 1:31; 2:1-3.

סַבְרִי מָרָנָן וְרַבּוֹתַי.

בָּרוּךְ אַתָּה, יְיָ אֱלֹהֵינוּ, מֶלֶךְ הָעוֹלָם, בּוֹרֵא פְּרִי הַגָּפֶן.

בָּרוּךְ אַתָּה, יְיָ אֱלֹהֵינוּ, מֶלֶךְ הָעוֹלָם, אֲשֶׁר בָּחַר בָּנוּ מִכָּל
עָם, וְרוֹמְמָנוּ מִכָּל לָשׁוֹן, וְקִדְּשָׁנוּ בְּמִצְוֹתָיו. וַתִּתֶּן לָנוּ, יְיָ
אֱלֹהֵינוּ, בְּאַהֲבָה אֶת יוֹם (הַשַּׁבָּת הַזֶּה וְאֶת יוֹם) הַזִּכָּרוֹן הַזֶּה,
יוֹם (זִכְרוֹן) תְּרוּעָה (בְּאַהֲבָה) מִקְרָא קֹדֶשׁ, זֵכֶר לִיצִיאַת
מִצְרָיִם. כִּי בָנוּ בָחַרְתָּ, וְאוֹתָנוּ קִדַּשְׁתָּ מִכָּל הָעַמִּים, וּדְבָרְךָ
אֱמֶת וְקַיָּם לָעַד. בָּרוּךְ אַתָּה, יְיָ, מֶלֶךְ עַל כָּל הָאָרֶץ, מְקַדֵּשׁ
(הַשַּׁבָּת וְ)יִשְׂרָאֵל וְיוֹם הַזִּכָּרוֹן.

On Saturday night add:

(בָּרוּךְ אַתָּה, יְיָ אֱלֹהֵינוּ, מֶלֶךְ הָעוֹלָם, בּוֹרֵא מְאוֹרֵי הָאֵשׁ.

בָּרוּךְ אַתָּה, יְיָ אֱלֹהֵינוּ, מֶלֶךְ הָעוֹלָם, הַמַּבְדִּיל בֵּין קֹדֶשׁ
לְחֹל, בֵּין אוֹר לְחֹשֶׁךְ, בֵּין יִשְׂרָאֵל לָעַמִּים, בֵּין יוֹם הַשְּׁבִיעִי
לְשֵׁשֶׁת יְמֵי הַמַּעֲשֶׂה. בֵּין קְדֻשַּׁת שַׁבָּת לִקְדֻשַּׁת יוֹם טוֹב
הִבְדַּלְתָּ, וְאֶת יוֹם הַשְּׁבִיעִי מִשֵּׁשֶׁת יְמֵי הַמַּעֲשֶׂה קִדַּשְׁתָּ; הִבְדַּלְתָּ
וְקִדַּשְׁתָּ אֶת עַמְּךָ יִשְׂרָאֵל בִּקְדֻשָּׁתֶךָ. בָּרוּךְ אַתָּה, יְיָ, הַמַּבְדִּיל
בֵּין קֹדֶשׁ לְקֹדֶשׁ.)

בָּרוּךְ אַתָּה, יְיָ אֱלֹהֵינוּ, מֶלֶךְ הָעוֹלָם, שֶׁהֶחֱיָנוּ וְקִיְּמָנוּ
וְהִגִּיעָנוּ לַזְּמַן הַזֶּה.

It is customary to eat an apple dipped in honey and to say:

יְהִי רָצוֹן מִלְּפָנֶיךָ, יְיָ אֱלֹהֵינוּ וֵאלֹהֵי אֲבוֹתֵינוּ, שֶׁתְּחַדֵּשׁ
עָלֵינוּ שָׁנָה טוֹבָה וּמְתוּקָה.

Blessed art thou, Lord our God, King of the universe, who createst the fruit of the vine.

Blessed art thou, Lord our God, King of the universe, who hast chosen and exalted us above all nations, and hast sanctified us with thy commandments. Thou, Lord our God, hast graciously given us (this Sabbath day and) this Day of Remembrance, a day for the blowing of the *Shofar*, a holy festival in remembrance of the exodus from Egypt. Indeed, thou hast chosen and sanctified us above all nations; thy word is true and permanent forever. Blessed art thou, O Lord, King over all the earth, who sanctifiest (the Sabbath,) Israel and the Day of Remembrance.

On Saturday night add:

(Blessed art thou, Lord our God, King of the universe, who createst the light of the fire.

Blessed art thou, Lord our God, King of the universe, who hast made a distinction between the sacred and the profane, between light and darkness, between Israel and the nations, between the seventh day and the six working days. Thou hast made a distinction between the holiness of the Sabbath and that of the festival, and hast hallowed the seventh day above the six working days; thou hast distinguished and sanctified thy people Israel with thy holiness. Blessed art thou, O Lord, who makest a distinction between the greater holiness and the lesser holiness.)

Blessed art thou, Lord our God, King of the universe, who hast granted us life and sustenance and permitted us to reach this season.

It is customary to eat an apple dipped in honey and to say:

May it be thy will, Lord our God and God of our fathers, to grant us a happy and pleasant New Year.

סברי מרנן is used to call attention to the blessing which is about to be pronounced over the wine, so that those present may answer Amen. This phrase was originally used in the form of a question, namely: "Gentlemen, what is your opinion?" Is it safe to drink of this wine? The response was ולחיים

תַּשְׁלִיךְ

Performed on the afternoon of the first day of *Rosh Hashanah*, or on the second, should Sabbath commence the festival. Processions are formed to the banks of a river, where the following is recited:

מִי אֵל כָּמוֹךָ, נֹשֵׂא עָוֹן וְעֹבֵר עַל פֶּשַׁע לִשְׁאֵרִית נַחֲלָתוֹ; לֹא הֶחֱזִיק לָעַד אַפּוֹ, כִּי חָפֵץ חֶסֶד הוּא. יָשׁוּב יְרַחֲמֵנוּ, יִכְבֹּשׁ עֲוֹנוֹתֵינוּ, וְתַשְׁלִיךְ בִּמְצֻלוֹת יָם כָּל חַטֹּאתָם. תִּתֵּן אֱמֶת לְיַעֲקֹב, חֶסֶד לְאַבְרָהָם, אֲשֶׁר נִשְׁבַּעְתָּ לַאֲבֹתֵינוּ מִימֵי קֶדֶם.

מִן הַמֵּצַר קָרָאתִי יָּהּ, עָנָנִי בַמֶּרְחָב יָהּ. יְיָ לִי, לֹא אִירָא; מַה יַּעֲשֶׂה לִי אָדָם. יְיָ לִי בְּעֹזְרָי, וַאֲנִי אֶרְאֶה בְשֹׂנְאָי. טוֹב לַחֲסוֹת בַּיְיָ מִבְּטֹחַ בָּאָדָם. טוֹב לַחֲסוֹת בַּיְיָ מִבְּטֹחַ בִּנְדִיבִים.

תהלים לג

רַנְּנוּ צַדִּיקִים בַּיְיָ, לַיְשָׁרִים נָאוָה תְהִלָּה. הוֹדוּ לַיְיָ בְּכִנּוֹר, בְּנֵבֶל עָשׂוֹר זַמְּרוּ לוֹ. שִׁירוּ לוֹ שִׁיר חָדָשׁ, הֵיטִיבוּ נַגֵּן בִּתְרוּעָה. כִּי יָשָׁר דְּבַר יְיָ, וְכָל מַעֲשֵׂהוּ בֶּאֱמוּנָה. אֹהֵב צְדָקָה וּמִשְׁפָּט, חֶסֶד יְיָ מָלְאָה הָאָרֶץ. בִּדְבַר יְיָ שָׁמַיִם נַעֲשׂוּ, וּבְרוּחַ פִּיו כָּל צְבָאָם. כֹּנֵס כַּנֵּד מֵי הַיָּם, נֹתֵן בְּאוֹצָרוֹת תְּהוֹמוֹת. יִירְאוּ מֵיְיָ כָּל הָאָרֶץ, מִמֶּנּוּ יָגוּרוּ כָּל יֹשְׁבֵי תֵבֵל. כִּי הוּא אָמַר וַיֶּהִי, הוּא צִוָּה וַיַּעֲמֹד. יְיָ הֵפִיר עֲצַת גּוֹיִם, הֵנִיא מַחְשְׁבוֹת עַמִּים. עֲצַת

תשליך, the custom of symbolically casting the sins into a running stream, presumably dates from the fourteenth century. It is mentioned for the first time in *Sefer Maharil* by Rabbi Jacob Moelin (1355-1427), the leading Jewish authority of his time. He explains it as a reminder of the *Akedah*, concerning which the Midrash relates that Satan, in an effort to prevent Abraham from sacrificing Isaac, transformed himself into a deep stream on the road leading to Mount Moriah. Plunging into the stream, Abraham and Isaac prayed for divine aid, whereupon the place became dry land again. The name תשליך ("thou wilt cast") is derived from Micah 7:19.

669

TASHLIKH

Performed on the afternoon of the first day of Rosh Hashanah, or on the second, should Sabbath commence the festival. Processions are formed to the banks of a river, where the following is recited:

Who is a God like thee? Thou forgivest iniquity and passest over transgression in the survivors of thy people. Thou dost not retain thy anger forever, for thou delightest in kindness. Thou wilt again show us mercy and subdue our iniquities; thou wilt cast all our sins into the depths of the sea. Thou wilt show kindness to Jacob and mercy to Abraham, as thou didst promise to our fathers from of old.[1]

Out of distress I called upon the Lord; he answered me by setting me free. The Lord is with me; I have no fear. What can man do to me? The Lord is my helper; I shall see the defeat of my foes. It is better to seek refuge in the Lord than to trust in man. It is better to seek refuge in the Lord than to trust in princes.[2]

Psalm 33

Rejoice in the Lord, you righteous; for the upright it is fitting to give praise. Give thanks to the Lord with harp; sing his praises with the ten-stringed lute. Sing to him a new song; play skilfully amid shouts of joy. The word of the Lord is right; all his work is done with faithfulness. He loves righteousness and justice; the earth is full of the Lord's kindness. By the word of the Lord the heavens were made, and all their host by the breath of his mouth. He gathers the waters of the sea as a heap; he lays up the deeps in storehouses. Let the earth revere the Lord; let all the inhabitants of the world stand in awe of him. For he but spoke, and it came into being; he but commanded, and it stood forth. The Lord annuls the counsel of nations; he frustrates the designs of peoples.

---

[1] *Micah* 7:18-20. [2] *Psalm* 118:5-9.

יְיָ לְעוֹלָם תַּעֲמֹד, מַחְשְׁבוֹת לִבּוֹ לְדֹר וָדֹר. אַשְׁרֵי הַגּוֹי אֲשֶׁר
יְיָ אֱלֹהָיו, הָעָם בָּחַר לְנַחֲלָה לוֹ. מִשָּׁמַיִם הִבִּיט יְיָ, רָאָה אֶת
כָּל בְּנֵי הָאָדָם. מִמְּכוֹן שִׁבְתּוֹ הִשְׁגִּיחַ, אֶל כָּל יֹשְׁבֵי הָאָרֶץ.
הַיֹּצֵר יַחַד לִבָּם, הַמֵּבִין אֶל כָּל מַעֲשֵׂיהֶם. אֵין הַמֶּלֶךְ נוֹשָׁע
בְּרָב־חָיִל, גִּבּוֹר לֹא יִנָּצֵל בְּרָב־כֹּחַ. שֶׁקֶר הַסּוּס לִתְשׁוּעָה,
וּבְרֹב חֵילוֹ לֹא יְמַלֵּט. הִנֵּה עֵין יְיָ אֶל יְרֵאָיו, לַמְיַחֲלִים
לְחַסְדּוֹ. לְהַצִּיל מִמָּוֶת נַפְשָׁם, וּלְחַיּוֹתָם בָּרָעָב. נַפְשֵׁנוּ חִכְּתָה
לַיְיָ, עֶזְרֵנוּ וּמָגִנֵּנוּ הוּא. כִּי בוֹ יִשְׂמַח לִבֵּנוּ, כִּי בְשֵׁם קָדְשׁוֹ
בָטָחְנוּ. יְהִי חַסְדְּךָ יְיָ עָלֵינוּ, כַּאֲשֶׁר יִחַלְנוּ לָךְ.

לֹא יָרֵעוּ וְלֹא יַשְׁחִיתוּ בְּכָל הַר קָדְשִׁי, כִּי מָלְאָה הָאָרֶץ
דֵעָה אֶת יְיָ, כַּמַּיִם לַיָּם מְכַסִּים.

שִׁיר הַמַּעֲלוֹת. מִמַּעֲמַקִּים קְרָאתִיךָ, יְיָ. אֲדֹנָי, שִׁמְעָה
בְקוֹלִי, תִּהְיֶינָה אָזְנֶיךָ קַשֻּׁבוֹת לְקוֹל תַּחֲנוּנָי. אִם עֲוֹנוֹת תִּשְׁמָר־
יָהּ, אֲדֹנָי, מִי יַעֲמֹד. כִּי עִמְּךָ הַסְּלִיחָה, לְמַעַן תִּוָּרֵא. קִוִּיתִי יְיָ,
קִוְּתָה נַפְשִׁי, וְלִדְבָרוֹ הוֹחָלְתִּי. נַפְשִׁי לַאדֹנָי מִשֹּׁמְרִים לַבֹּקֶר,
שֹׁמְרִים לַבֹּקֶר. יַחֵל יִשְׂרָאֵל אֶל יְיָ, כִּי עִם יְיָ הַחֶסֶד, וְהַרְבֵּה
עִמּוֹ פְדוּת. וְהוּא יִפְדֶּה אֶת יִשְׂרָאֵל מִכֹּל עֲוֹנוֹתָיו.

Psalm 33 contains a description of God's righteous rule and creative omnipotence. Israel's protection does not depend on military power but on God.
"He gathers the waters of the sea as a heap" refers to the appearance of the sea
from the shore. "He lays up the deeps in storehouses" refers to the vast sub-
terranean masses of water.

Psalm 130 is an expression of remorse for sin and a plea for forgiveness.
Since God reveals himself as a forgiving God, Israel can hope and trust.

מעמקים ("deep waters") is used in the sense of distress and danger.

But the counsel of the Lord stands forever; his plans last for all generations. Happy is the nation whose God is the Lord, the people he has chosen for his possession. From heaven the Lord looks down; he sees all of mankind. From his abode he looks intently on all the inhabitants of the earth, he who fashions the hearts of them all, who considers all their actions. A king is not saved by the size of an army; a warrior is not rescued by sheer strength. Vain is the horse for victory; nor does it afford escape by its great strength. The eye of the Lord rests on those who revere him, those who hope for his kindness, to save them from death and keep them alive in famine. Our soul has waited for the Lord; he is our help and our shield. In him our heart rejoices; in his holy name we trust. May thy kindness, O Lord, be upon us, even as we hope in thee.

None shall injure, none shall destroy anywhere on my holy mountain, for the land shall be full of the knowledge of the Lord as the waters cover the sea.[1]

Psalm 130

A Pilgrim Song. Out of the depths I call to thee, O Lord. O Lord, hear my voice; let thy ears be attentive to my supplicating voice. If thou, O Lord, shouldst keep strict account of iniquities, O Lord, who could live on? But with thee there is forgiveness, that thou mayest be revered. I look for the Lord, my whole being hopes; I wait for his word. My soul waits for the Lord more eagerly than watchmen for the dawn, than watchmen for the dawn. O Israel, put your hope in the Lord, for with the Lord there is kindness; with him there is great saving power. It is he who will redeem Israel from all its iniquities.

מי יעמד that is, no one can maintain his innocence when standing in judgment before God.

למען תורא God's forgiveness inspires man to revere him. The general idea here is that God forgives and does not keep strict account of our iniquities.

משמרים לבקר than impatient watchmen longing for the dawn to release them from their duty. The repetition of the phrase is for emphasis.

---

[1] *Isaiah* 11:9.

כַּפָּרוֹת

Consisting in waving a fowl three times around the head after the recitation of,
the following paragraph on the day previous to *Yom Kippur*

בְּנֵי אָדָם, יֹשְׁבֵי חֹשֶׁךְ וְצַלְמָוֶת, אֲסִירֵי עֳנִי וּבַרְזֶל. יוֹצִיאֵם
מֵחֹשֶׁךְ וְצַלְמָוֶת, וּמוֹסְרוֹתֵיהֶם יְנַתֵּק. אֱוִילִים מִדֶּרֶךְ פִּשְׁעָם,
וּמֵעֲוֹנֹתֵיהֶם יִתְעַנּוּ. כָּל אֹכֶל תְּתַעֵב נַפְשָׁם, וַיַּגִּיעוּ עַד שַׁעֲרֵי
מָוֶת. וַיִּזְעֲקוּ אֶל יְיָ בַּצַּר לָהֶם, מִמְּצוּקוֹתֵיהֶם יוֹשִׁיעֵם. יִשְׁלַח
דְּבָרוֹ וְיִרְפָּאֵם, וִימַלֵּט מִשְּׁחִיתוֹתָם. יוֹדוּ לַיָי חַסְדּוֹ, וְנִפְלְאוֹתָיו
לִבְנֵי אָדָם. אִם יֵשׁ עָלָיו מַלְאָךְ מֵלִיץ, אֶחָד מִנִּי אָלֶף, לְהַגִּיד
לְאָדָם יָשְׁרוֹ. וַיְחֻנֶּנּוּ, וַיֹּאמֶר: פְּדָעֵהוּ מֵרֶדֶת שַׁחַת, מָצָאתִי
כֹפֶר.

Waving a fowl over the heads:

זֶה חֲלִיפָתֵנוּ, זֶה תְּמוּרָתֵנוּ, זֶה כַּפָּרָתֵנוּ, זֶה הַתַּרְנְגֹל יֵלֵךְ
לְמִיתָה, וַאֲנַחְנוּ נִכָּנֵס וְנֵלֵךְ לְחַיִּים טוֹבִים אֲרֻכִּים וּלְשָׁלוֹם.

Feminine:

(זֹאת חֲלִיפָתֵנוּ, זֹאת תְּמוּרָתֵנוּ, זֹאת כַּפָּרָתֵנוּ, זֹאת הַתַּרְנְגֹלֶת
תֵּלֵךְ לְמִיתָה, וַאֲנַחְנוּ נִכָּנֵס וְנֵלֵךְ לְחַיִּים טוֹבִים אֲרֻכִּים
וּלְשָׁלוֹם.)

BLESSING OVER THE YOM KIPPUR LIGHTS

בָּרוּךְ אַתָּה, יְיָ אֱלֹהֵינוּ, מֶלֶךְ הָעוֹלָם, אֲשֶׁר קִדְּשָׁנוּ בְּמִצְוֹתָיו
וְצִוָּנוּ לְהַדְלִיק נֵר שֶׁל (שַׁבָּת וְשֶׁל) יוֹם הַכִּפּוּרִים.

בָּרוּךְ אַתָּה, יְיָ אֱלֹהֵינוּ, מֶלֶךְ הָעוֹלָם, שֶׁהֶחֱיָנוּ וְקִיְּמָנוּ,
וְהִגִּיעָנוּ לַזְּמַן הַזֶּה.

כפרות ("atonements"), the custom of symbolically transferring one's guilt
to the fowl on the day previous to *Yom Kippur*, is mentioned in Maḥzor Vitry

KAPPAROTH

Consisting in waving a fowl three times around the head after the recitation of the following paragraph on the day previous to Yom Kippur

Men who sit in darkness and in gloom, bound in misery and iron—he will take them out from the darkness and the gloom; he will break their chains. Fools are they who transgress; they are afflicted because of their iniquities. They loath every kind of food; they reach the gates of death. Then they cry out to the Lord in their trouble, and he delivers them from their distress. He sends his word and heals them; he frees them from their graves. Let them thank the Lord for his kindness, and for the wonderful things he does for men.[1] If one angel among a thousand pleads for a man, vouching for his uprightness, then God is gracious to him and says: "Deliver him from going down to the grave; I have found a ransom."[2]

Waving a fowl over the heads:

This is offered in exchange for us; this is our ransom; this is our atonement. This fowl shall meet death, but we shall find a long and pleasant life of peace.

BLESSING OVER THE YOM KIPPUR LIGHTS

Blessed art thou, Lord our God, King of the universe, who hast sanctified us with thy commandments, and commanded us to light the lights of (the Sabbath and of) the Day of Atonement.

Blessed art thou, Lord our God, King of the universe, who hast granted us life and sustenance and permitted us to reach this season.

(page 373) as related to the use of a scapegoat in Temple times. "This bird is a sacrifice in my stead" is the formula repeated three times as the fowl is held above the heads of the adults and children. This practice was instituted for the purpose of helping the poor, among whom the fowls are distributed. The authorities recommend the distribution of money instead. When money is used in the *Kapparoth* ceremony, זֶה הַכֶּסֶף יִתֵּן לִצְדָקָה should be said instead of זה התרנגול ילך למיתה.

The phrase בני אדם has been added to the heart-stirring biblical verses contained in this passage.

[1]*Psalm* 107:10, 14, 17-21.   [2]*Job* 33:23-24.

674

אֻשְׁפִּיזִין

Upon entering the *Sukkah*

יְהִי רָצוֹן מִלְּפָנֶיךָ, יְיָ אֱלֹהַי וֵאלֹהֵי אֲבוֹתַי, שֶׁתַּשְׁרֶה שְׁכִינָתְךָ
בֵּינֵינוּ, וְתִפְרֹשׂ עָלֵינוּ סֻכַּת שְׁלוֹמֶךָ, וְתַקִּיף אוֹתָנוּ מִזִּיו כְּבוֹדְךָ
הַקָּדוֹשׁ וְהַטָּהוֹר. וְלָרְעֵבִים גַּם צְמֵאִים, תֵּן לַחְמָם וּמֵימָם נֶאֱמָנִים.
וּתְזַכֵּנוּ לֵשֵׁב יָמִים רַבִּים עַל הָאֲדָמָה, אַדְמַת קֹדֶשׁ, בַּעֲבוֹדָתֶךָ
וּבְיִרְאָתֶךָ. בָּרוּךְ יְיָ לְעוֹלָם, אָמֵן וְאָמֵן.

אֲזַמֵּן לִסְעֻדָתִי אֻשְׁפִּיזִין עִלָּאִין: אַבְרָהָם יִצְחָק וְיַעֲקֹב, יוֹסֵף
מֹשֶׁה אַהֲרֹן וְדָוִד.

First day of *Sukkoth:*

בְּמָטוּ מִנָּךְ, אַבְרָהָם אֻשְׁפִּיזִי עִלָּאִי, דְּיֵתְבוּ עִמִּי וְעִמָּךְ כָּל
אֻשְׁפִּיזֵי עִלָּאֵי: יִצְחָק יַעֲקֹב יוֹסֵף, מֹשֶׁה אַהֲרֹן וְדָוִד.

Second day of *Sukkoth:*

בְּמָטוּ מִנָּךְ, יִצְחָק אֻשְׁפִּיזִי עִלָּאִי, דְּיֵתְבוּ עִמִּי וְעִמָּךְ כָּל
אֻשְׁפִּיזֵי עִלָּאֵי: אַבְרָהָם יַעֲקֹב יוֹסֵף, מֹשֶׁה אַהֲרֹן וְדָוִד.

Third day of *Sukkoth:*

בְּמָטוּ מִנָּךְ, יַעֲקֹב אֻשְׁפִּיזִי עִלָּאִי, דְּיֵתְבוּ עִמִּי וְעִמָּךְ כָּל
אֻשְׁפִּיזֵי עִלָּאֵי: אַבְרָהָם יִצְחָק יוֹסֵף, מֹשֶׁה אַהֲרֹן וְדָוִד.

Fourth day of *Sukkoth:*

בְּמָטוּ מִנָּךְ, יוֹסֵף אֻשְׁפִּיזִי עִלָּאִי, דְּיֵתְבוּ עִמִּי וְעִמָּךְ כָּל
אֻשְׁפִּיזֵי עִלָּאֵי: אַבְרָהָם יִצְחָק יַעֲקֹב, מֹשֶׁה אַהֲרֹן וְדָוִד.

Fifth day of *Sukkoth:*

בְּמָטוּ מִנָּךְ, מֹשֶׁה אֻשְׁפִּיזִי עִלָּאִי, דְּיֵתְבוּ עִמִּי וְעִמָּךְ כָּל
אֻשְׁפִּיזֵי עִלָּאֵי: אַבְרָהָם יִצְחָק יַעֲקֹב, יוֹסֵף אַהֲרֹן וְדָוִד.

אושפיזין, the custom of inviting the patriarchs to the *Sukkah*, is based
on a passage in the Zohar (section *Emor*) which reads: "When one sits in the

GUESTS IN THE SUKKAH

Upon entering the Sukkah:

May it be thy will, Lord my God and God of my fathers, to cause thy divine spirit to dwell in our midst. O spread over us thy shelter of peace, and encircle us with thy majestic glory, holy and pure. As for those who are hungry and thirsty, do thou grant them sufficient bread and water. O grant us long life in the Holy Land, that we may serve thee with reverence. Praised be the Lord forever. Amen, Amen.

I invite sublime guests to dinner—Abraham, Isaac, Jacob, Joseph, Moses, Aaron and David.

First day of Sukkoth:

O Abraham, my exalted guest, may it please you to have all the exalted guests dwell with us—Isaac, Jacob, Joseph, Moses, Aaron and David.

Second day of Sukkoth:

O Isaac, my exalted guest, may it please you to have all the exalted guests dwell with us—Abraham, Jacob, Joseph, Moses, Aaron and David.

Third day of Sukkoth:

O Jacob, my exalted guest, may it please you to have all the exalted guests dwell with us—Abraham, Isaac, Joseph, Moses, Aaron and David.

Fourth day of Sukkoth:

O Joseph, my exalted guest, may it please you to have all the exalted guests dwell with us—Abraham, Isaac, Jacob, Moses, Aaron and David.

Fifth day of Sukkoth:

O Moses, my exalted guest, may it please you to have all the exalted guests dwell with us—Abraham, Isaac, Jacob, Joseph, Aaron and David.

Sukkah . . . Abraham and six righteous men come to share his company . . . Everyone should try to invite an equal number of poor people to share his meals in the *Sukkah*. . ."

Sixth day of *Sukkoth:*

בְּמָטוּ מִנָּךְ, אַהֲרֹן אֻשְׁפִּיזִי עִלָּאִי דְּיֵיתְבוּ עִמִּי וְעִמָּךְ כָּל
אֻשְׁפִּיזֵי עִלָּאֵי: אַבְרָהָם יִצְחָק יַעֲקֹב, יוֹסֵף מֹשֶׁה וְדָוִד.

Seventh day of *Sukkoth:*

בְּמָטוּ מִנָּךְ, דָּוִד אֻשְׁפִּיזִי עִלָּאִי, דְּיֵיתְבוּ עִמִּי וְעִמָּךְ כָּל
אֻשְׁפִּיזֵי עִלָּאֵי: אַבְרָהָם יִצְחָק יַעֲקֹב, יוֹסֵף מֹשֶׁה וְאַהֲרֹן.

נְטִילַת לוּלָב

During *Sukkoth* (except Sabbath) the following is recited as the *lulav* (in the right hand) and the *ethrog* (in the left hand) are held together.

הֲרֵינִי מוּכָן וּמְזֻמָּן לְקַיֵּם מִצְוַת בּוֹרְאִי, שֶׁצִּוָּנוּ בְּתוֹרָתוֹ:
וּלְקַחְתֶּם לָכֶם בַּיּוֹם הָרִאשׁוֹן פְּרִי עֵץ הָדָר, כַּפֹּת תְּמָרִים,
וַעֲנַף עֵץ עָבֹת, וְעַרְבֵי־נָחַל. וּבְנַעֲנוּעִי אוֹתָם יַשְׁפִּיעַ עָלַי
שֶׁפַע בְּרָכוֹת וּמַחֲשָׁבוֹת קְדוֹשׁוֹת, שֶׁהוּא אֱלֹהֵי הָאֱלֹהִים וַאֲדוֹנֵי
הָאֲדוֹנִים, שַׁלִּיט בְּמַטָּה וּבְמַעַל, וּמַלְכוּתוֹ בַּכֹּל מָשָׁלָה. וּתְהֵא
חֲשׁוּבָה מִצְוַת אַרְבָּעָה מִינִים כְּאִלּוּ קִיַּמְתִּיהָ בְּכָל פְּרָטֶיהָ
וְדִקְדּוּקֶיהָ. וִיהִי נֹעַם יְיָ אֱלֹהֵינוּ עָלֵינוּ; וּמַעֲשֵׂה יָדֵינוּ כּוֹנְנָה
עָלֵינוּ, וּמַעֲשֵׂה יָדֵינוּ כּוֹנְנֵהוּ. בָּרוּךְ יְיָ לְעוֹלָם, אָמֵן וְאָמֵן.

בָּרוּךְ אַתָּה, יְיָ אֱלֹהֵינוּ, מֶלֶךְ הָעוֹלָם, אֲשֶׁר קִדְּשָׁנוּ בְּמִצְוֹתָיו
וְצִוָּנוּ עַל נְטִילַת לוּלָב.

On the first day of waving the *lulav* add:

בָּרוּךְ אַתָּה, יְיָ אֱלֹהֵינוּ, מֶלֶךְ הָעוֹלָם, שֶׁהֶחֱיָנוּ וְקִיְּמָנוּ
וְהִגִּיעָנוּ לַזְּמַן הַזֶּה.

נטילת לולב ("taking the *lulav*") is based on the traditional interpretation of Leviticus 23:40 regarding the celebration of *Sukkoth*: "You shall take . . .the fruit of a beautiful tree (אתרוג), branches of palm trees (לולב), boughs of leafy trees (הדסים), and water-willows (ערבות), and ·ejoice before the Lord your God for seven days." Since the *lulav* is the most prominent of the four

Sixth day of Sukkoth:

O Aaron, my exalted guest, may it please you to have all the exalted guests dwell with us—Abraham, Isaac, Jacob, Joseph, Moses and David.

Seventh day of Sukkoth:

O David, my exalted guest, may it please you to have all the exalted guests dwell with us—Abraham, Isaac, Jacob, Joseph, Moses and Aaron.

WAVING THE LULAV

During Sukkoth (except Sabbath) the following is recited as the lulav (in the right hand) and the ethrog (in the left hand) are held together.

I am ready and prepared to fulfill the command of my Creator, who has commanded us in his Torah: "On the first day you shall take for yourselves the fruit of the *hadar* tree, branches of palm trees, limbs of leafy trees, and water-willows."[1] As I wave them, may God shower me with blessings and imbue me with holy thoughts. He is the supreme God, the Lord of lords, Ruler of earth and heaven, whose majesty has dominion over all things. May my observance of this precept of [waving] the four species be considered as if I fulfilled it with all its particulars, details and implications. May the favor of the Lord our God rest on us. Do thou prosper all the work we undertake; do thou establish the work of our hands. Blessed be the Lord forever. Amen, Amen.[2]

Blessed art thou, Lord our God, King of the universe, who hast sanctified us with thy commandments, and commanded us about the waving of the palm branch.

On the first day of waving the lulav add:

Blessed art thou, Lord our God, King of the universe, who hast granted us life and sustenance and permitted us to reach this season.

---

plants (ארבעה מינים), it is held in the right hand and mentioned in the blessing. The wavings toward all directions (נענועים) symbolize the stream of abundance which comes from the sky and the four corners of the earth. The meditation preceeding the blessing over the *lulav* is taken from שערי ציון, a collection of kabbalistic prayers and reflections by Rabbi Nathan Hannover of the seventeenth century.

[1] *Leviticus* 23:40. [2] *Psalms* 90:17; 89:53.

הוֹשַׁעֲנוֹת

On *Sukkoth* after *Musaf*—numbered for special days of the week:

If Monday is the first day of *Sukkoth*, the order is: א, ב, ה, ג, ו, ח.

If Tuesday is the first day of *Sukkoth*, the order is: א, ב, ה, ו, ח, ד.

If Thursday is the first day of *Sukkoth*, the order is: א, ב, ח, ה, ו, ד.

If Sabbath is the first day of *Sukkoth*, the order is: ח, א, ה, ב, ו, ד.

Number ו is added on days other than Sabbath.

On the seventh day of *Sukkoth*, all the *Hoshanoth* are recited.

Responsively

הוֹשַׁע נָא

לְמַעַנְךָ אֱלֹהֵינוּ הוֹשַׁע נָא.

לְמַעַנְךָ בּוֹרְאֵנוּ הוֹשַׁע נָא.

לְמַעַנְךָ גּוֹאֲלֵנוּ הוֹשַׁע נָא.

לְמַעַנְךָ דּוֹרְשֵׁנוּ הוֹשַׁע נָא.

א לְמַעַן אֲמִתָּךְ, לְמַעַן בְּרִיתָךְ, לְמַעַן גָּדְלְךָ וְתִפְאַרְתָּךְ, לְמַעַן דָּתָךְ, לְמַעַן הוֹדָךְ, לְמַעַן וִעוּדָךְ, לְמַעַן זִכְרָךְ, לְמַעַן חַסְדָּךְ, לְמַעַן טוּבָךְ, לְמַעַן יִחוּדָךְ, לְמַעַן כְּבוֹדָךְ, לְמַעַן לִמּוּדָךְ, לְמַעַן מַלְכוּתָךְ, לְמַעַן נִצְחָךְ, לְמַעַן סוֹדָךְ, לְמַעַן עֻזָּךְ, לְמַעַן פְּאֵרָךְ, לְמַעַן צִדְקָתָךְ, לְמַעַן קְדֻשָּׁתָךְ, לְמַעַן רַחֲמֶיךָ הָרַבִּים, לְמַעַן שְׁכִינָתָךְ, הוֹשַׁע נָא; לְמַעַן תְּהִלָּתָךְ, הוֹשַׁע נָא.

*(כִּי אָמַרְתִּי עוֹלָם חֶסֶד יִבָּנֶה.)

* The verse marked by an asterisk is added on *Hoshana Rabbah*.

הושענות are prayers for deliverance, based on biblical and midrashic pass-ages. They were mainly composed by Elazar ha-Kallir who lived presumably in Palestine during the eighth century. Alphabetically arranged, each of these compositions contains as many verses or phrases as there are letters in the Hebrew alphabet.

679

ב אֶבֶן שְׁתִיָּה, בֵּית הַבְּחִירָה, גְּרֶן אָרְנָן, דְּבִיר הַמְּצְנָע, הַר הַמּוֹרִיָּה, וְהַר יֵרָאֶה, זְבוּל תִּפְאַרְתֶּךָ, חָנָה דָוִד, טוֹב הַלְּבָנוֹן, יְפֵה נוֹף מְשׂוֹשׂ כָּל הָאָרֶץ, כְּלִילַת יְפִי, לִינַת הַצֶּדֶק, מְכוֹן לְשִׁבְתֶּךָ, נָוֶה שַׁאֲנָן, סֻכַּת שָׁלֵם, עֲלִיַּת שְׁבָטִים, פִּנַּת יִקְרַת, צִיּוֹן הַמְּצֻיֶּנֶת, קֹדֶשׁ הַקֳּדָשִׁים, רָצוּף אַהֲבָה, שְׁכִינַת כְּבוֹדֶךָ, הוֹשַׁע נָא; תֵּל תַּלְפִּיּוֹת, הוֹשַׁע נָא.

*(לְךָ זְרוֹעַ עִם גְּבוּרָה; תָּעֹז יָדְךָ, תָּרוּם יְמִינֶךָ.)

ג אִם אֲנִי חוֹמָה, בָּרָה כַּחַמָּה, גּוֹלָה וְסוּרָה, דָּמְתָה לְתָמָר, הַהֲרוּגָה עָלֶיךָ, וְנֶחֱשֶׁבֶת כְּצֹאן טִבְחָה, זְרוּיָה בֵּין מַכְעִיסֶיהָ, חֲבוּקָה וּדְבוּקָה בָּךְ, טוֹעֶנֶת עֻלָּךְ, יְחִידָה לְיַחֲדָךְ, כְּבוּשָׁה בַּגּוֹלָה, לוֹמֶדֶת יִרְאָתֶךָ, מְרוּטַת לֶחִי, נְתוּנָה לְמַכִּים, סוֹבֶלֶת סִבְלָךְ, עֲנִיָּה סֹעֲרָה, פְּדוּיַת טוֹבִיָּה, צֹאן קָדָשִׁים, קְהִלּוֹת יַעֲקֹב, רְשׁוּמִים בְּשִׁמְךָ, שׁוֹאֲגִים הוֹשַׁע נָא; תְּמוּכִים עָלֶיךָ, הוֹשַׁע נָא.

*(תִּתֵּן אֱמֶת לְיַעֲקֹב, חֶסֶד לְאַבְרָהָם.)

ד אָדוֹן הַמּוֹשִׁיעַ, בִּלְתְּךָ אֵין לְהוֹשִׁיעַ, גִּבּוֹר וְרַב לְהוֹשִׁיעַ,

---

In Temple times, the people formed a procession around the altar on each of the first six days of *Sukkoth* while chanting אנא ה' הושיעה נא (Psalm 118:25). On the seventh day of *Sukkoth*, however, they formed seven such processions; hence the name *Hoshana Rabbah*. After the seven processions they would beat willow-sprigs against the ground, symbolically casting off sins as the leaves are beaten off (Mishnah Sukkah 4:5-6).

למען אמתך that is, save us for the sake of thy truth, thy covenant, thy glory, thy Torah ...

אבן שתיה ("the world's corner-stone") heads the alphabetic list of synonyms for the Temple.

אם אני חומה is an alphabetic description of Israel, "as firm as a rampart," who clings to God in spite of all oppression and suffering endured in exile.

אדון המושיע the saving Lord, being entreated to grant deliverance and prosperity.

דַּלְתִי וְלִי יְהוֹשִׁיעַ, הָאֵל הַמּוֹשִׁיעַ, וּמַצִּיל וּמוֹשִׁיעַ, זוֹעֲקֶיךָ
תּוֹשִׁיעַ, חוֹכֶיךָ הוֹשִׁיעַ, טָלָאֶיךָ תַּשְׂבִּיעַ, יְבוּל לְהַשְׁפִּיעַ, כָּל
שִׂיחַ תַּדְשֵׁא וְתוֹשִׁיעַ, לְגֶיא בַּל תַּרְשִׁיעַ, מְגָדִים תַּמְתִּיק וְתוֹשִׁיעַ,
נְשִׂיאִים לְהַסִּיעַ, שְׂעִירִים לְהָנִיעַ, עֲנָנִים מִלְּהַמְנִיעַ, פּוֹתֵחַ יָד
וּמַשְׂבִּיעַ, צְמֵאֶיךָ תַּשְׂבִּיעַ, קוֹרְאֶיךָ תּוֹשִׁיעַ, רְחוּמֶיךָ תּוֹשִׁיעַ,
שׁוֹחֲרֶיךָ הוֹשִׁיעַ, הוֹשַׁע נָא; תְּמִימֶיךָ תּוֹשִׁיעַ, הוֹשַׁע נָא.
*(נְעִמוֹת בִּימִינְךָ נֶצַח.)

אָדָם וּבְהֵמָה, בָּשָׂר וְרוּחַ וּנְשָׁמָה, גִּיד וְעֶצֶם וְקָרְמָה, דְּמוּת
וְצֶלֶם וְרִקְמָה, הוֹד לַהֶבֶל דָּמָה, וְנִמְשַׁל כַּבְּהֵמוֹת נִדְמָה, זִיו
וְתֹאַר וְקוֹמָה, חִדּוּשׁ פְּנֵי אֲדָמָה, טִיעַת עֲצֵי נְשַׁמָּה, יְקָבִים
וְקָמָה, כְּרָמִים וְשִׁקְמָה, לְתֵבֵל הַמְסַיְּמָה, מִטְּרוֹת עֹז לְסַמְּמָה,
נְשִׁיָּה לְקַיְּמָה, שִׂיחִים לְקוֹמְמָה, עֲדָנִים לְעָצְמָה, פְּרָחִים
לְהַעֲצִימָה, צְמָחִים לְנַשְּׁמָה, קָרִים לְזָרְמָה, רְבִיבִים לְשַׁלְּמָה,
שְׁתִיָּה לְרוֹמְמָה, הוֹשַׁע נָא; תְּלוּיָה עַל בְּלִימָה, הוֹשַׁע נָא.

*(יְיָ אֲדוֹנֵינוּ, מָה אַדִּיר שִׁמְךָ בְּכָל הָאָרֶץ; אֲשֶׁר תְּנָה הוֹדְךָ
עַל הַשָּׁמָיִם.)

אֲדָמָה מֵאֶרֶר, בְּהֵמָה מִמְּשַׁכֶּלֶת, גֹּרֶן מִזָּעָם, דָּגָן מִדַּלֶּקֶת,
הוֹן מִמְּאֵרָה, וְאֹכֶל מִמְּהוּמָה, זַיִת מִנְּשׁוֹל, חִטָּה מֵחָגָב, טֶרֶף
מִגּוֹבַי, יֶקֶב מִיֶּלֶק, כֶּרֶם מִתּוֹלַעַת, לֶקֶשׁ מֵאַרְבֶּה, מֶגֶד
מִצְּלָצַל, נֶפֶשׁ מִבֶּהָלָה, שֶׂבַע מִסָּלְעָם, עֲדָרִים מִדַּלּוּת, פֵּרוֹת
מִשִּׁדָּפוֹן, צֹאן מִצְּמִיתוּת, קָצִיר מִקְּלָלָה, רֹב מֵרָזוֹן, שִׁבֹּלֶת
מִצְּנָמוֹן, הוֹשַׁע נָא; תְּבוּאָה מֵחָסִיל, הוֹשַׁע נָא.
*(צַדִּיק יְיָ בְּכָל דְּרָכָיו, וְחָסִיד בְּכָל מַעֲשָׂיו.)

* The verse marked by an asterisk is added on *Hoshana Rabbah*.

אדם ובהמה is a plea for God's providence over animal and plant life.
אדמה מארר that is, may no harm come to animals or plants.

לְמַעַן אֵיתָן הַנִּזְרָק בְּלַהַב אֵשׁ, לְמַעַן בֶּן הַנֶּעֱקַד עַל עֵצִים
וָאֵשׁ, לְמַעַן גִּבּוֹר הַנֶּאֱבַק עִם שַׂר אֵשׁ, לְמַעַן דְּגָלִים נָחִיתָ בְּעָנָן
וָאוֹר אֵשׁ, לְמַעַן הָעֲלָה לַמָּרוֹם וְנִתְעַלָּה כְּמַלְאֲכֵי אֵשׁ, לְמַעַן
וְהוּא לָךְ כְּסֶגֶן בְּאֶרְאֶלֵּי אֵשׁ, לְמַעַן זֶבֶד דִּבְּרוֹת הַנְּתוּנוֹת מֵאֵשׁ,
לְמַעַן חִפּוּי יְרִיעוֹת וַעֲנַן אֵשׁ, לְמַעַן טֶכֶס הַר יָרַדְתָּ עָלָיו בָּאֵשׁ,
לְמַעַן יְדִידוּת אֲשֶׁר אָהַבְתָּ מִשְּׁמֵי אֵשׁ, לְמַעַן כָּמָהּ עַד שָׁקְעָה
הָאֵשׁ, לְמַעַן לָקַח מַחְתַּת אֵשׁ וְהֵסִיר חֲרוֹן אֵשׁ, לְמַעַן מְקַנֵּא
קִנְאָה גְדוֹלָה בָּאֵשׁ, לְמַעַן נָף יָדוֹ וְיָרְדוּ אַבְנֵי אֵשׁ, לְמַעַן שָׂם
טָלֶה חָלָב כְּלִיל אֵשׁ, לְמַעַן עָמַד בַּגֹּרֶן וְנִתְרַצָּה בָאֵשׁ, לְמַעַן
פִּלֵּל בָּעֲזָרָה וְיָרְדָה הָאֵשׁ, לְמַעַן צִיר עָלָה וְנִתְעַלָּה בְּרֶכֶב
וְסוּסֵי אֵשׁ, לְמַעַן קְדוֹשִׁים מֻשְׁלָכִים בָּאֵשׁ, לְמַעַן רִבּוֹ רִבְבָן
חָז וְנַחֲרֵי אֵשׁ, לְמַעַן שְׁמָמוֹת עִירְךָ הַשְּׂרוּפָה בָאֵשׁ, הוֹשַׁע נָא;
לְמַעַן תּוֹלְדוֹת אַלּוּפֵי יְהוּדָה תָּשִׂים כְּכִיּוֹר אֵשׁ, הוֹשַׁע נָא.

לָךְ יְיָ הַגְּדֻלָּה וְהַגְּבוּרָה, וְהַתִּפְאֶרֶת וְהַנֵּצַח וְהַהוֹד, כִּי כֹל
בַּשָּׁמַיִם וּבָאָרֶץ; לְךָ יְיָ הַמַּמְלָכָה, וְהַמִּתְנַשֵּׂא לְכֹל לְרֹאשׁ.
וְהָיָה יְיָ לְמֶלֶךְ עַל כָּל הָאָרֶץ; בַּיּוֹם הַהוּא יִהְיֶה יְיָ אֶחָד וּשְׁמוֹ
אֶחָד. וּבְתוֹרָתְךָ כָּתוּב לֵאמֹר: שְׁמַע יִשְׂרָאֵל, יְיָ אֱלֹהֵינוּ, יְיָ
אֶחָד. בָּרוּךְ שֵׁם כְּבוֹד מַלְכוּתוֹ לְעוֹלָם וָעֶד.

On *Hoshana Rabbah* omit the following two paragraphs.

ה אֶעֱרוֹךְ שׁוּעִי, בְּבֵית שַׁוְעִי, גִּלִּיתִי בַצּוֹם פִּשְׁעִי, דְּרַשְׁתִּיךָ בּוֹ
לְהוֹשִׁיעִי, הַקְשִׁיבָה לְקוֹל שַׁוְעִי, וְקוּמָה וְהוֹשִׁיעִי, זְכוֹר וְרַחֵם
מוֹשִׁיעִי, חַי בֶּן תְּשַׁעְשְׁעִי, טוֹב בְּאֶנֶק שְׁעִי, יָחִישׁ מוֹשִׁיעִי, כַּלֵּה

למען איתן save us for the sake of the three patriarchs and the twelve
tribes, for the sake of Moses, Aaron, Phineas, Joshua, Samuel, David, Solomon,
Hananiah, Mishael, Azariah and Daniel.

אערוך שׁוּעִי that is, I pray in the house of prayer, where on the fast of *Yom
Kippur* I confessed my sins. O hasten to send my deliverer.

מַרְשִׁיעִי, לְכָל עוֹד תַּרְשִׁיעִי, מַהֵר אֱלֹהֵי יִשְׁעִי, נֶצַח לְהוֹשִׁיעִי,
שָׂא נָא עֲוֹן רִשְׁעִי, עֲבוֹר עַל פִּשְׁעִי, פְּנֵה נָא לְהוֹשִׁיעִי, צוּר
צַדִּיק מוֹשִׁיעִי, קַבֵּל נָא שַׁוְעִי, רוֹמֵם קֶרֶן יִשְׁעִי, שַׁדַּי מוֹשִׁיעִי,
הוֹשַׁע נָא; תּוֹפִיעַ וְתוֹשִׁיעִי, הוֹשַׁע נָא.

ו אֵל לְמוֹשָׁעוֹת, בְּאַרְבַּע שְׁבוּעוֹת, גָּשִׁים בְּשַׁוְעוֹת, דּוֹפְקֵי
עֶרֶךְ שׁוּעוֹת, הוֹגֵי שַׁעֲשׁוּעוֹת, וְחִידוֹתָם מִשְׁתַּעַשְׁעוֹת, זוֹעֲקִים
לְהַשְׁעוֹת, חוֹכֵי יְשׁוּעוֹת, טְפוּלִים בָּךְ שָׁעוֹת, יוֹדְעֵי בִּין שָׁעוֹת,
כּוֹרְעֶךְ בְּשַׁוְעוֹת, לְהָבִין שְׁמוּעוֹת, מִפִּיךְ נִשְׁמָעוֹת, נוֹתֵן
תְּשׁוּעוֹת, סְפוּרוֹת מַשְׁמָעוֹת, עֵדוּת מַשְׁמִיעוֹת, פּוֹעֵל יְשׁוּעוֹת,
צַדִּיק נוֹשָׁעוֹת, קְרִיַּת תְּשׁוּעוֹת, רֶגֶשׁ תְּשׁוּאוֹת, שָׁלֹשׁ שָׁעוֹת,
הוֹשַׁע נָא; תָּחִישׁ לְתְשׁוּעוֹת, הוֹשַׁע נָא.
אֲנִי וָהוֹ הוֹשִׁיעָה נָא.

On days other than Sabbath add:

ז כְּהוֹשַׁעְתָּ אֵלִים בְּלוּד עִמָּךְ, בְּצֵאתְךָ לְיֵשַׁע עַמָּךְ, בֵּן הוֹשַׁע
נָא. כְּהוֹשַׁעְתָּ גּוֹי וֵאלֹהִים, דְּרוּשִׁים לְיֵשַׁע אֱלֹהִים, בֵּן הוֹשַׁע נָא.
כְּהוֹשַׁעְתָּ הֲמוֹן צְבָאוֹת, וְעִמָּם מַלְאֲכֵי צְבָאוֹת, בֵּן הוֹשַׁע נָא.
כְּהוֹשַׁעְתָּ זַכִּים מִבֵּית עֲבָדִים, חַנּוּן בְּיָדָם מַעֲבִידִים, בֵּן הוֹשַׁע
נָא. כְּהוֹשַׁעְתָּ טְבוּעִים בְּצוּל גְּזָרִים, יְקָרְךָ עִמָּם מַעֲבִירִים, בֵּן

אל למושעות O God, who didst seal thy promise for salvation by a four-fold oath, save thy prayerful people speedily.

אני והו has the numerical value of אנא ה', namely 78. אני והו was substituted for אנא ה' in order to avoid the repetition of God's four-letter name, the tetragrammaton, considered too sacred to pronounce (Mishnah Sukkah 4:5). Out of reverence for the divine name, the tetragrammaton was already in ancient times pronounced *Adonai* ("my Lord"), a substitute for its original pronunciation.

כהושעת אלים as thou didst save the faithful in Egypt, save thou also us. Lud and Egypt are here used synonymously on the basis of Genesis 10:13.

הוֹשַׁע נָא. כְּהוֹשַׁעְתָּ כַּנָּה מְשׁוֹרֶרֶת וַיּוֹשַׁע, לְנוֹחָה מְצֻיֶּנֶת וַיִּוָּשַׁע,
בֶּן הוֹשַׁע נָא. כְּהוֹשַׁעְתָּ מַאֲמַר וְהוֹצֵאתִי אֶתְכֶם, נָקוֹב וְהוֹצֵאתִי
אֶתְכֶם, בֶּן הוֹשַׁע נָא. כְּהוֹשַׁעְתָּ סוֹבְבֵי מִזְבֵּחַ, עוֹמְסֵי עֲרָבָה
לְהַקִּיף מִזְבֵּחַ, בֶּן הוֹשַׁע נָא. כְּהוֹשַׁעְתָּ פִּלְאֵי אָרוֹן כְּהָפְשַׁע,
צֹעַר פְּלֶשֶׁת בַּחֲרוֹן אַף וְנוֹשַׁע, בֶּן הוֹשַׁע נָא. כְּהוֹשַׁעְתָּ קְהִלּוֹת
בָּבֶלָה שָׁלַחְתָּ, רַחוּם לְמַעֲנָם שָׁלַחְתָּ, בֶּן הוֹשַׁע נָא. כְּהוֹשַׁעְתָּ
שְׁבוּת שִׁבְטֵי יַעֲקֹב, תָּשׁוּב וְתָשִׁיב שְׁבוּת אָהֳלֵי יַעֲקֹב, וְהוֹשִׁיעָה
נָא. כְּהוֹשַׁעְתָּ שׁוֹמְרֵי מִצְוֹת, וְחוֹכֵי יְשׁוּעוֹת, אֵל לְמוֹשָׁעוֹת,
וְהוֹשִׁיעָה נָא.

אֲנִי וָהוֹ הוֹשִׁיעָה נָא.

הוֹשִׁיעָה אֶת עַמֶּךָ, וּבָרֵךְ אֶת נַחֲלָתֶךָ, וּרְעֵם וְנַשְּׂאֵם עַד
הָעוֹלָם. וְיִהְיוּ דְבָרַי אֵלֶּה, אֲשֶׁר הִתְחַנַּנְתִּי לִפְנֵי יְיָ, קְרוֹבִים
אֶל יְיָ אֱלֹהֵינוּ יוֹמָם וָלָיְלָה, לַעֲשׂוֹת מִשְׁפַּט עַבְדּוֹ וּמִשְׁפַּט עַמּוֹ
יִשְׂרָאֵל דְּבַר יוֹם בְּיוֹמוֹ. לְמַעַן דַּעַת כָּל עַמֵּי הָאָרֶץ, כִּי יְיָ
הוּא הָאֱלֹהִים, אֵין עוֹד.

ON SABBATH

ח אִם נְצוּרָה כְּבָבַת, בּוֹנֶנֶת בְּדַת נֶפֶשׁ מְשִׁיבַת, גּוֹמֶרֶת הִלְכוֹת
שַׁבָּת, דּוֹרֶשֶׁת מַשְּׂאַת שַׁבָּת, הַקּוֹבַעַת אַלְפַּיִם תְּחוּם שַׁבָּת,
וּמְשִׁיבַת רֶגֶל מִשַּׁבָּת, זָכוֹר וְשָׁמוֹר מְקַיֶּמֶת בַּשַּׁבָּת, חָשָׁה לְמַהֵר
בִּיאַת שַׁבָּת, טוֹרַחַת כָּל מִשִּׁשָּׁה לַשַּׁבָּת, יוֹשֶׁבֶת וּמַמְתֶּנֶת עַד
כְּלוֹת שַׁבָּת, כָּבוֹד וָעֹנֶג קוֹרְאָה לַשַּׁבָּת, לְבוּשׁ וּכְסוּת מְחַלֶּפֶת
בַּשַּׁבָּת, מַאֲכָל וּמִשְׁתֶּה מְכִינָה לַשַּׁבָּת, נֹעַם מְגָדִים מַנְעֶמֶת
לַשַּׁבָּת, סְעוּדוֹת שָׁלשׁ מְקַיֶּמֶת בַּשַּׁבָּת, עַל שְׁתֵּי כִכָּרוֹת בּוֹצַעַת

אם נצורה כבבת the people of Israel, which has been guarded as one guards
the apple of his eye, studies the inspiring Torah and conscientiously observes
the precepts of the Sabbath.

בְּשַׁבָּת, פּוֹרֶטֶת אַרְבַּע רְשָׁיוֹת בַּשַׁבָּת, צִוּוּי הַדְלָקַת נֵר
מַדְלֶקֶת בַּשַׁבָּת, קִדּוּשׁ הַיּוֹם מְקַדֶּשֶׁת בַּשַׁבָּת, רֶנֶן שֶׁבַע
מְפַלֶּלֶת בַּשַׁבָּת, שִׁבְעָה בְּדָת קוֹרְאָה בַּשַׁבָּת, תַּנְחִילֶנָּה לְיוֹם
שֶׁכֻּלּוֹ שַׁבָּת, הוֹשַׁע נָא.

אֲנִי וָהוּ הוֹשִׁיעָה נָּא.

כְּהוֹשַׁעְתָּ אָדָם יְצִיר כַּפֶּיךָ לְגוֹנְנָה, בְּשַׁבַּת קֹדֶשׁ הִמְצֵאתוֹ
כֹּפֶר וַחֲנִינָה, כֵּן הוֹשַׁע נָא. כְּהוֹשַׁעְתָּ גּוֹי מְצֻיָּן מְקַוְּים חְפֶשׁ,
דֵּעָה כִּוְּנוּ לְבַר שְׁבִיעִי לְנָפֶשׁ, כֵּן הוֹשַׁע נָא. כְּהוֹשַׁעְתָּ הָעָם
נִהַגְתָּ כַּצֹּאן לְהַנְחוֹת, וְחֹק שַׂמְתָּ בְּמָרָה עַל מֵי מְנוּחוֹת, כֵּן
הוֹשַׁע נָא. כְּהוֹשַׁעְתָּ זְבוּדֶיךָ בְּמִדְבַּר סִין בַּמַּחֲנֶה, חָכְמוּ וְלָקְטוּ
בַּשִּׁשִּׁי לֶחֶם מִשְׁנֶה, כֵּן הוֹשַׁע נָא. כְּהוֹשַׁעְתָּ טִפּוּלֶיךָ הוֹרוּ הֲכָנָה
בְּמַדְעָם, יָשָׁר כֹּחָם וְהוֹדָה לָמוֹ רוֹעָם, כֵּן הוֹשַׁע נָא. כְּהוֹשַׁעְתָּ
כִּלְכְּלוּ בְּעָנְגָ מָן הַמְשֻׁמָּר, לֹא הָפַךְ עֵינוֹ וְרֵיחוֹ לֹא נָמָר, כֵּן
הוֹשַׁע נָא. כְּהוֹשַׁעְתָּ מִשְׁפְּטֵי מַשְׂאוֹת שַׁבָּת גָּמָרוּ, נָחוּ וְשָׁבְתוּ
רְשָׁיוֹת וּתְחוּמִים שָׁמָרוּ, כֵּן הוֹשַׁע נָא. כְּהוֹשַׁעְתָּ סִינַי הָשְׁמְעוּ
בְּדִבּוּר רְבִיעִי, עִנְיַן זָכוֹר וְשָׁמוֹר לְקַדֵּשׁ שְׁבִיעִי, כֵּן הוֹשַׁע נָא.
כְּהוֹשַׁעְתָּ פִּקְּדוּ יְרִיחוֹ שֶׁבַע לְהַקֵּף, צָרוּ עַד רִדְתָּהּ בַּשַׁבָּת
לְתַקֵּף, כֵּן הוֹשַׁע נָא. כְּהוֹשַׁעְתָּ קֹהֶלֶת וְעַמּוֹ בְּבֵית עוֹלָמִים,
רִצּוּךָ בְּחָגְגָם שִׁבְעָה וְשִׁבְעָה יָמִים, כֵּן הוֹשַׁע נָא. כְּהוֹשַׁעְתָּ
שָׁבִים עוֹלֵי גוֹלָה לְפִדְיוֹם, תּוֹרָתְךָ בְּקָרְאָם בְּחַג יוֹם יוֹם, כֵּן
הוֹשַׁע נָא. כְּהוֹשַׁעְתָּ מְשַׂמְּחֶיךָ בְּבִנְיַן שֵׁנִי הַמְחֻדָּשׁ, נוֹטְלִין לוּלָב
כָּל שִׁבְעָה בַּמִּקְדָּשׁ, כֵּן הוֹשַׁע נָא. כְּהוֹשַׁעְתָּ חִבּוּט עֲרָבָה שַׁבָּת

כהושעת אדם was composed in the eleventh century by Rabbi Menaḥem ben
Makhir, whose signature (מנחם ברבי מכיר) is given in the form of an acrostic
immediately after the alphabetical acrostic. This poem treats of the Sabbath and
the manner in which it was observed in Temple times.

מַדְחִים, מַרְבִּיוֹת מוֹצָא לִיסוֹד מִזְבֵּחַ מַנִּיחִים, בֶּן הוֹשַׁע נָא.
כְּהוֹשַׁעְתָּ בְּרַבּוֹת וַאֲרוּכוֹת וּגְבוֹהוֹת מְעַלְסִים, בִּפְטִירָתָן יְפִי
לָךְ מִזְבֵּחַ מְקַלְסִים, בֶּן הוֹשַׁע נָא. כְּהוֹשַׁעְתָּ מוֹדִים וּמְיַחֲלִים
וְלֹא מְשַׁנִּים, כֻּלָּנוּ אָנוּ לְיָהּ וְעֵינֵינוּ לְיָהּ שׁוֹנִים, בֶּן הוֹשַׁע נָא.
כְּהוֹשַׁעְתָּ יֶקֶב מֵחַצָּבֶיךָ סוֹבְבִים בְּרַעֲנָנָה, רוֹנְנִים אֲנִי וָהוֹ
הוֹשִׁיעָה נָּא, בֶּן הוֹשַׁע נָא. כְּהוֹשַׁעְתָּ חֵיל זְרִיזִים מְשָׁרְתִים
בִּמְנוּחָה, קָרְבַּן שַׁבָּת כָּפוּל עוֹלָה וּמִנְחָה, בֶּן הוֹשַׁע נָא.
כְּהוֹשַׁעְתָּ לְוִיֶּךָ עַל דּוּכָנָם לְהַרְבַּת, אוֹמְרִים מִזְמוֹר שִׁיר לְיוֹם
הַשַּׁבָּת, בֶּן הוֹשַׁע נָא. כְּהוֹשַׁעְתָּ נְחוּמֶיךָ בְּמִצְוֹתֶיךָ תָּמִיד
יִשְׁתַּעַשְׁעוּן, וּרְצֵם וְהַחֲלִיצֵם בְּשׁוּבָה וָנַחַת יִוָּשֵׁעוּן, בֶּן הוֹשַׁע
נָא. כְּהוֹשַׁעְתָּ שְׁבוּת שִׁבְטֵי יַעֲקֹב, תָּשׁוּב וְתָשִׁיב שְׁבוּת אָהֳלֵי
יַעֲקֹב, וְהוֹשִׁיעָה נָּא. כְּהוֹשַׁעְתָּ שׁוֹמְרֵי מִצְוֹת, וְחוֹכֵי יְשׁוּעוֹת,
אֵל לְמוֹשָׁעוֹת, וְהוֹשִׁיעָה נָּא.

אֲנִי וָהוֹ הוֹשִׁיעָה נָּא.

הוֹשִׁיעָה אֶת עַמֶּךָ, וּבָרֵךְ אֶת נַחֲלָתֶךָ, וּרְעֵם וְנַשְּׂאֵם עַד
הָעוֹלָם. וְיִהְיוּ דְבָרַי אֵלֶּה, אֲשֶׁר הִתְחַנַּנְתִּי לִפְנֵי יְיָ, קְרוֹבִים
אֶל יְיָ אֱלֹהֵינוּ יוֹמָם וָלָיְלָה, לַעֲשׂוֹת מִשְׁפַּט עַבְדּוֹ וּמִשְׁפַּט עַמּוֹ
יִשְׂרָאֵל דְּבַר יוֹם בְּיוֹמוֹ. לְמַעַן דַּעַת כָּל עַמֵּי הָאָרֶץ, כִּי יְיָ
הוּא הָאֱלֹהִים, אֵין עוֹד.

ON HOSHANA RABBAH

אֲנִי וָהוֹ הוֹשִׁיעָה נָּא.

תִּתְּנֵנוּ לְשֵׁם וְלִתְהִלָּה. תְּשִׁיבֵנוּ אֶל הַחֵבֶל וְאֶל הַנַּחֲלָה.
תְּרוֹמְמֵנוּ לְמַעְלָה לְמָעְלָה. תְּקַבְּצֵנוּ לְבֵית הַתְּפִלָּה. תַּצִּיבֵנוּ

תתנני לשם, a poem by Rabbi Elazar ha-Kallir, runs in a reversed alphabetic
acrostic. It begins with ת, the last letter of the alphabet, and ends with א, the
first letter. The acrostic אלעזר חזק is found in the concluding verse. This poem
contains a plea for the restoration of Zion and the liberation of Israel.

כְּעֵץ עַל פַּלְגֵי מַיִם שְׁתוּלָה. תִּפְדֵּנוּ מִכָּל נֶגַע וּמַחֲלָה. תְּעַטְּרֵנוּ
בְּאַהֲבָה כְּלוּלָה. תְּשַׂמְּחֵנוּ בְּבֵית הַתְּפִלָּה. תְּנַהֲלֵנוּ עַל מֵי
מְנוּחוֹת סֶלָה. תְּמַלְּאֵנוּ חָכְמָה וְשִׂכְלָה. תַּלְבִּישֵׁנוּ עֹז וְגֶדְלָה.
תַּבְחִירֵנוּ בְּכֶתֶר כְּלוּלָה. תְּיַשְּׁרֵנוּ בְּאֹרַח סְלוּלָה. תִּטָּעֵנוּ בְּיֹשֶׁר
מְסִלָּה. תְּחָנֵּנוּ בְּרַחֲמִים וּבְחֶמְלָה. תַּזְכִּירֵנוּ בְּמֵי זֹאת עוֹלָה.
תּוֹשִׁיעֵנוּ לְקֵץ הַגְּאֻלָּה. תְּהַדְּרֵנוּ בְּזִיו הַמְּלָה. תַּדְבִּיקֵנוּ כְּאֵזוֹר
חֲתֻלָּה. תְּגַדְּלֵנוּ בְּיָד הַגְּדוֹלָה. תְּבִיאֵנוּ לְבֵיתְךָ בְּרִנָּה וְצָהֳלָה.
תְּאַדְּרֵנוּ בְּיֶשַׁע וְגִילָה. תְּאַמְּצֵנוּ בְּרֶוַח וְהַצָּלָה. תְּלַבְּבֵנוּ בְּבִנְיַן
עִירְךָ בְּבַתְּחִלָּה. תְּעוֹרְרֵנוּ לְצִיּוֹן בְּשִׂכְלוּלָה. תְּזַכֵּנוּ בְּנִבְנָתָה
הָעִיר עַל תִּלָּה. תַּרְבִּיצֵנוּ בְּשָׂשׂוֹן וְגִילָה. הוֹשַׁע נָא. תְּחַזְּקֵנוּ
אֱלֹהֵי יַעֲקֹב סֶלָה. הוֹשַׁע נָא.

Reader and Congregation:

אָנָּא הוֹשִׁיעָה נָּא.

אָנָּא אֱזוֹן חִין תְּאֵבֵי יִשְׁעָךְ, בְּעַרְבֵי נַחַל לְשַׁעְשָׁעָךְ, וְהוֹשִׁיעָה נָּא.

אָנָּא גְּאַל כַּנַּת נִטְעָךְ, דּוּמָה בְּטַאטֵאָךְ, וְהוֹשִׁיעָה נָּא.

אָנָּא הַבֵּט לִבְרִית טִבְעָךְ, וּמַחֲשַׁבֵּי אֶרֶץ בְּהַטְבִּיעָךְ, וְהוֹשִׁיעָה נָּא.

אָנָּא זְכָר־לָנוּ אָב יְדָעָךְ, חַסְדְּךָ לָמוֹ בְּהוֹדִיעָךְ, וְהוֹשִׁיעָה נָּא.

אָנָּא טְהוֹרֵי לֵב בְּהַפְלִיאָךְ, יֻדַּע כִּי הוּא פִּלְאָךְ, וְהוֹשִׁיעָה נָּא.

אָנָּא כַּבִּיר כֹּחַ הֵן לָנוּ יִשְׁעָךְ, לַאֲבוֹתֵינוּ כְּהִשָּׁבְעָךְ, וְהוֹשִׁיעָה נָּא.

אָנָּא מַלֵּא מִשְׁאֲלוֹת עַם מְשַׁוְּעָךְ, נֶעֱקַד כְּמוֹ בְּהַר מוֹר
שׁוְעָךְ, וְהוֹשִׁיעָה נָּא.

אָנָּא שַׂגֵּב אֶשְׁלֵי נִטְעָךְ, עָרִיצִים בַּהֲנִיעָךְ, וְהוֹשִׁיעָה נָּא.

אנא אזון O hearken to the prayer of those who long for thy salvation; deliver
the stock of Israel thou hast planted; save us on the day when thou sweepest
the wicked away; give rain for the thirsty land, and sustain us.

אָנָּא פְּתַח לָנוּ אוֹצְרוֹת רִבְעֶךָ, צִיָּה מֵהֶם בְּהַרְבִּיעֶךָ,
וְהוֹשִׁיעָה נָּא.

אָנָּא קוֹרְאֶיךָ אֶרֶץ בְּרוֹעֲעֶךָ, רְעֵם בְּטוּב מִרְעֶךָ, וְהוֹשִׁיעָה נָּא.

אָנָּא שְׁעָרֶיךָ תַּעַל מִמְּשׁוֹאָךְ, תֵּל תַּלְפִּיּוֹת בְּהַשִּׂיאָךְ,
וְהוֹשִׁיעָה נָּא.

Reader and Congregation:

אָנָּא אֵל נָא, הוֹשַׁע נָא וְהוֹשִׁיעָה נָּא.

אֵל נָא תָּעִינוּ כְּשֶׂה אוֹבֵד, שְׁמֵנוּ מִסִּפְרְךָ אַל תְּאַבֵּד,
הוֹשַׁע נָא וְהוֹשִׁיעָה נָּא.

אֵל נָא רְעֵה אֶת צֹאן הַהֲרֵגָה, קְצוּפָה וְעָלֶיךָ הֲרוּגָה,
הוֹשַׁע נָא וְהוֹשִׁיעָה נָּא.

אֵל נָא צֹאנְךָ וְצֹאן מַרְעִיתֶךָ, פְּעֻלָּתְךָ וְרַעְיָתֶךָ,
הוֹשַׁע נָא וְהוֹשִׁיעָה נָּא.

אֵל נָא עֲנִיֵּי הַצֹּאן, שִׂיחָם עֲנֵה בְּעֵת רָצוֹן,
הוֹשַׁע נָא וְהוֹשִׁיעָה נָּא.

אֵל נָא נוֹשְׂאֵי לְךָ עַיִן, מִתְקוֹמְמֶיךָ יִהְיוּ כְאַיִן,
הוֹשַׁע נָא וְהוֹשִׁיעָה נָּא.

אֵל נָא לִמְנַסְּכֵי לְךָ מַיִם, כְּמִמַּעַיְנֵי הַיְשׁוּעָה יִשְׁאֲבוּן מַיִם,
הוֹשַׁע נָא וְהוֹשִׁיעָה נָּא.

אֵל נָא יַעֲלוּ לְצִיּוֹן מוֹשִׁיעִים, טְפוּלִים בְּךָ וּבְשִׁמְךָ נוֹשָׁעִים,
הוֹשַׁע נָא וְהוֹשִׁיעָה נָּא.

אֵל נָא חֲמוּץ בְּגָדִים, זָעוֹם לְנַעֵר כָּל בּוֹגְדִים,
הוֹשַׁע נָא וְהוֹשִׁיעָה נָּא.

תעינו כשה is a reversed alphabetic acrostic, beginning with the letter ת and ending with the letter א. We are like wandering sheep; do not erase our name from thy book of life.

אֵל נָא וְזָכוֹר תִּזְכּוֹר, הַנִּכּוּרִים בְּלֶחְתֵּךְ וָכוֹר,
הוֹשַׁע נָא וְהוֹשִׁיעָה נָא.

אֵל נָא דוֹרְשֶׁךָ בְּעַנְפֵי עֲרָבוֹת, נַּעִים שְׁעֵה מֵעֲרָבוֹת,
הוֹשַׁע נָא וְהוֹשִׁיעָה נָא.

אֵל נָא בָּרֵךְ בְּעִטוּר שָׁנָה, אֲמָרֵי רְצֵה בְּפִלּוּלִי
בְּיוֹם הוֹשַׁעְנָא, הוֹשַׁע נָא וְהוֹשִׁיעָה נָא.

Reader and Congregation:

אָנָּא אֵל נָא, הוֹשַׁע נָא וְהוֹשִׁיעָה נָא, אָבִינוּ אָתָּה.

לְמַעַן תָּמִים בְּדוֹרוֹתָיו, הַנִּמְלָט בְּרֹב צִדְקוֹתָיו, מֻצָּל מִשֶּׁטֶף
בְּבוֹא מַבּוּל מַיִם, לְאִם אֲנִי חוֹמָה הוֹשַׁע נָא וְהוֹשִׁיעָה נָא, אָבִינוּ
אָתָּה.

לְמַעַן שָׁלֵם בְּכָל מַעֲשִׂים, הַמְנֻסֶּה בַּעֲשָׂרָה נִסִּים, כְּשֻׂר
מַלְאָכִים נָם יֻקַּח נָא מְעַט מַיִם, לְבָרָה כַּחַמָּה הוֹשַׁע נָא
וְהוֹשִׁיעָה נָא, אָבִינוּ אָתָּה.

לְמַעַן רַךְ וְיָחִיד נֶחְנַט פְּרִי לְמֵאָה, זָעַק וְאַיֵּה הַשֶּׂה לְעוֹלָה,
בְּשֹׂרוּהוּ עֲבָדָיו מָצָאנוּ מַיִם, לְגוֹלָה וְסוּרָה הוֹשַׁע נָא וְהוֹשִׁיעָה
נָא, אָבִינוּ אָתָּה.

לְמַעַן קָדַם שְׂאֵת בְּרָכָה, הַנִּשְׁטָם וּלְשִׁמְךָ חִכָּה, מְיַחֵם
בְּמַקְלוֹת בְּשִׁקֲתוֹת הַמַּיִם, לְדָמְתָה לְתָמָר הוֹשַׁע נָא וְהוֹשִׁיעָה
נָא, אָבִינוּ אָתָּה.

לְמַעַן צָדַק הֱיוֹת לְךָ לְכֹהֵן, כְּחָתָן פְּאֵר יְכַהֵן, מְנֻסֶּה בְּמַסָּה

למען תמים consists of a twofold alphabetic acrostic, reversed and straight.
The first stanza, for example, begins with the letter ת (תמים) and ends with the
letter א (אם אני); the second stanza begins with ש (שלם) and ends with ב (גברה).

בְּמֵי מְרִיבַת מַיִם, לְהָהָר הַטּוֹב הוֹשַׁע נָא וְהוֹשִׁיעָה נָּא, אָבִינוּ
אָתָּה.

לְמַעַן פֹּאַר חֲיוֹת גְּבִיר לְאֶחָיו, יְהוּדָה אֲשֶׁר גָּבַר בְּאֶחָיו,
מִסְפַּר רֹבַע מִדָּלְיָו יִזַּל מַיִם, לֹא לָנוּ כִּי אִם לְמַעַנְךָ הוֹשַׁע נָא
וְהוֹשִׁיעָה נָּא, אָבִינוּ אָתָּה.

לְמַעַן עָנָו מִכֹּל וְנֶאֱמָן, אֲשֶׁר בְּצִדְקוֹ כִּלְכֵּל הַמָּן, מְשׁוּךְ
לְגוֹאֵל וּמָשׁוּי מִמַּיִם, לְזֹאת הַנִּשְׁקָפָה הוֹשַׁע נָא וְהוֹשִׁיעָה נָּא,
אָבִינוּ אָתָּה.

לְמַעַן שָׂמְתּוֹ כְּמַלְאֲכֵי מְרוֹמִים, הַלּוֹבֵשׁ אוּרִים וְתֻמִּים,
מְצֻוֶּה לָבֹא בַּמִּקְדָּשׁ בְּקִדּוּשׁ יָדַיִם וְרַגְלַיִם וּרְחִיצַת מַיִם,
לְחוֹלַת אַהֲבָה הוֹשַׁע נָא וְהוֹשִׁיעָה נָּא, אָבִינוּ אָתָּה.

לְמַעַן נְבִיאָה מְחוֹלַת מַחֲנָיִם, לִכְמֵהֵי לֵב הוּשְׂמָה עֵינָיִם,
לְרַגְלָהּ רָצָה עֲלוֹת וְרָדַת בְּאֵר מַיִם, לְטוֹבוּ אֹהָלָיו הוֹשַׁע נָא
וְהוֹשִׁיעָה נָּא, אָבִינוּ אָתָּה.

לְמַעַן מְשָׁרֵת לֹא מָשׁ מֵאֹהֶל, וְרוּחַ הַקֹּדֶשׁ עָלָיו אֹהֵל,
בְּעָבְרוֹ בַּיַּרְדֵּן נִכְרְתוּ הַמַּיִם, לְיָפָה וּבָרָה הוֹשַׁע נָא וְהוֹשִׁיעָה
נָּא, אָבִינוּ אָתָּה.

לְמַעַן לֻמַּד רְאוֹת לְטוֹבָה אוֹת, זָעַק אַיֵּה נִפְלָאוֹת, מִצָּה טַל
מִגִּזָּה מִלֵּא הַסֵּפֶל מַיִם, לְבַלַּת לְבָנוֹן הוֹשַׁע נָא וְהוֹשִׁיעָה נָּא,
אָבִינוּ אָתָּה.

לְמַעַן כְּלוּלֵי עֲשׂוֹת מִלְחַמְתֶּךָ, אֲשֶׁר בְּיָדָם תִּתָּה יְשׁוּעָתֶךָ,
צְרוּפֵי מִגּוֹי בְּלִקְקָם בְּיָדָם מַיִם, לְלֹא בָגְדוּ בָךְ הוֹשַׁע נָא
וְהוֹשִׁיעָה נָּא, אָבִינוּ אָתָּה.

This poem refers to Noah, Abraham, Isaac, Jacob, the tribe of Levi, the tribe
of Judah, Moses, Aaron, Miriam, Joshua, Gideon, Samson, Samuel, David,
Elijah, Elisha, Hezekiah, Daniel's three companions and contemporary Israel.

לְמַעַן יָחִיד צוֹרְרִים דָּשׁ, אֲשֶׁר מֵרֶחֶם לְנָזִיר הָקְדָּשׁ, מִמַּכְתֵּשׁ לֶחִי הִבְקַעְתָּ לוֹ מָיִם, לְמַעַן שֵׁם קָדְשֶׁךָ הוֹשַׁע נָא וְהוֹשִׁיעָה נָּא, אָבִינוּ אָתָּה.

לְמַעַן טוֹב הוֹלֵךְ וְגָדֵל, אֲשֶׁר מֵעֶשֶׁק עֵדָה חָדֵל, בְּשׁוּב עַם מֵחֵטְא צָו שְׁאָב־מָיִם, לְנָאוָה כִּירוּשָׁלַיִם הוֹשַׁע נָא וְהוֹשִׁיעָה נָּא, אָבִינוּ אָתָּה.

לְמַעַן חַיָּךְ מְכַרְכֵּר בְּשִׁיר, הַמְלַמֵּד תּוֹרָה בְּכָל כְּלֵי שִׁיר, מְנַסֵּךְ לְפָנֶיךָ כְּתָאֵב שְׁתוֹת מָיִם, לְשָׁמוּ בְךָ סִבְרָם הוֹשַׁע נָא וְהוֹשִׁיעָה נָּא, אָבִינוּ אָתָּה.

לְמַעַן זָךְ עָלָה בַּסְּעָרָה, הַמְקַנֵּא וּמֵשִׁיב עֶבְרָה, לְפִלּוּלוֹ יָרְדָה אֵשׁ וְלִחֲכָה עָפָר וּמָיִם, לְעֵינֶיךָ בְּרֵכוֹת הוֹשַׁע נָא וְהוֹשִׁיעָה נָּא, אָבִינוּ אָתָּה.

לְמַעַן וְשָׁרֵת בֶּאֱמֶת לְרַבּוֹ, פִּי שְׁנַיִם בְּרוּחוֹ נֶאֱצַל בּוֹ, בְּקַחְתּוֹ מִמֶּנּוּ נִתְמַלְּאוּ גֵבִים מַיִם, לְפָצוּ מִי כָמוֹךָ הוֹשַׁע נָא וְהוֹשִׁיעָה נָּא, אָבִינוּ אָתָּה.

לְמַעַן הִרְהֵר עֲשׂוֹת רְצוֹנֶךָ, הַמַּכְרִיז תְּשׁוּבָה לְצֹאנֶךָ, אָז בְּבוֹא מְחָרֵף סָתַם עֵינוֹת מָיִם, לְצִיּוֹן מִכְלָל יֹפִי הוֹשַׁע נָא וְהוֹשִׁיעָה נָּא, אָבִינוּ אָתָּה.

לְמַעַן דְּרָשׁוּךָ בְּתוֹךְ הַגּוֹלָה, וְסוֹדְךָ לָמוֹ נִגְלָה, בְּלִי לְהִתְגָּאֵל דָּרְשׁוּ זֵרְעוֹנִים וּמַיִם, לְקוֹרְאֶיךָ בַצָּר הוֹשַׁע נָא וְהוֹשִׁיעָה נָּא, אָבִינוּ אָתָּה.

לְמַעַן גָּמַר חָכְמָה וּבִינָה, סוֹפֵר מָהִיר מְפַלֵּשׁ אֲמָנָה, מֵחַכְמָנוּ אֲמָרִים הַמְּשׁוּלִים בְּרַחֲבֵי מָיִם, לְרַבָּתִי עָם הוֹשַׁע נָא וְהוֹשִׁיעָה נָּא, אָבִינוּ אָתָּה.

לְמַעַן בָּאֵי לְךָ הַיּוֹם בְּכָל לֵב, שׁוֹפְכִים לְךָ שִׂיחַ בְּלֹא לֵב
וָלֵב, שׁוֹאֲלִים מִמְּךָ עֹז מִטְרוֹת מַיִם, לְשׁוֹרְרוּ בַיָּם הוֹשַׁע נָא
וְהוֹשִׁיעָה נָא, אָבִינוּ אָתָּה.

לְמַעַן אוֹמְרֵי יִגְדַּל שְׂמֵחַ, וְהֵם נַחֲלָתְךָ וְעַמֶּךָ, צְמֵאִים
לְיִשְׁעֲךָ כְּאֶרֶץ עֲיֵפָה לַמַּיִם, לְתָרְתָּ לָמוֹ מְנוּחָה הוֹשַׁע נָא
וְהוֹשִׁיעָה נָא, אָבִינוּ אָתָּה.

Reader and Congregation:

הוֹשַׁע נָא אֵל נָא, אָנָּא הוֹשִׁיעָה נָא.

הוֹשַׁע נָא סְלַח נָא, וְהַצְלִיחָה נָא, וְהוֹשִׁיעֵנוּ אֵל מָעֻזֵּנוּ.

The *hoshana*, made of five willow-twigs, is taken in hand.

וְהוֹשִׁיעָה נָא.	תַּעֲנֶה אֱמוּנִים שׁוֹפְכִים לְךָ לֵב כַּמַּיִם
וְהַצְלִיחָה נָא.	לְמַעַן בָּא בָאֵשׁ וּבַמַּיִם
וְהוֹשִׁיעֵנוּ אֵל מָעֻזֵּנוּ.	גָּזַר וְנָם יָקַח נָא מְעַט מַיִם
וְהוֹשִׁיעָה נָא.	תַּעֲנֶה דְגָלִים גֵּזוּ גִזְרֵי מַיִם
וְהַצְלִיחָה נָא.	לְמַעַן הַנֶּעֱקַד בְּשַׁעַר הַשָּׁמַיִם
וְהוֹשִׁיעֵנוּ אֵל מָעֻזֵּנוּ.	וְשָׁב וְחָפַר בְּאֵרוֹת מַיִם
וְהוֹשִׁיעָה נָא.	תַּעֲנֶה זַכִּים חוֹנִים עֲלֵי מַיִם
וְהַצְלִיחָה נָא.	לְמַעַן חָלָק מְפַצֵּל מַקְלוֹת בְּשִׁקֲתוֹת הַמַּיִם
וְהוֹשִׁיעֵנוּ אֵל מָעֻזֵּנוּ.	טָעַן וְגָל אֶבֶן מִבְּאֵר מַיִם
וְהוֹשִׁיעָה נָא.	תַּעֲנֶה יְדִידִים נוֹחֲלֵי דָת מְשׁוּלַת מַיִם
וְהַצְלִיחָה נָא.	לְמַעַן כָּרוּ בְּמִשְׁעֲנוֹתָם מַיִם
וְהוֹשִׁיעֵנוּ אֵל מָעֻזֵּנוּ.	לְהָכִין לָמוֹ וּלְצֶאֱצָאֵימוֹ מַיִם

תענה אמונים mayest thou answer the faithful who pour out their heart like water; answer them for the sake of Abraham, Isaac, Jacob, Moses and David. This poem is a prayer for rain.

תַּעֲנֶה מִתְחַנְּנִים כְּבִישִׁמוֹן עֲלֵי מָיִם   וְהוֹשִׁיעָה נָא.

לְמַעַן נֶאֱמַן בַּיִת מַסְפִּיק לְעָם מַיִם   וְהַצְלִיחָה נָא.

סֶלַע הָךְ וַיָּזֻבוּ מַיִם   וְהוֹשִׁיעֵנוּ אֵל מָעֻזֵּנוּ.

תַּעֲנֶה עוֹנִים עֲלֵי בְאֵר מַיִם   וְהוֹשִׁיעָה נָא.

לְמַעַן פָּקַד בְּמֵי מְרִיבַת מַיִם   וְהַצְלִיחָה נָא.

צְמֵאִים לְהַשְׁקוֹתָם מַיִם   וְהוֹשִׁיעֵנוּ אֵל מָעֻזֵּנוּ.

תַּעֲנֶה קְדוֹשִׁים מְנַסְּכִים לְךָ מַיִם   וְהוֹשִׁיעָה נָא.

לְמַעַן רֹאשׁ מְשׁוֹרְרִים כְּתָאַב שְׁתוֹת מַיִם   וְהַצְלִיחָה נָא.

שָׁב וְנָסַךְ לְךָ מַיִם   וְהוֹשִׁיעֵנוּ אֵל מָעֻזֵּנוּ.

תַּעֲנֶה שׁוֹאֲלִים בְּרִבּוּעַ אֶשְׁלֵי מַיִם   וְהוֹשִׁיעָה נָא.

לְמַעַן תֵּל תַּלְפִּיּוֹת מוֹצָא מַיִם   וְהַצְלִיחָה נָא.

תִּפְתַּח אֶרֶץ וְתַרְעִיף שָׁמַיִם   וְהוֹשִׁיעֵנוּ אֵל מָעֻזֵּנוּ.

רַחֶם־נָא קְהַל עֲדַת יְשֻׁרוּן, סְלַח וּמְחַל עֲוֺנָם,
וְהוֹשִׁיעֵנוּ אֱלֹהֵי יִשְׁעֵנוּ.

אָז כְּעֵינֵי עֲבָדִים אֶל יַד אֲדוֹנִים

בָּאנוּ לְפָנֶיךָ נְדוֹנִים   וְהוֹשִׁיעֵנוּ אֱלֹהֵי יִשְׁעֵנוּ.

גֵּאֶה אֲדוֹנֵי הָאֲדוֹנִים, נִתְגָּרוּ בָנוּ מְדָנִים

דָּשׁוּנוּ וּבִלְעוּנוּ זוּלָתְךָ אֲדוֹנִים   וְהוֹשִׁיעֵנוּ אֱלֹהֵי יִשְׁעֵנוּ.

הֵן גֵּשְׁנוּ הַיּוֹם בְּתַחֲנוּן, עָרֶיךָ רַחוּם וְחַנּוּן

וְסִפַּרְנוּ נִפְלְאוֹתֶיךָ בְּשִׁנּוּן   וְהוֹשִׁיעֵנוּ אֱלֹהֵי יִשְׁעֵנוּ.

זָבַת חָלָב וּדְבָשׁ, נָא אַל תִּיבָשׁ

חַסְרַת מַיִם בְּאַבֵּיהָ תְּחֻבָּשׁ   וְהוֹשִׁיעֵנוּ אֱלֹהֵי יִשְׁעֵנוּ.

אז כעיני עבדים is another prayer for rain and ample sustenance.

טָעֵנוּ בְשָׁמֶנָה, בְּיַד שִׁבְעָה וּשְׁמֹנָה

יָשָׁר צַדִּיק אֵל אֱמוּנָה   וְהוֹשִׁיעֵנוּ אֱלֹהֵי יִשְׁעֵנוּ.

כָּרַתָּ בְרִית לָאָרֶץ, עוֹד כָּל יְמֵי הָאָרֶץ

לְבִלְתִּי פְּרָץ־בָּהּ פֶּרֶץ   וְהוֹשִׁיעֵנוּ אֱלֹהֵי יִשְׁעֵנוּ.

מִתְחַנְּנִים עָלֶי מַיִם, בַּעֲרָבִים עַל יִבְלֵי מָיִם

נָא זְכָר־לָנוּ נְסוּךְ הַמָּיִם   וְהוֹשִׁיעֵנוּ אֱלֹהֵי יִשְׁעֵנוּ.

שִׂיחִים בְּדֶרֶךְ מַטָּעָתָם, עוֹמְסִים בְּשַׁוְעָתָם

עֲנֵם בְּקוֹל פְּגִיעָתָם   וְהוֹשִׁיעֵנוּ אֱלֹהֵי יִשְׁעֵנוּ.

פּוֹעֵל יְשׁוּעוֹת, פְּנֵה לִפְלוּלָם שְׁעוֹת

צַדְּקֵם אֵל לְמוֹשָׁעוֹת   וְהוֹשִׁיעֵנוּ אֱלֹהֵי יִשְׁעֵנוּ.

קוֹל רְגָשָׁם תְּשַׁע, תִּפְתַּח אֶרֶץ וְיִפְרוּ יֶשַׁע

רַב לְהוֹשִׁיעַ וְלֹא חָפֵץ רֶשַׁע   וְהוֹשִׁיעֵנוּ אֱלֹהֵי יִשְׁעֵנוּ.

שַׁעֲרֵי שָׁמַיִם פְּתַח, וְאוֹצָרְךָ הַטּוֹב לָנוּ תִפְתַּח,

תּוֹשִׁיעֵנוּ וְרִיב אַל תִּמְתַּח, וְהוֹשִׁיעֵנוּ אֱלֹהֵי יִשְׁעֵנוּ.

Reader and Congregation:

קוֹל מְבַשֵּׂר, מְבַשֵּׂר וְאוֹמֵר.

אֹמֶץ יֶשְׁעֲךָ בָּא, קוֹל דּוֹדִי הִנֵּה זֶה בָּא,   מְבַשֵּׂר וְאוֹמֵר.

קוֹל בָּא בְּרִבְבוֹת כִּתִּים, לַעֲמוֹד עַל הַר הַזֵּיתִים,

מְבַשֵּׂר וְאוֹמֵר.

קוֹל גִּשְׁתּוֹ בַּשּׁוֹפָר לִתְקֹעַ, תַּחְתָּיו הַר יִבָּקֵעַ,   מְבַשֵּׂר וְאוֹמֵר.

קוֹל דָּפַק וְהֵצִיץ וְזָרַח, וּמָשׁ חֲצִי הָהָר מִמִּזְרָח,   מְבַשֵּׂר וְאוֹמֵר.

קוֹל הֵקִים מָלוּל נָאֲמוֹ, וּבָא הוּא וְכָל קְדוֹשִׁים עִמּוֹ,

מְבַשֵּׂר וְאוֹמֵר.

קול מבשר is based on Isaiah 52:7: ("How beautiful upon the mountains is the herald who brings good news of peace").

אמץ ישעך refers to prophetic promises of salvation and restoration.

קוֹל וּלְכָל בָּאֵי עוֹלָם, בַּת קוֹל יִשָּׁמַע בָּעוֹלָם, מְבַשֵּׂר וְאוֹמֵר.

קוֹל זֶרַע עֲמוּסֵי רַחֲמוֹ, נוֹלְדוּ כְּיֶלֶד מִמְּעֵי אִמּוֹ, מְבַשֵּׂר וְאוֹמֵר.

קוֹל חָלָה וְיָלְדָה מִי זֹאת, מִי שָׁמַע כָּזֹאת, מְבַשֵּׂר וְאוֹמֵר.

קוֹל טָהוֹר פָּעַל כָּל אֵלֶּה, וּמִי רָאָה כָּאֵלֶּה, מְבַשֵּׂר וְאוֹמֵר.

קוֹל יֶשַׁע וּזְמַן הוּחַד, הֲיוּחַל אֶרֶץ בְּיוֹם אֶחָד, מְבַשֵּׂר וְאוֹמֵר.

קוֹל כַּבִּיר רוֹם וָתַחַת, אִם יִוָּלֵד גּוֹי פַּעַם אֶחָת, מְבַשֵּׂר וְאוֹמֵר.

קוֹל לְעֵת יִגְאַל לְעַמּוֹ נָאוֹר, וְהָיָה לְעֵת עֶרֶב יִהְיֶה אוֹר, מְבַשֵּׂר וְאוֹמֵר.

קוֹל מוֹשִׁיעִים יַעֲלוּ בְּהַר צִיּוֹן, כִּי חָלָה גַּם יָלְדָה צִיּוֹן, מְבַשֵּׂר וְאוֹמֵר.

קוֹל נִשְׁמַע בְּכָל גְּבוּלֵךְ, הַרְחִיבִי מְקוֹם אָהֳלֵךְ, מְבַשֵּׂר וְאוֹמֵר.

קוֹל שִׂימִי עַד דַּמֶּשֶׂק מִשְׁכְּנוֹתַיִךְ, קַבְּלִי בָּנַיִךְ וּבְנוֹתַיִךְ, מְבַשֵּׂר וְאוֹמֵר.

קוֹל עִלְזוּ חֲבַצֶּלֶת הַשָּׁרוֹן, כִּי קָמוּ יְשֵׁנֵי חֶבְרוֹן, מְבַשֵּׂר וְאוֹמֵר.

קוֹל פְּנוּ אֵלַי וְהִוָּשְׁעוּ, הַיּוֹם אִם בְּקוֹלִי תִשְׁמָעוּ, מְבַשֵּׂר וְאוֹמֵר.

קוֹל צֶמַח אִישׁ צֶמַח שְׁמוֹ, הוּא דָוִד בְּעַצְמוֹ, מְבַשֵּׂר וְאוֹמֵר.

קוֹל קוּמוּ כְּפוּשֵׁי עָפָר, הָקִיצוּ וְרַנְּנוּ שׁוֹכְנֵי עָפָר, מְבַשֵּׂר וְאוֹמֵר.

קוֹל רַבָּתִי עָם בְּהַמְלִיכוֹ, מִגְדּוֹל יְשׁוּעוֹת מַלְכּוֹ, מְבַשֵּׂר וְאוֹמֵר.

קוֹל שֵׁם רְשָׁעִים לְהַאֲבִיד, עוֹשֶׂה חֶסֶד לִמְשִׁיחוֹ לְדָוִד, מְבַשֵּׂר וְאוֹמֵר.

קוֹל תִּנָּה יְשׁוּעוֹת לְעַם עוֹלָם, לְדָוִד וּלְזַרְעוֹ עַד עוֹלָם, מְבַשֵּׂר וְאוֹמֵר.

Reader and Congregation:

(three times)

קוֹל מְבַשֵּׂר, מְבַשֵּׂר וְאוֹמֵר.

הוֹשִׁיעָה אֶת עַמֶּךָ, וּבָרֵךְ אֶת נַחֲלָתֶךָ, וּרְעֵם וְנַשְּׂאֵם עַד הָעוֹלָם. וְיִהְיוּ דְבָרַי אֵלֶּה, אֲשֶׁר הִתְחַנַּנְתִּי לִפְנֵי יְיָ, קְרוֹבִים אֶל יְיָ אֱלֹהֵינוּ יוֹמָם וָלָיְלָה, לַעֲשׂוֹת מִשְׁפַּט עַבְדּוֹ וּמִשְׁפַּט עַמּוֹ יִשְׂרָאֵל דְּבַר יוֹם בְּיוֹמוֹ. לְמַעַן דַּעַת כָּל עַמֵּי הָאָרֶץ, כִּי יְיָ הוּא הָאֱלֹהִים, אֵין עוֹד.

The *hoshanas* are struck five times.

יְהִי רָצוֹן מִלְּפָנֶיךָ, יְיָ אֱלֹהֵינוּ וֵאלֹהֵי אֲבוֹתֵינוּ, הַבּוֹחֵר בִּנְבִיאִים טוֹבִים וּבְמִנְהֲגֵיהֶם הַטּוֹבִים, שֶׁתְּקַבֵּל בְּרַחֲמִים וּבְרָצוֹן אֶת תְּפִלָּתֵנוּ וְהַקָּפוֹתֵינוּ, וְתִזְכָּר־לָנוּ זְכוּת שִׁבְעַת תְּמִימֶיךָ, וְתָסִיר מְחִיצַת הַבַּרְזֶל הַמַּפְסֶקֶת בֵּינֵינוּ וּבֵינֶיךָ, וְתַאֲזִין שַׁוְעָתֵנוּ וְתֵיטִיב לָנוּ הַחֲתִימָה, תּוֹלֶה אֶרֶץ עַל בְּלִימָה; וְחָתְמֵנוּ בְּסֵפֶר חַיִּים טוֹבִים. וְאוֹצָרְךָ הַטּוֹב תִּפְתַּח לְהַשְׂבִּיעַ מַיִם נֶפֶשׁ שׁוֹקֵקָה, כְּמוֹ שֶׁכָּתוּב: יִפְתַּח יְיָ לְךָ אֶת אוֹצָרוֹ הַטּוֹב, אֶת הַשָּׁמַיִם, לָתֵת מְטַר אַרְצְךָ בְּעִתּוֹ, וּלְבָרֵךְ אֶת כָּל מַעֲשֵׂה יָדֶךָ. אָמֵן.

Full-*Kaddish* by the Reader on page 405, where the service is continued.

הושענא רבה is designated in Sukkah 4:6 as יום חיבוט חריות ("the day of striking the twigs"). The Mishnah relates that "they used to bring twigs and strike them against the ground at the sides of the altar." This symbol of casting off the sins is considered to be of very ancient origin.

יהי רצון expresses the belief that the seventh day of *Sukkoth, Hoshana Rabbah*, is the day of sealing the decree of judgment. Several customs and tunes on this festival are borrowed from the High Holydays.

תְּפִלַּת גֶּשֶׁם

Chanted on the eighth day of *Sukkoth* during *Musaf*

Reader:

בָּרוּךְ אַתָּה, יְיָ אֱלֹהֵינוּ וֵאלֹהֵי אֲבוֹתֵינוּ, אֱלֹהֵי אַבְרָהָם,
אֱלֹהֵי יִצְחָק, וֵאלֹהֵי יַעֲקֹב, הָאֵל הַגָּדוֹל הַגִּבּוֹר וְהַנּוֹרָא, אֵל
עֶלְיוֹן, גּוֹמֵל חֲסָדִים טוֹבִים, וְקוֹנֵה הַכֹּל, וְזוֹכֵר חַסְדֵי אָבוֹת,
וּמֵבִיא גוֹאֵל לִבְנֵי בְנֵיהֶם לְמַעַן שְׁמוֹ בְּאַהֲבָה. מֶלֶךְ עוֹזֵר
וּמוֹשִׁיעַ וּמָגֵן.

אַף־בְּרִי אֻתַּת שֵׁם שַׂר מָטָר, לְהַעֲבִיב וּלְהַעֲנִין לְהָרִיק
לְהַמְטִיר, מַיִם אַבִּים בָּם גֵּיא לַעֲטֵר, לְבַל יֵעָצְרוּ בְּנִשְׁיוֹן שְׁטָר,
אֱמוּנִים גְּנוֹן בָּם שׁוֹאֲלֵי מָטָר.

בָּרוּךְ אַתָּה, יְיָ, מָגֵן אַבְרָהָם.

אַתָּה גִבּוֹר לְעוֹלָם, אֲדֹנָי; מְחַיֵּה מֵתִים אַתָּה, רַב לְהוֹשִׁיעַ.

יַטְרִיחַ לְפַלֵּג מִפֶּלֶג גֶּשֶׁם, לְמוֹזֵג פְּנֵי נֶשִׁי בְּצַחוֹת לֶשֶׁם, מַיִם
לְאַדְּרָךְ כְּנִיתָ בְּרֶשֶׁם, לְהַרְגִּיעַ בְּרַעֲפָם לִנְפוּחֵי נֶשֶׁם, לְהַחֲיוֹת
מַזְכִּירִים גְּבוּרוֹת הַגֶּשֶׁם.

אֱלֹהֵינוּ וֵאלֹהֵי אֲבוֹתֵינוּ,
זְכוֹר אָב נִמְשַׁךְ אַחֲרֶיךָ כַּמַּיִם,
בֵּרַכְתּוֹ כְּעֵץ שָׁתוּל עַל פַּלְגֵי מָיִם,

תפלת גשם, the prayer for rain recited on the eighth day of *Sukkoth*, solemnly introduces the formula משיב הרוח ומוריד הגשם which is inserted into the
beginning of the *Amidah* during the period between *Sukkoth* and *Pesaḥ*. The
poems אף ברי and זכור אב were composed by Rabbi Elazar ha-Kallir of the
seventh century.

PRAYER FOR RAIN

Chanted on the eighth day of Sukkoth during Musaf

Reader:

Blessed art thou, Lord our God and God of our fathers, God of Abraham, God of Isaac and God of Jacob; great, mighty and revered God, sublime God, who bestowest loving kindness, and art Master of all things; who rememberest the good deeds of our fathers, and who wilt graciously bring a redeemer to their children's children for the sake of thy name. O King, Supporter, Savior and Shield!

Af-Bri is the title of the prince of rain,
Who gathers the clouds and makes them drop rain,
Water to adorn the earth with verdure.
Be it not held back because of unpaid debts;
O shield faithful Israel who prays for rain.

Blessed art thou, O Lord, Shield of Abraham.

Thou, O Lord, art mighty forever; thou revivest the dead; thou art powerful to save.

May he send rain from the heavenly source,
To soften the earth with its crystal drops.
Thou hast named water the symbol of thy might;
Its drops refresh all that have breath of life,
And revive those who praise thy powers of rain.

Our God and God of our fathers,

Remember Abraham who followed thee like water,
Whom thou didst bless like a tree planted near streams of water;

אַף בְּרִי presents an impressive picture of the importance and symbolical significance of rain.

זְכוֹר אָב, an alphabetic acrostic, refers to the pious deeds of Abraham, Isaac, Jacob, Moses, Aaron, the twelve tribes, and the miracles that were

גְּנַנְתּוֹ, הִצַּלְתּוֹ מֵאֵשׁ וּמִמַּיִם,
דְּרַשְׁתּוֹ בְּזָרְעוֹ עַל כָּל מָיִם.

Congregation:

בַּעֲבוּרוֹ אַל תִּמְנַע מָיִם.

זְכוֹר הַנּוֹלָד בִּבְשׂוֹרַת יֻקַּח נָא מְעַט מַיִם,
וְשַׂחְתָּ לְהוֹרוֹ לְשָׁחֲטוֹ, לִשְׁפּוֹךְ דָּמוֹ כַּמַּיִם,
זָהַר גַּם הוּא לִשְׁפּוֹךְ לֵב כַּמַּיִם,
חָפַר וּמָצָא בְּאֵרוֹת מָיִם.

Congregation:

בְּצִדְקוֹ חֹן חַשְׁרַת מָיִם.

זְכוֹר טָעַן מַקְלוֹ וְעָבַר יַרְדֵּן מַיִם,
יָחַד לֵב וְגָל אֶבֶן מִפִּי בְּאֵר מָיִם,
כְּנֶאֱבַק לוֹ שַׂר בָּלוּל מֵאֵשׁ וּמִמַּיִם,
לָכֵן הִבְטַחְתּוֹ הֱיוֹת עִמּוֹ בָּאֵשׁ וּבַמָּיִם.

Congregation:

בַּעֲבוּרוֹ אַל תִּמְנַע מָיִם.

זְכוֹר מָשׁוּי בְּתֵבַת גֹּמֶא מִן הַמַּיִם,
נָמוּ דָּלֹה דָלָה וְהִשְׁקָה צֹאן מָיִם,
סְגוּלֶיךָ עֵת צָמְאוּ לְמָיִם,
עַל הַסֶּלַע הָךְ וַיֵּצְאוּ מָיִם.

Congregation:

בְּצִדְקוֹ חֹן חַשְׁרַת מָיִם.

---

shown to them in connection with water. The alternating refrains of the poem are בצדקו חן חשרת מים and בעבורו אל תמנע מים.

The term water is often used symbolically. In Numbers 24:7, the constant flow of water is symbolic of numerous descendants. The Torah is frequently

Thou didst shield him, thou didst save him from fire and water;
Thou didst care for him when he sowed by all streams of water.

Congregation:

For his sake, do not refuse water.

Remember Isaac whose birth was foretold over a little water;
Thou didst tell his father to offer his blood like water;
Isaac was heedful in pouring out his heart like water;
Digging wells he did discover water.

Congregation:

For his righteousness' sake, grant abundant water.

Remember Jacob who, staff in hand, crossed the Jordan's water;
His heart trusted when he rolled the stone of the well of water;
When he wrestled with the prince of fire and water,
Thou didst promise to be with him through fire and water.

Congregation:

For his sake, do not refuse water.

Remember Moses in an ark of papyrus reeds drawn out of the water;
They said: He drew water for us and provided the flock with water;
And when thy chosen people thirsted for water,
He struck the rock and there gushed out water.

Congregation:

For his righteousness' sake, grant abundant water.

---

compared to water that purifies. In Temple times, the Water-Feast (שמחת בית
השואבה) began on the first day of *Sukkoth* at nightfall and lasted till the following morning. The outer court of the Temple was brilliantly illuminated
for the occasion. A torchlight procession, dances and singing followed, while
the women were looking on from their galleries. During the day the great

זְכוֹר פְּקִיד שָׁתוֹת טוֹבֵל חָמֵשׁ טְבִילוֹת בַּמָּיִם,

צוֹעֶה וּמַרְחִיץ כַּפָּיו בְּקִדּוּשׁ מָיִם,

קוֹרֵא וּמַזֶּה טָהֳרַת מָיִם,

רָחַק מֵעַם פַּחַז כַּמָּיִם.

Congregation:

בַּעֲבוּרוֹ אַל תִּמְנַע מָיִם.

זְכוֹר שְׁנֵים עָשָׂר שְׁבָטִים שֶׁהֶעֱבַרְתָּ בְּגִזְרַת מָיִם,

שֶׁהִמְתַּקְתָּ לָמוֹ מְרִירוּת מָיִם,

תּוֹלְדוֹתָם נִשְׁפַּךְ דָּמָם עָלֶיךָ כַּמָּיִם,

תֵּפֶן כִּי נַפְשֵׁנוּ אָפְפוּ מָיִם.

Congregation:

בְּצִדְקָם חֹן חַשְׁרַת מָיִם.

Reader:

שָׁאַתָּה הוּא יְיָ אֱלֹהֵינוּ, מַשִּׁיב הָרוּחַ וּמוֹרִיד הַגָּשֶׁם.

Congregation:	Congregation and Reader:
אָמֵן.	לִבְרָכָה וְלֹא לִקְלָלָה.
אָמֵן.	לְחַיִּים וְלֹא לְמָוֶת.
אָמֵן.	לְשֹׂבַע וְלֹא לְרָזוֹן.

מְכַלְכֵּל חַיִּים (page 609).

---

feature was the procession which accompanied the priest who had been al-
lotted the duty of drawing water for the libation ceremony from the pool of
Siloam at Jerusalem. According to tradition, "whoever has not witnessed
this celebration has never seen real rejoicing" (Sukkah 5:1). It was called
שמחת בית השואבה ("the joyous procession to and from the well") because

Remember the Temple-priest who bathed five times in water;

He removed sins when he washed his hands with sanctified water;

He read from the Scriptures when he sprinkled purifying water;

He was kept at a distance from a people as turbulent as water.

Congregation:

For his sake, do not refuse water.

Remember the twelve tribes thou didst bring across the water;

Thou didst sweeten for them the bitterness of the water;

For thy sake was the blood of their descendants spilt like water;

Turn to us, for our life is encircled by foes like water.

Congregation:

For their righteousness' sake, grant abundant water.

Reader:

For thou art the Lord our God, who causest the wind to blow and the rain to fall.

Congregation and Reader:	*Congregation:*
For a blessing and not for a curse.	Amen.
For life and not for death.	Amen.
For plenty and not for scarcity.	Amen.

"Thou sustainest the living" (*page* 610).

---

from there they drew inspiration. Compare Isaiah 12:3 ("With joy shall you draw water from the fountains of deliverance").

‫...משיב הרוח‬ is referred to in the Mishnah as ‫גבורות גשמים‬ ("the power of rain"), presumably because the reference to rain is inserted in the second benediction of the *Shemoneh Esreh*, beginning with the words ‫אתה גבור‬ ("thou art mighty"). This benediction is called ‫גבורות‬, since it recounts the omnipotence of God. According to a talmudic statement, the term ‫גבורות גשמים‬ is used because rain comes down by the power of God (Ta'anith 2a).

הַקָּפוֹת לְשִׂמְחַת תּוֹרָה

Responsively

אַתָּה הָרְאֵתָ לָדַעַת כִּי יְיָ הוּא הָאֱלֹהִים, אֵין עוֹד מִלְּבַדּוֹ.
לְעֹשֵׂה נִפְלָאוֹת גְּדֹלוֹת לְבַדּוֹ, כִּי לְעוֹלָם חַסְדּוֹ. אֵין כָּמוֹךָ
בָאֱלֹהִים, אֲדֹנָי, וְאֵין כְּמַעֲשֶׂיךָ. יְהִי כְבוֹד יְיָ לְעוֹלָם, יִשְׂמַח יְיָ
בְּמַעֲשָׂיו. יְהִי שֵׁם יְיָ מְבֹרָךְ, מֵעַתָּה וְעַד עוֹלָם. יְהִי יְיָ אֱלֹהֵינוּ
עִמָּנוּ, כַּאֲשֶׁר הָיָה עִם אֲבוֹתֵינוּ, אַל יַעַזְבֵנוּ וְאַל יִטְּשֵׁנוּ. וְאִמְרוּ:
הוֹשִׁיעֵנוּ, אֱלֹהֵי יִשְׁעֵנוּ, וְקַבְּצֵנוּ וְהַצִּילֵנוּ מִן הַגּוֹיִם, לְהוֹדוֹת
לְשֵׁם קָדְשֶׁךָ, לְהִשְׁתַּבֵּחַ בִּתְהִלָּתֶךָ. יְיָ מֶלֶךְ, יְיָ מָלָךְ, יְיָ יִמְלֹךְ
לְעוֹלָם וָעֶד. יְיָ עֹז לְעַמּוֹ יִתֵּן; יְיָ יְבָרֵךְ אֶת עַמּוֹ בַשָּׁלוֹם. וְיִהְיוּ
נָא אֲמָרֵינוּ לְרָצוֹן לִפְנֵי אֲדוֹן כֹּל. וַיְהִי בִּנְסֹעַ הָאָרֹן, וַיֹּאמֶר
מֹשֶׁה: קוּמָה יְיָ, וְיָפֻצוּ אֹיְבֶיךָ, וְיָנֻסוּ מְשַׂנְאֶיךָ מִפָּנֶיךָ. קוּמָה
יְיָ לִמְנוּחָתֶךָ, אַתָּה וַאֲרוֹן עֻזֶּךָ. כֹּהֲנֶיךָ יִלְבְּשׁוּ צֶדֶק, וַחֲסִידֶיךָ
יְרַנֵּנוּ. בַּעֲבוּר דָּוִד עַבְדֶּךָ, אַל תָּשֵׁב פְּנֵי מְשִׁיחֶךָ. וְאָמַר בַּיּוֹם
הַהוּא: הִנֵּה אֱלֹהֵינוּ זֶה קִוִּינוּ לוֹ וְיוֹשִׁיעֵנוּ; זֶה יְיָ קִוִּינוּ לוֹ, נָגִילָה
וְנִשְׂמְחָה בִּישׁוּעָתוֹ. מַלְכוּתְךָ מַלְכוּת כָּל עֹלָמִים, וּמֶמְשַׁלְתְּךָ
בְּכָל דּוֹר וָדוֹר. כִּי מִצִּיּוֹן תֵּצֵא תוֹרָה, וּדְבַר יְיָ מִירוּשָׁלָיִם.

שמחת תורה is celebrated in Eretz Yisrael on the eighth day of *Sukkoth*, on
Shemini Atsereth. The name *Simhath Torah* was not known in talmudic times.
It came into use presumably around the ninth century in Babylonia, where the
one-year cycle for the reading of the Five Books of Moses prevailed. The seven
processions with the Torah-scrolls on *Simhath Torah* became customary in the
sixteenth century.

HAKKAFOTH FOR SIMHATH TORAH

Responsively

You have learned to know that the Lord is God; there is none else besides him.[1]

To him who alone does great wonders; his mercy endures forever.[2]

There is no god like thee, O Lord; there are no deeds like thine.[3]

May the glory of the Lord be forever; may the Lord rejoice in his works.[4]

Blessed be the name of the Lord henceforth and forever.[5]

May the Lord our God be with us, as he was with our fathers; let him not leave us nor forsake us.[6]

Pray: Save us, our saving God; gather us, deliver us from the nations, to give thanks to thy holy name, to triumph in thy praise.[7]

The Lord is King; the Lord was King; the Lord will be King forever and ever.

The Lord will give strength to his people; the Lord will bless his people with peace.[8]

May our words please the Master of all things.

It came to pass, whenever the ark would start, Moses would say: "Arise, O Lord, and let thy enemies be scattered; let those who hate thee flee before thee."[9]

Arise, O Lord, to thy resting-place, thou and thy glorious ark.

May thy priests be clothed with righteousness; may thy devoted followers sing for joy.

For the sake of thy servant David, reject not thy anointed prince.[10]

It will be said on that day: "Lo, this is our God, for whom we waited that he might save us; this is the Lord for whom we were waiting—let us rejoice and be happy with his salvation."[11]

Thy kingdom is an everlasting kingdom, and thy dominion endures throughout all generations.[12]

Truly, out of Zion shall come Torah, and the word of the Lord out of Jerusalem.[13]

---

[1]*Deuteronomy* 4:35. [2]*Psalm* 136:4. [3]*Psalm* 86:8. [4]*Psalm* 104:31. [5]*Psalm* 113:2. [6]*I Kings* 8:57. [7]*I Chronicles* 16:35. [8]*Psalm* 29:11. [9]*Numbers* 10:35. [10]*Psalm* 132:8-10. [11]*Isaiah* 25:9. [12]*Psalm* 145:13. [13]*Isaiah* 2:3.

אַב הָרַחֲמִים, הֵיטִיבָה בִרְצוֹנְךָ אֶת צִיּוֹן, תִּבְנֶה חוֹמוֹת יְרוּשָׁלָיִם. כִּי בְךָ לְבַד בָּטֵחְנוּ, מֶלֶךְ אֵל רָם וְנִשָּׂא, אֲדוֹן עוֹלָמִים.

For each of the seven *Hakkafoth* a different group of worshipers is invited.

First Hakkafah

אָנָּא יְיָ, הוֹשִׁיעָה נָא; אָנָּא יְיָ, הַצְלִיחָה נָא; אָנָּא יְיָ, עֲנֵנוּ בְיוֹם קָרְאֵנוּ.

אֱלֹהֵי הָרוּחוֹת, הוֹשִׁיעָה נָא; בּוֹחֵן לְבָבוֹת, הַצְלִיחָה נָא; גּוֹאֵל חָזָק, עֲנֵנוּ בְיוֹם קָרְאֵנוּ.

Second Hakkafah

דּוֹבֵר צְדָקוֹת, הוֹשִׁיעָה נָא; הָדוּר בִּלְבוּשׁוֹ, הַצְלִיחָה נָא; וָתִיק וְחָסִיד, עֲנֵנוּ בְיוֹם קָרְאֵנוּ.

Third Hakkafah

זַךְ וְיָשָׁר, הוֹשִׁיעָה נָא; חוֹמֵל דַּלִּים, הַצְלִיחָה נָא; [טוֹב וּמֵטִיב, עֲנֵנוּ בְיוֹם קָרְאֵנוּ.

Fourth Hakkafah

יוֹדֵעַ מַחֲשָׁבוֹת, הוֹשִׁיעָה נָא; כַּבִּיר וְנָאוֹר, הַצְלִיחָה נָא; לוֹבֵשׁ צְדָקוֹת, עֲנֵנוּ בְיוֹם קָרְאֵנוּ.

Fifth Hakkafah

מֶלֶךְ עוֹלָמִים, הוֹשִׁיעָה נָא; נָאוֹר וְאַדִּיר, הַצְלִיחָה נָא; סוֹמֵךְ נוֹפְלִים, עֲנֵנוּ בְיוֹם קָרְאֵנוּ.

Sixth Hakkafah

עוֹזֵר דַּלִּים, הוֹשִׁיעָה נָא; פּוֹדֶה וּמַצִּיל, הַצְלִיחָה נָא; צוּר עוֹלָמִים, עֲנֵנוּ בְיוֹם קָרְאֵנוּ.

Merciful Father, may it be thy will to favor Zion with thy goodness; mayest thou rebuild the walls of Jerusalem. Truly, in thee alone we trust, high and exalted King and God, eternal Lord.

For each of the seven Hakkafoth a different group of worshipers is invited.

FIRST HAKKAFAH

O Lord, save us; O Lord, prosper us; O Lord, answer us when we call.

God of all souls, save us; Examiner of hearts, prosper us; mighty Redeemer, answer us when we call.

SECOND HAKKAFAH

Thou who speakest what is right, save us; thou who art arrayed in splendor, prosper us; thou who art ever kind, answer us when we call.

THIRD HAKKAFAH

Thou who art pure and upright, save us; thou who sparest the weak, prosper us; thou who art good and doest good, answer us when we call.

FOURTH HAKKAFAH

Thou who knowest our thoughts, save us; thou who art mighty and illustrious, prosper us; thou who art clothed with righteousness, answer us when we call.

FIFTH HAKKAFAH

Eternal King, save us; thou who art illustrious and majestic, prosper us; thou who supportest those who fall, answer us when we call.

SIXTH HAKKAFAH

Helper of the weak, save us; Redeemer and deliverer, prosper us; eternal Creator, answer us when we call.

SEVENTH HAKKAFAH

קָדוֹשׁ וְנוֹרָא, הוֹשִׁיעָה נָא; רַחוּם וְחַנּוּן, הַצְלִיחָה נָא; שׁוֹמֵר
הַבְּרִית, עֲנֵנוּ בְיוֹם קָרְאֵנוּ.

תּוֹמֵךְ תְּמִימִים, הוֹשִׁיעָה נָא; תַּקִּיף לָעַד, הַצְלִיחָה נָא;
תָּמִים בְּמַעֲשָׂיו, עֲנֵנוּ בְיוֹם קָרְאֵנוּ.

וּתְנוּ כָבוֹד לַתּוֹרָה.	שִׂישׂוּ וְשִׂמְחוּ בְּשִׂמְחַת תּוֹרָה
מִפָּז וּמִפְּנִינִים יְקָרָה.	כִּי טוֹב סַחְרָהּ מִכָּל סְחוֹרָה
כִּי הִיא לָנוּ עֹז וְאוֹרָה.	נָגִיל וְנָשִׂישׂ בְּזֹאת הַתּוֹרָה
וְאָשִׂימָה תִקְוָתִי בּוֹ.	אֲהַלְלָה אֱלֹהַי וְאֶשְׂמְחָה בּוֹ
אֱלֹהֵי צוּרִי אֶחֱסֶה בּוֹ.	אֲהוֹדֶנּוּ בְּסוֹד עַם קְרוֹבוֹ
וַאֲסַפְּרָה תְּהִלָּתֶךָ.	בְּכָל לֵב אֲרַנֵּן צִדְקוֹתֶיךָ
עַל חַסְדְּךָ וְעַל אֲמִתֶּךָ.	בְּעוֹדִי אַגִּיד נִפְלְאוֹתֶיךָ
כִּי הִיא לָנוּ עֹז וְאוֹרָה.	נָגִיל וְנָשִׂישׂ בְּזֹאת הַתּוֹרָה

The Torah-scrolls (except three) are returned to the ark.

[Reader and Congregation:

שְׁמַע יִשְׂרָאֵל, יְיָ אֱלֹהֵינוּ, יְיָ אֶחָד.

[Reader and Congregation:

אֶחָד אֱלֹהֵינוּ, גָּדוֹל אֲדוֹנֵינוּ, קָדוֹשׁ שְׁמוֹ.

Reader:

גַּדְּלוּ לַיְיָ אִתִּי, וּנְרוֹמְמָה שְׁמוֹ יַחְדָּו.

The service continues on page 365.

Seventh Hakkafah

Thou who art holy and awe-inspiring, save us; thou who art merciful and gracious, prosper us; thou who keepest the covenant, answer us when we call.

Thou who supportest men of integrity, save us; thou who art mighty forever, prosper us; thou who art blameless in thy deeds answer us when we call.

> Thrill with joy over the Torah!
> Render glory to the Torah!
> Her profits are richest of all;
> She is more precious than jewels.
> We exult over this Torah,
> For she is our strength and our light.

> I sing joyous praise to my God,
> And I place all my hope in him.
> I praise him amidst his people,
> My Creator, in whom I trust.

> With all my heart I sing thy faith,
> Ever rendering thy praises.
> As long as I live I will tell
> Of thy wonders and thy kindness.
> Let us exult in this Torah,
> For she is our strength and our light.

The Torah-scrolls (except three) are returned to the ark.

Reader and Congregation:

Hear, O Israel, the Lord is our God, the Lord is One.

Reader and Congregation:

One is our God; Great is our Lord; Holy is his name.

Reader:

Exalt the Lord with me, and let us extol his name together.

The service continues on page 366.

הַדְלָקַת נֵר שֶׁל חֲנֻכָּה

בָּרוּךְ אַתָּה, יְיָ אֱלֹהֵינוּ, מֶלֶךְ הָעוֹלָם, אֲשֶׁר קִדְּשָׁנוּ בְּמִצְוֹתָיו
וְצִוָּנוּ לְהַדְלִיק נֵר שֶׁל חֲנֻכָּה.

בָּרוּךְ אַתָּה, יְיָ אֱלֹהֵינוּ, מֶלֶךְ הָעוֹלָם, שֶׁעָשָׂה נִסִּים
לַאֲבוֹתֵינוּ בַּיָּמִים הָהֵם בַּזְּמַן הַזֶּה.

On the first night of *Ḥanukkah* add:

בָּרוּךְ אַתָּה, יְיָ אֱלֹהֵינוּ, מֶלֶךְ הָעוֹלָם, שֶׁהֶחֱיָנוּ וְקִיְּמָנוּ
וְהִגִּיעָנוּ לַזְּמַן הַזֶּה.

While kindling the lights from left to right:

הַנֵּרוֹת הַלָּלוּ אֲנַחְנוּ מַדְלִיקִין עַל הַנִּסִּים וְעַל הַנִּפְלָאוֹת,
וְעַל הַתְּשׁוּעוֹת וְעַל הַמִּלְחָמוֹת, שֶׁעָשִׂיתָ לַאֲבוֹתֵינוּ בַּיָּמִים הָהֵם
בַּזְּמַן הַזֶּה עַל יְדֵי כֹּהֲנֶיךָ הַקְּדוֹשִׁים. וְכָל שְׁמוֹנַת יְמֵי חֲנֻכָּה
הַנֵּרוֹת הַלָּלוּ קֹדֶשׁ הֵם, וְאֵין לָנוּ רְשׁוּת לְהִשְׁתַּמֵּשׁ בָּהֶם אֶלָּא
לִרְאוֹתָם בִּלְבָד, כְּדֵי לְהוֹדוֹת וּלְהַלֵּל לְשִׁמְךָ הַגָּדוֹל עַל נִסֶּיךָ
וְעַל נִפְלְאוֹתֶיךָ וְעַל יְשׁוּעָתֶךָ.

לְךָ נָאֶה לְשַׁבֵּחַ.	מָעוֹז צוּר יְשׁוּעָתִי
וְשָׁם תּוֹדָה נְזַבֵּחַ.	תִּכּוֹן בֵּית תְּפִלָּתִי
מִצָּר הַמְנַבֵּחַ.	לְעֵת תָּכִין מַטְבֵּחַ
חֲנֻכַּת הַמִּזְבֵּחַ.	אָז אֶגְמֹר בְּשִׁיר מִזְמוֹר

מעוז צור was composed presumably in the thirteenth century. The name
of the author (מרדכי) is given in the initial letters of the five stanzas. The poem
alludes to the deliverance from Egypt, Babylonia, Persia, and Syria.

709

LIGHTING THE ḤANUKKAH LIGHTS

Blessed art thou, Lord our God, King of the universe, who hast sanctified us with thy commandments, and commanded us to light Ḥanukkah lights.

Blessed art thou, Lord our God, King of the universe, who didst perform miracles for our fathers in those days, at this season.

On the first night of Ḥanukkah add:

Blessed art thou, Lord our God, King of the universe, who hast granted us life and sustenance and permitted us to reach this season.

While kindling the lights from left to right:

We light these lights on account of the miracles, and wonders, triumphs and battles, thou didst perform for our fathers through thy holy priests in those days, at this season. These lights are sacred throughout the eight days of Ḥanukkah; we are not permitted to make any other use of them except watching them, in order to praise thy great name for thy miracles, thy wonders and thy triumphs.

MAOZ TSUR.

O God, my saving Stronghold,
To praise thee is a delight!
Restore my house of prayer,
Where I will offer thee thanks;
When thou wilt prepare havoc
For the foe who maligns us,
I will gratify myself
With a song at the altar.

רָ עוֹת שָׂבְעָה נַפְשִׁי   בְּיָגוֹן כֹּחִי כָּלָה.

חַיַּי מֵרְרוּ בְּקשִׁי   בְּשִׁעְבּוּד מַלְכוּת עֶגְלָה.

וּבְיָדוֹ הַגְּדוֹלָה   הוֹצִיא אֶת הַסְּגֻלָּה.

חֵיל פַּרְעֹה וְכָל זַרְעוֹ   יָרְדוּ כְּאֶבֶן מְצוּלָה.

דְּ בִיר קָדְשׁוֹ הֱבִיאַנִי   וְגַם שָׁם לֹא שָׁקַטְתִּי.

וּבָא נוֹגֵשׂ וְהִגְלַנִי   כִּי זָרִים עָבַדְתִּי.

וְיֵין רַעַל מָסַכְתִּי   כִּמְעַט שֶׁעָבַרְתִּי.

קֵץ בָּבֶל, זְרֻבָּבֶל,   לְקֵץ שִׁבְעִים נוֹשָׁעְתִּי.

כְּ רֹת קוֹמַת בְּרוֹשׁ בִּקֵּשׁ   אֲגָגִי בֶּן הַמְּדָתָא.

וְנִהְיָתָה לוֹ לְפַח וּלְמוֹקֵשׁ   וְגַאֲוָתוֹ נִשְׁבָּתָה.

רֹאשׁ יְמִינִי נִשֵּׂאתָ   וְאוֹיֵב שְׁמוֹ מָחִיתָ.

רֹב בָּנָיו וְקִנְיָנָיו   עַל הָעֵץ תָּלִיתָ.

יְ וָנִים נִקְבְּצוּ עָלַי   אֲזַי בִּימֵי חַשְׁמַנִּים.

וּפָרְצוּ חוֹמוֹת מִגְדָּלַי   וְטִמְּאוּ כָּל הַשְּׁמָנִים.

וּמִנּוֹתַר קַנְקַנִּים   נַעֲשָׂה נֵס לְשׁוֹשַׁנִּים.

בְּנֵי בִינָה יְמֵי שְׁמוֹנָה   קָבְעוּ שִׁיר וּרְנָנִים.

The following stanza is a comparatively late addition.

חֲ שׂוֹף זְרוֹעַ קָדְשֶׁךָ   וְקָרֵב יוֹם הַיְשׁוּעָה.

נְקֹם נִקְמַת עֲבָדֶיךָ   מִמַּלְכוּת הָרְשָׁעָה.

כִּי אָרְכָה הַשָּׁעָה   וְאֵין קֵץ לִימֵי רָעָה.

דְּחֵה אַדְמוֹן בְּצֵל צַלְמוֹן   וְהָקֵם לָנוּ רוֹעִים שִׁבְעָה.

My soul is sated with trouble;
My strength is consumed with grief;
They made life bitter for me
With hard service in Egypt;
But God with his great power
Brought forth the chosen people,
While all the host of Pharaoh
Sank like stone into the deep.

He brought me to his holy shrine;
Even there I found no peace;
The foe came and exiled me,
Because I had served strange gods
And was dazed with poisoned wine.
Soon Babylon's end drew near!
Guided by Zerubbabel,
I was saved after seventy years.

To cut down Mordecai's tree
Was the design of Haman;
But it proved a snare to him,
And his arrogance was stilled.
Thou didst promote Mordecai
And didst blot out the foe's name;
His numerous progeny
Didst thou hang on the gallows.

Greeks gathered to attack me
In the Hasmonean days;
They demolished my towers
And polluted all the oils;
From the last remaining flask
A miracle was wrought for Israel.
Men of wisdom then decreed
Eight days for hymns of praise.

מְגִלַּת הַחַשְׁמוֹנָאִים

א וַיְהִי בִּימֵי אַנְטְיוֹכוֹס מֶלֶךְ יָוָן; מֶלֶךְ גָּדוֹל וְחָזָק הָיָה,

ב וְתַקִּיף בְּמֶמְשַׁלְתּוֹ, וְכָל הַמְּלָכִים יִשְׁמְעוּ לוֹ. הוּא כָבַשׁ מְדִינוֹת רַבּוֹת וּמְלָכִים חֲזָקִים, וְהֶחֱרִיב טִירוֹתָם, וְהֵיכְלֵיהֶם

ג שָׂרַף בָּאֵשׁ, וְאַנְשֵׁיהֶם בְּבֵית הָאֲסוּרִים אָסָר. מִימֵי אֲלֶכְּסַנְדְּרוֹס הַמֶּלֶךְ לֹא קָם מֶלֶךְ כָּמֹהוּ בְּכָל עֵבֶר הַנָּהָר.

ד הוּא בָּנָה מְדִינָה גְדוֹלָה עַל חוֹף הַיָּם לִהְיוֹת לוֹ לְבֵית

ה מַלְכוּת, וַיִּקְרָא לָהּ מְדִינַת אַנְטְיוֹכִיָּא עַל שְׁמוֹ. וְגַם בַּגְרַס מִשְׁנֵהוּ בָּנָה מְדִינָה אַחֶרֶת לְנֶגְדָּהּ, וַיִּקְרָא לָהּ מְדִינַת בַּגְרַס עַל שְׁמוֹ; וְכֵן שְׁמוֹתָן עַד הַיּוֹם הַזֶּה.

ו בִּשְׁנַת עֶשְׂרִים וְשָׁלֹשׁ שָׁנִים לְמָלְכוֹ, הִיא שְׁנַת מָאתַיִם וּשְׁלֹשׁ עֶשְׂרֵה שָׁנִים לְבִנְיַן בֵּית הָאֱלֹהִים, שָׂם פָּנָיו לַעֲלוֹת

ז לִירוּשָׁלָיִם. וַיַּעַן וַיֹּאמֶר לְשָׂרָיו: הֲלֹא יְדַעְתֶּם כִּי יֵשׁ עַם הַיְּהוּדִים אֲשֶׁר בִּירוּשָׁלַיִם בֵּינֵינוּ. לֵאלֹהֵינוּ אֵינָם מַקְרִיבִים, וְדָתֵינוּ אֵינָם עוֹשִׂים, וְדָתֵי הַמֶּלֶךְ הֵם עוֹזְבִים לַעֲשׂוֹת

ח דָּתָם. וְגַם הֵם מְיַחֲלִים לְיוֹם שִׁבְרוֹן הַמְּלָכִים וְהַשִּׁלְטוֹנִים, וְאוֹמְרִים: מָתַי יִמְלֹךְ עָלֵינוּ מַלְכֵּנוּ, וְנִשְׁלוֹט בַּיָּם וּבַיַּבָּשָׁה,

ט וְכָל הָעוֹלָם יִנָּתֵן בְּיָדֵנוּ. אֵין כָּבוֹד לַמַּלְכוּת לְהַנִּיחַ אֵלֶּה עַל פְּנֵי הָאֲדָמָה. עַתָּה, בּוֹאוּ וְנַעֲלֶה עֲלֵיהֶם וּנְבַטֵּל מֵהֶם אֶת הַבְּרִית אֲשֶׁר כָּרַת לָהֶם: שַׁבָּת, רֹאשׁ חֹדֶשׁ וּמִילָה.

י וַיִּיטַב הַדָּבָר בְּעֵינֵי שָׂרָיו וּבְעֵינֵי כָל חֵילוֹ.

מְגִלַּת הַחַשְׁמוֹנָאִים, known also as מְגִלַּת אַנְטְיוֹכוֹס, has come down to us in both Aramaic and Hebrew. The Hebrew version is a literal translation from the

THE SCROLL OF THE HASMONEANS

The Greek monarch Antiochus was a powerful ruler; all the kings heeded him. He subdued many provinces and mighty sovereigns; he destroyed their castles, burned their palaces and imprisoned their men. Since the reign of Alexander there had never been a king like him beyond the Euphrates. He erected a large city on the seacoast to serve as his royal residence, and called it Antioch after his own name. Opposite it his governor Bagris founded another city, and called it City of Bagris after himself. Such are their names to this day.

In the twenty-third year of his reign, the two hundred and thirteenth year after the Temple had been rebuilt, Antiochus determined to march on Jerusalem. He said to his officers: "You are aware that the Jews of Jerusalem are in our midst. They neither offer sacrifices to our gods nor observe our laws; they abandon the king's laws to practise their own. They hope moreover for the day when kings and tyrants shall be crushed, saying: 'O that our own king might reign over us, that we might rule the sea and the land, so that the entire world would be ours.' It is indeed a disgrace for the royal government to let them remain on the face of the earth. Come now, let us attack them and abolish the covenant made with them: sabbath, new moon festivals and circumcision." The proposal pleased his officers and all his host.

Aramaic original which was composed probably in the seventh century. During the Middle Ages this *Megillah* was read in the Italian synagogues on *Ḥanukkah* as the Book of Esther is read on *Purim*. It still forms part of the liturgy of the Yemenite Jews. Saadyah Gaon attributed its authorship to the five sons of Mattathias.

יא בְּאוֹתָהּ שָׁעָה קָם אַנְטִיוֹכוֹס הַמֶּלֶךְ וַיִּשְׁלַח אֶת נִיקָנוֹר מִשְׁנֵהוּ בְּחַיִל גָּדוֹל וְעַם רָב, וַיָּבֹא לְעִיר יְהוּדָה, לִירוּשָׁלַיִם,

יב וַיַּהֲרֹג בָּהּ הֶרֶג רָב. וַיִּבֶן בָּמָה בְּבֵית הַמִּקְדָּשׁ, בִּמְקוֹם אֲשֶׁר אָמַר אֱלֹהֵי יִשְׂרָאֵל לַעֲבָדָיו הַנְּבִיאִים: שָׁם אֲשַׁכֵּן שְׁכִינָתִי לְעוֹלָם; בַּמָּקוֹם הַהוּא שָׁחֲטוּ אֶת הַחֲזִיר, וַיָּבִיאוּ אֶת דָּמוֹ

יג לַעֲזָרַת הַקֹּדֶשׁ. וּבִהְיוֹת זֶה, כַּאֲשֶׁר שָׁמַע יוֹחָנָן בֶּן מַתִּתְיָה כִּי זֶה הַמַּעֲשֶׂה נַעֲשָׂה, נִמְלָא קֶצֶף וְחֵמָה, וְזִיו פָּנָיו נִשְׁתַּנָּה;

יד וַיִּוָּעֵץ בְּלִבּוֹ מַה שֶּׁיּוּכַל לַעֲשׂוֹת עַל זֶה. וְאָז יוֹחָנָן בֶּן מַתִּתְיָה עָשָׂה לוֹ חֶרֶב, שְׁתֵּי זְרָתוֹת אָרְכָּהּ וְזֶרֶת אַחַת רָחְבָּהּ, וְהִיא

טו תַּחַת בְּגָדָיו עֲטוּפָה. וַיָּבֹא לִירוּשָׁלַיִם, וַיַּעֲמֹד בְּשַׁעַר הַמֶּלֶךְ, וַיִּקְרָא לַשּׁוֹעֲרִים וַיֹּאמֶר לָהֶם: אֲנִי יוֹחָנָן בֶּן מַתִּתְיָה, הַכֹּהֵן

טז הַגָּדוֹל שֶׁל הַיְּהוּדִים, בָּאתִי לָבוֹא לִפְנֵי נִיקָנוֹר. וְאָז בָּאוּ הַשּׁוֹעֲרִים וְהַשּׁוֹמְרִים וַיֹּאמְרוּ לְנִיקָנוֹר: הַכֹּהֵן הַגָּדוֹל שֶׁל הַיְּהוּדִים עוֹמֵד בַּפֶּתַח. וַיַּעַן נִיקָנוֹר וַיֹּאמֶר לָהֶם: בּוֹא יָבוֹא.

יז אָז הוּבָא יוֹחָנָן לִפְנֵי נִיקָנוֹר. וַיַּעַן נִיקָנוֹר וַיֹּאמֶר לְיוֹחָנָן: אַתָּה הוּא אֶחָד מִן הַמּוֹרְדִים אֲשֶׁר מָרְדוּ בַּמֶּלֶךְ וְאֵינָם

יח רוֹצִים בִּשְׁלוֹם מַלְכוּתוֹ. וַיַּעַן יוֹחָנָן לִפְנֵי נִיקָנוֹר וַיֹּאמַר:

יט אֲדוֹנִי, עַתָּה בָאתִי לְפָנֶיךָ, אֲשֶׁר תִּרְצֶה אֶעֱשֶׂה. וַיַּעַן נִיקָנוֹר וַיֹּאמֶר לְיוֹחָנָן: אִם כִּרְצוֹנִי אַתָּה עוֹשֶׂה, קַח חֲזִיר וּשְׁחָטֵהוּ עַל הַבָּמָה, וְתִלְבַּשׁ בִּגְדֵי מַלְכוּת, וְתִרְכַּב עַל סוּס הַמֶּלֶךְ,

כ וּכְאַחַד מֵאוֹהֲבֵי הַמֶּלֶךְ תִּהְיֶה. וְכַאֲשֶׁר שָׁמַע יוֹחָנָן, הֱשִׁיבוֹ דָבָר: אֲדוֹנִי, אֲנִי יָרֵא מִבְּנֵי יִשְׂרָאֵל, פֶּן יִשְׁמְעוּ כִּי עָשִׂיתִי כֵן וְיִסְקְלוּנִי בָּאֲבָנִים; עַתָּה, יֵצֵא כָל אִישׁ מִלְּפָנֶיךָ, פֶּן יוֹדִיעוּ

כא לִבְנֵי יִשְׂרָאֵל. אָז הוֹצִיא נִיקָנוֹר מִלְּפָנָיו כָּל אִישׁ. בָּעֵת

כב הַהִיא נָשָׂא יוֹחָנָן בֶּן מַתִּתְיָה עֵינָיו לַשָּׁמַיִם, וְתִקֵּן תְּפִלָּתוֹ

Immediately king Antiochus dispatched his governor Nicanor with a large body of troops. He came to the Jewish city of Jerusalem and massacred many people; he set up a heathen altar in the Temple, concerning which the God of Israel had said to his faithful prophets: "There will I establish my residence forever." In that very place they slaughtered a swine and brought its blood into the holy court. When Yoḥanan ben Mattathias heard of this deed, he was filled with rage and his face changed color. In his heart he drew a plan of action. Whereupon he made himself a dagger, two spans long and one span wide, and concealed it under his clothes. He came to Jerusalem and stood at the royal gate, calling to the gate-keepers: "I am Yoḥanan ben Mattathias; I have come to appear before Nicanor." The guards informed Nicanor that the high priest of the Jews was standing at the door. "Let him enter!" Nicanor said.

Yoḥanan was admitted to Nicanor, who said: "You are one of the rebels who rebel against the king and do not care for the welfare of his government!" Yoḥanan replied: "My lord, I have come to you; whatever you demand I will do." "If you wish to do as I please," said Nicanor, "then take a swine and sacrifice it upon the altar. You shall wear royal clothes and ride the king's own horse; you shall be counted among the king's close friends." To this, Yoḥanan answered: "My lord, I am afraid of the Israelites; if they hear that I have done such a thing they will stone me. Let everyone leave your presence, so as not to inform them." Immediately Nicanor ordered everybody out.

At that moment Yoḥanan ben Mattathias raised his eyes to heaven and prayed: "My God and God of my fathers Abraham,

לִפְנֵי רִבּוֹן הָעוֹלָמִים וַיֹּאמַר: אֱלֹהַי וֵאלֹהֵי אֲבוֹתַי, אַבְרָהָם
יִצְחָק וְיַעֲקֹב, אַל נָא תִּתְּנֵנִי בְּיַד הֶעָרֵל הַזֶּה, כִּי אִם יַהַרְגֵנִי
יֵלֵךְ וְיִשְׁתַּבַּח בְּבֵית דָּגוֹן אֱלֹהָיו וְיֹאמַר: אֱלֹהַי נְתָנוּ בְיָדִי.

כג בְּאוֹתָהּ שָׁעָה פָּסַע עָלָיו שָׁלֹשׁ פְּסִיעוֹת, וַיִּתְקַע הַחֶרֶב
כד בְּלִבּוֹ, וַיַּשְׁלֵךְ אוֹתוֹ חָלָל בַּעֲזֶרֶת הַקֹּדֶשׁ. עָנָה יוֹחָנָן וְאָמַר
לִפְנֵי אֱלֹהֵי הַשָּׁמָיִם: אֱלֹהַי, אַל תָּשֵׂם עָלַי חֵטְא כִּי הֲרַגְתִּי
אֶת הֶעָרֵל הַזֶּה בְּבֵית הַמִּקְדָּשׁ; כֵּן תִּתֵּן עַתָּה אֶת כָּל הָעַמִּים
כה אֲשֶׁר בָּאוּ עִמּוֹ לְהָצֵר לִיהוּדָה וְלִירוּשָׁלָיִם. אָז יָצָא יוֹחָנָן
כו בַּיּוֹם הַהוּא וַיִּלָּחֶם בָּעַמִּים, וַיַּהֲרֹג בָּהֶם הֶרֶג רָב. מִסְפַּר
הַהֲרוּגִים אֲשֶׁר הָרַג בַּיּוֹם הַהוּא שִׁבְעַת אֲלָפִים, אֲשֶׁר הָיוּ
כז הוֹרְגִים אֵלֶּה לָאֵלֶּה. בְּשׁוּבוֹ בָּנָה עַמּוּד עַל שְׁמוֹ, וַיִּקְרָא
לוֹ: מַכַּבִּי מֵמִית הַחֲזָקִים.

כח וַיְהִי כַּאֲשֶׁר שָׁמַע אַנְטִיוֹכוֹס הַמֶּלֶךְ כִּי נֶהֱרַג נִיקָנוֹר
מִשְׁנֵהוּ, צַר לוֹ מְאֹד; וַיִּשְׁלַח לְהָבִיא בַּגְרַס הָרָשָׁע הַמַּטְעֶה
כט אֶת עַמּוֹ. וַיַּעַן אַנְטִיוֹכוֹס הַמֶּלֶךְ וַיֹּאמֶר לְבַגְרַס: הֲלֹא יָדַעְתָּ
אִם לֹא שָׁמַעְתָּ אֲשֶׁר עָשׂוּ לִי בְּנֵי יִשְׂרָאֵל; הָרְגוּ חֲיָלַי, וַיָּבֹזּוּ
ל מַחֲנוֹתַי וְשָׁרָי. עַתָּה עַל מָמוֹנְכֶם אַתֶּם בּוֹטְחִים, אוֹ עַל
בָּתֵּיכֶם לָכֶם הֵם; בֹּאוּ וְנַעֲלֶה עֲלֵיהֶם, וּנְבַטֵּל מֵהֶם
הַבְּרִית אֲשֶׁר כָּרַת לָהֶם אֱלֹהֵיהֶם: שַׁבָּת, רֹאשׁ חֹדֶשׁ וּמִילָה.
לא אָז קָם בַּגְרַס הָרָשָׁע וְכָל מַחֲנוֹתָיו, וַיָּבֹאוּ לִירוּשָׁלָיִם. וַיַּהֲרֹג
לב בָּהּ הֶרֶג רָב, וַיִּגְזֹר בָּהּ גְּזֵרָה גְמוּרָה עַל שַׁבָּת, רֹאשׁ חֹדֶשׁ
לג וּמִילָה. בִּהְיוֹת זֶה, כַּאֲשֶׁר הָיָה דְבַר הַמֶּלֶךְ נֶחְפָּז, מָצְאוּ
אִישׁ אֲשֶׁר מָל בְּנוֹ, וַיָּבִיאוּ הָאִישׁ וְאִשְׁתּוֹ, וַיִּתְלוּ אוֹתָם כְּנֶגֶד
לד הַיָּלֶד. וְגַם אִשָּׁה אֲשֶׁר יָלְדָה בֶן אַחֲרֵי מוֹת בַּעֲלָהּ, וַתָּמָל
אוֹתוֹ לִשְׁמֹנָה יָמִים, וַתַּעַל עַל חוֹמַת יְרוּשָׁלָיִם וּבְנָהּ הַמָּהוּל

Isaac and Jacob, do not hand me over to this heathen; for if he kills me, he will boast in the temple of Dagon that his god has handed me over to him." He advanced three steps toward Nicanor, thrust the dagger into his heart, and flung him fatally wounded into the court of the Temple. "My God," Yoḥanan prayed, "do not count it a sin that I killed this heathen in the sanctuary; punish thus all the foes who came with him to persecute Judea and Jerusalem." On that day Yoḥanan set out and fought the enemy, inflicting heavy slaughter on them. The number of those who were slain by him on that day totaled seven thousand. Upon returning, he erected a column with the inscription: "Maccabee, Destroyer of Tyrants."

When king Antiochus heard that his governor Nicanor had been slain, he was bitterly distressed. He sent for wicked Bagris, the deceiver of his people, and told him: "Do you not know, have you not heard, what the Israelites did to me? They massacred my troops and ransacked my camps! Can you now be sure of your wealth? Will your homes remain yours? Come, let us move against them and abolish the covenant which their God made with them: sabbath, new moon festivals and circumcision." Thereupon wicked Bagris and his hosts invaded Jerusalem, murdering the population and proclaiming an absolute decree against sabbath, new moon festivals and circumcision. So drastic was the king's edict that when a man was discovered to have circumcised his son, he and his wife were hanged along with the child. A woman gave birth to a son after her husband's death and had him circumcised when he was eight days old. With the child in her arms, she went up on top

לה בְּיָדָהּ. וַיַּעַן וַיֹּאמֶר: לְךָ אוֹמְרִים, בַּגְרֹס הָרָשָׁע, אַתֶּם חוֹשְׁבִים לְבַטֵּל מֵאִתָּנוּ הַבְּרִית אֲשֶׁר כָּרַת עִמָּנוּ; בְּרִית
לו אֲבוֹתֵינוּ לֹא נִבְטַל מִמֶּנּוּ וְלֹא מִבְּנֵי בָנֵינוּ. וַתִּפֹּל בִּנְךָ לָאָרֶץ וַתִּפֹּל אַחֲרָיו, וַיָּמוּתוּ שְׁנֵיהֶם כְּאֶחָד. וְרַבִּים מִבְּנֵי יִשְׂרָאֵל הָיוּ עוֹשִׂים כֵּן בַּיָּמִים הָהֵם, וְלֹא שִׁנּוּ בְּרִית אֲבוֹתָם.

לז בַּזְּמַן הַהוּא אָמְרוּ בְּנֵי יִשְׂרָאֵל אֵלֶּה לָאֵלֶּה: בֹּאוּ וְנִשְׁבֹּת בִּמְעָרָה, פֶּן נְחַלֵּל אֶת יוֹם הַשַּׁבָּת; וַיַּלְשִׁינוּ אוֹתָם לִפְנֵי
לח בַגְרֹס. אָז שָׁלַח בַּגְרֹס אֲנָשִׁים חֲלוּצִים, וַיָּבֹאוּ וַיֵּשְׁבוּ עַל פִּי הַמְּעָרָה וַיֹּאמְרוּ: בְּנֵי יִשְׂרָאֵל, צְאוּ אֵלֵינוּ; אִכְלוּ מִלַּחְמֵנוּ
לט וּשְׁתוּ מִיֵּינֵנוּ, וּמַעֲשֵׂינוּ תִּהְיוּ עוֹשִׂים. וַיַּעֲנוּ בְּנֵי יִשְׂרָאֵל וַיֹּאמְרוּ אֵלֶּה לָאֵלֶּה: זוֹכְרִים אֲנַחְנוּ אֶת אֲשֶׁר נִצְטַוֵּינוּ עַל הַר סִינַי: שֵׁשֶׁת יָמִים תַּעֲבֹד וְעָשִׂיתָ כָּל מְלַאכְתֶּךָ, וּבַיּוֹם הַשְּׁבִיעִי תִּשְׁבֹּת; עַתָּה, טוֹב לָנוּ אֲשֶׁר נָמוּת מֵאֲשֶׁר נְחַלֵּל אֶת יוֹם
מ הַשַּׁבָּת. בִּהְיוֹת זֶה, כַּאֲשֶׁר לֹא יָצְאוּ אֲלֵיהֶם הַיְּהוּדִים, וַיָּבִיאוּ עֵצִים וַיִּשְׂרְפוּ עַל פִּי הַמְּעָרָה, וַיָּמוּתוּ כְּאֶלֶף אִישׁ
מא וְאִשָּׁה. אַחֲרֵי כֵן יָצְאוּ חֲמֵשֶׁת בְּנֵי מַתִּתְיָה, יוֹחָנָן וְאַרְבַּעַת
מב אֶחָיו, וַיִּלָּחֲמוּ בָעַמִּים, וַיַּהַרְגוּ בָהֶם הֶרֶג רָב; וַיְגָרְשׁוּם לְאִיֵּי הַיָּם, כִּי בָטְחוּ בֵּאלֹהֵי הַשָּׁמָיִם.

מג אָז נִכְנַס בַּגְרֹס הָרָשָׁע בִּסְפִינָה וַיָּנָס אֶל אַנְטְיוֹכוֹס
מד הַמֶּלֶךְ, וְעִמּוֹ אֲנָשִׁים פְּלִיטֵי חָרֶב. וַיַּעַן בַּגְרֹס וַיֹּאמֶר לְאַנְטְיוֹכוֹס הַמֶּלֶךְ: אַתָּה, הַמֶּלֶךְ, שַׂמְתָּ צַו לְבַטֵּל מִן יְהוּדָה שַׁבָּת, רֹאשׁ חֹדֶשׁ וּמִילָה, וְהִנֵּה מֶרֶד גָּדוֹל בְּתוֹכָהּ, אֲשֶׁר אִם [לֹא] יֵלְכוּ כָל הָעַמִּים וְהָאֻמּוֹת וְהַלְּשׁוֹנוֹת לֹא יוּכְלוּ לַחֲמֵשֶׁת בְּנֵי מַתִּתְיָה; מֵאֲרָיוֹת הֵם חֲזָקִים, וּמִנְּשָׁרִים הֵם
מה קַלִּים, וּמִדֻּבִּים הֵם נִמְהָרִים. עַתָּה, הַמֶּלֶךְ, עֲצָתִי תִיטַב

of the wall of Jerusalem and cried out: "We say to you, wicked Bagris: This covenant of our fathers which you intend to destroy shall never cease from us nor from our children's children." She cast her son down to the ground and flung herself after him so that they died together. Many Israelites of that period did the same, refusing to renounce the covenant of their fathers.

Some of the Jews said to one another: "Come, let us keep the Sabbath in a cave lest we violate it." When they were betrayed to Bagris, he dispatched armed men who sat down at the entrance of the cave and said: "You Jews, surrender to us! Eat of our bread, drink of our wine, and do what we do!" But the Jews said to one another: "We remember what we were commanded on Mount Sinai: 'Six days you shall labor and do all your work; on the seventh day you shall rest.' It is better for us to die than to desecrate the Sabbath." When the Jews failed to come out, wood was brought and set on fire at the entrance of the cave. About a thousand men and women died there. Later the five sons of Mattathias, Yoḥanan and his four brothers, set out and routed the hostile forces, whom they drove to the coast; for they trusted in the God of heaven.

Wicked Bagris, accompanied by those who had escaped the sword, boarded a ship and fled to king Antiochus. "O king," he said, "you have issued a decree abolishing sabbath, new moon festivals and circumcision in Judea, and now there is complete rebellion there. The five sons of Mattathias cannot be defeated unless they are attacked by all the combined forces; they are stronger than lions, swifter than eagles, braver than bears. Be

עָלֶיךָ; אִם תִּלָּחֵם בָּהֶם בְּחַיִל זֶה, תֵּבוֹשׁ בְּעֵינֵי כָל הַמְּלָכִים.

מו לָכֵן שָׁלַח סְפָרִים בְּכָל מְדִינוֹת מַלְכוּתֶךָ, וַיָּבֹאוּ שָׂרֵי הַחֲיָלוֹת, וְלֹא יִשָּׁאֵר מֵהֶם אֶחָד; וְגַם פִּילִים מְלֻבָּשִׁים

מז שִׁרְיוֹנִים יִהְיוּ עִמָּהֶם. וַיִּיטַב הַדָּבָר בְּעֵינֵי אַנְטִיוֹכוֹס הַמֶּלֶךְ, וַיִּשְׁלַח סְפָרִים לְכָל מְדִינוֹת מַלְכוּתוֹ; וַיָּבֹאוּ שָׂרֵי עַם וָעָם,

מח וְעִמָּהֶם פִּילִים מְלֻבָּשִׁים שִׁרְיוֹנִים. שֵׁנִית קָם בַּגְרַס הָרָשָׁע וַיָּבֹא לִירוּשָׁלַיִם; בָּקַע הַחוֹמָה וַיְנַתֵּק הַמָּבוֹא וַיִּפְרֹץ בַּמִּקְדָּשׁ

מט שָׁלֹשׁ עֶשְׂרֵה פְרָצוֹת, וְגַם מִן הָאֲבָנִים שִׁבֵּר עַד אֲשֶׁר הָיוּ כֶעָפָר. וַיַּחֲשׁוֹב בְּלִבּוֹ וַיֹּאמַר: הַפַּעַם הַזֹּאת לֹא יוּכְלוּ לִי, כִּי רַב חֵילִי וְעָזָּה יָדִי; וֵאלֹהֵי הַשָּׁמַיִם לֹא חָשַׁב כֵּן.

נ   כְּשָׁמְעַ חֲמֵשֶׁת בְּנֵי מַתִּתְיָה, קָמוּ וַיָּבֹאוּ לְמִצְפֶּה גִלְעָד, אֲשֶׁר הָיְתָה שָׁם פְּלֵיטָה לְבֵית יִשְׂרָאֵל בִּימֵי שְׁמוּאֵל הַנָּבִיא.

נא צוֹם גָּזְרוּ, וַיֵּשְׁבוּ עַל הָאֵפֶר לְבַקֵּשׁ רַחֲמִים מִלִּפְנֵי אֱלֹהֵי

נב הַשָּׁמָיִם; אָז נָפְלָה בְלִבָּם עֵצָה טוֹבָה. וְהָיוּ שְׁמוֹתֵיהֶם: יְהוּדָה הַבְּכוֹר, שִׁמְעוֹן הַשֵּׁנִי, יוֹחָנָן הַשְּׁלִישִׁי, יוֹנָתָן הָרְבִיעִי,

נג אֶלְעָזָר הַחֲמִישִׁי. וַיְבָרֶךְ אוֹתָם אֲבִיהֶם קֹדֶם שֶׁשְּׁלָחָם לַמִּלְחָמָה, וַיֹּאמֶר לָהֶם: יְהוּדָה בְּנִי, אֲדַמֶּה אוֹתְךָ לִיהוּדָה

נד בֶּן יַעֲקֹב אֲשֶׁר הָיָה נִמְשָׁל לְאַרְיֵה. שִׁמְעוֹן בְּנִי, אֲדַמֶּה אוֹתְךָ

נה לְשִׁמְעוֹן בֶּן יַעֲקֹב אֲשֶׁר הָרַג יוֹשְׁבֵי שְׁכֶם. יוֹחָנָן בְּנִי, אֲדַמֶּה

נו אוֹתְךָ לְאַבְנֵר בֶּן נֵר, שַׂר צְבָא יִשְׂרָאֵל. יוֹנָתָן בְּנִי, אֲדַמֶּה

נז אוֹתְךָ לְיוֹנָתָן בֶּן שָׁאוּל אֲשֶׁר הָרַג עִם פְּלִשְׁתִּים. אֶלְעָזָר בְּנִי, אֲדַמֶּה אוֹתְךָ לְפִינְחָס בֶּן אֶלְעָזָר, אֲשֶׁר קִנֵּא לֵאלֹהָיו

נח וְהִצִּיל אֶת בְּנֵי יִשְׂרָאֵל. אַחַר זֶה קָמוּ חֲמֵשֶׁת בְּנֵי מַתִּתְיָה וַיִּלָּחֲמוּ בָּעַמִּים הָהֵם, וַיַּהַרְגוּ בָהֶם הֶרֶג רָב; וַיֵּהָרֵג מֵהֶם יְהוּדָה.

pleased to accept my advice, and do not fight them with this small army lest you be disgraced in the sight of all the kings. Send letters to all your royal provinces; let all the army officers without exception come with armored elephants." This pleased king Antiochus. He sent letters to all his royal domains, and the chieftains of various clans arrived with armored elephants. Wicked Bagris invaded Jerusalem for the second time. He broke through the wall, shattered the gateway, made thirteen breaches in the Temple, and ground the stones to dust. He thought to himself: "This time they shall not defeat me; my army is numerous, my hand is mighty." However, the God of heaven did not think so.

The five sons of Mattathias went to Mizpeh in Gilead, where the house of Israel had been saved in the days of Samuel the prophet. They fasted, sat in ashes and prayed to the God of heaven for mercy; then a good plan came to their mind. These were their names: Judah, the firstborn; Simeon, the second; Yoḥanan, the third; Jonathan, the fourth; Elazar, the fifth. Their father blessed them, saying: "Judah my son, I compare you to Judah the son of Jacob who was likened to a lion. Simeon my son, I compare you to Simeon the son of Jacob who slew the men of Shechem. Yoḥanan my son, I compare you to Abner the son of Ner, general of Israel's army. Jonathan my son, I compare you to Jonathan the son of Saul who defeated the Philistines. Elazar my son, I compare you to Phinehas the son of Elazar, who was zealous for his God and rescued the Israelites." Soon afterwards the five sons of Mattathias attacked the pagan forces, inflicting severe losses upon them. One of the brothers, Judah, was killed.

נט בְּאוֹתָהּ שָׁעָה, כַּאֲשֶׁר רָאוּ בְּנֵי מַתִּתְיָה כִּי נֶהֱרַג יְהוּדָה,

ס שָׁבוּ וַיָּבְאוּ אֶל אֲבִיהֶם; וַיֹּאמֶר לָהֶם: לָמָּה שַׁבְתֶּם. וַיַּעֲנוּ

סא וַיֹּאמְרוּ: נֶהֱרַג יְהוּדָה אָחִינוּ, אֲשֶׁר הָיָה חָשׁוּב כְּכֻלָּנוּ. וַיַּעַן מַתִּתְיָה וַיֹּאמֶר אֲלֵיהֶם: אֲנִי אֵצֵא עִמָּכֶם וְאֶלָּחֵם בָּעַמִּים,

סב פֶּן יֹאבְדוּ בֵּית יִשְׂרָאֵל; וְאַתֶּם נִבְהַלְתֶּם עַל אֲחִיכֶם. וַיֵּצֵא

סג מַתִּתְיָה בַּיּוֹם הַהוּא עִם בָּנָיו, וַיִּלָּחֲמוּ בָּעַמִּים. וֵאלֹהֵי הַשָּׁמַיִם נָתַן כָּל גִּבּוֹרֵי הָעַמִּים בְּיָדָם, וַיַּהַרְגוּ בָהֶם הֶרֶג רָב, כָּל שֹׁלֵף חֶרֶב וְכָל אוֹחֵז קֶשֶׁת, שָׂרֵי הַחַיִל וְהַסְּגָנִים, לֹא נוֹתַר בָּהֶם שָׂרִיד; וַיָּנוּסוּ שְׁאָר הָעַמִּים לִמְדִינוֹת הַיָּם.

סד וְאֶלְעָזָר הָיָה מִתְעַסֵּק לְהָמִית הַפִּילִים, וַיִּטְבַּע בְּפֶרֶשׁ הַפִּילִים; וַיְבַקְשׁוּהוּ אֶחָיו בֵּין הַחַיִּים וּבֵין הַמֵּתִים וְלֹא מְצָאוּהוּ, וְאַחֲרֵי כֵן מְצָאוּהוּ טוֹבֵעַ בְּפֶרֶשׁ הַפִּילִים.

סה וַיִּשְׂמְחוּ בְּנֵי יִשְׂרָאֵל כִּי נִתְּנוּ בִידֵיהֶם שׂוֹנְאֵיהֶם; מֵהֶם שָׂרְפוּ בָאֵשׁ, וּמֵהֶם תָּלוּ עַל הָעֵץ, וּבַגְּרַס הָרָשָׁע, הַמַּטְעֶה

סו אֶת עַמּוֹ, שָׂרְפוּ אוֹתוֹ בְּנֵי יִשְׂרָאֵל בָּאֵשׁ. וְאַנְטְיוֹכוּס הַמֶּלֶךְ, כַּאֲשֶׁר שָׁמַע אֲשֶׁר נֶהֶרְגוּ בַּגְּרַס מִשְׁנֵהוּ וְכָל שָׂרֵי הַחַיִל אֲשֶׁר

סז עִמּוֹ, נִכְנַס בִּסְפִינָה וַיָּנָס לִמְדִינוֹת הַיָּם. וַיְהִי, כָּל מָקוֹם אֲשֶׁר הָיָה בָא שָׁמָּה הָיוּ מוֹרְדִים בּוֹ וְקוֹרְאִים אוֹתוֹ הַבּוֹרֵחַ, וַיַּשְׁלֵךְ אֶת נַפְשׁוֹ הַיָּמָּה.

סח אַחֲרֵי כֵן בָּאוּ בְּנֵי חַשְׁמוֹנַי לְבֵית הַמִּקְדָּשׁ, וַיִּבְנוּ הַשְּׁעָרִים, וַיִּסְגְּרוּ הַפְּרָצוֹת, וַיְטַהֲרוּ אֶת הָעֲזָרָה מִן הַהֲרוּגִים

סט וּמִן הַטֻּמְאוֹת. וַיְבַקְשׁוּ שֶׁמֶן זַיִת זָךְ לְהַדְלִיק הַמְּנוֹרָה, וְלֹא מָצְאוּ כִּי אִם צְלוֹחִית אַחַת אֲשֶׁר הָיְתָה חֲתוּמָה בְּטַבַּעַת הַכֹּהֵן הַגָּדוֹל, וַיֵּדְעוּ כִּי הָיְתָה טְהוֹרָה, וְהָיָה בָהּ כְּשִׁעוּר

ע הַדְלָקַת יוֹם אֶחָד. וֵאלֹהֵי הַשָּׁמַיִם, אֲשֶׁר שִׁכֵּן שְׁמוֹ שָׁם, נָתַן

When the sons of Mattathias discovered that Judah had been slain, they returned to their father who asked: "Why did you come back?" They replied: "Our brother Judah, who alone equaled all of us, has been killed." "I will join you in the battle against the heathen," Mattathias said, "lest they destroy the house of Israel; why be so dismayed over your brother?" He joined his sons that same day and waged war against the enemy. The God of heaven delivered into their hands all swordsmen and archers, army officers and high officials. None of these survived. Others were compelled to seek refuge in the coastal cities. In attacking the elephants, Elazar was engulfed in their dung. His brothers searched for him among the living and the dead and could not find him. Eventually, however, they did find him.

The Jews rejoiced over the defeat of their enemies, some of whom were burned while others were hanged on the gallows. Wicked Bagris was included among those who were burned to death. When king Antiochus heard that his governor Bagris and the army officers had been killed, he boarded a ship and fled to the coastal cities. Wherever he came the people rebelled and called him "The Fugitive," so he drowned himself in the sea.

The Hasmoneans entered the sanctuary, rebuilt the gates, closed the breaches, and cleansed the Temple court from the slain and the impurities. They looked for pure olive oil to light the Menorah, and found only one bottle with the seal of the high priest so that they were sure of its purity. Though its quantity seemed sufficient only for one day's lighting, it lasted for eight days owing

עא בְּרָכָה וְהִדְלִיקוּ מִמֶּנָּה שְׁמֹנָה יָמִים. עַל כֵּן קִיְּמוּ בְּנֵי חַשְׁמוֹנַי
קִיּוּם, וְחִזְּקוּ אִסָּר, וּבְנֵי יִשְׂרָאֵל עִמָּהֶם כְּאֶחָד, לַעֲשׂוֹת
שְׁמוֹנַת הַיָּמִים הָאֵלֶּה יְמֵי מִשְׁתֶּה וְשִׂמְחָה כִּימֵי מוֹעֲדִים
הַכְּתוּבִים בַּתּוֹרָה, וּלְהַדְלִיק בָּהֶם נֵרוֹת לְהוֹדִיעַ אֲשֶׁר
עב עָשָׂה לָהֶם אֱלֹהֵי הַשָּׁמַיִם נִצּוּחִים. וּבָהֶם אֵין לִסְפּוֹד וְלֹא
לִגְזֹר צוֹם, זוּלָתִי אֲשֶׁר יִהְיֶה עָלָיו נֶדֶר יְשַׁלְּמֶנּוּ; אַךְ חַשְׁמוֹנַי
עג וּבָנָיו וַאֲחֵיהֶם לֹא גָזְרוּ בָהֶם לְבַטֵּל מְלָאכָה וַעֲבוֹדָה. וּמִן
הָעֵת הַהִיא לֹא הָיָה שָׁם לְמַלְכוּת יָוָן.

עד ‏ ‏ וַיְקַבְּלוּ הַמַּלְכוּת בְּנֵי חַשְׁמוֹנַי, הֵם וּבְנֵיהֶם וּבְנֵי בְנֵיהֶם,
מֵחָזֵת הַזֹּאת עַד חֻרְבַּן בֵּית הָאֱלֹהִים, מָאתַיִם וְשֵׁשׁ שָׁנִים.
עה עַל כֵּן שׁוֹמְרִים בְּנֵי יִשְׂרָאֵל הַיָּמִים הָאֵלֶּה בְּכָל גָּלוּתָם,
וְיִקְרְאוּ לָהֶם יְמֵי מִשְׁתֶּה וְשִׂמְחָה, מֵחֲמִשָּׁה וְעֶשְׂרִים לַחֹדֶשׁ
עו כִּסְלֵו שְׁמֹנָה יָמִים. וְהַיָּמִים הָאֵלֶּה קִיְּמוּ וְקִבְּלוּ עֲלֵיהֶם
וְעַל בְּנֵי בְנֵיהֶם עַד עוֹלָם הַכֹּהֲנִים וְהַלְוִיִּם וְהַחֲכָמִים אֲשֶׁר
הָיוּ בְּבֵית הַמִּקְדָּשׁ, וְלֹא יָסוּרוּ מִזַּרְעָם עַד עוֹלָם.

לְפוּרִים

Before the reading of the *Megillah*:

בָּרוּךְ אַתָּה, יְיָ אֱלֹהֵינוּ, מֶלֶךְ הָעוֹלָם, אֲשֶׁר קִדְּשָׁנוּ בְּמִצְוֹתָיו
וְצִוָּנוּ עַל מִקְרָא מְגִלָּה.

בָּרוּךְ אַתָּה, יְיָ אֱלֹהֵינוּ, מֶלֶךְ הָעוֹלָם, שֶׁעָשָׂה נִסִּים
לַאֲבוֹתֵינוּ בַּיָּמִים הָהֵם בַּזְּמַן הַזֶּה.

בָּרוּךְ אַתָּה, יְיָ אֱלֹהֵינוּ, מֶלֶךְ הָעוֹלָם, שֶׁהֶחֱיָנוּ וְקִיְּמָנוּ
וְהִגִּיעָנוּ לַזְּמַן הַזֶּה.

to the blessing of the God of heaven who had established his name there. Hence, the Hasmoneans and all the Jews alike instituted these eight days as a time of feasting and rejoicing, like any festival prescribed in the Torah, and of kindling lights to commemorate the victories God had given them. Mourning and fasting are forbidden on Ḥanukkah, except in the case of an individual's vow which must be discharged. Nevertheless, the Hasmoneans did not prohibit work on this holiday.

From that time on the Greek government was stripped of its renown. The Hasmoneans and their descendants ruled for two hundred and six years, until the destruction of the Temple.

And so the Jews everywhere observe this festival for eight days, beginning on the twenty-fifth of Kislev. These days, instituted by priests, Levites and sages of Temple times, shall be celebrated by their descendants forever.

FOR PURIM

Before the reading of the Megillah:

Blessed art thou, Lord our God, King of the universe, who hast sanctified us with thy commandments, and commanded us concerning the reading of the *Megillah*.

Blessed art thou, Lord our God, King of the universe, who didst perform miracles for our fathers in those days, at this season.

Blessed art thou, Lord our God, King of the universe, who hast granted us life and sustenance and permitted us to reach this season.

After the reading of the *Megillah:*

בָּרוּךְ אַתָּה, יְיָ אֱלֹהֵינוּ, מֶלֶךְ הָעוֹלָם, הָרָב אֶת רִיבֵנוּ,
וְהַדָּן אֶת דִּינֵנוּ, וְהַנּוֹקֵם אֶת נִקְמָתֵנוּ, וְהַנִּפְרָע לָנוּ מִצָּרֵינוּ,
וְהַמְשַׁלֵּם גְּמוּל לְכָל אֹיְבֵי נַפְשֵׁנוּ. בָּרוּךְ אַתָּה, יְיָ, הַנִּפְרָע
לְעַמּוֹ יִשְׂרָאֵל מִכָּל צָרֵיהֶם, הָאֵל הַמּוֹשִׁיעַ.

On *Purim* morning omit:

אֲשֶׁר הֵנִיא עֲצַת גּוֹיִם, וַיָּפֶר מַחְשְׁבוֹת עֲרוּמִים.

בְּקוּם עָלֵינוּ אָדָם רָשָׁע, נֵצֶר זָדוֹן מִזֶּרַע עֲמָלֵק.

גָּאָה בְעָשְׁרוֹ וְכָרָה לוֹ בוֹר, וּגְדֻלָּתוֹ יָקְשָׁה לוֹ לָכֶד.

דִּמָּה בְנַפְשׁוֹ לִלְכּוֹד וְנִלְכָּד, בִּקֵּשׁ לְהַשְׁמִיד וְנִשְׁמַד מְהֵרָה.

הָמָן הוֹדִיעַ אֵיבַת אֲבוֹתָיו, וְעוֹרֵר שִׂנְאַת אַחִים לַבָּנִים.

וְלֹא זָכַר רַחֲמֵי שָׁאוּל, כִּי בְחֶמְלָתוֹ עַל אֲגָג נוֹלַד אוֹיֵב.

זָמַם רָשָׁע לְהַכְרִית צַדִּיק, וְנִלְכַּד טָמֵא בִּידֵי טָהוֹר.

חֶסֶד גָּבַר עַל שִׁגְגַת אָב, וְרָשָׁע הוֹסִיף חֵטְא עַל חֲטָאָיו.

טָמַן בְּלִבּוֹ מַחְשְׁבוֹת עֲרוּמָיו, וַיִּתְמַכֵּר לַעֲשׂוֹת רָעָה.

יָדוֹ שָׁלַח בִּקְדוֹשֵׁי אֵל, כַּסְפּוֹ נָתַן לְהַכְרִית זִכְרָם.

כִּרְאוֹת מָרְדְּכַי כִּי יָצָא קֶצֶף וְדָתֵי הָמָן נִתְּנוּ בְשׁוּשָׁן,

לָבַשׁ שַׂק וְקָשַׁר מִסְפֵּד, וְגָזַר צוֹם וַיֵּשֶׁב עַל הָאֵפֶר.

מִי זֶה יַעֲמוֹד לְכַפֵּר שְׁגָגָה, וְלִמְחוֹל חַטַּאת עֲוֹן אֲבוֹתֵינוּ.

ברוך... הרב את ריבנו is quoted in the Talmud (Megillah 21b).

אשר הניא, an alphabetic acrostic, recounts the story of *Purim* with poetical embellishments and closes with a eulogy of Mordecai and Esther. This *piyyut*, found in Maḥzor Vitry (page 214), was composed during the geonic period.

קשר מספד is used in the sense of עשה מספד (Micah 1:8). The phrase קושרים הספד is repeatedly found in Midrash Rabbah (Introduction to the Book of Lamentations).

After the reading of the Megillah:

Blessed art thou, Lord our God, King of the universe, who dost champion our cause and vindicate our rights, taking revenge for us, repaying all our mortal enemies as they deserve, and punishing our oppressors. Blessed art thou, O Lord, who dealest out punishment to the oppressors of Israel thy people, O thou, redeeming God.

On Purim morning omit:

The Lord wrecked the counsel of heathen,
Frustrating the plans of the crafty,
When against us rose a wicked man.
A hateful offshoot of Amalek,
Who grew in wealth and dug his own grave.
It was his power that ensnared him!
He wished to entrap and was entrapped;
He sought to destroy and was destroyed.
Haman revealed his fathers' hatred,
And stirred Esau's enmity to Jacob.
He failed to recall that he, the foe,
Was born thanks to Saul's pity for Agag.
The wicked planned to cut off the righteous;
But the impure was caught by the pure.
Mordecai's kindness offset Saul's fault;
Wicked Haman heaped guilt upon guilt.
He hid his crafty plans in his heart,
And gave himself over to evil.
He laid his hands on godly people,
Spending his wealth to destroy their name.
When Mordecai saw that wrath had gone forth,
Haman's decrees issued in Shushan,
He put on sackcloth, sign of mourning,
Proclaimed a fast and sat in ashes.
Who would rise to atone for errors,
To gain pardon for our fathers' sins?

נֵץ פָּרַח מְלוּלָב, הֵן הֲדַסָּה עָמְדָה לְעוֹרֵר יְשֵׁנִים.

סָרִיסֶיהָ הִבְהִילוּ לְהָמָן, לְהַשְׁקוֹתוֹ יֵין חֲמַת תַּנִּינִים.

עָמַד בְּעָשְׁרוֹ וְנָפַל בְּרִשְׁעוֹ, עָשָׂה לוֹ עֵץ וְנִתְלָה עָלָיו.

פִּיהֶם פָּתְחוּ כָּל יוֹשְׁבֵי תֵבֵל, כִּי פוּר הָמָן נֶהְפַּךְ לְפוּרֵנוּ.

צַדִּיק נֶחֱלַץ מִיַּד רָשָׁע, אוֹיֵב נִתַּן תַּחַת נַפְשׁוֹ.

קִיְּמוּ עֲלֵיהֶם לַעֲשׂוֹת פוּרִים, וְלִשְׂמֹחַ בְּכָל שָׁנָה וְשָׁנָה.

רָאִיתָ אֶת תְּפִלַּת מָרְדְּכַי וְאֶסְתֵּר, הָמָן וּבָנָיו עַל הָעֵץ תָּלִיתָ.

On *Purim* morning:

שׁוֹשַׁנַּת יַעֲקֹב צָהֲלָה וְשָׂמֵחָה, בִּרְאוֹתָם יַחַד תְּכֵלֶת מָרְדְּכָי,

תְּשׁוּעָתָם הָיִיתָ לָנֶצַח, וְתִקְוָתָם בְּכָל דּוֹר וָדוֹר.

לְהוֹדִיעַ שֶׁכָּל קֹוֶיךָ לֹא יֵבֹשׁוּ,

וְלֹא יִכָּלְמוּ לָנֶצַח כָּל הַחוֹסִים בָּךְ.

אָרוּר הָמָן אֲשֶׁר בִּקֵּשׁ לְאַבְּדִי; בָּרוּךְ מָרְדְּכַי הַיְּהוּדִי.

אֲרוּרָה זֶרֶשׁ אֵשֶׁת מַפְחִידִי; בְּרוּכָה אֶסְתֵּר [מְגִנָּה] בַּעֲדִי.

וְגַם חַרְבוֹנָה זָכוּר לְטוֹב.

והעיר שושן צהלה ושמחה שושנת יעקב צהלה ושמחה alludes to the biblical verse
(Esther 8:15). The passage beginning with ארור המן is quoted in Sofrim 14:6.
The two phrases ארור המן and ברוך מרדכי have the same numerical value, 502.
This clearly explains the statement: מיחייב איניש לבסומי בפוריא עד דלא ידע בין
ארור המן לברוך מרדכי (Megillah 7b), "a man should cheer himself with wine
on Purim until he cannot tell the difference between the Hebrew phrases
ברוך מרדכי and ארור המן," since they seem to signify the same thing on numerical grounds. Similar reference to identical numerical values of Hebrew
words is applied to יין and סוד (70), on the basis of which the Talmud says:
נכנס יין יצא סוד, "when wine enters, counsel leaves" (Eruvin 65a). The term
adloyada, borrowed from the foregoing talmudic passage, has been applied to
the modern Purim carnivals in Israel.

A flower blossomed forth from a palm,
Hadassah rose to stir those who slept!
Her servants hastily brought Haman,
To make him drink the wine of poison.
He rose by wealth and sank by evil,
Being hanged on the gallows he made.
All the people of the world were agape
When Haman's *pur* became our Purim.
The upright were saved from evil men;
The enemies were put in their place.
The Jews undertook to make Purim,
To rejoice each and every year.
Thou didst hear Mordecai and Esther;
Thou didst hang Haman and his sons.

On Purim morning:

The Jews of Shushan shouted for joy
When they all saw Mordecai robed in purple.
Thou hast ever been their salvation,
Their hope in every generation,
To show that all who hope in thee
Shall never be shamed nor confounded.
Cursed be Haman who sought to slay me;
Blessed be Mordecai the Judean!
Cursed be Zeresh, my menacer's wife;
Blessed be Esther, my protectress!
Harbonah, too, be well remembered.

חרבונה, a chamberlain of Ahasuerus, was instrumental in the hanging of
Haman by telling the king: "In Haman's house gallows are standing... which
he erected for Mordecai, who did good service to the king" (Esther 7:9).

תְּפִלַת הַדֶּרֶךְ

יְהִי רָצוֹן מִלְּפָנֶיךָ, יְיָ אֱלֹהֵינוּ וֵאלֹהֵי אֲבוֹתֵינוּ, שֶׁתּוֹלִיכֵנוּ
לְשָׁלוֹם וְתַצְעִידֵנוּ לְשָׁלוֹם, וְתַגִּיעֵנוּ אֶל מְחוֹז חֶפְצֵנוּ לְחַיִּים
וּלְשִׂמְחָה וּלְשָׁלוֹם. וְתַצִּילֵנוּ מִכַּף כָּל אוֹיֵב וְאוֹרֵב וְאָסוֹן
בַּדֶּרֶךְ, וְתִתְּנֵנוּ לְחֵן וּלְחֶסֶד וּלְרַחֲמִים בְּעֵינֶיךָ וּבְעֵינֵי כָל
רוֹאֵינוּ. וְתִשְׁמַע קוֹל תַּחֲנוּנֵינוּ, כִּי אֵל שׁוֹמֵעַ תְּפִלָּה וְתַחֲנוּן
אָתָּה. בָּרוּךְ אַתָּה, יְיָ, שׁוֹמֵעַ תְּפִלָּה.

וְיַעֲקֹב הָלַךְ לְדַרְכּוֹ, וַיִּפְגְּעוּ בוֹ מַלְאֲכֵי אֱלֹהִים. וַיֹּאמֶר
יַעֲקֹב כַּאֲשֶׁר רָאָם, מַחֲנֵה אֱלֹהִים זֶה; וַיִּקְרָא שֵׁם הַמָּקוֹם הַהוּא
מַחֲנָיִם.

הִנֵּה אָנֹכִי שֹׁלֵחַ מַלְאָךְ לְפָנֶיךָ, לִשְׁמָרְךָ בַּדָּרֶךְ, וְלַהֲבִיאֲךָ
אֶל הַמָּקוֹם אֲשֶׁר הֲכִנֹתִי.

יְבָרֶכְךָ יְיָ וְיִשְׁמְרֶךָ. יָאֵר יְיָ פָּנָיו אֵלֶיךָ וִיחֻנֶּךָּ. יִשָּׂא יְיָ פָּנָיו
אֵלֶיךָ וְיָשֵׂם לְךָ שָׁלוֹם.

תהלים צא

יֹשֵׁב בְּסֵתֶר עֶלְיוֹן, בְּצֵל שַׁדַּי יִתְלוֹנָן. אֹמַר לַייָ, מַחְסִי
וּמְצוּדָתִי, אֱלֹהַי אֶבְטַח בּוֹ. כִּי הוּא יַצִּילְךָ מִפַּח יָקוּשׁ, מִדֶּבֶר
הַוּוֹת. בְּאֶבְרָתוֹ יָסֶךְ לָךְ, וְתַחַת כְּנָפָיו תֶּחְסֶה; צִנָּה וְסֹחֵרָה
אֲמִתּוֹ. לֹא תִירָא מִפַּחַד לָיְלָה, מֵחֵץ יָעוּף יוֹמָם. מִדֶּבֶר בָּאֹפֶל
יַהֲלֹךְ, מִקֶּטֶב יָשׁוּד צָהֳרָיִם. יִפֹּל מִצִּדְּךָ אֶלֶף, וּרְבָבָה מִימִינֶךָ,
אֵלֶיךָ לֹא יִגָּשׁ. רַק בְּעֵינֶיךָ תַבִּיט, וְשִׁלֻּמַת רְשָׁעִים תִּרְאֶה. כִּי
אַתָּה יְיָ מַחְסִי, עֶלְיוֹן שַׂמְתָּ מְעוֹנֶךָ. לֹא תְאֻנֶּה אֵלֶיךָ רָעָה,
וְנֶגַע לֹא יִקְרַב בְּאָהֳלֶךָ. כִּי מַלְאָכָיו יְצַוֶּה־לָךְ, לִשְׁמָרְךָ בְּכָל

תפלת הדרך is quoted in the Talmud (Berakhoth 29b).

731

PRAYER FOR A SAFE JOURNEY

May it be thy will, Lord our God and God of our fathers, to lead us in safety and direct our steps in safety; mayest thou bring us to our destination in life, happiness and peace. Deliver us from every lurking enemy and danger on the road. May we obtain favor, kindness and love from thee and from all whom we meet. Hear our supplication, for thou art God who hearest prayer and supplication. Blessed art thou, O Lord, who hearest prayer.

Jacob went his way and met the angels of God. On seeing them, Jacob said: "This is God's camp," and he called the name of that place Mahanaim.

I am sending an angel in front of you, to guard you as you go and to guide you to the place I have prepared.

May the Lord bless you and protect you; may the Lord countenance you and be gracious to you; may the Lord favor you and grant you peace.[1]

Psalm 91

He who dwells in the shelter of the Most High abides under the protection of the Almighty. I call the Lord: "My refuge and my fortress, my God in whom I trust." He saves you from the fowler's snare and from the destructive pestilence. With his pinions he covers you, and under his wings you find refuge; his truth is a shield and armor. Fear not the terror of the night, nor the arrow that flies by day, nor the pestilence that stalks in darkness, nor the destruction that ravages at noon. Though a thousand fall at your side, and a myriad at your right hand, it shall not come to you. You have only to look with your eyes and see how evil men are punished. Thou, O Lord, art my refuge! When you have made the Most High your shelter, no disaster shall befall you or come near your tent. For he will give his angels charge over you, to guard you

---

[1]*Genesis* 32:2-3; *Exodus* 23:20; *Numbers* 6:24-26.

דְּרָכֶיךָ. עַל כַּפַּיִם יִשָּׂאוּנְךָ, פֶּן תִּגֹּף בָּאֶבֶן רַגְלֶךָ. עַל שַׁחַל
וָפֶתֶן תִּדְרֹךְ, תִּרְמֹס כְּפִיר וְתַנִּין. כִּי בִי חָשַׁק וַאֲפַלְּטֵהוּ;
אֲשַׂגְּבֵהוּ כִּי יָדַע שְׁמִי. יִקְרָאֵנִי וְאֶעֱנֵהוּ, עִמּוֹ אָנֹכִי בְצָרָה;
אֲחַלְּצֵהוּ וַאֲכַבְּדֵהוּ. אֹרֶךְ יָמִים אַשְׂבִּיעֵהוּ, וְאַרְאֵהוּ בִּישׁוּעָתִי.

תְּפִלָּה לְחוֹלֶה

יְיָ, אַל בְּאַפְּךָ תוֹכִיחֵנִי, וְאַל בַּחֲמָתְךָ תְיַסְּרֵנִי. חָנֵּנִי, יְיָ, כִּי
אֻמְלַל אָנִי; רְפָאֵנִי, יְיָ, כִּי נִבְהֲלוּ עֲצָמָי. וְנַפְשִׁי נִבְהֲלָה מְאֹד;
וְאַתָּה יְיָ, עַד מָתָי. שׁוּבָה, יְיָ, חַלְּצָה נַפְשִׁי; הוֹשִׁיעֵנִי לְמַעַן
חַסְדֶּךָ. כִּי אֵין בַּמָּוֶת זִכְרֶךָ; בִּשְׁאוֹל מִי יוֹדֶה לָּךְ. יָגַעְתִּי
בְּאַנְחָתִי, אַשְׂחֶה בְכָל לַיְלָה מִטָּתִי; בְּדִמְעָתִי עַרְשִׂי אַמְסֶה.
עָשְׁשָׁה מִכַּעַס עֵינִי; עָתְקָה בְּכָל צוֹרְרָי. סוּרוּ מִמֶּנִּי, כָּל פֹּעֲלֵי
אָוֶן, כִּי שָׁמַע יְיָ קוֹל בִּכְיִי. שָׁמַע יְיָ תְּחִנָּתִי; יְיָ תְּפִלָּתִי יִקָּח.
יֵבֹשׁוּ וְיִבָּהֲלוּ מְאֹד כָּל אֹיְבָי; יָשֻׁבוּ יֵבֹשׁוּ רָגַע.

תהלים כג

מִזְמוֹר לְדָוִד. יְיָ רֹעִי, לֹא אֶחְסָר. בִּנְאוֹת דֶּשֶׁא יַרְבִּיצֵנִי,
עַל מֵי מְנֻחוֹת יְנַהֲלֵנִי. נַפְשִׁי יְשׁוֹבֵב, יַנְחֵנִי בְמַעְגְּלֵי צֶדֶק לְמַעַן
שְׁמוֹ. גַּם כִּי אֵלֵךְ בְּגֵיא צַלְמָוֶת לֹא אִירָא רָע, כִּי אַתָּה עִמָּדִי;
שִׁבְטְךָ וּמִשְׁעַנְתֶּךָ, הֵמָּה יְנַחֲמֻנִי. תַּעֲרֹךְ לְפָנַי שֻׁלְחָן נֶגֶד צֹרְרָי;
דִּשַּׁנְתָּ בַשֶּׁמֶן רֹאשִׁי, כּוֹסִי רְוָיָה. אַךְ טוֹב וָחֶסֶד יִרְדְּפוּנִי כָּל
יְמֵי חַיָּי; וְשַׁבְתִּי בְּבֵית יְיָ לְאֹרֶךְ יָמִים.

רְפָאֵנוּ יְיָ וְנֵרָפֵא, הוֹשִׁיעֵנוּ וְנִוָּשֵׁעָה, כִּי תְהִלָּתֵנוּ אָתָּה;
וְהַעֲלֵה רְפוּאָה שְׁלֵמָה לְכָל מַכּוֹתֵינוּ, כִּי אֵל מֶלֶךְ רוֹפֵא נֶאֱמָן
וְרַחֲמָן אָתָּה. בָּרוּךְ אַתָּה, יְיָ, רוֹפֵא חוֹלֵי עַמּוֹ יִשְׂרָאֵל.

in all your ways. They will bear you upon their hands, lest you strike your foot against a stone. You shall tread upon the lion and the asp; you shall trample the young lion and the serpent. "Because he clings to me, I deliver him; I protect him because he loves me. When he calls upon me, I answer him; I am with him when he is in trouble; I rescue him and bring him to honor. I enrich him with long life, and let him witness my deliverance."

PRAYER FOR THE SICK

O Lord, punish me not in thy anger; chastise me not in thy wrath. Have pity on me, O Lord, for I languish away; heal me, O Lord, for my health is shaken. My soul is severely troubled; and thou, O Lord, how long? O Lord, deliver my life once again; save me because of thy grace. For in death there is no thought of thee; in the grave who gives thanks to thee? I am worn out with my groaning; every night I flood my bed with tears; I cause my couch to melt with my weeping. My eye is dimmed from grief; it grows old because of all my foes. Depart from me, all you evildoers, for the Lord has heard the sound of my weeping. The Lord has heard my supplication; the Lord receives my prayer. All my foes shall be utterly ashamed and terrified; they shall turn back; they shall be suddenly ashamed.[1]

Psalm 23

A psalm of David. The Lord is my shepherd; I am not in want. He makes me lie down in green meadows; he leads me beside refreshing streams. He restores my life; he guides me by righteous paths for his own sake. Even though I walk through the darkest valley, I fear no harm; for thou art with me. Thy rod and thy staff —they comfort me. Thou spreadest a feast for me in the presence of my enemies. Thou hast perfumed my head with oil; my cup overflows. Only goodness and kindness shall follow me all the days of my life; I shall dwell in the house of the Lord forever.

Heal us, O Lord, and we shall be healed; save us and we shall be saved; for thou art our praise. Grant a perfect healing to all our wounds; for thou art a faithful and merciful God, King and Healer. Blessed art thou, O Lord, who healest the sick among thy people Israel.

---

[1] Psalm 6.

צִדּוּק הַדִּין

Burial service held on days when *Taḥanun* (page 103) is recited

הַצּוּר תָּמִים פָּעֳלוֹ, כִּי כָל דְּרָכָיו מִשְׁפָּט; אֵל אֱמוּנָה וְאֵין
עָוֶל, צַדִּיק וְיָשָׁר הוּא.

הַצּוּר תָּמִים בְּכָל פֹּעַל, מִי יֹאמַר לוֹ מַה תִּפְעָל; הַשַּׁלִּיט
בְּמַטָּה וּבְמַעַל, מֵמִית וּמְחַיֶּה, מוֹרִיד שְׁאוֹל וַיָּעַל.

הַצּוּר תָּמִים בְּכָל מַעֲשֶׂה, מִי יֹאמַר אֵלָיו מַה תַּעֲשֶׂה;
הָאוֹמֵר וְעֹשֶׂה, חֶסֶד חִנָּם לָנוּ תַעֲשֶׂה; וּבִזְכוּת הַנֶּעֱקָד כְּשֶׂה,
הַקְשִׁיבָה וַעֲשֵׂה.

צַדִּיק בְּכָל דְּרָכָיו, הַצּוּר תָּמִים, אֶרֶךְ אַפָּיִם וּמָלֵא רַחֲמִים,
חֲמָל־נָא וְחוּס נָא עַל אָבוֹת וּבָנִים, כִּי לְךָ אֲדוֹן הַסְּלִיחוֹת
וְהָרַחֲמִים.

צַדִּיק אַתָּה, יְיָ, לְהָמִית וּלְהַחֲיוֹת; אֲשֶׁר בְּיָדְךָ פִּקְדוֹן כָּל
רוּחוֹת, חָלִילָה לְךָ זִכְרוֹנֵנוּ לִמְחוֹת; וְיִהְיוּ נָא עֵינֶיךָ בְּרַחֲמִים
עָלֵינוּ פְּקוּחוֹת, כִּי לְךָ אֲדוֹן הָרַחֲמִים וְהַסְּלִיחוֹת.

אָדָם אִם בֶּן־שָׁנָה יִחְיֶה, אוֹ אֶלֶף שָׁנִים יִחְיֶה, מַה יִּתְרוֹן לוֹ;
כְּלֹא הָיָה יִהְיֶה; בָּרוּךְ דַּיַּן הָאֱמֶת, מֵמִית וּמְחַיֶּה.

בָּרוּךְ הוּא, כִּי אֱמֶת דִּינוֹ, וּמְשׁוֹטֵט הַכֹּל בְּעֵינוֹ, וּמְשַׁלֵּם
לְאָדָם חֶשְׁבּוֹנוֹ וְדִינוֹ, וְהַכֹּל לִשְׁמוֹ הוֹדָיָה יִתֵּנוּ.

צדוק הדין, the submission to the justice of the divine judgment, is mentioned in the Talmud (Abodah Zarah 18a) in connection with the martyrdom

735

ACKNOWLEDGMENT OF DIVINE JUSTICE

Burial service held on days when Taḥanan (page 104) is recited

He is God; what he does is right, for all his ways are just; God of faithfulness and without wrong, just and right is he.[1]

He is God, perfect in every deed; who can say to him: "What art thou doing?" He rules below and above; he causes death and life; he brings down to the grave and raises up.

He is God, perfect in every deed; who can say to him: "What art thou doing?" O thou who decreest and performest, show us unmerited kindness; for the sake of Isaac who was bound like a lamb, listen and take action.

O thou who art righteous in all thy ways, thou who art the perfect God, slow to anger and full of mercy, have compassion, have pity on parents and children; for thine, O Lord, is forgiveness and mercy.

Just art thou, O Lord, in causing death and life; thou in whose hand all living beings are kept, far be it from thee to blot out our remembrance; let thy eyes be open to us in mercy; for thine, O Lord, is mercy and forgiveness.

Whether one lives a year or a thousand years—what does he gain? He is as though he were non-existent. Blessed be the true Judge, who causes death and life.

Blessed be he, for his judgment is true; his eye ranges over all, and he punishes and rewards man according to strict account; all must render acknowledgment to him.

---

of Rabbi Ḥanina ben Teradyon and his family. Before the execution was carried out by the Romans, Rabbi Ḥanina quoted the biblical verse הצור תמים פעלו; his wife continued it: אל אמונה ואין עול, צדיק וישר הוא, כי כל דרכיו משפט (Deuteronomy 32:4); and the daughter quoted: ...גדול העצה ורב העליליה (Jeremiah 32:19). These passages were later embodied in the rhymed verses of *tsidduk ha-din*, the burial service.

---

[1] *Deuteronomy* 32:4.

736

יָדַעְנוּ, יְיָ, כִּי צֶדֶק מִשְׁפָּטֶיךָ, תִּצְדַּק בְּדָבְרֶךָ, וְתִזְכֶּה
בְּשָׁפְטֶךָ, וְאֵין לְהַרְהֵר אַחַר מִדַּת שָׁפְטֶךָ; צַדִּיק אַתָּה, יְיָ,
וְיָשָׁר מִשְׁפָּטֶךָ.

דַּיַּן אֱמֶת, שׁוֹפֵט צֶדֶק וֶאֱמֶת; בָּרוּךְ דַּיַּן הָאֱמֶת, שֶׁכָּל
מִשְׁפָּטָיו צֶדֶק וֶאֱמֶת.

נֶפֶשׁ כָּל חַי בְּיָדֶךָ, צֶדֶק מָלְאָה יְמִינְךָ וְיָדֶךָ, רַחֵם עַל
פְּלֵיטַת צֹאן יָדֶךָ, וְתֹאמַר לַמַּלְאָךְ הֶרֶף יָדֶךָ.

גְּדֹל הָעֵצָה וְרַב הָעֲלִילִיָּה, אֲשֶׁר עֵינֶיךָ פְּקֻחוֹת עַל כָּל
דַּרְכֵי בְּנֵי אָדָם, לָתֵת לְאִישׁ כִּדְרָכָיו וְכִפְרִי מַעֲלָלָיו.

לְהַגִּיד כִּי יָשָׁר יְיָ; צוּרִי, וְלֹא עַוְלָתָה בּוֹ.

יְיָ נָתַן, וַיְיָ לָקָח; יְהִי שֵׁם יְיָ מְבֹרָךְ.

וְהוּא רַחוּם, יְכַפֵּר עָוֹן וְלֹא יַשְׁחִית; וְהִרְבָּה לְהָשִׁיב אַפּוֹ,
וְלֹא יָעִיר כָּל חֲמָתוֹ.

MOURNERS' KADDISH

Recited after the burial

יִתְגַּדַּל וְיִתְקַדַּשׁ שְׁמֵהּ רַבָּא בְּעָלְמָא דְּהוּא עָתִיד
לְחַדָּתָא, וּלְאַחֲיָאָה מֵתַיָּא, וּלְאַסָּקָא יָתְהוֹן לְחַיֵּי עָלְמָא,
וּלְמִבְנֵא קַרְתָּא דִירוּשְׁלֵם וּלְשַׁכְלָלָא הֵיכְלֵהּ בְּגַוַּהּ, וּלְמֶעֱקַר
פֻּלְחָנָא נֻכְרָאָה מִן אַרְעָא, וְלַאֲתָבָא פֻּלְחָנָא דִשְׁמַיָּא לְאַתְרֵהּ.
וְיַמְלוֹךְ קֻדְשָׁא בְּרִיךְ הוּא בְּמַלְכוּתֵהּ וִיקָרֵהּ בְּחַיֵּיכוֹן
וּבְיוֹמֵיכוֹן, וּבְחַיֵּי דְכָל בֵּית יִשְׂרָאֵל, בַּעֲגָלָא וּבִזְמַן קָרִיב,
וְאִמְרוּ אָמֵן.

<hr>

קדִּישׁ ל(אתֹ)חֲדַתָּא refers to the restoration of the Holy Land. The Sephardic Jews recite this Kaddish on the fast of *Tish'ah b'Av*. Maimonides quotes it as the *Kaddish d'Rabbanan* to be recited at the conclusion of a talmudic discourse; compare Sofrim 19:12.

We know, O Lord, that thy judgment is just; thou art right when thou speakest, and justified when thou givest sentence; one must not find fault with thy manner of judging. Thou art righteous, O Lord, and thy judgment is right.

True and righteous Judge, blessed art thou, all whose judgments are righteous and true.

The life of every living being is in thy hand; thy right hand is full of righteousness. Have mercy on the remnant of thy own flock, and say to the angel: "Stay your hand."

Thou art great in counsel and mighty in action; thy eyes are open to all the ways of men, to give to every one according to his conduct and according to the results of his doings.[1]

We proclaim that the Lord is just. He is my stronghold, and there is no wrong in him.[2]

The Lord gave and the Lord has taken away; blessed be the name of the Lord.[3]

He being merciful, forgives iniquity and does not destroy; frequently he turns his anger away, and does not stir up all his wrath.[4]

MOURNERS' KADDISH

Recited after the burial

Glorified and sanctified be God's great name throughout the world which he will renew, reviving the dead and raising them to life eternal; rebuilding the city of Jerusalem and establishing his shrine therein; uprooting idolatry from the earth and restoring divine worship to its site. May the Holy One, blessed be he, reign in his majestic glory in your lifetime and during your days, and within the life of the entire house of Israel, speedily and soon; and say, Amen.

---

[1] *Jeremiah* 32:19. [2] *Psalm* 92:16 [3] *Job* 1:21. [4] *Psalm* 78:38.

יְהֵא שְׁמֵהּ רַבָּא מְבָרַךְ לְעָלַם וּלְעָלְמֵי עָלְמַיָּא.

יִתְבָּרַךְ וְיִשְׁתַּבַּח, וְיִתְפָּאַר וְיִתְרוֹמַם, וְיִתְנַשֵּׂא וְיִתְהַדָּר,
וְיִתְעַלֶּה וְיִתְהַלָּל שְׁמֵהּ דְּקֻדְשָׁא, בְּרִיךְ הוּא, לְעֵלָּא מִן כָּל
בִּרְכָתָא וְשִׁירָתָא, תֻּשְׁבְּחָתָא וְנֶחֱמָתָא, דַּאֲמִירָן בְּעָלְמָא,
וְאִמְרוּ אָמֵן.

יְהֵא שְׁלָמָא רַבָּא מִן שְׁמַיָּא, וְחַיִּים, עָלֵינוּ וְעַל כָּל יִשְׂרָאֵל,
וְאִמְרוּ אָמֵן.

עֹשֶׂה שָׁלוֹם בִּמְרוֹמָיו, הוּא יַעֲשֶׂה שָׁלוֹם עָלֵינוּ וְעַל כָּל
יִשְׂרָאֵל, וְאִמְרוּ אָמֵן.

On leaving the burial ground all wash their hands and say:

בִּלַּע הַמָּוֶת לָנֶצַח, וּמָחָה אֲדֹנָי אֱלֹהִים דִּמְעָה מֵעַל כָּל
פָּנִים; וְחֶרְפַּת עַמּוֹ יָסִיר מֵעַל כָּל הָאָרֶץ, כִּי יְיָ דִּבֵּר.

FUNERAL SERVICE AT THE CHAPEL

יְיָ, מָה אָדָם וַתֵּדָעֵהוּ, בֶּן־אֱנוֹשׁ וַתְּחַשְּׁבֵהוּ.

אָדָם לַהֶבֶל דָּמָה, יָמָיו כְּצֵל עוֹבֵר.

בַּבֹּקֶר יָצִיץ וְחָלָף, לָעֶרֶב יְמוֹלֵל וְיָבֵשׁ.

לִמְנוֹת יָמֵינוּ כֵּן הוֹדַע, וְנָבִא לְבַב חָכְמָה.

שְׁמָר־תָּם וּרְאֵה יָשָׁר, כִּי אַחֲרִית לְאִישׁ שָׁלוֹם.

אַךְ אֱלֹהִים יִפְדֶּה נַפְשִׁי מִיַּד שְׁאוֹל, כִּי יִקָּחֵנִי סֶלָה.

כָּלָה שְׁאֵרִי וּלְבָבִי, צוּר לְבָבִי וְחֶלְקִי אֱלֹהִים לְעוֹלָם.

וְיָשָׁב הֶעָפָר עַל הָאָרֶץ כְּשֶׁהָיָה, וְהָרוּחַ תָּשׁוּב אֶל
הָאֱלֹהִים אֲשֶׁר נְתָנָהּ.

Add Psalm 23 (page 733).

May his great name be blessed forever and to all eternity.

Blessed and praised, glorified and exalted, extolled and honored, adored and lauded be the name of the Holy One, blessed be he, beyond all the blessings and hymns, praises and consolations that are ever spoken in the world; and say, Amen.

May there be abundant peace from heaven, and life, for us and for all Israel; and say, Amen.

He who creates peace in his celestial heights, may he create peace for us and for all Israel; and say, Amen.

On leaving the burial ground all wash their hands and say:

He will destroy death forever; the Lord God will wipe away tears from every face, and will remove from all the earth all insult against his people; for the Lord has spoken.[1][7]

FUNERAL SERVICE AT THE CHAPEL

O Lord, what is man that thou shouldst notice him?
What is mortal man that thou shouldst consider him?

Man is like a breath;
His days are like a passing shadow.

He flourishes and grows in the morning;
He fades and withers in the evening.

O teach us how to number our days,
That we may attain a heart of wisdom.

Mark the innocent, look upon the upright;
For there is a future for the man of peace.

Surely God will free me from the grave;
He will receive me indeed.

My flesh and my heart fail,
Yet God is my strength forever.

The dust returns to the earth as it was,
But the spirit returns to God who gave it.[2]

Add Psalm 23 (page 734).

---

[1]*Isaiah* 25:8. [2]*Psalms* 144:3-4; 90:6,12; 37:37; 49:16; 73:26; *Ecclesiastes* 12:7.

בְּרִית מִילָה

When the child is brought for circumcision, the guests rise and say:

בָּרוּךְ הַבָּא.

The father of the child:

הִנְנִי מוּכָן וּמְזֻמָּן לְקַיֵּם מִצְוַת עֲשֵׂה, שֶׁצִּוָּנוּ הַבּוֹרֵא יִתְבָּרַךְ, לָמוּל אֶת בְּנִי, כַּכָּתוּב בַּתּוֹרָה: וּבֶן־שְׁמֹנַת יָמִים יִמּוֹל לָכֶם כָּל זָכָר לְדֹרֹתֵיכֶם.

The *Mohel*, placing the child upon the sandek's knees:

זֶה הַכִּסֵּא שֶׁל אֵלִיָּהוּ זָכוּר לַטּוֹב.

לִישׁוּעָתְךָ קִוִּיתִי, יְיָ. שִׂבַּרְתִּי לִישׁוּעָתְךָ, יְיָ, וּמִצְוֹתֶיךָ עָשִׂיתִי. שִׂבַּרְתִּי לִישׁוּעָתְךָ, יְיָ. שָׂשׂ אָנֹכִי עַל אִמְרָתֶךָ, כְּמוֹצֵא שָׁלָל רָב. שָׁלוֹם רָב לְאֹהֲבֵי תוֹרָתֶךָ, וְאֵין לָמוֹ מִכְשׁוֹל. אַשְׁרֵי תִּבְחַר וּתְקָרֵב, יִשְׁכֹּן חֲצֵרֶיךָ—

All:

נִשְׂבְּעָה בְּטוּב בֵּיתֶךָ, קְדֹשׁ הֵיכָלֶךָ.

The *Mohel*, before operating:

בָּרוּךְ אַתָּה, יְיָ אֱלֹהֵינוּ, מֶלֶךְ הָעוֹלָם, אֲשֶׁר קִדְּשָׁנוּ בְּמִצְוֹתָיו וְצִוָּנוּ עַל הַמִּילָה.

The father, after the circumcision:

בָּרוּךְ אַתָּה, יְיָ אֱלֹהֵינוּ, מֶלֶךְ הָעוֹלָם, אֲשֶׁר קִדְּשָׁנוּ בְּמִצְוֹתָיו וְצִוָּנוּ לְהַכְנִיסוֹ בִּבְרִיתוֹ שֶׁל אַבְרָהָם אָבִינוּ.

ברוך הבא, the greeting extended to the infant, is at the same time a welcome to Elijah, the "angel of the covenant" and protector of children, who is said to be the invisible participant at circumcisions. The word הבא is said to be composed of the initials of הנה בא אליהו and to allude to the eight-days-old boy to be circumcised (הבא numerically equals eight).

BRITH MILAH

When the child is brought for circumcision, the guests rise and say:

Blessed be he who enters.

The father of the child:

I am ready to perform the precept of circumcising my son. as the Creator, blessed be he, has commanded us in the Torah: "Every male among you, throughout your generations, shall be circumcised when he is eight days old."[1]

The Mohel, placing the child upon the sandek's knees:

This is the throne of Elijah, of blessed memory.

O Lord, I hope for thy salvation. I wait for thy deliverance, O Lord, and I do thy bidding. I delight in thy promise, like one who finds abundant wealth. Abundant peace have they who love thy Torah, and there is no stumbling for them. Happy is he whom thou choosest to dwell in thy courts, close to thee.

All:

May we fully enjoy the goodness of thy house, thy holy shrine.[2]

The Mohel, before operating:

Blessed art thou, Lord our God, King of the universe, who hast sanctified us with thy commandments, and commanded us concerning circumcision.

The father, after the circumcision:

Blessed art thou, Lord our God, King of the universe, who hast sanctified us with thy commandments, and commanded us to introduce my son into the covenant of Abraham our father.

כסא של אליהו, the special chair reserved for Elijah, is left in position for three days because the first three days after circumcision are a dangerous period for the child.

---

[1]*Genesis* 17:12.　[2]*Genesis* 49:18; *Psalms* 119:162-166; 65:5.

742

All:

כְּשֵׁם שֶׁנִּכְנַס לַבְּרִית, כֵּן יִכָּנֵס לְתוֹרָה וּלְחֻפָּה וּלְמַעֲשִׂים טוֹבִים.

The Mohel:

בָּרוּךְ אַתָּה, יְיָ אֱלֹהֵינוּ, מֶלֶךְ הָעוֹלָם, בּוֹרֵא פְּרִי הַגָּפֶן.

בָּרוּךְ אַתָּה, יְיָ אֱלֹהֵינוּ, מֶלֶךְ הָעוֹלָם, אֲשֶׁר קִדֵּשׁ יְדִיד מִבֶּטֶן, וְחֹק בִּשְׁאֵרוֹ שָׂם, וְצֶאֱצָאָיו חָתַם בְּאוֹת בְּרִית קֹדֶשׁ. עַל כֵּן, בִּשְׂכַר זֹאת, אֵל חַי, חֶלְקֵנוּ, צוּרֵנוּ, צַוֵּה לְהַצִּיל יְדִידוּת שְׁאֵרֵנוּ מִשַּׁחַת, לְמַעַן בְּרִיתוֹ אֲשֶׁר שָׂם בִּבְשָׂרֵנוּ. בָּרוּךְ אַתָּה, יְיָ, כּוֹרֵת הַבְּרִית.

אֱלֹהֵינוּ וֵאלֹהֵי אֲבוֹתֵינוּ, קַיֵּם אֶת הַיֶּלֶד הַזֶּה לְאָבִיו וּלְאִמּוֹ, וְיִקָּרֵא שְׁמוֹ בְּיִשְׂרָאֵל (פלוני בן פלוני). יִשְׂמַח הָאָב בְּיוֹצֵא חֲלָצָיו, וְתָגֵל אִמּוֹ בִּפְרִי בִטְנָה, כַּכָּתוּב: יִשְׂמַח אָבִיךָ וְאִמֶּךָ, וְתָגֵל יוֹלַדְתֶּךָ. וְנֶאֱמַר: וָאֶעֱבֹר עָלַיִךְ וָאֶרְאֵךְ מִתְבּוֹסֶסֶת בְּדָמָיִךְ, וָאֹמַר לָךְ בְּדָמַיִךְ חֲיִי; וָאֹמַר לָךְ בְּדָמַיִךְ חֲיִי. וְנֶאֱמַר: זָכַר לְעוֹלָם בְּרִיתוֹ, דָּבָר צִוָּה לְאֶלֶף דּוֹר. אֲשֶׁר כָּרַת אֶת אַבְרָהָם, וּשְׁבוּעָתוֹ לְיִצְחָק. וַיַּעֲמִידֶהָ לְיַעֲקֹב לְחֹק, לְיִשְׂרָאֵל בְּרִית עוֹלָם. וְנֶאֱמַר: וַיָּמָל אַבְרָהָם אֶת יִצְחָק בְּנוֹ בֶּן שְׁמֹנַת יָמִים, כַּאֲשֶׁר צִוָּה אֹתוֹ אֱלֹהִים. הוֹדוּ לַיְיָ כִּי טוֹב, כִּי לְעוֹלָם חַסְדּוֹ. זֶה הַקָּטֹן (פלוני) גָּדוֹל יִהְיֶה. כְּשֵׁם שֶׁנִּכְנַס לַבְּרִית, כֵּן יִכָּנֵס לְתוֹרָה וּלְחֻפָּה וּלְמַעֲשִׂים טוֹבִים.

כשם שנכנס לברית and the passages which follow are quoted in the Talmud (Shabbath 137b).

סנדק has been identified with the Greek term "synteknos" denoting literally "with the child." The *sandek*, whose privilege it is to hold the child on his knees during the operation, became known in medieval times as Gottvater, G'vater (Kwater). At a later period, the title "Kwater" was conferred upon the person handing the infant to the *Mohel*.

All:

Even as he has been introduced into the covenant, so may he be introduced to the Torah, to the marriage canopy, and to a life of good deeds.

The Mohel:

Blessed art thou, Lord our God, King of the universe, who createst the fruit of the vine.

Blessed art thou, Lord our God, King of the universe, who didst sanctify beloved Israel from birth, impressing thy statute in his flesh and marking his descendants with the sign of the holy covenant. Because of this, for the sake of the covenant thou didst impress in our flesh, O eternal God, our Stronghold, deliver our dearly beloved from destruction. Blessed art thou, O Lord, Author of the covenant.

Our God and God of our fathers, sustain this child for his father and mother. Let him be called in Israel . . . son of . . . May both husband and wife rejoice in their offspring, as it is written: "Let your parents be happy; let your mother thrill with joy."

"I passed by you and saw you weltering in your blood. Live through your blood—I said to you—live through your blood."

"He remembers his covenant forever, the word which he pledged for a thousand generations, the covenant he made with Abraham, and his oath to Isaac. He confirmed the same to Jacob as a statute, to Israel as an everlasting covenant."

"Abraham circumcised his son Isaac when he was eight days old, as God had commanded him."

"Give thanks to the Lord, for he is good; his mercy endures forever."[1] May this child, named . . . , become great. Even as he has been introduced into the covenant, so may he be introduced to the Torah, to the marriage canopy, and to a life of good deeds.

Proverbs 23:25; *Ezekiel* 16:6; *Psalm* 105:8-10; *Genesis* 21:4; *Psalm* 118:1.

Leader:

אֶפְתַּח בְּשִׁיר פִּי וּשְׂפָתַי   בִּרְשׁוּת מוֹרַי וְרַבּוֹתַי

בָּרוּךְ הַבָּא בְּשֵׁם יְיָ.   וְתֹאמַרְנָה עַצְמוֹתַי

All:

נוֹדֶה לְשִׁמְךָ בְּתוֹךְ אֱמוּנַי   בְּרוּכִים אַתֶּם לַיְיָ.

Grace is continued on page 759.

The following is inserted after בעיני אלהים ואדם (page 767).

הָרַחֲמָן, הוּא יְבָרֵךְ אֲבִי הַיֶּלֶד וְאִמּוֹ

וְיִזְכּוּ לְגַדְּלוֹ וּלְחַנְּכוֹ וּלְחַכְּמוֹ;

מִיּוֹם הַשְּׁמִינִי וָהָלְאָה יֵרָצֶה דָמוֹ

וִיהִי יְיָ אֱלֹהָיו עִמּוֹ.

הָרַחֲמָן, הוּא יְבָרֵךְ בַּעַל בְּרִית הַמִּילָה

אֲשֶׁר שָׂשׂ לַעֲשׂוֹת צֶדֶק בְּגִילָה;

וִישַׁלֵּם פָּעֳלוֹ וּמַשְׂכֻּרְתּוֹ כְּפוּלָה

וְיִתְּנֵהוּ לְמַעְלָה לְמָעְלָה.

הָרַחֲמָן, הוּא יְבָרֵךְ רַךְ הַנִּמּוֹל לִשְׁמוֹנָה

וְיִהְיוּ יָדָיו וְלִבּוֹ לְאֵל אֱמוּנָה;

וְיִזְכֶּה לִרְאוֹת פְּנֵי הַשְּׁכִינָה

שָׁלֹשׁ פְּעָמִים בַּשָּׁנָה.

הָרַחֲמָן, הוּא יְבָרֵךְ הַמָּל בְּשַׂר הָעָרְלָה

וּפָרַע וּמָצַץ דְּמֵי הַמִּילָה;

אִישׁ הַיָּרֵא וְרַךְ הַלֵּבָב עֲבוֹדָתוֹ פְּסוּלָה

אִם שְׁלָשׁ־אֵלֶּה לֹא יַעֲשֶׂה לָהּ.

הרחמן, inserted at the closing of grace, is a poem by Rabbi Abraham ben Isaac ha-Kohen who lived in Germany (eleventh century).

Leader:

On behalf of all those gathered here,
I open my lips with a poem,
And my entire being does exclaim:
Happy he who comes in the Lord's name.

All:

We praise his name amidst the faithful;
May the Lord's blessing rest upon you.

Grace is continued on page 760.

The following is inserted after "God and men" (page 768).

May God bless this child's father and mother;
May they bring him up and teach him wisdom.
Henceforth may his blood win favor for him;
May the Lord his God ever be with him.

May God bless the one who served as sandek,
And has performed a good deed joyously.
May God richly reward his services,
And place him ever higher and higher.

May God bless this tender child of eight days;
May his hands and his heart be firm with God.
May he be privileged to make visits
To Jerusalem three times every year.

May God bless him who removed the foreskin,
And did fulfill all that had been ordained.
One who is faint-hearted must not perform
This service which includes three essentials.

שלש פעמים בשנה and ידי אמונה are phrases borrowed from Exodus 17:12;
אם שלש-אלה לא and ,Deuteronomy 20:8 is taken from איש הירא ורך הלבב 23:17.
is based upon the expression חתני מולות דמים .from Exodus 21:11 יעשה לה
(Exodus 4·26). חתן דמים למולות

הָרַחֲמָן, הוּא יִשְׁלַח לָנוּ מְשִׁיחוֹ הוֹלֵךְ תָּמִים

בִּזְכוּת חַתְנֵי מוּלוֹת דָּמִים;

לְבַשֵּׂר בְּשׂוֹרוֹת טוֹבוֹת וְנִחוּמִים

לְעַם אֶחָד מְפֻזָּר וּמְפֹרָד בֵּין הָעַמִּים.

הָרַחֲמָן, הוּא יִשְׁלַח לָנוּ כֹּהֵן צֶדֶק אֲשֶׁר לֻקַּח לְעֵילוֹם

עַד הוּכַן כִּסְאוֹ כַּשֶּׁמֶשׁ וְיַהֲלוֹם;

וַיֵּלֶט פָּנָיו בְּאַדַּרְתּוֹ וַיִּגְלֹם

בְּרִיתִי הָיְתָה אִתּוֹ הַחַיִּים וְהַשָּׁלוֹם.

פִּדְיוֹן הַבֵּן

Performed on the thirty-first day after birth. Should the child's father be a kohen or a Levite, or the mother the daughter of a kohen or Levite, they are exempt from this duty. If the thirty-first day falls on a Sabbath or a major festival, the *Pidyon ha-Ben* is postponed until the following day.

Presenting the child to the *kohen*, the father says:

זֶה בְּנִי בְכוֹרִי הוּא פֶּטֶר רֶחֶם לְאִמּוֹ, וְהַקָּדוֹשׁ בָּרוּךְ הוּא צִוָּה לִפְדוֹתוֹ, שֶׁנֶּאֱמַר: וּפְדוּיָו מִבֶּן חֹדֶשׁ תִּפְדֶּה בְּעֶרְכְּךָ כֶּסֶף חֲמֵשֶׁת שְׁקָלִים, בְּשֶׁקֶל הַקֹּדֶשׁ, עֶשְׂרִים גֵּרָה הוּא. וְנֶאֱמַר: קַדֶּשׁ־לִי כָל בְּכוֹר; פֶּטֶר כָּל רֶחֶם בִּבְנֵי יִשְׂרָאֵל, בָּאָדָם וּבַבְּהֵמָה, לִי הוּא.

לֻקַּח לְעֵילוֹם refers to Elijah's translation to heaven (II Kings 2:1-12). The word לְעֵילוֹם (=לְעוֹלָם) occurs only once in the Bible (II Chronicles 33:7). The poet chose this word for a double connotation: eternity and concealment.

וַיֵּלֶט פָּנָיו בְּאַדַּרְתּוֹ וַיִּגְלֹם is a combination of two biblical verses concerning Elijah (I Kings 19:13; II Kings 2:8).

פדיון הבן, the redemption of the first-born son (of the mother), is based on Exodus 13:13 and Numbers 18:16. Originally, the first-born sons belonged to

May God send us his faultless Messiah
For the sake of our innocent children,
To bring good tidings and consolation
To a people dispersed among the nations.

May God send us Elijah the true priest,
Concealed till his bright throne be ready,
The prophet who wrapped his face in his mantle
When God's covenant was made for life and peace.

REDEMPTION OF THE FIRST-BORN SON

*Performed on the thirty-first day after birth. Should the child's father be a
kohen or a Levite, or the mother the daughter of a kohen or Levite, they are exempt
from this duty. If the thirty-first day falls on a Sabbath or a major festival, the
Pidyon ha-Ben is postponed until the following day.*

Presenting the child to the kohen, the father says:

This is my first-born son, the first-born of his mother. The Holy
One, blessed be he, has commanded to redeem him, as it is said:
"The redemption-price for each first-born son of the age of one
month shall be fixed at five sacred silver shekels at the rate of
twenty gerahs." And it is said: "Consecrate every first-born to me,
whatever is first-born in Israel, of man or beast, since it belongs
to me."[1]

---

the service of God. Later, instead of the first-born of all the tribes, the Levites
were chosen for service in connection with the sanctuary. In return for this,
every first-born Israelite was to be redeemed by paying five shekels to a *kohen*,
descendant of Levi. The two blessings recited by the father are found in
Pesaḥim 121b.

שקל הקדש may have received its name from the fact that the standard
weight of the silver shekel (=סלע in post-biblical Hebrew) was kept in the
Temple. Tradition has it that the sacred shekel had twice the value of a
common shekel.

---

[1] *Numbers* 18:16; *Exodus* 13:2.

Kohen:

מַאי בָּעִית טְפֵי לִתֶּן לִי, בִּנְךָ בְּכוֹרְךָ שֶׁהוּא פֶּטֶר רֶחֶם
לְאִמּוֹ, אוֹ בָּעִית לִפְדּוֹתוֹ בְּעַד חָמֵשׁ סְלָעִים, כְּדִמְחַיַּבְתְּ
מִדְּאוֹרַיְתָא.

Father:

חָפֵץ אֲנִי לִפְדּוֹת אֶת בְּנִי, וְהֵילָךְ דְּמֵי פִדְיוֹנוֹ, כְּדִמְחַיַּבְתִּי
מִדְּאוֹרַיְתָא.

בָּרוּךְ אַתָּה, יְיָ אֱלֹהֵינוּ, מֶלֶךְ הָעוֹלָם, אֲשֶׁר קִדְּשָׁנוּ בְּמִצְוֹתָיו
וְצִוָּנוּ עַל פִּדְיוֹן הַבֵּן.

בָּרוּךְ אַתָּה, יְיָ אֱלֹהֵינוּ, מֶלֶךְ הָעוֹלָם, שֶׁהֶחֱיָנוּ וְקִיְּמָנוּ
וְהִגִּיעָנוּ לַזְּמַן הַזֶּה.

Holding the redemption-money over the child's head, the *kohen* says:

זֶה תַּחַת זֶה, זֶה חִלּוּף זֶה, זֶה מָחוּל עַל זֶה; וְיִכָּנֵס זֶה הַבֵּן
לְחַיִּים, לְתוֹרָה וּלְיִרְאַת שָׁמָיִם. יְהִי רָצוֹן, שֶׁכְּשֵׁם שֶׁנִּכְנַס
לַפִּדְיוֹן, כֵּן יִכָּנֵס לְתוֹרָה וּלְחֻפָּה וּלְמַעֲשִׂים טוֹבִים. אָמֵן.

Placing his hand on the child's head:

יְשִׂמְךָ אֱלֹהִים כְּאֶפְרַיִם וְכִמְנַשֶּׁה. יְבָרֶכְךָ יְיָ וְיִשְׁמְרֶךָ. יָאֵר
יְיָ פָּנָיו אֵלֶיךָ וִיחֻנֶּךָּ. יִשָּׂא יְיָ פָּנָיו אֵלֶיךָ, וְיָשֵׂם לְךָ שָׁלוֹם.

יְיָ שׁוֹמְרֶךָ, יְיָ צִלְּךָ עַל יַד יְמִינֶךָ. כִּי אֹרֶךְ יָמִים וּשְׁנוֹת חַיִּים
וְשָׁלוֹם יוֹסִיפוּ לָךְ. יְיָ יִשְׁמָרְךָ מִכָּל רָע, יִשְׁמֹר אֶת נַפְשֶׁךָ. אָמֵן.

מאי בעית טפי, the question in Aramaic asked by the *kohen*, is quoted
by Abudarham in Hebrew: אִתָּה תִרְצֶה יוֹתֵר, בִּנְךָ בְּכוֹרְךָ זֶה אוֹ חָמֵשׁ סְלָעִים
שֶׁנִּתְחַיַּבְתָּ לִפְדּוֹתוֹ.

Kohen:

Do you prefer to give me your first-born son, the first-born of his mother, or would you rather redeem him for five shekels required by the Torah?

Father:

I prefer to redeem my son, and here is his redemption-price required by the Torah.

Blessed art thou, Lord our God, King of the universe, who hast sanctified us with thy commandments, and commanded us concerning the redemption of the first-born.

Blessed art thou, Lord our God, King of the universe, who hast granted us life and sustenance and permitted us to reach this season.

Holding the redemption-money over the child's head, the kohen says:

This instead of that, this in exchange for that, this is given up for that. May this child enjoy a life of Torah and godliness. Even as he has attained to redemption, so may he attain to the Torah, to the marriage canopy and to a life of good deeds. Amen.

Placing his hand on the child's head:

May God make you like Ephraim and like Manasseh. May the Lord bless you and protect you; may the Lord countenance you and be gracious to you; may the Lord favor you and grant you peace.[1]

The Lord guards you; the Lord at your right hand is your shelter. A long and happy life will be given you. The Lord will guard you from all evil; he will guard your life.[2] Amen.

With the Spanish and Portuguese Jews it is customary that the *kohen* officiating at a *Pidyon-ha-Ben* begins by directing several questions to the mother of the child in order to determine that the child is indeed her first-born; thereupon he makes the following declaration: זה הבן בכור הוא, והקדוש ברוך הוא צוה לפדותו ...

[1]*Genesis* 48:20; *Numbers* 6:24-26. [2]*Psalm* 121:5; *Proverbs* 3:2; *Psalm* 121:7.

אֵרוּסִין וְנִשּׂוּאִין

Rabbi:

מִי אַדִּיר עַל הַכֹּל,

מִי בָּרוּךְ עַל הַכֹּל,

מִי גָּדוֹל עַל הַכֹּל,

יְבָרֵךְ חָתָן וְכַלָּה.

בָּרוּךְ אַתָּה, יְיָ אֱלֹהֵינוּ, מֶלֶךְ הָעוֹלָם, בּוֹרֵא פְּרִי הַגָּפֶן.

בָּרוּךְ אַתָּה, יְיָ אֱלֹהֵינוּ, מֶלֶךְ הָעוֹלָם, אֲשֶׁר קִדְּשָׁנוּ בְּמִצְוֹתָיו

וְצִוָּנוּ עַל הָעֲרָיוֹת, וְאָסַר לָנוּ אֶת הָאֲרוּסוֹת, וְהִתִּיר לָנוּ אֶת

הַנְּשׂוּאוֹת לָנוּ עַל יְדֵי חֻפָּה וְקִדּוּשִׁין. בָּרוּךְ אַתָּה, יְיָ, מְקַדֵּשׁ

עַמּוֹ יִשְׂרָאֵל עַל יְדֵי חֻפָּה וְקִדּוּשִׁין.

The groom, placing the ring on the forefinger of the bride's right hand:

הֲרֵי אַתְּ מְקֻדֶּשֶׁת לִי בְּטַבַּעַת זוֹ כְּדַת מֹשֶׁה וְיִשְׂרָאֵל.

After the reading of the kethubah the seven blessings are chanted:

בָּרוּךְ אַתָּה, יְיָ אֱלֹהֵינוּ, מֶלֶךְ הָעוֹלָם, בּוֹרֵא פְּרִי הַגָּפֶן.

בָּרוּךְ אַתָּה, יְיָ אֱלֹהֵינוּ, מֶלֶךְ הָעוֹלָם, שֶׁהַכֹּל בָּרָא לִכְבוֹדוֹ.

ארוסין ("betrothal") and נשואין ("marriage") were in talmudic times celebrated as two separate events. The formal betrothal was performed in the house of the bride months before the actual marriage took place in the home of the groom. Hence, two cups of wine are used in modern wedding ceremonies, one for *erusin* and one for *nissuin*. The two celebrations are now separated only by the reading of the Aramaic *Kethubah*, the marriage contract specifying the mutual obligations between husband and wife (Tosafoth, Kethuboth 7b). Since the fourteenth century it has been customary to have a rabbi perform the ceremony under a *huppah*, representing symbolically the future home of the couple. The use of a wedding ring, symbolic of attachment and fidelity, dates from the seventh century. The custom of breaking a glass under the *huppah* is

753

MARRIAGE SERVICE

Rabbi:

He who is supremely mighty,
He who is supremely blessed,
He who is supremely sublime,
May he bless the groom and the bride.

Blessed art thou, Lord our God, King of the universe, who createst the fruit of the vine.

Blessed art thou, Lord our God, King of the universe, who hast sanctified us with thy commandments, and commanded us concerning illicit relations; thou hast forbidden us those who are merely betrothed, and permitted us those who are married to us through consecrated wedlock. Blessed art thou, O Lord, who sanctifiest thy people Israel by consecrated wedlock.

The groom, placing the ring on the forefinger of the bride's right hand:

With this ring, you are wedded to me in accordance with the law of Moses and Israel.

After the reading of the kethubah the seven blessings are chanted:

Blessed art thou, Lord our God, King of the universe, who createst the fruit of the vine.

Blessed art thou, Lord our God, King of the universe, who hast created everything for thy glory.

---

derived from Berakhoth 31a, where it is related that in the course of a wedding feast one of the rabbis broke a costly vase in order to curb the spirits of those present and warn them against excessive joy (Tosafoth).

הרי את מקודשת לי is mentioned in the Talmud (Kiddushin 5b). The phrase כדת משה וישראל signifies the traditional interpretation of the laws of Moses. The word וישראל is added because the regulations of *erusin* are not directly biblical.

שבע ברכות, the seven blessings which are recited when a *minyan* is present, are quoted in the Talmud (Kethuboth 8a) where they are called ברכת חתנים. The fourth benediction refers to the perpetual renewal of the human being in the

בָּרוּךְ אַתָּה, יְיָ אֱלֹהֵינוּ, מֶלֶךְ הָעוֹלָם, יוֹצֵר הָאָדָם.

בָּרוּךְ אַתָּה, יְיָ אֱלֹהֵינוּ, מֶלֶךְ הָעוֹלָם, אֲשֶׁר יָצַר אֶת הָאָדָם בְּצַלְמוֹ, בְּצֶלֶם דְּמוּת תַּבְנִיתוֹ, וְהִתְקִין לוֹ מִמֶּנּוּ בִּנְיַן עֲדֵי עַד. בָּרוּךְ אַתָּה, יְיָ, יוֹצֵר הָאָדָם.

שׂוֹשׂ תָּשִׂישׂ וְתָגֵל הָעֲקָרָה, בְּקִבּוּץ בָּנֶיהָ לְתוֹכָהּ בְּשִׂמְחָה. בָּרוּךְ אַתָּה, יְיָ, מְשַׂמֵּחַ צִיּוֹן בְּבָנֶיהָ.

שַׂמֵּחַ תְּשַׂמַּח רֵעִים הָאֲהוּבִים, כְּשַׂמֵּחֲךָ יְצִירְךָ בְּגַן עֵדֶן מִקֶּדֶם. בָּרוּךְ אַתָּה, יְיָ, מְשַׂמֵּחַ חָתָן וְכַלָּה.

בָּרוּךְ אַתָּה, יְיָ אֱלֹהֵינוּ, מֶלֶךְ הָעוֹלָם, אֲשֶׁר בָּרָא שָׂשׂוֹן וְשִׂמְחָה, חָתָן וְכַלָּה, גִּילָה רִנָּה, דִּיצָה וְחֶדְוָה, אַהֲבָה וְאַחֲוָה, וְשָׁלוֹם וְרֵעוּת. מְהֵרָה, יְיָ אֱלֹהֵינוּ, יִשָּׁמַע בְּעָרֵי יְהוּדָה וּבְחוּצוֹת יְרוּשָׁלָיִם קוֹל שָׂשׂוֹן וְקוֹל שִׂמְחָה, קוֹל חָתָן וְקוֹל כַּלָּה, קוֹל מִצְהֲלוֹת חֲתָנִים מֵחֻפָּתָם וּנְעָרִים מִמִּשְׁתֵּה נְגִינָתָם. בָּרוּךְ אַתָּה, יְיָ, מְשַׂמֵּחַ חָתָן עִם הַכַּלָּה.

GRACE AFTER THE WEDDING MEAL

Leader:

וְאִם אִלֵּם בְּשִׁיר יָרָן;   דְּוַי הָסֵר וְגַם חָרוֹן

שְׁעֵה בִרְכַּת בְּנֵי אַהֲרֹן.   נְחֶנּוּ מַעְגְּלֵי צֶדֶק

בִּרְשׁוּת מָרָנָן וְרַבָּנָן וְרַבּוֹתַי, נְבָרֵךְ אֱלֹהֵינוּ שֶׁהַשִּׂמְחָה בִּמְעוֹנוֹ וְשֶׁאָכַלְנוּ מִשֶּׁלּוֹ.

Company, then Leader:

בָּרוּךְ אֱלֹהֵינוּ שֶׁהַשִּׂמְחָה בִּמְעוֹנוֹ וְשֶׁאָכַלְנוּ מִשֶּׁלּוֹ וּבְטוּבוֹ חָיִינוּ.

After the grace (page 759) the seven wedding blessings are repeated.

---

divine form. In the last three benedictions a prayer is uttered that God may comfort Zion, cause happiness to the young couple like the happiness of the

Blessed art thou, Lord our God, King of the universe, Creator of men.

Blessed art thou, Lord our God, King of the universe, who hast created man in thy image, and didst forever form woman out of his frame to be beside him. Blessed art thou, O Lord, Creator of man.

May Zion exult at the joyful reunion of her children in Jerusalem. Blessed art thou, O Lord, who causest Zion to rejoice in her children.

O give abundant joy to these loved companions, even as thou didst gladden thy creation of old in the Garden of Eden. Blessed art thou, O Lord, who givest joy to groom and bride.

Blessed art thou, O Lord, King of the universe, who hast created groom and bride, joy and gladness, delight and cheer, love and harmony, peace and companionship. Lord our God, may there soon be heard in the cities of Judah, in the streets of Jerusalem, the sound of joy and gladness, the sound of joyous wedding celebrations, the sound of young people feasting and singing. Blessed art thou, O Lord, who makest the groom rejoice with the bride.

GRACE AFTER THE WEDDING MEAL

Leader:

Banish grief and anguish;
Let the speechless exult.
Guide us in the righteous paths;
Heed the blessings of priests.

With your permission, gentlemen, let us now bless our God in whose abode is joy and of whose food we have eaten.

Company, then Leader:

Blessed be our God in whose abode is joy, of whose food we have eaten and through whose goodness we live.

After the grace (page 760) the seven wedding blessings are repeated.

---

first couple in Eden, and bring about complete exultation in restored Judea and Jerusalem. The seventh benediction contains phrases from Jeremiah 33:10-11. The marriage service thus combines individual with communal hopes.

דוי הסר is a poem by Dunash ben Labrat, the renowned poet and grammarian of the tenth century. His name דונש forms the acrostic of the four lines.

Upon washing the hands before meals:

בָּרוּךְ אַתָּה, יְיָ אֱלֹהֵינוּ, מֶלֶךְ הָעוֹלָם, אֲשֶׁר קִדְּשָׁנוּ בְּמִצְוֹתָיו
וְצִוָּנוּ עַל נְטִילַת יָדָיִם.

Over bread:

בָּרוּךְ אַתָּה, יְיָ אֱלֹהֵינוּ, מֶלֶךְ הָעוֹלָם, הַמּוֹצִיא לֶחֶם מִן
הָאָרֶץ.

Before grace on weekdays:

תהלים קלז

עַל נַהֲרוֹת בָּבֶל, שָׁם יָשַׁבְנוּ גַּם בָּכִינוּ בְּזָכְרֵנוּ אֶת צִיּוֹן. עַל
עֲרָבִים בְּתוֹכָהּ תָּלִינוּ כִּנֹּרוֹתֵינוּ. כִּי שָׁם שְׁאֵלוּנוּ שׁוֹבֵינוּ דִּבְרֵי
שִׁיר, וְתוֹלָלֵינוּ שִׂמְחָה; שִׁירוּ לָנוּ מִשִּׁיר צִיּוֹן. אֵיךְ נָשִׁיר אֶת שִׁיר
יְיָ עַל אַדְמַת נֵכָר. אִם אֶשְׁכָּחֵךְ יְרוּשָׁלָיִם, תִּשְׁכַּח יְמִינִי. תִּדְבַּק
לְשׁוֹנִי לְחִכִּי, אִם לֹא אֶזְכְּרֵכִי, אִם לֹא אַעֲלֶה אֶת יְרוּשָׁלַיִם
עַל רֹאשׁ שִׂמְחָתִי. זְכֹר יְיָ לִבְנֵי אֱדוֹם אֵת יוֹם יְרוּשָׁלָיִם;
הָאוֹמְרִים עָרוּ עָרוּ, עַד הַיְסוֹד בָּהּ. בַּת בָּבֶל הַשְּׁדוּדָה, אַשְׁרֵי
שֶׁיְשַׁלֶּם־לָךְ אֶת גְּמוּלֵךְ שֶׁגָּמַלְתְּ לָנוּ. אַשְׁרֵי שֶׁיֹּאחֵז וְנִפֵּץ אֶת
עֹלָלַיִךְ אֶל הַסָּלַע.

Before grace on Sabbaths and festivals:

תהלים קכו

שִׁיר הַמַּעֲלוֹת. בְּשׁוּב יְיָ אֶת שִׁיבַת צִיּוֹן הָיִינוּ כְּחֹלְמִים. אָז
יִמָּלֵא שְׂחוֹק פִּינוּ, וּלְשׁוֹנֵנוּ רִנָּה; אָז יֹאמְרוּ בַגּוֹיִם, הִגְדִּיל יְיָ
לַעֲשׂוֹת עִם אֵלֶּה. הִגְדִּיל יְיָ לַעֲשׂוֹת עִמָּנוּ, הָיִינוּ שְׂמֵחִים. שׁוּבָה
יְיָ אֶת שְׁבִיתֵנוּ, כַּאֲפִיקִים בַּנֶּגֶב. הַזֹּרְעִים בְּדִמְעָה, בְּרִנָּה
יִקְצֹרוּ. הָלוֹךְ יֵלֵךְ וּבָכֹה נֹשֵׂא מֶשֶׁךְ הַזָּרַע; בֹּא יָבֹא בְרִנָּה נֹשֵׂא
אֲלֻמֹּתָיו.

עַל נהרות בבל is recited in order to remember the desolation of Zion. After
enjoying a meal, says the Zohar (section *Terumah*), one ought to keep in mind

Upon washing the hands before meals:

Blessed art thou, Lord our God, King of the universe, who hast sanctified us with thy commandments, and commanded us concerning the washing of the hands.

Over bread:

Blessed art thou, Lord our God, King of the universe, who bringest forth bread from the earth.

Before grace on weekdays:

Psalm 137

By the rivers of Babylon we sat down and wept when we remembered Zion. Upon the willows there we hung up our harps, when our captors demanded of us songs; our tormentors asked of us mirth: "Sing us some of the songs of Zion!" How shall we sing the Lord's song in a foreign land? If ever I forget you, O Jerusalem, withered be my right hand! May my tongue cleave to my palate, if ever I think not of you, if ever I set not Jerusalem above my highest joy!

Remember, O Lord, the day of Jerusalem's fall against the Edomites, who said: "Raze it, raze it, to its very foundation!" O Babylon, you are to be destroyed! Happy be he who repays you all that you have dealt to us! Happy be he who takes and dashes your little ones against the rocks!

Before grace on Sabbaths and festivals:

Psalm 126

A Pilgrim Song. When the Lord brought the exiles back to Zion, we were like those who dream. Our mouth was filled with laughter, and our tongue with ringing song; then it was said among the nations: "The Lord has done great things for them." The Lord had done great things for us, and we rejoiced. Restore our fortunes, O Lord, like streams in the Negev. Those are who sowing in tears shall reap in joy. Sadly the farmer bears the bag of seed to the field; he shall come home with joy, bearing his sheaves.

---

the destruction of the Holy Land. On Sabbaths and festivals, however, שיר המעלות is recited instead, because this psalm cheerfully describes the restoration of Zion and is therefore appropriate for days when one ought to be full of joy.

בִּרְכַּת הַמָּזוֹן

When three men or more have eaten together, the following is used as an introduction to the grace. The word in parentheses is included when a *minyan* is present.

Leader:

רַבּוֹתַי נְבָרֵךְ.

Company, then Leader:

יְהִי שֵׁם יְיָ מְבֹרָךְ מֵעַתָּה וְעַד עוֹלָם.

Leader:

בִּרְשׁוּת מָרָנָן וְרַבָּנָן וְרַבּוֹתַי נְבָרֵךְ (אֱלֹהֵינוּ) שֶׁאָכַלְנוּ מִשֶּׁלוֹ.

Company, then Leader:

בָּרוּךְ (אֱלֹהֵינוּ) שֶׁאָכַלְנוּ מִשֶּׁלוֹ וּבְטוּבוֹ חָיִינוּ.

All:

בָּרוּךְ הוּא וּבָרוּךְ שְׁמוֹ.

בָּרוּךְ אַתָּה, יְיָ אֱלֹהֵינוּ, מֶלֶךְ הָעוֹלָם, הַזָּן אֶת הָעוֹלָם כֻּלוֹ בְּטוּבוֹ, בְּחֵן בְּחֶסֶד וּבְרַחֲמִים. הוּא נוֹתֵן לֶחֶם לְכָל בָּשָׂר, כִּי לְעוֹלָם חַסְדּוֹ. וּבְטוּבוֹ הַגָּדוֹל תָּמִיד לֹא חָסַר לָנוּ, וְאַל יֶחְסַר לָנוּ מָזוֹן לְעוֹלָם וָעֶד בַּעֲבוּר שְׁמוֹ הַגָּדוֹל. כִּי הוּא אֵל זָן וּמְפַרְנֵס לַכֹּל, וּמֵטִיב לַכֹּל, וּמֵכִין מָזוֹן לְכָל בְּרִיּוֹתָיו אֲשֶׁר בָּרָא. בָּרוּךְ אַתָּה, יְיָ, הַזָּן אֶת הַכֹּל.

ברכת המזון is of high antiquity. According to the Talmud, the first benediction of grace after meals (הזן) was composed by Moses, the second (עודה) by Joshua, the third (רחם) by David and Solomon, and the fourth (הטוב והמטיב) by the sages shortly after Bar Kokhba's defeat (Berakhoth 48b). The petitions beginning with הרחמן are later additions. The third benediction ends with אמן so as to mark the end of the three benedictions which are based on the

GRACE AFTER MEALS

When three men or more have eaten together, the following is used as an introduction to the grace. The word in parentheses is included when a minyan is present.

Leader:

Gentlemen, let us say grace.

Company, then Leader:

Blessed be the name of the Lord henceforth and forever.

Leader:

With your consent, let us now bless (our) God whose food we have eaten.

Company, then Leader:

Blessed be (our) God whose food we have eaten and through whose goodness we live.

All:

Blessed be he and blessed be his name.

Blessed art thou, Lord our God, King of the universe, who sustainest the whole world with goodness, kindness and mercy. Thou givest food to all creatures, for thy mercy endures forever. Through thy abundant goodness we have never yet been in want; may we never be in want of sustenance for thy great name's sake. Thou, O God, sustainest all, doest good to all, and providest food for all the creatures thou hast created. Blessed art thou, O Lord, who dost sustain all.

---

biblical command: "You shall eat... and you shall bless the Lord for the good land he has given you" (Deuteronomy 8:10).

The introductory formula used when three or more men recite grace jointly (ברכת הזימון) is taken from the Mishnah (Berakhoth 7:3). The duty of inviting the table-companions to recite grace jointly is derived from Psalm 34:4 ("Exalt the Lord with me, and let us extol the Lord together").

וְעַד זָקֵן, טַף וְנָשִׁים, בְּיוֹם אֶחָד, בִּשְׁלוֹשָׁה עָשָׂר לְחֹדֶשׁ שְׁנֵים
עָשָׂר, הוּא חֹדֶשׁ אֲדָר, וּשְׁלָלָם לָבוֹז. וְאַתָּה בְּרַחֲמֶיךָ הָרַבִּים
הֵפַרְתָּ אֶת עֲצָתוֹ, וְקִלְקַלְתָּ אֶת מַחֲשַׁבְתּוֹ, וַהֲשֵׁבוֹתָ גְּמוּלוֹ
בְּרֹאשׁוֹ, וְתָלוּ אוֹתוֹ וְאֶת בָּנָיו עַל הָעֵץ.)

וְעַל הַכֹּל, יְיָ אֱלֹהֵינוּ, אֲנַחְנוּ מוֹדִים לָךְ וּמְבָרְכִים אוֹתָךְ,
יִתְבָּרַךְ שִׁמְךָ בְּפִי כָל חַי תָּמִיד לְעוֹלָם וָעֶד, כַּכָּתוּב: וְאָכַלְתָּ
וְשָׂבָעְתָּ, וּבֵרַכְתָּ אֶת יְיָ אֱלֹהֶיךָ עַל הָאָרֶץ הַטֹּבָה אֲשֶׁר נָתַן לָךְ.
בָּרוּךְ אַתָּה, יְיָ, עַל הָאָרֶץ וְעַל הַמָּזוֹן.

רַחֵם, יְיָ אֱלֹהֵינוּ, עַל יִשְׂרָאֵל עַמֶּךָ, וְעַל יְרוּשָׁלַיִם עִירֶךָ,
וְעַל צִיּוֹן מִשְׁכַּן כְּבוֹדֶךָ, וְעַל מַלְכוּת בֵּית דָּוִד מְשִׁיחֶךָ, וְעַל
הַבַּיִת הַגָּדוֹל וְהַקָּדוֹשׁ שֶׁנִּקְרָא שִׁמְךָ עָלָיו. אֱלֹהֵינוּ אָבִינוּ,
רְעֵנוּ זוּנֵנוּ, פַּרְנְסֵנוּ וְכַלְכְּלֵנוּ וְהַרְוִיחֵנוּ, וְהַרְוַח לָנוּ, יְיָ אֱלֹהֵינוּ,
מְהֵרָה מִכָּל צָרוֹתֵינוּ. וְנָא, אַל תַּצְרִיכֵנוּ, יְיָ אֱלֹהֵינוּ, לֹא לִידֵי
מַתְּנַת בָּשָׂר וָדָם וְלֹא לִידֵי הַלְוָאָתָם, כִּי אִם לְיָדְךָ הַמְּלֵאָה
הַפְּתוּחָה, הַקְּדוֹשָׁה וְהָרְחָבָה, שֶׁלֹּא נֵבוֹשׁ וְלֹא נִכָּלֵם לְעוֹלָם
וָעֶד.

On Sabbath add:

(רְצֵה וְהַחֲלִיצֵנוּ, יְיָ אֱלֹהֵינוּ, בְּמִצְוֹתֶיךָ וּבְמִצְוַת יוֹם הַשְּׁבִיעִי,
הַשַּׁבָּת הַגָּדוֹל וְהַקָּדוֹשׁ הַזֶּה; כִּי יוֹם זֶה גָּדוֹל וְקָדוֹשׁ הוּא
לְפָנֶיךָ, לִשְׁבָּת בּוֹ וְלָנוּחַ בּוֹ בְּאַהֲבָה כְּמִצְוַת רְצוֹנֶךָ. וּבִרְצוֹנְךָ
הָנַח לָנוּ, יְיָ אֱלֹהֵינוּ, שֶׁלֹּא תְהֵא צָרָה, וְיָגוֹן וַאֲנָחָה, בְּיוֹם
מְנוּחָתֵנוּ. וְהַרְאֵנוּ, יְיָ אֱלֹהֵינוּ, בְּנֶחָמַת צִיּוֹן עִירֶךָ, וּבְבִנְיַן
יְרוּשָׁלַיִם עִיר קָדְשֶׁךָ, כִּי אַתָּה הוּא בַּעַל הַיְשׁוּעוֹת וּבַעַל
הַנֶּחָמוֹת.)

הקדושה is a variant of הגדושה ("superabundant"). The context supports
הגדושה. The reading in the Spanish *Siddur* is העשירה. It has therefore been
suggested to read לידך המלאה, הפתוחה, הגדושה והרחבה.

infants and women, in one day, on the thirteenth of the twelfth month Adar, and to plunder their wealth. Thou in thy great mercy didst frustrate his counsel and upset his plan; thou didst cause his mischief to recoil on his own head, so that he and his sons were hanged upon the gallows.)

For everything, Lord our God, we thank thee and bless thee—be thy name forever blessed by all—as it is written: "When you have eaten and are satisfied, you shall bless the Lord your God for the good land he has given you."[1] Blessed art thou, O Lord, for the land and the sustenance.

Have mercy, Lord our God, on Israel thy people, on Jerusalem thy city, on Zion the abode of thy majesty, on the royal house of David thy chosen one, and on the great and holy Temple that bears thy name. Our God, our Father, tend and nourish us; sustain and maintain us; grant us deliverance. Speedily, Lord our God, grant us relief from all our troubles. Lord our God, O make us not dependent on the gifts and loans of men but rather on thy full, open and generous hand, that we may never be put to shame and disgrace.

On Sabbath add:

(O strengthen us, Lord our God, with thy commandments—with the commandment concerning the seventh day, this great and holy Sabbath. This day is indeed great and holy to thee; on it we are to abstain from work and rest on it with delight according to thy will. In thy grace, Lord our God, grant us rest; may there be no sorrow and grief on our day of rest. Let us, Lord our God, live to see Zion thy city comforted, Jerusalem thy holy city rebuilt, for thou art Lord of all salvation and consolation.)

נשבת בו וננוח בו, the reading in the Sephardic *Siddur*, makes better sense.

[1] *Deuteronomy* 8:10.

On *Rosh Ḥodesh* and festivals add:

(אֱלֹהֵינוּ וֵאלֹהֵי אֲבוֹתֵינוּ, יַעֲלֶה וְיָבֹא, וְיַגִּיעַ וְיֵרָאֶה, וְיֵרָצֶה
וְיִשָּׁמַע, וְיִפָּקֵד וְיִזָּכֵר זִכְרוֹנֵנוּ וּפִקְדוֹנֵנוּ, וְזִכְרוֹן אֲבוֹתֵינוּ, וְזִכְרוֹן
מָשִׁיחַ בֶּן דָּוִד עַבְדֶּךָ, וְזִכְרוֹן יְרוּשָׁלַיִם עִיר קָדְשֶׁךָ, וְזִכְרוֹן כָּל
עַמְּךָ בֵּית יִשְׂרָאֵל לְפָנֶיךָ, לִפְלֵיטָה וּלְטוֹבָה, לְחֵן וּלְחֶסֶד
וּלְרַחֲמִים, לְחַיִּים וּלְשָׁלוֹם, בְּיוֹם

Shavuoth	Pesaḥ	Rosh Ḥodesh
חַג הַשָּׁבֻעוֹת	חַג הַמַּצּוֹת	רֹאשׁ הַחֹדֶשׁ

Shemini Atsereth	Sukkoth	Rosh Hashanah
הַשְּׁמִינִי, חַג הָעֲצֶרֶת	חַג הַסֻּכּוֹת	הַזִּכָּרוֹן

הַזֶּה. זָכְרֵנוּ, יְיָ אֱלֹהֵינוּ, בּוֹ לְטוֹבָה, וּפָקְדֵנוּ בוֹ לִבְרָכָה,
וְהוֹשִׁיעֵנוּ בוֹ לְחַיִּים. וּבִדְבַר יְשׁוּעָה וְרַחֲמִים חוּס וְחָנֵּנוּ, וְרַחֵם
עָלֵינוּ וְהוֹשִׁיעֵנוּ כִּי אֵלֶיךָ עֵינֵינוּ, כִּי אֵל מֶלֶךְ חַנּוּן וְרַחוּם אָתָּה.)
וּבְנֵה יְרוּשָׁלַיִם עִיר הַקֹּדֶשׁ בִּמְהֵרָה בְיָמֵינוּ. בָּרוּךְ אַתָּה,
יְיָ, בּוֹנֵה בְרַחֲמָיו יְרוּשָׁלָיִם, אָמֵן.

בָּרוּךְ אַתָּה, יְיָ אֱלֹהֵינוּ, מֶלֶךְ הָעוֹלָם, הָאֵל, אָבִינוּ, מַלְכֵּנוּ,
אַדִּירֵנוּ, בּוֹרְאֵנוּ, גּוֹאֲלֵנוּ, יוֹצְרֵנוּ, קְדוֹשֵׁנוּ, קְדוֹשׁ יַעֲקֹב, רוֹעֵנוּ,
רוֹעֵה יִשְׂרָאֵל, הַמֶּלֶךְ הַטּוֹב וְהַמֵּטִיב לַכֹּל, שֶׁבְּכָל יוֹם וָיוֹם
הוּא הֵטִיב, הוּא מֵטִיב, הוּא יֵיטִיב לָנוּ. הוּא גְמָלָנוּ, הוּא
גוֹמְלֵנוּ, הוּא יִגְמְלֵנוּ לָעַד, לְחֵן וּלְחֶסֶד וּלְרַחֲמִים וּלְרֶוַח,
הַצָּלָה וְהַצְלָחָה, בְּרָכָה וִישׁוּעָה, נֶחָמָה פַּרְנָסָה וְכַלְכָּלָה,
וְרַחֲמִים וְחַיִּים וְשָׁלוֹם וְכָל טוֹב, וּמִכָּל טוֹב לְעוֹלָם אַל יְחַסְּרֵנוּ.
הָרַחֲמָן, הוּא יִמְלוֹךְ עָלֵינוּ לְעוֹלָם וָעֶד.
הָרַחֲמָן, הוּא יִתְבָּרַךְ בַּשָּׁמַיִם וּבָאָרֶץ.
הָרַחֲמָן, הוּא יִשְׁתַּבַּח לְדוֹר דּוֹרִים, וְיִתְפָּאַר בָּנוּ לָעַד
וּלְנֵצַח נְצָחִים, וְיִתְהַדַּר בָּנוּ לָעַד וּלְעוֹלְמֵי עוֹלָמִים.

On Rosh Ḥodesh and festivals add:

(Our God and God of our fathers, may the remembrance of us, of our fathers, of Messiah the son of David thy servant, of Jerusalem thy holy city, and of all thy people the house of Israel, ascend and come and be accepted before thee for deliverance and happiness, for grace, kindness and mercy, for life and peace, on this day of the

Rosh Ḥodesh	*Pesaḥ*	*Shavuoth*
New Moon.	Feast of Unleavened Bread.	Feast of Weeks.
Rosh Hashanah	*Sukkoth*	*Shemini Atsereth*
Remembrance.	Feast of Tabernacles.	Eighth Day Feast.

Remember us this day, Lord our God, for happiness; be mindful of us for blessing; save us to enjoy life. With a promise of salvation and mercy spare us and be gracious to us; have pity on us and save us, for we look to thee, for thou art a gracious and merciful God and King.)

Rebuild Jerusalem the holy city speedily in our days. Blessed art thou, O Lord, merciful Restorer of Jerusalem. Amen.

Blessed art thou, Lord our God, King of the universe. O God, thou art our Father, our King, our Creator, our Redeemer, the Holy One of Jacob, the Shepherd of Israel, the good King who doest good to all. Thou bestowest favors on us continuously; thou dost ever confer on us kindness and mercy, relief and deliverance, prosperity and blessing, life and peace and all goodness. Mayest thou never deprive us of any good thing.

May the Merciful One reign over us forever and ever.

May the Merciful One be worshiped in heaven and on earth.

May the Merciful One be praised for countless generations; may he be glorified in us forever and ever; may he be honored in us to to all eternity.

הָרַחֲמָן, הוּא יְפַרְנְסֵנוּ בְּכָבוֹד.

הָרַחֲמָן, הוּא יִשְׁבּוֹר עֻלֵנוּ מֵעַל צַוָּארֵנוּ, וְהוּא יוֹלִיכֵנוּ
קוֹמְמִיּוּת לְאַרְצֵנוּ.

הָרַחֲמָן, הוּא יִשְׁלַח בְּרָכָה מְרֻבָּה בַּבַּיִת הַזֶּה, וְעַל שֻׁלְחָן
זֶה שֶׁאָכַלְנוּ עָלָיו.

הָרַחֲמָן, הוּא יִשְׁלַח לָנוּ אֶת אֵלִיָּהוּ הַנָּבִיא, זָכוּר לַטּוֹב,
וִיבַשֶּׂר־לָנוּ בְּשׂוֹרוֹת טוֹבוֹת, יְשׁוּעוֹת וְנֶחָמוֹת.

Variations suitable to different occasions:

הָרַחֲמָן, הוּא יְבָרֵךְ אוֹתִי (וְאֶת אִשְׁתִּי וְאֶת זַרְעִי) וְאֶת כָּל
אֲשֶׁר לִי.

הָרַחֲמָן, הוּא יְבָרֵךְ־אֶת (אָבִי מוֹרִי) בַּעַל הַבַּיִת הַזֶּה
וְאֶת (אִמִּי מוֹרָתִי) בַּעֲלַת הַבַּיִת הַזֶּה, אוֹתָם וְאֶת בֵּיתָם וְאֶת
זַרְעָם וְאֶת כָּל אֲשֶׁר לָהֶם־אוֹתָנוּ וְאֶת כָּל אֲשֶׁר לָנוּ. כְּמוֹ
שֶׁנִּתְבָּרְכוּ אֲבוֹתֵינוּ אַבְרָהָם יִצְחָק וְיַעֲקֹב בַּכֹּל מִכֹּל כֹּל, כֵּן
יְבָרֵךְ אוֹתָנוּ, כֻּלָּנוּ יַחַד, בִּבְרָכָה שְׁלֵמָה, וְנֹאמַר אָמֵן.

בַּמָּרוֹם יְלַמְּדוּ (עֲלֵיהֶם וְ)עָלֵינוּ זְכוּת, שֶׁתְּהֵא לְמִשְׁמֶרֶת
שָׁלוֹם. וְנִשָּׂא בְרָכָה מֵאֵת יְיָ, וּצְדָקָה מֵאֱלֹהֵי יִשְׁעֵנוּ, וְנִמְצָא חֵן
וְשֵׂכֶל טוֹב בְּעֵינֵי אֱלֹהִים וְאָדָם.

On Sabbath:

הָרַחֲמָן, הוּא יַנְחִילֵנוּ יוֹם שֶׁכֻּלּוֹ שַׁבָּת וּמְנוּחָה לְחַיֵּי
הָעוֹלָמִים.

On *Rosh Ḥodesh*:

הָרַחֲמָן, הוּא יְחַדֵּשׁ עָלֵינוּ אֶת הַחֹדֶשׁ הַזֶּה לְטוֹבָה וְלִבְרָכָה.

בכל מכל כל were the words used in connection with the three patriarchs,
respectively (Genesis 24:1; 27:33; 33:11). The Talmud (Baba Bathra 17a)
states that the use of בכל מכל כל with reference to Abraham, Isaac and Jacob,
shows that they were completely righteous.

May the Merciful One grant us a respectable livelihood.

May the Merciful One break the yoke from our neck; may he lead us securely into our land.

May the Merciful One send abundant blessings into this house and upon this table at which we have eaten.

May the Merciful One send us Elijah the prophet—of blessed memory—to bring us the good tidings of deliverance and comfort.

Variations suitable to different occasions:

May the Merciful One bless me, (my wife, my children) and all that is mine.

May the Merciful One bless (my dear father) the master of this house and (my dear mother) the mistress of this house, their entire family and all that is theirs.

May he bless us and all that is ours; may he bless us all alike with a perfect blessing even as our forefathers Abraham, Isaac and Jacob were blessed in every way; and let us say, Amen.

May they in heaven plead for all of us that we may have enduring peace. May we receive gifts from the Lord, justice from our saving God; may we be in the good graces of God and men.

On Sabbath:

May the Merciful One grant us the day which will be all Sabbath and rest in life everlasting.

On Rosh Ḥodesh:

May the Merciful One renew for us this month for happiness and blessedness.

במרום expresses the idea found in the Talmud (Hullin 92b) that the angels on high plead the cause of Israel. עליהם refers to the hosts who entertain the guests. ונשא ברכה and ונמצא חן are somewhat modified quotations from Psalm 24:5 and Proverbs 3:4.

יום שכולו שבת... is borrowed from the Mishnah (Tamid, end).

On festivals:

הָרַחֲמָן, הוּא יַנְחִילֵנוּ יוֹם שֶׁכֻּלּוֹ טוֹב.

On *Rosh Hashanah*:

הָרַחֲמָן, הוּא יְחַדֵּשׁ עָלֵינוּ אֶת הַשָּׁנָה הַזֹּאת לְטוֹבָה
וְלִבְרָכָה.

On *Sukkoth*:

הָרַחֲמָן, הוּא יָקִים לָנוּ אֶת סֻכַּת דָּוִד הַנּוֹפָלֶת.

הָרַחֲמָן, הוּא יְזַכֵּנוּ לִימוֹת הַמָּשִׁיחַ וּלְחַיֵּי הָעוֹלָם הַבָּא.
מַגְדִּיל (מִגְדּוֹל (on the days when *Musaf* is recited: יְשׁוּעוֹת מַלְכּוֹ
וְעֹשֶׂה חֶסֶד לִמְשִׁיחוֹ, לְדָוִד וּלְזַרְעוֹ עַד עוֹלָם. עֹשֶׂה שָׁלוֹם
בִּמְרוֹמָיו, הוּא יַעֲשֶׂה שָׁלוֹם עָלֵינוּ וְעַל כָּל יִשְׂרָאֵל, וְאִמְרוּ
אָמֵן.

יְראוּ אֶת יְיָ, קְדֹשָׁיו, כִּי אֵין מַחְסוֹר לִירֵאָיו. כְּפִירִים רָשׁוּ
וְרָעֵבוּ, וְדֹרְשֵׁי יְיָ לֹא יַחְסְרוּ כָל טוֹב. הוֹדוּ לַייָ כִּי טוֹב, כִּי
לְעוֹלָם חַסְדּוֹ. פּוֹתֵחַ אֶת יָדֶךָ, וּמַשְׂבִּיעַ לְכָל חַי רָצוֹן. בָּרוּךְ
הַגֶּבֶר אֲשֶׁר יִבְטַח בַּייָ, וְהָיָה יְיָ מִבְטַחוֹ. נַעַר הָיִיתִי גַּם זָקַנְתִּי,
וְלֹא רָאִיתִי צַדִּיק נֶעֱזָב, וְזַרְעוֹ מְבַקֶּשׁ־לָחֶם. יְיָ עֹז לְעַמּוֹ יִתֵּן;
יְיָ יְבָרֵךְ אֶת עַמּוֹ בַשָּׁלוֹם.

מגדיל ישועות מלכו is found in Psalm 18:51. The same verse occurs in
II Samuel 22:51, where the reading is **מגדול** instead of **מגדיל**. For the sake of
compromise, both readings have been inserted here, one for weekdays and one
for Sabbaths and festivals. The verse **חדש ושבת קרא מקרא** (Isaiah 1:13) was
fancifully introduced in support of the use of **מגדול** on Sabbaths, festivals
and *Rosh Ḥodesh*.

יראו is pronounced **יְרוּ** just as **קוֹראִיט** (page 241) is pronounced **קוֹרִים**: compare the mishnaic use of **קוֹרִין** in place of **קוֹראִין**.

On festivals:

May the Merciful One grant us the day of unmixed happiness.

On Rosh Hashanah:

May the Merciful One renew for us this year for happiness and blessedness.

On Sukkoth:

May the Merciful One restore for us the fallen *Sukkah* of David.

––––––––––

May the Merciful One grant us life in the days of the Messiah and in the world to come.

He gives great victories to his chosen king, and shows kindness to his anointed prince, to David and his dynasty forever.[1]

He who creates peace in his celestial heights, may he create peace for us and for all Israel; and say, Amen.

Revere the Lord, you his holy ones; those who revere him suffer no want. Lions may be famishing and starving, but those who seek the Lord are not in want of any good thing. Give thanks to the Lord, for he is good; his mercy endures forever. Thou openest thy hand and satisfiest every living thing with favor. Blessed is the man who trusts in the Lord, ever relying on the Lord. I have been young and now I am old, but never have I seen the righteous man forsaken, nor his children begging bread. The Lord will give strength to his people; the Lord will bless his people with peace.[2]

––––––––––

סכת דוד הנופלת is taken from Amos 9:11 and connotes the ruined state of David.

לא ראיתי צדיק נעזב that is, the poor and needy among the righteous are never completely abandoned. Sooner or later, righteouness is vindicated

––––––––––

[1]*Psalm* 18:51. [2]*Psalms* 34:10-11; 118:1; 145:16; *Jeremiah* 17:7; *Psalms* 37:25; 29:11.

ABRIDGED FORM OF GRACE

After cake or Palestinian fruits (grapes, figs, pommegranates, olives and dates)

בָּרוּךְ אַתָּה, יְיָ אֱלֹהֵינוּ, מֶלֶךְ הָעוֹלָם,

Cake and wine	Cake	Fruit	Wine
עַל הַמִּחְיָה וְעַל	עַל הַמִּחְיָה	עַל הָעֵץ	עַל הַגֶּפֶן
הַכַּלְכָּלָה וְעַל הַגֶּפֶן	וְעַל	וְעַל פְּרִי	וְעַל פְּרִי
וְעַל פְּרִי הַגֶּפֶן,	הַכַּלְכָּלָה,	הָעֵץ,	הַגֶּפֶן,

וְעַל תְּנוּבַת הַשָּׂדֶה, וְעַל אֶרֶץ חֶמְדָּה טוֹבָה וּרְחָבָה שֶׁרָצִיתָ
וְהִנְחַלְתָּ לַאֲבוֹתֵינוּ לֶאֱכֹל מִפִּרְיָה וְלִשְׂבֹּעַ מִטּוּבָהּ. רַחֶם־נָא,
יְיָ אֱלֹהֵינוּ, עַל יִשְׂרָאֵל עַמֶּךָ, וְעַל יְרוּשָׁלַיִם עִירֶךָ, וְעַל צִיּוֹן
מִשְׁכַּן כְּבוֹדֶךָ, וְעַל מִזְבַּחַךְ וְעַל הֵיכָלֶךָ. וּבְנֵה יְרוּשָׁלַיִם עִיר
הַקֹּדֶשׁ בִּמְהֵרָה בְיָמֵינוּ, וְהַעֲלֵנוּ לְתוֹכָהּ וְשַׂמְּחֵנוּ בְּבִנְיָנָהּ, וְנֹאכַל
מִפִּרְיָה וְנִשְׂבַּע מִטּוּבָהּ, וּנְבָרֶכְךָ עָלֶיהָ בִּקְדֻשָׁה וּבְטָהֳרָה.

On Sabbath:

רְצֵה וְהַחֲלִיצֵנוּ בְּיוֹם הַשַּׁבָּת הַזֶּה.

On Rosh Ḥodesh:

זָכְרֵנוּ לְטוֹבָה בְּיוֹם רֹאשׁ הַחֹדֶשׁ הַזֶּה.

On Rosh Hashanah:

זָכְרֵנוּ לְטוֹבָה בְּיוֹם הַזִּכָּרוֹן הַזֶּה.

On festivals:

שַׂמְּחֵנוּ בְּיוֹם חַג

Shemini Atsereth	Sukkoth	Shavuoth	Pesaḥ
הַשְּׁמִינִי, חַג הָעֲצֶרֶת	הַסֻּכּוֹת	הַשָּׁבֻעוֹת	הַמַּצּוֹת

הַזֶּה.   כִּי אַתָּה, יְיָ, טוֹב וּמֵטִיב לַכֹּל, וְנוֹדֶה לְּךָ עַל הָאָרֶץ

Fruit	Wine
וְעַל פְּרִי הַגֶּפֶן. בָּרוּךְ אַתָּה, יְיָ,	וְעַל הַפֵּרוֹת. בָּרוּךְ אַתָּה, יְיָ,
יְיָ, עַל הָאָרֶץ וְעַל פְּרִי הַגֶּפֶן.	עַל הָאָרֶץ וְעַל הַפֵּרוֹת.

ABRIDGED FORM OF GRACE

After cake or Palestinian fruits (grapes, figs, pommegranates, olives and dates)

Blessed art thou, Lord our God, King of the universe, for all the nourishment and produce of the field, for the lovely and spacious land which thou didst grant to our fathers as a heritage to eat of its fruit and enjoy its good gifts. Have mercy, Lord our God, on Israel thy people, on Jerusalem thy city, on Zion the abode of thy majesty, on thy altar and thy shrine. Rebuild the holy city of Jerusalem speedily in our days. Bring us there and gladden us with the restoration of our land; may we eat of its fruit and enjoy its good gifts; may we bless thee for it in holiness and purity.

On Sabbath:

Be pleased to strengthen us on this Sabbath day.

On Rosh Ḥodesh:

Be mindful of us on this New Moon festival.

On Rosh Hashanah:

Be mindful of us on this Day of Remembrance.

On festivals:

Grant us joy on this Festival of

Pesaḥ	*Shavuoth*	*Sukkoth*	*Shemini Atsereth*
Unleavened Bread.	Weeks.	Tabernacles.	Eighth Day Feast.

For thou, O Lord, art good and beneficent to all; we thank thee for our land and all the nourishment. Blessed art thou, O Lord, for the land and all the sustenance.

Cake

וְעַל הַמִּחְיָה. בָּרוּךְ אַתָּה, יְיָ, עַל הָאָרֶץ וְעַל הַמִּחְיָה.

Cake and wine

וְעַל הַמִּחְיָה וְעַל פְּרִי הַגָּֽפֶן. בָּרוּךְ אַתָּה, יְיָ, עַל הָאָרֶץ
וְעַל הַמִּחְיָה וְעַל פְּרִי הַגָּֽפֶן.

After any food or liquids requiring the blessing שֶׁהַכֹּל:

בָּרוּךְ אַתָּה, יְיָ אֱלֹהֵינוּ, מֶלֶךְ הָעוֹלָם, בּוֹרֵא נְפָשׁוֹת רַבּוֹת וְחֶסְרוֹנָן, עַל כָּל מַה שֶׁבָּרָאתָ לְהַחֲיוֹת בָּהֶם נֶפֶשׁ כָּל חָי. בָּרוּךְ חֵי הָעוֹלָמִים.

בְּרָכוֹת

Recited on various occasions

Over bread:

בָּרוּךְ אַתָּה, יְיָ אֱלֹהֵינוּ, מֶלֶךְ הָעוֹלָם, הַמּוֹצִיא לֶחֶם מִן הָאָרֶץ.

Over wine:

בָּרוּךְ אַתָּה, יְיָ אֱלֹהֵינוּ, מֶלֶךְ הָעוֹלָם, בּוֹרֵא פְּרִי הַגָּפֶן.

Over cakes and pastry:

בָּרוּךְ אַתָּה, יְיָ אֱלֹהֵינוּ, מֶלֶךְ הָעוֹלָם, בּוֹרֵא מִינֵי מְזוֹנוֹת.

Over liquids other than wine and food other than plants:

בָּרוּךְ אַתָּה, יְיָ אֱלֹהֵינוּ, מֶלֶךְ הָעוֹלָם, שֶׁהַכֹּל נִהְיָה בִּדְבָרוֹ.

Over fruits that grow on trees:

בָּרוּךְ אַתָּה, יְיָ אֱלֹהֵינוּ, מֶלֶךְ הָעוֹלָם, בּוֹרֵא פְּרִי הָעֵץ.

Over fruits that grow in the soil:

בָּרוּךְ אַתָּה, יְיָ אֱלֹהֵינוּ, מֶלֶךְ הָעוֹלָם, בּוֹרֵא פְּרִי הָאֲדָמָה.

Over fragrant spices:

בָּרוּךְ אַתָּה, יְיָ אֱלֹהֵינוּ, מֶלֶךְ הָעוֹלָם, בּוֹרֵא מִינֵי בְשָׂמִים.

ברכות, the blessings on various occasions, are attributed to the men of the Great Assembly, the spiritual leaders in the time of Ezra the Scribe, who are considered the successors of the prophets in that they kept alive the knowledge of the Torah and Jewish traditions. The word ברכה is derived from the verb ברך in the sense of bending the knees, worshiping; compare נברכה (Psalm 95:6) and ויברך על ברכיו (IIChronicles 6:13). לפני ה'

After liquids other than wine and food other than plants:

Blessed art thou, Lord our God, King of the universe, Creator of all life and its needs, for all the things thou hast created to sustain every living being. Blessed art thou who art the life of the universe.

BLESSINGS

Recited on various occasions

Over bread:

Blessed art thou, Lord our God, King of the universe, who bringest forth bread from the earth.

Over wine:

Blessed art thou, Lord our God, King of the universe, who createst the fruit of the vine.

Over cakes and pastry:

Blessed art thou, Lord our God, King of the universe, who createst various kinds of food.

Over liquids other than wine and food other than plants:

Blessed art thou, Lord our God, King of the universe, by whose word all things come into being.

Over fruits that grow on trees:

Blessed art thou, Lord our God, King of the universe, who createst the fruit of the tree.

Over fruits that grow in the soil:

Blessed art thou, Lord our God, King of the universe, who createst the fruit of the earth.

Over fragrant spices:

Blessed art thou, Lord our God, King of the universe, who createst various kinds of spices.

The blessings here are taken from the Mishnah (Berakhoth 6:1-2,8; 9:2-3), the Babylonian Talmud (Berakhoth 36-37; 40; 43-44; 58-59) and the Palestinian Talmud (Berakhoth 6:1; 9:3).

On attaching a *mezuzah*:

בָּרוּךְ אַתָּה, יְיָ אֱלֹהֵינוּ, מֶלֶךְ הָעוֹלָם, אֲשֶׁר קִדְּשָׁנוּ בְּמִצְוֹתָיו וְצִוָּנוּ לִקְבְּוֹעַ מְזוּזָה.

On tasting fruit for the first time in the season:

בָּרוּךְ אַתָּה, יְיָ אֱלֹהֵינוּ, מֶלֶךְ הָעוֹלָם, שֶׁהֶחֱיָנוּ וְקִיְּמָנוּ וְהִגִּיעָנוּ לַזְּמַן הַזֶּה.

On seeing the wonders of nature:

בָּרוּךְ אַתָּה, יְיָ אֱלֹהֵינוּ, מֶלֶךְ הָעוֹלָם, עֹשֶׂה מַעֲשֵׂה בְרֵאשִׁית.

On seeing an electrical storm:

בָּרוּךְ אַתָּה, יְיָ אֱלֹהֵינוּ, מֶלֶךְ הָעוֹלָם, שֶׁכֹּחוֹ וּגְבוּרָתוֹ מָלֵא עוֹלָם.

On seeing a rainbow:

בָּרוּךְ אַתָּה, יְיָ אֱלֹהֵינוּ, מֶלֶךְ הָעוֹלָם, זוֹכֵר הַבְּרִית וְנֶאֱמָן בִּבְרִיתוֹ וְקַיָּם בְּמַאֲמָרוֹ.

On seeing the ocean:

בָּרוּךְ אַתָּה, יְיָ אֱלֹהֵינוּ, מֶלֶךְ הָעוֹלָם, שֶׁעָשָׂה אֶת הַיָּם הַגָּדוֹל.

On seeing beauties of nature.

בָּרוּךְ אַתָּה, יְיָ אֱלֹהֵינוּ, מֶלֶךְ הָעוֹלָם, שֶׁכָּכָה לוֹ בְּעוֹלָמוֹ.

On seeing trees blossoming:

בָּרוּךְ אַתָּה, יְיָ אֱלֹהֵינוּ, מֶלֶךְ הָעוֹלָם, שֶׁלֹּא חִסַּר בְּעוֹלָמוֹ דָּבָר, וּבָרָא בוֹ בְּרִיּוֹת טוֹבוֹת וְאִילָנוֹת טוֹבִים לְהַנּוֹת בָּהֶם בְּנֵי אָדָם.

On seeing an exalted ruler:

בָּרוּךְ אַתָּה, יְיָ אֱלֹהֵינוּ, מֶלֶךְ הָעוֹלָם, שֶׁנָּתַן מִכְּבוֹדוֹ לְבָשָׂר וָדָם.

On attaching a mezuzah:

Blessed art thou, Lord our God, King of the universe, who hast sanctified us with thy commandments, and commanded us to attach a mezuzah.

On tasting fruit for the first time in the season:

Blessed art thou, Lord our God, King of the universe, who hast granted us life and sustenance and permitted us to reach this season.

On seeing the wonders of nature:

Blessed art thou, Lord our God, King of the universe, who didst create the universe.

On seeing an electrical storm:

Blessed art thou, Lord our God, King of the universe, whose might and power fill the world.

On seeing a rainbow:

Blessed art thou, Lord our God, King of the universe, who rememberest the covenant, and keepest thy promise faithfully.

On seeing the ocean:

Blessed art thou, Lord our God, King of the universe, who hast made the great sea.

On seeing beauties of nature:

Blessed art thou, Lord our God, King of the universe, who hast such as these in thy world.

On seeing trees blossoming:

Blessed art thou, Lord our God, King of the universe, who hast withheld nothing from thy world; and hast created therein beautiful creatures and goodly trees for the enjoyment of mankind.

On seeing an exalted ruler:

Blessed art thou, Lord our God, King of the universe, who hast given of thy glory to mortal man.

On seeing a person of abnormal appearance:

בָּרוּךְ אַתָּה, יְיָ אֱלֹהֵינוּ, מֶלֶךְ הָעוֹלָם, מְשַׁנֶּה הַבְּרִיּוֹת.

On seeing a person of profound Torah wisdom:

בָּרוּךְ אַתָּה, יְיָ אֱלֹהֵינוּ, מֶלֶךְ הָעוֹלָם, שֶׁחָלַק מֵחָכְמָתוֹ לִירֵאָיו.

On seeing a person of profound secular learning:

בָּרוּךְ אַתָּה, יְיָ אֱלֹהֵינוּ, מֶלֶךְ הָעוֹלָם, שֶׁנָּתַן מֵחָכְמָתוֹ לְבָשָׂר וָדָם.

On hearing bad tidings:

בָּרוּךְ אַתָּה, יְיָ אֱלֹהֵינוּ, מֶלֶךְ הָעוֹלָם, דַּיַּן הָאֱמֶת.

On hearing good tidings:

בָּרוּךְ אַתָּה, יְיָ אֱלֹהֵינוּ, מֶלֶךְ הָעוֹלָם, הַטּוֹב וְהַמֵּטִיב.

קְרִיאַת שְׁמַע עַל הַמִּטָּה

Recited before retiring

בָּרוּךְ אַתָּה, יְיָ אֱלֹהֵינוּ, מֶלֶךְ הָעוֹלָם, הַמַּפִּיל חֶבְלֵי שֵׁנָה עַל עֵינַי, וּתְנוּמָה עַל עַפְעַפָּי. וִיהִי רָצוֹן מִלְּפָנֶיךָ, יְיָ אֱלֹהַי וֵאלֹהֵי אֲבוֹתַי, שֶׁתַּשְׁכִּיבֵנִי לְשָׁלוֹם וְתַעֲמִידֵנִי לְשָׁלוֹם; וְאַל יְבַהֲלוּנִי רַעְיוֹנַי, וַחֲלוֹמוֹת רָעִים וְהִרְהוּרִים רָעִים; וּתְהִי מִטָּתִי שְׁלֵמָה לְפָנֶיךָ. וְהָאֵר עֵינַי פֶּן אִישַׁן הַמָּוֶת, כִּי אַתָּה הַמֵּאִיר לְאִישׁוֹן בַּת עָיִן. בָּרוּךְ אַתָּה, יְיָ, הַמֵּאִיר לָעוֹלָם כֻּלּוֹ בִּכְבוֹדוֹ.

המפּיל is an abbreviation from a passage cited in Berakhoth 60b. The prayer recited before going to bed is called קריאת שמע because the *Shema* forms its chief element. According to the Talmud, one ought to read the *Shema* before retiring at night in addition to its recital in the evening service (Berakhoth 4b.)

המפּיל חבלי שנה... literally means "who lets down the cords, or chains, of sleep upon my eyes." The reference is to the whole body, metaphorically represented as chained in sleep.

On seeing a person of abnormal appearance:

Blessed art thou, Lord our God, King of the universe, who dost vary the aspect of thy creatures.

On seeing a person of profound Torah wisdom:

Blessed art thou, Lord our God, King of the universe, who hast imparted of thy wisdom to those who revere thee.

On seeing a person of profound secular learning:

Blessed art thou, Lord our God, King of the universe, who hast imparted of thy wisdom to flesh and blood.

On hearing bad tidings:

Blessed art thou, Lord our God, King of the universe, the true Judge.

On hearing good tidings:

Blessed art thou, Lord our God, King of the universe, who art good and beneficent.

NIGHT PRAYER

Recited before retiring

Blessed art thou, Lord our God, King of the universe, who closest my eyes in sleep, my eyelids in slumber. May it be thy will, Lord my God and God of my fathers, to grant that I lie down in peace and that I rise up in peace. Let not my thoughts upset me— nor evil dreams, nor sinful fancies. May my family ever be perfect in thy sight. Grant me light, lest I sleep the sleep of death; for it is thou who givest light to the eyes. Blessed art thou, O Lord, whose majesty gives light to the whole world.

מטתי is here used figuratively in the sense of my offspring; compare the expressions שהיתה מטתו שלימה and שהיתה מטתי פסול שמא חס ושלום יש במטתי (Pesaḥim 56a). אישון and בת עין are synonyms denoting the apple of the eye.

אֵל מֶלֶךְ נֶאֱמָן.

שְׁמַע יִשְׂרָאֵל, יְיָ אֱלֹהֵינוּ, יְיָ אֶחָד.

בָּרוּךְ שֵׁם כְּבוֹד מַלְכוּתוֹ לְעוֹלָם וָעֶד.

וְאָהַבְתָּ אֵת יְיָ אֱלֹהֶיךָ בְּכָל לְבָבְךָ וּבְכָל נַפְשְׁךָ וּבְכָל מְאֹדֶךָ. וְהָיוּ הַדְּבָרִים הָאֵלֶּה, אֲשֶׁר אָנֹכִי מְצַוְּךָ הַיּוֹם, עַל לְבָבֶךָ. וְשִׁנַּנְתָּם לְבָנֶיךָ, וְדִבַּרְתָּ בָּם בְּשִׁבְתְּךָ בְּבֵיתֶךָ, וּבְלֶכְתְּךָ בַדֶּרֶךְ, וּבְשָׁכְבְּךָ וּבְקוּמֶךָ. וּקְשַׁרְתָּם לְאוֹת עַל יָדֶךָ, וְהָיוּ לְטֹטָפֹת בֵּין עֵינֶיךָ. וּכְתַבְתָּם עַל מְזֻזוֹת בֵּיתֶךָ וּבִשְׁעָרֶיךָ.

וִיהִי נֹעַם אֲדֹנָי אֱלֹהֵינוּ עָלֵינוּ, וּמַעֲשֵׂה יָדֵינוּ כּוֹנְנָה עָלֵינוּ; וּמַעֲשֵׂה יָדֵינוּ כּוֹנְנֵהוּ.

תהלים צא

יֹשֵׁב בְּסֵתֶר עֶלְיוֹן, בְּצֵל שַׁדַּי יִתְלוֹנָן. אֹמַר לַיְיָ, מַחְסִי וּמְצוּדָתִי; אֱלֹהַי אֶבְטַח בּוֹ. כִּי הוּא יַצִּילְךָ מִפַּח יָקוּשׁ, מִדֶּבֶר הַוּוֹת. בְּאֶבְרָתוֹ יָסֶךְ לָךְ, וְתַחַת כְּנָפָיו תֶּחְסֶה; צִנָּה וְסֹחֵרָה אֲמִתּוֹ. לֹא תִירָא מִפַּחַד לָיְלָה, מֵחֵץ יָעוּף יוֹמָם. מִדֶּבֶר בָּאֹפֶל יַהֲלֹךְ, מִקֶּטֶב יָשׁוּד צָהֳרָיִם. יִפֹּל מִצִּדְּךָ אֶלֶף, וּרְבָבָה מִימִינֶךָ; אֵלֶיךָ לֹא יִגָּשׁ. רַק בְּעֵינֶיךָ תַבִּיט, וְשִׁלֻּמַת רְשָׁעִים תִּרְאֶה. כִּי אַתָּה, יְיָ, מַחְסִי; עֶלְיוֹן שַׂמְתָּ מְעוֹנֶךָ. לֹא תְאֻנֶּה אֵלֶיךָ רָעָה, וְנֶגַע לֹא יִקְרַב בְּאָהֳלֶךָ. כִּי מַלְאָכָיו יְצַוֶּה לָּךְ, לִשְׁמָרְךָ בְּכָל דְּרָכֶיךָ. עַל כַּפַּיִם יִשָּׂאוּנְךָ, פֶּן תִּגֹּף בָּאֶבֶן רַגְלֶךָ. עַל שַׁחַל וָפֶתֶן תִּדְרֹךְ, תִּרְמֹס כְּפִיר וְתַנִּין. כִּי בִי חָשַׁק וַאֲפַלְּטֵהוּ, אֲשַׂגְּבֵהוּ, כִּי יָדַע שְׁמִי. יִקְרָאֵנִי וְאֶעֱנֵהוּ, עִמּוֹ אָנֹכִי בְצָרָה, אֲחַלְּצֵהוּ וַאֲכַבְּדֵהוּ. אֹרֶךְ יָמִים אַשְׂבִּיעֵהוּ, וְאַרְאֵהוּ בִּישׁוּעָתִי. אֹרֶךְ יָמִים אַשְׂבִּיעֵהוּ, וְאַרְאֵהוּ בִּישׁוּעָתִי.

God is a faithful King.

Hear, O Israel, the Lord is our God, the Lord is One.

Blessed be the name of his glorious majesty forever and ever.

You shall love the Lord your God with all your heart, and with all your soul, and with all your might. And these words which I command you today shall be in your heart. You shall teach them diligently to your children, and you shall speak of them when you are sitting at home and when you go on a journey, when you lie down and when you rise up. You shall bind them for a sign on your hand, and they shall be for frontlets between your eyes. You shall inscribe them on the doorposts of your house and on your gates.[1]

May the favor of the Lord our God rest on us; establish thou for us the work of our hands; the work of our hands establish thou.[2]

Psalm 91

He who dwells in the shelter of the Most High abides under the protection of the Almighty. I call the Lord "My refuge and my fortress, my God in whom I trust." He saves you from the fowler's snare and from the destructive pestilence. With his pinions he covers you, and under his wings you find refuge; his truth is a shield and armor. Fear not the terror of the night, nor the arrow that flies by day, nor the pestilence that stalks in darkness, nor the destruction that ravages at noon. Though a thousand fall at your side, and a myriad at your right hand, it shall not come to you. You have only to look with your eyes and see how evil men are punished. Thou, O Lord, art my refuge! When you have made the Most High your shelter, no disaster shall befall you or come near your tent. For he will give his angels charge over you, to guard you in all your ways. They will bear you upon their hands, lest you strike your foot against a stone. You shall tread upon the lion and the asp; you shall trample the young lion and the serpent. "Because he clings to me, I deliver him; I protect him because he loves me. When he calls upon me, I answer him; I am with him when he is in trouble; I rescue him and bring him to honor. I enrich him with long life, and let him witness my deliverance."

[1] *Deuteronomy* 6:4-9. [2] *Psalm* 90:17.

תהלים ג

יְיָ, מָה רַבּוּ צָרָי; רַבִּים קָמִים עָלָי. רַבִּים אוֹמְרִים לְנַפְשִׁי,
אֵין יְשׁוּעָתָה לּוֹ בֵאלֹהִים, סֶלָה. וְאַתָּה, יְיָ, מָגֵן בַּעֲדִי, כְּבוֹדִי
וּמֵרִים רֹאשִׁי. קוֹלִי אֶל יְיָ אֶקְרָא, וַיַּעֲנֵנִי מֵהַר קָדְשׁוֹ, סֶלָה.
אֲנִי שָׁכַבְתִּי וָאִישָׁנָה, הֱקִיצוֹתִי, כִּי יְיָ יִסְמְכֵנִי. לֹא אִירָא
מֵרִבְבוֹת עָם, אֲשֶׁר סָבִיב שָׁתוּ עָלָי. קוּמָה, יְיָ; הוֹשִׁיעֵנִי, אֱלֹהַי;
כִּי הִכִּיתָ אֶת כָּל אֹיְבַי לֶחִי; שִׁנֵּי רְשָׁעִים שִׁבַּרְתָּ. לַיְיָ הַיְשׁוּעָה,
עַל עַמְּךָ בִרְכָתֶךָ סֶּלָה.

הַשְׁכִּיבֵנוּ, יְיָ אֱלֹהֵינוּ, לְשָׁלוֹם, וְהַעֲמִידֵנוּ, מַלְכֵּנוּ, לְחַיִּים;
וּפְרוֹשׂ עָלֵינוּ סֻכַּת שְׁלוֹמֶךָ, וְתַקְּנֵנוּ בְּעֵצָה טוֹבָה מִלְּפָנֶיךָ,
וְהוֹשִׁיעֵנוּ לְמַעַן שְׁמֶךָ; וְהָגֵן בַּעֲדֵנוּ, וְהָסֵר מֵעָלֵינוּ אוֹיֵב, דֶּבֶר
וְחֶרֶב וְרָעָב וְיָגוֹן; וְהָסֵר שָׂטָן מִלְּפָנֵינוּ וּמֵאַחֲרֵינוּ, וּבְצֵל כְּנָפֶיךָ
תַּסְתִּירֵנוּ; כִּי אֵל שׁוֹמְרֵנוּ וּמַצִּילֵנוּ אָתָּה, כִּי אֵל מֶלֶךְ חַנּוּן
וְרַחוּם אָתָּה. וּשְׁמוֹר צֵאתֵנוּ וּבוֹאֵנוּ לְחַיִּים וּלְשָׁלוֹם, מֵעַתָּה
וְעַד עוֹלָם.

בָּרוּךְ יְיָ בַּיּוֹם, בָּרוּךְ יְיָ בַּלָּיְלָה; בָּרוּךְ יְיָ בְּשָׁכְבֵנוּ, בָּרוּךְ
יְיָ בְּקוּמֵנוּ, כִּי בְיָדְךָ נַפְשׁוֹת הַחַיִּים וְהַמֵּתִים. אֲשֶׁר בְּיָדוֹ נֶפֶשׁ
כָּל חָי, וְרוּחַ כָּל בְּשַׂר אִישׁ. בְּיָדְךָ אַפְקִיד רוּחִי; פָּדִיתָה אוֹתִי,
יְיָ, אֵל אֱמֶת. אֱלֹהֵינוּ שֶׁבַּשָּׁמַיִם, יַחֵד שִׁמְךָ וְקַיֵּם מַלְכוּתְךָ
תָּמִיד, וּמְלוֹךְ עָלֵינוּ לְעוֹלָם וָעֶד.

יִרְאוּ עֵינֵינוּ וְיִשְׂמַח לִבֵּנוּ, וְתָגֵל נַפְשֵׁנוּ בִּישׁוּעָתְךָ בֶּאֱמֶת,
בֶּאֱמֹר לְצִיּוֹן מָלַךְ אֱלֹהָיִךְ. יְיָ מֶלֶךְ, יְיָ מָלָךְ, יְיָ יִמְלֹךְ לְעוֹלָם
וָעֶד. כִּי הַמַּלְכוּת שֶׁלְּךָ הִיא, וּלְעוֹלְמֵי עַד תִּמְלוֹךְ בְּכָבוֹד, כִּי
אֵין לָנוּ מֶלֶךְ אֶלָּא אָתָּה.

Psalm 3

O Lord, how my foes have increased! Many are rising against me. Many are saying concerning me: "There is no help for him in God." But thou, O Lord, art my shield, my glory, my uplifter. When I call out to the Lord, he answers me from his holy mountain. When I lie down I sleep, I awake; for the Lord sustains me. I am not afraid of the thousands of people that have set upon me all around. Arise, O Lord; save me, O my God. Thou dost strike all my foes on the cheek; thou dost break the teeth of the wicked. Salvation belongs to the Lord. Upon thy people be thy blessing!

Grant, Lord our God, that we lie down in peace, and that we rise again, O our King, to life. Spread over us thy shelter of peace, and direct us with good counsel of thy own. Save us for thy name's sake; shield us, and remove from us the enemy and pestilence, the sword and famine and grief; remove the adversary from before us and from behind us; shelter us in the shadow of thy wings; for thou art our guarding and saving God, indeed, a gracious and merciful God and King. Guard thou our going out and our coming in, for life and peace henceforth and forever.

Blessed be the Lord by day; blessed be the Lord by night; blessed be the Lord when we lie down; blessed be the Lord when we rise up. In thy hand are the souls of the living and the dead, *as it is written*: "In his hand is the soul of every living thing, and the spirit of every human being."[1] Into thy hand I commit my spirit; O Lord, faithful God, thou savest me.[2] Our God who art in heaven, reveal thy Oneness and establish thy kingdom forever; do thou reign over us forever and ever.

May our eyes behold, our heart rejoice, and our soul exult in thy true salvation, when it will be said to Zion: "Your God is King." The Lord is King, the Lord was King, the Lord will be King forever and ever. For the kingdom is thine, and to all eternity thou wilt reign in glory; we have no king except thee.

---

[1] *Job* 12:10.   [2] *Psalm* 31:6.

הַמַּלְאָךְ הַגֹּאֵל אֹתִי מִכָּל רָע יְבָרֵךְ אֶת הַנְּעָרִים, וְיִקָּרֵא
בָהֶם שְׁמִי וְשֵׁם אֲבֹתַי אַבְרָהָם וְיִצְחָק; וְיִדְגּוּ לָרֹב בְּקֶרֶב
הָאָרֶץ. וַיֹּאמֶר: אִם שָׁמְוֹעַ תִּשְׁמַע לְקוֹל יְיָ אֱלֹהֶיךָ וְהַיָּשָׁר
בְּעֵינָיו תַּעֲשֶׂה, וְהַאֲזַנְתָּ לְמִצְוֹתָיו, וְשָׁמַרְתָּ כָּל חֻקָּיו, כָּל
הַמַּחֲלָה אֲשֶׁר שַׂמְתִּי בְמִצְרַיִם לֹא אָשִׂים עָלֶיךָ, כִּי אֲנִי יְיָ
רֹפְאֶךָ. וַיֹּאמֶר יְיָ אֶל הַשָּׂטָן: יִגְעַר יְיָ בְּךָ, הַשָּׂטָן; וְיִגְעַר יְיָ בְּךָ
הַבֹּחֵר בִּירוּשָׁלָיִם; הֲלוֹא זֶה אוּד מֻצָּל מֵאֵשׁ. הִנֵּה מִטָּתוֹ
שֶׁלִּשְׁלֹמֹה, שִׁשִּׁים גִּבֹּרִים סָבִיב לָהּ מִגִּבֹּרֵי יִשְׂרָאֵל. כֻּלָּם אֲחֻזֵי
חֶרֶב, מְלֻמְּדֵי מִלְחָמָה, אִישׁ חַרְבּוֹ עַל יְרֵכוֹ מִפַּחַד בַּלֵּילוֹת.
יְבָרֶכְךָ יְיָ וְיִשְׁמְרֶךָ. יָאֵר יְיָ פָּנָיו אֵלֶיךָ וִיחֻנֶּךָּ. יִשָּׂא יְיָ פָּנָיו
אֵלֶיךָ, וְיָשֵׂם לְךָ שָׁלוֹם.

הִנֵּה לֹא יָנוּם וְלֹא יִישָׁן שׁוֹמֵר יִשְׂרָאֵל.

לִישׁוּעָתְךָ קִוִּיתִי, יְיָ. קִוִּיתִי, יְיָ, לִישׁוּעָתְךָ. יְיָ, לִישׁוּעָתְךָ
קִוִּיתִי.

בְּשֵׁם יְיָ אֱלֹהֵי יִשְׂרָאֵל, מִימִינִי מִיכָאֵל וּמִשְּׂמֹאלִי גַּבְרִיאֵל,
וּמִלְּפָנַי אוּרִיאֵל וּמֵאֲחוֹרַי רְפָאֵל, וְעַל רֹאשִׁי שְׁכִינַת אֵל.

תהלים קכח

שִׁיר הַמַּעֲלוֹת. אַשְׁרֵי כָּל יְרֵא יְיָ, הַהֹלֵךְ בִּדְרָכָיו. יְגִיעַ
כַּפֶּיךָ כִּי תֹאכֵל, אַשְׁרֶיךָ וְטוֹב לָךְ. אֶשְׁתְּךָ כְּגֶפֶן פֹּרִיָּה בְּיַרְכְּתֵי
בֵיתֶךָ, בָּנֶיךָ כִּשְׁתִלֵי זֵיתִים סָבִיב לְשֻׁלְחָנֶךָ. הִנֵּה כִי כֵן יְבֹרַךְ
גָּבֶר, יְרֵא יְיָ. יְבָרֶכְךָ יְיָ מִצִּיּוֹן, וּרְאֵה בְּטוּב יְרוּשָׁלָם כֹּל יְמֵי
חַיֶּיךָ. וּרְאֵה בָנִים לְבָנֶיךָ; שָׁלוֹם עַל יִשְׂרָאֵל.

אוד מצל מאש refers to Israel saved from the fire of exile.

The angel who redeemed me from all evil bless the lads; may they carry on my name and the name of my fathers Abraham and Isaac; may they grow into a multitude on earth.[1]

And he said: "If you will listen carefully to the voice of the Lord your God, and do what is right in his eyes, and heed his commands, and observe all his laws, then I will inflict none of the diseases on you which I inflicted on the Egyptians, for I am the Lord who heals you."[2]

[The angel of] the Lord said to Satan: "The Lord rebuke you, O Satan! May the Lord who has chosen Jerusalem rebuke you! This is indeed a piece of wood snatched from the fire."[3]

Solomon's bed—sixty heroes are around it, heroes of Israel. All of them are armed with swords, and are trained in war; each has his sword on his hip, because of danger at night.[4]

May the Lord bless you and protect you; may the Lord countenance you and be gracious to you; may the Lord favor you and give you peace.[5]

Behold, the Guardian of Israel neither slumbers nor sleeps.[6]

For thy salvation I hope, O Lord. I hope, O Lord, for thy salvation. O Lord, for thy salvation I hope.[7]

In the name of the Lord God of Israel, may Michael be at my right hand, and Gabriel at my left; before me Uriel; behind me Raphael; and above my head the divine presence.

Psalm 128

A Pilgrim Song. Happy is everyone who reveres the Lord, who walks in his ways. When you eat of the toil of your hands, you shall be happy and at ease. Your wife shall be like a fruitful vine in the interior of your house; your children like olive plants, around your table. Behold, thus indeed shall the man be blessed who reveres the Lord. The Lord bless you from Zion; may you see the welfare of Jerusalem all the days of your life; may you live to see your children's children. Peace be upon Israel!

---

[1]*Genesis* 48:16. [2]*Exodus* 15:26. [3]*Zechariah* 3:2. [4]*Song of Songs* 3:7-8. [5]*Numbers* 6:24-26. [6]*Psalm* 121:4. [7]*Genesis* 49:18.

רִגְזוּ וְאַל תֶּחֱטָאוּ; אִמְרוּ בִלְבַבְכֶם עַל מִשְׁכַּבְכֶם וְדֹמּוּ. סֶלָה.

אֲדוֹן עוֹלָם

בְּטֶרֶם כָּל יְצִיר נִבְרָא.	אֲדוֹן עוֹלָם אֲשֶׁר מָלַךְ
אֲזַי מֶלֶךְ שְׁמוֹ נִקְרָא.	לְעֵת נַעֲשָׂה בְחֶפְצוֹ כֹּל
לְבַדּוֹ יִמְלֹךְ נוֹרָא.	וְאַחֲרֵי כִּכְלוֹת הַכֹּל
וְהוּא יִהְיֶה בְּתִפְאָרָה.	וְהוּא הָיָה, וְהוּא הֹוֶה
לְהַמְשִׁיל לוֹ לְהַחְבִּירָה.	וְהוּא אֶחָד וְאֵין שֵׁנִי
וְלוֹ הָעֹז וְהַמִּשְׂרָה.	בְּלִי רֵאשִׁית בְּלִי תַכְלִית
וְצוּר חֶבְלִי בְּעֵת צָרָה.	וְהוּא אֵלִי וְחַי גֹּאֲלִי
מְנָת כּוֹסִי בְּיוֹם אֶקְרָא.	וְהוּא נִסִּי וּמָנוֹס לִי
בְּעֵת אִישַׁן וְאָעִירָה.	בְּיָדוֹ אַפְקִיד רוּחִי
יְיָ לִי וְלֹא אִירָא.	וְעִם רוּחִי גְּוִיָּתִי

רגזו fear God; אמרו בלבבכם על משכבכם that is, let the voice of your conscience make itself heard in the silence of the night; ודמו put an end to your striving after vanity, and repent.

סלה occurs seventy-one times in the Book of Psalms. It is derived from סלל ("to lift up"). In Psalm 68:5, the word סלו is used synonymously with שירו and זמרו in the sense of "extol, exalt." Hence, it is safe to assume that סלה was a direction to the singers to raise their voices before certain pauses. In the writings of medieval Hebrew poets, however, סלה frequently connotes "forever."

אדון עולם treats of God's omnipotence and providence. This noble hymn has been attributed to various poets, particularly to Solomon ibn Gabirol who flourished in Spain during the eleventh century. It has been part of the

Tremble, and do not sin; commune with your own heart upon your bed, and be still.[1]

ADON OLAM

He is the eternal Lord who reigned
Before any being was created.

At the time when all was made by his will,
He was at once acknowledged as King.

And at the end, when all shall cease to be,
The revered God alone shall still be King.

He was, he is, and he shall be
In glorious eternity.

He is One, and there is no other
To compare to him, to place beside him.

He is without beginning, without end;
Power and dominion belong to him.

He is my God, my living Redeemer,
My stronghold in times of distress.

He is my guide and my refuge,
My share of bliss the day I call.

To him I entrust my spirit
When I sleep and when I wake.

As long as my soul is with my body
The Lord is with me; I am not afraid.

---

morning service since the fifteenth century. It is composed of ten lines, each of which consists of twelve syllables. A single rhyme runs through it. שכל זמן conveys the idea expressed in Sifré, section 139: ...ועם רוחי גויתי שאדם נתון בחיים, נפשו פקודה ביד קונו ... מת, נתונה באוצר...

---

[1] *Psalm* 4:5.

קְרִיאַת שְׁמַע לִילָדִים

בָּרוּךְ אַתָּה, יְיָ אֱלֹהֵינוּ, מֶלֶךְ הָעוֹלָם, הַמַּפִּיל חֶבְלֵי שֵׁנָה עַל עֵינַי, וּתְנוּמָה עַל עַפְעַפָּי.

וִיהִי רָצוֹן מִלְּפָנֶיךָ, יְיָ אֱלֹהַי וֵאלֹהֵי אֲבוֹתַי, שֶׁתַּשְׁכִּיבֵנִי לְשָׁלוֹם וְתַעֲמִידֵנִי לְשָׁלוֹם.

שְׁמַע יִשְׂרָאֵל, יְיָ אֱלֹהֵינוּ, יְיָ אֶחָד.

בָּרוּךְ שֵׁם כְּבוֹד מַלְכוּתוֹ לְעוֹלָם וָעֶד.

וְאָהַבְתָּ אֵת יְיָ אֱלֹהֶיךָ בְּכָל לְבָבְךָ וּבְכָל נַפְשְׁךָ וּבְכָל מְאֹדֶךָ. וְהָיוּ הַדְּבָרִים הָאֵלֶּה, אֲשֶׁר אָנֹכִי מְצַוְּךָ הַיּוֹם, עַל לְבָבֶךָ. וְשִׁנַּנְתָּם לְבָנֶיךָ, וְדִבַּרְתָּ בָּם בְּשִׁבְתְּךָ בְּבֵיתֶךָ וּבְלֶכְתְּךָ בַדֶּרֶךְ, וּבְשָׁכְבְּךָ וּבְקוּמֶךָ. וּקְשַׁרְתָּם לְאוֹת עַל יָדֶךָ, וְהָיוּ לְטֹטָפֹת בֵּין עֵינֶיךָ, וּכְתַבְתָּם עַל מְזֻזוֹת בֵּיתֶךָ וּבִשְׁעָרֶיךָ.

בָּרוּךְ יְיָ בַּיּוֹם, בָּרוּךְ יְיָ בַּלָּיְלָה; בָּרוּךְ יְיָ בְּשָׁכְבֵּנוּ, בָּרוּךְ יְיָ בְּקוּמֵנוּ.

הִנֵּה לֹא יָנוּם וְלֹא יִישָׁן שׁוֹמֵר יִשְׂרָאֵל.

בְּיָדְךָ אַפְקִיד רוּחִי; פָּדִיתָה אוֹתִי, יְיָ, אֵל אֱמֶת.
לִישׁוּעָתְךָ קִוִּיתִי, יְיָ.

787

NIGHT PRAYER FOR CHILDREN

Blessed art thou, Lord our God, King of the universe, who closest my eyes in sleep, my eyelids in slumber.

May it be thy will, Lord my God and God of my fathers, to grant that I lie down in peace and that I rise again to life.

Hear, O Israel, the Lord is our God, the Lord is One.

Blessed be the name of his glorious majesty forever and ever.

You shall love the Lord your God with all your heart, and with all your soul, and with all your might. And these words which I command you today shall be in your heart. You shall teach them diligently to your children, and you shall speak of them when you are sitting at home and when you go on a journey, when you lie down and when you rise up. You shall bind them for a sign on your hand, and they shall be for frontlets between your eyes. You shall inscribe them on the doorposts of your house and on your gates.

Blessed be the Lord by day; blessed be the Lord by night; blessed be the Lord when we lie down; blessed be the Lord when we rise up.

The Guardian of Israel neither slumbers nor sleeps.

Into thy hand I commit my spirit; O Lord, faithful God, thou savest me.

For thy salvation I hope, O Lord.

תְּפִלָּה לִשְׁלוֹם מְדִינַת יִשְׂרָאֵל

מאת הרבנים הראשיים שבארץ ישראל

אָבִינוּ שֶׁבַּשָּׁמַיִם, צוּר יִשְׂרָאֵל וְגוֹאֲלוֹ, בָּרֵךְ אֶת מְדִינַת יִשְׂרָאֵל, רֵאשִׁית צְמִיחַת גְּאֻלָּתֵנוּ. הָגֵן עָלֶיהָ בְּאֶבְרַת חַסְדֶּךָ, וּפְרוֹשׂ עָלֶיהָ סֻכַּת שְׁלוֹמֶךָ; וּשְׁלַח אוֹרְךָ וַאֲמִתְּךָ לְרָאשֶׁיהָ, שָׂרֶיהָ וְיוֹעֲצֶיהָ, וְתַקְּנֵם בְּעֵצָה טוֹבָה מִלְּפָנֶיךָ.

חַזֵּק אֶת יְדֵי מְגִנֵּי אֶרֶץ קָדְשֵׁנוּ, וְהַנְחִילֵם אֱלֹהֵינוּ יְשׁוּעָה, וַעֲטֶרֶת נִצָּחוֹן תְּעַטְּרֵם; וְנָתַתָּ שָׁלוֹם בָּאָרֶץ, וְשִׂמְחַת עוֹלָם לְיוֹשְׁבֶיהָ.

וְאֶת אַחֵינוּ, כָּל בֵּית יִשְׂרָאֵל, פְּקָד-נָא בְּכָל אַרְצוֹת פְּזוּרֵיהֶם, וְתוֹלִיכֵם מְהֵרָה קוֹמְמִיּוּת לְצִיּוֹן עִירֶךָ, וְלִירוּשָׁלַיִם מִשְׁכַּן שְׁמֶךָ, כַּכָּתוּב בְּתוֹרַת מֹשֶׁה עַבְדֶּךָ: אִם יִהְיֶה נִדַּחֲךָ בִּקְצֵה הַשָּׁמַיִם, מִשָּׁם יְקַבֶּצְךָ יְיָ אֱלֹהֶיךָ וּמִשָּׁם יִקָּחֶךָ. וֶהֱבִיאֲךָ יְיָ אֱלֹהֶיךָ אֶל הָאָרֶץ אֲשֶׁר יָרְשׁוּ אֲבוֹתֶיךָ, וִירִשְׁתָּהּ.

וְיַחֵד לְבָבֵנוּ לְאַהֲבָה וּלְיִרְאָה אֶת שְׁמֶךָ, וְלִשְׁמוֹר אֶת כָּל דִּבְרֵי תוֹרָתֶךָ. הוֹפַע בַּהֲדַר גְּאוֹן עֻזֶּךָ עַל כָּל יוֹשְׁבֵי תֵּבֵל אַרְצֶךָ, וְיֹאמַר כֹּל אֲשֶׁר נְשָׁמָה בְאַפּוֹ: יְיָ אֱלֹהֵי יִשְׂרָאֵל מֶלֶךְ, וּמַלְכוּתוֹ בַּכֹּל מָשָׁלָה. אָמֵן סֶלָה.

PRAYER FOR THE WELFARE OF THE STATE OF ISRAEL

By the Chief Rabbinate of Israel

Our Father who art in heaven, Protector and Redeemer of Israel, bless thou the State of Israel which marks the dawn of our deliverance. Shield it beneath the wings of thy love; spread over it thy canopy of peace; send thy light and thy truth to its leaders, officers and counselors, and direct them with thy good counsel.

O God, strengthen the defenders of our Holy Land; grant them salvation and crown them with victory. Establish peace in the land, and everlasting joy for its inhabitants.

Remember our brethren, the whole house of Israel, in all the lands of their dispersion. Speedily let them walk upright to Zion thy city, to Jerusalem thy dwelling-place, as it is written in the Torah of thy servant Moses: "Even if you are dispersed in the uttermost parts of the world, from there the Lord your God will gather and fetch you. The Lord your God will bring you into the land which your fathers possessed, and you shall possess it."[1]

Unite our heart to love and revere thy name, and to observe all the precepts of thy Torah. Shine forth in thy glorious majesty over all the inhabitants of thy world. Let everything that breathes proclaim: "The Lord God of Israel is King; his majesty rules over all." Amen.

---

[1] *Deuteronomy* 30:4-5.

MOURNERS' KADDISH

Yisgaddal v'yiskaddash shmey rabboh
B'olmoh dee v'roh chir-usey
V'yamlich malchusey
B'cha-yeychon uvyo-meychon
Uvcha-yey d'chol beys yisro-eyl
Ba-agoloh uvizman koreev
V'imru omeyn.

Y'hey shmey rabboh m'vorach
L'olam ul'olmey olmayoh.

Yisborach v'yishtabbach
V'yispo-ar v'yisromam
V'yisnassey v'yis-haddar
V'yis-alleh v'yis-hallal
Shmey d'kudshoh b'reech hu
L'eyloh min kol birchosoh v'shirosoh
Tush-b'chosoh v'nechemosoh
Da-amiron b'olmo
V'imru omeyn.

Y'hey shlomoh rabboh min sh'mah-yoh
V'cha-yeem, oleynu v'al kol yisro-eyl
V'imru omeyn.
O-seh sholom bimromov
Hu ya-aseh sholom
Oleynu v'al kol yisro-eyl
V'imru omeyn.